THE ORIGIN AND DEVELOPMENT
OF THE MORAL IDEAS

VOL. II

MACMILLAN AND CO., Limited
LONDON . BOMBAY . CALCUTTA
MELBOURNE

THE MACMILLAN COMPANY
NEW YORK . BOSTON . CHICAGO
DALLAS . SAN FRANCISCO

THE MACMILLAN CO. OF CANADA, Ltd.
TORONTO

THE ORIGIN

AND DEVELOPMENT

OF THE

MORAL IDEAS

BY

EDWARD WESTERMARCK

Ph.D., LL.D. (Aberdeen)

MARTIN WHITE PROFESSOR OF SOCIOLOGY IN THE UNIVERSITY OF LONDON
PROFESSOR OF MORAL PHILOSOPHY AT THE UNIVERSITY OF FINLAND, HELSINFORS
AUTHOR OF "THE HISTORY OF HUMAN MARRIAGE," "MARRIAGE CEREMONIES IN MOROCCO," ETC

IN TWO VOLUMES

VOL. II

SECOND EDITION

MACMILLAN AND CO., LIMITED
ST. MARTIN'S STREET, LONDON

1917

JOHNSON REPRINT CORPORATION
New York • London
1971

Landmarks in Anthropology, a series of reprints in cultural anthropology
General Editor: Weston La Barre

Library of Congress Catalog Card Number: 79-184262

113716

COPYRIGHT

First Edition, 1903
Second Edition, 1917

First reprinting 1971, Johnson Reprint Corporation

Johnson Reprint Corporation   Johnson Reprint Company Ltd.
111 Fifth Avenue   24/28 Oval Road
New York, N.Y. 10003   London, NW1 7DD, England

Printed in the U.S.A.

PREFACE

TO THE SECOND EDITION OF VOL. II

WHILE the text of the first edition has been left almost unchanged, some notes have been added at the end of it.

E. W.

LONDON,
September, 1916.

CONTENTS

CHAPTER XXVIII

THE RIGHT OF PROPERTY

CHAPTER XXIX

THE RIGHT OF PROPERTY (*concluded*)

CHAPTER XXX

THE REGARD FOR TRUTH AND GOOD FAITH

CHAPTER XXXI

THE REGARD FOR TRUTH AND GOOD FAITH (*concluded*)

CONTENTS

CHAPTER XXXII

THE RESPECT FOR OTHER MEN'S HONOUR AND SELF-REGARDING PRIDE—POLITENESS

CHAPTER XXXIII

REGARD FOR OTHER PERSONS' HAPPINESS IN GENERAL—GRATITUDE—PATRIOTISM AND COSMOPOLITANISM

CONTENTS

CHAPTER XXXIV

THE ORIGIN AND DEVELOPMENT OF THE ALTRUISTIC SENTIMENT

CHAPTER XXXV

SUICIDE

CHAPTER XXXVI

SELF-REGARDING DUTIES AND VIRTUES—INDUSTRY—REST

CHAPTER XXXVII

RESTRICTIONS IN DIET

CHAPTER XXXVIII

RESTRICTIONS IN DIET (*concluded*)

CHAPTER XXXIX

CLEANLINESS AND UNCLEANLINESS—ASCETICISM IN GENERAL

CONTENTS

CHAPTER XL

MARRIAGE

CHAPTER XLI

CELIBACY

CHAPTER XLII

FREE LOVE—ADULTERY

CHAPTER XLIII

HOMOSEXUAL LOVE

CHAPTER XLIV

REGARD FOR THE LOWER ANIMALS

CHAPTER XLV

REGARD FOR THE DEAD

CHAPTER XLVI

CANNIBALISM

CHAPTER XLVII

THE BELIEF IN SUPERNATURAL BEINGS

CONTENTS

CHAPTER XLVIII

DUTIES TO GODS

CHAPTER XLIX

DUTIES TO GODS (concluded)

CHAPTER L

GODS AS GUARDIANS OF MORALITY

CHAPTER LI

GODS AS GUARDIANS OF MORALITY (*continued*)

CHAPTER LII

GODS AS GUARDIANS OF MORALITY (*concluded*)

CHAPTER LIII

CONCLUSION

Recapitulation of the theory of the moral consciousness set forth in vol. I., pp. 738–741.—This theory supported by the fact that not only moral emotions but non-moral retributive emotions are felt with reference to phenomena exactly similar in their general nature to those on which moral judgments are passed, p. 741.—As also by the circumstance that the very acts, forbearances, and omissions which are condemned as wrong are also apt to call forth anger and revenge, and that the acts and forbearances which are praised as morally good are apt to call forth gratitude, p. 741 *sq.*—The variations of the moral ideas partly due to different external conditions, p. 742.—But chiefly to psychical causes, pp. 742–746.—The duties to neighbours have gradually become more expansive owing to the expansion of the altruistic sentiment, p. 743 *sq.*—The influence of reflection upon moral judgments has been increasing, p. 744 *sq.*—The influence of sentimental antipathies and likings has been decreasing, *ibid.*—The influence which the belief in supernatural forces or beings or in a future state has exercised upon the moral ideas of mankind, p. 745 *sq.*—Remarks as to the future development of the moral ideas, p. 746.

THE ORIGIN AND DEVELOPMENT
OF THE MORAL IDEAS

CHAPTER XXVIII

THE RIGHT OF PROPERTY

THE right of property implies that a certain person or certain persons are recognised as having a right to the exclusive disposal of a certain thing. The owner is not necessarily allowed to do with his property whatever he likes ; but whether absolute or limited, his right to disposal is not shared by anybody else, save under very exceptional circumstances, as in the case of " compulsion by necessity."[1] Property in a thing thus means not only that the owner of it is allowed, at least within certain limits, to use or deal with it at his discretion, but also that other persons are forbidden to prevent him from using or dealing with it in any manner he is entitled to.

The most common offence against property is illicit appropriation of other persons' belongings. Not the mere fact that individuals are in actual possession of certain objects, but the public disapproval of acts by which they are deprived of such possession, shows that they have proprietary rights over those objects. Hence the universal condemnation of what we call theft or robbery proves that the right of property exists among all races of men known to us.

[1] *Supra,* i. 285 *sqq.*

B

Travellers often accuse savages of thievishness.[1] But then their judgments are commonly based upon the treatment to which they have been subject themselves, and from this no conclusions must be drawn as regards intratribal morality. Nor can races who have had much to do with foreigners be taken as fair representatives of savage honesty, as such contact has proved the origin of thievish propensities.[2] In the majority of cases uncivilised peoples seem to respect proprietary rights within their own communities, and not infrequently even in their dealings

---

[1] Beni, ' Notizie sopra gli indigeni di Mexico,' in *Archivio per l'antropologia e la etnologia*, xii. 15 (Apaches). Burton, *City of the Saints*, p. 125 (Dacotahs and Prairie Indians). Powers, *Tribes of California*, p. 127 (Yuki). Macfie, *Vancouver Island and British Columbia*, p. 468. Heriot, *Travels through the Canadas*, p. 22 (Newfoundland Eskimo). Coxe, *Russian Discoveries between Asia and America*, p. 300 (Kinaighi). Georgi, *Russia*, iv. 22 (Kalmucks), 133 (Buriats). Scott Robertson, *Káfirs of the Hindu-Kush*, p. 193 *sq.* Modigliani, *Viaggio a Nías*, p. 468. Powell, *Wanderings in a Wild Country*, p. 23 (South Sea Islanders). Romilly, *From my Verandah in New Guinea*, p. 50; Comrie, ' Anthropological Notes on New Guinea,' in *Jour. Anthr. Inst.* vi. 109 *sq.* de Labillardière, *Voyage in Search of La Pérouse*, i. 275; Moseley, *Notes by a Naturalist on the "Challenger,"* p. 391 (Admiralty Islanders). Brenchley, *Jottings during the Cruise of H.M.S. Curaçoa*, p. 58 (natives of Tutuila). Lisiansky, *Voyage round the World*, p. 88 *sq.* (Nukahivans). Williams, *Missionary Enterprises in the South Sea Islands*, p. 126 (natives of Rarotonga). Cooke, *Journal of a Voyage round the World*, p. 40; Montgomery, *Journal of Voyages and Travels by Tyerman and Bennet*, ii. 11 (Society Islanders). Barrington, *History of New South Wales*, p. 22; Breton, *Excursions in New South Wales*, p. 221; Collins, *Account of the English Colony in New South Wales*, i. 599 *sq.*; Hodgson, *Reminiscences of Australia*,

p. 79; Mitchell, *Expeditions into the Interior of Eastern Australia*, i. 264, 304; Lumholtz, *Among Cannibals*, p. 71 *sq.* (Australian tribes). Reade, *Savage Africa*, p. 579 (West African Negroes). Bosman, *Description of the Coast of Guinea*, p. 324 *sq.* (Negroes of Fida and the Gold Coast). Caillié, *Travels through Central Africa*, i. 353 (Mandingoes). Beltrame, *Il Fiume Bianco*, p. 83 (Shilluk). Wilson and Felkin, *Uganda and the Egyptian Soudan*, ii. 310 (Gowane people of Kordofan). Krapf, *Travels, Researches and Missionary Labours in Eastern Africa*, p. 355 (Wakamba). Burton, *Zanzibar*, ii. 92 (Wanika). Bonfanti, ' L'incivilimento dei negri nell' Africa intertropicale,' in *Archivio per l'antropologia e la etnologia*, xv. 133 (Bantu races). Arbousset and Daumas, *Exploratory Tour to the North-East of the Colony of the Cape of Good Hope*, p. 323 (Bechuanas). Andersson, *Lake Ngami*, pp. 468 *sq.* (Bechuanas), 499 (Bayeye). Leslie, *Among the Zulus and Amatongas*, p. 256. Fritsch, *Die Eingeborenen Süd-Afrika's*, pp. 53 (Kafirs), 372, 419 (Hottentots and Bushmans).

[2] Domenech, *Great Deserts of North America*, ii. 321. Mackenzie, *Voyages to the Frozen and Pacific Oceans*, p. xcvi. note (Crees). Burton, *Highlands of the Brazil*, i. 403 *sq.* Moorcroft and Trebeck, *Travels in the Himalayan Provinces*, i. 321 (Ladakhis). Anderson, *Mandalay to Momien*, p. 151 (Kakhyens). Earl, *Papuans*, p. 80. Tyler, *Forty Years among the Zulus*, p. 192.

with strangers. Many of them are expressly said to condemn or abhor theft, at any rate when committed among
themselves. And that all of them disapprove of it may
be inferred from the universal custom of subjecting a
detected thief to punishment or revenge, or, at the very
least, of compelling him to restore the stolen property to
its owner.

The Fuegians have shown themselves enterprising thieves
on board European vessels visiting their shores ;[1] but, when
presents were given to them, a traveller noticed that " if any
present was designed for one canoe, and it fell near another, it
was invariably given to the right owner."[2] The boys are
taught by their fathers not to steal ;[3] and in case a theft has
been committed, " quand le coupable est découvert et châtié,
l'opinion publique est satisfaite."[4] In his dealings with the
Tehuelches Lieutenant Musters was always treated with fair-
ness, and the greatest care was taken of his belongings, though
they were borrowed at times. He gives the following advice
to the traveller :—" Never show distrust of the Indians ; be as
free with your goods and chattels as they are to each other. . . .
As you treat them so they will treat you."[5] Among the
Abipones doors, locks, and other things with which civilised
men protect their possessions from thieves, were as unnecessary
as they were unknown ; and if children pilfered melons grown
in the gardens of the missionaries or chickens reared in their
houses, " they falsely imagined that these things were free to
all, or might be taken not much against the will of the
owner."[6] Among the Brazilian Indians theft and robbery
were extremely rare, and are so still in places where strangers have
not settled.[7] We are told that the greatest insult which could
be offered to an Indian was to accuse him of stealing, and that
the wild women preferred the epithet of a prostitute to that of a

[1] Weddell, Voyage towards the South
Pole, pp. 151, 154, 182. King and
Fitzroy, Voyages of the "Adventure"
and "Beagle," i. 128 ; ii. 188.
[2] Darwin, Journal of Researches, p.
242. See also Snow, ' Wild Tribes of
Tierra del Fuego,' in Jour. Ethn.
Soc. London, N.S. i. 264.
[3] Bridges, in A Voice for South
America, xiii. 204.
[4] Hyades and Deniker, Mission
scientifique du Cap Horn, vii. 243.
[5] Musters, At Home with the Pata-

gonians, pp. 195, 197 sq.
[6] Dobrizhoffer, Account of the Abipones, ii. 148 sq.
[7] von Martius, Beiträge zur Ethnographie Amerika's, i. 85, 87 sq. Idem,
in Jour. Roy. Geo. Soc. ii. 196. von
Spix and von Martius, Travels in
Brazil, ii. 242. Southey, History of
Brazil, i. 247. von den Steinen,
Unter den Naturvölkern Zentral-Brasiliens, p. 332. Burton, Highlands of
the Brazil, i. 403 sq.

thief.[1] When detected a thief was not only obliged to restore
the property he had stolen, but was punished with stripes and
wounds, the chief often acting as executioner.[2] Among the
Indians of British Guiana theft and pilfering rarely occur ; "if
they happen to take anything, they do it before one's eyes,
under the notion of having some claim to it, which, when
called to an account, they are always prepared to substantiate."[3]
If anything is stolen from his house during his absence, the
Guiana Indian thinks that the missing article has been carried
off by people of some other race than his own.[4] Formerly,
when the Caribs lost anything, they used to say, "The
Christians have been here."[5] In Hayti the punishment of a
thief was to be eaten.[6]

It is known that many North American tribes had a very
high standard of honesty among themselves. Domenech
wrote :—"The Indians who do not come in contact with the
Palefaces never appropriate what belongs to others ; they have
no law against theft, as it is a crime unknown among them. They
never close their doors."[7] According to Colonel Dodge, theft
was the sole unpardonable crime amongst them ; a man found
guilty of stealing even the most trifling article from a member
of his own band was whipped almost to death, deprived of
his property, and together with his wives and children driven
away from the band to starve or live as best he could.[8]
Among the Rocky Mountains Indians visited by Harmon
theft was frequently punished with death.[9] Among the
Omahas, "when the suspected thief did not confess his offence,
some of his property was taken from him until he told the
truth. When he restored what he had stolen, one-half of his
own property was returned to him, and the rest was given to
the man from whom he had stolen. Sometimes all of the
policemen whipped the thief. But when the thief fled from
the tribe, and remained away for a year or two, the offence was
not remembered."[10] Among the Wyandots the punishment for
theft is twofold restitution.[11] The Iroquois looked down upon

[1] Burton, *Highlands of the Brazil*,
i. 404.
[2] von Martius, *Beiträge*, i. 88.
Idem, in *Jour. Roy. Geo. Soc.* ii. 196.
[3] Bernau, *Missionary Labours in
British Guiana*, p. 51.
[4] Brett, *Indian Tribes of Guiana*, p.
348.
[5] Kames, *Sketches of the History of
Man*, iv. 133 *sq.*
[6] von Martius, *Beiträge*, i. 88, n.*

[7] Domenech, *op. cit.* ii. 320.
[8] Dodge, *Our Wild Indians*, pp.
64, 79. *Cf.* Charlevoix, *Journal of a
Voyage to North America*, ii. 26, 28
(Hurons).
[9] Harmon, *Voyages and Travels in
the Interior of North America*, p. 348.
[10] Dorsey, ' Omaha Sociology,' in
Ann. Rep. Bur. Ethn. iii. 367.
[11] Powell, 'Wyandot Government,'
in *Ann. Rep. Bur. Ethn.* i. 66.

theft with the greatest disdain, although the lash of public indignation was the only penalty attached to it.[1] The Potawatomis considered it one of the most atrocious crimes.[2] Among the Chippewas Keating found a few individuals who were addicted to thieving, but these were held in disrepute.[3] Richardson praises the Chippewyans for their honesty, no precautions for the safety of his and his companions' property being required during their stay among them.[4] Mackenzie was struck by the remarkable honesty of the Beaver Indians; "in the whole tribe there were only two women and a man who had been known to have swerved from that virtue, and they were considered as objects of disregard and reprobation."[5] Among the Ahts "larceny of a fellow-tribesman's property is rarely heard of, and the aggravation of taking it from the house or person is almost unknown"; nay, "anything left under an Indian's charge, in reliance on his good faith, is perfectly safe."[6] The Thlinkets generally respect the property of their fellow-tribesmen; but although they admit that theft is wrong they do not regard it as a very serious offence, which disgraces the perpetrator, and if a thief is caught he is only required to return the stolen article or to pay its value.[7] Among the Aleuts "theft was not only a crime but a disgrace"; for the first offence of this kind corporal punishment was inflicted, for the fourth the penalty was death.[8] According to Egede, the Greenlanders had as great an abhorrence of stealing among themselves as any nation upon earth;[9] according to Cranz, they considered such an act "excessively disgraceful."[10] Similar views still prevail among them, as also among other Eskimo tribes.[11] A Greenlander never touches driftwood which another

[1] Colden, in Schoolcraft, *Indian Tribes of the United States*, iii. 191. Morgan, *League of the Iroquois*, p. 333 *sq.* Loskiel, *History of the Mission of the United Brethren among the Indians*, i. 16.
[2] Keating, *Expedition to the Source of St. Peter's River*, i. 127.
[3] *Ibid.* ii. 168.
[4] Richardson, *Arctic Searching Expedition*, ii. 19 *sq.*
[5] Mackenzie, *Voyages to the Frozen and Pacific Oceans*, p. 148.
[6] Sproat, *Scenes and Studies of Savage Life*, p. 159.
[7] Krause, *Die Tlinkit-Indianer*, p. 167. Holmberg, 'Ethnographische Skizzen über die Völker des russischen Amerika,' in *Acta Soc. Scient.*

Fennicæ, iv. 322. Petroff, *Report on Alaska,* p. 170. Dall, *Alaska*, p. 416.
[8] Veniaminof, quoted by Petroff, *op. cit.* pp. 155, 152.
[9] Egede, *Description of Greenland*, p. 124. See also Dalager,*Grønlandske Relationer*, p. 69.
[10] Cranz, *History of Greenland*, i. 160.
[11] Nansen, *First Crossing of Greenland*, ii. 335. *Idem, Eskimo Life*, p. 158. Rink, *Danish Greenland*, p. 224. Hall, *Arctic Researches*, pp. 567, 571. Richardson, *Arctic Searching Expedition,* i. 352. Parry, *Second Voyage for the Discovery of a North-West Passage*, p. 522; Lyon, *Private Journal*, p. 347 (Eskimo of Igloolik). Seemann, *Voyage of "Herald*," ii. 65

has placed above high-water mark, though it would often be easy to appropriate it without fear of detection.[1] Parry states that, during his stay at Igloolik and Winter Island, a great many instances occurred in which the Eskimo scrupulously returned articles that did not belong to them, even though detection of a theft, or at least of the offender, would have been next to impossible.[2]

Among the Chukchi it is held criminal to thieve " in the family and race to which a person belongs " ;[3] and incorrigible thieves are sometimes banished from the village.[4] In Kamchatka, if anybody was found to be a thief he was beaten by the person from whom he had stolen, without being allowed to make resistance, and no one would ever after be friends with him.[5] The three principal precepts of the Ainu are to honour old age, not to steal, not to lie ;[6] theft is also uncommon among them, and is severely punished.[7] Among the Kirghiz " whoever commits a robbery on any of the nation must make restitution to nine times the value."[8] Among the Tunguses a thief is punished by a certain number of strokes ; he is besides obliged to restore the things stolen, and remains covered with ignominy all the rest of his life.[9] The Jakuts,[10] Ostyaks,[11] Mordvins,[12] Samoyedes,[13] and Lapps,[14] are praised for their honesty, at least among their own people ; and so are the Butias,[15] Kukis,[16] Santals,[17] the hill people in the Central Provinces of India,[18] and the Chittagong Hill tribes.[19] The Kurubars of the Dekhan are of such known honesty, that on all occasions they are entrusted with the custody of produce by the farmers, who know that they would rather starve than take one grain of what was given them in

(Western Eskimo). Nelson, 'Eskimo about Bering Strait,' in *Ann. Rep. Bur. Ethn.* xviii. 293. Among the Point Barrow Eskimo, however, " men who were said to be thieves did not appear to lose any social consideration " (Murdoch, ' Ethnological Results of the Point Barrow Expedition,' in *Ann. Rep. Bur. Ethn.* ix. 41).

[1] Nansen, *Eskimo Life*, p. 162.
[2] Parry, *op. cit.* p. 521.
[3] Georgi, *op. cit.* iii. 183.
[4] Dall, *op. cit.* p. 382.
[5] Steller, *Beschreibung von Kamtschatka*, p. 356. See also *supra*, i. 311 *sq.*
[6] von Siebold, *Die Aino auf der Insel Yesso*, p. 25.
[7] *Ibid.* pp. 11, 34 *sq.* See also *supra*, i. 312.
[8] Georgi, *op. cit.* ii. 262.

[9] *Ibid.* iii. 83 *sq. Cf. ibid.* iii. 78.
[10] *Ibid.* ii. 397. Sauer, *Expedition to the Northern Parts of Russia*, p. 122.
[11] Castrén, *Nordiska resor och forskningar*, i. 319.
[12] Georgi, *op. cit.* i. 113.
[13] *Ibid.* iii. 13. von Struve, in *Das Ausland*, 1880, p. 796.
[14] Jessen, *Afhandling om de Norske Finners og Lappers Hedenske Religion*, p. 72. Castrén, *op. cit.* i. 118 *sq.*
[15] Fraser, *Tour through the Himālā Mountains*, p. 335.
[16] Lewin, *Wild Races of South-Eastern India*, p. 256. *Cf.* Butler, *Travels in Assam*, p. 94.
[17] Man, *Sonthalia*, p. 20.
[18] Hislop, *Papers relating to the Aboriginal Tribes of the Central Provinces*, p. 1.
[19] Lewin, *Wild Races of South-Eastern India*, p. 341.

charge.[1] "Honest as a Pahari," is a proverbial expression. In fact, among these mountaineers theft is almost unknown, and the men "carry treasures, which to them would be priceless, for days and days, along wild mountain tracks, whence at any moment they might diverge, and never be traced. Even money is safely entrusted to them, and is invariably delivered into the right hands."[2] Harkness says of the Todas :—"I never saw a people, civilised or uncivilised, who seemed to have a more religious respect for the rights of *meum et tuum*. This feeling is taught to their children from the tenderest age."[3] Among the Chukmas "theft is unknown."[4] Among the Karens habitual thieves are sold into slavery.[5] Among the Shans theft of valuable property is punishable with death, though it may be expiated by a money payment ; but in cases of culprits who cannot pay, or whose relatives cannot pay, death is looked upon as a fitting punishment even for petty thefts.[6] At Zimmé, "if a theft is proved, three times the value of the article is decreed to the owner ; and if not paid, the offender, after suffering imprisonment in irons, is made over with his family, to be dealt with as in cases of debt."[7] Among the hill tribes of North Aracan a person who commits theft is bound to return the property or its value and pay a fine not exceeding Rs. 30.[8] Among the Kandhs, on the other hand, the restitution of the property abstracted or the substitution of an equivalent is alone required by ancient usage ; but this leniency extends to the first offence only, a repetition of it being followed by expulsion from the community.[9] The Andaman Islanders call theft a *yūbda*, or sin.[10] Among those Veddahs who live in their natural state, theft and robbery are not known at all.[11] They think it perfectly inconceivable that any person should ever take that which does not belong to him,[12] and death only would, in their opinion, be the punishment for such an offence.[13]

[1] Buchanan, quoted by Elliot, ' Characteristics of the Population of Central and Southern India,' in *Jour. Ethn. Soc. London*, N.S. i. 105.
[2] Cumming, *In the Himalayas*, p. 356.
[3] Harkness,*Description of a Singular Aboriginal Race inhabiting the Neilgherry Hills*, p. 17 sq.
[4] Lewin, *Wild Races of South-Eastern India*, p. 188.
[5] Mason, ' Dwellings, &c., of the Karens,' in *Jour. Asiatic Soc. Bengal*, xxxvii. pt. ii. p. 146 sq. Smeaton, *Loyal Karens of Burma*, p. 86.
[6] Woodthorpe, in *Jour. Anthr.Inst.* xxvi. 21.
[7] Colquhoun, *Amongst the Shans*, p. 131.
[8] St. John, in *Jour. Anthr. Inst.* ii. 241.
[9] Macpherson, *Memorials of Service in India*, p. 82.
[10] Man,in *Jour. Anthr. Inst.* xii.112.
[11] Sarasin, *Ergebnisse naturwissenschaftlicher Forschungen auf Ceylon*, iii. 548. Deschamps, *Carnet d'un voyageur*, p. 385. Nevill, ' Vaeddas of Ceylon,' in *Taprobanian*, i. 192.
[12] Hartshorne, 'Weddas,' in *Indian Antiquary*, viii. 320.
[13] Sarasin, *op. cit.* iii. 549.

In the Malay Archipelago native custom punishes theft with a fine, most frequently equivalent to twice the value of the stolen article,[1] or with slavery,[2] mutilation,[3] or even death ;[4] and in many islands it was lawful to kill a thief caught in the act.[5] Among the Malays of Perak,[6] Dyaks,[7] Kyans,[8] Bataks, [9] and the natives of Ambon and Uliase,[10] theft is said to be unknown or almost so, at least within their own communities. Many of the South Sea Islanders have been described as honest among themselves, and some of them as honest even towards Europeans.[11] In the opinion of Captain Cook the light-coloured Polynesians have thievish propensities, but the dark-coloured not.[12] In the Tonga Islands theft was considered

[1] Wilken, ' Het strafrecht bij de volken van het maleische ras,' in *Bijdragen tot de taal- land- en volkenkunde van Nederlandsch-Indië*, 1883, Land- en volkenkunde, p. 109 *sq.* Crawfurd,*History of the Indian Archipelago*, iii. 117. Marsden, *History of Sumatra*, pp. 221 (Rejangs), 389 (Bataks). von Brenner, *Besuch bei den Kannibalen Sumatras*, p. 213 (Bataks). Junghuhn,*Die Battaländer auf Sumatra*, ii. 145 (Bataks), 308 (natives of Passumah in Central Sumatra),317(Timorese),339(natives of Bali and Lombok). Modigliani, *op. cit.* ᴨ. 496 ; von Rosenberg, *Der malayische Archipel*, p. 166 (Niase). Worcester,*Philippine Islands*, p.108 (Tagbanuas of Palawan).

[2] Wilken, *loc. cit.* p. 108 *sq.* Junghuhn, *op. cit.* ii. 145 *sq.* (Bataks). Raffles,*History of Java*,ii. p. ccxxxv. (people of Bali). Forbes, *A Naturalist's Wanderings in the Eastern Archipelago*, p. 320 (people of Timor-laut). von Rosenberg, *op. cit.*p. 166 (Niase).

[3] St. John,*Life in the Forests of the Far East*, ii. 297 (natives of the kingdom of Borneo, formerly). Low, *Sarawak*, p. 133. Marsden,*op. cit.* p. 404 (Achinese of Sumatra). Hickson, *A Naturalist in North Celebes*,p. 198 (Sangirese). Crawfurd, *op. cit.* iii. 107, 115. Crawfurd thinks (*ibid.* iii. 107) that the punishment of mutilation was introduced by Muhammedanism.

[4] Crawfurd,*op.cit.*iii.115(Javanese) Kükenthal, *Ergebnisse einer zoologischen Forschungsreise in den Molukken und Borneo*, i. 188 (Alfura of Halmahera). Marsden, *op. cit.* p.471 (Poggi Islanders). Among the Bataks

(von Brenner, *op. cit.* p. 212) and Achinese of Sumatra (Marsden, *op. cit.* p. 404) robbery is punished with death.
[5] Wilken, *loc. cit.* p. 88 *sqq.* von Rosenberg, *op. cit.* p. 166 ; Modigliani, *op. cit.* p. 496 (Niase).
[6] McNair, *Perak and the Malays*, p. 204.
[7] Boyle, *Adventures among the Dyaks of Borneo*, p. 235. Bock, *Head-Hunters of Borneo*, p. 209. Selenka, *Sonnige Welten*, p. 19. Ling Roth, *Natives of Sarawak*, i. 81, 82, 92.
[8] Low, *op. cit.* p. 336.
[9] Marsden, *op. cit.* p. 389. Junghuhn, *op. cit.* ii. 148.
[10] Martin, *Reisen in den Molukken*, p. 63.
[11] Earl, *Papuans*, pp. 49, 80, 105. Seemann, *Viti*, p. 46 *sq.* ; Anderson, *Travel in Fiji*, p. 130. Hale, *U. S. Exploring Expedition.* Vol. VI. *Ethnography and Philology*, p. 73 (Micronesians). Melville, *Typee*, pp. 294 (Marquesas Islanders), 295 n. 1 (various Polynesians). Williams, *Missionary Enterprises in the South Sea Islands*, p. 530 (Samoans). von Kotzebue, *Voyage of Discovery into the South Sea*, iii. 164 (people of Radack), 255 (Sandwich Islanders). Lisiansky, *op. cit.* p. 125 (Sandwich Islanders). Dieffenbach, *Travels in New Zealand*, ii. 105 ; Meade, *Ride through the disturbed Districts of New Zealand*, p. 162 *sq.* ; Thomson, *Story of New Zealand*, i. 86 ; Colenso, *Maori Races*, p. 43. Bonwick, *Daily Life and Origin of the Tasmanians*, p. 9.
[12] Seemann, *Viti*, p. 47.

an act of meanness rather than a crime,[1] whereas in many other islands it was regarded as a very grave offence.[2] Sometimes the delinquent was subject to private retaliation,[3] sometimes to a fine,[4] or blows,[5] or the loss of a finger,[6] or the penalty of death.[7] Among the natives of Herbert River, Northern Queensland, there is " considerable respect for the right of property, and they do not steal from one another to any great extent. . . . If they hunt they will not take another person's game, all the members of the same tribe having apparently full confidence in each other."[8] When a theft does occur, " the thief is challenged by his victim to a duel with wooden swords and shields ; and the matter is settled sometimes privately, the relatives of both parties serving as witnesses, sometimes publicly at the borboby, where two hundred to three hundred meet from various tribes to decide all their disputes. The victor in the duel wins in the dispute."[9] So also among the Dieyerie tribe, " should any native steal from another, and the offender be known, he is challenged to fight by the person he has robbed, and this settles the matter."[10] Of the Bangerang tribe of Victoria we are told that, amongst themselves, they were scrupulously honest ;[11] and, speaking of West Australian natives, Mr. Chauncy expresses his belief that " the members of a tribe never pilfer from each other."[12] In their relations to Europeans, again, Australian blacks have been sometimes accused of thievishness,[13] sometimes praised for their

---

[1] Mariner, *Natives of the Tonga Islands*, ii. 162. In Ponapé (Christian, *Caroline Islands*, p. 72) and among the Maoris (Meade, *op. cit.* p. 162) thieves are said to be despised.
[2] Earl, *op. cit.* p. 80 (Papuans of Dorey). Ellis, *Tour through Hawaii*, p. 429 ; &c.
[3] Turner, *Samoa*, pp. 278 (natives of Humphrey's Island), 343 (New Caledonians). Lisiansky, *op. cit.* p.80 *sq.* (Nukahivans). Williams, *Missionary Enterprises*, p. 127 (natives of Rarotonga). Ellis, *Polynesian Researches*, iv. 420 (Sandwich Islanders).
[4] Earl, *op. cit.* p. 83 (Papuans of Dorey). Sorge, in Steinmetz, *Rechtsverhältnisse von eingeborenen Völkern in Afrika und Ozeanien*, p. 421 (Nissan Islanders of the Bismarck Archipelago). Williams and Calvert, *Fiji*, p. 22. Turner, *Samoa*, p. 281 (natives of the Mitchell Group).
[5] Cook, *Journal of a Voyage round the World*, p. 42 (Tahitians). Yate,

Account of New Zealand, p. 104.
[6] Williams and Calvert, *Fiji*, p. 23.
[7] Gill, *Life in the Southern Isles*, p. 47. Turner, *Samoa*, pp. 290 (natives of Hudson's Island), 295 (natives of Arorae), 297 (natives of Nikumau of the Gilbert Group), 300 (natives of Francis Island), 337 (Efatese, of the New Hebrides). Tutuila, in *Jour. Polynesian Soc.* i. 268 (Line Islanders). Ellis, *Polynesian Researches*, iv. 421 (Sandwich Islanders). Cook, *Journal of a Voyage round the World*, p. 41 *sq.* (Tahitians).
[8] Lumholtz, *Among Cannibals*, p. 147.
[9] *Ibid.* p. 126.
[10] Gason, in Woods, *Native Tribes of South Australia*, p. 266.
[11] Curr, *Recollections of Squatting in Victoria*, p. 298.
[12] Chauncy, in Brough Smyth, *Aborigines of Victoria*, ii. 278.
[13] *Supra*, ii. 2, n. 1.

honesty.[1] From his own observation Mr. Curr has no doubt that they feel that theft is wrong.[2] Of the aborigines of West Australia we are told that they occasionally speared the sheep and robbed the potato gardens of the early settlers simply because they did not understand the settlers' views regarding property, having themselves no separate property in any living animal except their dogs or in any produce of the soil. But " only entrust a native with property, and he will invariably be faithful to the trust. Lend him your gun to shoot game, and he will bring you the result of his day's sport ; send him a long journey with provisions for your shepherd, and he will certainly deliver them safely. Entrust him with a flock of sheep through a rugged country to a distant run, and he and his wife will take them generally more safely than a white man would." [3]

" The Arab," says Burckhardt, " robs his enemies, his friends, and his neighbours, provided that they are not actually in his own tent, where their property is sacred. To rob in the camp, or among friendly tribes, is not reckoned creditable to a man ; yet no stain remains upon him for such an action, which, in fact, is of daily occurrence. But the Arab chiefly prides himself on robbing his enemies." [4] This, however, seems to hold true only of Bedouin tribes inhabiting rich pasture plains, who are much exposed to attacks from others, whereas in more sheltered territories a person who " attempts to steal in the tents of his own tribe, is for ever dishonoured among his friends." Thus among the Arabs of Sinai robberies are wholly unknown ; any articles of dress or of furniture may be left upon a rock without the least risk of their being taken away.[5] According to Waháby law, a robber is obliged to return the stolen goods or their value, but if the offence is not attended with circumstances of violence he escapes without further punishment, except a fine to the treasury.[6] Among some Bedouins of Ḥadhramaut theft from a tribesman is punished with banishment from the tribe.[7] Lady Anne and Mr. Blunt state that, with regard to honesty, the pure Bedouin stands in marked contrast to his half-bred brethren. Whilst the Kurdish and semi-Kurdish tribes of Upper Mesopotamia make it almost a point of honour to steal, the genuine Arab accounts theft disgraceful, although he holds

[1] Howitt, in Brough Smyth, *op. cit.* ii. 306. Fraser, *Aborigines of New South Wales*, p. 90.
[2] Curr, *The Australian Race*, i. 100.
[3] Chauncy, in Brough Smyth, *op. cit.* ii. 278.
[4] Burckhardt, *Notes on the Be-*douins and Wahábys, p. 90.
[5] *Ibid.* p. 184 *sq.* Wallin, *Första resa från Cairo till Arabiska öknen*, p. 64.
[6] Burckhardt, *op. cit.* p. 301.
[7] von Wrede, *Reise in Hadhramaut*, p. 51.

highway robbery to be a right. In the large tribes persons of known dishonesty are not tolerated.[1]

In Africa honesty between members of the same tribe is no uncommon characteristic of the native races, and some of them have displayed the same quality in their dealings with European travellers.[2] Andersson, for instance, tells us that the Ovambo, so far as they came under his observation, were strictly honest and appeared to entertain great horror of theft. "Without permission," he says, "the natives would not even *touch* anything; and we could leave our camp free from the least apprehension of being plundered. As a proof of their honesty, I may mention, that, when we left the Ovambo country, the servants forgot some trifles; and such was the integrity of the people, that messengers actually came after us a very considerable distance to restore the articles left behind."[3] A few African peoples are said to look upon petty larceny almost with indifference.[4] Among others thieves are only compelled to restore stolen property, or to return an equivalent for it,[5] but at the same time they are disgraced or laughed at.[6] In Africa, as elsewhere, theft is frequently punished with a fine.[7] Thus

[1] Blunt, *Bedouin Tribes of the Euphrates*, ii. 204, 225.
[2] St. John, *Village Life in Egypt*, ii. 198. Tristram, *The Great Sahara*, p. 193 *sq.* (Beni Mzab). Nachtigal, *Sahara und Sudan*, i. 188 (inhabitants of Fezzân). Dyveyrier, *Exploration du Sahara*, p. 385 (Touareg); *cf.* Chavanne, *Die Sahara*, p. 188. Munzinger, *Ostafrikanische Studien*, p. 531 *sq.* (Barea and Kunáma). Scaramucci and Giglioli, 'Notizie sui Danakil,' in *Archivio per l'antropologia e la etnologia* xiv. 25. Baumann, *Durch Massailand zur Nilquelle*, pp. 165 (Masai), 179 (Wafiomi). Thomson, *Through Masai Land*, p. 64 (Wakwafi of the Taveta). Baker, *Ismailia*, p. 56; Petherick, *Travels in Central Africa*, ii. 3 (Shilluk). Macdonald, *Africana*, i. 182 (Eastern Central Africans). Mungo Park, *Travels in the Interior of Africa*, p. 239; Caillié, *Travels through Central Africa to Timbuctoo*, i. 353 (Mandingoes). Ward, *Five Years with the Congo Cannibals*, p. 93; Tuckey, *Expedition to explore the River Zaire*, p. 374. Johnston, *Uganda Protectorate*, ii. 590 (Wanyoro). Kolben, *Present State of the Cape of Good Hope*, i. 326; Hahn, *The Supreme Being of the Khoi-Khoi*, p.

32 (Hottentots); *cf.* Fritsch, *Die Eingeborenen Süd-Afrika's*, p. 307. Tyler, *Forty Years among the Zulus*, p. 191 *sq.*
[3] Andersson, *Lake Ngami*, p. 197. *Cf. Idem, Notes on Travel in South Africa*, p. 236.
[4] Monrad, *Skildring af Guinea-Kysten*, p. 6, n.*; Reade, *Savage Africa*, p. 580 (West African Negroes). Ellis, *History of Madagascar*, i. 144.
[5] Munzinger, *Ostafrikanische Studien*, pp. 389 (inhabitants of Saraë), 494 (Barea and Kunáma). Arbousset and Daumas, *op. cit.* p. 66 (Mantetis). Cunningham, *Uganda*, p. 293 (Baziba). Rautanen, in Steinmetz, *Rechtsverhältnisse*, p. 343 (Ondonga). Warner, in Maclean, *Compendium of Kafir Laws and Customs*, pp. 65, 67. Post, *Afrikanische Jurisprudenz*, ii. 84.
[6] Munzinger, *Ostafrikanische Studien*, pp. 386 (inhabitants of Saraë), 531 (Barea and Kunáma). Arbousset and Daumas, *op. cit.* p. 66 (Mantetis).
[7] Scaramucci and Giglioli, in *Archivio per l'antropologia e la etnologia*, xiv. 39 (Danakil). Nachtigal, *op. cit.* i. 449 (Tedâ). Bosman, *Description of the Coast of Guinea*, p. 142 (Negroes of Axim, on the Gold Coast). Ellis,

among the Bahima,[1] Wadshagga,[2] and Tanala of Madagascar,[3] thieves are made to pay twice the value of the stolen goods ; among the Takue,[4] Rendile,[5] and Herero,[6] three times their value ; among the Bechuanas double or fourfold.[7] Among the Taveta, if a man commits a theft, he has to refund what he has robbed, and five times the value of the stolen property can be claimed by the person who has suffered the loss.[8] Among the Kafirs, " in cases of cattle stealing, the law allows a fine of ten head, though but one may have been stolen, provided the animal has been slaughtered, or cannot be restored." [9] Among the Masai, according to Herr Merker, the fine for stealing cattle is likewise a tenfold one ; [10] whilst, according to another authority, " if a man steals one cow, or more than one cow, all his property is given to the man from whom he has stolen." [11] Among the Basukuma all thieves, it seems, are punished with the confiscation of everything they possess.[12] Other punishments for theft are imprisonment,[13] banishment,[14] slavery,[15] flogging,[16] mutilation,[17] and, especially under aggravating circumstances, death.[18]

Tshi-speaking Peoples of the Gold Coast, p. 303. Idem, Ewe-speaking Peoples of the Slave Coast, p. 225. Emin Pasha in Central Africa, p. 86 (Wanyoro). Cunningham, Uganda, p. 322 (Manyema). Steinmetz, Rechtsverhältnisse, p. 52 (Banaka and Bapuku). Beverley, ibid. p. 215 (Wagogo). Lang, ibid. p. 259 (Washambala). Wandrer, ibid. p. 325 (Hottentots). Post, Afrikanische Jurisprudenz, ii. 85 sq.
[1] Cunningham, Uganda, p. 20.
[2] Volkens, Der Kilimandscharo, p. 250.
[3] Richardson, 'Tanala Customs,' in Antananarivo Annual, ii. 95 sq.
[4] Munzinger, Ostafrikanische Studien, p. 208.
[5] Chanler, Through Jungle and Desert, p. 317.
[6] François, Nama und Damara, p. 174.
[7] Holub, Seven Years in South Africa, i. 395. Casalis, Basutos, p. 228.
[8] Hollis, in Jour. African Soc. i. 123.
[9] Dugmore, in Maclean, Compendium of Kafir Laws and Customs, p. 36. Cf. ibid. pp. 112, 143.
[10] Merker, Die Masai, p. 208.
[11] Hinde, The Last of the Masai, p. 107.

[12] Cunningham, Uganda, p. 304.
[13] Mademba, in Steinmetz, Rechtsverhältnisse, p. 90 (inhabitants of the Sansanding States).
[14] Chavanne, Die Sahara, p. 315 (Beni Mzab).
[15] Bowdich, Mission to Ashantee, p. 258, n.* (Fantis). Petherick, op. cit. ii. 3 (Shilluk of the White Nile). Post, Afrikanische Jurisprudenz, ii. 87.
[16] Reade, Savage Africa, p. 261 (West Equatorial Africans). Ellis, Yoruba-speaking Peoples of the Slave Coast, p. 191. Volkens, op. cit. p. 250 (Wadshagga). Velten, Sitten und Gebräuche der Suaheli, p. 363. Campbell, Travels in South Africa, p. 519. Post, Afrikanische Jurisprudenz, ii. 88.
[17] de Abreu, Discovery and Conquest of the Canary Islands, p. 27 (aborigines of Ferro). Ellis, Yoruba-speaking Peoples, p. 191. Beltrame, Il Fiume Bianco, p. 280 (Dinka). Casati, Ten Years in Equatoria, i. 163 (Mambettu and Wanyoro). Wilson and Felkin, Uganda and the Egyptian Soudan, i. 201 (Waganda). Holub, op. cit. i. 395 sq. (Bechuanas). Post, Afrikanische Jurisprudenz, ii. 87 sq.
[18] Ellis, Yoruba-speaking Peoples, p. 191 ; Burton, Abeokuta, i. 304 (Yoruba). Ellis, Tshi-speaking Peoples, p. 303. Bosman, op. cit. p. 143

In some African countries a thief caught in the act may be killed with impunity.[1]

The condemnation of theft, in one and the same people, varies in degree according to a variety of circumstances. It is influenced by the value of the goods stolen, as appears from the different punishments inflicted in cases where the value differs.[2] Thus, when the penalty consists of a fine, its amount is often strictly proportioned to the loss suffered by the owner, the thief being compelled to pay twice, or three, or four, or five, or ten times the worth of the appropriated article.[3] Among the Aztecs a petty thief became the slave of the person from whom he had stolen, whilst theft of a large amount was almost invariably punished with death.[4] According to the Koran, theft is to be punished by cutting off the offender's right hand for the first offence ; but a Sunneh law ordains that this punishment shall not be inflicted if the value of the stolen property is less than a quarter of a deenár.[5] Ancient Scotch law proportioned the punishment of theft to the value of the goods stolen, heightening it gradually from a slight corporal to a capital punishment, if the value

(Negroes of Axim). Cunningham, *Uganda*, pp. 69 (Banabuddu), 102 (Bakoki), 346 (Karamojo). François, *op. cit.* p. 175 (Herero). Andersson, *Lake Ngami*, p. 197 (Ovambo). Casalis, *op. cit.* p. 228 (Basutos). Shooter, *Kafirs of Natal*, p. 155. Tyler, *op. cit.* p. 192 (Zulus). Kolben, *op. cit.* i. 158 (Hottentots). Post, *Afrikanische Jurisprudenz*, ii. 88 *sq.*
[1] Hübbe-Schleiden, *Ethiopien*, p. 143 (Mpongwe). Cunningham, *Uganda*, p. 333 (Lendu). Burton, *Zanzibar*, ii. 94 (Wanika). Macdonald, *Africana*, i. 162, 183 (Eastern Central Africans). Macdonald, 'East Central African Customs,' in *Jour. Anthr. Inst.* xxii. 109. *Supra*, i. 289.
[2] Steinmetz, *Rechtsverhältnisse*, p. 52 (Banaka and Bapuku). Nicole, *ibid.* p. 133 (Diakité-Sarracolese): Beverley, *ibid.* p. 215 (Wagogo). Bosman, *op. cit.* p. 142 (Negroes of Axim). Hinde, *op. cit.* p. 107 (Masai). Post, *Afrikanische Juris-*

prudenz, ii. 91. *Idem, Grundriss der ethnologischen Jurisprudenz*, ii. 420. *Ta Tsing Leu Lee*, sec. cclxix. *sqq.* p. 284 *sqq.* (Chinese). Keil, *Manual of Biblical Archæology*, ii. 366. *Laws of Manu*, viii. 320 *sqq.* Wilda, *Das Strafrecht der Germanen*, p. 870 *sqq.* ; Nordström, *Bidrag till den svenska samhälls-författningens historia*, ii. 296 *sqq.*; Stemann, *Den danske Retshistorie indtil Christian V.'s Lov*, pp. 621, 677 *sq.* ; Brunner, *Deutsche Rechtsgeschichte*, ii. 639 *sqq.* (ancient Teutons). Du Boys, *Histoire du droit criminel de l'Espagne*, p. 721.
[3] *Supra*, ii. 4, 6-8, 12.
[4] Bancroft, *Native Races of the Pacific States*, ii. 456.
[5] *Koran*, v. 42. Lane, *Manners and Customs of the Modern Egyptians*, p. 120 *sq.* *Idem, Arabian Society in the Middle Ages*, p.20. Sachau, *Muhammedanisches Recht*, pp. 810, 811, 825 *sqq.*

amounted to thirty-two pennies Scots, which in the reign of David I. was the price of two sheep.[1] In England a distinction was made between " grand " and " petty larceny," the line between them being drawn at twelve pence, and grand larceny was capital at least as early as the time of Edward I.[2] Among various peoples custom or law punishes with particular severity the stealing of objects of a certain kind, such as cattle, horses, agricultural implements, corn, precious metals, or arms.[3] The Negroes of Axim, says Bosman, " will rather put a man to death for stealing a sheep, than killing a man."[4] The Kalmucks regard horse-stealing as the greatest of all crimes.[5] The ancient Teutons held cattle-lifting and robbery of crops to be particularly disgraceful.[6] According to Roman law, people who stole an ox or horse from the pastures or from a stable, or ten sheep, or four or five swine, might be punished even with death.[7] The natives of Danger Island, in the South Seas, punished with drowning anyone who was caught stealing food, " the most valuable property they knew of."[8] In Tahiti, on the other hand, those who stole clothes or arms were commonly put to death, whereas those who stole provisions were bastinadoed.[9] Among other peoples the appropriation of a small quantity of food belonging to somebody else is not punished at all.[10] The Masai do not punish a person for stealing milk or meat.[11] Among the Bakoki " it was not a crime to steal bananas."[12] In ancient Mexico " every poor traveller was permitted to

[1] Erskine, *Principles of the Law of Scotland*, p. 568. Innes, *Scotland in the Middle Ages*, p. 190. Mackintosh, *History of Civilisation in Scotland*, i. 231.
[2] Pollock and Maitland, *History of English Law before the Time of Edward I.* ii. 495 *sq.* Brunner, *Deutsche Rechtsgeschichte*, ii. 640. Stephen, *History of the Criminal Law of England*, iii. 129.
[3] Post, *Grundriss der ethnologischen Jurisprudenz*, ii. 421 *sqq.*
[4] Bosman, *op. cit.* p. 143.
[5] Bergmann, *Nomadische Streifereien unter den Kalmüken*, ii. 297.

[6] Grimm, *Deutsche Rechtsalterthümer*, p. 636 *sq.* Wilda, *op. cit.* p. 875 *sq.* Nordström, *op.cit.* ii.307. Brunner, *Deutsche Rechtsgeschichte*, ii. 645 *sq.*
[7] *Digesta*, xlvii. 14. 1. pr., 1, 3 ; xlvii. 14. 3.
[8] Gill, *Life in the Southern Isles*, p. 47.
[9] Cook, *Journal of a Voyage round the World*, p. 41 *sq.*
[10] *Supra*, i. 286 *sq.* Post, *Grundriss der ethnol. Jurisprudenz*, ii. 426. Ellis, *History of Madagascar*, i. 385.
[11] Hollis, *Masai*, p. 310.
[12] Cunningham, *Uganda*, p. 102 *sq.*

take of the maize, or the fruit-bearing trees, which were
planted by the side of the highway, as much as was
sufficient to satisfy immediate hunger."[1] Among the
Hebrews a person was allowed to go into his neighbour's
vineyard and eat grapes at his own pleasure, or to pluck
ears in his field, but the visitor was forbidden to put any
grapes in his vessel or to move a sickle into the standing
corn.[2] It is said in the Laws of Manu that " a twice-born
man, who is travelling and whose provisions are exhausted,
shall not be fined, if he takes two stalks of sugar-cane or
two esculent roots from the field of another man."[3]
According to ancient Swedish laws, a passer-by could take
a handful of peas, beans, turnips, and so forth, from
another person's field, and a traveller could give to his
fatigued horse some hay from any barn he found in the
wood.[4] However, whilst the punishment of theft is
commonly, to some extent, influenced by the worth or
nature of the appropriated property, there are peoples who
punish thieves with the same severity whether they have
stolen little or much. Among the North American
Indians described by Colonel Dodge " the value of the
article stolen is not considered. The crime is the theft." [5]
Among the Yleou, a Manchurian tribe mentioned by
ancient Chinese chroniclers, theft of any kind was punished
with death.[6] The Beni Mzab in the Sahara sentence a
thief to two years' banishment and the payment of fifty
francs, independently of the value of the thing he has
stolen.[7]

The degree of criminality attached to theft also depends
on the place where it is committed. To steal from a house,
especially after breaking the door, is frequently regarded
as an aggravated form of theft.[8] According to Muham-

---

[1] Clavigero, *History of Mexico*, i.
358.
[2] *Deuteronomy*, xxiii. 24 *sq.*
[3] *Laws of Manu*, viii. 341. *Cf.*
ibid. viii. 339.
[4] Nordström, *op. cit.* ii. 297.
[5] Dodge, *op. cit.* p. 64.
[6] Castrén, *op. cit.* iv. 27.

[7] Chavanne, *Die Sahara*, p. 315.
[8] Post, *Grundriss der ethnol. Juris-
prudenz*, ii. 423 *sq.* von Rosenberg,
Der malayische Archipel, p. 166
(Niase). Riedel, *De sluik- en kroes-
harige rassen tusschen Selebes en
Papua*, p. 103 (Serangese). Lang, in
Steinmetz, *Rechtsverhältnisse*, p. 259

medan law, the punishment of cutting off the right hand
of the thief is inflicted on him only if the stolen property
was deposited in a place to which he had not ordinary or
easy access ; hence a man who steals in the house of a near
relative is not subject to this punishment, nor a slave who
robs the house of his master.[1] Among some peoples a
theft committed by night is punished more heavily than
one committed by day.[2]

A distinction is further made between ordinary theft and
robbery. The robber is treated sometimes more severely,[3]
sometimes more leniently than the thief, and is not infrequently regarded with admiration. Among the Wanyamwezi thieves are despised, but robbers are honoured,
especially by the women, on account of their courage.[4] In
Uganda robbery is not thought shameful, although it is
rigorously punished.[5] In Sindh no disgrace is attached to
larceny when the perpetrators are armed.[6] Among the
Ossetes, " where open robbery has been committed outside
a village, the court merely requires the stolen article or an
equivalent to be restored ; but in cases of secret theft, five
times the value must be paid. Robbery and theft within
the boundaries of a village are rated much higher. A
proverb says, ' What a man finds on the high-road is God's
gift ' ; and in fact highway robbery is hardly regarded as a
crime." [7] The Kazak Kirghiz go so far as to consider it
almost dishonourable for a man never to have taken part
in a *baranta*, or cattle-lifting exploit.[8] According to

(Washambala). Wilda, *op. cit.* p.
878 *sq.*; Brunner, *Deutsche Rechtsgeschichte*, ii. 646 (ancient Teutonic
law). *Digesta*, xlvii. 11. 7 ; xlvii. 18.2.
[1] Lane, *Modern Egyptians*, p. 121.
Cf. Burckhardt, *Bedouins and
Wahábys*, p. 301.
[2] Wilken, *loc. cit.* p. 109 (people of
Bali). *Digesta*, xlvii. 17. 1. *Lex
Saxonum*, 32, 34 ; Wilda, *op. cit.* p.
877 ; Grimm, *Deutsche Rechtsalterthümer*, p. 637 ; Brunner, *Deutsche
Rechtsgeschichte*, ii. 646 (ancient Teutonic law).
[3] *Ta Tsing Leu Lee*, sec. cclxviii.

p. 283 (Chinese law). *Digesta*, xlviii.
19. 28. 10. Erskine, *Principles of the
Law of Scotland*, p. 566.   Post,
*Grundriss der ethnologischen Juris-
prudenz*, ii. 455 *sq.*
[4] Reichardt, quoted by Steinmetz,
Rechtsverhältnisse, p. 281.
[5] Ashe, *Two Kings of Uganda*, p.
294.
[6] Burton, *Sindh*, p. 195.
[7] von Haxthausen, *Transcaucasia*,
p. 411. *Cf.* Kovalewsky, *Coutume
contemporaine*, p. 342.
[8] Vámbéry, *Das Türkenvolk*, p.306.
Cf. Georgi, *op.cit.*ii.270 *sq.* (Kirghiz).

Bedouin notions, there is a clear distinction between " taking and stealing." To steal is to abstract clandestinely, " whereas to take, in the sense of depriving another of his property, generally implies to take from him openly, by right of superior force.".[1] The Arabian robber, says Burckhardt, considers his profession honourable, and " the term *haràmy* (robber) is one of the most flattering titles that could be conferred on a youthful hero." [2] In ancient Teutonic law theft and robbery were kept apart ; the one was the secret, the other the open crime. In most lawbooks robbery was subject to a milder punishment than theft, and was undoubtedly regarded as far less dishonourable. Indeed, however illegal the mode of acquiring property may have been, publicity was looked upon as a palliation of the offence, if not as a species of justification, even though the injured party was a fellow-countryman.[3] This difference between theft and robbery seems still to have been felt in the thirteenth century, when Bracton had to argue that the robber is a thief.[4] But in later times robbery was regarded by the law of England as an aggravated kind of theft.[5]

A line has been drawn between manifest and non-manifest theft. Among many peoples thieves who are caught in the act may be killed with impunity,[6] or are punished much more heavily than other thieves, frequently with death.[7] We also hear that the worst part of the offence

[1] Ayrton, in Wallin, *Notes taken during a Journey through Part of Northern Arabia*, p. 29, n.‡ (in *Jour. Roy. Geo. Soc.* xx. 317, n.‡).

[2] Burckhardt,*Bedouins and Wahdbys*, p. 90. *Cf.* Burton, *Pilgrimage to Al-Madinah & Meccah*, ii. 101 ; Blunt, *op. cit.* ii. 204 *sq.*

[3] Wilda, *op. cit.* pp. 860, 911, 914. Grimm, *Deutsche Rechtsalterthümer*, p. 634 *sq.* Nordström, *op. cit.* ii. 314 *sq.* Maurer, *Bekehrung des Norwegischen Stammes*, ii. 173 *sq.* Brunner, *Deutsche Rechtsgeschichte*, ii. 647 *sq.* Thrupp, *The Anglo-Saxon Home*, p. 288. Pollock and Maitland, *op. cit.* ii. 493 *sq.*

[4] Bracton, *De Legibus et Consue-* *tudinibus Angliæ*, fol. 150 b, vol. ii. 508 *sqq.* Pollock and Maitland, *op. cit.* ii. 494.

[5] Coke, *Third Part of the Institutes of the Laws of England*, p. 68. Blackstone, *Commentaries on the Laws of England*, iv. 252. Stephen, *History of the Criminal Law of England*, iii. 149. Pollock and Maitland, *op. cit.* ii. 493. *Cf.* Wilda, *op. cit.* p. 914.

[6] *Supra*, i. 293 ; ii. 8, 13. Brunner, *Deutsche Rechtsgeschichte*, ii. 642. Post, *Grundriss der ethnologischen Jurisprudenz*, ii. 441 *sq.*

[7] Mommsen, *Römisches Strafrecht*, p. 750 *sq.* Du Boys, *Histoire du droit criminel de l'Espagne*, p. 378. Brunner, *Deutsche Rechtsgeschichte*, ii.

consists in being detected, and that a successful thief is admired rather than disapproved of.

It is said of the Navahos that "the time is evidently not long gone by when with them, as among the Spartans, adroit theft was deemed honourable."[1] Among the Californian Yuki "thieving is a virtue . . . , provided the thief is sly enough not to get caught."[2] The Ahts "have a tendency to sympathise with some forms of theft, in which dexterity is required."[3] Among the Thlinkets "theft does not seem to be considered a disgrace ; the detected thief is at most ashamed of his want of skill."[4] The Chukchi "have but a bad opinion of a young girl who has never acquitted herself cleverly in some theft ; and without such testimony of her dexterity and address she will scarcely find a husband."[5] In Mongolia "known thieves are treated as respectable members of society. As long as they manage well and are successful, little or no odium seems to attach to them ; and it is no uncommon thing to hear them spoken of in terms of high praise. Success seems to be regarded as a kind of palliation of their crimes."[6] Among the Kukis, according to early notices, the accomplishment most esteemed was dexterity in thieving, whilst the most contemptible person was a thief caught in the act.[7] The Persians say that "it is no shame to steal, only to be found out."[8] The same view seems to be held by the Motu tribe of New Guinea,[9] the natives of Tana (New Hebrides),[10] the Maoris,[11] and several African peoples.[12] In Fiji "success, without discovery, is deemed quite enough to make thieving virtuous, and a participation in the ill-gotten gain honourable."[13] Among the Matabele

642 sq. ; Dareste, *Études d'histoire du droit*, p. 299 sq. Pollock and Maitland, *op. cit.* ii.' 495 (ancient Teutonic law). Post, *Grundriss der ethnologischen Jurisprudenz*, ii. 443.

[1] Matthews, ' Study of Ethics among the Lower Races,' in *Journal of American Folk-Lore*, xii. 4.

[2] Powers, *Tribes of California*, p. 133.

[3] Sproat, *op. cit.* p. 158 sq.

[4] Krause, *op. cit.* p. 167.

[5] Georgi, *op. cit.* iii. 183. Krasheninnikoff, *History of Kamschatka*, p. 232.

[6] Gilmour, *Among the Mongols*, p. 291.

[7] Dalton, *Descriptive Ethnology of Bengal*, p. 45.

[8] Polak, *Persien*, ii. 81.

[9] Stone, *A few Months in New Guinea*, p. 95.

[10] Brenchley, *op. cit.* p. 208.

[11] Shortland, *Traditions and Superstitions of the New Zealanders*, p. 224. Waitz-Gerland, *Anthropologie der Naturvölker*, vi. 224. Dieffenbach *Travels in New Zealand*, ii. 111.

[12] Zöller, *Forschungsreisen in der deutschen Colonie Kamerun*, ii. 64 (Dualla). Wilson and Felkin, *op. cit.* i. 224 (Waganda). Leslie, *op. cit.* p. 256 (Amatongas).

[13] Williams and Calvert, *op. cit.* p. 110.

" the thief is not despised because he has stolen, but because he has allowed himself to be caught, and if his crime remains undetected he is admired by all."[1]   Among the aborigines of Palma, in the Canary Islands, " he was esteemed the cleverest fellow who could steal with such address as not to be discovered."[2]

The moral valuation of theft varies according to the social position of the thief and of the person robbed. Among the Marea a nobleman who commits theft is only obliged to restore the appropriated article ; but if a commoner steals from another commoner, the whole of his property may be confiscated by the latter's master, and if he steals from a nobleman he becomes the nobleman's serf.[3] Among the Káfirs of the Hindu-Kush the penalty for theft is theoretically a fine of seven or eight times the value of the thing stolen ; " but such a punishment in ordinary cases would only be inflicted on a man of inferior mark, unless it were accompanied by circumstances which aggravated the original offence."[4]   In Rome, according to an old law, a freeman caught in the act of thieving was scourged and delivered over to the party aggrieved, whereas a slave in similar circumstances was scourged and then hurled from the Tarpeian rock ;[5] and according to an enactment of Hadrian, the punishment for stealing an ox or horse from the pastures or from a stable was only relegation if the offender was a person of rank, though ordinary persons might have to suffer death for the same offence.[6]   In ancient India, on the other hand, the punishment increased with the rank of the criminal. According to the Laws of Manu, " in a case of theft the guilt of a Sûdra shall be eightfold, that of a Vaisya sixteen-fold, that of a Kshatriya two-and-thirtyfold, that of a Brâhmana sixty-fourfold, or quite a hundredfold, or even twice four-and-sixtyfold ; each of them knowing the nature

[1] Decle, *Three Years in Savage Africa*, p. 165.
[2] de Abreu, *op. cit.* p. 138.
[3] Munzinger, *Ostafrikanische Studien*, p. 243 *sq.*

[4] Scott Robertson, *Káfirs of the Hindu-Kush*, p. 440.
[5] Mommsen, *Römisches Strafrecht*, p. 751.
[6] *Digesta*, xlvii. 14. 1. pr., 3.

of the offence." [1] In other cases, again, the degree of guilt is determined by the station of the person robbed.[2] Among the Gaika tribe of the Kafirs, for instance, the fine by which a theft is punished " is fixed according to the rank of the person against whom the offence is committed, confiscation of property being the general punishment imposed for offences against chiefs." [3] Among many other peoples theft or robbery committed on the property of a chief or king is treated with exceptional severity.[4] Sometimes difference in religion affects the criminality of the thief. According to modern Buddhism, " to take that which belongs to a sceptic is an inferior crime, and the guilt rises in magnitude in proportion to the merit of the individual upon whom the theft is perpetrated. To take that which belongs to the associated priesthood, or to a supreme Buddha, is the highest crime." [5] But the commonest and most important personal distinction influencing the moral valuation of theft and robbery is that between a tribesman or fellow-countryman and a stranger.

Among uncivilised races intra-tribal theft is carefully distinguished from extra-tribal theft. Whilst the former is forbidden, the latter is commonly allowed, and robbery committed on a stranger is an object of praise.[6]

The Tehuelches of Patagonia, " although honest enough as regards each other, will, nevertheless, not scruple to steal from any one not belonging to their party." [7] The Abipones, who never took anything from their own countrymen, " used to rob and murder the Spaniards whilst they thought them their enemies." [8] Among the Mbayás the law, Thou shalt not steal, " applies only to tribesmen and

[1] Laws of Manu, viii. 337 sq.
[2] Crawfurd, op. cit. iii. 115 (Javanese). Desoignies, in Steinmetz, Rechtsverhältnisse, p. 281 (Msalala). Maclean, Compendium of Kafir Laws and Customs, p. 143.
[3] Brownlee, in Maclean, op. cit. p. 112.
[4] Ellis, Tour through Hawaii, p. 429 sq. Ellis, Ewe-speaking Peoples of the Slave Coast, p. 225 (Dahomans). Decle, Three Years in Savage Africa, p. 73. Post, Afrikanische Jurisprudenz, ii. 91. Laws of Æthelbirht, 4, 9 (Anglo-Saxons).
[5] Hardy, Manual of Budhism, p. 483.
[6] Cf. Tylor, 'Primitive Society,' in Contemporary Review, xxi. 715 sq.; Anthropology, p. 413 sq.
[7] Musters, op. cit. p. 195.
[8] Dobrizhoffer, op. cit. ii. 148.

allies, not to strangers and enemies."[1]   The high standard of
honesty which prevailed among the North American Indians
did not refer to foreigners, especially white men, whom they
thought it no shame to rob or cheat.[2]   " A theft from an
individual of another band," says Colonel Dodge, " is no crime.
A theft from one of the same band is the greatest of all crimes."[3]
Among the Californian Indians, for instance, who are proverbially honest in their own neighbourhood, " a stranger in the gates
who seems to be friendless may lose the very blankets off him in
the night."[4]   Among the Ahts thieving " is a common vice
where the property of other tribes, or white men, is concerned."[5]
Of the Dacotahs we read that, though the men think it undignified for them to steal even from white people, " they send
their wives thus unlawfully to procure what they want."[6]   Of
the Greenlanders the old missionary Egede writes :—" If they
can lay hands upon any thing belonging to us foreigners, they
make no great scruple of conscience about it.   But, as we now
have lived some time in the country amongst them, and are
look'd upon as true inhabitants of the land, they at last have for-
borne to molest us any more that way."[7]   Another early
authority states, " If they can purloin or even forcibly seize the
property of a foreigner, it is a feather in their cap " ;[8] and,
according to Dr. Nansen, it is still held by the Greenlanders
" to be far less objectionable to rob Europeans than their own
fellow-countrymen."[9]   Many travellers have complained of the
pilfering tendencies of Eskimo tribes with whom they have
come into contact.[10]   Richardson believes that, in the opinion of
an Eskimo, " to steal boldly and adroitly from a stranger is an
act of heroism."[11]   Of the Eskimo about Behring Strait Mr.
Nelson writes :—" Stealing from people of the same village or
tribe is regarded as wrong. . . . To steal from a stranger or
from people of another tribe is not considered wrong so long as
it does not bring trouble on the community."[12]

[1] Tylor, in *Contemporary Review*, xxi. 716.
[2] *Ibid.* p. 716.
[3] Dodge, *op. cit.* p. 79.
[4] Powers, *Tribes of California*, p. 410 *sq.*
[5] Sproat, *op. cit.* p. 159.   *Cf.* Macfie, *Vancouver Island and British Columbia*, p. 468.
[6] Eastman, *Dacotah*, p. xvii.
[7] Egede, *op. cit.* p. 124 *sq.*
[8] Cranz, *op. cit.* i. 175.   See also Dalager, *op. cit.* p. 69.
[9] Nansen, *First Crossing of Green-*land, ii. 335 *sq.*   *Cf. Idem, Eskimo Life*, p. 159 *sq.*
[10] Murdoch, ' Ethnological Results of the Point Barrow Expedition,' in *Ann. Rep. Bur. Ethn.* ix. 41.   See-mann, *Voyage of "Herald,"* ii. 65 ; Armstrong, *Discovery of the North-West Passage*, p. 196 (Western Es-kimo).
[11] Richardson, *Arctic Searching Expedition*, i. 352.
[12] Nelson, in *Ann. Rep. Bur. Ethn.* xviii. 293.

The Chukchi [1] and Koriaks [2] consider theft reputable or glorious if committed on a stranger, though criminal if committed in their own communities. The hill people of the Central Provinces of India, whilst observant of the rights of property among themselves, do not scruple to plunder those to whom they are under no obligation of fidelity.[3] The Bataks of Sumatra, who hardly ever steal among themselves, are expert at pilfering from strangers when not restrained by the laws of hospitality, and think it no moral offence to do so.[4] Other tribes in the Malay Archipelago likewise hold it allowable to plunder the same stranger or traveller who, when forlorn and destitute, would find a hospitable reception among them.[5] " The strict honesty," says Mr. Melville, " which the inhabitants of nearly all the Polynesian Islands manifest towards each other is in striking contrast with the thieving propensities some of them evince in their intercourse with foreigners. It would almost seem that, according to their peculiar code of morals, the pilfering of a hatchet or a wrought nail from a European is looked upon as a praiseworthy action. Or rather, it may be presumed, that, bearing in mind the wholesale forays made upon them by their nautical visitors, they consider the property of the latter as a fair object of reprisal."[6] In Fiji theft is regarded as no offence at all when practised on a foreigner.[7] The Savage Islanders consider theft from a tribesman a vice, but theft from a member of another tribe a virtue.[8] Of the Sandwich Islanders, again, we are told that they stole from rich strangers on board well loaded ships, whereas Europeans settled among them left their doors and shops unlocked without apprehension.[9] Speaking of the honesty of the Herbert River natives, Northern Queensland, Mr. Lumholtz adds :—" It is, of course, solely among members of the same tribe that there is so great a difference between mine and thine ; strange tribes look upon each other as wild beasts." [10] The aborigines of West Australia " would not consider the act of pillaging base when practised on another people, or carried on beyond the limits of their own tribe." [11]

Among the For tribe of Central Africa " it is not considered

[1] Georgi, op. cit. iii. 183.
[2] Ibid. iii. 170.   Krasheninnikoff, op. cit. p. 232.
[3] Hislop, op. cit. p. 1.
[4] Marsden, op. cit. p. 389.
[5] Crawfurd, op. cit. i. 72.
[6] Melville, Typee, p. 295, n. 1. See also Williams, Missionary Enterprises, p. 530 (Samoans) ; Hale, op.

cit. p. 73 (Micronesians).
[7] Williams and Calvert, op. cit. p. 110.
[8] Thomson, Savage Island, p. 94.
[9] von Kotzebue, op. cit. iii. 255.
[10] Lumholtz, Among Cannibals, p. 148.
[11] Chauncy, in Brough Smyth, op. cit. ii. 278 sq.

right to rob strangers, but the chiefs wink at this offence, and the stranger runs but a poor chance of obtaining justice."[1] Of the Mandingoes Caillié observes that, while they do not steal from each other, "their probity with respect to others is very equivocal and in particular towards strangers, who would be very imprudent to shew them any thing that might tempt their cupidity."[2] When an Eastern Central African is plundered by a companion, he may be heard exclaiming, "If you had stolen from a white man, then I could have understood it, but to steal from a black man——."[3] Among the Masai the warriors and old men have a profound contempt for a thief, but "cattle-raiding from neighbouring tribes they do not consider stealing."[4] The Wafiomi[5] and Shilluk[6] regard theft or robbery committed on a stranger as a praiseworthy action, though they never or rarely practise it on members of their own people. The Barea and Kunáma[7] and the inhabitants of Saraë[8] consider it honourable for a man to rob an enemy of his tribe. The Kabyles of Djurdjura, who demand strict mutual honesty from members of the same village, see nothing wrong in stealing from a stranger.[9] Among the Bedouins "travellers passing without proper escort from or introduction to the tribes, may expect to lose their beasts, goods, clothes, and all they possess. There is no kind of shame attached to such acts of rapine. . . . By desert law, the act of passing through the desert entails forfeiture of goods to whoever can seize them."[10] Indeed, the Arab is proud of robbing his enemies, and of bringing away by stealth what he could not have taken by open force.[11] The Ossetes "distinguent . . . le vol commis au préjudice d'une personne étrangère à la famille, et le vol commis au préjudice d'un parent. Le premier, à proprement parler, n'est pas un acte criminel ; le second, au contraire, est tenu pour un délit."[12]

Similar views prevailed among the ancient Teutons. "Robberies," says Caesar, "which are committed beyond

[1] Felkin, 'Notes on the For Tribe of Central Africa,' in *Proceed. Roy. Soc. Edinburgh*, xiii. 234.

[2] Caillié, *op. cit.* i. 353. *Cf.* Mungo Park, *op. cit.* p. 239 *sq.*

[3] Macdonald, *Africana*, i. 182.

[4] Hinde, *op. cit.* p. 104. *Cf.* Johnston, *Kilima-njaro Expedition*, p. 419.

[5] Baumann, *Durch Massailand*, p. 179.

[6] Petherick, *Travels in Central Africa*, ii. 3. Beltrame, *Il Fiume Bianco*, p. 83.

[7] Munzinger, *Ostafrikanische Studien*, p. 531.

[8] *Ibid.* p. 386.

[9] Kobelt, *Reiseerinnerungen aus Algerien und Tunis*, p. 223.

[10] Blunt, *op. cit.* ii. 204 *sq.*

[11] Burckhardt, *Bedouins and Wahábys*, p. 90.

[12] Kovalewsky, *Coutume contemporaine*, p. 343.

the boundaries of each state bear no infamy, and they avow that these are committed for the purpose of disciplining their youth and of preventing sloth." [1] The same was the case with the Highlanders of Scotland until they were brought into subjection after the rebellion of 1745.[2] " Regarding every Lowlander as an alien, and his cattle as fair spoil of war," says Major-General Stewart, " they considered no law for his protection as binding. . . . Yet, except against the Lowlanders or a hostile clan, these freebooters maintained, in general, the strictest honesty towards one another, and inspired confidence in their integrity. . . . In the interior of their own society all property was safe, without the usual security of bolts, bars, and locks." [3] In the Commentary to the Irish Senchus Mór it is stated that, whilst an ordinary thief loses his full honour-price at once, committing theft in another territory deprives a person of only half his honour-price, until it is committed the third time.[4] Throughout the Middle Ages all Europe seems to have tacitly agreed that foreigners were created for the purpose of being robbed.[5] In the thirteenth century there were still several places in France in which a stranger who fixed his residence for a year and a day became the serf of the lord of the manor.[6] In England, till upwards of two centuries after the Conquest, foreign merchants were considered only as sojourners coming to a fair or market, and were obliged to employ their landlords as brokers to buy and sell their commodities ; and one stranger was often arrested for the debt, or punished for the misdemeanour, of another.[7] In a later age the old habit of oppression was still so strong that, when the State suddenly wanted a sum of money, it seemed quite natural that foreigners should be called upon to

[1] Caesar, *De bello Gallico*, vi. 23.

[2] Tylor, in *Contemporary Review*, xxi. 716.

[3] Stewart, *Sketches of the Character, &c., of the Highlanders of Scotland*, p. 42 *sq.*

[4] *Ancient Laws of Ireland*, i. 57.

[5] *Cf.* Marshall, *International Vanities*, p. 285.

[6] Beaumanoir, *Les coutumes du Beauvoisis*, xlv. 19, vol. ii. p. 226.

[7] Chitty, *Treatise on the Laws of Commerce and Manufactures*, i. 131. *Cf.* Cibrario, *Della economia politica del medio eve*, i. 192.

provide a part of it.[1] The custom of seizing the goods of
persons who had been shipwrecked, and of confiscating
them as the property of the lord on whose manor they
were thrown, seems to have been universal ; [2] and in some
European countries the laws even permitted the inhabitants of maritime provinces to reduce to servitude people
who were shipwrecked on their coast.[3] The sea laws of
Oléron, which probably date from the twelfth century, tell
us that in many places shipwrecked sailors meet with
people more inhuman, barbarous, and cruel than mad
dogs, who slaughter those unhappy mariners in order to
obtain possession of their money, clothes, and other
property.[4] In the latter part of the Middle Ages attempts
were incessantly made by sovereigns and councils to
abolish this ancient right, so far as Christian sailors
were concerned,[5] whereas the robbing of shipwrecked
infidels was not prohibited.[6] But for a long time these
endeavours were far from being successful ; [7] and it was
even argued that, as shipwrecks were punishments sent by
God, it was impious to be merciful to the victims.[8]

The readiness with which wars are waged, and the
destruction of property held legitimate in warfare, are
other instances of the little regard felt for the proprietary
rights of foreigners. Grotius maintained that " such ravage
is tolerable as in a short time reduces the enemy to seek
peace " ; [9] and in the practice of his time devastation was

[1] See Marshall, *International Vanities*, p. 291 *sq.*
[2] Du Cange, *Glossarium ad scriptores mediæ et infimæ Latinitatis*, iv.
22 *sq.* Robertson, *History of the
Reign of Charles V.* i. 395.
[3] Du Cange, *op. cit.* iv. 23 *sq.*
Cleffelius, *Antiquitates Germanorum
potissimum septentrionalium*, x. 4, p.
362. Dreyer, *Specimen juris publici
Lubecensis*, p. cxcii. Potgiesser,
*Commentarii juris Germanici de
statu servorum*, i. 1. 17, p. 18 *sq.*
[4] *Ancient Sea-Laws of Oleron*, art.
30, p. 11.
[5] Du Cange, *op. cit.* iv. 24 *sqq.*
Pardessus, *Collection de lois mari-

times*, ii. p. cxv. *sqq.* ; iii. p. clxxix.
von Eicken, *Geschichte und System
der mittelalterlichen Weltanschauung*,
p. 569 *sqq. Constitutiones Neapolitanæ sive Siculæ*, i. 28. *Concilium
Romanum IV.* A.D. 1078 (Labbe-
Mansi, *Sacrorum Conciliorum collectio*, xx. 505 *sq.*).
[6] Laurent, *Études sur l'histoire de
l'humanité*, vii. 323, 413 n. 3. von
Eicken, *op. cit.* p. 570.
[7] Pardessus, *op. cit.* ii. p. cxv. Laurent, *op. cit.* vii. 314. Marshall,
International Vanities, pp. 287, 295.
[8] von Eicken, *op. cit.* p. 570 *sq.*
[9] Grotius, *De jure belli et pacis*, iii.
12. 1. 3.

constantly used independently of any immediate military advantage accruing from it.[1] In the eighteenth century the alliance of devastation with strategical objects became more close, but it was still regarded as an independent means of attack by Wolff,[2] Vattel,[3] and others ; [4] and even at the beginning of the nineteenth century instances of devastation of a not necessary kind occasionally occurred.[5] In later days opinion has decisively laid down that the measure of permissible devastation is to be found in the strict necessities of war.[6] Yet there is an exception to this rule: during the siege of a fortified town custom still permits the houses of the town itself to be bombarded, with a view to inducing the commandant to surrender on account of the misery suffered by the inhabitants.[7] Under the old customs of war a belligerent possessed a right to seize and appropriate all property belonging to a hostile state or its subjects, of whatever kind it might be and in any place where acts of war were permissible.[8] Subsequently this extreme right has been tempered by usage, and in a few directions it has disappeared.[9] Thus the principle proclaimed, but not always acted on, by the Revolutionary Government of France, that private property should be respected on a hostile as on a friendly soil,[10] is favoured by present opinion and usage,[11] and pillage by the soldiers of an invading army is expressly forbidden.[12] At the same time there is unfortunately no

[1] Hall, *Treatise on International Law*, p. 533.

[2] Wolff, *Jus Gentium*, §823, p. 300.

[3] Vattel, *Le droit des gens*, iii. 9. 167, vol. ii. 76 *sq.*

[4] Hall, *op. cit.* p. 533 *sq.*

[5] *Ibid.* p. 534 *sq.*

[6] *Ibid.* p. 535. Bluntschli, *Le droit international*, §663, p. 385. Heffter, *Das europäische Völkerrecht*, §125, p. 262. Wheaton, *Elements of International Law*, p. 473. *Conférence de Bruxelles*, art. 13, *g*. *Conférence internationale de la paix*, *La Haye* 1899, ' Règlement concernant les lois et coutumes de la guerre sur terre,' art. 23 *g*, pt. i. 245.

[7] Hall, *op. cit.* p. 536 *sq.*

[8] Grotius, *op. cit.* iii. 6. 2. Hall, *op. cit.* pp. 417, 438.

[9] Hall, *op. cit.* p. 419 *sqq.*

[10] Bernard, ' Growth of Laws and Usages of War,' in *Oxford Essays*, 1856, p. 109.

[11] *Conférence de Bruxelles*, art. 38. *Instructions for the Government of Armies of the United States in the Field*, art. 37. *Conférence de La Haye*, ' Règlement concernant la guerre sur terre,' art. 46, pt. i. 248. Hall, *op. cit.* p. 441. Geffken, in Heffter, *op. cit.* §140, p. 297, n. 5.

[12] *Conférence de Bruxelles*, art. 39. *Instructions of the United States*, art. 44. *Conférence de La Haye*, ' Règlement concernant la guerre sur terre,' art. 28, 47, pt. i. 246, 248.

doubt that in all wars pillage does continue with impunity ;[1] and we sometimes hear of a captured town being sacked, and the houses of the inhabitants being plundered, on the plea that it was impossible for the general to restrain his soldiers.[2] Moreover, private property taken from the enemy on the field of battle, in the operations of a siege, or in the storming of a place which refuses to capitulate, is usually regarded as legitimate spoils of war.[3] Military contributions and requisitions are levied upon the inhabitants of the hostile territory.[4] And whilst the progress of civilisation has slowly tended to soften the extreme severity of the operations of war by land, it still remains unrelaxed in respect to maritime warfare, the private property of the enemy taken at sea or afloat in port being indiscriminately liable to capture and confiscation. In justification of this it is said that the object of maritime wars is the destruction of the enemy's commerce and navigation, and that this object can only be attained by the seizure of private property.[5]

Not only does the respect in which the right of property is held vary according to the *status* of the owner, but in many instances certain persons are deemed incapable of possessing such a right.

The father's power over his children may imply that the latter, even when grown-up, have no property of their own, the father having a right to the disposal of their earnings. This is the case among some African peoples,[6] and the

---

[1] Maine, *International Law*, p. 199. Halleck, *International Law*, ii. 73, note.

[2] Halleck, *op. cit.* ii. 32. If we may believe Garcilasso de la Vega (*First Part of the Royal Commentaries of the Yncas*, i. 151) the officers of the Incas in ancient Peru were more humane, never allowing the pillage of a captured town.

[3] Halleck, *op. cit.* ii. 73 *sq.* Wheaton, *op. cit.* p. 467.

[4] Wheaton, *op. cit.* p. 467. Hall, *op. cit.* p. 427 *sqq. Conférence de La Haye*, 'Règlement concernant la guerre sur terre,' art. 49, 52, pt. i. 248.

[5] Wheaton, *op. cit.* p. 483. Twiss,

Law of Nations, p. 141. Heffter, *op. cit.* §137, p. 287. Hall, *op. cit.* p. 443 *sqq.*

[6] Sarbah, *Fanti Customary Laws*, p. 51. Kraft, in Steinmetz, *Rechtsverhältnisse*, p. 285 (Wapokomo). Munzinger, *Ueber die Sitten und das Recht der Bogos*, p. 36. Among the Barea and Kunáma a man's earnings belong to his father until he builds a house for himself, that is, until he marries (Munzinger, *Ostafrikanische Studien*, p. 477). Among the Basutos parents can deprive their sons of their earnings at pleasure (Endemann, 'Mittheilungen über die Sotho-Neger,' in *Zeitschr. f. Ethnol.* vi. 39).

Kandhs of India.[1] In the Laws of Manu, the mythical
legislator of the Hindus, it is said, " A wife, a son, and a
slave, these three are declared to have no property ; the
wealth they earn is acquired for him to whom they
belong." [2] But according to the standard commentators
this only means that the persons mentioned are unable to
dispose of their property independently ; [3] and it is
expressly stipulated that property acquired by learning
belongs exclusively to the person to whom it was given,
and so also the gift of a friend.[4] In Rome the *peculium*,
or separate property, allowed to a son was originally
subject to the authority of the house-father, should he
choose to exercise such authority ; and it was only by very
late legislation that sons were secured the independent
holding of their *peculium*.[5] Even now it is the law in
many European countries that, during the minority of a
child, the father or mother has the usufruct of its property,
with the exception of certain kinds of property expressly
specified.[6]

Among some uncivilised peoples women are said to be
incapable of holding property ; [7] but this is certainly not
the rule among savage tribes, not even among the very
lowest. When Mr. Snow wished to buy a canoe from
some Fuegians, his request was refused on the ground that
the object in question belonged to an old woman, who
would not part with it ; [8] and among the blacks of
Australia Mr. Curr has often heard husbands ask permission of their wives to take something out of their bags.[9]
There are instances in which the property owned by a

[1] Macpherson, *Memorials of Service in India*, p. 62.
[2] *Laws of Manu*, viii. 416. See also *Nârada*, v. 41.
[3] Buehler, in his translation of the Laws of Manu, *Sacred Books of the East*, xxv. 326, n. 416.
[4] *Laws of Manu*, ix. 206.
[5] Hunter, *Exposition of Roman Law*, p. 292 *sqq.* Maine, *Dissertations on Early Law and Custom*, p. 252. Girard, *Manuel élémentaire de droit romain*, pp. 135, 138 *sqq.*
[6] Bridel, *Le droit des femmes et le mariage*, p. 156.
[7] Nassau, *Fetichism in West Africa*, p. 13 (tribes of the Cameroons). Marshall, *A Phrenologist amongst the Todas*, p. 206. Waitz, *Anthropologie der Naturvölker*, iii. 129 (some Indian tribes of North America).
[8] Snow, 'Wild Tribes of Tierra del Fuego,' in *Jour. Ethn. Soc. London*, N.S. i. 264.
[9] Curr, *The Australian Race*, i. 66.

woman is by marriage transferred to her husband;[1] but
more commonly, it seems, the wife remains mistress of her
own property during the existence of the marriage relation.[2]
Among many savages considerable proprietary privileges
are granted to the female sex. We have seen that the
household goods are frequently regarded as the special
property of the wife.[3] Among the Navahos of New
Mexico everything, except horses and cattle, practically
belongs to the married women.[4] Among the Kafirs
of Natal, " when a man takes his first wife, all the cows he
possesses are regarded as her property," and the husband
can, theoretically, neither sell nor otherwise dispose of
them without his wife's consent.[5] The Mandans of North
America have a custom that all the horses which a young
man steals or captures in war belong to his sisters.[6]
Among the Koch of India, we are told, " the men are so
gallant as to have made over all property to the women." [7]
As regards woman's right of ownership, nations of a higher
culture compare unfavourably with many savages. In
Japan the husband formerly had full rights over the
property of his wife.[8] We have already noticed the
disabilities in point of ownership to which women were
once subject in India; but the development of the *strīdhana*,
or *peculium* of the female members of a family, shows that
they gradually became less dependent on their husbands in

[1] Mason, in *Jour. Asiatic Soc. Bengal*,
xxxvii. pt. ii. 142 (Karens). Sumner,
in *Jour. Anthr. Inst.* xxxi. 94 (Jakuts).
Post, *Studien zur Entwicklungsge-
schichte des Familienrechts*, p. 291.
[2] von den Steinen, *Unter den Natur-
völkern Zentral-Brasiliens*, p. 330
(Bakaïri). Morgan, *League of the
Iroquois*, p. 326. Lala, *Philippine
Islands*, p. 91. Hagen, *Unter den
Papua's*, pp. 226, 243 (Papuans of
Bogadjim, Kaiser Wilhelm Land).
Kubary, ' Die Palau-Inseln in der
Südsee,' in *Jour. des Museum Godef-
froy*, iv. 54. Ratzel, *History of Man-
kind*, i. 279 (various South Sea
Islanders). Kingsley, *West African
Studies*, p. 373. Bosman, *op. cit.* p.

172 (Gold Coast natives). Ellis, *Tshi-
speaking Peoples of the Gold Coast*, p.
298. Sarbah, *Fanti Customary Laws*,
p. 5. Lang, in Steinmetz, *Rechtsverhältnisse*, p. 223 (Washambala).
Burton, *Lake Regions of Central
Africa*, ii. 25 (Wanyamwezi). Post,
*Entwicklungsgeschichte des Familien-
rechts*, p. 292 *sqq.*
[3] *Supra*, i. 637 *sqq.*
[4] Mindeleff, ' Navaho Houses,' in
Ann. Rep. Bur. Ethn. xvii. 485.
[5] Shooter, *Kafirs of Natal*, p. 84.
[6] Wied-Neuwied, *Travels in the
Interior of North America*, p. 350.
[7] Buchanan, quoted by Hodgson,
Miscellaneous Essays, i. 110.
[8] Rein, *Japan*, p. 424.

matters relating to property.[1]   Among the ancient
Hebrews women appear to have been in every respect
regarded as minors so far as proprietary rights were concerned.[2]   In Rome a marriage with *conventio in manum*,
which was the regular form of marriage in early times,
gave the husband a right to all the property which the
wife had when she married, and entitled him to all
she might acquire afterwards whether by gift or by her
own labour.[3]   Later on marriage without *manus* became
the ordinary Roman marriage, and this, together with the
downfall of the ancient *patria potestas*, led to the result
that finally all the wife's property was practically under
her own control, save when a part of it had been converted
by settlement into a fund for contributing to the expenses
of the conjugal household.[4]   But, as we have noticed in
another place, the new religion was not favourable to the
remarkable liberty granted to married women during the
pagan Empire ; [5] and the combined influence of Teutonic
custom and Canon law led to those proprietary incapacities
of wives which up to quite recent times have disfigured the
lawbooks of Christian Europe.[6]   In England, before 1857,
even a man who had abandoned his wife and left her
unaided to support his family might at any time return to
appropriate her earnings and to sell everything she had
acquired, and he might again and again desert her,
and again and again repeat the process of spoliation.   In
1870 a law was passed securing to women the legal control
of their own earnings, but all other female property, with
some insignificant exceptions, was left absolutely unpro-
tected.   And it was not until the Married Women's

[1] Jolly, ' Recht und Sitte,' in Buehler, *Grundriss der indo-arischen Philologie*, ii. 78, 79, 87 *sqq.* Kohler, 'Indisches Ehe- und Familienrecht,' in *Zeitschr. f. vergl. Rechtswiss.* iii. 424 *sqq.*
[2] Benzinger, ' Law and Justice,' in Cheyne and Black, *Encyclopædia Biblica*, iii. 2724.
[3] Hunter, *Roman Law*, p. 295. Maine, *Early History of Institutions*,

p. 312. Bryce, *Studies in History and Jurisprudence*, ii. 387. Girard, *op. cit.* p. 163.
[4] Hunter, *Roman Law*, p. 295 *sqq.* Maine, *Early History of Institutions*, p. 317 *sqq.* Friedlaender, *Darstellungen aus der Sittengeschichte Roms*, i. 252. Girard, *op. cit.* p. 164.
[5] *Supra*, i. 653 *sq.*
[6] Maine, *Ancient Law*, p. 157 *sqq.*

Property Act of 1882 that a full right to their own property was given to English wives.[1]

A third class of persons who in many cases are considered incapable of holding property of their own is the slave class.[2] It may indeed be asked whether a slave ever has the right of ownership in the full sense of the term. Yet slaves are frequently said to be owners of property ; and though this " ownership " may have originally been a mere privilege granted to them by their masters and subject to withdrawal at the discretion of the latter,[3] it is undoubtedly in several cases a genuine right guaranteed by custom. Among the Káfirs of the Hindu-Kush, if the slaves work for others, they do not hand the wages over to their masters, but keep the pay themselves.[4] In Africa, in particular, it is a common thing for slaves to have private property ;[5] in Southern Guinea there are slaves who are wealthier than their masters.[6] In some African countries, as we have seen, the slave is obliged to work for his master only on certain days of the week or a certain number of hours, and has the rest of his time free.[7] So also in ancient Mexico the slave was allowed a certain amount of time to labour for his own advantage.[8] A Babylonian slave had his *peculium*, of which, at least under normal circumstances, he was in safe possession.[9] In Rome any-

---

[1] Lecky, *Democracy and Liberty*, ii. 536 *sq.* Cleveland, *Woman under the English Law*, p. 279 *sqq.* For the laws of other European countries see Bridel, *op. cit.* p. 61 *sqq.*, and for the history of the subject see Gide, *Étude sur la condition de la femme, passim.*

[2] Post, *Grundriss der ethnol. Jurisprudenz*, i. 370, 381. Holmberg, in *Acta Soc. Scientiarum Fennicæ*, iv. 330 *sq.* (Thlinkets). Kohler, ' Recht der Marschallinsulaner,' in *Zeitschr. f. vergl. Rechtswiss.* xiv. 428 *sq.* Volkens, *op. cit.* p. 249 (Wadshagga). Lang, in Steinmetz, *Rechtsverhältnisse*, p. 241 (Washambala).

[3] Nicole, in Steinmetz, *Rechtsverhältnisse*, p. 119 (Diakité-Sarracolese). Senfft, *ibid.* p. 442 (Marshall Islanders).

[4] Scott Robertson, *op. cit.* p. 100.

[5] Kingsley, *West African Studies*, p. 366. Ellis, *Ewe-speaking Peoples of the Slave Coast*, p. 219. Steinmetz, *Rechtsverhältnisse*, p. 43 (Banaka and Bapuku). Tellier, *ibid.* pp. 169, 171 (Kreis Kita). Baskerville, *ibid.* p. 193 (Waganda). Beverley, *ibid.* p. 213 (Wagogo). Dale, in *Jour. Anthr. Inst.* xxv. 230 (Wabondei). Munzinger, *Die Sitten und das Recht der Bogos*, p. 43. *Idem, Ostafrikanische Studien*, p. 309 *sq.* (Beni Amer).

[6] Wilson, *Western Africa*, p. 271.

[7] *Supra*, i. 677.

[8] Bancroft, *op. cit.* ii. 221.

[9] Kohler and Peiser, *Aus dem babylonischen Rechtsleben*, i. 1. See also *supra*, i. 684.

thing a slave acquired was legally his master's ; but he was in practice permitted to enjoy and accumulate chance earnings or savings or a share of what he produced, which was regarded not as his property in the full sense of the term, but as his *peculium*.[1] In the Middle Ages slaves, and in many instances serfs also, were, strictly speaking, destitute of proprietary rights.[2] In England it was held that whatever was acquired by a villein was acquired by his lord. At the same time his chattels did not *eo ipso* lapse into the lord's possession, but only if the latter actually seized them ; and if he for some reason or other refrained from doing so the villein was practically their owner in respect of all persons but his lord.[3] In the British and French colonies and the American Slave States the negro slaves had no legal rights of property in things real or personal.[4] According to the laws of Georgia, masters must not permit their slaves to labour for their own benefit, at a penalty of thirty dollars for every such weekly offence ;[5] and in other States they were expressly forbidden to suffer their slaves to hire out themselves.[6] In some places, however, negro slaves might hold a *peculium*. In Arkansas a statute was passed granting masters the right of allowing their slaves to do work on their own behalf on Sundays ;[7] and in the British colonies Sunday was made a marketing day for the slaves so as to encourage them to labour for themselves.[8] In the Civil Code of Louisiana

[1] *Digesta*, xv. 1. 39. Wallon, *Histoire de l'esclavage dans l'antiquité*, ii. 181 *sq*. Ingram, *History of Slavery*, p. 44. Hunter, *Roman Law*, pp. 157, 290 *sq*. Girard, *op. cit.* p. 95.

[2] *Supra*, i. 697. Guérard, *Cartulaire de l'Abbaye de Saint-Père de Chartres*, i. p. xlvii.

[3] Vinogradoff, *Villainage in England*, p. 67 *sq*. Pollock and Maitland, *op. cit.* i. 416, 419.

[4] Stephen, *Slavery of the British West India Colonies*, i. 58. *Code Noir*, Édit du mois de Mars 1685, art. 28, p. 42 *sq*.; Édit donné au mois de Mars 1724, art. 22, p. 295 *sq*. Stroud, *Sketch of the Laws relating to Slavery in the several States of the United States of America*, p. 74. Goodell, *American Slave Code*, p. 89 *sqq*.

[5] Prince, *Digest of the Laws of Georgia*, p. 788.

[6] Caruthers and Nicholson, *Compilation of the Statutes of Tennessee*, p. 675. Alden and van Hoesen, *Digest of the Laws of Mississippi*, p. 751. Morehead and Brown, *Digest of the Statute Laws of Kentucky*, ii. 1480 *sq*.

[7] Ball and Roane, *Revised Statutes of Arkansas*, xliv. 7. 2. 8, p. 276 *sq*.

[8] Edwards, *History of the British West Indies*, ii. 181.

it is said that the slave " possesses nothing of his own, except his *peculium*, that is to say, the sum of money, or movable estate, which his master chooses he should possess." [1] The Spanish and Portuguese slave laws were more humane. According to them the money and effects which a slave acquired by his labour at times set apart for his own use or by any other means, were legally his own and could not be seized by the master. [2]

Among many peoples, finally, we find the theory that nobody but the chief or king has proprietary rights, and that it is only by his sufferance that his subjects hold their possessions. [3] The soil, in particular, is regarded as his. [4] But even autocrats are tied by custom, [5] and in practice the right of ownership is not denied to their subjects.

In the next chapter we shall try to explain all these facts :—the existence of proprietary rights, the refusal of such rights to certain classes of persons, the different

---

[1] Morgan, *Civil Code of Louisiana*, art. 175.

[2] Stephen, *op. cit.* i. 60. Couty, *L'esclavage au Brésil*, p. 9.

[3] Butler, *Travels in Assam*, p. 94 (Kukis). Beecham, *Ashantee*, p. 96. Spencer, *Descriptive Sociology*, African Races, p. 12 (Abyssinians). Decle, *op. cit.* p. 70 *sqq.* (Barotse). Kidd, *The Essential Kafir*, p. 353. Ellis, *History of Madagascar*, i. 342. Post, *Afrikanische Jurisprudenz*, ii. 171. Percy Smith, 'Uea, Western Pacific,' in *Jour. Polynesian Soc.* i. 112. Tregear, 'Easter Island,' *ibid.* i. 99. In Samoa it is a maxim that a chief cannot steal; he is merely considered to "take" the thing which he covets (Pritchard, *Polynesian Reminiscences*, p. 104). In Uea, when a chief enters a house, he enjoys the right to take all in it that he pleases (Percy Smith, in *Jour. Polynesian Soc.* i. 113). Among the Kafirs no case can be brought against a chief for theft, except if it be committed on the property of a person belonging to another tribe ; and even the children of chiefs are permitted to steal from

their own people (Brownlee, in Maclean, *Compendium of Kafir Laws and Customs*, p. 112 *sq.* Trollope, *South Africa*, ii. 303. Holden, *Past and Future of the Kaffir Races*, p. 338).

[4] Waitz, *op. cit.* iii. 128 (Indian tribes of North America) ; v. pt. i. 153 (Malays). Ellis, *Polynesian Researches*, iii. 115 (Sandwich Islanders). Bory de St. Vincent, *Essais sur les Isles Fortunées*, p. 64 (Guanches). Nicole, in Steinmetz, *Rechtsverhältnisse*, p. 136 (Diakité-Sarracolese). Baskerville, *ibid.* p. 201 (Waganda). Beverley, *ibid.* p. 216 (Wagogo). Lang, *ibid.* p. 262 (Washambala). Rautanen, *ibid.* p. 343 (Ondonga). Stuhlmann, *Mit Emin Pasha ins Herz von Africa*, p. 75 (Wanyamwezi). Post, *Afrikanische Jurisprudenz*, ii. 170 *sq.*; Ratzel, *op. cit.* i. 126; de Laveleye-Bücher, *Das Ureigenthum*, p. 275 (various African peoples). Kohler, *Rechtsvergleichende Studien*, p. 235 (Kandian law). Giles, *Strange Stories from a Chinese Studio*, ii. 369, n. 21 (Chinese).

[5] *Supra*, i. 162.

degrees of condemnation attending theft under different circumstances. But before we can understand the psychological origin of the right of ownership and the regard in which it is held, it is necessary to examine the methods by which it is acquired, the external facts which give to certain individuals a right to the exclusive disposal of certain things.

CHAPTER XXIX

THE RIGHT OF PROPERTY (*concluded*)

ACCORDING to an old theory set forth by Roman jurists, and afterwards much emphasised by Grotius,[1] the original mode of acquisition is occupation, that is, a person's taking possession of that which at the moment belongs to nobody (*res nullius*), with the intention of keeping it as his property. That occupation very largely, though by no means exclusively, is at the bottom of the right of ownership seems obvious enough, and it is only by means of strained constructions that Locke and others have been able to trace the origin of this right to labour alone.[2] The principle of occupation is illustrated by innumerable facts from all quarters of the world—by the hunter's right to the game which he has killed or captured;[3] by the nomad's or settler's right to the previously unoccupied place where

---

[1] Grotius, *De jure belli et pacis*, ii. 3. 3.

[2] Locke, *Treatises of Government*, ii. 5. 27 *sqq.*, p. 200 *sqq.* Thiers, *De la propriété*, p. 94 *sqq.* Hume remarks (*Treatise of Human Nature*, ii. 3 [*Philosophical Works*, ii. 276, n. 1]) : —" There are several kinds of occupation, where we cannot be said to join our labour to the object we acquire ; as when we possess a meadow by grazing our cattle upon it."

[3] Curr, *Recollections of Squatting in Victoria*, p. 265 (Bangerang tribe). Murdoch, 'Ethnol. Results of the Point Barrow Expedition,' in *Ann. Rep. Bur. Ethn.* ix. 428 (Point Barrow Eskimo). Ahlqvist, ' Unter Wogulen und Ostjaken,' in *Acta Soc. Scientiarum Fennicæ*, xiv. 166 (Voguls). Steinmetz, *Rechtsverhältnisse*, p. 53 (Banaka and Bapuku). Post, *Afrikanische Jurisprudenz*, ii. 162 *sq.* Andree, ' Ethnogr. Bemerkungen zu einigen Rechtsgebräuchen,' in *Globus*, xxxviii. 287. Among some Indian tibes of North America it was customary for individuals to mark their arrows, in order that the stricken game might fall to the man by whose arrow it had been despatched (Powell, in *Ann. Rep. Bur. Ethn.* iii. p. lvii.).

he has pitched his tent or built his dwelling ;[1] by the agriculturist's right to the land of which he has taken possession by cultivating the soil ;[2] by a tribe's or community's right to the territory which it has occupied.[3] Among the Kandhs of India " the right. of possession of land is simply founded in the case of tribes upon priority of appropriation, and in the case of individuals upon priority of culture."[4] Among the Herero, " notwithstanding the loose notions generally entertained by them as to *meum* and *tuum*, there is an understanding that he who arrives first at any given locality is the master of it as long as he chooses to remain there, and no one will intrude upon him without having previously asked and obtained his permission. The same," our authority adds, "is observed even with regard to strangers."[5] Again, among some of the Australian natives a man who had found a bees' nest and did not wish to rob it for some time, would mark the tree in some way or other, and " it was a crime to rob a nest thus indicated."[6] In Greenland anyone picking up pieces

---

[1] von Martius, *Von dem Rechtszustande unter den Ureinwohnern Brasiliens*, p. 34 (Brazilian aborigines). Dalager, *Grønlandske Relationer*, p. 15 ; Nansen, *Eskimo Life*, p. 109 (Greenlanders). Marsden, *History of Sumatra*, pp. 68, 244 (Rejangs). Steinmetz, *Rechtsverhältnisse*, p. 53 (Banaka and Bapuku). Kraft, *ibid.* p. 293 (Wapokomo). Decle, *Three Years in Savage Africa*, p. 487 (Wakamba). Robertson Smith, *Religion of the Semites*, pp. 95, 96, 143 (ancient Semitic custom and Muhammedan law).

[2] Thomson, *Savage Island,* p. 137. Polack, *Manners and Customs of the New Zealanders,* ii.69; Thomson, *Story of New Zealand,* i.97. Munzinger, *Die Sitten und das Recht der Bogos*, p. 69. Cruickshank, *Eighteen Years on the Gold Coast*, ii. 277. Leuschner, in Steinmetz, *Rechtsverhältnisse*, p. 24 (Bakwiri). *Ibid.* p. 53 (Banaka and Bapuku). Tellier, *ibid.* p. 178 (Kreis Kita). Dale, in *Jour. Anthr. Inst.* xxv. 230 (Wabondei). *Laws of Manu*, ix. 44. Wellhausen, *Reste arabischen*

Heidentums, p. 108. Robertson Smith, *Religion of the Semites*, pp. 95, 96, 143 (ancient Semitic custom and Muhammedan law). Waitz, *Anthropologie der Naturvölker*, i. 440. Dargun, ' Ursprung und Entwicklungs-Geschichte des Eigenthums,' in *Zeitschr. f. vergl. Rechtswiss.* v. 71 *sqq.* Post, *Entwicklungsgeschichte des Familienrechts*, p. 283 *sqq. Idem*, *Grundriss der ethnol. Jurisprudenz*, i. 342 *sqq.* See also *infra*, p. 39 *sq.*

[3] Thomson, *Story of New Zealand*, i. 96; Polack, *op. cit.* ii. 71 (Maoris). Mademba, in Steinmetz, *Rechtsverhältnisse*, p. 90 (natives of the Sansanding States).

[4] Macpherson, *Memorials of Service in India*, p. 62.

[5] Andersson, *Lake Ngami*, p. 115. See also Viehe, in Steinmetz, *Rechtsverhältnisse*, p. 310.

[6] Mathew, in Curr, *The Australian Race*, iii. 162. On the finder's right to wild honey see Munzinger, *Die Sitten und das Recht der Bogos*, p. 70; Steinmetz, *Rechtsverhältnisse*, p. 53 (Banaka and Bapuku); Post, *Afrika-*

of driftwood or goods lost at sea or on land was considered
the rightful owner of them ; and to make good his
possession he had only to carry them up above high-water
mark and put stones upon them, no matter where his
homestead might be.[1] But the finder's right to the discovered article is not always restricted to objects which
have no owner or the owner of which is unknown : in
some instances his occupation of it makes it his property
in all circumstances,[2] whilst in other cases he at any rate
has a claim to part of its value.[3] Among the Hurons
" every thing found, tho' it had been lost but a moment,
belonged to the person that found it, provided the loser
had not claimed it before." [4] The Kafirs " are not
bound by their law to give up anything they may
have found, which has been lost by some one else.
The loser should have taken better care of his property,
is their moral theory." [5] Among the Chippewyans
any unsuccessful hunter passing by a trap where a deer
is caught may take the animal, if only he leaves the
head, skin, and saddle for the owner ; [6] and among the
Tunguses whoever finds a beast in another man's trap may
take half the meat.[7] Among the Maoris boats or canoes
which were cast adrift became the property of the captors.
" Even a canoe . . . of friends and relatives upsetting off
a village, and drifting on shore where a village was, became
the property of the people of that village ; although it
might be that the people in the canoe had all got safely to
land or were coming by special invitation to visit that very

---

nische Jurisprudenz, ii. 165 ; Hyde
Clarke, 'Right of Property in Trees
on the Land of Another,' in Jour.
Anthr. Inst. xix. 201.
[1] Dalager, op. cit. p. 23. Rink,
Tales and Traditions of the Eskimo,
p. 28.
[2] Nicole, in Steinmetz, Rechtsverhältnisse, p. 137 (Diakité-Sarracolese). Beverley, ibid. p. 216 (Wagogo). Walter, ibid. p. 395 (natives
of Nossi-Bé and Mayotte). Sorge,
ibid. p. 423 (Nissan Islanders).

[3] Merker, Die Masai, p. 204.
Desoignies, in Steinmetz, Rechtsverhältnisse, p. 281 (Msalala). Post,
Grundriss der ethnol. Jurisprudenz,
ii. 605.
[4] Charlevoix, Voyage to North-
America, ii. 26 sq.
[5] Leslie, Among the Zulus and
Amatongas, p. 202.
[6] Schoolcraft, Archives of Aboriginal Knowledge, v. 177.
[7] Ratzel, History of Mankind, ii.
226.

village." [1] We have previously noticed the customary treatment of shipwrecked mariners in mediæval Europe. And another instance of occupation establishing a right of property in things which already have an owner is conquest or capture made in war. The Romans regarded spoils taken from an enemy as the most excellent kind of property. [2]

The occupation of a thing may take place in various ways. Hegel says that " taking possession is partly the simple bodily grasp, partly the forming and partly the marking or designating of the object." [3] But there are still other methods of occupation, in which the bodily contact with the object is involuntary, or in which there is no bodily contact at all. Among the Maoris a man acquired a peculiar right to land " by having been born on it (or, in their expressive language, 'where his navel-string was cut'), as his first blood (ever sacred in their eyes) had been shed there"; [4] or, generally, "by having had his blood shed upon it " ; or " by having had the body, or bones, of his deceased father, or mother, or uterine brother or sister, deposited or resting on it " ; or " by having had a near relative killed, or roasted on it, or a portion of his body stuck up or thrown away upon it." [5] Among many peoples an animal belongs entirely or chiefly to the person who first wounded it,

[1] Colenso, *Maori Races of New Zealand*, p. 34. Polack, *op. cit.* p. 68 sq.

[2] "Maxima sua esse credebant quae ab hostibus cepissent " (quoted by Ahrens, *Naturrecht*, ii. 137).

[3] Hegel, *Grundlinien der Philosophie des Rechts*, § 54, p. 54 ; English translation, p. 59.

[4] Of certain tribes of Western Victoria we are likewise told that, " should a child of another family have been born on the estate, it is looked upon as one of the family, and it has an equal right with them to a share of the land, if it has attained the age of six months at the death of the proprietor" (Dawson, *Australian Aborigines*, p. 7). The Rev. John Bulmer (quoted by Brough Smyth, *Aborigines o Victoria*, i. 146) testifies the prevalence of such a birth-right among the Murray tribes, and suspects it is common to most of the tribes of Australia :—"The fact that an aboriginal is born in a certain locality constitutes a right to that part, and it would be considered a breach of privilege for any one to hunt over it without his permission. Should another black have been born in the same place, he, with the former, would have a joint right to the land. Otherwise, no native seems to have made a claim to any particular portion of the territory of his tribe." *Cf.* Schurtz, 'Die Anfänge des Landbesitzes,' in *Zeitschr. f. Socialwissenschaft*, iii. 357 *sqq.*

[5] Colenso, *op. cit.* p. 31. See also Polack, *op. cit.* ii. 82.

however slightly,[1] or who first saw it,[2] even though it was killed by somebody else. Thus among the Greenlanders, if a seal or some other sea-animal escapes with the javelin sticking in it, and is afterwards killed, it belongs to him who threw the first dart ; [3] if a bear is killed, it belongs to. him who first discovered it ; [4] and when a whale is taken, the very spectators have an equal right to it with the harpooners.[5]

Besides occupation, or the taking possession of a thing, the keeping possession of it may establish a right of ownership. That these principles, though closely connected with each other, are not identical is obvious from two groups of facts. First, a proprietary right which is based on occupation may disappear if the object has ceased to remain in the possession of the person who had appropriated it. The place occupied by a nomad is his only so long as he continues to stay there ; [6] and among agricultural savages the cultivator frequently loses his right to the field when he makes no more use of it[7]—though, on the other hand, instances are not wanting in which cultivation gives pro-

---

[1] Dalager, *op. cit.* p. 24 *sq.* (Greenlanders). Boas, ' Central Eskimo,' in *Ann. Rep. Bur. Ethn.* vi. 582. Dall, *Alaska,* p. 394 (Aleuts). Ratzel, *op. cit.* ii. 227 (Asiatic Hyperboreans). Campbell, *Second Journey in the Interior of South Africa,* ii. 212 (Bechuanas). Livingstone, *Missionary Travels,* p. 599 (natives of South Africa). von Heuglin, *Reise nach Abessinien,* p. 290 *sq.* (Woitos). *Laws of Manu,* ix. 44. Post, *Afrikanische Jurisprudenz,* ii. 163. *Idem, Grundriss der ethnol. Jurisprudenz,* ii. 707 *sq.* Andree, in *Globus,* xxxviii. 287 *sq.*
[2] Boas, ' Central Eskimo,' in *Ann. Rep. Bur. Ethn.* vi. 582. Ratzel, *op. cit.* ii. 227 (Asiatic Hyperboreans). See also Semper, *Die Palau-Inseln,* p. 86.
[3] Dalager, *op. cit.* p. 24.
[4] Rink, *Tales and Traditions of the Eskimo,* p. 29.
[5] Dalager, *op. cit.* p. 25.
[6] *Cf.* Post, *Afrikanische Jurisprudenz,* ii. 167.

[7] Morgan, *League of the Iroquois,* p. 326. Dorsey, ' Omaha Sociology,' in *Ann. Rep. Bur. Ethn.* iii. 366. Bourke, *Snake-Dance of the Moquis,* p. 261. Shooter, *Kafirs of Natal,* p. 16; Lichtenstein, *Travels in Southern Africa,* i. 271 (Kafirs). MacGregor, in *Jour. African Soc.* 1904, p. 474 (Yoruba). Leuschner, in Steinmetz, *Rechtsverhältnisse,* p. 25. Lang, *ibid.* p. 264. (Washambala). Marx, *ibid.* p. 358 (Amahlubi). Sorge, *ibid.* p. 422 (Nissan Islanders). Waitz, *op. cit.* i. 440. Dargun, in *Zeitschr. f. vergl. Rechtswiss.* v. 71 *sqq.* Post, *Entwicklungsgeschichte des Familienrechts,* p. 283 *sqq. Idem, Grundriss der ethnol. Jurisprudenz,* i. 343 *sq.* de Laveleye-Bücher, *Das Ureigenthum,* ch. xiv. p. 270 *sqq.* Among the Rejangs of Sumatra a planter of fruit-trees or his descendants may claim the ground as long as any of the trees subsist, but when they disappear "the land reverts to the public" (Marsden, *op. cit.* p. 245).

prietary rights of a more lasting nature.[1] Loss of possession may, indeed, annul or weaken ownership gained by any method of acquisition. In the Hindu work Panchatantra it is said that the property in " tanks, wells, ponds, temples, and choultries " will no longer rest with persons who once have left them.[2] Among the natives of the Sansanding States the right to a house is lost by its being abandoned.[3] In Greenland, if a man makes a fox trap and neglects it for some time, another may set it and claim the captured animal.[4] So also the finder's title to the discovered article springs from the fact that the original owner's right has been relaxed by his losing the possession of it. Secondly, the retaining possession of an object for a certain length of time may make it the property of the possessor, even though the occupation of that object conferred on him no such right, nay though the acquisition of it was actually wrongful.[5] According to the Roman Law of the Twelve Tables, commodities which had been uninterruptedly possessed for a certain period—movables for a year, and land or houses for two years—became the property of the person possessing them.[6] This principle, known to the Romans as *usucapio*, has descended to modern jurisprudence under the name of " prescription." It also prevailed in India since ancient times. The older law-books laid down the rule that, if the owner of a thing is neither an idiot nor a minor and if his chattel is enjoyed

---

[1] von Martius, *Von dem Rechtszustande unter den Ureinwohnern Brasiliens*, p. 35 *sq.* (Brazilian aborigines). Steinmetz, *Rechtsverhältnisse*, p. 53 (Banaka and Bapuku). Kohler, 'Banturecht in Ostafrika,' in *Zeitschr. f. vergl. Rechtswiss.* xv. 48 (natives of Lindi). Trollope, *op. cit.* ii. 302 (Kafirs). Post, *Afrikanische Jurisprudenz*, ii. 169. *Idem, Entwicklungsgeschichte des Familienrechts*, p. 285 *sq.* Schurtz, in *Zeitschrift für Socialwissenschaft*, iii. 255. Among the Angami Nagas any member of a village "may choose to leave his fields untilled for one year and cannot be compelled to grow his crops during the next, but after that, if illness or idle-ness prevent him from overtaking the work, his village insists on the fields being let " (Prain, ' Angami Nagas,' in *Revue coloniale internationale*, v. 484).

[2] *Panchatantram*, iii. p. 15.

[3] Mademba, in Steinmetz, *Rechtsverhältnisse*, p. 91.

[4] Dalager, *op. cit.* p. 27.

[5] See Mill, *Principles of Political Economy*, i. 272 ; Thiers, *op. cit.* p. 108 ; Waitz-Gerland, *op. cit.* vi. 228 (Maoris).

[6] Hunter, *Roman Law*, p. 265 *sqq.* Maine, *Ancient Law*, p. 284. Girard, *Manuel élémentaire de droit romain*, p. 296 *sqq.* Puchta, *Cursus der Institutionen*, ii. 202 *sqq.*

by another before his eyes during ten years and he says nothing, it is lost to him, and the adverse possessor shall retain it as his own property;[1] but it seems that later on the period of prescription was extended to thirty years or even more.[2] In this connection it should also be noticed that the division of labour, implying the use of certain articles, often confers proprietary rights to those articles upon the persons who make habitual use of them, as in the case of women becoming the owners of the household goods.[3]

A further source of ownership lies in the principle that a person has a title to the products of his own labour. Grotius—in criticising the Roman jurist Paulus, who long before Locke had made labour a justification of property,—[4] argues that this is no special mode of acquisition, but that the labourer's claim to what he produces is based on occupation. " Since in the course of nature," Grotius says, " nothing can be made except but of pre-existing matter, if that matter was ours, the ownership continues when it assumes a new form ; if the matter was no one's property, this acquisition comes under occupation ; if the matter belonged to another, the thing made is not ours alone." [5] This argument contains its own refutation. If a thing which we make of matter belonging to another person is not " ours alone," our partial right to it can be due only to our labour. Again, if we make a thing of materials belonging to ourselves, our right to it is certainly held to be increased by our exertions in producing it. It should, moreover, be remembered that there is ownership in the products not only of manual but of mental labour, and in the latter case the ownership can hardly be considered to be due to occupation at all. We may say with Mr. Spencer that from the beginning things identified as products of a man's labour are recognised as his. Even

[1] *Gautama*, xii. 39. *Vasishtha*, xvi. 16 *sq.*. *Laws of Manu*, viii. 147 *sq.*. See also *Panchatantram*, iii. p. 15 ; Benfey's translation, vol. ii. 233.
[2] *Brihaspati*, ix. 7. Jolly, ' Recht und Sitte,' in Buehler, *Grundriss der indo-arischen Philologie,* ii. 92. For the rules of prescription in ancient India see also Jolly, p. 91 *sqq.*, and Kohler, *Altindisches Prozessrecht,* p. 55 *sq.*
[3] *Supra,* i. 637 *sqq.*
[4] *Cf.* Girard, *op. cit.* p. 316.
[5] Grotius, *op. cit.* ii. 3. 3.

among the rudest peoples there is property in weapons, implements, dress, decorations, and other things in which the value given by labour bears a specially large proportion to the value of the raw material.[1] If a Greenlander finds a dead seal with a harpoon in it, he keeps the seal, but restores the harpoon to its owner.[2] Among the same people, when somebody has built dams across salmon-rivers to catch the fish, it is not considered proper for strangers to come and meddle with them.[3] In various parts of Africa he who has dug a well has a right to the exclusive disposal of it.[4] In West Africa, according to Miss Kingsley, that which is acquired or made by a man or woman by their personal exertions is regarded as his or her private property.[5] The Moquis of Arizona " are co-operative in all their labours, whether as hunters, herders, or tillers of the soil ; but each man gathers the spoils of his individual skill and daring, or the fruits of his own industry." [6] In the Nicobars, whilst everything which the village as a whole makes or purchases is common property, the result of individual work belongs to the individual.[7] In old Hindu law-books the performance of labour is specified as one of the lawful modes of acquiring property.[8] According to Nârada, when the owner of a field is unable to cultivate it, or dead, or gone no one knows whither, any stranger who undertakes its cultivation unchecked by the owner shall be allowed to keep the produce ; and if the owner returns while the stranger is engaged in cultivation, the owner, in order to recover his field, has to pay to the cultivator the whole expense incurred in tilling the waste.[9] Thus, though cultivation does not give a right to the land, it gives a right to the produce

[1] Spencer, *Principles of Sociology,* ii. 646. *Idem, Principles of Ethics,* ii. 98. *Cf.* Waitz, *op. cit.* i. 440 *sq.*

[2] Dalager, *op. cit.* p. 25.

[3] Nansen, *First Crossing of Greenland,* ii. 299.

[4] Munzinger, *Die Sitten und das Recht der Bogos,* p. 70. Lang, in Steinmetz, *Rechtsverhältnisse,* p. 264 (Washambala). von François, *Nama und Damara,* p. 175 (Herero).

[5] Kingsley, *West African Studies,* p. 366.

[6] Bourke, *Snake-dance of the Moquis,* p. 260 *sq.*

[7] Kloss, *In the Andamans and Nicobars,* p. 240.

[8] *Gautama,* x. 42. *Laws of Manu,* x. 115.

[9] *Nârada,* xi. 32 *sq.*

of the labour performed. Among uncivilised races we frequently find that the land itself and the crops or trees growing on it have different owners, the latter belonging to the person who planted them.[1]

The right of ownership may, further, be established by a transfer of property by its owner, either by way of gift or by sale or exchange or some other form of contract. The conditions necessary for this method of acquisition are, that the owner shall have a right to alienate the article in question, and that the other party shall be capable of owning such property. As has been said before, ownership does not necessarily imply an unrestricted power of disposition. Property in land, for instance, is frequently considered inalienable ;[2] and, to take another example, the power of testation, if recognised at all, is often subject to restrictions.[3] The customary law of the Fantis of West Africa does not permit any person to bequeath to an outsider a greater portion of his property than is left for his family.[4] Among the Maoris land obtained by purchase or conquest may be given away or willed by the owner to anybody he thinks fit, but the case is different with patrimony.[5] With regard to the so-called Aryan peoples Sir Henry Maine thinks " it is doubtful whether a true power of testation was known to any original society except the Roman." [6] Even in Rome bequest seems not to have been permitted in pre-historic times, and afterwards a *legitima portio* was compulsorily reserved for each child.[7] Such is still the law of some continental nations.

---

[1] Colenso, *op. cit.* p. 31 (Maoris). Leuschner, in Steinmetz, *Rechtsverhältnisse*, p. 25 (Bakwiri). Lang, *ibid.* p. 264 (Washambala). Munzinger, *Die Sitten und das Recht der Bogos*, p. 69. Hanoteau and Letourneux, *La Kabylie*, ii. 230 ; Kobelt, *Reiseerinnerungen aus Algerien und Tunis*, p. 293 (Kabyles of Jurjura). Hyde Clarke, in *Jour. Anthr. Inst.* xix. 199 *sqq.* Post, *Afrikanische Jurisprudenz*, ii. 172. Schurtz, in *Zeitschr. f. Socialwissenschaft*, iii. 250 *sq.*

[2] Post, *Entwicklungsgeschichte des Familienrechts*, p. 286 *sqq.* Avebury, *Origin of Civilisation*, p. 483 *sq.*

[3] Post, *Grundriss der ethnol. Jurisprudenz*, ii. 200 *sqq. Idem, Afrikanische Jurisprudenz*, ii. 19.

[4] Sarbah, *op. cit.* p. 85.

[5] Polack, *op. cit.* ii. 69.

[6] Maine, *Ancient Law*, p. 196. See also Fustel de Coulanges, *La cité antique*, p. 95.

[7] Fustel de Coulanges, *op. cit.* p. 96. Hunter, *Roman Law*, p. 780 *sqq.* Girard, *op. cit.* p. 854 *sqq.*

Closely connected with the restrictions imposed on a proprietor's power of testation is the rule of inheritance, one of the most common methods of acquiring property. At the earlier stages of civilisation the property of a deceased person is not in every case subject to this rule. Apart from the practice of testation, which, though hardly primitive, is not infrequently found among savages,[1] there are other ways of dealing with it besides inheritance. The private belongings of the dead, or part of them, are destroyed or buried with him, or his dwelling is burned or abandoned ;[2] but Dr. Dargun goes too far when saying that among rude savages this custom is generally practised to such an extent as to exclude heirship in property altogether.[3] Nor must we infer the general prevalence of a stage where there were no definite rules of inheritance[4] from the fact that among some North American tribes, when a man dies leaving young children who are unable to defend themselves, grown-up relatives or other persons come in and seize whatever they please.[5] The ordinary custom of savages is that the dead man's property is inherited either by his own children, if kinship is reckoned through the father, or by his sister's children or other relatives on the mother's side, if kinship is reckoned through females only.[6] Sometimes the rules of inheritance make little or no distinction between men and women ;[7] sometimes a decided preference is given to the

[1] Ellis, *Polynesian Researches*, iii. 115 *sq.* (Tahitians). Wilkin, in *Reports of the Cambridge Anthrop. Expedition to Torres Straits*, v. 286 (natives of Mabuiag). Kingsley, *West African Studies*, p. 373. Lang, in Steinmetz, *Rechtsverhältnisse*, p. 238 (Washambala). Desoignies, *ibid.* p. 277 (Msalala). Rautanen, *ibid.* p. 336 (Ondonga). Dale, in *Jour. Anthr. Inst.* xxv. 224. Post, *Grundriss der ethnol. Jurisprudenz*, ii. 199.
[2] See *infra*, on Regard for the Dead.
[3] Dargun, in *Zeitschr. f. vergl. Rechtswiss.* v. 99 *sqq.*
[4] *Ibid.* p. 102 *sq.*
[5] Prescott, in Schoolcraft, *Indian Tribes of the United States*, ii. 194 *sq.*

(Dacotahs). Hale, *U.S. Exploring Expedition. Vol. VI. Ethnography and Philology*, p. 208 (Salish). Dalager, *op. cit.* p. 30 *sq.* ; Cranz, *op. cit.* i. 176 (Greenlanders).
[6] See Westermarck, *op. cit.* p. 97 *sqq.*
[7] Kloss, *op. cit.* p. 241 (Nicobarese). Wilkin, in *Rep. Cambridge Anthr. Exped.* v. 285 *sq.* (natives of Mabuiag). Wilkes, *U.S. Exploring Expedition*, v. 85 (Kingsmill Islanders). Senfft, in Steinmetz, *Rechtsverhältnisse*, p. 441 (Marshall Islanders). Dawson, *op. cit.* p. 7 (certain tribes of Western Victoria). Post, *Afrikanische Jurisprudenz*, ii. 14. *Idem, Entwicklungsgeschichte des Familienrechts*, p. 299. *Idem, Grundriss der ethnol. Jurisprudenz*, i. 225.

men;[1] sometimes the women inherit nothing;[2] whereas in a few exceptional cases the women are the only inheritors.[3] Among various savages the widow also has a share in the inheritance, or at any rate has the usufruct of property left by her deceased husband.[4] Very frequently the eldest son,[5] or, where the maternal system of descent prevails in

[1] Sarbah, *Fanti Customary Laws*, p.87. Post,*AfrikanischeJurisprudenz* ii. 13 *sq. Idem, Entwicklungsgeschichte des Familienrechts*, p. 298 *sq. Idem, Grundriss der ethnol. Jurisprudenz*, i. 222 *sqq.* Among several uncivilised peoples landed property descends exclusively (Macpherson, *Memorials of Service in India*, p. 62 [Kandhs]; Sumner, in *Jour. Anthr. Inst.* xxxi. 79 [Jakuts]; Curr, *The Australian Race*, i. 64; Johnston, *Uganda Protectorate*, ii. 694; Post, *Entwicklungsgeschichte des Familienrechts*, p. 298 *sq.* ; *Idem, Grundriss der ethnol. Jurisprudenz*, i. 224)or by preference (Thomson, *Story of New Zealand*, i. 96; Post, *Grundriss der ethnol. Jurisprudenz*, i. 224 *sq.*) to men.

[2] Castrén, *Nordiska resor och forskningar*, i. 312 (Ostyaks). Marshall, *A Phrenologistamongsthe Todas*, p.206. Hodgson, *Miscellaneous Essays*, i. 122 (Bódo and Dhimáls). Hislop, *Papersrelating tothe AboriginalTribes of the Central Provinces*, p. 12, n. † (Gonds). Soppitt, *Account of the Kuki-Lushai Tribes*, p. 16; Stewart, 'Notes on Northern Cachar,' in *Jour. AsiaticSoc.Bengal,*xxiv.640(Kukis). Risley, *Census of India*, 1901, vol. i. Ethnographic Appendices, pp. 146 (Santals), 156 (Mundas), 209 (most of the Angami Nagas). Fryer, *Khyeng People of the Sandoway District*, p. 6. Marsden, *op. cit.* p. 244 (Rejangs). Eyre, *Expeditions of Discovery into CentralAustralia*, ii. 297. Munzinger, *Die Sitten und das Recht der Bogos*, p. 73. Hinde, *Last of the Masai*, p. 105; Johnston, *Uganda Protectorate*, ii. 828 (Masai). Dale, in *Jour. Anthr. Inst.* xxv. 224 (Wabondei). Kingsley, *Travels in West Africa*, p. 485 (some West Africantribes). Nassau,*Fetichism in WestAfrica*,p.13(nativesofthe Cameroons).Leuschner,inSteinmetz, *Rechtsverhältnisse*, p. 20 (Bakwiri).

Mademba,*ibid*.p.81(paganBambara). Lang, *ibid.* p. 238 (Washambala). Kraft, *ibid.* p. 289 (Wapokomo). Rautanen, *ibid.* p. 335 (Ondonga). Decle, *op. cit.* p. 486 (Wakamba). Campbell, *Travels in South Africa*, p. 520 (Kafirs). Post, *Afrikanische Jurisprudenz*, ii. 5. *Idem, Entwicklungsgeschichte des Familienrechts*, p. 296 *sqq. Idem, Grundriss der ethnol. Jurisprudenz*, i. 218 *sq.*

[3] Hamy, in *Bull. Soc. d'Anthr.. Paris*, ser. ii. vol. xii. (1877), 535 (Penong Piâk of Cambodia). Buchanan, quoted by Hodgson, *Miscellaneous Essays*, i. 110 (Kócch). Post, *Grundriss der ethnol. Jurisprudenz*, i. 213.

[4] Nelson, ' Eskimo about Bering Strait,' in *Ann. Rep. Bur. Ethn.* xviii. 307. Dawson, *Australian Aborigines*, p. 7 (certain tribes of Western Victoria). Hunt,'Ethnogr. Notes on the Murray Islands, Torres Straits,' in *Jour. Anthr. Inst.* xxviii. 7. Grange, ' Journal of an Expedition into the Naga Hills,' in *Jour. Asiatic Soc. Bengal*, ix. pt. ii. 964. Mason, *ibid.* xxxvii. pt. ii. (Karens). Post, *Entwicklungsgeschichtedes Familienrechts*,p. 303 *sqq.*

[5] Dalager, *op. cit.* pp. 29, 31; Cranz, *op. cit.* i. 176 (Greenlanders). Risley, *op. cit.* p. 203 (Limbus of Nepal). Macpherson, *op. cit.* p. 62 (Kandhs). Soppitt, *op. cit.* p. 16 (Kukis). Fryer, *op. cit.* p. 6 (Khyens). Junghuhn, *op. cit.* ii. 147 (Bataks). Gill, *Life in the Southern Isles*, p. 46. Polack, *op. cit.* ii. 69; Colenso, *op. cit.* p. 33 (Maoris). Munzinger, *Die Sitten und das Recht der Bogos*, pp. 69, 73 *sq.* Paulitschke, *op. cit.* p. 192 (Gallas). Hollis, *Masai*, p. 309; Hinde, *op. cit.* pp. 51, 105 (Masai). Volkens, *Der Kilimandscharo*, p. 253 (Wadshagga). Kingsley, *Travels in West Africa*, p. 485 (some West

full, the eldest uterine brother[1] or the eldest son of
the eldest uterine sister,[2] is the chief or even the only heir.
But there are also several instances in which this privilege
is granted to the youngest son.[3] Thus, among the Hos of
India he apparently inherits all the property of his father ;[4]
among the Limbus of Nepal, though an extra share is set
apart for the eldest son, the youngest one is allowed
to choose his share first ;[5] among the Eskimo of Behring
Strait, " if there are several sons the eldest gets the least,
the most valuable things being given to the youngest." [6]
In Greenland a foster-son inherits all the property of his
foster-father, if the latter dies without offspring or if his
sons are still young children ;[7] and of the West African
Fulah we are told that, though they have sons and
daughters, the adopted child becomes heir to all that they
leave behind.[8] Among the Kukis, in default of legitimate
issue, a natural son succeeds to his father's property before
all other male relations ;[9] among the Bódo and Dhimáls
sons by concubinage or adoption get equal shares with sons
born in wedlock ;[10] the Wanyamwezi of Eastern Africa
have the habit of leaving property to their illegitimate
children by slave girls or concubines even to the exclusion
of their issue by wives.[11] Among other uncivilised peoples,

African tribes). Bosman, *op. cit.* pp.
173 (natives of the Gold Coast), 322
(natives of the Slave Coast).
Leuschner, in Steinmetz, *Rechtsverhältnisse*, p. 20 (Bakwiri). Mademba,
ibid. p. 81 (pagan Bambara). Desoignies, *ibid.* p. 276 (Msalala). Marx,
ibid. p. 355 (Amahlubi), Chanler,
Through Jungle and Desert, p. 316
(Rendile). Post, *Afrikanische Jurisprudenz*, ii. 12 *sqq. Idem, Grundriss
der ethnol. Jurisprudenz*, i. 217, 218,
220 *sq.*

[1] Proyart, ' History of Loango,' in
Pinkerton, *Collection of Voyages and
Travels*, xvi. 571.

[2] Kingsley, *West African Studies*,
p. 373 *sq.* (some West African tribes).
Sorge, in Steinmetz, *Rechtsverhältnisse*, p. 413 (Nissan Islanders).

[3] Risley, *op. cit.* p. 227 (Lusheis).
Avebury, *Origin of Civilisation*, p.

493 *sqq.* Post, *Grundriss, der ethnol.
Jurisprudenz*, i. 218, 221 *sq.* Liebrecht, *Zur Volkskunde*, p. 432.

[4] Tickell, ' Memoir on the
Hodésum,' in *Jour. Asiatic Soc.
Bengal*, xix. pt. ii. 794, n.*

[5] Risley, *op. cit.* p. 203. *Cf.*
Mason, in *Jour. Asiatic Soc. Bengal*,
xxxvii. pt. ii. 142 (Karens).

[6] Nelson, in *Ann. Rep. Bur. Ethn.*
xviii. 307.

[7] Dalager, *op. cit.* p. 33.

[8] Denham and Clapperton, quoted
in Spencer's *Descriptive Sociology*,
African Races, p. 8.

[9] Stewart, in *Jour. Asiatic Soc.
Bengal*, xxiv. 640.

[10] Hodgson, *Miscellaneous Essays*,
i. 122.

[11] Burton, *Lake Regions of Central
Africa*, ii. 23 *sq. Cf.* Post, *Afrikanische Jurisprudenz*, ii. 6.

again, slaves cannot inherit at all,[1] and where they are allowed to possess property the master is sometimes the legitimate heir of his slave.[2]

At higher stages of civilisation the rules of inheritance present the same characteristics as among many savages. During historic times, at least, the nations of culture have reckoned kinship through the father, and succession has been agnatic.[3] In China women only inherit in the very last resort, failing all male relatives.[4] Among the Hebrews, in ancient times, only sons, not daughters, still less wives, could inherit ; [5] but the later law conferred on daughters the right of heirship in the absence of sons.[6] The Muham- medan law of inheritance in most cases awards to a female a share equal to half that of a male of the same degree of relationship to the deceased ; [7] but according to the old law of Medina women could not inherit at all.[8] Of all the ancient nations with whose rules of inheritance we are acquainted, the Romans seem to have been the only one who gave daughters the same right of inheritance as sons.[9] In India women had originally no such right at all, but in this, as in other matters relating to property, their position subsequently improved.[10] In Attic law sons excluded

[1] Nicole, in Steinmetz, *Rechtsver- hältnisse*, pp. 115, 119 (Diakité- Sarracolese). Lang, *ibid.* pp. 238, 242 (Washambala). Kraft, *ibid.* pp. 289, 291 (Wapokomo). Rautanen, *ibid.* p. 335 (Ondonga). Post, *Grund- riss der ethnol. Jurisprudenz*, i. 383.

[2] Munzinger, *Die Sitten und das Recht der Bogos*, p. 73. Steinmetz, *Rechtsverhältnisse*, p. 43 (Banaka and Bapuku). Mademba, *ibid.* p. 83 natives of the Sansanding States). Post, *Grundriss der ethnol. Juris- prudenz*, i. 383.

[3] See Westermarck, *op. cit.* p. 104.

[4] Alabaster, 'Law of Inheritance,' in *China Review*, v. 193. 'Inheritance and " Patria Potestas " in China,' *ibid.* v. 406.

[5] *Genesis*, xxxi. 14 *sq. Numbers*, xxvii. 4. Gans, *Das Erbrecht in weltgeschichtlicher Entwickelung*, i.

147. Benzinger, ' Law and Justice,' in Cheyne and Black, *Encyclopædia Biblica*, iii. 2728.

[6] *Numbers*, xxvii. 8. Gans, *op. cit.* i. 147. Benzinger, *loc. cit.* p. 2729. It is only by exceptional favour that the daughters inherit along with the sons (*Job*, xlii. 15).

[7] *Koran*, iv. 12, 175. Lane, *Manners and Customs of the Modern Egyptians*, p. 116 *sq.* Kohler, *Rechts- vergleichende Studien*, p. 102 *sqq.*

[8] Robertson Smith, *Kinship and Marriage in Early Arabia*, pp. 65, 117.

[9] Gans, *op. cit.* ii. 367 *sq.* Gide, *Étude sur la condition privée de la femme*, p. 102.

[10] Jolly, *loc. cit.* pp. 83, 86. Kohler, 'Indisches Ehe- und Familienrecht,' in *Zeitschr. f. vergl. Rechtswiss.* iii. 424 *sqq.* Leist, *Alt-arisches Jus Civile*, ii. 48.

daughters from succession,[1] and the same was the case among the Scandinavian peoples still in the later Middle Ages.[2] In England women are even to this day postponed to men in the order of succession to real property.[3] Special privileges in the division of the father's property were granted to the eldest son by the Hebrews [4] and Hindus,[5] and traces of primogeniture are met with in ancient Greek legislation.[6] In the history of English law we find not only primogeniture, but ultimogeniture as well.[7] As regards the question of legitimacy, we notice that in China all sons born in the household have an equal share in the inheritance, whether born of the principal wife or a concubine or a domestic slave.[8] Among the Hebrews the sons of concubines had a right of inheritance,[9] but whether on an equality with the other sons we do not know.[10] According to Muhammedan law no distinction in point of inheritance is made between the child of a wife and that borne by a slave to her master, if the master acknowledge the child to be his own.[11] In Hindu legislation the legiti-

---

[1] Gans, *op. cit.* i. 338, 341. Gide, *op. cit.* p. 79.

[2] Nordström, *Bidrag till den svenska samhälls-författningens historia*, ii. 95, 190. Stemann, *Den danske Retshistorie indtil Christian V.'s Lov*, p. 311 *sq.* Keyser, *Efterladte Skrifter*, ii. pt. i. 330, 339.

[3] Renton, *Encyclopædia of the Laws of England*, xi. 75.

[4] *Deuteronomy*, xxi. 17. Gans, *op. cit.* i. 148. Benzinger, in Cheyne and Black, *Encyclopædia Biblica*, iii. 2729. Mr. Jacobs suggests (*Studies in Biblical Archæology*, p. 49 *sqq.*) that ultimogeniture was once the rule in early Hebrew society, and was succeeded by primogeniture only when the Israelites exchanged their roving life for one in which sons became more stay-at-home.

[5] *Apastamba*, ii. 6. 14. 6, 12. *Laws of Manu*, ix. 114. Jolly, *loc. cit.* pp. 77, 82. Maine, *Dissertations on Early Law and Custom*, p. 89 *sq.* In China, though sons inherit in equal shares, "it is not uncommon for the brothers to temporarily yield up their share to

the elder brother, either in whole or in part, for the glory of the House " ('Inheritance and " Patria Potestas" in China,' in *China Review*, v. 406 ; *cf.* Doolittle, *Social Life of the Chinese*, ii. 224 ; Davis, *China*, i. 343).

[6] Fustel de Coulanges, *op. cit.* p. 99.

[7] Elton, *Origins of English History*, p. 178 *sqq.* Pollock and Maitland, *History of English Law till the Time of Edward I*. ii. 263 *sqq.* The custom of ultimogeniture has also been traced in Wales, parts of France, Germany, Friesland, Scandinavia, Russia, and Hungary (Elton, *op. cit.* p. 180 *sqq.*; Liebrecht, *op. cit.* p. 431 *sq.*).

[8] Parker, ' Comparative Chinese Family Law,' in *China Review*, viii. 79. ' Inheritance and " Patria Potestas " in China,' *ibid.* v. 406. Medhurst, ' Marriage, Affinity, and Inheritance in China,' in *Trans. Roy. Asiatic Soc. China Branch*, iv. 31. Simcox, *Primitive Civilizations*, ii. 351.

[9] *Genesis*, xxi. 10 *sqq.*

[10] Benzinger, in Cheyne and Black, *Encyclopædia Biblica*, iii. 2729.

[11] Lane, *Modern Egyptians*, p. 118.

mate sons have the nearest right to the inheritance of their
father, but a son begotten by a Sûdra on a female slave
may, if permitted by his father, take a share of it.[1] The
Roman law on the subject may be summed up thus :—
With regard to its father a natural child has no right at all,
and differs in no respect from a stranger ; with regard to
its mother it has the same right as a legitimate child.[2] In
Teutonic countries the position of illegitimate children as to
succession was much more favourable in earlier times than
later on when Christianity made its influence felt, depriving
them of all title to inheritance.[3] Strangers were formerly
unable both to inherit and to transmit property. For a long
time it was the custom in Europe to confiscate their effects
on their death ; and not only persons who were born in a
foreign country were subject to this *droit d'aubaine*, as it
was called in France, but in some countries it was applied
even to persons who removed from one diocese to another,
or from the lands of one baron to another.[4] Indeed, it is
only in recent times that foreigners have been placed on a
footing of equality with citizens with regard to inheritance.
In 1790 the French National Assembly abolished the right
of *aubaine* as being contrary to the principle of a human
brotherhood.[5] Later on, when the Code Napoléon was
drawn up, a backward step was taken by restricting the
abolition of this right to nations who acted with reciprocity;
but this limitation only lasted till 1819, when all
inequalities were finally removed in France.[6] In England
it was not until 1870 that foreigners were authorised
to inherit and bequeath like British subjects.[7]

Besides acquisition by occupation, possession for a
certain length of time, labour, voluntary transfer, and
inheritance, there are instances in which ownership in a

[1] Jolly, *loc. cit.* p. 85. *Laws of
Manu*, ix. 179.
[2] Gide, *op. cit.* p. 567 *sqq.*
[3] Nordström, *op. cit.* ii. 67, 200 *sqq.*
See also Alard, *Condition et droits des
enfants naturels*, pp. 9, 11 ; *supra*,
i. 47.
[4] Brussel, *Nouvel examen de l'usage*
général des fiefs en France, ii. 944 *sqq.*
de Laurière, *Glossaire du droit
françois*, p. 47 *sq.* Demangeat,
*Histoire de la condition civile des
étrangers en France*, p. 107 *sqq.*
[5] Demangeat, *op. cit.* p. 239.
[6] *Ibid.* p. 250 *sqq.*
[7] *Naturalisation Act*, 1870, § 2.

thing directly follows from ownership in another thing. It is a general rule that the owner of an object also owns what develops from or is produced by it.[1] The owner of a cow owns her calf, the owner of a tree its fruits, the owner of a piece of land anything growing on it, at least if no labour has been necessary for its production. Ownership in land also gives a certain right to the wild animals which are found there. Among the Fantis, for instance, if anybody kills game on another person's land, its proprietor is entitled to the shoulder or a quarter of such game.[2] In this connection we have further to notice the mode of acquisition which the Roman jurists called *accessio*. When that which belongs to one person is so intermixed with the property of another, that either it cannot be separated at all, or cannot be separated without inflicting damage out of proportion to the gain, the owner of the principal becomes the owner of the accessory, though, as a rule, he would have to pay compensation for it.[3]

All these methods of acquisition apply not only to individual property, but to common property as well. Occupation may establish ownership whether there be many occupants or only one ; joint labour may lead to joint ownership in the produce ; property may be transferred to a body of persons as well as to a single individual. But the custom which prescribes community of goods may also itself be an independent method of acquisition : by belonging to an association of people who hold property in common a person may be part owner of a thing which has been occupied or produced by some other member of the association. Communism of one kind or another is undoubtedly a very ancient institution,[4] though its prevalence at the lower stages of civilisation has often been exaggerated.[5] But the whole question of

[1] See Post, *Grundriss der ethnol. Jurisprudenz*, ii. 612; Goos, *Forelæsninger over den almindelige Retslære*, ii. 159 *sqq.*

[2] Sarbah, *op. cit.* p. 48.

[3] Hunter, *Roman Law*, p. 247 *sq.*

[4] *Cf.* Kovalewsky, *Tableau des origines et de l'évolution de la famille et de la propriété*, p. 51 *sqq.*

[5] Dr. Dargun (in *Zeitschr. f. vergl. Rechtswiss.* v. 76, &c.) even goes so far as to say that savages know of no

common ownership is too complicated and lies too much apart from our special subject to admit of a detailed treatment.

From the statement of facts we shall now proceed to an explanation of these facts. First, why do men recognise proprietary rights at all ? Why do the moral feelings of mankind grant to certain persons a right to the exclusive disposal of certain things, in other words, why does the disposal of an object without the consent of the person called its owner give rise to moral disapproval ? The " right of property," it is true, is generally used as a term for a legal right. But in this, as in so many other cases, the legal right is essentially a formulated expression of moral feelings.

As Mr. Spencer observes, the desire to appropriate, and to keep that which has been appropriated, lies deep not only in human but in animal nature, being, indeed, a condition of survival.[1] Sticklebacks show obvious signs of anger when their territory is invaded by other sticklebacks.[2] Birds defend their nests against the attacks of intruders.[3] The dog fights for his kennel or for the prey he has caught. A monkey in the Zoological Gardens of London, which made use of a stone to open nuts, always hid it in the straw after using it, and would not allow any other monkey to touch it.[4] We find the same propensity in man from his earliest years. At the age of two, Tiedemann's son did not let his sister sit on his chair or take any of his clothes, though he had no scruples against appropriating things which belonged to her.[5] Owing to this tendency to keep an appropriated object, and to resist its abstraction, it is dangerous for an individual to try to seize anything held by another of about equal strength ;

other property but such as belongs to individuals ; but this statement is hardly justified by facts.

[1] Spencer, *Principles of Sociology*, ii. 644.

[2] *Supra*, i. 22.

[3] Perty, *Das Seelenleben der Thiere*, p. 68.

[4] Darwin, *Descent of Man*, i. 125. See also Fischer, ' Notes sur l'intelligence des singes,' in *Revue scientifique*, xxxiii. 618.

[5] Compayré, *L'évolution intellectuelle et morale de l'enfant*, p. 312.

and in human societies this naturally led to the habit of leaving each in possession of whatever he had attained, especially in early times when the objects possessed were of little value, and there was no great inequality of wealth.[1] This habit was further strengthened by various circumstances, all of which tended to make interference with other persons' possessions the subject of moral censure. From both prudential and altruistic motives parents taught their children to abstain from such interference, and this, by itself, would readily give rise to the notion of theft as a moral wrong. Society at large also tried to prevent acts of this kind, partly in order to preserve peace and order, partly out of sympathy with the possessor. Resentment is felt not only by him who is deprived of his possession, but by others on his behalf. This is seen even among some of the lower animals. The Pomeranian dogs of German carters watch the goods of their masters;[2] Mr. Romanes's terrier protected meat from other terriers, his offspring, which lived in the same house with him, and with which he was on the very best of terms;[3] Captain Gordon Stables's cat, which had her place on the table at meals, never allowed any unauthorised interference with the viands.[4] In men such sympathetic resentment naturally develops into genuine moral disapproval.

All this applies not only to proprietary rights based on occupation, but also to the principle of continued possession as a ground of ownership. Indeed, the longer a person is in possession of a certain object, the more apt are both he and other individuals to resent its alienation; whereas the loss or abandonment of a thing has a tendency to loosen the connection between the thing and its owner.[5] This is undoubtedly the chief source of the rule of pre-

---

[1] *Cf.* Spencer, *Principles of Sociology,* ii. 634, 644 ; Dargun, in *Zeitschr. f. vergl. Rechtswiss.* v. 79 *sq.* ; von Martius, *Beiträge zur Ethnographie Amerika's,* i. 88, 90.

[2] Peschel, *Races of Man,* p. 240.

[3] Romanes, 'Conscience in Animals,' in *Quarterly Journal of Science,* xiii. 156, n.*

[4] 'Studies in Animal Life,' in *Chambers's Journal,* 1884, p. 824.

[5] *Cf.* Hume, *Treatise of Human Nature,* ii. 3 (*Philosophical Works,* ii. 274) :—"What has long lain under our eye, and has often been employed to our advantage, *that* we are always the most unwilling to part with."

scription, though there may be other circumstances as well which help to justify it. Thus it has been said that it is necessary to the security of rightful possessors that they should not be molested by charges of wrongful acquisition when by the lapse of time witnesses must have perished or been lost sight of, and the real character of the transaction can no longer be cleared up;[1] whilst another argument adduced in favour of prescription is, that long possession generally implies labour and that labour gives ownership.[2] The reason why property is gained by labour is obvious enough. Not only do exertions in producing an object make the producer desirous to keep it and to have the exclusive disposal of it, but an encroachment upon the fruit of his labour arouses sympathetic resentment in outsiders, who feel that an effort deserves its reward.

As the recognition of ownership thus ultimately springs from a desire in the owner to keep and dispose of what he has appropriated or produced, it is evident that, in ordinary circumstances, there would be no moral disapproval of a voluntary transfer of property to another person. But the case is different if such a transfer is injurious to the interests of persons who have a special claim to consideration. Thus testation is frequently held to be inconsistent with the duties which parents owe to their children or other near relatives to one another. The father, though the lord of the family's possessions, may indeed be regarded only as the first magistrate of an association, and in such a case his share in the division naturally devolves on the member of the family who succeeds to his authority.[3] The right of inheritance, then, may be intimately connected with the idea that the heir was, in a manner, joint owner of the deceased person's property already during his lifetime.[4] But there are

[1] Mill, *Principles of Political Economy*, i. 272.
[2] Thiers, *op. cit.* p. 103 *sqq.*
[3] Plato, *Leges*, xi. 923. Maine, *Ancient Law*, p. 184. Fustel de Coulanges, *op. cit.* p. 85. Leist, *Alt-arisches Jus Civile*, ii. 48. Mill, *op. cit.* i. 274. Kovalewsky, *Coutume contemporaine et loi ancienne*, p. 198 (Ossetes).
[4] It is interesting to note that in the Chinese penal code stealing from a relative is punished less severely than other cases of theft, and that the

various other facts which account for the existence of this right. In early civilisation the rule of succession is part of a comprehensive system of rights and duties which unite persons of the same kin. Professor Robertson Smith observes that in ancient Arabia all persons on whom the duty of blood-revenge lay originally had the right of inheritance ; [1] and a similar connection between inheritance and blood-revenge is found among other peoples. This system of mutual rights and duties is generally one-sided, it has reference either to paternal or to maternal relatives, but not to both at once. Now, whatever be the reason why the one or the other method of reckoning kinship prevails among a certain people, it is in the present place sufficient to point out the influence which the idea of a common descent exercises upon the right of inheritance owing to its power of knitting together the persons to whom it refers. Besides, the duty connected with this right may also be of such a nature as to require a certain amount of wealth for its performance ; among the Hindus, Greeks, and Romans, the right to inherit a dead man's property was exactly co-extensive with the duty of performing his obsequies and offering sacrifices to his spirit.[2] A further cause of children inheriting their father's property may be that they, to some extent, have previously been in joint possession of it ; for, as we know, possession readily leads to ownership. They would have an additional claim to succeed to his property when it had been gathered by their labour, as well as his, or when they stood in need of the support which it had been the father's duty to give them had he been alive. Moreover, where a person's children are present on the spot at his death, they are apt to be the first occupants of his

---

mitigation of the punishment is proportionate to the nearness of the relationship (*Ta Tsing Leu Lee*, sec. cclxxii. p. 287). The reason for this is that, "according to the Chinese patriarchal system, a theft is not in this case a violation of an exclusive right, but only of the qualified interest which each individual has in his share of the

family property " (Staunton, *ibid.* p. 287, n.*).

[1] Robertson Smith, *Kinship and Marriage in Early Arabia*, pp. 55, 56, 66 *sq.*

[2] *Laws of Manu*, ix. 186 *sq.* Isaeus, *Oratio de Philoctemonis hereditate*, 51. Cicero, *De legibus*, ii. 19 *sq.* Fustel de Coulanges, *op. cit.* p. 84. Maine, *Ancient Law*, p. 191 *sq.*

property ;[1] and we have noticed the importance of first occupancy as a means of establishing proprietary rights. The influence of these latter considerations, which are independent of the method of tracing descent, is apparent from the fact that among several peoples inheritance runs in the male line even though children take the mother's name and are considered to belong to her clan.[2] It may be added that a reason which modern writers often have assigned for giving the property of a person who dies intestate to his children or other near relatives is the supposition that in so disposing of it the law is only likely to do what the proprietor himself would have done, if he had done anything.[3]

In details the rules of succession are influenced by a variety of circumstances. Women may be excluded from inheritance or receive a smaller share than the men because the latter, being the stronger party, appropriate everything or the larger portion of the property for themselves ;[4] or because the women are less in need of property, being supported by their male relatives or husbands ;[5] or because they are exempt from the heaviest duties connected with kinship, as the duty of blood-revenge ;[6] or, as was the case in the feudal system, because a female tenant is naturally unable to attend the lord in his wars ;[7] or for the purpose of preventing the estate from passing to another family or tribe.[8] The idea of keeping together the property of the house also largely is at the bottom of the rule of primo-

---

[1] Cf. Mill, op. cit. i. 274.

[2] Westermarck, History of Human Marriage, pp. 104, 111.

[3] Hume, Treatise of Human Nature, ii. 3 (Philosophical Works, ii. 280). Godwin, Enquiry concerning Political Justice, ii. 438. Mill, op. cit. i. 275.

[4] Cf. Campbell, Travels in South Africa, p. 520 (Kafirs).

[5] Cf. Cranz, op. cit. i. 176 (Greenlanders) ; Macpherson, Memorials of Service in India, p. 62 (Kandhs) ; Hinde, op. cit. p. 51 (Masai) ; 'Inheritance and "Patria Potestas" in China,' in China Review, v. 406; Jolly, loc. cit. p. 83 (ancient Hindus) ; Post,

Entwicklungsgeschichte des Familienrechts, p. 296 sq. ; Idem, Grundriss der ethnol. Jurisprudenz, i. 218 sq.

[6] Cf. Robertson Smith, Kinship and Marriage in Early Arabia, p. 65 sq. ; Stemann, Den danske Retshistorie indtil Christian V.'s Lov, p. 311 sq.

[7] Cf. Cleveland, Woman under the English Law, p. 83.

[8] Shortland, Traditions and Superstitions of the New Zealanders, p. 256. Kingsley, Travels in West Africa, p. 485. Post, Grundriss der ethnol. Jurisprudenz, i. 214. Cf. Numbers, xxxvi. 1 sqq.

geniture. Besides, the eldest son is the most respected among the children, sometimes he is regarded quite as a sacred being.[1] On the death of the head of the family he is generally better suited than anybody else to take his place; and his privileged position with regard to inheritance is justified by the duties connected with it, especially the duty of looking after and supporting the other members of the household.[2] In feudalism, where tenancy implied duties as well as rights, it was also, from the lord's point of view, the simplest arrangement that when a tenant died a single person should fill the vacant place.[3] But there are many other points of view which may determine the rules of succession. It may be thought just that each child should have an equal share in the inheritance, and that something should be given also to the widow, whose maintenance devolved on the husband and who, whilst he was alive, had been in joint possession of many of his belongings. Or the youngest son may be the chief or the exclusive heir, partly perhaps for the sake of preventing a division of the property, or because the lord would have but one tenant,[4] but partly also because he had remained with his father till his death,[5] or " on the plea of his being less able to help himself on the death of the parents than his elder brethren, who have had their father's assistance in settling themselves in the world during his lifetime." [6] The Wanyamwezi, again, justify the practice of leaving property

---

[1] *Supra*, i. 605, 606, 614. Gill, *Life in the Southern Isles*, p. 46 *sq.*
[2] Dalager, *op. cit.* pp. 29, 31 ; Cranz, *op. cit.* i. 176 (Greenlanders). Munzinger, *Die Sitten und das Recht der Bogos*, p. 74. Hinde, *op. cit.* p. 51 (Masai). Of the Bāgdis of Bengal Mr. Risley expressly says (*op. cit.* p. 183) that the extra share which is given to the eldest son " seems to be intended to enable him to support the female members of the family, who remain under his care."
[3] Pollock and Maitland, *op. cit.* ii. 274.
[4] *Ibid.* ii. 280.
[5] Risley, *op. cit.* p. 227 (Lusheis). Among the Angami Nagas the

youngest son nearly always inherits his father's house, because sons, when marrying, leave the paternal mansion and build houses of their own (*ibid.* p. 209). It has been suggested that the custom of ultimogeniture " would naturally arise during the latter stages of the pastoral period, when the elder sons would in the ordinary course of events have ' set up for themselves ' by the time of the father's death " (Jacobs, *Studies in Biblical Archæology*, p. 47 ; Gomme, quoted *ibid.* p. 47, n. 1 ; Blackstone, *Commentaries on the Laws of England*, ii. 70 *sq.*).
[6] Tickell, in *Jour. Asiatic Soc. Bengal*, ix. pt. ii. 794, n.*

to their illegitimate children by slave girls or concubines, to the exclusion of their legitimate offspring, " by the fact of the former requiring their assistance more than the latter, who have friends and relatives to aid them." [1] Generally there seems to be a close connection between illegitimate children's right to inheritance and the legal recognition of polygamous practices. This is indicated by a comparison between Oriental and Roman legislation on the subject, and, in Teutonic countries, between ancient custom and the later law, which was influenced by Christianity's horror of sexual acts falling outside the monogamous marriage relation. The privileges which Hindu law grants to the illegitimate children of Sûdras are due to the notion that the marriage of a member of this caste is itself considered to be of so low a nature as to be on a par with irregular connections.[2]

Of the incapacity of children, wives, and slaves to acquire property for themselves little needs to be said, in the present connection, by way of explanation. Their exclusion from the right of independent ownership is an incident of their subjection to their parents, husbands, or masters. But we must remember that, whilst the latter have a right to dispose of the earnings of their subordinates, they also have the duty of supporting them, and that in early civilisation the child and the wife, sometimes even the slave,[3] are practically, as it were, joint owners of goods which in theory belong to the head of the family alone.

We have still to explain the variations of moral judgments with regard to different acts of theft. That the condemnation of the offence varies in degree according to the value of the stolen goods follows from the fact that theft is disapproved of on account of the injury done to the owner. But in many cases, when the injury is very slight, the appropriation of another person's property is

---

[1] Burton, *Lake Regions of Central Africa*, ii. 23 *sq.*
[2] Jolly, *loc. cit.* p. 85.
[3] Volkens, *op. cit.* p. 249 (Wadshagga).

justified by the needs of him who took it. And frequently, also, the condemnation of the thief is more concerned with his encroachment upon a neighbour's right than with measuring the exact amount of harm inflicted. Among the Basutos, says Casalis, " the idea of theft is expressed by a generic word which refers to the violation of right, much more than to the damage caused." [1] Burglary is regarded as an aggravated form of theft partly because it adds a fresh offence, the illicit entering into another person's house, to that against property, partly because it proves great premeditation in the offender.[2] Robbery is likewise a double offence, implying, as it does, an act of violence, and may on that account be more severely censured than ordinary theft ; but in other cases the courage and strength displayed by the robber is looked upon as a mitigating circumstance, and sometimes substitutes admiration for disapproval, whereas the secret offender is despised as a coward. So, too, the secrecy of nocturnal theft may aggravate the crime, whilst at the same time the difficulty in providing against it may induce society to increase the punishment. But men are apt to admire not only bravery and force, but also dexterity and pluck, hence the appreciation of adroit theft. The same tendency in some measure accounts for the distinction between manifest and non-manifest theft ; but here we have in the first place to remember that strong emotions are more easily aroused by the sight of an act than by the mere knowledge of its commission.[3] That the moral valuation of theft varies according to the station of the thief and the person robbed is due to the same causes as are similar variations with regard to other injuries ; and so is the distinction between offences against the property of a tribesman or fellow-countryman and offences against the property of a stranger. The theory of the Roman jurists according to which the property of an enemy in war belongs to nobody as long as the hostilities last, and therefore becomes the property of the

---

[1] Casalis, *Basutos*, p. 304.
[2] *Cf*. Wilda, *op. cit*. p. 878 (ancient Teutons).
[3] *Supra*, i. 294.

captor by the right of occupation,[1] is only a play with words
intended to give a reasonable justification to a practice
which is really due to lack of regard for the feelings
of strangers. When men at an early stage of civilisation
respect a stranger's property the motive is undoubtedly in
the main prudential. Savages may be anxious to prevent
theft from a neighbouring tribe in order to avoid disagreeable consequences.[2] And I venture to think that the
honesty they often display with regard to objects belonging
to strangers who visit them, and especially with regard
to things left in their charge,[3] largely springs from superstitious fear. We have noticed before that even the
acceptance of gifts is supposed to be connected with
supernatural danger, owing to the baneful magic energy
with which the gift is suspected to be saturated.[4] Would
not the same apply to the illicit appropriation of a
stranger's belongings, and especially to trusts, which
naturally call for great precaution on the part of the
owner ? This leads us to a subject of considerable importance in the history of property, namely, the influence which
magic and religious beliefs have exercised on the regard for
proprietary rights.

Theft is not only punished by men, but is supposed to be
avenged by supernatural powers. The Alfura of Halmahera
are said to be honest only because they fear that they otherwise would be subject to the punishment of spirits.[5] The
natives of Efate, in the New Hebrides, maintained that
theft was condemned by their gods.[6] In Aneiteum, another
island belonging to the same group, thieves were supposed
to be punished after death.[7] In Netherland Island they

---

[1] Hunter, *Roman Law*, p. 257.
Puchta, *op. cit.* ii. 220.
[2] Sproat, *Scenes and Studies of
Savage Life*, p. 159 (Ahts). Scott
Robertson, *Káfirs of the Hindu-
Kush*, p. 440.
[3] See, besides statements referred to
above, Lumholtz, *Unknown Mexico*,
i. 420, and ii. 477 ; Nordenskiöld,
Vegas färd kring Asien och Europa, ii.
140 *sq.* (Chukchi) ; Worcester, *Philip-*

pine Islands, p. 413 (Mangyans) ;
Colenso, *op. cit.* p. 43 (Maoris) ;
Macdonald, *Light in Africa*, p. 212
(Bantu) ; Campbell, *Travels in South
Africa*, p. 517, and Leslie, *Among the
Zulus and Amatongas*, p. 201 (Kafirs).
[4] *Supra*, i. 593 *sq.*
[5] Kükenthal, *Forschungsreise in
den Molukken*, p. 188.
[6] Macdonald, *Oceania*, p. 208.
[7] Turner, *Samoa*, p. 326.

were said to go to a prison of darkness under the earth ;[1] according to the beliefs of the Banks' Islanders they were excluded from the true Panoi or Paradise.[2] On the Gold Coast, "if a man had property stolen from his house, he might go to the priest of the local deity he was accustomed to worship, state the loss that had befallen him, make an offering of a fowl, rum, and eggs, and ask the priest to supplicate the god to punish the thief."[3] In Southern Guinea fetishes are inaugurated to detect and punish certain kinds of theft, and persons who are cognisant of such crimes and do not give information about them are also liable to be punished by the fetish.[4] The Bechuanas speak of an unknown being, vaguely called by the name of Lord and Master of things (Mongalinto), who punishes theft. One of them said :—" When it thunders every one trembles ; if there are several together, one asks the other with uneasiness, Is there any one amongst us who devours the wealth of others ? All then spit on the ground saying, We do not devour the wealth of others. If a thunderbolt strikes and kills one of them, no one complains, no one weeps ; instead of being grieved, all unite in saying that the Lord is delighted (that is to say, he has done right) with killing that man ; we also say that the thief eats thunderbolts, that is to say, does things which draw down upon men such judgments."[5]

According to the Zoroastrian Yasts, Rashnu Razista was " the best killer, smiter, destroyer of thieves and bandits." [6] In Greece Zeus κτήσιος was a guardian of the family property ;[7] and according to a Roman tradition the domestic god repulsed the robber and kept off the enemy.[8] The removing of landmarks

[1] *Ibid.* p. 301.

[2] Codrington, *Melanesians*, p. 274.

[3] Ellis, *Tshi-speaking Peoples of the Gold Coast*, p. 75. See also Cruickshank, *op. cit.* ii. 152, 160, 184 ; Schultze, *Der Fetischismus*, p. 91.

[4] Wilson, *Western Africa*, p. 275.

[5] Arbousset and Daumas, *Exploratory Tour to the North-East of the Colony of the Cape of Good Hope*, p. 322 sq.

[6] *Yasts*, xii. 8.

[7] Aeschylus, *Supplices*, 445. Farnell, *Cults of the Greek States*, i. 55.

[8] Ovid, *Fasti*, v. 141.

has frequently been regarded as sacrilegious.[1] It was strictly prohibited by the religious law of the Hebrews.[2] In Greece boundaries were protected by Zeus ὅριος. Plato says in his 'Laws':—"Let no one shift the boundary line either of a fellow-citizen who is a neighbour, or, if he dwells at the extremity of the land, of any stranger who is conterminous with him. . . . Every one should be more willing to move the largest rock which is not a landmark, than the least stone which is the sworn mark of friendship and hatred between neighbours; for Zeus, the god of kindred, is the witness of the citizen, and Zeus, the god of strangers, of the stranger, and when aroused terrible are the wars which they stir up. He who obeys the law will never know the fatal consequences of disobedience, but he who despises the law shall be liable to a double penalty, the first coming from the Gods, and the second from the law."[3] The Romans worshipped Terminus or Jupiter Terminalis as the god of boundaries.[4] According to an old tradition, Numa directed that every one should mark the bounds of his landed property by stones consecrated to Jupiter, that yearly sacrifices should be offered to them at the festival of the Terminalia, and that, " if any person demolished or displaced these bound-stones, he should be looked upon as devoted to this god, to the end that anybody might kill him as a sacrilegious person with impunity and without being defiled with guilt." [5] In the higher religions theft of any kind is frequently condemned as a sin.

This religious sanction given to ownership is no doubt in some measure due to the same circumstances as, in certain cases, make morality in general a matter of divine

<hr/>

[1] Trumbull, *The Threshold Covenant*, p. 166 sqq.
[2] *Deuteronomy*, xix. 14; xxvii. 17. *Proverbs*, xxii. 28; xxiii. 10 sq. *Hosea*, v. 10. *Cf. Job*, xxiv. 2.
[3] Plato, *Leges*, viii. 842 sq. Demosthenes, *Oratio de Halonneso*, 39, p. 86. See also Hermann, *Disputatio de terminis eorumque religione apud Græcos, passim.*
[4] Ovid, *Fasti*, ii. 639 sqq. Festus, *De verborum significatione* 'Ter-

mino.' Lactantius, *Divinæ Institutiones*, i. 10 (Migne, *Patrologiæ cursus*, vi. 227 sqq.). Pauly, *Real-Encyclopädie der classischen Alterthumswissenschaft*, vi. pt. ii. 1707 sqq. Fowler, *Roman Festivals of the Period of the Republic*, p. 324 sqq.
[5] Dionysius of Halicarnassus, *Antiquitates Romanæ*, ii. 74. Plutarch, *Numa*, xvi. 1. Festus, *op. cit.* ' Termino.'

concern—a subject which will be dealt with in a future chapter. But there are also special reasons which account for it. Partly it has its origin in magic practices, particularly in the curse.

Cursing is a frequent method of punishing criminals who cannot be reached in any other way.[1] In the Book of Judges we read of Micah's mother who had pronounced a curse with reference to the money stolen from her, and afterwards, when her son had confessed his guilt, hastened to render it ineffective by a blessing.[2] In early Arabia the owner of stolen property had recourse to cursing in order to recover what he had lost.[3] In Samoa " the party from whom anything had been stolen, if he knew not the thief, would seek satisfaction in sitting down and deliberately cursing him." [4] The Kamchadales " think they can punish an undiscovered theft by burning the sinews of the stone-buck in a publick meeting with great ceremonies of conjuration, believing that as these sinews are contracted by the fire so the thief will have all his limbs contracted." [5] Among the Ossetes, if an object has been secretly stolen, its owner secures the assistance of a sorcerer. They proceed together to the house of any person whom they suspect, the sorcerer carrying under his arm a cat, which is regarded as a particularly enchanted animal. He exclaims, " If thou hast stolen the article and dost not restore it to its owner, may this cat torment the souls of thy ancestors ! " And such an imprecation is generally followed by a speedy restitution of the stolen property. Again, if their suspicions rest upon no particular individual, they proceed in the same manner from house to house, and the thief then, knowing that his turn must come, frequently confesses his guilt at once.[6] A common mode of detecting the perpetrator of a theft is to compel the suspected individual to make oath,

[1] See, e.g., Mason, in Jour. Asiatic Soc. Bengal, xxxvii. pt. ii. 149 (Karens).
[2] Judges, xvii. 2.
[3] Wellhausen, Reste arabischen Heidentums, p. 192.

[4] Turner, Nineteen Years in Polynesia, p. 318.
[5] Krasheninnikoff, History of Kamschatka, p. 179 sq.
[6] von Haxthausen, Transcaucasia, p. 398 sq.

that is to say, to pronounce a conditional curse upon himself.[1]

Cursing is resorted to not only for the purpose of punishing thieves or compelling them to restore what they have stolen, but also as a means of preventing theft. In the South Sea Islands it is a common practice to protect property by making it *taboo*, and the tabooing of an object is, as Dr. Codrington puts it, " a prohibition with a curse expressed or implied."[2] The curse is then, in many cases, deposited in some article which is attached to the thing or place it is intended to protect. The mark of taboo, in Polynesia called *rahui* or *raui*, sometimes consists of a cocoa-nut leaf plaited in a particular way,[3] sometimes of a wooden image of a man or a carved post stuck in the ground,[4] sometimes of a bunch of human hair or a piece of an old mat,[5] and so forth. In Samoa there were various forms of taboo which formed a powerful check on stealing, especially from plantations and fruit-trees, and each was known by a special name indicating the sort of curse which the owner wished would fall on the thief. Thus, if a man desired that a sea-pike should run into the body of the person who attempted to steal, say, his bread-fruits, he would plait some cocoa-nut leaflets in the form of a sea-pike, and suspend it from one or more of the trees which he wanted to protect. This was called the " sea-pike taboo " ; and any ordinary thief would be terrified to touch a tree from which this was suspended, believing that, if he did so, a fish of the said description would dart up and mortally wound him the next time he went to the sea. The " white shark taboo " was done by plaiting a cocoa-nut leaf in the form of a shark, and was tantamount to an

[1] von Struve, in *Das Ausland*, 1880, p. 796 (Samoyedes). Worcester, *Philippine Islands*, p. 412 (Mangyans of Mindoro). Turner, *Nineteen Years in Polynesia*, p. 292 *sq.* (Samoans). Bosman, *op. cit.* p. 125 (Negroes of the Gold Coast). Bowdich, *Mission to Ashantee*, p. 267 ; &c.

[2] Codrington, *Melanesians*, p. 215.

[3] Taylor White, in *Jour. Polynesian Soc.* i. 275.

[4] Hamilton, *Maori Art*, p. 102 ; Thomson, *Story of New Zealand*, i. 102 ; Polack, *op. cit.* ii. 70 (Maoris). Ellis, *Polynesian Researches*, iii. 116 (Tahitians).

[5] Thomson, *op. cit.* i. 102 (Maoris). See also Colenso, *op. cit.* p. 34 (Maoris) ; Ellis, *Polynesian Researches*, iii. 201 (Tahitians).

expressed imprecation that the thief might be devoured by the white shark when he went to fish. The " cross-stick taboo," again, consisted of a stick suspended horizontally from the tree, and meant that any thief touching the tree would have a disease running right across his body and remaining fixed there till he died.[1] Exactly equivalent to the taboo of the Pacific Islanders is the *pomali* of the natives of Timor ; " a few palm leaves stuck outside a garden as a sign of the *pomali* will preserve its produce from thieves as effectually as the threatening notice of man-traps, spring-guns, or a savage dog, would do with us." [2] Among the Santals, whenever a person " is desirous of pro-tecting a patch of jungle from the axes of the villagers, or a patch of grass from being grazed over, or a newly-sown field from being trespassed upon, he erects a bamboo in his patch of grass or field, to which is affixed a tuft of straw, or in the case of jungle some prominent and lofty tree has the same prohibitory mark attached, which mark is well understood and strictly observed by all parties interested."[3] So also in Madagascar " on rencontre sur les chemins, on voit dans les champs de longs bâtons munis à leur sommet d'un paquet d'herbes et qui sont plantés en terre soit pour interdire le passage du terrain soit pour indiquer que les récoltes sont réservées à l'usage d'individus déterminés." [4] Among the Washambala the owner of a field sometimes puts a stick wound round with a banana leaf on the road to it, believing that anybody who without permission enters the field " will be subject to the curse of this charm." [5] The Wadshagga protect a doorless hut against burglars by placing a banana leaf over the threshold, and any mali-ciously inclined person who dares to step over it is sup-posed to get ill or die.[6] The Akka " stick an arrow in a bunch of bananas still on the stalk to mark it as their own

[1] Turner, *Nineteen Years in Poly-nesia*, p. 294 *sqq*.

[2] Wallace, *Malay Archipelago*, p. 149 *sq*.

[3] Sherwill, ' Tour through the Ráj-mahal Hills,' in *Jour. Asiatic Soc.* Bengal, xx. 568.

[4] van Gennep, *Tabou et totémisme à Madagascar*, p. 184 *sqq*.

[5] Lang, in Steinmetz, *Rechtverhält-nisse*, p. 263.

[6] Volkens, *op. cit.* p. 254.

when ripe," and then not even the owner of the tree would think of touching the fruit so claimed by others.[1] Of the Barotse we are told that " when they do not want a thing touched they spit on straws and stick them all about the object."[2] When a Balonda has placed a beehive on a tree, he ties a " piece of medicine " round the trunk, and this will prove sufficient protection against thieves.[3] Jacob of Edessa tells us of a Syrian priest who wrote a curse and hung it on a tree, that nobody might eat the fruit.[4] In the early days of Islam a masterful man reserved water for his own use by hanging pieces of fringe of his red blanket on a tree beside it, or by throwing them into the pool ;[5] and in modern Palestine nobody dares to touch the piles of stones which are placed on the boundaries of landed property.[6] The old inhabitants of Cumaná on the Caribbean Sea used to mark off their plantations by a single cotton thread, in the belief that anybody tampering with these boundary marks would speedily die.[7] A similar idea seems still to prevail among the Indians of the Amazon. Among the Juris a traveller noticed that in places where the hedge surrounding a field was broken, it was replaced by a cotton string ; and when Brazilian Indians leave their huts they often wind a piece of the same material round the latch of the door.[8] Sometimes they also hang baskets, rags, or flaps of bark on their landmarks.[9] In these and in various other instances just referred to it is not expressly stated that the taboo mark embodies a curse, but their similarity to cases in which it does so is striking enough to

[1] Junker, *Travels in Africa during the Years* 1882–1886, p. 86.

[2] Decle, *op. cit.* p. 77.

[3] Livingstone, *Missionary Travels*, p. 285.

[4] Robertson Smith, *Religion of the Semites*, p. 164, n. 1.

[5] *Ibid.* p. 336, n. 1.

[6] Pierotti, *Customs and Traditions of Palestine*, p. 95 sq. According to Roman sources (*Digesta*, xlvii. 11. 9), there was in the province of Arabia an offence called σκοπελισμός, which consisted in laying stones on an enemy's ground as a threat that if the owner cultivated the land "malo leto periturus esset insidiis eorum, qui scopulos posuissent"; and so great was the fear of such stones that nobody would go near a field where they had been put.

[7] Gomara, *Primera parte de la historia general de las Indias*, ch. 79 (*Biblioteca de autores españoles*, xxii. 206).

[8] von Martius, *Von dem Rechtszustande unter den Ureinwohnern Brasiliens*, p. 37 sq.

[9] *Ibid.* p. 34.

preclude much doubt about their real meaning. It is true that an object which is sacred by itself may, on that account, protect everything in its neighbourhood;[1] in Morocco any article deposited in the *horm* of a saint is safe, and among pagan Africans the same effect is produced by using fetishes as protectors of fields or houses.[2] But a thing of inherent holiness may also be chosen for taboo purposes for the reason that its sanctity is supposed to give particular efficacy to any curse with which it may be loaded.

We have previously noticed another method of charging a curse with magic energy, namely, by giving it the form of an appeal to a supernatural being.[3] So also spirits or gods are frequently invoked in curses referring to theft. On the Gold Coast, " when the owner of land sees that some one has been making a clearing on his land, he cuts the young inner branches of the palm tree and hangs them about the place where the trespass has been committed. As he hangs each leaf he says something to the following effect : ' The person who did this and did not make it known to me before he did it, if he comes here to do any other thing, may fetish Katawere (or Tanor or Fofie or other fetish) kill him and all his family.' " [4] In Samoa, in the case of a theft, the suspected persons had to swear before the chiefs, each one invoking the village god to send swift destruction if he had committed the crime ; and if all had sworn and the culprit was still undiscovered, the chiefs solemnly made a similar invocation on behalf of the

---

[1] *Cf.* van Gennep, *op. cit.* p. 185 (natives of Madagascar). It was an ancient Roman usage to inter the dead in the field belonging to the family, and in the works of the elder Cato there is a formula according to which the Italian labourer prayed to the manes to take good care against thieves (Fustel de Coulanges, *op. cit.* p. 75). Cicero says (*Pro domo*, 41) that the house of each citizen was sacred because his household gods were there.

[2] Rowley, *Africa Unveiled*, p. 174. Bastian, *Afrikanische Reisen*, p. 78 *sq.* Nassau, *Fetichism in West Africa*, p. 85. *Cf.* Schneider, *Die Religion* *der afrikanischen Naturvölker*, p. 230. If we knew the ceremonies with which magicians transform ordinary material objects into fetishes, we might perhaps find that they charge them with curses. Dr. Nassau says (*op. cit.* p. 85):—"For every human passion or desire of every part of our nature, for our thousand necessities or wishes, a fetich can be made, its operation being directed to the attainment of one specified wish." See also Schultze, *Der Fetischismus*, p. 109.

[3] *Supra*, i. 564.

[4] *Jour. African Soc.* no. xviii. January, 1906, p. 203.

thief.[1] The Hawaiians seem likewise to have appealed to an avenging deity in certain cursing ceremonies, which they performed for the purpose of detecting or punishing thieves.[2] In ancient Greece it was a custom to dedicate a lost article to a deity, with a curse for those who kept it.[3] Of the Melanesian taboo, again, Dr. Codrington observes that the power at the back of it " is that of the ghost or spirit in whose name, or in reliance upon whom, it is pronounced." [4] In Ceylon, " to prevent fruit being stolen, the people hang up certain grotesque figures around the orchard and dedicate it to the devils, after which none of the native Ceylonese will dare even to touch the fruit on any account. Even the owner will not venture to use it till it be first liberated from the dedication." [5] On the landmarks of the ancient Babylonians, generally consisting of stone pillars in the form of a phallus, imprecations were inscribed with appeals to various deities. One of these boundary stones contains the following curse directed against the violator of its sacredness :—" Upon this man may the great gods Anu, Bêl, Ea, and Nusku, look wrathfully, uproot his foundation, and destroy his off-spring " ; and similar invocations are then made to many other gods.[6]

Now we can understand why gods so frequently take notice of offences against property. They are invoked in curses uttered against thieves ; the invocation in a curse easily develops into a genuine prayer, and where this is the case the god is supposed to punish the offender of his own free will. Besides, he may be induced to do so by offerings. And when often appealed to in connection with theft, a supernatural being may finally come to be looked upon as a guardian of property. This, for instance, I take to be the explanation of the belief prevalent among the Berbers

[1] Turner, *Samoa*, p. 19. *Idem, Nineteen Years in Polynesia*, p. 292 sq.
[2] Jarves, *History of the Hawaiian Islands*, p. 20.
[3] Rouse, *Greek Votive Offerings*, p. 339.
[4] Codrington, *op. cit.* p. 215.
[5] Percival, *Account of the Island of Ceylon*, p. 198.
[6] Trumbull, *The Threshold Covenant*, p. 166 sq. Hilprecht, quoted *ibid.* p. 167 *sqq.*

of Haha, in Southern Morocco, that some of the local saints punish thieves who approach their sanctuaries, even though the theft was committed elsewhere ; being constantly appealed to in oaths taken by persons suspected of theft, they have become the permanent enemies of thieves. We can, further, understand why in some cases certain offences against property have actually assumed the character of a sacrilege, even apart from such as are committed in the proximity of a supernatural being. Curses are sometimes personified and elevated to the rank of divine agents ; this, as we have seen, is the origin of the Erinyes of parents, beggars, and strangers, and of the Roman *divi parentum* and *dii hospitales* ; and this is also in all probability the origin of the god Terminus.[1] Or the curse may be transformed into an attribute of the chief god, not only because he is frequently appealed to in connection with offences of a certain kind, but also because such a god has a tendency to attract supernatural forces which are in harmony with his general nature. This explains the origin of conceptions such as Zeus ὅριος and Jupiter Terminalis, as well as the extreme severity with which Yahweh treated the removal of landmarks. In all these cases there are indications of a connection between the god and a curse. Apart from other evidence to be found in Semitic antiquities, there is the anathema of Deuteronomy, " Cursed be he that removeth his neighbour's landmark." [2] That the boundary stones dedicated to Zeus ὅριος were originally charged with imprecations appears from a passage in Plato's ' Laws ' quoted above,[3] as also from inscriptions made on them.[4] The Etruscans cursed anyone who should touch or displace a boundary mark :—Such a person shall be condemned by the gods ; his house shall disappear ; his race shall be extinguished ; his limbs shall be covered with ulcers and waste away ; his land shall no longer produce

---

[1] *Cf.* Festus, *op. cit.* 'Termino' :— "Numa Pompilius statuit eum, qui terminum exarasset, et ipsum, et boves sacros esse."

[2] *Deuteronomy*, xxvii. 17. *Cf. Genesis*, xxxi. 44 *sqq.*

[3] Plato, *Leges*, viii. 843 : ". . . ἢ σμικρὸν λίθον ὁρίζοντα φιλαἰν καὶ ἐχθραν ἔνορκον παρὰ θεῶν."

[4] Xenophon, *Anabasis*, v. 3. 13. Hermann, *Disputatio de terminis apud Græcos*, p. 11.

fruits ; hail, rust, and the fires of the dog-star shall destroy his harvests.[1] Considering the important part played by blood as a conductor of imprecations, it is not improbable that the Roman ceremony of letting the blood of a sacrificial animal flow into the hole where the landmark was to be placed [2] was intended to give efficacy to a curse. In some parts of England a custom of annually " beating the bounds " of a parish has survived up to the present time, and this ceremony was formerly accompanied by religious services, in which a clergyman invoked curses on him who should transgress the bounds of his neighbour, and blessings on him who should regard the landmarks.[3]

The practice of cursing a thief may possibly even be at the bottom of the belief of some savages that such a person will be punished after death. In a following chapter we shall notice instances where the efficacy of a curse is supposed to extend beyond the grave. But we shall also find other reasons for savage doctrines of retribution in the world to come. In the cases referred to above it is not expressly said that the *post mortem* punishment of the thief is inflicted by a god.

I have here only dealt with rules relating to property which have been recognised by custom or law. But the established principles of ownership have not always been admitted to be just : in the civilised countries of the West they have called forth an opposition which is rapidly gaining in strength. The limited scope of the present work does not allow me to attempt a detailed account of this movement, with its variety of arguments and its multitudinous schemes of reform. The main reasons for complaint are :—first, that our actual law of property does not ensure to every labourer the whole produce of his labour ; secondly, that it does not provide for every want

---

[1] *Rei agrariæ auctores legesque variæ*, edited by Gœsius, p. 258 *sq.*
[2] Siculus Flaccus, 'De conditionibus agrorum,' in *Rei agrariæ auctores*, p. 5.

[3] Dibbs, 'Beating the Bounds,' in *Chambers's Edinburgh Journal*, N.S. xx. (1853) 49 *sqq.* Trumbull, *The Threshold Covenant*, p. 174 *sq.*

a satisfaction proportionate to the available means. However much the opinions of the different schools of socialists may vary, every socialist organisation of property aims either at guaranteeing to the working-classes the entire product of their industry, or at reducing to just proportions individual needs and existing means of satisfaction by recognising the claim of every member of society to the commodities and services necessary to support existence, in preference to the satisfaction of the less pressing wants of others.[1] These aims are greatly hampered by the present system, in which land and capital are the property of private individuals freely struggling for increase of wealth, and especially by the legally recognised existence of unearned income[2]—the " rent " of the Saint-Simonians, the " surplus value " (*Mehrwert*) of Thompson and Marx,—for which the favoured recipient returns no personal equivalent to society, and which he is able to pocket because the wage labourer receives in money-wages less than the full value of the produce of his work. We have here a conflict between different principles of acquisition. Both the rule that the owner of a thing also owns what results from it, and the law of inheritance, leading as they do to unearned income, are intruding upon the principle of labour as a source of property. They, moreover, interfere with the right to subsistence, which in some measure, though often insufficiently, is recognised in all human societies ;[3] for, as Marx observed, the accumulation of wealth at one pole means the accumulation of misery at the opposite pole.[4] This conflict between different principles or rights, all of which have deep foundations in human nature and the conditions of social life, has been brought about by certain

[1] See Menger, *Right to the whole Produce of Labour*, p. 5 *sqq.* ; Goos, *op. cit.* ii. 61.

[2] The term "unearned income" (*arbeitsloses Einkommen*) has been proposed by Menger (*op. cit.* p. 3).

[3] See *supra*, ch. xxiii.,vol. i. 526 *sqq.* Among the Eskimo about Behring Strait (Nelson, in *Ann. Rep. Bur.*

Ethn. xviii. 294) and the Greenlanders (Rink, *Eskimo Tales*, p. 29 *sq.*), if a man borrows an article from another and fails to return it, the owner is not entitled to claim it back, as they consider that when a person has enough property to enable him to lend some of it he has more than he needs.

[4] Marx, *Capital*, p. 661.

facts inherent in progressive civilisation. In simple societies the unearned income is small, because no fortunes exist, and the wants of those who are incapable of earning their own livelihood are provided for by the system of mutual aid. Progress in culture, on the other hand, has been accompanied by a more unequal distribution of wealth, and also by a decrease of social solidarity as a result of the increase and greater differentiation of the social unit. The unearned income has grown larger, the disproportion between the returns on capital and the reward for labour has in many cases become enormous, and hand in hand with the opulence of some goes the destitution of others. At the same time the injustice of prerogatives based on birth or fortune is keenly felt, the dignity of labour is recognised, and the working-classes are every day becoming more conscious both of their power and their rights. All this has resulted in a strong and wide-spread conviction that the actual law of property greatly differs from the ideal law. But much struggle will no doubt be required to bring them in harmony with one another. The present rights of property are supported not only by personal interests, but also by a deep-rooted feeling, trained in the school of tradition, that it would be iniquitous of the State to interfere with individuals' long-established claims to use at their pleasure the objects of wealth. The new scheme, on the other hand, derives strength from the fact that it aims at rectifying legal rights in accordance with existing needs, and that it lays stress on a method of acquisition which more than any other seems to appeal to the natural sense of justice in man. We are utterly unable to foresee in detail the issue of this struggle. But that the law of property will sooner or later undergo a radical change must be obvious to every one who realises that, though ideas of right and wrong may for some time outlive the conditions from which they sprang, they cannot do so for ever.

CHAPTER XXX

THE REGARD FOR TRUTH AND GOOD FAITH

THE regard for truth implies in the first place that we ought to abstain from lying, that is, a wilful misrepresentation of facts, by word or deed, with the intention of producing a false belief. Closely connected with this duty is that of good faith or fidelity to promises, which requires that we should make facts correspond with our emphatic assertions as to our conduct in the future. Within certain limits these duties seem to be universally recognised, though the censure passed on the transgressor varies extremely in degree. But there are also many cases in which untruthfulness and bad faith are looked upon with indifference, or even held laudable or obligatory.

Various uncivilised races are conspicuous for their great regard for truth ; of some savages it is said that not even the most trying circumstances can induce them to tell a lie. Among others, again, falsehood is found to be a prevailing vice and the successful lie a matter of popular admiration.

All authorities agree that the Veddahs of Ceylon are models of veracity. They "are proverbially truthful and honest." [1] They think it perfectly inconceivable that any person should say anything which is not true.[2] Mr. Nevill writes, " I never knew a true Vaedda to tell a lie, and the Sinhalese give them the same character." [3] Messrs. Sarasin had a similar ex-

[1] Bailey, ' Wild Tribes of the Veddahs of Ceylon,' in *Trans. Ethn. Soc.* N.S. ii. 291.

[2] Hartshorne, in *Indian Antiquary,* viii. 320.

[3] Nevill, in *Taprobanian,* i. 193.

perience :—" The genuine Wood-Wedda always speaks the truth ; we never heard a lie from any of them ; all their statements are short and true." [1]   A Veddah who had committed murder and was tried for it, instead of telling a lie in order to escape punishment, said simply nothing.[2]

Other instances of extreme truthfulness are provided by various uncivilised tribes in India.   The Saoras of the province of Madras, " like most of the hill people, . . . are not inclined to lying.   If one Saora kill another he admits it at once and tells why he killed him." [3]   The highlander of Central India is described as " the most truthful of beings, and rarely denies either a money obligation or a crime really chargeable against him." [4]   A true Gond " will commit a murder, but he will not tell a lie." [5]   The Kandhs, says Macpherson, " are, I believe, inferior in veracity to no people in the world. . . . It is in all cases imperative to tell the truth, except when deception is necessary to save the life of a guest." [6]   And to break a solemn pledge of friendship is, in their opinion, one of the greatest sins a man can commit.[7]   The Korwás inhabiting the highlands of Sirgúja—though they show great cruelty in committing robberies, putting to death the whole of the party attacked, even when unresisting—" have what one might call the savage virtue of truthfulness to an extraordinary degree, and, rightly accused, will at once confess and give you every required detail of the crime." [8]   The Santals are noted for veracity and fidelity to their word even in the most trying circumstances.[9]   A Kurubar " always speaks the truth." [10]   Among the Hos " a reflection on a man's honesty or veracity may be sufficient to send him to self-destruction." [11]   Among the Angami Nagas simple truth is highly regarded ; it is rare for a statement to be made on oath, and rarer still for it to be false.[12]   In the Chittagong Hills the Tipperahs are the only people among whom Captain Lewin

[1] Sarasin, *Forschungen auf Ceylon*, iii. 541. *Cf. ibid.* iii. 542 *sq.* ; Schmidt, *Ceylon*, p. 276.

[2] Sarasin, *op. cit.* iii. 543.

[3] Fawcett, *Saoras*, p. 17.

[4] Forsyth, *Highlands of Central India*, p. 164. *Cf. ibid.* p. 361 ; Sleeman, *Rambles and Recollections of an Indian Official*, ii. 109 ; Hislop, *Aboriginal Tribes of the Central Provinces*, p. 1.

[5] Dalton, *Ethnology of Bengal*, p. 284. *Cf.* Forsyth, *op. cit.* p. 155.

[6] Macpherson, ' Religious Opinions and Observances of the Khonds,' in *Jour. Roy. Asiatic Soc.* vii. 196.

[7] Macpherson, *Memorials of Service in India*, p. 94.

[8] Dalton, *op. cit.* p. 230.

[9] Elliot, ' Characteristics of the Population of Central and Southern India,' in *Jour. Ethn. Soc. London*, N.S. i. 106 *sq.*

[10] *Ibid.* i. 105.

[11] Dalton, *op. cit.* p. 206. *Cf. ibid.* p. 204 *sq.* ; Bradley-Birt, *Chota Nagpore*, p. 103.

[12] Prain, 'Angami Nagas,' in *Revue coloniale internationale*, v. 490.

has met with meanness and lying ;[1] and they, too, have previously been said to be, "as a rule, truthful and simple-minded.[2] The Karens of Burma have the following traditional precept :—" Do not speak falsehood. What you do not know, do not speak. Liars shall have their tongues cut out."[3] Among the Bannavs of Cambodia "severe penalties, such as slavery or exile, are imposed for lying."[4]

The Andaman Islanders call falsehood *yubda*, that is, sin or wrong-doing.[5] The natives of Car Nicobar are not only very honest,[6] but "the accusation of untruthfulness brings them up in arms immediately."[7] The Dyaks of Borneo are praised for their honesty and great regard for truth.[8] Mr. Bock states that if they could not satisfactorily reply to his questions they hesitated to answer at all, and that if he did not always get the whole truth he always got at least nothing but the truth from them.[9] Veracity is a characteristic of the Alfura of Halmahera[10] and the Bataks of Sumatra, who only in cases of urgent necessity have recourse to a lie.[11] The Javanese, says Crawfurd, "are honourably distinguished from all the civilised nations of Asia by a regard for truth."[12] "In their intercourse with society," Raffles observes, "they display, in a high degree, the virtues of honesty, plain dealing, and candour. Their ingenuousness is such that, as the first Dutch authorities have acknowledged, prisoners brought to the bar on criminal charges, if really guilty, nine times out of ten confess, without disguise or equivocation, the full extent and exact circumstances of their offences, and communicate, when required, more information on the matter at issue than all the rest of the evidence."[13] Among the natives

[1] Lewin, *Wild Races of South-Eastern India*, p. 191.

[2] Browne, quoted by Dalton, *op. cit.* p. 110.

[3] Smeaton, *Loyal Karens of India*, p. 254.

[4] Comte, quoted by Mouhot, *Travels in Indo-China, Cambodia, and Laos*, ii. 27. For the truthfulness of the uncivilised races of India see also Sleeman, *op. cit.* ii. 110 *sqq.*; Dalton, *op. cit.* p. 256 (Oraons) ; Crooke, *Tribes and Castes of the North-Western Provinces*, ii. 478 (Hâbûra) ; Fraser, *Tour through the Himālā Mountains*, pp. 264 (inhabitants of Kunawur), 335 (Bhoteas) ; Iyer, in the Madras Government Museum's *Bulletin*, iv. 73 (Nayādis of Malabar) ; Walhouse, Account of a Leaf-wearing Tribe on the Western Coast of India,' in *Jour. Anthr. Inst.* iv. 370 (Koragars).

[5] Man, in *Jour. Anthr. Inst.* xii. 112.

[6] Distant, in *Jour. Anthr. Inst.* iii. 4.

[7] Kloss, *In the Andamans and Nicobars*, p. 227 *sq.*

[8] Ling Roth, *Natives of Sarawak*, i. 66–68, 82. Boyle, *Adventures among the Dyaks of Borneo*, p. 215. Selenka, *Sonnige Welten*, p. 47.

[9] Bock, *Head-Hunters of Borneo*, p. 209.

[10] Kükenthal, *Forschungsreise in den Molukken*, p. 188.

[11] Junghuhn, *Battaländer auf Sumatra*, ii. 239.

[12] Crawfurd, *History of the Indian Archipelago*, i. 50.

[13] Raffles, *History of Java*, i. 248.

of the Malay Archipelago there are some further instances of
trustworthy and truthful peoples ;[1] whereas others are described
as distrustful and regardless of truth.[2] Thus the natives of
Timor-laut lie without compunction when they think they can
escape detection,[3] and of the Niase it is said that "truth is
their bitter enemy."[4]

Veracity and probity were conspicuous virtues among various
uncivilised peoples belonging to the Russian Empire. Georgi,
whose work dates from the eighteenth century, says of the
Chuvashes that they "content themselves with a simple
affirmation or denial, and always keep their word ";[5] of the
Barabinzes, that "lying, duplicity, and fraud, are unknown
among them ";[6] of the Tunguses, that they "always appear
to be what they really are," and that "lying seems to them
the absurdest thing in the world, which prevents them being
either suspicious or necessitated to accompany their affirmations
by oaths or solemn protestations " ;[7] of the Kurilians, that
they always speak the truth "with the most scrupulous
fidelity."[8] Castrén states that the Zyrians, like the Finnish
tribes generally, are trustworthy and honest,[9] and that the
Ostyaks have no other oaths but those of purgation. Among
them "witnesses never take the oath, but their words are
unconditionally believed in, and everybody, with the exception
of lunatics, is allowed to give evidence. Children may witness
against their parents, brothers against brothers, a husband
against his wife, and a wife against her husband."[10]

The Aleuts were highly praised by Father Veniaminof for
their truthfulness :—"These people detest lying, and never
spread false rumours. . . . They are very much offended if any
one doubts their word." They "despise hypocrisy in every
respect," and "do not flatter nor make empty promises, even in
order to escape reproof."[11] The regard in which truth is held
by the Eskimo seems to vary among different tribes.
Armstrong blames the Western Eskimo for being much

[1] Riedel, De sluik- en kroesharige
rassen tusschen Selebes en Papua, p.
96 (Serangese). St. John, Life in the
Forests of the Far East, ii. 322
(Malays of Sarawak).

[2] Marsden, History of Sumatra,
p. 209 (natives of the interior of
Sumatra). Riedel, op. cit. p. 314
(natives of the Luang-Sermata
group). Steller, De Sangi-Archipel,
p. 23.

[3] Forbes, A Naturalist's Wanderings
in the Eastern Archipelago, p. 320.

[4] Modigliani, Viaggio a Nías, p.467.

[5] Georgi, Russia, i. 110.

[6] Ibid. ii. 229.

[7] Ibid. iii. 78. Cf. ibid. iii. 109.

[8] Ibid. iii. 192. Cf. Krasheninnikoff,
History of Kamschatka, p. 236.

[9] Castrén, Nordiska resor och forskningar, i. 257.

[10] Ibid. i. 309 sq.

[11] Veniaminof, quoted by Dall,
Alaska, pp. 396, 395.

addicted to falsehood, and for seldom telling the truth, if there be anything to gain by a lie.[1] The Point Barrow Eskimo "are in the main truthful, though a detected lie is hardly considered more than a good joke, and considerable trickery is practised in trading."[2] Of the Eskimo at Igloolik, an island near Melville Peninsula, we are told that "their lies consist only of vilifying each other's character, with false accusations of theft or ill behaviour. When asking questions of an individual, it is but rarely that he will either advance or persist in an untruth. . . . Lying among them is almost exclusively confined to the ladies."[3] In his description of the Eskimo on the western side of Davis Strait and in the region of Frobisher Bay, Mr. Hall says that they despise and shun one who will *shag-la-voo*, that is, "tell a lie," and that they are rarely troubled by any of this class.[4] The Greenlanders are generally truthful towards each other, at least the men.[5] But if he can help it, a Greenlander will not tell a truth which he thinks may be unpleasant to the hearer, as he is anxious to stand on as good a footing as possible with his fellow-men.[6]

The Thompson River Indians of British Columbia maintain that it is bad to lie, that if you do so people will laugh at you and call you a "liar."[7] Speaking of the Iroquois, Mr. Morgan says that the love of truth was a marked trait of the Indian character. "This inborn sentiment flourished in the period of their highest prosperity, in all the freshness of its primeval purity. On all occasions and at whatever peril, the Iroquois spoke the truth without fear and without hesitation. Dissimulation was not an Indian habit. . . . The Iroquois prided themselves upon their sacred regard for the public faith, and punished the want of it with severity when an occasion presented itself."[8] Loskiel likewise states that they considered lying and cheating heinous and scandalous offences.[9] Among the Chippewas there were a few persons addicted to lying, but these

[1] Armstrong, *Discovery of the North-West Passage*, p. 196 *sq.*

[2] Murdoch, 'Ethnological Results of the Point Barrow Expedition,' in *Ann. Rep. Bur. Ethn.* ix. 41.

[3] Lyon, *Private Journal during the Voyage of Discovery under Captain Parry*, p. 349.

[4] Hall, *Arctic Researches*, p. 567.

[5] Dalager, *Grønlandske Relationer*, p. 69. Cranz, *History of Greenland*, i. 171, 175. Nansen, *Eskimo Life*, p. 158.

[6] Nansen, *Eskimo Life*, p. 101. *Idem*, *First Crossing of Greenland*, ii. 334 *sq.*

[7] Teit, 'Thompson Indians of British Columbia,' in *Memoirs of the American Museum of Natural History*, Anthropology, i. 366.

[8] Morgan, *League of the Iroquois*, pp. 335, 338.

[9] Loskiel, *History of the Mission of the United Brethren among the Indians in North America*, i. 16.

were held in disrepute.[1]   The Shoshones, a tribe of the Snake
Indians, were frank and communicative in their intercourse
with strangers, and perfectly fair in their dealings.[2]   The
Seminole Indians of Florida are commended for their truthfulness.[3]   With special reference to the Navahos, Mr. Matthews
observes, " As the result of over thirty years' experience among
Indians, I must say that I have not found them less truthful
than the average of our own race."[4]   Among the Dacotahs
lying " is considered very bad " ; yet in this respect "every one
sees the mote in his brother's eye, but does not discover the
beam that is in his own," [5] want of truthfulness and habitual
dishonesty in little things being prevalent traits in their
character.[6]   So, also, the Thlinkets admit that falsehood is
criminal, although they have recourse to it without hesitation
whenever it suits their purpose.[7]   Of the Chippewyans, again,
it is said that they carry the habit of lying to such an extent,
even among themselves, that they can scarcely be said to
esteem truth a virtue.[8]   The Crees are " not very strict in
their adherence to truth, being great boasters." [9]   Heriot [10] and
Adair [11] speak of the treacherous or deceitful disposition of the
North American Indians ; but the latter adds that, though
" privately dishonest," they are " very faithful indeed to their
own tribe."

Of the regard in which truth is held by the Indians of South
America the authorities I have consulted have little to say.
The Coroados are not deceitful.[12]   The Tehuelches of Patagonia nearly always lie in minor affairs, and will invent stories
for sheer amusement.   "In anything of importance, however,
such as guaranteeing the safety of a person, they were very
truthful, as long as faith was kept with them.   After a time,"
Lieutenant Musters adds, "when they ascertained that I invariably avoided deviating in any way from the truth, they left
off lying to me even in minor matters.   This will serve to
show that they are not of the treacherous nature assigned to

[1] Keating, *Expedition to the Source
of St. Peter's River,* ii. 168.
[2] Lewis and Clarke, *Travels to the
Source of the Missouri River,* p. 306.
[3] Maccauley, ' Seminole Indians of
Florida,' in *Ann. Rep. Bur. Ethn.* v.
491.
[4] Matthews, ' Study of Ethics
among the Lower Races,' in *Jour. of
American Folk-Lore,* xii. 5.
[5] Schoolcraft, *Indian Tribes of the
United States,* ii. 196.
[6] Eastman, *Dacotah,* p. xvii.

[7] Douglas, quoted by Petroff, *Report on Alaska,* p. 177.
[8] Richardson, *Arctic Searching Expedition,* ii. 18. *Cf. ibid.* ii. 19.
[9] Richardson, in Franklin, *Journey
to the Shores of the Polar Sea,* p. 63.
[10] Heriot, *Travels through the Canadas,* p. 319.
[11] Adair, *History of the American
Indians,* p. 4.
[12] von Spix and von Martius,
Travels in Brazil, ii. 242.

them by some ignorant writers."[1] Among the Fuegians, according to Mr. Bridge, no one can trust another, lying tales of slander are very common, great exaggeration is used, and it is not even considered wrong to tell a lie.[2] Snow, however, speaks of "the honesty they undoubtedly evince in many of their transactions";[3] and Darwin states that the Fuegian boy on board the Beagle "showed, by going into the most violent passion, that he quite understood the reproach of being called a liar, which in truth he was."[4]

Of the Australian aborigines we are told that some tribes and families display on nearly all occasions honesty and truthfulness, whereas others "seem almost destitute of the better qualities."[5] According to Mr. Mathew, they are not wantonly untruthful, although one can rely on them being faithful to a trust only on condition that they are exempt from strong temptation.[6] Mr. Curr admits that under some circumstances they are treacherous, and that it costs them little pain to lie ; but from his own observations he has no doubt that the black feels, in the commencement of his career at least, that lying is wrong.[7] Mr. Howitt has found the South Australian Kurnai "to compare not unfavourably with our own people in their narration of occurrences, or as witnesses in courts of justice as to facts. Among them a person known to disregard truth is branded as a liar (*jet-bolan*)."[8] Among the aborigines of New South Wales people who cause strife by lying are punished, and "liars are much disliked"; Dr. Fraser was assured by a person who had had much intercourse with them for thirty years that he never knew them to tell a lie.[9] Among the tribes of Western Victoria described by Mr. Dawson liars are detested ; should any man, through lying, get others into trouble, he is punished with the boomerang, whilst women and young people, for the same fault, are beaten with a stick.[10] In his description of his expeditions into Central Australia Eyre writes, "In their intercourse with each other I

[1] Musters, *At Home with the Patagonians*, p. 195 sq.

[2] Bridges, in *A Voice for South America*, xiii. 202 sq. Cf. Hyades and Deniker, *Mission scientifique du Cap Horn*, vii. 242 ; King and Fitzroy, *Voyages of the "Adventure" and "Beagle,"* ii. 188.

[3] Snow, *Two Years' Cruise off Tierra del Fuego*, i. 347.

[4] Darwin, *Journal of Researches*, p. 227.

[5] Brough Smyth, *Aborigines of Victoria*, i. 25.

[6] Mathew, 'Australian Aborigines,' in *Jour. and Proceed. Roy. Soc. N.S. Wales*, xxiii. 387.

[7] Curr, *Australian Race*, i. 43, 100.

[8] Fison and Howitt, *Kamilaroi and Kurnai*, p. 256.

[9] Fraser, *Aborigines of New South Wales*, pp. 41, 90.

[10] Dawson, *Australian Aborigines*, p. 76.

have generally found the natives to speak the truth and act with honesty, and they will usually do the same with Europeans if on friendly terms with them." [1] With regard to West Australian tribes Mr. Chauncy states that they are certainly not remarkable for their treachery, and that he has very seldom known any of them accused of it. He adds that they are "habitually honest among themselves, if not truthful," and that, during his many years' acquaintance with them, he does not remember ever hearing a native utter a falsehood with a definite idea of gaining anything by it. "If questioned on any subject, he would form his reply rather with the view of pleasing the enquirer than of its being true; but this was attributable to his politeness." [2] According to a late Advocate-General of West Australia, "when a native is accused of any crime, he often acknowledges his share in the transaction with perfect candour." [3] Very different from these accounts is Mr. Gason's statement concerning the Dieyerie in South Australia. "A more treacherous race," he says, "I do not believe exists. They imbibe treachery in infancy, and practise it until death, and have no sense of wrong in it. . . . They seem to take a delight in lying, especially if they think it will please you. Should you ask them any question, be prepared for a falsehood, as a matter of course. They not only lie to the white man, but to each other, and do not appear to see any wrong in it." [4] The natives of Botany Bay and Port Jackson in New South Wales are by older writers described as no strangers to falsehood.[5] And speaking of a tribe in North Queensland, Mr. Lumholtz observed that "an Australian native can betray anybody," and that "there is not one among them who will not lie if it is to his advantage." [6]

According to Mr. Hale, the Polynesians are not naturally treacherous, by no means from a horror of deception, but apparently from a mere inaptitude at dissembling; and it is said that the word of a Micronesian may generally be relied upon.[7] To the Tonga Islanders a false accusation appeared more horrible than deliberate murder does to us, and they also put this

[1] Eyre, *Expeditions of Discovery into Central Australia*, ii. 385.
[2] Chauncy, quoted by Brough Smyth, *op. cit.* ii. 275, 281. *Cf.* Oldfield, 'Aborigines of Australia,' in *Trans. Ethn. Soc.* N.S. iii. 255.
[3] Moore, quoted by Brough Smyth, *op. cit.* ii. 278.
[4] Gason, 'Dieyerie Tribe of Australian Aborigines,' in Woods, *Native Tribes of South Australia*, p. 257 sq.
[5] Collins, *English Colony in New South Wales*, i. 600. Barrington, *History of New South Wales*, p. 22.
[6] Lumholtz, *Among Cannibals*, p. 100.
[7] Hale, *U.S. Exploring Expedition, Vol. VI. Ethnography and Philology*, pp. 16, 73.

principle into practice.[1]   We are told by Polack that among the Maoris of New Zealand lying is universally practised by all classes, and that an accomplished liar is accounted a man of consummate ability.[2]   But Dieffenbach found that, if treated with honesty, they were always ready to reciprocate such treatment ; [3] and, according to another authority, they believed in an evil spirit whom they said was "a liar and the father of lies." [4] The broad statement made by von Jhering, that among the South Sea Islanders lying is regarded as a harmless and innocent play of the imagination,[5] is certainly not correct.   The treacherous disposition attributed to the Caroline Islanders [6] and the natives of New Britain [7] does not imply so much as that.   The New Caledonians are, comparatively speaking, "not naturally dishonest." [8]   The Solomon Islanders are praised as faithful and reliable workmen and servants,[9] though cheating in trade is nowadays very common among some of them.[10]   Of the people of Erromanga, in the New Hebrides, the Rev. H. A. Robertson states that "truth, in heathenism, was told only when it suited best, but," he adds, "it is not that natives are always reckless about the truth so much as that they seem utterly incapable of stating anything definitely, or stating a thing just as it really occurred." [11]   In the opinion of some authorities, the Fijians are very untruthful and regard adroit lying as an accomplishment.[12] Their propensity to lie, says the missionary Williams, "is so strong that they seem to have no wish to deny its existence, or very little shame when convicted of a falsehood."   The universal prevalence of the habit of lying is so thoroughly taken for granted, "that it is common to hear, after the most ordinary statement, the rejoinder, 'That's a lie,' or something to the same effect, at which the accused person does not think of taking offence."   But the same writer adds :—"Natives have often told me lies, manifestly without any ill-will, and when it would have been far more to their advantage to have spoken the truth.   The Fijians hail as agreeable companions those who are

---

[1] Mariner, *Natives of the Tonga Islands*, ii. 163 *sq.*

[2] Polack, *Manners and Customs of the New Zealanders*, ii. 102 *sq.* See also Colenso, *Maori Races of New Zealand*, pp. 44, 46.

[3] Dieffenbach, *Travels in New Zealand*, ii. 109.

[4] Yate, *Account of New Zealand*, p. 145.

[5] von Jhering, *Der Zweck im Recht*, ii. 606.

[6] Angas, *Polynesia*, p. 386.

[7] Powell, *Wanderings in a Wild Country*, p. 262.

[8] Anderson, *Travel in Fiji and New Caledonia*, p. 233.

[9] Parkinson, *Zur Ethnographie der nordwestlichen Salomo Inseln*, p. 4.

[10] Sommerville, 'Ethnogr. Notes in New Georgia,' in *Jour. Anthr. Inst.* xxvi. 393.

[11] Robertson, *Erromanga*, p. 384 *sq.*

[12] Wilkes, *U.S. Exploring Expedition*, iii. 76.

skilful in making tales, but, under some circumstances, strongly condemn the practice of falsehood. . . . On matters most lied about by civilised people, the native is the readiest to speak the truth. Thus, when convicted of some offence, he rarely attempts to deny it, but will generally confess all to any one he esteems. . . . The following incident shows that lying *per se* is condemned and considered disreputable. A white man, notorious for falsehood, had displeased a powerful chief, and wrote asking me to intercede for him. I did so ; when the chief dismissed the case briefly, saying, ' Tell—that no one hates a foreigner ; but tell him that every one hates a liar ! ' " [1] Other writers even deny that the Fijians were habitual liars ; [2] and Erskine found that those chiefs with whom he had to deal were so open to appeals to their good faith as to convince him " that they had a due appreciation of the virtue of truth." [3]

Nowhere in the savage world is truth held in less estimation than among many of the African races. The Negroes are described as cunning and liars by nature.[4] They " tell a lie more readily than they tell the truth," and falsehood " is not re- cognised amongst them as a fault." [5] They lie not only for the sake of gaining some advantage by it, or in order to please or amuse, but their lies are often said to be absolutely without purpose.[6] Of the natives of the Gold Coast the old traveller Bosman says, " The Negroes are all, without exception, crafty, villainous and fraudulent, and very seldom to be trusted, being sure to slip no opportunity of cheating an European, nor indeed one another." [7] Among all the Bakalai tribes " lying is thought an enviable accomplishment." [8] The Bakongo, in their answers, " will generally try and tell the questioner what they think will please him most, quite ignoring the truthfulness we consider it necessary to observe in our replies." [9] Miss Kingsley's experience of West African natives is likewise that they " will say ' Yes ' to any mortal thing, if they think you want them to." [10] The Wakamba are described as great liars.[11]

---

[1] Williams and Calvert, *Fiji*, p. 107 sq.
[2] Erskine, *Cruise among the Islands of the Western Pacific*, p. 264. Ander- son, *Travel in Fiji and New Cale- donia*, p. 130.
[3] Erskine, *op. cit.* p. 264.
[4] Baker, *Albert N'yanza*, i. 289. Burton, *Mission to Gelele*, ii. 199.
[5] Reade, *Savage Africa*, p. 580.
[6] Hübbe-Schleiden, *Ethiopien, Stu- dien über West-Afrika*, p. 186 sq.

[7] Bosman, *New Description of the Coast of Guinea*, p. 100.
[8] Du Chaillu, *Explorations and Adventures in Equatorial Africa*, p. 390. *Cf. ibid.* p. 331.
[9] Ward, *Five Years with the Congo Cannibals*, p. 47.
[10] Kingsley, *Travels in West Africa*, p. 525.
[11] Krapf, *Travels in Eastern Africa*, p. 355.

Among the Waganda "truth is held in very low estimation, and it is never considered wrong to tell lies; indeed, a successful liar is considered a smart, clever fellow, and rather admired." [1] Untruthfulness is said to be " a national characteristic " of the tribes inhabiting the region of Lake Nyassa.[2] From his experience of the Eastern Central Africans, the Rev. D. Macdonald writes :—" ' Telling lies ' is much practised and is seldom considered a fault. . . . The negro often thinks that he is flattered by being accused of falsehood. So, when natives wish to pay a high compliment to a European who has told them an interesting story, they look into his face and say, ' O father, you are a great liar.' " [3] To the Wanika, says Mr. New, lying is " almost as the very breath of their nostrils, and all classes, young and old, male and female, indulge in it. A great deal of their lying is without cause or object; it is lying for lying's sake. You ask a man his name, his tribe, where he lives, or any other simple question of like nature, and the answer he gives you will, as a rule, be the very opposite to the truth ; yet he has nothing to evade or gain by so doing. Lying seems to be more natural to him than speaking the truth. He lies when detection is evident, and laughs at it as though he thought it a good joke. He hears himself called a *mulongo* (liar) a score of times a day, but he notices it not, for there is no opprobrium in the term to him. To hide a fault he lies with the most barefaced audacity and blindest obstinacy. . . . When his object is gain, he will invent falsehoods wholesale. . . . He boasts that *ulongo* (lying) is his *pesa* (piece, ha'pence), and holds bare truth to be the most unprofitable commodity in the world. But while he lies causelessly, objectlessly, recklessly in self-defence or for self-interest, he is not a malicious liar. He does not lie with express intent to do others harm ; this he would consider immoral, and he has sufficient goodness of heart to avoid indulging therein. . . . I have often been struck with the manner in which he has controlled his tongue when the character and interest of others have been at stake." [4] If a Bantu of South-Eastern Africa " undertakes the charge of any form of property, he accounts for it with as great fidelity as if he were the Keeper of the Great Seal. But, on the other hand, there are many circumstances in which falsehood is not reckoned even a disgrace, and if a man could

[1] Wilson and Felkin, *Uganda*, i. 224. *Cf.* Felkin, ' Notes on the Waganda Tribe,' in *Proceed. Roy. Soc. Edinburgh*, xiii. 722 ; Ashe, *Two Kings of Uganda*, p. 295.
[2] Macdonald, 'East Central African Customs,' in *Jour. Anthr. Inst.* xxii. 119.
[3] Macdonald, *Africana*, i. 262 *sq.*
[4] New, *Life, Wanderings, and Labours in Eastern Africa*, p. 96 *sqq.*

extricate himself from difficulties by lying and did not do so, he would be simply thought a fool."[1] Andersson speaks of the "lying habits" of the Herero.[2] Of the Bachapins, a Bechuana tribe, Burchell observes that among their vices a universal disregard for truth and a want of honourable adherence to their promise stand high above the rest, the consequence of this habitual practice of lying being "the absence of shame, even on being detected."[3] Among the Kafirs "deception is a practised art from early childhood; even the children will not answer a plain question."[4] It is considered a smart thing to deceive so long as a person is not found out, but it is awkward to be detected; hence a native father will enjoy seeing his children deceive people cleverly.[5] "In trading with them, you may make up your mind that all they tell you is untrue, and act accordingly. . . . Your own natives, on the other hand, if they like you, will lie for your benefit as strongly as the opposite party against you; and both sides think it all fair trade."[6] And in a Kafir lawsuit "defendant, plaintiff, and witnesses are allowed to tell as many lies as they like, in order to make the best of their case."[7] But we also hear that Kafirs do not tell lies to their chiefs, and that there are many among them who would never deceive a white man whom they are fond of or respect.[8] Among the Bushmans veracity is said to be too often, yet not always, disregarded, "and the neglect of it considered a mere venial offence."[9] "The first version of what a Bushman or any native has to say can never be relied on; whatever you ask him about, he invariably says first, 'I don't know,' and then promises to tell you all he does know. Ask him for news, and he says, 'No; we have got no news,' and shortly afterwards he will tell you news of perhaps great interest."[10] In Madagascar there was no stigma attached to deceit or fraud; they "were rather admired as proofs of superior cunning, as things to be imitated, so far at least as they would not bring the offender within the penalties of the native laws."[11] Ellis says that "the best sign of genius in children is esteemed a quickness to deceive,

---

[1] Macdonald, *Light in Africa*, p. 211.
[2] Andersson, *Lake Ngami*, p. 217. Cf. *ibid.* p. 499 (Bayeye).
[3] Burchell, *Travels in the Interior of Southern Africa*, ii. 553 *sq.*
[4] Holden, *The Past and Future of the Kaffir Races*, p. 179.
[5] Kidd, *The Essential Kafir*, p. 285.
[6] Leslie, *Among the Zulus and Amatongas*, p. 199. *Cf. ibid.* p. 202.
[7] Maclean, *Compendium of Kafir Laws and Customs*, p. 58.
[8] Kidd, *The Essential Kafir*, p. 286.
[9] Burchell, *op. cit.* ii. 54.
[10] Chapman, *Travels in the Interior of South Africa*, i. 76 *sq.*
[11] Sibree, *The Great African Island*, p. 338.

overreach and cheat. The people delight in fabulous tales, but in none so much or universally as in those that relate instances of successful deceit or fraud. . . . Their constant aim is, in business to swindle, in professed friendship to extort, and in mere conversation to exaggerate and fabricate." [1] These statements refer to the Hovas ; but among the Betsileo, inhabiting the same island, lying and cheating are equally rife, and "neither appears to have been thought a sin, so long as it remained undiscovered." [2] At the same time many of the Madagascar proverbs are designed to put down lying, and to show that truth is always best.[3]

But in Africa, also, there are many peoples who have been described as regardful of truth and hostile to falsehood. Early travellers speak very highly of the sincerity of the Hottentots. Father Tachart says that they have more honesty than is almost anywhere found among Christians ; [4] and Kolben agrees with him, asserting that the word of a Hottentot is sacred, and that there is hardly anything upon earth which he looks upon as a fouler crime than breach of engagement.[5] According to Barrow, the Hottentots are perfectly honest and faithful, and, " if accused of crimes of which they have been guilty, they generally divulge the truth." [6] Of the Manansas Dr. Holub states that, so far as his experience goes, they are beyond the average for honesty and fidelity, and are consequently laughed at by the more powerful tribes as "the simpletons of the North." [7] The Bahima in the Uganda Protectorate are usually very honest and truthful, and most of the Nandi think it very wicked to tell a lie.[8] Among the For tribe of Central Africa "lying is held to be a great crime ; even the youngest children are severely beaten for it, and any one over fifteen or sixteen who is an habitual liar suffers the loss of one lip as a penalty." [9] Speaking of the natives of Sierra Leone, Winterbottom remarks that, in proportion as we advance into the interior of the country, the people are found to be more devoid of art and more free from suspicion.[10] " Those who have dealings with the Fán univers-

[1] Ellis, *History of Madagascar*, i. 143 *sq.*

[2] Sibree, *op. cit.* p. 125. Shaw, ' Betsileo,' in *Antananarivo Annual*, iii. 79.

[3] Clemes, ' Malagasy Proverbs,' *ibid.* iv. 29.

[4] Tachart, quoted by Kolben, *Present State of the Cape of Good Hope*, i. 167.

[5] *Ibid.* i. 59.

[6] Barrow, *Travels into the Interior of Southern Africa*, i. 151 *sq.*

[7] Holub, *Seven Years in South Africa*, ii. 209.

[8] Johnston, *Uganda Protectorate*, ii. 630, 879.

[9] Felkin, in *Proceed. Roy. Soc. Edinburgh*, xiii. 232.

[10] Winterbottom, *Account of the*

ally prefer them in point of honesty and manliness to the Mpongwe and Coast races," and it is an insult to call one of them a liar or coward.[1] Monrad, who wrote in the beginning of the nineteenth century, asserts that among the Negroes of Accra lying is by no means common and that they are as a rule honest towards their own people.[2] According to an early authority, the people of Great Benin were very straightforward and did not cheat each other.[3] Mr. and Mrs. Hinde write that the Masai are as a race truthful, and that a grown-up person among them will not lie ; "he may refuse to answer a question, but, once given, his word can be depended on."[4] Dr. Baumann, on the other hand, says that they often lie, but that they regard lying as a great fault.[5] The Guanches of the Canary Islands are stated to have been "slaves to their word."[6] Of the Berbers of Morocco Leo Africanus writes :—"Most honest people they are, and destitute of all fraud and guile.... They keep their couenant most faithfully ; insomuch that they had rather die than breake promise."[7] M. Dyveyrier found the same virtue among the Touareg, another Berber people :—"La fidélité aux promesses, aux traités, est poussée si loin par les Touâreg, qu'il est difficile d'obtenir d'eux des engagements.... Il est de maxime chez les Touâreg, en matière de contrat, de ne s'engager que pour la moitié de ce qu'on peut tenir, afin de ne pas s'exposer au reproche d'infidélité. . . . Le mensonge, le vol domestique et l'abus de confiance sont inconnus des Touâreg."[8] As regards the truthfulness of the African Arabs opinions vary. Parkyns asks, "Who is more trustworthy than the desert Arab ?"[9] According to Rohlfs and Chavanne, on the other hand, the Arabs of the Sahara are much addicted to lying ;[10] and of the Arabs of Egypt Mr. St. John observes :— "There is no general appreciation of a man's word.... 'Liar' is a playful appellative scarcely reproachful ; and 'I have told a lie' a confession that may be made without a blush."[11] Herodotus' statement that "the Arabs observe pledges as religiously as any people,"[12] is true of the Bedouins of Arabia in the

Native Africans in the Neighbourhood of Sierra Leone, i. 206 *sq.*

[1] Burton, *Two Trips to Gorilla Land*, i. 225 *sq.*

[2] Monrad, *Guinea-Kysten og dens Indbyggere*, p. 6.

[3] Quoted by Ling Roth, *Great Benin*, p. 45.

[4] Hinde, *The Last of the Masai*, p. 34.

[5] Baumann, *Durch Massailand*, p. 165.

[6] Bory de St. Vincent, *Essais sur les Isles Fortunées*, p. 70.

[7] Leo Africanus, *History and Description of Africa*, i. 183.

[8] Dyveyrier, *Exploration du Sahara*, p. 384 *sq.*

[9] Parkyns, *Life in Abyssinia*, ii. 182.

[10] Chavanne, *Die Sahara*, p. 392.

[11] St. John, *Adventures in the Lybian Desert*, p. 31.

[12] Herodotus, iii. 8.

present day. " No vice or crime is more deservedly stigmatised
as infamous among Bedouins than treachery. An individual in
the great Arabian Desert will be forgiven if he should kill a
stranger on the road, but eternal disgrace would be attached to
his name, if it were known that he had robbed his companion,
or his protected guest, even of a handkerchief." [1] Wallin
affirms that you may put perfect trust in the promise of a
Bedouin, as soon as you have eaten salt and bread with him.[2]
But whilst faithfulness to a tacit or express promise is thus
regarded by him as a sacred duty, lying and cheating are as
prevalent in the desert as in the market-towns of Syria.[3]
Speaking of the Bedouins of the Euphrates, Mr. Blunt
observes :—" Truth, in ordinary matters, is not regarded as a
virtue by the Bedouins, nor is lying held shameful. Every
man, they say, has a right to conceal his own thought. In
matters of importance, the simple affirmation is confirmed by
an oath, and then the fact stated may be relied on. There is
only one exception to the general rule of lying among them.
The Bedouin, if questioned on the breed of his mare, will not
give a false answer. He may refuse to say, or he may answer
that he does not know ; but he will not name another breed
than that to which she really belongs. . . . The rule, however,
does not hold good on any other point of horse dealing. The
age, the qualities, and the ownership of the horse may be all
falsely stated." [4]

Various statements of travellers thus directly contradict
the common opinion that want of truthfulness is mostly a
characteristic of uncivilised races.[5] And we have much
reason to assume that a foreigner visiting a savage tribe is
apt rather to underrate than to overestimate its veracity.
Mr. Savage Landor gives us a curious insight into an
explorer's method of testing it. " If you were to say to
an Ainu, ' You are old, are you not ? ' he would answer

[1] Burckhardt, *Notes on the Be-
douins and Wahábys*, p. 190 sq.
[2] Wallin, *Reseanteckningar från
Orienten*, iii. 116.
[3] Burckhardt, *op. cit.* p. 104 sq.
Cf. Wallin, *op. cit.* iv. 89 sq. ;
Doughty, *Arabia Deserta*, i. 241.
[4] Blunt, *Bedouin Tribes of the
Euphrates*, ii. 203 sq. Cf. Niebuhr,
Travels through Arabia, ii. 302 :—
" There is no instance of false testi-

mony given in respect to the descent
of a horse. Every Arabian is persuaded that himself and his whole
family would be ruined, if he should
prevaricate in giving his oath in an
affair of such consequence."
[5] Burton, *City of the Saints*, p. 130.
Vierkandt, *Naturvölker und Kulturvölker*, p. 273. von Jhering, *Der
Zweck im Recht*, ii. 606.

' Yes ' ; but if you asked the same man, ' You are not old, are you ? ' he would equally answer ' Yes.' " And then comes the conclusion :—" Knowingly speaking the truth is not one of their characteristics ; indeed, they do not know the difference between falsehood and truth." [1] It is hardly surprising to hear from other authorities that the Ainu are remarkably honest, and regard veracity as one of the most imperative duties.[2] Speaking of the Uaupés and other Brazilian tribes, Mr. Wallace observes : —" In my communications and inquiries among the Indians on various matters, I have always found the greatest caution necessary, to prevent one's arriving at wrong conclusions. They are always apt to affirm that which they see you wish to believe, and, when they do not at all comprehend your question, will unhesitatingly answer, ' Yes.' " [3] Savages who are inclined to give inaccurate answers to questions made by strangers, may nevertheless be truthful towards each other. As the regard for life and property, so the regard for truth varies according as the person concerned is a foreigner or a tribesman. " Perfidy and faithlessness," says Crawfurd, " are vices of the Indian islanders, and those vices of which they have been most frequently accused by strangers. This sentence against them must, however, be understood with some allowances. In their domestic and social inter-course, they are far from being a deceitful people, but in reality possess more integrity than it is reasonable to look for with so much misgovernment and barbarity. It is in their intercourse with strangers and with enemies that, like other barbarians, the treachery of their character is dis-played." [4] The natives of the interior of Sumatra are " dis-honest in their dealings with strangers, which they esteem no moral defect." [5] Dalager states that the same Green-landers who, among themselves, in the sale of an object

[1] Landor, *Alone with the Hairy Ainu*, p. 283.
[2] Holland, in *Jour. Anthr. Inst.* iii. 237. von Siebold, *Aino auf der Insel Yesso*, p. 25.
[3] Wallace, *Travels on the Amazon*, p. 494 *sq*.
[4] Crawfurd, *op. cit.* i. 71 *sq*. Cf. Christian, *Caroline Islands*, p. 71 *sq*.
[5] Marsden, *op. cit.* p. 208.

which the buyer had not seen, would depreciate it rather than overpraise it—even though the seller was anxious to get rid of it—told frightful lies in their transactions with Danish traders.[1] The Touareg, whilst scrupulously faithful to a promise given to one of their own people, do not regard as binding a promise given to a Christian ;[2] and their Arab neighbours say that their word, " like water fallen on the sand, is never to be found again." [3] The Masai, according to Herr Merker, hold any kind of deceit to be allowable in their relations with persons of another race.[4] The Hovas of Madagascar even considered it a duty for anyone speaking with foreigners on political matters to state the exact opposite to the truth, and punished him who did otherwise.[5]

In point of truthfulness savages are in many cases superior to nations more advanced in culture. " A Chinese," says Mr. Wells Williams, " requires but little motive to falsify, and he is constantly sharpening his wits to cozen his customer—wheedle him by promises and cheat him in goods or work." [6] His ordinary speech is said to be so full of insincerity that it is very difficult to learn the truth in almost any case.[7] He feels no shame at being detected in a lie, nor does he fear any punishment from his gods for it ; [8] if you call him a liar, " you arouse in him no sense of outrage, no sentiment of degradation." [9] Yet the moral teachings of the Chinese inculcate truthfulness as a stringent duty. One of their injunctions is, " Let children always be taught to speak the simple truth." [10] Many sayings may be quoted from Confucius in which sincerity is celebrated as highly and demanded as urgently as it ever was by any

[1] Dalager, op. cit. p. 69 sq.
[2] von Bary, quoted by Chavanne, Die Sahara, p. 186.
[3] Dubois, Timbuctoo, p. 231.
[4] Merker, Die Masai, p. 115.
[5] Ellis, History of Madagascar, i. 144. Professor Stanley Hall observes ('Children's Lies,' in American Journal of Psychology, iii. 62) that "truth for our friends and lies for our enemies is a practical, though not distinctly conscious rule widely current with children."
[6] Wells Williams, The Middle Kingdom, i. 834.
[7] Smith, Chinese Characteristics, p. 271.
[8] Cooke, China, p. 414. Edkins, Religion in China, p. 122. Bowring, Siam, i. 106. Wells Williams, op. cit. i. 834.
[9] Smith, Chinese Characteristics, p. 271.
[10] Wells Williams, op. cit. i. 522.

Christian moralist. Faithfulness and sincerity, he said, should be held as first principles. Sincerity is the way of Heaven, the end and beginning of things, without which there would be nothing. It is as necessary to truly virtuous conduct as a boat is to a man wishing to cross a river, or as oars are to a boat. The superior man ought to feel shame when his conduct is not in accord with his words.[1] But there are instances in which sincerity has to yield to family duties : a father should conceal the misconduct of his son, and a son that of his father.[2] Moreover, the great moralists themselves did not always act up to their lofty principles. Confucius and Mencius sometimes did not hesitate to tell a lie for the sake of convenience.[3] The former could excuse himself from seeing an unwelcome visitor on the ground that he was sick, when there was nothing the matter with him ; [4] and he deliberately broke an oath which he had sworn, because it had been forced from him.[5] In Japan, Burma, and Siam, truth is more respected than in China. " In love of truth," says Professor Rein, " the Japanese, so far as my experience goes, are not inferior to us Europeans." [6] The Burmese, though partial to much exaggeration, are generally truthful.[7] And " the mendacity so characteristic of Orientals is not a national defect among the Siamese. Lying, no doubt, is often resorted to as a protection against injustice and oppression, but the chances are greatly in favour of truth when evidence is sought." [8]

Lying has been called the national vice of the Hindus.[9] " It is not too much to assert that the mass of Bengalis have no notion of truth and falsehood." [10] A gentleman

[1] *Lun Yü*, i. 8. 2 ; vii. 24 ; ix. 24 ; xii. 10. 1 ; xv. 5. 2. *Chung Yung*, xx. 18. Douglas, *Confucianism and Taouism*, pp. 103, 114, 146. Legge, *Chinese Classics*, i. 100.
[2] *Lun Yü*, xiii. 18. 2.
[3] Legge, *Chinese Classics*, i. 100. Smith, *Chinese Characteristics*, p. 267.
[4] *Lun Yü*, vi. 13.
[5] *Lun Yü*, xvii. 20.
[6] Rein, *Japan*, p. 393.
[7] MacMahon, *Far Cathay and Farther India*, p. 62. Forbes, *British Burma*, p. 45. Fytche, *Burma Past and Present*, ii. 67.
[8] Bowring, *Siam*, i. 105.
[9] Caldwell, *Tinnevelly Shanars*, p. 38. *Cf.* Kearns, *Tribes of South India*, pp. 64 (Reddies and Hindus generally), 68 (Reddies and Naickers) ; Burton, *Sindh*, pp. 197, 284 ; *Idem, Sind Revisited*, i. 314.
[10] Trevelyan, quoted by Wilkins, *Modern Hinduism*, p. 401.

who has been brought into the closest intimacy with natives of all classes, declares " that when a question is asked, the full bearing of which on themselves or those connected with them they cannot see, you may rely upon it that the first answer you receive is false ; but that, when they see that the truth cannot injure themselves or any one they care for, they will speak the truth." [1] The testimony of a Hindu is not generally regarded as evidence.[2] Forgery is frequently resorted to, cheating is rife. " In almost all business transactions of the smallest kind a written agreement must be made on both sides, and this must be stamped and registered, because it is believed that a man's word is not binding." [3] Nor is a lie held disreputable, especially if not found out.[4] But in India, as elsewhere, the question whether truth or falsehood is to be spoken depends on the relationship between the speaker and the party addressed. In their relations with each other, says Sir W. H. Sleeman, members of a village community spoke as much truth as those of any other community in the world, but in their relations with the government they told as many lies ; " if a man had told a lie to *cheat* his neighbour, he would have become an object of hatred and contempt—if he had told a lie to *save* his neighbour's fields from an increase of rent or tax, he would have become an object of esteem and respect." [5] Of the Sûdra inhabitants of Central India Sir John Malcolm likewise observes that " they may be said, in their intercourse with strangers and with officers of government, to evade the truth, and often to assert positive falsehoods"; whereas, " in their intercourse with each other, falsehood is not common, and many (particularly some of the cultivators) are distinguished by their adherence to truth." [6] The ancient Hindus were praised for their veracity and good faith ;

[1] Wilkins, *Modern Hinduism*, p. 399 *sq.*
[2] Percival, *Land of the Veda*, p. 288.
[3] Wilkins, *op. cit.* p. 407 *sq.*
[4] *Ibid.* p. 400. Caldwell, *op. cit.* p. 40.
[5] Sleeman, *op. cit.* ii. 123. *Cf.*
ibid. ii. 118, 129 *sq.* ; Crooke, *Tribes and Castes of the North-Western Provinces and Oudh*, ii. 478 (Hâbûra).
[6] Malcolm, *Memoir of Central India*, ii. 171. *Cf.* Hislop, *op. cit.* p. 1.

in his History of India, written in the second century of
the Christian era, Arrian states that no Indian was ever
known to tell an untruth.[1]   In the sacred books of
India truthfulness is highly celebrated.   " If veracity and
a thousand horse-sacrifices are weighed against each other,
it is found that truth ranks even higher than a thousand
horse-sacrifices." [2]   " Verily the gods are the truth, and
man is the untruth." [3]   " There is one law which the gods
do keep, namely, the truth.   It is through this that their
conquest, their glory is unassailable: and so, forsooth, is his
conquest, his glory unassailable whosoever, knowing this,
speaks the truth." [4]   Attendance on, or the worship of,
the sacred fire means speaking the truth :—" Whosoever
speaks the truth, acts as if he sprinkled that lighted fire
with ghee ; for even so does he enkindle it : and ever the
more increases his own vital energy, and day by day does
he become better.   And whosoever speaks the untruth,
acts as if he sprinkled that lighted fire with water ; for even
so does he enfeeble it : and ever the less becomes his own
vital energy, and day by day does he become more wicked.
Let him, therefore, speak nothing but the truth." [5] Fearful denunciations are particularly pronounced against those
who deliver false testimony in a court of justice.[6]   By
giving false evidence concerning small cattle, a witness
commits the sin of killing ten men ; by false evidence concerning cows, horses, and men, he commits the sin of killing a hundred, a thousand, and ten thousand men respectively ; but by false evidence concerning land, he commits
the sin of killing the whole human race.[7]   The sin of
falsehood thus admits of different degrees according to the
magnitude of the injury inflicted by it.   Indeed, " in some
cases a man who, though knowing the facts to be different,
gives such false evidence from a pious motive, does not lose
heaven ; such evidence they call the speech of the gods." [8]

---

[1] Arrian, *Historia Indica*, xii. 5.
[2] *Institutes of Vishnu*, viii. 36.
[3] *Satapatha-Brâhmana*, i. 1. 1. 4 ;
iii. 3. 2. 2.
[4] *Ibid.* iii. 4. 2. 8. *Cf. ibid.* i. 1. 1. 5.
[5] *Ibid.* ii. 2. 2. 19.
[6] *Laws of Manu*, viii. 82.
[7] *Gautama*, xiii. 14 *sqq.*
[8] *Laws of Manu*, viii. 103.

Moreover, " whenever the death of a Sûdra, of a Vaisya, of a Kshatriya, or of a Brâhmana would be caused by a declaration of the truth, a falsehood may be spoken ; for such falsehood is preferable to the truth." [1] According to Buddhist conceptions of lying, " the magnitude of the crime increases in proportion to the value of the article, or the importance of the matter, about which the lie is told."[2] And it is a lesser wrong to lie in self-defence than to lie with a view to procuring an advantage by injuring one's neighbour. Thus, to deny the possession of any article, in order to retain it, is not a lie of a heinous description, whereas to bear false witness in order that the proper owner may be deprived of that which he possesses, is a lie to which a greater degree of culpability is attached.[3] The Buddhist precept of truthfulness is more restricted than that laid down by Brahmanism :—" It is said by the Brahmans that it is not a crime to tell a lie on behalf of the guru, or on account of cattle, or to save the person's own life, or to gain the victory in any contest ; but this is contrary to the precept." [4] One of the conditions that make a Buddha is, never, under the influence of desire and other passions, to utter a conscious lie, for the sake of wealth or any other advantage.[5] From the time that Gautama became a Bodhisattva, or claimant for the Buddhaship, through all his births until the attainment of the Buddhaship, he never told a lie ; and " it were easier for the sakwala [or system of worlds] to be blown away than for a supreme Buddha to utter an untruth." [6] His followers are not equally scrupulous. The Buddhists of Ceylon, we are told, lie without compunction, and are not ashamed to be detected in a lie.[7] And religious Mongols " do not hesitate to tell lies even when saying their prayers." [8]

[1] *Laws of Manu*, viii. 104.
[2] Hardy, *Manual of Budhism*, p. 486.
[3] *Ibid.* p. 485.
[4] *Ibid.* p. 486.
[5] *Jātaka Tales*, p. 23.
[6] Hardy, *op. cit.* p. 486.
[7] Knox, quoted by Schmidt, *Ceylon*, p. 317. Hæckel, *Visit to Ceylon*, p. 239.
[8] Gilmour, *Among the Mongols*, p. 259.

According to Zoroastrianism, truthfulness is a most
sacred duty. Lying is a creation of the evil spirits, and
the most efficacious weapon against it is the holy religion
revealed to man by Zarathustra.[1] In one of the Pahlavi
texts it is said that when the Spirit of Wisdom was asked,
" Through how many ways and motives and good works
do people arrive most at heaven ? " he answered thus :
" The first good work is liberality, the second truth." [2]
Contracts are inviolable, both those which are pledged
with hand or pawn, and those by a mere word.[3] It is a
duty to keep faith even with an unbeliever :—" Break not
the contract, O Spitama, neither the one that thou hadst
entered into with one of the unfaithful, nor the one that
thou hadst entered into with one of the faithful who
is one of thy own faith." [4] Greek historians and cuneiform inscriptions also bear witness to the great detestation
in which falsehood was held by the ancient Persians.
Herodotus writes :—" Their sons are carefully instructed
from their fifth to their twentieth year in three things
alone—to ride, to draw the bow, and to speak the truth.
. . . The most disgraceful thing in the world, they think,
is to tell a lie ; the next worse, to owe a debt : because,
among other reasons, the debtor is obliged to tell lies." [5]
In the inscriptions of Darius lying is taken as representative of all evil. He is favoured by Ormuzd " because he was not a heretic, nor a liar, nor a tyrant." His
great fear is lest it may be thought that any part of the
record which he has set up has been falsely related ; and
he even abstains from narrating certain events of his reign
" lest to him who may hereafter peruse the tablet, the
many deeds that have been done by him may seem to be
falsely recorded." [6] Professor Spiegel tries to prove that

---

[1] *Bundahis*, i. 24 ; xxviii. 14, 16.
Dînâ-î Maînôg-î Khirad, xix. 4, 6 ;
xxx. 5 ; xxxvi. 29. Darmesteter, in
Sacred Books of the East, iv. p. lxii.
Spiegel, *Erânische Alterthumskunde*,
iii. 684 *sq.* Geiger, *Civilization of the
Eastern Irânians*, i. 164 *sq.* Meyer,
Geschichte des Alterthums, i. 534,
536.

[2] *Dînâ-î Maînôg-î Khirad*, xxxvii.
2 *sqq.*
[3] *Vendîdâd*, iv. 5 *sqq.*
[4] *Yasts*, x. 2.
[5] Herodotus, i. 136, 138. *Cf.*
Stobæus, *Florilegium*, 44, vol. ii. 227 ;
Xenophon, *Cyri Institutio*, i. 6. 33.
[6] Rawlinson, in his translation of
Herodotus, i. 262 *sq.* n. 3.

falsehood, not truthfulness, was a national characteristic
of the ancient Eranians, to which their noblest men
offered fruitless resistance ;[1] but the facts he quotes in
support of his opinion refer to their dealings with foreign
nations, and have consequently little bearing on the subject. The modern Persians are notorious liars, who do
not even claim to be believed, and smile when detected in
a lie.[2] The nomad alone is faithful to his word ; the expression, " I am a nomad," means, " You may trust me." [3]
    Falsehood is a prevailing vice in other Muhammedan
countries also. " Constant veracity," says Mr. Lane, " is
a virtue extremely rare in modern Egypt " ; and a deceitful disposition in commercial transactions is one of the
most notorious faults of the Egyptian.[4] Mr. Lane partly
ascribes this habit to the influence of Islam, which allows,
and even commands, falsehood in certain cases. The
common Moslem doctrine is, that a lie is permissible when
told in order to save one's own life, or to reconcile persons
at variance with each other, or to please or persuade one's
wife, or to obtain any advantage in a war with the enemies
of the faith.[5] But in other cases lying was highly reprobated by the Prophet ; and that the people have not
forgotten its sinfulness appears from the phrase, " No, I
beg forgiveness of God, it was so and so," which they
seldom omit when retracting an unintentional mis-state-
ment.[6] I think it is erroneous to regard the want of
truthfulness among Muhammedan nations as a result of
their religion. The Eastern Christians and Buddhists are
no less addicted to falsehood than the Muhammedans.[7]
    The Homeric poems make us acquainted with gods and
men who have recourse to fraud and lying whenever it
suits their purpose.[8] The great Zeus makes no difficulty

[1] Spiegel, op. cit. iii. 686.
[2] Polak, Persien, i. 10. Wallin,
Reseanteckningar från Orienten, iv.
192, 247. Wilson, Persian Life and
Customs, p. 229 sqq.
[3] Polak, op. cit. ii. 95.
[4] Lane, Manners and Customs of the
Modern Egyptians, i. 382 sq. Cf.
Burckhardt, Arabic Proverbs, p. 100.

[5] Lane, Modern Egyptians, i. 383.
Muir, Life of Mahomet, i. p. lxxiii.
sq. n. †.
[6] Lane, Modern Egyptians, i. 383 sq.
[7] Vámbéry, Der Islam im neunzehnten Jahrhundert, p. 232.
[8] Cf. Kames, Sketches of the History
of Man, iv. 150 sq. ; Mahaffy, Social
Life in Greece, p. 26 sqq.

in sending a lying dream to Agamemnon. Pallas Athene
is guilty of gross deceit and treachery to Hector ; she
expressly recommends dissimulation, and loves Odysseus
on account of his deceitful character.[1] No man deals
more in feigned stories than this master of cunning, who
makes a boast of his falsehood.[2] In the period which lies
between the Homeric age and the Persian wars veracity
made perhaps some progress among the Greeks,[3] but it
never became one of their national virtues.[4] Yet in the
Greek literature deceit is frequently condemned as a vice,
and truthfulness praised as a virtue.[5] Achilles expresses
his horror of lying.[6] " Not to tell a lie," was one of the
maxims of Solon.[7] Pindar strongly censures a character
like that of Odysseus,[8] and ends up his eulogy on Psaumis
by the assurance that he never would contaminate his
speech with a lie.[9] According to Pythagoras, men become like gods when they speak the truth.[10] According to
Plato, the habit of lying makes the soul ugly[11] ; " truth
is the beginning of every good thing, both to gods and
men." [12] Yet a distinction should be made between
different kinds of untruth. Though the many are too
fond of saying that at proper times and places falsehood
may often be right,[13] it must be admitted that a lie is in
certain cases useful and not hateful, as in dealing with
enemies, or when those whom we call our friends in a fit
of madness or illusion are going to do some harm.[14] Moreover, the rulers of the State are allowed to lie for the
public good, just as physicians make use of medicines ;
and they will find a considerable dose of falsehood and
deceit necessary for this purpose.[15] On the other hand, if
the ruler catches anybody besides himself lying in the

[1] *Odyssey*, xiii. 331 *sq.*
[2] *Ibid.* ix. 19 *sq.*
[3] Schmidt, *Die Ethik der alten Griechen*, ii. 413.
[4] *Cf.* Thucydides, iii. 83.
[5] See Schmidt, *op. cit.* ii. 403 *sqq.*
[6] *Iliad*, ix. 312 *sq.*
[7] Diogenes Laertius, *Vitæ philosophorum*, i. 2 (60).

[8] Pindar, *Nemea*, viii. 26.
[9] *Idem, Olympia*, iv. 17.
[10] Stobæus, *op. cit.* xi. 25, vol. i. 312.
[11] Plato, *Gorgias*, p. 524 *sq.*
[12] *Idem, Leges*, v. 730.
[13] *Ibid.* xi. 916.
[14] Plato, *Respublica*, ii. 382.
[15] *Ibid.* iii. 389 ; v. 459.

State, he will punish him for introducing a practice "which is equally subversive and destructive of ships or State."[1] Next to him who takes a false oath, he who tells a falsehood in the presence of his superiors—elders, parents, or rulers—is most hateful to the gods.[2]

Not without reason did the Romans of the republican age contrast their own *fides* with the mendacity of the Greeks and the perfidy of the Phœnicians. " The goddess of faith (of human and social faith)," says Gibbon, " was worshipped, not only in her temples, but in the lives of the Romans ; and if that nation was deficient in the more amiable qualities of benevolence and generosity, they astonished the Greeks by their sincere and simple performance of the most burdensome engagements."[3] Their annals are adorned with signal examples of uprightness, which, though to a great extent fictitious, yet bear testimony to the estimation in which that quality was held.[4] The Greeks had no Regulus who " chose to deliver himself up to a cruel death rather than to falsify his word to the enemy."[5] The basest forms of falsehood were severely punished by law. According to the Twelve Tables, anyone who had slandered or libelled another by imputing to him a wrongful or immoral act, was to be scourged to death,[6] and capital punishment was also inflicted on false witnesses[7] and corrupt judges.[8] However, already before the end of the Republic dishonesty, perjuries, and forgeries became common in Rome.[9]

The ancient Scandinavians considered it disgraceful for a man to tell a lie, to break a promise, or to commit a treacherous act.[10] To kill or rob openly was a pardonable offence, if an offence at all ; but he who did it secretly was a *nithinger*, a " hateful man;" unless indeed he after-

[1] Plato, *Respublica*, iii. 389.
[2] *Idem, Leges*, xi. 917. *Idem, Respublica*, iii. 389.
[3] Gibbon, *History of the Decline and Fall of the Roman Empire*, v. 311.
[4] Cf. Inge, *Society in Rome under the Cæsars*, p. 33 sq.
[5] Cicero, *De officiis*, i. 13.
[6] *Lex Duodecim Tabularum*, viii. 1.
[7] *Ibid.* viii. 23. Aulus Gellius, *Noctes Atticæ*, xx. i. 53.
[8] *Lex Duodecim Tabularum*, ix. 3. Aulus Gellius, *op. cit.* xx. i. 7.
[9] Inge, *op. cit.* p. 35.
[10] Maurer, *Bekehrung des Norwegischen Stammes*, ii. 154, 183 sq. Rosenberg, *Nordboernes Aandsliv*, i. 487.

wards openly declared his deed.[1] In the Irish Senchus
Mór it is said that not only false witness, but lying in
general, deprives the guilty person of " half his honour-
price up to the third time " ; [2] and, according to the
commentary to the Book of Aicill, the double of his own
full honour-price is due from each person who commits
the crime of secret murder.[3]

In the Old Testament there are recorded, from the
patriarchal age, some cases of lying, which, far from being
condemned, in no way prevented the liar being a special
object of divine favour. It must be admitted, however,
that undue importance has been attached to some of these
acts of falsehood,[4] which were committed among foreigners
with a view to escaping an impending danger.[5] For
instance, when Isaac, dwelling in Gerar, said of his wife
that she was his sister, for fear lest the men of the place
should kill him,[6] he did a thing which few conscientious
men under similar circumstances would hesitate to do. As
for Jacob's long course of double-dealing with his father-
in-law, who was equally greedy and unscrupulous, it
should be remembered that they were natives of different
lands.[7] Again, when Jacob, at the instigation of his
mother, grossly deceived his own blind father, the in-
triguers, as has been pointed out,[8] manifestly felt that the
blessing extorted from Isaac ought to descend upon Jacob
rather than upon Esau, and inasmuch as the word of the
father was held to carry with it divine validity and potency,
the securing of it by fair means or foul was deemed an
urgent necessity. It is obvious that the ancient Hebrews
did not condemn deceit as wrong in the abstract, and that
they were very unscrupulous in the use of means. When-

---

[1] Wilda, *Strafrecht der Germanen*, p.
569. Nordström, *Bidrag till den svenska samhälls-författningens historia*,
ii. 320 *sqq.* Keyser, *Efterladte Skrifter*,
ii. pt. i. 361. Rosenberg, *Nordboernes
Aandsliv*, i. 487. von Amira, 'Recht,'
in Paul's *Grundriss der germanischen
Philologie*, ii. pt. ii. 173.
[2] *Ancient Laws of Ireland*, i. 57.
[3] *Ibid.* iii. 99.

[4] *E.g.*, by McCurdy, ' Moral Evolution of the Old Testament,' in *American Journal of Theology*, i. 665 *sq.* ;
von Jhering, *Zweck im Recht*, ii. 606
sq. ; Spencer, *Principles of Ethics*, i.
402.
[5] *Genesis*, xii. 12 *sq.* ; xx. 2.
[6] *Ibid.* xxvi. 7.
[7] *Ibid.* ch. xxix. *sqq.*
[8] McCurdy, *loc. cit.* p. 666.

ever David was threatened by any danger, he immediately employed a falsehood which served his turn ; though not incapable of generosity, he deceived enemies and friends indifferently, and there is probably no record of treachery and lying consistently pursued which surpasses in baseness his affair with his faithful servant Uriah the Hittite.[1] It is true that his conduct towards Uriah was condemned ; " the thing that David had done displeased the Lord." [2] But it is significant that Yahveh himself occasionally had recourse to deceit for the purpose of carrying out his plans. In order to ruin Ahab he commissioned a lying spirit to deceive his prophets ; [3] and once he threatened to use deception as a means of taking revenge upon idolaters.[4] But to bear false witness against a neighbour was strictly prohibited ; [5] the false witness should suffer the punishment which he was minded to bring upon the person whom he calumniated.[6] In Ecclesiasticus lying is severely censured : —" A lie is a foul blot in a man, yet it is continually in the mouth of the untaught.   A thief is better than a man that is accustomed to lie : but they both shall have destruction to heritage.   The disposition of a liar is dishonourable, and his shame is ever with him." [7]   " Lying lips are abomination to the Lord : but they that deal truly are his delight." [8]   According to the Talmud, " four shall not enter Paradise : the scoffer, the liar, the hypocrite, and the slanderer." [9]   Only for the sake of peace, and especially domestic peace, may a man tell a lie without sinning ; [10] but he who changes his word commits as heavy a sin as he who worships idols.[11]   The duty of truthfulness was particularly emphasised by the Essenes.[12]   He who entered their sect had to pledge himself always to love

---

[1] Cf. Kuenen, Religion of Israel, i. 327 ; McCurdy, loc. cit. p. 681.
[2] 2 Samuel, xi. 27 ; xii. 1 sqq.
[3] 1 Kings, xxii. 20 sqq.
[4] Ezekiel, xiv. 7 sqq. Cf. Spencer, Principles of Ethics, i. 402.
[5] Deuteronomy, v. 20.
[6] Ibid. xix. 16 sqq.
[7] Ecclesiasticus, xx. 24 sqq.
[8] Proverbs, xii. 22.

[9] Deutsch, Literary Remains, p. 57.
[10] Hershon, Treasures of the Talmud, p. 69 sq.
[11] Sanhedrin, fol. 92 A, quoted by Montefiore, Hibbert Lectures on the Religion of the Ancient Hebrews, p. 558.
[12] Philo Judæus, Quod liber sit quisque virtuti studet, p. 877 (Opera, ii. 458).

truth and strive to reclaim all liars.[1] " They are eminent
for fidelity," says Josephus. " Whatsoever they say also is
firmer than an oath ; but swearing is avoided by them,
and they esteem it worse than perjury ; for they say that
he who cannot be believed without [swearing by] God is
already condemned." [2]

" Speak every man truth with his neighbour," [3] was
from early times regarded as one of the most imperative
of Christian maxims.[4] According to St. Augustine, a
lie is not permissible even when told with a view to saving
the life of a neighbour ; " since by lying eternal life is
lost, never for any man's temporal life must a lie be
told." [5] Yet all lies are not equally sinful ; the degree of
sinfulness depends on the mind of the liar and on the
nature of the subject on which the lie is told.[6] This
became the authorised doctrine of the Church.[7] Thomas
Aquinas says that, although lying is always sinful, it is
not a mortal sin if the end intended be not contrary
to charity, " as appears in a jocose lie, that is intended
to create some slight amusement, and in an officious lie,
in which is intended even the advantage of our neighbour." [8] Yet from early times we meet within the Christian Church a much less rigorous doctrine, which soon
came to exercise a more powerful influence on the practice
and feelings of men than did St. Augustine's uncom-
promising love of truth. The Greek Fathers maintained
that an untruth is not a lie when there is a " just cause "

---

[1] Josephus, *De bello Judaico*, ii. 8. 7.
[2] *Ibid*. ii. 8. 6.
[3] *Ephesians*, iv. 25.
[4] Gass, *Geschichte der christlichen Ethik*, i. 90.
[5] St. Augustine, *De mendacio*, 6 (Migne, *Patrologiæ cursus*, xl. 494 sq.).
[6] *Idem*, *Enchiridion*, 18 (Migne, *op. cit.* xl. 240) ; *Idem*, *De mendacio*, 21 (Migne, xl. 516). For St. Augustine's views on lying see also his treatise *Contra mendacium*, addressed to Consentius (Migne, xl. 517 *sqq.*), and Bindemann, *Der heilige Augustinus*, ii. 465 *sqq*.

[7] Gratian, *Decretum*, ii. 22. 2. 12, 17. *Catechism of the Council of Trent*, iii. 9. 23.
[8] Thomas Aquinas, *Summa theologica*, ii.–ii. 100. 3 sq. St. Augustine says (*De mendacio*, 2 [Migne, *op. cit.* xl. 487 sq.]; *Quæstiones in Genesim*, 145, *ad Gen*. xliv. 15 [Migne, xxxiv. 587]) that jokes which "bear with them in the tone of voice, and in the very mood of the joker a most evident indication that he means no deceit," are not accounted lies, though the thing he utters be not true. This statement is also incorporated in Gratian's *Decretum* (ii. 22. 2. 18).

for it ; and as a just cause they regarded not only self-
defence, but also zeal for God's honour.[1] This zeal,
together with an indiscriminate devotion to the Church,
led to those " pious frauds," those innumerable falsifica-
tions of documents, inventions of legends, and forgeries
of every description, which made the Catholic Church
a veritable seat of lying, and most seriously impaired the
sense of truth in the minds of Christians.[2] By a fiction,
Papacy, as a divine institution, was traced back to the age
of the Apostles, and in virtue of another fiction Constantine
was alleged to have abdicated his imperial authority in
Italy in favour of the successor of St. Peter.[3] The Bishop
of Rome assumed the privilege of disengaging men from
their oaths and promises. An oath which was contrary
to the good of the Church was declared not to be binding.[4]
The theory was laid down that, as faith was not to be
kept with a tyrant, pirate, or robber, who kills the body,
it was still less to be kept with an heretic, who kills the
soul.[5] Private protestations were thought sufficient to
relieve men in conscience from being bound by a solemn
treaty or from the duty of speaking the truth ; and an
equivocation, or play upon words in which one sense is
taken by the speaker and another sense intended by him
for the hearer, was in some cases held permissible.[6] According to Alfonso de' Liguori—who lived in the eighteenth century and was beatified in the nineteenth, and
whose writings were declared by high authority not to
contain a word that could be justly found fault with,[7]—

---

[1] Gass, *op. cit.* i. 91, 92, 236 *sqq.*
Newman, *Apologia pro vita sua,*
p. 349 *sq.*

[2] von Mosheim, *Institutes of Eccle-
siastical History,* i. 275. Middleton,
*Free Inquiry into the Miraculous
Powers, which are supposed to have
subsisted in the Christian Church,*
passim. Lecky, *Rise and Influence of
Rationalism in Europe,* i. 396 *sqq.*
Gass, *op. cit.* i. 91, 235. von Eicken,
*System der mittelalterlichen Weltan-
schauung,* pp. 654–656, 663.

[3] von Eicken, *op. cit.* p. 656. Poole,
Illustrations of the History of Medi-

eval Thought, p. 249.

[4] Gregory IX. *Decretales,* ii. 24. 27.

[5] Simancas, *De catholicis institutionibus,* xlvi. 52 *sq.* p. 365 *sq.*

[6] Alagona, *Compendium manualis
D. Navarri,* xii. 88, p. 94 *sq.*:—"Fur,
qui est furatus aliquid, si interro-
getur a judice non competenti, vel
non juridice, an sit furatus tale quid,
potest secura conscientia respondere
simpliciter, non sum furatus, intelli-
gendo intra se in tali die, vel anno."
See also Kames, *op. cit.* iv. 158 *sq.*

[7] Meyrick, *Moral and Devotional
Theology of the Church of Rome,* i. 3.

there are three sorts of equivocation which may be
employed for a good reason, even with the addition of
a solemn oath. We are allowed to use ambiguously words
having two senses, as the word *volo*, which means both to
" wish " and to " fly " ; sentences bearing two main mean-
ings, as " This book is Peter's," which may mean
either that the book belongs to Peter or that Peter is
the author of it ; words having two senses, one more
common than the other or one literal and the other
metaphorical—for instance, if a man is asked about
something which it is in his interest to conceal, he may
answer, " No, I say," that is " I say the word ' no.' " [1]
As for mental restrictions, again, such as are " purely
mental," and on that account cannot in any manner
be discovered by other persons, are not permissible ; but
we may, for a good reason, make use of a " non-pure
mental restriction," which, in the nature of things, is
discoverable, although it is not discovered by the person
with whom we are dealing.[2] Thus it would be wrong
secretly to insert the word " no " in an affirmative oath
without any external sign ; but it would not be wrong to
insert it in a whispering voice or under the cover of a
cough. The " good reason " for which equivocations
and non-pure mental restrictions may be employed is
defined as " any honest object, such as keeping our goods
spiritual or temporal." [3] In support of this casuistry it is
uniformly said by Catholic apologists that each man has a
right to act upon the defensive, that he has a right to
keep guard over the knowledge which he possesses in the
same way as he may defend his goods ; and as for there
being any deceit in the matter—why, soldiers use stratagems in war, and opponents use feints in fencing.[4]

Adherence to truth and especially perfect fidelity to a
promise were strongly insisted upon by the code of
Chivalry.[5] However exacting or absurd the vow might

---

[1] Alfonso de' Liguori, *Theologia
moralis*, iii. 151, vol. i. 249.
[2] *Ibid*. iii. 152, vol. i. 249.
[3] *Ibid*. iii. 151, vol. i. 249.

[4] Meyrick, *op. cit.* i. 25.
[5] *Book of the Ordre of Chyualry*
foll. 18 b, 31 b, 34 b. Robertson, *History of the Reign of Charles V.* i. 84.

be, a knight was compelled to perform it in all the strictness of the letter. A man frequently promised to grant whatever another should ask, and he would have lost the honour of his knighthood if he had declined from his word.[1] We are told by Lancelot du Lac that when King Artus had given his word to a knight to make him a present of his wife, he would neither listen to the lamentations of the unfortunate woman, nor to any representations which could be made him ; he replied that a king must not go from his word, and the queen was accordingly delivered to the knight.[2] The knights taken in war were readily allowed liberty for the time they asked, on their word of honour that they would return of their own accord, whenever it should be required.[3] So great, it is said, was the knights' respect for an oath, a promise, or a vow, that when they lay under any of these restrictions, they appeared everywhere with little chains attached to their arms or habits to show all the world that they were slaves to their word ; nor were these chains taken off till their promise had been performed, which sometimes extended to a term of four or five years.[4] It cannot be expected, of course, that reality should have always come up to the ideal. In the thirteenth century the Count of Champagne declared that he confided more in the lowest of his subjects than in his knights.[5] Moreover, the knightly duty of sincerity seems to have gone little beyond the formal fulfilment of an engagement. " The age of Chivalry was an age of chicane, and fraud, and trickery, which were not least conspicuous among the knightly classes." [6] It is significant that the English law of the thirteenth century, though quite willing to admit in vague phrase that no one should be suffered to gain anything by fraud, was inclined to hold that a man has himself to thank if he is misled by deceit, the king's court generally providing no remedy for him who to

Sainte-Palaye, *Mémoires sur l'an-cienne chevalerie*, i. 76 sq.
[1] Mills, *History of Chivalry*, p. 152.
[2] Lancelot du Lac, vol. ii. fol. 2 a.
[3] Sainte-Palaye, *op. cit.* i. 135.
[4] *Ibid.* i. 236 sq.
[5] *Ibid.* ii. 47. *Cf.* Kames, *op. cit.* iv. 157.
[6] Pike, *History of Crime in England*, i. 283.

his disadvantage had trusted the word of a liar.[1] Towards
the end of the Middle Ages and later, crimes against the
Mint and the offence of counterfeiting seals, usually accompanied by that of forging letters or official documents,
were extremely common in England ; [2] and false weights,
false measures, and false pretences of all kinds were ordinary instruments of commerce.[3]

In modern times, according to Mr. Pike, the Public
Records testify a decrease of deception in England.[4] Commercial honesty has improved, and those mean arts to
which, during the reigns of the Tudors, even men in the
highest positions frequently had recourse, have now, at
any rate, descended to a lower grade of society.[5]   At
present, in the civilised countries of the West, opinion
as to what the duty of sincerity implies varies not only in
different individuals, but among different classes or groups
of people, as also among different nations.   Duplicity is
held more reprehensible in a gentleman than in a shopkeeper
or a peasant.   The notion which seems to be common in
England, that an advocate is over-scrupulous who refuses
to say what he knows to be false if he is instructed to say
it,[6] appears strange at least to some foreigners ; [7] and in
certain countries it is commonly regarded as blamable if a
person ostensibly professes a religion in which he does not
believe, say, by going to church.   The Quakers deem all
complimentary modes of speech, for instance in addressing
people, to be objectionable as being inconsistent with
truth[8].   Certain philosophers have expressed the opinion
that veracity is an unconditional duty, which is not to be
limited by any expediency, but must be respected in all
circumstances.   According to Kant, it would be a crime
to tell a falsehood to a murderer who asked us whether

[1] Pollock and Maitland, *History of English Law before the Time of Edward I.* ii. 535 *sq.*
[2] Pike, *op. cit.* i. 265, 269 ; ii. 392.
[3] *Ibid.* i. 142 ; ii. 238.
[4] *Ibid.* i. 264. *Cf. ibid.* ii. 474.
[5] *Ibid.* ii. 14 *sq.*
[6] Sidgwick, *Methods of Ethics*, p.

316. Paley, *Principles of Moral and Political Philosophy*, iii. 15 (*Complete Works*, ii. 117). The same view was expressed by Cicero (*De officiis*, ii. 14).
[7] See also Dymond, *Essays on the Principles of Morals*, ii. 5, p. 50 *sqq.*
[8] Gurney, *Views and Practices of the Society of Friends*, p. 401.

our friend, of whom he was in pursuit, had taken refuge in our house.[1] Fichte maintains that the defence of so-called necessary lies is " the most wicked argument possible amongst men." [2] Dymond says, " If I may tell a falsehood to a robber in order to save my property, I may commit parricide for the same purpose." [3] But this rigorous view is not shared by common sense, nor by orthodox Protestant theology.[4] Jeremy Taylor asks, " Who will not tell a harmless lie to save the life of his friend, of his child, of himself, of a good and brave man ? " [5] Where deception is designed to benefit the person deceived, says Professor Sidgwick, " common sense seems to concede that it may sometimes be right : for example, most persons would not hesitate to speak falsely to an invalid, if this seemed the only way of concealing facts that might produce a dangerous shock : nor do I perceive that any one shrinks from telling fictions to children, on matters upon which it is thought well that they should not know the truth." [6] In the case of grown-up people, how-ever, this principle seems to require the modification made by Hutcheson, that there is no wrong in false speech when the party deceived himself does not consider it an injury to be deceived.[7] Otherwise it might easily be supposed to give support to " pious fraud," which in its crudest form is nowadays generally disapproved of, but which in subtle disguise still has many advocates among religious partisans. It is argued that the most important truths of religion cannot be conveyed into the minds of ordinary men, except by being enclosed, as it were, in a shell of fiction, and that by relating such fictions as if they were facts we are really performing an act of substantial veracity.[8] But this argument seems chiefly to have been invented for the

---

[1] Kant, ' Ueber ein vermeintes Recht, aus Menschenliebe zu Lügen,' in *Sämmtliche Werke*, vii. 309.

[2] Fichte, *Das System der Sittenlehre*, p. 371 ; English translation, p. 303 *sq.*

[3] Dymond, *op. cit.* ii. 6, p. 57.

[4] Reinhard, *System der Christ-lichen Moral*, iii. 193 *sqq.* Martensen,

Christian Ethics, 'Individual Ethics,' p. 216 *sqq.* Newman, *Apologia pro vita sua*, p. 274.

[5] Taylor, *Whole Works*, xii. 162.

[6] Sidgwick, *op. cit.* p. 316.

[7] Hutcheson, *System of Moral Philosophy*, ii. 32.

[8] Sidgwick, *op. cit.* p. 316

purpose of supporting a dilapidated structure of theological teaching, and can hardly be accepted by any person un-prejudiced by religious bias. As a means of self-defence deviation from truth has been justified not only in the case of grosser injuries, but in the case of illegitimate curiosity, as it seems unreasonable that a person should be obliged to supply another with information which he has no right to exact.[1] The obligation of keeping a promise, again, is qualified in various ways. Thoughtful persons would commonly admit that such an obligation is relative to the promisee, and may be annulled by him.[2] A promise to do an immoral act is held not to be binding, because the prior obligation not to do the act is paramount.[3] If, before the time comes to fulfil a promise, circumstances have altered so much that the effects of keeping it are quite different from those which were foreseen when it was made, all would agree that the promisee ought to release the promiser ; but if he declines to do so, some would say that the latter is in every case bound by his promise, whilst others would maintain that a considerable alteration of circumstances has removed the obligation.[4] How far promises obtained by force or fraud are binding is a much disputed question.[5] According to Hutcheson, for instance, no regard is due to a promise which has been extorted by unjust violence.[6] Adam Smith, on the other hand, considers that whenever such a promise is violated, though for the most necessary reason, it is always with some degree of dishonour to the person who made it, and that " a brave man ought to die rather than make a promise

---

[1] Schopenhauer, *Die Grundlage der Moral*, § 17 (*Sämmtliche Werke*, vi. 247 *sqq.*).

[2] Whewell, *Elements of Morality*, p. 156. Sidgwick, *op. cit.* p. 305.

[3] Dymond, *op. cit.* ii. 6, p. 55. Whewell, *op. cit.* p. 156 *sq.* Sidgwick, *op. cit.* p. 305. This is also the opinion of Thomas Aquinas (*op. cit.* ii.-ii. 110. 3. 5).

[4] Sidgwick, *op. cit.* p. 306 *sq.* Thomas Aquinas says (*op. cit.* ii.-ii. 110. 3. 5) that a person who does not do what he has promised is excused " if the conditions of persons and things are changed."

[5] Dymond, *op. cit.* ii. 6, p. 55 *sq.* Whewell, *op. cit.* pp. 155, 159 *sqq.* Sidgwick, *op. cit.* p. 305 *sq.* Adam Smith, *Theory of Moral Sentiments*, p. 486 *sqq.*

[6] Hutcheson, *System of Moral Philosophy*, ii. 34.

which he can neither keep without folly nor violate without ignominy." [1]

In point of veracity and good faith the old distinction between duties which we owe to our fellow-countrymen and such as we owe to foreigners is still preserved in various cases. It is particularly conspicuous in the relations between different states, in peace or war. Stratagems and the employment of deceptive means necessary to procure intelligence respecting the enemy or the country are held allowable in warfare, independently of the question whether the war is defensive or aggressive.[2] Deceit has, in fact, often constituted a great share of the glory of the most celebrated commanders; and particularly in the eighteenth century it was a common opinion that successes gained through a spy are more creditable to the skill of a general than successes in regular battles.[3] Lord Wolseley writes :—" As a nation we are bred up to feel it a disgrace even to succeed by falsehood ; the word spy conveys something as repulsive as slave ; we will keep hammering along with the conviction that ' honesty is the best policy,' and that truth always wins in the long run. These pretty little sentences do well for a child's copy-book, but the man who acts upon them in war had better sheathe his sword for ever." [4] At the same time, there are some exceptions to the general rule that deceit is permitted against an enemy. Under the customs of war it has been agreed that particular acts and signs shall have a specific meaning in order that belligerents

[1] Adam Smith, *op. cit.* p. 489.

[2] *Conférence de Bruxelles*, art. 14. *Instructions for the Government of Armies of the United States in the Field*, art. 16, 101. *Conférence internationale de la paix, La Haye*, 1899, ' Règlement concernant les lois de la guerre sur terre,' art. 24, pt. i. p.245. Roman Catholicism admits the employment of stratagems in wars which are just (Gratian, *op. cit.* ii. 23. 2. 2 ; Ayala, *De jure et officiis bellicis et disciplina militari*, i. 8. 1 *sq.*; Ferraris, quoted by Adds, *Catholic Dictionary*, p. 945 ; Nys, *Le droit de la guerre et les précurseurs de Grotius*, p. 128 *sq.*), on the authority of St. Augustine, the great advocate of general truthfulness (*Quæstiones in Jesum Nave*, 10, *ad Jos.* viii. 2 [Migne, *op. cit.* xxxiv. 781]:—"Cum autem justum bellum susceperit, utrum aperta pugna utrum insidiis vincat, nihil ad justitiam interest ").

[3] Halleck, *International Law*, i. 567. Maine, *International Law*, p. 149 *sqq.*

[4] Wolseley, *Soldier's Pocket-Book for Field Service*, p. 169.

may carry on certain necessary intercourse, and it is forbidden to employ such acts or signs in deceiving an enemy. Thus information must not be surreptitiously obtained under the shelter of a flag of truce ; buildings not used as hospitals must not be marked with an hospital flag ; and persons not covered by the provisions of the Geneva Convention must not be protected by its cross.[1] A curious arbitrary rule affects one class of stratagems by forbidding certain permitted means of deception from the moment at which they cease to deceive. It is perfectly legitimate to use the distinctive emblems of an enemy in order to escape from him or to draw his forces into action ; but it is held that soldiers clothed in the uniforms of their enemy must put on a conspicuous mark by which they can be recognised before attacking, and that a vessel using the enemy's flag must hoist its own flag before firing with shot or shell.[2] Disobedience to this rule is considered to entail grave dishonour ; for " in actual battle enemies are bound to combat loyally, and are not free to ensure victory by putting on a mask of friendship." [3] But, as Mr. Hall observes, it is not easy to see why it is more disloyal to wear a disguise when it is obviously useless, than when it serves its purpose.[4] Finally, it is universally agreed that promises given to the enemy ought to be kept ; [5] this was admitted even by Machiavelli [6] and Bynkershoek,[7] who did not in general burden belligerents with particularly heavy duties. But the restrictions which " international law "

---

[1] *Conférence de Bruxelles*, art. 13 sq. *Instructions for the Government of Armies of the United States in the Field*, art. 101, 114, 117. *Manual of the Laws of War on Land*, prepared by the Institute of International Law, art. 8 (d). Hall, *Treatise on International Law*, p. 537 sq.

[2] Hall, *op. cit.* p. 538 sq. Bluntschli, *Droit international*, § 565, p. 328 sq.

[3] Bluntschli, *op. cit.* § 565, p. 329.

[4] Hall, *op. cit.* p. 539.

[5] Heffter, *Das Europäische Völkerrecht der Gegenwart*, § 125, p. 262.

[6] Machiavelli, *Discorsi*, iii. 40 (*Opere*, iii. 164).

[7] Bynkershoek, *Quæstiones juris publici*, i. 1, p. 4. The maxim of Canon Law, "Fides servanda hosti" (Gratian, *Decretum*, ii. 23. i. 3), however, was greatly impaired by the principle, "Juramentum contra utilitatem ecclesiasticam praestitum non tenet" (Gregory IX. *Decretales*, ii. 24, 27. See Nys, *Le droit de la guerre et les précurseurs de Grotius*, p. 126 sq.).

lays on deceit against enemies do not seem to be taken
very seriously. Treaties between nations and promises
given by one state to another, either in war or peace, are
hardly meant to be kept longer than it is convenient
to keep them. And when an excuse for the breach of
faith is felt necessary, that excuse itself is generally
a lie.

CHAPTER XXXI

THE REGARD FOR TRUTH AND GOOD FAITH
(*concluded*)

THE condemnation of untruthfulness and bad faith springs from a variety of sources. In the first place, he who tells a lie, or who breaks a promise, generally commits an injury against another person. His act consequently calls forth sympathetic resentment, and becomes an object of moral censure.

Men have a natural disposition to believe what they are told. This disposition is particularly obvious in young children ; it is acquired wisdom and experience only that teach incredulity, and, as Adam Smith observes, they very seldom teach it enough.[1] Even people who are themselves pre-eminent liars are often deceived by the falsehoods of others.[2] When detected a deception always implies a conflict between two irreconcilable ideas ; and such a conflict gives rise to a feeling of pain,[3] which may call forth resentment against its volitional cause, the deceiver.

But men are not only ready to believe what they are told, they also like to know the truth. Curiosity, or the love of truth, is coeval with the first operations of the intellect ; it seems to be an ultimate fact in the human

---

[1] Reid, *Inquiry into the Human Mind*, vi. 24, p. 430 *sqq.* Adam Smith, *Theory of Moral Sentiments*, p.494 *sq.* Dugald Stewart, *Philosophy of the Active and Moral Powers of Man*, ii. 340 *sq.*

[2] Burton, *Two Trips to Gorilla Land*, i. 106 (Mpongwe).

[3] Lehmann, *Hovedlovene for det menneskelige Følelseliv*, p. 181. *Cf.* Bain, *Emotions and the Will*, p. 218.

frame.[1]   In our endeavour to learn the truth we are
frustrated by him who deceives us, and he becomes an
object of our resentment.

Nor are we injured by a deception merely because we
like to know the truth, but, chiefly, because it is of much
importance for us that we should know it. Our conduct
is based upon our ideas ; hence the erroneous notion as
regards some fact in the past, present, or future, which is
produced by a lie or false promise, may lead to unforeseen
events detrimental to our interests. Moreover, on discovering that we have been deceived, we have the humiliating feeling that another person has impertinently made our
conduct subject to his will. This is a wound on our pride,
a blot on our honour. Francis I. of France laid down as
a principle, " that the lie was never to be put up with
without satisfaction, but by a base-born fellow." [2] " The
lie," says Sainte-Palaye, " has always been considered the
most fatal and irreparable affront that a man of honour
could receive." [3]

How largely the condemnation of falsehood and bad
faith is due to the harm suffered by the victim appears
from the fact that a lie or breach of faith is held more
condemnable in proportion to the magnitude of the harm
caused by it. But even in apparently trifling cases the
reflective mind strongly insists upon the necessity of
truthfulness and fidelity to a given word. Every lie and
every unfulfilled promise has a tendency to lessen mutual
confidence, to predispose the perpetrator to commit a
similar offence in the future, and to serve as a bad example
for others. " The importance of truth," says Bentham,
" is so great, that the least violation of its laws, even in
frivolous matters, is always attended with a certain degree
of danger. The slightest deviation from it is an attack
upon the respect we owe to it. It is a first transgression
which facilitates a second, and familiarises the odious ideal

---

[1] Dugald Stewart, *op. cit.* ii. 334,
340.
[2] Millingen, *History of Duelling,*

i. 71.
[3] Sainte-Palaye, *Mémoires sur
l'ancienne chevalerie,* i. 78.

TRUTH AND GOOD FAITH III

of falsehood." [1] Contrariwise, as Aristotle observes, he who is truthful in unimportant matters will be all the more so in important ones.[2] Similar considerations, however, require a certain amount of reflection and farsightedness ; hence intellectual development tends to increase the emphasis laid on the duties of sincerity and good faith. At the earlier stages of civilisation it is frequently considered good form to tell an untruth to a person in order to please him, and ill-mannered to contradict him, however much he be mistaken,[3] for the reason that farther consequences are left out of account. The utilitarian basis of the duty of truthfulness also accounts for those extreme cases in which a deception is held permissible or even a duty, when promoting the true interests of the person subject to it.

The detestation of falsehood is in a very large measure due to the motive which commonly is at the bottom of a lie. It is doubtful whether a lie ever is told simply from love of falsehood.[4] The intention to produce a wrong belief has a deeper motive than the mere desire to produce such a belief ; and in most cases this motive is the deceiver's hope of benefiting himself at the expense of the person deceived. A better motive makes the act less detestable, or may even serve as a justification. But the broad doctrine that the end sanctifies the means is generally rejected ; and the principle which sometimes allows

[1] Bentham, *Theory of Legislation*, p. 260.
[2] Aristotle, *Ethica Nicomachea*, iv. 7. 8.
[3] Besides statements referred to above, see Dobrizhoffer, *Account of the Abipones*, ii. 137; Hennepin, *New Discovery of a Vast Country in America between New France and New Mexico*, ii. 70 ; Dall, *Alaska*, p. 398 (Aleuts) ; Oldfield, in *Trans. Ethn. Soc.* N.S. iii. 255 (West Australian natives). "The natives of Africa," says Livingstone (*Expedition to the Zambesi*, p. 309), "have an amiable desire to please, and often tell what they imagine will be gratifying, rather than the uninteresting naked truth." An English sportsman, after firing at an antelope, inquired of his dark attendant, "Is it wounded?" The answer was, "Yes! the ball went right into his heart." These mortal wounds never proving fatal, he asked a friend, who understood the language, to explain to the man that he preferred the truth in every case. "He is my father," replied the native, "and I thought he would be displeased if I told him that he never hits at all." The wish to please is likewise a fertile source of untruth in children, especially girls (Sully, *Studies of Childhood*, p. 256).
[4] Dugald Stewart, *op. cit.* ii. 342.

deceit from a benevolent motive has been restricted within very narrow limits by a higher conception of individual freedom and individual rights. Thus the emancipation of morality from theology has brought discredit on the old theory that religious deception is permissible when it serves the object of saving human souls from eternal perdition. The opinion that no motive whatsoever can justify an act of falsehood has been advocated not only by intuitional moralists, but on utilitarian grounds.[1] But it certainly seems absurd to the common sense of mankind that we should be allowed to save our own life or the life of a fellow-man by killing the person who wants to take it, but not by deceiving him.

It is easy to see why falsehood is so frequently held permissible, praiseworthy, or even obligatory, when directed against a stranger. In early society an injury inflicted on a stranger calls forth no sympathetic resentment. On the contrary, being looked upon with suspicion or hated as an enemy, he is considered a proper object of deception. Among the Bushmans " no one dare give any information in the absence of the chief or father of the clan." [2] " A Bedouin," says Burckhardt, " who does not know the person interrogating him, will seldom answer with truth to questions concerning his family or tribe. The children are taught never to answer similar questions, lest the interrogator may be a secret enemy and come for purposes of revenge." [3] Among the Beni Amer a stranger can never trust a man's word on account of " their contempt for everything foreign." [4] That even civilised nations allow stratagem in warfare is the natural consequence of war itself being allowed ; and if good faith is to be preserved between enemies, that is because only thereby useless cruelty can be avoided and an end be put to hostilities.

However, deceit is not condemned merely because it is

---

[1] Macmillan, *Promotion of General Happiness*, p. 166 sq.
[2] Chapman, *Travels in the Interior of South Africa*, i. 76.
[3] Burckhardt, *Notes on the Bedouins and Wahábys*, p. 210.
[4] Munzinger, *Ostafrikanische Studien*, p. 337.

an injury to the party deceived and as such apt to arouse sympathetic resentment, but it is an object of disinterested, moral resentment also because it is intrinsically antipathetic. Lying is a cheap and cowardly method of gaining an undue advantage, and is consequently despised where courage is respected.[1] It is the weapon of the weak, the woman,[2] and the slave.[3] Fraud, says Cicero, is the property of a fox, force that of a lion ; " both are utterly repugnant to society, but fraud is the more detestable." [4] " To lie is servile," says Plutarch, " and most hateful in all men, hardly to be pardoned even in poor slaves." [5] On account of its cowardliness, lying was incompatible with Teutonic and knightly notions of manly honour ; and among ourselves the epithets " liar " and " coward " are equally disgraceful to a man. " All . . . in the rank and station of gentlemen," Sir Walter Scott observes, " are forcibly called upon to remember that they must resent the imputation of a voluntary falsehood as the most gross injury." [6] Fichte asks, " Whence comes that internal shame for one's self which manifests itself even stronger in the case of a lie than in the case of any other violation of conscience ? " And his answer is, that the lie is accompanied by cowardice, and that nothing so much dishonours us in our own eyes as want of courage.[7] According to Kant, " a lie is the abandonment, and, as it were, the annihilation, of the dignity of a man." [8]

[1] *Cf.* Schopenhauer, *Die Grundlage der Moral*, § 17 (*Sämmtliche Werke*, vi. 250); Grote, *Treatise on the Moral Ideals*, p. 254.

[2] Women are commonly said to be particularly addicted to falsehood (Schopenhauer, *Parerga und Paralipomena*, ii. 497 *sq.* Galton, *Inquiries into Human Faculty*, p. 56 *sq.* Krauss, *Sitte und Brauch der Südslaven*, pp. 508, 514. Maurer, *Bekehrung des Norwegischen Stammes*, ii. 159 [ancient Scandinavians]. Döllinger, *The Gentile and the Jew*, ii. 234 [ancient Greeks]. Lane, *Arabian Society in the Middle Ages*, p. 219. Le Bon, *La civilisation des Arabes*, p. 433. Loskiel,

History of the Mission of the United Brethren, i. 16 [Iroquois]. Hearne, *Journey to the Northern Ocean*, p. 307 *sq.* [Northern Indians]. Lyon, *Private Journal*, p. 349 [Eskimo of Igloolik]. Dalager, *Grønlandske Relationer*, p. 69 ; Cranz, *History of Greenland*, i. 175).

[3] See *infra*, p. 129 *sq.*

[4] Cicero, *De officiis*, i. 13.

[5] Plutarch, *De educatione puerorum*, 14.

[6] Scott, 'Essay on Chivalry,' in *Miscellaneous Prose Works*, vi. 58.

[7] Fichte, *Das System der Sittenlehre*, p. 370 ; English translation, p. 302 *sq.*

[8] Kant, *Metaphysische Anfangsgründe der Tugendlehre*, p. 84.

But a lie may also be judged of from a very different point of view. It may be not only a sign of cowardice, but a sign of cleverness. Hence a successful lie may excite admiration, a disinterested kindly feeling towards the liar, genuine moral approval ; whereas to be detected in a lie is considered shameful. And not only is the clever liar an object of admiration, but the person whom he deceives is an object of ridicule. To the mind of a West African native, Miss Kingsley observes, there is no intrinsic harm in lying, " because a man is a fool who believes another man on an important matter unless he puts on the oath." [1] A Syrian proverb says, " Lying is the salt (goodness) of men, and shameful only to one who believes." [2]

The duties of sincerity and good faith are also to some extent, and in certain cases principally, founded on prudential considerations. Although, as the *Märchen* tells us, it happens every day in the world that the fraudulent is successful,[3] there is a widespread notion that, after all, " honesty is the best policy." " Nothing that is false can be lasting," says Cicero.[4] " The liar is short-lived " (that is, soon detected), say the Arabs.[5] According to a Wolof proverb, " lies, however numerous, will be caught by truth when it rises up." [6] The Basutos have a saying that " cunning devours its master." [7] It has been remarked that " if there were no such thing as honesty, it would be a good speculation to invent it, as a means of making one's fortune." [8]

Moreover, lying is attended not only with social disadvantages, but with supernatural danger. The West African Fjort have a tale about a fisherman who every day used to catch and smuggle into his house great quantities of fish,

[1] Kingsley, *West African Studies*, p. 414. *Cf.* Sommerville, 'Ethnogr. Notes in New Georgia,' *Jour. Anthr. Inst.* xxvi. 394.

[2] Burton and Drake, *Unexplored Syria*, i. 275. See also Burckhardt, *Arabic Proverbs*, p. 44 *sq.*

[3] Grimm, *Kinder und Hausmärchen*, 'Katze und Maus in Gesellschaft,' 'Die drei Spinnerinnen,' 'Das tapfere Schneiderlein,' &c.

[4] Cicero, *De officiis*, ii. 12.

[5] Burckhardt, *Arabic Proverbs*, p. 119.

[6] Burton, *Wit and Wisdom from West Africa*, p. 15.

[7] Casalis, *Basutos*, p. 307.

[8] Quoted by Bentham, *Theory of Legislation*, p. 64.

but denied to his brother and relatives that he had caught
anything. All this time the fetish Sunga was watching, and
was grieved to hear him lie thus. The fetish punished him
by depriving him of the power of speech, that he might lie
no more, and so for the future he could only make his
wants known by signs.[1] In another instance, the Fjort
tell us, the earth-spirit turned into a pillar of clay a woman
who said that she had no peas for sale, when she had her
basket full of them.[2] The Nandi of the Uganda Protectorate believe that " God punishes lying by striking the untruthful person with lightning." [3] The Dyaks of Borneo
think that the lightning god is made angry even by the
most nonsensical untruth, such as the statement that a man
has a cat for his mother or that vermin can dance.[4] In
Aneiteum, of the New Hebrides, the belief prevailed that
liars would be punished in the life to come ; [5] according
to the Banks Islanders, they were excluded from the true
Panoi or Paradise after death.[6] We have already noticed
the emphasis which some of the higher religions lay on
veracity and good faith, and other statements may be added
testifying the interest which gods of a more civilised type
take in the fulfilment of these duties. In ancient Egypt
Amon Ra, " the chief of all the gods," was invoked as
" Lord of Truth " ; [7] and Maā, or Maat, represented as
his daughter, was the goddess of truth and righteousness.[8]
In a Babylonian hymn the moon god is appealed to as the
guardian of truth.[9] The Vedic gods are described as
" true " and " not deceitful," as friends of honesty and
righteousness ; [10] and Agni was the lord of vows.[11] The

---

[1] Dennett, *Folklore of the Fjort*,
p. 88 *sq.*
[2] *Ibid.* p. 5.
[3] Johnston, *Uganda Protectorate*, ii.
879.
[4] Selenka, *Sonnige Welten*, p. 47.
[5] Turner, *Samoa*, p. 326.
[6] Codrington, *Melanesians*, p. 274.
[7] Wiedemann, *Religion of the
Ancient Egyptians*, p. 112. *Cf.*
Brugsch, *Die Aegyptologie*, pp. 49,
91, 92, 97 ; Amélineau, *Essai sur*

*l'évolution des idées morales dans
l'Égypte Ancienne*, pp. 182, 188, 251.
[8] Wiedemann, ' Maā, déesse de la
vérité,' in *Annales du Musée Guimet*,
x. 561 *sqq.* Amélineau, *op. cit.* p.
187. *Infra*, p. 699.
[9] Mürdter-Delitzsch, *Geschichte Babyloniens und Assyriens*, p. 37.
[10] Bergaigne, *La religion védique*, iii.
199. Macdonell, *Vedic Mythology*,
p. 18.
[11] *Satapatha-Brâhmana*, iii. 2. 2. 24.

Zoroastrian Mithra was a protector of truth, fidelity, and covenants;[1] and Rashnu Razista, "the truest true," was the genius of truth.[2] According to the Iliad, Zeus is " no abettor of falsehoods " ;[3] according to Plato, a lie is hateful not only to men but to gods.[4] Among the Romans Jupiter and Dius Fidius were gods of treaties,[5] and Fides was worshipped as the deity of faithfulness.[6] How shall we explain this connection between religious beliefs and the duties of veracity and fidelity to promises ?

Apart from the circumstances which in some cases make gods vindicators of the moral law in general, as conceived of by their worshippers, there are quite special reasons for their disapproval of insincerity and bad faith. Here again we notice the influence of magic beliefs on the religious sanction of morality.

There is something uncanny in the untrue word itself. As Professor Stanley Hall points out, children not infrequently regard every deviation from the most painfully literal truth as alike heinous, with no perspective or degrees of difference between the most barefaced intended and unintended lies. In some children this fear of telling an untruth becomes so neurotic that to every statement, even to yes or no, a " perhaps " or " I think " is added mentally, whispered, or aloud. One boy had a long period of fear that, like Ananias and Sapphira, he might some moment drop down dead for a chance and perhaps unconscious lie.[7] On the other hand, an acted lie is felt to be much less harmful than a spoken one ; to point the wrong way when asked where some one is gone is less objectionable than to speak wrongly, to nod is less sinful than to say yes. Indeed, acted lies are for the most

[1] Darmesteter, *Ormazd et Ahriman,* p. 78. Geiger, *Civilization of the Eastern Irānians,* pp. lvii., 164. Spiegel, *Erânische Alterthumskunde,* iii. 685.

[2] Darmesteter, in *Sacred Books of the East,* xxiii. 168.

[3] *Iliad,* iv. 235.

[4] Plato, *Respublica,* ii. 382.

[5] Fowler, *Roman Festivals of the* *Period of the Republic,* pp. 141, 229 *sq.*

[6] Cicero, *De officiis,* iii. 29. *Idem, De natura deorum,* ii. 23 ; iii. 18. *Idem, De legibus,* ii. 8, 11. Dionysius of Halicarnassus, *Antiquitates Romanæ,* ii. 75.

[7] Stanley Hall, ' Children's Lies,' in *American Journal of Psychology,* iii. 59 *sq.*

part easily gotten away with, whereas some mysterious baneful energy seems to be attributed to the spoken untruth. That its evil influence is looked upon as quite mechanical appears from the palliatives used for it. Many American children are of opinion that a lie may be reversed by putting the left hand on the right shoulder and that even an oath may be neutralised or taken in an opposite sense by raising the left instead of the right hand.[1] Among children in New York " it was sufficient to cross the fingers, elbows, or legs, though the act might not be noticed by the companion accosted, and under such circumstances no blame attached to a falsehood." [2] To think " I do not mean it," or to attach to a statement a meaning quite different from the current one, is a form of reservation which is repeatedly found in children.[3] Nor are feelings and ideas of this kind restricted to the young ; they are fairly common among grown-up people, and have even found expression in ethical doctrines. They lie at the root of the Jesuit theory of mental reservations. According to Thomas Aquinas, again, though it is wrong to tell a lie for the purpose of delivering another from any danger whatever, it is lawful " to hide the truth prudently under some dissimulation, as Augustine says." [4] It is not uncommonly argued that in defence of a secret we may not " lie," that is, produce directly beliefs contrary to facts ; but that we may " turn a question aside," that is, produce indirectly, by natural inference from our answer, a negatively false belief ; or that we may " throw the inquirer on a wrong scent," that is, produce similarly a positively false belief.[5] This extreme formalism may no doubt to some extent be traced to the influence of early training. From the day we learned to speak, the duty of telling the truth has been strenuously enjoined upon us, and the word " lie " has been associated with sin of the

[1] Stanley Hall, ' Children's Lies,' in *American Journal of Psychology*, iii. 68 *sq.*

[2] Bergen and Newell, ' Current Superstitions,' in *Journal of American Folk-lore*, ii. 111.

[3] Stanley Hall, *loc. cit.* p. 68.

[4] Thomas Aquinas, *Summa theologica*, ii.–ii. 110. 3. 4.

[5] See Sidgwick, *Methods of Ethics*, p. 317.

blackest hue ; whereas other forms of falsehood, being less frequent, less obvious, and less easy to define, have also been less emphasised. But after full allowance is made for this influence, the fact still remains that a mystic efficacy is very commonly ascribed to the spoken word. Even among ourselves many persons would not dare to praise their health or fortune for fear lest some evil should result from their speech ; and among less civilised peoples much greater significance is given to a word than among us. Herodotus, after mentioning the extreme importance which the ancient Persians attached to the duty of speaking the truth, adds that they held it unlawful even " to talk of anything which it is unlawful to do."[1] I think, then, we may assume that, if for some reason or other, falsehood is stigmatised, the mysterious tendency inherent in the word easily develops into an avenging power which, as often happens in similar cases, is associated with the activity of a god.

The punishing power of a word is particularly conspicuous in the case of an oath. But the evil attending perjury does not come from the lie as such : it is in the first place a result of the curse which constitutes the oath. An oath is essentially a conditional self-imprecation, a curse by which a person calls down upon himself some evil in the event of what he says not being true. The efficacy of the oath is originally entirely magical, it is due to the magic power inherent in the cursing words. In order to charge them with supernatural energy various methods are adopted. Sometimes the person who takes the oath puts himself in contact with some object which represents the state referred to in the oath, so that the oath may absorb, as it were, its quality and communicate it to the perjurer. Thus the Kandhs swear upon the lizard's skin, " whose scaliness they pray may be their lot if forsworn," or upon the earth of an ant-hill, " like which they desire that, if false, they may be reduced to powder."[2] The Tunguses regard it as the most dreadful

---

[2] Herodotus, i. 139.   [2] Macpherson, *Memorials of Service in India*, p. 83.

of all their oaths when an accused person is compelled to
drink some of the blood of a dog which, after its throat
has been cut, is impaled near a fire and burnt, or has its
flesh scattered about piece-meal, and to swear :—" I speak
the truth, and that is as true as it is that I drink this blood.
If I lie, let me perish, burn, or be dried up like this
dog." [1] In other cases the person who is to swear takes
hold of a certain object and calls it to inflict on him some
injury if he perjure himself. The Kandhs frequently take
oath upon the skin of a tiger, " from which animal destruction to the perjured is invoked." [2] The Angami Nagas, when
they swear to keep the peace, or to perform any promise,
" place the barrel of a gun, or a spear, between their teeth,
signifying by this ceremony that, if they do not act up to
their agreement, they are prepared to fall by either of the
two weapons." [3] The Chuvashes, again, put a piece of
bread and a little salt in the mouth and swear, " May I
be in want of these, if I say not true ! " or " if I do not
keep my word ! " [4] Another method of charging an oath
with supernatural energy is to touch, or to establish some
kind of contact with, a holy object on the occasion when
the oath is taken. The Iowa have a mysterious iron or
stone, wrapped in seven skins, by which they make men
swear to speak the truth. [5] The people of Kesam, in the
highlands of Palembang, swear by an old sacred knife, [6]
the Bataks of South Tóba on their village idols, [7] the
Ostyaks on the nose of a bear, which is regarded by them
as an animal endowed with supernatural power. [8] Among
the Tunguses a criminal may be compelled to climb one

[1] Georgi, *Russia*, iii. 86.
[2] Macpherson, *op. cit.* p. 83. *Cf.*
Hose, ' Natives of Borneo,' in *Jour.
Anthr. Inst.* xxiii. 165 (Kayans).
[3] Butler, *Travels in Assam*, p. 154.
Mac Mahon, *Far Cathay*, p. 253.
Prain, 'Angami Nagas,' in *Revue
coloniale internationale*, v. 490. *Cf.*
Lewin, *Wild Races of South-Eastern
India*, pp. 193 (Toungtha), 244 *sq.*
(Pankhos and Bunjogees) ; St. John,
' Hill Tribes of North Aracan,' in
Jour. Anthr. Inst. ii. 242.

[4] Georgi, *op. cit.* i. 110.
[5] Hamilton, quoted by Dorsey,
' Siouan Cults,' in *Ann. Rep. Bur.
Ethn.* xi. 427.
[6] *Glimpses of the Eastern Archipelago*, p. 104.
[7] von Brenner, *Besuch bei den Kannibalen Sumatras*, p. 213.
[8] Castrén, *Nordiska resor och forskningar*, i. 307, 309 ; iv. 123 *sq.* *Cf.*
Ahlqvist, ' Unter Wogulen und
Ostjaken,' in *Acta Societatis Scientiarum Fennicæ*, xiv. 298.

of their sacred mountains, repeating as he mounts, " May
I die if I am guilty," or, " May I lose my children and my
cattle," or, " I renounce for ever all success in hunting
and fishing if I am guilty." [1] In Tibetan law-courts, when
the great oath is taken, " it is done by the person placing
a holy scripture on his head, and sitting on the reeking
hide of an ox and eating part of the ox's heart." [2] Hindus
swear on a copy of the Sanskrit *haribans*, or with Ganges
water in their hands, or touch the legs of a Brâhmana in
taking an oath.[3] Muhammedans swear on the Koran,
as Christians do on the Bible.   In Morocco an oath
derives efficacy from contact with, or the presence of,
any lifeless object, animal, or person endowed with
baraka, or holiness, such as a saint-house or a mosque,
corn or wool, a flock of sheep or a horse, or a shereef.
In mediæval Christendom sacred relics were generally
adopted as the most effective means of adding security to
oaths, and " so little respect was felt for the simple oath
that, ere long, the adjuncts came to be looked upon as the
essential feature, and the imprecation itself to be divested
of binding force without them." [4]

Finally, as an ordinary curse, so an oath is made efficacious by bringing in the name of a supernatural being,
to whom an appeal is made.   When the Comanches
of Texas make a sacred pledge or promise, " they call
upon the great spirit as their father, and the earth as their
mother, to testify to the truth of their asseverations." [5]
Of the Chukchi we are told that " as often as they would
certify the truth of any thing by oath or solemn protestations they take the sun for their guarantee and security." [6]
Among the Tunguses an accused person takes a knife in
his hand, brandishes it towards the sun, and says, " If I

[1] Georgi, *op. cit.* iii. 86.
[2] Waddell, *Buddhism of Tibet*, p.
569, n. 7.
[3] Grierson, *Bihār Peasant Life*, p.
401. Sleeman, *Rambles and Recollections of an Indian Official*, ii. 116.
[4] Lea, *Superstition and Force*, p.
29. See also Kaufmann, *Deutsche*

Geschichte, ii. 297 ; Ellinger, *Das
Verhältniss der öffentlichen Meinung
zu Wahrheit und Lüge im 10. 11. und
12. Jahrhundert*, pp. 30, 111.
[5] Neighbors, in Schoolcraft,
Indian Tribes of the United States,
i. 132.
[6] Georgi, *op. cit.* iii. 183.

am guilty, may the sun send diseases into my bowels as mortal as a stab with this knife would be ! " [1]   An Arab from the province of Dukkâla in Morocco presses a dagger against his chest, saying, " By this poison, may God thrust it into my heart if I did so or so ! "   If a Masai is accused of having done something wrong, he drinks some blood, which is given him by the spokesman, and says, " If I have done this deed may God kill me " ; and it is believed that if he has committed the crime he dies, whereas no harm befalls him if he is innocent. [2] Among the Tshi-speaking peoples of the Gold Coast, " to make an oath binding on the person who takes it, it is usual to give him something to eat or to drink which in some way appertains to a deity, who is then invoked to visit a breach of faith with punishment." [3]   Among the Shekani and Bakele people of Southern Guinea, when a covenant between different tribes is about to be formed, their great spirit, Mwetyi, " is always invoked as a witness, and is commissioned with the duty of visiting vengeance upon the party who shall violate the engagement." [4]   It seems to be a common practice in certain parts of Africa to swear by some fetish. [5]   The Efatese, of the New Hebrides, invoked punishment from the gods in their oaths. [6]   In Florida, of the Solomon Group, a man will deny an accusation by some *tindalo* (that is, the disembodied spirit of some man who already in his lifetime was supposed to be endowed with supernatural power), or by the ghostly frigate-bird, or by the ghostly shark. [7]   When an ancient Egyptian wished to give assurance of his honesty and good faith, he called Thoth to witness, the advocate in the heavenly court of justice, without whose justification no soul could stand in the day of judgment. [8]   The Eranians swore by Mithra, [9] the Greeks by Zeus, [10] the

[1] Georgi, *op. cit.* iii. 85 *sq.*
[2] Hollis, *Masai*, p. 345.
[3] Ellis, *Tshi-speaking Peoples of the Gold Coast*, p. 196.
[4] Wilson, *Western Africa*, p. 392.
[5] Schultze, *Der Fetischismus*, p. 111.
[6] Turner, *Samoa*, p. 334.
[7] Codrington, *op. cit.* p. 217.
[8] Tiele, *History of the Egyptian Religion*, p. 229. Amélineau, *op. cit.* p. 251.
[9] *Yasts*, x.
[10] *Iliad*, iii. 276 *sqq.* Farnell, *Cults of the Greek States*, i. 70.

Romans by Jupiter and Dius Fidius.[1] A god is more
able than ordinary mortals to master the processes of
nature, and he may also better know whether the sworn
word be true or false.[2] It is undoubtedly on account of
their superior knowledge that sun or moon or light gods
are so frequently appealed to in oaths. The Egyptian
god Ra is a solar,[3] and Thoth a lunar[4] deity. The Zoroastrian Mithra, who " has a thousand senses, and sees every
man that tells a lie," [5] is closely connected with the sun ; [6]
and Rashnu Razista, according to M. Darmesteter, is an
offshoot either of Mithra or Ahura Mazda himself.[7] Dius
Fidius seems originally to have been a spirit of the heaven,
and a wielder of the lightning, closely allied to the great
Jupiter.[8] Zeus is all-seeing, the infallible spy of both gods
and men.[9] Now, even though the oath has the form of
an appeal to a god, it may nevertheless be of a chiefly
magic character, being an imprecation rather than a prayer.
The oaths which the Moors swear by Allah are otherwise
exactly similar in nature to those in which he is not mentioned at all. But the more the belief in magic was shaken,
the more the spoken word was divested of that mysterious
power which had been attributed to it by minds too apt
to confound words with facts, the more prominent became
the religious element in the oath. The fulfilment of the
self-imprecation was made dependent upon the free will of
the deity appealed to, and was regarded as the punishment
for an offence committed by the perjurer against the god
himself.[10]

[1] von Lasaulx, Der Eid bei den
Römern, p. 9.
[2] Cf. James, Expedition from Pitts-
burg to the Rocky Mountains, i. 267
(Omahas) ; Tylor, Primitive Culture,
ii. 231 (Ostyaks).
[3] Maspero, Dawn of Civilization,
p. 87 sq. Wiedemann, Religion of the
Ancient Egyptians, p. 14. Erman,
Handbook of Egyptian Religion, p.10.
[4] Maspero, op. cit. p. 145. Erman,
op. cit. p. 11.
[5] Yasts, x. 107.
[6] Darmesteter, in Sacred Books of
the East, xxiii. 122, n. 4. Meyer, Geschichte des Alterthums, i. 541 sq.
Geiger, op. cit. i. p. lvi.
[7] Darmesteter, in Sacred Books of
the East, xxiii. 168.
[8] Fowler, Roman Festivals, p. 141.
[9] Cf. Iliad, iii. 277 ; Ovid, Metamorphoses, iv. 172 ; Darmesteter,
Essais orientaux, p. 107 ; Usener,
Götternamen, p. 177 sqq.
[10] Grotius says (De jure belli et pacis,
ii. 13. 12) that even he who swears by
false gods is bound, "because, though
under false notions, he refers to the
general idea of Godhead, and therefore the true God will interpret it

Owing to its invocation of supernatural sanction, perjury is considered the most heinous of all acts of falsehood.[1] But it has a tendency to make even the ordinary lie or breach of faith a matter of religious concern. If a god is frequently appealed to in oaths, a general hatred of lying and unfaithfulness may become one of his attributes, as is suggested by various facts quoted above. There is every reason to believe that a god is not, in the first place, appealed to because he is looked upon as a guardian of veracity and good faith, but that he has come to be looked upon as a guardian of these duties because he has been frequently appealed to in connection with them.

It seems that sometimes the habit of oath-taking has, in another respect also, made it prudential for men to speak the simple truth in all circumstances. Sir W. H. Sleeman

as a wrong to himself if perjury be committed."

[1] Among various peoples perjury is punished even by custom or law. Thus among the Gaika tribe of the Kafirs a person may be fined for taking a false oath in a law case (Brownlee, in Maclean, *Compendium of Kafir Laws and Customs*, p. 124). In Abyssinia a man convicted of perjury "would not only lose his reputation, and be for ever incapacitated from being witness even on the most trivial question, but he would likewise in all probability be bound and severely fined, and might indeed think himself fortunate if he got off with all his limbs in their proper places, or without his hide being scored " (Parkyns, *Life in Abyssinia*, ii. 258 *sq.*). The laws of the Malays punish perjury (Crawfurd, *History of the Indian Archipelago*, iii. 90). In India, according to the Laws of Manu (viii. 219 *sq.*), he who broke an agreement after swearing to it was to be banished, imprisoned, and fined. Mediæval law-books punished perjurers with the loss of the right hand, by which the oath was sworn (Wilda, *Das Strafrecht der Germanen*, p. 983 *sq.*; Pollock and Maitland, *History of English Law before the Time of Edward I*. ii. 541). In a Danish law of 1537 it is said that the perjurer shall lose the two offending fingers so as to appease the wrath of God (Stemann, *Den danske Retshistorie indtil Christian V.'s Lov*, p. 645). In other cases, again, no civil punishment is affixed to a false oath—for instance, among the Rejangs (Marsden, *History of Sumatra*, p. 240) and Bataks of Sumatra (*Glimpses of the Eastern Archipelago*, p. 86), the Ossetes (Kovalewsky, *Coutume contemporaine*, p. 324), Persians (Polak, *Persien*, ii. 83), and, as it seems, the ancient Hebrews (Keil, *Manual of Biblical Archæology*, ii. 348; Greenstone, 'Perjury,' in *Jewish Encyclopedia*, ix. 640), Greeks (Rohde, *Psyche*, p. 245, note), and Teutons in early times (Wilda, *op. cit.* p. 982 ; Brunner, *Deutsche Rechtsgeschichte*, ii. 681). Cicero says (*De legibus*, ii. 9) that "the divine punishment of perjury is destruction, the human punishment infamy " ; but though perjury *per se* was not punished in Rome, the law appears from very early times to have contained provisions for punishing false testimony (Hunter, *Roman Law*, p. 1063 ; see also Mommsen, *Römisches Strafrecht*, p. 681). However, the fact that perjury is not treated as a crime by no means implies that it is not regarded as a sin. The punishment of it is left to the offended deity (Marsden, *op. cit.* p. 219; *Glimpses of the Eastern Archipelago*, p. 86; Crawfurd, *op. cit.* iii. 90 [Javanese]).

observes that among the woods and hills of India the cotton and other trees are supposed by the natives to be occupied by deities who are vested with a local super-intendence over the affairs of a district, or perhaps of a single village. "These," he says, "are always in the view of the people, and every man knows that he is every moment liable to be taken to their court, and to be made to invoke their vengeance upon himself or those dear to him, if he has told a falsehood in what he has stated, or tells one in what he is about to state. Men so situated adhere habitually, and I may say religiously, to the truth ; and I have had before me hundreds of cases in which a man's property, liberty, or life, has depended upon his telling a lie, and he has refused to tell it to save either." [1] On the other hand, there are peoples among whom a person's word can hardly be trusted unless confirmed by an oath.[2] And one of the arguments adduced by the Quakers against the taking of oaths is that, if on any particular occasion a man swear in addition to his yea or nay, in order to make it more obligatory or convincing, its force becomes comparatively weak at other times when it receives no such confirmation.[3]

Modes of conduct which are recommended by prudence tend on that account in various ways to be regarded as morally compulsory or praiseworthy. This subject will be discussed in connection with duties and virtues which are called " self-regarding," but in the present place it is necessary to remind ourselves of the share which early education has in making prudence a matter of moral consideration. Few duties owe so much to the training of parents and teachers as does veracity. Children easily resort to falsehood, in self-defence or otherwise, and truthfulness is therefore enjoined on them with particular emphasis.[4]

---

[1] Sleeman, op. cit. ii. 111 sq.
[2] See, besides supra, Kingsley, West African Studies, p. 414 ; Chanler, Through Jungle and Desert, p. 186 sq. (Wamsara).

[3] Gurney, Views and Practices of the Society of Friends, p. 327.
[4] Cf. Priestley, in ' Essay III.' introductory to Hartley's Theory of the Human Mind, p. xlix. sq.

The moral ideas referring to truthfulness are, finally, much influenced by the force of habit. Where lying is frequent it is, other things being equal, less strenuously condemned, if condemned at all, than in communities which are strictly truthful. It is natural to speak the truth. Von Jhering's suggestion that man was originally a liar, and that veracity is the result of human progress,[1] is not consistent with facts. Language was not invented to disguise the truth, but to express it. As Hutcheson remarked long ago, " truth is the natural production of the mind when it gets the capacity of communicating it, dissimulation and disguise are plainly artificial effects of design and reflection." [2] It may be doubted whether there are any other mendacious creatures in the world than men.[3] It is said that " lies are told, if not in speech yet in acts, by dogs " ; [4] but the instances reported of canine deceitfulness [5] are hardly conclusive. As a cautious writer observes, the question is not whether there may be " objective deceitfulness " in the dog's conduct, but whether the motive is deceit ; and " the deceitful intent is a piece, not of the observed fact, but of the observer's inference." [6] Nor is the child, strictly speaking, a born liar. M. Compayré even goes so far as to say that, if the child has not been subjected to bad influences, or if a discipline of repression and constraint has not driven him to seek a refuge in dissimulation, he is usually frankness and sincerity itself.[7] Montaigne remarked that the falsehood of a child grows with its growth.[8] According to M. Perez, useful dissimulations are practised by children already at the age of two years, but generally it is only after they are three or four years old that fear of being scolded or punished will lead

---

[1] von Jhering, *Zweck im Recht*, ii. 606.

[2] Hutcheson, *System of Moral Philosophy*, ii. 28. *Cf.* Reid, *op. cit.* vi. 24, p. 428 *sqq.* ; Dugald Stewart, *op. cit.* ii. 333.

[3] *Cf.* Schopenhauer, *Essays*, p. 145.

[4] Spencer, *Principles of Ethics*, i. 405.

[5] Romanes, *Animal Intelligence*, pp. 443, 444, 451.

[6] Lloyd Morgan, *Animal Life and Intelligence*, p. 400.

[7] Compayré, *L'évolution intellectuelle et morale de l'enfant*, p. 309. See also Sully, *Studies of Childhood*, p. 263 *sq.*

[8] Montaigne, *Essais*, i. 9 (*Œuvres*, p. 16).

them into falsehood.[1] We are even told that certain
savages are too stupid or too ignorant to tell lies. A
Hindu gentleman of the plains, in the valley of the
Nerbudda, when asked what made the uncultured people
of the woods to the north and south so truthful, replied,
" They have not yet learned the value of a lie." [2] But as
we know how readily truthful savages become liars when
their social conditions change, we may conclude that their
veracity was due rather to absence of temptation than to
lack of intelligence. In a small community of savages
living by themselves, there is no need for lying, nor much
opportunity to practise it. There is little scope for those
motives which most commonly induce people to practise
falsehood—fear and love of gain, combined with a hope of
success.[3] Harmony and sympathy generally prevail
between the members of the group, and deception is
hardly possible since secrets do not exist.

The case is different when savages come into frequent contact with foreigners. To deceive a stranger is easy, and no
scruple is made of doing so. On the contrary, as we
have seen, he is regarded as a proper object of deception,
and this opinion is only too often justified by his own
behaviour. But when commonly practised in relation to
strangers, falsehood easily becomes a habit which affects the
general conduct of the man. Hamzé, the teacher of the
Druses, said, " When a man once gets into the way of
speaking falsely, it is to be apprehended that, in spite of
himself, and by the mere force of habit, he will get to
speak falsely towards the brethren " ; hence it is advisable
to speak the truth at all times and before all men.[4]
There is indeed abundant evidence that intercourse with
strangers, and especially with people of a different race,
has had a destructive influence on savage veracity.

This has been noticed among many of the uncivilised tribes
of India. " Formerly," says Mr. Man, " a Sonthal, as a rule,

[1] Perez, *First Three Years of Childhood*, pp. 87, 89.
[2] Sleeman, *op. cit.* ii. 110.
[3] *Cf.* Sarasin, *Forschungen auf*
Ceylon, iii. 543 (Veddahs).
[4] Churchill, *Mount Lebanon*, iii.
225 *sq.*

disdained to tell a falsehood, but the influences of civilisation, transfused through the contagious ethics of his Bengali neighbours, have somewhat impaired his truthfulness. In the last four or five years a great change for the worse has become evident, although even now, as a people, they are glorious exceptions to the prevailing idiosyncrasy of the lower class of natives in Bengal. With the latter, speaking the truth has been always an accident; with the Sonthal it was a characteristic principle."[1] Indeed, the Santals in Singbhúm, who live much to themselves, are still described by Colonel Dalton as "a very simple-minded people, almost incapable of deception."[2] The Tipperah, "where he is brought into contact with, or under the influence of the Bengallee, easily acquires their worst vices and superstitions, losing at the same time the leading characteristic of the primitive man—the love of truth."[3] Other tribes, like the Garos and Bhúmij, have likewise been partly contaminated by their intercourse with Bengalis, and acquired from them a propensity to lie, which, in former days, was altogether foreign to them.[4] The Kakhyens are at the present time lazy, thievish, and untrustworthy, "whether their character has been deteriorated by knavish injustice on the part of Chinese traders, or high-handed extortion and wrong on the part of Burmese."[5] The Ladakhis are, in general, "frank, honest, and moral when not corrupted by communication with the dissolute Kashmiris."[6] Of the Pahárias, who according to an earlier authority would sooner die than lie,[7] it is now reported that "those who have most to do with them say they cannot rely on their word, and that they not only lie without scruple, but are scarcely annoyed at being detected."[8] The Todas, whilst they call falsehood one of the worst vices and have a temple dedicated to Truth, seem nowadays only too often to forget both the temple and its object;[9] and we are told that the dissimulation they practise in their dealings with Europeans has been brought about by the habit of paying them for every insignificant item of information.[10] According to an

---

[1] Man, *Sonthalia*, p. 14. *Cf. ibid.* p. 20.
[2] Dalton, *Ethnology of Bengal*, *op. cit.* p. 217.
[3] Lewin, *Wild Races of South-Eastern India*, p. 216.
[4] Dalton, *op. cit.* pp. 68, 177.
[5] Anderson, *Mandalay to Momien*, p. 151.
[6] Moorcroft and Trebeck, *Travels in the Himalayan Provinces of Hindustan*, i. 321.
[7] Shaw, quoted by Dalton, *op. cit.* p. 274.
[8] Cumming, *In the Himalayas*, p. 404 *sq.*
[9] Harkness, *A Singular Aboriginal Race inhabiting the Neilgherry Hills*, p. 18.
[10] Metz, *Tribes inhabiting the Neilgherry Hills*, p. 13.

Indian civil servant quoted by Mr. Spencer, various other hill tribes, originally distinguished by their veracity, have afterwards been rendered less veracious by contact with the whites.[1]

Of the Andaman Islanders Mr. Man observes :—"It has been remarked with regret by all interested in the race, that intercourse with the alien population has, generally speaking, prejudicially affected their morals ; and that the candour, veracity, and self-reliance they manifest in their savage and untutored state are, when they become associated with foreigners, to a great extent lost, and habits of untruthfulness, dependence, and sloth engendered."[2] Riedel makes a similar remark with reference to the natives of Ambon and Uliase.[3] Mr. Sommerville believes that the natives of New Georgia, in the Solomon Islands, learned their practice of cheating from European traders.[4]

Among the Ostyaks increasing civilisation has proved injurious to their ancient honesty, and those who live in the neighbourhood of towns or large villages have become even more deceitful than the colonists.[5] A similar change has taken place with other tribes belonging to the Russian Empire, for instance the Tunguses[6] and Kamchadales.[7]

We hear the same story from America.[8] Among the Omahas "formerly only two or three were notorious liars ; but now, there are about twenty who do not lie."[9] The old men of the Ojibwas all agree in saying that before the white man came and resided among them there was less lying than there is now.[10] The Indians of Mexico, Lumholtz writes, "do not tell the truth unless it suits them."[11] But with reference to some of them, the Tarahumares, he adds that, where they have had little or nothing to do with the whites, they are trustworthy, and profit is no inducement to them, as they believe

---

[1] Spencer, *Principles of Sociology*, ii. 234. See also Hodgson, *Miscellaneous Essays*, i. 152. (Bódo and Dhimáls) ; Dalton, *op. cit.* p. 206 (Múndas).
[2] Man, in *Jour. Anthr. Inst.* xii. 92.
[3] Riedel, *De sluik- en kroesharige rassen tusschen Selebes en Papua*, p. 41.
[4] Sommerville, in *Jour. Anthr. Inst.* xxvi. 394.
[5] Castrén, *op. cit.* ii. 121.
[6] Dall, *Alaska*, p. 518.
[7] Steller, *Beschreibung von dem Lande Kamtschatka*, p. 285. Sary-

tchew, 'Voyage of Discovery to the North-East of Siberia,' in *Collection of Modern and Contemporary Voyages*, v. 67.
[8] Domenech, *Seven Years' Residence in the Great Deserts of North America*, ii. 69. *Cf.* Hearne, *Journey to the Northern Ocean*, pp. 307, 308, 310 (Chippewyans) ; Morgan, *League of the Iroquois*, p. 335 *sq.*
[9] Dorsey, 'Omaha Sociology,' in *Ann. Rep. Bur. Ethn.* iii. 370.
[10] Schoolcraft, *Indian Tribes of the United States*, ii. 139.
[11] Lumholtz, *Unknown Mexico*, ii. 477.

that their gods would be angry with them for charging an undue price.[1]

The deceitfulness of many African peoples is undoubtedly in some degree a result of their intercourse with foreigners. In Sierra Leone, says Winterbottom, the natives on the sea coast, who are chiefly engaged in commerce, "are in general shrewd and artful, sometimes malevolent and perfidious. Their long connection with European slave traders has tutored them in the arts of deceit."[2] The Yorubas, according to Burton, are eminently dishonest only "in and around the cities."[3] Among the Kalunda those who live near the great caravan roads and have had much to do with foreign traders are suspicious and false.[4] And the Hottentots, of whose truthfulness earlier writers spoke very highly, are nowadays said to be addicted to lying.[5]

It has also been noticed that mendacity is favoured among children by much intercourse with strangers, when "first impressions" are consciously made, as also by frequent change of environment, or of school or residence, as such changes give rise to a feeling that "new leaves" can be easily turned.[6]

When a social unit is composed of loosely connected sub-groups, the intercourse between members of different sub-groups resembles in many respects that between foreigners. Social incoherence is thus apt to lead to deceitful habits, as was the case in the Middle Ages. The same phenomenon is to be observed in the East; perhaps also among the Desert Arabs and the Fuegians, who live in small parties which only occasionally meet and soon again separate.

Another factor which has favoured deception is social differentiation. The different classes of society have often little sympathy for each other, their interests are not infrequently conflicting, deceit is a means of procuring advantages, and, for the inferior classes especially, a means of self-protection. As Euripides observes, slaves are in

---

[1] Lumholtz, *Unknown Mexico*, i. 244, 418.
[2] Winterbottom, *Native Africans in the Neighbourhood of Sierra Leone*, i. 206.
[3] Burton, *Abeokuta*, i. 303.

[4] Pogge, *Im Reiche des Muata Jamwo*, p. 236.
[5] Fritsch, *Die Eingeborenen Süd-Afrika's*, p. 307 sq.
[6] Stanley Hall, in *American Journal of Psychology*, iii. 70.

the habit of concealing the truth.[1] In Eastern Africa, says Livingstone, falsehood is a vice prevailing among the free, but still more among the slaves ; " one can scarcely induce a slave to translate anything truly : he is so intent on thinking of what will please." [2]

Hardly anything has been a greater inducement to falsehood than oppression. Whilst the old Makololo were truthful, this is not the case with their sons, " who, having been brought up among the subjected tribes, have acquired some of the vices peculiar to a menial and degraded race." [3] The Wanyoro, who are described as " splendid liars," exercised deception chiefly to evade the intolerable exactions of their own chiefs, whereas they are fairly truthful in contact with Europeans who attempt to treat them justly.[4] The duplicity and cunning of the Malagasy are " the natural result of centuries of superstition, ignorance, and submission to the rule of tyrannical despots, with whom the spy system has always been a necessity." [5] In Morocco the independent Jbâla, or mountaineers of the North, are more to be trusted than the Arabs of the plains, who have long been suffering from the extortions of rapacious officials. The duplicity of Orientals is very largely due to their despotic form of government.[6] In India, Mr. Percival observes, " despotism in one form or other that has so long prevailed, and the consequent oppression attendant thereon, must have rendered it difficult to make way without fraud. Deception and arts of cunning, under such circumstances, being the only means at the command of the inferior portions of the community for gaining their ends, and securing the plainest rights, they would resort to them as the only way of avoiding certain ruin." [7] The Chinese habit of lying has

[1] Euripides, *Phœnissœ*, 392. *Cf.* Burton, *Arabian Nights*, i. 176, n. 1.

[2] Livingstone, *Expedition to the Zambesi*, p. 309. See also Polack, *Manners and Customs of the New Zealanders*, ii. 59.

[3] Livingstone, *Expedition to the Zambesi*, p. 283.

[4] Johnston, *Uganda Protectorate*, ii.

591.

[5] Little, *Madagascar*, p. 72.

[6] Vámbéry, *Der Islam im neunzehnten Jahrhundert*, p. 231.

[7] Percival, *Land of the Veda*, p. 288. *Cf.* Malcolm, *Memoir of Central India*, ii. 171 ; Hodgson, *Miscellaneous Essays*, i. 152.

been attributed partly to the truckling fear of officers.[1] In China and many other parts of the East, says Sir J. Bowring, " there is a fear of truth *as* truth, lest its discovery should lead to consequences of which the inquirer never dreams, but which are present to the mind of the person under interrogation." [2]

The regard for truth displays itself not only in the condemnation of falsehood, but in the idea that, under certain circumstances, it is a person's duty to inform others of the truth, although there is no deception in withholding it. This duty is limited by utilitarian considerations, and it is less insisted on than the duty of refraining from falsehood ; positive commandments, as we have seen, are generally less stringent than the corresponding negative commandments.[3] But to disclose the truth for the benefit of others, when it is attended with injurious consequences for the person who discloses it, can hardly fail to evoke moral approval, and may be deemed a merit of the highest order.

The regard for truth goes a step further still. It may be obligatory or praiseworthy not only to spread the knowledge of truth, but to seek for it. The possession of knowledge, of some kind or other, is universally respected. A Wolof proverb says, " Not to know is bad, not to wish to know is worse." [4] In the moral and religious systems of the East knowledge is one of the chief pursuits of man. Confucius described virtue as consisting of knowledge, magnanimity, and valour.[5] The ancients, he says, "wishing to rectify their hearts, . . . first desired to be sincere in their thoughts. Wishing to be sincere in their thoughts, they first extended to the utmost their knowledge. Such extension of knowledge lay in the investigation of things."[6] Knowledge is to be pursued not for theoretical, but for

---

[1] Wells Williams, *The Middle Kingdom*, i. 835.
[2] Bowring, *Siam*, i. 105 *sq.*
[3] *Supra*, i. 303 *sqq.*
[4] Burton, *Wit and Wisdom from West Africa*, p. 6.
[5] *Chung Yung*, xx. 8. Douglas, *Confucianism and Taouism*, p. 105.
[6] *Tâ Hsio*, 4.

moral purposes ; the Master said, " It is not easy to find
a man who has learned for three years without coming to
be good." [1] The Hindus maintain that ignorance is the
greatest of evils, and that the sole and ultimate object of
life should be to give and receive instruction.[2] It is said
in the Laws of Manu, " A man is not therefore considered venerable because his head is gray ; him who,
though young, has learned the Veda, the gods consider to
be venerable." [3] According to the Mahabharata, it is by
knowledge that a creature is liberated, by knowledge that
he becomes the Eternal, Imperceptible, and Undecaying.[4]
Buddhism regards sin as folly and delusion as the cause
of crime ; [5] " the unwise man cannot discover the difference between that which is evil and that which is good, as
a child knows not the value of a coin that is placed before
him." [6] And the highest of all gifts, the source of abiding salvation, is the knowledge of the identity between
the individual and God, in whom and by whom the
individual lives, and moves, and has his being. [7] According to one of the Pahlavi texts, wisdom is better than
wealth of any kind ; [8] through the power of wisdom it is
possible to do every duty and good work ;[9] the religion
of the Mazda-worshippers is apprehended more fully by
means of the most perfect wisdom, and " even the struggle
and warfare of Irân with foreigners, and the smiting of
Aharman and the demons it is possible to effect through
the power of wisdom." [10] A strong dash of intellectualism
is a prominent feature in the Rabbinic religion. The
highest virtue lies not only in the fulfilment but in the
study of the law. There is a special merit bound up in it
that will assist man both in this world and in the world to
come ; and it is said that even a bastard who is learned in

---

[1] *Lun Yü*, viii. 12.   *Cf.* Faber,
Digest of the Doctrines of Confucius,
p. 60 ; de Lanessan, *La morale des
philosophes chinois,* p. 27.

[2] Percival, *Land of the Veda,* p.
263.

[3] *Laws of Manu,* ii. 156.

[4] Muir, *Original Sanskrit Texts,* v.
327.

[5] Rhys Davids, *Hibbert Lectures on
the History of Buddhism,* p. 208.

[6] Hardy, *Manual of Budhism,* p.
505.

[7] Rhys Davids, *op. cit.* p. 209.

[8] *Dînâ-î Maînôg-î Khirad,* xlvii. 6.

[9] *Ibid.* i. 54.

[10] *Ibid.* lvii. 15 *sq.*

the law is more honoured than a high-priest who is not.[1]
Among Muhammedans, also, great respect is shown to
men of learning.[2] Knowledge, the Prophet said, " lights
the way to Heaven "—" He dies not who gives life to
learning "—" With knowledge the servant of God rises to
the heights of goodness and to a noble position "—" The
ink of the scholar is more holy than the blood of the
martyr." [3]

In Christianity the knowledge of truth became a necessary requirement of salvation. But here, as in the East,
the truth which alone was valued was religious truth. All
knowledge that was not useful to salvation was, indeed,
despised, and science was regarded not only as valueless,
but as sinful.[4] " The wisdom of this world is foolishness
with God." [5] If it happened that any one gave himself to
letters, or lifted up his mind to the contemplation of the
heavenly bodies, he passed instantly for a magician or a
heretic.[6] So also every mental disposition which is essential to scientific research was for centuries stigmatised as
offensive to the Almighty ; it was a sin to doubt the
opinions which had been instilled in childhood before they
had been examined, to notice any objection to those
opinions, to resolve to follow the light of evidence wherever it might lead.[7] Yet we are told, even by highly
respectable writers, that the modern world owes its scientific spirit to the extreme importance which Christianity

---

[1] Montefiore, *Hibbert Lectures on
the Religion of the Ancient Hebrews*,
p. 495. Deutsch, *Literary Remains*,
p. 35.
[2] Lane, *Manners and Customs of
the Modern Egyptians*, p. 301 *sq.*
[3] Ameer Ali, *Ethics of Islâm*, pp.
47, 49.
[4] Gibbon, *Decline and Fall of the
Roman Empire*, ii. 185. von Eicken,
*Geschichte der mittelalterlichen Welt-
anschauung*, pp. 128–130, 589 *sqq.*
[5] 1 *Corinthians*, iii. 19. *Cf.* Lactantius, *Divinæ Institutiones*, iii. 3
(Migne, *Patrologiæ cursus*, vi. 354
sqq.) ; St. Augustine, *De Civitate Dei*,
viii. 10 (Migne, xli. 234).

[6] Chapelain, *De la lecture des vieux
romans*, p. 20. As late as the middle
of the seventeenth century a powerful party was rising in England who
said that all learning was unfavourable to religion, and that it was
sufficient for everyone to be acquainted with his mother-tongue
alone (Twells, *Life of Pocock*, p. 176).
The Duke de Saint Simon, who in
1721 and 1722 was the French am-
bassador in Madrid, states (*Mémoires*, xxxv. 209) that in Spain
science was a crime, and ignorance
and stupidity the chief virtues.
[7] Lecky, *Rationalism in Europe*, ii.
87 *sq.*

assigned to the possession of truth, of *the* truth.[1] According to M. Réville, " it was the orthodox intolerance of the Church in the Middle Ages which impressed on Christian society this disposition to seek truth at any price, of which the modern scientific spirit is only the application. The more importance the Church attached to the profession of the truth—to the extent even of considering involuntary error as in the highest degree a damnable crime—so much the more the sentiment of the immense value of this truth arose in the general persuasion, along with a resolve to conquer it wherever it was felt not to be possessed. How otherwise," M. Réville asks, " can we explain that science was not developed and has not been pursued with constancy, except in the midst of Christian societies ? "[2] This statement is characteristic of the common tendency to attribute to the influence of the Christian religion almost anything good which may be found among Christian nations. But, surely, the patient and impartial search after hidden truth, for the sake of truth, which constitutes the essence of scientific research, is not congenial to, but the very opposite of, that ready acceptance of a revealed truth for the sake of eternal salvation, which was insisted upon by the Church. And what about that singular love of abstract knowledge which flourished in ancient Athens, where Aristotle declared it a sacred duty to prefer truth to everything else,[3] and Socrates sacrificed his life on its altar ? It seems that the modern scientific spirit is only a revival and development of a mental disposition which was for ages suppressed by the persecuting tendencies of the Church and the extreme contempt for learning displayed by the barbarian invaders and their descendants. Even when they had settled in the countries which they had conquered, the

---

[1] Ritchie, *Natural Rights*, p. 172. *Cf.* Kuenen, *Hibbert Lectures on National Religions and Universal Religions*, p. 290.

[2] Réville, *Prolegomena of the History of Religions*, p. 226.

[3] Aristotle, *Ethica Nicomachea*, i. 6. 1. Prof. Ritchie argues (*op. cit.* p. 172 *sq.*) that a devotion to truth as such was in the ancient world known only to a few philosophers. Prof. Fowler is probably more correct in saying (*Principles of Morals*, ii. 45, 220 *sq.* ; *Progressive Morality*, p. 114) that it was more common amongst the Greeks than amongst ourselves.

Teutons would not permit their children to be instructed
in any science, for fear lest they should become effeminate
and averse from war ;[1] and long afterwards it was held
that a nobleman ought not to know letters, and that to
write and read was a shame to gentry.[2]

The regard for knowledge springs in the first instance
from the love of it. As Aristotle said, " all men are by
nature desirous of knowledge."[3] But this feeling is not
equally strong, nor equally deep, in all. The curiosity of
savages, however great it often may be,[4] has chiefly reference to objects or events which immediately concern their
welfare or appear to them alarming, or to trifles which
attract attention on account of their novelty. If their curiosity were more penetrating, they would no longer remain
savages ; an extended desire of knowledge leads to civilisation. But curiosity or love of knowledge, whether in
savage or civilised men, is not resolvable merely into
views of utility ; as Dr. Brown observed, we feel it without
reflecting on the pleasure which we are to enjoy or the
pain which we are to suffer.[5] When highly developed, it
drives men to scientific investigations even though no
practical benefits are expected from the results. This
devotion to truth for its own sake, pure and disinterested
as it is, has a singular tendency to excite regard and
admiration in everyone who has come under its influence.
From the utilitarian point of view it has been defended on

[1] Procopius, *De bello Gothorum*, i.
2. Robertson, *History of the Reign of
Charles V.* i. 234. Millingen, *op. cit.*
i. 22 *sq.* n.†
[2] Alain Chartier, quoted by Sainte-
Palaye, *op. cit.* ii. 104. See also De la
Noüe, *Discours politiques et militaires*, p. 238 ; Lyttleton, *Life of
Henry II.* ii. 246 *sq.* The ignorance
of the mediæval clergy has been
somewhat exaggerated by Robertson (*op. cit.* pp. 21, 22, 278 *sq.*).
Even in the dark ages it was not a
very uncommon thing for the clergy
to be able to read and write (Maitland, *The Dark Ages*, p. 16 *sqq.*).
[3] Aristotle, *Metaphysica*, i. 1. 1, p.
980. *Cf.* Cicero, *De officiis*, i. 4.

[4] Murdoch, ' Ethnological Results
of the Point Barrow Expedition,' in
Ann. Rep. Bur. Ethn. ix. 42 (Eskimo). Krasheninnikoff, *History of
Kamschatka*, p. 177. Anderson,
Mandalay to Momien, p.151 (Kakhyens). Foreman, *Philippine Islands*, p. 188 (Tagálog natives of the
North). Bock, *Head Hunters of
Borneo*, p. 209 (Dyaks). Forbes, *A
Naturalist's Wanderings in the
Eastern Archipelago*, p. 320 (natives
of Timor-laut). Dieffenbach, *Travels
in New Zealand*, ii. 108.
[5] Dugald Stewart, *op. cit.* ii. 336.
Brown, *Lectures on the Philosophy of
the Human Mind*, lec. 67, p. 451.

the ground that, on the whole, every truth is in the long run useful and every error harmful, and that we can never exactly tell in advance what benefits may accrue even from a knowledge which is apparently fruitless.   But it seems that our love of truth is somewhat apt to mislead our moral judgment. When duly reflecting on the matter, we cannot help making a moral distinction between him who pursues his studies merely from an instinctive craving for knowledge, and him who devotes his life to the search of truth from a conviction that he may thereby promote human welfare.

CHAPTER XXXII

THE RESPECT FOR OTHER MEN'S HONOUR AND SELF-REGARDING PRIDE—POLITENESS

THERE are many acts, forbearances, and omissions, the offensiveness of which mainly or exclusively springs from men's desire to be respected by their fellow-men and their dislike of being looked down upon. Foremost among these are attacks upon people's honour and good name. A man's honour may be defined as the moral worth he possesses in the eyes of the society of which he is a member, and it behoves other persons to acknowledge this worth and, especially, not to detract from it by imputing to him, on insufficient grounds, such behaviour as is generally considered degrading. The censure to which he is subject or the contempt in which he is held may no doubt affect his welfare in various ways, but it is chiefly painful as a violation of his personal dignity. Hence the duty of respecting a man's honour is on the whole contained in the more comprehensive obligation of showing deference, in words and deeds, for his feeling of self-regarding pride.

This feeling, or at least the germ of it, is found already in some of the lower animals. Among " high-life " dogs, says Professor Romanes, " wounded sensibilities and loss of esteem are capable of producing much keener suffering than is mere physical pain." A reproachful word or look from any of his friends made a

Skye terrier miserable for a whole day ; and another terrier, who when in good humour used to perform various tricks, was never so pleased as when his joke was duly appreciated, whereas " nothing displeased him so much as being laughed at when he did not intend to be ridiculous."[1] Monkeys also, according to Dr. Brehm, are " very sensitive to every kind of treatment they may receive, to love and dislike, to encouraging praise and chilling blame, to pleasant flattery and wounding ridicule, to caresses and chastisement." [2]

Among the savage races of men, as among civilised peoples, self-regarding pride is universal, and in many of them it is a very conspicuous trait of character.[3] The Veddah of Ceylon, says Mr. Nevill, " is proud in the extreme, and considers himself no man's inferior. Hence he is keenly sensitive to ridicule, contempt, and even patronage. There is nothing he dreads more than being laughed at as a savage, because he dislikes clothes and cultivation." [4] Australian aborigines are described as " extravagantly proud," [5] as "vain and fond of approbation." [6] In Fiji " anything like a slight deeply offends a native, and is not soon forgotten."[7] The Negroes of Sierra Leone " possess a great share of pride, and are easily affected by an insult : they cannot hear even a harsh expression, or a raised tone of voice, without shewing that

[1] Romanes, *Animal Intelligence*, pp. 439, 444.

[2] Brehm, *From North Pole to Equator*, p. 299. *Cf. ibid.* pp. 304–306, 312, 314 ; Brehm, *Thierleben*, i. 75, 157 ; Schultze, *Vergleichende Seelenkunde*, i. pt. i. 110; Perty, *Das Seelenleben der Thiere*, p. 66.

[3] Dieffenbach, *Travels in New Zealand*, ii. 107 ; Colenso, *Maori Races of New Zealand*, p. 56. Crawfurd, *History of the Indian Archipelago*, i. 54. Raffles, *History of Java*, i. 249. St. John, *Life in the Forests of the Far East*, ii. 323 (Malays of Sarawak). Man, 'Aboriginal Inhabitants of the Andaman Islands,' in *Jour. Anthr. Inst.* xii. 94. Stewart, 'Notes on Northern Cachar,' in *Jour. Asiatic*

Soc. Bengal, xxiv. 609 (Nagas). Bergmann, *Nomadische Streifereien unter den Kalmüken*, ii. 290, 295, 296, 312. Högström, *Beskrifning öfver de til Sveriges Krona lydande Lapmarker*, p. 152 (Lapps). Dall, *Alaska*, p. 392 *sq.* (Aleuts). Brett, *Indian Tribes of Guiana*, p. 103.

[4] Nevill, 'Vaeddas of Ceylon,' in *Taprobanian*, i. 192. *Cf.* Sarasin, *Ergebnisse naturwissenschaftlicher Forschungen auf Ceylon*, iii. 537.

[5] Hale, *U.S. Exploring Expedition. Vol. VI. Ethnography and Philology*, p. 109.

[6] Mathew, in Curr, *The Australian Race*, iii. 155.

[7] Williams and Calvert, *Fiji*, p. 105. *Cf. ibid.* p. 103 *sq.*

they feel it."[1] The Araucanians, inhabiting parts of Chili,
" are naturally fond of honourable distinction, and there is
nothing they can endure with less patience than contempt
or inattention."[2] The North American Indians, says
Perrot, " ont généralement touts beaucoup de vaine gloire
dans leurs actions bonnes ou mauvaises. . . . L'ambition
est en un mot une des plus fortes passions qui les anime."[3]
The Indian of British Columbia, for instance, " watches
that he may receive his proper share of honour at
festivals ; he cannot endure to be ridiculed for even the
slightest mistake ; he carefully guards all his actions, and
looks for due honour to be paid to him by friends,
strangers, and subordinates. This peculiarity appears
most clearly in great festivals."[4] Thus, in numerous
instances, " persons who have been hoarding up property
for ten, fifteen, or twenty years (at the same time almost
starving themselves for want of clothing), have given it all
away to make a show for a few hours, and to be thought
of consequence."[5] Speaking of the Eskimo about
Behring Strait, Mr. Nelson observes, "As with all
savages, the Eskimo are extremely sensitive to ridicule
and are very quick to take offence at real or seeming
slights."[6] Among the Atkha Aleuts it has happened that
men have committed suicide from disappointment at the
failure of an undertaking, fearing that they would become
the laughing-stock of the village.[7] Among many other
savages shame or wounded pride is not uncommonly a cause
of suicide.[8] The Hos of Chota Nagpore have a saying
that for a wife who has been reproved by her husband

[1] Winterbottom, *Native Africans in
the Neighbourhood of Sierra Leone*, i.
211.
[2] Molina, *History of Chili*, ii. 113.
[3] Perrot, *Memoire sur les mœurs,
coustumes et relligion des sauvages de
l'Amerique septentrionale*, p. 76. *Cf.*
Buchanan, *Sketches of the History,
Manners, and Customs of the North
American Indians*, p. 165; Matthews, *Ethnography and Philology
of the Hidatsa Indians*, p. 41.
[4] Boas, in *Fifth Report on the North-*

Western Tribes of Canada, p. 19.
[5] Duncan, quoted by Mayne, *Four
Years in British Columbia*, p. 295.
[6] Nelson, ' Eskimo about Bering
Strait,' in *Ann. Rep. Bur. Ethn.*
xviii. 300.
[7] Yakof, quoted by Petroff, *Report
on Alaska*, p. 158. *Cf.* Dall, *op. cit.*
p. 391 (Aleuts).
[8] See *infra*, on Suicide; Lasch, ' Besitzen die Naturvölker ein persönliches Ehrgefühl ? ' in *Zeitschr. f.
Socialwissenschaft*, iii. 837 *sqq.*

" nothing remains but the water at the bottom of the well " ; [1] and in New Zealand native women sometimes killed themselves because they had been rebuked for negligence in cooking or for want of care towards a child.[2]

Like other injuries, an insult not only affects the feelings of the victim, but arouses sympathetic resentment in outsiders, and is consequently disapproved of as wrong. Among the Maoris, if anybody wantonly tried to hurt another's feelings, it was immediately repressed, and " such a person was spoken of as having had no parents, or, as having been born (laid) by a bird." [3] In the Malay Archipelago, " among some of the tribes, abusive language cannot with impunity be used even to a slave. Blows are still more intolerable, and considered such grievous affronts, that, by law, the person who receives them is considered justified in putting the offender to death." [4] The natives of the Tonga Islands hold no bad moral habit to be more " ridiculous, depraved, and unjust, than publishing the faults of one's acquaintances and friends . . . . ; and as to downright calumny or false accusation, it appears to them more horrible than deliberate murder does to us : for it is better, they think, to assassinate a man's person than to attack his reputation." [5] According to the customary laws of the Fantis in West Africa, " where a person has been found guilty of using slanderous words, he is bound to retract his words publicly, in addition to paying a small fine by way of compensation to the aggrieved party. Words imputing witchcraft, adultery, immoral conduct, crime, and all words which sound to the disreputation of a person of whom they are spoken are actionable." [6]

Among the Aztecs of ancient Mexico he who wilfully calumniated another, thereby seriously injuring his

[1] Bradley-Birt, *Chota Nagpore*, p. 104. Cf. Dalton, *Descriptive Ethnology of Bengal*, p. 206.
[2] Colenso, *op. cit.* p. 57.
[3] *Ibid.* p. 53.

[4] Crawfurd, *op. cit.* iii. 119 *sq.*
[5] Mariner, *Natives of the Tonga Islands*, ii. 163 *sq.*
[6] Sarbah, *Fanti Customary Laws*, p. 94.

reputation, was condemned to have his lips cut off, and sometimes his ears also ; whilst in Tezcuco the slanderer suffered death.[1] In the Chinese penal code a special book is provided for the prevention and punishment of opprobrious and insulting language, as " having naturally a tendency to produce quarrels and affrays." [2] Among Arabs all insulting expressions have their respective fines ascertained in the *kady's* court.[3] It is said in the Talmud :—" Let the honour of thy neighbour be to thee like thine own. Rather be thrown into a fiery furnace than bring any one to public shame." [4]

The Roman Law of the Twelve Tables contained provisions against libellers,[5] and throughout the whole history of Roman law an attack upon honour or reputation was deemed a serious crime.[6] As for wrongful prosecution, which may be regarded as an aggravated form of defamation, the law of the later Empire required that any one bringing a criminal charge should bind himself to suffer in case of failure the penalty that he had endeavoured to call down upon his adversary.[7] Among Teutonic peoples defamatory words and libelling were already at an early date punished with a fine.[8] The Salic Law decrees that a person who calls a freeborn man a " fox " or a " hare " or a " dirty fellow," or says that he has thrown away his shield, must pay him three solidi ;[9] whilst, according to one text of the same law, it cost 188 solidi (or nearly as much as was paid for the murder of a Frankish freeman) [10] to call a freeborn woman a witch or a harlot, in case the truth of the charge could not be proved.[11]

---

[1] Bancroft, *Native Races of the Pacific States*, ii. 463.
[2] *Ta Tsing Leu Lee*, p. 354 n.*
[3] Burckhardt, *Notes on the Bedouins and Wahábys*, p. 70 sq.
[4] Deutsch, *Literary Remains*, p. 57.
[5] *Lex Duodecim Tabularum*, viii. 1.
[6] *Digesta*, xlvii. 10. 15. 25. *Codex Justinianus*, ix. 36. Hunter, *Exposition of Roman Law*, p. 1069 sq. Mommsen, *Römisches Strafrecht*, p. 794 sq.
[7] Günther, *Die Idee der Wieder-*

vergeltung, i. 141 sqq. Mommsen, *op. cit.* p. 496 sq.
[8] Wilda, *Strafrecht der Germanen*, p. 776 sqq. Nordström, *Bidrag till den svenska samhälls-författningens historia*, ii. 293 sqq. Stemann, *Den danske Retshistorie indtil Christian V.'s Lov*, p. 686 sq. Brunner, *Deutsche Rechtsgeschichte*, ii. 672 sqq.
[9] *Lex Salica*, xxx. 4, 5, 2 ; Hessel's edition, col. 181 sqq.
[10] *Ibid.* xv. col. 91 sqq.
[11] *Ibid.* lxvii. 2, col. 403.

The oldest English laws exacted *bót* and *wíte* from persons who attacked others with abusive words.[1] In the thirteenth century, in almost every action before an English local court, the plaintiff claimed compensation not only for the " damage," but also for the " shame " which had been done him.[2] We further find that regular actions for defamation were common in the local courts ; whereas in later days the ecclesiastical procedure against defamatory speech seems to have been regarded as the usual, if not the only, engine which could be brought to bear upon cases of libel and slander.[3] In England, as in Rome, there was a strong feeling that men should not make charges which they could not prove : before the Conquest a person might lose his tongue, or have to redeem it with his full *wer*, if he brought a false and scandalous accusation ; and under Edward I. a statute decreed that if the appellee was acquitted his accuser should lie in prison for a year and pay damages by way of recompense for the imprisonment and infamy which he had brought upon the innocent.[4]

The condemnation of an insult is greatly influenced by the *status* of, or the relations between, the parties concerned. Among the Goajiro Indians of Colombia a poor man may be insulted with impunity, when the same treatment to a rich man would cause certain bloodshed.[5] In Nias an affront is punished with a fine, which varies according to the rank of the parties.[6] The Chinese penal code lays down that a person who is guilty of addressing abusive language to his or her father or mother, or father's parents, or a wife who rails at her husband's parents or grandparents, shall be strangled ;[7] and the same punishment is prescribed for a slave who abuses his master.[8]

[1] *Laws of Hlothhaere and Eadric,* 11.
[2] Pollock and Maitland, *History of English Law till the Time of Edward I.* ii. 537.
[3] *Ibid.* ii. 538. Stephen, *History of the Criminal Law of England,* ii. 409.
[4] Pollock and Maitland, *op. cit.* ii. 539.

[5] Simons, 'Exploration of the Goajira Peninsula,' in *Proceed. Roy. Geo. Soc.* N.S. vii. 786.
[6] von Rosenberg, *Der malayische Archipel,* p. 167.
[7] *Ta Tsing Leu Lee,* sec. cccxxix. p. 357.
[8] *Ibid.* sec. cccxxvii. p. 356.

According to the Laws of Manu, a Kshatriya shall be fined
one hundred *panas* for defaming a Brâhmana, a Vaisya
shall be fined one hundred and fifty or two hundred *panas*,
and a Sûdra shall suffer corporal punishment ; whereas a
Brâhmana shall pay only fifty *panas* for defaming a
Kshatriya, twenty-five for defaming a Vaisya, and twelve
for defaming a Sûdra.[1] In ancient Teutonic law the fines
for insulting behaviour were graduated according to the
rank of the person offended.[2] The starting-point of the
Roman law was that an *injuria*—which was pre-eminently
an affront to the dignity of the person—could not be
done to a slave as such, only to the master through the
medium of his slave ;[3] and even in later times, in the case
of trifling injuries, such as mere verbal insults, the master
had no action, unless by leave of the Praetor, or unless
the insult were meant for the master himself.[4] These and
similar variations spring from the same causes as do corresponding variations in the case of other injuries dealt with
above. But there are also special reasons why social
superiority or inferiority influences moral opinions concerning offences against persons' self-regarding pride. The
respect due to a man is closely connected with his station,
and in the case of defamation the injury suffered by the
loss of honour or reputation is naturally proportionate to
the esteem in which the offended party is held. At the
same time the harmfulness of an insult also depends upon
the reputation of the person who offers it. According
to the Gotlands Lag, one of the ancient provincial laws of
Sweden, a slave can not only be insulted with impunity,
but has himself to pay no fine for insulting another person[5]
—obviously because he was too degraded a being to be
able to detract from anybody's honour or good name.

---

[1] *Laws of Manu*, viii. 267 sq. *Cf.
Gautama*, xii. 8 *sqq.* It is also said
that "a once-born man (a Sûdra),
who insults a twice-born man with
gross invective, shall have his
tongue cut out ; for he is of low
origin" (*ibid.* viii. 270. See also *Institutes of Vishnu*, v. 23 ; *Gautama*,
xii. 1 ; *Âpastamba*, ii. 10. 27. 14).

[2] Keyser, *Efterladte Skrifter*, ii. pt.
i. 295.
[3] Hunter, *Exposition of Roman
Law*, p. 164. Mommsen, *Römisches
Strafrecht*, p. 786, n. 3.
[4] *Digesta*, xlvii. 10. 15. 35.
Hunter, *op. cit.* p. 165.
[5] *Gotlands-Lagen*, i. 19. 37.

The condemnation of such conduct as is offensive to other persons' self-regarding pride includes condemnation of pride itself, when displayed in an excessive degree ; whereas the opposite disposition—modesty—which implies regard for other people's " self-feeling," is praised as a virtue. The Fijians say of a boasting person, " You are like the *kaka* (parrot) ; you only speak to shout your own name." [1] On the other hand, among the Tonga Islanders " a modest opinion of oneself is esteemed a great virtue, and is also put in practice." [2] Confucius taught that humility belongs to the characteristics of a superior man.[3] Such a man, he said, is modest in his speech, though he exceeds in his actions ; [4] he has dignified ease without pride, whereas the mean man has pride without a dignified ease ;[5] he prefers the concealment of his virtue, when it daily becomes more illustrious, whereas the mean man seeks notoriety when he daily goes more and more to ruin.[6] So also humility has a distinguished place in the teachings of Lao-tsze :—" I have three precious things which I hold fast and prize, namely, compassion, economy, and humility " ; " He who knows the glory, and at the same time keeps to shame, will be the whole world's valley . . . , eternal virtue will fill him, and he will return home to Taou." [7] In the Book of the Dead the soul of the ancient Egyptian pleads, " I am not swollen with pride."[8] According to Zoroastrianism, the sin of pride has been created by Ahriman.[9] Overbearingness was censured in ancient Scandinavia,[10] Greece,[11] and Rome. During our prosperity, says Cicero, " we ought with great care to

[1] Williams and Calvert, *op. cit.* p. 107.
[2] Mariner, *op. cit.* ii. 164.
[3] *Lun Yü*, v. 15. *Chung Yung*, xxvii. 7.
[4] *Lun Yü*, xiv. 29.
[5] *Ibid.* xiii. 26. *Cf. ibid.* xx. 2. 1.
[6] *Chung Yung*, xxxiii. 1.
[7] Douglas, *Confucianism and Taouism*, p. 194 *sq*. *Tâo Teh King*, xxviii. 1.
[8] *Book of the Dead*, ch. 125, p. 216. *Cf.* Amélineau, *Essai sur l'évolution des idées morales dans l'Égypt Ancienne*, p. 353.
[9] *Vendîdâd*, i. 11.
[10] Maurer, *Die Bekehrung des Norwegischen Stammes zum Christenthume*, ii. 150.
[11] Schmidt, *Die Ethik der alten Griechen*, i. 253. Hermann, *Lehrbuch der Griechischen Antiquitäten*, ii. pt. i. 34 *sq*. Blümner, *Ueber die Idee des Schicksals in den Tragödien des Aischylos*, p. 131.

avoid pride and arrogance." [1]   The Hebrew prophets
condemned not only pride but eminence, because an
eminent man is apt to be proud.[2]   We read in the
Talmud :—" He who humiliates himself will be lifted
up ; he who raises himself up will be humiliated.   Whosoever runs after greatness, greatness runs away from
him ; he who runs from greatness, greatness follows him." [3]
Christianity enjoined humility as a cardinal duty in every
man.[4]   In the Koran it is said, " God loves not him who
is proud and boastful." [5]   Pride has thus come to be
stigmatised not only as a vice, but as a sin of great
magnitude.   One reason for this is that it is regarded as
even more offensive to the " self-feeling " of a great god
or the Supreme Being than it is to that of a man.   But
pride must also appear as irreligious arrogance to those
who maintain that man is by nature altogether corrupt,
and that everything good in him is a gift of God.[6]

At the same time, whilst pride is held blamable, humility
may also go too far to be approved of, and may even be an
object of censure.   In early ethics, as we have noticed
above, revenge is enjoined as a duty and forgiveness of
enemies is despised ; and this is the case not only among
savages. [7]   The device of Chivalry was, " It is better to die
than to be avenged by shame " ;[8] and side by side with the
nominal acceptance of the Christian doctrine of absolute
placability the idea still prevails, in many European
countries, that an assault upon honour shall be followed
by a challenge to mortal combat.   Too great humility is
regarded as a sign of weakness, cowardice, hypocrisy, or a
defective sense of honour.   We are not allowed to be
indifferent to the estimation in which we are held by our
neighbours.   Such indifference springs either from a feeble
moral constitution and absence of moral shame, or from

[1] Cicero, *De officiis*, i. 26.
[2] *Cf.* Kuenen, *Religion of Israel*,
i. 62 *sq.*
[3] Deutsch, *Literary Remains*, p. 58.
[4] *St. Matthew*, v. 11, 12, 39 ; vi.
25, 26, 30 *sqq.* ; xviii. 4 ; &c.

[5] *Koran*, iv. 40.   *Cf.* Ameer Ali,
Ethics of Islâm, p. 44.
[6] *Cf.* Manzoni, *Osservazioni sulla
morale cattolica*, p. 182 *sqq.*
[7] *Supra*, i. 73 *sq.*
[8] Laurent, *Études sur l'histoire de
l'Humanité*, vii. 184.

a depreciation of other people's opinions in comparison with our own, and this is offensive to their *amour-propre*. Outward humility may thus suggest inward pride and appear arrogant.

A person's "self-feeling" may be violated in innumerable ways, by words and deeds. Almost any deviation from what is usual may arouse a suspicion of arrogance. This largely accounts for the fact mentioned in a previous chapter that habits have a tendency to become true customs, that is, rules of duty. Transgressions of the established forms of social intercourse are particularly apt to be offensive to people's self-regarding pride. Many of these forms originated in a desire to please, but by becoming habitual they at the same time became obligatory. Politeness is a duty rather than a virtue.

There is probably no people on earth which does not recognise some rules of politeness. Many savages are conspicuous for their civility.[1] It has been observed that Christian missionaries working among uncivilised races often are in manners much inferior to those they are teaching, and thus lower the native standard of refinement.[2] The Samoans, we are told, " are a nation of gentlemen," and contrast most favourably with the generality of Europeans who come amongst them.[3] On their first intercourse with Europeans, the Maoris " always manifest a degree of politeness which would do honour to a more civilised people " ; but by continued intercourse they lose a great part of this characteristic.[4] Among the Fijians " the rules of politeness are minute, and receive scrupulous attention. They affect the language, and are seen in forms of salutation, in attention to strangers, at meals, in dress, and, indeed, influence their manners in-doors and

---

[1] Waitz-Gerland, *Anthropologie der Naturvölker*, vi. 143 *sqq.* (Polynesians). Macdonald, *Oceania*, p. 195 (Efatese). Cranz, *History of Greenland*, i. 157. MacGregor, 'Lagos, Abeokuta and the Alake,' in *Jour. African Soc.* July, 1904, p. 466 (Yorubas).

[2] Brenchley, *Jottings during the Cruise of H.M.S. 'Curaçoa' among the South Sea Islands*, p. 349.
[3] Hood, *Cruise in H.M.S. 'Fawn' in the Western Pacific*, p. 59 *sq.*
[4] Dieffenbach, *op. cit.* ii. 108 *sqq.* See also Colenso, *op. cit.* p. 53 *sqq.*

out. None but the very lowest are ill-behaved, and their confusion on committing themselves shows that they are not impudently so." [1] The Malagasy " are a very polite people, and look with contempt upon those who neglect the ordinary usages and salutations " ; [2] " even the most ragged and tattered slave possesses a natural dignity and ease of manner, which contrasts favourably with the rude conduct and boorish manners of the lower class at home." [3] Of the Point Barrow Eskimo Mr. Murdoch observes that " many of them show a grace of manner and a natural delicacy and politeness which is quite surprising " ; and he mentions the instance of a young Eskimo being so polite in conversing with an American officer that " he would take pains to mispronounce his words in the same way as the latter did, so as not to hurt his feelings by correcting him bluntly." [4] The forms of Kafir politeness " are very strictly adhered to, and are many." [5] Of the Negroes of Fida Bosman wrote, " They are so civil to each other and the inferior so respectful to the superior, that at first I was very much surprised at it." [6] Monrad found the Negroes of Accra surpass many civilised people in politeness. [7] So also in Morocco even country-folks are much more civil in their general behaviour than the large majority of Europeans. " The conversations of the Arabs," says d'Arvieux, " are full of civilities ; one never hears anything there that they think rude and unbecoming." [8] Politeness is a characteristic of all the great nations of the East. The Chinese have brought the practice of it " to a pitch of perfection which is not only unknown in Western lands, but, previous to experience, is unthought of and almost unimaginable. The rules of ceremony, we are reminded in the Classics, are three

[1] Williams and Calvert, *op. cit.* p. 129. *Cf. ibid.* pp. 128, 131 *sq.* ; Anderson, *Notes of Travel in Fiji*, p. 135.
[2] Sibree, *The Great African Island*, p. 325.
[3] Little, *Madagascar*, p. 71.
[4] Murdoch, 'Ethn. Results of the Point Barrow Expedition,' in *Ann. Rep. Bur. Ethn.* ix. 42.

[5] Leslie, *Among the Zulus and Amatongas*, p. 203.
[6] Bosman, *Description of the Coast of Guinea*, p. 317.
[7] Monrad, *Skildring af Guinea-Kysten*, p. 9.
[8] d'Arvieux, *Travels in Arabia the Desart,* p. 141.

L 2

hundred, and the rules of behaviour three thousand." [1]
In Europe courtesy was recommended as the most amiable
of knightly qualities ; and from " the wild and over-
strained courtesies of Chivalry " has been derived our
present system of manners.[2]

The rules of politeness and good manners refer to all
sorts of social intercourse and vary indefinitely in detail.
They tell people how to sit or stand in each other's
presence, or how to pass through a door ; a Zulu wou'd
be fined for going out of a hut back first.[3] They prescribe
how to behave at a meal ; the Indians of British Columbia
consider it improper to talk on such an occasion,[4] and it
appears that in England also, in the fifteenth century,
" people did not hold conversation while eating, but that
the talk and mirth began with the liquor."[5] Politeness
demands that a person should never interrupt another
while speaking ;[6] or that he should avoid contradicting a
statement ;[7] or, not infrequently, that he should rather tell
a pleasant untruth than an unpleasant truth.[8] At times it
requires the use of certain phrases, words of thanks,
flattery, or expressions of self-humiliation. In Chinese
there is " a whole vocabulary of words which are indispensable to one who wishes to pose as a ' polite ' person,
words in which whatever belongs to the speaker is treated
with scorn and contempt, and whatever relates to the
person addressed is honourable. The ' polite ' Chinese
will refer to his wife, if driven to the extremity of referring

---

[1] Smith, *Chinese Characteristics*, p. 35.

[2] *Ordre of Chyualry*, fol. 46. Robertson, *History of the Reign of Charles V.* i. 84. Milman, *History of Latin Christianity*, iv. 211. Turner, *History of England*, iii. 473. Mills, *History of Chivalry*, i. 161 *sq.* Scott, 'Essay on Chivalry,' in *Miscellaneous Prose Works*, vi. 58.

[3] Tyler, *Forty Years among the Zulus*, p. 190 *sq.*

[4] Woldt, *Kaptein Jacobsens Reiser til Nordamerikas Nordvestkyst*, p. 99.

[5] Wright, *Domestic Manners and Sentiments in England during the Middle Ages*, p. 396.

[6] Domenech, *Seven Years' Residence in the Great Deserts o North America*, ii. 72. Richardson, *Arctic Searching Expedition*, i. 385 (Kutchin). Cranz, *History of Greenland*, i. 157. Dobrizhoffer, *Account of the Abipones*, ii. 136 *sq.* d'Arvieux, *op. cit.* p. 139 *sq.*; Wallin, *Reseanteckningar från Orienten*, iii. 259 (Bedouins).

[7] Nansen, *First Crossing of Greenland*, ii. 334 *sq.*; Cranz, *op. cit.* i. 157 (Greenlanders). Dobrizhoffer, *op. cit.* ii. 137 (Abipones). d'Arvieux, *op. cit.* p. 141 (Bedouins).

[8] *Supra*, ii. 111.

to her at all, as his ' dull thorn,' or in some similar elegant figure of speech." [1]

Politeness enjoins the performance of certain ceremonies upon persons who meet or part. The custom of salutation is of world-wide prevalence, though there are certain savages who are said to have no greetings except when they have learnt the practice from the whites.[2] As a ceremony prescribed by public opinion it is an obligatory tribute paid to another person's " self-feeling," whatever be the original nature of the act which has been adopted for the purpose. The form of salutation has sometimes been borrowed from questions springing from curiosity or suspicion. Among the Californian Miwok, when anybody meets a stranger he generally salutes him, " Whence do you come ? What are you at ? " [3] The Abipones " would think it quite contrary to the laws of good-breeding, were they to meet any one and not ask him where he was going " ; [4] and a similar question is also a very common mode of greeting among the Berbers of Southern Morocco. Very frequently a salutation consists of some phrase which is expressive of goodwill. It may be an inquiry about the other person's health or welfare, as the English " How are you ? " " How do you do ? " Among the Burmese two relatives or friends who meet begin a conversation by the expressions, " Are you well ? I am well," if they have been some time separated ; whereas those who are daily accustomed to meet say, " Where are you going ? " [5] The Moors ask, " What is your news ? " or, " Is nothing wrong ? " The ordinary salutation of the Zulus is, " I see you, are you well ? " after which the snuffbox, the token of friendship, is passed round.[6] Among several tribes of California, again, a person when greeting another

[1] Smith, *Chinese Characteristics*, p. 274.

[2] Krasheninnikoff, *History of Kamschatka*, p. 177. Dall, *op. cit.* p. 397 (Aleuts). Egede, *Description of Greenland*, p. 125 ; Rink, *Danish Greenland*, p. 223 ; Cranz, *op. cit.* i. 157 (Greenlanders). Prescott, in Schoolcraft, *Indian Tribes of the United States*, iii. 244 (Dacotahs). Lewin, *Wild Races of South-Eastern India*, pp. 230 (Kumi), 256 (Kukis).

[3] Powers, *Tribes of California*, p. 347.

[4] Dobrizhoffer, *op. cit.* ii. 138.

[5] Forbes, *British Burma*, p. 69.

[6] Tyler, *op. cit.* p. 190.

simply utters a word which means " friendship." [1] The
goodwill is often directly expressed in the form of a wish,
like our " Good day ! " " Good night ! "   Among the
Hebrews the salutation at meeting or entering another's
house seems at first to have consisted most commonly in
an inquiry after mutual welfare,[2] but in later times
" Health ! " or " Peace to thee ! " became the current
greeting.[3] According to the Laws of Manu, a Brâhmana
should be saluted, " May thou be long-lived, O gentle
one ! " [4]   The Greeks said χαῖρε (" Be joyful ! "); the
Romans, Salve ! (" Be in health ! ") especially on meeting,
and Vale ! (" Be well ! ") on parting. The good wish may
have the form of a prayer. The Moors say, " May God
give thee peace ! " " May God give thee a good night ! "
and the English " Good-bye " and the French Adieu are
prayers curtailed by the progress of time.   But there is
no foundation for Professor Wundt's assertion that " the
words employed in greeting are one and all prayer formulæ
in a more or less rudimentary state." [5] A salutation may,
finally, be a verbal profession of subjection, as the Swedish
" Ödmjukaste tjänare," that is, (I am your) " most humble
servant.'

Salutations may consist not only in words spoken, but
in conventional gestures, either accompanied by some
verbal expression or performed silently.[6] They may be
tokens of submission or reverence, as cowering, crouching,
and bowing. Or they may originally have been signs of
disarming or defencelessness, as uncovering some particular
portion of the body.   Von Jhering suggests that the offering of the hand belongs to the same group of salutations,
its object being to indicate that the other person has
nothing to fear ; [7] but in many cases at least handshaking
seems to have the same origin as other ceremonies con-

---

[1] Powers, op. cit. p. 58.

[2] Genesis, xliii. 27. Exodus, xviii. 7.

[3] Judges, xix. 20. 1 Chronicles, xii. 18.   Cf. Keil, Manual of Biblical Archæology, ii. 183.

[4] Laws of Manu, ii. 125.

[5] Wundt, Ethik, p. 179.

[6] See Tylor, ' Salutations,' in Encyclopædia Britannica, xxi. 235 sqq.; Ling Roth, ' Salutations,' in Jour. Anthr. Inst. xix. 166 sqq.

[7] von Jhering, Der Zweck im Recht, ii. 649 sqq.

sisting in bodily contact. Salutatory gestures may express
not only absence of evil intentions but positive friendliness ; among respectable Moors it is a common mode of
greeting that each party places his right hand on his heart
to indicate, as Jackson puts it, " that part to be the
residence of the friend." [1] Various forms of salutation by
contact, such as clasping, embracing, kissing, and sniffing,
are obviously direct expressions of affection ; [2] and we can
hardly doubt that the joining of hands serves a similar
object when we find it combined with other tokens of
goodwill. Among some of the Australian natives, friends,
on meeting after an absence, " will kiss, shake hands, and
sometimes cry over one another." [3] In Morocco equals
salute each other by joining their hands with a quick
motion, separating them immediately, and kissing each
his own hand. The Soolimas, again, place the palms
of the right hands together, carry them then to the
forehead, and from thence to the left side of the chest.[4]
But bodily union is also employed as a method of
transferring either blessings or conditional curses, and
it seems probable that certain salutatory acts have vaguely
or distinctly such transference in view. Among the Masai,
who spit on each other both when they meet and when
they part, spitting " expresses the greatest goodwill and
the best of wishes " ;[5] and in a previous chapter I have
endeavoured to show that the object of certain reception
ceremonies is to transfer a conditional curse to the stranger
who is received as a guest.[6] On the same principle as
underlies these ceremonies, handshaking may be a means
of joining in compact, analogous to a common meal [7] and
the blood-covenant.[8]

Being an homage rendered to other persons' self-regard-

[1] Jackson, *Account of Timbuctoo,
&c.* p. 235.
[2] See *infra*, on the Origin and Development of the Altruistic Sentiment.
[3] Hackett, ' Ballardong or Baller-
dokking Tribe,' in Curr, *The
Australian Race*, i. 343.
[4] Laing, *Travels in the Timannee,
Kooranko, and Soolima Countries*, p.
368.
[5] Thomson, *Through Masai Land*,
p. 166.
[6] *Supra*, i. 590 *sq.*
[7] *Supra*, i. 587.
[8] See *infra*, on the Origin and Development of the Altruistic Sentiment.

ing pride, the rule of politeness is naturally most exacting in relation to superiors. Many of its forms have, in fact, originated in humble or respectful behaviour towards rulers, masters, or elders, and, often in a modified shape, become common between equals after they have lost their original meaning.[1] It has been noticed that the cruelty of despots always engenders politeness, whereas the freest nations are generally the rudest in manners.[2] Politeness is further in a special degree shown by men to women, not only among ourselves, but even among many savages ;[3] in this case courtesy is connected with courtship. Strangers or remote acquaintances, also, have particular claims to be treated with civility, whereas politeness is of little moment in the intercourse of friends ; it imitates kindness, and is resorted to where the genuine feeling is wanting.[4] And in the capacity of guest, the stranger is often for the time being flattered with exquisite marks of honour, for reasons which have been stated in another connection.

[1] See Spencer, *Principles of Sociology*, ii. ' Ceremonial Institutions,' *passim*.

[2] Johnston, *Uganda*, ii. 685.

[3] Dorsey, ' Omaha Sociology,' in *Ann. Rep. Bur Ethn.* iii. 270.

Chanler, *Through Jungle and Desert*, p. 485 (Wakamba). See also *supra*, i. ch. xxvi.

[4] *Cf.* Tucker, *Light of Nature*, ii. 599 *sqq.* ; Joubert, *Pensées*, i. 243.

CHAPTER XXXIII

REGARD FOR OTHER PERSONS' HAPPINESS IN GENERAL—
GRATITUDE—PATRIOTISM AND COSMOPOLITANISM

In previous chapters we have dealt with moral ideas concerning various modes of conduct which have reference to other men's welfare—to their life or bodily comfort, their liberty, property, knowledge of truth, or self-regarding pride. But the list of duties which we owe to our fellow-creatures is as yet by no means complete. Any act, forbearance, or omission, which in some way or other diminishes or increases their happiness may on that account become a subject of moral blame or praise, being apt to call forth sympathetic retributive emotions.

To do good to others is a rule which has been inculcated by all the great teachers of morality. According to Confucius, benevolence is the root of righteousness and a leading characteristic of perfect virtue.[1] In the Taouist ' Book of Secret Blessings ' men are enjoined to be compassionate and loving, and to devote their wealth to the good of their fellow-men.[2] The moralists of ancient India teach that we should with our life, means, understanding, and speech, seek to advance the welfare of other creatures in this world ; that we should do so without expecting reciprocity ; and that we should enjoy the prosperity of others even though ourselves unprosperous.[3] The writers

[1] *Lun Yü*, xvii. 6. Douglas, *Confucianism and Taouism*, p. 108.
[2] Douglas, *op. cit.* p. 272 *sq.*
[3] Muir, *Religious and Moral Sentiments rendered from Sanskrit Writers*, p. 107 *sq.* Monier Williams, *Indian Wisdom*, p. 448.

of classical antiquity repeatedly give expression to the idea that man is not born for himself alone, but should assist his fellow-men to the best of his ability.[1] In the Old Testament we meet with the injunction, " Thou shalt love thy neighbour as thyself " ; [2] and this was declared by Christ to be of equal importance with the commandment, " Thou shalt love the Lord thy God." [3]

To a reflecting mind it is obvious that the moral value of beneficence exclusively lies in the benevolent motive, and that there is nothing praiseworthy in promoting the happiness of others from selfish considerations. Confucius taught that self must be conquered before a man can be perfectly virtuous.[4] According to Lao-tsze, self-abnegation is the cardinal rule for both the sovereign and the people.[5] Self-denial is the chief demand of the Gospel, and is emphasised as a supreme duty by Islam.[6] Generally speaking, the merit attached to a good action is proportionate to the self-denial which it costs the agent. This follows from the nature of moral approval in its capacity of a retributive emotion, as is proved by the fact that the degree of gratitude felt towards a benefactor is in a similar way influenced by the deprivation to which he subjects himself. On the other hand, there is considerable variety of opinion, even among ourselves, as to the dictates of duty, in cases where our own interests conflict with those of our fellow-men. To Professor Sidgwick it is a moral axiom that " I ought not to prefer my own lesser good to the greater good of another."[7] According to Hutcheson, we do not condemn those as evil who will not sacrifice their private interest to the advancement of the positive good of others, " unless the private interest be very small, and the publick good very great."[8]

The idea that it is bad to cause harm to others and

---

[1] Schmidt, *Die Ethik der alten Griechen*, ii. 275 *sqq.*
[2] *Leviticus*, xix. 18.
[3] *St. Matthew*, xxii. 39.
[4] *Lun Yü*, xii. 1. 1.
[5] Douglas, *Confucianism and Taouism*, p. 192.

[6] Ameer Ali, *Ethics of Islâm*, p. 32.
[7] Sidgwick, *Methods of Ethics*, p. 383.
[8] Hutcheson, *Essay on the Nature and Conduct of the Passions, &c.* p. 312.

good or obligatory to promote their happiness, is in different ways influenced by the relationship between the
parties ; and to many cases it does not apply at all. We
have previously noticed that according to early ethics an
enemy is a proper object of hatred, not of love ; [1] and
according to more advanced ideas a person who treats us
badly has at all events little claim upon our kindness. The
very opposite is the case with a benefactor or friend. To
requite a benefit, or to be grateful to him who bestows it,
is probably everywhere, at least under certain circumstances, regarded as a duty. This is a subject which
in the present connection calls for special consideration.

The duty of gratefulness presupposes a disposition for
gratitude.[2] According to travellers' accounts, this feeling
is lacking in many uncivilised races.[3] Lyon writes of the
Eskimo of Igloolik :—" Gratitude is not only rare, but
absolutely unknown amongst them, either by action, word,
or look, beyond the first outcry of satisfaction. Nursing
their sick, burying the dead, clothing and feeding the
whole tribe, furnishing the men with weapons, and the
women and children with ornaments, are insufficient to
awaken a grateful feeling, and the very people who relieved
their distresses when starving are laughed at in time of
plenty for the quantity and quality of the food which
was bestowed in charity." [4] Various other tribes in

---

[1] *Supra*, i. 73 *sq.*

[2] For the definition of gratitude,
see *supra*, i. 93.

[3] Steller, *Beschreibung von Kamtschatka*, p. 292. Bergmann, *Nomadische Streifereien unter den Kalmüken*,
ii. 310, 316. Foreman, *Philippine
Islands*, p. 183. Modigliani, *Viaggio
a Nías*, p. 467. Selenka, *Sonnige
Welten*, p. 286 (Malays). Marsden,
History of Sumatra, p. 207 (Malays
of Sumatra). Forbes, *A Naturalist's
Wanderings in the Eastern Archipelago*, p. 320 (natives of Timor-
laut). Mrs. Forbes, *Insulinde*, p. 178
(natives of Ritabel). Hagen, *Unter
den Papua's*, p. 266 (Papuans of
Bogadjim). Romilly, *Western Pacific
and New Guinea*, p. 239. La Pérouse,
Voyage round the World, ii. 109
(Samoans). Colenso, *Maori Races of
New Zealand*, p. 48 ; Dieffenbach,
Travels in New Zealand, ii. 110.
Ling Roth, *Aborigines of Tasmania*,
p. 63. Gason, ' Manners and Customs
of the Dieyerie Tribe,' in Woods,
Native Tribes of South Australia,
p. 258.   Baker, *Albert N'yanza*, i.
242 (Latukas), 289 (Negroes). von
François, *Nama und Damara*, p. 191
(Herero).

[4] Lyon, *Private Journal during the
Voyage of Discovery under Captain
Parry*, p. 348 *sq.* See also Parry,
*Journal of a Second Voyage for the
Discovery of a North-West Passage*,
p. 524 *sq.*

North America have been accused of ingratitude ;[1] and of some South American savages we are told that they evinced no thankfulness for the presents which were given them.[2] The Fijians are described as utterly indifferent to their benefactors. The Rev. Th. Williams writes :— " If one of them, when sick, obtained medicine from me, he thought me bound to give him food ; the reception of food he considered as giving him a claim on me for covering ; and, that being secured, he deemed himself at liberty to beg anything he wanted, and abuse me if I refused his unreasonable request." [3] Mr. Lumholtz had a similar experience with regard to the natives of Herbert River, Northern Queensland :—" If you give one thing to a black man, he finds ten other things to ask for, and he is not ashamed to ask for all that you have, and more too. He is never satisfied. Gratitude does not exist in his breast." [4] In several languages there is no word expressive of what we term gratitude or no phrase corresponding to our " thank you " ;[5] and on this fact much stress has been

[1] Cranz, *History of Greenland*, i. 174. Sarytschew, ' Voyage of Discovery to the North-East of Siberia,' in *Collection of Modern Voyages*, vi. 78 (Aleuts). Harmon, *Voyages and Travels in the Interior of North America*, p. 291 (Tacullies). Heriot, *Travels through the Canadas*, p. 319. Lafitau, *Mœurs des sauvages ameriquains*, i. 106. Burton, *City of the Saints*, p. 125 (Sioux and prairie tribes generally).

[2] von Spix and von Martius, *Travels in Brazil*, ii. 228, 241 *sq.* (Coroados). Stokes, quoted by King and Fitzroy, *Voyages of the ' Adventure ' and ' Beagle,'* i. 77 (Fuegians).

[3] Williams and Calvert, *Fiji*, p. 111. See also Anderson, *Notes of Travel in Fiji and New Caledonia*, pp. 124, 131.

[4] Lumholtz, *Among Cannibals*, p. 100.

[5] Southey, *History of Brazil*, iii. 399 (Abipones, Guaranies). Hearne, *Journey to the Northern Ocean*, p. 307 (Northern Indians). Lewin, *Wild Races of South-Eastern India*, p. 192 (Toungtha). Foreman, *op. cit.* p. 182 *sq.* (Bisayans). Modigliani, *Viaggio a Nías*, p. 467. Ling Roth, *Natives of Sarawak*, i. 74 (Dyaks). Chalmers, *Pioneering in New Guinea*, p. 187 ; Romilly, *Western Pacific and New Guinea*, p. 239 *sq.* (However, Mr Romilly's statement that " in all the known New Guinea languages there is not even a word for 'thank you,' " is not quite correct, as appears from Chalmers, *op. cit.* p. 187.) Wilson, *Missionary Voyage to the Southern Pacific Ocean*, p. 365 ; Waitz-Gerland, *Anthropologie der Naturvölker*, vi. 116 (Tahitians). Colenso, *op. cit.* p. 48 (Maoris). New, *Life and Labours in Eastern Africa*, p. 100 (Wanika). von François, *op. cit.* p. 191 (Herero). In the Vedic language, also, there was no word for " thanks " (Oldenberg, *Die Religion des Veda*, p. 305); and many Eastern languages of the present day lack an equivalent for "thank you" (Ward, *View of the History, &c. of the Hindoos*, ii. 81, n. *a.* ; Pool, *Studies in Muhammedanism*, p. 176 ; Polak,

laid, the deficiency of language being regarded as an
indication of a corresponding deficiency in feelings.

Here again we must distinguish between a traveller's
actual experience and the conclusions which he draws from
it ; and it seems that in many cases our authorities have
been too ready to charge savages with a total lack of
grateful feelings, because they have been wanting in
gratitude on certain occasions. It is too much to expect
that a savage should show himself thankful to any stranger
who gives him a present. Speaking of the Ahts of British
Columbia, Mr Sproat remarks that the Indian's suspicion
prevents a ready gratitude, as he is prone to see, in apparent
kindness extended to him, some under-current of selfish
motive. " He is accustomed, among his own people, to
gifts made for purposes of guile, and also to presents
made merely to show the greatness and richness of the
giver ; but, I imagine," our author adds, " when the Aht
ceases to suspect such motives—when he does not detect
pride, craft, or carelessness—he is grateful, and probably
grateful in proportion to the trouble taken to serve him." [1]
As for the ingratitude of the Northern Queensland natives,
Mr. Lumholtz himself admits that " they assume that the
gift is bestowed out of fear " ; [2] and of the New Zealanders
we are told that their total want of gratitude was particularly due to the fact that " no New Zealander ever did any
kindness, or gave anything, to another, without mainly
having an eye to himself in the transaction." [3] Moreover,
gratitude often requires not only the absence of a selfish
motive in the benefactor, but some degree of self-sacrifice.
" A person," says Mr. Sproat, " may keep an Indian from
starving all the winter through, yet, when summer comes,
very likely he will not walk a yard for his preserver without payment. The savage does not, in this instance,

---

Persien, i. 9). When one of the
missionaries in India was engaged in
the translation of the Scriptures into
Bengali, he found no common word
in that language suitable to express
the idea of gratitude (Wilkins,

Modern Hinduism, p. 397).
[1] Sproat, Scenes and Studies of
Savage Life, p. 165 sq.
[2] Lumholtz, Among Cannibals, p.
159.
[3] Colenso, op. cit. p. 48.

recognise any obligation ; but thinks that a person who
had so much more than he could himself consume might
well, and without any claim for after services, part with
some of it for the advantage of another in want."[1] Mr.
Powers makes a similar observation with reference to the
aborigines of California :—" White men," he says, " who
have had dealings with Indians, in conversation with me
have often bitterly accused them of ingratitude. ' Do
everything in your power for an Indian,' they say, ' and
he will accept it all as a matter of course ; but for the
slightest service you require of him he will demand pay.'
These men do not enter into the Indian's ideas. This
' ingratitude ' is really an unconscious compliment to our
power. The savage feels, vaguely, the unapproachable
elevation on which the American stands above him. He
feels that we had much and he had little, and we took
away from him even his little. In his view giving does
not impoverish us, nor withholding enrich us. Gratitude
is a sentiment not in place between master and slave ;
it is a sentiment for equals. The Indians are grateful to
one another."[2] Nor are men very apt to feel grateful
for benefits to which they consider themselves to have a
right. Thus, according to Mr. Howitt, the want of
gratitude among the South Australian Kurnai for kind-
nesses shown them by the whites is due to the principle
of community, which is so strong a feature of the domestic
and social life of these aborigines. " For a supply of food,
or for nursing when sick, the Kurnai would not feel grateful
to his family group. There would be a common obligation
upon all to share food, and to afford personal aid and
succour. This principle would also come into play as
regards the simple personal property they possess, and
would extend to the before-unknown articles procured
from the whites. The food, the clothes, the medical
attendance which the Kurnai receive from the whites,
they take in the accustomed manner ; and, in addition to

---

[1] Sproat, *op. cit.* p. 165 *sq.*   [2] Powers, *Tribes of California*,
p. 411.

this, we must remember that the donors are regarded as
having unlimited resources. They cannot be supposed by
the Kurnai to be doing anything but giving out of their
abundance."[1] Mr. Guppy found the same principle at
work among the Solomon Islanders :—" Often when
during my excursions I have come upon some man who was
preparing a meal for himself and his family, I have been
surprised at the open-handed way in which he dispensed
the food to my party of hungry natives. No gratitude was
shown towards the giver, who apparently expected none."[2]
It has also been observed that the want of gratitude with
which Arabs have often been charged by Europeans has
arisen " from the very common practice of hospitality and
generosity, and from the prevailing opinion that these
virtues are absolute duties which it would be disgraceful
and sinful to neglect." [3]

We should further remember that savages often take
care not to display their emotions. Among the Melanesians, according to Dr. Codrington, "it is not the custom to
say anything by way of thanks ; it is rather improper to
show emotion when anything is given, or when friends
meet again ; silence with the eyes cast down is the sign of
the inward trembling or shyness which they feel, or think
they ought to feel, under these circumstances. There is
no lack of a word which may be fairly translated ' thank ' ;
and certainly no one who has given cause for it will say
that Melanesians have no gratitude ; others probably are
ready enough to say it." [4] Of the North American
Chippewas Major Strickland writes :—" If an Indian
makes a present, it is always expected that one equally
valuable should be given in return. No matter what you
give them, or how valuable or rich the present, they seldom betray the least emotion or appearance of gratitude,
it being considered beneath the dignity of a red man to
betray his feelings. For all this seeming indifference,

Fison and Howitt, *Kamilaroi and
Kurnai*, p. 257.
[2] Guppy, *Solomon Islands*, p. 127.
[3] Lane, *Manners and Customs of*
the Modern Egyptians, p. 298. See
also Burton, *Pilgrimage to Al-
Madinah and Meccah*, i. 51.
[4] Codrington, *Melanesians*, p. 354.

they are in reality as grateful, and, I believe, even more so than our own peasantry." [1] The Aleuts also, although they are chary of expressions of thanks, " do not forget kindness, and endeavour to express their thankfulness by deeds. If anyone assists an Aleut, and afterwards offends him, he does not forget the former favour, and in his mind it often cancels the offence." [2] From the want of a word for a feeling we must not conclude that the feeling itself is wanting. Mr. Sproat observes :—" The Ahts have, it is true, no word for gratitude, but a defect in language does not absolutely imply defect in heart ; and the Indian who, in return for a benefit received, says, with glistening eyes, that ' his heart is good ' towards his benefactor, expresses his gratitude quite as well perhaps as the Englishman who says ' Thank you.' " [3]

It is not surprising, then, that in various cases a people which to one traveller appears to be quite destitute of gratitude is by another described as being by no means lacking in this feeling ; [4] and sometimes contradictory statements are made even by the same writer. Thus Mr. Lumholtz, who gives such a gloomy picture of the character of the Northern Queensland natives, nevertheless tells us of a native who, though himself very hungry, threw the animals which the traveller had shot for him to an old man—his wife's uncle—whom they met, in order to give some proof of the gratitude he owed the person from whom he had received his wife ; [5] and regarding the Fijians Mr. Williams himself states that thanks for presents " are always expressed aloud, and generally with a kind wish for the giver." [6] As we have noticed before, retributive kindly emotions, of which gratitude is only the most developed form, are commonly found among gregarious animals, social affection being not only a friendly

---

[1] Strickland, *Twenty-seven Years in Canada West*, ii. 58.
[2] Veniaminof, quoted by Dall, *Alaska*, p. 395.
[3] Sproat, *op. cit.* p. 165. See also Ling Roth, *Natives of Sarawak*, i. 74 (Dyaks).

[4] *E.g.*, the Fuegians, Sioux, Ahts, Aleuts, Kamchadales, Tasmanians, Zulus (see *supra* and *infra*).
[5] Lumholtz, *Among Cannibals*, p. 221.
[6] Williams and Calvert, *op. cit.* p. 132.

sentiment towards another individual, but towards an individual who is conceived of as a friend.[1] And it is all the more difficult to believe in the absolute want of gratitude in some savage races, as the majority of them—to judge from my collection of facts—are expressly acquitted of such a defect, and several are described as remarkably grateful for benefits bestowed upon them.

The Fuegians use the word *chapakouta*, which means glad, satisfied, affectionate, grateful, to express thanks.[2] Jemmy Button, the young Fuegian who was brought to England on board the *Beagle*, gave proofs of sincere gratitude ;[3] and Admiral Fitzroy also mentions a Patagonian boy who appeared thankful for kindness shown to him.[4] Of the Mapuchés of Chili Mr. E. R. Smith observes :—"Whatever present is made, or favour conferred, is considered as something to be returned ; and the Indian never fails, though months and years may intervene, to repay what he conscientiously thinks an exact equivalent for the thing received."[5] The Botocudos do not readily forget kind treatment ;[6] and the Tupis " were a grateful race, and remembered that they had received gifts, after the giver had forgotten it."[7] The Guiana Indians "are grateful for any kindness."[8] The Navahos of New Mexico have a word for thanks, and employ it on all occasions which we would consider appropriate.[9] The Sioux " evinced the warmest gratitude to any who had ever displayed kind feelings towards them."[10] In his 'Voyages from Montreal to the Frozen and Pacific Oceans,' Mackenzie mentions the gratitude shown him by a young Indian whom he had cured of a bad wound. When well enough to engage in a hunting party, the young man brought to his physician the tongue of an elk, and when they parted both he and his relatives expressed the heartiest acknowledgment for the care bestowed on him.[11] If an Aleut receives a gift he accepts it, saying *Akh !* which means " thanks."[12] Some of the Point Barrow Eskimo visited by Mr. Murdoch " seem to feel truly

---

[1] *Supra*, i. 94.
[2] Hyades and Deniker, *Mission scientifique du Cap Horn*, vii. 314.
[3] King and Fitzroy, *op. cit.* ii. 327.
[4] *Ibid.* ii. 173.
[5] Smith, *Araucanians*, p. 258.
[6] Wied-Neuwied, *Reise nach Brasilien*, ii. 16.
[7] Southey, *op. cit.* i. 247.
[8] Im Thurn, *Among the Indians of Guiana*, p. 213.
[9] Matthews, 'Study of Ethics among the Lower Races,' in *Journal of American Folk-Lore*, xii. 9.
[10] Eastman, *Dacotah*, p. ix.
[11] Mackenzie, *Voyages from Montreal to the Frozen and Pacific Oceans*, p. 137 *sq*.
[12] Veniaminof, quoted by Dall, *op. cit.* p. 395.

grateful for the benefits and gifts received, and endeavoured by their general behaviour, as well as in more substantial ways, to make some adequate return " ; whereas others appeared to think only of what they might receive.[1]

Of the Tunguses it is said, " If you make them a present, they hardly thank you ; but though so unpolite, they are exceedingly grateful."[2] The Jakuts never forget a benefit received ; " for they not only make restitution, but recommend to their offspring the ties of friendship and gratitude to their benefactors."[3] The Veddah of Ceylon is described as very grateful for attention or assistance.[4] " A little kindly sympathy makes him an attached friend, and for his friend . . . . he will readily give his life."[5] Mr. Bennett once had an interview with two village Veddahs, and on that occasion gave them presents. Two months after a couple of elephant's tusks found their way into his front verandah at night, but the Veddahs who had brought them never gave him an opportunity to reward them. " What a lesson in gratitude and delicacy," he exclaims, " even a Veddah may teach ! "[6]

The Alfura of Halmahera,[7] the Bataks of Sumatra,[8] and the Dyaks of Borneo[9] are praised for their grateful disposition of mind. Of the Hill Dyaks Mr. Low observes that gratitude " eminently adorns the character of these simple people, and the smallest benefit conferred upon them calls forth its vigorous and continued exercise."[10] The Motu people of New Guinea are " capable of appreciating kindness,"[11] and have words for expressing thanks.[12] Chamisso speaks highly of the gratitude evinced by the natives of Ulea, Caroline Islands :—" Any thing, a useful instrument, for example, which they have received as a gift from a friend, retains and bears among them as a lasting memorial the name of the friend who bestowed it."[13] When Professor Moseley at Dentrecasteaux Island, of the Admiralty Group, gave a hatchet as pay to his guide, according

---

[1] Murdoch, ' Ethnol. Results of the Point Barrow Expedition,' in *Ann. Rep. Bur. Ethn.* ix. 42. See also Seemann, *Voyage of ' Herald,'* ii. 67 (Western Eskimo).
[2] Georgi, *Russia,* iii. 111.
[3] Sauer, *Expedition to the Northern Parts of Russia, performed by Billings,* p. 124.
[4] Tennent, *Ceylon,* ii. 445. Sarasin, *Forschungen auf Ceylon,* iii. 546.
[5] Nevill, ' Vaeddas of Ceylon,' in *Taprobanian,* i. 192.
[6] Pridham, *Account of Ceylon,* i. 460 *sq.*
[7] Kükenthal, *Forschungsreise in den Molukken und Borneo,* i. 188.
[8] Junghuhn, *Die Battaländer auf Sumatra,* ii. 239.
[9] Ling Roth, *Natives of Sarawak,* i. 74, 76.
[10] Low, *Sarawak,* p. 246.
[11] Stone, *A Few Months in New Guinea,* p. 95.
[12] Chalmers, *Pioneering in New Guinea,* p. 187.
[13] von Kotzebue, *Voyage of Discovery into the South Sea,* iii. 214.

to promise, the guide seemed grateful, and presented him with his own shell adze in return.[1] Though the Tahitians never return thanks nor seem to have a word in their language expressive of gratitude, they are not devoid of the feeling itself.[2] Backhouse tells us of a Tasmanian native who, having been nursed through an illness, showed many demonstrations of gratitude ; and he adds that this virtue was often exhibited among these people—a statement which is corroborated by the accounts of other travellers.[3] Of the Australian aborigines Mr. Ridley writes :—" I believe they are as a people remarkably susceptible of impressions from kind treatment. They recognised me as one who sought their good, and were evidently pleased and thankful to see that I thought them worth looking after."[4] The Adelaide and Encounter Bay blacks are said to display attachment to persons who are kind to them.[5] Speaking of the Central Australian tribes, Messrs. Spencer and Gillen observe that, though they are not in the habit of showing anything like excessive gratitude on receiving gifts from the white man, they are in reality by no means incapable of that feeling ; [6] and other writers report instances of gratitude displayed by natives of West Australia [7] and Queensland.[8]

Concerning the people of Madagascar the missionary Ellis writes :—" Whether the noble and generous feeling of gratitude has much place amongst the Malagasy has been questioned. Though often characterised by extreme apathy, they are certainly susceptible of tenderness of feeling, and their customs furnish various modes of testifying their sense of any acts of kindness shewn them, and their language contains many forms of speech expressive of thankfulness. The following are among those in most general use : ' May you live to grow old—may you live long—may you live sacred—may you see, or obtain, justice from the sovereign.' " Moreover, with all their expressions of thankfulness, considerable action is used : sometimes the two hands are extended open as if to make a present ; or the party stoops down to the ground, and clasps the legs, or touches the knee and the feet of the person he is thanking.[9] Ingratitude,

---

[1] Moseley, ' Inhabitants of the Admiralty Islands,' in *Jour. Anthr. Inst.* vi. 416.

[2] Waitz-Gerland, *op. cit.* vi. 116.

[3] Ling Roth, *Aborigines of Tasmania*, pp. 47, 62, 64.

[4] Ridley, *Aborigines of Australia*, p. 24. See also *ibid.* p. 20 *sqq.*

[5] Wyatt, ' Manners and Superstitions of the Adelaide and Encounter Bay Aboriginal Tribes,' in Woods, *Native Tribes of South Australia*, p. 162.

[6] Spencer and Gillen, *Native Tribes of Central Australia*, p. 48 *sqq.*

[7] Salvado, *Mémoires historiques sur l'Australie*, p. 146.

[8] Fraser, *Aborigines of New South Wales*, p. 44.

[9] Ellis, *History of Madagascar*,

again, is expressed by many strong metaphors, such as "son of a thunderbolt," or "offspring of a wild boar." [1] The Bushmans, according to Burchell, are not incapable of gratitude. [2] The statement made by certain travellers or colonists that the Zulus are devoid of this feeling, is contradicted by Mr. Tyler, who asserts that "many instances might be related in which a thankful spirit has been manifested, and gifts bestowed for favours received." [3] The Basutos have words to express gratitude. [4] Among the Bakongo, says Mr. Ward, "evidences of gratitude are rare indeed, although occasionally one meets with this sentiment in odd guises. Once, by a happy chance, I saved a baby's life. The child was brought to me by its mother in convulsions, and I was fortunate enough to find in my medicine chest a drug that effected an almost immediate cure. Yet the service I rendered to this woman, instead of meeting with any appreciation, only procured for me the whispered reputation of being a witch." But twenty months afterwards, at midnight when all the people were sleeping, the same woman came to Mr. Ward and gave him some fowl's eggs in payment. " I come," she said, " in the darkness that my people may not know, for they would jeer at me if they knew of this gift." [5] A traveller tells us that the inhabitants of Great Benin "if given any trifles expressed their thanks." [6] Writing on the natives of Accra, Monrad states that gratitude is among the virtues of the Negroes, and induces them even to give their lives in return for benefits conferred on them. [7] The Feloops, bordering on the Gambia, "display the utmost gratitude and affection towards their benefactors." [8] As regards the Eastern Central Africans, Mr. Macdonald affirms without any hesitation that they have gratitude, " even though we define gratitude as being much more than an 'acute sense of favours to come.' " [9] The Masai and Wadshagga have " a curious habit of spitting on things or people as a compliment or sign of gratitude " [10]—originally, I presume, with a view to transferring to them a blessing. The Barea are said to be thankful for benefits. [11] According to Palgrave, " gratitude is no

i. 258. See also Rochon, *Voyage to Madagascar*, p. 56.

[1] Ellis, *op. cit.* i. 139 *sq.*

[2] Burchell, *Travels in the Interior of Southern Africa*, ii. 68, 86, 447.

[3] Tyler, *Forty Years among the Zulus*, p. 194.

[4] Casalis, *Basutos*, p. 306.

[5] Ward, *Five Years with the Congo Cannibals*, p. 47 *sqq.*

[6] Punch, quoted by Ling Roth, *Great Benin*, p. 45.

[7] Monrad, *Skildring af Guinea-Kysten*, p. 8.

[8] Mungo Park, *Travels in the Interior of Africa*, p. 14.

[9] Macdonald, *Africana*, i. 10.

[10] Johnston, *Kilima-njaro Expedition*, p. 438.

[11] Munzinger, *Ostafrikanische Studien*, p. 533.

less an Arab than a European virtue, whatever the ignorance or
the prejudices of some foreigners may have affirmed to the contrary ";[1] and Burckhardt says that an Arab never forgets the
generosity shown to him even by an enemy.[2]

In other statements gratitude is directly represented as
an object of praise, or its absence as an object of disapproval. Among the Atkha Aleuts, according to Father
Yakof, gratitude to benefactors was considered a virtue.[3]
Among the Omahas, if a man receives a favour and does
not manifest his thankfulness, the people exclaim :—" He
does not appreciate the gift ! He has no manners." [4] The
Kamchadales " are not only grateful for favours, but they
think it absolutely necessary to make some return for a
present." [5] The Chinese say that " kindness is more binding than a loan." [6] According to the ' Divine Panorama,'
a well-known Taouist work, those who forget kindness and
are guilty of ingratitude shall be tormented after death and
" shall not escape one jot of their punishments." [7] In one
of the Pahlavi texts gratitude is represented as a means of
arriving at heaven, whilst ingratitude is stigmatised as a
heinous sin ;[8] and according to Ammian ungrateful persons
were even punished by law in ancient Persia.[9] The same,
we are told, was the case in Macedonia.[10] The duty of
gratitude was strongly inculcated by Greek and Roman
moralists.[11] Aristotle observes that we ought, as a general
rule, rather to return a kindness to our benefactor than to
confer a gratuitous favour upon a brother in arms, just as
we ought rather to repay a loan to a creditor than to spend
the same sum upon a present to a friend.[12] According to

---

[1] Palgrave, quoted in Spencer's
Descriptive Sociology, ' Asiatic
Races,' p. 31.
[2] Burckhardt, *Notes on the Bedouins and Wahábys,* p. 105.
[3] Yakof, quoted by Petroff, *Report
on the Population, &c. of Alaska,*
p. 158.
[4] 'Dorsey, ' Omaha Sociology,' in
Ann. Rep. Bur. Ethn. iii. 270.
[5] Dobell, *Travels in Kamtschatka,*
i. 75.
[6] Davis, *China,* ii. 123.

[7] Giles, *Strange Stories from a
Chinese Studio,* ii. 374 *sq.* See also
Thâi-Shang, 4.
[8] *Dînâ-î Maînôg-î Khirad,* xxxvi.
28 ; xxxvii. 6 ; xliii. 9.
[9] Ammianus Marcellinus, xxiii.
6. 81.
[10] Seneca, *De beneficiis,* iii. 6. 2.
[11] See Schmidt, *Die Ethik der alten
Griechen,* ii. 305 *sqq.*
[12] Aristotle, *Ethica Nicomachea,*
x. 2. 3.

Xenophon the requital of benefits is enjoined by a divine law.[1] " There is no duty more indispensable than that of returning a kindness," says Cicero ; " all men detest one forgetful of a benefit." [2] Seneca calls ingratitude a most odious vice, which it is difficult to punish by law, but which we refer for judgment to the gods.[3] The ancient Scandinavians considered it dishonourable for a man to kill even an enemy in blood-revenge if he had received a benefit from him.[4]

We may assume that among beings capable of feeling moral emotions the general disposition to be kind to a benefactor will inevitably lead to the notion that ungrateful behaviour is wrong. Such behaviour is offensive to the benefactor ; as Spinoza observes, " he who has conferred a benefit on anyone from motives of love or honour will feel pain, if he sees that the benefit is received without gratitude." [5] This by itself tends to evoke in the bystander sympathetic resentment towards the offender ; but his resentment is much increased by the retributive kindliness which he is apt to feel, sympathetically, towards the benefactor. He wants to see the latter's kindness rewarded ; and he is shocked by the absence of a similar desire in the very person who may be naturally expected to feel it more strongly than anybody else.—

The moral ideas concerning conduct which affects other persons' welfare vary according as the parties are members of the same or different families, or of the same or different communities. For reasons which have been stated in previous chapters parents have in this respect special duties towards their children, and children towards their parents ; and a tribesman or a fellow-countryman has claims which are not shared by a foreigner. But there are duties not only to particular individuals, but also to

[1] Xenophon, *Memorabilia*, iv. 4. 24.
[2] Cicero, *De officiis*, i. 15 (47) ; ii. 18 (63).
[3] Seneca, *De beneficiis*, iii. 6. 1 *sq.*
[4] Maurer, *Die Bekehrung des Nor-* *wegischen Stammes*, ii. 174.
[5] Spinoza, *Ethica*, iii. 42. A Japanese proverb says that " thankless labour brings fatigue " (Reed, *Japan*, ii. 109).

whole social aggregates.   Foremost among these is the duty of patriotism.

The duty of patriotism is rooted in the patriotic senti-ment, in a person's love of the social body of which he is himself a member, and which is attached to the territory he calls his country.   It involves a desire to promote its welfare, a wish that it may prosper for the time being and for all future.   This desire is the outcome of a variety of sentiments : of men's affection for the people among whom they live, of attachment to the places where they have grown up or spent part of their lives, of devotion to their race and language, and to the traditions, customs, laws, and institutions of the society in which they were born and to which they belong.

Genuine patriotism presupposes a power of abstraction which the lower savages can hardly be supposed to possess.   But it seems to be far from unknown among uncultured peoples of a higher type.   North American Indians are praised for their truly patriotic spirit, for their strong attachment to their tribe and their country.[1] Carver says of the Naudowessies :—" The honour of their tribe, and the welfare of their nation, is the first and most predominant emotion of their hearts ; and from hence proceed in a great measure all their virtues and their vices.   Actuated by this, they brave every danger, endure the most exquisite torments, and expire triumphing in their fortitude, not as a personal qualification, but as a national characteristic." [2]   Patriotism and public spirit were often strongly manifested by the Tahitians.[3]   The Maori " loves his country and the rights of his ancestors, and he will fight for his children's land." [4]   Of the Guanches of Teneriffe we are told that patriotism was

---

[1] Adair, *History of the American Indians*, p. 378 *sq.* Heriot, *Travels through the Canadas*, p. 317. Loskiel, *History of the Mission of the United Brethren among the Indians*, i. 17 (Iroquois).

[2] Carver, *Travels through the Interior Parts of North America*, p. 412.

[3] Ellis, *Polynesian Researches*, i. 128.

[4] Angas, *Savage Life and Scenes in Australia and New Zealand*, i. 338. See also Travers, ' Life and Times of Te Rauparaha,' in *Trans. and Proceed. New Zealand Institute*, v. 22.

their chief virtue.[1] The same quality distinguishes the Yorubas of West Africa ; " no race of men," says Mr. MacGregor, " could be more devoted to their country." [2] Burckhardt writes :—" As to the attachment which a Bedouin entertains for his own tribe, the deep-felt interest he takes in its power and fame, and the sacrifices of every kind he is ready to make for its prosperity— these are feelings rarely operating with equal force in any other nation ; and it is with an exulting pride of conscious patriotism, not inferior to any which ennobled the history of Grecian or Helvetian republics, that an Aeneze, should he be suddenly attacked, seizes his lance, and waving it over his head exclaims, ' I am an Aeneze.' " [3]

Many of the elements out of which patriotism proper has grown are clearly distinguishable among savages, even the very lowest. We have previously noticed the savage's attachment to members of his own community or tribe. Combined with this is his love of his native place, and of the mode of life to which he is habituated. There is a touching illustration of this feeling in the behaviour of the wild boy who had been found in the woods near Aveyron—where he had spent most part of his young life in perfect isolation from all human beings—when he, after being removed to Paris, was once taken back to the country, to the vale of Montmorence. Joy was painted in his eyes, in all the motions and postures of his body, at the view of the hills and the woods of the charming valley ; he appeared more than ever restless and savage, and " in spite of the most assiduous attention that was paid to his wishes, and the most affectionate regard that was expressed for him, he seemed to be occupied only with an anxious desire of taking his flight." [4] How much greater must not the love of home be in him who has there his relatives and friends ! Mr. Howitt tells us of

[1] Bory de St. Vincent, *Essais sur es Isles Fortunées*, p. 70.

[2] MacGregor, ' Lagos, Abeokuta, and the Alake,' in *Jour. African Soc.* 1904, p. 466.

[3] Burckhardt, *Notes on the Bedouins and Wahábys*, p. 205.

[4] Itard, *Account of the Discovery and Education of a Savage Man*, p. 70 *sqq.*

an Australian native who, on leaving his camp with him
for a trip of about a week, burst into tears, saying to
himself once and again, " My country, my people, I shall
not see them." [1] The Veddahs of Ceylon " would
exchange their wild forest life for none other, and it was
with the utmost difficulty that they could be induced to
quit even for a short time their favourite solitude." [2] The
Stiêns of Cambodia are so strongly attached to their
forests and mountains that to leave them seems almost
like death.[3] Solomon Islanders not seldom die from
home-sickness on their way to the Fiji or Queensland
plantations.[4] The Hovas of Madagascar, when setting
out on a journey, often take with them a small portion of
their native earth, on which they gaze during their
absence, invoking their god that they may be permitted to
return to restore it to the place from which it was taken.[5]
Mr. Crawfurd observes that in the Malay Archipelago the
attachment to the native spot is strongest with the agricultural tribes ;[6] but, though a settled life is naturally
most favourable to its development, this feeling is not
inconsistent with nomadism. The Nishinam, who are the
most nomadic of all the Californian tribes, have very
great attachment for the valley or flat which they count
their home. [7]

[1] Brough Smyth, *Aborigines of Victoria*, ii. 305.
[2] Hartshorne, 'Weddas,' in *Indian Antiquary*, viii. 317.
[3] Mouhot, *Travels in the Central Parts of Indo-China*, i. 243.
[4] Guppy, *op. cit.* p. 167.
[5] Ellis, *History of Madagascar*, i. 141.
[6] Crawfurd, *History of the Indian Archipelago*, i. 84.
[7] Powers, *op. cit.* p. 318 *sq.* For other instances of love of home among uncivilised races see von Spix and von Martius, *op. cit.* ii. 242, note (Coroados); von Kotzebue, *op. cit.* iii. 45 (Indians of California); Gibbs, *Tribes of Western Washington and North-Western Oregon*, p. 187 ; Elliott, *Report of the Seal Islands of Alaska*, p. 240 ; Hooper, *Ten Months among the Tents of the Tuski*, p. 209;

von Siebold, *Aino auf der Insel Yesso*, p. 11 ; Mallat, *Les Philippines*, ii. 95 (Negritos); von Brenner, *Besuch bei den Kannibalen Sumatras*, p. 194 (Bataks); Earl, *Papuans*, p. 126 (natives of Rotti, near Timor) ; Ling Roth, *Aborigines of Tasmania*, p. 46 ; Dieffenbach, *Travels in New Zealand*, ii. 174 ; Cumming, *In the Himalayas*, p. 404 (Paharis); Lane, *Manners and Customs of the Modern Egyptians*, p. 302 (Bedawees); Tristram, *Great Sahara*, p. 193 *sq.* (Beni M'zab); Burton, *Zanzibar*, ii. 96 (Wanika); *Emin Pasha in Central Africa*, p. 315 (Monbuttu); Andersson, *Lake Ngami*, p. 198 (Ovambo) ; Rowley, *Africa Unveiled*, p. 63 *sq.* (Kroos of the Grain Coast below Liberia); Price, 'Quissama Tribe,' in *Jour. Anthr. Inst.* i. 187.

Moreover, as we have noticed above, savages have the greatest regard for their native customs and institutions.[1] Many of them have displayed that love of national independence which gives to patriotism its highest fervour.[2] And among some uncivilised peoples, at least, the force of racial and linguistic unity shows itself even outside the social or political unit. Burckhardt observes that the Bedouins are not only solicitous for the honour of their own respective tribes, but consider the interests of all other tribes as more or less attached to their own, and frequently evince a general *esprit de corps*, lamenting " the losses of any of their tribes occasioned by attacks from settlers or foreign troops, even though at war with those tribes." [3] A Tongan " loves the island on which he was born, in particular, and all the Tonga islands generally, as being one country, and speaking one language." [4] Travellers have noticed how gratifying it is, when visiting an uncultured people, to know a little of their language ; there is at once a sympathetic link between the native and the stranger.[5] Even the almost inaccessible Berber of the Great Atlas, in spite of his excessive hatred of the European, will at once give you a kindly glance as soon as you, to his astonishment, utter to him a few words in his own tongue.

Like other species of the altruistic sentiment, patriotism is apt to overestimate the qualities of the object for which it is felt ; and it does so all the more readily as love of one's country is almost inseparably intermingled with love of one's self. The ordinary, typical patriot has a strong will to believe that his nation is the best. If, as many

[1] See *supra*, i. 118 *sq.*

[2] *Cf.* Dobrizhoffer, *Account of the Abipones*, ii. 95, 105 ; Lomonaco, ' Sulle razze indigene del Brasile,' in *Archivio per l'antropologia e la etnologia*, xix. 57 (Tupis) ; Brett, *Indian Tribes of Guiana*, p. 348 ; Schoolcraft, *Indian Tribes of the United States*, iii. 189 (Iroquois) ; Nansen, *Eskimo Life*, p. 323 (Greenlanders); Macpherson, *Memorials of Service in India*, p. 81 (Kandhs) ;

Sarasin, *op. cit.* iii. 530 (Veddahs) ; Casati, *Ten Years in Equatoria*, i. 188, 304 (Negroes of Central Africa); Fritsch, *Die Eingeborenen Süd-Afrika's*, p. 422 *sq.* (Bushmans).

[3] Burckhardt, *Bedouins and Wahábys*, p. 205.

[4] Mariner, *Natives of the Tonga Islands*, ii. 156.

[5] See Stokes, *Discoveries in Australia*, ii. 25.

people nowadays seem to maintain, such a will to believe
is an essential characteristic of true patriotism, savages are
as good patriots as anybody. In their intercourse with
white men they have often with astonishment noticed the
arrogant air of superiority adopted by the latter ; in their
own opinion they are themselves vastly superior to the
whites. According to Eskimo beliefs, the first man, though
made by the Great Being, was a failure, and was consequently cast aside and called *kob-lu-na*, which means "white
man " ; but a second attempt of the Great Being resulted
in the formation of a perfect man, and he was called *in-nu*,
the name which the Eskimo give to themselves.[1] Australian
natives, on being asked to work, have often replied,
" White fellow works, not black fellow ; black fellow
gentleman." [2] When anything foolish is done, the Chippewas use an expression which means " as stupid as a white
man." [3] If a South Sea Islander sees a very awkward person, he says, " How stupid you are ; perhaps you are an
Englishman." [4] Mr. Williams tells us of a Fijian who,
having been to the United States, was ordered by his chiefs
to say whether the country of the white man was better
than Fiji, and in what respects. He had not, however,
gone far in telling the truth, when one cried out, " He is
a prating fellow " ; another, " He is impudent " ; and
some said, "Kill him." [5] The Koriaks are more argumentative ; in order to prove that the accounts they hear of
the advantages of other countries are so many lies, they
say to the stranger, " If you could enjoy these advantages
at home, what made you take so much trouble to come to
us ? " [6] But the Koriaks, in their turn are looked down
upon by their neighbours, the Chukchi, who call the surrounding peoples old women, only fit to guard their flocks,
and to be their attendants. [7] The Ainu despise the Japanese

[1] Hall, *Arctic Researches*, p. 566
sq.
[2] Hale, *U.S. Exploring Expedition.
Vol. VI. Ethnography and Philology*, p. 109.
[3] Keating, *Expedition to the Source
of St. Peter's River*, ii. 168. See also

Boller, *Among the Indians*, p. 54 *sq.*
[4] Williams, *Missionary Enterprises
in the South Sea Islands*, p. 514.
[5] Williams and Calvert, *Fiji*, p. 105.
[6] Krasheninnikoff, *History of
Kamschatka*, p. 224.
[7] Sauer, *op. cit.* p. 255.

just as much as the Japanese despise them, and are convinced of " the superiority of their own blood and descent over that of all other peoples in the world."[1] Even the miserable Veddah of Ceylon has a very high opinion of himself, and regards his civilised neighbours with contempt.[2] As is often the case with civilised men, savages attribute to their own people all kinds of virtue in perfection. The South American Mbayás, according to Azara, " se croient la nation la plus noble du monde, la plus généreuse, la plus exacte à tenir sa parole avec loyauté, et la plus vaillante."[3] The Eskimo of Norton Sound speak of themselves as yu'-$p\~ik$, meaning fine or complete people, whereas an Indian is termed $i\~n$-$k\~i'$-$l\~ik$, from a word which means " a louse egg."[4] When a Greenlander saw a foreigner of gentle and modest manners, his usual remark was, " He is almost as well-bred as we," or, " He begins to be a man," that is, a Greenlander.[5] The savage regards his people as *the* people, as the root of all others, and as occupying the middle of the earth. The Hottentots love to call themselves " the men of men."[6] The Indians of the Ungava district, Hudson Bay, give themselves the name *nenenot*, that is, true or ideal red men.[7] In the language of the Illinois Indians the word *illinois* means " men "—" as if they looked upon all other Indians as beasts."[8] The aborigines of Hayti believed that their island was the first of all things, that the sun and moon issued from one of its caverns, and men from another.[9] Each Australian tribe, says Mr. Curr, regards its country as the centre of the earth, which in most cases is believed not to extend more than a couple of hundred miles or so in any direction.[10]

[1] Batchelor, 'Notes on the Ainu,' in *Trans. Asiatic Soc. Japan*, x. 211 *sq.* Howard, *Life with Trans-Siberian Savages*, p. 182.

[2] Nevill, in *Taprobanian*, i. 192. Sarasin, *op. cit.* iii. 530, 534, 553.

[3] Azara, *Voyages dans l'Amérique méridionale*, ii. 107.

[4] Nelson, ' Eskimo about Bering Strait,' in *Ann. Rep. Bur. Ethn.* xviii. 306 *sq.*

[5] Cranz, *History of Greenland*, i. 126.

[6] Kidd, *The Essential Kafir*, p. 92.

[7] Turner, ' Ethnology of the Ungava District,' in *Ann. Rep. Bur. Ethn.* xi. 267.

[8] Marquette, *Recit des voyages*, p. 47 *sq.*

[9] Brett, *Indian Tribes of Guiana*, p. 376.

[10] Curr, *The Australian Race*, i. 50. For other instances of national con-

We meet with similar feelings and ideas among the
nations of archaic culture. The Chinese are taught to
think themselves superior to all other peoples. In their
writings, ancient and modern, the word " foreigner " is
regularly joined with some disrespectful epithet, implying
or expressing the ignorance, brutality, obstinacy, or meanness of alien nations, and their obligations to or dependence
upon China.[1] To Confucius himself China was " the
middle kingdom," " the multitude of great states," " all
under heaven," beyond which were only rude and barbarous tribes.[2] According to Japanese ideas, Nippon was the
first country created, and the centre of the world.[3] The
ancient Egyptians considered themselves as the peculiar
people, specially loved by the gods. They alone were
termed " men " (*romet*) ; other nations were negroes,
Asiatics, or Libyans, but not men; and according to the
myth these nations were descended from the enemies of
the gods.[4] The national pride of the Assyrians, so often
referred to by the Hebrew prophets,[5] is conspicuous everywhere in their cuneiform inscriptions : they are the wise,
the brave, the powerful, who, like the deluge, carry away
all resistance ; their kings are the " matchless, irresistible ";
and their gods are much exalted above the gods of all
other nations.[6] To the Hebrews their own land was " an
exceeding good land," " flowing with milk and honey,"
" the glory of all lands " ;[7] and its inhabitants were a holy

---

ceit or pride among savages see
Darwin, *Journal of Researches*, p.
207 (Fuegians) ; von den Steinen,
*Unter den Naturvölkern Zentral-
Brasiliens*, p. 332 (Bakaïri) ; von
Humboldt, *Personal Narrative of
Travels to the Equinoctial Regions of
the New Continent*, v. 423, and Brett,
op. cit. p. 128 (Guiana Indians) ;
James, *Expedition to the Rocky
Mountains*, i. 320 (Omahas); Murdoch, in *Ann. Rep. Bur. Ethn.* ix.
42 (Point Barrow Eskimo); Krasheninnikoff, *op. cit.* p. 180 (Kamchadales); Brough Smyth, *op. cit.* ii.
284 (Australian natives); Macpherson, *op. cit.* p. 67 (Kandhs) ;
Munzinger, *Ueber die Sitten und das*

Recht der Bogos, p. 94 ; Andersson,
Lake Ngami, p. 198 (Ovambo).
[1] Philip, *Li e and Opinions of the
Rev. W. Milne*, p. 257. *Cf.* Staunton, in *Narrative of the Chinese
Embassy to the Khan of the Tourgouth Tartars*, p. viii.
[2] Legge, *Chinese Classics*, i. 107.
See also Giles, *op. cit.* ii. 116, n. 2.
[3] Griffis, *Religions of Japan*, p. 207.
[4] Erman, *Life in Ancient Egypt*, p.
32.
[5] *Isaiah*, x. 7 *sqq.*; xxxvii. 24 *sqq.*
Ezekiel, xxxi. 10 *sq. Zephaniah*, ii. 15.
[6] Mürdter-Delitzsch,   *Geschichte
Babyloniens und Assyriens*, p. 104.
[7] *Numbers*, xiii. 27 ; xiv. 7.
Ezekiel, xx. 6, 15.

people which the Lord had chosen " to be a special people unto Himself, above all people that are upon the face of the earth."[1] Concerning the ancient Persians, Herodotus writes :—" They look upon themselves as very greatly superior in all respects to the rest of mankind, regarding others as approaching to excellence in proportion as they dwell nearer to them ; whence it comes to pass that those who are the farthest off must be the most degraded of mankind." [2] To this day the monarch of Persia retains the title of " the Centre of the Universe " ; and it is not easy to persuade a native of Isfahan that any European capital can be superior to his native city.[3] The Greeks called Delphi—or rather the round stone in the Delphic temple—" the navel " or " middle point of the earth " ; [4] and they considered the natural relation between themselves and barbarians to be that between master and slave.[5]

In the archaic State the national feeling is in some cases greatly strengthened by the religious feeling ; whilst in other instances religion inspires devotion to the family, clan, or caste rather than to the nation, or constitutes a tie not only between compatriots but between members of different political communities. The ancestor-worship of the Chinese has hardly been conducive to genuine patriotism. Whatever devotion to the common weal may have prevailed among the Vedic Aryans, it has certainly passed away beneath the influence of Brahmanism, or been narrowed down to the caste, the village, or the family.[6] The Zoroastrian Ahura-Mazda was not a national god, but " the god of the Aryans," that is, of all the peoples who inhabited ancient Iran ; and these were constantly at war

---

[1] *Deuteronomy*, vii. 6.

[2] Herodotus, i. 134.

[3] Rawlinson, in his translation of Herodotus, i. 260, n. 5.

[4] Pindar, *Pythia*, vi. 3 *sq. Idem, Nemea*, vii. 33 *sq.* Aeschylus, *Eumenides*, 40, 166. Sophocles, *Œdipus Tyrannus*, 480, 898. Livy, xxxviii. 48. *Cf.* Herodotus' theory of " extremities " (iii. 115 *sq.*), and Rawlinson's commentary, in his translation of Herodotus, i. 260 *sq.* n. 6.

[5] Euripides, *Iphigenia in Aulide*, 1400 *sq.* Aristotle, *Politica*, i. 2, 6, pp. 1252 b, 1255 a.

[6] Wheeler, *History of India*, ii. 586 *sq.* See also Leist, *Alt-arisches Jus Gentium*, p. 529.

with one another.[1] Muhammedans, whilst animated with
a common hatred towards the Christians, show little public
spirit in relation to their respective countries,[2] composed
as they are of a variety of loosely connected, often very
heterogeneous elements, ruled over by a monarch whose
power is in many districts more nominal than real. In
ancient Greece and Rome patriotism no doubt contained a
religious element—each state and town had its tutelary
gods and heroes, who were considered its proper masters ; [3]
but in the first place it was free citizens' love of their native
institutions, a civic virtue which grew up on the soil of
liberty. When the two Spartans who were sent to Xerxes
to be put to death were advised by one of his governors to
surrender themselves to the king, their answer was, " Had
you known what freedom is, you would have bidden us
fight for it, not with the spear only, but with the battle-
axe." [4] And of the Athenians who lived at the time of
the Persian wars, Demosthenes said that they were ready to
die for their country rather than to see it enslaved, and
that they considered the outrages and insults which befell
him who lived in a subjugated city to be more terrible
than death.[5] In classical antiquity " the influence of
patriotism thrilled through every fibre of moral and
intellectual life." [6] In some Greek cities emigration was
prohibited by law, at Argos even on penalty of death.[7]
Plato, in the Republic, sacrificed the family to the interests
of the State. Cicero placed our duty to our country next
after our duty to the immortal gods and before our duty
to our parents.[8] " Of all connections," he says, " none is
more weighty, none is more dear, than that between every
individual and his country. Our parents are dear to us ;

---

[1] Meyer, *Geschichte des Alterthums*,
i. 540. Spiegel, *Erânische Alterthumskunde*, iii. 687 *sqq.*
[2] Polak, *Persien*, i. 12. Urquhart,
Spirit of the East, ii. 427, 439 (Turks).
Burckhardt, *Bedouins and Wahâbys*,
p. 204 *sq.* (Turks and Arab settlers).
[3] Leist, *Alt-arisches Jus Gentium*,
p. 529. Schmidt, *Die Ethik der alten
Griechen*, ii. 221.

[4] Herodotus, vii. 134 *sq.*
[5] Demosthenes, *De Corona*, 205, p.
296.
[6] Lecky, *History of European
Morals*, i. 200.
[7] Plutarch, *Lycurgus*, xxvii. 5.
Ovid, *Metamorphoses*, xv. 29.
[8] Cicero, *De officiis*, i. 45 (160).
Cf. ibid. iii. 23 (90).

our children, our kinsmen, our friends, are dear to us ; but our country comprehends alone all the endearments of us all. What good man would hesitate to die for her if he could do her service ? " [1]

The duty of patriotism springs, in the first instance, from the patriotic feeling ; when the love of country is common in a nation public resentment is felt towards him who does not act as that sentiment requires him to act. Moreover, lack of patriotism in a person may also be resented by his fellow-countrymen as an injury done to themselves ; and as we have seen before, anger, and especially anger felt by a whole community, has a tendency to lead to moral disapproval. For analogous reasons deeds of patriotism are apt to evoke moral praise. However, in benefiting his own people the patriot may cause harm to other people ; and where the altruistic sentiment is broad enough to extend beyond the limits of the State and strong enough to make its voice heard even in competition with the love of country and the love of self, his conduct may consequently be an object of reproach. At the lower stages of civilisation the interests of foreigners are not regarded at all, except when sheltered by the rule of hospitality ; but gradually, owing to circumstances which will be discussed in the following chapter, altruism tends to expand, and men are at last considered to have duties to mankind at large. The Chinese moralists inculcated benevolence to all men without making any reference to national distinctions.[2] Mih-tsze, who lived in the interval between Confucius and Mencius, even taught that we ought to love all men equally ; but this doctrine called forth protests as abnegating the peculiar devotion due to relatives.[3] In Thâi-Shang it is said that a good man will feel kindly towards every creature, and should not hurt even the insect tribes, grass, and trees.[4] Buddhism

[1] Ibid. i. 17 (57). Cf. Cicero, De legibus, ii. 2 (5).
[2] Lun Yü, xii. 22. Mencius, vii. 1. 45. Douglas, Confucianism and Taoism, pp. 108, 205.
[3] Edkins, Religion in China, p. 119. Legge, Chinese Classics, ii. 476, n. 45. de Groot, Religious System of China, (vol. ii. book) i. 684.
[4] Thâi-Shang, 3.

enjoins the duty of universal love :—". As a mother, even at the risk of her own life, protects her son, her only son, so let a man cultivate goodwill without measure toward all beings, . . . unhindered love and friendliness toward the whole world, above, below, around." [1] According to the Hindu work Panchatantra it is the thought of little-minded persons to consider whether a man is one of our-selves or an alien, the whole earth being of kin to him who is generously disposed.[2]   In Greece and Rome philosophers arose who opposed national narrowness and prejudice.   Democritus of Abdera said that every country is accessible to a wise man, and that a good soul's father-land is the whole earth.[3]   The same view was expressed by Theodorus, one of the later Cyrenaics, who denounced devotion to country as ridiculous.[4]   The Cynics, in particular, attached slight value to the citizenship of any special state, declaring themselves to be citizens of the world.[5]   But, as Zeller observes, in the mouth of the Cynic this doctrine was meant to express not so much the essential oneness of all mankind, as the philosopher's independence of country and home.[6]   It was the Stoic philosophy that first gave to the idea of a world-citizenship a definite positive meaning, and raised it to historical importance.   The citizen of Alexander's huge empire had in a way become a citizen of the world ; and national dislikes were so much more readily overcome as the various nationalities comprised in it were united not only under a common government but also in a common culture.[7]   Indeed, the founder of Stoicism was himself only half a Greek.   But there is also an obvious connection between the cosmopolitan idea and the Stoic

---

[1] Quoted by Rhys Davids, *Hibbert Lectures on the History of Buddhism*, p. 111.

[2] Muir, *Religious and Moral Sentiments rendered from Sanskrit Writers*, p. 109.

[3] Stobæus, *Florilegium*, xl. 7, vol. ii. 80. *Cf.* Natorp, *Die Ethika des Demokritos*, p. 117, n. 41.

[4] Diogenes Laertius, *Vitæ philosophorum*, ii. 98 *sq.*

[5] *Ibid.* vi. 12, 63, 72, 98. Epictetus, *Dissertationes*, iii. 24. 66. Stobæus, xlv. 28. vol. ii. 252.

[6] Zeller, *Socrates and the Socratic Schools*, p. 326 *sq. Idem, Stoics, Epicureans, and Sceptics*, p. 327.

[7] *Cf.* Plutarch, *De Alexandri Magni ortuna aut virtute*, i. 6, p. 329.

system in general.[1]   According to the Stoics, human society has for its basis the identity of reason in individuals ; hence we have no ground for limiting this society to a single nation. We are all, says Seneca, members of one great body, the universe ; " we are all akin by Nature, who has formed us of the same elements, and placed us here together for the same end."[2]   " If our reason is common," says Marcus Aurelius, " there is a common law, as reason commands us what to do and what not to do ; and if there is a common law we are fellow-citizens ; if this is so, we are members of sóme political community—the world is in a manner a state."[3]   To this great state, which includes all rational beings, the individual states are related as the houses of a city are to the city collectively ;[4] and the wise man will esteem it far above any particular community in which the accident of birth has placed him.[5]

But the Roman ideal of patriotism, with its utter disregard for foreign nations,[6] was not opposed by philosophy alone : it met with an even more formidable antagonist in the new religion. The Christian and the Stoic rejected it on different grounds : whilst the Stoic felt himself as a citizen of the world, the Christian felt himself as a citizen of heaven, to whom this planet was only a place of exile. Christianity was not hostile to the State.[7] At the very time when Nero committed his worst atrocities, St. Paul declared that there is no power but of God, and that whosoever resists the power resists the ordinance of God and shall be condemned ;[8] and Tertullian says that all Christians send up their prayers for the life of the emperors, for their ministers, for magistrates, for the good of the

---

[1] See Zeller, *Stoics, &c.* p. 327 *sq.*
[2] Seneca, *Epistulæ*, xcv. 52.
[3] Marcus Aurelius, *Commentarii*, iv. 4. *Cf. ibid.* vi. 44, and ix. 9 ; Cicero, *De legibus*, i. 7 (23) ; Epictetus, *Dissertationes*, i. 13. 3.
[4] Marcus Aurelius, iii. 11.
[5] Seneca, *De otio*, iv. 1.   *Idem, Epistulæ*, lxviii. 2. Epictetus. *Dis-*

sertationes, iii. 22. 83 *sqq.*
[6] *Cf.* Lactantius, *Divinæ Institutiones*, vi. (' De vero cultu '), 6 (Migne, *Patrologiæ cursus,* vi. 655).
[7] *St. Matthew*, xxii. 21   1 *Peter*, ii. 13 *sq.*
[8] *Romans*, xiii. 1 *sq.* See also *Tilus*, iii. 1.

State and the peace of the Empire.[1] But the emperor
should be obeyed only so long as his commands do not
conflict with the law of God—a Christian ought rather to
suffer like Daniel in the lions' den than sin against his
religion ;[2] and nothing is more entirely foreign to him
than affairs of State.[3] Indeed, in the whole Roman Empire
there were no men who so entirely lacked patriotism as the
early Christians. They had no affection for Judea, they
soon forgot Galilee, they cared nothing for the glory of
Greece and Rome.[4] When the judges asked them which
was their country they said in answer," I am a Christian." [5]
And long after Christianity had become the religion of the
Empire, St. Augustine declared that it matters not, in
respect of this short and transitory life, under whose dominion a mortal man lives, if only he be not compelled to
acts of impiety or injustice.[6] Later on, when the Church
grew into a political power independent of the State, she
became a positive enemy of national interests. In the
seventeenth century a Jesuit general called patriotism " a
plague and the most certain death of Christian love." [7]

With the fall of the Roman Empire patriotism died out
in Europe, and remained extinct for centuries. It was a
feeling hardly compatible either with the migratory life of
the Teutonic tribes or with the feudal system, which grew
up wherever they fixed their residence. The knights, it is
true, were not destitute of the natural affection for home.
When Aliaumes is mortally wounded by Géri li Sors he
exclaims, " Holy Virgin, I shall never more see Saint-
Quentin nor Néèle " ;[8] and the troubadour Bernard de
Ventadour touchingly sings, " Quan la doussa aura venta—
Deves nostre païs,—M'es veiaire que senta—Odor de

[1] Tertullian, *Apologeticus*, 39 (Migne, *op. cit.* i. 468). See also Ludwig, *Tertullian's Ethik*, p. 153 *sqq.*; Nielsen, *Tertullian's Ethik*, p. 98 *sq.*
[2] Tertullian, *De idololatria*, 15 (Migne, *op. cit.* i. 684).
[3] Tertullian, *Apologeticus*, 38 (Migne, *op. cit.* i. 465):—" Nec ulla magis res aliena, quam publica."
[4] See Renan, *Hibber Lectures on the Influence of Rome on Christianity*, p. 28.
[5] Le Blant, *Inscriptions chrétiennes*, i. 128.
[6] St. Augustine, *De Civitate Dei*, v. 17.
[7] von Eicken, *Geschichte und System der mittelalterlichen Weltan-schauung*, p. 809.
[8] *Li Romans de Raoul de Cambrai*, 210, p. 185.

Paradis." [1]   But to a man of the Middle Ages "his country" meant little more than the neighbourhood in which he lived.[2] Kingdoms existed, but no nations. The first duty of a vassal was to be loyal to his lord ; [3] but no national spirit bound together the various barons of one country. A man might be the vassal of the king of France and of the king of England at the same time ; and often, from caprice, passion, or sordid interest, the barons sold their services to the enemies of the kingdom. The character of his knighthood was also perpetually pressing the knight to a course of conduct distinct from all national objects.[4] The cause of a distressed lady was in many instances preferable to that of the country to which he belonged—as when the Captal de Bouche, though an English subject, did not hesitate to unite his troops with those of the Compte de Foix to relieve the ladies in a French town, where they were besieged and threatened with violence by the insurgent peasantry.[5] When a knight's duties towards his country are mentioned in the rules of Chivalry they are spoken of as duties towards his lord :— " The wicked knight," it is said, " that aids not his earthly lord and natural country against another prince, is a knight without office." [6] Far from being, as M. Gautier asserts, [7] the object of an express command in the code of Chivalry, true patriotism had there no place at all. It was not known as an ideal, still less did it exist as a reality, among either knights or commoners. As a duke of Orleans could bind himself by a fraternity of arms and alliance to a duke of Lancaster,[8] so English merchants were in the habit of supplying nations at war against England with provisions bought at English fairs, and weapons wrought by English hands.[9] If, as M. Gaston Paris maintains, a

---

[1] Quoted by Gautier, *La Cheval-erie*, p. 64.

[2] See Cibrario, *Della economia poli-tica del medio eve*, i. 263 ; de Crozals, *Histoire de la civilization*, ii. 287.

[3] *Ordre of Chyualry*, foll. 13 b. 32 b.

[4] See Mills, *History of Chivalry*, i.

140 *sq.*

[5] Scott, *Essay on Chivalry*, p. 31.

[6] *Ordre of Chyualry*, fol. 14 b.

[7] Gautier, *op. cit.* p. 33.

[8] Sainte-Palaye, *Mémoires sur l'an-cienne Chevalerie*, ii. 72.

[9] Pike, *History of Crime in England*, i. 264 *sq.*

deep feeling of national union had inspired the Chanson de Roland,[1] it is a strange, yet undeniable, fact that no distinct trace of this feeling displayed itself in the mediæval history of France before the English wars.

Besides feudalism and the want of political cohesion, there were other factors that contributed to hinder the development of national personality and patriotic devotion. This sentiment presupposes not only that the various parts of which a country is composed shall have a vivid feeling of their unity, but also that they, united, shall feel themselves as a nation clearly distinct from other nations. In the Middle Ages national differences were largely obscured by the preponderance of the Universal Church, by the creation of the Holy Roman Empire, by the prevalence of a common language as the sole vehicle of mental culture, and by the undeveloped state of the vernacular tongues. To make use of the native dialect was a sign of ignorance, and to place worldly interests above the claims of the Church was impious. When Macchiavelli declared that he preferred his country to the safety of his soul, people considered him guilty of blasphemy ; and when the Venetians defied the Papal thunders by averring that they were Venetians in the first place, and only Christians in the second, the world heard them with amazement.[2]

In England the national feeling developed earlier than on the Continent, no doubt owing to her insular position and freer institutions ; as Montesquieu observes, patriotism thrives best in democracies.[3] At the time of the English Reformation the sense of corporate national life had evidently gained considerable strength, and the love of England has never been expressed in more exquisite form than it was by Shakespeare. At the same time the sense of patriotism was often grossly perverted by religious

---

[1] Paris, *La poésie du moyen age*, p. 107. M. Gautier says (*op. cit.* p. 61) that Roland is " la France faite homme."

[2] 'National Personality,' in *Edinburgh Review*, cxciv. 133.

[3] Montesquieu, *De l'esprit des Lois,* iv. 5 (*Œuvres*, p 206 *sq.*).

bigotry and party. spirit.[1] Even champions of liberty, like Lord Russell and Algernon Sidney, accepted French gold in the hope of embarrassing the King; and Sidney went so far as to try to instigate De Witt to invade England. Loyalism, in particular, proved a much stronger incentive than love of country. A loyalist like Strafford would have employed half-savage Irish troops against his own countrymen, and the Scotch Jacobites invited a French invasion.

In France the development of the national feeling was closely connected with the strengthening of the royal power and its gradual victory over feudalism. The word *patrie* was for the first time used by Charles VII.'s chronicler, Jean Chartier, and he also condemned as *renégats* those Frenchmen who, at the end of the hundred years' war, fought on the side of the English.[2] But patriotism was for a long time inseparably confounded with loyalty to the sovereign. According to Bossuet " tout l'État est en la personne du prince " ;[3] and Abbé Coyer observes that Colbert believed *royaume* and *patrie* to signify one and the same thing.[4] In the eighteenth century the spirit of rebellion succeeded that of devotion to the king; but the key-note of the great movement which led to the Revolution was the liberty and equality of the individual, not the glory or welfare of the nation. Men were looked upon as members of the human race, rather than as citizens of any particular country. To be a citizen of every nation, and not to belong to one's native country alone, was the dream of French writers in the eighteenth century.[5] " The true sage is a cosmopolitan," says a writer of comedy.[6] Diderot asks which is the greater merit, to enlighten the human race, which remains for ever, or to save one's fatherland, which is

---

[1] See *Edinburgh Review*, cxciv. 133, 136 *sq.* ; Pearson, *National Life and Character*, p. 190.

[2] Guibal, *Histoire du sentiment national en France pendant la guerre de Cent ans*, p. 526 *sq.*

[3] Legrand, *L'idée de patrie*, p. 20.

[4] Block, *Dictionnaire général de la politique*, ii. 518.

[5] Texte, *Jean-Jacques Rousseau and the Cosmopolitan Spirit in Literature*, p. 79.

[6] Palissot de Montenoy, *Les philosophes*, iii. 4, p. 75.

perishable.[1] According to Voltaire patriotism is composed of self-love and prejudice,[2] and only too often makes us the enemies of our fellow-men :— ' Il est clair qu'un pays ne peut gagner sans qu'un autre perde, et qu'il ne peut vaincre sans faire des malheureux. Telle est donc la condition humaine, que souhaiter la grandeur de son pays, c'est souhaiter du mal à ses voisins.'' [3]   In Germany, Lessing, Goethe, and Schiller felt themselves as citizens of the world, not of the German Empire, still less as Saxons or Suabians ; and Klopstock, with his enthusiasm for German nationality and language, almost appeared eccentric.[4] Lessing writes point-blank :—" The praise of being an ardent patriot is to my mind the very last thing that I should covet ; . . . I have no idea at all of love of the Fatherland, and it seems to me at best but an heroical weakness, which I can very readily dispense with." [5]

The first French revolution marks the beginning of a new era in the history of patriotism. It inspired the masses with passion for the unity of the fatherland, the Republic " one and indivisible." At the same time it declared all nations to be brothers, and when it made war on foreign nations the object was only to deliver them from their oppressors.[6] But gradually the interest in the affairs of other countries grew more and more selfish, the attempt to emancipate was absorbed in the desire to subjugate ; and this awoke throughout Europe a feeling which was destined to become the most powerful force in the history of the nineteenth century, the feeling of nationality. When Napoleon introduced French administration in the countries whose sovereigns he had deposed or degraded, the people resisted the change. The resistance was popular, as the rulers were absent or helpless, and it was national, being directed against foreign institu-

---

[1] Diderot, *Essai sur. es règnes de Claude et de Néron*, ii. 75 (*Œuvres*, vi. 244).

[2] Voltaire, *Pensées sur l'administration publique*, 14 (*Œuvres complètes*, v. 351).

[3] *Idem, Dictionnaire philosophique*, art. Patrie (*Œuvres complètes*, viii. 118).

[4] See Strauss, *Der alte und der neue Glaube*, p. 259 *sq.*

[5] Lessing, quoted by Ziegler, *Social Ethics*, p. 121.

[6] Block, *op. cit.* ii. 376.

tions. It was stirred by the feeling of national rather than political unity, it was a protest against the dominion of race over race. The national element in this movement had in a manner been anticipated by the French Revolution itself. The French people was regarded by it as an ethnological, not as an historic, unit ; descent was put in the place of tradition ; the idea of the sovereignty of the people uncontrolled by the past gave birth to the idea of nationality independent of the political influence of history. But, as has been truly remarked, men were made conscious of the national element of the revolution by its conquests, not in its rise.[1]

Ever since, the racial feeling has been the most vigorous force in European patriotism, and has gradually become a true danger to humanity. Beginning as a protest against the dominion of one race over another, this feeling led to a condemnation of every state which included different races, and finally developed into the complete doctrine that state and nationality should so far as possible be coextensive.[2] According to this theory the dominant nationality cannot admit the inferior nationalities dwelling within the boundaries of the state to an equality with itself, because, if it did, the state would cease to be national, and this would be contrary to the principle of its existence ; or the weaker nationalities are compelled to change their language, institutions, and individuality, so as to be absorbed in the dominant race. And not only does the leading nationality assert its superiority in relation to all others within the body politic, but it also wants to assert itself at the expense of foreign nations and races. To the nationalist all this is true patriotism ; love of country often stands for a feeling which has been well described as love of more country.[3] But at the same time opposite ideals are at work. The fervour of nineteenth century nationalism has not been able to quench the

[1] See ' Nationality,' in *Home and Foreign Review,* i. 6 *sqq.*
[2] *Ibid.* p. 13 *sq.*

[3] Robertson, *Patriotism and Empire,* p. 138.

cosmopolitan spirit. In spite of loud appeals made to racial instincts and the sense of national solidarity, the idea has been gaining ground that the aims of a nation must not conflict with the interests of humanity at large ; that our love of country should be controlled by other countries' right to prosper and to develop their own individuality ; and that the oppression of weaker nation-alities inside the state and aggressiveness towards foreign nations, being mainly the outcome of vainglory and greed, are inconsistent with the aspirations of a good patriot, as well as of a good man.

Our long discussion of moral ideas regarding such modes of conduct as directly concern other men's welfare has at last come to an end. We have seen that they may be ultimately traced to a variety of sources : to the influence of habit or education, to egoistic considerations of some kind or other which have given rise to moral feelings, to notions of social expediency, to disinterested likings or dislikes, and, above all, to sympathetic resentment or sympathetic approval springing from an altruistic disposi-tion of mind. But how to account for this disposition ? Our explanation of that group of moral ideas which we have been hitherto investigating is not complete until we have found an answer to this important question. I shall therefore in the next chapter examine the origin and development of the altruistic sentiment.

CHAPTER XXXIV

THE ORIGIN AND DEVELOPMENT OF THE ALTRUISTIC
SENTIMENT

THERE is one form of the altruistic sentiment which man shares with all mammals and many other animals, namely, maternal affection. As regards its origin various theories have been set forth.

According to Aristotle, parents love their children as being portions of themselves.[1] A similar explanation of maternal affection has been given by some modern writers.[2] Thus Professor Espinas regards this sentiment as modified self-love and love of property. The female, he says, at the moment when she gives birth to little ones resembling herself, has no difficulty in recognising them as the flesh of her flesh ; the feeling she experiences towards them is made up of sympathy and pity, but we cannot exclude from it an idea of property which is the most solid support of sympathy. She feels and understands up to a certain point that these young ones which are herself at the same time belong to her ; the love of herself, extended to those who have gone out from her, changes egoism into sympathy and the proprietary instinct into an affectionate impulse.[3] This hypothesis, however, seems to me to be very inadequate. It does not explain why, for instance, a bird takes more care of her eggs than of other matter segregated from

[1] Aristotle, *Ethica Nicomachea*, viii. 12. 2 *sq.*
[2] Hartley, *Observations on Man*, i. 496 *sq.* Fichte, *Das System der Sittenlehre*, p. 433.

[3] Espinas, *Des sociétés animales* (2nd ed.), p. 444 *sq.*, quoted by Ribot, *Psychology of the Emotions*, p. 280.

her body, which may equally well be regarded as a part of herself. Nor does it account for a foster-mother's affection for her adopted offspring.[1] Of this many instances have been noticed in the lower animals; and among some savage peoples adopted children are said to be treated by their foster-parents with the same affection as if they were their own flesh and blood.[2]

A very different explanation of maternal love has been given by Professor Bain. He derives parental affection from the " intense pleasure in the embrace of the young." He observes that " such a pleasure once created would associate itself with the prevailing features and aspects of the young, and give to all of these their very great interest. For the sake of the pleasure, the parent discovers the necessity of nourishing the subject of it, and comes to regard the ministering function as a part or condition of the delight." [3] But if the satisfaction in animal contact were at the bottom of the maternal feeling, conjugal affection ought by far to surpass it in intensity; and yet, among the lower races at least, the case is exactly the reverse, conjugal affection being vastly inferior in degree to a mother's love of her child. It may indeed be fairly doubted whether there is any " intense pleasure " at all in embracing a new-born baby—unless it be one's own. It seems much more likely that parents like to touch their children because they love them, than that they love them because they like to touch them. Attraction, showing itself either by elementary movements of approach, or by contact, or by the embrace, is the outward *expression* of tenderness.[4] Professor Bain himself observes that as anger reaches a satisfying term by knocking some one down, love is completed and satisfied with an embrace.[5] But this by no means implies that the embrace is the cause of love; it

[1] *Cf.* Spencer, *Principles of Psychology*, ii. 624.

[2] Murdoch, ' Ethnol. Results of the Point Barrow Expedition,' in *Ann. Rep. Bur. Ethn.* ix. 419 (Point Barrow Eskimo). Thomson, *Savage Island*, p. 135.

[3] Bain, *Emotions and the Will*, p. 140.

[4] Ribot, *op. cit.* p. 234.

[5] Bain, *op. cit.* p. 126.

only means that love has a tendency to express itself out-
wardly in an act of embrace.

In the opinion of Mr. Spencer, again, parental love is
essentially love of the weak or helpless. This instinct,
he remarks, is not adequately defined as that which
attaches a creature to its young. Though most frequently
and most strongly displayed in this relation, the so-called
parental feeling is really excitable apart from parenthood ;
and the common trait of the objects which arouse it is
always relative weakness or helplessness.[1] This hypothesis
undoubtedly contains part of the truth. That the maternal
instinct is in some degree love of the helpless is obvious
from the fact that, among those of the lower animals
which are not gregarious, mother and young separate as
soon as the latter are able to shift for themselves ; nay, in
many cases they are actually driven away by her. Moreover, in species which are so constituted that the young
from the very outset can help themselves there is no
maternal love. These facts indicate where we have to
look for the source of this sentiment. When the young
are born in a state of utter helplessness somebody must
take care of them, or the species cannot survive, or, rather,
such a species could never have come into existence. The
maternal instinct may thus be assumed to owe its origin
to the survival of the fittest, to the natural selection of
useful spontaneous variations.

This is also recognised by Mr. Spencer ;[2] but his theory
fails to explain the indisputable fact that there is a
difference between maternal love and the mere love of the
helpless. Even in a gregarious species mothers make a
distinction between their own offspring and other young.
During my stay among the mountaineers of Morocco I
was often struck by the extreme eagerness with which in
the evening, when the flock of ewes and the flock of
lambs were reunited, each mother sought for her own
lamb, and each lamb for its own mother. A similar

---

[1] Spencer, *Principles of Psychology*,   i. 497.
ii. 623 *sq*. See also Hartley, *op. cit.*   [2] Spencer, *op. cit.* ii. 623.

discrimination has been noticed even in cases of conscious adoption. Brehm tells us of a female baboon which had so capacious a heart that she not only adopted young monkeys of other species, but stole young dogs and cats which she continually carried about ; yet her kindness did not go so far as to share food with her adopted offspring, although she divided everything quite fairly with her own young ones.[1] To account for the maternal sentiment we must therefore assume the existence of some other stimulus besides the signs of helplessness, which produces, or at least strengthens, the instinctive motor response in the mother. This stimulus, so far as I can see, is rooted in the external relationship in which the offspring from the beginning stand to the mother. She is in close proximity to her helpless young from their tenderest age ; and she loves them because they are to her a cause of pleasure.

In various animal species the young are cared for not only by the mother, but by the father as well. This is the general rule among birds : whilst the hatching of the eggs and the chief part of the rearing-duties belong to the mother, the father acts as a protector, and provides food for the family. Among most of the mammals, on the other hand, the connections between the sexes are restricted to the time of the rut, hence the father may not even see his young. But there are also some mammalian species in which male and female remain together even after the birth of the offspring and the father defends his family against enemies.[2] Among the Quadrumana this seems to be the rule.[3] All the best authorities agree that the Gorilla and the Chimpanzee live in families. When the female is pregnant the male builds a rude nest in a tree, where she is delivered ; and he spends the night crouching at the foot of the tree, protecting the female and their young one, which are in the nest above, from the nocturnal attacks of leopards. Passing from the

[1] Darwin, *Descent of Man*, p. 70. Westermarck, *History of Human* *Marriage*, p. 11 *sq.*
[3] *Ibid.* p. 12 *sqq.*

highest monkeys to the savage and barbarous races of
men, we meet with the same phenomenon. In the human
race the family consisting of father, mother, and offspring
is probably a universal institution, whether founded on
a monogamous, polygynous, or polyandrous marriage.
And, as among the lower animals having the same habit,
whilst the immediate care of the children chiefly belongs
to the mother, the father is the guardian of the family.[1]

The stimuli to which the paternal instinct responds are
apparently derived from the same circumstances as those
which call into activity the maternal instinct, that is, the
helplessness and the nearness of the offspring. Wherever
this instinct exists, the father is near his young from the
beginning, living together with the mother. And here
again the sentimental response is in all probability the
result of a process of natural selection, which has preserved a mental disposition necessary for the existence of
the species. Among birds paternal care is indispensable.
Equal and continual warmth is the first requirement for
the development of the embryo and the preservation of
the young ones ; and for this the mother almost always
wants the assistance of the father, who provides her with
necessaries, and sometimes relieves her of the brooding.
Among mammals, again, whilst the young at their
tenderest age can never do without the mother, the
father's aid is generally not required. That the Primates
form an exception to this rule is probably due to the
small number of young, the female bringing forth but
one at a time, and besides, among the highest apes and
in man, to the long period of infancy.[2] If this is true
we may assume that the paternal instinct occurred in
primitive man, as it occurs, more or less strongly
developed, among the anthropoid apes and among existing
savages.

By origin closely allied to the paternal feeling is the
attachment between individuals of different sex, which

[1] Westermarck, *History of Human Marriage*, p. 14 *sqq.*

[2] See *ibid.* p. 20 *sqq.*; Fiske, *Outlines of Cosmic Philosophy*, ii. 342 *sq.*

induces male and female to remain with one another beyond the mere act of propagation till after the birth of the offspring.   It is obvious that, where the generative power is restricted to a certain season—a peculiarity which primitive man seems to have shared with other mammals [1] —it cannot be the sexual instinct that causes the prolonged union of the sexes, nor can I conceive any other egoistic motive that could account for this habit.   Considering that the union lasts till after the birth of the offspring and that it is accompanied with parental care, I conclude that it is for the benefit of the young that male and female continue to live together.   The tie which joins them seems therefore, like parental affection, to be an instinct developed through natural selection.   The tendency to feel some attachment to a being which has been the cause of pleasure—in this case sexual pleasure—is undoubtedly at the bottom of this instinct.   Such a feeling may originally have induced the sexes to remain united and the male to protect the female even after the sexual desire was gratified ; and if procuring great advantage to the species in the struggle for existence, conjugal attachment would naturally have developed into a specific characteristic.

We have reason to believe that the germ of this sentiment occurred already in our earliest human ancestors, that marriage, in the natural history sense of the term, is a habit transmitted to man from some ape-like progenitor.[2]   In the course of evolution conjugal affection has increased both in intensity and complexity ; but advancement in civilisation has not at every step been favourable to its development.   When restricted to men only, a higher culture on the contrary tends to alienate husband and wife, as is the case in Eastern countries and as was the case in ancient Greece.   Another fact leading to conjugal apathy is the custom which compels the women before marriage to live strictly apart from the men.   In China it often happens that the parties have not even seen each

[1] Westermarck, *op. cit.* ch. ii.   [2] *Ibid. op. cit.* chs. i., iii.

other till the wedding day ;[1] and in Greece Plato urged in vain that young men and women should be more frequently permitted to meet one another, so that there should be less enmity and indifference in the married life.[2] Conjugal love is both a cause and an effect of monogamy ; but, as we shall see subsequently, the course of civilisation does not involve a steady progress towards stricter monogamy.   The notions about women also influence the emotions felt towards them ; and we have noticed that the great religions of the world have generally held them in little regard.[3]   In its fully developed form the passion which unites the sexes is perhaps the most compound of all human feelings.   Mr. Spencer thus sums up the masterly analysis he has given of it :—" Round the physical feeling forming the nucleus of the whole, are gathered the feelings produced by personal beauty, that constituting simple attachment, those of reverence, of love, of approbation, of self-esteem, of property, of love of freedom, of sympathy.   These, all greatly exalted, and severally tending to reflect their excitements on one another, unite to form the mental state we call love." [4]

The duration of conjugal and parental feelings varies extremely.   Most birds, with the exception of those belonging to the Gallinaceous family, when pairing do so once for all till either one or the other dies ;[5] whereas among the mammals man and possibly some apes [6] are the only species whose conjugal unions last any considerable time after the birth of the offspring.   Among many of the lower races of men lifelong marriages seem to be the rule, and among a few separation is said to be entirely unknown ; but there is abundant evidence that marriage has, upon the whole, become more durable with advancing civilisation.[7]   One cause of this is that conjugal affection has become more lasting.   And the greater duration of this sentiment may be explained partly from the refine-

[1] Katscher, *Bilder aus dem chinesischen Leben*, pp. 71, 84.
[2] Plato, *Leges*, vi. 771 *sq.*
[3] *Supra*, i. 662 *sqq.*
[4] Spencer, *Principles of Psychology*,
i. 488.
[5] Westermarck, *op. cit.* p. 11.
[6] *Ibid.* pp. 13, 14, 535.
[7] *Ibid.* ch. xxiii.

ment of the uniting passion, involving appreciation of mental qualities which last long after youth and beauty have passed away, and partly also from the greater durability of parental feelings, which form a tie not only between parents and children, but between husband and wife.

The parental feelings originally only last as long as the young are unable to shift for themselves—the paternal feeling possibly less. As Mr. Fiske observes, " where the infancy is very short, the parental feeling, though intense while it lasts, presently disappears, and the offspring cease to be distinguished from strangers of the same species. And in general the duration of the feelings which insure the protection of the offspring is determined by the duration of the infancy."[1]   Among certain savages parental love is still said to be restricted to the age of helplessness. We are told that the affection of a Fuegian mother for her child gradually decreases in proportion as the child grows older, and ceases entirely when it reaches the age of seven or eight ; thenceforth the parents in no way meddle with the affairs of their son, who may leave them if he likes.[2] When the parental feelings became more complex, through the association of other feelings, as those of property and pride, they naturally tended to extend themselves beyond the limits of infancy and childhood.   But the chief cause of this extension seems to lie in the same circumstances as made man a gregarious animal.   Where the grown-up children continued to stay with their parents, parental affection naturally tended to be prolonged, not only by the infusion into it of new elements, but by the direct influence of close living together.   It was, moreover, extended to more distant descendants.   The same stimuli as call forth kindly emotions towards a person's own children evoke similar emotions towards his grand- and great-grandchildren.

[1] Fiske, *op. cit.* ii. 343.
[2] Bove, *Patagonia, Terra del Fuoco*, p. 133. See also Wied-Neuwied, *Reise nach Brasilien*, ii. 40 (Botocudos); Im Thurn, *Among the Indians of Guiana*, p. 219 ; Scaramucci and Giglioli, 'Notizie sui Danakil,' in *Archivio per l'antropologia e la etnologia*, xiv. 35.

It is an old truth that children's love of their parents is generally much weaker than the parents' love of their children. The latter is absolutely necessary for the subsistence of the species, the former is not ;[1] though, when a richer food-supply favoured the formation of larger communities, filial attachment must have been of advantage to the race.[2] No individual is born with filial love. However, Aristotle goes too far when saying that, whilst parents love their children from their birth upward, " children do not begin to love their parents until they are of a considerable age, and have got full possession of their wits and faculties."[3] Under normal circumstances the infant from an early age displays some attachment to its parents. Professor Sully tells us of a girl, about seventeen months old, who received her father after a few days' absence with special marks of affection, " rushing up to him, smoothing and stroking his face and giving him all the toys in the room."[4] Filial love is retributive ; the agreeable feeling produced by benefits received makes the individual look with pleasure and kindliness upon the giver. And here again the affection is strengthened by close living together, as appears from the cooling effect of long separation of children from their parents. But the filial feeling is not affection pure and simple, it is affection mingled with regard for the physical and mental superiority of the parent.[5] As the parental feeling is partly love of the weak and young, so the filial feeling is partly regard for the strong and (comparatively) old.

Besides parental, conjugal, and filial attachment we find among all existing races of men altruism of the fraternal

[1] This observation was made already by Hutcheson (*Inquiry into the Original of our Ideas of Beauty and Virtue*, p. 219) and Adam Smith (*Theory of Moral Sentiments*, p. 199). The latter wrote, a hundred years before the publication of ' The Origin of Species,' that parental tenderness is a much stronger affection than filial piety, because " the continuance and propagation of the species depend altogether upon the former, and not upon the latter."

[2] Darwin maintains (*Descent of Man*, p. 105) that the filial affections have been to a large extent gained through natural selection.

[3] Aristotle, *Ethica Nicomachea*, viii. 12. 2.

[4] Sully, *Studies of Childhood*, p. 243.

[5] See *supra*, i. 618 *sq.*

type, binding together children of the same parents, relatives more remotely allied, and, generally, members of the same social unit. But I am inclined to suppose that man was not originally a gregarious animal, in the proper sense of the word, that he originally lived in families rather than in tribes, and that the tribe arose as the result of increasing food-supply, allowing the formation of larger communities, combined with the advantages which under such circumstances accrued from a gregarious life. The man-like apes are not gregarious ; and considering that some of them are reported to be encountered in greater numbers in the season when most fruits come to maturity,[1] we may infer that the solitary life generally led by them is due chiefly to the difficulty they experience in getting food at other times of the year. That our earliest human or half-human ancestors lived on the same kind of food, and required about the same quantities of it as the man-like apes, seems to me a fairly legitimate supposition ; and from this I conclude that they were probably not more gregarious than these apes. Subsequently man became carnivorous ; but even when getting his living by fishing or hunting, he may still have continued as a rule this solitary kind of life, or gregariousness may have become his habit only in part. " An animal of a predatory kind," Mr. Spencer observes, " which has prey that can be caught and killed without help, profits by living alone : especially if its prey is much scattered, and is secured by stealthy approach or by lying in ambush. Gregariousness would here be a positive disadvantage. Hence the tendency of large carnivores, and also of small carnivores that have feeble and widely-distributed prey, to lead solitary lives." [2] It is certainly a noteworthy fact that even now there are rude savages who live rather in separate families than in tribes ; and that their solitary life is due to want of

[1] Savage,' Observations on the External Characters and Habits of the *Troglodytes Niger*,' in *Boston Journal of Natural History*, iv. 384. *Cf.* von Koppenfels, ' Meine Jagden auf Gorillas,' in *Die Gartenlaube*, 1877, p. 419.

[2] Spencer, *Principles of Psychology*, ii. 558.

sufficient food is obvious from several facts which I have
stated in full in another place.[1] These facts, as it seems to
me, give much support to the supposition that the kind
of food man subsisted upon, together with the large
quantities of it which he wanted, formed in olden times
a hindrance to a true gregarious manner of living, except
perhaps in some unusually rich places.

But man finally overcame this obstacle. " He has,"
to quote Darwin, " invented and is able to use various
weapons, tools, traps, &c., with which he defends himself,
kills or catches prey, and otherwise obtains food. He
has made rafts or canoes for fishing or crossing over
to neighbouring fertile islands. He has discovered the
art of making fire, by which hard and stringy roots
can be rendered digestible, and poisonous roots or
herbs innocuous." [2] In short, man gradually found
out new ways of earning his living and more and more
emancipated himself from direct dependence on surrounding nature. The chief obstacle to a gregarious
life was by this means surmounted, and the advantages of
such a life were considerable. Living together in larger
groups, men could resist the dangers of life and defend
themselves much better than when solitary—all the more
so as the physical strength of man, and especially savage
man, is comparatively slight. The extension of the
small family group may have taken place in two different
ways : either by adhesion, or by natural growth and
cohesion. In other words, new elements—whether other
family groups or single individuals—may have united
with it from without, or the children, instead of
separating from their parents, may have remained with
them and increased the group by forming new families
themselves. There can be little doubt that the latter
was the normal mode of extension. When gregariousness
became an advantage to man, he would feel inclined to
remain with those with whom he was living even after
the family had fulfilled its object—the preservation of

[1] Westermarck, *op. cit.* p. 43 *sqq.*   [2] Darwin, *Descent of Man*, p. 48 *sq.*

the helpless offspring. And he would be induced to do so not only from egoistic considerations, but by an instinct which, owing to its usefulness, would gradually develop, practically within the limits of kinship—the gregarious instinct.

By the gregarious instinct I understand an animal's proneness to live together with other members of its own species, apart from parental, conjugal, and filial attachment. It involves, or leads to, pleasure in the consciousness of their presence. The members of a herd are at ease in each other's company, suffer when they are separated, and rejoice when they are reunited. By actual living together the instinct is individualised,[1] and it is strengthened by habit. The pleasure with which one individual looks upon another is further increased by the solidarity of interests. Not only have they enjoyments in common, but they have the same enemies to resist, the same dangers to encounter, the same difficulties to overcome. Hence acts which are beneficial to the agent are at the same time beneficial to his companions, and the distinction between *ego* and *alter* loses much of its importance.

But the members of the group do not merely take pleasure in each other's company. Associated animals very frequently display a feeling of affection for each other—defend each other, help each other in distress and danger, perform various other services for each other.[2] Considering that the very object of the gregarious instinct is the preservation of the species, I think we are obliged to regard the mutual affection of associated animals as a development of this instinct. With the pleasure they take in each other's company is intimately connected kindliness towards its cause, the companion himself. In this explanation of social affection I believe no further step can be made. Professor Bain asks why a more lively feeling should grow up towards a fellow-being than towards an

---

[1] In mankind we very early recognise the child's tendency to sympathise with persons who are familiar to it (Compayré, *L'évolution intellectuelle et morale de l'enfant*, p. 288).

[2] Darwin, *op. cit.* p. 100 *sqq.* Kropotkin, *Mutual Aid*, ch. i. *sq.*

inanimate source of pleasure ; and to account for this he suggests, curiously enough, " the primary and independent pleasure of the animal embrace " [1]—although embrace even as an outward expression of affection plays a very insignificant part in the social relations of gregarious animals. It might as well be asked why there should be a more lively feeling towards a sentient creature which inflicts pain than towards an inanimate cause of pain. Both cases call for a similar explanation. The animal distinguishes between a living being and a lifeless thing, and affection proper, like anger proper, is according to its very nature felt towards the former only. The object of anger is normally an enemy, the object of social affection is normally a friend. Social affection is not only greatly increased by reciprocity of feeling, but could never have come into existence without such reciprocity. The being to which an animal attaches itself is conceived of as kindly disposed towards it ; hence among wild animals social affection is found only in connection with the gregarious instinct, which is reciprocal in nature.

Among men the members of the same social unit are tied to each other with various bonds of a distinctly human character—the same customs, laws, institutions, magic or religious ceremonies and beliefs, or notions of a common descent. As men generally are fond of that to which they are used or which is their own, they are also naturally apt to have likings for other individuals whose habits or ideas are similar to theirs. The intensity and extensiveness of social affection thus in the first place depend upon the coherence and size of the social aggregate, and its development must consequently be studied in connection with the evolution of such aggregates.

This evolution is largely influenced by economic conditions. Savages who know neither cattle-rearing nor agriculture, but subsist on what nature gives them—game, fish, fruit, roots, and so forth—mostly live in single families consisting of parents and children, or in larger

---

[1] Bain, *op. cit.* p. 132.

family groups including in addition a few other individuals closely allied.[1] But even among these savages the isolation of the families is not complete. Persons of the same stock inhabiting neighbouring districts hold friendly relations with one another, and unite for the purpose of common defence. When the younger branches of a family are obliged to disperse in search of food, at least some of them remain in the neighbourhood of the parent family, preserve their language, and never quite lose the idea of belonging to one and the same social group. And in some cases we find that people in the hunting or fishing stage actually live in larger communities, and have a well-developed social organisation. This is the case with many or most of the Australian aborigines. Though in Australia, also, isolated families are often met with,[2] the rule seems to be that the blacks live in hordes. Thus the Arunta of Central Australia are distributed in a large number of small local groups, each of which occupies a given area of country and has its own headman.[3] Every family, consisting of a man and one or more wives and children, has a separate lean-to of shrubs ;[4] but clusters of these shelters are always found in spots where food is more or less easily obtainable,[5] and the members of each group are bound together by a strong " local feeling."[6] The local influence makes itself felt even outside the horde. " Without belonging to the same group," say Messrs. Spencer and Gillen, " men who inhabit localities close to one another are more closely associated than men living at a distance from one another, and, as a matter of fact, this local bond is strongly marked. . . . Groups which are contiguous locally are constantly meeting to perform ceremonies."[7] At the time when the series of initiation ceremonies called the *Engwura* are performed, men and women gather together from all parts of the tribe, councils of the elder

[1] Westermarck, *op. cit.* p. 43 *sqq.*
Hildebrand, *Recht und Sitte*, p. 1 *sqq.*
[2] Westermarck, *op. cit.* p. 45.
[3] Spencer and Gillen, *Native Tribes of Central Australia*, p. 8 *sqq.*
[4] *Ibid.* p. 18.
[5] *Ibid.* p. 31.
[6] *Ibid.* p. 544.
[7] *Ibid.* p. 14.

men are held day by day, the old traditions of the tribe are repeated and discussed, and " it is by means of meetings such as this, that a knowledge of the unwritten history of the tribe and of its leading members is passed on from generation to generation." [1]   Nay, even members of different tribes often have friendly intercourse with each other ; in Central Australia, when two tribes come into contact with one another on the border-land of their respective territories, the same amicable feelings as prevail within the tribe are maintained between the members of the two.[2]   Now it seems extremely probable that Australian blacks are so much more sociable than most other hunting people because the food-supply of their country is naturally more plentiful, or, partly thanks to their boomerangs, more easily attainable. A Central Australian native is, as a general rule, well nourished ; " kangaroo, rock-wallabies, emus, and other forms of game are not scarce, and often fall a prey to his spear and boomerang, while smaller animals, such as rats and lizards, are constantly caught without any difficulty by the women." [3]   Circumstances of an economic character also account for the gregariousness of the various peoples on the northwest coast of North America who are neither pastoral nor agricultural—the Thlinkets, Haidas, Nootkas, and others. On the shore of the sea or some river they have permanent houses, each of which is inhabited by a number of families ;[4] the houses are grouped in villages, some of which are very populous ;[5] and though the tribal bond is not conspicuous for its strength, there are councils which discuss and decide all important questions concerning the tribe.[6] The territory inhabited by these peoples, with its bays, sounds, and rivers, supplies them with food in abundance ; " its enormous wealth of fish allows its inhabitants to enjoy a pampered existence." [7]

[1] Spencer and Gillen, *Native Tribes of Central Australia*, p. 272.

[2] *Ibid.* p. 32.

[3] *Ibid.* pp. 7, 44.

[4] Boas, in *Fifth Report on the North-Western Tribes of Canada*, p. 22.

[5] Krause (*Die Tlinkit-Indianer*, p. 100) speaks of a Thlinket village which consisted of sixty-five houses and five or six hundred inhabitants.

[6] Boas, *loc. cit.* p. 36 *sq.*

[7] Ratzel, *History of Mankind*, ii. 92.

To pastoral people sociality, up to a certain degree, is of great importance. They have not only to defend their own persons against their enemies, but they have also to protect valuable property, their cattle. Moreover, they are often anxious to increase their wealth by robbing their neighbours of cattle, and this is best done in company. But at the same time a pastoral community is never large, and, though cohesive so long as it exists, it is liable to break up into sections. The reason for this is that a certain spot can pasture only a limited stock of cattle. The thirteenth chapter of Genesis well illustrates the social difficulties experienced by pastoral peoples. Abraham went up out of Egypt together with his wife and all that he had, and Lot went with him. Abraham was very rich in cattle, and Lot also had flocks, and herds, and tents. But " the land was not able to bear them, that they might dwell together : for their substance was great, so that they could not dwell together " ; they were obliged to separate.[1]

The case is different with people subsisting on agriculture. A certain piece of land can support a much larger number of persons when it is cultivated than when it consists merely of pasture ground. Its resources largely depend on the labour bestowed on it, and the more people the more labour. The soil also constitutes a tie which cannot be loosened. It is a kind of property which, unlike cattle, is immovable ; hence even where individual ownership in land prevails, the heirs to an estate have to remain together. As a matter of fact, the social union of agricultural communities is very close, and the households are often enormous.[2]

But living together is not the only factor which, among savages, establishes a social unit. Such a unit may be based not only on local proximity, but on marriage or a common descent ; it may consist not only of persons who live together in the same district, but of persons who are of the same family, or who are, or consider themselves to be,

---

[1] *Genesis*, xiii. 1 *sqq.* See Hildebrand, *op. cit.* p. 29 *sq.* ; Grosse, *Die Formen der Familie*, pp. 99, 100, 124 *sq.*

[2] See Grosse, *op. cit.* p. 136 *sqq.*

of the same kin. These different modes of organisation often, in a large measure, coincide. The family is a social unit made up of persons who are either married or related by blood, and at the same time, in normal cases, live together. The tribe is a social unit, though often a very incoherent one,[1] consisting of persons who inhabit the same district and also, at least in many cases, regard themselves as descendants of some common ancestor. The clan, which is essentially a body of kindred having a common name, may likewise on the whole coincide with the population of a certain territory, with the members of one or more hordes or villages. This is the case where the husband takes his wife to his own community and descent is reckoned through the father, or where he goes to live in his wife's community and descent is reckoned through the mother. But frequently the system of maternal descent is combined with the custom of the husband taking his wife to his own home, and this, in connection with the rule of clan-exogamy, occasions a great discrepancy between the horde and the clan. The local group is then by no means a group of clansmen ; the children live in their father's community, but belong to their mother's clan, whilst the next generation of children within the community must belong to another clan.[2]

Kinship certainly gives rise to special rights and duties, but when unsupported by local proximity it loses much of its social force. Among the Australian natives, for instance, the clan rules seem generally to be concerned with little or nothing else than marriage, sexual intercourse, and, perhaps, blood-revenge.[3] " The object of caste " (clan), says Mr. Curr, " is not to create or define a bond of union, but to secure the absence of any blood relationship between

---

[1] See Cunow, *Die Verwandtschafts-Organisationen der Australneger*, p. 121, n. 1.
[2] *Cf.* Giddings, *Principles of Sociology*, p. 259.
[3] Cunow, *op. cit.* pp. 97, 136. Dr. Stirling says (*Report of the Horn Expedition to Central Australia*, 'An-

thropology,' p. 43) that the laws arising out of the "class" (clan) divisions "have extraordinary force and are, in general, implicitly obeyed whether in respect of actual marriage, illicit connections, or social relations"; but I find no further reference to these "social relations."

persons proposed to marry. So far from being a bond of
friendship, no Black ever hesitates to kill one of another
tribe because he happens to bear the same caste- (clan-)
name as himself." [1] It appears that the system of descent
itself is largely influenced by local connections.[2] Sir E. B.
Tylor has found by means of his statistical method that
the number of coincidences between peoples among whom
the husband lives with the wife's family and peoples who
reckon kinship through the mother only, is proportionally
large, and that the full maternal system never appears
among peoples whose exclusive custom is for the husband
to take his wife to his own home ; [3] and I have myself
drawn attention to the fact that where the two customs,
the woman receiving her husband in her own hut and the
man taking his wife to his, occur side by side among the
same people, descent in the former case is traced through
the mother, in the latter through the father.[4] Nay, even
where kinship constitutes a tie between persons belonging
to different local groups, its social force is ultimately
derived not merely from the idea of a common origin, but
from near relatives' habit of living together. Men became
gregarious by remaining in the circle where they were
born ; if, instead of keeping together with their kindred,
they had preferred to isolate themselves or to unite with
strangers, there would certainly be no blood-bond at all.
The mutual attachment and the social rights and duties
which resulted from this gregarious condition were associated with the relation in which members of the group
stood to one another—the relation of kinship as expressed
by a common name,—and these associations might last
even after the local tie was broken. By means of the name
former connections were kept up. Even we ourselves are
generally more disposed to count kin with distant relatives
who have our own surname than with relatives who have a
different name ; and still greater is the influence which
language in this respect exercises on the mind of a savage,

---

[1] Curr, *The Australian Race*, i. 69.   the Development of Institutions,' in
[2] Westermarck, *op. cit.* p. 107 *sqq.*   *Jour. Anthr. Inst.* xviii. 258.
[3] Tylor, 'Method of Investigating   [4] Westermarck, *op. cit.* p. 110.

to whom a person's name is part of his personality. The derivative origin of the social force in kinship accounts for its formal character, when personal intercourse is wanting ; it may enjoin duties, but hardly inspires much affection. If in modern society much less importance is attached to kinship than at earlier stages of civilisation, this is largely due to the fact that relatives, except the nearest, have little communication with each other. And if, as Aristotle observes, friendship between kinsfolk varies according to the degree of relationship,[1] it does so in the first instance on account of the varying intimacy of their mutual intercourse.

A very different explanation of the social influence of kinship has been given by Mr. Hartland. He connects it with primitive superstition. A clan, he says, " is regarded as an unity, literally and not metaphorically one body, the individual members of which are as truly portions as the fingers or the legs are portions of the external, visible body of each of them." Now, a severed limb or lock of hair is believed by the savage to remain in some invisible but real union with the body whereof it once, in outward appearance also, formed a part, and any injury done to it is supposed to affect the organism to which it belonged. " The individual member of a clan was in exactly the same position as a lock of hair cut from the head, or an amputated limb. He had no separate significance, no value apart from his kin. . ... Injury inflicted on him was inflicted on, and was felt by, the whole kin, just as an injury inflicted on the severed lock or limb was felt by the bulk."[2] Mr. Hartland insists upon a literal interpretation of his words ;[3] and this implies that the members of a clan are in their behaviour influenced by the idea that what happens to one of them reacts upon all.

In support of his theory Mr. Hartland makes reference to the belief of some savages, that charms may be made from dead bodies against the surviving relatives of the deceased,[4] and to certain rites of healing in which, besides the patient himself, " other members of his tribe, presumably kinsmen," take part.[5] But the former belief is a superstition connected with the wonder of death, from which no conclusion must be drawn as

[1] Aristotle, *Ethica Nicomachea,* viii. 12. 7.
[2] Hartland, *Legend of Perseus,* ii. 277.
[3] *Ibid.* ii. 236, 398, 444.
[4] *Ibid.* ii. 437 *sq.*
[5] *Ibid.* ii. 432 *sqq.*

to relations between the living ; and in the ceremonies of healing the medicine-man plays a much more prominent part than
the other bystanders—whose relationship to the patient, besides,
is so little marked that Mr. Hartland only presumes them to be
kindred.   He further observes that in the wide-spread custom of
the Couvade we meet with the idea that the child, being a part
of the father, is liable to be affected by various acts committed
by him.[1] And from Sir J. G. Frazer's ' Golden Bough ' might be
quoted many instances of a belief in some mysterious bond of
sympathy knitting together absent friends and relations—
especially at critical times of life—which has, in particular, led
to rules regulating the conduct of persons left at home while a
party of their friends is out fishing or hunting or on the war-
path.[2] But all these rules are taboo restrictions of a definite and
altogether special kind, generally, it seems, referring to members
of the same family, and frequently to wives in their husbands'
absence.   In order to make his hypothesis acceptable, Mr.
Hartland ought to have produced a fair number of facts proving
that the members of the same clan really are believed to be connected with each other in such a manner, that whatever affects
one of them at the same time in a mysterious way affects the
rest.   But we look in vain for a single well-established instance
of such a belief.

It seems that the importance which savages attach to a
common blood has been much exaggerated.   Clanship is based
on a method of counting descent by means of names, either
through the father or through the mother, but not through
both at once.   This, however, by no means implies that the
other line is not recognised as a line of blood-relationship.   The
paternal system of descent is not necessarily associated with the
idea that the mother has no share in parentage, nor is the
maternal system necessarily associated with unconsciousness of
the child's relation to its father ; [3] even the Couvade, which
assumes the recognition of a most intimate relationship between
the child and its father, has been found to prevail among some
peoples who regard the child as a member of the mother's clan.[4]
Nay, there are instances in which the clan-bond is obviously

[1] Hartland, *Legend of Perseus*, ii.
406.
[2] Frazer, *Golden Bough*, i. 27 *sqq.*
See also Haddon, *Magic and Fetishism*, p. 11 *sq.*
[3] Mr. Swan informs me that the
Waguha of West Tanganyika, among
whom children are generally named
after their father, recognise the part

taken by both parents in generation;
and Archdeacon Hodgson writes the
same concerning certain other tribes
of Eastern Central Africa, who trace
descent through the mother.
[4] Ling Roth, ' Signification of Couvade,' in *Jour. Anthr. Inst.* xxii. 227,
238.

not regarded as a blood-bond at all, in the strict sense of the word. Of some tribes in New South Wales Mr. Cameron tells us that, although a daughter belongs not to her father's clan but to that of her mother's brother, they believe that she emanates from her father solely, being only nurtured by her mother;[1] and the Arunta of Central Australia, who have the paternal system of descent, maintain that a child really descends neither from its father nor from its mother, but is the reincarnation of a mythical totem-ancestor.[2] Their theory is " that the child is not the direct result of intercourse, that it may come without this, which merely, as it were, prepares the mother for the reception and birth also of an already-formed spirit child who inhabits one of the local totem centres " ;[3] and its totem-name, which is derived from the spot where it is supposed to have been conceived,[4] is different from its clan-name. It is useful to scrutinise Mr. Hartland's theory in the light of this class of facts. They evidently prove that clanship and what we are used to call the system of counting " descent," is not necessarily based on the notion of actual blood-relationship, but on kinship as a fact combined with a name ; whereas Mr. Hartland's hypothesis presupposes, not that the members of a clan really are, but that they consider themselves to be all of one blood.

Yet another practice has been adduced as evidence of the supreme importance which the primitive clan is supposed to attach to unity in blood—the so-called blood-covenant. The members of a clan, Mr. Hartland observes, may not be all descended from a common ancestry. Though descent is the normal, the typical cause of kinship and a common blood, kinship may also be acquired. " To acquire kinship, the blood of the candidate for admission into the kin must be mingled with that of the kin. In this way he enters into the brotherhood, is reckoned as of the same stock, obtains the full privileges of a kinsman."[5] As Professor Robertson Smith puts it, " he who has drunk a clansman's blood is no longer a stranger but a brother, and included in the mystic circle of those who have a share in the life-blood that is common to all the clan."[6] Mr. Hartland gives us a short account of the rite :—" It is sufficient that an incision be made in the neophyte's arm and the flowing blood sucked from it by one of the clansmen, upon whom the

[1] Cameron, ' Notes on some Tribes of New South Wales,' in *Jour. Anthr. Inst.* xiv. 352.
[2] Spencer and Gillen, *Native Tribes of Central Australia*, ch. iv. especially pp. 121, 124.
[3] *Ibid.* p. 265.
[4] *Ibid.* p. 124 *sqq.*
[5] Hartland, *op. cit.* ii. 237.
[6] Robertson Smith, *Religion of the Semites*, p. 315.

operation is repeated in turn by the neophyte. Originally, perhaps, the clansmen all assembled and partook of the rite ; but if so, the necessity has ceased to be recognised almost everywhere. The form, indeed, has undergone numberless variations. . . . But, whatever may be the exact form adopted, the essence of the rite is the same, and its range is world-wide." Then there follows a list of peoples from various quarters of the world among whom it is said to prevail.[1]

From this the reader undoubtedly gets the impression that the mingling of blood is a frequently practised ceremony of adoption, by which a person is admitted into a strange clan. But the facts stated by the chief authorities on the subject, to whom Mr. Hartland refers, prove nothing of the kind. In most cases with which we are acquainted the mingling of blood is a form of covenant between individuals, although an engagement with a chief or king naturally embraces his subjects also ; and sometimes the covenanters are tribes or kingdoms. But of the "world-wide" adoption rite there is hardly a single instance which corresponds to Mr. Hartland's description. He admits himself that "in the same measure as the clan relaxed its hold upon the individual members, blood-brotherhood assumed a personal aspect, until, having no longer any social force, it came to be regarded as merely the most solemn and binding form of covenant between man and man."[2] His account of the blood-covenant is, in fact, only an inference based on the assumption that the existing rite is a survival from times when the clan was literally one body and the individual nothing but an amputated limb. But to regard the present blood-covenant as a survival of a previous rite of adoption into the clan is not justified by facts. So far as I know, there is no record of a blood-covenant among savages of the lowest type, unless the aborigines of Australia be included among them ; and in Australia it is certainly not a ceremony of adoption. Among the Arunta it is intended to prevent treachery : "if, for example, an Alice Springs party wanted to go on an avenging expedition to the Burt country, and they had with them in camp a man of that locality, he would be forced to drink blood with them, and, having partaken of it, would be bound not to aid his friends by giving them warning of their danger."[3] This instance is instructive. The Australian native is obliged to help those with whom he has drunk blood against his own relatives, nay, against members of his own totem group. So also " the tie

---

[1] Hartland, *op. cit.* 237 *sqq.*
[2] *Ibid.* ii. 240.

[3] Spencer and Gillen, *Native Tribes of Central Australia*, p. 461.

of blood-covenanting is reckoned in the East even a closer tie than that of natural descent," [1] and the same was the case among the ancient Scandinavians. [2] I do not see how Mr. Hartland's theory can account for this.

Mingling of blood is sometimes supposed to be a direct cause of mutual sympathy and agreement, in accordance with the principle of transmission of properties by contact ; [3] even in Europe there are traces of the belief that a few drops of blood transferred from one person to another inspire the recipient with friendly feelings towards him with whose blood he is inoculated. [4] But the genuine blood-covenant imposes duties on both parties, and also contains the potential punishment for their transgression. It involves a promise, and the transference of blood is vaguely or distinctly supposed to convey to the person who drinks it, or who is inoculated with it, a conditional curse which will injure or destroy him should he break his promise. That this is the main idea underlying the blood-covenant appears from the fact that it is regularly accompanied by curses or self-imprecations. [5] In Madagascar, for instance, when two or more persons have agreed on forming the bond of fraternity, a fowl is procured, its head is nearly cut off, and it is left in this state to continue bleeding during the ceremony. The parties then pronounce a long imprecation and mutual vow over the blood, saying, *inter alia*, "O this miserable fowl weltering in its blood ! thy liver do we eat, thy liver do we eat ; and should either of us retract from the terms of this oath, let him instantly become a fool, let him instantly become blind, let this covenant prove a curse to him." A small portion of blood is then drawn from each individual and drunk by the covenanting parties with execrations of vengeance on each other in case of either violating the sacred oath. [6] According to another description the parties, after they have drunk each other's blood, drink a mixture from the same bowl, praying that it may turn into

Trumbull, *Blood Covenant*, p. 10.

[2] Maurer, *Bekehrung des Norwegischen Stammes*, ii. 171.

[3] *Cf.* Crawley, *Mystic Rose*, p. 236 sq.

[4] von Wlislocki, 'Menschenblut im Glauben der Zigeuner,' in *Am Ur-Quell*, iii. 64. Dörfler, 'Das Blut im magyarischen Volkglauben,' *ibid.* iii. 269 sq.

[5] Forbes, *A Naturalist's Wanderings in the Eastern Archipelago*, p. 452 (natives of Timor). Burns, 'Kayans of the North-West of Borneo,' in *Jour. of the Indian Archipelago*, iii. 146 sq. New, *Life, Wanderings, and Labours in Eastern Africa*, p. 364 (Taveta). Decle, *Three Years in Savage Africa*, p. 494 (Wakamba). Trumbull, *op. cit.* pp. 9, 20, 31, 42, 45–47, 53, 61 sq. For the practice of sealing an agreement by transference of blood accompanied by an oath, see also Partridge, *Cross River Natives*, p. 191 (pagans of Obubura Hill district in Southern Nigeria).

[6] Ellis, *History of Madagascar*, i. 187 sqq.

poison for him who fails to keep the oath.[1] As we have seen
before, blood is commonly regarded as a particularly efficient
conductor of curses, and what could in this respect be more
excellent than the blood of the very person who utters the
curse ?   But the blood of a victim sacrificed on the occasion
may serve the same purpose, or some other suitable vehicle may
be chosen to transfer the imprecation. The Masai in the old
days "spat at a man with whom they swore eternal friendship " ;[2] and the meaning of this seems clear when we heaı
that they spit copiously when cursing, and that " if a man while
cursing spits in his enemy's eyes, blindness is supposed to
follow." [3] The ancient Arabs, besides swearing alliance and protection by dipping their hands in a pan of blood and tasting the
contents, had a covenant known as the *ḥilf al-foḍûl*, which was
made by taking Zemzem water and washing the corners of the
Ka'ba with it, whereafter it was drunk by the parties concerned.[4]
The blood-covenant is essentially based on the same idea
as underlies the Moorish custom of sealing a compact of friendship by a common meal at the tomb of some saint, the meaning
of which is obvious from the phrase that " the food will repay "
him who breaks the compact.[5]

Besides marriage, local proximity, and a common
descent, a common worship may tie people together into

[1] Dumont d'Urville, *Voyage pittoresque autour du monde*, i. 81.

[2] Hinde, *Last of the Masai*, p. 47.
See also Johnston, *Uganda*, ii. 833.

[3] Hinde, *op. cit.* p. 48.

[4] Robertson Smith, *Marriage and
Kinship in Early Arabia*, p. 56 *sqq.*
Cf. Herodotus, iii. 8.

[5] See *supra*, i. 587. According to
another theory the inoculated blood
is regarded as a pledge or deposit,
which compels the person from whom
it was drawn to be faithful to the
person to whom it was transferred.
Suppose that two individuals, A and
B, become "blood-brothers " by
mutual inoculation. Each, then, Mr.
Crawley argues (*Mystic Rose*, p. 236
sq.), has a part of the other in his
keeping, each has " given himself
away " to the other in a very real
sense ; and the possibility of mutual
treachery or wrong is prevented
both by the fact that injury done
to B by A is considered equivalent to
injury done by A to himself, and also
by the belief that if B is wronged he

may work vengeance by injuring the
part of A which he possesses. To this
explanation, however, serious objections may be raised. The belief in
sympathetic magic does not imply
that injury done to B by A is *eo
ipso* supposed to affect A himself
through that part of him which
has been deposited in B ; it does not
imply that two things which have
once been conjoined remain, when
quite dissevered from each other,
in such a relation that "whatever is
done to the one must similarly
affect the other " (Frazer, *Golden
Bough*, i. 49), unless there is an intention to this effect in the agent.
The severed part then serves as a
medium by which magic influence is
transferred to the whole. Again, it is
difficult to see how B could injure
A through the part of him which
he possesses when that part has been
absorbed into his own system, as
must be the case with those few
drops of A's blood with which he
was inoculated.

social union. But among savages a religious community
generally coincides with a community of some other kind.
There are tutelary gods of families, clans, and tribes ;[1]
and a purely local group may also form a religious
community by itself. Major Ellis observes that with
some two or three exceptions all the gods worshipped by
the Tshi-speaking tribes on the Gold Coast are exclusively
local and have a limited area of worship. If they are
nature-gods they are bound up with the natural objects
they animate, if they are ghost-gods they are localised by
the place of sepulture, and if they are tutelary deities
whose origin has been forgotten their position is necessarily
fixed by that of the town, village, or family they protect ;
in any case they are worshipped only by those who live in
the neighbourhood, the only exceptions being the sky-god,
the earthquake-god, and the goddess of the silkcotton
trees, who are worshipped everywhere.[2]

When the religious community is thus at the same time
a family, clan, village, or tribe, it is of course impossible
exactly to distinguish the social influence of the common
religion from that exercised by marriage, local proximity,
or a common descent. It seems, however, that the importance of the religious bond, or at least of the totem bond,
has been somewhat exaggerated by a certain school of
anthropologists. We are told that in early society " each
member of the kin testifies and renews his union with the
rest " by taking part in a sacrificial meal in which the
totem god is eaten by his worshippers.[3] But no satisfactory evidence has ever been given in support of this
theory. Sir J. G. Frazer knows only one certain case of
a totem sacrament, namely, that prevalent among the
Arunta and some other tribes in Central Australia,[4] who
at the time of Intichiuma are in the habit of killing and
eating totem animals ; and this practice has nothing what-

[1] See *infra*, ch. l.
[2] Ellis, *Yoruba-speaking Peoples of the Slave Coast*, p. 284 *sq.* For various instances of village gods see Turner, *Samoa*, p. 18 ; Crozet, *Voyage to Tasmania, &c.* p. 45 (Maoris); Christian, *Caroline Islands*, p. 75 (natives of Ponape); Grierson, *Bihār Peasant Life*, p. 403 *sqq.*
[3] Hartland, *op. cit.* ii. 236.
[4] Frazer, *Golden Bough*, i. p. xix. Cf. *Idem, Totemism and Exogamy*, iv. 230 *sqq.*

ever to do with the mutual relations between kindred. Its object is only to multiply in a magic manner the animals of certain species for the purpose of increasing the food-supply for other totemic groups.[1] In his book on Totemism Frazer writes :—" The totem bond is stronger than the bond of blood or family in the modern sense. This is expressly stated of the clans of western Australia and of north-western America, and is probably true of all societies where totemism exists in full force. Hence in totem tribes every local group, being necessarily composed (owing to exogamy) of members of at least two totem clans, is liable to be dissolved at any moment into its totem elements by the outbreak of a blood feud, in which husband and wife must always (if the feud is between their clans) be arrayed on opposite sides, and in which the children will be arrayed against either their father or their mother, according as descent is traced through the mother, or through the father." [2] In the two or three cases which Frazer quotes in support of his statement [3] the totemic group is identical with the clan ; hence it is impossible to decide whether the strength of the tie which unites its members is due to the totem relationship or to the common descent. But even the combined clan and totem systems seem at most only in exceptional cases to lead to such consequences as are indicated by Frazer's authorities. With reference to the Australian aborigines Mr. Curr observes :—" Of the children of one father being at war with him, or with each other, on the ground of maternal relationship, or any other ground, my inquiries and experience supply no instances. To Captain Grey's statements, indeed, there are several objections." [4]

[1] Spencer and Gillen, *Native Tribes of Central Australia*, ch. vi. *Iidem, Northern Tribes of Central Australia*, ch. ix. *sq.*

[2] Frazer, *Totemism*, p. 57.

[3] Grey, *Journals of Expeditions in North-West and Western Australia*, ii. 230. Petroff, *Report on Alaska*, p. 165. Hardisty, ' Loucheux Indians,'

in *Smithsonian Report*, 1866, p. 315.

[4] Curr, *The Australian Race*, i. 67. In Hardisty's statement, referring to the Loucheux Indians, there is a conspicuous lack of definiteness. He says :—" In war it was not tribe against tribe, but division against division, and as the children were never of the same caste (clan) as the

Among the Arunta and some other Central Australian tribes we have fortunately an opportunity of studying the social influence of totemism apart from that of clanship, the division into totems being quite independent of the clan system. The whole district of a tribe may be mapped out into a large number of areas of various sizes, each of which centres in one or more spots where, in the dim past, certain mythical ancestors are said to have originated or camped during their wanderings, and where their spirits are still supposed to remain, associated with sacred stones, which the ancestors used to carry about with them. From these spirits have sprung, and still continue to spring, actual men and women, the members of the various totems being their reincarnations. At the spots where they remained, the ancestral spirits enter the bodies of women, and in consequence a child must belong to the totem of the spot at which the mother believes that it was conceived. A result of this is that no one totem is confined to the members of a particular clan or sub-clan,[1] and that though most members of a given horde or local group belong to the same totemic group, there is no absolute coincidence between these two kinds of organisation.[2] How, then, does the fact that two persons belong to the same totem influence their social relationships ? " In these tribes," say Messrs. Spencer and Gillen, " there is no such thing as the members of one totem being bound together in such a way that they must combine to fight on behalf of a member of the totem to which they belong. . . . The men to assist a particular man in a quarrel are those of his locality, and not of necessity those of the same totem as himself, indeed the latter consideration does not enter into account and in this as in other matters we see the strong

father, the children would, of course, be against the father and the father against the children. . . . This, however, was not likely to occur very often, as the worst of parents would have naturally preferred peace to war with his own children." Petroff's passage concerning the Thlinkets,

referred to by Sir J.G. Frazer,simply runs :—"The ties of the totem or clanship are considered far stronger than those of blood relationship."

[1] Spencer and Gillen, *Native Tribes of Central Australia*, ch. iv.

[2] *Ibid.* pp. 9, 32, 34.

development of what we have called the ' local influence.'
. . . The men who assist him are his brothers, blood and
tribal, the sons of his mother's brothers, blood and tribal.
That is, if he be a Panunga man he will have the
assistance of the Panunga and Ungalla men of his
locality, while if it comes to a general fight he will have
the help of the whole of his local group. . . . It is only
indeed during the performance of certain ceremonies that
the existence of a mutual relationship, consequent upon
the possession of a common totemic name, stands out at
all prominently. In fact, it is perfectly easy to spend a
considerable time amongst the Arunta tribe without even
being aware that each individual has a totemic name." [1]

When from the savage and barbarous races of men we
pass to peoples of a higher culture, as they first appear to
us in the light of history, we meet among them social
units similar in kind to those prevalent at lower stages of
civilisation : the family, clan, village, tribe. We also find
among them, side by side with the family consisting of
parents and children, a larger family organisation, which,
though not unknown among the lower races, assumes
particular prominence in the archaic State.

In China the family generally remains undivided till
the children of the younger sons are beginning to grow
up. Then the younger branches of the family separate,
and form their own households. But the new house-
holders continue to take part in the ancestral worship of
the old home ; and mourning is worn in theory for four
generations of ascendants and descendants in the direct
line, and for contemporaries descended in the same fifth
generation from the " honoured head " of the family.[2]
At the same time we find in China at least traces of a clan
organisation. Large bodies of persons bear the same
surname, and a penalty is inflicted on anyone who
marries a person with the same surname as his own,
whilst a man is strictly forbidden to nominate as his heir

---

[1] Spencer and Gillen, *Native Tribes of Central Australia*, pp. 34, 544.

[2] Simcox, *Primitive Civilizations*, ii. 303, 493, 69.

an individual of a different surname.[1] Moreover, there
are whole villages composed of relatives all bearing the
same ancestral name. "In many cases," says Mr.
Doolittle, "for a long period of time no division of
inherited property is made in rural districts, the descendants of a common ancestor living or working together,
enjoying and sharing the profits of their labours under the
general direction and supervision of the head of the clan
and the heads of the family branches. . . . There may
be only one head of the clan. Under him there are
several heads of families."[2]

The "four generations" of the Chinese, comprising
those who are regarded as near relatives, have their
counterpart in the family organisation of most so-called
Aryan peoples. The Roman Propinqui—that is, parents
and children, brothers and sisters, uncles and aunts,
nephews and nieces, first cousins (*consobrini*) and second
cousins (*sobrini*)—exactly corresponded to the Anchisteis
of the Greeks, the Sapindas of the Hindus,[3] and the
"Syngeneis" of the Persians.[4] The persons belonging
to these four generations stood in a particularly close
relationship to each other. They had mutual rights
and duties of various kinds. In early times, if one of
them was killed, the survivors had to avenge his death.
They were expected to assist each other whenever it
was needed, especially before the court. They celebrated
in common feasts of rejoicing and feasts for the dead.
They had a common cult and common mourning. In
short, they formed an enlarged family unit of which the
individual families were merely sub-branches, even though

[1] Medhurst, 'Marriage, Affinity,
and Inheritance in China,' in *Trans.
Roy. Asiatic Soc. China Branch*, iv.
21, 22, 29.
[2] Doolittle, *Social Life of the
Chinese*, ii. 225 *sqq.*
[3] *Baudhâyana*, i. 5. 11. 9 :—" The
great-grandfather, the grandfather,
the father, oneself, the uterine brothers, the son by a wife of equal caste,
the grandson, and the great-grandson—these they call Sapindas, but

not the great-grandson's son." *Laws
of Manu*, ix. 186:—"To three ancestors water must be offered, to three
the funeral cake is given, the fourth
descendant is the giver of these
oblations, the fifth has no connection
with them." *Cf.* Jolly, 'Recht und
Sitte,' in Bühler, *Grundriss der indo-
arischen Philologie*, ii. 85.
[4] Brissonius, *De regio Persarum
principatu*, i. 207, p. 279. Leist,
Alt-arisches Jus Civile, i. 47 *sqq.*

they did not necessarily live in the same house.[1] In India we still meet with a perishable survival of this organisation. "In the Joint Family of the Hindus," says Sir Henry Maine, " . . . . the agnatic group of the Romans absolutely survives—or rather, but for the English law and English courts, it would survive. Here there is a real, thoroughly ascertained common ancestor, a genuine consanguinity, a common fund of property, a common dwelling." [2] The Gwentian, Dimetian, and Venedotian codes likewise represent the homestead and land of the free Welshman as a family holding. "So long as the head of the family lived," says Mr. Seebohm, " all his descendants lived with him, apparently in the same homestead, unless new ones had already been built for them on the family land. In any case, they still formed part of the joint household of which he was the head. When a free tribesman, the head of a household, died, his holding was not broken up. It was held by his heirs for three generations as one joint holding." [3]   So also among the subdivisions of ancient Irish society there was one which comprised the " near relatives," the Propinqui of the Romans.[4] Many of the South Slavonians to this day live in house communities each consisting of a body of from ten to sixty members or even more, who are blood-relations to the second or third degree on the male side, and who associate in a common dwelling or group of dwellings, having their land in common, following a common occupation, and being governed by a common chief.[5]   Among the Russians,

---

[1] Klenze, 'Die Cognaten und Affinen nach Römischem Rechte in Vergleichung mit andern verwandten Rechten,' in Zeitschr. f. geschichtliche Rechtswiss. vi. 5 sqq. Leist, Alt-arisches Jus Civile, i. 231 sqq. Rivier, Précis du droit de famille romain, p. 34 sqq.

[2] Maine, Dissertations on Early Law and Custom, p. 240.

[3] Seebohm, English Village Community, p. 193. Idem, Tribal System in Wales, p. 89 sqq.

[4] Maine, Early History of Institutions, p. 90 sq. Leist, Alt-arisches Jus Civile, i. Anhang i.

[5] Krauss, Sitte und Brauch der Südslaven, pp. 75, 79 sqq. Maine, Dissertations on Early Law and Custom, p. 241 sqq. Utiešenović, Die Hauskommunionen der Südslaven, p. 20 sqq. Miler, 'Die Hauskommunion der Südslaven,' in Jahrbuch d. internat. Vereinigung f. vergl. Rechtswiss. iii. 199 sqq.

too, there are households of this kind, containing the representatives of three generations ; and previous to the emancipation of the serfs in 1861 such households were much more common than they are now.[1] The ancient Teutons are the only "Aryan" race among whom the joint family organisation cannot be proved to have prevailed.[2]

Among all these peoples a number of kindred families or joint families were united into a larger social group forming a village community or a cluster of households. The Vedic people called such a body of kindred *janmanā* or simply *grāma*, which means " village " ;[3] and the same organisation still survives in India, though in a modified form. The type of Indian village communities which has been described by Sir Henry Maine is at once an assemblage of co-proprietors and an organised patriarchal society, providing for the management of the common fund and generally also for internal government, police, the administration of justice, and the apportionment of taxes and public duties. Unlike the joint family, the related families of the village community no longer hold their land as an indistinguishable common fund : they have portioned it out, at most they redistribute it periodically, and are thus on the high road to modern landed proprietorship. And whilst the joint family is a narrow circle of persons actually related to each other, the village community has very generally been adulterated by the admission of strangers, especially purchasers of shares, who have from time to time been engrafted on the original stock of blood-relatives. Yet in all such cases there is the assumption of an original common parentage ; hence the Hindu village community of the type indicated, whenever it is not actually an association of kinsmen, is always a body of co-proprietors formed on the model of such an association.[4]

[1] Mackenzie Wallace, *Russia*, i.134. von Hellwald, *Die menschliche Familie*, p. 506 *sq.* Kovalewsky, *Modern Customs and Ancient Laws of Russia*, p. 53 *sq.*
[2] See Leist, *Alt-arisches Jus Civile*, i. Anhang i.
[3] Zimmer, *Altindisches Leben*, p. 159 *sq.*
[4] Maine, *Ancient Law*, p. 260 *sqq.* Idem, *Dissertations on Early Law and Custom*, p. 240. Elphinstone, *His-*

Corresponding to the Vedic *grāma* there were the Iranian *viç*, the Greek *genos*, and the Roman *gens ;* and as among the Vedic people several *grāmas* formed a *viç* and several *viçs* a *jana*,[1] so the Iranian *viç*, the Greek *genos*, and the Roman *gens* were, respectively, subdivisions of a *zantu, phratria*, and *curia* ; and these again were subdivisions of a still more comprehensive unit, a *daqyu, phyle*, and *tribus*.[2] The Roman territory was in earliest times divided into a number of clan-districts, each inhabited by a particular *gens*, which was thus a group associated at once by locality and by a common descent. Whilst each household had its own portion of land, the clan-household or village had a clan-land belonging to it, and this clan-land was managed up to a comparatively late period after the analogy of household-land, that is, on the system of joint-possession, each clan tilling its own land and thereafter distributing the produce among the several households belonging to it. Even the traditions of Roman law furnish the information that wealth consisted at first in cattle and the usufruct of the soil, and that it was not till later that land came to be distributed among the burgesses as their own special property.[3] Still in historical times, if a person left no sons or agnates living at his death, the inheritance escheated to the *gentiles*, or entire body of Roman citizens bearing the same name with the deceased, whereas no part of it was given to any relative united, however closely, with the dead man through female descent.[4] But as the Hindu village community, so also the Roman *gens*, though originally a group of blood-relatives inhabiting a common district, was already in early times recruited from men of alien extraction who were assumed to be descended from a common ancestor. And it is difficult to believe

tory of India, p. 68 *sqq.* Mr. Baden-Powell (*Indian Village Community*, p. 3 *sqq.*) has shown that Sir Henry Maine's general description of Indian village communities holds true only of a certain class of villages in India.
[1] Zimmer, *op. cit.* p. 159 *sq.*

[2] Leist, *Græco-italische Rechtsgeschichte*, p. 104 *sq.*
[3] Mommsen, *History of Rome*, i. 45, 46, 238.
[4] Maine, *Ancient Law*, p. 220 *sq.* Fustel de Coulanges, *La Cité antique*, p. 126.

that either in Rome or Greece even the fiction of a common origin could be preserved for long when the organisation of the people into gentes, phratries, and tribes was adopted by the State as a system of political division and their numbers were fixed.[1] When the *genos* and *gens* first appear to us in history they were mere dwindling survivals, except in one respect : they remained, as they had been from the outset,[2] religious communities long after they had lost all other practical importance. This was especially the case at Athens, where certain reputed gentes for centuries continued to play a prominent part in the religious cult ; [3] and the Romans seem to have preserved their *gentilicia sacra* still in Cicero's time.[4]

In ancient Wales districts were occupied by tribes under their petty kings or chiefs, and the tribe (*cenedl*) was a bundle of kindreds " bound together and interlocked by common interests and frequent intermarriages, as well as by the necessity of mutual protection against foreign foes."[5] A group of households, again, corresponding to the Roman *gens* formed a *trev*, which was a cluster of scattered households, " not necessarily a village in the modern sense." [6] The same seems to have been the case with the Teutonic *vici*, spoken of by Tacitus ;[7] but that among the Teutons, also, the people of the same neighbourhood were blood-relatives may be directly inferred from a statement made by Cæsar.[8] They were not much addicted to agriculture,[9] and " the dreary world " they inhabited, with its desert aspect, its harsh climate, its lack of cultivation, was not

---

[1] Leist, *Græco-italische Rechtsgeschichte*, p. 150 *sqq*. It is expressly said that at Athens the members of the same γένος were not necessarily regarded as blood-relations (see Bunsen, *De jure hereditario Atheniensium*, p. 104, n. 28).

[2] Schoemann, *Griechische Alterthümer*, ii. 548 *sqq*. Marquardt, *Römische Staatsverwaltung*, iii. 126, 130. Fustel de Coulanges, *op. cit.* p. 124 *sqq*.

[3] Leist, *Græco-italische Rechtsgeschichte*, p. 159 *sq*.

[4] Cicero, *Pro domo*, 13 (34).

[5] Seebohm, *English Village Community*, p. 190. *Idem, Tribal System in Wales*, p. 61.

[6] *Idem, English Village Community*, p. 343.

[7] Tacitus, *Germania*, 16. Cf. Hildebrand, *op. cit.* p. 105 *sqq*.

[8] Cæsar, *De bello Gallico*, vi. 22 :— " Magistratus ac princeps in annos singulos gentibus cognationibusque hominum, qui una coierint, quantum, et quo loco visum est, agri attribuunt."

[9] *Ibid.* vi. 22.

favourable to the formation of permanent large social
bodies of great cohesiveness. However, we meet among
them social units which Cæsar calls *regiones* or *pagi*,[1] of
which the *vici* may be assumed to have been subdivisions.
Among the highly agricultural Slavonians, on the other
hand, we find even in the present time a social organisation very similar to that of the Hindus. The South
Slavonians, as we have seen, live in house communities
corresponding to the joint families in India. Now, when
the members of a house community, or *zadruga*—as it is
often called—become too numerous, a separation takes
place, and the emigrants form new households by themselves. A *zadruga* is thus gradually expanded into a
bratstvo, or brotherhood—a group of related house communities which not only feel themselves as branches of
the same stock, but still have certain practical interests in
common and a common chief. Several *bratstva*, finally,
form a *pleme*, or tribe.[2] Among the Russians, again, the
family, or joint family, has developed into a *mir*, or village
community, composed of an assemblage of separate houses
each ruled by its own head, but with a common village
chief elected by the heads of the various households. The
Russian *mir* is an institution very similar to the Hindu
village community described above. The land belongs
to the community, and in earlier days it was probably
cultivated in common. At present it is divided between
the component families, the lots shifting among them
periodically, or perhaps vesting in them as their property,
but always subject to a power in the collective body of
villagers to veto its sale. Originally the *mir* was also a
group of kindred ; but, as in the Hindu village community, the tie of blood has been greatly weakened by all
sorts of fictions and the admission of so many strangers
that the tradition of a common origin is dim or lost.[3]

In the social organisation of all these peoples there is

[1] Cæsar, *De bello Gallico*, vi. 23.
[2] Krauss, *op. cit.* pp. 2, 32 *sqq.*
von Hellwald, *op. cit.* p. 502 *sq.*
Grosse, *op. cit.* p. 204 *sq.*
[3] de Laveleye, *De la propriété*, p.
12 *sqq.* Maine, *Dissertations on
Early Law and Custom*, p. 261 *sq.*

thus originally a general congruity between the principle of local proximity and the principle of descent. On the one hand, all freemen, all true members of the society, who belong to the same local group, are at the same time kinsmen ; on the other hand, all persons who are united by the tie of a common descent belong to the same or neighbouring local groups. The cause of this congruity is the universal prevalence of the paternal system of descent. Whether the case was different in prehistoric times is an open question. That the ancient Chinese reckoned kinship through the mother, not through the father, has been conjectured on philological grounds,[1] as to the plausibility of which I can express no opinion. Several writers have also endeavoured to prove that the uterine line of descent prevailed among the primitive Aryans, but the evidence is far from being conclusive. I agree with Professor Leist that all so-called survivals of a system of maternal descent in the prehistoric antiquity of the " Aryan " races are doubtful, if not false.[2] As regards the Teutons, much importance has been attributed to the specially close connection which, according to Tacitus, existed between a sister's children and their mother's brothers ;[3] but, as Professor Schrader remarks, in spite of the prominent position of the maternal uncle among Teutonic peoples, the *patruus* distinctly came before the *avunculus*, the agnates before the cognates, in testamentary succession.[4] The existence of a custom which in some respect recognises uterine relationship does not prove the earlier prevalence of the full maternal system of descent, to the exclusion of the paternal.

Progress in civilisation is up to a certain point connected with social expansion. Among savages the largest permanent social unit is generally the tribe, and even the tribal bond is often very loose, if not entirely wanting. It is true that associations of tribes occur even among so

[1] Puini, quoted by Grosse, *op. cit.* p. 193.
[2] Leist, *Alt-arisches Jus Gentium*, p. 58. *Idem, Alt-arisches Jus Civile*, i. 490.
[3] Tacitus, *Germania*, 20.
[4] Schrader, *Prehistoric Antiquities of the Aryan Peoples*, p. 395.

low a race as the Australian aborigines, but unaccompanied by any kind of political organisation.[1] At a somewhat higher stage we meet with the famous league of the Iroquois—a federation on republican principles of five distinct tribes, which could point to three centuries of uninterrupted domestic unity and peace [2]—and the kingdoms of various African potentates. Civilisation only thrives in states. From small beginnings round the lake of Mexico the Aztecs gradually succeeded, through conquest, in forming an empire which covered probably almost sixteen thousand square leagues. However, between the various tribes lay broad belts of uninhabited territory, which enabled them to keep up a shy and exclusive attitude towards each other ; and at the time of the Spanish conquest the empire of Mexico was, in fact, little more than " a chain of intimidated Indian tribes, who, kept apart from each other under the influence of mutual timidity, were held down by dread of attacks from an unassailable robber-stronghold in their midst." [3] In South America, in a long course of ages, six nations inhabited the region which extends from the water-parting between the basins of the Huallaga and Ucayali to that between the basins of the Ucayali and Lake Titicaca. When increasing population brought them in contact with each other, a struggle for supremacy ended in the mastery of the fittest—the Incas ; and the empire of the latter was subsequently extended by the subjugation of a variety of other nations or tribes.[4] The extent of territory claimed for ancient China by the earliest records is more than double the size of modern France, and, though it was often divided into different states, the great dynasties ruled over the whole of it.[5] The two crowns of Upper and Lower Egypt were united at a

---

[1] Curr, *The Australian Race*, i. 62 *sq.*
[2] Morgan, *League of the Iroquois*, p. 141.
[3] Scheppig, 'Ancient Mexicans,' &c. p. 6, in Spencer's *Descriptive Sociology*. Prescott, *History of the* *Conquest of Mexico*, p. 4. Ratzel, *History of Mankind*, ii. 199, 202.
[4] Markham, 'Geographical Positions of the Tribes which formed the Empire of the Yncas,' in *Jour. Roy. Geo. Soc.* xli. 287 *sqq.*
[5] Simcox, *op. cit.* ii. 10, 13.

very early date ; and no less imposing was the great kingdom of Babylon and Assur. We may assume that all
these empires were formed by an association, either
voluntary or forcible, of different tribes, as was the case
with those states with whose origin and early growth we
are somewhat better acquainted. As late as the time of
the Judges the tribes of Israel either stood each entirely
alone or formed smaller groups, and there was no such
thing as an Israelitish nation in a political sense until the
unity of the people came into being under Samuel and the
first kings.[1] The Vedic people consisted of a great
number of independent tribes, between which only
temporary alliances were made for the sake of defence or
attack. But gradually the alliances grew more permanent ;
war-kings united several tribes, surrounded themselves
with a military nobility, and founded great kingdoms.[2]
In Greece and Italy the states grew out of forts which had
been built on elevated places to serve as common strong-
holds or places of refuge in case of war. Several tribes
united so as to be better able to resist dangerous enemies,
and one of the fortified towns in time gained supremacy
over all others in the neighbourhood, as Athens did in
Attica and Alba Longa in Latium. Similar districts, ruled
by a town, were called *poleis* or *civitates*.[3] In historical
times attempts were made to carry this process further by
joining several of the small states under the rule of one.
In this Sparta and Athens failed, whereas the efforts of
Rome met with unequalled success.

The development of the State tended to weaken or
destroy the smaller units of which it was composed. The
central power, hostile to separatism, naturally endeavoured
to appropriate the authority invested in the latter, and in
a well-governed state these on their part had little reason
to resist. The main object of the clan, phratry, and tribe
was to protect their respective members ; hence they
became superfluous in the presence of a powerful national

[1] Kuenen, *Religion of Israel*, i. 133.   [3] Leist, *Græco-italische Rechtsge-*
[2] Zimmer, *Altindisches Leben*, pp.   *schichte*, p. 109 *sqq.*
158, 192 *sq.*

government which unselfishly and impartially looked after the interests of its various subjects. Adam Smith contrasts the strong clan-feeling which still in the eighteenth century prevailed among the Scotch Highlanders with the little regard felt for remote relatives by the English, and observes that in countries where the authority of the law is not sufficiently strong to give security to every member of the State the different branches of the same family choose to live in the neighbourhood of one another, their association being frequently necessary for their common defence ; whereas in a country like England, where the authority of the law was well established, " the descendants of the same family, having no such motive for keeping together, naturally separate and disperse, as interest or inclination may direct." [1] It seems also probable that the persistency of the village community or the gentile system among the Hindus and Slavs has been largely due to the weakness of the State or to the badness of the government.

As the larger units, so the family also was influenced by the rise of the State, but originally in quite the opposite direction. Whilst the former dwindled away, the family grew in importance. Nowhere do we find the family-tie stronger, nowhere does the father or eldest male ascendant possess greater power than in the archaic State. In a previous chapter I have already tried to explain this singular fact. I pointed out that in early society there seems to be a certain antagonism between the family and the clan, that the family was strengthened because the clan was weakened, that the father became a patriarch only as the inheritor of the authority which formerly belonged to the clan. But we have also noticed that at a higher stage the family again lost in importance. [2]

It seems that the tribes which united into one nation or state were normally, in the first instance, branches of the same stock, living in the same neighbourhood and speaking

[1] Smith, *Theory of Moral Sentiments*, p. 326 *sq.*   [2] *Supra*, i. 627 *sq.*

the same language, though with dialectic differences. Like the smaller units, such a state was no doubt frequently adulterated by the amalgamation of aliens, but here again fictions were substituted for realities, and the foreign extraction was forgotten. The case was different, however, when the commonwealth was formed or aggrandised by the subjugation of a strange race. Instead of being adopted into the circle of the conquerors, the subdued people were treated as their inferiors in blood, civic rights were denied to them, and in many cases they were kept in servitude ; thus even here the principle of a common origin as the base of citizenship was preserved, the conquerors being the only citizens in the full sense of the term. But however strong and durable similar barriers may be, they are not imperishable. The different races inhabiting the same country under the same government tend to draw nearer each other, the inferior race is incorporated with the nation, and local proximity instead of descent at last becomes the basis of community in political functions. This change, however, was neither so radical nor so startling as it has been represented to be ; [1] fictions on a large scale still formed a bridge between ancient and modern ideas. Sir Henry Maine says that we cannot now hope to understand the good faith of the fiction by which in early times the incoming population were assumed to be descended from the same stock as the people on whom they were engrafted.[2] But is this good faith more astonishing than the readiness with which a common language, in spite of the most obvious facts to the contrary, is even now constantly taken as the sign of a common origin ? Though identity of language, even in the case of whole peoples, proves nothing more than contact or neighbourhood, a person's mother-tongue popularly decides his race, and language and nationality are regarded almost as synonymous. Genealogical fictions, then, are not merely a thing of the past, nor have they ceased to influence political ideas. The modern theory of

[1] Maine, *Ancient Law*, p. 129.   [2] *Ibid.* p. 131.

nationalism vindicates the right of the strongest nationality to absorb the other nationalities living within the
same state by a method of compulsory engraftment, and
this can be effected only by their accepting its language.
But this theory is not so much concerned with language
as such, as with language as an emblem of nationality.
At the bottom of it is the narrow feeling of racial intolerance, quite ready however to be appeased by a fiction.
The doctrine of nationalism is the spectre of the same
political principle—the principle of a common descent,
either real or fictitious—on which states were founded
and governed when civilisation was in its cradle.

Like the smaller units, the archaic State was not
only a political but at the same time a religious community. Over and above all separate cults there was
one religion common to all its citizens. In ancient
Mexico and Peru it was the religion of the dominant
people, the worship of the god of war or of the sun ;
and the sovereigns themselves were regarded as incarnations or children of this god.[1] In other cases the state
religion arose by a fusion of different cults. The gods
of the communities which united into a state not only
continued to receive the worship of their old believers,
but were elevated to the rank of national deities, and
formed together a heavenly commonwealth to which the
earthly commonwealth jointly paid its homage. In this
way, it seems, the Roman,[2] Egyptian,[3] Assyrian, and
Babylonian [4] pantheons were recruited ; whilst the Greeks
went a step further and, already in prehistoric times,
constructed a Pan-Hellenic Olympus.[5] Sometimes also,
as Professor Robertson Smith points out, different gods
were themselves fused into one, as when the mass of the
Israelites in their local worship of Yahveh identified him
with the Baalim of the Canaanite high places, and carried

---

[1] Ratzel, *op. cit.* ii. 199 *sq.* Markham, *History of Peru*, p. 23.
[2] *Cf.* von Jhering, *Geist des römischen Rechts*, i. 269.
[3] Wiedemann, *Religion of the Ancient Egyptians*, p. 148.

[4] Mürdter-Delitzsch, *Geschichte
Babyloniens und Assyriens*, p. 24.
Robertson Smith, *Religion of the
Semites*, p. 39.
[5] *Cf.* Rohde, *Psyche*, p. 36.

over into his worship the ritual of the Canaanite shrines, not deeming that in so doing they were less truly Yahveh-worshippers than before.[1]

Nobody will deny that the common religion added strength to the State, but it seems that its national importance has often been overrated. On the one hand, the political fusion between different communities took place before the religious fusion and was obviously the cause of it ; on the other hand, the mere tie of a common religion has never proved sufficient to bind together neighbouring tribes or peoples so as to form one nation. The Greek states had both the same religion and the same language, but nevertheless remained distinct states. Professor Seeley's assertion that " in the East to this day nationality and religion are almost convertible terms,"[2] is very far from the truth. Wallin, who had exceptional opportunities to study the feelings of different Muhammedan nationalities, observes that " every Oriental people has a certain national aversion to every other, and even the inhabitants of one province to those of another. The Turk does not readily tolerate the Arab, nor the Persian, and these feel similarly towards the Turk ; the Arab does not get on well with the Persian, nor the Persian with the Arab ; the Syrian does not like the Egyptian, whom he calls inhuman, and the latter does not willingly associate with the Syrian, whom he calls simple-minded and stupid ; and the son of the desert condemns both."[3] It sometimes seems as if the national spirit of a people rather influenced its religion than was influenced by it. Patriotism has even succeeded in nationalising the greatest enemy of nationalities, Christianity, and has well nigh revived the old notion of a national god, whose chief business is to look after his own people and, especially, to fight its battles.

It is obvious that the various aspects of social develop-

---

[1] Robertson Smith, *op. cit.* p. 38.   [3] Wallin, *Anteckningar från*
[2] Seeley, *Natural Religion,* p. 229.   *Orienten,* iv. 181 *sq.*

ment which we have now considered have exercised much influence upon the altruistic sentiment. The combination of local proximity and political unity, the notion of a common descent, and the fellowship of a common religion, tend to engender friendly feelings between the members of each respective group. Hence, when the political unit grew larger, when the idea of kinship developed into that of racial affinity, and when the same religion became common to all the citizens of the State, or, as happened in several cases, extended beyond the limits of any particular country or nation, the altruistic sentiment underwent a corresponding expansion—unless, of course, it was checked by some rival influence. The increasing coherence of the political aggregate, again, added to the strength of this sentiment ; and so did the antagonism towards foreign communities and the natural antipathy or hatred to their members. As people like that to which they are used or which is their own, they dislike that which is strange or unfamiliar. Among ourselves we notice this particularly in children [1] and uneducated persons, whose anger may be aroused by the sight of a black skin or an oriental dress or the sounds of a strange language. Antipathies of this kind have directly influenced the moral valuation of conduct towards foreigners ; but at the same time they have also strengthened the feelings of mutual goodwill between tribesmen or compatriots. For likes and dislikes are increased by the contrast ; to hate a thing makes us better love its opposite. So also the competition and enmity which prevail between different communities tend within each community to intensify its members' devotion to the common goal and their friendly feelings towards one another.

But the altruistic sentiment has not necessarily reference only to individuals belonging to the same social unit.

---

[1] Compayré, *op. cit.* p. 100 :— " Tout ce qui est inattendu, imprévu, est insupportable à l'enfant, et provoque soit la peur, soit plus tard la colère. J'ai vu un de mes fils, à quatre ans et demi, entrer dans de véritables rages, toutes les fois que je lui parlais dans le patois de mon pays."

Gregarious animals may be kindly disposed to any member of their species which is not an object of their anger or their fear. Savages have shown themselves capable of tender feelings towards suffering and harmless strangers.[1] The sensibility of little children sometimes goes beyond the circle of the family ; Madame Manacéine tells us of a girl two years old who, in the Zoological Gardens at St. Petersburg, began to cry bitterly when she saw an elephant walking over the keeper's body, although the other spectators were quietly watching the trick.[2] In mankind altruism has been narrowed by social isolation, by differences in race, language, habits, and customs, by enmity and suspicion. But increased intercourse has gradually led to conditions favourable to its expansion. As Buckle remarks, ignorance is the most powerful of all the causes of national hatred ; " when you increase the contact, you remove the ignorance, and thus you diminish the hatred." [3] People of different nationalities feel that in spite of all dissimilarities between them there is much that they have in common ; and frequent intercourse makes the differences less marked, or obliterates many of them altogether. There can be no doubt that this process will go on in the future. And equally certain it is that similar causes will produce similar effects—that altruism will continue to expand, and that the notion of a human brotherhood will receive more support from the actual feelings of mankind than it does at present.

[1] See *supra*, i. 570–572, 581. See also Compayré, *op. cit.* p. 323.
[2] Manacéine, *Le surmenage mental dans la civilisation moderne*, p. 248. [3] Buckle, *History of Civilization in England*, i. 222

CHAPTER XXXV

SUICIDE

IN previous chapters we have discussed the moral valuation of acts, forbearances, and omissions, which directly concern the interests of other men ; we shall now proceed to consider moral ideas regarding such modes of conduct as chiefly concern a man's own welfare. Among these we notice, in the first place, acts affecting his existence.

Suicide, or intentional self-destruction, has often been represented as a fruit of a higher civilisation ; Dr. Steinmetz, on the other hand, in his essay on ' Suicide among Primitive Peoples,' thinks it probable that " there is a greater propensity to suicide among savage than among civilised peoples." [1] The former view is obviously erroneous ; the latter probably holds good of certain savages as compared with certain peoples of culture, but cannot claim general validity.

Among several uncivilised races suicide is said to be unknown.[2] To these belong some of the lower savages—the Yahgans of Tierra del Fuego,[3] the Andaman Islanders,[4]

[1] Steinmetz,' Suicide among Primitive Peoples,' in *American Anthropologist*, vii. 60.
[2] Paulitschke, *Ethnographie Nordost-Afrikas*, p. 205 (Danakil and Galla). Munzinger, *Ostafrikanische Studien*, p. 532 (Barea and Kunáma). New, *Life, Wanderings, and Labours in Eastern Africa*, p. 99 (Wanika).

Felkin, ' Notes on the For Tribe of Central Africa,' in *Proceed. Roy. Soc. Edinburgh*, xiii. 231. Lumholtz (*Unknown Mexico*, i. 243) thinks it is doubtful whether a pagan Tarahumare ever killed himself.
[3] Bridge, in *South American Missionary Magazine*, xiii. 211.
[4] Man, *Jour. Anthr. Inst.* xii. 111.

and various Australian tribes ;[1] whilst as regards most other tribes at about the same stage of culture information seems to be wanting. Of the natives in Western and Central Australia Sir G. Grey writes, " Whenever I have interrogated them on this point, they have invariably laughed at me, and treated my question as a joke."[2] When a Caroline Islander was told of suicides committed by Europeans, he thought that he had not grasped what was said to him, as he never in his life had heard of anything so ridiculous.[3] The Káfirs of the Hindu-Kush, though they have no intense fear of death, cannot understand suicide ; " the idea of a man killing himself strikes them as inexplicable."[4]

Among many savages and barbarians suicide is stated to be very rare,[5] or to occur only occasionally ;[6] whereas

[1] Grey, *Expeditions of Discovery in North-West and Western Australia*, ii. 248. Curr, *Recollections of Squatting in Victoria*, p. 277 (Bangerang). Among the tribes of Western Victoria described by Mr. Dawson (*Australian Aborigines*, p. 62) suicide is not unknown, though it is uncommon ; " if a native wishes to die, and cannot get any one to kill him, he will sometimes put himself in the way of a venomous snake, that he may be bitten by it."

[2] Grey, *op. cit.* ii. 248.

[3] von Kotzebue, *Voyage of Discovery into the South Sea*, iii. 195.

[4] Scott Robertson, *Káfirs of the Hindu-Kush*, p. 381.

[5] Nansen, *Eskimo Life*, p. 267 (Greenlanders). Murdoch, ' Ethnol. Results of the Point Barrow Expedition,' in *Ann. Rep. Bur. Ethn.* ix. 41 (Point Barrow Eskimo). von Siebold, *Die Aino auf der Insel Yesso*, p. 35. von Stenin, ' Die Kirgisen des Kreises Saissansk im Gebiete von Ssemipalatinsk,' in *Globus*, lxix. 230. Beltrame, *Il Fiume Bianco*, p. 51 (Arabs). Felkin, ' Waganda Tribe of Central Africa,' in *Proceed. Roy. Soc. Edinburgh*, xiii. 723. Schwarz, quoted by Steinmetz, *Rechtsverhältnisse*, p. 24 (Bakwiri). *Ibid.* p. 52 (Banaka and Bapuku). Wandrer, *ibid.* p. 325 (Hottentots). Fritsch,

Die Eingeborenen Süd-Afrika's, p. 221 (Bantu race). Sorge, in Steinmetz, *Rechtsverhältnisse*, p. 421 (Nissan Islanders in the Bismarck Archipelago). Kubary, ' Die Verbrechen und das Strafverfahren auf den Pelau-Inseln,' in *Original-Mittheilungen aus der ethnol. Abtheil. d. königl. Museen zu Berlin*, i.78 (Pelew Islanders). Among the Malays suicide is reported to be extremely rare (Brooke, *Ten Years in Saráwak*, i. 56 ; Ellis, ' The Amok of the Malays,' in *Journal of Mental Science*, xxxix. 331) ; but Dr. Gilmore Ellis has been told by many Malays that they consider Amok a kind of suicide. If a man wishes to die, he " amoks " in the hope of being killed, rather than kills himself, suicide being a most heinous sin according to the ethics of Muhammedanism (*ibid.* p. 331). In Siam suicide is rare (Bowring, *Siam*, i. 106). Of the Western Islanders of Torres Straits Dr. Haddon says (in *Reports of the Cambridge Anthrop. Expedition to Torres Straits*, v. 278) that he does not remember to have heard of a case of suicide in real life, though there are some instances of it in their folk-tales.

[6] Comte, quoted by Mouhot, *Travels in the Central Parts of Indo-China*, ii. 27 *sq.* (Bannavs in Cam-

among others it is represented as either common or extremely prevalent.[1] Of the Kamchadales we are told that the least apprehension of danger drives them to despair, and that they fly to suicide as a relief, not only from present, but even from imaginary evil ; " not only those who are confined for some offence, but such as are discontented with their lot, prefer a voluntary death to an uneasy life, and the pains of disease." [2] Among the Hos, an Indian hill tribe, suicide is reported to be so frightfully prevalent as to afford no parallel in any known country : —" If a girl appears mortified by anything that has been said, it is not safe to let her go away till she is soothed. A reflection on a man's honesty or veracity may be sufficient to send him to self-destruction. In a recent case, a young woman attempted to poison herself because her uncle would not partake of the food she had cooked for him." [3] Among the Karens of Burma suicide is likewise very common where Christianity has not been introduced. If a man has some incurable or painful disease, he says in a matter-of-fact way that he will hang himself, and he does as he says ; if a girl's parents compel her to marry the man she does not love, she hangs herself ; wives sometimes hang themselves through jealousy, sometimes because they quarrel with their husbands, and sometimes out of mere

bodia). Kloss, *In the Andamans and Nicobars*, p. 316 (Nicobarese). Among the Bakongo cases of suicide occur, "although much less frequently than in civilised countries " (Ward, *Five Years with the Congo Cannibals*, p. 45).
[1] Veniaminof, quoted by Petroff, *Report on Alaska*, p. 158 (Atkha Aleuts). Steller, *Beschreibung von Kamtschatka*, p. 293 *sq.*; Krasheninnikoff, *History of Kamschatka*, pp. 176, 200. Georgi, *Russia*, iii. 133 *sq.* (Kamchadales), 184 (Chukchi), 205 (Aleuts). Brooke, *op. cit.* i. 55 (Sea Dyaks). Williams and Calvert, *Fiji*, p. 106. Turner, *Samoa*, p. 305 ; Tregear, 'Niue,' in *Jour. Polynesian Soc.* ii. 14 ; Thomson, *Savage Island*, p. 109 ; Hood, *Cruise in the Western Pacific*, p. 22 (Savage Islanders).

Dieffenbach, *Travels in New Zealand*, ii. 111 *sq.*; Collins, *English Colony in New South Wales*, i. 524 (Maoris). Reade, *Savage Africa*, p. 553 *sq.*; *Idem*, quoted by Darwin, *Descent of Man*, p. 117, n. 33 (West African Negroes). Monrad, *Skildring af Guinea-Kysten*, p. 23. Decle, *Three Years in Savage Africa*, p. 74 (Barotse). In Tana, of the New Hebrides (Gray, in *Jour. Anthr. Inst.* xxviii. 132) and Nias (Rosenberg, *Der malayische Archipel*, p. 146) suicides are said to be not infrequent.
[2] Georgi, *op. cit.* iii. 133 *sq.* Cf. Krasheninnikoff, *op. cit.* p. 176.
[3] Tickell, ' Memoir on the Hodésum,' in *Jour. Asiatic Soc. Bengal*, ix. 807. Dalton, *Descriptive Ethnology of Bengal*, p. 206.

chagrin, because they are subject to depreciating comparisons ; and it is a favourite threat with a wife or daughter, when not allowed to have her own way, that she will hang herself.[1] Among some uncivilised peoples suicide is frequently practised by women, though rarely by men.[2]

The causes which, among savages, lead to suicide are manifold :—disappointed love or jealousy ; [3] illness [4] or old age ;[5] grief over the death of a child,[6] a husband,[7] or a

[1] Mason, ' Dwellings, &c., of the Karens,' in *Jour. Asiatic Soc. Bengal*, xxxvii. pt. ii. 141.

[2] Keating, *Expedition to the Source of St. Peter's River*, i. 394 (Dacotahs); ii. 171 *sq.* (Chippewas). Bradbury, *Travels in the Interior of America*, p. 87 (Dacotahs). Brooke Low, quoted by Ling Roth, *Natives of Sarawak*, i. 117 (Sea Dyaks). Munzinger, *Die Sitten und das Recht der Bogos*, p. 93.

[3] Lasch, ' Der Selbstmord aus erotischen Motiven bei den primitiven Völkern,' in *Zeitschrift für Socialwissenschaft*, ii. 579 *sqq.* Westermarck, *History of Human Marriage*, p. 503. Keating, *op. cit.* ii. 172 (Chippewas). Eastman, *Dacotah*, pp. 89 *sqq.*, 168 *sq.* ; Dodge, *Our Wild Indians*, p. 321 *sq.* (Dacotahs). Turner, ' Ethnology of the Ungava District, Hudson Bay Territory,' in *Ann. Rep. Bur. Ethn.* xi. 187 (Koksoagmyut). Mason, in *Jour. Asiatic Soc. Bengal*, xxxvii. pt. ii. 141 (Karens). Brooke Low, quoted by Ling Roth, *Natives of Sarawak*, i. 115 (Sea Dyaks). Kubary, 'Religion der Pelauer,' in Bastian, *Allerlei aus Volks- und Menschenkunde*, i. 3 (Pelew Islanders). Senfft, in Steinmetz, *Rechtsverhältnisse*, p. 452 (Marshall Islanders). Codrington, *Melanesians*, p. 243 *sq.* (natives of the Banks' Islands and Northern New Hebrides). Waitz, *Anthropologie der Naturvölker*, vi. 115 ; Malone, *Three Years' Cruise in the Australasian Colonies*, p. 72 *sq.* (Maoris). Reade, *Savage Africa*, p. 554 (West African Negroes). Munzinger, *Die Sitten und das Recht der Bogos*, p. 93 *sq.*

[4] Dodge, *op. cit.* p. 321 *sq.* (North American Indians). Holm, ' Ethno-

logisk Skizze af Angmagsalikerne,' in *Meddelelser om Grönland*, x. 181 (Angmagsaliks of Eastern Greenland). Georgi, *op. cit.* iii. 134 (Kamchadales). Mason, in *Jour. Asiatic Soc. Bengal*, xxxvii. pt. ii. 141 (Karens). Gray, in *Jour. Anthr. Inst.* xxviii. 132 (natives of Tana, New Hebrides). Sartori, ' Die Sitte der Alten- und Krankentötung,' in *Globus*, lxvii. 109 *sq.*

[5] Perrin du Lac, *Voyage dans les deux Louisianes*, p. 346. Nansen, *First Crossing of Greenland*, ii. 331 ; Idem, *Eskimo Life*, pp. 170, 267 (Greenlanders). Steller, *Beschreibung von Kamtschatka*, p. 294. Wilkes, *U.S. Exploring Expedition*, iii. 96 ; Hale, *U.S. Exploring Expedition. Vol. VI. Ethnography and Philology*, p. 65 (Fijians). Diodorus Siculus, *Bibliotheca historica*, iii. 33.5 (Troglodytes). Pomponius Mela, *De situ orbis*, iii. 7 (Seres). Hartknoch, *Alt- und Neues Preussen*, i. 181 (ancient Prussians). Mareschalcus, *Annales Herulorum ac Vandalorum*, i. 8 (*Monumenta inedita rerum Germanicarum*, i. 191) ; Procopius, *De bello Gothico*, ii. 14 (Heruli). Maurer, *Die Bekehrung des Norwegischen Stammes zum Christenthume*, ii. 79, n. 48 (ancient Scandinavians).

[6] Veniaminof, quoted by Petroff, *op. cit.* p. 158 (Atkha Aleuts). Keating, *op. cit.* ii. 172 (Chippewas). Colenso, *Maori Races*, pp. 46, 57 ; Dieffenbach, *op. cit.* ii. 112 (Maoris).

[7] Veniaminof, quoted by Petroff, *op. cit.* p. 158 (Atkha Aleuts). Haddon, in *Rep. Cambridge Anthr. Exped. to Torres Straits*, v. 17 (Western Islanders, according to a Kauralaig folk-tale). Colenso, *op. cit.* pp. 46, 57 ; Dieffenbach, *op. cit.* ii. 112 (Maoris).

wife ;[1] fear of punishment ;[2] slavery[3] or brutal treatment by a husband ;[4] remorse,[5] shame or wounded
pride, anger or revenge.[6] In various cases an offended
person kills himself for the express purpose of taking
revenge upon the offender.[7] Thus among the Tshi-
speaking peoples of the Gold Coast, "should a person
commit suicide, and before so doing attribute the act to
the conduct of another person, that other person is
required by native law to undergo a like fate. The practice
is termed 'killing oneself upon the head of another,' and
the person whose conduct is supposed to have driven the
suicide to commit the rash act is visited with a death of an
exactly similar nature "—unless, indeed, the family of the
suicide be pacified with a money compensation.[8] With
reference to the Savage Islanders, who especially in heathen

[1] Veniaminof, quoted by Petroff,
op. cit. p. 158 (Atkha Aleuts). Fawcett, *Saoras*, p. 17. Dieffenbach, *op.
cit.* ii. 112 (Maoris).

[2] Steller, *Beschreibung von Kamtschatka*, p. 293. Dieffenbach, *op. cit.*
ii. 112 (Maoris).

[3] Modigliani, *Viaggio a Nías*, p.
473. Decle, *op. cit.* p. 74 (Barotse).
Monrad, *op. cit.* p. 25 (Negroes of
Accra). Donne, *Biathanatos*, p. 56
(American Indians).

[4] Wied-Neuwied, *Travels in the
Interior of North America*, p. 349
(Mandans).

[5] Turner, in *Ann. Rep. Bur. Ethn.*
xi. 187 (Koksoagmyut). Mr. Dawson
(*Australian Aborigines*, p. 62 *sq.*)
tells us of a native of Western Victoria who decided to commit suicide
because, being intoxicated, he had
killed his wife, and was so sorry for
it. He besought the tribe to kill him,
and seeing his determination to
starve himself to death, his friends
at last sent for the tribal executioner,
who pushed a spear through him.

[6] Veniaminof, quoted by Petroff,
op. cit. p. 158 (Atkha Aleuts). Keat-
ing, *op. cit.* ii. 171 (Chippewas).
Dalton, *op. cit.* p. 206; Jickell, in
Jour. Asiatic Soc. Bengal, ix. 807
(Hos). Colquhoun, *Amongst the
Shans*, p. 76 *sq.* (Lethtas). Mac
Mahon, *Far Cathay*, p. 241 (Tarus,
one of the Chino-Burmese border

tribes). Brooke, *op. cit.* i. 55 (Sea
Dyaks). Chalmers, *Pioneer Life and
Work in New Guinea*, p. 227 (a
woman at Port Moresby ; Mr. Abel
[*Savage Life in New Guinea*, p. 102]
speaks of a New Guinea woman who
was so annoyed because her old
village friends had not visited her
during her illness that she attempted
to commit suicide). Codrington, *op.
cit.* p. 243 *sq.* (natives of the Banks'
Islands and Northern New Hebrides).
Williams and Calvert, *op. cit.* p. 106
(Fijians). Tregear, in *Jour. Poly-
nesian Soc.* ii. 14 (Savage Islanders).
Dieffenbach, *op. cit.* ii. 111 sq. ;
Collins, *op. cit.* i. 524 ; Angas, *Savage
Life in Australia and New Zealand*,
ii. 45 ; Colenso, *op. cit.* p. 56 *sq.*
(Maoris). Ward, *Five Years with the
Congo Cannibals*, p. 45 (Bakongo).
Lasch, 'Besitzen die Naturvölker
ein persönliches Ehrgefühl?' in *Zeit-
schr. f. Socialwissenschaft*, iii. 837 *sqq.*

[7] See Lasch, 'Rache als Selbstmordmotiv,' in *Globus*, lxxiv. 37 *sqq.* ;
Steinmetz, 'Gli antichi scongiuri
giuridici contro i creditori,' in *Rivista italiana di sociologia*, ii. 49 *sqq.*

[8] Ellis, *Tshi-speaking Peoples of the
Gold Coast*, p. 302. The same custom
is mentioned by Monrad (*op. cit.* p.
23 *sq.*), Bowdich (*Mission to Ashantee*, pp. 256, 257, 259 n. ‡), and
Reade (*Savage Africa*, p. 554).

times were much addicted to suicide, we are told that, " like angry children, they are tempted to avenge themselves by picturing the trouble that they will bring upon the friends who have offended them." [1] Among the Thlinkets an offended person who is unable to take revenge in any other way commits suicide in order to expose the person who gave the offence to the vengeance of his surviving relatives and friends. [2] Among the Chuvashes it was formerly the custom for enraged persons to hang themselves at the doors of their enemies. [3] A similar method of taking revenge is still not infrequently resorted to by the Votyaks, who believe that the ghost of the deceased will then persecute the offender. [4] Sometimes a suicide has the character of a human sacrifice. [5] In the times of epidemics or great calamities the Chukchi sacrifice their own lives in order to appease evil spirits and the souls of departed relatives. [6] Among some savages it is common for a woman, especially if married to a man of importance, to commit suicide on the death of her husband, [7] or to demand to be buried with him ; [8] and many Brazilian Indians killed themselves on the graves of their chiefs. [9]

In various other cases, besides the voluntary sacrifices of widows or slaves, the suicides of savages are connected with their notions of a future life. [10] The belief in the new

[1] Thomson, *Savage Island*, p. 109.
[2] Krause, *Die Tlinkit-Indianer*, p. 222.
[3] Lebedew, ' Die simbirskischen Tschuwaschen,' in Erman's *Archiv für wissenschaftliche Kunde von Russland*, ix. 586 n.**
[4] Buch, ' Die Wotjäken,' in *Acta Soc. Scient. Fennicæ*, xii. 611 *sq.*
[5] See Lasch, 'Religiöser Selbstmord und seine Beziehung zum Menschenopfer,' in *Globus*, lxxv. 69 *sqq.*
[6] Skrzyncki, ' Der Selbstmord bei den Tschuktschen,' in *Am Ur-Quell*, v. 207 *sq.*
[7] Ashe, *Two Kings of Uganda*, p. 342 (Wahuma). Johnston, *Uganda Protectorate*, ii. 610 (Bairo). Junghuhn, *Die Battaländer auf Sumatra*, ii. 340 (natives of Bali and Lombok).
[8] Westermarck, *History of Human Marriage*, p. 125 (Fijians). Codring-

ton, *op. cit.* p. 289 (natives of Aurora Island, New Hebrides).
[9] Dorman, *Origin of Primitive Superstitions*, p. 211. *Cf. ibid.* p. 209. Of the Niger Delta tribes M. le Comte de Cardi writes (in *Jour. Anthr. Inst.* xxix. 55) :—" On the deportation of a king or a chief by the British or other European government for some offence I have seen the wives of the deported man throw themselves into the river and fight like mad women with the people who went to their rescue ; I have also seen some of the male retainers both free and slaves of a deported king or chief attempt their own lives at the moment when the vessel carrying away their chief disappeared from their sight."
[10] *Cf.* Steinmetz, in *American Anthropologist*, vii. 60 ; Vierkandt,

human birth of the departed soul has led West African
negroes to take their own lives when in distant slavery,
that they may awaken in their native land.[1] Among the
Chukchi there are persons who kill themselves for the
purpose of effecting an earlier reunion with their deceased
relatives.[2] Among the Samoyedes it happens that a young
girl who is sold to an old man strangles herself in the hope
of getting a more suitable bridegroom in the other world.[3]
We are told that the Kamchadales inflict death on themselves with the utmost coolness because they maintain that
" the future life is a continuation of the present, but much
better and more perfect, where they expect to have all
their desires more completely satisfied than here." [4] The
suicides of old people, again, are in some cases due to the
belief that a man enters into the other world in the same
condition in which he left this one, and that it consequently is best for him to die before he grows too old and
feeble [5]

The notions of savages concerning life after death also
influence their moral valuation of suicide. Where men
are supposed to require wives not only during their lifetime, but after their death, it may be a praiseworthy thing,
or even a duty, for a widow to accompany her husband to
the land of souls. According to Fijian beliefs, the woman
who at the funeral of her husband met death with the
greatest devotedness would become the favourite wife in
the abode of spirits, whereas a widow who did not permit
herself to be killed was considered an adulteress.[6] Among
the Central African Bairo those women who refrained
from destroying themselves over their husbands' graves
were regarded as outcasts.[7] On the Gold Coast a man of
low rank who has married one of the king's sisters is

Naturvölker und Kulturvölker, p.
284 ; Lasch, in Zeitschrift für Socialwissenschaft, ii. 585.
[1] Tylor, Primitive Culture, ii. 5.
[2] Skrzyncki, in Am Ur-Quell,
v. 207.
[3] von Struve, ' Die Samojeden im
Norden von Sibirien,' in Ausland,
1880, p. 777.

[4] Georgi, op. cit. iii. 265. Cf. Steller,
Beschreibung von Kamtschatka, p.
294.
[5] Hale, op. cit. p. 65 (Fijians). Cf.
supra, i. 390.
[6] Westermarck, op. cit. p. 125 sq.
[7] Johnston, Uganda Protectorate,
i. 610.

expected to make away with himself when his wife dies, or upon the death of an only male child ; and " should he outrage native custom and neglect to do so, a hint is conveyed to him that he will be put to death, which usually produces the desired effect." [1] The customary suicides of the Chukchi are solemnly performed in the presence and with the assistance of relatives and neighbours.[2] The Samoyedes maintain that suicide by strangulation " is pleasing to God, who looks upon it as a voluntary sacrifice, which deserves reward." [3] The opinion of the Kamchadales that it is " allowable and praiseworthy " for a man to take his own life,[4] was probably connected with their optimistic notions about their fate after death. And that the habitual suicides of old persons have the sanction of public opinion is particularly obvious where they may choose between killing themselves and being killed.[5]

Whilst in some cases suicide opens the door to a happy land beyond the grave, it in other cases entails consequences of a very different kind. The Omahas believe that a self-murderer ceases to exist.[6] According to the Thompson Indians in British Columbia, " the souls of people who commit suicide do not go to the land of souls. The shamans declare they never saw such people there ; and some say that they have looked for the souls of such people, but could not find their tracks. Some shamans say they cannot locate the place where the souls of suicides go, but think they must be lost, because they seem to disappear altogether. Others say that these souls die, and cease to exist. Still others claim that the souls never leave the earth, but wander around aimlessly." [7] So also the Jakuts believe that the ghost of a self-murderer never

[1] Ellis, *Tshi-speaking Peoples of the Gold Coast*, p. 287.
[2] Skrzyncki, in *Am Ur-Quell*, v. 208.
[3] von Struve, in *Ausland*, 1880, p. 777.
[4] Steller, *op. cit.* p. 269. *Cf.* Krasheninnikoff, *op. cit.* p. 204.
[5] *Supra*, i. 389 *sq.* (Fijians). Nansen, *First Crossing of Greenland*, ii.

331. Steller, *op. cit.* p. 294 (Kamchadales).
[6] La Flesche, ' Death and Funeral Customs among the Omahas,' in *Jour. of American Folk-Lore*, ii. 11.
[7] Teit, ' Thompson Indians of British Columbia,' in *Memoirs of the American Museum of Natural History*, Anthropology, i. 358 *sq.*

comes to rest.[1] Sometimes the fate of suicides after death
is represented as a punishment which they suffer for their
deed. Thus the Dacotahs, among whom women not
infrequently put an end to their existence by hanging
themselves, are of opinion that suicide is displeasing to the
" Father of Life," and will be punished in the land of
spirits by the ghost being doomed for ever to drag the
tree on which the person hanged herself ; hence the
women always suspend themselves to as small a tree as
can possibly sustain their weight.[2] The Pahárias of the
Rájmahal Hills, in India, say that " suicide is a crime in
God's eyes," and that " the soul of one who so offends
shall not be admitted into heaven, but must hover eternally
as a ghost between heaven and earth." [3] The Kayans of
Borneo maintain that self-murderers are sent to a place
called *Tan Tekkan*, where they will be very poor and
wretched, subsisting on leaves, roots, or anything they can
pick up in the forests, and being easily distinguished by
their miserable appearance.[4] According to Dyak beliefs,
they go to a special place, where those who have drowned
themselves must thenceforth live up to their waists in
water, and those who have poisoned themselves must live
in houses built of poisonous woods and surrounded by
noxious plants, the exhalations of which are painful to the
spirits.[5] In other instances we are simply told that the
souls of suicides, together with those of persons who have
been killed in war,[6] or who have died a violent death,[7]
are not permitted to live with the rest of the souls, to
whom their presence would cause uneasiness. Among the
Hidatsa Indians some people say that the ghosts of men

[1] Sumner, in *Jour. Anthr. Inst.*
xxxi. 101.
[2] Bradbury, *Travels in the Interior
of America*, p. 89. *Cf.* Keating, *op.
cit.* i. 394.
[3] Dalton, *Descriptive Ethnology of
Bengal*, p. 268. *Cf.* Sherwill, ' Tour
through the Rájmahal Hills,' in
Jour. Asiatic Soc. Bengal, xx. 556.
[4] Hose, ' Journey up the Baram
River to Mount Dulit and the Highlands of Borneo,' in *Geographical

Journal*, i. 199.
[5] Wilken, *Het animisme bij de
volken van den Indischen Archipel*,
i. 44.
[6] Brebeuf, ' Relation de ce qui
s'est passé dans le pays des Hurons,'
in *Relations des Jésuites*, 1636, p.
104 *sq.* Hewitt, ' The Iroquoian
Concept of the Soul,' in *Jour. of
American Folk-Lore*, viii. 109.
[7] Steinmetz, in *American Anthropologist*, vii. 58 (Niase).

who have made away with themselves occupy a separate part of the village of the dead, but that their condition in no other wise differs from that of the other ghosts.[1]

It is, however, hard to believe that the fate of the self-murderer, whether it be annihilation, a vagrant existence on earth, or separation in the other world, was originally meant as a punishment; for a similar lot is assigned to the souls of persons who have been drowned,[2] or who have died by accident or violence.[3] It seems that the suicide's future state is in the first place supposed to depend upon the treatment of his corpse. Frequently he is denied burial, or at least the ordinary funeral rites,[4] and this may give rise to the notion that his soul never comes to rest or, possibly, even ceases to exist. Or he is buried by himself, apart from the other dead,[5] in which case his soul must naturally remain equally isolated. Among the Alabama Indians, for instance, " when a man kills himself, either in despair or in a sickness, he is deprived of burial, and thrown into the river."[6] In Dahomey ".the body of any person committing suicide is not allowed to be buried, but thrown out into the fields to be devoured by wild beasts."[7] Among the Fantis of the Gold Coast " il y a des places réservées aux suicidés et à ceux qui sont morts de la petite vérole. Ils sont enterrés à l'écart loin de toute

---

[1] Matthews, *Ethnography and Philology of the Hidatsa Indians*, p. 49.

[2] Teit, *loc. cit.* p. 359 (Thompson Indians).

[3] Soppitt, *Kuki-Lushai Tribes*, p. 12. Anderson, *Mandalay to Momien*, p. 146 (Kakhyens). Müller, *Geschichte der Amerikanischen Urreligionen*, p. 287 (Brazilian Indians). *Supra*, ii. 237. The Central Eskimo believe that all who die by accident or by violence, and women who die in childbirth, are taken to the upper, happier world (Boas, ' Central Eskimo,' in *Ann. Rep. Bur. Ethn.* vi. 590). According to the belief of the Behring Strait Eskimo, the shades of shamans, or persons who die by accident, violence, or starva-

tion, go to a land of plenty in the sky, where there is light, food, and water in abundance; whereas the shades of people who die from natural causes go to the underground land of the dead (Nelson, ' Eskimo about Bering Strait,' in *Ann. Rep. Bur. Ethn.* xviii. 423).

[4] See Lasch, 'Die Behandlung der Leiche des Selbstmörders,' in *Globus*, lxxvi. 63 *sqq.*

[5] *Ibid.* p. 65.

[6] Bossu, *Travels through Louisiana*, i. 258.

[7] M'Leod, *Voyage to Africa*, p. 48 *sq.* I am indebted to Mr. N. W. Thomas for drawing my attention to this and a few other statements in the present chapter.

habitation et de tout chemin public."[1] In the Pelew
Islands a self-murderer is buried not with his own deceased
relatives, but in the place where he ended his life, as are
also the corpses of those who fall in war.[2] Among the
Bannavs of Cambodia " anyone who perishes by his own
hand is buried in a corner of the forest far from the graves
of his brethren."[3] Among the Sea Dyaks " those who
commit suicide are buried in different places from others,
as it is supposed that they will not be allowed to mix in
the seven-storied heaven with such of their fellow-countrymen as come by their death in a natural manner or from
the influence of the spirits."[4] The motive for thus treat-
ing self-murderers' bodies is superstitious fear. Their
ghosts, as the ghosts of persons who have died by any
other violent means or by accident, are supposed to be
particularly malevolent,[5] owing to their unnatural mode of
death[6] or to the desperate or angry state of mind in which
they left this life. If they are not buried at all, or if they
are buried in the spot where they died or in a separate
place, that is either because nobody dares to interfere with
them, or in order to prevent them from mixing with the
other dead. So also murdered persons are sometimes left
unburied,[7] and people who are supposed to have been
killed by evil spirits are buried apart ;[8] whilst those struck
with lightning are either denied interment,[9] or buried
where they fell and in the position in which they died.[10]
We sometimes hear of a connection between the way in
which a suicide's body is treated and the moral opinion as
regards his deed. Among the Alabama Indians his corpse

---

[1] Gallaud, 'A la Côte d'Or,' in
Les missions catholiques, xxv. 347.
[2] Kubary, in Original-Mittheil. aus
der ethnol. Abtheil. d. königl. Museen
zu Berlin, i. 78.
[3] Comte, quoted by Mouhot, op.
cit. ii. 28. See also ' Das Volk der
Bannar,' in Mittheil. d. Geogr. Ges.
zu Jena, iii. 9.
[4] St. John, Life in the Forests of the
Far East, i. 69.
[5] Lasch, in Globus, lxxvi. 65. Cf.
Liebrecht, Zur Volkskunde, p. 414 sq.

[6] Lippert, Der Seelencult, p. 11.
Kubary, in Original-Mittheil. aus
der ethnol. Abtheil. d. königl. Museen
zu Berlin, i. 78.
[7] Rosenberg, Der malayische
Archipel, p. 461 (Papuans of Dorey).
[8] Hodson, ' Native Tribes of Mani-
pur,' in Jour. Anthr. Inst. xxxi.
305 sq.
[9] Burton, Mission to Gelele, ii. 142
sq. (Dahomans).
[10] La Flesche, in Jour. American
Folk-Lore, ii. 11 (Omahas).

is said to be thrown into the river " because he is looked upon as a coward " ;[1] and of the Ossetes M. Kovalewsky states that they bury suicides far away from other dead persons because they regard their act as sinful.[2] But we may be sure that moral condemnation is not the original cause of these practices.

It is comparatively seldom that savages are reported to attach any stigma to suicide. To the instances mentioned above a few others may be added. The Waganda, we are told, greatly condemn the act.[3] Among the Bogos " a man never despairs, never gives himself up, and considers suicide as the greatest indignity." [4] The Karens of Burma deem it an act of cowardice ; but at the same time they have no command against it, they " seem to see little or no guilt in it," and " we are nowhere told that it is displeasing to the God of heaven and earth." [5] The Dacotahs said of a girl who had destroyed herself because her parents had turned her beloved from the wigwam, and would force her to marry a man she hated, that her spirit did not watch over her earthly remains, being offended when she brought trouble upon her aged mother and father.[6] In Dahomey " it is criminal to attempt to commit suicide, because every man is the property of the king. The bodies of suicides are exposed to public execration, and the head is always struck off and sent to Agbomi ; at the expense of the family if the suicide were a free man, at that of his master if he were a slave." [7] On the other hand, it is expressly stated of various savages that they do not punish attempts to commit suicide.[8] The negroes of Accra see nothing wrong in the act. " Why," they would ask, " should a person not be

[1] Bossu, *op. cit.* i. 258.
[2] Kovalewsky, *Coutume contemporaine et loi ancienne*, p. 327.
[3] Felkin, in *Proceed. Roy. Soc. Edinburgh*, xiii. 723.
[4] Munzinger, *Die Sitten und das Recht der Bogos*, p. 93.
[5] Mason, in *Jour. Asiatic Soc. Bengal*, xxxvii. pt. ii. 141.
[6] Eastman, *op. cit.* p. 169.

[7] Ellis, *Ewe-speaking Peoples*, p. 224.
[8] Leuschner, in Steinmetz, *Rechtsverhältnisse*, p. 24 (Bakwiri). Nicole, *ibid.* p. 135 (Diakité-Sarracolese). Lang, *ibid.* p. 262 (Washambala). Rautanen, *ibid.* p. 343 (Ondonga). Sorge, *ibid.* p. 421 (Nissan Islanders). Senfft, *ibid.* p. 452 (Marshall Islanders).

allowed to die, when he no longer desires to live ? " But
they inflict cruel punishments upon slaves who try to put
an end to themselves, in order to deter other slaves from
doing the same.[1] Among the Pelew Islanders suicide " is
neither praised nor blamed." [2] The Eskimo around
Northumberland Inlet and Davis Strait believe that anyone who has been killed by accident, or who has taken
his own life, certainly goes to the happy place after
death.[3] The Chippewas hold suicide " to be a foolish, not
a reprehensible action," and do not believe it to entail
any punishment in the other world.[4] In his sketches of
the manners and customs of the North American Indians,
Buchanan writes :—" Suicide is not considered by the
Indians either as an act of heroism or of cowardice, nor is
it with them a subject of praise or blame. They view
this desperate act as the consequence of mental derangement, and the person who destroys himself is to them an
object of pity." [5]

From the opinions on suicide held by uncivilised races
we shall pass to those prevalent among peoples of a higher
culture. In China suicide is extremely common among
all classes and among persons of all ages.[6] For those who
have been impelled to this course by a sense of honour
the gates of heaven open wide, and tablets bearing their
names are erected in the temples in honour of virtuous
men or women. As honourable self-murderers are
regarded servants or officers of state who choose not to
survive a defeat in battle or an insult offered to the
sovereign of their country ; young men who, when an
insult has been paid to their parents which they are unable
to avenge, prefer not to survive it ; and women who kill

[1] Monrad, op. cit. pp. 23, 25.
[2] Kubary, in Original-Mittheil. aus
der ethnol. Abtheil. d. königl. Museen
zu Berlin, i. 78.
[3] Hall, Arctic Researches, p. 572.
Cf. supra, ii. 238, n. 3.
[4] Keating, op. cit. ii. 172.
[5] Buchanan, Sketches of the History,
&c. of the North American Indians,
p. 184.
[6] Gray, China, i. 329. Huc, The
Chinese Empire, p. 181. Matignon,
' Le suicide en Chine,' in Archives
d'anthropologie criminelle, xii. 367
sqq. Cathonay, 'Aux environs de
Foutchéon,' in Les missions catholiques, xxxi. 341 sq. Ball, Things
Chinese, p. 564 sqq.

themselves on the death of their husbands or *fiancés*.[1] In spite of imperial prohibitions, sutteeism of widowed wives and brides has continued to flourish in China down to this day, and meets with the same public applause as ever ;[2] whilst those widowed wives and brides who have lost their lives in preserving their chastity, are entitled both to an honorary gate and to a place in a temple of the State as an object of worship.[3] Another common form of suicide which is admired as heroic in China is that committed for the purpose of taking revenge upon an enemy who is otherwise out of reach—according to Chinese ideas a most effective mode of revenge, not only because the law throws the responsibility of the deed on him who occasioned it, but also because the disembodied soul is supposed to be better able than the living man to persecute the enemy.[4] The Chinese have a firm belief in the wandering spirits of persons who have died by violence ; thus self-murderers are supposed to haunt the places where they committed the fatal deed and endeavour to persuade others to follow their example, at times even attempting to play executioner by strangling those who reject their advances.[5] "Violent deaths," says Mr. Giles, "are regarded with horror by the Chinese ";[6] and suicides committed from meaner motives are reprobated.[7] It is said in the Yü Li, or "Divine Panorama"— a Taouist work which is very popular all over the Chinese Empire—that whilst persons who kill themselves out of loyalty, filial piety, chastity, or friendship, will go to heaven, those who do so "in a trivial burst of rage, or fearing the consequences of a crime which would not amount to death, or in the hope of falsely injuring a

[1] Gray, *op. cit.* i. 337 *sqq.*

[2] de Groot, *Religious System of China*, (vol. ii. book) i. 748. Ball, *op. cit.* p. 565. Cathonay, in *Les missions catholiques*, xxxi. 341.

[3] de Groot, *op. cit.* (vol. ii. book) i. 792.

[4] Huc, *op. cit.* p. 181. Matignon, in *Archives d'anthropologie crimin-* *elle*, xii. 371 *sqq.* de Groot, *op. cit.* (vol. iv. book) ii. 450 *sq.* Cathonay, in *Les missions catholiques*, xxxi. 341 *sq.* Ball, *op. cit.* p. 566 *sq.*

[5] Davis, *China*, ii. 94. Dennys, *Folk-Lore of China*, p. 74 *sq.*

[6] Giles, *Strange Stories from a Chinese Studio*, ii. 363, n. 9.

[7] Gray, *op. cit.* i. 337.

fellow-creature," will be severely punished in the infernal
regions.[1] No pardon will be granted them ; they are
not, like other sinners, allowed to claim their good works
as a set-off against evil, whereby they might partly escape
the agonies of hell and receive some reward for their
virtuous deeds.[2] Sometimes suicide is classified by the
Chinese as an offence against religion, on the ground that
a person owes his being to Heaven, and is therefore
responsible to Heaven for due care of the gift.[3]

"The Japanese calendar of saints," says Mr. Griffis,
" is not filled with reformers, alms-givers, and founders of
hospitals or orphanages, but is overcrowded with canonised
suicides and committers of *harakiri*. Even to-day, no man
more . . . surely draws homage to his tomb, securing even
apotheosis, than the suicide, though he may have committed a crime." [4] There were two kinds of *harakiri*, or
" belly-cutting," one obligatory and the other voluntary.
The former was a boon granted by government, who
graciously permitted criminals of the Samurai, or military,
class thus to destroy themselves instead of being handed
over to the common executioner ; but this custom is now
quite extinct. Voluntary *harakiri*, again, was practised
out of loyalty to a dead superior, or in order to protest,
when other protests might be unavailing, against the
erroneous conduct of a living superior, or to avoid
beheading by the enemy in a lost battle, or to restore
injured honour if revenge was impossible. Under any
circumstances *harakiri* cleansed from every stain, and en-
sured an honourable interment and a respected memory.[5]
It is said in a Japanese manuscript, " To slay his enemy
against whom he has cause of hatred, and then to kill
himself, is the part of a noble Samurai, and it is sheer
nonsense to look upon the place where he has disem-

---

[1] Giles, *op. cit.* ii. 365.
[2] *Ibid.* ii. 363.
[3] Alabaster, *Notes and Commen-taries on Chinese Criminal Law*, p. 304.
[4] Griffis, *Religions of Japan*, p. 112.
[5] Chamberlain, *Things Japanese*,
p. 219 *sqq.* Rein, *Japan*, p. 328. Kühne, in *Globus*, lxxiv. 166 *sq.* A very full account of the ceremony of *harakiri* is given in Mitford's *Tales of Old Japan*, ii. 193 *sqq.*, from a rare Japanese manuscript.

bowelled himself as polluted." [1] In old days the ceremony used to be performed in a temple. [2]

Among the Hindus we meet with the practice of self-immolation of widows—until recently very prevalent in many parts of India [3]—and various forms of self-destruction for religious purposes. Suicide has always been considered by the Hindus to be one of the most acceptable rites that can be offered to their deities. According to the Ayen Akbery, there were five kinds of suicide held to be meritorious in the Hindu, namely :—starving ; covering himself with cow-dung and setting it on fire and consuming himself therein ; burying himself in snow ; immersing himself in the water at the extremity of Bengal, where the Ganges discharges itself into the sea through a thousand channels, enumerating his sins, and praying till the alligators come and devour him ; cutting his throat at Allahabad, at the confluence of the Ganges and Jumna. [4] To these might be added drowning at Hurdwar, Allahabad, and Saugor ; perishing in the cold of the Himalayas ; the practice of dying under the wheels of Juggurnath's car ; [5] and the custom of men throwing themselves down from certain rocks to fulfil the vows of their mothers, or to receive forgiveness for sins, or to be re-born rajas in their next state of transmigration. [6] It is also common for persons who are afflicted with leprosy or any other incurable disease to bury or drown themselves with due ceremonies, by which they are considered acceptable sacrifices to the deity, [7] or to roll themselves into fires with the notion that thus purified they will receive a happy transmigration into a healthy body. [8] Suicide was further

---

[1] Mitford, *op. cit.* ii. 201.

[2] *Ibid.* ii. 196.

[3] Malcolm, *Memoir of Central India*, ii. 206 *sqq.* Chevers, *Manual of Medical Jurisprudence for India*, p. 665. *Cf. supra*, i. 473 *sq.* Sir John Malcolm observes (*op. cit.* ii. 206, n. ‡) that the practice of *suttee* was not always confined to widows, but that sometimes mothers burned themselves on the death of their only sons.

[4] Chevers, *op. cit.* p. 664. *Cf. Laws of Manu*, vi. 31.

[5] *Ibid.* p. 664. Ward, *View of the History, &c. of the Hindoos*, ii. 115 *sqq.* Rájendralála Mitra, *Indo-Aryans*, ii. 70.

[6] Sleeman, *Rambles and Recollections of an Indian Official*, i. 132 *sq.* Malcolm, *Memoir of Central India*, ii. 209 *sqq.* Forsyth, *Highlands of Central India*, p. 172 *sq.*

[7] Sleeman, *op. cit.* ii. 344 *sq.*

[8] Ward, *op. cit.* ii. 119.

resorted to by Brâhmans for the purpose of avenging an
injury, as it was believed that the ghost of the deceased
would persecute the offender, and, presumably, also
because of the great efficacy which was attributed to the
curse of a dying Brâhman.[1] When one of the Rajput rajas
once levied a war-subsidy on the Brâhmans, some of the
wealthiest, having expostulated in vain, poniarded themselves in his presence, pouring maledictions on his head
with their last breath ; and thus cursed, the raja laboured
under a ban of excommunication even amongst his personal friends.[2] We are told of a Brâhman girl who, having
been seduced by a certain raja, burned herself to death,
and in dying imprecated the most fearful curses on the
raja's kindred, after which they were visited with such a
succession of disasters that they abandoned their family
settlement at Baliya, where the woman's tomb is worshipped
to this day.[3] Once when a raja ordered the house of a
Brâhman to be demolished and resumed the lands which
had been conferred upon him, the latter fasted till he died
at the palace gate, and became thus a Brahm, or malignant
Brâhman ghost, who avenged the injury he had suffered by
destroying the raja and his house.[4] At Azimghur, in 1835,
a Brâhman " threw himself down a well, that his ghost
might haunt his neighbour."[5] The same idea undoubtedly
underlies the custom of " sitting *dharna*," which was
practised by creditors who sat down before the doors of
their debtors threatening to starve themselves to death if
their claims were not paid ;[6] and the sin attached to
causing the death of a Brâhman would further increase the
efficacy of the creditor's threats.[7] At the same time
religious suicide is said to be a crime in a Brâhman.[8] And
in the sacred books we read that for him who destroys

---

[1] Chevers, *op. cit.* p. 659 *sqq.*
Crooke, *Popular Religion and Folk-
Lore of Northern India*, i. 191 *sqq.*
van Mökern, *Ostindien*, i. 319 *sqq.*
[2] Tod, quoted by Chevers, *op. cit.*
p. 659 *sq.*
[3] Crooke, *op. cit.* i. 193.
[4] *Ibid.* i. 191 *sq.*
[5] Chevers, *op. cit.* p. 663.
[6] *Cf.* Steinmetz, ' Gli antichi

scongiuri giuridici contro i creditori,'
in *Rivista italiana di sociologia*, ii.
58. For the practice of *dharna* see
ibid. p. 37 *sqq.* ; Balfour, *Cyclopædia of India*, i. 934 *sq.* ; van
Mökern, *op. cit.* i. 322 *sq.*
[7] *Cf.* Jones, quoted by Balfour,
op. cit. i. 935.
[8] Ward, *op. cit.* ii. 115. Forsyth,
op. cit. p. 173.

himself by means of wood, water, clods of earth, stones, weapons, poison, or a rope, no funeral rites shall be performed by his relatives ; [1] that he who resolves to die by his own hand shall fast for three days ; and that he who attempts suicide, but remains alive, shall perform severe penance.[2] The Buddhists allow a man under certain circumstances to take his own life, but maintain that generally dire miseries are in store for the self-murderer, and look upon him as one who must have sinned deeply in a former state of existence.[3] It should be added that in India, as elsewhere, the souls of those who have killed themselves or met death by any other violent means are regarded as particularly malevolent and troublesome.[4]

The Old Testament mentions a few cases of suicide.[5] In none of them is any censure passed on the perpetrator of the deed, nor is there any text which expressly forbids a man to die by his own hand ; and of Ahithophel it is said that he was buried in the sepulchre of his father.[6] It seems, however, that according to Jewish custom persons who had killed themselves should be left unburied till sunset,[7] perhaps for fear lest the spirit of the deceased otherwise might find its way back to the old home.[8] Josephus, who mentions this custom, denounces suicide as an act of cowardice, as a crime most remote from the common nature of all animals, as impiety against the Creator ; and he maintains that the souls of those who have thus acted madly against themselves will go to the darkest place in Hades.[9] The Talmud considers suicide justifiable, if not meritorious, in the case of the chief of a vanquished army who is sure of disgrace and death at the hands of the exulting conqueror,[10] or when a person has

[1] *Vasishtha*, xxiii. 14 *sq.*
[2] *Ibid.* xxiii. 18 *sqq.*
[3] Hardy, *Manual of Budhism*, p. 479.
[4] Crooke, *Popular Religion and Folk-Lore of Northern India*, i. 269. Fawcett, ' Nâyars of Malabar,' in the Madras Government Museum's *Bulletin*, iii. 253.
[5] I *Samuel*, xxxi. 4 *sq.* 2 *Samuel*, xvii. 23. I *Kings*, xvi. 18. 2 *Mac-*

cabees, xiv. 4 *sqq.*
[6] 2 *Samuel*, xvii. 23.
[7] Josephus, *De bello Judaico*, iii. 8. 5.
[8] *Cf.* Frazer, ' Burial Customs as illustrative of the Primitive Theory of the Soul,' in *Jour. Anthr. Inst.* xv. 72.
[9] Josephus, *op. cit.* iii. 8. 5.
[10] *Cf.* I *Samuel*, xxxi. 4.

reason to fear being forced to renounce his religion.[1] In all other circumstances the Rabbis consider it criminal for a person to shorten his own life, even when he is undergoing tortures which must soon end his earthly career ; [2] and they forbid all marks of mourning for a self-murderer, such as wearing sombre apparel and eulogising him.[3] Islam prohibits suicide, as an act which interferes with the decrees of God.[4] Muhammedans say that it is a greater sin for a person to kill himself than to kill a fellow-man ; [5] and, as a matter of fact, suicide is very rare in the Moslem world.[6]

Ancient Greece had its honourable suicides. The Milesian and Corinthian women, who by a voluntary death escaped from falling into the hands of the enemy, were praised in epigrams.[7] The story that Themistocles preferred death to bearing arms against his native country was circulated with a view to doing honour to his memory.[8] The tragedians frequently give expression to the idea that suicide is in certain circumstances becoming to a noble mind.[9] Hecuba blames Helena for not putting an end to her life by a rope or a sword.[10] Phaedra [11] and Leda [12] kill themselves out of shame, Haemon from violent remorse.[13] Ajax decides to die after having in vain attempted to kill the Atreidae, maintaining that " one of generous strain should nobly live, or forthwith nobly die." [14] Instances are, moreover, mentioned of women killing themselves on the death of their husbands ; [15] and in Cheos it was the custom to prevent

[1] Guittin, 57 B, quoted by Mendelsohn, Criminal Jurisprudence of the Ancient Hebrews, p. 77, n. 163. Cf. 2 Maccabees, xiv. 37 sqq.

[2] Ab Zara, 18 A, quoted by Mendelsohn, op. cit. p. 78, n. 163.

[3] Mendelsohn, op. cit. p. 77.

[4] Koran, iv. 33.

[5] I have often heard this myself. Cf. Westcott, Suicide, p. 12.

[6] Lisle, Du suicide, pp. 305, 345 sq. Legoyt, Le suicide ancien et moderne, p. 7. Morselli, Il suicidio, p. 33. Westcott, op. cit. p. 12.

[7] Schmidt, Die Ethik der alten Griechen, ii. 443.

[8] Diodorus Siculus, Bibliotheca historica, xi. 58. 2 sq.

[9] See Schmidt, op. cit. ii. 442 sqq.

[10] Euripides, Troades, 1012 sqq.

[11] Idem, Hippolytus, 715 sqq.

[12] Idem, Helena, 134 sqq.

[13] Sophocles, Antigone, 1234 sqq.

[14] Idem, Ajax, 470 sqq. Cf. ibid. 654 sqq.

[15] Euripides, Supplices, 1000 sqq. Pausanias, iv. 2. 7.

the decrepitude of old age by a voluntary death.[1] At
Athens the right hand of a person who had taken his own
life was struck off and buried apart from the rest of the
body,[2] evidently in order to make him harmless after death.[3]
Plato says in his ' Laws,' probably in agreement with
Attic custom, that those who inflict death upon themselves " from sloth or want of manliness," shall be buried
alone in such places as are uncultivated and nameless, and
that no column or inscription shall mark the spot where
they are interred.[4] At Thebes self-murderers were
deprived of the accustomed funeral ceremonies,[5] and in
Cyprus they were left unburied.[6] The objections which
philosophers raised against the commission of suicide were
no doubt to some extent shared by popular sentiments.
Pythagoras is represented as saying that we should not
abandon our station in life without the orders of our
commander, that is, God.[7] According to the Platonic
Socrates, the gods are our guardians and we are a possession of theirs, hence " there may be reason in saying that
a man should wait, and not take his own life until God
summons him."[8] Aristotle, again, maintains that he who
from rage kills himself commits a wrong against the
State, and that therefore the State punishes him and civil
infamy is attached to him.[9] The religious argument
could not be foreign to a people who regarded it as
impious interference in the order of nature to make a
bridge over the Hellespont and to separate a landscape
from the continent ;[10] and the idea that suicide is a matter
of public concern evidently prevailed in Massilia, where
no man was allowed to make away with himself unless the
magistrates had given him permission to do so.[11] But the

[1] Strabo, *Geographica*, x. 5. 6, p.
486. Aelian, *Varia historia*, iii. 37.
Cf. Boeckh, *Gesammelte kleine Schriften*, vii. 345 *sqq.*; Welcker, *Kleine
Schriften*, ii. 502 *sq.*
   [2] Aeschines, *In Ctesiphontem*, 244.
   [3] Some Australian natives cut off
the thumb of the right hand of a
dead foe in order to make his spirit
unable to throw the spear efficiently
(Oldfield, in *Trans. Ethn. Soc.* N.S.
iii. 287).

[4] Plato, *Leges*, ix. 873.
[5] Schmidt, *op. cit.* ii. 104.
[6] Dio Chrysostom, *Orationes*, lxiv.
3.
[7] Cicero, *Cato Major*, 20 (73).
[8] Plato, *Phædro*, p. 62.
[9] Aristotle, *Ethica Nicomachea*, v.
11. 3.
[10] See Schmidt, *op. cit.* ii. 83, 441 ;
Rohde, *Psyche*, p. 202, n. 1.
[11] Valerius Maximus, *Factorum dictorumque memorabilia*, ii. 6. 7.

opinions of the philosophers were anything but
unanimous.[1] Plato himself, in his ' Laws,' has no word
of censure for him who deprives himself by violence of his
appointed share of life under the compulsion of some
painful and inevitable misfortune, or out of irremediable
and intolerable shame.[2] Hegesias, surnamed the " death-
persuader," who belonged to the Cyrenaic school, tried to
prove the utter worthlessness and unprofitableness of life.[3]
According to Epicurus we ought to consider " whether it
be better that death should come to us, or we go to
him." [4] The Stoics, especially, advocated suicide as a
relief from all kinds of misery.[5] Seneca remarks that it
is a man's own fault if he suffers, as, by putting an end to
himself, he can put an end to his misery :—" As I would
choose a ship to sail in, or a house to live in, so would I
choose the most tolerable death when about to die. . . .
Human affairs are in such a happy situation, that no one
need be wretched but by choice. Do you like to be
wretched ? Live. Do you like it not ? It is in your
power to return from whence you came." [6] The Stoics
did not deny that it is wrong to commit suicide in cases
where the act would be an injury to society ;[7] Seneca
himself points out that Socrates lived thirty days in prison
in expectation of death, so as to submit to the laws of his
country, and to give his friends the enjoyment of his conversation to the last.[8] Epictetus opposes indiscriminate
suicide on religious grounds :—" Friends, wait for God ;
when he shall give the signal and release you from this
service, then go to him ; but for the present endure to
dwell in the place where he has put you."[9] Such a signal,
however, is given often enough : it may consist in incurable disease, intolerable pain, or misery of any kind.
" Remember this : the door is open ; be not more timid

[1] See Geiger, *Der Selbstmord im
klassischen Altertum*, p. 5 *sqq.*
[2] Plato, *Leges*, ix. 873.
[3] Cicero, *Tusculanæ quæstiones*, i.
34 (83 *sq.*). Valerius Maximus, viii.
9. Externa 3.
[4] Epicurus, quoted by Seneca,
Epistulæ, 26.

[5] See Geiger, *op. cit.* p. 15 *sqq.*
[6] Seneca, *Epistulæ*, 70. See also
Idem, De ira, iii. 15; *Idem, Con-
solatio ad Marciam*, 20.
[7] Lecky, *History of European
Morals*, i. 214, n. 1.
[8] Seneca, *Epistulæ*, 70.
[9] Epictetus, *Dissertationes*, i. 9. 16.

than little children, but as they say, when the thing does
not please them, ' I will play no longer,' so do you,
when things seem to you of such a kind, say I will no
longer play, and be gone : but if you stay, do not
complain." [1] Pliny says that the power of dying when
you please is the best thing that God has given to man
amidst all the sufferings of life. [2]

It seems that the Roman people, before the influence of
Christianity made itself felt, regarded suicide with considerable moral indifference. According to Servius, it was
provided by the Pontifical laws that whoever hanged himself should be cast out unburied ; [3] but from what has
been said before it is probable that this practice only owed
its origin to fear of the dead man's ghost. Vergil
enumerates self-murderers not among the guilty, but
among the unfortunate, confounding them with infants
who have died prematurely and persons who have been
condemned to die on a false charge. [4] Throughout the
whole history of pagan Rome there was no statute declaring it to be a crime for an ordinary citizen to take his
own life. The self-murderer's rights were in no way
affected by his deed, his memory was no less honoured than
if he had died a natural death, his will was recognised by
law, and the regular order of succession was not interfered
with. [5] In Roman law there are only two noteworthy
exceptions to the rule that suicide is a matter with which
the State has nothing to do : it was prohibited in the case
of soldiers, [6] and the enactment was made that the suicide
of an accused person should entail the same consequences
as his condemnation ; but in the latter instance the deed
was admitted as a confession of guilt. [7] On the other

[1] *Ibid.* i. 24. 20 ; i. 25. 20 *sq.* ; ii.
16. 37 *sqq.* ; iii. 13. 14 ; iii. 24. 95
sqq.
[2] Pliny, *Historia naturalis*, ii.5 (7).
[3] Servius, *Commentarii in Virgilii
Æneidos*, xii. 603.
[4] Vergil, *Æneis*, vi. 426 *sqq.*
[5] Bourquelot, ' Recherches sur les
opinions et la législation en matière
de mort volontaire pendant le moyen

age,' in *Bibliothèque de l'École des
Chartes*, iii. 544. Geiger, *op. cit.*
p. 64 *sqq.* Bynkershoek, *Observa-
tiones Juris Romani*, iv. 4, p. 350.
[6] *Digesta*, xlix. 16. 6. 7.
[7] *Ibid.* xlviii. 21. 3 pr. *Cf.* Bourquelot, *op. cit.* iii. 543 *sq.*; Gibbon,
*Decline and Fall of the Roman
Empire*, v. 326 ; Lecky, *History of
European Morals*, i. 219,

hand, it seems to have been the general opinion in Rome
that suicide under certain circumstances is an heroic and
praiseworthy act.[1] Even Cicero, who professed the
doctrine of Pythagoras,[2] approved of the death of Cato.[3]

In no question of morality was there a greater difference
between classical and Christian doctrines than in regard to
suicide. The earlier Fathers of the Church still allowed,
or even approved of, suicide in certain cases, namely,
when committed in order to procure martyrdom,[4] or to
avoid apostacy, or to retain the crown of virginity. To
bring death upon ourselves voluntarily, says Lactantius, is
a wicked and impious deed ; " but when urged to the
alternative, either of forsaking God and relinquishing
faith, or of expecting all torture and death, then it is
that undaunted in spirit we defy that death with all
its previous threats and terrors which others fear." [5]
Eusebius and other ecclesiastical writers mention several
instances of Christian women putting an end to their lives
when their chastity was in danger, and their acts are
spoken of with tenderness, if not approbation ; indeed,
some of them were admitted into the calendar of saints.[6]
This admission was due to the extreme honour in which
virginity was held by the Fathers ; St. Jerome, who
denied that it was lawful in times of persecution to die by
one's own hands, made an exception for cases in which a
person's chastity was at stake.[7] But even this exception
was abolished by St. Augustine. He allows that the
virgins who laid violent hands upon themselves are
worthy of compassion, but declares that there was no
necessity for their doing so, since chastity is a virtue of

[1] Stäudlin, *Geschichte der Vorstellungen und Lehren vom Selbstmorde,*
p. 62 *sq.*
[2] Cicero, *Cato Major,* 20 (72 *sq.*).
[3] *Idem, De officiis,* i. 31 (112).
[4] See Barbeyrac, *Traité de la morale
des Pères de l'Église,* pp. 18, 122 *sq.* ;
Buonafede, *Istoria critica e filosofica
del suicidio,* p. 135 *sqq.* ; Lecky, *op.
cit.* ii. 45 *sq.*
[5] Lactantius, *Divinæ Institutiones,*
vi. (' De vero cultu ') 17 (Migne,

Patrologiæ cursus, vi. 697).
[6] Eusebius, *Historia ecclesiastica,*
viii. 12 (Migne, *op. cit.* Ser. Graeca,
xx. 769 *sqq.*), 14 (*ibid.* col. 785 *sqq.*).
St. Ambrose, *De virginibus,* xiii. 7
(Migne, *op. cit.* xvi. 229 *sqq.*). St.
Chrysostom, *Homilia encomiastica in
S. Martyrem Pelagiam* (Migne, *op.
cit.* Ser. Graeca, l. 579 *sqq.*).
[7] St. Jerome, *Commentarii in Jonam,* i. 12 (Migne, *op. cit.* xxv. 1129)

the mind which is not lost by the body being in captivity to the will and superior force of another. He argues that there is no passage in the canonical Scriptures which permits us to destroy ourselves either with a view to obtaining immortality or to avoiding calamity. On the contrary, suicide is prohibited in the commandment, " Thou shalt not kill," namely, " neither thyself nor another " ; for he who kills himself kills no other but a man.[1] This doctrine, which assimilates suicide with murder, was adopted by the Church.[2] Nay, self-murder was declared to be the worst form of murder, " the most grievous thing of all " ; [3] already St. Chrysostom had declared that " if it is base to destroy others, much more is it to destroy one's self." [4] The self-murderer was deprived of rights which were granted to all other criminals. In the sixth century a Council at Orleans enjoined that " the oblations of those who were killed in the commission of any crime may be received, except of such as laid violent hands on themselves " ; [5] and a subsequent Council denied self-murderers the usual rites of Christian burial.[6] It was even said that Judas committed a greater sin in killing himself than in betraying his master Christ to a certain death. [7]

According to the Christian doctrine, as formulated by Thomas Aquinas, suicide is utterly unlawful for three reasons. First, everything naturally loves itself and preserves itself in being ; suicide is against a natural inclination and contrary to the charity which a man ought to bear towards himself, and consequently a mortal sin.

---

[1] St. Augustine, *De Civitate Dei*, i. 16 *sqq.*

[2] Gratian, *Decretum*, ii. 23. 5. 9. 3.

[3] Thomas Aquinas, *Summa theologica*, ii.–ii. 64. 5. 3.

[4] St. Chrysostom, *In Epistolam ad Galatas commentarius*, i. 4 (Migne, *op. cit.* Ser. Graeca, lxi. 618 *sq.*).

[5] *Concilium Aurelianense II.* A.D. 533, can. 15 (Labbe-Mansi, *Sacrorum Conciliorum collectio*, viii. 837). See also *Concilium Autisiodorense*, A.D. 578, can. 17 (Labbe-Mansi, ix. 913).

[6] *Concilium Bracarense II.* A.D. 563, cap. 16 (Labbe-Mansi, *op. cit.* ix. 779).

[7] Damhouder, *Praxis rerum criminalium*, lviii. 2 *sq.*, p. 258. See Gratian, *op. cit.* ii. 33. 3. 3. 38. At the trial of the Marquise de Brinvilliers in 1676, the presiding judge said to the prisoner that " the greatest of all her crimes, horrible as they were, was, not the poisoning of her father and brothers, but her attempt to poison herself " (Ives, *Classification of Crimes*, p. 36).

Secondly, by killing himself a person does an injury to
the community of which he is a part. Thirdly, " life is
a gift divinely bestowed on man, and subject to His power
who ' killeth and maketh alive ' ; and therefore he who
takes his own life sins against God, as he who kills another
man's slave sins against the master to whom the slave
belongs, and as he sins who usurps the office of judge on
a point not referred to him ; for to God alone belongs
judgment of life and death." [1] The second of these
arguments is borrowed from Aristotle, and is entirely
foreign to the spirit of early Christianity. The notion of
patriotism being a moral duty was habitually discouraged
by it, and, as Mr. Lecky observes, " it was impossible to
urge the civic argument against suicide without at the
same time condemning the hermit life, which in the third
century became the ideal of the Church." [2] But the other
arguments are deeply rooted in some of the fundamental
doctrines of Christianity—in the sacredness of human life,
in the duty of absolute submission to God's will, and in
the extreme importance attached to the moment of death.
The earthly life is a preparation for eternity ; sufferings
which are sent by God are not to be evaded, but to be
endured.[3] The man who deliberately takes away the life
which was given him by the Creator displays the utmost
disregard for the will and authority of his Master ; and,
worst of all, he does so in the very last minute of his life,
when his doom is sealed for ever. His deed, as Thomas
Aquinas says, is " the most dangerous thing of all, because
no time is left to expiate it by repentance." [4] He who
kills a fellow-creature does not in the same degree
renounce the protection of God ; he kills only the body,
whereas the self-murderer kills both the body and the
soul.[5] By denying the latter the right of Christian

---

[1] Thomas Aquinas, *op. cit.* ii.–ii.
64. 5.
[2] Lecky, *History of European
Morals*, ii. 44.
[3] *Cf.* St. Augustine, *De Civitate Dei*,
i. 23.

[4] Thomas Aquinas, *op. cit.* ii.–ii.
64. 5. 3. *Cf.* St. Augustine, *De
Civitate Dei*, i. 25.
[5] Damhouder, *op. cit.* lxxxviii. 1
sq., p. 258.

burial the Church recognises that he has placed himself outside her pale.

The condemnation of the Church influenced the secular legislation. The provisions of the Councils were introduced into the law-books. In France Louis IX. enforced the penalty of confiscating the self-murderer's property,[1] and laws to the same effect were passed in other European countries.[2] Louis XIV. assimilated the crime of suicide to that of *lèze majesté.*[3] According to the law of Scotland, " self-murder is as highly criminal as the killing our neighbour." [4] In England suicide is still regarded by the law as murder committed by a man on himself ; [5] and, unless declared insane, the self-murderer forfeited his property as late as the year 1870, when forfeitures for felony were abolished.[6] In Russia, to this day, the testamentary dispositions of a suicide are deemed void by the law. [7]

The horror of suicide also found a vent in outrages committed on the dead body. Of a woman who drowned herself in Edinburgh in 1598, we are told that her body was " harled through the town backwards, and thereafter hanged on the gallows."[8] In France, as late as the middle of the eighteenth century, self-murderers were dragged upon a hurdle through the streets with the face turned to the ground ; they were then hanged up with the head downwards, and finally thrown into the common sewer.[9] However, in most cases the treatment to which suicides' bodies were subject was not originally meant as a punishment, but was intended to prevent their spirits

[1] *Les Établissements de Saint Louis,* i. 92, vol. ii. 150.
[2] Bourquelot, *op. cit.* iv. 263. Morselli, *op. cit.* p. 196 *sq.*
[3] Louis XIV., 'Ordonnance criminelle,' A.D. 1670, xxii. 1, in Isambert, Decrusy, and Taillandier, *Recueil général des anciennes lois françaises,* xviii. 414.
[4] Erskine-Rankine, *Principles of the Law of Scotland,* p. 559.
[5] Stephen, *History of the Criminal Law of England,* iii. 104. For earlier times see Bracton, *De Legibus et*

Consuetudinibus Angliæ, fol. 150, vol. ii. 504 *sq.*
[6] Stephen, *op. cit.* iii. 105.
[7] Foinitzki, in von Liszt, *La législation pénale comparée,* p. 548.
[8] Ross, 'Superstitions as to burying Suicides in the Highlands,' in *Celtic Magazine,* xii. 354.
[9] Serpillon, *Code Criminel,* ii. 223. Cf. Louis XIV., ' Ordonnance criminelle,' A.D. 1670, xxii. 1, in Isambert, Decrusy, and Taillandier, *op. cit.* xviii. 414.

from causing mischief. All over Europe wandering
tendencies have been ascribed to their ghosts.[1] In some
countries the corpse of a suicide is supposed to make
barren the earth with which it comes in contact,[2] or to
produce hailstorms or tempests [3] or drought.[4] At
Lochbroom, in the North-West of Scotland, the people
believe that if the remains of a self-murderer be taken to
any burying-ground which is within sight of the sea or
of cultivated land, this would prove disastrous both to
fishing and agriculture, or, in the words of the people,
would cause " famine (or dearth) on sea and land " ; hence
the custom has been to inter suicides in out-of-the-way
places among the lonely solitudes of the mountains.[5] The
practice of burying them apart from other dead has been
very wide-spread in Europe, and in many cases there are
obvious indications that it arose from fear.[6] In the
North-East of Scotland a suicide was buried outside a
churchyard, close beneath the wall, and the grave was
marked by a single large stone, or by a small cairn, to which
the passing traveller was bound to cast a stone ; and afterwards, when the suicide's body was allowed to rest in the
churchyard, it was laid below the wall in such a position
that no one could walk over the grave, as the people
believed that if a woman enceinte stepped over such a

[1] Ross, in *Celtic Magazine*, xii. 352
(Highlanders of Scotland). Atkin-
son, *Forty Years in a Moorland
Parish*, p. 217. Hyltén-Cavallius,
Wärend och Wirdarne, i. 472 *sq.*
(Swedes). Allardt, ' Nyländska folk-
seder och bruk,' in *Nyland*, iv. 114
(Swedish Finlanders). Wuttke, *Der
deutsche Volksaberglaube der Gegen-
wart*, §756, p. 474 *sq.* Schiffer,
' Totenfetische bei den Polen,' in
Am Ur-Quell, iii. 50 (Polanders), 52
(Lithuanians). Volkov, ' Der Selbst-
mörder in Lithauen,' *ibid.* v. 87.
von Wlislocki, ' Tod und Toten-
fetische im Volkglauben der Sieben-
bürger Sachsen,' *ibid.* iv. 53.
Lippert, *Christenthum, Volksglaube
und Volksbrauch*, p. 391. Dyer, *The
Ghost World*, pp. 53, 151. Gaidoz,
' Le suicide,' in *Mélusine*, iv. 12.

[2] Schiffer, in *Am Ur-Quell*, iii. 52
(Lithuanians).

[3] *Ibid.* pp. 50 (Polanders), 53
(Lithuanians). von Wlislocki, *Volksglaube und religiöser Brauch der Magyaren*, p. 61. Strausz, *Die Bulgaren*,
p. 455. Prexl, 'Geburts- und Todtengebräuche der Rumänen in Siebenbürgen,' in *Globus*, lvii. 30.

[4] Strausz, *op. cit.* p. 455 (Bulgarians).

[5] Ross, in *Celtic Magazine*, xii.
350 *sq.*

[6] Gaidoz, in *Mélusine*, iv. 12.
Frank, *System einer vollständigen
medicinischen Polizey*, iv. 499.
Moore, *op. cit.* i. 310 (Danes).
Schiffer, in *Am Ur-Quell*, iii. 50
(Polanders), 53 (Lithuanians). Vol-
kov, *ibid.* v. 87 (Lithuanians).
Strausz, *op. cit.* p. 455 (Bulgarians).

grave, her child would quit this earth by its own act.[1] In England persons against whom a coroner's jury had found a verdict of *felo de se* were buried at cross-roads, with a stake driven through the body so as to prevent their ghosts from walking.[2] For the same purpose the bodies of

[1] Gregor, *Folk-Lore of the North-East of Scotland*, p. 213 *sq.*

[2] Stephen, *History of the Criminal Law of England*, iii. 105. Atkinson, *op. cit.* p. 217. This custom was formally abolished in 1823 by 4 Geo. IV. c. 52 (Stephen, *op. cit.* iii. 105). Why were suicides buried at cross-roads ? Possibly because the cross was supposed to disperse the evil energy ascribed to their bodies. Both in Europe and India the cross-road has, since ancient times, been a favourite place to divest oneself of diseases or other influences (Wuttke, *Der deutsche Volksaberglaube der Gegenwart*, §§ 483, 484, 492, 508, 514, 522, 545, pp. 325, 326, 331, 341, 345, 349, 361. *Hymns of the Atharva-Veda*, pp. 272, 473, 519. Oldenberg, *Die Religion des Veda*, pp. 267, 268 n. 1). In the sacred books of India it is said that "a student who has broken the vow of chastity shall offer an ass to Nirriti on a cross-road " (*Gautama*, xxiii. 17), and that a person who has previously undergone certain other purification ceremonies "is freed from all crimes, even mortal sins, after looking on a cross-road at a pot filled with water, and reciting the text, ' Simhe me manyuh ' " (*Baudhâyana*, iv. 7. 7). In the hills of Northern India and as far as Madras, an approved charm for getting rid of a disease of demoniacal origin is to plant a stake where four roads meet, and to bury grains underneath, which crows disinter and eat (*North Indian Notes and Queries*, i. § 652, p. 100 ; Madden, ' The Turaee and Outer Mountains of Kumaoon,' in *Jour. Asiatic Soc. Bengal*, xvii. pt. i. 583 ; Crooke, *Popular Religion and Folk-Lore of Northern India*, i. 290). In the Province of Bihār, "in cases of sickness various articles are exposed in a saucer at a cross-road " (Grierson, *Bihār Peasant Life*, p. 407). According to a Bulgarian tale, Lot was enjoined by the priest to plant on a cross-road three charred twigs in order to free himself from his sin (Strausz, *op. cit.* p. 115). The Gypsies of Servia believe that a thief may divert from himself all suspicions by painting with blood a cross and a dot above it on the spot where he committed the theft (von Wlislocki, ' Menschenblut im Glauben der Zigeuner,' in *Am Ur-Quell*, iii. 64 *sq.*). In Morocco the cross is used as a charm against the evil eye, and the chief reason for this is, I believe, that it is regarded as a conductor of the baneful energy emanating from the eye, dispersing it in all the quarters of the wind and thus preventing it from injuring the person or object looked at (Westermarck, ' Magic Origin of Moorish Designs,' in *Jour. Anthr. Inst.* xxxiv. 214). In Japan, if a criminal belonging to one of the lower classes commits suicide, his body is crucified (*Globus*, xviii. 197). When, under Tarquinius Priscus (or Tarquinius Superbus), many Romans preferred voluntary death to compulsory labour in the *cloaca*, or artificial canals by which the sewage was carried into the Tiber, the king ordered that their bodies should be crucified and abandoned to birds and beasts of prey (Pliny, *Historia naturalis*, xxxvi. 24 ; Servius, *Commentarii in Virgilii Æneidos*, xii. 603). The reason for thus crucifying the bodies of self-murderers is not stated ; but it is interesting to notice, in this connection, the idea expressed by some Christian writers that the cross of the Saviour symbolised the distribution of his benign influence in all directions (d'Ancona, *Origini del teatro italiano*, i. 646 ; Tauler, quoted by Peltzer, *Deutsche Mystik und deutsche Kunst*, p. 191. I am indebted to my friend Dr. Yrjö Hirn for drawing my attention to this idea). With reference to persons who had killed a father, mother, brother, or child, Plato says in his ' Laws ' (ix. 873) :—"If he be convicted, the ser-

suicides were in many cases burned.[1] And when removed
from the house where the act had been committed, they
were commonly carried out, not by the door, but by a
window,[2] or through a perforation specially made for the
occasion in the door,[3] or through a hole under the threshold,[4] in order that the ghost should not find its way back
into the house, or perhaps with a view to keeping the
entrance of the house free from dangerous infection.[5]

However, side by side with the extreme severity with
which suicide is viewed by the Christian Church, we find,
even in the Middle Ages, instances of more humane feelings towards its perpetrator. In mediæval tales and
ballads true lovers die together and are buried in the
same grave ; two roses spring through the turf and twine
lovingly together.[6] In the later Middle Ages, says M.

vants of the judges and the magistrates shall slay him at an appointed
place without the city where three
ways meet, and there expose his
body naked, and each of the magistrates on behalf of the whole city
shall take a stone and cast it upon
the head of the dead man, and so
deliver the city from pollution ;
after that, they shall bear him to
the borders of the land, and cast him
forth unburied, according to law."
The duels by which the ancient
Swedes were legally compelled to
repair their wounded honour were
to be fought on a place where three
roads met (Leffler, *Om den fornsvenska hednalagen*, p. 40 *sq.*; *supra*,
1. 502). In various countries it has
been the custom to bury the dead
at cross-roads (Grimm, ' Ueber das
Verbrennen der Leichen,' in *Kleinere
Schriften*, ii. 288 (Bohemians).
Lippert, *Die Religionen der europäischen Culturvölker*, p. 310 (Slavonians) ; Winternitz, *Das altindische
Hochzeitsrituell*, p.68; Oldenberg, *Die
Religion des Veda*, pp. 267, 268, 562
n. 3)—a custom which may have
given rise to the idea that cross-
roads are haunted (Winternitz, *op.
cit.* p.68; Oldenberg, *op. cit.* p. 267 *sq.*;
cf. Wuttke, *op. cit.* § 108, p. 89 *sq.*).
[1] Bourquelot, *loc. cit.* iv. 263.
Hyltén-Cavallius, *op. cit.* i. 459 ;
Nordström, *Bidrag till den svenska*

samhälls-författningens historia, ii.
331 (Swedes). von Wlislocki, ' Tod
und Totenfetische im Volkglauben
der Siebenbürger Sachsen,' in *Am
Ur-Quell*, iv. 53.
[2] Wuttke, *op. cit.* § 756, p. 474 ;
Frank, *op. cit.* iv. 498 *sq.* ; Lippert,
Der Seelencult, p. 11 (people in
various parts of Germany). Schiffer,
in *Am Ur-Quell*, iii. 50 (Polanders).
[3] Bourquelot, *loc. cit.* iv. 264 (at
Abbeville).
[4] Grimm, *Deutsche Rechtsalterthümer*, p. 726 *sqq.* Hyltén-Cavallius,
op. cit. i. 472 *sq.* (Swedes).
[5] See *infra*, on Regard for the Dead.
Contact with a self-murderer's
body is considered polluting (Prexl,
'Geburts- und Todtengebräuche der
Rumänen in Siebenbürgen,' in
Globus, lvii. 30 ; Hyltén-Cavallius,
Wärend och Wirdarne, i. 459, 460,
and ii. 412). We are told that in the
eighteenth century people did not
dare to cut down a person who had
hanged himself, though he was found
still alive (Frank, *op. cit.* iv. 499).
Among the Bannavs of Cambodia
everbody who takes part in the
burial of a self-murderer is obliged to
undergo a certain ceremony of purification, whereas no such ceremony is
prescribed in the case of other burials
(*Mittheil. d. Geogr. Ges. zu Jena*, iii. 9).
[6] See Bourquelot, *loc. cit.* iv. 248 ;
Gummere, *Germanic Origins*, p. 322.

Bourquelot, " on voit qu'à mesure qu'on avance, l'antagonisme devient plus prononcé entre l'esprit religieux et les idées mondaines relativement à la mort volontaire. Le clergé continue à suivre la route qui a été tracée par Saint Augustin et à déclarer le suicide criminel et impie ; mais la tristesse et le désespoir n'entendent pas sa voix, ne se souviennent pas de ses prescriptions." [1] The revival of classical learning, accompanied as it was by admiration for antiquity and a desire to imitate its great men, not only increased the number of suicides, but influenced popular sentiments on the subject.[2] Even the Catholic casuists, and later on philosophers of the school of Grotius and others, began to distinguish certain cases of legitimate suicide, such as that committed to avoid dishonour or probable sin, or that of a condemned person saving himself from torture by anticipating an inevitable death, or that of a man offering himself to death for the sake of his friend.[3] Sir Thomas More, in his Utopia, permits a person who is suffering from an incurable and painful disease to take his own life, provided that he does so with the agreement of the priests and magistrates ; nay, he even maintains that these should exhort such a man to put an end to a life which is only a burden to himself and others.[4] Donne, the well-known Dean of St. Paul's, wrote in his younger days a book in defence of suicide, " a Declaration," as he called it, " of that paradoxe, or thesis, that Self-homicide is not so naturally sin, that it may never be otherwise." He there pointed out the fact— which ought never to be overlooked by those who derive their arguments from " nature "—that some things may be natural to the species, and yet not natural to every individual member of it.[5] In one of his essays Montaigne pictures classical cases of suicide with colours of unmistakable sympathy. " La plus volontaire mort," he

[1] Bourquelot, loc. cit. iv. 253.
[2] Ibid. iv. 464. Morselli, op. cit. p. 35.
[3] Buonafede, op. cit. p. 148 sqq. Lecky, op. cit. ii. 55.

[4] More, Utopia, p. 122.
[5] Donne, Biathanatos, p. 45. Donne's book was first committed to the press in 1644, by his son.

observes, "c'est la plus belle. La vie despend de la volonté d'aultruy; la mort, de la nostre."[1] The rationalism of the eighteenth century led to numerous attacks both upon the views of the Church and upon the laws of the State concerning suicide. Montesquieu advocated its legitimacy :—" La société est fondée sur un avantage mutuel ; mais lorsqu'elle me devient onéreuse, qui m'empêche d'y renoncer ? La vie m'a été donnée comme une faveur ; je puis donc la rendre lorsqu'elle ne l'est plus : la cause cesse, l'effet doit donc cesser aussi."[2] Voltaire strongly opposed the cruel laws which subjected a suicide's body to outrage and deprived his children of their heritage.[3] If his act is a wrong against society, what is to be said of the voluntary homicides committed in war, which are permitted by the laws of all countries ? Are they not much more harmful to the human race than self-murder, which nature prevents from ever being practised by any large number of men ?[4] Beccaria pointed out that the State is more wronged by the emigrant than by the suicide, since the former takes his property with him, whereas the latter leaves his behind.[5] According to Holbach, he who kills himself is guilty of no outrage on nature or its author ; on the contrary, he follows an indication given by nature when he parts from his sufferings through the only door which has been left open. Nor has his country or his family any right to complain of a member whom it has no means of rendering happy, and from whom it consequently has nothing more to hope.[6] Others eulogised suicide when committed for a noble end,[7] or recommended it on certain occasions. "Suppose," says Hume, " that it is no longer in my

---

[1] Montaigne, *Essais*, ii. 3 (*Œuvres*, p. 187).

[2] Montesquieu, *Lettres Persanes*, 76 (*Œuvres*, p. 53).

[3] Voltaire, *Commentaire sur le livre Des délits et des peines*, 19 (*Œuvres complètes*, v. 416). *Idem*, *Prix de la justice et de l'humanité*, 5 (*ibid.* v. 424).

[4] *Idem*, *Note to Olympie acte v. scène 7* (*Œuvres complètes*, i. 826,

n. *b*). *Idem*, *Dictionnaire Philosophique*, art. Suicide (*ibid.* viii. 236).

[5] Beccaria, *Dei delitti e delle pene*, § 35 (*Opere*, i. 101).

[6] Holbach, *Système de la nature*, i. 369.

[7] In the early part of the nineteenth century this was done by Fries, *Neue oder anthropologische Kritik der Vernunft*, iii. 197.

power to promote the interest of society ; suppose that I
am a burthen to it ; suppose that my life hinders some
person from being much more useful to society. In such
cases my resignation of life must not only be innocent
but laudable."[1]   Hume also attacks the doctrine that
suicide is a transgression of our duty to God.   " If it
would be no crime in me to divert the Nile from its
course, were I able to do so, how could it be a crime to
turn a few ounces of blood from their natural channel ?
Were the disposal of human life so much reserved as the
peculiar province of the Almighty that it were an encroachment on his right for men to dispose of their own lives,
would it not be equally wrong of them to lengthen out
their lives beyond the period which by the general laws of
nature he had assigned to it ?   My death, however
voluntary, does not happen without the consent of
Providence ; when I fall upon my own sword, I receive
my death equally from the hands of the Deity as if it
had proceeded from a lion, a precipice, or a fever."[2]
Thus the main arguments against suicide which had
been set forth by pagan philosophers and Christian theologians were scrutinised and found unsatisfactory or at least
insufficient to justify that severe and wholesale censure
which was passed on it by the Church and the State. But
a doctrine which has for ages been inculcated by the leading authorities on morals is not easily overthrown ; and
when the old arguments are found fault with new ones are
invented. Kant maintained that a person who disposes of
his own life degrades the humanity subsisting in his person
and entrusted to him to the end that he might uphold it.[3]
Fichte argued that it is our duty to preserve our life and
to will to live, not for the sake of life, but because our
life is the exclusive condition of the realisation of the moral
law through us.[4] According to Hegel it is a contradiction
to speak of a person's right over his life, since this would

---

[1] Hume, ' Suicide,' in *Philosophical Works*, iv. 413.
[2] *Ibid.* p. 407 *sqq.*
[3] Kant, *Metaphysische Anfangungs-*

gründe der Tugendlehre, p. 73.
[4] Fichte, *Das System der Sitten-lehre*, p. 339 *sqq.* See also *ibid.* pp. 360, 391.

imply a right of a person over himself, and no one can stand
above and execute himself.[1] Paley, again, feared that if
religion and morality allowed us to kill ourselves in any
case, mankind would have to live in continual alarm for
the fate of their friends and dearest relations [2]—just as if
there were a very strong temptation for men to shorten
their lives. But common sense is neither a metaphysician
nor a sophist. When not restrained by the yoke of a narrow
theology, it is inclined in most cases to regard the self-
murderer as a proper object of compassion rather than of
condemnation, and in some instances to admire him as a
hero. The legislation on the subject therefore changed as
soon as the religious influence was weakened. The laws
against suicide were abolished in France by the Revolution,[3] and afterwards in various other continental countries ; [4] whilst in England it became the custom of
jurymen to presume absence of a sound mind in the
self-murderer—perjury, as Bentham said, being the
penance which prevented an outrage on humanity.[5]
These measures undoubtedly indicate not only a greater
regard for the innocent relatives of the self-murderer,
but also a change in the moral ideas concerning the act
itself.—

As appears from this survey of facts, the moral valuation
of suicide varies to an extreme degree. It depends partly
on the circumstances in which the act is committed,
partly on the point of view from which it is regarded and
the notions held about the future life. When a person
sacrifices his life for the benefit of a fellow-man or for the
sake of his country or to gratify the supposed desire of a
god, his deed may be an object of the highest praise. It
may, further, call forth approval or admiration as indicating a keen sense of honour or as a test of courage ; in
Japan, says Professor Chamberlain, " the courage to ·take

[1] Hegel, *Grundlinien der Philosophie des Rechts*, § 70, Zusatz, p. 72.
[2] Paley, *Principles of Moral and
Political Philosophy*, iv. 3 (*Complete
Works*, ii. 230).
[3] Legoyt, *op. cit.* p. 109.
[4] Bourquelot, *loc. cit.* iv. 475.
[5] Bentham, *Principles of Penal
Law*, ii. 4. 4 (*Works*, i. 479 *sq.*).

life—be it one's own or that of others—ranks extraordinarily high in public esteem."[1] In other cases suicide
is regarded with indifference as an act which concerns the
agent alone. But for various reasons it is also apt to give
rise to moral disapproval. The injury which the person
committing it inflicts upon himself may excite sympathetic
resentment towards him ; he may be looked upon as
injurer and injured at the same time. Plato asks in his
' Laws ' :—" What ought he to suffer who murders his
nearest and so-called dearest friend ? I mean, he who
kills himself."[2] And the same point of view is conspicuous
in St. Augustine's argument, that the more innocent
the self-murderer was before he committed his deed the
greater is his guilt in taking his life[3]—an argument of
particular force in connection with a theology which
condemns suicides to everlasting torments and which
regards it as a man's first duty to save his soul. The condemnation of killing others may by an association of ideas
lead to a condemnation of killing one's self,[4] as is suggested
by the Christian doctrine that suicide is prohibited in
the commandment, " Thou shalt not kill." The horror
which the act inspires, the fear of the malignant ghost, and
the defiling effect attributed to the shedding of blood, also
tend to make suicide an object of moral reprobation or to
increase the disapproval of it ;[5] and the same is the case
with the exceptional treatment to which the self-murderer's
body is subject and his supposed annihilation or miserable existence after death, which easily come to be looked
upon in the light of a punishment.[6] Suicide is, moreover,
blamed as an act of moral cowardice,[7] and, especially, as an
injury inflicted upon other persons, to whom the agent

[1] Chamberlain, *Things Japanese*, p.
221.
[2] Plato, *Leges*, ix. 873.
[3] St. Augustine, *De Civitate Dei*, i.
17.
[4] See Simmel, *Einleitung in die
Moralwissenschaft*, i. 187.
[5] *Cf. supra*, i. 377.

[6] See *supra*, ii. 237 *sqq.* ; Josephus,
De bello Judaico, iii. 8. 5 ; Plato,
Leges, ix. 873 ; Aristotle, *Ethica
Nicomachea*, v. 11. 2 *sq.*
[7] Hegel, *Grundlinien der Philo-
sophie des Rechts*, § 70, Zusatz, p. 72 ;
Fowler, *Progressive Morality*, p.
151 ; &c.

owed duties from which he withdrew by shortening his
life.[1] Even among savages we meet with the notion that a
person is not entitled to treat himself just as he pleases.
Among the Goajiro Indians of Colombia, if anybody accidentally cuts himself, say with his own knife, or breaks a
limb, or otherwise does himself an injury, his family on the
mother's side immediately demands blood-money, since,
being of their blood, he is not allowed to spill it without
paying for it ; the father's relatives demand tear-money,
and friends present claim compensation to repay their
sorrow at seeing a friend in pain.[2] That a similar view is
sometimes taken by savages with regard to suicide appears
from a few statements quoted above.[3] The opinion that
suicide is an offence against society at large is particularly
likely to prevail in communities where the interests of the
individual are considered entirely subordinate to the
interests of the State. The religious argument, again, that
suicide is a sin against the Creator, an illegitimate interference with his work and decrees, comes to prominence in
proportion as the moral consciousness is influenced by
theological considerations. In Europe this influence is
certainly becoming less and less. And considering that the
religious view of suicide has been the chief cause of the
extreme severity with which it has been treated in Christian countries, I am unable to subscribe to the opinion
expressed by Professor Durkheim, that the more lenient
judgment passed on it by the public conscience of the
present time is merely accidental and transient. The
argument adduced in support of this opinion leaves out of
account the real causes to which the valuation of suicide
is due : it is said that the moral evolution is not likely to
be retrogressive in this particular point after it has followed

---

[1] English lawyers have represented
suicide as an offence both against
God and against the sovereign, who
"has an interest in the preservation
of all his subjects" (Plowden, Commentaries, i. 261 ; Blackstone, Commentaries on the Laws of England, iv.
190. Cf. Ives, op. cit. p. 40 sq.).

[2] Simons, 'Exploration of the
Goajira Peninsula,' in Proceed. Roy.
Geo. Soc. N. Ser. vii. 790.

[3] Supra, ii. 240 sq.

a certain course for centuries.[1] It is true that moral progress has a tendency to increase our sense of duty towards
our fellow-men.   But at the same time it also makes us
more considerate as regards the motives of conduct ; and—
not to speak of suicides committed for the benefit of
others—the despair of the self-murderer will largely serve
as a palliation of the wrong which he may possibly inflict
upon his neighbour.

[1] Durkheim, *Le suicide*, p. 377.

CHAPTER XXXVI

SELF-REGARDING DUTIES AND VIRTUES—INDUSTRY—
REST

ACCORDING to current ideas men owe to themselves a variety of duties similar in kind to those which they owe to their fellow-creatures. They are not only forbidden to take their own lives, but are also in some measure considered to be under an obligation to support their existence, to take care of their bodies, to preserve a certain amount of personal freedom, not to waste their property, to exhibit self-respect, and, in general, to promote their own happiness. And closely related to these self-regarding duties there are self-regarding virtues, such as diligence, thrift, temperance. In all these cases, however, the moral judgment is greatly influenced by the question whether the act, forbearance, or omission, which increases the person's own welfare, conflicts or not with the interests of other people. If it does conflict, opinions vary as to the degree of selfishness which is recognised as allowable. But judgments containing moral praise or the inculcation of duty are most commonly passed upon conduct which involves some degree of self-sacrifice, not on such as involves self-indulgence.

Moreover, the duties which we owe to ourselves are generally much less emphasised than those which we owe to others. " Nature," says Butler, " has not given us so sensible a disapprobation of imprudence and folly, either in ourselves or others, as of falsehood, injustice, and cruelty." [1] Nor does a prudential virtue receive the same praise as one springing from a desire to promote the happiness of a fellow-man. Many moralists even maintain that, properly speaking, there are no self-regarding duties and virtues at all ; that useful action which is useful to ourselves alone is not matter for moral notice ; that in every case duties towards one's self may be reduced into duties towards others ; that intemperance and extravagant luxury, for instance, are blamable only because they tend to the public detriment, and that prudence is a virtue only in so far as it is employed in promoting public interest.[2] But this opinion is hardly in agreement with the ordinary moral consciousness.

It is undoubtedly true that no mode of conduct is exclusively self-regarding. No man is an entirely isolated being, hence anything which immediately affects a person's own welfare affects at the same time, in some degree, the welfare of other individuals. It is also true that the moral ideas concerning such conduct as is called self-regarding are more or less influenced by considerations as to its bearing upon others. But this is certainly not the only factor which determines the judgment passed on it. In the education of children various modes of self-regarding conduct are strenuously insisted upon by parents and teachers. What they censure or punish is regarded as wrong, what they praise or reward is regarded as good ; for, as we have noticed above, men have a tendency to sympathise with the retributive emotions of persons for whom they feel regard.[3] Moreover, as in the case of suicide,[4] so also in other instances of self-inflicted harm, the injury committed may excite sympathetic resentment towards the agent, although the victim of it is his own self. Disinterested likes or dislikes often give rise to moral

[1] Butler, 'Dissertation on the Nature of Virtue,' in *Analogy of Religion, &c.* p. 339.
[2] Hutcheson, *Inquiry into the Original of our Ideas of Beauty and Virtue*, pp. 133, 201. Grote, *Treatise on the Moral Ideals*, p. 77 *sqq.* Clifford, *Lectures and Essays*, pp. 298, 335. von Jhering, *Der Zweck im Recht*, ii. 225.
[3] *Supra*, i. 114 *sq.*
[4] *Supra*, ii. 262.

approval or disapproval of conduct which is essentially self-regarding.[1] It has also been argued that no man has a right to trifle with his own well-being even where other persons' interests are not visibly affected by it, for the reason that he is not entitled wantonly to waste " what is not at his unconditional disposal." [2] And in various other ways—as will be seen directly—religious, as well as magical, ideas have influenced moral opinions relating to self-regarding conduct. But at the same time it is not difficult to see why self-regarding duties and virtues only occupy a subordinate place in our moral consciousness. The influence they exercise upon other persons' welfare is generally too remote to attract much attention. In education there is no need to emphasise any other self-regarding duties and virtues but those which, for the sake of the individual's general welfare, require some sacrifice of his immediate comfort or happiness. The compassion which we are apt to feel for the victim of an injury is naturally lessened by the fact that it is self-inflicted. And, on the other hand, indignation against the offender is disarmed by pity, imprudence commonly carrying its own punishment along with it.[3]

Being so little noticed by custom and public opinion, and still less by law, most self-regarding duties hardly admit of a detailed treatment. In a general way it may be said that progress in intellectual culture has, in some respects, been favourable to their evolution ; Darwin even maintains that, with a few exceptions, self-regarding virtues are not esteemed by savages.[4] The less developed the intellect, the less apt it is to recognise the remoter consequences of men's behaviour ; hence more reflection than that exercised by the savage may be needed to see that modes of conduct which immediately concern a person's own welfare at the same time affect the well-being

---

[1] *Cf. supra*, i. 116 *sq.*
[2] Martineau, *Types of Ethical Theory*, ii. 126.
[3] *Cf.* Butler, *op. cit.* p. 339 *sq.* ; Dugald Stewart, *Philosophy of the*

Active and Moral Powers of Man, ii. 346 *sq.*
[4] Darwin, *Descent of Man*, p. 118 *sq.*

of his neighbours or the whole community of which he is a member. So also, owing to his want of foresight, the savage would often fail to notice how important it may be to subject one's self to some temporary deprivation or discomfort in order to attain greater happiness in the future. We have noticed above that many savages hardly ever correct their children,[1] and this means that one of the chief sources from which the notions of self-regarding duties spring is almost absent among them. But on the other hand it must also be remembered that disinterested antipathies, another cause of such notions, exercise more influence upon the unreflecting than upon the reflecting moral consciousness, and that many magical and religious ideas which at the lower stages of civilisation give rise to duties of a self-regarding character are no longer held by people more advanced in culture.

These general statements referring to the nature and origin of self-regarding duties and virtues I shall now illustrate by a short survey of moral ideas concerning some representative modes of self-regarding conduct :— industry and rest ; temperance, fasting, and abstinence from certain kinds of food and drink ; cleanliness and uncleanliness ; and ascetic practices generally.

Man is naturally inclined to idleness, not because he is averse from muscular activity as such, but because he dislikes the monotony of regular labour and the mental exertion it implies.[2] In general he is induced to work only by some special motive which makes him think the trouble worth his while. Among savages, who have little care for the morrow,[3] who have few comforts of life to provide for, and whose property is often of such a kind as to prevent any great accumulation of it, almost the sole inducement to industry is either necessity or compulsion. Men are lazy or industrious according as the necessaries of life are easy

[1] *Supra*, i. 513 *sq.*
[2] *Cf.* Ferrero, ' Les formes primitives du travail,' in *Revue scienti-fique*, ser. iv. vol. v. 331 *sqq.*
[3] Buecher, *Die Entstehung der Volkswirtschaft*, p. 21 *sqq.*

or difficult to procure, and they prefer being idle if they can compel other persons to work for them as their servants or slaves.

Australian natives " can exert themselves vigorously when hunting or fishing or fighting or dancing, or at any time when there is a prospect of an immediate reward ; but prolonged labour with the object of securing ultimate gain is distasteful to them." [1] With reference to the Polynesians Mr. Hale observes that in those islands which are situated nearest the equator, where the heat with little or no aid from human labour calls into existence fruits serving to support human life, the inhabitants are an indolent and listless race ; whilst " a severer clime and ruder soil are favourable to industry, foresight, and a hardy temperament. These opposite effects are manifested in the Samoans, Nukahivans, and Tahitians, on the one side, and the Sandwich Islanders and New Zealanders on the other." [2] Mr. Yate likewise contrasts the industry of the Maoris with the proverbial idleness of the Tonga Islanders : the former " are obliged to work, if they would eat," whereas " in the luxurious climate of the Friendly Islands, there is scarcely any need of labour, to obtain the necessaries, and even many of the luxuries, of life." [3] The Malays are described as fond of a life of slothful ease, because " persevering toil is unnecessary, or would bring them no additional enjoyments." [4] The natives of Sumatra, says Marsden, " are careless and improvident of the future, because their wants are few ; for though poor

---

[1] Brough Smyth, *Aborigines of Victoria*, i. 29 *sq.* See also *ibid.* ii. 248 ; Collins, *English Colony in New South Wales*, i. 601 ; Fison and Howitt, *Kamilaroi and Kurnai*, p. 259 *sq.*
[2] Hale, *U.S. Exploring Expedition. Vol. VI. Ethnography and Philology*, p. 17. See also Williams, *Missionary Enterprises in the South Sea Islands*, p. 534 (Samoans) ; Ellis, *Polynesian Researches*, i. 130 *sq.* (Tahitians) ; Brenchley, *Cruise of H.M.S. Curaçoa among the South Sea Islands*, p. 58 (natives of Tutuila) ; Melville, *Typee*, p. 287 (some Marquesas Islanders) ; Anderson, *Notes of Travel in Fiji and New Caledonia*, p. 236 (New Caledonians) ; Penny, *Ten Years in Melanesia*, p. 74 (Solomon Islanders).
[3] Yate, *Account of New Zealand*, p. 105 *sq.*
[4] McNair, *Perak and the Malays*, p. 201. Bock, *Head-Hunters of Borneo*, p. 275. Raffles, *History of Java*, i. 251.. St. John, *Life in the Forests of the Far East*, ii. 323.

they are not necessitous, nature supplying, with extraordinary facility, whatever she has made requisite for their existence."[1] The Toda of the Neilgherry Hills will not " work one iota more than circumstances compel him to do " ;[2] and indolence seems to be a characteristic of most peoples of India,[3] though there are exceptions to the rule.[4] Burckhardt observes that it is not the southern sun, as Montesquieu imagined, but the luxuriance of the southern soil and the abundance of provisions that relax the exertions of the inhabitants and cause apathy :—" By the fertility of Egypt, Mesopotamia, and India, which yield their produce almost spontaneously, the people are lulled into indolence ; while in neighbouring countries, of a temperature equally warm, as among the mountains of Yemen and Syria, where hard labour is necessary to ensure a good harvest, we find a race as superior in industry to the former as the inhabitants of Northern Europe are to those of Spain or Italy."[5] Indolence is a common,[6] though not universal,[7] trait of the African character. Of the Negroes on the Gold Coast Bosman says that " nothing

[1] Marsden, *History of Sumatra*, p. 209. See also *Glimpses of the Eastern Archipelago*, pp. 76, 87 (Bataks).

[2] Marshall, *A Phrenologist amongst the Todas*, p. 88. See also *ibid.* p. 86 ; Shortt, ' Hill Tribes of the Neilgherries,' in *Trans. Ethn. Soc.* N.S. vii. 241 ; Mantegazza, ' Studii sull' etnologia dell' India,' in *Archivio per l'antropologia e la etnologia*, xiii. 406.

[3] Cooper, *Mishmee Hills*, p. 100 (Assamese). Tickell, ' Memoir on the Hodésum,' in *Jour. Asiatic Soc. Bengal*, ix. 808 (Hos). Dalton, *Ethnology of Bengal*, pp. 57 (Jyntias and Kasias), 101 (Lepchas). Burton, *Sindh*, p. 284. Moorcroft and Trebeck, *Travels in the Himalayan Provinces of Hindustan*, i. 321 (Ladakhis). Caldwell, *Tinnevelly Shanars*, p. 58.

[4] Man, *Sonthalia*, p. 19. Hodgson, *Miscellaneous Essays*, i. 152 (Bódo and Dhimáls). Macpherson, *Memorials of Service in India*, p. 81 (Kandhs).

[5] Burckhardt, *Arabic Proverbs*, p. 219.

[6] Beltrame, *Il Sènnaar*, i. 166. Tuckey, *Expedition to Explore the River Zaire*, p. 369. Johnston, *The River Congo*, p. 402 (Bakongo). Casati, *Ten Years in Equatoria*, i. 85 (Abaka Negroes). Wilson and Felkin, *Uganda*, ii. 310 (Gowane people). Burton, *Zanzibar*, ii. 96 (Wanika). Bonfanti, ' L'incivilimento dei negri nell' Africa intertropicale,' in *Archivio per l'antropologia e la etnologia*, xv. 133 (Bantu). Andersson, *Lake Ngami*, p. 231 (Herero). Magyar, *Reisen in Süd-Afrika*, p. 290 (Kimbunda). Kropf, *Das Volk der Xosa-Kaffern*, p. 89. Tyler, *Forty Years among the Zulus*, p. 194. Ellis, *History of Madagascar*, i. 140. Shaw, ' Betsileo Country and People,' in *Antananarivo Annual*, iii. 81.

[7] Baker, *Ismailia*, p. 56 (Shilluk). Baumann, *Usambara*, p. 244 (Wapare). Bosman, *Description of the Coast of Guinea*, p. 318 (Negroes of Fida). Andersson, *Notes on Travel in South Africa*, p. 235 (Ovambo). See also *infra*, p. 272.

but the utmost necessity can force them to labour." [1]
The Waganda are represented as excessively indolent, in
consequence of the ease with which they can obtain all
the necessaries of life.[2] Of the Namaquas we are told
that "they may be seen basking in the sun for days
together, in listless inactivity, frequently almost perishing
from thirst or hunger, when with very little exertion they
may have it in their power to satisfy the cravings of
nature. If urged to work, they have been heard to say :
' Why should we resemble the worms of the ground ? ' " [3]
Most of the American Indians are said to have a slothful
disposition, because they can procure a livelihood with but
little labour.[4] But the case is different with the Greenlanders and other Eskimo, who have to struggle hard for
their existence.[5]

We have seen that savages consider it a duty for a
married man to support his family,[6] and this in most cases
implies that he is under an obligation to do a certain
amount of work. We have also seen that the various
occupations of life are divided between the sexes according
to rules fixed by custom,[7] and this means that absolute
idleness is not generally tolerated in either men or women,
though the drudgeries of life are often imposed upon the
latter. Of some uncivilised peoples we are directly told
that they enjoin work as a duty or regard industry as a
virtue. The Greenlanders esteem addiction to labour as
the chief of virtues and believe that the industrious man

---

[1] Bosman, op. cit. p. 101.
[2] Wilson and Felkin, op. cit. i. 225.
[3] Andersson, Lake Ngami, p. 335.
See also Kolben, Present State of the
Cape of Good-Hope, i. 46, 324 ;
Barrow, Travels into the Interior of
Southern Africa, i. 152 ; Fritsch,
Die Eingeborenen Süd-Afrika's, p.
324 (Hottentots).
[4] Bridges, 'Manners and Customs
of the Firelanders,' in A Voice for
South America, xiii. 203 (Fuegians).
Dobrizhoffer, Account of the Abi-
pones, ii. 151 ; but he praises the
Abiponian women for their un-
wearied industry (ibid. ii. 151 sq.).
Brett, Indian Tribes of Guiana, p.

343 ; Kirke, Twenty-five Years in
British Guiana, p. 150. Domenech,
Seven Years' Residence in the Great
Deserts of North America, ii. 190. Bur-
ton, City of the Saints, p. 126 (Sioux).
Harmon, Voyages and Travels in the
Interior of North America, p. 285
(Tacullies). Meares, Voyages to the
North-West Coast of America, p. 265
(Nootkas).
[5] Cranz, History of Greenland, i.
126. Armstrong, Narrative of the
Discovery of the North-West Passage,
p. 196 (Western Eskimo).
[6] Supra, i. 526 sqq.
[7] Supra, i. 634 sqq.

will have a very happy existence after death.[1] The Atkha Aleuts prohibited laziness.[2] Mr. Batchelor relates an Ainu fable which encourages diligence and discourages idleness in young people.[3] The Karens of Burma have a traditional precept which runs, " Be not idle, but labour diligently, that you may not become slaves." [4] The Maoris say, " Let industry be rewarded, lest idleness gets the advantage." [5] The Malagasy likewise inculcate industry in many of their proverbs.[6] The Basutos have a saying that " perseverance always triumphs."[7] Among the Bachapins, a Bechuana tribe conspicuous for its activity, " a man's merit is estimated principally by his industry, and the words *múnŏnă usinăachă* (an industrious man) are an expression of high approbation and praise ; while he who is seldom seen to hunt, to prepare skins for clothing, or to sew koboes, is accounted a worthless and disgraceful member of society."[8] Among the Beni M'zab in the Sahara—an industrious people inhabiting a sterile country —boys are already at the age of six years compelled by law to begin to work, either in driving a camel or ass, or in drawing water for the gardens.[9] We may expect to find industry especially insisted upon by uncivilised peoples who are habitually addicted to it, partly because it is a necessity among them, partly owing to the influence of habit.

But instead of being regarded as a duty, industrial activity is not infrequently looked down upon as disreputable for a free man. This is especially the case among warlike nations, nomadic tribes, and peoples who have many slaves. In Uganda, for instance, the prevalence of slavery " causes all manual labour to be looked upon as derogatory to the dignity of a free man." [10] The

[1] Cranz, *op. cit.* i. 186.
[2] Yakof, quoted by Petroff, *Report on Alaska*, p. 158.
[3] Batchelor, *Ainu of Japan*, p. 111.
[4] Smeaton, *Loyal Karens of Burma*, p. 255.
[5] Taylor, *Te Ika a Maui*, p. 293. See also Johnston, *Maoria*, p. 43.
[6] Clemes, ' Malagasy Proverbs,' in *Antananarivo Annual*, iv. 29.
[7] Casalis, *Basutos*, p. 310.
[8] Burchell, *Travels in the Interior of Southern Africa*, ii. 557.
[9] Tristram, *The Great Sahara*, p. 207 *sq.*
[10] Wilson and Felkin, *op. cit.* i. 186.

Masai [1] and Matabele [2] consider that the only occupation
which becomes a man is warfare. The Arabs of the
desert hold labour humiliating to anybody but a slave.[3]
Speaking of the Turkomans, Vámbéry observes that " in
his domestic circle, the nomad presents us a picture of the
most absolute indolence. In his eyes it is the greatest
shame for a man to apply his hand to any domestic
occupation." [4] The Chippewas " have ever looked upon
agricultural and mechanical labours as degrading," and
" have regarded the use of the bow and arrow, the war-
club and spear, as the noblest employments of man." [5]
Among the Iroquois " the warrior despised the toil of
husbandry, and held all labour beneath him." [6] Though an
industrious race, the Maoris considered it more honourable, as well as more desirable, to acquire property by war
and plunder than by labour. [7] Among the Line Islanders it
is undignified for a landholder to do work of any kind,
except to make weapons, hence he employs persons of the
lower class to work for him.[8] In Nukahiva the people of
distinction " suffer the nails on the fingers to grow very
long, that it may be evident they are not accustomed to
hard labour." [9] This contempt for industrial activity is
easy to explain. A man who earns his livelihood by
labour is considered to be lacking in those qualities which
are alone admired—courage and strength ;—or work is
associated with the idea of servile subjection. It is also
universally held degrading for a man to engage in any
occupation which belongs to the women.[10] Thus among
hunting and pastoral peoples it would be quite out of
place for him to supply the household with vegetable
food.[11] On the other hand, when agriculture became an

[1] Merker, *Die Masai*, p. 117.
[2] Holub, ' Die Ma-Atabele,' in
Zeitschr. f. Ethnol. xxv. 198.
[3] Burton, *Pilgrimage to Al-Madinah & Meccah*, ii. 10.
[4] Vámbéry, *Travels in Central Asia*,
p. 320.
[5] Schoolcraft, *Archives of Aboriginal Knowledge*, v. 150.
[6] Morgan, *League of the Iroquois*,

p. 329.
[7] Travers, ' Life and Times of Te
Rauparaha,' in *Trans. New Zealand
Inst.* v. 29.
[8] Tutuila, ' Line Islanders,' in
Jour. Polynesian Soc. i. 266.
[9] von Langsdorf, *Voyages and
Travels*, i. 174.
[10] *Supra*, i. 636 sq.
[11] *Supra*, i. 634.

indispensable means to maintenance of life it at the same time became respectable. But trade was scorned, probably, as Mr. Spencer suggests, because it was carried on chiefly by unsettled persons, who were detached, untrustworthy members of a community in which most men had fixed positions.[1] The Kandhs " consider it beneath their dignity to barter or traffic, and . . . . regard as base and plebeian all who are not either warriors or tillers of the soil." [2] The Javans " have a contempt for trade, and those of higher rank esteem it disgraceful to be engaged in it ; but the common people are ever ready to engage in the labours of agriculture, and the chiefs to honour and encourage agricultural industry." [3]

Progress in civilisation implies an increase of industry. Both the necessities and the comforts of life grow more numerous ; hence more labour is required to provide for them, and at the same time there is more inducement to accumulate wealth. The advantages, both private and public, accruing from diligence are more clearly recognised, and the government, in particular, is anxious that the people should work so as to be able to pay their taxes. All this leads to condemnation of idleness and approbation of industry ; and the influence of habit must operate in the same direction among a nation whose industrial propensities have been the cause of its civilisation. But in the archaic State war is still regarded as a nobler occupation than labour ; and whilst agriculture is held in honour, trade and handicraft are frequently despised.

In the kingdom of the Peruvian Incas there was a law that no one should be idle. " Children of five years old were employed at very light work, suitable to their age. Even the blind and lame, if they had no other infirmity, were provided with certain kinds of work. The rest of the people, while they were healthy, were occupied each at his own labour, and it was a most infamous and degrading

---

[1] Spencer, *Principles of Ethics*, i. 429.
[2] Campbell, *Wild Tribes of* *Khondistan*, p. 50.
[3] Raffles, *op. cit.* i. 246 *sq.*

thing among these people to be chastised in public for idleness." [1] If any of them was slothful, or slept in the day, he was whipped or had to carry the stone. [2] The reason for these measures was that the whole duty of defraying the expenses of the government belonged to the people, and that, without money and with little property, they paid their taxes in labour ; hence to be idle was, in a manner, to rob the exchequer. [3]

One of the characteristics of Zoroastrianism is its appreciation of labour. [4] The faithful man must be vigilant, alert, and active ; sleep itself is merely a concession to the demons, and should therefore be kept within the limits of necessity. [5] The lazy man is the most unworthy of men, because he eats his food through impropriety and injustice. [6] And of all kinds of labour the most necessary is husbandry. [7] Man has been placed upon earth to preserve Ahura Mazda's good creation, and this can only be done by careful tilling of the soil, eradication of thorns and weeds, and reclamation of the tracks over which Angra Mainyu has spread the curse of barrenness. Zoroaster asked, "What is the food that fills the Religion of Mazda ? " and Ahura Mazda answered, " It is sowing corn again and again, O Spitama Zarathustra ! He who sows corn sows righteousness." [8] According to Xenophon, the king of the Persians considered the art of agriculture and that of war to be the most honourable and necessary occupations, and paid the greatest attention to both. [9] He appointed officers to overlook the tillers of the ground, as well as to collect tribute from them ; for " those who

[1] Blas Valera, quoted by Garcilasso de la Vega, *First Part of the Royal Commentaries of the Yncas*, ii. 34. See also *ibid*. ii. 14 ; Acosta, *Natural and Moral History of the Indies*, ii. 413.

[2] Herrera, *General History of the West Indies*, iv. 339.

[3] Prescott, *History of the Conquest of Peru*, i. 57.

[4] See Darmesteter, in *Sacred Books of the East*, iv. p. lxvii. ; Geiger,

Civilization of the Eastern Iranians, i. 70 ; Rawlinson, *Religions of the Ancient World*, p. 108 ; *Dînâ-î Maînôg-î Khirad*, ii. 29, xxxvi. 15, xxxvii. 14, &c.

[5] *Vendîdâd*, xviii. 16.

[6] *Dînâ-î Maînôg-î Khirad*, xxi. 27.

[7] See *Vendîdâd*, iii. 23 *sqq*.

[8] *Ibid*. iii. 30 *sq*.

[9] Xenophon, *Œconomicus*, iv. 4, 8 *sqq*.

cultivate the ground inefficiently will neither maintain the garrisons, nor be able to pay their tribute." [1]

In his description of ancient Egypt Herodotus tells us that one of its kings made a law to the effect that every Egyptian should annually declare to the governor of his district by what means he maintained himself, and that, if he failed to do this, or did not show that he lived by honest means, he should be punished with death.[2] Whether this statement be correct or not,[3] it seems certain that the Egyptians were anxious to encourage industry.[4] An ostracon which has often been quoted contains the maxim, " Do not spare thy body whilst thou art young, for food cometh by the arms and provisions by the legs." [5]

A law against idleness resembling that which is reported to have existed in Egypt was established at Athens, according to some writers by Draco or Pisistratus,[6] according to others by Solon, who is said to have borrowed it from the Egyptians.[7] Plutarch states that, as the city was filled with persons who assembled from all parts on account of the great security which prevailed in Attica and the country withal was poor and barren, Solon turned the attention of the citizens to manufactures. For this purpose he ordered that trades should be accounted honourable, that the council of the Areopagus should examine into every man's means of subsisting and chastise the idle, and that no son should be obliged to maintain his father if the father had not taught him a trade.[8] Thucydides puts the following words in the mouth of Pericles :—" To avow poverty with us is no disgrace ; the true disgrace is in doing nothing to avoid it. An Athenian citizen does not neglect the State because he takes care of his own house-

[1] Xenophon, Œconomicus, iv. 9, 11.
[2] Herodotus, ii. 177. Cf. Diodorus Siculus, Bibliotheca historica, i. 77. 5.
[3] Cf. Wiedemann, Herodots zweites Buch, p. 605.
[4] See Amélineau, Essai sur l'évolution des idées morales dans l'Égypte Ancienne, p. 329.
[5] Gardiner, ' Egyptian Ethics,' in Hastings' Encyclopædia of Religion and Ethics, v. 484.
[6] Pollux, Onomasticum, viii. 42. Diogenes Laertius, Vitæ philosophorum, i. 55. Plutarch, Solon, xxxi. 6.
[7] Herodotus, ii. 177. Diodorus Siculus, i. 77. 5.
[8] Plutarch, Solon, xxii. 1, 3 sq.

hold ; and even those of us who are engaged in business have a very fair idea of politics." [1]   In Xenophon's ' Memorabilia ' Socrates recommends industry as a means of supporting life, of maintaining the health and strength of the body, of promoting temperance and honesty.[2] According to Plato idleness is the mother of wantonness, whereas by labour the aliment of passion is diverted into other parts of the body.[3] Agriculture was highly praised. It is the best of all the occupations and arts by which men procure the means of living.[4]   Where it flourishes all other pursuits are in full vigour, but when the ground is allowed to lie barren other occupations are almost stopped.[5] It is an exercise for the body, and strengthens it for discharging the duties that become a man of honourable birth.[6]   It requires people to accustom themselves to endure the colds of winter and the heats of summer.[7] It renders them fit for running, throwing, leaping.[8] It gives them the greatest gratification for their labour, it is the most attractive of all employments.[9] It receives strangers with the richest hospitality.[10] It offers the most pleasing first-fruits to the gods, and the richest banquets on festival days.[11] It teaches men justice, for it is those who treat the earth best that she recompenses with the most numerous benefits.[12]   It instructs people to assist one another, for it cannot be conducted without the aid of other men.[13] It does not give such constant occupation to a person's mind as to prevent him from attending to the interests of his friends or his native land.[14] The possession of an estate stimulates men to defend their country in arms.[15]   In short, agriculture renders citizens most useful, most virtuous, and best affected towards the commonwealth.[16]

[1] Thucydides, *Historia belli Peloponnesiaci*, ii. 40. 1 *sq.*
[2] Xenophon, *Memorabilia*, ii. 7. 7 *sq.*
[3] Plato, *Leges*, viii. 835, 841.
[4] Xenophon, *Œconomicus*, vi. 8.
[5] *Ibid.* v. 17.
[6] *Ibid.* v. 1 ; vi. 9.
[7] *Ibid.* v. 4.
[8] *Ibid.* v. 8.
[9] *Ibid.* v. 8, 11.
[10] *Ibid.* v. 8.
[11] *Ibid.* v. 10.
[12] *Ibid.* v. 12.
[13] *Ibid.* v. 14.
[14] *Ibid.* vi. 9.
[15] *Ibid.* v. 7.
[16] *Ibid.* vi. 10.

The argumentative manner in which these views were expressed by the philosophers indicates, however, that industrial occupations were deficient in public appreciation.[1] Herodotus says that not only among most barbarians but also throughout Greece those who are given wholly to war are honoured above others.[2] This was especially the case at Sparta, where a freeman was forbidden to engage in any industrial occupation.[3] Contrasting Lycurgus' legislation with that of Solon, Plutarch observes that in a state where the earth was sufficient to support twice the number of inhabitants and where there were a multitude of Helots to be worn out by servitude, it was right to set the citizens free from laborious and mechanic arts and to employ them in arms as the only art fit for them to learn and exercise.[4] At Thebes there was a law that no man could hold office who had not retired from business for ten years, because it was looked upon as a mean employment.[5] Even at Athens, in spite of its democratic institutions and its laws against idleness, trade and handicrafts were despised, both by the general public and by the philosophers. Xenophon's Socrates said that the industrial arts are objectionable and justly held in little repute in communities, because they weaken the bodies of those who work at them by compelling them to sit and to live indoors and in some cases to pass whole days by the fire ; for when the body becomes effeminate the mind loses its strength.[6] Moreover, mechanical occupations leave those who practise them no leisure to attend to the interests of their friends or the commonwealth, hence men of that class seem unsuited alike to be of advantage to their connections and to be defenders of their country.[7] Plato maintains that manual arts are a reproach because they " imply a natural weakness of the higher principle " ;[8] by

---

[1] *Cf.* Schmidt, *Die Ethik der alten Griechen*, ii. 435 *sqq.*
[2] Herodotus, ii. 167.
[3] *Ibid.* ii. 167. Xenophon, *Lacedæmoniorum respublica*, vii. 2.   Plutarch, *Lycurgus*, xxiv. 2.   *Idem, Agesilaus*, xxvi. 6.   Aelian, *Varia*

historia, vi. 6.
[4] Plutarch, *Solon*, xxii. 2.
[5] Aristotle, *Politica*, iii. 5. 7, p. 1278 a ; vi. 7. 4, p. 1321 a.
[6] Xenophon, *Œconomicus*, iv. 2.
[7] *Ibid.* iv. 3.
[8] Plato, *Respublica*, ix. 590.

their meanness they maim and disfigure the souls as well
as the bodies of those who are employed in them.[1] When
Hesiod said that " work is no disgrace," [2] he could certainly
not have meant that there was no disgrace for example
in the manufacture of shoes or in selling pickles.[3] And
in his ' Laws ' Plato lays down the regulation that no
citizen or servant of a citizen should be occupied in
handicraft arts ; " for he who is to secure and preserve
the public order of the State has an art which requires
much study and many kinds of knowledge, and does not
admit of being made a secondary occupation." [4] Aristotle,
again, observes that in a community which has an aristo-
cratic form of government the mechanic and the labourer
will not be citizens, because honours are there given
according to virtue and merit, and " no man can practise
virtue who is living the life of a mechanic or labourer." [5]
Corinth was the place in Greece where the mechanic's
occupation was least despised [6]—no doubt because its
situation naturally led to extensive trade and thence to
that splendour of living by which the useful and orna-
mental arts are most encouraged.[7]

The Roman views on the subject were very similar to
those of the Greeks. With regard to what arts and means
of acquiring wealth are to be regarded as worthy and what
disreputable, says Cicero, we have been taught as follows.
In the first place, those sources of emolument which incur
public hatred, such as those of tax-gatherers and usurers,
are condemned. We are likewise to account as mean the
gains of hired workmen, whose source of profit is not their
art but their labour ; for their very wages are the consideration of their servitude. We are further to despise
all who retail from merchants goods for prompt sale ; for
they never can succeed unless they lie most abominably,

---

[1] *Ibid*. vi. 495.
[2] Hesiod, *Opera et dies*, 311.
[3] Plato, *Charmides*, p. 163.
[4] *Idem, Leges*, viii. 846.
[5] Aristotle, *Politica*, iii. 5. 5, p.
1278 a. See also *ibid*. vi. 4. 12, p.

1319 a ; vii. 8. 3, p. 1328 b ; viii. 2.
4 *sq.* p. 1337 b.
[6] Herodotus, ii. 167.
[7] See Rawlinson's note in his translation of Herodotus, ii. 252, n. 7.

and nothing is more disgraceful than insincerity. All mechanical labourers are by their profession mean ; for a workshop can contain nothing befitting a gentleman. Least of all are those trades to be approved that serve the purposes of sensuality, such as the occupations of butchers, cooks, and fishermen. But those professions that involve a higher degree of intelligence or a greater amount of utility, such as medicine, architecture, and the teaching of the liberal arts, are honourable in those to whose rank in life they are suited. As to merchandising, if on a small scale it is mean, but if it is extensive and rich, if it brings numerous commodities from all parts of the world, and gives bread to a multitude of people without fraud, it is not so despicable. However, if a merchant, satisfied with his profits, steps from the harbour into an estate, such a man seems most justly deserving of praise. For of all gainful professions nothing is better, nothing is more pleasing and more delightful, nothing is more befitting a well-bred man than agriculture.[1]

The contempt in which manual labour was held by the ancient pagans could hardly be shared by early Christianity. Christ had been born in a carpenter's family, his apostles belonged to the working class, and so did originally most of his followers. Origen accepts with pride the reproach of Celsus, when he accuses Christians of worshipping the son of a poor workwoman, who had earned her bread by spinning,[2] and contrasts with the wisdom of Plato that of Paul, the tent-maker, of Peter, the fisherman, of John, who had abandoned his father's nets.[3] St. Paul presses on the Thessalonians the duty of personal industry ; " if any one would not work, neither should he eat."[4] But at the same time the spirit of Christianity was not consistent with much anxiety about earthly matters. The aim of a true disciple of Christ was not to prosper in the world but

---

[1] Cicero, De officiis, i. 42. See also Idem, Cato Major, ch. 15 sqq.
[2] Origen, Contra Celsum, i. 28 sq. (Migne, Patrologiæ cursus, Ser. Graeca, xi. 714 sq.).

[3] Ibid. vi. 7 (Migne, Ser. Gr. xi. 1298 sq.).
[4] 1 Thessalonians, iv. 11 ; 2 Thessalonians, iii. 10.

to seek the kingdom of God, not to lay up for himself treasures upon earth but to lay up for himself treasures in heaven.[1] Poverty became an ideal, in conformity with both the example and teachings of Christ. It was associated with godliness, whilst wealth was associated with godlessness.[2] " The love of money," says St. Paul, " is the root of all evil " ;[3] and the same idea was over and again expressed by Christian moralists.[4] In the original sinless state of mankind property was unknown, and so was labour. It was to punish man for his disobedience that God caused him to eat daily bread in the sweat of his face.[5] Since then work is a necessity ; but the contemplative life is better than the active life.[6] Bonaventura points out that Jesus preferred the meditating Mary to the busy Martha,[7] and that he himself seems to have done no work till his thirtieth year.[8] Work is of no value by itself ; its highest object is to further contemplation, to macerate the body, to curb concupiscence.[9] For this purpose, indeed, it was strongly insisted upon by several founders of religious orders. According to St. Benedict, " idleness is an enemy to the soul ; and hence at certain seasons the brethren ought to occupy themselves in the labour of their hands, and at others in holy reading."[10] St. Bernard writes :— " The handmaid of Christ ought always to pray, to read, to work, lest haply the spirit of uncleanness should lead astray the slothful mind. The delight of the flesh is overcome by labour. . . . The body tired by work is less delighted with vice."[11] But the active life must not be pursued to such an extent as to hinder what it is intended to promote ;

---

[1] St. Luke, xii. 22 sqq. St. Matthew, vi. 19 sq.

[2] St. Luke, xvi. 19 sqq. St. Matthew, xix. 24.

[3] 1 Timothy, vi. 10.

[4] von Eicken, Geschichte der mittelalterlichen Weltanschauung, p. 498 sqq. Thomas Aquinas, Summa theologica, ii.–ii. 186. 3.

[5] Genesis, iii. 19.

[6] Thomas Aquinas, op. cit. ii.–ii. 182. 1 sq. von Eicken, op. cit. p. 488 sqq.

[7] Bonaventura, Meditationes vitæ Christi, ch. 45 (Opera, xii. 452).

[8] Ibid. ch. 15 (Opera, xii. 405).

[9] Guigo, Epistola ad Fratres de Monte-Dei, i. 8 (in St. Bernard, Opera omnia, ii. 214) :—" Non spiritualia exercitia sunt propter corporalia, sed corporalia propter spiritualia." von Eicken, op. cit. p. 491 sqq.

[10] St. Benedict, Regula Monachorum, 48.

[11] St. Bernard, De modo bene vivendi, ch. 51 (Opera omnia, ii. 883 sq.).

for it is impossible for any man to be at once occupied with exterior actions and at the same time apply himself to divine contemplation.[1] And whilst he who has nothing else to live upon is bound to work, it is a sin to try to acquire riches beyond the limit which necessity has fixed.[2]

This doctrine was more or less realised in the monastic life, but was hardly held applicable to laymen. The mediæval baron and knight resembled the Teutonic warrior described by Tacitus, who regarded it as "a dull and stupid thing to accumulate painfully by the sweat of the brow what might be won by a little blood."[3] In England, after the Conquest, the aristocracy in general lived a life of idleness but indulged eagerly in hunting, and its members continually sallied forth in parties to plunder.[4] For a long time the lower classes, constituting the mass of society, existed only for the benefit of the upper.class. It was considered honourable to live in sloth supported by the exertions of others, it was held degrading to depend on the gains of industry. The degradation really attached to the gains of labour rather than labour itself ; for labour ceased to be degrading if not prosecuted for gain. " Louis XVI. may make locks, the ladies of his court may make butter and cheese, provided it is only for amusement. Lord Rosse may build a telescope as an amateur in the interest of science, and still be noble. But if the locks, the butter, or the telescope are sold, the makers are degraded to the level of the tradesman."[5] However, as Mr. Spencer observes, trade, while at first relatively unessential (since essential things were mostly made at home) and consequently lacking the sanction of necessity and of ancestral custom, ceased to be despised when it grew in importance.[6] Among ourselves the respect in which a certain occupation is held is

---

[1] *Speculum Monachorum*, in St. Bernard, *Opera omnia*, ii. 818. von Eicken, *op. cit.* p. 494 *sq.* Cf. Thomas Aquinas, *op.cit.* ii.–ii.182. 3.
[2] Thomas Aquinas, *op. cit.* ii.–ii. 187. 3 ; 118. 1.
[3] Tacitus, *Germania*, 14.
[4] Wright, *Domestic Manners and Sentiments in England during the Middle Ages*, p. 102.
[5] Harris,'The Christian Doctrine of Labor,' in *New Englander*, xxiv. 245.
[6] Spencer, *Principles of Ethics*, i. 429.

largely determined by the degree of mental power implied
in it ; hence manual labour, and especially unskilled labour,
is still in some degree looked down upon. But we do not
regard as dishonourable any kind of work which is not
opposed to the ordinary rules of morality. We distinguish
more clearly than the ancients did between social and moral
inferiority. Our moral judgments are less influenced by
class antipathies. We recognise that a high standard of
duty is compatible even with the humblest station in life.
And when we duly reflect upon the matter, we admit that
the moral value of industry depends, not on the occupation
in which it is displayed, but on the purpose of the labourer.

But though industry is applauded or insisted on, rest is
also in certain circumstances regarded as a duty. By doing
too much work a person may injure himself and indirectly
other persons as well. In early society there is little inducement to overwork, but the case is very different in modern
civilisation. This accounts for the persistence and general
popularity of an institution which originally sprang from
quite different sources, namely, the Sunday rest.

Among various peoples it is the custom to abstain from
work, or from some special kind of work, on certain occasions or days which are regarded as defiling or inauspicious.
Work is often suspended after a death, partly perhaps
because inactivity is a natural accompaniment of sorrow,[1]
or because a mourner is supposed to be in a delicate state
requiring rest,[2] but chiefly, I presume, from fear lest the
work done should be contaminated by the pollution of
death. Among the Arabs of Morocco no work must be performed in the village till the dead is buried. In Greenland
everyone who had lived in the same house with the deceased was obliged to be idle for a certain period, according
to the directions of the priests or wizards.[3] Among the
Eskimo of Behring Strait none of the relatives of the dead
must do any work during the time in which the shade is

---

[1] Cf. infra, p. 308.
[2] Cf. infra, p. 307.

[3] Egede, Description of Greenland,
p. 149 sq.

believed to remain with the body, that is, for four or five days.[1] Among the Seminole Indians of Florida the relatives remained at home and refrained from work during the day of the burial and for three days thereafter, when the dead was supposed to stay in his grave.[2] The Kar Nicobarese abstain from work as a sign of mourning.[3] In Samoa all labour was suspended in the settlement on the death of a chief.[4] So also the Basutos do no work on the day when an influential person dies. They, moreover, refrain from going to their fields, or hasten to leave them, at the approach of clouds which give promise of rain, " in order quietly to await the desired benediction, fearing to disturb Nature in her operations. This idea is carried to such an extent, that most of the natives believe that, if they obstinately persist in their labour at such a moment, the clouds are irritated and retire, or send hail instead of rain. Days of sacrifice, or great purification, are also holidays. Hence it is that the law relative to the repose of the seventh day, so far from finding any objection in the minds of the natives, appears to them very natural, and perhaps even more fundamental, than it seems to certain Christians." [5]

Changes in the moon are frequently considered unfavourable for work. Among the Bechuanas, " when the new moon appears, all must cease from work, and keep what is called in England a holiday." [6] The people of Thermia, in the Cyclades, maintain that all work, so far as possible, should be suspended on the days immediately preceding the full moon.[7] In the Vishnu Purana it is said that one who attends to secular affairs on the days of the full or new moon goes to the Rudhirándha hell, whose wells are blood.[8] In Northern India it is considered bad to undertake any business of importance at the new moon

[1] Nelson, ' Eskimo about Bering Strait,' in *Ann. Rep. Bur. Ethn.* xviii. 319.

[2] Maccauley, ' Seminole Indians of Florida,' in *Ann. Rep. Bur. Ethn.* v. 52.

[3] Kloss, *In the Andamans and Nicobars*, p. 305.

[4] Turner, *Nineteen Years in Polynesia*, p. 229. *Idem, Samoa*, p. 146.

[5] Casalis, *Basutos*, p. 260 *sq.*

[6] Campbell, *Second Journey in the Interior of South Africa*, ii. 205.

[7] Bent, *Cyclades*, p. 438.

[8] *Vishńu Puráńa*, p. 209.

or at an eclipse.[1] According to the ' Laws of Manu,' a
Brâhmana is not allowed to study " on the new-moon
day, nor on the fourteenth and the eighth days of each
half-month, nor on the full-moon day." It is said
that " the new-moon day destroys the teacher, the
fourteenth day the pupil, the eighth and the full-moon
days destroy all remembrance of the Veda ; let him therefore avoid reading on those days." [2] The Buddhists have
their Sabbath, or *Uposatha*, which occurs four times in
the month, namely, on the day of full moon, on the day
when there is no moon, and on the two days which are
eighth from the full and new moon. On these days selling
and buying, work and business, hunting and fishing, are
forbidden, and all schools and law-courts are closed.[3] In
Ashantee and neighbouring districts, where the people
reckon time by moons, there is a weekly " fetish-day "
or sabbath, which seems to be of native origin. " In all
the countries along the coast, the regular fetish-day is
Tuesday, the day which is observed by the king of
Ashantee. Other days in the week are held sacred in the
bush. On this weekly sabbath, or fetish-day, the people
generally dress themselves in white garments, and mark
their faces, and sometimes their arms, with white clay.
They also rest from labour. The fishermen would expect,
that were they to go out on that day, the fetish would be
angry, and spoil their fishing." [4] The natives of Coomassie,
on the Gold Coast, have a law according to which no
agricultural work may be done on a Thursday.[5] In
Hawaii, where each month contained thirty nights and
the different days and nights derived their names from the
varying aspects of the moon according to her age, there
were during every month four periods lasting from two to
four nights in which the nights were consecrated or made
taboo. So also there were tabooed seasons on certain other

[1] Crooke, *Popular Religion of
Northern India*, i. 23.
[2] *Laws of Manu*, iv. 113 *sq.*
[3] Childers, *Dictionary of the Pali
Language*, p. 535. Kern, *Der
Buddhismus*, ii. 258.

[4] Beecham, *Ashantee*, p. 185 *sq.*
Cf. Bosman, *op. cit.* p. 131 (Gold
Coast natives).
[5] Ellis, *Tshi-speaking Peoples of
the Gold Coast*, p. 304.

occasions, as when a high chief was ill, or preparations were made for war, or on the approach of important religious ceremonies. These taboos were either " common " or " strict." In the case of the former men were only required to abstain from their common pursuits and to attend prayers morning and evening, whereas when the season of strict taboo was in force a general gloom and silence pervaded the whole district or island. " Not a fire or light was to be seen, or canoe launched ; none bathed ; the mouths of dogs were tied up, and fowls put under calabashes, or their heads enveloped in cloth ; for no noise of man or animal must be heard. No persons, excepting those who officiated at the temple, were allowed to leave the shelter of their roofs. Were but one of these rules broken, the taboo would fail and the gods be displeased." [1]

The peoples of Semitic stock or with Semitic culture also have their tabooed days. In Morocco work, or certain kinds of work, are avoided on holy days or in holy periods, as being unsuccessful or, in some cases, even dangerous to him who performs it ; there is a saying that " work at a feast are like the stab of a dagger." Nobody likes to start on a journey on a Friday before the midday prayer has been said, and it is considered bad to commence any work on that day.[2] I was also told that clothes will not remain clean if they are washed on a Saturday. Among the modern Egyptians Saturday is held to be the most unfortunate of days, and particularly unfavourable for shaving, cutting the nails, and starting on a journey.[3] At Kheybar, in Arabia, again, Sunday is considered an unlucky day for beginning any kind of work.[4] There can be little doubt that the Jewish Sabbath originated in the belief that it was inauspicious or dangerous to work on the seventh day, and that the reason for this belief was the mystic connection which in

---

[1] Jarves, *History of the Hawaiian Islands*, pp. 40, 28. The word *tapuaʻi* means "to abstain from all work, games, &c." (Tregear, *Maori-Polynesian Dictionary*, p. 472).
[2] See Westermarck, *The Moorish Conception of Holiness (Baraka)*, p. 140 *sqq.*
[3] Lane, *Modern Egyptians*, p. 272.
[4] Doughty, *Arabia Deserta*, ii. 197 *sq.*

the opinion of the ancient Hebrews, as of so many other peoples, existed between human activity and the changes in the moon.[1] It has been sufficiently demonstrated that the Sabbath originally depended upon the new moon, and this carries with it the assumption that the Hebrews must at one time have observed a Sabbath at intervals of seven days corresponding with the moon's phases.[2] In the Old Testament the new moon and Sabbath are repeatedly mentioned side by side;[3] thus the oppressors of the poor are represented as saying, "When will the new moon be gone, that we may sell corn ? and the Sabbath, that we may set forth wheat ? "[4] Among modern Jews, at the feast of the New Moon, which is held every month on the first or on the first and second days of the month, the women are obliged to suspend all servile work, though the men are not required to interrupt their secular employments.[5] That the superstitious fear of doing work on the seventh day developed into a religious prohibition, is only another instance of a tendency which we have noticed often before—the tendency of magic forces to be transformed into divine volitions.[6] Like the ancient Hebrews, the Assyrians and Babylonians looked upon the seventh day as an " evil day " ; and though they do not seem generally to have abstained from work on that day, there were various royal taboos connected with it.   The

---

[1] See Jastrow, ' Original Character of the Hebrew Sabbath,' in *American Journal of Theology*, ii. 321 *sqq.*

[2] Wellhausen, *Prolegomena to the History of Israel*, p. 112 *sqq.* Jastrow, *loc. cit.* pp. 314, 327.

[3] 2 *Kings*, iv. 23. *Isaiah*, i. 13. *Hosea*, ii. 11.

[4] *Amos*, viii. 5.

[5] Allen, *Modern Judaism*, p. 390 *sq.*

[6] Prof. Jastrow seems to have failed to see this when he says (*loc. cit.* p. 323) that " if the Sabbath was originally an 'unfavourable ' day on which one must avoid showing one's self before Yahwe, it would naturally be regarded as dangerous to provoke his anger by endeavouring to secure on that day personal benefits through the usual forms of activity." Wellhausen, again, suggests (*op. cit.* p. 114) that the rest on the Sabbath was originally the consequence of that day being the festal and sacrificial day of the week, and only gradually became its essential attribute on account of the regularity with which it every eighth day interrupted the round of everyday work. He argues that the Sabbath as a day of rest cannot be very primitive, because such a day " presupposes agriculture and a tolerably hard-pressed working-day life." But this argument appears very futile when we consider how commonly changes in the moon are believed to exercise an unfavourable influence upon work of any kind. See *infra*, Additional Notes.

King was not to show himself in his chariot, not to hold court, not to bring sacrifices, not to change his clothes, not to eat a good dinner, and not even to curse his enemies.[1]

The Jewish Sabbath was abolished by Christ. " The Sabbath was made for man, and not man for the Sabbath";[2] " My father worketh [on it] hitherto, and I work."[3] Jewish converts no doubt continued to observe the Sabbath, but this met with disapproval. In one of the Epistles of Ignatius we find the exhortation not to " sabbatise," which was expanded by the subsequent paraphraser of these compositions into a warning against keeping the Sabbath, after the manner of the Jews, " as if delighting in idleness."[4] And in the fourth century a Council of the Church enacted " that the Christians ought not to judaise, and rest on the Sabbath, but ought to work on that day."[5] On the other hand, it was from early times a recognised custom among the Christians to celebrate the first day of the week in memory of Christ's resurrection, by holding a form of religious service ; but there was no sabbatic regard for it, and it was chiefly looked upon as a day of rejoicing.[6] Tertullian is the first writer who speaks of abstinence from secular care and labour on Sunday as a duty incumbent upon Christians, lest they should " give place to the devil."[7] But it is extremely doubtful whether the earliest Sunday law really had a Christian origin. In 321 the Emperor Constantine issued an edict to the effect that all judges and all city people and tradesmen should rest on " the venerable Day of the Sun," whereas those living in the country should have full liberty to attend to the culture of their fields, " since it frequently happens

---

[1] Schrader, *Die Keilinschriften und das Alte Testament*, p. 592 *sq.* Hirschfeld, 'Remarks on the Etymology of Šabbāth,' in *Jour. Roy. Asiatic Soc.* 1896, p. 358. Jastrow, *loc. cit.* pp. 320, 328.

[2] *St. Mark*, ii. 27.

[3] *St. John*, v. 17.

[4] Ignatius, *Epistola ad Magnesios*, 9 (Migne, *op. cit.* Ser. Graeca, v. 768). Neale, *Feasts and Fasts*, p. 89.

[5] *Concilium Laodicenum*, can. 29 (Labbe-Mansi, *Sacrorum Conciliorum collectio*, ii. 580).

[6] Justin Martyr, *Apologia I. pro Christianis*, 67 (Migne, *op. cit.* Ser. Graeca, vi. 429). Schaff, *History of the Christian Church*, ' Ante-Nicene Christianity,' p. 202 *sqq.* Hessey, *Sunday*, p. 29 *sqq.*

[7] Tertullian, *De oratione*, 23 (Migne, *op. cit.* i. 1191).

that no other day is so fit for the sowing of grain or the planting of vines."[1] In this rescript nothing is said of any relation to Christianity, nor do we know that it in any way was due to Christian influence.[2] It seems that Constantine, in his capacity of Pontifex Maximus, only added the day of the sun—whose worship was the characteristic of the new paganism—to those inauspicious days, *religiosi dies*, which the Romans of old regarded as unsuitable for worldly business and especially for judicial proceedings.[3] But though the obligatory Sunday rest in no case was a continuance of the Jewish Sabbath, it gradually was confounded with it, owing to the recognition of the decalogue, with its injunction of a weekly day of rest, as the code of divine morality. From the sixth century upwards vexatious restrictions were made by civil rulers, councils, and ecclesiastical writers;[4] until in Puritanism the Christian Sunday became a perfect image of the pharisaic Sabbath, or even excelled it in the rigour with which abstinence from every kind of worldly activity was insisted upon. The theory that the keeping holy of one day out of seven is the essence of the Fourth Commandment reconciled people to the fact that the Jewish Sabbath was the seventh day and Sunday the first. In England, in the seventeenth century, persons were punished for carrying coal on Sunday, for hanging out clothes to dry, for travelling on horseback, for rural strolls and walking about.[5] And Scotch clergymen taught their congregations that on that day it was sinful to save a vessel in distress, and that it was proof of religion to leave ship and crew to perish.[6]

[1] *Codex Justinianus*, iii. 12. 2 (3).
[2] *Cf.* Lewis, *Critical History of Sunday Legislation*, p. 18 *sqq.*; Milman, *History of Christianity*, ii. 291 *sq.*
[3] Gellius, *Noctes Atticæ*, iv. 9. 5; vi. 9. 10. Varro, *De lingua Latina*, vi. 30. Neale, *op. cit.* pp. 5, 6, 86, 87, 206. Fowler, *Roman Festivals of the Period of the Republic*, p. 8 *sq.* The Greeks, also, had "unblest and in-auspicious" days, when no court or assembly was to be held, and work was to be abstained from (Plato, *Leges*, vii. 800; Karsten, *Studies in Primitive Greek Religion*, p. 90).
[4] Hessey, *op. cit.* p. 87 *sqq.*
[5] Roberts, *Social History of the People of the Southern Counties of England*, p. 244 *sqq.*
[6] Buckle, *History of Civilization in England*, iii. 276.

CHAPTER XXXVII

RESTRICTIONS IN DIET

TRAVELLERS have often noticed with astonishment the immense quantities of food which uncivilised people are able to consume. Sir George Grey has described the orgies which follow the stranding of a whale in Australia, when the natives remain by the carcase for many days, fairly eating their way into it.[1] The Rocky Mountain Indians, though they often subsist for a great length of time on a very little food, will at their feasts " gorge down an incredible quantity."[2] A Mongol " will eat more than ten pounds of meat at one sitting, but some have been known to devour an average-sized sheep in the course of twenty-four hours."[3] The Waganda in Central Africa " sometimes gorge themselves to such an extent that they are unable to move, and appear just as if intoxicated."[4] It has been justly observed that what would among ourselves be condemned as disgusting gluttony is, under the conditions to which certain races of men are exposed, quite normal and in fact necessary. As Mr. Spencer observes, " where the habitat is such as at one time to supply very little food and at another time food in great abundance, survival depends on the ability to consume immense quantities when the opportunities occur."[5] When this is the case gluttony can hardly be

---

[1] Grey, *Journals of Expeditions in North-West and Western Australia,* ii. 277 *sqq.*

[2] Harmon, *Journal of Voyages in the Interior of North America,* p. 329.

[3] Prejevalsky, *Mongolia,* i. 55.

[4] Wilson and Felkin, *Uganda,* i. 185.

[5] Spencer, *Principles of Ethics,* i. 436.

stigmatised as a vice ; and I find no direct evidence that it is so even among savages who are described as generally moderate in their diet. The lack of foresight, which is a characteristic of uncivilised peoples, must prevent them from attaching much moral value to temperance. On the other hand, gluttony is sometimes said to be regarded with admiration. Mr. Torday informs me that the Bambala in South-Western Congo, when praising a man for his strength, are in the habit of saying, " He eats a whole goat with its skin."

At higher stages of culture intemperance is often subject to censure—because it is detrimental to health or prosperity, or because it calls forth an instinctive feeling of disgust, or because indulgence in sensual pleasures is considered degrading, or, generally, because it is inconsistent with an ascetic ideal of life. It is said in the Proverbs that " the glutton shall come to poverty."[1] According to the Laws of Manu, " excessive eating is prejudicial to health, to fame, and to bliss in heaven ; it prevents the acquisition of spiritual merit, and is odious among men ; one ought, for these reasons, to avoid it carefully."[2] Aristotle maintains that the pleasure with which intemperance is concerned is justly held in disgrace, " since it belongs to us in that we are animals, not in that we are men."[3] Cicero observes that, as mere corporeal pleasure is unworthy the excellency of man's nature, the nourishment of our bodies " should be with a view not to our pleasure, but to our health and our strength."[4] The same opinion is at least nominally shared by many among ourselves ; whereas others, though denying that the gratification of appetite is to be sought for its own sake, admit as legitimate ends for it not only the maintenance of health and strength but also " cheerfulness and the cultivation of the social affections."[5] But most of us are undoubtedly less exacting, if not in theory at least in practice, and really find nothing blamable in pleasures of the

[1] *Proverbs*, xxiii. 21.
[2] *Laws of Manu*, ii. 57.
[3] Aristotle, *Ethica Nicomachea*, iii. 10. 10.
[4] Cicero, *De officiis*, i. 30.
[5] Whewell, *Elements of Morality*, p. 124 *sq.*

table which neither impair health, nor involve a perceptible loss of some greater gratification, nor interfere with duties towards neighbours.[1]

Sometimes temperance has been inculcated on grounds which in other cases lead to the duty of fasting, that is, abstinence from all food and drink, or at least (in a looser sense of the word) from certain kinds of food, for a determined period. The custom of fasting is wide-spread, and deserves special attention in a study of moral ideas.

Fasting is practised or enjoined for a variety of purposes. It is frequently adopted as a means of having supernatural converse, or acquiring supernatural powers.[2] He who fasts sees in dreams or visions things that no ordinary eye can see. The Hudson Bay Eskimo " discovered that a period of fasting and abstinence from contact with other people endowed a person with supernatural powers and enabled him to learn the secrets of Tung ak [the great spirit]. This is accomplished by repairing to some lonely spot, where, for a greater or less period, the hermit abstains from food or water until the imagination is so worked upon that he believes himself imbued with the power to heal the sick and control all the destinies of life. Tung ak is supposed to stand near and reveal those things while the person is undergoing the test." [3] The Naudowessies totally abstain from every kind of either victuals or drink before a hunting expedition, because they think that " it enables them freely to dream, in which dreams they are informed where they shall find the greatest plenty of game." [4] The Tsimshian of British Columbia, if a special object is to be attained,

---

[1] See Sidgwick, *Methods of Ethics*, p. 328 *sq.*

[2] Tylor, *Primitive Culture*, ii. 410 *sqq.* Spencer, *Principles of Sociology*, i. 261. Avebury, *Origin of Civilisation*, p. 266 *sqq.* Landtman, *Origin of Priesthood*, pp. 118–123, 158 *sqq.* Müller, *Geschichte der Amerikanischen Urreligionen*, pp. 285, 651. Dorsey, 'Siouan Cults,' in *Ann. Rep. Bur. Ethn.* xi. 390. Mooney, 'Myths

of the Cherokee,' *ibid.* xix. 480. Herrera, *General History of the West Indies*, i. 165 (ancient natives of Hispaniola). Niebuhr, *Travels through Arabia*, ii. 282.

[3] Turner, 'Ethnology of the Ungava District,' in *Ann. Rep. Bur. Ethn.* xi. 195.

[4] Carver, *Travels through the Interior Parts of North America*, p. 285.

believe they can compel the deity to grant it by a rigid fasting.[1] The Amazulu have a saying that " the continually stuffed body cannot see secret things," and, in accordance with this belief, put no faith in a fat diviner.[2] A Tungus shaman, who is summoned to treat a sick person, will for several days abstain from food and maintain silence till he becomes inspired.[3] Among the Santals the person or persons who have to offer sacrifices at their feasts prepare themselves for this duty by fasting and prayer and by placing themselves for some time in a position of apparent mental absorption.[4] The savage, as Sir E. B. Tylor remarks, has many a time, for days and weeks together, to try involuntarily the effects of fasting, accompanied with other privations and with prolonged solitary contemplation in the desert or the forest. Under these circumstances he soon comes to see and talk with phantoms, which are to him visible personal spirits, and, having thus learnt the secret of spiritual intercourse, he thenceforth reproduces the cause in order to renew the effects.[5] The Hindus believe that a fasting person will ascend to the heaven of that god in whose name he observes the fast.[6] The Hebrews associated fasting with divine revelations.[7] St. Chrysostom says that fasting " makes the soul brighter, and gives it wings to mount up and soar on high."[8]

Ideas of this kind partly underlie the common practice of abstaining from food before or in connection with the performance of a magical or religious ceremony ;[9] but there

[1] Boas, in *Fifth Report on the North-Western Tribes of Canada*, p. 50.
[2] Callaway, *Religious System of the Amazulu*, p. 387, n. 41.
[3] Krivoshapkin, quoted by Landtman, *op. cit.* p. 159.
[4] Dalton, *Ethnology of Bengal*, p. 213. See also Rowney, *Wild Tribes of India*, p. 77.
[5] Tylor, *Primitive Culture*, ii. 410.
[6] Ward, *View of the History, &c. of the Hindoos*, ii. 77.
[7] *Exodus*, xxxiv. 28. *Deuteronomy*, ix. 9. *Daniel*, ix. 3.

[8] St. Chrysostom, *In Cap. I. Genes. Homil. X.* (Migne, *Patrologiæ cursus*, Ser. Graeca, liii. 83). *Cf.* Tertullian, *De jejuniis*, 6 *sqq.* (Migne, ii. 960, 961, 963) ; Haug, *Alterthümmer der Christen*, pp. 476, 482.
[9] Bossu, *Travels through Louisiana*, i. 38 (Natchez). Clavigero, *History of Mexico*, i. 285 *sq.* ; Bancroft, *Native Races of the Pacific States*, iii. 440 *sq.* (ancient Mexicans). Landa, *Relacion de las cosas de Yucatan*, p. 156. Junghuhn, *Die Battaländer auf Sumatra*, ii. 311 *sq.* (natives of

is yet another ground for this practice. The effect attributed to fasting is not merely psychical, but it also prevents pollution. Food may cause defilement, and, like other polluting matter, be detrimental to sanctity. Among the Maoris " no food is permitted to touch the head or hair of a chief, which is sacred ; and if food is mentioned in connection with anything sacred (or ' tapu ') it is considered as an insult, and revenged as such." [1] So also a full stomach may be polluting.[2] This is obviously the reason why in Morocco and elsewhere [3] certain magical practices, in order to be efficacious, have to be performed before breakfast. The Masai use strong purges before they venture to eat holy meat.[4] The Caribs purified their bodies by purging, bloodletting, and fasting ; and the natives of the Antilles, at certain religious festivals, cleansed themselves by vomiting before they approached the sanctuary.[5] The true object of fasting often appears from the fact that it is practised hand in hand with other ceremonies of a purificatory character. A Lappish *noaide*, or wizard, prepares himself for the offering of a sacrifice by abstinence from food and ablutions.[6] Herodotus tells us that the ancient Egyptians fasted before making a sacrifice to Isis, and beat their bodies while the victims were burnt.[7] When a Hindu resolves to visit a sacred place, he has his head shaved two days preceding the commencement of his journey, and fasts the next day ; on the last day of his journey he fasts again, and on his

Tjumba). Beauchamp, in the Madras Government Museum's *Bulletin*, iv. 56 (Hindus of Southern India). Ward, *op. cit.* ii. 76 *sq.* (Hindu). Wassiljew, quoted by Haberland, ' Gebräuche und Aberglauben beim Essen,' in *Zeitschrift für Völkerpsychologie*, xviii. 30 (Buddhists). Porphyry, *De abstinentia ab esu animalium*, ii. 44 ; Wachsmuth, *Hellenische Alterthumskunde*, ii. 560, 576 ; Hermann-Stark, *Lehrbuch der gottesdienstlichen Alterthümer der Griechen*, p. 381 ; Anrich, *Das antike Mysterienwesen*, p. 25 ; Diels, ' Ein orphischer Demeterhymnus,' in *Fest-*

schrift Theodor Gomperz dargebracht, p. 6 *sqq.* Chwolsohn, *Die Ssabier und der Ssabismus*, ii. 23, 74.
[1] Angas, *Polynesia*, p. 149.
[2] See Robertson Smith, *Religion of the Semites*, p. 434 *sq.*; Westermarck, *The Moorish Conception of Holiness*, p. 127.
[3] Wuttke, *Der deutsche Volksaberglaube der Gegenwart*, § 219, p. 161.
[4] Thomson, *Masai Land*, p. 430.
[5] Waitz, *Anthropologie der Naturvölker*, iv. 330 ; iii. 384.
[6] von Düben, *Lappland*, p. 256. Friis, *Lappisk Mythologi*, p. 145 *sq.*
[7] Herodotus, ii. 40.

arrival at the sacred spot he has his whole body shaved, after which he bathes.[1] In Christianity we likewise meet with fasting as a rite of purification. At least as early as the time of Tertullian it was usual for communicants to prepare themselves by fasting for receiving the Eucharist ;[2] and to this day Roman Catholicism regards it as unlawful to consecrate or partake of it after food or drink.[3] The Lent fast itself was partly interpreted as a purifying preparation for the holy table.[4] And in the early Church catechumens were accustomed to fast before baptism.[5]

In the case of a sacrifice it is considered necessary not only that he who offers it, but that the victim also, should be free from pollution. In ancient Egypt a sacrificial animal had to be perfectly clean.[6] According to Hindu notions the gods enjoy pure sacrifices only.[7] In the Kalika-Purana, a work supposed to have been written under the direction of Siva, it is said that if a man is offered he must be free from corporal defect and unstained with great crimes, and that if an animal is offered it must have exceeded its third year and be without blemish or disease ; and in no case must the victim be a woman or a she animal, because, as it seems, females are regarded as naturally unclean.[8] According to the religious law of the Hebrews, no leaven or honey should be used in connection with vegetable offerings, on the ground that these articles have the effect of producing fermentation and tend to acidify and spoil anything with which they are mixed ;[9] and the animal which was intended for sacrifice should be absolutely free from blemish [10] and at least eight days old,[11] that is, untainted with the impurity of birth. Quite in harmony with these prescriptions is the notion that human or

---

[1] Ward, *op. cit.* ii. 130 *sq.* *Cf. Institutes of Vishnu*, xlvi. 17, 24 *sq.*
[2] Tertullian, *De oratione*, 19 (Migne, *op. cit.* i. 1182).
[3] *Catechism of the Council of Trent*, ii. 4. 6.
[4] St. Jerome, *In Jonam*, 3 (Migne, *op. cit.* xxv. 1140).
[5] Justin Martyr, *Apologia I. pro Christianis*, 61 (Migne, *op. cit.* Ser.

Graeca, vi. 420). St. Augustine, *De fide et operibus*, vi. 8 (Migne, xl. 202).
[6] Herodotus, ii. 38.
[7] *Baudhâyana*, i. 6. 13. 1 *sq.*
[8] Dubois, *Description of the Character, &c. of the People of India*, p. 491.
[9] Keil, *Manual of Biblical Archæology*, i. 262.
[10] *Leviticus*, xxii. 19 *sqq.*
[11] *Ibid.* xxii. 27.

animal victims have to abstain from food for some time
before they are offered up. Among the Kandhs the man
who was destined to be sacrificed was kept fasting from
the preceding evening, but on the day of the sacrifice he
was refreshed with a little milk and palm-sago ; and
before he was led forth from the village in solemn
procession he was carefully washed and dressed in a new
garment.[1] In Morocco it is not only considered meritorious for the people to fast on the day previous to the
celebration of the yearly sacrificial feast, *l-ʿăîd l-kbîr*, but
in several parts of the country the sheep which is going to
be sacrificed has to fast on that day or at least on the
following morning, till some food is given it immediately
before it is slaughtered. The Jewish custom which
compels the firstborn to fast on the eve of Passover [2] may
also perhaps be a survival from a time when all the first-
born belonged to the Lord.[3]

In some cases the custom of fasting before the performance of a sacrifice may be due to the idea that it is
dangerous or improper for the worshipper to partake of
food before the god has had his share.[4] In India a regular
performance of two half-monthly sacrifices is enjoined on
the Brahmanical householder for a period of thirty years
from the time when he has set up a fire of his own—
according to some authorities even for the rest of his life.
The ceremony usually occupies two consecutive days, the
first of which is chiefly taken up with preparatory rites
and the vow of abstinence (*vrata*) by the sacrificer and his
wife, whilst the second day is reserved for the main
performance of the sacrifice. The *vrata* includes the
abstention from certain kinds of food, especially meat,
which will be offered to the gods on the following day,
as also from other carnal pleasures. The Satapatha-
Brâhmana gives the following explanation of it :—" The
gods see through the mind of man ; they know that, when

[1] Macpherson; *Memorials of Service in India*, p. 118.
[2] Greenstone, ' Fasting,' in *Jewish
Encyclopedia*, v. 348. Allen, *Modern*
Judaism, p. 394.
[3] *Supra*, i. 459.
[4] *Cf.* Oldenberg, *Die Religion des
Veda*, p. 414.

he enters on this vow, he means to sacrifice to them the next morning. Therefore all the gods betake themselves to his house, and abide by him or the fires (*upa-vas*) in his house ; whence this day is called *upa-vasatha*. Now, as it would even be unbecoming for him to take food before men who are staying with him as his guests have eaten ; how much more would it be so, if he were to take food before the gods who are staying with him have eaten : let him therefore take no food at all."[1] It is hardly probable, however, that this is the original meaning of the abstinence in question. It occurs about the time of new moon and full moon ; according to some native authorities the abstinence and sacrifice take place on the last two days of each half of the lunar month, whilst the generality of ritualistic writers consider the first day of the half-month —that is, the first and sixteenth days of the month—to be the proper time for the sacrifice.[2] We shall presently see how frequently fasting is observed on these occasions, presumably for fear of eating food which is supposed to have been polluted by the moon ; hence it seems to me by no means improbable that the *vrata* has a similar origin, instead of being merely a rite preparatory to the sacrifice which follows it. But at the same time the idea that spirits or gods should have the first share of a meal is certainly very ancient, and may lead to actual fasting in case the offering for some reason or other is to be delayed. A Polynesian legend tells us that a man by name Maui once caught an immense fish. Then he left his brothers, saying to them :—" After I am gone, be courageous and patient ; do not eat food until I return, and do not let our fish be cut up, but rather leave it until I have carried an offering to the gods from this great haul of fish, and until I have found a priest, that fitting prayers and sacrifices may be offered to the god, and the necessary rites be completed in order. We shall thus all be purified. I will then

---

[1] *Satapatha-Bráhmana*, i. 1. 1. 7 *sq.* Eggeling, in *Sacred Books of the East*, xii. 1 *sq.* Oldenberg, *op. cit.* p. 413, n. 1.

[2] Eggeling, in *Sacred Books of the East*, xii. 1.

return, and we can cut up this fish in safety, and it shall be fairly portioned out to this one, and to that one, and to that other." But as soon as Maui had gone, his brothers began at once to eat food, and to cut up the fish. Had Maui previously reached the sacred place, the heart of the deity would have been appeased with the offering of a portion of the fish which had been caught by his disciples, and all the male and female deities would have partaken of their portions of the sacrifice. But now the gods turned with wrath upon them, on account of the fish which they had thus cut up without having made a fitting sacrifice.[1]

Among many peoples custom prescribes fasting after a death. Lucian says that at the funeral feast the parents of the deceased are prevailed upon by their relatives to take food, being almost prostrated by a three days' fast.[2] We are told that among the Hindus children fast three days after the death of a parent, and a wife the same period after the death of her husband;[3] but according to a more recent statement, to be quoted presently, they do not altogether abstain from food. In one of the sacred books of India it is said that mourners shall fast during three days, and that, if they are unable to do so, they shall subsist on food bought in the market or given unasked.[4] Among the Nayādis of Malabar "from the time of death until the funeral is over, all the relations must fast."[5] Among the Irulas of the Neilgherries "the relatives of the deceased fast during the first day, that is, if . . . . the death occur after the morning meal, they refrain from the evening one, and eat nothing till the next morning. If it occur during the night, or before the morning meal, they refrain from all food till the evening. Similar fasting is observed on every return of the same day of the week, till the obsequies take place."[6] Among

[1] Grey, *Polynesian Mythology*, p. 26 *sq.*
[2] Lucian, *De luctu*, 24.
[3] Ward, *View of the History, &c. of the Hindoos*, ii. 76 *sq.*
[4] *Vasishtha*, iv. 14 *sq.* Cf. *Institutes of Vishnu*, xix. 14.
[5] Thurston, in the Madras Government Museum's *Bulletin*, iv. 76.
[6] Harkness, *Description of a Singular Race inhabiting the Neilgherry Hills*, p. 97.

the Bogos of Eastern Africa a son must fast three days after the death of his father.[1]   On the Gold Coast it is the custom for the near relatives of the deceased to perform a long and painful fast, and sometimes they can only with difficulty be induced to have recourse to food again.[2] So also in Dahomey they must fast during the " corpse time," or mourning.[3]   Among the Brazilian Paressí the relatives of a dead person remain for six days at his grave, carefully refraining from taking food.[4]   Among the aborigines of the Antilles children used to fast after the death of a parent, a husband after the death of his wife, and a wife after the death of her husband.[5]   In some Indian tribes of North America it is the custom for the relatives of the deceased to fast till the funeral is over.[6] Among the Snanaimuq, a tribe of the Coast Salish, after the death of a husband or wife the surviving partner must not eat anything for three or four days.[7]   In one of the interior divisions of the Salish of British Columbia, the Stlatlumh, the next four days after a funeral feast are spent by the members of the household of the deceased person in fasting, lamenting and ceremonial ablutions.[8] Among the Upper Thompson Indians in British Columbia, again, those who handled the dead body and who dug the grave had to fast until the corpse was buried.[9]

   In several instances fasting after a death is observed only in the daytime.

   David and his people fasted for Saul and Jonathan until even on the day when the news of their death arrived.[10]   Among the Arabs of Morocco it is the custom that if a death takes place in the morning everyone in the village refrains from food until

---

[1] Munzinger, *Die Sitten und das Recht der Bogos*, p. 29.
[2] Cruickshank, *Eighteen Years on the Gold Coast*, ii. 218.
[3] Burton, *Mission to Gelele*, ii. 163.
[4] von den Steinen, *Unter den Naturvölkern Zentral-Brasiliens*, p. 435. *Cf. ibid.* p. 339 (Bakaïri).
[5] Du Tertre, *Histoire générale des Antilles*, ii. 371.
[6] Charlevoix, *Voyage to North-America*, ii. 187.
[7] Boas, in *Fifth Report on the North-Western Tribes of Canada*, p. 45.
[8] Tout, ' Ethnology of the Stlatlumh of British Columbia,' in *Jour. Anthr. Inst.* xxxv. 138.
[9] Teit, ' Thompson Indians of British Columbia,' in *Memoirs of the American Museum of Natural History*, Anthropology, i. 331.
[10] 2 Samuel, i. 12. *Cf. ibid.* iii. 35.

the deceased is buried in the afternoon or evening ; but if a person dies so late that he cannot be buried till the next morning the people eat at night.   In the Pelew Islands, as long as the dead is unburied, fasting is observed in the daytime but not in the evening.[1]   In Fiji after a burial the *kana-bogi*, or fasting till evening, is practised for ten or twenty days.[2]   In Samoa it was common for those who attended the deceased to eat nothing during the day, but to have a meal at night.[3]   In the Tuhoe tribe of the Maoris, " when a chief of distinction died his widow and children would remain for some time within the *whare potae* [that is, mourning house], eating food during the night time only, never during the day." [4]   The Sacs and Foxes in Nebraska formerly required that children should fast for three months after the death of a parent, except that they every day about sunset were allowed to partake of a meal made entirely of hominy.[5]   Among the Kansas a man who loses his wife must fast from sunrise to sunset for a year and a half, and a woman who loses her husband must observe a similar fast for a year.[6]   In some tribes of British Columbia and among the Thlinkets, until the dead body is buried the relatives of the deceased may eat a little at night but have to fast during the day.[7]   Among the Upper Thompson Indians a different custom prevailed : " nobody was allowed to eat, drink, or smoke in the open air after sunset (others say after dusk) before the burial, else the ghost would harm them." [8]

Very frequently mourners have to abstain from certain victuals only, especially flesh or fish, or some other staple or favourite food.

In Greenland everybody who had lived in the same house with the dead, or who had touched his corpse, was for some time forbidden to partake of certain kinds of food.[9]   Among the Upper Thompson Indians " parents bereft of a child did not eat fresh meat for several months." [10]   Among the Stlatlumh of

[1] Waitz, *op. cit.* v. 153.

[2] Williams and Calvert, *Fiji*, p. 169.

[3] Turner, *Nineteen Years in Polynesia*, p. 228. *Idem, Samoa*, p. 145.

[4] Best, ' Tuhoe Land,' in *Trans. and Proceed. of the New Zealand Institute*, xxx. 38.

[5] Yarrow, ' Mortuary Customs of the North American Indians,' in *Ann. Rep. Bur. Ethn.* i. 95.

[6] Dorsey, ' Mourning and War Customs of the Kansas,' in *American Naturalist*, xix. 679 *sq.*

[7] Boas, *loc. cit.* p. 41.

[8] Teit, *loc. cit.* p. 328.

[9] Egede, *Description of Greenland*, p. 149 *sq.* Cranz, *History of Greenland*, i. 218.

[10] Teit, *loc. cit.* p. 332.

British Columbia a widow might eat no fresh food for a whole
year, whilst the other members of the deceased person's family
abstained from such food for a period of from four days to as
many months. A widower was likewise forbidden to eat fresh
meats for a certain period, the length of which varied with the
age of the person—the younger the man, the longer his abstention.[1] In some of the Goajiro clans of Colombia a person is
prohibited from eating flesh during the mourning time, which
lasts nine days.[2] Among the Abipones, when a chief died, the
whole tribe abstained for a month from eating fish, their principal dainty.[3] While in mourning, the Northern Queensland
aborigines carefully avoid certain victuals, believing that the
forbidden food, if eaten, would burn up their bowels.[4] In
Easter Island the nearest relatives of the dead are for a year or
even longer obliged to abstain from eating potatoes, their chief
article of food, or some other victuals of which they are particularly fond.[5] Certain Papuans and various tribes in the Malay
Archipelago prohibit persons in mourning from eating rice or
sago.[6] In the Andaman Islands mourners refuse to partake of
their favourite viands.[7] After the death of a relative the
Tipperahs abstain from flesh for a week.[8] The same is the
case with the Arakh, a tribe in Oudh, during the fifteen days
in the month of Kuâr which are sacred to the worship of the
dead.[9] Among the Nayādis of Malabar the relatives of the
deceased are not allowed to eat meat for ten days after his
death.[10] According to Toda custom the near relatives must
not eat rice, milk, honey, or gram until the funeral is over.[11]
Among the Hindus described by Mr. Chunder Bose a widow is
restricted to one scanty meal a day, and this is of the coarsest
description and always devoid of fish, the most esteemed article
of food in a Hindu lady's bill of fare. The son, again, from

[1] Tout, in *Jour. Anthr. Inst.* xxxv.
138 *sq.*
[2] Candelier, *Rio-Hacha*, p. 220.
[3] Charlevoix, *History of Paraguay*,
i. 405.
[4] Lumholtz, *Among Cannibals*,
p. 203.
[5] Geiseler, *Die Oster-Insel*, pp. 28,
30.
[6] Wilken, ' Ueber das Haaropfer,
und einige andere Trauergebräuche
bei den Völkern Indonesien's,' in
Revue coloniale internationale, iv.
348 *sq.*
[7] Man, 'Aboriginal Inhabitants of
the Andaman Islands,' in *Jour.
Anthr. Inst.* xii. 142, 353.

[8] Browne, quoted by Dalton, *op.
cit.* p. 110.
[9] Crooke, *Tribes and Castes of the
North-Western Provinces and Oudh*,
i. 84.
[10] Thurston, in the Madras Government Museum's *Bulletin*, iv. 76.
[11] *Idem, ibid.* i. 174. Dr. Rivers
says (*Todas*, p. 370) that, among the
Todas, a widower is not allowed to
eat rice nor drink milk, and that on
every return of the day of the week
on which his wife died he takes no
food in the morning but only has
his evening meal. The same holds
good for a widow.

the hour of his father's death to the conclusion of the funeral ceremony, is allowed to take only a meal consisting of *atab* rice, a sort of inferior pulse, milk, ghee, sugar, and a few fruits, and at night a little milk, sugar, and fruits—a *régime* which lasts ten days in the case of a Brahmin and thirty-one days in the case of a Sûdra.[1] In some of the sacred books of India it is said that, during the period of impurity, all the mourners shall abstain from eating meat.[2] In China " meat, must, and spirits were forbidden even in the last month of the deepest mourning, when other sorts of food had long been allowed already." [3]

The custom of fasting after a death has been ascribed to different causes by different writers. Mr. Spencer believes that it has resulted from the habit of making excessive provision for the dead.[4] But although among some peoples the funeral offerings no doubt are so extensive as to reduce the survivors to poverty and starvation,[5] I have met with no statement to the effect that they are anxious to give to the deceased all the eatables which they possess, or that the mourning fast is a matter of actual necessity. It is always restricted to some fixed period, often to a few days only, and it prevails among many peoples who have never been known to be profuse in their sacrifices to the dead. With reference to the Chinese, Dr. de Groot maintains that the mourners originally fasted with a view to being able to sacrifice so much the more at the tomb ; and he bases this conclusion on the fact that the articles of food which were forbidden till the end of the deepest mourning were the very same as those which in ancient China played the principal part at every burial sacrifice.[6] But this prohibition may also perhaps be due to a belief that the offering of certain victuals to the dead pollutes all food belonging to the same species.

Professor Wilken, again, suggests that the mourners abstain from food till they have given the dead his due, in

[1] Bose, *The Hindoos as they are,* pp. 244, 254 *sq.*
[2] *Gautama,* xiv. 39.   *Institutes of Vishnu,* xix. 15.
[3] de Groot, *Religious System of China,* (vol. ii. book) i. 651.
[4] Spencer, *Principles of Sociology,* i. 261 *sqq.*
[5] *Ibid.* i. 262.
[6] de Groot, *op. cit.* (vol. ii. book) i. 652.

order to show that they do not wish to keep him waiting longer than is necessary and thus make him kindly disposed towards them.[1] This explanation presupposes that the fast is immediately followed by offerings or a feast for the dead. In some instances this is expressly said to be the case ; [2] the ancient Chinese, for instance, observed a special fast as an introductory rite to the sacrifices which they offered to the manes at regular periods after the demise and even after the close of the mourning.[3] But generally there is no indication of the mourning fast being an essential preliminary to a sacrifice to the dead, and in an instance mentioned above the funeral feast regularly precedes it.[4]

It seems that Sir J. G. Frazer comes much nearer the truth when he observes that people originally fasted after a death " just in those circumstances in which they considered that they might possibly in eating devour a ghost."[5] Yet I think it would generally be more correct to say that they were afraid of swallowing, not the ghost, but food polluted with the contagion of death. The dead body is regarded as a seat of infection, which defiles anything in its immediate neighbourhood, and this infection is of course considered particularly dangerous if it is allowed to enter into the bowels. In certain cases the length of the mourning fast is obviously determined by the belief in the polluting presence of the ghost. The six days' fast of the Paressí coincides with the period after which the dead is supposed to have arrived in heaven no longer to return ; and they say that anybody who should fail to observe this fast would " eat the mouth of the dead " and die himself.[6] Frequently the fasting lasts till the corpse is buried ; and burial is a common safeguard against the return of the ghost.[7] The custom

---

[1] Wilken, in *Revue coloniale internationale*, iv. 347, 348, 350 sq. n. 32.
[2] Selenka, *Sonnige Welten*, p. 90 (Dyaks). Black, ' Fasting,' in *Encyclopædia Britannica*, ix. 44.
[3] de Groot, *op. cit.* (vol. ii. book) i. 656.
[4] *Supra*, ii. 299.

[5] Frazer, ' Certain Burial Customs as illustrative of the Primitive Theory of the Soul,' in *Jour. Anthr. Inst.* xv. 94. See also Oldenberg, *Die Religion des Veda*, pp. 270, 590.
[6] von den Steinen, *op. cit.* p. 434 *sq.*
[7] *Infra*, on Regard for the Dead.

of restricting the fast to the daytime probably springs from the idea that a ghost cannot see in the dark, and is consequently unable to come and pollute the food at night. That the object of the fast is to prevent pollution is also suggested by its resemblance to some other practices, which are evidently intended to serve this purpose. The Maoris were not allowed to eat on or near any spot where a dead body had been buried, or to take a meal in a canoe while passing opposite to such a place.[1] In Samoa, while a dead body is in the house, no food is eaten under the same roof; hence the family have their meals outside, or in another house.[2] The Todas, who fast on the day when a death has taken place, have on the following day their meals served in another hut.[3] In one of the sacred books of India it is said that a Brâhmana " shall not eat in the house of a relation within six degrees where a person has died, before the ten days of impurity have elapsed "; in a house " where a lying-in woman has not yet come out of the lying-in chamber "; nor in a house where a corpse lies;[4] and in connection with this last injunction we are told that, when a person who is not a relation has died, it is customary to place at the distance of " one hundred bows " a lamp and water-vessel, and to eat beyond that distance.[5] In one of the Zoroastrian books Órmuzd is represented as saying, " In a house when a person shall die, until three nights are completed . . . nothing whatever of meat is to be eaten by his relations ";[6] and the obvious reason for this rule was the belief that the soul of the dead was hovering about the body for the first three nights after death.[7] Closely related to this custom is that of the modern Parsis, which forbids for three days all cooking under a roof where a death has occurred, but allows the inmates to obtain food from their neighbours

---

[1] Polack, *Manners and Customs of the New Zealanders*, i. 239.
[2] Turner, *Nineteen Years in Polynesia*, p. 228. *Idem, Samoa*, p. 145.
[3] Thurston, in the Madras Government Museum's *Bulletin*, i. 174.

[4] *Âpastamba*, i. 5. 16. 18 *sqq.*
[5] Haradatta, quoted by Bühler, in *Sacred Books of the East*, ii. 59, n. 20.
[6] *Shâyast Lâ-Shâyast*, xvii. 2.
[7] West, in *Sacred Books of the East*, v. 382, n. 3.

and friends.[1]   Among the Agariya, a Dravidian tribe in
the hilly parts of Mirzápur, no fire is lit and no cooking
is done in the house of a dead person on the day when he
is cremated, the food being cooked in the house of the
brother-in-law of the deceased.[2]   In Mykonos, one of the
Cyclades, it is considered wrong to cook in the house of
mourning ; hence friends and relatives come laden with
food, and lay the " bitter table." [3]   Among the Albanians
there is no cooking in the house for three days after a
death, and the family are fed by friends.[4]   So also the
Maronites of Syria " dress no victuals for some time in
the house of the deceased, but their relations and friends
supply them." [5]   When a Jew dies all the water in the
same and adjoining houses is instantly thrown away ; [6]
nobody may eat in the same room with the corpse, unless
there is only one room in the house, in which case the
inhabitants may take food in it if they interpose a screen,
so that in eating they do not see the corpse ; they must
abstain from flesh and wine so long as the dead body is in
the house ; [7] and on the evening of mourning the
members of the family may not eat their own food, but
are supplied with food by their friends.[8]   Among the
Arabs of Morocco, if a person has died in the morning, no
fire is made in the whole village until he is buried, and in
some parts of the country the inmates of a house or
tent where a death has occurred, abstain from making fire
for two or three days.   In Algeria " dès que quelqu'un est
mort, on ne doit pas allumer de feu dans la maison
pendant trois jours, et il est défendu de toucher à de la
viande rôtie, grillée ou bouillie, à moins qu'elle ne vienne
de quelqu'un de dehors."[9]   In China, for seven days
after a death " no food is cooked in the house, and friends

---

[1] West, *ibid.* v. 382, n. 2.
[2] Crooke, *Tribes and Castes of the North-Western Provinces*, i. 7.
[3] Bent, *Cyclades*, p. 221.
[4] von Hahn, *Albanesische Studien*, p. 151.
[5] Dandini, 'Voyage to Mount Libanus,' in Pinkerton, *Collection of Voyages*, x. 290.
[6] Allen, *Modern Judaism,* p. 435.
[7] Bodenschatz, *Kirchliche Verfassung der heutigen Juden*, iv. 177.
[8] Buxtorf, *Synagoga Judaica*, p. 707.
[9] Certeux and Carnoy, *L'Algérie traditionelle*, p. 220.

and neighbours are trusted to supply the common necessaries of life."[1] There is no sufficient reason to assume that this practice of abstaining from cooking food after a death is a survival of a previous mourning fast, but the two customs seem partly to have a similar origin. The cooking may contaminate the food if done in a polluted house, or by a polluted individual. The relatives of the dead, or persons who have handled the corpse, are regarded as defiled ; hence they have to abstain from cooking food, as they have to abstain from any kind of work,[2] and from sexual intercourse.[3] Hence, also, they are often prohibited from touching food ; and this may in some cases have led to fasting, whilst in other instances they have to be fed by their neighbours.[4]

However, an unclean individual may be supposed to pollute a piece of food not only by touching it with his hand, but in some cases by eating it ; and, in accordance with the principle of *pars pro toto*, the pollution may then spread to all victuals belonging to the same species. Ideas of this kind are sometimes conspicuous in connection with the restrictions in diet after a death. Thus the Siciatl of British Columbia believe that a dead body, or anything connected with the dead, is inimical to the salmon, and therefore the relatives of a deceased person must abstain from eating salmon in the early stages of the run, as also from entering a creek where salmon are found.[5] Among the Stlatlumh, a neighbouring people, not even elderly widowers, for whom the period of abstention is compara-

---

[1] Gray, *China*, i. 287 *sq.*

[2] *Supra*, ii. 283 *sq.*

[3] Teit, *loc. cit.* p. 331 (Upper Thompson Indians). Tout, in *Jour. Anthr. Inst.* xxxv. 139 (Stlatlumh of British Columbia). Oldenberg, *Die Religion des Veda*, pp. 578, 590 ; Caland, *Die Altindischen Todten- und Bestattungsgebräuche*, p. 81. de Groot, *op. cit.* (vol. ii. book) i. 609 (Chinese). Wilken, in *Revue internationale coloniale*, iv. 352, n. 41.

[4] Turner, *Samoa*, p. 145 ; *Idem, Nineteen Years in Polynesia*, p. 228

(Samoans). Ellis, *Polynesian Researches*, i. 403 (Tahitians). Frazer, *Golden Bough*, i. 323 (Maoris). Williams and Calvert, *Fiji*, p. 169. Among the Upper Thompson Indians the persons who handled the dead body would not touch the food with their hands, but must put it into their mouths with sharp-pointed sticks (Teit, *loc. cit.* p. 331).

[5] Tout, ' Ethnology of the Siciatl of British Columbia,' in *Jour. Anthr. Inst.* xxxiv. 33.

tively short, are allowed to eat fresh salmon till the first of the run is over and the fish have arrived in such numbers that there is no danger of their being driven away.[1] It is not unlikely that if the motives for the restrictions in diet after a death were sufficiently known in each case, a similar fear lest the unclean mourner should pollute the whole species by polluting some individual member of it would be found to be a common cause of those rules which prohibit the eating of staple or favourite food.[2] But it would seem that such rules also may spring from the idea that this kind of food is particularly sought for by the dead and therefore defiled.

Moreover, unclean individuals are not only a danger to others, but are themselves in danger. As Sir J. G. Frazer has shown, they are supposed to be in a delicate condition, which imposes upon them various precautions ;[3] and one of these may be restrictions in their diet. Among the Thlinkets and some peoples in British Columbia the relatives of the deceased not only fast till the body is buried, but have their faces blackened, cover their heads with ragged mats, and must speak but little, confining themselves to answering questions, as it is believed that they would else become chatterboxes.[4] According to early ideas, mourners are in a state very similar to that of girls at puberty, who also, among various peoples, are obliged to fast or abstain from certain kinds of food on account of their uncleanness.[5] Among the Stlatlumh, for instance,

---

[1] Tout, in *Jour. Anthr. Inst.* xxxv. 139.

[2] In the Arunta tribe, Central Australia, no menstruous woman is allowed to gather the Irriakura bulbs, which form a staple article of diet for both men and women, the idea being that any infringement of the restriction would result in the failure of the supply of the bulb (Spencer and Gillen, *Northern Tribes of Central Australia*, p. 615).

[3] Frazer, *Golden Bough*, i. 343, &c.

[4] Boas, *loc. cit.* p. 41.

[5] Boas, *loc. cit.* p. 40 *sqq.* (various tribes in British Columbia). Tout, in *Jour. Anthr. Inst.* xxxiv. 33 (Siciatl).

Sproat, *Scenes and Studies of Savage Life*, p. 93 *sq.* (Ahts). Bourke, 'Medicine-Men of the Apache,' in *Ann. Rep. Bur. Ethn.* ix. 501. Du Tertre, *Histoire générale des Antilles*, ii. 371. Schomburgk, 'Natives of Guiana,' in *Jour. Ethn. Soc. London*, i. 269 *sq.* von Martius, *Beiträge zur Ethnographie Amerika's*, i. 644 (Macusís). Seligmann, in *Reports of the Cambridge Expedition to Torres Straits*, v. 200 *sqq.* (Western Islanders). Man, 'Aboriginal Inhabitants of the Andaman Islands,' in *Jour. Anthr. Inst.* xii. 94. See Frazer, *op. cit.* iii. 205 *sqq.*

when a girl reaches puberty, she fasts for the first four days and abstains from fresh meats of any kind throughout the whole period of her seclusion. "There was a two-fold object in this abstention. First, the girl, it was thought, would be harmed by the fresh meat in her peculiar condition ; and second, the game animals would take offence if she partook of their meat in these circumstances," and would not permit her father to kill them.[1]

It should finally be noticed that, though the custom of fasting after a death in the main has a superstitious origin, there may at the same time be a physiological motive for it.[2] Even the rudest savage feels afflicted at the death of a friend, and grief is accompanied by a loss of appetite. This natural disinclination to partake of food may, combined with superstitious fear, have given rise to prohibitory rules, nay, may even in the first instance have suggested the idea that there is danger in taking food. The mourning observances so commonly coincide with the natural expressions of sorrow, that we are almost bound to assume the existence of some connection between them, even though in their developed forms the superstitious motive be the most prominent.

An important survival of the mourning fast is the Lent fast. It originally lasted for forty hours only, that is, the time when Christ lay in the grave.[3] Irenaeus speaks of the fast of forty hours before Easter,[4] and Tertullian, when a Montanist disputing against the Catholics, says that the only legitimate days for Christian fasting were those in which the Bridegroom was taken away.[5] Subsequently, however, the forty hours were extended to forty

---

[1] Tout, in *Jour. Anthr. Inst.* xxxv. 136.

[2] *Cf.* Mallery, ' Manners and Meals,' in *American Anthropologist*, i. 202 ; Brinton, *Religions of Primitive Peoples*, p. 213 ; Schurtz, *Urgeschichte der Kultur*, p. 587.

[3] *Cf. St. Matthew*, ix. 15 ; *St. Mark*, ii. 20 ; *St. Luke*, v. 35.

[4] Irenaeus, quoted by Eusebius, *Historia ecclesiastica*, v. 24 (Migne, *Patrologiœ cursus*, Ser. Graeca, xx. 501). *Cf.* Funk, ' Die Entwicklung des Osterfastens,' in *Theologische Quartalschrift*, lxxv. 181 *sqq.*; Duchesne, *Christian Worship*, p. 241.

[5] Tertullian, *De jejuniis*, 2 (Migne, *op. cit.* ii. 956).

days, in imitation of the forty days' fasts of Moses, Elijah, and Christ.[1]

Not only on a death, but on certain other occasions, food is supposed to pollute or injure him who partakes of it, and is therefore to be avoided. In Pfalz the people maintain that no food should be taken at an eclipse of the sun ; [2] and all over Germany there is a popular belief that anybody who eats during a thunderstorm will be struck by the lightning.[3] When the Todas know that there is going to be an eclipse of the sun or the moon, they abstain from food.[4] Among the Hindus, while an eclipse is going on, " drinking water, eating food, and all household business, as well as the worship of the gods, are all prohibited " ; high-caste Hindus do not even eat food which has remained in the house during an eclipse, but give it away, and all earthen vessels in use in their houses at the time must be broken.[5] Among the rules laid down for Snâtakas, that is, Brâhmanas who have completed their studentship, there is one which forbids them to eat, travel, and sleep during the twilight ; [6] and in one of the Zoroastrian Pahlavi texts it is said that " in the dark it is not allowable to eat food, for the demons and fiends seize upon one-third of the wisdom and glory of him who eats food in the dark."[7] Many Hindus who revere the sun do not break their fast in the morning till they catch a clear view of it, and do not eat at all on days when it is obscured by clouds [8]— a custom to which there is a parallel among some North American sun-worshippers, the Snanaimuq Indians belonging to the Coast Salish, who must not partake of any food until the sun is well up in the sky.[9] Brahmins

---

[1] St. Jerome, *Commentarii in Jonam*, 3 (Migne, *op. cit.* xxv. 1140). St. Augustine, *Epistola LV (alias CXIX)*, ' Ad inquisitiones Januarii,' 15 (Migne, xxxiii. 217 *sq.*). Funk, *loc. cit.* p. 209.

[2] Schönwerth, *Aus der Oberpfalz*, iii. 55.

[3] Haberland, in *Zeitschr. f. Völkerpsychologie*, xviii. 258.

[4] Rivers, *op. cit.* p. 592 *sq.*

[5] Crooke, *Popular Religion of Northern India*, i. 21 *sq.*

[6] *Laws of Manu*, iv. 55.

[7] *Shâyast Lâ-Shâyast*, ix. 8.

[8] Wilson, *Works*, i. 266. Hunter, *Annals of Rural Bengal*, ii. 285. Crooke, *Things Indian*, p. 214.

[9] Boas, *loc. cit.* p. 51.

fast at the equinoxes, solstices, conjunctions of planets, and on the days of the new and full moon.[1] The Buddhist Sabbath, or *Uposatha*, which, as we have noticed above, occurs on the day of full moon, on the day when there is no moon, and on the two days which are eighth from the full and new moon, is not only a day of rest, but has also from ancient times been a fast-day. He who keeps the Sabbath rigorously abstains from all food between sunrise and sunset, and, as no cooking must be done during the *Uposatha*, he prepares his evening meal in the early morning before the rise of the sun.[2]

Among the Jews there are many who abstain from food on the day of an eclipse of the moon, which they regard as an evil omen.[3] We have also reason to believe that the Jews were once in the habit of observing the new moons and Sabbaths not only as days of rest, but as fast-days ; and the Hebrew Sabbath, as we have seen, in all probability owes its origin to superstitious fear of the changes in the moon.[4] Or how shall we explain the curious rule which forbids fasting on a new moon and on the seventh day,[5] if not as a protest against a fast once in vogue among the Jews on these occasions, but afterwards regarded as an illegitimate rite ?[6] This theory is not new, for Hooker in his ' Ecclesiastical Polity ' observes that " it may be a question, whether in some sort they did not always fast on the Sabbath." He refers to a statement of Josephus, according to which the sixth hour " was wont on the Sabbath always to call them home unto meat," and to certain pagan writers who upbraided them with fasting on that day.[7] In Nehemiah there is an indication that it was a custom to fast on the first day of the seventh month,[8]

[1] Dubois, *Description of the People of India*, p. 160. See also *supra*, ii. 297.
[2] Childers, *Dictionary of the Pali Language*, p. 535. Kern, *Der Buddhismus*, ii. 258.
[3] Buxtorf, *op. cit.* p. 477.
[4] *Supra*, ii. 286 *sq.*
[5] *Judith*, viii. 6. *Schulchan Aruch*, i. 91, 117.

[6] See Jastrow, ' Original Character of the Hebrew Sabbath,' in *American Journal of Theology*, ii. 325.
[7] Hooker, *Ecclesiastical Polity*, v. 72, vol. ii. 338.
[8] *Nehemiah*, viii. 2, 10 :—" Then he said unto them, Go your way, eat the fat, and drink the sweet, and send portions unto them *for whom nothing is prepared.*"

which is " holy unto the Lord " ;[1] and on the tenth day
of the same month there was the great fast of atonement,
combined with abstinence from every kind of work.[2]   I
venture to think that all these fasts may be ultimately
traced to a belief that the changes in the moon not only
are unfavourable for work, but also make it dangerous to
partake of food.   The fact of the seventh day being a
day of rest established the number seven as a sabbatical
number.   In the seventh month there are several days,
besides Saturdays, which are to be observed as days of rest,[3]
and in the seventh year there shall be " a sabbath of rest
unto the land." [4] In these sabbatarian regulations the day
of atonement plays a particularly prominent part.   The
severest punishment is prescribed for him who does not
rest and fast on that day " from even unto even " ;[5] and it
is on the same day that, after the lapse of seven times
seven years, the trumpet of the jubilee shall be caused to
sound throughout the land.[6]   Most of the rules concerning the day of atonement are undoubtedly post-exilic.
But the fact that no other regular days of fasting but
those mentioned by Zechariah are referred to by the
prophets or in earlier books, hardly justifies the conclusion
drawn by many scholars that no such fast existed.   It is
extremely probable that the fast of the tenth day of the
seventh month *as a fast of atonement* is of a comparatively
modern date ; but it is perhaps not too bold to suggest
that the idea of atonement is a later interpretation of a
previously existing fast, which was originally observed for
fear of the dangerous quality attributed to the number
seven.   Why this fast was enjoined on the tenth day of
the seventh month remains obscure ; but it seems that the
order of the month was considered more important than
that of the day.   Nehemiah speaks of a fast which

---

[1] *Nehemiah*, viii. 9 *sqq.* See also
Leviticus, xxiii. 24 *sq.* ; *Numbers*,
xxix. 1.   Among the Babylonians,
too, the seventh month had a sacred
character (Jastrow, *Religion of Babylonia and Assyria*, pp. 681, 683, 686).
[2] *Leviticus*, xvi. 29, 31 ; xxiii. 27

sqq. Numbers, xxix. 7.
[3] *Leviticus*, xxiii. 24, 25, 35, 36, 39.
Numbers, xxix. 1, 12, 35.
[4] *Leviticus*,   xxv. 4.   See also
Exodus, xxiii. 10 *sq.*
[5] *Leviticus*, xxiii. 29 *sq.*
[6] *Ibid.* xxv. 9.

was kept on the twenty-fourth day of the seventh month.[1]

In other Semitic religions we meet with various fasts which are in some way or other connected with astronomical changes. According to En-Nedîm, the Harranians, or " Sabians," observed a thirty days' fast in honour of the moon, commencing on the eighth day after the new moon of Adsâr (March) ; a nine days' fast in honour of " the Lord of Good Luck" (probably Jupiter),[2] commencing on the ninth day before the new moon of the first Kânûn (December) ; and a seven days' fast in honour of the sun, commencing on the eighth or ninth day after the new moon of Shobâth (February).[3] The thirty days' fast seems to have implied abstinence from every kind of food and drink between sunrise and sunset,[4] whereas the seven days' fast is expressly said to have consisted in abstinence from fat and wine.[5] In Manichæism—which is essentially based upon the ancient nature religion of Babylonia, though modified by Christian and Persian elements and elevated into a gnosis[6] —we meet with a great number of fasts. There is a continuous fast for two days when the sun is in Sagittarius (which it enters about the 22nd November) and the moon has its full light ; another fast when the sun has entered Capricornus (which it does about the 21st December) and the moon first becomes visible ; and a thirty days' fast between sunrise and sunset commencing on the day " when the new moon begins to shine, the sun is in Aquarius (where it is from about the 20th January), and eight days of the month have passed," which seems to imply that the fast cannot begin until eight days after the sun has entered Aquarius and that consequently, if the new moon

[1] *Nehemiah*, ix. 1.

[2] Chwolsohn, *Die Ssabier*, ii. 226, n. 247.

[3] En-Nedîm, *Fihrist*, (book ix. ch. i.) i. 4 ; v. 8, 11 *sq.* (Chwolsohn, *op. cit.* ii. 6, 7, 32, 35 *sq.*). See also Chwolsohn, i. 533 *sqq.* ; ii. 75 *sq.*

[4] Chwolsohn, *op. cit.* ii. 71 *sq.* Cf. Abûlfedâ, 6 (*ibid.* ii. 500).

[5] En-Nedîm, *op. cit.* v. 11 (Chwolsohn, *op. cit.* ii. 36).

[6] Kessler, ' Mani, Manichäer,' in Herzog-Hauck, *Realencyclopädie f. protestantische Theologie*, xii. 198 *sq.* Harnack, *History of Dogma*, iii. 330. *Idem*, 'Manichæism,' in *Encyclopædia Britannica*, xv. 485.

appears during that period, the commencement of the fast
has to be postponed till the following new moon. The
Manichæans also fasted for two days at every new moon ;
and our chief authority on the subject, En-Nedîm, states
that they had seven fast-days in each month. They fasted
on Sundays, and some of them, the *electi* or " perfect
ones," on Mondays also.[1] We are told by Leo the
Great that they observed these weekly fasts in honour of
the sun and the moon ;[2] but according to the Armenian
Bishop Ebedjesu their abstinence on Sunday was occasioned by their belief that the destruction of the world
was going to take place on that day.[3] There can be little
doubt that the Harranian and Manichæan fasts were
originally due, not to reverence, but to fear of evil
influences ; reverence can never be the primitive motive
for a customary rite of fasting. The thirty days' fast
which the Harranians observed in the month of Adsâr
finds perhaps its explanation in the fact that, according to
Babylonian beliefs, the month Adar was presided over by
the seven evil spirits, who knew neither compassion nor
mercy, who heard no prayer or supplication, and to
whose baneful influence the popular faith attributed the
eclipse of the moon.[4] But it may also be worth noticing
that the Harranian fast took place about the vernal
equinox—a time at which, as we have seen, the Brahmins
of India are wont to fast, though only for a day or two.

It is highly probable that the thirty days' fast of
the Harranians and Manichæans is the prototype of
the Muhammedan fast of Ramaḍân. During the whole
ninth month of the Muhammedan year the complete
abstinence from food, drink and cohabitation from
sunrise till sunset is enjoined upon every Moslem, with
the exception of young children and idiots, as also sick
persons and travellers, who are allowed to postpone the

[1] En-Nedîm, *Fihrist*, in Flügel,
Mani, pp. 95, 97. Flügel, p. 311
sqq. Kessler, *loc. cit.* p. 212 *sq.*
[2] Leo the Great, *Sermo XLII.* (*al.*

XLI.) 5 (Migne, *op. cit.* liv. 279).
[3] Flügel, *op. cit.* p. 312 *sq.*
[4] Jastrow, *Religion of Babylonia
and Assyria*, pp. 263, 276, 463.

fast to another time.[1] This fast is said to be a fourth
part of Faith, the other cardinal duties of religious
practice being prayer, almsgiving, and pilgrimage. But,
as a matter of fact, modern Muhammedans regard the
fast of Ramadân as of more importance than any other
religious observance;[2] many of them neglect their
prayers, but anybody who should openly disregard the
rule of fasting would be subject to a very severe punishment.[3] Even the privilege granted to travellers and sick
persons is not readily taken advantage of. During their
marches in the middle of summer nothing but the apprehension of death can induce the Aeneze to interrupt the
fast;[4] and when Burton, in the disguise of a Muhammedan doctor, was in Cairo making preparations for his
pilgrimage to Mecca, he found among all those who
suffered severely from such total abstinence only one
patient who would eat even to save his life.[5] There is
no evidence that the fast of Ramadan was an ancient,
pre-Muhammedan custom.[6] On the other hand, its
similarity with the Harranian and Manichæan fasts is
so striking that we are almost compelled to regard them
all as fundamentally the same institution; and if this
assumption is correct, Muhammed must have borrowed
his fast from the Harranians or Manichæans or both.

[1] *Koran*, ii. 180, 181, 183.
[2] *Cf.* Lane, *Modern Egyptians*, p. 106.
[3] von Kremer, *Culturgeschichte des Orients*, i. 460.
[4] Burckhardt, *Bedouins and Wahâbys*, p. 57.
[5] Burton, *Pilgrimage to Al-Madinah and Meccah*, i. 74.
[6] We can hardly regard as such the passage in the Koran (ii. 179) where it is said, "O ye who believe! There is prescribed for you the fast as it was prescribed for those before you; haply ye may fear." The traditionists say that Muhammed was in the habit of spending the month of Ramadân every year in the cave at Hirâ, meditating and feeding all the poor who resorted to him, and that he did so in accordance with

a religious practice which the Koreish used to perform in the days of their heathenism. Others add that 'Abd al-Muttalib commenced the practice, saying "that it was the worship of God which that patriarch used to begin with the new moon of Ramadân, and continue during the whole of the month" (Muir, *Life of Mahomet*, ii. 56, n.* Sell, *Faith of Islâm*, p. 316). But, as Muir remarks (*op. cit.* ii. 56, n.*), it is the tendency of the traditionists to foreshadow the customs and precepts of Islam as if some of them had existed prior to Muhammed, and constituted part of "the religion of Abraham." See Jacob, 'Der muslimische Fasten-monat Ramadân,' in *VI. Jahresbericht der Geographischen Gesellsch. zu Greifswald*, pt. i. 1893–96, p. 2 *sqq.*

Indeed, Dr. Jacob has shown that in the year 623, when
this fast seems to have been instituted, Ramaḍân exactly
coincided with the Harranian fast-month.[1] In its Muhammedan form the fast extending over a whole month is
looked upon as a means of expiation. It is said that by
the observance of it a person will be pardoned all his past
venial sins, and that only those who keep it will be allowed
to enter through the gate of heaven called Rayyân.[2] But
this is only another instance of the common fact that
customs often for an incalculable period survive the
motives from which they sprang.

In various religions we meet with fasting as a form
of penance, as a means of appeasing an angry or indignant
God, as an expiation for sin.[3] The voluntary suffering
involved in it is regarded as an expression of sorrow
and repentance pleasing to God, as a substitute for the
punishment which He otherwise would inflict upon the
sinner; and at the same time it may be thought to
excite His compassion, an idea noticeable in many Jewish
fasts.[4] Among the Jews individuals fasted in cases of
private distress or danger: Ahab, for instance, when
Elijah predicted his downfall,[5] Ezra and his companions
before their journey to Palestine,[6] the pious Israelite when
his friends were sick.[7] Moreover, fasts were instituted
for the whole community when it believed itself to be
under divine displeasure, when danger threatened, when
a great calamity befell the land, when pestilence raged
or drought set in, or there was a reverse in war.[8] Four

[1] Jacob, loc. cit. p. 5.
[2] Sell, op. cit. p. 317.
[3] Wasserschleben, Die Bussordnungen der abendländischen Kirche,
passim (Christianity). Koran, ii.
192; iv. 94; v. 91, 96; lviii. 5.
Jolly, 'Recht und Sitte,' in Bühler,
Grundriss der indo-arischen Philologie, p. 117; Dubois, Description of
the Character, &c. of the People of
India, p. 160 (Brahmanism). Clavigero, History of Mexico, i. 285. On
the occasion of any public calamity
the Mexican high-priest retired to a
wood, where he constructed a hut
for himself, and shut up in this hut

he passed nine or ten months in constant prayer and frequent effusions
of blood, eating only raw maize and
water (Torquemada, Monarchia Indiana, ix. 25, vol. ii. 212 sq.).
[4] Cf. Benzinger, 'Fasting,' in Encyclopædia Biblica, ii. 1508; Schwally,
Das Leben nach dem Tode nach den
Vorstellungen des alten Israel. p. 26.
[5] 1 Kings, xxi. 27.
[6] Ezra, viii. 21.
[7] Psalms, xxxv. 13.
[8] Judges, xx. 26. 1 Samuel, vii. 6.
2 Chronicles, xx. 3. Nehemiah, ix. 1.
Jeremiah, xxxvi. 9. Joel, i. 14; ii. 12.

regular fast-days were established in commemoration of various sad events that had befallen Israel during the captivity ;[1] and in the course of time many other fasts were added, in memory of certain national troubles, though they were not regarded as obligatory.[2] The law itself enjoined fasting for the great day of atonement only.

It may be asked why this particular kind of self-mortification became such a frequent and popular form of penance as it did both in Judaism and in several other religions. One reason is, no doubt, that fasting is a natural expression of contrition, owing to the depressing effect which sorrow has upon the appetite. Another reason is that the idea of penitence, as we have just observed, may be a later interpretation put upon a fast which originally sprang from fear of contamination. Nay, even when fasting is resorted to as a cure in the case of distress or danger, as also when it is practised in commemoration of a calamity, there may be a vague belief that the food is polluted and should therefore be avoided. But in several cases fasting is distinctly a survival of an expiatory sacrifice. The sacrifice of food offered to the deity was changed into the " sacrifice " involved in the abstinence from food on the part of the worshipper. We find that among the Jews the decay of sacrifice was accompanied by a greater frequency of fasts. It was only in the period immediately before the exile that fasting began to acquire special importance ; and the popular estimation of it went on increasing during and after the exile, partly at least from a feeling of the need of religious exercises to take the place of the suspended temple services.[3] Like sacrifice, fasting was a regular appendage to prayer, as a means of giving special efficacy to the supplication ;[4] fasting and praying became in fact a constant combination of words.[5] And equally close is the

[1] *Zechariah*, viii. 19.
[2] Greenstone, in *Jewish Encyclopedia*, v. 347.
[3] Benzinger, in *Encyclopædia Biblica*, ii. 1508. Nowack, *Lehrbuch der hebräischen Archäologie*, ii. 271.
[4] Löw, *Gesammelte Schriften*, i. 108. Nowack, *op. cit.* ii. 271. Benzinger, in *Encyclopædia Biblica*, ii. 1507.
[5] *Judith*, iv. 9, 11. *Tobit*, xii. 8 *Ecclesiasticus*, xxxiv. 26. *St. Luke*, ii. 37.

connection between fasting and almsgiving—a circumstance which deserves special notice where almsgiving is
regarded as a form of sacrifice or has taken the place of it.[1]
In the penitential regulations of Brahmanism we repeatedly meet with the combination " sacrifice, fasting, giving
gifts " ; [2] or also fasting and giving gifts, without mention
being made of sacrifice.[3] Among the Jews each fast-day
was virtually an occasion for almsgiving,[4] in accordance
with the rabbinic saying that " the reward of the fast-day
is in the amount of charity distributed " ; [5] but fasting was
sometimes declared to be even more meritorious than charity, because the former affects the body and the latter the
purse only.[6] And from Judaism this combination of fasting
and almsgiving passed over into Christianity and Muhammedanism. According to Islam, it is a religious duty to
give alms after a fast ; [7] if a person through the infirmity of
old age is not able to keep the fast, he must feed a poor
person ; [8] and the violation of an inconsiderate oath may be
expiated either by once feeding or clothing ten poor men,
or liberating a Muhammedan slave or captive, or fasting
three days.[9] In the Christian Church fasting was not only
looked upon as a necessary accompaniment of prayer, but
whatever a person saved by means of it was to be given to
the poor.[10] St. Augustine says that man's righteousness in
this life consists in fasting, alms, and prayer, that alms and
fasting are the two wings which enable his prayer to fly
upward to God.[11] But fasting without almsgiving " is not

---

[1] *Supra*, i. 565 *sqq.*
[2] *Gautama*, xix. 11. *Vasishtha*,
xxii. 8. *Baudhâyana*, iii. 10. 9.
[3] *Vasishtha*, xx. 47.
[4] Kohler, 'Alms,' in *Jewish Encyclopedia*, i. 435. Löw, *op. cit.* i. 108.
Cf. *Tobit*, xii. 8 ; Katz, *Der wahre
Talmudjude*, p. 43.
[5] *Ibid.* fol. 6 b, quoted by Greenstone, in *Jewish Encyclopedia*, v.349.
[6] *Berakhoth*, fol. 32 b, quoted by
Hershon, *Treasures of the Talmud*,
p. 124.
[7] Sell, *op. cit.* p. 251.
[8] *Ibid.* p. 281. This opinion is
based on a sentence in the Koran

(ii. 180) which has caused a great
deal of dispute. It is said there that
"those who are fit to fast may
redeem it by feeding a poor man."
But the expression " those who are
fit to fast " has been understood to
mean those who can do so only with
great difficulty.
[9] *Koran*, v. 91. Lane, *Modern
Egyptians*, p. 313 *sq.* See also *Koran*,
ii. 192 ; iv. 94 ; v. 96 ; lviii. 5.
[10] Harnack, *History of Dogma*, i.
205, n. 5. Löw, *op. cit.* i. 108.
[11] St. Augustine, *Enarratio in
Psalmum XLII.* 8 (Migne, *Patrologiæ cursus*, xxxvi. 482).

so much as counted for fasting " ;[1] that which is gained
by the fast at dinner ought not to be turned into a feast at
supper, but should be expended on the bellies of the
poor.[2] And if a person was too weak to fast without
injuring his health he was admonished to give the more
plentiful alms.[3]   Tertullian expressly calls fastings
" sacrifices which are acceptable to God."[4] They assumed
the character of reverence offerings, they were said to
be works of reverence towards God.[5]   But fasting, as
well as temperance, has also from early times been
advocated by Christian writers on the ground that it is
" the beginning of chastity,"[6] whereas " through love of
eating love of impurity finds passage."[7]

[1] St. Chrysostom, *In Matthæum Homil. LXXVII.* (*al. LXXVIII.*) 6 (Migne, *op. cit.* Ser. Graeca, lviii. 710).   St. Augustine, *Sermones supposititii*, cxlii. 2, 6 (Migne, xxxix. 2023 *sq.*).

[2] St. Augustine, *Sermones supposititii*, cxli. 4 (Migne, *op. cit.* xxxix. 2021).   See also *Canons enacted under King Edgar*, ' Of Powerful Men,' 3 (*Ancient Laws of England*, p. 415) ; *Ecclesiastical Institutes*, 38 (*ibid.* p. 486).

[3] St. Chrysostom, *In Cap. I. Genes. Homil. X.* 2 (Migne, *op. cit.* Ser.

Graeca, liii. 83).   St. Augustine, *Sermones supposititii*, cxlii. 1 (Migne, xxxix. 2022 *sq.*).

[4] Tertullian, *De resurrectione carnis*, 8 (Migne, *op. cit.* ii. 806).

[5] Hooker, *Ecclesiastical Polity*, v. 72, vol. ii. 334.

[6] St. Chrysostom, *In Epist. II. ad Thessal. Cap. I. Homil. I.* 2 (Migne, *op. cit.* Ser. Gr. lxii. 470).

[7] Tertullian, *De jejuniis*, 1 (Migne, *op. cit.* ii. 953).   See also Manzoni, *Osservazioni sulla morale cattolica*, p. 175.

CHAPTER XXXVIII

RESTRICTIONS IN DIET (*concluded*)

BESIDES the occasional abstinence from certain victuals, which was noticed in the last chapter, there are restrictions in diet of a more durable character.

Thus among the Australian aborigines the younger members of a tribe are, as it seems universally, subject to a variety of such restrictions, from which they are only gradually released as they grow older.[1] In the Wotjobaluk tribe in South-Eastern Australia, for instance, boys are forbidden to eat of the kangaroo and the padi-melon, being told that if they transgress these rules they will fall sick, break out all over with eruptions, and perhaps die. If a man under forty eats the tail part of the emu or bustard, he will turn grey, and if he eats the freshwater turtle he will be killed by lightning. If young men or women of the Wakelbura tribe eat emu, black-headed snake, or porcupine, they will become sick and probably die, uttering the sounds peculiar to the creature in question, the spirit of which is believed to have entered into their bodies.[2] In the Warramunga tribe in Central Australia a man is usually well in the middle age before he

[1] Curr, *The Australian Race*, i. 81. Fraser, *Aborigines of New South Wales*, p. 53. Howitt, *Native Tribes of South-East Australia*, p. 769 *sq*. Brough Smyth, *Aborigines of Victoria*, i. p. xxxv. Taplin, 'Narrinyeri,' in Woods, *Native Tribes of South Australia*, p. 137. Jung, 'Die Mündungsgegend des Murray und ihre Bewohner,' in *Mittheil. d. Vereins f. Erdkunde zu Halle*, 1877, p. 32. Spencer and Gillen, *Native Tribes of Central Australia*, p. 470 *sqq*. Iidem, *Northern Tribes of Central Australia*, p. 611 *sq*. Eyre, *Expeditions of Discovery into Central Australia*, ii. 293.

[2] Howitt, *op. cit.* p. 769.

is allowed to eat wild turkey, rabbit-bandicoot, and emu.[1]
According to certain writers, the object of these restrictions is to reserve the best things for the use of the elders,
and, more especially, of the older men ; [2] but, on the other
hand, it has been remarked that, in looking over the list of
animals prohibited, one fails to see any good reasons for
the selection, unless they may be assumed to have chiefly
sprung from superstitious beliefs.[3] Among the Land
Dyaks the young men and warriors are debarred from
venison for fear it should render them as timid as the
hind.[4] The Moors believe that if a young person before
the age of puberty eats wolf's flesh he will have troubles
afterwards.

There are, further, numerous instances of certain kinds
of food being permanently forbidden to certain individuals.
In Unyamwezi, south of Victoria Nyanza, women are not
permitted to eat fowl, a food which is reserved for the men.[5]
Among the Mandingoes of Teesee no woman is allowed to
eat an egg, and this prohibition is so rigidly adhered to
that " nothing will more affront a woman of Teesee than
to offer her an egg " ; the men, on the other hand, eat eggs
without scruple, even in the presence of their wives.[6]
Among the Bayaka, a Bantu people in the Congo Free
State, both fowls and eggs are forbidden to women ; " if
a woman eats an egg she is supposed to become mad, tear
off her clothes and run away into the bush." [7] The Bahima
of Enkole, in the Uganda Protectorate, allow men to eat
beef and the meat of certain antelopes and of buffalo,
whereas women are generally allowed to eat beef only.[8]
The people of Darfur, in Central Africa, prohibit their
women from eating an animal's liver, because they think

[1] Spencer and Gillen, *Northern Tribes of Central Australia*, p. 612.
[2] *Iidem, Native Tribes of Central Australia*, p. 470 *sq. Iidem, Northern Tribes of Central Australia*, p. 613. Jung, in *Mittheil. d. Vereins f. Erdkunde zu Halle*, 1877, p. 32.
[3] Brough Smyth, *op. cit.* i. 234.
[4] St. John, *Life in the Forests of the Far East*, i. 186.

[5] Reichard, ' Die Wanjamuesi,' in *Zeitschr. d. Gesellsch. f. Erdkunde zu Berlin*, xxiv. 321.
[6] Park, *Travels in the Interior of Africa*, i. 114.
[7] Torday and Joyce, ' Ethnography of the Ba-Yaka,' in *Jour. Anthr. Inst.* xxxvi. 41, 42, 51.
[8] Roscoe, ' Bahima,' in *Jour. Anthr. Inst.* xxxvii. 101.

that a person may increase his soul by partaking of it, and
women are believed to have no souls.[1] The Miris of
Northern India prize tiger's flesh as food for men, but
consider it unsuitable for women, as " it would make them
too strong-minded." [2] In the Australian tribes some
articles of food are entirely interdicted to females.[3] The
natives inhabiting the neighbourhood of Cape York forbid
women to eat various kinds of fish, including some of
the best, " on the pretence of causing disease in women,
although not injurious to the men." [4] In the Sandwich
Islands, again, women were not allowed to eat hog's flesh,
turtle, and certain kinds of fruit, as cocoa and banana.[5]
Many of these prohibitions have been represented as signs
of the low condition of the female sex ; but a more
intimate knowledge of the facts connected with them
would perhaps show that they have some other foundation
than the mere selfishness of the men. For sometimes the
latter also are subject to very similar restrictions. Among
the Bahuana, in the Congo Free State, " women are
forbidden to eat owls or other birds of prey, but are
permitted to eat frogs, from which men are obliged to
abstain under penalty of becoming ill." [6] With reference
to the natives of New Britain, Mr. Powell states that,
whilst in one place the women are prohibited from eating
pigs or tortoises, the men are, in another place, prohibited
from eating anything but human flesh, fowls, or fish.[7] In
the Caroline Islands the men are forbidden to eat a common blackbird, *Lamprothornis*—which is a favourite food
of the women—because it is believed that anyone who did
so, and afterwards climbed a cocoa-tree, would fall down
and perish.[8] In some Dyak tribes on the Western branch

[1] Felkin, ' Notes on the For Tribe,'
in *Proceed. Roy. Soc. Edinburgh*,
xiii. 218.
[2] Dalton, *Ethnology of Bengal*, p. 33.
[3] Curr, *The Australian Race*, i. 81.
Brough Smyth, *op. cit.* i. xxxv.
[4] Macgillivray, *Voyage of Rattlesnake*, ii. 10.
[5] von Kotzebue, *Voyage of Discovery into the South Sea*, iii. 249,
note. Cook, quoted by Buckle, *Miscellaneous and Posthumous Works*, iii.
355.
[6] Torday and Joyce, 'Ethnography of the Ba-Huana,' in *Jour.
Anthr. Inst.* xxxvi. 279.
[7] Powell, *Wanderings in a Wild
Country*, p. 173.
[8] von Kittlitz, *Reise nach dem russischen Amerika, &c.* ii. 103 *sq.*

of the river of Sarawak, goats, fowls, and the fine kind
of fern (*paku*), which forms an excellent vegetable, are
forbidden food to the men, though the women and boys
are allowed to partake of them.[1]

Among various peoples certain foods are forbidden to
priests or magicians. The priests of the ancient Egyptians
were not allowed to eat fish,[2] nor to meddle with the
esculent or potable substances which were produced out of
Egypt ;[3] and, according to Plutarch, they so greatly
disliked the nature of excrementitious things that they
not only rejected most kinds of pulse, but also the flesh
of sheep and swine, because it produced much superfluity
of nutriment.[4] The lamas of Mongolia will touch no
meat of goats, horses, or camels.[5] Among the Semang
of the Malay Peninsula the medicine-men will not eat goat
or buffalo flesh and but rarely that of fowl.[6] The dairymen
of the Todas may drink milk from certain buffaloes only,
and are altogether forbidden to eat chillies.[7] These and
similar restraints laid upon priests or wizards are probably
connected with the idea that holiness is a delicate quality
which calls for special precautions.[8] Schomburgk states
that the conjurers of the British Guiana Indians partake
but seldom of the native hog, because they consider the
eating of it injurious to the efficacy of their skill.[9] And
the Ulád Bu 'Azîz in Morocco believe that if a scribe or
a saint eats wolf's flesh the charms he writes will have no
effect, and the saliva of the saint will lose its curative
power.

There are still other cases in which certain persons are
permanently required to abstain from certain kinds of
food. Thus in the Andaman Islands every man and
woman " is prohibited all through life from eating some

---

[1] Low, *Sarawak*, p. 266.
[2] Herodotus, ii. 37. Plutarch, *De
Iside et Osiride*, 7. Porphyry, *De
abstinentia ab esu animalium*, iv. 7.
[3] Porphyry, *op. cit.* iv. 7.
[4] Plutarch, *De Iside et Osiride*, 5.
[5] Prejevalsky, *Mongolia*, i. 56.
[6] Skeat and Blagden, *Pagan Races*

of the Malay Peninsula, ii. 226.
[7] Rivers, *Todas*, p. 102 *sq.* For
some other instances see Landtman,
Origin of Priesthood, p. 161 *sq.*
[8] *Cf.* Frazer, *Golden Bough*, i. 391.
[9] Schomburgk, ' Expedition to the
Upper Corentyne,' in *Jour. Roy.
Geograph. Soc. London*, xv. 30.

one (or more) fish or animal : in most cases the forbidden dainty is one which in childhood was observed (or imagined) by the mother to occasion some functional derangement ; when of an age to understand it the circumstance is explained, and cause and effect being clearly demonstrated, the individual in question thenceforth considers that particular meat his *yât-tūb*, and avoids it carefully. In cases where no evil consequences have resulted from partaking of any kind of food, the fortunate person is privileged to select his own *yât-tūb*, and is, of course, shrewd enough to decide upon some fish, such as shark or skate, which is little relished, and to abstain from which consequently entails no exercise of self-denial." It is believed that the god Puluga would punish severely any person who might be guilty of eating his *yât-tūb*, either by causing his skin to peel off, or by turning his hair white, and flaying him alive.[1] In Samoa each man had generally his god in the shape of some species of animal ; and if he ate one of these divine animals it was supposed that the god avenged the insult by taking up his abode in the eater's body and there generating an animal of the same kind until it caused his death.[2] The members of a totem clan are usually forbidden to eat the particular animal or plant whose name they bear.[3] Thus among the Omaha Indians men whose totem is the elk believe that if they ate the flesh of the male elk they would break out in boils and white spots in different parts of their bodies ; and men whose totem is the red corn think that if they ate red corn they would have running sores all round their mouths.[4] Yet, however general, prohibitions of this kind cannot be said to be a universal characteristic of totemism.[5] Sir J. G. Frazer even suggests that the original custom was perhaps to eat the totem and the

[1] Man, 'Aboriginal Inhabitants of the Andaman Islands,' in *Jour. Anthr. Inst.* xii. 354.

[2] Turner, *Samoa*, p. 17 *sq.*

[3] Frazer, *Totemism*, p. 7 *sqq. Idem, Totemism and Exogamy*, iv. 6.

[4] Dorsey, 'Omaha Sociology,' in *Ann. Rep. Bur. Ethn.* iii. 225, 231. *Idem,* 'Siouan Folk-Lore,' in *American Antiquarian*, vii. 107.

[5] Frazer, *Totemism*, p. 19. *Idem, Totemism and Exogamy,* iv. 6 *sq.*

latter custom to abstain from it.[1]   But this is hardly
more than a guess.

There are, finally, restrictions in eating which refer to
the whole people or tribe. In early society certain things
which might serve as food are often not only universally
abstained from, but actually prohibited by custom or law.
The majority of these prohibitions have reference to
animals or animal products, which are naturally more
apt to cause disgust than is vegetable food—probably
because our ancestors in early days, by instinct, subsisted
chiefly on a vegetable diet, and only subsequently acquired
a more general taste for animal nourishment.[2]   Certain
animals excite a feeling of disgust by their very appearance, and are therefore abstained from. This I take to
be a reason for the aversion to eating reptiles. It is
said that snakes are avoided as food because their flesh
is supposed to be as poisonous as their bite ;[3] but this
explanation is hardly relevant to harmless reptiles, which
are likewise in some cases forbidden food.[4] The abstinence from fish seems generally to have a similar origin,
though some peoples say that they refuse to eat certain
species because the soul of a relative might be in the fish.[5]
The Navahoes of New Mexico " must never touch fish,
and nothing will induce them to taste one." [6] The
Mongols consider them unclean animals.[7] The South
Siberian Kachinzes are said to refrain from them because
they believe that " the evil principle lives in the water
and eats fish." [8] The Kâfirs on the North-Western
frontier of India " detest fish, though their rivers abound
in them."[9] The same aversion is common in the South

[1] Frazer, *Totemism and Exogamy,*
iv. 6 *sq.*
[2] *Cf.* Schurtz, *Die Speiseverbote,* p.
17.
[3] Skeat and Blagden, *Pagan Races
of the Malay Peninsula,* i. 130
(Berembun). Schurtz, *op. cit.* p. 22.
[4] *Leviticus,* xi. 29 *sq.* Sayce, *Hibbert Lectures on the Religion of the
Ancient Babylonians,* p. 83.
[5] Frazer, *Golden Bough,* ii. 430, 432.

[6] Stephen, ' Navajo,' in *American
Anthropologist,* vi. 357.
[7] Prejevalsky, *op. cit.* i. 56.
[8] von Strümpell, ' Der·Volksstamm
der Katschinzen,' in *Mittheil. d.
Vereins f. Erdkunde zu Leipzig,*
1875, p. 23.
[9] Fosberry, ' Some of the Mountain
Tribes of the N.W. Frontier of
India,' in *Jour. Ethn. Soc. London,*
N.S. i. 192.

African tribes[1] and among most Hamitic peoples of East Africa ;[2] when asked for an explanation of it, they say that fish are akin to snakes. Fish, or at least certain species of fish, were forbidden to the ancient Syrians ;[3] and the Hebrews were prohibited from eating all fish that have not fins and scales.[4] It is curious to note that various peoples who detest fish also abstain from fowl.[5] The Navahoes are strictly forbidden to eat the wild turkey with which their forests abound ;[6] and the Mongols' dislike of fowl is so great that one of Prejevalsky's guides nearly turned sick on seeing him eat boiled duck.[7] Some peoples have a great aversion to eggs,[8] which are said to be excrements, and therefore unfit for food.[9] There may be a similar reason for the abstinence from milk among peoples who have domesticated animals able to supply them with it.[10] The Dravidian aborigines of the hills of

[1] Fritsch, *Drei Jahre in Süd-Afrika*, p. 338. Shooter, *Kafirs of Natal and the Zulu Country*, p. 215 (Zulus). Kropf, *Das Volk der Xosa-Kaffern*, p. 102. Campbell, *Second Journey in the Interior of South Africa*, ii. 203 (Bechuanas). The Hottentots, however, eat fish (Fritsch, p. 339). [2] Hildebrandt, 'Wakamba und ihre Nachbarn,' in *Zeitschr. f. Ethnol.* x. 378. Paulitschke, *Ethnographie Nordost-Afrikas*, i. 155 (Somals, Gallas). Schurtz, *op. cit.* p. 23.
[3] Porphyry, *op. cit.* iv. 15. Plutarch, *De superstitione*, 10.
[4] *Leviticus*, xi. 10 *sqq.*
[5] Hildebrandt, in *Zeitschr. f. Ethnol.* x. 378 (Gallas, Wadshagga, Waikuyu, &c.). Paulitschke, *op. cit.* i. 153 *sqq.* (Gallas, Somals). Burton, *Two Trips to Gorilla Land*, i. 95 (Somals). Meldon, 'Bahima of Ankole,' in *Jour. African Soc.* vi. 146 ; Ashe, *Two Kings of Uganda*, p. 303 (Bahima). Kropf, *Das Volk der Xosa-Kaffern*, p. 102. Among the Zulus domestic fowls are eaten by none except young persons and old (Shooter, *op. cit.* p. 215). For other peoples who abstain from fowl, see Bastian, *Die deutsche Expedition an der Loango-Küste*, i. 185 ; Casati, *Ten Years in Equatoria*, i. 165 (Mon-

buttu); Salt, *Voyage to Abyssinia*, p. 179 (Danakil); Skeat and Blagden, *Pagan Races of the Malay Peninsula*, i. 135 (Sabimba), 136 (Orang Muka Kuning); *Globus*, l. 330 (inhabitants of Hainan); Ehrenreich, quoted by Schurtz, *op. cit.* p. 20 (Karaya of Goyaz); von den Steinen, *Durch Central-Brasilien*, p. 262 (Yuruna) ; Cæsar, *De bello Gallico*, v. 12 (ancient Britons).
[6] Stephen, in *American Anthropologist*, vi. 357.
[7] Prejevalsky, *op. cit.* i. 56.
[8] The Kafirs formerly abstained from eggs (Kropf, *op. cit.* p. 102). Among the Zulus eggs are eaten by young and old persons only (Shooter, *op. cit.* p. 215). The Bahima refuse this kind of food (Ashe, *op. cit.* p. 303), and so do generally the Waganda, especially the women (Felkin, 'Notes on the Waganda Tribe,' in *Proceed. Roy. Soc. Edinburgh*, xiii. 716; Ashe, p. 303). See also Andree, *Ethnographische Parallelen*, p. 126 *sq.*; Schurtz, *op. cit.* p. 23 *sq.*
[9] Reichard, 'Die Wanjamuesi,' in *Zeitschr. d. Gesellsch. f. Erdkunde zu Berlin*, xxiv. 321. Hildebrandt, 'Wakamba und ihre Nachbarn,' in *Zeitschr. f. Ethnol.* x. 378.
[10] See Westermarck, *History of Human Marriage*, p. 484.

Central India, who never use milk, are expressly said to regard it as an excrement.[1] The ancient Caribs had a horror of eggs and never drank milk.[2] The Ashantees are " forbidden eggs by the fetish, and cannot be persuaded to taste milk." [3] The Kimbunda in South-Western Africa detest milk, and consider it inconceivable how a grown-up person can enjoy it ; they believe that the Kilulu, or spirit, would punish him who partook of it.[4] The Dyaks of Borneo, the Javanese, and the Malays abstain from milk.[5] To the Chinese milk and butter are insupportably odious.[6]

The meat of certain animals may also be regarded with disgust on account of their filthy habits or the nasty food on which they live. In the Warramunga tribe, in Central Australia, there is a general restriction applying to eagle-hawks, and the reason assigned for it is that this bird feeds on the bodies of dead natives.[7] It seems that the abstinence from swine's flesh, at least in part, belongs to the same group of facts. Various tribes in South Africa hold it in abomination.[8] In some districts of Madagascar, according to Drury, the eating of pork was accounted a very contemptible thing.[9] It is, or was, abstained from by the Jakuts of Siberia, the Votyaks of the Government of Vologda,[10] and the Lapps.[11] The disgust for pork has likewise been met with in many American tribes. The Koniagas will eat almost any digestible substance except pork.[12] The Navahoes of New Mexico abominate it " as if they were the devoutest of Hebrews " ; [13] it is not forbidden by their religion, but " they say they will not eat the flesh of the hog simply because the animal is filthy in

[1] Crooke, *Things Indian*, p. 92.

[2] Du Tertre, *Histoire générale des Antilles*, ii. 389.

[3] Bowdich, *Mission to Ashantee*, p. 319.

[4] Magyar, *Reisen in Süd-Afrika*, i. 303, 321.

[5] Low, *op. cit.* p. 267.

[6] Huc, *Travels in Tartary*, i. 281. Westermarck, *op. cit.* p. 484.

[7] Spencer and Gillen, *Northern Tribes of Central Australia*, p. 612.

[8] Fritsch, *Drei Jahre in Süd-Afrika*, p. 339. Kropf, *op. cit.* p. 102 (Kafirs).

[9] Drury, *Madagascar*, p. 143.

[10] Latham, *Descriptive Ethnology*, i. 363.

[11] Leem, *Beskrivelse over Finmarkens Lapper*, p. 501.

[12] Bancroft, *Native Races of the Pacific States*, i. 75.

[13] Stephen, in *American Anthropologist*, vi. 357.

its habits, because it is the scavenger of the town." [1]   In
his description of the Indians of the South-Eastern States
Adair writes :—" They reckon all those animals to be
unclean that are either carnivorous, or live on nasty food,
as hogs, wolves, panthers, foxes, cats, mice, rats. . . .
When swine were first brought among them, they deemed
it such a horrid abomination in any of their people to eat
that filthy and impure food, that they excluded the criminal from all religious communion in their circular town-
house. . . . They still affix vicious and contemptible ideas
to the eating of swine's flesh ; insomuch that *Shúkàpa*,
' swine eater,' is the most opprobrious epithet that they
can use to brand us with ; they commonly subjoin *Akang-
gàpa*, ' eater of dunghill fowls.' Both together signify
' filthy, helpless animals.' " [2]   So also those Indians in
British Guiana who have kept aloof from intercourse
with the colonists reject pork with the greatest loathing.
Schomburgk tells us that an old Indian permitted his
children to accompany him on a journey only on the
condition that they were never to eat any viands prepared
by his cook, for fear lest pork should have been used in their
preparation.   But this objection does not extend to the
native hog, which, though generally abstained from by
wizards, is eaten by the laity indiscriminately, with the
exception of women who are pregnant or who have just
given birth to a child.[3] This suggests that the aversion to
the domestic pig partly springs from the fact that it is a
foreign animal.   Indeed, the Guiana Indians refuse to eat
the flesh of all animals that are not indigenous to their
country, but were introduced from abroad, such as oxen,
sheep, and fowls, apparently on the principle " that any
strange and abnormal object is especially likely to be
possessed of a harmful spirit." [4] The Kafirs, also, abstain

[1] Matthews, ' Study of Ethics
among the Lower Races,' in *Jour.
American Folk-Lore*, xii. 5.
[2] Adair, *History of the American
Indians*, p. 132 *sqq.*
[3] Schomburgk, in *Jour. Roy. Geograph. Soc. London*, xv. 29 *sq.*

[4] Im Thurn, *Indians of Guiana*, p.
368. Dr. Schurtz suggests (*op. cit.*
p. 19 *sqq.*) that some other peoples,
as the Indians of Brazil, abstain
from fowls because they are not
indigenous to their country.

from the domestic swine, though they eat the wild hog.[1]
Some writers maintain that pork has been prohibited on
the ground that it is prejudicial to health in hot countries;[2]
but, as we have seen, this prohibition is found among
various northern peoples as well, and it seems besides that
the unwholesomeness of pork in good condition has been
rather assumed than proved. Sir J. G. Frazer, again, believes that the ancient Egyptians, Semites, and some of the
Greeks abstained from this food not because the pig was
looked upon simply as a filthy and disgusting creature, but
because it was considered to be endowed with high supernatural powers.[3] In Greece the pig was used in purificatory ceremonies.[4] Lucian says that the worshippers of
the Syrian goddess abstained from eating pigs, some
because they held them in abomination, others because
they thought them holy.[5] The heathen Harranians
sacrificed the swine and ate swine's flesh once a year.[6]
According to Greek writers, the Egyptians abhorred the
pig as a foul and loathsome animal, and to drink its milk
was believed to cause leprosy and itchy eruptions ;[7] but
once a year they sacrificed pigs to the moon and to Osiris
and ate of the flesh of the victims, though at any other
time they would not so much as taste pork.[8]

Of the abhorrence of cannibalism I shall speak in a
separate chapter, but in this connection it is worth
noticing that the eating of certain animals is regarded
with horror or disgust either because they are supposed
to be metamorphosed ancestors[9] or on account of their
resemblance to men. Various peoples refrain from

[1] Müller, *Allgemeine Ethnographie*, p. 189.
[2] Ramsay, *Historical Geography of Asia Minor*, p. 32. Wiener, 'Die alttestamentarischen Speiseverbote,' in *Zeitschr. f. Ethnol.* viii. 103. See also Buckle, *Miscellaneous and Posthumous Works*, iii. 354 *sq.*
[3] Frazer, *Golden Bough*, ii. 304 *sqq.* Idem, *Pausanias's Description of Greece*, iv. 137 *sq.*
[4] Ramsay, *op. cit.* p. 31 *sq.* Frazer, *Pausanias's Description of Greece*, iii. 277, 593.
[5] Lucian, *De dea Syria*, 54.
[6] Robertson Smith, *Religion of the Semites*, p. 290. Cf. Isaiah, lxv. 4, and lxvi. 3, 17, where this sacrifice is alluded to as a heathen abomination.
[7] Herodotus, ii. 47. Plutarch, *De Iside et Osiride*, 8. Aelian, *De natura animalium*, x. 16.
[8] Herodotus, ii. 47. Plutarch, *De Iside et Osiride*, 8.
[9] Frazer, *Golden Bough*, ii. 430 *sqq.* St. John, *op. cit.* i. 186 (Land Dyaks).

monkey's flesh ;[1] and European travellers mention their
own instinctive repugnance to it and their aversion to
shooting monkeys.[2]   The Indians of Lower California
will eat any animal, except men and monkeys, " the
latter because they so much resemble the former."[3]
According to an ancient writer quoted by Porphyry, the
Egyptian priests rejected those animals which " verged
to a similitude to the human form."[4]   The Kafirs say
that elephants are forbidden food because their intelligence resembles that of men.[5]

Moreover, intimacy with an animal easily takes away
the appetite for its flesh. Among ourselves, as Mandeville
observes, " some people are not to be persuaded to taste
of any creatures they have daily seen and been acquainted
with, whilst they were alive ; others extend their scruple
no further than to their own poultry, and refuse to eat
what they fed and took care of themselves ; yet all of
them will feed heartily and without remorse on beef,
mutton, and fowls, when they are bought in the
market."[6]   Among other races we meet with feelings
no less refined. Mencius, the Chinese moralist, said :—
" So is the superior man affected towards animals, that,
having seen them alive, he cannot bear to see them die ;
having heard their dying cries, he cannot bear to eat
their flesh. Therefore he keeps away from his slaughter-
house and cook-room."[7]   The abstinence from domestic
fowls and their eggs, as also from the tame pig, may
occasionally have sprung from sympathy.   Dr. von den
Steinen states that the Brazilian Yuruna cannot be
induced to eat any animal which they have bred themselves, and that they apparently considered it very
immoral when he and his party ate hen-eggs.[8]   In the

---

[1] Shooter, *op. cit.* p. 215 (Zulus).
Schurtz, *op. cit.* p. 28 (Abyssinians).
Skeat and Blagden, *op. cit.* i. 134
(Orang Sletar). In the *Institutes of
Vishnu* (li. 3) the eating of apes is
particularly stigmatised.

[2] Schurtz, *op. cit.* p. 28. *Infra*, on
Regard for the Lower Animals.

[3] Bancroft, *op. cit.* i. 560.

[4] Porphyry, *op. cit.* iv. 7.

[5] Müller, *Ethnographie*, p. 189.

[6] Mandeville, *Fable of the Bees*, p.
188.

[7] Mencius, i. 1. 7. 8.

[8] von den Steinen, *Durch Central-
Brasilien*, p. 262. See also Juan and
Ulloa, *Voyage to South America*, i.
426 (Indians of Quito).

sacred books of India it is represented as a particularly bad action to eat certain domestic animals, including village pigs and tame cocks ; a twice-born man who does so knowingly will ·become an outcast.[1] Among the Bechuanas in South Africa dogs and tame cats are not eaten, though wild cats are.[2] The Arabs of Dukkâla in Morocco eat their neighbours' cats but not their own. Among the Dinka only such cows as die naturally or by an accident are used for food ; but a dead cow is never eaten by the bereaved owner himself, who is too much afflicted at the loss to be able to touch a morsel of the carcase of his departed beast.[3] Herodotus says that the Libyans would not taste the flesh of the cow, though they ate oxen ;[4] and the same rule prevailed among the Egyptians and Phœnicians, who would sooner have partaken of human flesh than of the meat of a cow.[5] The eating of cow's flesh is prohibited by the law of Brahmanism.[6] According to Dr. Rájendralála Mitra, the idea of beef as an article of food " is so shocking to the Hindus, that thousands over thousands of the more orthodox among them never repeat the counterpart of the word in their vernaculars, and many and dire have been the sanguinary conflicts which the shedding of the blood of cows has caused."[7] In China " the slaughter of buffaloes for food is unlawful, according to the assertions of the people, and the abstaining from the eating of beef is regarded as very meritorious."[8] It is said in the ' Divine Panorama ' that he who partakes of beef or dog's flesh will be punished by the deity.[9] In Japan neither cattle nor sheep were in former days killed for food ;[10] and in the rural districts many people still think it wrong to eat beef.[11] In Rome the slaughter of

[1] Institutes of Vishnu, li. 3. Laws of Manu, v. 19.
[2] Campbell, Second Journey in the Interior of South Africa, ii. 203.
[3] Schweinfurth, Heart of Africa, i. 163 sq.
[4] Herodotus, iv. 186.
[5] Ibid. ii. 41. Porphyry, op. cit. ii. 11.
[6] Institutes of Vishnu, li. 3.
[7] Rájendralála Mitra, Indo-Aryans, i. 354.
[8] Doolittle, Social Life of the Chinese, ii. 187.
[9] Giles, Strange Stories from a Chinese Studio, ii. 376.
[10] Reed, Japan, i. 61.
[11] Griffis, Mikado's Empire, p. 472.

a labouring ox was in olden days punished with ex-communication ;[1] and at Athens and in Peloponnesus it was prohibited even on penalty of death.[2] Indeed, the ancient idea has survived up to modern times in Greece, where it has been held as a maxim that the animal which tills the ground ought not to be used for food.[3] These prohibitions are no doubt to some extent expressions of kindly feelings towards the animals to which they refer.[4] A Dinka is said to be fonder of his cattle than of his wife and children ;[5] and according to classical writers, the ploughing ox is not allowed to be slaughtered because he is himself an agriculturist, the servant of Ceres, and a companion to the labourer in his work.[6] But at the same time the restrictions in question are very largely due to prudential motives. Peoples who live chiefly on the products of their cattle show a strong disinclination to reduce their herds, especially by killing cows or calves ;[7] and agricultural races are naturally anxious to preserve the animal which is used for work on the field. With reference to the Egyptian and Phœnician custom of eating bulls but abstaining from cows, Porphyry observes that " for the sake of utility in one and the same species of animals distinction is made between that which is pious and that which is impious," cows being spared on account of their progeny.[8] Until quite recently in Egypt no one was allowed to kill a calf, and permission from the government was required for the slaughter of a bull.[9] Moreover, domestic animals are frequently regarded as sacred in consequence of their utility, and for that reason also abstained from. The Dinka pay a

[1] Pliny, *Historia naturalis*, viii. 70.
[2] Varro, *De re rustica*, ii. 5. 3. *sq.* Aelian, *Varia historia*, v. 14.
[3] Mariti, *Travels through Cyprus*, i. 35.
[4] See *infra*, on Regard for the Lower Animals.
[5] Schweinfurth, *op. cit.* i. 164.
[6] Aelian, *Varia historia*, v. 14. Varro, *De re rustica*, ii. 5. 3.
[7] Fritsch, *Die Eingeborenen Süd-Afrika's*, p. 86; Kropf, *op. cit.* p. 102 (Kafirs). Merker, *Die Masai*, p. 169.

Paulitschke, *Ethnographie Nordost-Afrikas*, i. 153. Ratzel, *History of Mankind*, ii. 411 (pastoral races of Africa). Erman, *Reise um die Erde*, i. 515 (Kirghiz). Andree, *Ethnographische Parallelen*, p. 122 *sq.* Robertson Smith, *Religion of the Semites*, p. 297. Schurtz, *op. cit.* p. 30 *sq.*
[8] Porphyry, *op. cit.* ii. 11.
[9] Wilkinson, in Rawlinson's translation of Herodotus, ii. 72 *sq.* n. 7.

kind of reverence to their cattle.[1] In Egypt, according to Herodotus, the cow was sacred to Isis.[2] In India she has been the object of a special worship.[3]

Certain foods, then, are generally abjured, not merely because they excite disgust, or as the case may be, because they have a disagreeable taste, but also from utilitarian considerations. To the instances just mentioned may be added the custom prevalent among the Tonga Islanders of setting a temporary prohibition or taboo on certain eatables in order to prevent them from growing scarce.[4] But the most important prudential motive underlying the general restrictions in diet is no doubt fear lest the food should have an injurious effect upon him who partakes of it. The harm caused by it may only be imaginary ; indeed, forbidden food is commonly regarded as unwholesome, whatever be the original ground on which it was prohibited.[5] The Negroes of the Loango Coast say that they abstain from goat-flesh because otherwise their skin would scale off, and from fowl so as not to lose their hair.[6] Some tribes of the Malay Peninsula refuse to eat the flesh of elephants under the pretext that it would occasion sickness.[7] The tribes inhabiting the hills of Assam think that " the penalty for eating the flesh of a cat is loss of speech, while those who infringe a special rule forbidding the flesh of a dog are believed to die of boils."[8] The worshippers of the Syrian goddess maintained that the eating of sprats or anchovies would fill the body with ulcers and wither up the liver.[9] In Russia veal is considered by many to be very unwholesome food, and is entirely rejected by pious people.[10] It is not probable that these ideas are in the first instance derived from experience ; but there can be no doubt that fear of evil consequences is in many cases a

[1] Schweinfurth, op. cit. i. 163.
[2] Herodotus, ii. 41.
[3] Barth, Religions of India, p. 264.
[4] Mariner, Natives of the Tonga Islands, ii. 233.
[5] Cf. Schurtz, op. cit. p. 23.
[6] Bastian, Die deutsche Expedition an der Loango-Küste, i. 185.
[7] Skeat and Blagden, op. cit. i. 132.
[8] Hodson, ' The " Genna " amongst the Tribes of Assam,' in Jour. Anthr. Inst. xxxvi. 98.
[9] Plutarch, De superstitione, 10.
[10] Erman, Reise um die Erde, i. 515.

primary motive for the abstinence from a certain kind of food. Mr. Im Thurn supposes that the Guiana Indian avoids eating the flesh of various animals because he thinks they are particularly malignant.[1] Animals that present some unusual or uncanny peculiarity are rejected because they are objects of superstitious fear. The Egyptian priests, we are told, did not eat oxen which were twins or which were speckled, nor animals that had only one eye.[2] The North American Indians of the South-Eastern States abstained from all birds of night, believing that if they ate them they would fall ill.[3] Another cause of rejecting the flesh of certain animals is the idea that anybody who partook of it would at the same time acquire some undesirable quality inherent in the animal.[4] The Záparo Indians of Ecuador " will, unless from necessity, in most cases not eat any heavy meats such as tapir and peccary, but confine themselves to birds, monkeys, deer, fish, &c., principally because they argue that the heavier meats make them also un-wieldy, like the animals who supply the flesh, impeding their agility and unfitting them for the chase." [5] For a similar reason the ancient Caribs are said to have refrained from turtles ;[6] and some North American Indians state that in former days their greatest chieftains " seldom ate of any animal of gross quality, or heavy motion of body, fancying it conveyed a dullness through the whole system, and disabled them from exerting them-selves with proper vigour in their martial, civil, and religious duties." [7] The Namaquas of South Africa, again, pretend not to eat the flesh of the hare, because they think it would make them as faint-hearted as that animal.[8] Among the Kafirs only children may eat hares, whereas the men partake of the flesh of the

---

[1] Im Thurn, *op. cit.* p. 368.
[2] Porphyry, *op. cit.* iv. 7.
[3] Adair, *op. cit.* p. 130 *sq.*
[4] See Frazer, *Golden Bough,* ii. 353 *sqq.*
[5] Simson, *Travels in the Wilds of*

Ecuador, p. 168.
[6] Waitz, *Anthropologie der Natur-völker,* iii. 384.
[7] Adair, *op. cit.* p. 133.
[8] Hahn, *Supreme Being of the Khoi-Khoi,* p. 106.

leopard in order to get its strength.[1] Among some other
peoples the hare is forbidden food,[2] possibly owing to a
similar superstition. The blood of an animal is avoided
because it is believed to contain its life or soul. We
meet with this custom in several North American tribes,[3]
as well as in the Old Testament ; [4] and from the Jews it
passed into early Christianity.[5]

The general abstinence from certain kinds of food has
thus sprung from a great variety of causes. Of these I have
been able to point out only some of the more general and
obvious. As Sir J. G. Frazer justly remarks, to explain
the ultimate reason why any particular food is prohibited
to a whole tribe or to certain of its members would
commonly require a far more intimate knowledge of the
history and beliefs of the tribe than we possess.[6] Even
explanations given by the natives themselves may be misleading, since the original motive for a custom may have
been forgotten, while the custom itself is still preserved.
But I think that, broadly speaking, the general avoidance
of a certain food may be traced to one or several of
the following sources :—its disagreeable taste ; disgust
caused, in the case of animal food, either by the external
appearance of the animal, or by its unclean habits, or by
sympathy, or by associations of some kind or other, or
even by the mere fact that it is commonly abstained from ;
the disinclination to kill an animal for food, or, generally,
to reduce the supply of a certain kind of victuals ; the
idea, whether correct or false, that the food would injure

[1] Kropf, *op. cit.* p. 102.
[2] *Leviticus*, xi. 6, 8. Cæsar, *De bello Gallico*, v. 12 (ancient Britons). The Chinese have a deep-rooted pre-judice against eating the flesh of the hare, which they have always re-garded as an animal endowed with mysterious properties (Dennis, *Folk-Lore of China*, p. 64). With refer-ence to the Biblical prohibition of eating camel's flesh, old exegetes observed that the camel is a very revengeful animal, and that its vindictiveness would be transferred to him who partook of its meat (Wiener, in *Zeitschr. f. Ethnol.* viii. 104) ; but whether the prohibition in question originated in such a belief is open to doubt.
[3] Adair, *op. cit.* p. 134. Frazer, *Golden Bough*, i. 353.
[4] *Leviticus*, iii. 17 ; vii. 25 *sqq.* ; xvii. 10 *sqq.* ; xix. 26. *Deuter-onomy*, xii. 16, 23 *sqq.* ; xv. 23.
[5] Haberland, 'Gebräuche und Aber-glauben beim Essen,' in *Zeitschr. f. Völkerpsychologie*, xvii. 363 *sq.*
[6] Frazer, *Golden Bough*, i. 391 *sq.*

him who partook of it. From what has been said in
previous chapters it is obvious that any of these factors,
if influencing the manners of a whole community and
especially when supported by the force of habit, may lead
not only to actual abstinence but to prohibitory rules the
transgression of which is apt to call forth moral disapproval. This is particularly the case at the earlier
stages of culture, where a people's tastes and habits are
most uniform, where the sway of custom is most powerful, where instinctive aversion most readily develops into
moral indignation, and where man in almost every branch
of action thinks he has to be on his guard against supernatural dangers. And in this, as in other cases of moral
concern, the prohibition may easily be sanctioned by
religion, especially when the abstinence is due to fear of
some mysterious force or quality in the thing avoided.
The religious aspect assumed particular prominence in
Hebrewism and Brahmanism. It is said in the ' Institutes of Vishnu ' that the eating of pure food is more
essential than all external means of purification ; " he
who eats pure food only is truly pure, not he who is
only purified with earth and water." [1] The Koran forbids
the eating of " what is dead, and blood, and flesh of
swine, and whatsoever has been consecrated to other than
God." [2] Mediæval Christianity prohibited the eating of
various animals, especially horses, which were not used
as food in the South of Europe, but which the pagan
Teutons sacrificed and ate at their religious feasts.[3] The
idea that it is " unchristian " to eat horseflesh has
survived even to the present day, and has, together with
the aversion to feeding on a pet animal, been responsible
for the loss of enormous quantities of nourishing food.
Among ourselves the only eatable thing the partaking of
which is generally condemned as immoral is human flesh.
But there are a considerable number of people who think

[1] *Institutes of Vishnu,* xxii. 89.
[2] *Koran,* ii. 168.
[3] Langkavel, ' Pferde und Naturvölker,' in *Internationales Archiv*
für Ethnographie, i. 53. Schurtz, *op.
cit.* p. 32 *sq.* Maurer, *Die Bekehrung
des Norwegischen Stammes zum
Christenthume,* ii. 198.

that we ought to abstain from all animal meat, not only for sanitary reasons, but because man is held to have no right to subject any living being to suffering and death for the purpose of gratifying his appetite.

On similar grounds vegetarianism has been advocated as a moral duty among Eastern races, as also in classical antiquity. The regard for life in general, which is characteristic of Taouism, Buddhism, Jainism, and Brahmanism,[1] led to the condemnation of the use of animals as food. It is a very common feeling among the Chinese of all classes that the eating of flesh is sensual and sinful, or at least quite incompatible with the highest degree of sincerity and purity.[2] In Japan many persons abstain from meat, owing to Buddhistic influence.[3] In India animal food was not avoided in early times ; the epic characters shoot deer and eat cows.[4] Even in the sacred law-books the eating of meat is permitted in certain circumstances : —" On offering the honey-mixture to a guest, at a sacrifice and at the rites in honour of the manes, but on these occasions only, may an animal be slain." [5] Nay, some particular animals are expressly declared eatable.[6] The total abstinence from meat is in fact represented as something meritorious rather than as a strict duty ;[7] it is said that " by avoiding the use of flesh one gains a greater reward than by subsisting on pure fruit and roots, and by eating food fit for ascetics in the forest." [8] But on the other hand we also read that " there is no greater sinner than that man who, though not worshipping the gods or the manes, seeks to increase the bulk of his own flesh by the flesh of other beings." [9] As a matter of fact, meat is nowadays commonly, though by no means universally, abstained from by high caste Hindus, whereas

---

[1] See *infra*, on Regard for the Lower Animals.
[2] Doolittle, *op. cit.* ii. 183.
[3] Chamberlain, *Things Japanese*, p. 175 *sq.*
[4] Hopkins, *Religions of India*, p. 200.
[5] *Laws of Manu*, v. 41. See also *Vasishtha*, iv. 5.

[6] *Institutes of Vishnu*, li. 6. *Laws of Manu*, v. 18.
[7] See Jolly, 'Recht und Sitte,' in Bühler, *Grundriss der indo-arischen Philologie*, ii. 157.
[8] *Laws of Manu*, v. 54. See also *ibid.* v. 53, 56.
[9] *Ibid.* v. 52.

most low caste natives are only vegetarian when flesh food is not within their reach ;[1] and we are told that the views which many Hindus entertain of people who indulge in such food are not very unlike the opinions which Europeans have about cannibals.[2] The immediate origin of these restrictions seems obvious enough. They were not introduced—as has been supposed—either as mere sumptuary measures,[3] or because meat was found to be an aliment too rich and heavy in a warm climate,[4] but they were the natural outcome of a system which enjoins regard for life in general and kindness towards all living beings. In the ' Laws of Manu ' it is expressly said that the use of meat should be shunned for the reason that " meat can never be obtained without injury to living creatures, and injury to sentient beings is detrimental to the attainment of heavenly bliss." [5] That the prohibition of eating animals resulted from the prohibition of killing them is also suggested by other facts. If Hindu Pariahs eat the flesh of animals which have died naturally, it " is not visited upon them as a crime, but they are considered to be wretches as filthy and disgusting as their food is revolting." [6] Buddhism allows the eating of fish and meat if it is pure in three respects, to wit—if one has not seen, nor heard, nor suspected that it has been procured for the purpose ;[7] and among the Buddhists of Burma even the most strictly religious have no scruples in eating the flesh of an animal killed by another person, " as then, they consider, the sin of its destruction does not rest upon them, but on the person who actually caused it."[8]

Vegetarianism is, further, said to have been practised by the first and most learned class of the Persian Magi, who, according to Eubulus, neither slew nor ate anything

---

[1] Kipling, *Beast and Man in India*, p. 6. Crooke, *Things Indian*, p. 228.
[2] Percival, *Land of the Veda*, p. 272.
[3] Hopkins, *op. cit.* p. 200.
[4] Dubois, *Description of the Character, &c. of the People of India*, p. 120.

[5] *Laws of Manu*, v. 48. See also *ibid.* v. 45, 49.
[6] Dubois, *op. cit.* p. 121.
[7] Kern, *Manual of Indian Buddhism*, p. 71, n. 5.
[8] Fytche, *Burma Past and Present*, ii. 78.

animated ;[1] and many of the Egyptian priests are reported
to have abstained entirely from animal food.[2] In ancient
legends we are told that the earliest men, who were pure
and free from sin, killed no animal but lived exclusively
on the fruits of the earth.[3] In Greece the Pythagoreans
opposed the killing and eating of animals, " as having a
right to live in common with mankind," [4] or in consequence of their theory that the souls of men after death
transmigrate into animals.[5] According to Porphyry, a
fleshless diet not only contributes to the health of the
body and to the preservation of the power and purity of
the mind, but is required by justice. Animals, he said,
are allied to men, and he must be considered an impious
person who does not abstain from acting unjustly towards
his kindred.[6]

There still remains a group of restrictions in diet which
call for our consideration, namely, such as refer to the
use of intoxicating drinks, either only prohibiting im-
moderation or also demanding total abstinence.

Among a large number of peoples drunkenness is so
common that it can hardly be looked upon as a vice by
the community ; on the contrary, it is sometimes an
object of pride, or is regarded almost as a religious duty.
An old traveller on the West African Gold Coast says
that the natives teach their children drunkenness at the
age of three or four years, " as if it were a virtue." [7]
The Negroes of Accra, according to Monrad, take a
pride in getting drunk, and praise the happiness of a
person who is so intoxicated that he can hardly walk.[8]
In ancient Yucatan he who dropped down senseless from
drink in a banquet was allowed to remain where he fell,

---

[1] Porphyry, *op. cit.* iv. 16.
[2] *Ibid.* iv. 7.
[3] *Genesis*, i. 29. *Bundahis*, xv. 6
sqq. ; *cf.* Windischmann, *Zoroastrische Studien*, p. 212. Hesiod,
Opera et dies, 109 *sqq.* Plato,
Politicus, p. 272. Porphyry, *op. cit.*
iv. 2.
[4] Diogenes Laertius, *Vitæ philoso-*

phorum, viii. 1. 12 (13). Plutarch,
De carnium esu oratio I. 1.
[5] Seneca, *Epistulæ*, cviii. 19.
[6] Porphyry, *op. cit.* i. 2 ; iii. 26 *sq.*
[7] Bosman, *Description of the Coast
of Guinea*, p. 107.
[8] Monrad, *Skildring af Guinea-
Kysten*, p. 242.

and was regarded by his companions with feelings of
envy.[1] Among the Pueblo Indians in New Mexico, who
are otherwise a sober people, drunkenness forms a part of
their religious festivals.[2] So also in the hill tribes of the
Central Provinces of India a large quantity of liquor is an
essential element in their religious rites, and their acts of
worship invariably end in intoxication.[3] Of the Ainu in
Japan we are told that " to drink for the god " is their chief
act of worship ; the more *saké* they drink the more devout
they are, whereas the gods will be angry with a person
who abstains from the intoxicating drink.[4] The ancient
Scandinavians regularly concluded their religious ceremonies with filling and emptying stoops in honour of
their gods ; and even after their conversion to Christianity
they were allowed to continue this practice at the end of
their services, with the difference that they were now
required in their toast-drinking to substitute for the
names of their false deities those of the true God and his
saints.[5] Of the Germans Tacitus states that " to pass an
entire day and night in drinking disgraces no one " ;[6] and
this habit of intoxication the Anglo-Saxons brought with
them to England, where it was nourished by a damp
climate and a marshy soil. In the seventh and eighth
centuries some efforts were made to check drunkenness
on the initiative of Theodore, archbishop of Canterbury,
and Egbert, archbishop of York, and these exertions were
supported by the kings from a political desire to prevent
riots and bloodshed.[7] The Penitentials tell us the tale of
universal intemperance more effectively than any description of it could do. A bishop who was so drunk as to
vomit while administering the holy sacrament was condemned to eighty or ninety days' penance, a presbyter to

[1] Bancroft, *op. cit.* ii. 725.
[2] *Ibid.* i. 555.
[3] Hislop, *Aboriginal Tribes of the Central Provinces*, p. 1. Campbell, *Wild Tribes of Khondistan*, p. 164 *sq.* (Kandhs).
[4] Bird, *Unbeaten Tracks in Japan*, ii. 68, 96. *Cf.* Batchelor, *Ainu of Japan*, p. 31.

[5] Maurer, *op. cit.* ii. 200. Bartho-linus, *Antiquitates Danicæ*, i. 8, p. 128 *sqq.* Mallet, *Northern Anti-quities*, p. 196.
[6] Tacitus, *Germania*, 22.
[7] *Laws of Hlothhære and Eadric*, 12 *sq.* Thrupp, *The Anglo-Saxon Home*, p. 297.

seventy, a deacon or monk to sixty, a clerk to forty ;[1] and if a person was so intoxicated that, pending the rite, he dropped the sacred elements into the fire or into a river, he was required to chant a hundred psalms.[2] A bishop or priest who persevered in the habit of drunkenness was to be degraded from his office ;[3] whilst single cases of intoxication, if accompanied by vomiting, incurred penance for a certain number of days—forty for a presbyter or deacon,[4] thirty for a monk,[5] fifteen for a layman.[6] However, these rules admitted of exceptions : if anybody in joy and glory of our Saviour's natal day, or of Easter, or in honour of any saint, vomited through being drunk, and in so doing had taken no more than he was ordered by his elders, it mattered nothing ; and if a bishop had commanded him to be drunk he was likewise innocent, unless indeed the bishop was in the same state himself.[7] If these attempts to encourage soberness produced any change for the better, it could only have been temporary ; for some time afterwards intemperance was carried to its greatest excess through the practice and example of the Danes.[8] Under the influence of the Normans, who were a more temperate race, drunkenness for a time decreased in England ; but after a few reigns the Saxons seem rather to have corrupted their conquerors than to have been benefited by their example.[9] As late as the eighteenth century drunkenness was universal among all classes in England. It was then as uncommon for a party to separate while any member of it remained sober

---

[1] *Pœnitentiale Pseudo - Theodori,* xxvi. 4 (Wasserschleben, *Die Bussordnungen der abendländischen Kirche,* p. 594). *Pœnitentiale Egberti,* xi. 7 (Wasserschleben, p. 242).

[2] *Pœnitentiale Pseudo - Theodori,* xxvi. 5 (Wasserschleben, *op. cit.* p. 594). *Pœnitentiale Egberti,* xi. 9 (Wasserschleben, p. 242).

[3] *Pœnitentiale Theodori,* i. 1. 1 (Wasserschleben, *op. cit.* p. 184). *Pœnitentiale Egberti,* xi. 1 (Wasserschleben, p. 242).

[4] *Pœnitentiale Theodori,* i. 1. 3

(Wasserschleben, *op. cit.* p. 184). *Pœnitentiale Egberti,* xi. 3 (Wasserschleben, p. 242).

[5] *Pœnitentiale Theodori,* i. 1. 2 (Wasserschleben, *op. cit.* p. 184). *Pœnitentiale Egberti,* xi. 2 (Wasserschleben, p. 242).

[6] *Pœnitentiale Theodori,* i. 1. 5 (Wasserschleben, *op. cit.* p. 184).

[7] *Pœnitentiale Theodori,* i. 1. 4 (Wasserschleben, *op. cit.* p. 184).

[8] Thrupp, *op. cit.* p. 299 *sqq.*

[9] *Ibid.* p. 301 *sq.*

as it is now for any one in such a party to degrade himself through intoxication. No loss of character was incurred by habitual excess. Men in the position of gentlemen congratulated each other upon the number of bottles emptied ; and it would have been considered a very frivolous objection to a citizen who aspired to the dignity of Alderman or Mayor that he was an habitual drunkard.[1]

Though of late years drunkenness has been decreasing among those European nations who have been most addicted to it, and is nowadays generally recognised as a vice, our civilisation is still, as it has always been, the great source from which the poison of intoxication is pouring over the earth in all directions, infecting or killing races who previously knew nothing of alcohol or looked upon it with abhorrence. Eastern religions have emphatically insisted upon sobriety or even total abstinence from intoxicating liquors. In the sacred law-books of Brahmanism thirteen different kinds of alcoholic drinks are mentioned, all of which are forbidden to Brâhmanas and three to Kshatriyas and Vaisyas ;[2] yet, though there be no sin in drinking spirituous liquor, "abstention brings greater reward."[3] A twice-born man who drinks the liquor called Surâ commits a mortal sin, which will be punished both in this life and in the life to come ;[4] the most proper penalty for such a person is to drink that liquor boiling-hot, and only when his body has been completely scalded by it is he freed from his guilt.[5] Among the modern Hindus drunkenness is said to be detested by all but the very lowest castes in the agricultural districts and some high caste people residing in the great towns, who have learned it from Europeans ; it is supposed to be destructive of caste purity ; hence a notorious drunkard is, or at least

[1] Porter, *Progress of the Nation*, p. 239. Pike, *History of Crime in England*, ii. 587. Massey, *History of England during the Reign of George III*. ii.60.
[2] *Institutes of Vishnu*, xxii. 82, 84.
Gautama, ii. 20. *Laws of Manu*, xi. 94 *sq.*
[3] *Laws of Manu*, v. 56.
[4] *Ibid.* ix. 235, 237 ; xi. 49, 55 ; xii. 56.
[5] *Ibid.* xi. 91.

used to be, expelled from his caste.[1] Buddhism interdicts
altogether the use of alcohol ; [2] " of the five crimes, the
taking of life, theft, adultery, lying, and drinking, the last
is the worst." [3] Taouism condemns the love of wine.[4] In
Zoroastrianism the holy Sraosha is represented as fighting
against the demon of drunkenness,[5] and it is said that the
sacred beings are not pleased with him who drinks wine
more than moderately ;[6] but it seems that the ancient
Persians nevertheless were much addicted to intoxication. [7]
According to classical writers, some of the Egyptian
priests abstained entirely from wine, whilst others drank
very little of it ;[8] and before the reign of Psammetichus
the kings neither drank wine, nor made libation of it as a
thing acceptable to the gods.[9] The use of wine and
other inebriating drinks is forbidden by Islam,[10] and was
punished by Muhammed with flogging.[11] It may also be
said of his followers that they for the most part have
obeyed this command, at least in country districts,[12] and
that the exceptions to the rule are directly or indirectly
attributable to the influence of Christians.

The condemnation of drunkenness is, of course, in the
first place due to its injurious consequences. The Basutos
of South Africa say that " there is blood in the dregs "—
that is, intoxication ends in bloody quarrels.[13] The Omaha
Indians made drunkenness a crime punishable with flogging and loss of property, because it often led to murders.[14]
Sahagun tells us of a Mexican king who severely admonished his people to abstain from intoxication, as
being the cause of troubles and disorders in villages and

[1] Caldwell, Tinnevelly Shanars, p.
38. Dubois, op. cit. p. 116. Samuelson, History of Drink, p. 46.
[2] Oldenberg, Buddha, p. 290.
Monier-Williams, Buddhism, p. 126.
[3] Hardy, Manual of Budhism,
p. 491.
[4] Douglas, Confucianism and Taouism, p. 266.
[5] Vendîdâd, xix. 41.
[6] Dînâ-î Maînôg-î Khirad, xvi. 62.
[7] Herodotus, i. 133.
[8] Porphyry, op. cit. iv. 6. Plutarch,
De Iside et Osiride, 6.
[9] Plutarch, De Iside et Osiride, 6.
[10] Koran, ii. 216.
[11] Lane, Modern Egyptians, p. 122.
[12] Burton, Pilgrimage to Al-Madinah and Meccah, ii. 118. Blunt,
Bedouin Tribes of the Euphrates, ii.
213. Polak, Persien, ii. 268. Lane,
Modern Egyptians, p. 298 sq. Pool,
Studies in Mohammedanism, p. 283.
[13] Casalis, Basutos, p. 307.
[14] Dorsey, 'Omaha Sociology,' in
Ann. Rep. Bur. Ethn. iii. 370.

kingdoms, of misery, sorrow, and poverty.[1] Of him who
drinks immoderately it is said in one of the Pahlavi
texts that infamy comes to his body and wickedness to
his soul.[2]   According to Ecclesiasticus, " drunkenness
increaseth the rage of a fool till he offend : it diminisheth
strength and maketh wounds." [3] We read in the Talmud,
" Drink not, and you will not sin." [4]   Muhammed said
that in wine there is both sin and profit, but that the sin
is greater than the profit.[5] Buddhism stigmatises drinking
as the worst of crimes because it leads to all other sins ;
from the continued use of intoxicating drink six evil consequences are said to follow—namely, the loss of wealth ;
the arising of disputes that lead to blows and battles ;
the production of various diseases, as soreness of the eyes
and others ; the bringing of disgrace, from the rebuke of
parents and superiors ; the exposure to shame, from going
hither and thither unclothed ; the loss of the judgment
required for the carrying on of the affairs of the world.[6]
That drunkenness, in spite of the evils resulting from it,
nevertheless so frequently escapes censure, is due partly to
the pleasures connected with it, partly to lack of foresight,[7] and in a large measure to the influence of
intemperate habits. Why such habits should have grown
up in one country and not in another we are often unable
to tell.   The climate has no doubt something to do with
it, although it is impossible to agree with the statement
made by Montesquieu that the prevalence of intoxication
in different parts of the earth is proportionate to the coldness and humidity of the air.[8] A gloomy temperament
and a cheerless life are apt to induce people to resort to
the artificial pleasures produced by drink. The dreariness
of the Puritan Sunday has much to answer for ; the evidence given by a spirit merchant before the Commission
on the Forbes Mackenzie Act was " that there is a great

[1] Sahagun, *Historia general de las
cosas de Nueva España*, ii. 94 *sqq.*
[2] *Dînâ-î Maînôg-î Khirad*, xvi. 63.
[3] *Ecclesiasticus*, xxxi. 30.
[4] Deutsch, *Literary Remains*, p. 58.
[5] *Koran*, ii. 216.
[6] Hardy, *op. cit.* p. 491 *sq.*
[7] *Cf. supra*, i. 281, 309 *sq.*
[8] Montesquieu, *De l'esprit des lois*,
xiv. 10 (*Œuvres*, p. 303 *sq.*).

demand for drink on Sunday," and that " this demand *must* be supplied." [1] *Ennui* was probably a cause of the prevailing inebriety in Europe in former days, when there was difficulty in passing the time not occupied in fighting or hunting ; [2] and the monotony of life in the lower ranks of an industrial community still tends to produce a similar effect. Other causes of drunkenness are miserable homes and wretched cooking. Mr. Lecky is of opinion that if the wives of the poor in Great Britain and Ireland could cook as they can cook in France and in Holland, a much smaller proportion of the husbands would seek a refuge in the public-house. [3]

The evil consequences of intoxication have led not only to the condemnation of an immoderate use of alcoholic drink, but also to the demand for total abstinence, in consideration of the difficulty many people have in avoiding excess. But this hardly accounts in full for the religious prohibition of drink which we meet with in the East. Wine or spirituous liquor inspires mysterious fear. The abnormal mental state which it produces suggests the idea that there is something supernatural in it, that it contains a spirit, or is perhaps itself a spirit. [4] Moreover, the juice of the grape is conceived as the blood of the vine [5]—in Ecclesiasticus the wine which was poured out at the foot of the altar is even called " the blood of the grape " ; [6] and in the blood is the soul. The law of Brahmanism not only prohibits the drinking of wine, but also commands that " one should carefully avoid red exudations from trees and juices flowing from incisions." [7] That spirituous liquor is believed to contain baneful mysterious energy is obvious from the statement that if the Brahman (the Veda) which dwells in the body of a Brâhmana is even once deluged with it, his Brahmanhood forsakes him, and he becomes a Sûdra ; [8] holy persons are, of

---

[1] Hessey, *Sunday*, p. 378.
[2] *Cf.* Spencer, *Principles of Ethics*, i. 445.
[3] Lecky, *Democracy and Liberty*, ii. 138.
[4] See *supra*, i. 278, 281 ; *infra*, on the Belief in Supernatural Beings ; Frazer, *Golden Bough*, i. 359.
[5] Frazer, *op. cit.* i. 358 *sq.*
[6] *Ecclesiasticus*, l. 15.
[7] *Laws of Manu*, v. 6.
[8] *Ibid.* xi. 98.

course, most easily affected by the mysterious drink, owing
to the delicate nature of holiness. Muhammedans likewise
regard wine as " unclean " and polluting ;[1] some of them
dread it so much that if a single drop were to fall upon a
clean garment it would be rendered unfit to wear until
washed.[2] In Morocco it is said that by drinking alcohol
a Muhammedan loses the *baraka*, or holiness, of " the
faith " and a scribe the memory of the Koran, and that
if a person who drinks alcohol has a charm on him, its
baraka is spoiled. The fact that wine was forbidden by
the Prophet might perhaps by itself be a sufficient reason
for the notion that it is unclean. But already in pre-
Muhammedan times it seems to have been scrupulously
avoided by some of the Arabs,[3] though among others it
was much in use and was highly praised by their poets.[4]

As for the Muhammedan prohibition of wine, the suggestion has been made by Palgrave that it mainly arose
from the Prophet's antipathy to Christianity and his desire
to broaden the line of demarcation between his followers
and those of Christ. Wine was raised by the founder of
Christianity to a dignity of the highest religious import.
It became well-nigh typical of Christianity and in a
manner its badge. To declare it " unclean," an " abomination," and " the work of the devil," was to set up for
the Faithful a counter-badge.[5] This view derives much
probability from the fact that there are several unequivo-
cal indications of the same bent of policy in Muhammed's
system, showing a distinct tendency to oppose Islam to
other religions. But at the same time both a desire to
prevent intoxication and the notion that wine is polluting
may very well have been co-operating motives for the
prohibition.

[1] Lane, *Modern Egyptians*, p. 299.
[2] Winterbottom, *Native Africans in the Neighbourhood of Sierra Leone*, i. 72.
[3] Diodorus Siculus, *Bibliotheca historica*, xix. 94. 3. Zöckler, *Askese und Mönchtum*, i. 93.
[4] Goldziher, *Muhammedanische Studien*, i. 21 *sqq.*
[5] Palgrave, *Journey through Central and Eastern Arabia*, i. 428 *sqq.*

CHAPTER XXXIX

CLEANLINESS AND UNCLEANLINESS—ASCETICISM IN GENERAL

IT seems that man, like many other animals, is naturally endowed with a certain tendency to cleanliness or aversion to filth. Of Caspar Hauser—the boy who had been kept in a dungeon separated from all communication with the world from early childhood to about the age of seventeen —Feuerbach tells us that " uncleanliness, or whatever he considered as such, whether in his own person or in others, was an abomination to him." [1] And the savage boy of Aveyron, though filthy at first, soon became so scrupulously clean in his habits that " he constantly threw away, in a pet, the contents of his plate, if any particle of dirt or dust had fallen upon it ; and, after he had broken his walnuts under his feet, he took pains to clean them in the nicest and most delicate manner." [2]

Many savages are praised for their cleanliness.[3] The Veddahs of Ceylon wash their bodies every few days, as opportunity occurs.[4] Among the South Sea Islanders

[1] Feuerbach, *Caspar Hauser,* p. 62.
[2] Itard, *Account of the Discovery and Education of a Savage Man,* p. 58.
[3] Colquhoun, *Amongst the Shans,* p. 298 *sq.* Man, *Sonthalia and the Sonthals,* p. 84. Foreman, *Philippine Islands,* p. 189 (domesticated natives). Boyle, *Dyaks of Borneo,* p. 242.

Erskine, *Cruise among the Islands of the Western Pacific,* pp. 110 (Samoans ; cf. Turner, *Nineteen Years in Polynesia,* p. 205), 262, 264 (Fijians). Percy Smith, ' Futuna,' in *Jour. Polynesian Soc.* i. 35. Markham, *Cruise of the " Rosario,"* p. 136 (Polynesians).
[4] Nevill, ' Vaeddas of Ceylon,' in *Taprobanian,* i. 187.

bathing is a very common practice ; the Tahitians bathe in fresh water once or twice a day,[1] and the natives of Ni-afu, in the Tonga Islands, are said to spend half their life in the water.[2] So, also, many Indian tribes both in North, Central, and South America are very fond of bathing.[3] The Omahas generally bathe every day in warm weather, early in the morning and at night, and some of them also at noon.[4] Among the Guiana Indians it is a custom for men and women to troop down together to the nearest water early in the morning and many times during the day.[5] The Tehuelches of Patagonia not only make morning ablutions and, when encamped near a river, enjoy bathing for hours, but are also scrupulously careful as to the cleanliness of their houses and utensils, and will, if they can obtain soap, wash up everything they may be possessed of.[6] The Moquis and Pueblos of New Mexico are remarkable both for their personal cleanliness and the neatness of their dwellings.[7] Cleanliness is a common characteristic of many natives of Africa.[8] The Negroes of the Gold Coast wash their whole persons once, if not oftener, during the day.[9] The Megé, a people subject to the Monbuttu, wash two or three times a day, and when engaged in work constantly adjourn to a neighbouring stream to cleanse themselves.[10] The Marutse-Mabundas, rather than lose their bath, are always ready

[1] Ellis, *Polynesian Researches* (ed. 1829), ii. 113 *sq.*

[2] Romilly, *Western Pacific*, p. 145.

[3] Bancroft, *Native Races of the Pacific States*, i. 83, 696, 722, 760. Domenech, *Seven Years' Residence in the Great Deserts of North America*, ii. 337. von Humboldt, *Personal Narrative of Travels to the Equinoctial Regions of the New Continent*, iii. 237 (Chaymas). von Martius, *Beiträge zur Ethnographie Amerika's*, i. 600 (Uaupés), 643 (Macusís). Molina, *History of Chili*, ii. 118 ; Smith, *Araucanians*, p. 184. Dobrizhoffer, *Account of the Abipones*, ii. 53.

[4] Dorsey, ' Omaha Sociology,' in *Ann. Rep. Bur. Ethn.* iii. 269.

[5] Im Thurn, *Among the Indians of Guiana*, p. 191.

[6] Musters, *At Home with the Patagonians*, p. 173.

[7] Bancroft, *op. cit.* i. 540. See also *ibid.* i. 267 (some Inland Columbians).

[8] Waitz, *Anthropologie der Naturvölker*, ii. 86 (Negroes of Accra, Krus), 464 (Western Fulahs). Torday and Joyce, ' Ethnography of the Ba-Huana,' in *Jour. Anthr. Inst.* xxxvi. 292. Rowley, *Africa Unveiled*, p. 153. Ashe, *Two Kings of Uganda*, p. 305 ; Wilson and Felkin, *Uganda*, i. 184. Casati, *Ten Years in Equatoria*, i. 122 (Monbuttu). Holub, *Seven Years in South Africa*, ii. 208 (Manansas).

[9] Cruickshank, *Eighteen Years on the Gold Coast*, ii. 283 *sq.*

[10] Burrows, *Land of the Pigmies*, p. 119.

to run the risk of being snapped up by crocodiles, and they are in the habit of keeping their materials in well-washed wooden or earthenware bowls or in suitable baskets or calabashes.[1] The cleanliness of the Dinka in everything that concerns the preparation of food is said to be absolutely exemplary.[2] Among the Bari tribes the dwellings " are the perfection of cleanliness." [3] So also the Bachapins, a Bechuana tribe, are remarkable for the cleanliness of their dwellings, showing the greatest carefulness to remove all rubbish and everything unsightly ; but at the same time they are lacking in personal cleanliness.[4]

We commonly find that savages who are clean in certain respects are dirty in others. The Wanyoro bathe frequently and always wash their hands before and after eating, but their dwellings are very filthy and swarm with vermin.[5] The Nagas of India [6] and the natives of the interior of Sumatra,[7] though cleanly in their persons, are very dirty in their apparel. The Mayas of Central America make frequent use of cold water, but neither in their persons nor in their dwellings do they present an appearance of cleanliness.[8] So also the Californian Indians, whilst exceedingly fond of bathing, are unclean about their lodges and clothing.[9] The Aleuts, though they wash daily, allow dirt to be piled up close to their dwellings, prepare their food very carelessly, and never wash their household utensils.[10] The New Zealander, again, whilst not over-clean in his person, is very particular respecting his food and also keeps his dwelling in as much order as possible.[11] On the other hand there are very many uncivilised peoples who are described as generally filthy in their habits—for instance, the Fuegians,[12] many

[1] Holub, op. cit. ii. 309.
[2] Casati, op. cit. i. 44.
[3] Baker, Albert N'yanza, i. 89.
[4] Burchell, Travels in the Interior of Southern Africa, ii. 521, 553.
[5] Wilson and Felkin, op. cit. ii. 46. Baker, Albert N'yanza, ii. 58.
[6] Stewart, ' Northern Cachar,' in Jour. Asiatic Soc. Bengal, xxiv. 616.
[7] Marsden, History of Sumatra, p. 209.

[8] Bancroft, op. cit. i. 654.
[9] Powers, Tribes of California, p. 403. Bancroft, op. cit. i. 377, 407.
[10] Veniaminof, quoted by Dall, Alaska, p. 398. See also Bancroft, op. cit. i. 267 (Flatheads).
[11] Dieffenbach, Travels in New Zealand, ii. 58.
[12] Snow, Two Years' Cruise off Tierra del Fuego, i. 345.

Indian tribes in the Pacific States,[1] several Eskimo tribes,[2] various Siberian peoples,[3] the Ainu of Japan,[4] most hill tribes in India,[5] many Australian tribes,[6] the Bushmans,[7] and, generally, the dwarf races of Africa.[8] But although these peoples never or hardly ever wash their bodies, or do not change their dress until it is worn to pieces, or eat out of the same vessels as their dogs without cleaning them, or feed on disgusting substances, or regard vermin as a delicacy—we may assume that their toleration of filth is not absolutely boundless.

The prevalence of cleanly or dirty habits among a certain people may depend on a variety of circumstances : the occupations of life, sufficiency or want of water, climatic conditions, industry or laziness, wealth or poverty, religious or superstitious beliefs. Castrén observes that filthiness is a characteristic of fishing peoples ; among the Ostyaks only those who live by fishing are conspicuous for their uncleanliness, whereas the nomads and owners of

[1] Bancroft, op. cit. i. 83, 102, 184, 231, 492, 626.

[2] Ibid. i. 51. Seemann, Voyage of "Herald," ii. 61 sq. (Western Eskimo). Kane, Arctic Explorations, ii. 116 (Eskimo of Etah). Cranz, History of Greenland, i. 155.

[3] Sarytschew, 'Voyage of Discovery to the North-East of Siberia,' in Collection of Modern and Contemporary Voyages, v. 67 (Kamchadales). Krasheninnikoff, History of Kamschatka, pp. 176 (Kamchadales), 226 (Koriaks). Sauer, Expedition to the Northern Parts of Russia performed by Billings, p. 125 (Jakuts). Georgi, Russia, ii. 398 (Jakuts) ; iii. 59 (Kotoftzes), 112 (Tunguses) ; iv. 37 (Kalmucks), 134 (Burats). Liadov, in Jour. Anthr. Inst. i. 401 ; Bergmann, Nomadische Streifereien unter den Kalmüken, ii. 102, 123 sq. ; Pallas, quoted in Spencer's Descriptive Sociology, ' Asiatic Races,' p. 29 (Kalmucks).

[4] Batchelor, Ainu of Japan, p. 24 sqq. Mac Ritchie, Ainos, p. 12 sq.

[5] Spencer, Descriptive Sociology, ' Asiatic Races,' p. 29. Grange, ' Expedition into the Naga Hills,' in

Jour. Asiatic Soc. Bengal, ix. 962. Stewart, ibid. xxiv. 637 (Kukis). Mason, ' Physical Character of the Karens,' ibid. xxxv. pt. ii. 25. Butler, Travels in Assam, p. 98. Anderson, Mandalay to Momien, p. 131 (Kakhyens). Moorcroft and Trebeck, Travels in the Himalayan Provinces, i. 321 (Ladakhis).

[6] Breton, Excursions in New South Wales, p. 197. Barrington, History of New South Wales, p. 19 (natives of Botany Bay). Angas, Savage Life in Australia, i. 80 (South Australian aborigines). Chauncy, in Brough Smyth, Aborigines of Victoria, ii. 284 (West Australian aborigines).

[7] Moffat, Missionary Labours in Southern Africa, p. 15. Barrow, Travels into the Interior of Southern Africa, i. 288.

[8] Stuhlmann, Mit Emin Pascha ins Herz von Afrika, p. 451. For other instances of uncleanliness in savages see Crawfurd, History of the Indian Archipelago, i. 39 ; St. John, Life in the Forests of the Far East, i. 147 (some of the Land Dyaks) ; Andersson, Lake Ngami, pp. 50 (Herero), 470 (Bechuanas).

reindeer are not.[1] It has been observed that the inland
negro is clean when he dwells in the neighbourhood of
rivers.[2] In West Australia those tribes only which live
by large rivers or near the sea are said to have an idea of
cleanliness.[3] Concerning the filthy habits of the Kukis
and other hill peoples in India, Major Butler remarks that
they may probably be accounted for by the scarcity
of water in the neighbourhood of the villages, as also by
the coldness of the climate.[4] Dr. Kane believes that
the indifference of many Eskimo to dirt or filth is largely
due to the extreme cold, which by rapid freezing resists
putrefaction and thus prevents the household, with its
numerous dogs, from being intolerable.[5] Their well-known
habit of washing themselves with freshly passed urine
arises partly from scarcity of water and the difficulty of
heating it, but partly also from the fact that the ammonia
of the urine is an excellent substitute for soap in
removing the grease with which the skin necessarily
becomes soiled.[6] A cold climate, moreover, leads to
uncleanliness because it makes garments necessary ;[7] and
among some savages the practice of greasing their bodies
to protect the skin from the effects of a parching air
produces a similar result.[8] Lord Kames maintains that
the greatest promoter of cleanliness is industry, whereas
its greatest antagonist is indolence. In Holland, he
observes, the people were cleaner than all their neighbours
because they were more industrious, at a time when in
England industry was as great a stranger as cleanliness.[9]
Kolben says that the general laziness of the Hottentots
accounts for the fact that " they are in the matter of diet

[1] Castrén, *Nordiska resor och forskningar*, i. 319 *sq.*

[2] Bastian, *Der Mensch in der Geschichte*, iii. 75. Mr. Torday, who speaks from extensive experience, tells me the same.

[3] Chauncy, quoted by Brough Smyth, *op. cit.* ii. 284.

[4] Butler, *Travels in Assam*, p. 98 *sq.* Cf. Stewart, in *Jour. Asiatic Soc. Bengal*, xxiv. 616.

[5] Kane, *Arctic Explorations*, ii. 116.

[6] Murdoch, ' Ethnol. Results of the Point Barrow Expedition,' in *Ann. Rep. Bur. Ethn.* ix. 421. Dall, *op. cit.* p. 20.

[7] *Cf.* von Humboldt, *op. cit.* iii. 237.

[8] Burchell, *op. cit.* ii. 553 (Bachapins of Litakun).

[9] Kames, *Sketches of the History of Man*, i. 323, 327 *sqq.*

the filthiest people in the world."[1] Of the Siberian
Burats Georgi writes that " from their laziness they are
as dirty as swine " ;[2] and the Kamchadales are described
as a " dirty, lazy race."[3] Poverty, also, is for obvious
reasons a cause of uncleanliness;[4] " a starving vulture
neglects to polish his feathers, and a famished dog has a
ragged coat."[5] Very commonly cleanliness is a class
distinction.[6] Thus among the Point Barrow Eskimo the
poorer people are often careless about their clothes and
persons, whereas most of the wealthier individuals appear
to take pride in being well clad, and, except when actually
engaged in some dirty work, always have their faces and
hands scrupulously clean and their hair neatly combed.[7]
Dr. Schweinfurth maintains that domestic cleanliness and
care in the preparation of food are everywhere signs of a
higher grade of external culture and answer to a certain
degree of intellectual superiority.[8] But already Lord
Kames pointed out the fact indicated above, that
" cleanness is remarkable in several nations which have
made little progress in the arts of life."[9]

The factors which determine the cleanliness of a people
also naturally influence the moral valuation of it.
Aversion to dirt not only leads to cleanly habits, but
makes a filthy person an object of disgust and disapprobation ; indeed, this aversion is generally stronger with
reference to other individuals than with reference to one's
own person. But where for some reason or other
dirtiness becomes habitual, it at the same time ceases to
be disgusting ; and it is often astonishing how soon

[1] Kolben, *Present State of the Cape
of Good Hope*, i. 47.
[2] Georgi, *op. cit.* iv. 134.
[3] *Ibid.* iii. 152. See also Sarytschew, in *Collection of Modern and
Contemporary Voyages*, v. 67.
[4] See Marshall, *A Phrenologist
amongst the Todas*, p. 50 ; Veniaminof, quoted by Dall, *op. cit.* p.
398 (Aleuts).
[5] St. John, *Village Life in Egypt*,
i. 187.
[6] Tickell, ' Memoir on the Hodé-

sum,' in *Jour. Asiatic Soc. Bengal*,
ix. 808 (Hos). Rowlatt, ' Expedition
into the Mishmee Hills,' *ibid.* xiv.
489. Williams and Calvert, *Fiji*, p.
117. Waitz, *op. cit.* ii. 86 (Ashantees). Arnot, *Garenganze*, p. 76 (Barotse). Lane, *Modern Egyptians*,
p. 299.
[7] Murdoch, in *Ann. Rep. Bur.
Ethn.* ix. 421.
[8] Schweinfurth, *Heart of Africa*,
i. 156.
[9] Kames, *op. cit.* i. 321.

people get used to filthy surroundings. Thus, when
cleanliness is insisted upon it is so in the first instance
because dirt is directly disagreeable to other persons, and
when uncleanness is tolerated it is so because it gives
no offence to the senses of the public. But at the higher
stages of civilisation, at least, cleanliness is besides inculcated on hygienic grounds.

In many cases cleanliness, either temporary or
habitual, is also practised and enjoined from religious or
superstitious motives. A Lappish *noaide*, or wizard, had
to wash all his body before he offered a sacrifice.[1] The
Siberian shamans have compulsory water purifications
once a year, sometimes every month, as also on special
occasions when they feel themselves defiled by contact
with unclean things.[2] The Shinto priests in Japan bathed
and put on clean garments before making the sacred
offerings or chanting the liturgies.[3] Herodotus speaks of
the cleanliness observed by the Egyptian priests when
engaged in the service of the gods.[4] As a preliminary
to an act of worship the ancient Greeks washed their
hands or bathed and put on clean clothes.[5] One of the
legal maxims of the Romans required that men should
approach the deity in a state of purity.[6] According to
Zoroastrianism it is the great business of life to avoid
impurity, and, when it is involuntarily contracted, to
remove it in the correct manner as quickly as possible ;
and by impurity is then understood not an inward state
of the soul, but mainly a physical state of the body,
everything going out of the human body being considered
polluting.[7] For a Brahmin bathing is the chief part of
the minute ceremonial of daily worship, whilst further
washings and aspersions enter into more solemn religious
acts ;[8] and not only Brahmins but most Hindus regard

[1] Friis, *Lappisk Mythologie*, p. 145
sq. von Düben, *Lappland*, p. 256.
[2] *Jour. Anthr. Inst.* xxiv. 88.
[3] Griffis, *Religions of Japan*, p. 85.
[4] Herodotus, ii. 37. *Cf.* Wiedemann, *Herodots zweites Buch*, p. 154.
[5] *Iliad*, i. 449 ; iii. 270 ; vi. 266 ;
ix. 171, 174 ; xvi. 229 *sq.* ; xxiii. 41;
xxiv. 302 *sqq. Odyssey*, ii. 261 ; iv.
750 ; xvii. 58. Keller, *Homeric
Society*, p. 141. Stengel, *Die griechischen Kultusaltertümer*, p. 106.
[6] Cicero, *De legibus*, ii. 10.
[7] Darmesteter, in *Sacred Books of
the East*, iv. p. lxxii. *sqq.*
[8] Ward, *View of the History, &c. of*

it as a religious duty to bathe daily if this is at all convenient.[1] Lamaism enjoins personal ablution as a sacerdotal rite preparatory to worship, though the ceremony seldom extends to more than dipping the tips of the fingers in water.[2] Jewish Rabbis are compelled to wash their hands before they begin to pray.[3] Tertullian mentions that a similar ablution was practised by the Christians before prayer.[4] According to Islam, the clothes and person of the worshipper should be clean, and so also the ground, mat, carpet, or whatever else it be, upon which he prays ; and every act of worship must be preceded by an ablution, though, where water cannot be got, sand may be used as a substitute.[5] But a polluting influence is not ascribed to everything which we regard as dirt. For instance, Muhammedans consider the excrements of men and dogs defiling, but not the dung of cows and sheep ; cow-dung is even used as a means of purification.

These practices and rules spring from the idea that the contact of a polluting substance with anything holy is followed by injurious consequences—an idea which will be more fully discussed in connection with sexual abstinences. Such contact is supposed to deprive a deity or holy being of its holiness, or otherwise be detrimental to it, and therefore to excite its anger against him who causes the defilement. So also a sacred act is believed to lose its sacredness by being performed by an unclean individual. Moreover, as a polluting substance is itself held to contain mysterious energy of a baneful kind, it is looked upon as a direct danger even to persons who are not engaged in religious worship. We have previously noticed the rites of purification which a manslayer has to undergo in order to get rid of the blood-pollution.[6] We have also seen that ablutions and other purificatory cere-

the Hindoos, ii. 61 sq. Colebrooke, Miscellaneous Essays, ii. 142 sqq. Dubois, People of India, p. 113 sq.
[1] Wilkins, Modern Hinduism, p. 201.
[2] Waddell, Buddhism of Tibet, p. 423.
[3] Chwolsohn, Die Ssabier, ii. 71.
[4] Tertullian, De Oratione, 13 (Migne, Patrologiæ cursus, ii. 1167 sq.).
[5] Sell, Faith of Islám, p. 252 sqq. Lane, Modern Egyptians, i. 84 sqq.
[6] Supra, i. 375 sqq.

monies are performed for the purpose of removing sins and misfortunes.[1] And bathing or sprinkling with water is a common method of clearing mourners or persons who have come in contact with a corpse from the contagion of death.[2]

But whilst religious or superstitious beliefs have thus led to ablutions and cleanliness, they have in other instances had the very opposite effect. Among Arabs young children are often left dirty and ill-dressed purposely, to preserve them from the evil eye.[3] The Obbo natives in Central Africa declare that if they do not wash their hands with cow's urine before milking, the cow will lose her milk; and with the same fluid they wash the milk-bowl, and even mix some of it with the milk.[4] The Jakuts " never wash any of their eating or drinking utensils; but, as soon as a dish is emptied, they clean it with the fore and middle finger; for they think it a great sin to wash away any part of their food, and apprehend that the consequence will be a scarcity." [5] A similar custom prevails among the Kirghiz [6] and Kalmucks. The latter " are forbidden by the laws of their faith " to wash their vessels in river-water, and therefore " do no more than wipe them with a piece of an old sheep-skin shube, which they use also for cleaning their hands upon when dirty." [7] They, moreover, abstain from washing their

[1] *Supra*, i. 54 *sqq.*
[2] Teit, ' Thompson Indians of British Columbia,' in *Memoirs of the American Museum of Natural History*, ' Anthropology,' i. 331. Cruickshank, *op. cit.* ii. 218 (Negroes of the Gold Coast). Ellis, *Ewe-speaking Peoples of the Slave Coast*, p. 160. Turner, *Samoa*, p. 145; *Idem, Nineteen Years in Polynesia*, p. 228 (Samoans). Ellis, *Polynesian Researches*, i. 403 (Society Islanders). Kloss, *In the Andamans and Nicobars*, p. 305 (Kar Nicobarese). Joinville, ' Religion and Manners of the People of Ceylon,' in *Asiatick Researches*, vii. 437 (Sinhalese). Iyer, ' Nayādis of Malabar,' in the Madras Government Museum's *Bulletin*, iv. 71; Thurston, *ibid.* iv. 76 *sq.* (Na-

yādis). Crooke, *Tribes and Castes of the North-Western Provinces and Oudh*, i. 83 (Arakh, a tribe in Oudh). Ward, *View of the History, &c. of the Hindoos*, ii. 147, iii. 275; Dubois, *Manners and Customs of the People of India*, p. 108 *sq.*; Bose, *Hindoos as they are*, p. 257. Caland, *Die Altindischen Todten- und Bestattungsgebräuche*, p. 79 *sq.*
[3] Blunt, *Bedouin Tribes of the Euphrates*, ii. 214. Klunzinger, *Upper Egypt*, p. 391.
[4] Baker, *Albert N'yanza*, i. 381.
[5] Sauer, *op. cit.* p. 125.
[6] Valikhanof, &c., *Russians in Central Asia*, p. 80.
[7] Georgi, *op. cit.* iv. 37. Bergmann, *op. cit.* ii. 123.

clothes; and so did the Huns and Mongols.[1] The
ancient Turks never washed themselves, because they
believed that their gods punished ablutions with thunder
and lightning; and the same belief still prevails among
kindred peoples in Central Asia.[2] Among the Bahima of
Enkole, in the Uganda Protectorate, a man may smear
his body with butter or clay as often as he wishes, but
" to wash with water is bad for him, and is a sure way of
bringing sickness into his family and amongst his cattle." [3]
The dread of water may be due partly to ill effects
experienced after using it, partly to superstition. The
Moors dare not wash their bodies with cold water in the
afternoon and evening after the *'âṣar*, because all such
water is then supposed to be haunted by *jnûn*, or evil
spirits. In various religions the odour of sanctity is associated with filth. Muhammedan dervishes are recognised by
their appearance of untidiness and uncleanness. Among
the rules laid down for Buddhist monks there is one
which prescribes that their dress shall be made of
rags taken from a dust or refuse heap.[4] In the early
days of Christian monasticism " the cleanliness of the
body was regarded as a pollution of the soul." The
saints who were most admired were those who had
become one hideous mass of clotted filth. St. Atha-
nasius relates with enthusiasm how St. Antony, the
patriarch of monachism, had never, to extreme old age,
been guilty of washing his feet. A famous virgin,
though bodily sickness was a consequence of her habits,
resolutely refused, on religious principles, to wash any
part of her body except her fingers. And St. Simeon
Stylites, who was generally pronounced to be the highest
model of a Christian saint, bound a rope round himself
so that it became imbedded in his flesh and caused putrefaction; and it is said that " a horrible stench, intolerable

---

[1] Neumann, *Die Völker des süd-*
lichen Russlands, p. 27. For the excessive dirtiness of the present
Mongols, see Prejevalsky, *Mongolia*,
i. 51 *sq.*

[2] Castrén, *op. cit.* iv. 61.
[3] Roscoe, ' Bahima,' in *Jour.*
Anthr. Inst. xxxvii. 111.
[4] Kern, *Manual of Indian Bud-*
dhism, p. 75.

to the bystanders, exhaled from his body, and worms dropped from him whenever he moved, and they filled his bed." [1] In mediæval Christianity abstinence from every species of cleanliness was also enjoined as a penance, the penitent being required to go with foul mouth, filthy hands and neck, undressed hair and beard, unpared nails, and clothes as dirty as his person. In these cases uncleanliness is a form of asceticism, a subject which we have already touched upon in dealing with industry and fasting, but the principles of which still call for our consideration.

In various religions we meet with the idea that a person appeases or gives pleasure to the deity by subjecting himself to suffering or deprivation. This belief finds expression in all sorts of ascetic practices. We read of Christian ascetics who lived in deserted dens of wild beasts, or in dried-up wells, or in tombs ; who disdained all clothes, and crawled abroad like animals covered only by their matted hair ; who ate nothing but corn which had become rotten by remaining for a month in water ; who spent forty days and nights in the middle of thornbushes, and for forty years never lay down.[2] Hindu ascetics remain in immovable attitudes with their faces or their arms raised to heaven, until the sinews shrink and the posture assumed stiffens into rigidity ; or they expose themselves to the inclemency of the weather in a state of absolute nudity, or tear their bodies with knives, or feed on carrion and excrement.[3] Among the Muhammedans of India there are fakirs who have been seen dragging heavy chains or cannon balls, or crawling upon their hands and knees for years ; others have been found lying upon iron spikes for a bed ; and others, again, have been swinging for months before a slow fire with a

[1] Lecky, History of European Morals, ii. 109 sqq.
[2] Ibid. ii. 108 sq.
[3] Barth, Religions of India, p. 214 sq. Hopkins, Religions of India, p. 352. Monier-Williams, Brahmanism and Hinduism, p. 395.

tropical sun blazing overhead.[1] Among modern Jews
some of the more sanctimonious members of the
synagogue have been known to undergo the penance of
voluntary flagellation before the commencement of the
fast of atonement, two persons successively inflicting
upon each other thirty-nine stripes or thirteen lashes with
a triple scourge.[2] According to the Zoroastrian Yasts,
thirty strokes with the Sraoshô-karana is an expiation
which purges people from their sins, and makes them fit
for offering a sacrifice.[3] Herodotus tells us that the
ancient Egyptians beat themselves while the things offered
by them as sacrifices were being burned, and that the
Carian dwellers in Egypt on such occasions cut their
faces with knives.[4] Among the ancient Mexicans blood-
drawing was a favourite and most common mode of
expiating sin and showing devotion. " It makes one
shudder," says Clavigero, " to read the austerities which
they exercised upon themselves, either in atonement of
their transgressions or in preparation for their festivals.
They mangled their flesh as if it had been insensible, and
let their blood run in such profusion, that it appeared to
be a superfluous fluid of the body." [5] Self-mortification
also formed part of the religious cult in many uncivilised
tribes in North America.[6] " The Indian," Colonel Dodge
observes, " believes, with many Christians, that self-
torture is an act most acceptable to God, and the extent
of pleasure that he can give his god is exactly measured
by the amount of suffering that he can bear without
flinching." [7]

The idea underlying religious asceticism has no doubt

[1] Pool, *Studies in Mohammedanism*, p. 305. For similar practices
among the modern Egyptians, see
Lane, *Modern Egyptians*, p. 244.
[2] Allen, *Modern Judaism*, p. 407.
[3] *Yasts*, x. 122. Darmesteter, in
Sacred Books of the East, xxiii. 151,
n. 3.
[4] Herodotus, ii. 40, 61.
[5] Clavigero, *History of Mexico*, i.
284. See also Bancroft, *op. cit.* iii.
441 *sq.* ; Réville, *Hibbert Lectures on*

the Native Religions of Mexico and
Peru*, p. 100.
[6] Domenech, *Seven Years' Resi-
dence in the Great Deserts of North
America*, ii. 380. Catlin, *North
American Indians*, ii. 243. James,
Expedition to the Rocky Mountains,
i. 276 *sqq.* (Omahas). McGee,
' Siouan Indians,' in *Ann. Rep. Bur.
Ethn.* xv. 184.
[7] Dodge, *Our Wild Indians*, p. 149.

been derived from several different sources. It should first be noticed that certain ascetic practices have originally been performed for another purpose, and only afterwards come to be regarded as means of propitiating or pleasing the deity through the suffering involved in them. This, as we have seen, is the case with certain fasts, and also with sexual asceticism.[1] When an act is supposed to be connected with supernatural danger, the evil (real or imaginary) resulting from it is readily interpreted as a sign of divine anger and the act itself is regarded as being forbidden by a god. If then the abstinence from it implies suffering, as is in some degree the case with fasting and sexual continence, the conclusion is drawn that the god delights in such suffering. The same inference is, moreover, made from the fact that such abstinences are enjoined in connection with religious worship, though the primary motive for this injunction was fear of pollution. Beating or scourging, again, was in certain cases originally a mode of purification, intended to wipe off and drive away a dangerous contagion either personified as demoniacal or otherwise of a magical character. And although the pain inflicted on the person beaten was at first not the object of the act but only incidental to it, it became subsequently the chief purpose of the ceremony, which was now regarded as a mortification well pleasing to the god.[2] This change of ideas seems likewise to be due both to the tendency of the supernatural contagion to develop into a divine punishment in case it is not removed by the painful rite, and also to the circumstance that purification is held to be a necessary accompaniment of acts of religious worship. The Egyptian sacrifice described by Herodotus was combined with purificatory fasting as well as beating.[3] Among the Jews, before the commencement of the fast of atonement, whilst a few very religious persons undergo the penance of flagellation, " some purify themselves by

---

[1] See *infra*, p. 420 *sq.*   [3] Herodotus, ii. 40.
[2] Frazer, *Golden Bough*, iii. 217 *sq.*

ablutions." [1] And that the original object of the scourging mentioned in the Yasts was to purify the worshipper
is suggested by the fact that he on the same occasion had
to wash his body three days and three nights.[2] But it
should also be remembered that religious exaltation,
when it has reached its highest stage, may express itself
in self-laceration ; [3] and the deity is naturally supposed to
be pleased with the outward expression of such an emotion
in his devotees.

An ascetic practice may also be the survival of an
earlier sacrifice. We have seen that this is frequently
the case with fasting and almsgiving, and the same may
hold true of other forms of asceticism.[4] The essence of
the act then no longer lies in the benefit which the god
derives from it, but in the self-denial or self-mortification
which it costs the worshipper. In the sacred books of
India "austerity" is mentioned as a means of expiation
side by side with sacrifice, fasting, and giving gifts.[5]

When an ascetic practice develops out of a previous
custom of a different origin, it may be combined with an
idea which by itself has been a frequent source of self-
inflicted pain, to wit, the belief that such pain is an expiation for sin, that it may serve as a substitute for a punishment which would otherwise be inflicted by the offended
god ; and almost inseparably connected with this belief
there may be that desire to suffer which is so often,
vaguely or distinctly, involved in genuine repentance.[6]
The idea of expiation very largely underlies the penitential discipline of the Christian Church and the
asceticism of its saints. From the days of Tertullian
and Cyprian the Latins were familiar with the notion that
the Christian has to propitiate God, that cries of pain,
sufferings, and deprivations are means of appeasing his
anger, that God takes strict account of the quantity of

[1] Allen, *op. cit.* p. 407.
[2] *Yasts*, x. 122.
[3] See Hirn, *Origins of Art*, p. 64.
[4] *Cf.* Tertullian, *De resurrectione carnis*, 8 (Migne, *op. cit.* ii. 806).
[5] *Gautama*, xix. 11.   *Vasishtha*, xx. 47 ; xxii. 8.   *Baudhâyana*, iii. 10. 9.
[6] See *supra*, i. 105 *sq.*

the atonement, and that, where there is no guilt to have blotted out, those very means are regarded as merits.[1] According to the doctrine of the Church, penance should in all grave cases be preceded by sorrow for the sin and also by confession, either public or private ; repentance, as we have noticed above, is the only ground on which pardon can be given by a scrupulous judge.[2] But the notion was only too often adopted that the penitential practice itself was a compensation for sin, that a man was at liberty to do whatever he pleased provided he was prepared to do penance afterwards, and that a person who, conscious of his frailty, had laid in a large stock of vicarious penance in anticipation of future necessity, had a right "to work it out," and spend it in sins.[3] The idea that sins may be expiated by certain acts of self-mortification is familiar both to Muhammedans[4] and Jews.[5] According to Zoroastrian beliefs, it is possible to wipe out by peculiarly severe atonements not only the special sin on account of which the atonement is performed, but also other offences committed in former times or unconsciously.[6] In the sacred books of the Hindus we meet with a strong conviction that pain suffered in this life will redeem the sufferer from punishment in a future existence. It is said that "men who have committed crimes and have been punished by the king go to heaven, being pure like those who performed meritorious deeds " ;[7] and the same idea is at the bottom of their penitential system.[8] But in Brahmanism, as in Catholicism, the effect of ascetic practices is supposed to go beyond mere expiation. They are regarded as means of accumulating religious merit or attaining superhuman powers. Brahmanical poems tell of marvellous self-

[1] Tertullian, De jejuniis, 7 (Migne, op. cit. ii. 962). Idem, De resurrectione carnis, 8 (Migne, ii. 806 sq.). Harnack, History of Dogma, ii. 110, 132 ; iii. 311.
[2] Supra, i. 85.
[3] See Thrupp, The Anglo-Saxon Home, p. 259.

[4] Supra, ii. 315, 317. Pool, op. cit. p. 264.
[5] Supra, ii. 315 sqq. Allen, op. cit. p. 130.
[6] Geiger, Civilization of the Eastern Irānians, i. 163.
[7] Laws of Manu, viii. 318.
[8] Ibid. xi. 228.

mortifications by which sages of the past obtained influence over the gods themselves ; nay, even the power wielded by certain archdemons over men and gods is supposed to have been acquired by the practice of religious austerities.[1] How largely ascetic practices are due to the idea of expiation is indicated by the fact that they hardly occur among nations who have no vivid sense of sin, like the Chinese before the introduction of Taouism and Buddhism,[2] and the ancient Greeks, Romans, and Scandinavians. In Greece, however, people sometimes voluntarily sacrificed a part of their happiness in order to avoid the envy of the gods, who would not allow to man more than a moderate share of good fortune.[3]

Self-mortification is also sometimes resorted to not so much to appease the anger of a god as rather to excite his compassion. In some of the Jewish fasts, as we have seen before, these two objects are closely interwoven.[4] The Jewish custom of fasting in the case of a drought is in a way parallel to the Moorish practice of tying holy men and throwing them into a pond in order that their pitiful condition may induce God to send rain. Mr. Williams tells us of a Fijian priest who, " after supplicating his god for rain in the usual way without success, slept for several successive nights exposed on the top of a rock, without mat or pillow, hoping thus to move the obdurate deity to send a shower." [5]

Not only is suffering voluntarily sought as a means of wiping off sins committed, but it is also endured with a view to preventing the commission of sin. This is the second or, in importance, the first great idea upon which Christian asceticism rests. The gratification of every worldly desire is sinful, the flesh should be the abject slave of the spirit intent upon unearthly things. Man was created for a life in spiritual communion with God,

---

[1] Monier-Williams, *Brāhmanism and Hindūism*, pp. 231, 427. Oldenberg, *Buddha*, p. 302.

[2] Réville, *La religion Chinoise*, p. 221.

[3] Aeschylus, *Agamemnon*, 1008 sqq. Schmidt, *Die Ethik der alten Griechen*, i. 82.

[4] *Supra*, ii. 315.

[5] Williams and Calvert, *Fiji*, p. 196.

but he yielded to the seduction of evil demons, who availed themselves of the sensuous side of his nature to draw him away from the contemplation of the divine and lead him to the earthly. Moral goodness, therefore, consists in renouncing all sensuous pleasures, in separating from the world, in living solely after the spirit, in imitating the perfection and purity of God. The contrast between good and evil is the contrast between God and the world, and the conception of the world includes not only the objects of bodily appetites but all human institutions, as well as science and art.[1] And still more than any theoretical doctrine, the personal example of Christ led to the glorification of spiritual joy and bodily suffering.

The antithesis of spirit and body was not peculiar to Christianity. It was an old Platonic conception, which was regarded by the Fathers of the Church as the contrast between that which was precious and that which was to be mortified. The doctrine that bodily enjoyments are low and degrading was taught by many pagan philosophers ; even a man like Cicero says that all corporeal pleasure is opposed to virtue and ought to be rejected.[2] And in the Neo-Platonic and Neo-Pythagorean schools of Alexandria an ascetic ideal of life was the natural outcome of their theory that God alone is pure and good, and matter impure and evil. Renunciation of the world was taught and practised by the Jewish sects of the Essenes and Therapeutæ. In India, Professor Kern observes, " climate, institutions, the contemplative bent of the native mind, all tended to facilitate the growth of a persuasion that the highest aims of human life and real felicity cannot be obtained but by the seclusion from the busy world, by undisturbed pious exercises, and by a certain amount of mortification." [3] We read in the Hitopadesa, " Subjection to the senses has been called the road to ruin, and

---

[1] Harnack, *op. cit.* ii. 214 *sqq.* ; iii. 258 *sqq.* von Eicken, *Geschichte der mittelalterlichen Weltanschauung,* p. 313 *sqq.*

[2] Cicero, *De officiis,* i. 30 ; iii. 33.
[3] Kern, *Manual of Indian Buddhism,* p. 73.

their subjugation the path to fortune." [1] The Jain regards
pleasure in itself as sinful :—" What is discontent, and
what is pleasure ? One should live subject to neither.
Giving up all gaiety, circumspect, restrained, one should
lead a religious life." [2] According to Buddhism, there
are two causes of the misery with which life is inseparably
bound up—lust and ignorance ; and so there are two
cures—the suppression of lust and desire and the removal
of ignorance.[3] It is said in the Dhammapada, " There is
no satisfying lusts, even by a shower of gold pieces ; he
who knows that lusts have a short taste and cause pain, he
is wise." [4] Penances, as they were practised among the
ascetics of India, were discarded by Buddha as vexatious,
unworthy, unprofitable. " Not nakedness, not platted
hair, not dirt, not fasting, or lying on the earth, not
rubbing with dust, not sitting motionless, can purify a
mortal who has not overcome desires."[5] Where all contact with the earthly ceases, there, and there only, are
deliverance and freedom.

The idea that man ·ought to liberate himself from the
bondage of earthly desires is the conclusion of a contemplative mind reflecting upon the short duration and
emptiness of all bodily pleasures and the allurements by
which they lead men into misery and sin. And separation from the material world is the ideal of the religious
enthusiast whose highest aspiration is union with God
conceived as an immaterial being, as pure spirit.

[1] Hitopadesa, quoted by Monier-
Williams, *Indian Wisdom*, p. 538.
[2] Hopkins, *op. cit.* p. 291.
[3] Oldenberg, *op. cit.* p. 212 *sq.*

Monier-Williams, *Buddhism*, p. 99.
[4] *Dhammapada*, 186 *sq.*
[5] *Ibid.* 141. See also Oldenberg,
op. cit. p. 301 *sq.*

CHAPTER XL

MARRIAGE

MAN's sexual nature gives rise to various modes of conduct on which moral judgments are passed. We shall first consider such relations between the sexes as are comprised under the heading Marriage.

In a previous work I have endeavoured to show that in all probability there has been no stage in the social history of mankind where marriage has not existed, human marriage apparently being an inheritance from some ape-like progenitor.[1] I then defined marriage as a more or less durable connection between male and female, lasting beyond the mere act of propagation till after the birth of the offspring. This is marriage in the natural history sense of the term. As a social institution, on the other hand, it has a somewhat different meaning : it is a union regulated by custom or law.[2] Society lays down rules relating to the selection of partners, to the mode of contracting marriage, to its form, and to its duration. These rules are essentially expressions of moral feelings.

There is, first, a circle of persons within which marriage is prohibited. It seems that the horror of incest is well-nigh universal in the human race, and that the few cases in which this feeling is said to be absent can only be regarded

---

[1] Westermarck, *History of Human Marriage*, ch. iii. *sqq.*

[2] The best definition of marriage as a social institution which I have met with is the following one given by Dr. Friedrichs (' Einzeluntersuch-ungen zur vergleichenden Rechts-wissenschaft,' in *Zeitschr. f. vergl. Rechtswiss.* x. 255) :—" Eine von der Rechtsordnung anerkannte und privilegirte Vereinigung geschlechts-differenter Personen, entweder zur Führung eines gemeinsamen Haus-standes und zum Geschlechtsver-kehr, oder zum ausschliesslichen Ge-schlechtsverkehr."

as abnormalities. But the degrees of kinship within which marriage is forbidden are by no means the same everywhere. It is most, and almost universally, abominated between parents and children. It is also held in general abhorrence between brothers and sisters who are children of the same mother as well as of the same father. Most of the exceptions to this rule refer to royal persons, for whom it is considered improper to contract marriage with individuals of less exalted birth ; but among a few peoples incestuous unions are practised on a larger scale on account of extreme isolation or as a result of vitiated instincts.[1] It seems, however, that habitual marriages between brothers and sisters have been imputed to certain peoples without sufficient reason.[2] This is obviously true of the Veddahs of Ceylon, who have long been supposed to regard the marriage of a man with his younger sister as *the* proper marriage.[3] " Such incest," says Mr. Nevill, " never was allowed, and never could be, while the Vaedda

[1] Westermarck, *op. cit.* ch. xiv. *sq.*

[2] This is apparently the case with various peoples mentioned by Sir J. G. Frazer (*Pausanias's Description of Greece*, ii. 84 *sq.*) as being addicted to incestuous unions. Mr. Turner's short statement (*Samoa*, p. 341) that among the New Caledonians no laws of consanguinity were observed in their marriages, and that even the nearest relatives united, radically differs from M. de Rochas' description of the same people. " Les Néo-Calédoniens," he says (*Nouvelle Calédonie*, p. 232), " ne se marient pas entre proches parents du côté paternel ; mais du côté maternel, ils se marient à tous les degrés de cousinage." Brothers and sisters, after they have reached years of maturity, are no longer permitted to entertain any social intercourse with each other ; they are prohibited from keeping each other company even in the presence of a third person ; and if they casually meet they must instantly go out of the way or, if that is impossible, the sister must throw herself on the ground with her face downwards. " Cet éloignement," M. de Rochas adds (*ibid.* p. 239), " qui n'est certes l'effet ni du mépris ni de l'inimitié, me paraît né d'une exagération déraisonnable d'un sentiment naturel, l'horreur de l'inceste." Sir J. G. Frazer says that, according to Mr. Thomson, the marriage of brothers with sisters has been practised among the Masai ; but a later and, as it seems, better informed authority tells us that " the Masai do not marry their near relations " and that " incest is unknown among them" (Hinde, *The Last of the Masai*, p. 76). Again, the statement that among the Obongos, a dwarf race in West Africa, sisters marry with brothers, is only based on information derived from another people, the Ashangos, who have a strong antipathy to them (Du Chaillu, *Journey to Ashango-Land*, p. 320). Liebich's assertion (*Die Zigeuner*, p. 49) that the Gypsies allow a brother to marry his sister is certainly not true of the Gypsies of Finland, who greatly abhor incest (Thesleff, 'Zigenarlif i Finland,' in *Nya Pressen*, 1897, no. 331 B).

[3] Bailey, ' Wild Tribes of the Veddahs of Ceylon,' in *Trans. Ethn. Soc.* N.S. ii. 294 *sq.*

customs lingered. Incest is regarded as worse than murder.
So positive is this feeling, that the Tamils have based a
legend upon the instant murder of his sister by a Vaedda to
whom she had made undue advances. The mistake arose
from gross ignorance of Vaedda usages. The title of a
cousin with whom marriage ought to be contracted, that is,
mother's brother's daughter, or father's sister's daughter,
is *nagâ* or *nangî*. This, in Sinhalese, is applied to a younger
sister. Hence if you ask a Vaedda, ' Do you marry
your sisters ? ' the Sinhalese interpreter is apt to say, ' Do
you marry your nagâ ? ' The reply is (I have often tested
it), ' Yes—we always did formerly, but now it is not always
observed.' You say then, ' What ? marry your own-sister-
nagâ ? ' and the reply is an angry and insulted denial, the
very question appearing a gross insult." The same writer
adds :—" In no case did a person marry one of the same
family, even though the relationship was lost in remote
antiquity. Such a marriage is incest. The penalty for
incest was death." [1]

As a rule, the prohibited degrees are more numerous
among peoples unaffected by modern civilisation than they
are in more advanced communities, the prohibitions in a
great many cases referring even to all the members of the
tribe or clan ; and the violation of these rules is regarded
as a most heinous crime.[2]

The Algonquins speak of cases where men have been put to
death by their nearest kinsfolk for marrying women of their own
clan.[3] Among the Asiniboin, a Siouan tribe, a chief can commit
murder with impunity if the murdered person be without
friends, but if he married within his *gens* he would be dismissed,
on account of the general disgust which such a union would
arouse.[4] The Hottentots used to punish alliances between first
or second cousins with death.[5] A Bantu of the coast region
considers similar unions to be "something horrible, something
unutterably disgraceful."[6] The Busoga of the Uganda

[1] Nevill, ' Vaeddas of Ceylon,' in *Taprobanian*, i. 178.
[2] Westermarck, *op. cit.* p. 297 *sqq.*
[3] Frazer, *Totemism*, p. 59.
[4] Dorsey, ' Siouan Sociology,' in *Ann. Rep. Bur. Ethn.* xv. 224.
[5] Kolben, *Present State of the Cape of Good Hope*, i. 155 *sq.*
[6] Theal, *History of the Boers in South Africa*, p. 16.

Protectorate held in great abhorrence anything like incest even amongst domestic animals.[1] Among the Kandhs of India "inter-marriage between persons of the same tribe, however large or scattered, is considered incestuous and punishable with death." [2] In the Malay Archipelago submersion is a common punishment for incest,[3] but among certain tribes the guilty parties are killed and eaten [4] or buried alive.[5] · In Efate, of the New Hebrides, it would be a crime punishable with death for a man or woman to marry a person belonging to his or her mother's clan ; [6] and the Mortlock Islanders are said to inflict the same punishment upon anybody who has sexual intercourse with a relative belonging to his own "tribe." [7] Nowhere has marriage been bound by more severe laws than among the Australian aborigines. Their tribes are grouped in exogamous subdivisions, the number of which varies ; and at least before the occupation of the country by the whites the regular punishment for marriage or sexual inter-course with a person belonging to a forbidden division was death.[8]

Not less intense is the horror of incest among nations that have passed beyond savagery and barbarism. Among the Chinese incest with a grand-uncle, a father's first cousin, a brother, or a nephew, is punishable by death, and a man who marries his mother's sister is strangled ; nay, punishment is inflicted even on him who marries a person with the same surname as his own, sixty blows being the penalty.[9] So also incest was held in the utmost horror by the so-called Aryan peoples in ancient times.[10] In the ' Institutes of Vishnu ' it is said that sexual intercourse

[1] Johnston, *Uganda Protectorate*, ii. 719.

[2] Macpherson, quoted by Percival, *Land of the Veda*, p. 345. *Cf.* Hunter, *Annals of Rural Bengal*, iii. 81.

[3] Wilken, *Huwelijken tusschen bloedverwanten*, p. 26 *sq.* Riedel, *De sluik- en kroesharige rassen tusschen Selebes en Papua*, p. 460.

[4] Wilken, *Over de verwantschap en het huwelijks- en erfrecht bij de volken van het maleische ras*, p. 18.

[5] *Glimpses of the Eastern Archipelago*, p. 105.

[6] Macdonald, *Oceania*, p. 181 *sq.*

[7] Kubary, ' Die Bewohner der Mortlock Inseln,' in *Mittheil. d. Geogr. Gesellsch. in Hamburg*, 1878–9, p. 251.

[8] Westermarck, *op. cit.* p. 299 *sq.* See, besides the authorities quoted there, Roth, *Ethnol. Studies among the North-West-Central Queensland Aborigines*, p. 182 ; Spencer and Gillen, *Native Tribes of Central Australia*, p. 15.

[9] Medhurst, ' Marriage, Affinity, and Inheritance in China,' in *Trans. Roy. Asiatic Soc. China Branch*, iv. 21 *sqq.*

[10] Leist, *Alt-arisches Jus Gentium*, p. 394 *sq.*

with one's mother or daughter or daughter-in-law is a crime of the highest degree, for which there is no other atonement than to proceed into the flames.[1]

Various theories have been set forth to account for the prohibition of marriage between near kin. I criticised some of them in my book on the ' History of Human Marriage,' and ventured at the same time on an explanation of my own.[2] I pointed out that there is an innate aversion to sexual intercourse between persons living very closely together from early youth, and that, as such persons are in most cases related by blood, this feeling would naturally display itself in custom and law as a horror of intercourse between near kin. Indeed, an abundance of ethnographical facts seem to indicate that it is not in the first place by the degree of consanguinity, but by the close living together, that prohibitory laws against inter-marriage are determined. Thus many peoples have a rule of " exogamy " which does not depend on kinship at all, but on purely local considerations, all the members of a horde or village, though not related by blood, being forbidden to intermarry.[3] The prohibited degrees are very differently defined in the customs or laws of different nations, and it appears that the extent to which relatives are prohibited from intermarrying is nearly connected with their close living together. Very often the prohibitions against incest are more or less one-sided, applying more extensively either to the relatives on the father's side or to those on the mother's, according as descent is reckoned through men or women. Now, since

[1] *Institutes of Vishnu*, xxxiv. 1 *sq.*
[2] Westermarck, *op. cit.* p. 310 *sqq.*
[3] Herr Cunow (*Die Verwandtschafts-Organisationen der Australneger*, p. 187) finds this argument " rather peculiar," and offers himself a different explanation of the rule in question. He writes :—" In der Wirklichkeit erklärt sich das Verbot einfach daraus, dass sehr oft die Lokalgruppe mit dem Geschlechts-verband beziehungsweise dem To-temverband kongruirt, und dem-nach das was für die Gens gilt, zug-leich auch für die Lokalgruppe Gel-tung hat." This, however, is only Herr Cunow's own inference. And it may be asked why it is more " pecu-liar " to suppose that the prohibition of marriage between near kin has sprung from aversion to sexual in-tercourse between persons living closely together, than to assume that the rule which forbids marriage between unrelated persons living in the same community has sprung from the prohibition of marriage between kindred.

the line of descent is largely connected with local relationships, we may reasonably infer that the same local relationships exercise a considerable influence on the table of prohibited degrees. However, in a large number of cases prohibitions of intermarriage are only indirectly influenced by the close living together.[1] Aversion to the intermarriage of persons who live in intimate connection with one another has called forth prohibitions of the intermarriage of relations ; and, as kinship is traced by means of a system of names, the name comes to be considered identical with relationship. This system is necessarily one-sided. Though it will keep up the record of descent either on the male or female side, it cannot do both at once ;[2] and the line which has not been kept up by such means of record, even where it is recognised as a line of relationship, is naturally more or less neglected and soon forgotten. Hence the prohibited degrees frequently extend very far on the one side—to the whole clan—but not on the other. It should also be remembered that, according to primitive ideas, the name itself constitutes a mystic link between those who have it in common. " In Greenland, as everywhere else," says Dr. Nansen, " the name is of great importance ; it is believed that there is a spiritual affinity between two people of the same name."[3] Generally speaking, the feeling that two persons are intimately connected in some way or other may, through an association of ideas, give rise to the notion that marriage or sexual intercourse between them is incestuous. Hence the prohibitions of marriage between relations by alliance and by adoption. Hence, too, the prohibitions of the Roman and Greek Churches on the ground of what is called " spiritual relationship."

---

[1] I do not understand how any reader of my book can, like Herr Cunow (*op. cit.* p. 186 *sqq.*), attribute to me the statement that the group within which intermarriage is prohibited is identical with the group of people who live closely together. If he had read a little more carefully what I have said, he might have saved himself the trouble he has taken to prove my great ignorance of early social organisations.

[2] *Cf.* Tylor, *Early History of Mankind*, p. 285 *sq.*

[3] Nansen, *Eskimo Life*, p. 230.

The question arises :—How has this instinctive aversion to marriage and sexual intercourse in general between persons living closely together from early youth originated ? I have suggested that it may be the result of natural selection. Darwin's careful studies of the effects of cross- and self-fertilisation in the vegetable kingdom, the consensus of opinion among eminent breeders, and experiments made with rats, rabbits, and other animals, seem to have proved that self-fertilisation of plants and close inter-breeding of animals are more or less injurious to the species ; and it is probable that the evil chiefly results from the fact that the uniting sexual elements were not sufficiently differentiated. Now it is impossible to believe that a physiological law which holds good of the rest of the animal kingdom, as also of plants, would not apply to man as well. But it is difficult to adduce direct evidence for the evil effects of consanguineous marriages. We cannot expect very conspicuous results from other alliances than those between the nearest relatives—between brothers and sisters, parents and children,—and the injurious results even of such unions would not necessarily appear at once. The closest kind of intermarriage which we have opportunities of studying is that between first cousins. Unfortunately, the observations hitherto made on the subject are far from decisive. Yet it is noteworthy that of all the writers who have discussed it the majority, and certainly not the least able of them, have expressed their belief in marriages between first cousins being more or less unfavourable to the offspring ; and no evidence which can stand the test of scientific investigation has hitherto been adduced against this view. Moreover, we have reason to believe that consanguineous marriages are much more injurious in savage regions, where the struggle for existence is often very severe, than they have proved to be in civilised societies, especially as it is among the well-to-do classes that such marriages occur most frequently.

Taking all these facts into consideration, I am inclined to think that consanguineous marriages are in some way or

other detrimental to the species. And here I find a quite
sufficient explanation of the horror of incest ; not because
man at an early stage recognised the injurious influence of
close intermarriage, but because the law of natural selection must inevitably have operated. Among the ancestors
of man, as among other animals, there was no doubt a time
when blood-relationship was no bar to sexual intercourse.
But variations, here as elsewhere, would naturally present
themselves—we know how extremely liable to variations
the sexual instinct is ; and those of our ancestors who
avoided in-and-in breeding would survive, while the others
would gradually decay and ultimately perish. Thus a
sentiment would be developed which would be powerful
enough, as a rule, to prevent injurious unions. Of course
it would display itself, not as an innate aversion to sexual
connections with near relatives as such, but as an aversion
on the part of individuals to union with others with whom
they lived ; but these, as a matter of fact, would be blood-
relations, so that the result would be the survival of
the fittest. Whether man inherited this sentiment from
the predecessors from whom he sprang, or whether it was
developed after the evolution of distinctly human qualities,
we cannot know. It must have arisen at a stage when
family ties became comparatively strong, and children
remained with their parents until the age of puberty or
even longer. And exogamy, resulting from a natural
extension of this sentiment to a larger group, would arise
when single families united into hordes.

This attempt to explain the prohibition of marriage
between kindred and exogamy has not lacked sympathetic
support,[1] but more commonly, I think, it has been rejected.
Yet after a careful consideration of the various objections
raised against it I find no reason to alter my opinion.
Some of my opponents have evidently failed to grasp the

[1] A. R. Wallace, in his ' Introductory Note ' to my *History of Human
Marriage*, p. vi.   Giddings, *Principles of Sociology*, p. 267. Howard,
History of Matrimonial Institutions, i.
125 *sqq*. Sir E. B. Tylor (in *Academy*,
xl. 289) says with regard to my
theory that, at any rate, I am " well
on the track."   See also Crooke,
*Tribes and Castes of the North-
Western Provinces and Oudh*, i. pp.
clxxix, clxxx, ccii.

argument on which the theory is based. Thus Professor Robertson Smith argued that it begins by presupposing the very custom which it professes to explain, the custom of exogamy ; that " it postulates the existence of groups which through many generations (for the survival of the fittest implies this) avoided wiving within the group." [1] But what my theory postulates is not the existence of exogamous groups, but the spontaneous appearance of individual sentiments of aversion. And if, as Mr. Andrew Lang maintains, my whole argument is a "vicious circle," [2] then the theory of natural selection itself is a vicious circle, since there never could be a selection of qualities that did not exist before.

It has been argued that if close living together calls forth aversion to sexual intercourse, such aversion ought to display itself between husband and wife as well as between near relatives.[3] But these cases are certainly not identical. The feeling of which I have spoken is aversion associated with the idea of sexual intercourse between persons who have lived in a long-continued intimate relationship from a period of life when the action of sexual desire is naturally out of the question.[4] On the other hand, when a man marries a woman his feeling towards her is of a very different kind, and his love impulse may remain, nay increase, during the conjugal union ; though even in this case long living together has undoubtedly a tendency to lead to sexual indifference and sometimes to positive aversion. The opinion that the home is kept free from incestuous intercourse only by law, custom, and educa-

[1] Robertson Smith. in *Nature*, xliv. 271.

[2] Lang, *Social Origins*, p. 33.

[3] Durkheim, ' La prohibition de l'inceste et ses origines,' in *L'année sociologique*, i. 64. Professor Durkheim refers in this connection to an article by Dr. Simmel, ' Die Verwandtenehe,' in *Vossische Zeitung*, June 3rd and 10th, 1894. But I cannot find that Dr. Simmel is really opposed to my view. He only says, " Das intime Beisammenleben wirkt keineswegs nur abstumpfend, son-

dern in vie'en Fällen gerade anreizend, sonst würde die alte Erfahrung nicht gelten, dass die Liebe, wo sie beim Eingehen der Ehe fehlte, oft im Laufe derselben entsteht."

[4] *Cf.* Bentham, *Theory of Legislation*, p. 220 :—" Individuals accustomed to see each other and to know each other, from an age which is neither capable of conceiving the desire nor of inspiring it, will see each other with the same eyes to the end of life."

tion,[1] shows lack of discrimination. Law may forbid a son
to marry his mother, a brother to marry his sister, but it
could not prevent him from *desiring* such a union. Have
the most draconic codes ever been able to suppress, say,
homosexual love ? As Plato observed, an unwritten law
defends as sufficiently as possible parents from incestuous
intercourse with their children, brothers from intercourse
with their sisters ; " nor does the thought of such a thing
ever enter at all into the minds of most of them." [2]
Considering the extreme variability to which the sexual
impulse is subject, it is not astonishing that cases of what
we consider incestuous intercourse sometimes do occur. It
seems to me more remarkable that the abhorrence of incest
should be so general, and the exceptions to the rule so few.

Dr. Havelock Ellis, again, objects that my theory
assumes the existence of a kind of instinct which can with
difficulty be accepted. " An innate tendency," he says,
" at once so specific and so merely negative, involving at
the same time deliberate intellectual processes, can only
with a certain force be introduced into the accepted class of
instincts. It is as awkward and artificial an instinct as
would be, let us say, an instinct to avoid eating the apples
that grew in one's own orchard. The explanation of the
abhorrence of incest is really, however, exceedingly simple.
. . . The normal failure of the pairing instinct to manifest
itself in the case of brothers and sisters, or of boys and
girls brought up together from infancy, is a merely negative phenomenon due to the inevitable absence under those
circumstances of the conditions which evoke the pairing
impulse. . . . Between those who have been brought up
together from childhood all the sensory stimuli of vision,
hearing, and touch have been dulled by use, trained to the
calm level of affection, and deprived of their potency to

---

[1] For advocates of such a view see
Westermarck, *op. cit.* p. 310 *sqq.*
More recently it has been expressed
by Krauss, in *Am Ur-Quell*, iv. 151,
and Finck, *Primitive Love*, p. 49.
[2] Plato, *Leges*, viii. 838. Among
the Maoris of New Zealand, according to Mr. Colenso (*Maori Races*, p.
47 *sq.*), adult brothers and sisters
slept together, as they had always
done from their birth, " not only
without sin, but without thought of
it."

arouse the erethistic excitement which produces sexual tumescence."[1]   I think that Dr. Ellis has considerably exaggerated the difference between my theory and his own. The " instinct " of which I have spoken is simply aversion to sexual intercourse with certain persons, and this is a no more complicated mental phenomenon than, for instance, an animal's aversion to eating certain kinds of substances. Indeed, Dr. Ellis himself, in his excellent ' Studies in the Psychology of Sex,' gives us many instances not only of sexual indifference, but of sexual aversion, quite instinctive in character.[2] Thus the largest proportion of male inverts described by him experience what is called *horror feminæ*, that is to say, " woman as an object of sexual desire is disgusting " (not merely indifferent) to them.[3]   And Dr. Ellis also repeatedly speaks of the " abhorrence " of incest.

The objection has been raised that, if my explanation of the prohibition of incest were correct, connections between unrelated persons who have been brought up together should be as repulsive as connections between near kin ; whereas, as a matter of fact, the two cases are regarded in a very different light, the latter, only, being held incestuous.[4] Much, of course, depends on the closeness of the union, and Dr. Steinmetz's argument that " the very sensual Frenchmen often seem to marry the lady friends of their earliest youth,"[5] is certainly not to the point.   I believe that sexual love between a man and his foster-daughter is almost as great an abnormality as sexual love between a father and his daughter ; and among some peoples marriages between persons who have been brought up together in the same family or who

---

[1] Havelock Ellis, *Studies in the Psychology of Sex,* ' Sexual Selection in Man,' p. 205 *sq.*

[2] I have been blamed for making an illegitimate use of the word " instinct " (Crawley, *The Mystic Rose* p. 446). But if, as Dr. Ellis says, " an instinct is fundamentally a more or less complicated series of reflexes set in action by a definite stimulus," or as Mr. Crawley puts it (*op. cit.* p.

446), instinct " has nothing in its content except response of function to environment," then the aversion I speak of may certainly be called an instinct.

[3] Havelock Ellis, *op. cit.* p. 164.

[4] Steinmetz, ' Die neueren Forschungen zur Geschichte der menschlichen Familie,' in *Zeitschr. f. Socialwiss.* ii. 818 *sq.*

[5] *Ibid.* ii. 818.

belong to the same local group, without being related to each other by blood, are held blamable or are actually prohibited.[1] Even between lads and girls who have been educated in the same school there is a remarkable absence of erotic feelings, as appears from an interesting communication by a person who has for many years been the head-mistress of such a school in Finland. One youth assured her that neither he nor any of his friends would ever think of marrying a girl who had been their schoolfellow ;[2] and I heard of a lad who made a great distinction between girls of his own school and other, " real," girls, as he called them. Yet however objectionable and unnatural unions between foster-parents and foster-children or between foster-brothers and foster-sisters may appear to us, I do not deny that unions between the nearest blood-relatives inspire a horror of their own ; and it seems natural that they should do so considering that from earliest times the aversion to sexual intercourse between persons living closely together has been expressed in prohibitions against unions between kindred. Such unions have been stigmatised by custom, law, and religion, whilst much less notice has been taken of intercourse between unrelated persons who may occasionally have grown up in the same household. The belief in the supernatural, especially, has played a very important part in the ideas referring to incest, as in other points of sexual morality, owing to the mystery which surrounds everything connected with the function of reproduction.[3] The Aleuts in early times believed that incest, which they considered the gravest crime, was always followed by the birth of monsters with walrus tusks, beards, and other disfigurations.[4] The Kafirs

[1] Westermarck, op. cit. p. 321 sqq. Among the Western Islanders of Torres Straits marriage was forbidden, " with a remarkable delicacy of feeling, to the sister of a man's particular friend " (Haddon, 'Ethnology of the Western Tribe of Torres Straits,' in Jour. Anthr. Inst. xix. 315).
[2] Lucina Hagman, ' Från samskolan,' in Humanitas, ii. 188 sq.

[3] For the connection between religious feelings and the sexual impulse, see Vallon and Marie, ' Des psychoses religieuses,' in Archives de Neurologie, ser. ii. vol. iii. 184 sq.; Gadelius, Om tvångstankar, p. 120 sq. ; Starbuck, Psychology of Religion, p. 401 sqq.
[4] Veniaminof, quoted by Petroff, Report on Alaska, p. 155.

likewise maintain that the offspring of an incestuous union will be a monster, as "a punishment inflicted by the ancestral spirit."[1] The Bataks of Sumatra regard a long drought as a decisive proof that two cousins have had criminal intercourse with each other.[2] The Galelarese think that incest calls forth alarming natural phenomena, such as earthquakes, the eruption of a volcano, or torrents of rain.[3] So also the higher religions have branded incest as a heinous sin. As for Christianity's views on the subject, it is sufficient to notice that the prohibited degrees were extended by the Church,[4] and that the jurisdiction over incest, as over all sexual offences, was exercised by the ecclesiastical courts.[5]

It has, finally, been argued that my theory utterly fails to explain the fact that prohibitions of inter-marriage frequently refer to all the members of a clan, even those who live in different localities.[6] In addition to what I have previously observed on this point, I desire to emphasise that every hypothesis pretending to give a full explanation of prohibitions of incest must assume the operation of the very same mental law—that of association—which in my opinion accounts for clan-exogamy. Thus Professor Durkheim, while maintaining that my theory as regards the horror of incest could not apply to exogamy because the members of the same totem do not live together, is himself quite ready to resort to analogy to explain prohibitions extending outside the totem clan. He tries to show that clan-exogamy is the source of all other prohibitions against incest, and that clan-exogamy itself springs from totemism.[7] According

[1] Shooter, *Kafirs of Natal*, p. 45.

[2] von Brenner, *Besuch bei den Kannibalen Sumatras*, p. 212.

[3] van Baarda, ' Fabelen, verhalen en overleveringen der Galelareezen,' in *Bijdragen tot de taal-, land- en volkenkunde van Nederlandsch-Indië*, xlv. (ser. vi. vol. i.) p. 514. See also Frazer, *Golden Bough*, ii. 212 *sq.*

[4] Westermarck, *op. cit.* p. 308. Katz, *Grundriss des kanonischen Strafrechts*, p. 116 *sq.*

[5] Stephen, *History of the Criminal Law of England*, ii. 411.

[6] Cunow, *op. cit.* p. 185. Durkheim, in *L'année sociologique*, i. 39, n. 2. Steinmetz, in *Zeitschr. f. Socialwiss.* ii. 819.

[7] Prof. Durkheim says (*L'année sociologique*, i. 50) :—" Le sang est tabou d'une manière générale et il taboue tout ce qui entre en rapports avec lui. . . . La femme est, d'une manière chronique, le théâtre de

to him the rule of clan-exogamy has been extended to near relatives belonging to different clans, because they are in no less intimate contact with each other than are the members of the same clan. According to my own theory, again, the prohibition of marriage between near relatives living closely together has been extended to all the members of the clan on account of the notion of intimacy connected with the idea of a common descent and with a common name. If I consider Professor Durkheim's hypothesis extremely unsatisfactory,[1] it is certainly not because he has called in the law of association to explain the rules against incest. How could anybody deny the operation of this law for instance in the Roman Catholic prohibition of marriage between co-sponsors, or in the rule prevalent in Eastern Europe according to which the groomsman at the wedding is forbidden to intermarry with the family of the bride,[2] or in laws prohibiting marriage between relatives by alliance ? And why might not the

manifestations sanglantes. . . . La femme est donc, elle aussi, et d'une manière également chronique, tabou pour les autres membres du clan." However, the taboo is not restricted to the members of the clan, but refers also to near relatives belonging to different clans, and this has to be explained. M. Durkheim writes (*ibid.* p. 19):—"Quand on a pris l'habitude de regarder comme incestueux et abominables les rapports conjugaux de sujets qui sont nominalement du même clan, les rapports similaires d'individus qui, tout en ressortissant verbalement à des clans différents, sont pourtant en contact aussi ou plus intime que les précédents, ne peuvent manquer de prendre le même caractère." And further (*ibid.* p. 58) :—" Quand le totémisme disparaît, et avec lui la parenté spéciale au clan, l'exogamie devient solidaire des nouveaux types de famille qui se constituent et qui reposent sur d'autres bases, et comme ces familles sont plus restreintes que n'était le clan, elle se circonscrit, elle aussi, dans un cercle moins étendu ; le nombre des individus entre lesquels le mariage est prohibé diminue.

C'est ainsi que, par une évolution graduelle, elle en est arrivée à l'état actuel où les mariages entre ascendants et descendants, entre frères et sœurs, sont à peu près les seuls qui soient radicalement interdits."

[1] Professor Durkheim tries to explain a phenomenon of universal prevalence through an institution which has been proved to exist among certain peoples only. How does Professor Durkheim know that totem clans once prevailed among all peoples who now prohibit the intermarriage of near relatives ? If the rules which prevent parents from marrying their children and brothers from marrying their sisters are survivals of ancient totemism, how shall we explain the normal aversion to such unions ? Ancient totemism can certainly not account for this. But then the coincidence between these two facts—the legal prohibition of incest and the psychical aversion to it—is merely accidental ; and this seems to me a preposterous supposition. See *infra*, Additional Notes.

[2] Maine, *Dissertations*, p. 257 *sq.*

same law be applied to other relationships also, such as those constituted by a common descent or a common name ?

There is not only an inner circle within which no marriage is allowed, but also an outer circle outside of which marriage is either prohibited or at least disapproved of. Like the inner circle, the outer one varies greatly in extent.[1] Probably every people considers it a disgrace, if not a crime, for its men, and even more so for its women, to marry within a race very different from its own, especially if it be an inferior race. The Romans were prohibited from marrying barbarians—the emperor Valentinian inflicted the penalty of death for such unions ;[2] and a modern European girl who married an Australian native would no doubt be regarded as an outcast by her own society. Among many peoples marriage very seldom or never takes place outside the limits of the tribe or community. In India there are several instances of this. The Tipperahs and Abors view with abhorrence the idea of their girls marrying out of their clan ;[3] and Colonel Dalton was gravely assured that, " when one of the daughters of Pádam so demeans herself, the sun and moon refuse to shine, and there is such a strife in the elements that all labour is necessarily suspended, till by sacrifice and oblation the stain is washed away." [4] In ancient Peru it was not lawful for the natives of one province or village to intermarry with those of another.[5] Marriage with foreign women was unlawful at Sparta and Athens.[6] At Rome any marriage of a citizen with a woman who was not herself a Roman citizen, or did not belong to a community possessing the privilege of *connubium* with Rome, was invalid, and no legitimate children could be born of such a union. [7]

---

[1] Westermarck, *op. cit.* p. 363 *sqq.*
[2] Rossbach, *Römische Ehe*, p. 465.
[3] Lewin, *Wild Races of South-Eastern India*, p. 201.
[4] Dalton, *Ethnology of Bengal*, p.28.
[5] Garcilasso de la Vega, *First Part of the Royal Commentaries of the Yncas*, i. 308.
[6] Müller, *History of the Doric Race*, ii. 302. Hearn, *The Aryan Household*, p. 156 *sq.*
[7] Gaius, *Institutiones*, i. 56.

Prohibitions of intermarriage also very often relate to persons belonging to different classes or castes of the same community.[1] To mention a few instances. The wild tribes of Brazil consider alliances between slaves and freemen highly disgraceful.[2] In Tahiti, if a woman of condition chose an inferior person as her husband, the children he had by her were killed.[3] In the Malay Archipelago marriages between persons of different rank are, as a rule, disapproved of, and in some places prohibited.[4] In India intermarriage between different castes, though formerly permissible, is now altogether prohibited.[5] In Rome plebeians and patricians could not intermarry till the year 445 B.C., nor were marriages allowed between patricians and clients ; and Cicero himself disapproved of intermarriages of *ingenui* and freedmen.[6] Among the Teutonic peoples in ancient times any freeman who married a slave became a slave himself.[7] As late as the thirteenth century a German woman who had intercourse with a serf lost her liberty ; [8] and both in Germany and Scandinavia, when the nobility emerged as a distinct order from the class of freemen, marriages between persons of noble birth and persons who, although free, were not noble came to be considered misalliances.[9] Even in modern Europe there survive traces of the former class endogamy. According to German Civil Law, the marriage of a man belonging to the high nobility with a woman of inferior birth is still regarded as a *disparagium*, and the woman is not entitled to the rank of her husband, nor is the full right of inheritance possessed by her or her children.[10] Although in no way prevented by law, marriages out of

[1] Westermarck, *op. cit.* p. 368 *sqq.*
[2] von Martius, *Beiträge zur Ethnographie Amerika's*, i. 71. von Spix and von Martius, *Travels in Brazil*, ii. 74.
[3] Ellis, *Polynesian Researches*, i. 256. Cook, *Voyage to the Pacific Ocean*, ii. 171 *sq.*
[4] Westermarck, *op. cit.* p. 371.
[5] Monier-Williams, *Hinduism*, p. 155.

[6] Mommsen, *History of Rome*, i. 371. Rossbach, *op. cit.* pp. 249, 456 *sq.*
[7] Winroth, *Äktenskapshindren*, p. 227.
[8] *Ibid.* p. 230 *sq.* Weinhold, *Deutsche Frauen in dem Mittelalter*, i. 349, 353 *sq.*
[9] Weinhold, *op. cit.* i. 349 *sq.*
[10] Behrend, in von Holtzendorff, *Encyclopädie der Rechtswissenschaft*, i. 478.

the class are generally avoided by custom. As Sir Henry Maine observes, " the outer or endogamous limit, within which a man or woman must marry, has been mostly taken under the shelter of fashion or prejudice. It is but faintly traced in England, though not wholly obscured. It is (or perhaps was) rather more distinctly marked in the United States, through prejudices against the blending of white and coloured blood. But in Germany certain hereditary dignities are still forfeited by a marriage beyond the forbidden limits ; and in France, in spite of all formal institutions, marriages between a person belonging to the *noblesse* and a person belonging to the *bourgeoisie* (distinguished roughly from one another by the particle ' de ') are wonderfully rare, though they are not unknown." [1]

Religion, also, has formed a great bar to intermarriage. Among Muhammedans a marriage between a Christian man and a Muhammedan woman is not permitted under any circumstances, whereas it is held lawful for a Muhammedan to marry a Christian or a Jewish, but not a heathen, woman, if induced to do so by excessive love of her, or if he cannot obtain a wife of his own religion.[2] The Jewish law does not recognise marriage with a person of another belief ;[3] and during the Middle Ages marriage between Jews and Christians was prohibited by the Christians also.[4] St. Paul indicates that a Christian was not allowed to marry a heathen.[5] Tertullian calls such an alliance fornication ;[6] and in the fourth century the Council of Elvira forbade Christian parents to give their daughters in marriage to heathens.[7] Even the adherents of different Christian confessions have been prohibited from intermarrying. In

[1] Maine, *Dissertations on Early Law and Custom*, p. 224 *sq.*

[2] Lane, *Manners and Customs of the Modern Egyptians*, i. 123. d'Escayrac de Lauture, *Die afrikanische Wüste*, p. 68.

[3] Frankel, *Grundlinien des mosaisch-talmudischen Eherechts*, p. xx. Ritter, *Philo und die Halacha*, p. 71.

[4] Andree, *Zur Volkskunde der Juden*, p. 48. Neubauer, ' Notes on the Race-Types of the Jews,' in *Jour. Anthr. Inst.* xv. 19.

[5] 1 *Corinthians*, vii. 39.

[6] Tertullian, *Ad uxorem*, ii. 3 (Migne, *Patrologiæ cursus*, i. 1292 *sq.*).

[7] *Concilium Eliberitanum*, cap. 15 *sq.* (Labbe-Mansi, *Sacrorum Conciliorum collectio*, ii. 8). See also Müller, *Das sexuelle Leben der christlichen Kulturvölker*, p. 54.

the Roman Catholic Church the prohibition of marriage
with heathens and Jews was soon followed by the prohibition of " mixed marriages," and Protestants likewise
forbade such unions.[1]   Mixed marriages are not now
contrary to the civil law either among Roman Catholic or
Protestant nations, but in countries belonging to the
Orthodox Greek Church ecclesiastical restrictions have
been adopted, and are still recognised, by the State.[2]

The endogamous rules are in the first place due to the
proud antipathy people feel to races, nations, classes, or
religions different from their own. He who breaks such a
rule is regarded as an offender against the circle to which
he belongs. He hurts its feelings, he disgraces it at the
same time as he disgraces himself. Irregular connections
outside the endogamous circle are often looked upon with
less intolerance than marriage, which places the parties on
a more equal footing. A traveller relates that at Djidda,
where sexual morality is held in little respect, a Bedouin
woman may yield herself for money to a Turk or European,
but would think herself for ever dishonoured if she were
joined to him in lawful wedlock.[3] In Rome *contubernium*,
but not marriage, could take place between freemen and
slaves.[4] And among ourselves public opinion regards it
as a much more lenient offence if a royal person keeps a
woman of inferior rank as his concubine than if he
marries her.

Modern civilisation tends more or less to pull down the
barriers which separate races, nations, the various classes of
society, and the adherents of different religions. The endogamous rules have thus become less stringent and less
restricted. Whilst civilisation has narrowed the inner limit
within which a man or woman must not marry, it has
widened the outer limit within which a man or woman
may marry, and generally marries. The latter of these
processes has been one of vast importance in man's history.

---

[1] Winroth, *op. cit.* p. 213 *sqq.*
[2] *Ibid.* p. 220 *sq.*
[3] de Gobineau, *Moral and Intellectual Diversity of Races*, p. 174, n. 1.

Cf. d'Escayrac de Lauture, *op. cit.*
p. 155.
[4] Westermarck, *op. cit.* p. 372.

Originating in race- or class-pride, or in religious intolerance, the endogamous rules have in their turn helped to keep up and to strengthen these feelings. Frequent intermarriages, on the other hand, must have the very opposite effect.

Like the rules referring to the choice of partners, so the modes of contracting marriage and the ideas as to what in this respect is right and proper have undergone successive changes. The practice of capturing wives prevails in certain parts of the world, and traces of it are met with in the marriage ceremonies of several peoples, indicating that it occurred more frequently in past ages.[1] This practice, as it seems to me, has chiefly sprung from the aversion to close intermarriage, together with the difficulty a savage man may have in procuring a wife in a friendly manner, without giving compensation for the loss he inflicts on her family. We may imagine that it chiefly occurred at a stage of social growth where family ties had become stronger, and man lived in small groups of nearly related persons, but where the idea of barter had scarcely presented itself to his mind. Yet there is no reason to think that capture was at any period the exclusive form of contracting marriage ; its prevalence seems to have been much exaggerated by McLennan and his school.[2] It is impossible to believe that there ever was a time when friendly negotiations between families who could intermarry were altogether unknown. The custom prevalent among many savage tribes of a husband taking up his abode in his wife's family seems to have arisen very early in man's history.

Among most uncivilised peoples now existing a man has, in some way or other, to give compensation for his bride.[3] The simplest way of purchasing a wife is to give a kinswoman in exchange for her—a practice prevalent among

---

[1] Westermarck, *op. cit.* ch. xvii.

[2] Dr. Grosse (*Die Formen der Familie*, p. 105) goes so far as to believe that marriage by capture has never been a form of marriage recognised by custom or law, but only an occasional and punishable act of violence. But, as Dr. Havelock Ellis justly observes (*Studies in the Psychology of Sex*, ' Analysis of the Sexual Impulse,' p. 62, n. 2), this position is too extreme.

[3] Westermarck, *op. cit.* p. 390 *sqq.*

Australian tribes. Much more common is the custom of
obtaining a wife by services rendered to her father, the man
taking up his abode with the family of the girl for a certain
time, during which he works as a servant. But the ordinary
compensation for a girl is property paid to her father, or in
some cases to her uncle, or to some other relatives as well
as to the father. Marriage by exchange or purchase is not
only general among existing lower races ; it occurs, or
formerly occurred, among semi-civilised nations of a higher
culture as well—in Central America and Peru, in China
and Japan, in the various branches of the Semitic race, in
the past history of all so-called Aryan peoples. We have
no evidence that it is a stage through which every race has
passed ; we notice its absence among some of the rudest
races with whom we are acquainted. Yet with much more
reason than marriage by capture, purchase of wives may be
said to form a general stage in the social history of mankind. Although the two practices may occur simultaneously, the former seems more often to have succeeded
the latter, as barter in general has followed upon robbery.
It has been suggested that the transition from marriage by
capture to marriage by purchase was brought about in the
following way : abduction, in spite of parents, was the
primary form ; then there came the offering of compensation to escape vengeance ; and this grew eventually into
the making of presents or paying a sum beforehand.[1] The
price was a compensation for the loss sustained in the
giving up of the girl and a remuneration for the expenses
incurred in her maintenance till the time of her marriage.
The girl was regarded more or less in the light of property,
to take her away from her owner without his consent was
theft. To claim a compensation for her was his right, or
even his duty. The Indians in Columbia consider it in the
highest degree disgraceful to the girl's family if she is given
away without a price ;[2] and in certain tribes of California

[1] Koenigswarter, Études historiques
sur le développement de la société
humaine, p. 53. Spencer, Principles
of Sociology, i. 625.

[2] Bancroft, Native Races of the
Pacific States, i. 277. Cf. von Weber,
Vier Jahre in Afrika, ii. 215 sq.
(Kafirs).

" the children of a woman for whom no money was paid are accounted no better than bastards, and the whole family are condemned." [1]

With progressing civilisation, however, the practice of purchasing wives has been gradually abandoned, and come to be looked upon as infamous. The wealthier classes took the first step, and poorer and ruder persons subsequently followed their examples. Thus in India, in ancient times, the Âsura form, or marriage by purchase, was lawful for all the four castes. Afterwards it fell into disrepute, and was prohibited among the Brâhmanas and Kshatriyas, whereas it was still approved of in the case of a Vaisya and a Sûdra. But in the 'Laws of Manu' it is forbidden altogether.[2] It is said there, " No father who knows the law must take even the smallest gratuity for his daughter ; for a man who, through avarice, takes a gratuity, is a seller of his offspring." [3] The Greeks of the historical age had ceased to buy their wives. In Rome *confarreatio*, which suggested no idea of purchase, was in the very earliest known time the form of marriage in force among the patricians ; and among clients and plebeians, also, the purchase of wives came to an end in remote antiquity, surviving as a mere symbol in their *coëmptio*.[4] Among the Germans marriage by purchase was abolished only after their conversion to Christianity.[5] In the Talmudic law the purchase of wives appears as merely symbolical, the bride-price being fixed at a nominal amount.[6] In China, although marriage presents correspond exactly to purchase-money in a contract of sale, the people will not hear of their being called a " price " ;[7] which shows that here, too, some feeling of shame is attached to the idea of selling a daughter.

We may discern two different ways in which this

[1] Powers, *Tribes of California*, pp. 22, 56.

[2] *Laws of Manu*, iii. 23 *sqq*.

[3] *Ibid*. iii. 51. *Cf. ibid*. ix. 93, 98.

[4] Rossbach, *op. cit*. pp. 92, 146, 248, 250, &c.

[5] Grimm, *Deutsche Rechtsalterthümer*, p. 424.

[6] Gans, *Erbrecht*, i. 138.

[7] Jamieson, ' Marriage Laws,' in *China Review*, x. 78 n.*

gradual disappearance of marriage by purchase has taken place. On the one hand, the purchase became a symbol, appearing as a sham sale in the marriage ceremonies or as an exchange of presents ; on the other hand, the purchase sum was transformed into the morning gift and the dotal portion, a part—afterwards the whole—being given to the bride either directly by the bridegroom or by her father. These transformations of marriage by purchase have taken place not only in the history of the civilised nations, but among several peoples who are still in a savage or semi-civilised state ; and of a few of them it is expressly stated that they consider marriage by purchase a disgraceful practice.[1]

From marriage by purchase we have thus come to the practice of dower, which is apparently the very reverse of it. But whilst the marriage portion partly derives its origin from the purchase of wives, it does not do so in every case. It serves different ends, often indissolubly mixed up together. It may have the meaning of a return gift. It may imply that the wife as well as the husband is expected to contribute to the expenses of the joint household. It is also very often intended to be a settlement for the wife in case the marriage be dissolved through the husband's death or otherwise.[2] In the social history of the civilised races the marriage portion has played so prominent a part, that, as we have spoken of a stage of marriage by purchase, we may speak of another and later stage where fathers are bound by custom or law to portion their daughters. The Jews [3] and Muhammedans [4] consider it a religious duty for a man to give a dower to his daughter. In Greece the dowry came to be thought almost necessary to make the distinction between a wife and a concubine.[5] Isaeus says that no decent man would give his legitimate daughter less than a tenth of his

[1] Westermarck, *op. cit.* p. 405 *sqq.*
[2] *Ibid.* p. 411 *sqq.*
[3] Mayer, *Rechte der Israeliten,* ii. 344.
[4] *Koran,* iv. 3.
[5] Cauvet, ' L'organisation de la

famille à Athènes,' in *Revue de législation et de jurisprudence,* xxiv. 152. Potter, *Archæologia Græca,* ii. 268. *Cf.* Meier and Schömann, *Der attische Process,* p. 513 *sq.*

property ;[1] indeed, so great were the dowers given that in the time of Aristotle nearly two fifths of the whole territory of Sparta were supposed to belong to women.[2] In Rome, even more than in Greece, the marriage portion became a mark of distinction for a legitimate wife ;[3] and though later on Justinian in several of his constitutions declares that *dos* is obligatory for persons of high rank only,[4] the old custom did not fall into desuetude.[5] The Prussian ' Landrecht ' still prescribes that the father, or eventually the mother, shall arrange about the wedding and fit up the house of the newly-married couple.[6] According to the ' Code Napoléon,' on the other hand, parents are not bound to give a dower to their daughters,[7] and the same principle is generally adopted by modern legislation. It is true that especially in the so-called Latin countries there is still a strong tendency to dotation,[8] but another feeling, in some measure opposed to it, is gaining ground everywhere. In a society where monogamy is prescribed by law, where the adult women outnumber the adult men, where many men never marry, and where married women too often lead an indolent life—in such a society the marriage portion in many cases becomes a purchase-sum by means of which a father buys a husband for his daughter, as formerly a man bought a wife from her father. But, as Mr. Sutherland observes, " that pecuniary interests, either on one side or on the other, should conspicuously enter into the motives which lead to marriage, becomes repulsive to the increasing delicacy of feeling ; and so we find that in cultured communities the dowry dies out, just as the purchase-money declined in the civilised stages."[9]

[1] Isaeus, *Oratio de Pyrrhi hereditate*, 51, p. 43.

[2] Aristotle, *Politica*, ii. 9, p. 1270 a.

[3] Laboulaye, *Recherches sur la condition civile et politique des femmes*, p. 38 sq. Ginoulhiac, *Histoire du régime dotal*, p. 66. Meier and Schömann, *op. cit.* p. 513 sq.

[4] Ginoulhiac, *op. cit.* p. 103.

[5] For *dos necessaria* in Germany during the Middle Ages, see Mittermaier, *Grundsätze des gemeinen deutschen Privatrechts*, ii. 3.

[6] Eccius, in von Holtzendorff, *Encyclopädie der Rechtswissenschaft*, ii. 414.

[7] *Code Napoléon*, art. 204.

[8] See Maine, *Early History of Institutions*, p. 339.

[9] Sutherland, *Origin and Growth of the Moral Instinct*, i. 243.

Whilst most of the lower animal species are by instinct either monogamous or polygynous, with man every possible form of marriage occurs. There are marriages of one man with one woman (monogamy), of one man with many women (polygyny), of many men with one woman (polyandry), and, in a few exceptional cases, of many men with many women.[1] •

Among the causes by which the forms of marriage are influenced the numerical proportion between the sexes plays an important part. Polyandry seems to be due chiefly to a surplus of men, though it prevails only where the circumstances are otherwise in favour of it.[2] It presupposes an abnormally feeble disposition to jealousy, and has probably at all times been exceptional in the human race. There is no solid evidence for the theory set forth by McLennan that it was the rule in early times.[3] On the contrary, this form of marriage seems to require a certain degree of civilisation ; we have no trustworthy account of its occurrence among the lowest savages. In polyandrous families the husbands are most frequently brothers, and the eldest brother, at least in many cases, has the superiority. It seems a fair conclusion that in such instances polyandry was originally an expression of fraternal benevolence on the part of the eldest brother, or of urgent demands on the part of the younger ones, who otherwise, on account of the scarcity of women, would have to live unmarried. If additional wives were afterwards acquired, they would naturally be considered the common property of all the brothers ; and in this way the group marriage of the Toda type seems to have evolved.[4] Polygyny, also, is to some extent dependent upon the proportion between the sexes. It has been observed in India that polyandry occurs in those parts of the country where the males outnumber the females, polygyny in those

---

[1] Westermarck, *op. cit.* ch. xx.
[2] *Ibid.* p. 482.
[3] McLennan, ' The Levirate and Polyandry,' in *Fortnightly Review,* N.S. xxi. 703 *sqq. Idem, Studies in Ancient History,* p. 112 *sq.*
[4] Westermarck, *op. cit.* p. 510 *sqq.* See also Rivers, *Todas,* pp. 515, 519, 521.

where the reverse is the case.[1] Indeed, in countries unaffected by European civilisation polygyny is likely to prevail wherever there is a majority of women. But the proportion between the sexes is only one cause out of many to which polygyny is due.

There are several reasons why a man may desire to possess more than one wife.[2] Monogamy requires from him periodical continence, not only for a certain time every month, but among many peoples during the pregnancy of his wife, and as long as she suckles her child. One of the chief causes of polygyny is the attraction which female youth and beauty exercise upon a man ; and at the lower stages of civilisation women generally become old much sooner than in more advanced communities. The liking of men for variety is also a potent factor ; the Negroes of Angola asserted that they " were not able to eat always of the same dish." [3] We must further take into account men's desire for offspring, wealth, and authority. The barrenness of a wife is a very common reason for the choice of a new partner ; the polygyny of the ancient Hindus seems to have been due chiefly to the fact that men dreaded the idea of dying childless, and even now in the East the desire for offspring is one of the principal causes of polygyny.[4] The more wives, the more children ; and the more children, the greater power. In early civilisation a man's relations and connections are often his only friends ; and where slavery does not prevail, next to a man's wives the real servant, the only to be counted upon, is the child. Moreover, a man's fortune is increased by a multitude of wives not only through their children, but through their work. Manual labour among savages is undertaken largely by women ; and when neither slaves nor persons who will work for hire can be procured,

[1] Goehlert, ' Die Geschlechtsver-schiedenheit der Kinder in den Ehen,' in *Zeitschr. f. Ethnologie,* xiii. 127.

[2] Westermarck, *op. cit.* p. 483 *sqq.*

[3] Merolla da Sorrento, ' Voyage to Congo,' in Pinkerton, *Collection of Voyages,* xvi. 299.

[4] Wallin, *Reseanteckningar från Orienten,* iii. 267. Le Bon, *La civilisation des Arabes,* p. 424. Gray, *China,* i. 184.

it becomes necessary for any man who requires many servants to have many wives.

Nevertheless, however desirable polygyny may be from the man's point of view, it is altogether prohibited among many peoples, and in countries where it is an established institution it is practised—as a rule to which there are few exceptions—only by a comparatively small class.[1] The proportion between the sexes partly accounts for this, but there are other causes of no less importance.[2] Where the amount of female labour is limited and no accumulated property exists, it may be very difficult for a man to keep a plurality of wives. Again, where female labour is of considerable value, the necessity of paying the purchase-sum for a wife is a hindrance to polygyny which can be overcome only by the wealthier men. There are, more-over, certain factors of a psychical character which are unfavourable to polygyny. When love depends on external attractions only, it is necessarily fickle ; but when it implies sympathy arising from mental qualities, there is a tie between husband and wife which lasts long after youth and beauty are gone. As another obstacle to polygyny we have to note the true monogamous sentiment, the absorbing passion for one, which is not unknown even among savage races. Polygyny is finally checked by the respect in which women are held by men. Jealousy is not exclusively a masculine passion, and it is the ambition of every wife to be the mistress of her husband's house. Hence where women have succeeded in obtaining some power over their husbands, or where the altruistic feelings of men have become refined enough to lead them to respect the feelings of those weaker than themselves, monogamy is frequently the result.

It is certain that polygyny has been less prevalent at the lowest stages of civilisation—where wars do not seriously disturb the proportion of the sexes, where life is chiefly supported by hunting and female labour is consequently of slight value, and where there is no accumulation of wealth

[1] Westermarck, *op. cit.* p. 435 *sqq.*   [2] *Ibid.* p. 493 *sqq.*

and no distinction of class—than it is at somewhat higher stages.[1] The more advanced savages and barbarians seem to indulge in this practice to a greater extent than the lower ones, many, or most, of whom are either little addicted to polygyny or strictly monogamous. Various forest tribes in Brazil are monogamous,[2] and so are several of the Californian tribes—" a humble and a lowly race, . . . one of the lowest on earth." [3] Thus the Karok do not allow bigamy even to a chief ; and though a man may own as many women for slaves as he can purchase, he brings obloquy on himself if he cohabits with more than one.[4] Among the Veddahs [5] and Andaman Islanders [6] monogamy is as rigidly insisted upon as anywhere in Europe. The natives of Kar Nicobar " have but one wife, and look upon unchastity as a very deadly sin." [7] Among the Koch and Old Kukis polygyny and concubinage are forbidden ;[8] whilst among some other aboriginal tribes in India a man, though not expressly forbidden to have many wives, is blamed if he has more than one.[9] Among the Karens of Burma [10] and certain tribes of Indo-China, the Malay Peninsula, and the Indian Archipelago, polygyny is said either to be prohibited or unknown.[11] The Hill Dyaks marry but one wife, and a chief who once broke through this custom lost all his influence.[12] In Australia there are said to be some truly monogamous tribes ; [13] in the Birria tribe, for instance, " the possession of more than one wife is absolutely forbidden, or was so before the coming of the whites." [14]

[1] Westermarck, op. cit. p. 505 sqq.
[2] von Martius, op. cit. i. 274, 298. Wallace, Travels on the Amazon, pp. 509, 515 sqq. Waitz, Anthropologie der Naturvölker, iii. 472.
[3] Powers, op. cit. pp. 5, 56, 406. Wilkes, U. S. Exploring Expedition, v. 188.
[4] Powers, op. cit. p. 22.
[5] Bailey, in Trans. Ethn. Soc. N.S. ii. 291 sq. Hartshorne, in Indian Antiquary, viii. 320.
[6] Man, in Jour. Anthr. Inst. xii. 135.
[7] Distant, ibid. iii. 4.

[8] Dalton, op. cit. p. 91. Stewart, ' Notes on Northern Cachar,' in Jour. As. Soc. Bengal, xxiv. 621.
[9] Dalton, op. cit. pp. 28, 54. Jellinghaus, ' Munda-Kolhs in Chota Nagpore,' in Zeitschr. f. Ethnol. iii. 370.
[10] Smeaton, Loyal Karens of Burma, p. 81.
[11] Westermarck, op. cit. p. 436 sq.
[12] Low, Sarawak, p. 300.
[13] Curr, Australian Race, i. 402; ii. 371.
[14] Ibid. ii. 378.

Monogamy is all the more likely to have been the general
rule among our earliest human ancestors as it seems to be
so among the man-like apes. Darwin certainly mentions
the gorilla as a polygamist ; [1] but the majority of statements we have regarding this animal are to the opposite
effect. Relying on the most trustworthy authorities,
Professor Hartmann says, " The gorilla lives in a society
consisting of male and female and their young of varying
ages." [2]

Whilst civilisation is thus up to a certain point favourable to polygyny, it leads in its higher forms to
monogamy. Owing to the decrease of wars, the death-rate
of the men becomes less, and the considerable disproportion between the sexes which among many warlike peoples
makes polygyny almost a law of nature no longer exists
among the most advanced nations. No superstitious belief
keeps the civilised man apart from his wife during her
pregnancy and while she suckles her child ; and the
suckling time has become much shorter since the introduction of domesticated animals and the use of milk. To a
cultivated mind youth and beauty are by no.means the
only attractions of a woman ; and civilisation has made
female beauty more durable. The desire for offspring
becomes less intense. A large family, instead of being a
help in the struggle for existence, is often considered an
insufferable burden. A man's kinsfolk are no longer his
only friends, and his wealth and power do not depend
upon the number of his wives and children. A wife
ceases to be a mere labourer, and manual labour is to a
large extent replaced by the work of domesticated animals
and the use of implements and machines. Moreover, the
sentiment of love becomes more refined, the passion for
one more absorbing. The feelings of the weaker sex are
frequently held in higher regard. And the better education bestowed on women enables them to live comfortably
without the support of a husband.

---

[1] Darwin, *Descent of Man*, pp. 217,
590 *sq.*

[2] Hartmann, *Die menschenähnlichen Affen*, p. 214.

As for the moral valuation of the various forms of marriage, it should be noticed that even among polygynous and polyandrous peoples monogamy is permitted by custom or law, although in some instances it is associated with poverty and considered mean, whereas polygyny, as associated with greatness, is thought praiseworthy.[1] Again, the notion that monogamy is the only proper form of marriage, and that any other form is immoral, is due either to the mere force of habit ; or, possibly, to the notion that it is wrong of some men to appropriate a plurality of wives when others in consequence can get none ; or to the feeling that polygyny is an offence against the female sex ; or to the condemnation of lust. As regards the obligatory monogamy of Christian nations, we have to remember that monogamy was the only recognised form of marriage in the societies on which Christianity was first engrafted, and that it was the only form that could be tolerated by a religion which regarded every gratification of the sexual impulse with suspicion and incontinence as the gravest sin. In its early days the Church showed little respect for women but its horror of sensuality was immense.

A few words still remain to be said of a form of marriage which has of late been the subject of much discussion in connection with Australian ethnology. Many years ago attention was drawn to the fact that the Kamilaroi tribes in South Australia are divided into four classes, in which brothers and sisters are respectively Ipai and Ipătha, Kŭbi and Kubĭtha, Mŭri and Mătha, Kumbu and Bŭtha ; and that the members of one class are forbidden to marry among themselves, but bound to marry into a certain other class. Thus Ipai may only marry Kubĭtha ; Kŭbi, Ipătha ; Kumbu, Mătha ; and Mŭri, Bŭtha. In a certain sense, we were told, every Ipai is regarded as married, not by any individual contract, but by organic law, to every Kubĭtha ; every Kŭbi to every Ipătha, and so forth. If, for instance, a Kŭbi meet a stranger Ipătha, they address

---

[1] Spencer, *Principles of Sociology*, i. 657.

each other as " spouse " ; and " a Kŭbi thus meeting an
Ipātha, though she were of another tribe, would treat her
as his wife, and his right to do so would be recognised by
her tribe." [1] The institution according to which the
men of one division have as wives the women of another
division, the Rev. L. Fison called " group marriage."
He contends that among the natives of South Australia it
has given way in later times, in some measure, to individual marriage. But theoretically, he says, marriage is still
communal : " it is based upon the marriage of all the
males in one division of a tribe to all the females of
the same generation in another division." The chief
argument advanced by Mr. Fison in support of his theory
is grounded on the terms of relationship in use in the
tribes. These terms belong to the " classificatory system "
of Mr. Morgan ; [2] but he admits that he is not aware of
any tribe in which the actual practice is to its full extent
what the terms of relationship imply. " Present usage,"
he says, " is everywhere in advance of the system so implied,
and the terms are survivals of an ancient right, not precise
indications of custom as it is." [3] The same is granted by
Mr. Howitt. [4] Yet I have pointed out, in my criticism of
the classificatory system, to what absurd results we must be
led if, guided by such terms, we begin to speculate upon
early marriage. [5] Moreover, as I have said, " if a Kŭbi
and an Ipātha address each other as spouse, this does not
imply that in former times every Kŭbi was married to
every Ipātha indiscriminately. On the contrary, the
application of such a familiar term might be explained
from the fact that the women who may be a man's wives,
and those who cannot possibly be so, stand in a widely
different relation to him." [6] This suggestion derives
support from the following statement made by Dr.
Codrington with reference to the Melanesians :—" Speak-

---

[1] Ridley, *Kámilarói*, p. 161 *sq.*
(edit. 1866, p. 35 *sqq.*). Fison and
Howitt, *Kamilaroi and Kurnai*, pp.
36, 51, 53.
[2] Fison and Howitt, *op. cit.* p. 60.
[3] *Ibid.* p. 159 *sq.*

[4] Howitt, ' Australian Group Relations,' in *Smithsonian Report*, 1883,
p. 817.
[5] Westermarck, *op. cit.* ch. v.
[6] *Ibid.* p. 56.

ing generally, it may be said that to a Melanesian man all
women, of his own generation at least, are either sisters or
wives, to the Melanesian woman all men are either
brothers or husbands. . . . It must not be understood
that a Melanesian regards all women who are not of his
own division as, in fact, his wives, or conceives himself to
have rights which he may exercise in regard to those
women of them who are unmarried ; but the women who
may be his wives by marriage and those who cannot
possibly be so, stand in a widely different relation to
him." [1]

More recently Messrs. Spencer and Gillen have shown
that a marriage system essentially similar to that of the
South Australian natives prevails in Central Australia ;
and they, also, regard it as a later modification of genuine
group marriage. Nowadays, they say, the system of individual wives prevails—" modified, however, by the practice of customs according to which, at certain times, much
wider marital relations are allowed." But to this rule there
is one exception :—" In the Urabunna tribe group marriage actually exists at the present day, a group of men of a
certain designation having, not merely nominally but in
actual reality, and under normal conditions, marital relations with a group of women of another special designation " ; here " individual marriage does not exist either in
name or in practice." [2] But, after all, it appears that even
among the Urabunna every woman is the special *Nupa* of
one man, and that certain other men, her *Piraungaru*, only
have a secondary right to her. Thus, if the Nupa man (the
real, or at all events the chief, husband) be present, the
Piraungaru (accessory husbands) are allowed to have intercourse with her only in case the Nupa man consents.[3] Is
this modification of the Urabunna group marriage a later
development from a previous system according to which
all the men of a certain group had an equal right to all the

[1] Codrington,*Melanesians*, p. 22 *sq.*
[2] Spencer and Gillen, *Northern
Tribes of Central Australia*, p. 140.

*Iidem, Native Tribes of Central Aus-
tralia*, p. 62 *sq.*
[3] *Iidem, Native Tribes*, p. 110.

women of another group ? Here we are on dangerous
ground ; nothing is more difficult than to decide whether
certain customs are survivals or not. We find modifications resembling those connected with the group marriage
of the Urabunna both in polyandry and in polygyny ; the
first husband in a polyandrous family is usually the chief
husband, and the first wife in a polygynous family is very
frequently the chief wife. We must certainly not conclude
that these restrictions have been preceded by an earlier
custom which gave equal rights to all the husbands or all
the wives ; on the contrary, it is more likely that the
higher position granted to the first husband or to the first
wife is due to the fact that monogamy was the usual form
of marriage.[1] Similarly the Urabunna custom may very
well have developed out of ordinary individual marriage,[2]
and the cause of it may perhaps be, as Mr. N. W. Thomas
has suggested,[3] the difficulties which an Australian native
often experiences in getting a wife.[4] As for other facts
which have been adduced as evidence of Australian group
marriage in the past, such as the *jus primæ noctis*, &c., I
only desire to emphasise the circumstance that extra-
matrimonial intercourse is practised by the Australian
natives in a variety of cases the real meaning of which
seems obscure. In some instances at least, a magic
significance appears to be attributed to it ; [5] and that it is
a survival of group marriage, in the strict sense of the
term, is again only a conjecture.

I must admit, therefore, that the facts produced by
Messrs. Spencer and Gillen, and the severe criticism which
they have passed on my sceptical attitude towards Mr.
Fison's group marriage theory have not been able to convince me that among the Australian aborigines individual
marriage has evolved out of a previous system of marriage
between groups of men and women. Nor has Mr. Howitt,

[1] Westermarck, *op. cit.* pp. 443–
448, 457, 458, 508.
[2] *Cf.* Crawley, *op. cit.* p. 482 ;
Lang, *Social Origins*, p. 105 *sq.*
[3] Thomas, in a paper read before
the Anthropological Institute in
1905. *Cf. Idem, Kinship and Marriage in Australia*, p. 138.
[4] See Westermarck, *op. cit.* p. 132
sq. ; *infra*, p. 460.
[5] See, *e.g.*, Spencer and Gillen,
Northern Tribes, p. 137 *sq.*

in his recent work on the ' Native Tribes of South-East Australia,' in my opinion, sufficiently proved that such an evolution has taken place.[1] He blames certain " ethnologists of the study " for not being willing " to take the opinion of men who have first-hand knowledge of the natives " ;[2] but I think we do well in distinguishing between statements based on direct observation and the observer's interpretation of the stated facts. Even suppose, however, that group marriage really was once common in Australia, would that prove that it was once common among mankind at large ? Mr. Howitt's supposition that the practice of group marriage " will be ultimately accepted as one of the primitive conditions of mankind "[3] is no doubt shared by a host of anthropologists. The group marriage theory will probably for some time to come remain the residuary legatee of the old theory of promiscuity ; the important works which have lately been published on the Australian aborigines have made people inclined to view the early history of mankind through Australian spectacles. But even the most ardent advocate of Australian group marriage should remember that the existence of kangurus in Australia does not prove that there were once kangurus in England.

The time during which marriage lasts varies extremely in the human race.[4] There are unions which, though legally recognised as marriages, do not endure long enough to deserve to be so called in the natural history sense of the term ; there are others which are dissolved only by

[1] Mr. Thomas has come to the same result in his book on ' Kinship and Marriage in' Australia,' which appeared when the present chapter was already in type. A detailed examination of the facts which have been adduced as evidence of Australian group marriage (p. 127 *sqq.*) has led him to the conclusion (p. 147) that prevailing customs in Australia, far from proving the present or former existence of group marriage in that continent, do not even render it probable, and that on the terms of relationship no argument of any sort can be founded which assumes them to refer to consanguinity, kinship, or affinity. " It is therefore not rash to say that the case for group marriage, so far as Australia is concerned, falls to the ground." See *infra*, Addit. Notes.

[2] Howitt, ' Native Tribes of South-East Australia,' in *Folk-Lore*, xvii. 185.

[3] *Idem, Native Tribes of South-East Australia*, p. 281.

[4] Westermarck, *op. cit.* ch. xxiii.

death. As has already been pointed out, it is probable that among primitive men the union of the sexes lasted till after the birth of the offspring, and we have perhaps some reason to believe that the connection lasted for years. On the whole, progress in civilisation has tended to make marriage more durable. It is evident that at the early stage of development at which women first became valuable as labourers, a wife was united with her husband by a new bond more lasting than youth and beauty. The tie was strengthened by the bride-price and the marriage portion. And a higher development of the paternal feeling, better forethought for the children's welfare, in some instances greater consideration for women, and a more refined love passion have gradually made it stronger, until it has become in many cases indissoluble. Yet we must not conclude that divorce will in the future be less frequent and more restricted by law than it is now in European countries. It should be remembered that the laws of divorce in Christian Europe owe their origin to an idealistic religious commandment which, interpreted in its literal sense, gave rise to legal prescriptions far from harmonising with the mental and social life of the mass of the people. The powerful authority of the Roman Church was necessary to enforce the dogma that marriage is indissoluble. The Reformation introduced somewhat greater liberty in this respect, and modern legislation has gone further in the same direction. In those Christian states of Europe where absolute divorce is permitted the grounds on which it may be sued for are nearly the same for the man and the woman, except in England, where the husband must be accused of one or other of several offences besides adultery. In Italy, Spain, and Portugal, a judicial separation may always be decreed on the ground of the adultery of the wife, but, on the ground of the adultery of the husband, only if it has been committed under certain aggravating circumstances.[1] These laws imply that marriage is not yet a contract on the footing of perfect equality between the sexes ; but there is

[1] Glasson, *Le mariage civil et le divorce*, pp. 291, 298, 304.

a growing opinion that, where it is not, it ought to be so. Again, when both husband and wife desire to separate, it seems to many enlightened minds that the State has no right to prevent them from dissolving the marriage contract, provided the children are properly cared for ; and that for the children, also, it is better to have the supervision of one parent only than of two who cannot agree.

CHAPTER XLI

CELIBACY

AMONG savage and barbarous races of men nearly every individual endeavours to marry as soon as he, or she, reaches the age of puberty.[1] Marriage seems to them indispensable, and a person who abstains from it is looked upon as an unnatural being and is disdained. Among the Santals a man who remains single " is at once despised by both sexes, and is classed next to a thief, or a witch : they term the unhappy wretch ' No man.' "[2] Among the Kafirs a bachelor has no voice in the kraal.[3] In the Tupi tribes of Brazil no man was suffered to partake in the drinking-feast while he remained single.[4] The natives of Futuna in the Western Pacific maintained that it was necessary to be married in order to hold a part in the happy future life, and that the celibates, both men and women, had to submit to a chastisement of their own before entering the *fale-mate*, or " home of the dead." [5] According to Fijian beliefs, he who died wifeless was stopped by the god Nangganangga on the road to Paradise, and smashed to atoms.[6]

Among peoples of archaic culture celibacy is likewise a great exception and marriage regarded as a duty. In

[1] Westermarck, *History of Human Marriage*, p. 134 *sqq.*
[2] Man, *Sonthalia*, p. 101.
[3] von Weber, *Vier Jahre in Afrika*, ii. 215.
[4] Southey, *History of Brazil*, i. 240.
[5] Percy Smith, ' Futuna,' in *Jour. Polynesian Soc.* i. 39 *sq.*

[6] Pritchard, *Polynesian Reminiscences*, pp. 368, 372. Seemann, *Viti*, p. 399 *sq.* Fison, ' Fijian Burial Customs,' in *Jour. Anthr. Inst.* x. 139. Williams and Calvert, *Fiji*, p. 206. For other instances see Westermarck, *op. cit.* p. 136, n. 10.

ancient Peru marriage was compulsory at a certain age.[1]
Among the Aztecs no young man lived single till his
twenty-second year, unless he intended to become a priest,
and for girls the customary marrying-age was from eleven
to eighteen. In Tlascala, we are told, the unmarried state
was so despised that a grown-up man who would not
marry had his hair cut off for shame.[2]

" Almost all Chinese," says Dr. Gray, " robust or infirm,
well-formed or deformed, are called upon by their parents
to marry as soon as they have attained the age of puberty.
Were a grown-up son or daughter to die unmarried, the
parents would regard it as most deplorable." Hence a
young man of marriageable age, whom consumption or
any other lingering disease had marked for its own, would
be compelled by his parents or guardians to marry at
once.[3] So indispensable is marriage considered by the
Chinese, that even the dead are married, the spirits of all
males who die in infancy or in boyhood being in due time
married to the spirits of females who have been cut off at
a like early age.[4] There is a maxim by Mencius, re-
echoed by the whole nation, that it is a heavy sin to have
no sons, as this would doom father, mother, and the whole
ancestry in the Nether-world to a pitiable existence
without descendants enough to serve them properly, to
worship at the ancestral tombs, to take care of the ancestral
tablets, and duly to perform all rites and ceremonies
connected with the departed dead. For a man whose
wife has reached her fortieth year without bringing him a
son, it is an imperative duty to take a concubine.[5] In
Corea " the male human being who is unmarried is never
called a ' man,' whatever his age, but goes by the name of
' yatow,' a name given by the Chinese to unmarriageable
young girls ; and the ' man ' of thirteen or fourteen has a

[1] Garcilasso de la Vega, *First Part
of the Royal Commentaries of the
Yncas*, i. 306 *sq.*
[2] Klemm, *Allgemeine Cultur-Geschichte der Menschheit*, v. 46 *sq.*
Bancroft, *Native Races of the Pacific
States*, ii. 251 *sq.*

[3] Gray, *China*, i. 186.
[4] *Ibid.* i. 216 *sq.*
[5] Giles, *Strange Stories from a
Chinese Studio*, i. 64, n. 10. de
Groot, *Religious System of China*,
(vol. ii. book) i. 617. *Indo-Chinese
Gleaner*, iii. 58.

perfect right to strike, abuse, order about the ' yatow ' of thirty, who dares not as much as open his lips to complain." [1]

Among the Semites, also, we meet with the idea that a dead man who has no children will miss something in Shĕol through not receiving that kind of worship which ancestors in early times appear to have received.[2] The Hebrews looked upon marriage as a religious duty.[3] According to the Shulchan Aruch, he who abstains from marrying is guilty of bloodshed, diminishes the image of God, and causes the divine presence to withdraw from Israel ; hence a single man past twenty may be compelled by the court to take a wife.[4] Muhammedanism likewise regards marriage as a duty for men and women ; to neglect it without a sufficient excuse subjects a man to severe reproach.[5] " When a servant [of God] marries," said the Prophet, " verily he perfects half his religion." [6]

The so-called Aryan nations in ancient times, as M. Fustel de Coulanges and others have pointed out, regarded celibacy as an impiety and a misfortune : " an impiety, because one who did not marry put the happiness of the manes of the family in peril ; a misfortune, because he himself would receive no worship after his death." A man's happiness in the next world depended upon his having a continuous line of male descendants, whose duty it would be to make the periodical offerings for the repose of his soul. [7] According to the ' Laws of Manu,' marriage is the twelfth Sanskāra, and as such a religious duty incumbent upon all.[8] Among the Hindus of the present day a

[1] Ross, *History of Corea*, p. 313.
[2] Cheyne, ' Harlot,' in Cheyne and Black, *Encyclopædia Biblica*, ii. 1964.
[3] Mayer, *Rechte der Israeliten*, pp. 286, 353. Lichtschein, *Ehe nach mosaisch-talmudischer Auffassung*, p. 5 sqq. Klugmann, *Die Frau im Talmud*, p. 39 sq.
[4] *Schulchan Aruch*, iv. (' Eben haezer ') i. 1, 3. See also *Yebamoth*, fol. 63 b sq., quoted by Margolis, ' Celibacy,' in *Jewish Encyclopedia*, iii. 636.

[5] Lane, *Manners and Customs of the Modern Egyptians*, i. 197.
[6] *Idem*, *Arabian Society in the Middle Ages*, p. 221.
[7] Fustel de Coulanges, *La cité antique*, p. 54 sq. Hearn, *The Aryan Household*, pp. 69, 71. Mayne, *Treatise on Hindu Law and Usage*, p. 68 sq.
[8] *Laws of Manu*, ii. 66 sq. Monier-Williams, *Indian Wisdom*, p. 246. Cf. Mayne, *op. cit.* p. 69.

man who is not married is generally considered to be almost a useless member of the community, and is indeed looked upon as beyond the pale of nature ;[1] and the spirits of young men who have died without becoming fathers are believed to wander about in a restless miserable manner, like people burdened with an enormous debt which they are quite unable to discharge.[2] Similar views are expressed in Zoroastrianism. Ahura Mazda said to Zoroaster :—" The man who has a wife is far above him who lives in continence ; he who keeps a house is far above him who has none ; he who has children is far above the childless man."[3] The greatest misfortune which could befall an ancient Persian was to be childless.[4] To him who has no child the bridge of Paradise shall be barred ; the first question the angels there will ask him is, whether he has left in this world a substitute for himself, and if the answer be " No " they will pass by and he will stay at the head of the bridge, full of grief. The primitive meaning of this is plain : the man without a son cannot enter Paradise because there is nobody to pay him the family worship.[5] Ashi Vanguhi, a feminine impersonification of piety, and the source of all the good and riches that are connected with piety, rejects the offerings of barren people—old men, courtesans, and children.[6] It is said in the Yasts, " This is the worst deed that men and tyrants do, namely, when they deprive maids that have been barren for a long time of marrying and bringing forth children."[7] And in the eyes of all good Parsis of the present day, as in the time of king Darius and the contemporaries of Herodotus, the two greatest merits of a citizen are the begetting and rearing of a numerous family, and the fruitful tilling of the soil.[8]

[1] Dubois, *Description of the Character, &c. of the People of India*, p. 132.
[2] Monier-Williams, *Brāhmanism and Hindūism*, p. 243 sq.
[3] *Vendîdâd*, iv. 47.
[4] Rawlinson, in his translation of Herodotus, i. 262, n. 1. Cf. Herodotus, i. 133, 136 ; *Dînâ-î Maînôg-î*

Khirad, xxxv. 19.
[5] Darmesteter, in *Sacred Books of the East*, iv. 47. Cf. Idem, *Ormazd et Ahriman*, p. 294.
[6] *Yasts*, xvii. 54.
[7] *Ibid.* xvii. 59.
[8] Darmesteter, in *Sacred Books of the East*, iv. p. lxii. Cf. Ploss-Bartels, *Das Weib*, i. 173.

The ancient Greeks regarded marriage as a matter both of public and private importance.[1] In various places criminal proceedings might be taken against celibates.[2] Plato remarks that every individual is bound to provide for a continuance of representatives to succeed himself as ministers of the Divinity ;[3] and Isaeus says, " All those who think their end approaching look forward with a prudent care that their houses may not become desolate, but that there may be some person to attend to their funeral rites and to perform the legal ceremonies at their tombs." [4] So also the conviction that the founding of a house and the begetting of children constituted a moral necessity and a public duty had a deep hold of the Roman mind in early times.[5] Cicero's treatise ' De Legibus '— which generally reproduces in a philosophical form the ancient laws of Rome—contains a law according to which the Censors had to impose a tax upon unmarried men.[6] But in later periods, when sexual morality reached a very low ebb in Rome, celibacy—as to which grave complaints were made as early as 520 B.C.—naturally increased in proportion, especially among the upper classes. Among these marriage came to be regarded as a burden which people took upon themselves at the best in the public interest. Indeed, how it fared with marriage and the rearing of children is shown by the Gracchan agrarian laws, which first placed a premium thereon ;[7] and later the Lex Julia et Papia Poppaea imposed various penalties on those who lived in a state of celibacy after a certain age,[8] though with little or no result.[9]

Celibacy is thus disapproved of for various reasons. It

[1] Müller, *History and Antiquities of the Doric Race*, ii. 300 sq. Fustel de Coulanges, *op. cit.* p. 55. Hearn, *op. cit.* p. 72. Döllinger, *The Gentile and the Jew*, ii. 234 sq.
[2] Pollux, *Onomasticum*, iii. 48.
[3] Plato, *Leges*, vi. 773.
[4] Isaeus, *Oratio de Apollodori hereditate*, 30, p. 66. Rohde observes (*Psyche*, p. 228), however, that such a belief did not exist in the Homeric age, when the departed souls in Hades were supposed to be in no way dependent upon the survivors.
[5] Mommsen, *History of Rome*, i. 74.
[6] Cicero, *De legibus*, iii. 3. Fustel de Coulanges, *op. cit.* p. 55.
[7] Mommsen, *op. cit.* iii. 121 ; iv. 186 sq.
[8] Rossbach, *Römische Ehe*, p. 418.
[9] Mackenzie, *Studies in Roman Law*, p. 104.

appears unnatural. It is taken as an indication of licentious habits. Where ancestors are worshipped after their death it inspires religious horror : the man who leaves himself without offspring shows reckless indifference to the religion of his people, to his own fate after death, and to the duties he owes the dead, whose spirits depend upon the offerings of their descendants for their comfort. The last point of view, as we have seen, is particularly prominent among peoples of archaic culture, but it is not unknown at a lower stage of civilisation. Thus the Eskimo about Behring Strait " appear to have great dread of dying without being assured that their shades will be remembered during the festivals, fearing if neglected that they would thereby suffer destitution in the future life " ; hence a pair of childless Eskimo frequently adopt a child, so that when they die there will be some one left whose duty it will be to make the customary feast and offerings to their shades at the festival of the dead.[1] Finally, in communities with a keen public spirit, especially in ambitious states frequently engaged in war, celibacy is regarded as a wrong committed against the State.

Modern civilisation looks upon celibacy in a different light. The religious motive for marriage has ceased to exist, the lot of the dead being no longer supposed to depend upon the devotion of the living. It is said, in a general way, that marriage is a duty to the nation or the race, but this argument is hardly applied to individual cases. According to modern ideas the union between man and woman is too much a matter of sentiment to be properly classified among civic duties. Nor does the unmarried state strike us as particularly unnatural. The proportion of unmarried people is gradually growing larger and the age at which people marry is rising.[2] The chief causes of this increasing celibacy are the difficulty of supporting a family under present conditions of life, and the luxurious

---

[1] Nelson, ' Eskimo about Bering Strait,' in *Ann. Rep. Bur. Ethn.* xviii. 290.

[2] Westermarck, *op. cit.* p. 146.

habits of living in the upper classes of society. Another
reason is that the domestic circle does not fill so large a
place in life as it did formerly ; the married state has in
some measure lost its advantage over the single state, and
there are many more pleasures now that can be enjoyed as
well or even better in celibacy. Moreover, by the diffusion
of a finer culture throughout the community, men and
women can less easily find any one whom they are willing
to take as a partner for life ; their requirements are more
exacting, they have a livelier sense of the serious character
of the marriage union, and they are less willing to contract
it from any lower motives.[1]

Nay, far from enjoining marriage as a duty incumbent
upon all, enlightened opinion seems to agree that it is a
duty for many people never to marry. In some European
countries the marriages of persons in receipt of poor-law
relief have been legally prohibited, and in certain cases the
legislators have gone further still and prohibited all marriages until the contracting parties can prove that they
possess the means of supporting a family.[2] The opinion
has also been expressed that the State ought to forbid the
unions of persons suffering from certain kinds of disease,
which in all probability would be transmitted to the offspring. People are beginning to feel that it entails a
heavy responsibility to bring a new being into existence,
and that many persons are wholly unfit for such a
task.[3] Future generations will probably with a kind of
horror look back at a period when the most important, and
in its consequences the most far-reaching, function which
has fallen to the lot of man was entirely left to individual
caprice and lust.

Side by side with the opinion that marriage is a duty for
all ordinary men and women we find among many peoples

[1] *Ibid.* p. 147 *sqq.* ' Why is Single
Life becoming more General ? ' in
The Nation, vi. 190 *sq.*
[2] Lecky, *Democracy and Liberty,*
ii. 181.

[3] See Mr. Galton's papers on
" Eugenics " and the discussions of
the subject in *Sociological Papers,*
vols. i. and ii.

the notion that persons whose function it is to perform religious or magical rites must be celibates.[1] The Thlinkets believe that if a shaman does not observe continuous chastity his own guardian spirits will kill him.[2] In Patagonia the male wizards were not allowed to marry.[3] In some tribes of the Guaranies of Paraguay " the female Payes were bound to chastity, or they no longer obtained credit." [4] Celibacy was compulsory on the priests of the Chibchas in Bogota.[5] The Tohil priests in Guatemala were vowed to perpetual continence.[6] In Ichcatlan the high-priest was obliged to live constantly within the temple, and to abstain from commerce with any woman whatsoever ; and if he failed in this duty he was cut in pieces, and the bloody limbs were given as a warning to his successor.[7] Of the women who held positions in the temples of ancient Mexico we are told that their chastity was most zealously guarded ; during the performance of their duties they were required to keep at a proper distance from the male assistants, at whom they did not even dare to glance. The punishment to be inflicted upon those who violated their vow of chastity was death ; whilst, if their trespass remained entirely secret, they endeavoured to appease the anger of the gods by fasting and austerity of life, dreading that in punishment of their crime their flesh would rot.[8] In Yucatan there was, connected with the worship of the sun, an order of vestals the members of which generally enrolled themselves for a certain time, but were afterwards allowed to leave and enter the married state. Some of them, however, remained for ever in the service of the temple and were apotheosised. Their duty was to attend to the sacred fire, and to keep strictly chaste,

---

[1] Some instances of this are stated by Landtman, *Origin of Priesthood*, p. 156 *sq.*

[2] Veniaminof, quoted by Landtman, *op. cit.* p. 156.

[3] Falkner, *Description of Patagonia*, p. 117.

[4] Southey, *History of Brazil*, ii. 371.

[5] Simon, quoted by Dorman, *Origin of Primitive Superstitions*, p. 384.

[6] Bancroft, *op. cit.* iii. 489.

[7] Clavigero, *History of Mexico*, i. 274.

[8] *Ibid.* i. 275 *sq.* Torquemada, *Monarchia Indiana*, ii. 188 *sqq.* Bancroft, *op. cit.* iii. 435 *sq. Cf.* Acosta, *History of the Indies*, ii. 333 *sq.*

those who broke their vows being shot to death with arrows.[1] In Peru there were likewise virgins dedicated to the sun, who lived in perpetual seclusion to the end of their lives, who preserved their virginity and were forbidden to converse or have sexual intercourse with or to see any man, or even any woman who was not one of themselves.[2] And besides the virgins who thus professed perpetual virginity in the monasteries, there were other women, of the blood royal, who led the same life in their own houses, having taken a vow of continence. These women " were held in great veneration for their chastity and purity, and, as a mark of worship and respect, they were called *Ocllo*, which was a name held sacred in their idolatry " ; but if they lost their virtue, they were burnt alive or cast into " the lake of lions." [3]

Among the Guanches of the Canary Islands there were virgins, called Magades or Harimagades, who presided over the cult under the direction of the high-priest, and there were other virgins, highly respected, whose function was to pour water over the heads of newborn children, and who could abandon their office and marry whenever they pleased.[4] The priestesses of the Tshi- and Ewe-speaking peoples on the West Coast of Africa are forbidden to marry.[5] In a wood near Cape Padron, in Lower Guinea, lives a priestly king who is allowed neither to leave his house nor to touch a woman.[6]

In ancient Persia there were sun priestesses who were obliged to refrain from intercourse with men.[7] The nine priestesses of the oracle of a Gallic deity in Sena were devoted to perpetual virginity.[8] The Romans had their Vestal virgins, whose office, according to tradition, was instituted by Numa. They were compelled to continue

---

[1] Bancroft, *op. cit.* iii. 473. Lopez Cogolludo, *Historia de Yucathan*, p. 198.
[2] Garcilasso de la Vega, *op. cit.* i. 291 *sqq.*
[3] *Ibid.* i. 305.
[4] Bory de St. Vincent, *Essais sur les Isles Fortunées*, p. 96 *sq.*
[5] Ellis, *Tshi-speaking Peoples*, p.

121. *Idem, Ewe-speaking Peoples*, p. 142.
[6] Bastian, *Die deutsche Expedition an der Loango-Küste*, i. 287 *sq.*
[7] Justin, quoted by Justi, ' Die Weltgeschichte des Tabari,' in *Das Ausland*, 1875, p. 307.
[8] Pomponius Mela, *De situ orbis*, iii. 6.

unmarried during thirty years, which time they employed in offering sacrifices and performing other rites ordained by the law ; and if they suffered themselves to be debauched they were delivered up to the most miserable death, being placed in a subterraneous cell, in their funeral attire, without any sepulchral column, funeral rites, or other customary solemnities.[1] After the expiration of the term of thirty years they might marry on quitting the ensigns of their priesthood ; but we are told that very few did this, as those who did suffered calamities which were regarded as ominous by the rest, and induced them to remain virgins in the temple of the goddess till their death.[2] In Greece priestesses were not infrequently required to be virgins, if not for their whole life, at any rate for the duration of their priesthood.[3] Tertullian writes :—— " To the Achaean Juno, at the town Aegium, a virgin is allotted ; and the priestesses who rave at Delphi know not marriage. We know that widows minister to the African Ceres ; they not only withdraw from their still living husbands, but they even introduce other wives to them in their own room, all contact with males, even as far as the kiss of their sons, being forbidden them. . . . We have heard, too, of continent men, and among others the priests of the famous Egyptian bull." [4] There were eunuch priests connected with the cults of the Ephesian Artemis,[5] the Phrygian Cybele,[6] and the Syrian Astarte.[7]

Among the Todas of the Neilgherry Hills the " dairyman " or priest is bound to a celibate existence ;[8] and

[1] Dionysius of Halicarnassus, *Antiquitates Romanæ*, ii. 64 *sqq.* Plutarch, *Numa*, x. 7 *sqq.*

[2] Dionysius of Halicarnassus, ii. 67.

[3] Strabo, xiv. 1. 23. Müller, *Das sexuelle Leben der alten Kulturvölker*, p. 44 *sqq.* Blümner, *Home Life of the Ancient Greeks*, p. 325. Götte, *Das Delphische Orakel*, p. 78 *sq.*

[4] Tertullian, *Ad uxorem*, i. 6 (Migne, *Patrologiæ cursus*, i. 1284). *Idem, De exhortatione castitatis*, 13 (Migne, ii. 928 *sq.*). Cf. *Idem, De monogamia*, 17 (Migne, ii. 953).

[5] Strabo, xiv. 1. 23.

[6] Arnobius, *Adversus gentes*, v. 7 (Migne, *op. cit.* v. 1095 *sqq.*). Farnell, ' Sociological Hypotheses concerning the Position of Women in Ancient Religion,' in *Archiv f. Religionswiss.* vii. 78.

[7] Lucian, *De dea Syria*, 15, 27, 50 *sqq.*

[8] Thurston, ' Anthropology of the Todas and Kotas,' in the Madras Government Museum's *Bulletin*, i. 169, 170, 193. Rivers, *Todas*, pp. 80, 99, 236.

among the Hindus, in spite of the great honour in which
marriage is held, celibacy has always commanded respect in
instances of extraordinary sanctity.[1] Those of the Sann-
yāsis who are known to lead their lives in perfect celibacy
receive on that account marks of distinguished honour and
respect.[2] Already the time-honoured Indian institution of
the four Āśramas contained the germ of monastic celibacy,
the Brahmacārin, or student, being obliged to observe
absolute chastity during the whole course of his study.[3]
The idea was further developed in Jainism and Buddhism.
The Jain monk was to renounce all sexual pleasures,
" either with gods, or men, or animals " ; not to give way
to sensuality ; not to discuss topics relating to women ; not
to contemplate the forms of women.[4] Buddhism regards
sensuality as altogether incompatible with wisdom and
holiness ; it is said that " a wise man should avoid married
life as if it were a burning pit of live coals." [5] According
to the legend, Buddha's mother, who was the best and
purest of the daughters of men, had no other sons, and her
conception was due to supernatural causes.[6] One of the
fundamental duties of monastic life, by an infringement of
which the guilty person brings about his inevitable
expulsion from Buddha's order, is that " an ordained monk
may not have sexual intercourse,not even with an animal."[7]
In Tibet some sects of the Lamas are allowed to marry,
but those who do not are considered more holy ; and in
every sect the nuns must take a vow of absolute continence.[8]
The Buddhist priests of Ceylon are totally debarred from
women.[9] Chinese law enjoins celibacy on all priests,
Buddhist or Taouist.[10] And among the immortals of

[1] Monier-Williams, *Buddhism*, p.
88.
[2] Dubois, *op. cit.* p. 133. Cf.
Monier-Williams, *Brāhmanism and
Hindūism*, p. 261.
[3] Kern, *Manual of Indian Buddhism*, p. 73.
[4] Hopkins, *Religions of India*, p.
294.
[5] Dhammika-Sutta, 21, quoted by
Monier-Williams, *Buddhism*, p. 88.

[6] Rhys Davids, *Hibbert Lectures on
Buddhism*, p. 148.
[7] Oldenberg, *Buddha*, p. 350 sq.
[8] Wilson, *Abode of Snow*, p. 213.
[9] Percival, *Account of the Island of
Ceylon*, p. 202.
[10] *Ta Tsing Leu Lee*, sec. cxiv. p.
118. Medhurst, ' Marriage in China,'
in *Trans. Roy. Asiatic Soc. China
Branch*, iv. 18. Davis, *China*, ii. 53.

Taouism there are some women also, who have led an extraordinarily ascetic life.[1]

A small class of Hebrews held the idea that marriage is impure. The Essenes, says Josephus, " reject pleasure as an evil, but esteem continence and the conquest over our passions to be virtue. They neglect wedlock." [2] This doctrine exercised no influence on Judaism, but probably much upon Christianity. St. Paul considered celibacy to be preferable to marriage. " He that giveth her (his virgin) in marriage doeth well ; but he that giveth her not in marriage doeth better." [3] " It is good for a man not to touch a woman. Nevertheless, to avoid fornication, let each man have his own wife, and let each woman have her own husband." [4] If the unmarried and widows cannot contain let them marry, " for it is better to marry than to burn."[5] These and other passages [6] in the New Testament inspired a general enthusiasm for virginity. Commenting on the words of the Apostle, Tertullian points out that what is better is not necessarily good. It is better to lose one eye than two, but neither is good ; so also, though it is better to marry than to burn, it is far better neither to marry nor to burn.[7] Marriage " consists of that which is the essence of fornication " ;[8] whereas continence " is a means whereby a man will traffic in a mighty substance of sanctity."[9] The body which our Lord wore and in which He carried on the conflict of life in this world He put on from a holy virgin ; and John the Baptist, Paul, and all the others " whose names are in the book of life " [10] cherished and loved virginity.[11] Virginity works miracles : Mary, the sister of Moses, leading the female band, passed on

---

[1] Réville, *La Religion Chinoise*, p. 451 *sq.*
[2] Josephus, *De bello Judaico*, ii. 8. 2. See also Solinus, *Collectanea rerum memorabilium*, xxxv. 9 *sq.*
[3] I *Corinthians*, vii. 38.
[4] *Ibid.* vii. 1 *sq.*
[5] *Ibid.* vii. 9.
[6] *St. Matthew*, xix. 12. *Revelation*, xiv. 4 ; &c.
[7] Tertullian, *Ad uxorem*, i. 3

(Migne, *op. cit.* i. 1278 *sq.*). *Idem, De monogamia*, 3 (Migne, ii. 932 *sq.*).
[8] *Idem, De exhortatione castitatis*, 9 (Migne, *op. cit.* ii. 925).
[9] *Idem, De exhortatione castitatis*, 10 (Migne, *op. cit.* ii. 925).
[10] *Philippians*, iv. 3.
[11] St. Clement of Rome, *Epistola I. ad virgines*, 6 (Migne, *op. cit.* Ser. Græca, i. 392).

foot over the straits of the sea, and by the same grace
Thecla was reverenced even by lions, so that the unfed
beasts, lying at the feet of their prey, underwent a holy
fast, neither with wanton look nor sharp claw venturing to
harm the virgin.[1] Virginity is like a spring flower, always
softly exhaling immortality from its white petals.[2] The
Lord himself opens the kingdoms of the heavens to
eunuchs.[3] If Adam had preserved his obedience to the
Creator he would have lived for ever in a state of virgin
purity, and some harmless mode of vegetation would have
peopled paradise with a race of innocent and immortal
beings.[4] It is true that, though virginity is the shortest
way to the camp of the faithful, the way of matrimony
also arrives there, by a longer circuit.[5] Tertullian himself
opposed the Marcionites, who prohibited marriage among
themselves and compelled those who were married to
separate before they were received by baptism into the
community.[6] And in the earlier part of the fourth century
the Council of Gangra expressly condemned anyone who
maintained that marriage prevented a Christian from
entering the kingdom of God.[7] But, at the end of the
same century, a council also excommunicated the monk
Jovinian because he denied that virginity was more
meritorious than marriage.[8] The use of marriage was
permitted to man only as a necessary expedient for the
continuance of the human species, and as a restraint,

---

[1] St. Ambrose, *Epistola LXIII.*
34 (Migne, *op. cit.* xvi. 1198 *sq.*).
[2] Methodius, *Convivium decem virginum*, vii. 1 (Migne, *op. cit.* Ser.
Græca, xviii. 125).
[3] Tertullian, *De monogamia*, 3
(Migne, *op. cit.* ii. 932).
[4] This opinion was held by Gregory
of Nyssa and, in a later time, by
John of Damascus. It was opposed
by Thomas Aquinas, who maintained that the human race was
from the beginning propagated by
means of sexual intercourse, but
that such intercourse was originally
free from all carnal desire (von
Eicken, *Geschichte der mittelalterlichen Weltanschauung*, p. 437 *sq.* ;
see also Gibbon, *History of the*

*Decline and Fall of the Roman
Empire*, ii. 186).
[5] St. Ambrose, *Epistola LXIII.* 40
(Migne, *op. cit.* xvi. 1200).
[6] Tertullian, *Adversus Marcionem*,
i. 1, 29 ; iv. 11 ; &c. (Migne, *op. cit.*
ii. 247, 280 *sqq.*, 382). *Idem, De
monogamia*, 1, 15 (Migne, ii. 931,
950). *Cf.* Irenaeus, *Contra Hæreses*,
i. 28. 1 (Migne, *op. cit.* Ser. Græca,
vii. 690 *sq.*) ; Clement of Alexandria, *Stromata*, iii. 3 (Migne, *op. cit.*
Ser. Græca, viii. 1113 *sqq.*).
[7] *Concilium Gangrense*, can. 1
(Labbe-Mansi, *Sacrorum Conciliorum collectio*, ii. 1106).
[8] *Concilium Mediolanense*, A.D. 390
(Labbe-Mansi, *op. cit.* iii. 689 *sq.*).

however imperfect, on the natural licentiousness of desire.[1] The procreation of children is the measure of a Christian's indulgence in appetite, just as the husbandman throwing the seed into the ground awaits the harvest, not sowing more upon it.[2]

These opinions led by degrees to the obligatory celibacy of the secular and regular clergy. The conviction that a second marriage of a priest, or the marriage of a priest with a widow, is unlawful, seems to have existed from the earliest period of the Church ;[3] and as early as the beginning of the fourth century a synod held in Elvira in Spain insisted on the absolute continence of the higher ecclesiastics.[4] The celibacy of the clergy in general was prescribed by Gregory VII., who "looked with abhorrence on the contamination of the holy sacerdotal character, even in its lowest degree, by any sexual connection." But in many countries this prescription was so strenuously resisted, that it could not be carried through till late in the thirteenth century.[5]

The practice of religious celibacy may be traced to several sources. In many cases the priestess is obviously regarded as married to the god whom she is serving, and is therefore forbidden to marry anybody else. In ancient Peru the Sun was the husband of the virgins dedicated to him.[6] They were obliged to be of the same blood as their consort, that is to say, daughters of the Incas. "For though they imagined that the Sun had children, they considered that they ought not to be bastards, with mixed divine and human blood. So the

---

[1] St. Justin, *Apologia I. pro Christianis*, 29 (Migne, *op. cit.* Ser. Græca, vi. 373). Clement of Alexandria, *Stromata*, ii. 23 (Migne, *op. cit.* Ser. Græca, viii. 1089). Gibbon, *op. cit.* ii. 186.

[2] Athenagoras, *Legatio pro Christianis*, 33 (Migne, *op. cit.* Ser. Græca, vi. 966).

[3] Lea, *Sacerdotal Celibacy in the Christian Church*, p. 37. Lecky, *History of European Morals*, ii. 328 *sq.*

[4] *Concilium Eliberitanum*, A.D. 305,

ch. 33 (Labbe-Mansi, *op. cit.* ii. 11) :—" Placuit in totum prohiberi episcopis, presbyteris, et diaconibus, vel omnibus clericis positis in ministerio, abstinere se a conjugibus suis, et non generare filios : quicumque vero fecerit, ab honore clericatus exterminetur."

[5] Gieseler, *Text-Book of Ecclesiastical History*, ii. 275. Milman, *History of Latin Christianity*, ii. 150.

[6] Garcilasso de la Vega, *op. cit.* i. 297.

virgins were of necessity legitimate and of the blood royal, which was the same as being of the family of the Sun."[1] And the crime of violating the virgins dedicated to the Sun was the same and punished in the same severe manner as the crime of violating the women of the Inca.[2] Concerning the priestesses of the Tshi-speaking peoples of the Gold Coast, Major Ellis remarks that the reason for their celibacy appears to be that " a priestess belongs to the god she serves, and therefore cannot become the property of a man, as would be the case if she married one."[3] So also the Ewe-speaking peoples of the Slave Coast regard the women dedicated to a god as his wives.[4] In the great temple of Jupiter Belus, we are told, a single woman used to sleep, whom the god had chosen for himself out of all the women of the land ; and it was believed that he came down in person to sleep with her. " This," Herodotus says, " is like the story told by the Egyptians of what takes place in their city of Thebes, where a woman always passes the night in the temple of the Theban Jupiter. In each case the woman is said to be debarred all intercourse with men."[5] In the Egyptian texts there are frequent references to " the divine consort," *neter hemt*, a position which was generally occupied by the ruling queen, and the king was believed to be the offspring of such a union.[6] As Plutarch states, the Egyptians thought it quite possible for a woman to be impregnated by the approach of some divine spirit, though they denied that a man could have corporeal intercourse with a goddess.[7] Nor was the idea of a nuptial relation between a woman and the deity foreign to the early Christians. St. Cyprian speaks of women who had no husband and lord but Christ, with whom they lived in a spiritual matrimony—who had " dedicated themselves to Christ, and, retiring from carnal

[1] *Ibid.* i. 292.
[2] *Ibid.* i. 300.
[3] Ellis, *Tshi-speaking Peoples*, p. 121.
[4] *Idem, Ewe-speaking Peoples*, pp. 140, 142.

[5] Herodotus, i. 181 *sq.*
[6] Wiedemann, *Herodots zweites Buch*, p. 268. *Cf.* Erman, *Life in Ancient Egypt*, p. 295 *sq.*
[7] Plutarch, *Numa*, iv. 5. *Idem, Symposiaca problemata*, viii. 1. 6 *sq.*

lust, vowed themselves to God in flesh and spirit."[1] In the following words he condemns the cohabitation of such virgins with unmarried ecclesiastics, under the pretence of a purely spiritual connection:—" If a husband come and see his wife lying with another man, is he not indignant and maddened, and does he not in the violence of his jealousy perhaps even seize the sword ? What ? How indignant and angered then must Christ our Lord and Judge be, when He sees a virgin, dedicated to Himself, and consecrated to His holiness, lying with a man ! and what punishments does He threaten against such impure connections. . . . She who has been guilty of this crime is an adulteress, not against a husband, but Christ."[2] According to the gospel of Pseudo-Matthew, the Virgin Mary had in a similar manner dedicated herself as a virgin to God.[3] The idea that the deity is jealous of the chastity of his or her servants may also perhaps be at the bottom of the Greek custom according to which the hierophant and the other priests of Demeter were restrained from conjugal intercourse and washed their bodies with hemlock-juice in order to kill their passions,[4] as also of the rule which required the priests of certain goddesses to be eunuchs.[5]

Religious celibacy is further connected with the idea that sexual intercourse is defiling. In Efate, of the New Hebrides, it is regarded as something unclean.[6] The Tahitians believed that if a man refrained from all connections with women some months before death, he passed

[1] St. Cyprian, *De habitu virginum*, 4, 22 (Migne, *op. cit.* iv. 443, 462). *Cf.* Methodius, *Convivium decem virginum*, vii. 1 (Migne, *op. cit.* Ser. Græca, xviii. 125).

[2] St. Cyprian, *Epistola LXII.*, *ad Pomponium de virginibus*, 3 *sq.* (Migne, *op. cit.* iv. 368 *sqq.*). See also Neander, *General History of the Christian Religion and Church*, i. 378. The Council of Elvira decreed that such fallen virgins, if they refused to return back to their former condition, should be denied communion even at the moment of death (*Concilium Eliberitanum*, A.D. 305, ch. 13 [Labbe-Mansi, *op. cit.*

ii. 8]).

[3] *Gospel of Pseudo-Matthew*, 8 (*Ante-Nicene Christian Library*, xvi. 25). See also *Gospel of the Nativity of Mary*, 7 (*ibid.* xvi. 57 *sq.*).

[4] Wachsmuth, *Hellenische Alterthumskunde*, ii. 560.

[5] *Cf.* Lactantius, *Divinæ Institutiones*, i. 17 (Migne, *op. cit.* vi. 206) : —" Deum mater et amavit formosum adolescentem, et eumdem cum pellice deprehensum exsectis virilibus semivirum reddidit ; et ideo nunc sacra ejus a Gallis sacerdotibus celebrantur."

[6] Macdonald, *Oceania*, p. 181.

immediately into his eternal mansion without any purification.[1] Herodotus writes :—" As often as a Babylonian
has had intercourse with his wife, he sits down before a
censer of burning incense, and the woman sits opposite to
him. At dawn of day they wash ; for till they are washed
they will not touch any of their common vessels. This
practice is also observed by the Arabs." [2] Among the
Hebrews both the man and woman had to bathe themselves in water, and were " unclean until the even." [3] The
idea that sexual intercourse is unclean implies that some
degree of supernatural danger is connected with it ; [4] and,
as Mr. Crawley has pointed out, the notion of danger may
develop into that of sinfulness.[5] Where woman is regarded
as an unclean being [6] it is obvious that intercourse with
her should be considered polluting, but this is not a
sufficient explanation of the idea of sexual uncleanness. A
polluting effect is ascribed to any discharge of sexual
matter[7]—originally no doubt on account of its mysterious propensities and the veil of mystery which
surrounds the whole sexual nature of man.

The idea of sexual defilement is particularly conspicuous
in connection with religious observances. It is a common
rule that he who performs a sacred act or enters a holy
place must be ceremonially clean,[8] and no kind of uncleanness is to be avoided more carefully than sexual pollution.
Among the Chippewyans, " if a chief is anxious to know
the disposition of his people towards him, or if he wishes
to settle any difference between them, he announces his
intention of opening his medicine-bag and smoking in his

[1] Cook, *Voyage to the Pacific Ocean*, ii. 164.
[2] Herodotus, i. 198.
[3] *Leviticus*, xv. 18.
[4] The danger attributed to sexual intercourse has been much empha-sised by Mr. Crawley in *The Mystic Rose*. See also Westermarck, *Marriage Ceremonies in Morocco*.
[5] Crawley, *op. cit.* p. 214.
[6] See *supra*, i. 663 *sqq.*
[7] Gregory III., *Judicia congrua pœnitentibus*, ch. 24 (Labbe-Mansi,

op. cit. xii. 293) :—" In somno pec-cans, si ex cogitatione pollutus, viginti duos psalmos cantet : si in somno peccans sine cogitatione, duo-decim psalmos cantet." *Pœnitentiale Pseudo-Theodori*, xxviii. 25 (Wasser-schleben, *Bussordnungen der abend-ländischen Kirche*, p. 600) :—" Qui in somno, non voluntate, pollutus sit, surgat, cantetque vii. psalmos pœnitentiales." *Cf. ibid.* xxviii. 6, 33 (Wasserschleben, p. 559 *sq.*).
[8] See *supra*, ii. 294, 295, 352 *sq.*

sacred stem. . . . No one can avoid attending on these occasions ; but a person may attend and be excused from assisting at the ceremonies, by acknowledging that he has not undergone the necessary purification. The having cohabited with his wife, or any other woman, within twenty-four hours preceding the ceremony, renders him unclean, and, consequently, disqualifies him from performing any part of it." [1] Herodotus tells us that the Egyptians, like the Greeks, " made it a point of religion to have no converse with women in the sacred places, and not to enter them without washing, after such converse." [2] This statement is corroborated by a passage in the ' Book of the Dead.' [3] In Greece [4] and India [5] those who took part in certain religious festivals were obliged to be continent for some time previously. Before entering the sanctuary of Mên Tyrannos, whose worship was extended over the whole of Asia Minor, the worshipper had to abstain from garlic, pork, and women, and had to wash his head.[6] Among the Hebrews it was a duty incumbent upon all to be ritually clean before entering the temple— to be free from sexual defilement,[7] leprosy,[8] and the pollution produced by the association with corpses of human beings, of all animals not permitted for food, and of those permitted animals which had died a natural death or been killed by wild beasts ;[9] and eating of the consecrated bread was interdicted to persons who had not been continent for some time previously.[10] A Muhammedan would remove any defiled garment before he commences his prayer, or otherwise abstain from praying altogether ; he would not dare to approach the sanctuary of a saint in a state of sexual uncleanness; and sexual intercourse is forbidden for those who make the pilgrimage to Mecca.[11]

[1] Mackenzie, *Voyages to the Frozen and Pacific Oceans*, p. cii. *sq.*
[2] Herodotus, ii. 64.
[3] Wiedemann, *Herodots zweites Buch*, p. 269 *sq.*
[4] Wachsmuth, *op. cit.* ii. 560.
[5] Oldenberg, *Die Religion des Veda*, p. 411.
[6] Foucart, *Des associations reli-*
gieuses chez les Grecs, pp. 119, 123 *sq.*
[7] *Leviticus*, chs. xii., xv.
[8] *Ibid.* ch. xiii. *sq.*
[9] *Ibid.* xi. 24 *sqq.* ; xvii. 15. *Numbers*, xix. 14 *sqq.* Montefiore, *Hibbert Lectures on the Religion of the Ancient Hebrews*, p. 476.
[10] 1 *Samuel*, xxi. 4 *sq.*
[11] *Koran*, ii. 193.

The Christians prescribed strict continence as a preparation for baptism [1] and the partaking of the Eucharist.[2]
They further enjoined that no married persons should
participate in any of the great festivals of the Church if
the night before they had lain together ; [3] and in the
' Vision ' of Alberic, dating from the twelfth century, a
special place of torture, consisting of a lake of mingled lead,
pitch, and resin, is represented as existing in hell for the
punishment of married people who have had intercourse
on Sundays, church festivals, or fast-days.[4] They abstained
from the marriage-bed at other times also, when they were
disposed more freely to give themselves to prayer.[5] Newly
married couples were admonished to practise continence
during the wedding day and the night following, out of
reverence for the sacrament ; and in some instances their
abstinence lasted even for two or three days.[6]

Holiness is a delicate quality which is easily destroyed
if anything polluting is brought into contact with the
holy object or person. The Moors believe that if anybody who is sexually unclean enters a granary the grain
will lose its *baraka*, or holiness. A similar idea probably
underlies the belief prevalent among various peoples that
incontinence, and especially illicit love, injures the
harvest. [7] In Efate, *namim*, or uncleanness, supposed to be
contracted in various emergencies, was especially avoided

[1] St. Augustine, *De fide et operibus*,
vi. 8 (Migne, *op. cit.* xl. 202).
[2] St. Jerome, *Epistola XLVIII.* 15
(Migne, *op. cit.* xxii. 505 *sq.*).
[3] Lecky, *History of European
Morals*, ii. 324. St. Gregory the
Great, *Dialogi*, i. 10 (Migne, *op. cit.*
lxxvii. 200 *sq.*).
[4] Albericus, *Visio*, ch. 5, p. 17.
Delepierre, *L'enfer décrit par ceux
qui l'ont vu*, p. 57 *sq.* On this subject see also Müller, *Das sexuelle
Leben der christlichen Kulturvölker*,
pp. 52, 53, 120 *sq.*
[5] St. Jerome, *Epistola XLVIII.* 15
(Migne, *op. cit.* xxii. 505). Fleury,
*Manners and Behaviour of the
Christians*, p. 75.
[6] Muratori, *Dissertazioni sopra le
antichità italiane*, 20, vol. i. 347.

[7] Frazer, *Golden Bough*, ii. 209 *sqq.*
This is in my opinion a more natural
explanation than the one suggested
by Sir J. G. Frazer, namely, that uncivilised man imagines " that the
vigour which he refuses to expend in
reproducing his own kind, will form
as it were a store of energy whereby
other creatures, whether vegetable
or animal, will somehow benefit in
propagating their species." This
theory entirely fails to account for
the fact that illicit love, by preference, is supposed to mar the fertility
of the earth and to blight the crops
—a belief which is in full accordance
with my own explanation, in so far
as such love is considered particularly polluting.

by the sacred men, because it was believed to destroy their sacredness.[1] The priestly taboos, of which Sir J. G. Frazer has given such an exhaustive account in 'The Golden Bough,' have undoubtedly in a large measure a similar origin. Nay, it seems that pollution not only deprives the holy person of his holiness, but is also supposed to injure him in a more positive way. When the supreme pontiff in the kingdom of Congo left his residence to visit other places within his jurisdiction, all married people had to observe strict continence the whole time he was out, as it was believed that any act of incontinence would prove fatal to him.[2] In self-defence, therefore, gods and holy persons try to prevent polluted individuals from approaching them, and their worshippers are naturally anxious to do the same. But apart from the resentment which the sacred being would feel against the defiler, it appears that holiness is supposed to react quite mechanically against pollution, to the destruction or discomfort of the polluted individual. All Moors are convinced that anyone who in a state of sexual uncleanness dared to visit a saint's tomb would be struck by the saint; but the Arabs of Dukkâla, in Southern Morocco, also believe that if an unclean person rides a horse some accident will happen to him on account of the *baraka* with which the horse is endowed. It should further be noticed that, owing to the injurious effect of pollution upon holiness, an act generally regarded as sacred would, if performed by an unclean individual, lack that magic efficacy which otherwise would be ascribed to it. Muhammed represented ceremonial cleanliness as " one-half of the faith and the key of prayer."[3] The Moors say that a scribe is afraid of evil spirits only when he is sexually unclean, because then his reciting of passages of the Koran—the most powerful weapon against such spirits —would be of no avail. The Syrian philosopher Jam-

[1] Macdonald, *Oceania*, p. 181.
[2] Labat, *Relation historique de l'Ethiopie occidentale*, i. 259 sq.
[3] Pool, *Studies in Mohammedanism*, p. 27.

blichus speaks of the belief that " the gods do not hear him who invokes them, if he is impure from venereal connections." [1] A similar notion prevailed among the early Christians ; with reference to a passage in the First Epistle of the Corinthians,[2] Tertullian remarks that the Apostle added the recommendation of a temporary abstinence for the sake of adding an efficacy to prayers.[3] To the same class of beliefs belongs the notion that a sacrificial victim should be clean and without blemish.[4] The Chibchas of Bogota considered that the most valuable sacrifice they could offer was that of a youth who had never had intercourse with a woman.[5]

If ceremonial cleanliness is required even of the ordinary worshipper it is all the more indispensable in the case of a priest ;[6] and of all kinds of uncleanness none is to be more carefully avoided than sexual pollution. Sometimes admission into the priesthood is to be preceded by a period of continence.[7] In the Marquesas Islands no one could become a priest without having lived chastely for several years previously.[8] Among the Tshi-speaking peoples of the Gold Coast men and women, in order to become members of the priesthood, have to pass through a long novitiate, generally from two to three years, during which they live in retirement and are instructed by the priests in the secrets of the craft ; and " the people believe that, during this period of retirement and study, the novices must keep their bodies pure, and refrain from all commerce with the other sex."[9] The Huichols of Mexico, again, are of opinion that a man who wishes to become a shaman must be faithful to his wife for five years, and that, if he violates this rule, he is sure to be taken ill and will lose the power of healing.[10] In ancient Mexico the priests, all

---

[1] Jamblichus, De mysteriis, iv. 11.
[2] 1 Corinthians, vii. 5.
[3] Tertullian, De exhortatione castitatis, 10 (Migne, op. cit. ii. 926).
[4] See supra, ii. 295 sq.
[5] Simon, quoted by Waitz, Anthropologie der Naturvölker, iv. 363. See infra, Additional Notes.

[6] Cf. supra, ii. 352 sq.
[7] Cf. Landtman, op. cit. p. 118 sqq.
[8] Waitz - Gerland, Anthropologie der Naturvölker, vi. 387.
[9] Ellis, Tshi-speaking Peoples, p. 120.
[10] Lumholtz, Unknown Mexico, ii. 236.

the time that they were employed in the service of the temple, abstained from all other women but their wives, and " even affected so much modesty and reserve, that when they met a woman they fixed their eyes on the ground that they might not see her. Any incontinence amongst the priests was severely punished. The priest who, at Teohuacan, was convicted of having violated his chastity, was delivered up by the priests to the people, who at night killed him by the bastinado." [1] Among the Kotas of the Neilgherry Hills the priests—who, unlike the " dairymen " of their Toda neighbours are not celibates— are at the great festival in honour of Kāmatarāya forbidden to live or hold intercourse with their wives for fear of pollution, and are then even obliged to cook their meals themselves.[2] It seems that, according to the Anatolian religion, married *hieroi* had to separate from their wives during the period they were serving at the temple.[3] The Hebrew priest should avoid all unchastity ; he was not allowed to marry a harlot, or a profane, or a divorced wife,[4] and the high-priest was also forbidden to marry a widow.[5] Nay, even in a priest's daughter unchastity was punished with excessive severity, because she had profaned her father ; she was to be burned.[6]

Carried further, the idea underlying all these rules and practices led to the notions that celibacy is more pleasing to God than marriage,[7] and that it is a religious duty for those members of the community whose special office is to attend to the sacred cult. For a nation like the Jews, whose ambition was to live and to multiply, celibacy could never become an ideal ; whereas the Christians, who pro- fessed the most perfect indifference to all earthly matters, found no difficulty in glorifying a state which, however opposed it was to the interests of the race and the nation, made men pre-eminently fit to approach their god. Indeed,

[1] Clavigero, *op. cit.* i. 274.
[2] Thurston, in the Madras Govern- ment Museum's *Bulletin,* i. 193.
[3] Ramsay, *Cities and Bishoprics of Ph ygia,* i. 136, 137, 150 *sq.*

[4] *Leviticus,* xxi. 7.
[5] *Ibid.* xxi. 14.
[6] *Ibid.* xxi. 9.
[7] *Cf. supra,* ii. 358.

far from being a benefit to the kingdom of God by propagating the species, sexual intercourse was on the contrary
detrimental to it by being the great transmitter of the sin
of our first parents. This argument, however, was of a
comparatively late origin. Pelagius himself almost rivalled
St. Augustine in his praise of virginity, which he considered
the great test of that strength of free-will which he asserted to be at most only weakened by the fall of Adam.[1]

Religious celibacy is, moreover, enjoined or commended
as a means of self-mortification supposed to appease an
angry god, or with a view to raising the spiritual nature
of man by suppressing one of the strongest of all sensual
appetites. Thus we find in various religions celibacy side
by side with other ascetic observances practised for similar
purposes. Among the early Christians those young
women who took a vow of chastity " did not look upon
virginity as any thing if it were not attended with great
mortification, with silence, retirement, poverty, labour,
fastings, watchings, and continual praying. They were
not esteemed as virgins who would not deny themselves
the common diversions of the world, even the most
innocent." [2] Tertullian enumerates virginity, widowhood,
and the modest restraint in secret on the marriage-bed
among those fragrant offerings acceptable to God which
the flesh performs to its own especial suffering.[3] Finally,
it was argued that marriage prevents a person from
serving God perfectly, because it induces him to occupy
himself too much with worldly things.[4] Though not
contrary to the act of charity or the love of God, says
Thomas Aquinas, it is nevertheless an obstacle to it.[5]
This was one, but certainly not the only, cause of the
obligatory celibacy which the Christian Church imposed
upon her clergy.

[1] Milman, *op. cit.* i. 151, 153.
[2] Fleury, *op. cit.* p. 128 *sq.*
[3] Tertullian, *De resurrectione carnis*, 8 (Migne, *op. cit.* ii. 806).
[4] Vincentius Bellovacensis, *Speculum naturale*, xxx. 43. See also von
Eicken, *op. cit.* p. 445.
[5] Thomas Aquinas, *Summa theologica*, ii.-ii. 184. 3.

CHAPTER XLII

FREE LOVE—ADULTERY

HARDLY less variable than the moral ideas relating to marriage are those concerning sexual relations of a non-matrimonial character.

Among many uncivilised peoples both sexes enjoy perfect freedom previous to marriage, and in some cases it is considered almost dishonourable for a girl to have no lover.

The East African Barea and Kunáma do not regard it as in the least disreputable for a girl to become pregnant, nor do they punish nor censure the seducer.[1] Among the Wanyoro "it constantly happens that young girls spend the night with their lovers, only returning to their father's house in the morning, and this is not considered scandalous.[2] The Wadigo regard it as disgraceful, or at least as ridiculous, for a girl to enter into marriage as a virgin.[3] Among the Bakongo, "womanly chastity is unknown, and a woman's honour is measured by the price she costs." [4] Over nearly the whole of British Central Africa, says Sir H. Johnston, "before a girl is become a woman (that is to say before she is able to conceive) it is a matter of absolute indifference what she does, and scarcely any girl remains a virgin after about five years of age." [5] Among the Baronga "l'opinion publique se moque des gens continents plus qu'elle ne les admire." [6] According to Mr. Warner, "seduction of virgins, and cohabiting with unmarried women and

[1] Munzinger, *Ostafrikanische Stu-ien*, p. 524.
[2] *Emin Pasha in Central Africa*, p. 82. *Cf. ibid.* p. 208 (Monbuttu).
[3] Baumann, *Usambara*, p. 152.

[4] Johnston, *British Central Africa*, p. 405.
[5] *Ibid.* p. 409, note.
[6] Junod, *Les Ba-Ronga*, p. 29.

widows, are not punishable by Kafir law, neither does any disgrace attach to either sex by committing such acts."[1] In Madagascar " continence is not supposed to exist in either sex before marriage, . . . and its absence is not regarded as a vice."[2] Among the Maoris of New Zealand " girls were at perfect liberty to act as they pleased until married," and chastity in single women was held of little account.[3] In the Tonga Islands unmarried women might bestow their favours upon whomsoever they pleased without any opprobrium, although it was thought shameful for a woman frequently to change her lover.[4] In the Solomon Islands " female chastity is a virtue that would sound strangely in the ear of the native " ; and in St. Christoval and the adjacent islands, " for two or three years after a girl has become eligible for marriage she distributes her favours amongst all the young men of the village."[5] In the Malay Archipelago intercourse between unmarried people is very commonly considered neither a crime nor a disgrace ;[6] and the same is perhaps even more generally the case among the uncivilised races of India and Indo-China.[7] Among the Angami Nagas, for instance, " girls consider short hair, the symbol of virginity, a disgrace, and are anxious to become entitled to wear it long ; men are desirous before marriage to have proof that their wives will not be barren. . . . Chastity begins with marriage."[8] The Jakuts see nothing immoral in free love, provided only that nobody suffers material loss by it.[9] Among the Votyaks it is disgraceful for a girl to be little sought after by the young men, and it is honourable for her to have children ; she then gets a wealthier husband, and a higher price is paid for her to her father.[10] The Kamchadales set no great value on the virginity of their brides.[11] Of the Point Barrow Eskimo Mr. Murdoch writes :—" As to the relations between the sexes there seems to be the most complete absence of what we consider moral feelings. Promiscuous sexual

[1] Warner, in Maclean, *Compendium of Kafir Laws*, p. 63.
[2] Ellis, *History of Madagascar*, i. 137 *sq.*
[3] Taylor, *Te Ika a Maui*, p. 33. Gisborne, *Colony of New Zealand*, p. 27.
[4] Mariner, *Natives of the Tonga Islands*, ii. 174.
[5] Guppy, *Solomon Islands*, p. 43.
[6] Wilken, ' Plechtigheden en gebruiken bij verlovingen en huwelijken bij de volken van den Indischen Archipel,' in *Bijdragen tot de taal- land- en volkenkunde van Nederlandsch-Indië*, ser. v. vol. iv. 434 *sqq.*
[7] Westermarck, *History of Human Marriage*, p. 71. Crooke, *Tribes and Castes of the North-Western Provinces and Oudh*, i. p. clxxxiv.
[8] Prain, ' Angami Nagas,' in *Revue coloniale internationale*, v. 491 *sq.*
[9] Sumner, in *Jour. Anthr. Inst.* xxxi. 96.
[10] Buch, ' Die Wotjäken,' in *Acta Soc. Scientiarum Fennicæ*, xii. 509.
[11] Georgi, *Russia*, iii. 156.

intercourse between married or unmarried people, or even among children, appears to be looked upon simply as a matter for amusement. As far as we could learn, unchastity in a girl was considered nothing against her. The immorality of these people among themselves, as we witnessed it, seems too purely animal and natural to be of recent growth or the result of foreign influence. Moreover, a similar state of affairs has been observed among Eskimo elsewhere." [1]

Yet however commonly chastity is disregarded in the savage world, we must not suppose that such disregard is anything like a universal characteristic of the lower races. In a previous work I have given a list of numerous savage and barbarous peoples among whom unchastity before marriage is looked upon as a disgrace or a crime for a woman, sometimes punishable with banishment from the community or even with death ; [2] and it is noteworthy that to this group of peoples belong savages of so low a type as the Veddahs of Ceylon,[3] the Igorrotes of Luzon,[4] and certain Australian tribes.[5] I have also called attention to facts which seem to prove that in several cases the wantonness of savages is largely due to foreign influence. The pioneers of a " higher civilisation" are very frequently unmarried men who go out to make their living in un-civilised lands, and, though unwilling to contract regular marriages with native women, they have no objection to corrupting their morals.[6] Moreover, in many tribes the

[1] Murdoch, ' Ethnological Results of the Point Barrow Expedition,' in *Ann. Rep. Bur. Ethn.* ix. 419 *sq.* See also Turner, ' Ethnology of the Ungava District,' in *Ann. Rep. Bur. Ethn.* xi. 189 (Koksoagmyut) ; Parry, *Second Voyage for the Discovery of a North-West Passage*, p. 529 (Eskimo of Igloolik and Winter Island).

[2] Westermarck, *op. cit.* p. 61 *sqq.*

[3] Nevill, ' Vaeddas of Ceylon,' in *Taprobanian*, i. 178.

[4] Meyer, ' Igorrotes von Luzon,' in *Verhandl. Berliner Gesellsch. f. Anthrop.* 1883, p. 384 *sq.* Blumentritt, *Ethnographie der Philippinen*, p. 27.

[5] Westermarck, *op. cit.* p. 64 *sq.* Holden, in Taplin, *Folklore of the South Australian Aborigines,* p. 19.

[6] It is strange to hear from a modern student of anthropology, and especially from an Australian writer, that in sexual licence the savage has never anything to learn and that " all that the lower fringe of civilised men can do to harm the uncivilised is to stoop to the level of the latter instead of teaching them a better way " (Sutherland, *Origin and Growth of the Moral Instinct*, i. 186). Mr. Edward Stephens (' Aborigines of Australia,' in *Jour. & Proceed. Royal Soc. N. S. Wales*, xxiii. 480) has a very different story to tell with reference to the tribes which once inhabited the Adelaide Plains in South Australia and whose acquaintance he made more than half a century ago.

free intercourse which prevails between unmarried people is not of a promiscuous nature, and leads necessarily to marriage should the girl prove with child.[1] Nay, among various uncivilised races not only the girl, but the man who seduces her is subject to punishment or censure.

Among the East African Takue a seducer may have to pay the same sum as if he had killed the girl, although the fine is generally reduced to fifty cows.[2] Among the Beni Amer and Marea he is killed, together with the girl and the child.[3] In Tessaua a fine of 100,000 kurdi is imposed on the father of a bastard child.[4] Among the Beni Mzab a man who seduces a girl has to pay two hundred francs and is banished for four years.[5] Among the Tedâ he is exposed to the revenge of her father.[6] The Baziba look upon illegitimate intercourse between the sexes as the most serious offence, though no action is taken until the birth of a child ; "then the man and woman are bound hand and foot and thrown into Lake Victoria."[7] Among the Bakoki, whilst the girl was driven from home and remained for ever after an outcast, the man was fined three cows to her father and one to the chief.[8] Certain West African savages described by Mr. Winwood Reade, who banish from the clan a girl guilty of wantonness, inflict severe flogging on the seducer.[9] In Dahomey a man who seduces a girl is compelled by law to marry her and to pay eighty cowries to the parent or master.[10] Among some Kafir tribes the father or guardian of a woman who becomes pregnant can demand a fine of one head of cattle from the father of the child ;[11] whilst in the Gaika tribe the mere seduction of a virgin incurs the fine of three or four head of cattle.[12] Casalis mentions an interesting custom prevalent among the Basutos, which on the one hand illustrates the belief that sexual intercourse in certain circumstances exposes a person to supernatural danger, and on the other hand indicates that unchastity in unmarried men is not looked upon with perfect indifference :—Immediately after the birth of a child the fire of the dwelling was kindled afresh. " For this purpose it was necessary that a young man of chaste habits should rub two

[1] Westermarck, op. cit. pp. 23, 24, 71.
[2] Munzinger, Ostafrikanische Studien, p. 208.
[3] Ibid. p. 322.
[4] Barth, Reisen in Nord- und Central-Afrika, ii. 18.
[5] Chavanne, Die Sahara, p. 315.
[6] Nachtigal, Sahara und Sudan, i. 449.
[7] Cunningham, Uganda, p. 290.
[8] Ibid. p. 102.
[9] Reade, Savage Africa, p. 261.
[10] Forbes, Dahomey, i. 26.
[11] Warner, in Maclean, op. cit. p. 64.
[12] Brownlee, ibid. p. 112.

pieces of wood quickly one against another, until a flame sprung up, pure as himself. It was firmly believed that a premature death awaited him who should dare to take upon himself this office, after having lost his innocence. As soon, therefore, as a birth was proclaimed in the village, the fathers took their sons to undergo the ordeal. Those who felt themselves guilty confessed their crime, and submitted to be scourged rather than expose themselves to the consequences of a fatal temerity." [1] Livingstone, speaking of the good name which was given to him by the Bakwains, observes :—" No one ever gains much influence in this country without purity and uprightness. The acts of a stranger are keenly scrutinised by both young and old, and seldom is the judgment pronounced, even by the heathen, unfair or uncharitable. I have heard women speaking in admiration of a white man, because he was pure, and never was guilty of any secret immorality. Had he been, they would have known it, and, untutored heathen though they be, would have despised him in consequence." [2]

Of the Australian Maroura tribe, Lower Darling, we are told that before the advent of the whites " their laws were strict, especially those regarding young men and young women. It was almost death to a young lad or man who had sexual intercourse till married." [3] Among various tribes in Western Victoria " illegitimacy is rare, and is looked upon with such abhorrence that the mother is always severely beaten by her relatives, and sometimes put to death and burned. Her child is occasionally killed and burned with her. The father of the child is also punished with the greatest severity, and occasionally killed." [4]

In Nias the pregnancy of an unmarried girl is punished with death, inflicted not only upon her but upon the seducer as well.[5] Among the Bódo and Dhimáls of India chastity is prized in man and woman, married and unmarried.[6] Among the Tunguses " in irregular amours only the men are punished," the seducer being obliged either to purchase the girl at a certain price or, if he refuses, to submit to corporal punishment.[7] Among the Thlinkets, " if unmarried women prove frail the partner of their guilt, if discovered, is bound to make reparation to the parents, soothing their wounded honour with handsome

---

[1] Casalis, *Basutos*, p. 267 *sq.*
[2] Livingstone, *Missionary Travels*, p. 513.
[3] Holden, in Taplin, *Folklore of the South Australian Aborigines*, p. 19.
[4] Dawson, *Australian Aborigines*, p. 28.

[5] Wilken, in *Bijdragen tot de taal-land- en volkenkunde van Nederlandsch-Indië*, ser. v. vol. iv. 444.
[6] Hodgson, *Miscellaneous Essays*, i. 123.
[7] Georgi, *op. cit.* iii. 84.

presents." [1]   In certain North American tribes the seducer is said to be viewed with even more contempt than the girl whom he has dishonoured. [2]

Passing to more advanced races, we find that chastity is regarded as a duty for unmarried women, whilst a different standard of morality is generally applied to men. " Confucianism," says Mr. Griffis, " virtually admits two standards of morality, one for man, another for woman. . . . Chastity is a female virtue, it is a part of womanly duty, it has little or no relation to man personally." [3] Yet it is held up as an ideal even to men. It is said that in youth, when the physical powers are not yet settled, the superior man guards against lust. [4] Though licentious in their habits, the Chinese exalt and dignify chastity as a means of bringing the soul and body nearer to the highest excellence ; [5] one of their proverbs even maintains that " of the myriad vices, lust is the worst." [6] Chastity for its own sake, when defended by a woman at the expense of her life, meets with a reward at the hands of the Government. " If a woman "—so the Ordinances run—" be compelled by her husband to prostitute herself for money, and takes her own life in order to preserve her chastity, or if an unmarried virgin loses her life in defending herself against violation, an honorary gate shall be erected in each case near the door of the paternal dwelling." [7] According to the Chinese Penal Code, " criminal intercourse by mutual consent with an unmarried woman shall be punished with seventy blows," whilst the punishment for such intercourse with a married woman is eighty blows. [8]

Among the ancient Hebrews fornication was forbidden to women [9] but not to men. The action of Judah towards the supposed harlot on the way to Timnath is mentioned

[1] Douglas, quoted by Petroff, *Report on Alaska*, p. 177.
[2] Westermarck, *op. cit.* p. 66.
[3] Griffis, *Religions of Japan*, p. 149.
[4] *Lun Yü*, xvi. 7.
[5] Wells Williams, *Middle Kingdom*, ii. 193.
[6] Smith, *Proverbs of the Chinese*, p. 256.
[7] de Groot, *Religious System of China*, (vol. ii. book) i. 752 *sq.*
[8] *Ta Tsing Leu Lee*, sec. ccclxvi. p. 404.
[9] *Leviticus*, xix. 29. *Deuteronomy*, xxiii. 18.

as the most natural thing in the world,[1] even though
the perpetrator was a man of wealth and position, a man
whom his brethren " shall praise " and before whom his
" father's children shall bow down." [2] Throughout the
Muhammedan world chastity is regarded as an essential
duty for a woman.[3] In Persia an unmarried girl who
gàve birth to a child would surely be killed.[4] Among the
Fellaheen of Egypt a father or brother in most instances
punishes an unmarried daughter or sister who has been
guilty of incontinence by throwing her into the Nile with
a stone tied to her neck, or cutting her to pieces, and then
throwing her remains into the river.[5] Among the Jbâla
and Rif Berbers of Morocco she is also frequently killed.
For unmarried men, on the other hand, chastity is by
Muhammedans at most looked upon as an ideal, almost
out of reach. The Caliph Ali said that "with a man who is
modest and chaste nobody should find fault." [6] We are told
that the Muhammedans of India consider it inconceivable
that a Moslem should have illicit intercourse with a free
Muhammedan woman ;[7] but connections with slave girls
are regarded in a different light.

Among the Hindus sexual impurity is scarcely considered a sin in the men, but " in females nothing is
held more execrable or abominable. The unhappy
inhabitants of houses of ill fame are looked upon as the
most degraded of the human species." [8] In one of the
Pahlavi texts continence is recommended from the point
of view of prudence :—" Commit no lustfulness, so that
harm and regret may not reach thee from thine own
actions." [9] But in Zoroastrianism, also, chastity is chiefly
a female duty. It is written in the Avesta, " Any woman
that has given up her body to two men in one day is
sooner to be killed than a wolf, a lion, or a snake." [10]

---

[1] Genesis, xxxviii. 15 sqq.
[2] Ibid. xlix. 8.
[3] Burton, Sindh, p. 295.
[4] Polak, Persien, i. 217.
[5] Lane, Manners and Customs of the Modern Egyptians, p. 209.
[6] Ameer Ali, Ethics of Islâm, p. 30.
[7] Lane-Poole, Studies in a Mosque, p. 106.
[8] Calcutta Review, ii. 23. Dubois, Description of the Character, &c. of the People of India, p. 193. Cf. Laws of Manu, ix. 51 sq.
[9] Dînâ-î-Maînôgî Khirad, ii. 23 sq.
[10] Darmesteter, in Sacred Books of the East, iv. 206, n. 1.

Among the ancient Teutons an unmarried woman who belonged to an honourable family was severely punished for going wrong, and the seducer was exposed to the revenge of her family, or had to pay compensation for his deed.[1] The yet un-Romanised Saxons, down to the days of St. Boniface, compelled a maiden who had dishonoured her father's house, as well as an adulteress, to hang herself, after which her body was burned and her paramour hung over the blazing pile ; or she was scourged or cut with knives by all the women of the village till she was dead.[2]

In Greece the chastity of an unmarried girl was anxiously guarded.[3] According to Athenian law, the relatives of a maiden who had lost her virtue could with impunity kill the seducer on the spot.[4] Virginity was an object of worship. Chastity was the pre-eminent attribute of sanctity ascribed to Athene and Artemis, and the Parthenon, or virgin's temple, was the noblest religious edifice of Athens.[5] It is true that a certain class of courtesans occupied a remarkably high position in the social life of Greece, being admired and sought after even by the principal men. But they did so on account of their extraordinary beauty or their intellectual superiority; to the Greek mind the moral standard was by no means the only standard of excellence. The Romans, on the other hand, regarded the courtesan class with much contempt.[6] In A.D. 19 the profligacy of women was checked by stringent enactments, and it was provided that no woman whose grandfather, father, or husband had been a Roman knight should get money by prostitution.[7] The names of prostitutes had to be published on the aedile's list, as Tacitus says, " according to a recognised custom

[1] Brunner, *Deutsche Rechtsgeschichte*, ii. 659 *sqq.* Wilda, *Strafrecht der Germanen*, p. 799 *sqq.* Nordström, *Bidrag till den svenska samhälls-författningens historia*,ii.67. Maurer, *Bekehrung des Norwegischen Stammes*, ii. 154.
[2] Milman, *History of Latin Chrisanity*, ii. 54.

[3] See Denis, *Histoire des théories et des idées morales dans l'antiquité*, i. 69 *sq.*
[4] Schmidt, *Die Ethik der alten Griechen*, ii. 193.
[5] See Lecky, *History of European Morals*, i. 105.
[6] *Ibid.* ii. 300.
[7] Tacitus, *Annales*, ii. 85.

of our ancestors, who considered it a sufficient punishment
on unchaste women to have to profess their shame." [1]
But both in Rome and Greece pre-nuptial unchastity in
men, when it was not excessive [2] or did not take some
especially offensive form, was hardly censured by public
opinion.[3] The elder Cato expressly justified it.[4] Cicero
says :—" If there be any one who thinks that youth is to
be wholly interdicted from amours with courtesans, he
certainly is very strict indeed. I cannot deny what he
says ; but still he is at variance not only with the licence
of the present age, but even with the habits of our
ancestors, and with what they used to consider allowable. For when was the time that men were not used
to act in this manner ? When was such conduct found
fault with ? When was it not permitted ? When, in
short, was the time when that which is lawful was not
lawful ? " [5] Epictetus only went a little step further.
He said to his disciples :—" Concerning sexual pleasures,
it is right to be pure before marriage, as much as in you
lies. But if you indulge in them, let it be according
to what is lawful. But do not in any case make yourself disagreeable to those who use such pleasures, nor be
fond of reproving them, nor of putting yourself forward
as not using them." [6] Here chastity in men is at all
events recognised as an ideal. But even in pagan antiquity there were a few who enjoined it as a duty.[7]
Musonius Rufus emphatically asserted that no union of
the sexes other than marriage was permissible,[8] and Dio
Chrysostom desired prostitution to be suppressed by
law.[9] Similar opinions grew up in connection with the
Neo-Platonic and Neo-Pythagorean philosophies, and
may be traced back to the ancient masters themselves.
We are told that Pythagoras inculcated the virtue of

[1] Tacitus, *Annales*, ii. 85.
[2] Valerius Maximus (*Facta dictaque memorabilia*, ii. 5. 6) praises
" frugalitas " as " immoderato Ven-
eris usu aversa."
[3] Lecky, *op. cit.* ii. 314.
[4] Horace, *Satiræ*, i. 2. 31 *sq.*

[5] Cicero, *Pro Cœlio*, 20 (48).
[6] Epictetus, *Enchiridion*, xxxiii. 8.
[7] Denis, *op. cit.* ii. 133 *sqq.*
[8] Musonius Rufus, quoted by Stobæus, *Florilegium*, vi. 61.
[9] Denis, *op. cit.* ii. 149 *sqq.*

chastity so successfully that when ten of his disciples, being attacked, might have escaped by crossing a bean-field, they died to a man rather than tread down the beans, which were supposed to have a mystic affinity with the seat of impure desires.[1] Plato, again, is in favour of a law to the effect that " no one shall venture to touch any person of the freeborn or noble class except his wedded wife, or sow the unconsecrated and bastard seed among harlots, or in barren and un-natural lusts." Our citizens, he says, ought not to be worse than birds and beasts, which live without inter-course, pure and chaste, until the age for procreation, and afterwards, when they have arrived at that period and the male has paired with the female and the female with the male, " live the rest of their lives in holiness and innocence, abiding firmly in their original compact." [2]

Much stronger was the censure which Christianity passed on pre-nuptial connections. While looking with suspicion even on the life-long union of one man with one woman, the Church pronounced all other forms of sexual intercourse to be mortal sins. In its Penitentials sins of unchastity were the favourite topic ; and its horror of them finds an echo in the secular legislation of the first Christian emperors. Panders were condemned to have molten lead poured down their throats.[3] In the case of forcible seduction both the man and woman, if she consented to the act, were put to death.[4] Even the innocent offspring of illicit intercourse were punished for their parents' sins with ignominy and loss of certain rights which belonged to other, more respectable, members of the Church and the State.[5] Persons of different sex

[1] Jamblichus, *De Pythagorica vita*, 31 (191). *Cf.* Jevons, in Plutarch's *Romane Questions*, p. lxxxviii. *sq.*
[2] Plato, *Leges*, viii. 840 *sq. Cf.* Xenophon, *Memorabilia*, i. 3. 8.
[3] Lecky, *op. cit.* ii. 316.
[4] *Codex Theodosianus*, ix. 24. 1.
[5] *Concilium Claromontanum*, A.D.

1095, can. 11 (Labbe-Mansi, *Sacrorum Conciliorum collectio*, xx. 817):—"Ut nulli filii concubinarum ad ordines vel aliquos honores ecclesiasticos promoveantur, nisi monchaliter vel canonice vixerint in ecclesia." See also *supra*, i. 47.

who were not united in wedlock were forbidden by the
Church to kiss each other ; nay, the sexual desire itself,
though unaccompanied by any external act, was regarded
as sinful in the unmarried.[1] In this standard of purity
no difference of sex was recognised, the same obligations
being imposed upon man and woman.[2]

In this, as in so many other points of morals, however,
there is a considerable discrepancy between Christian
doctrine and public opinion in Christian countries. The
gross and open immorality of the Middle Ages indicates
how little the idea of sexual purity entered into the
manners and opinions of the people. The influence of
the ascetic doctrine of the Church was in fact quite
contrary to its aspirations. The institution of clerical
celibacy lowered the estimation of virtue by promoting
vice. During the Middle Ages unchastity was regarded
as an object of ridicule rather than censure, and in the
comic literature of that period the clergy are universally
represented as the great corrupters of domestic virtue.[3]
Whether the tenet of chastity laid down by the code of
Chivalry was taken more seriously may be fairly doubted.
A knight, it was said, should be abstinent and chaste ;[4] he
should love only the virtues, talents, and graces of his
lady ;[5] and love was defined as the " chaste union of two
hearts by virtue wrought." [6] But whilst the knight had
certain claims as regards the virtue of his lady, whilst he
probably was inclined to draw his sword only for a woman
of fair reputation, and whilst he himself professed to
aspire only to her lip or hand, we have reason to believe
that the amours in which he indulged with her were of a
far less delicate kind. Sainte-Palaye observes, " Jamais

---

[1] " Perit ergo et ipsa mente
virginitas." Katz, *Grundriss des
kanonischen Strafrechts*, p. 114 *sq.*
For the subject of kissing see also
Thomas Aquinas, *Summa theologica*,
ii.-ii. 154. 4.

[2] Laurent, *Études sur l'histoire de
l'Humanité*, iv. 114.

[3] Wright, *Essays on Archæological
Subjects*, ii. 238. *Cf. Idem, History*

*of Domestic Manners and Sentiments
in England during the Middle Ages*,
pp. 54, 281, 420.

[4] *Book of the Ordre of Chyualry*,
fol. 40.

[5] Sainte - Palaye, *Mémoires sur
l'ancienne Chevalerie*, ii. 17.

[6] Mills, *History of Chivalry*, i.
214 *sq.*

on ne vit les mœurs plus corrompues que du temps de nos Chevaliers, et jamais le règne de la débauche ne fut plus universel."[1] For a mediæval knight the chief object of life was love. He who did not understand how to win a lady was but half a man ; and the difference between a lover and a seducer was apparently slight. The character of the seducer, as Mr. Lecky remarks, and especially of the passionless seducer who pursues his career simply as a kind of sport, and under the influence of no stronger motive than vanity or a spirit of adventure, has for many centuries been glorified and idealised in the popular literature of Christendom in a manner to which there is no parallel in antiquity.[2]

The Reformation brought about some change for the better, if in no other respect at least by making marriage lawful for a large class of people to whom illicit love had previously been the only means of gratifying a natural desire, and by abolishing the monasteries. In fits of religious enthusiasm even the secular legislators busied themselves with acts of incontinence in which two unmarried adults of different sex were consenting parties. In the days of the Commonwealth, according to an act of 1650, in cases of less serious breach of chastity than adultery and incest, each man or woman was for each offence to be committed to the common gaol for three months, and to find sureties for good behaviour during a whole year afterwards.[3] In Scotland, after the Reformation, fornication was punished with a severity nearly equal to that which attended the infraction of the marriage vow.[4] But the fate of these and similar laws has been either to be repealed or to become inactive.[5] For ordinary acts of incontinence public opinion is, practically at least, the only judge. In the case of female unchastity its sentence is

---

[1] Sainte-Palaye, *op. cit.* ii. 19. *Cf.* Walter Scott, ' Essay on Chivalry,' in *Miscellaneous Prose Works,* vi. 48 *sq.*
[2] Lecky, *op. cit.* ii. 346. *Cf.* Delécluze, *Roland ou la Chevalerie,* i. 356.

[3] Pike, *History of Crime in England,* ii. 182.
[4] Rogers *Social Life in Scotland,* ii. 242.
[5] See Pike, *op. cit.* ii. 582 ; Hume, *Commentaries on the Law of Scotland,* ii. 333.

severe enough among the upper ranks of society, whilst, so far as the lower classes are concerned, it varies considerably even in different parts of the same country, and is in many cases regarded as venial. As to similar acts committed by unmarried men, the words which Cicero uttered on behalf of Cœlius might be repeated by any modern advocate who, in defending his client, ventured frankly to express the popular opinion on the subject. It seems to me that with regard to sexual relations between unmarried men and women Christianity has done little more than establish a standard which, though accepted perhaps in theory, is hardly recognised by the feelings of the large majority of people—or at least of men—in Christian communities, and has introduced the vice of hypocrisy, which apparently was little known in sexual matters by pagan antiquity.

Why has sexual intercourse between unmarried people, if both parties consent, come to be regarded as wrong ? Why are the moral opinions relating to it subject to so great variations ? Why is the standard commonly so different for man and woman ? We shall now try to find an answer to these questions.

If marriage, as I am inclined to suppose, is based on an instinct derived from some ape-like progenitor, it would from the beginning be regarded as the natural form of sexual intercourse in the human race, whilst other more transitory connections would appear abnormal and consequently be disapproved of. I am not certain whether some feeling of this sort, however vague, is not still very general in the race. But it has been more or less or almost totally suppressed by social conditions which make it in most cases impossible for men to marry at the first outbreak of the sexual passion. We have thus to seek for some other explanation of the severe censure passed on pre-nuptial connections.

It seems to me obvious that this censure is chiefly due to the preference which a man gives to a virgin bride. As I have shown in another place, such a preference is a

fact of very common occurrence.[1] It partly springs from
a feeling akin to jealousy towards women who have had
previous connections with other men, partly from the
warm response a man expects from a woman whose
appetites he is the first to gratify, and largely from an
instinctive appreciation of female coyness. Each sex is
attracted by the distinctive characteristics of the opposite
sex, and coyness is a female quality. In mankind, as
among other mammals, the female requires to be courted,
often endeavouring for a long time to escape from the
male. Not only in civilised countries may courtship mean
a prolonged making of love to the woman. Mariner's
words with reference to the women of Tonga hold true
of a great many, if not all, savage and barbarous races of
men. " It must not be supposed," he says, " that these
women are always easily won ; the greatest attentions and
most fervent solicitations are sometimes requisite, even
though there be no other lover in the way." [2] The
marriage ceremonies of many peoples bear testimony to
the same fact. One origin of the form of capture is the
resistance of the pursued woman, due to coyness,
partly real and partly assumed.[3] On the East Coast of
Greenland, for instance, the only method of contracting a
marriage is for a man to go to the girl's tent, catch her
by her hair or anything else which offers a hold, and drag
her off to his dwelling without further ado ; violent scenes
are often the result, as single women always affect the
utmost bashfulness and aversion to any proposal of
marriage, lest they should lose their reputation for
modesty.[4] It is certainly not the woman who most
readily yields to the desires of a man that is most
attractive to him ; as an ancient writer puts it, all men
love seasoned dishes, not plain meats, or plainly dressed

[1] Westermarck, *op. cit.* p. 123 *sq.*
[2] Mariner, *op. cit.* ii. 174. *Cf.*
Fritsch, *Die Eingeborenen Süd-
Afrika's*, p. 445 (Bushmans).
[3] *Cf.* Spencer, *Principles of Sociology*, i. 623 *sq.* ; *Idem*, in *Fortnightly*

Review, xxi. 897 *sq.* ; Westermarck,
op. cit. p. 388 ; Grosse, *Die Formen
der Familie*, p. 107 ; Crawley, *The
Mystic Rose*, p. 305 *sq.*
[4] Nansen, *First Crossing of Greenland*, i. 316 *sqq.*

fish, and it is modesty that gives the bloom to beauty.[1] Conspicuous eagerness in a woman appears to a man unwomanly, repulsive, contemptible. His ideal is the virgin ; the libertine he despises.

Where marriage is the customary form of sexual intercourse pre-nuptial incontinence in a woman, as suggesting lack of coyness and modesty, is therefore apt to disgrace her. At the same time it is a disgrace to, and consequently an offence against, her family, especially where the ties of kinship are strong. Moreover, where wives are purchased the unchaste girl, by lowering her market value, deprives her father or parents of part of their property. Among the Tshi-speaking peoples of the Gold Coast, says Major Ellis, " chastity *per se* is not understood. An unmarried girl is expected to be chaste because virginity possesses a marketable value, and were she to be unchaste her parents would receive little and perhaps no head-money for her." [2] Among the Rendile of Eastern Africa, we are told, the unchastity of unmarried girls meets with severe retribution, the girl invariably being driven out from her home, for the sole and simple reason that her market value to her parents has been decreased.[3] The same commercial point of view is expressed in the Mosaic rule :—" If a man entice a maid that is not betrothed, and lie with her, he shall surely endow her to be his wife. If her father utterly refuse to give her unto him, he shall pay money according to the dowry of virgins." [4] But the girl is not the only offender. Whilst the disgrace of incontinence falls on her alone, the offence against her relatives is divided between her and the seducer. Speaking of the presents which, among the Thlinkets, a man is bound to give to the parents of the girl whom he has seduced, Sir James Douglas observes, " The offender is simply regarded as a robber, who has committed depredation on their merchandise, their only anxiety being to make the

[1] Athenæus, *Deipnosophistæ*, xiii. 16.
[2] Ellis, *Tshi - speaking Peoples*, p. 286.
[3] Chanler, *Through Jungle and Desert*, p. 317.
[4] *Exodus*, xxii. 16 *sq*.

damages exacted as heavy as possible." [1] Marriage by
purchase has thus raised the standard of female chastity,
and also, to some extent, checked the incontinence of the
men. But it can certainly not be regarded as the
sole cause of the duty of chastity where such a duty
is recognised by savages. Among the Veddahs, who
do not make their daughters objects of traffic,[2] the
unmarried girls are nevertheless protected by their natural
guardians " with the keenest sense of honour." [3] In many
of the instances quoted above where a seduction is followed
by more or less serious consequences for the seducer,
the penalty he has to pay is evidently something else
than the mere market value of the girl.

Thus the men, by demanding that the women whom
they marry shall be virgins, indirectly give rise to the
demand that they themselves shall abstain from certain
forms of incontinence. From my collection of facts
relating to savages I find that in the majority of cases
where chastity is required of unmarried girls the seducer
also is considered guilty of a crime. But, as was just
pointed out, his act is judged from a more limited point
of view. It is chiefly, if not exclusively, regarded as
an offence against the parents or family of the girl;
chastity *per se* is hardly required of savage men. Where
prostitution exists they may without censure gratify their
passions among its victims. Now, to anybody who
duly reflects upon the matter it is clear that the seducer
does a wrong to the woman also; but I find no indication that this idea occurs at all to the savage mind.
Where the seducer is censured the girl also is censured,
being regarded not as the injured party but as an
injurer. Even in the case of rape the harm done to the
girl herself is little thought of. Among the Tonga
Islanders " rape, providing it be not upon a married
woman or one to whom respect is due on the score of

---

[1] Douglas, quoted by Petroff, *op.
cit.* p. 177.
[2] Le Mesurier, ' Veddás of Ceylon,'
in *Jour. Roy. Asiatic Soc. Ceylon*
Branch, ix. 340. Hartshorne, ' Weddas,' in *Indian Antiquary*, viii. 320.
[3] Nevill, ' Vaeddas of Ceylon,' in
Taprobanian, i. 178.

superior rank from the perpetrator, is considered not as a crime but as a matter of indifference."[1] The same is the case in the Pelew Islands.[2] In the laws of the Rejangs of Sumatra referring to this offence, " there is hardly anything considered but the value of the girl's person to her relations, as a mere vendible commodity."[3] Among the Asiniboin, a Siouan tribe, the punishment for rape is based on the principle that the price of the woman has been depreciated, that the chances of marriage have been lessened, and that the act is an insult to her kindred, as implying contempt of their feelings and their power of protection.[4] Even the Teutons in early days hardly severed rape from abduction, the kinsmen of the woman feeling themselves equally wronged in either case.[5] If the girl's feelings are thus disregarded when she is an unwilling victim of violence, it can hardly be expected that she should be an object of pity when she is a consenting partner. Does not public opinion in the midst of civilisation turn against the dishonoured rather than the dishonourer ?

There is yet another party to be considered, namely, the offspring. One would imagine that to every thinking mind, not altogether destitute of sympathetic feelings, the question what is likely to happen to the child if the woman becomes pregnant should present itself as one of the greatest gravity. But in judging of matters relating to sexual morality men have generally made little use of their reason and been guilty of much thoughtless cruelty. Although marriage has come into existence solely for the sake of the offspring, it rarely happens that in sexual relations much unselfish thought is bestowed upon unborn

---

[1] Mariner, *op. cit.* ii. 107.

[2] Kubary, 'Die Verbrechen und das Strafverfahren auf den Pelau-Inseln,' in *Original-Mittheil. aus der ethnol. Abtheil. der königl. Museen zu Berlin*, i. 78.

[3] Crawfurd, *History of the Indian Archipelago*, iii. 130.

[4] Dorsey, ' Siouan Sociology,' in *Ann. Rep. Bur. Ethn.* xv. 226.

[5] Brunner, *Deutsche Rechtsgeschichte* ii. 666. Pollock and Maitland, *History of English Law before the Time of Edward I.* ii. 490. According to Salic law, the fine for the rape of an *ingenua puella* was 62½ solidi, or only a little higher than the fine for a connection with her to which she herself consented (*Lex Salica*, Herold's text, xiv. 4 ; xv. 3) ; whereas the fine for adultery with a free woman was 200 solidi (*ibid.* xv. 1).

individuals. Legal provisions in favour of illegitimate
children have made men somewhat more careful, for their
own sake, but they have also nourished the idea that the
responsibility of fatherhood may be bought off by the
small sum the man has to pay for the support of his
natural child. Custom or law may exempt him even from
this duty. We are told that in Tahiti the father might
kill a bastard child, but that, if he suffered it to live, he
was *eo ipso* considered to be married to its mother.[1] This
custom, it would seem, is hardly more inhuman than the
famous law according to which " la recherche de la pater-
nité est interdite." [2]

The great authority on the ethics of Roman Catholicism tries to prove that simple fornication is a mortal sin
chiefly because it " tends to the hurt of the life of the
child who is to be born of such intercourse," or more
generally, because " it is contrary to the good of the offspring." [3] But this tender care for the welfare of illegitimate children seems strange when we consider the manner
in which such children have been treated by the Roman
Catholic Church herself. It is obvious that the extreme
horror of fornication which is expressed in the Christian
doctrine is in the main a result of the same ascetic
principle which declared celibacy superior to marriage and
tolerated marriage only because it could not be suppressed.

Moral ideas concerning unchastity have also been influenced by the close association which exists in a refined
mind between the sexual impulse and a sentiment of affection which lasts long after the gratification of the bodily
desire. We find the germ of this feeling in the
abhorrence with which prostitution is regarded by savage
tribes who have no objection to ordinary sexual intercourse
previous to marriage,[4] and in the distinction which among
ourselves is drawn between the prostitute and the woman

---

[1] Cook, *Voyage to the Pacific Ocean*,
ii. 157.
[2] *Code Napoléon*, § 340.
[3] Thomas Aquinas, *Summa theologica*, ii.-ii. 154. 2.

[4] *E.g.*, the Chittagong Hill tribes
(Lewin, *Wild Races of South-Eastern
India*, p. 348). *Cf.* Westermarck,
op. cit. p. 70 *sq.*

who yields to temptation because she loves. To indulge in mere sexual pleasure, unaccompanied by higher feelings, appears brutal and disgusting in the case of a man, and still more so in the case of a woman. After all, love is generally only an episode in a man's life, whereas for a woman it is the whole of her life.[1] The Greek orator said that in the moment when a woman loses her chastity her mind is changed.[2] On the other hand, when a man and a woman, tied to each other by deep and genuine affection, decide to live together as husband and wife, though not joined in legal wedlock, the censure which public opinion passes upon their conduct seems to an unprejudiced mind justifiable at most only in so far as it may be considered to have been their duty to comply with the laws of their country and to submit to a rule of some social importance.

Sexual intercourse between unmarried persons of opposite sex is thus regarded as wrong from different points of view under different conditions, social or psychical, and all of these conditions are not in any considerable degree combined at any special stage of civilisation. Sometimes the opinions on the subject are greatly influenced by the institution of marriage by purchase, sometimes they are influenced by the refinement of love ; and between such causes there can be no co-operation. This is one reason for the singular complexity which characterises the evolution of the duty of chastity ; but there is another reason perhaps even more important. The causes to which this duty may be traced are frequently checked by circumstances operating in an opposite direction. Thus the preference which a man is naturally disposed to give to a virgin bride may be overcome by his desire for offspring, inducing him to marry a woman who has proved capable of gratifying this desire.[3] It may also be ineffective for the simple reason that no virgin bride is to be found. Nothing has more generally prevented chastity

---

[1] *Cf.* Simmel, *Einleitung in die Moralwissenschaft*, i. 201 ; Paulsen, *System der Ethik*, ii. 274.

[2] Lysias, quoted by Schmidt, *Die Ethik der alten Griechen*, i. 273.

[3] See *supra*, ii. 423.

from being recognised as a duty than social conditions
promoting licentious habits.   Even in savage society,
where almost every man and every woman marry and most
of them marry early in life, there are always a great
number of unmarried people of both sexes above the age
of puberty ; and, generally speaking, the number of the
unmarried increases along with the progress of civilisation.
This state of things easily leads to incontinence in men and
women, and where such incontinence becomes habitual
it can hardly incur much censure.   Again, where the
general standard of female chastity is high, the standard
of male chastity may nevertheless be the lowest possible.
This is the case where there is a class of women who can
no longer be dishonoured, because they have already been
dishonoured, whose virtue is of no value either to themselves or their families because they have lost their virtue,
and who make incontinence their livelihood. Prostitution,
being a safeguard of female chastity, has facilitated the
enforcement of the rule which enjoins it as a duty, but at
the same time it has increased the inequality of obligations
imposed on men and women.   It has begun to exercise
this influence already at the lower stages of culture.
Prostitution is by no means unknown in the savage world.[1]
It is a recognised institution in many of the Melanesian
islands ; " at Santa Cruz," says Dr. Codrington, " where
the separation of the sexes is so carefully maintained,
there are certainly public courtesans." [2]   Prostitution
prevails in many or most Negro countries ;[3] and so
favourably, we are told, is this institution sometimes
regarded, that rich Negro ladies on their death-beds buy
female slaves and present them to the public, " in the
same manner as in England they would have left a legacy
to some public charity." [4] The Wanyoro even have a

---

[1] See, e.g., Tutuila, 'Line Islanders,'
in *Jour. Polynesian Soc.* i. 270 ;
Powell, *Wanderings in a Wild
Country*, p. 261 (natives of New
Britain) ; Davis, *El Gringo*, p. 221
(Indians of New Mexico) ; Ploss-

Bartels, *Das Weib*, i. 536, 540 *sqq.*
[2] Codrington, *Melanesians*, p. 234
sqq.
[3] *Emin Pasha in Central Africa*,
p. 88.
[4] Reade, *Savage Africa*, p. 547 *sq.*

definite system of prostitution, governed by stringent laws which seem to be very old.[1] In Greenland, where it was " reckoned the greatest of infamies " for an unmarried woman to become pregnant,[2] there were professional harlots already in early times ;[3] and the same was the case among many of the North American Indians.[4] Thus among the Omahas extra-matrimonial intercourse is, as a rule, practised only with public women, called *minckeda* ; and " so strict are the Omahas about these matters, that a young girl or even a married woman walking or riding alone, would be ruined in character, being liable to be taken for a *minckeda*, and addressed as such." [5] Public prostitution was tolerated, if not encouraged, among all the Maya nations, whilst intercourse with other unmarried women was punished with a fine or, if the affronted relatives insisted, with death.[6] " In order to avoid greater evils," the Incas of Peru permitted public prostitutes, who were treated with extreme contempt ;[7] but, with this exception, " to be lewd with single women was capital." [8] Among all the civilised nations of the Old World prostitution has existed, and still exists, as a tolerated institution, even where legislators have endeavoured to suppress it.[9] Its prevalence in our modern society greatly increases the perplexity of public opinion in regard to sexual morality. Its victims are degraded and despised beyond description. At the same time their male custo-

[1] *Emin Pasha in Central Africa*, p. 87. Wilson and Felkin, *Uganda*, ii. 49.

[2] Egede, *Description of Greenland*, p. 141.

[3] Cranz, *History of Greenland*, i. 176.

[4] Carver, *Travels through the Interior Parts of North America*, p. 375.

[5] Dorsey, ' Omaha Sociology,' in *Ann. Rep. Bur. Ethn.* iii. 365.

[6] Bancroft, *Native Races of the Pacific States*, ii. 676, 659.

[7] Garcilasso de la Vega, *First Part of the Royal Commentaries of the Yncas*, i. 321 *sq.*

[8] Herrera, *General History of the West Indies*, iv. 340.

[9] Dufour, *Histoire de la prostitution*, *passim*. Doolittle, *Social Life of the Chinese*, i. 348. Wilkins, *Modern Hinduism*, p. 412. Polak, ' Die Prostitution in Persien,' in *Wiener Medizinische Wochenschrift*, xi. 516, 517, 563 *sqq.* Lane, *Modern Egyptians*, i. 150. Weinhold, *Altnordisches Leben*, p. 259 (ancient Scandinavians). Desmaze, *Les pénalités anciennes*, p. 61 *sq.* n. 4 ; Mackintosh, *History of Civilisation in Scotland*, i. 428 (Middle Ages) ; &c. Since the thirteenth century even the Church tolerated the establishment of brothels in the larger cities (Müller, *Das sexuelle Leben der christlichen Kulturvölker*, p. 149).

mers are tacitly allowed to support the trade. That the
demand for a merchandise increases the production of it is
in this case seldom thought of. But secrecy must be
observed. In sexual matters openness is indecent, and the
chief crime is to be found out.

There is, moreover, a form of religious prostitution,
just as there is religious celibacy. In fact, the two customs
are sometimes very closely connected with one another.
Among the Ewe-speaking peoples of the Slave Coast the
chief business of the female *kosi*, or wife of the god to
whom she is dedicated, is prostitution. " In every town
there is at least one institution in which the best-looking
girls, between ten and twelve years of age, are received.
Here they remain for three years, learning the chants and
dances peculiar to the worship of the gods, and prostituting
themselves to the priests and the inmates of the male
seminaries ; and at the termination of their novitiate they
become public prostitutes. This condition, however, is
not regarded as one for reproach ; they are considered to
be married to the god, and their excesses are supposed to
be caused and directed by him. Properly speaking, their
libertinage should be confined to the male worshippers at
the temple of the god, but practically it is indiscriminate.
Children who are born from such unions belong to the
god." [1] So also the priestesses on the Gold Coast, though
not allowed to marry, are by no means debarred from
sexual intercourse. They " are ordinarily most licentious,
and custom allows them to gratify their passions with any
man who may chance to take their fancy. A priestess who
is favourably impressed by a man sends for him to her
house, and this command he is sure to obey, through fear
of the consequences of exciting her anger. She then tells
him that the god she serves has directed her to love him,
and the man thereupon lives with her until she grows
tired of him, or a new object takes her fancy. Some
priestesses have as many as half a dozen men in their train
at one time, and may on great occasions be seen walking

[1] Ellis, *Ewe-speaking Peoples*, p. 141.

in state, followed by them. Their life is one continual record of debauchery and sensuality, and when excited by the dance they frequently abandon themselves to the wildest excesses."[1] It seems that the " wife " of the Egyptian god at Thebes also in time became a libertine ; Strabo tells us that the beautiful woman who was dedicated to him had sexual intercourse with any man she chose " till the natural purification of her body took place," after which she was given to a man.[2] In India every Hindu temple of any importance has its dancing girls, whose position is inferior only to that of the sacrificers.[3] Thus at Jŭgŭnnat'hŭ-kshŭtrŭ in Orissa a number of women of infamous character are employed to dance and sing before the god. They live in separate houses, not at the temple. The Brahmins who officiate there continually have adulterous connections with them, and these women also prostitute themselves to visitors.[4] In the Canaanitish cults there were women, called kedẽshōth, who were consecrated to the deity with whose temple they were associated, and who at the same time acted as prostitutes.[5] At the local shrines of North Israel the worship of Yahveh itself was deeply affected by these practices ;[6] but they were forbidden in the Deuteronomic code.[7] Perhaps this temple prostitution may be accounted for by a belief that it bestowed blessings upon the worshippers. According to notions which prevail to this day in countries with Semitic culture, sexual intercourse with a holy person is regarded as beneficial to him or her who indulges in it.[8]

Of a somewhat different character was the religious prostitution which prevailed in ancient Babylonia, in connection with the worship of Ishtar. Herodotus says that every woman born in that country was obliged once in her

[1] Ellis, *Tshi-speaking Peoples*, p. 121 *sq.*
[2] Strabo, *Geographica*, xvii. 1. 46. *Cf.* Wiedemann, *Herodots zweites Buch*, p. 269.
[3] Warneck, quoted by Ploss-Bartels, *op. cit.* i. 534.
[4] Ward, *View of the History, &c. of the Hindoos*, ii. 134.
[5] Driver, *Commentary on Deuteronomy*, p. 264. Cheyne, ' Harlot,' in Cheyne and Black, *Encyclopædia Biblica*, ii. 1965.
[6] *Hosea*, iv. 14. *Cf.* Cheyne, in *Encyclopædia Biblica*, ii. 1965.
[7] *Deuteronomy*, xxiii. 17 *sq.*
[8] See Westermarck, *The Moorish Conception of Holiness (Baraka)*, p. 85.

life to go and sit down in the precinct of Aphrodite, and
there consort with a stranger. A woman who had once
taken her seat was not allowed to return home till one of
the strangers threw a silver coin into her lap, and took her
with him beyond the holy ground. The silver coin could
not be refused because, since once thrown, it was sacred.
The woman went with the first man who threw her money,
rejecting no one. When she had gone with him, and so
satisfied the goddess, she returned home, and from that
time forth no gift, however great, would prevail with her.[1]
Several allusions in cuneiform literature to the sacred prostitution carried on at Babylonian temples confirm Herodotus' statement in general.[2] A cult very similar to this
was also found in certain parts of the island of Cyprus,[3] at
Heliopolis in Syria,[4] and at Byblus.[5] In the worship of
Anaitis the Armenians even of the highest families prostituted their own daughters at least once in their lives, nor
was this regarded as any bar to an honourable marriage
afterwards.[6] Although such practices were generally
excluded from the ordinary Greek worships of Aphrodite,
unchastity in the temple cult of that goddess is reported
to have occurred at Corinth[7] and in the city of the Locri
Epizephyrii, who, according to the story, vowed to consecrate their daughters to this service in order to gain
the goddess's aid in a war.[8]

Various theories have been set forth to explain the
religious prostitution of the Babylonian type. It has
been interpreted as an expiation for individual marriage,
as a temporary recognition of pre-existing communal
rights at a time when " communal marriage " in the
full sense of the term had already ceased to exist.[9] It

---

[1] Herodotus, i. 199.
[2] Jeremias, *Izdubar-Nimrod*, p. 59
sq. Jastrow, *Religion of Babylonia
and Assyria*, p. 475 *sq.* Mürdter-
Delitzsch, *Geschichte Babyloniens*,
p. 41.
[3] Herodotus, i. 199.   Athenæus,
Deipnosophistæ, xii. 11, p. 516 a.
[4] Socrates, *Historia ecclesiastica*, i.
18 (Migne, *op. cit.* Ser. Græca, lxvii.
123). Sozomen, *Historia ecclesiastica*,

v. 10 (Migne, Ser. Græca, lxvii. 1243).
Eusebius, *Vita Constantini*, iii. 58
(Migne, Ser. Græca, xx. 1124).
[5] Lucian, *De Syria Dea*, 6.
[6] Strabo, xi. 14. 16.
[7] *Ibid.* viii. 6. 20.
[8] Farnell, *Cults of the Greek States*,
ii. 636. Athenæus, xii. 11, p. 516 a.
[9] Avebury, *Origin of Civilisation*,
p. 559.

has been supposed to be nothing but ordinary immorality practised under the cloak of religion.[1] It has been represented as a form of sacrifice, either as a first-fruit offering[2] or as an act by which a worshipper sacrifices her most precious possession to the deity.[3] To Dr. Farnell it seems to be " a special modification of a wide-spread custom, the custom of destroying virginity before marriage so that the bridegroom's intercourse should be safe from a peril that is much dreaded by men in a certain stage of culture ; and here, as in other ritual," he adds, " it is the stranger that takes the peril upon himself." [4] But why should the stranger have been more willing than the bridegroom to expose himself to this danger ? Considering that the act was performed at the temple of the goddess of fecundity, I think its object most probably was to ensure fertility in the woman ; this, in fact, is directly indicated by the words which the stranger, according to Herodotus, uttered when he threw the silver coin into her lap :—" The goddess Mylitta prosper thee ! " [5] And from what has been said in a previous chapter about the semi-supernatural character ascribed to strangers, about the efficacy of their blessings and the benefits expected from their love,[6] we can see why a stranger was appointed to confer the blessing upon the girl.[7]

Among ourselves an act of incontinence assumes a

[1] Jeremias, *Izdubar-Nimrod*, p. 60.
[2] Wiedemann, *Herodots zweites Buch*, p. 267 *sq.*
[3] Curtiss, *Primitive Semitic Religion To-day*, p. 155.
[4] Farnell, ' Sociological Hypotheses concerning the Position of Women in Ancient Religion,' in *Archiv f. Religionswiss.* vii. 88.
[5] Herodotus, i. 199.
[6] *Supra*, i. ch. xxiv.
[7] Since the present chapter was in type, some fresh attempts have been made to explain this religious prostitution. Sir J. G. Frazer (*Adonis Attis Osiris*, p. 23 *sq.*) regards it as a rite intended to ensure the fruitfulness of the ground and the increase of man and beast on the principle of homœopathic magic. A very similar opinion has been expressed by Dr. Havelock Ellis (' Ursprung und Entwicklung der Prostitution,' in *Mutterschutz*, iii. fasc. 1 *sq.*). According to Mr. Hartland, again (' Concerning the Rite at the Temple of Mylitta,' in *Anthropological Essays presented to E. B. Tylor*, p. 189 *sqq.*), it was a puberty rite involving a sacrifice of virginity to which every woman was subjected. [My own theory has subsequently been accepted by van Gennep, *Les rites de passage*, p. 242 *sq.*]

different aspect if one of the parties, either the man or the woman, is married. Involving a breach of faith, adultery is an offence against him or her to whom faith is due, and at the same time the seducer commits an offence against the husband of the adulteress. But here again our own views are not universally shared.

Although it is hard to understand that the seducer could ever be regarded as guiltless, we are told that among a few peoples adultery is not held to be wrong ; [1] and Mr. Morgan states that among the Iroquois " punishment was inflicted upon the woman alone, who was supposed to be the only offender." [2] But these cases are certainly quite exceptional. In a savage tribe a seducer may be thankful if he escapes by paying to the injured husband the value of the bride or some other fine, or if the penalty is reduced to a flogging, to his head being shaved, his ears cut off, one of his eyes destroyed, or his legs speared. Very commonly he has to pay with his life. We have seen that even among many peoples who generally prohibit self-redress an adulterer may be put to death by the aggrieved husband, especially if he be caught *flagrante delicto* ; [3] and in other cases he may be subject to capital punishment, in the proper sense of the word.[4] In Albania, even in our days, custom not only allows, but compels, the injured husband to kill the adulterer.[5] Hebrew law enjoined the man who committed adultery with another man's wife to be put to death ; [6] and Christian legislators followed the example. Constantine celebrated his new zeal for the sacramental idea of marriage by establishing the punishment of death for the seducer ; [7] adultery was in point of

---

[1] Davis, *El Gringo*, p. 221 *sq.* (Indians of New Mexico). Adair, *History of the American Indians*, p. 146 (Cherokees). Krasheninnikoff, *History of Kamschatka*, p. 204. Prejevalsky, *Mongolia*, i. 70 (Mongols). Colquhoun, *Amongst the Shans*, p. 75 (Yendalines, one of the Karen tribes). Chanler, *op. cit.* p. 317 (Rendile in Eastern Africa). Lichtenstein, *Travels in Southern Africa*, ii. 48 (Bushmans)

[2] Morgan, *League of the Iroquois*, p. 331.

[3] *Supra*, i. 290 *sqq.*

[4] *Supra*, i. 189.

[5] Hahn, *Albanesische Studien*, i. 177.

[6] *Leviticus*, xx. 10. *Deuteronomy*, xxii. 22.

[7] *Codex Justinianus*, ix. 9. 29. 4.

heinousness assimilated to murder, idolatry, and sorcery.[1] Various mediæval law-books punished the seducer with death ;[2] whilst in Scotland notorious and manifest adultery was made capital as late as 1563.[3] This extreme severity, however, has been followed by extreme leniency. In Scotland, though adultery kept its place in the statute-book as a heinous and in some cases a capital crime, prosecution for it had ceased for many years before the time of Baron Hume ;[4] and in England it is no crime at all in the eyes of the law, only an ecclesiastical offence.

The punishment of the seducer often varies according to his rank, or according to that of the husband, or according to the relative rank of both, or according to the rank of the adulteress. Among the Monbuttu, if the guilty woman belongs to the royal household, the adulterer is put to death, whereas otherwise he is only compelled to pay an indemnity to the offended husband.[5] Among the Ewe-speaking peoples of the Slave Coast the fine imposed for adultery depends on the rank of the injured husband ;[6] and the same principle is found in Anglo-Saxon law.[7] Among the Bakongo, again, the penalties for adultery " vary from capital punishment to a trifling fine, according to the station of the offender or the district he lives in."[8] Drury tells us that in the country of Anterndroea in Madagascar, " if a man lies with another man's wife who is superior to him, he forfeits thirty head of cattle besides beads and shovels a great number," whereas " if the men are of an equal rank, then twenty beasts are the fine."[9] According to the Chinese Penal Code, a slave who is guilty of criminal intercourse with the wife or daughter of a freeman, shall be punished at the least one degree more

[1] *Codex Theodosianus*, xi. 36. 1. St. Basil, quoted by Bingham, *Works*, vi. 432 *sq.*

[2] Du Boys, *Histoire du droit criminel des peuples modernes*, ii. 606. *Idem, Histoire du droit criminel de l'Espagne*, p. 391.

[3] Erskine-Rankine, *Principles of the Law of Scotland*, p. 563.

[4] Hume, *Commentaries on the Law of Scotland*, ii. 302.

[5] Casati, *Ten Years in Equatoria*, i. 163.

[6] Ellis, *Ewe-speaking Peoples*, p. 202.

[7] *Laws of Alfred*, ii. 10.

[8] Johnston, *River Congo*, p. 404.

[9] Drury, *Journal*, p. 183.

severely than a freeman would have been under the same circumstances.[1] In India a man of one of the first three castes who committed adultery with a Sûdra woman was banished, but a Sûdra who committed adultery with a woman of one of the first three castes suffered capital punishment ;[2] and an opinion is also quoted that for a Brâhmana who once was guilty of adultery with a married woman of equal class, the penance was one-fourth of that prescribed for an outcast.[3] In ancient Peru " an adulterer was punish'd with death, if the woman was of note, or else with the rack." [4]

We find no difficulty in explaining all these facts. In early civilisation a husband has often extreme rights over his wife. The seducer encroaches upon a right of which he is most jealous, and with regard to which his passions are most easily inflamed. Adultery is regarded as an illegitimate appropriation of the exclusive claims which the husband has acquired by the purchase of his wife, as an offence against property.[5] It is said in the ' Laws of Manu ' that " seed must not be sown by any man on that which belongs to another." [6] How closely the seducer is associated with a thief is illustrated by the fact that among some peoples he is punished as such, having his hands, or one of them, cut off.[7] Yet even among savages the offence is something more than a mere infringement of the right of ownership. The Kurile Islanders, says Krasheninnikoff, have an extraordinary way of punishing adultery : the husband of the adulteress challenges the adulterer to a combat. The result is generally the death of both the combatants ; but it is held to be " as great dishonour to refuse this combat as to refuse an invitation to a duel among the people of Europe." [8] The passion of jealousy, the feeling of ownership, and the sense of honour,

[1] *Ta Tsing Leu Lee*, sec. ccclxxiii. p. 409.
[2] *Âpastamba*, ii. 10. 27. 8 *sq.*
[3] *Ibid.* ii. 10. 27. 11.
[4] Herrera, *op. cit.* iv. 338.
[5] See, *e.g.*,Casalis, *Basutos*, p. 225 ; Burton, *Two Trips to Gorilla Land*, i. 77 ; Monrad, *Skildring af Guinea-*

Kysten, p. 5 ; Letourneau,*L'évolution de la morale*, p. 154 *sq.*
[6] *Laws of Manu*, ix. 42.
[7] Westermarck, *History of Human Marriage*, p. 130.
[8] Krasheninnikoff, *History of Kamschatka*, p. 238.

thus combine to make the seducer's act an offence, and often a heinous offence, in the eyes of custom or law ; and for the same reasons as in other offences the magnitude of guilt is here also influenced by the rank of the parties concerned. Modern legislation, on the other hand, does not to the same extent as early law and custom allow a man to give free vent to his angry passion ; it regards the dishonour of the aggrieved husband as a matter of too private a character to be publicly avenged ; and the faithfulness which a wife owes her husband is no longer connected with any idea of ownership. Moreover, the severity of earlier European laws against adultery was closely connected with Christianity's abhorrence of all kinds of irregular sexual intercourse ; and secular legislation has more and more freed itself from the bondage of religious doctrine.

Among some savage peoples it is the seducer only who suffers, whilst the unfaithful wife escapes without punishment.[1] Jealousy, in the first place, turns against the rival, and the seducer is the dishonourer and the thief. But, as a general rule, the unfaithful wife is also looked upon as an offender, and the punishment falls on both. She is discarded, beaten, or ill-treated in some way or other, and not infrequently she is killed. Often, too, she is disfigured by her enraged husband, so that no man may fall in love with her ever after.[2] Indeed, so strong is the idea that a wife belongs exclusively to her husband, that among several peoples she has to die with him ; [3] and frequently a widow is prohibited from remarrying either for ever or for a certain period after the husband's death.[4] In ancient Peru widows generally continued to live single, as " this virtue was much commended in their laws and ordinances." [5] Nor is it in China considered proper

---

[1] Westermarck, *op. cit.* p. 122. Macpherson, *Memorials of Service in India*, p. 133 (Kandhs). Batchelor, *Ainu of Japan*, p. 189 *sq.* Scaramucci and Giglioli, ' Notizie sui Danakil,' in *Archivio per l'antropologia e la etnologia*, xiv. 26.

[2] Westermarck, *op. cit.* p. 122.
[3] *Ibid.* p. 125 *sq. Supra*, i. 472 *sqq.*
[4] Westermarck, *History of Human Marriage*, p. 127 *sqq.*
[5] Garcilasso de la Vega, *op. cit.* i. 305.

for a woman to contract a second marriage after her husband's death, and a lady of rank, by doing so, exposes herself to a penalty of eighty blows.[1] " As a faithful minister does not serve two lords, neither may a faithful woman marry a second husband "—this is to the Chinese a principle of life, a maxim generally received as gospel.[2] Among so-called Aryan peoples the ancient custom which ordained sacrifice of widows survived in the prohibitions issued against their marrying a second time.[3] Even now the bare mention of a second marriage for a Hindu woman would be considered the greatest of insults, and, if she married again, " she would be hunted out of society, and no decent person would venture at any time to have the slightest intercourse with her." [4] In Greece [5] and Rome [6] a widow's remarriage was regarded as an insult to her former husband ; and so it is still regarded among the Southern Slavs. [7] The early Christians, especially the Montanists and Novatians, strongly disapproved of second marriages by persons of either sex ;[8] a second marriage was described by them as a " kind of fornication," [9] or as a " specious adultery." [10] It was looked upon as a manifest sign of incontinence, and also as inconsistent with the doctrine that marriage is an emblem of the union of Christ with the Church.[11]

Conjugal fidelity, whilst considered a stringent duty in the wife, is not generally considered so in the husband. This is obviously the rule among savage and barbarous tribes ; but there are interesting exceptions to the rule. The Igorrotes of Luzon are so strictly monogamous that

---

[1] Gray, *China*, i. 215.
[2] de Groot, *Religious System of China*, (vol. ii. book) i. 745.
[3] Schrader, *Prehistoric Antiquities of the Aryan Peoples*, p. 391.
[4] Dubois, *People of India*, p. 132.
[5] Pausanias, ii. 21. 7.
[6] Rossbach, *Römische Ehe*, p. 262.
[7] Krauss, *Sitte und Brauch der Südslaven*, p. 578. *Cf.* Ralston, *Songs of the Russian People*, p. 115 (Bulgarians).
[8] Mayer, *Die Rechte der Israeliten,*

Athener und Römer, ii. 290. Bingham, *op. cit.* vi. 427 *sq.* ; viii. 13 *sq.*
[9] Tertullian, *De exhortatione castitatis*, 9 (Migne, *Patrologiæ cursus*, ii. 924).
[10] Athenagoras, *Legatio pro Christianis*, 33 (Migne, *op. cit.* Ser. Graeca, vi. 967).
[11] Gibbon, *History of the Decline and Fall of the Roman Empire*, ii. 187. Lecky, *History of European Morals*, ii. 326.

in case of adultery the guilty party can be compelled to leave the hut and the family for ever,[1] and among various other monogamous savages adultery is said to be unknown.[2] The Dyak husband " preserves his vow of fidelity with a rectitude which makes jealousy a farce." [3] The Toungtha, who marry only one wife, do not consider it right for a master to take advantage of his position even with regard to the female slaves in his house.[4] Nay, the duty of fidelity in the husband has been recognised even by some savage peoples who allow polygamy. The Abipones, we are told, thought it both wicked and disgraceful to have any illicit intercourse with other women than their wives ; hence adultery was almost unheard of among them.[5] Among the Omaha Indians, " if a woman's husband be guilty of adultery with another woman she may strike him or the guilty female in her anger," though she cannot claim damages.[6] In several tribes of Western Victoria a wife whose husband has been unfaithful to her " may make a complaint to the chief, who can punish the man by sending him away from his tribe for two or three moons " ;[7] and among some aborigines in New South Wales similar complaints may be made to the elders of the tribe, with the result that the adulterous husband may have to suffer for his conduct.[8] The Kandhs of India deny the married man certain prerogatives which are granted to his wife : whilst constancy to her husband is so far from being re-quired in a wife, " that her pretensions do not, at least, suffer diminution in the eyes of either sex when fines are levied on her convicted lovers," infidelity in a married man is held to be highly dishonourable, and

[1] Meyer, in *Verhandl. Berliner Gesellsch. f. Anthrop.* 1883, p. 385.
[2] Bailey, in *Trans. Ethn. Soc.* N. S. ii. 291 *sq.* Hartshorne, in *Indian Antiquary*, viii. 320 (Veddahs). Finsch, *Neu-Guinea*, p. 101 ; Earl, *Papuans*, p. 81 (Papuans of Dorey).
[3] Boyle, *Adventures among the Dyaks of Borneo*, p. 236. See also Low, *Sarawak*, p. 300 (Hill Dyaks).

[4] Lewin, *Wild Races of South-Eastern India*, p. 193 *sq.*
[5] Dobrizhoffer, *Account of the Abipones*, ii. 138.
[6] Dorsey, ' Omaha Sociology,' in *Ann. Rep. Bur. Ethn.* iii. 364.
[7] Dawson, *Australian Aborigines*, p. 33.
[8] Nieboer, *Slavery as an Industrial System*, p. 18.

is often punished with deprivation of many social privileges.[1]

The duty which savages thus in certain instances have imposed on the husband is hardly at all recognised in the archaic State. The Mexicans " did not consider, nor did they punish, as adultery the trespass of a husband with any woman who was free, or not joined in matrimony ; wherefore the husband was not bound to so much fidelity as was exacted from the wife," adultery in her being inevitably punished with death.[2] In China, where adultery in a woman is branded as one of the vilest crimes and the guilty wife is oftentimes " cut into small pieces," concubinage is a recognised institution of the country.[3] In Corea " conjugal fidelity—obligatory on the woman— is not required of the husband. . . . Among the nobles, the young bridegroom spends three or four days with his bride, and then absents himself from her for a considerable time, to prove that he does not esteem her too highly. Etiquette dooms her to a species of widowhood, while he spends his hours of relaxation in the society of his concubines. To act otherwise would be considered in very bad taste, and highly unfashionable." [4] In Japan, " while the man is allowed a loose foot, the woman is expected not only to be absolutely spotless, but also never to show any jealousy, however wide the husband may roam, or however numerous may be the concubines in his family." [5] According to Hebrew law adultery was a capital offence, but it presupposed that the guilty woman was another man's wife.[6] The " Aryan " nations in early times generally saw nothing objectionable in the unfaith-fulness of a married man, whereas an adulterous wife was subject to the severest penalties.[7] Until some time after the introduction of Christianity among the Teutons their

---

[1] Macpherson, *Memorials of Service in India*, p. 133.
[2] Clavigero, *History of Mexico*, i. 356.
[3] Doolittle, *op. cit.* i. 339. Griffis, *Religions of Japan*, p. 149.

[4] Griffis, *Corea*, p. 251 *sq.*
[5] *Idem, Religions of Japan*, p. 320.
[6] *Leviticus*, xx. 10. *Deuteronomy*, xxii. 22.
[7] Schrader, *Prehistoric Antiquities of the Aryan Peoples*, p. 388.

law-books made no mention of the infidelity of husbands, because it was permitted by custom.[1] The Romans defined adultery as sexual intercourse with another man's wife ; on the other hand, the intercourse of a married man with an unmarried woman was not regarded as adultery.[2] The ordinary Greek feeling on the subject is expressed in the oration against Neæra, ascribed to Demosthenes, where the licence accorded to husbands is spoken of as a matter of course :—" We keep mistresses for our pleasures, concubines for constant attendance, and wives to bear us legitimate children and to be our faithful housekeepers." [3]

At the same time the idea that fidelity in marriage ought to be reciprocal was not altogether unknown in classical antiquity.[4] In a lost chapter of his ' Economics,' which has come to us only through a Latin translation, Aristotle points out that it for various reasons is prudent for a man to be faithful to his wife, but that nothing is so peculiarly the property of a wife as a chaste and hallowed intercourse.[5] Plutarch condemns the man who, lustful and dissolute, goes astray with a courtesan or maid-servant ; though at the same time he admonishes the wife not to be vexed or impatient, considering that " it is out of respect to her that he bestows upon another all his wanton depravity."[6] Plautus argues that it is unjust of a husband to exact a fidelity which he does not keep himself.[7]

In its condemnation of adultery Christianity made no distinction between husband and wife.[8] If continence is a stringent duty for unmarried persons independently of

---

[1] Wilda, *Strafrecht der Germanen*, p. 821. Nordström, *op. cit.* ii. 67 *sq.* Stemann, *Den danske Retshistorie indtil Christian V.'s Lov*, pp. 324, 633. Keyser, *Efterladte Skrifter*, vol. ii. pt. ii. 32 *sq.* Brunner, *Deutsche Rechtsgeschichte*, ii. 662.

[2] Vinnius, *In quatuor libros institutionum imperialium commentarius*, iv. 18. 4, p. 993. Cf. *Digesta*, l. 16. 101. 1 ; Mommsen, *Römisches Strafrecht*, p. 688 *sq.*

[3] *Oratio in Neæram*, p. 1386. Cf. Schmidt, *Die Ethik der alten Griechen*, ii. 196 *sq.*

[4] Lecky, *op. cit.* ii. 312 *sq.* Schmidt, *op. cit.* ii. 195 *sq.*

[5] Aristotle, *Œconomica*, p. 341, vol. ii. 679. Cf. Isocrates, *Nicocles sive Cyprii*, 40.

[6] Plutarch, *Conjugalia præcepta*, 16.

[7] Plautus, *Mercator*, iv. 5.

[8] Laurent, *op. cit.* iv. 114. Gratian, *Decretum*, ii. 35. 5. 23.

their sex, the observance of the sacred marriage vow must be so in a still higher degree. But here again there is a considerable discrepancy between the actual feelings of Christian peoples and the standard of their religion. Even in the laws of various European countries relating to divorce or judicial separation we find an echo of the popular notion that adultery is a smaller offence in a husband than in a wife.[1]

The judgment pronounced upon an unfaithful husband is of course influenced by the opinion about extra-matrimonial connections in general. Where it is considered wrong for a man to have intercourse with either an unmarried woman or another man's wife, adultery in a husband is *eo ipso* condemned. But whether, or how far, infidelity on his part is stigmatised as an offence against his wife, chiefly depends upon the degree of regard which is paid to the feelings of women. That a married man generally enjoys more liberty than a married woman is largely due to the same causes as make him the more privileged partner in other respects; but there are also special reasons for this inequality between the sexes. It was a doctrine of the Roman jurists that adultery is a crime in the wife, and in the wife only, on account of the danger of introducing strange children to the husband.[2] Moreover, the temptation to infidelity and the facility in indulging in it are commonly greater in the case of the husband than in that of the wife; and, as we have often noticed before, actual practice is always apt to influence moral opinion. And a still more important reason for the inequality in question is undoubtedly the general notion that unchastity of any kind is more discreditable for a woman than for a man.

[1] See *supra*, ii. 397.

[2] Hunter, *Exposition of Roman Law*, p. 1071.

CHAPTER XLIII

HOMOSEXUAL LOVE

OUR review of the moral ideas concerning sexual relations has not yet come to an end. The gratification of the sexual instinct assumes forms which fall outside the ordinary pale of nature. Of these there is one which, on account of the *rôle* which it has played in the moral history of mankind, cannot be passed over in silence, namely, intercourse between individuals of the same sex, what is nowadays commonly called homosexual love.

It is frequently met with among the lower animals.[1] It probably occurs, at least sporadically, among every race of mankind.[2] And among some peoples it has assumed such proportions as to form a true national habit.

In America homosexual customs have been observed among a great number of the native tribes. In nearly every part of the continent there seem to have been, since ancient times, men dressing themselves in the clothes and performing the functions of women, and living with other men as their concubines or wives.[3] Moreover, between

[1] Karsch, 'Päderastie und Tribadie bei den Tieren,' in *Jahrbuch für sexuelle Zwischenstufen,* ii. 126 *sqq.* Havelock Ellis, *Studies in the Psychology of Sex,* 'Sexual Inversion,' p. 2 *sqq.*

[2] Cf. Ives, *Classification of Crimes,* p. 49. The statement that it is unknown among a certain people cannot reasonably mean that it may not be practised in secret.

[3] von Spix and von Martius, *Travels in Brazil,* ii. 246 ; von Martius, *Von dem Rechtszustande unter den Ureinwohnern Brasiliens,* p. 27 *sq.* ; Lomonaco, 'Sulle razze indigene del Brasile,' in *Archivio per l'antropologia e la etnologia,* xix. 46; Burton, *Arabian Nights,* x. 246 (Brazilian Indians). Garcilasso de la Vega, *First Part of the Royal Commentaries of the Yncas,* ii. 441 *sqq.*; Cieza de Leon, 'La crónica del Perú [primera parte],' ch. 49, in

young men who are comrades in arms there are *liaisons d'amitié*, which, according to Lafitau, " ne laissent aucun soupçon de vice apparent, quoiqu'il y ait, ou qu'il puisse y avoir, beaucoup de vice réel." [1]

Homosexual practices are, or have been, very prominent among the peoples in the neighbourhood of Behring Sea. [2] In Kadiak it was the custom for parents who had a girl-like son to dress and rear him as a girl, teaching him only domestic duties, keeping him at woman's work, and letting him associate only with women and girls. Arriving at the age of ten or fifteen years, he was married to some wealthy man and was then called an *achnuchik* or *shoopan*. [3] Dr. Bogoraz gives the following account of a

Biblioteca de autores españoles, xxvi. 403 (Peruvian Indians at the time of the Spanish conquest). Oviedo y Valdés, ' Sumario de la natural historia de las Indias,' ch. 81, in *Biblioteca de autores españoles*, xxii. 508 (Isthmians). Bancroft, *Native Races of the Pacific States*, i. 585 (Indians of New Mexico); ii. 467 *sq.* (ancient Mexicans). Diaz del Castillo, ' Conquista de Nueva-España,' ch. 208, in *Biblioteca de autores españoles*, xxvi. 309 (ancient Mexicans). Landa, *Relacion de las cosas de Yucatan*, p. 178 (ancient Yucatans). Nuñez Cabeza de Vaca, ' Naufragios y relacion de la jornada que hizo a la Florida,' ch. 26, in *Biblioteca de autores españoles*, xxii. 538; Coreal, *Voyages aux Indes Occidentales*, i. 33 *sq.* (Indians of Florida). Perrin du Lac, *Voyage dans les deux Louisianes et chez les nations sauvages du Missouri*, p. 352; Bossu, *Travels through Louisiana*, i. 303. Hennepin, *Nouvelle Découverte d'un très Grand Pays Situé dans l'Amerique*, p. 219 *sq.*; ' La Salle's Last Expedition and Discoveries in North America,' in *Collections of the New-York Historical Society*, ii. 237 *sq.*; de Lahontan, *Mémoires de l'Amérique septentrionale*, p. 142 (Illinois). Marquette, *Recit des voyages*, p. 52 *sq.* (Illinois and Naudowessies). Wied-Neuwied, *Travels in the Interior of North America*, p. 351 (Manitaries, Mandans, &c.). McCoy, *History of*

Baptist Indian Missions, p. 360 *sq.* (Osages). Heriot, *Travels through the Canadas*, p. 278; Catlin, *North American Indians*, ii. 214 *sq.* (Sioux). Dorsey, 'Omaha Sociology,' in *Ann. Rep. Bur. Ethn.* iii. 365; James, *Expedition from Pittsburgh to the Rocky Mountains*, i. 267 (Omahas). Loskiel, *History of the Mission of the United Brethren among the Indians*, i. 14 (Iroquois). Richardson, *Arctic Searching Expedition*, ii. 42 (Crees). Oswald, quoted by Bastian, *Der Mensch in der Geschichte*, iii. 314 (Indians of California). Holder, in *New York Medical Journal*, December 7th, 1889, quoted by Havelock Ellis, *op. cit.* p. 9 *sq.* (Indians of Washington and other tribes in the North-Western United States). See also Karsch, 'Uranismus oder Päderastie und Tribadie bei den Naturvölkern,' in *Jahrbuch für sexuelle Zwischenstufen*, iii. 112 *sqq.*

[1] Lafitau, *Moeurs des sauvages ameriquains*, i. 603, 607 *sqq.*
[2] Dall, *Alaska*, p. 402; Bancroft, *op. cit.* i. 92; Waitz, *Anthropologie der Naturvölker*, iii. 314 (Aleuts). von Langsdorf, *Voyages and Travels*, ii. 48 (natives of Oonalaska). Steller, *Kamtschatka*, p. 289, n.*a*; Georgi, *Russia*, iii. 132 *sq.* (Kamchadales).
[3] Davydow, quoted by Holmberg, ' Ethnographische Skizzen über die Völker des russischen Amerika,' in *Acta Soc. Scientiarum Fennicæ*, iv. 400 *sq.* Lisiansky, *Voyage Round the World*, p. 199. von Langsdorf. *op. cit.*

similar practice prevalent among the Chukchi :—"It happens frequently that, under the supernatural influence of one of their shamans, or priests, a Chukchi lad at sixteen years of age will suddenly relinquish his sex and imagine himself to be a woman. He adopts a woman's attire, lets his hair grow, and devotes himself altogether to female occupation. Furthermore, this disowner of his sex takes a husband into the *yurt* and does all the work which is usually incumbent on the wife in most unnatural and voluntary subjection. Thus it frequently happens in a *yurt* that the husband is a woman, while the wife is a man ! These abnormal changes of sex imply the most abject immorality in the community, and appear to be strongly encouraged by the shamans, who interpret such cases as an injunction of their individual deity." The change of sex was usually accompanied by future shaman-ship ; indeed, nearly all the shamans were former delin-quents of their sex.[1] Among the Chukchi male shamans who are clothed in woman's attire and are believed to be transformed physically into women are still quite common; and traces of the change of a shaman's sex into that of a woman may be found among many other Siberian tribes.[2] In some cases at least there can be no doubt that these transformations were connected with homosexual prac-tices. In his description of the Koriaks, Krasheninnikoff makes mention of the *ke'yev*, that is, men occupying the position of concubines ; and he compares them with the Kamchadale *koe'kĕuĕ*, as he calls them, that is, men trans-formed into women. Every *koe'kĕuĕ*, he says, is regarded as a magician and interpreter of dreams ; but from his confused description Mr. Jochelson thinks it may be inferred that the most important feature of the institution of the *koe'kĕuĕ* lay, not in their shamanistic power, but in their position with regard to the satisfaction of the

ii. 64. Sauer, *Billing's Expedition to the Northern Parts of Russia*, p. 176. Sarytschew, 'Voyage of Discovery to the North-East of Siberia,' in *Collection of Modern and Contemporary*

Voyages, vi. 16.
[1] Bogoraz, quoted by Demidoff, *Shooting Trip to Kamchatka*, p. 74 *sq.*
[2] Jochelson, *Koryak Religion and Myth*, pp. 52, 53 n. 3.

unnatural inclinations of the Kamchadales. The *koe'kčuč* wore women's clothes, did women's work, and were in the position of wives or concubines.[1]

In the Malay Archipelago homosexual love is common,[2] though not in all of the islands.[3] It is widely spread among the Bataks of Sumatra.[4] In Bali it is practised openly, and there are persons who make it a profession.[5] The *basir* of the Dyaks are men who make their living by witchcraft and debauchery. They " are dressed as women, they are made use of at idolatrous feasts and for sodomitic abominations, and many of them are formally married to other men." [6]   Dr. Haddon says that he never heard of any unnatural offences in Torres Straits ;[7] but in the Rigo district of British New Guinea several instances of pederasty have been met with,[8] and at Mowat in Daudai it is regularly indulged in.[9]   Homosexual love is reported as common among the Marshall Islanders[10] and in Hawaii.[11] From Tahiti we hear of a set of men called by the natives *mahoos*, who " assume the dress, attitude, and manners, of women, and affect all the fantastic oddities and coquetries of the vainest of females. They mostly associate with the women, who court their acquaintance. With the manners of the women, they adopt their peculiar employments. . . . The encouragement of this abomination is almost solely

[1] Jochelson, *op. cit.* p. 52 *sq.*

[2] Wilken, ' Plechtigheden en gebruiken bij verlovingen en huwelijken bij de volken van den Indischen Archipel,' in *Bijdragen tot de taal- land- en volkenkunde van Nederlandsch-Indië*, xxxiii. (ser. v. vol. iv.) p. 457 *sqq.*

[3] Crawfurd, *History of the Indian Archipelago*, iii. 139. Marsden, *History of Sumatra*, p. 261.

[4] Junghuhn, *Die Battaländer auf Sumatra*, ii. 157, n.*

[5] Jacobs, *Eenigen tijd onder de Baliërs*, pp. 14, 134 *sq.*

[6] Hardeland, *Dajacksch-deutsches Wörterbuch*, p. 53 *sq.*   Schwaner, *Borneo*, i. 186.   Perelaer, *Ethnographische beschrijving der Dajaks*, p. 32.

[7] Haddon, ' Ethnography of the Western Tribe of Torres Straits,' in *Jour. Anthr. Inst.* xix. 315.

[8] Seligmann, ' Sexual Inversion among Primitive Races,' in *The Alienist and Neurologist*, xxiii. 3 *sqq.*

[9] Beardmore, ' Natives of Mowat, Daudai, New Guinea,' in *Jour. Anthr. Inst.* xix. 464. Haddon, *ibid.* xix. 315.

[10] Hernsheim, *Beitrag zur Sprache der Marshall-Inseln*, p. 40. A different opinion is expressed by Senfft, in Steinmetz, *Rechtsverhältnisse von eingeborenen Völkern in Afrika und Ozeanien*, p. 437.

[11] Remy, *Ka Mooolelo Hawaii*, p. xliii.

confined to the chiefs." [1] Of the New Caledonians M. Foley writes :—" La plus grande fraternité n'est pas chez eux la fraternité utérine, mais la fraternité des armes. Il en est ainsi surtout au village de Poepo. Il est vrai que cette fraternité des armes est compliquée de pédérastie." [2]

Among the natives of the Kimberley District in West Australia, if a young man on reaching a marriageable age can find no wife, he is presented with a boy-wife, known as *chookadoo*. In this case, also, the ordinary exogamic rules are observed, and the " husband " has to avoid his " mother-in-law," just as if he were married to a woman. The *chookadoo* is a boy of five years to about ten, when he is initiated. " The relations which exist between him and his protecting *billalu*," says Mr. Hardman, " are somewhat doubtful. There is no doubt they have connection, but the natives repudiate with horror and disgust the idea of sodomy." [3] Such marriages are evidently exceedingly common. As the women are generally monopolised by the older and more influential men of the tribe, it is rare to find a man under thirty or forty who has a wife ; hence it is the rule that, when a boy becomes five years old, he is given as a boy-wife to one of the young men.[4] According to Mr. Purcell's description of the natives of the same district, " every useless member of the tribe " gets a boy, about five or seven years old ; and these boys, who are called *mullawongahs*, are used for sexual purposes.[5] Among the Chingalee of South Australia, Northern Territory, old men are often noticed with no wives but accompanied by one or two boys, whom they jealously guard and with whom they have sodomitic intercourse.[6]

[1] Turnbull, *Voyage Round the World*, p. 382. See also Wilson, *Missionary Voyage to the Southern Pacific*, pp. 333, 361 ; Ellis, *Polynesian Researches*, i. 246, 258.

[2] Foley, ' Sur les habitations et les mœurs des Néo-Calédoniens,' in *Bull. Soc. d'Anthrop. Paris*, ser. iii. vol. ii. 606. See also de Rochas, *Nouvelle Calédonie*, p. 235.

[3] Hardman, ' Notes on some Habits and Customs of the Natives of the Kimberley District,' in *Proceed. Roy. Irish Academy*, ser. iii. vol. i. 74.

[4] *Ibid.* pp. 71, 73.

[5] Purcell, ' Rites and Customs of Australian Aborigines,' in *Verhandl. Berliner Gesellsch. Anthrop.* 1893, p. 287.

[6] Ravenscroft, ' Some Habits and Customs of the Chingalee Tribe,' in *Trans. Roy. Soc. South Australia*, xv.

That homosexual practices are not unknown among other Australian tribes may be inferred from Mr. Howitt's statement relating to South-Eastern natives, that unnatural offences are forbidden to the novices by the old men and guardians after leaving the initiation camp.[1]

In Madagascar there are certain boys who live like women and have intercourse with men, paying those men who please them.[2] In an old account of that island, dating from the seventeenth century, it is said : " Il y a . . . quelques hommes qu'ils appellent Tsecats, qui sont hommes effeminez et impuissans, qui recherchent les garçons, et font mine d'en estre amoureux, en contrefaisans les filles et se vestans ainsi qu'elles leurs font des presents pour dormir auec eux, et mesmes se donnent des noms de filles, en faisant les honteuses et les modestes. . . . Ils haïssent les femmes et ne les veulent point hanter." [3] Men behaving like women have also been observed among the Ondonga in German South-West Africa [4] and the Diakité-Sarracolese in the French Soudan,[5] but as regards their sexual habits details are wanting. Homosexual practices are common among the Banaka and Bapuku in the Cameroons.[6] But among the natives of Africa generally such practices seem to be comparatively rare,[7] except among Arabic-

---

122. I am indebted to Mr. N. W. Thomas for drawing my attention to these statements.
[1] Howitt, ' Some Australian Ceremonies of Initiation,' in *Jour. Anthr. Inst.* xiii. 450.
[2] Lasnet, in *Annales d'hygiène et de médecine coloniales*, 1899, p. 494, quoted by Havelock Ellis, *op. cit.* p. 10. *Cf.* Rencurel, in *Annales d'hygiène*, 1900, p. 562, quoted *ibid.* p. 11 *sq.* See also Leguével de Lacombe, *Voyage à Madagascar*, i. 97 *sq.* Pederasty prevails to some extent in the island of Nossi-Bé, close to Madagascar, and is very common at Ankisimane, opposite to it, on Jassandava Bay (Walter, in Steinmetz, *Rechtsverhältnisse*, p. 376).
[3] de Flacourt, *Histoire de la grande isle Madagascar*, p. 86.
[4] Rautanen, in Steinmetz, *Rechtsverhältnisse*, p. 333.

[5] Nicole, *ibid.* p. 111.
[6] *Ibid.* p. 38.
[7] Munzinger, *Ostafrikanische Studien*, p. 525 (Barea and Kunáma). Baumann, ' Conträre Sexual-Erscheinungen bei der Neger-Bevölkerung Zanzibars,' in *Verhandl. der Berliner Gesellsch. für Anthropologie*, 1899, p. 668. Felkin, ' Notes on the Waganda Tribe of Central Africa,' in *Proceed. Roy. Soc. Edinburgh*, xiii. 723. Johnston, *British Central Africa*, p. 404 (Bakongo). Monrad, *Skildring af Guinea-Kysten*, p. 57 (Negroes of Accra). Torday and Joyce, ' Ethnography of the Ba-Mbala,' in *Jour. Anthr. Inst.* xxxv. 410. Nicole, in Steinmetz, *Rechtsverhältnisse*, p. 111 (Muhammedan Negroes). Tellier, *ibid.* p. 159 (Kreis Kita in the French Soudan). Beverley, *ibid.* p. 210 (Wagogo). Kraft, *ibid.* p. 288 (Wapokomo).

speaking peoples and in countries like Zanzibar,[1] where there has been a strong Arab influence. In North Africa they are not restricted to the inhabitants of towns ; they are frequent among the peasants of Egypt [2] and universal among the Jbâla inhabiting the Northern mountains of Morocco. On the other hand, they are much less common or even rare among the Berbers and the nomadic Bedouins,[3] and it is reported that the Bedouins of Arabia are quite exempt from them.[4]

Homosexual love is spread over Asia Minor and Mesopotamia.[5] It is very prevalent among the Tartars and Karatchai of the Caucasus,[6] the Persians,[7] Sikhs,[8] and Afghans ; in Kaubul a bazaar or street is set apart for it.[9] Old travellers make reference to its enormous frequency among the Muhammedans of India,[10] and in this respect time seems to have produced no change.[11] In China, where it is also extremely common, there are special houses devoted to male prostitution, and boys are sold by their parents about the age of four, to be trained for this occupation.[12] In Japan pederasty is said by some to have prevailed from the most ancient times, whereas others are of opinion that it was introduced by Buddhism about the sixth century of our era. The monks used to live with handsome youths, to whom they were often passionately devoted ; and in feudal times nearly every knight had as

[1] Baumann, in *Verhandl. Berliner Gesellsch. Anthrop.* 1899, p. 668 *sq.*
[2] Burckhardt, *Travels in Nubia*, p. 135.
[3] d'Escayrac de Lauture, *Afrikanische Wüste*, p. 93.
[4] Burckhardt, *Travels in Arabia*, i. 364. See also von Kremer, *Culturgeschichte des Orients*, ii. 269.
[5] Burton, *Arabian Nights*, x. 232.
[6] Kovalewsky, *Coutume contemporaine*, p. 340.
[7] Polak, ' Die Prostitution in Persien,' in *Wiener Medizinische Wochenschrift*, xi. 627 *sqq*. *Idem*, *Persien*, i. 237. Burton, *Arabian Nights*, x. 233 *sq*. Wilson, *Persian Life and Customs*, p. 229.
[8] Malcolm, *Sketch of the Sikhs*, p.

140. Havelock Ellis, *op. cit.* p. 5, n. 2. Burton, *Arabian Nights*, x. 236.
[9] Wilson, *Abode of Snow*, p. 420. Burton, *Arabian Nights*, x. 236.
[10] Stavorinus, *Voyages to the East-Indies*, i. 456. Fryer, *New Account of East-India*, p. 97. Chevers, *Manual of Medical Jurisprudence for India*, p. 705.
[11] Chevers, *op. cit.* p. 708.
[12] *Indo-Chinese Gleaner*, iii. 193. Wells Williams, *The Middle Kingdom*, i. 836. Matignon, ' Deux mots sur la pédérastie en Chine,' in *Archives d'anthropologie criminelle*, xiv. 38 *sqq*. Karsch, *Das gleichgeschlechtliche Leben der Ostasiaten*, p. 6 *sqq*.

his favourite a young man with whom he entertained relations of the most intimate kind, and on behalf of whom
he was always ready to fight a duel when occasion occurred.
Tea-houses with male *gheishas* were found in Japan till the
middle of the nineteenth century. Nowadays pederasty
seems to be more prevalent in the Southern than in the
Northern provinces of the country, but there are also
districts where it is hardly known.[1]

No reference is made to pederasty either in the Homeric
poems or by Hesiod, but later on we meet with it almost
as a national institution in Greece. It was known in Rome
and other parts of Italy at an early period ;[2] but here also
it became much more frequent in the course of time. At
the close of the sixth century, Polybius tells us, many
Romans paid a talent for the possession of a beautiful
youth.[3] During the Empire " il était d'usage, dans les
familles patriciennes, de donner au jeune homme pubère
un esclave du même âge comme compagnon de lit, afin
qu'il pût satisfaire . . . ' ses premiers élans' génésiques ";[4]
and formal marriages between men were introduced with
all the solemnities of ordinary nuptials.[5] Homosexual
practices occurred among the Celts,[6] and were by no
means unknown to the ancient Scandinavians, who had a
whole nomenclature on the subject.[7]

Of late years a voluminous and constantly increasing
literature on homosexuality[8] has revealed its frequency in
modern Europe. No country and no class of society is
free from it. In certain parts of Albania it even exists as
a popular custom, the young men from the age of sixteen

[1] Jwaya, ' Nan sho k,' in *Jahrbuch für sexuelle Zwischenstufen*, iv. 266, 268, 270. Karsch, *op. cit.* p. 71 *sqq.*
[2] Dionysius of Halicarnassus, *Antiquitates Romanæ*, vii. 2. Athenæus, *Deipnosophistæ*, xii. 14, p. 518 (Etruscans). Rein, *Criminalrecht der Römer*, p. 863.
[3] Polybius, *Historiæ*, xxxii. 11. 5.
[4] Buret, *La syphilis aujourd'hui et chez les anciens*, p. 197 *sqq.* Catullus, *Carmina*, lxi. (' In Nuptias Juliæ et Manlii '), 128 *sqq.* *Cf.* Martial, *Epigrammata*, viii. 44. 16 *sq.*
[5] Juvenal, *Satiræ*, ii. 117 *sqq.* Martial, *op. cit.* xii. 42.
[6] Diodorus Siculus, *Bibliotheca historica*, v. 32. 7. Aristotle, *Politica*, ii. 9, p. 1269 b.
[7] ' Spuren von Konträrsexualität bei den alten Skandinaviern,' in *Jahrbuch für sexuelle Zwischenstufen*, iv. 244 *sqq.*
[8] *See infra*, Additional Notes.

upwards regularly having boy favourites of between twelve and seventeen.[1]

The above statements chiefly refer to homosexual practices between men, but similar practices also occur between women.[2] Among the American aborigines there are not only men who behave like women, but women who behave like men. Thus in certain Brazilian tribes women are found who abstain from every womanly occupation and imitate the men in everything, who wear their hair in a masculine fashion, who go to war with a bow and arrows, who hunt together with the men, and who would rather allow themselves to be killed than have sexual intercourse with a man. " Each of these women has a woman who serves her and with whom she says she is married ; they live together as husband and wife." [3] So also there are among the Eastern Eskimo some women who refuse to accept husbands, preferring to adopt masculine manners, following the deer on the mountains, trapping and fishing for themselves.[4] Homosexual practices are said to be common among Hottentot [5] and Herero [6] women. In Zanzibar there are women who wear men's clothes in private, show a preference for masculine occupations, and seek sexual satisfaction among women who have the same inclination, or else among normal women who are won over by presents or other means.[7] In Egyptian harems every woman is said to have a " friend."[8] In Bali homosexuality is almost as common among women as among men, though it is exercised more secretly ;[9] and the same seems to be the case in India.[10] From Greek antiquity we

[1] Hahn, *Albanesische Studien*, i. 168.

[2] Karsch, in *Jahrbuch für sexuelle Zwischenstufen*, iii. 85 sqq. Ploss-Bartels, *Das Weib*, i. 517 sqq. von Krafft-Ebing, *Psychopathia sexualis*, p. 278 sqq. Moll, *Die Conträre Sexualempfindung*, p. 247 sqq. Havelock Ellis, *op. cit.* p. 118 sqq.

[3] Magalhanes de Gandavo, *Histoire de la Province de Sancta-Cruz*, p. 116 sq.

[4] Dall, *op. cit.* p. 139.

[5] Fritsch, quoted by Karsch, in *Jahrbuch für sexuelle Zwischenstufen*, iii. 87 sq.

[6] Fritsch, *Die Eingeborenen Süd-Afrika's*, p. 227. Cf. Schinz, *Deutsch-Südwest-Afrika*, pp. 173, 177.

[7] Baumann, in *Verhandl. Berliner Gesellsch. Anthrop.* 1899, p. 668 sq.

[8] Havelock Ellis, *op. cit.* p. 123.

[9] Jacobs, *Eenigen tijd onder de Baliërs*, p. 134 sq.

[10] Havelock Ellis, *op. cit.* p. 124 sq.

hear of " Lesbian " love. The fact that homosexuality has been much more frequently noticed in men than in women does not imply that the latter are less addicted to it. For various reasons the sexual abnormalities of women have attracted much less attention,[1] and moral opinion has generally taken little notice of them.

Homosexual practices are due sometimes to instinctive preference, sometimes to external conditions unfavourable to normal intercourse.[2] A frequent cause is congenital sexual inversion, that is, " sexual instinct turned by inborn constitutional abnormality toward persons of the same sex." [3] It seems likely that the feminine men and the masculine women referred to above are, at least in many instances, sexual inverts ; though, in the case of shamans, the change of sex may also result from the belief that such transformed shamans, like their female colleagues, are particularly powerful.[4] Dr. Holder affirms the existence of congenital inversion among the North-Western tribes of the United States,[5] Dr. Baumann among the people of Zanzibar ; [6] and in Morocco, also, I believe it is common enough. But as regards its prevalence among non-European peoples we have mostly to resort to mere conjectures ; our real knowledge of congenital inversion is derived from the voluntary confessions of inverts. The large majority of travellers are totally ignorant of the psychological side of the subject, and even to an expert it must very often be impossible to decide whether a certain case of inversion is congenital or acquired. Indeed, acquired inversion itself presupposes an innate disposition which under certain circumstances develops into actual inversion.[7] Even between inversion and normal sexuality

---

[1] See *ibid.* p. 121 *sq.*
[2] Another reason for such practices is given by Mr. Beardmore (in *Jour. Anthr. Inst.* xix. 464), with reference to the Papuans of Mowat. He says that they indulge in sodomy because too great increase of population is undesired amongst the younger portion of the married

people. *Cf. infra*, p. 484 *sqq.*
[3] Havelock Ellis, *op. cit.* p. 1.
[4] Jochelson, *op. cit.* p. 52 *sq.*
[5] Holder, quoted by Havelock Ellis, *op. cit.* p. 9 *sq.*
[6] Baumann, in *Verhandl. Berliner Gesellsch. Anthrop.* 1899, p. 668 *sq.*
[7] *Cf.* Féré, *L'instinct sexuel*, quoted by Havelock Ellis, *op. cit.* p. 41.

there seem to be all shades of variation. Professor James thinks that inversion is "a kind of sexual appetite, of which very likely most men possess the germinal possibility."[1] This is certainly the case in early puberty.[2]

A very important cause of homosexual practices is absence of the other sex. There are many instances of this among the lower animals.[3] Buffon long ago observed that, if male or female birds of various species were shut up together, they would soon begin to have sexual relations among themselves, the males sooner than the females.[4] The West Australian boy-marriage is a substitute for ordinary marriage in cases when women are not obtainable. Among the Bororó of Brazil homosexual intercourse is said to occur in their men-houses only when the scarcity of accessible girls is unusually great.[5] Its prevalence in Tahiti may perhaps be connected with the fact that there was only one woman to four or five men, owing to the habit of female infanticide.[6] Among the Chinese in certain regions, for instance Java, the lack of accessible women is the principal cause of homosexual practices.[7] According to some writers such practices are the results of polygamy.[8] In Muhammedan countries they are no doubt largely due to the seclusion of women, preventing free intercourse between the sexes and compelling the unmarried people to associate almost exclusively with members of their own sex. Among the mountaineers of Northern Morocco the excessive indulgence in pederasty thus goes hand in hand with great isolation of the women

---

[1] James, *Principles of Psychology*, ii. 439. See also Ives, *op. cit.* p. 56 *sqq.*

[2] Dr. Dessoir ('Zur Psychologie der Vita sexualis,' in *Allgemeine Zeitschrift für Psychiatrie*, l. 942) even goes so far as to conclude that "an undifferentiated sexual feeling is normal, on the average, during the first years of puberty." But this is certainly an exaggeration (*cf.* Havelock Ellis, *op. cit.* p. 47 *sq.*).

[3] Karsch, in *Jahrbuch für sexuelle Zwischenstufen*, ii. 126 *sqq.* Havelock Ellis, *op. cit.* p. 2 *sq.*

[4] Havelock Ellis, *op. cit.* p. 2.

[5] von den Steinen, *Unter den Naturvölkern Zentral-Brasiliens*, p. 502.

[6] Ellis, *Polynesian Researches*, i. 257 *sq.*

[7] Matignon, in *Archives d'anthropologie criminelle*, xiv. 42. Karsch, *op. cit.* p. 32 *sqq.*

[8] Waitz, *Anthropologie der Naturvölker*, iii. 113. Bastian, *Der Mensch in der Geschichte*, iii. 305 (Dahomans).

and a very high standard of female chastity, whereas among the Arabs of the plains, who are little addicted to boy-love, the unmarried girls enjoy considerable freedom. Both in Asia [1] and Europe [2] the obligatory celibacy of the monks and priests has been a cause of homosexual practices, though it must not be forgotten that a profession which imposes abstinence from marriage is likely to attract a comparatively large number of congenital inverts. The temporary separation of the sexes involved in a military mode of life no doubt accounts for the extreme prevalence of homosexual love among warlike races,[3] like the Sikhs, Afghans, Dorians, and Normans.[4] In Persia[5] and Morocco it is particularly common among soldiers. In Japan it was an incident of knighthood, in New Caledonia and North America of brotherhood in arms. At least in some of the North American tribes men who were dressed as women accompanied the other men as servants in war and the chase.[6] Among the Banaka and Bapuku in the Cameroons pederasty is practised especially by men who are long absent from their wives.[7] In Morocco I have heard it advocated on account of the convenience it affords to persons who are travelling.

Dr. Havelock Ellis justly observes that when homosexual attraction is due simply to the absence of the other sex we are not concerned with sexual inversion, but merely with the accidental turning of the sexual instinct into an abnormal channel, the instinct being called out by an approximate substitute, or even by diffused emotional excitement, in the absence of the normal object.[8] But it seems to me probable that in such cases the homosexual

---

[1] *Supra*, ii. 462. Karsch, *op. cit.* pp. 7. (China), 76 *sqq.* (Japan), 132 (Corea).

[2] See Voltaire, *Dictionnaire philosophique*, ' Amour Socratique' (*Œuvres*, vii. 82) ; Buret, *Syphilis in the Middle Ages and in Modern Times*, p. 88 *sq.*

[3] *Cf.* Havelock Ellis, *op. cit.* p. 5.

[4] Freeman, *Reign of Willam Rufus*, i. 159.

[5] Polak, in *Wiener Medizinische Wochenschrift*, xi. 628.

[6] Marquette, *op. cit.* p. 53 (Illinois). Perrin du Lac, *Voyage dans les deux Louisianes et chez les nations sauvages du Missouri*, p. 352. *Cf.* Nuñez Cabeza de Vaca, *loc. cit.* p. 538 (concerning the Indians of Florida) :—" . . . tiran arco y llevan muy gran carga."

[7] Steinmetz, *Rechtsverhältnisse*, p. 38.

[8] Havelock Ellis, *op. cit.* p. 3.

attraction in the course of time quite easily develops into genuine inversion. I cannot but think that our chief authorities on homosexuality have underestimated the modifying influence which habit may exercise on the sexual instinct. Professor Krafft-Ebing[1] and Dr. Moll[2] deny the existence of acquired inversion except in occasional instances ; and Dr. Havelock Ellis takes a similar view, if putting aside those cases of a more or less morbid character in which old men with failing sexual powers, or younger men exhausted by heterosexual debauchery, are attracted to members of their own sex.[3] But how is it that in some parts of Morocco such a very large proportion of the men are distinctly sexual inverts, in the sense in which this word is used by Dr. Havelock Ellis,[4] that is, persons who for the gratification of their sexual desire prefer their own sex to the opposite one ? It may be that in Morocco and in Oriental countries generally, where almost every individual marries, congenital inversion, through the influence of heredity, is more frequent than in Europe, where inverts so commonly abstain from marrying. But that this could not be an adequate explanation of the fact in question becomes at once apparent when we consider the extremely unequal distribution of inverts among different neighbouring tribes of the same stock, some of which are very little or hardly at all addicted to pederasty. I take the case to be, that homosexual practices in early youth have had a lasting effect on the sexual instinct, which at its first appearance, being somewhat indefinite, is easily turned into a homosexual direction.[5] In Morocco inversion is most prevalent among the scribes, who from childhood have lived in very close association with their fellow-students. Of course, influences of this kind " require a favourable organic predisposition to act on " ;[6] but this predisposition is probably no abnormality at all, only a

---

[1] Krafft-Ebing, op. cit. p. 211 sq.
[2] Moll, op. cit. p. 157 sqq.
[3] Havelock Ellis, op. cit. p. 50 sq. Cf. ibid. p. 181 sqq.
[4] Ibid. p. 3.

[5] Cf. Norman, ' Sexual Perversion,' in Tuke's Dictionary of Psychological Medicine, ii. 1156.
[6] Havelock Ellis, op. cit. p. 191.

feature in the ordinary sexual constitution of man.[1] It
should be noticed that the most common form of inversion, at least in Muhammedan countries, is love of boys or
youths not yet in the age of puberty, that is, of male
individuals who are physically very like girls. Voltaire
observes :—" Souvent un jeune garçon, par la fraîcheur de
son teint, par l'éclat de ses couleurs, et par la douceur de
ses yeux, ressemble pendant deux ou trois ans à une belle
fille ; si on l'aime, c'est parce que la nature se méprend." [2]
Moreover, in normal cases sexual attraction depends not
only on sex, but on a youthful appearance as well ; and
there are persons so constituted that to them the latter
factor is of chief importance, whilst the question of sex
is almost a matter of indifference.

In ancient Greece, also, not only homosexual intercourse
but actual inversion, seems to have been very common ;
and although this, like every form of love, must have
contained a congenital element, there can be little doubt,
I think, that it was largely due to external circumstances
of a social character. It may, in the first place, be traced
to the methods of training the youth. In Sparta it seems
to have been the practice for every youth of good character
to have his lover, or " inspirator," [3] and for every well-
educated man to be the lover of some youth.[4] The relations between the " inspirator " and the " listener " were
extremely intimate : at home the youth was constantly
under the eyes of his lover, who was supposed to be to
him a model and pattern of life ; [5] in battle they stood
near one another and their fidelity and affection were often
shown till death ; [6] if his relatives were absent, the youth

[1] Dr. Havelock Ellis also admits
(op. cit. p. 190) that, if in early life
the sexual instincts are less definitely determined than when
adolescence is complete, " it is con-
ceivable, though unproved, that a
very strong impression, acting even
on a normal organism, may cause
arrest of sexual development on the
psychic side. It is a question," he
adds, " I am not in a position to
settle."

[2] Voltaire, Dictionnaire Philosophique, art. ' Amour Socratique,'
(Œuvres, vii. 81). Cf. Ovid, Metamorphoses, x. 84 sq.

[3] Servius, In Vergilii Æneidos, x.
325. For the whole subject of pederasty among the Dorians see
Mueller, History and Antiquities of
the Doric Race, ii. 307 sq.

[4] Aelian, Varia historia, iii. 10.

[5] Mueller, op. cit. ii. 308.

[6] Xenophon, Historia Græca, iv. 8.
39.

might be represented in the public assembly by his lover ; [1] and for many faults, particularly want of ambition, the lover could be punished instead of the " listener." [2] This ancient custom prevailed with still greater force in Crete, which island was hence by many persons considered to be the place of its birth.[3] Whatever may have been the case originally, there can be no doubt that in later times the relations between the youth and his lover implied unchaste intercourse.[4] And in other Greek states the education of the youth was accompanied by similar consequences. At an early age the boy was taken away from his mother, and spent thenceforth all his time in the company of men, until he reached the age when marriage became for him a civic duty.[5] According to Plato, the gymnasia and common meals among the youth " seem always to have had a tendency to degrade the ancient and natural custom of love below the level, not only of man, but of the beasts." [6] Plato also mentions the effect which these habits had on the sexual instincts of the men : when they reached manhood they were lovers of youths and not naturally inclined to marry or beget children, but, if at all, they did so only in obedience to the law.[7] Is not this, in all probability, an instance of acquired inversion ? But besides the influence of education there was another factor which, co-operating with it, favoured the development of homosexual tendencies, namely, the great gulf which mentally separated the sexes. Nowhere else has the difference in culture between men and women been so immense as in the fully developed Greek civilisation. The lot of a wife in Greece was retirement and ignorance. She lived in almost absolute seclusion, in a separate part of the house, together with her female slaves, deprived of all the educating influence of male society, and having no place at those public spectacles

---

[1] Plutarch, *Lycurgus*, xxv. 1.
[2] *Ibid.* xviii. 8. Aelian, *op. cit.* iii. 10.
[3] Aelian, *op. cit.* iii. 9. Athenaeus, *Deipnosophistæ*, xiii. 77, p. 601.
[4] *Cf.* Symonds, ' Die Homosexualität in Griechenland,' in Havelock Ellis and Symonds, *Das konträre Geschlechtsgefühl*, p. 55.
[5] *Ibid.* p. 116. Döllinger, *The Gentile and the Jew*, ii. 244.
[6] Plato, *Leges*, i. 636. *Cf.* Plutarch, *Amatorius*, v. 9.
[7] Plato, *Symposium*, p. 192.

which were the chief means of culture.[1] In such circumstances it is not difficult to understand that men so highly
intellectual as those of Athens regarded the love of women
as the offspring of the common Aphrodite, who " is of the
body rather than of the soul." [2] They had reached a stage
of mental culture at which the sexual instinct normally has
a craving for refinement, at which the gratification of mere
physical lust appears brutal. In the eyes of the most
refined among them those who were inspired by the
heavenly Aphrodite loved neither women nor boys, but
intelligent beings whose reason was beginning to be developed, much about the time at which their beards began to
grow.[3] In present China we meet with a parallel case.
Dr. Matignon observes :—" Il y a tout lieu de supposer
que certains Chinois, raffinés au point de vue intellectuel,
recherchent dans la pédérastie la satisfaction des sens et de
l'esprit. La femme chinoise est peu cultivée, ignorante
même, quelle que soit sa condition, honnête femme ou
prostituée. Or le Chinois a souvent l'âme poétique : il
aime les vers, la musique, les belles sentences des philosophes, autant de choses qu'il ne peut trouver chez le beau
sexe de l'Empire du Milieu." [4] So also it seems that the
ignorance and dullness of Muhammedan women, which is
a result of their total lack of education and their secluded
life, is a cause of homosexual practices ; Moors are
sometimes heard to defend pederasty on the plea that the
company of boys, who have always news to tell, is so much
more entertaining than the company of women.

We have hitherto dealt with homosexual love as a fact ;
we shall now pass to the moral valuation to which it is
subject. Where it occurs as a national habit we may
assume that no censure, or no severe censure, is passed on
it. Among the Bataks of Sumatra there is no punishment

---

[1] 'State of Female Society in
Greece,' in *Quarterly Review*, xxii.
172 *sqq.* Lecky, *History of European
Morals*, ii. 287. Döllinger, *op. cit.*
ii. 234.
[2] Plato, *Symposium*, p. 181. That
the low state of the Greek women

was instrumental to pederasty has
been pointed out by Döllinger (*op.
cit.* ii. 244) and Symonds (*loc. cit.*
pp. 77, 100, 101, 116 *sqq.*).
[3] Plato, *Symposium*, p. 181.
[4] Matignon, in *Archives d'anthropologie criminelle*, xiv. 41.

for it.[1] Of the *bazirs* among the Ngajus of Pula Patak, in Borneo, Dr. Schwaner says that " in spite of their loathsome calling they escape well-merited contempt." [2] The Society Islanders had for their homosexual practices " not only the sanction of their priests, but the direct example of their respective deities." [3] The *tsekats* of Madagascar maintained that they were serving the deity by leading a feminine life ; [4] but we are told that at Ankisimane and in Nossi-Bé, opposite to it, pederasts are objects of public contempt.[5] Father Veniaminof says of the Atkha Aleuts that " sodomy and too early cohabitation with a betrothed or intended wife are called among them grave sins " ; [6] but apart from the fact that his account of these natives in general gives the impression of being somewhat eulogistic, the details stated by him only show that the acts in question were considered to require a simple ceremony of purification.[7] There is no indication that the North American aborigines attached any opprobrium to men who had intercourse with those members of their own sex who had assumed the dress and habits of women. In Kadiak such a companion was on the contrary regarded as a great acquisition ; and the effeminate men themselves, far from being despised, were held in repute by the people, most of them being wizards.[8] We have previously noticed the connection between homosexual practices and shamanism among various Siberian peoples ; and it is said that such shamans as had changed their sex were greatly feared by the people, being regarded as very powerful.[9] Among the Illinois and Naudowessies the

[1] Junghuhn, *op. cit.* ii. 157, n.
[2] Schwaner, *op. cit.* i. 186.
[3] Ellis, *Polynesian Researches*, i. 258. *Cf.* Moerenhout, *Voyages aux îles du Grand Océan*, ii. 167 *sq.*
[4] de Flacourt, *op. cit.* p. 86.
[5] Walter, in Steinmetz, *Rechtsver-hältnisse*, p. 376.
[6] Veniaminof, quoted by Petroff, *Report on Alaska*, p. 158.
[7] *Ibid.* p. 158 :—" The offender desirous of unburdening himself selected a time when the sun was clear and unobscured ; he picked up

certain weeds and carried them about his person ; then deposited them and threw his sin upon them, calling the sun as a witness, and, when he had eased his heart of all that had weighed upon it, he threw the grass or weeds into the fire, and after that considered himself cleansed of his sin."
[8] Davydow, quoted by Holmberg, *loc. cit.* p. 400 *sq.* Lisianski, *op. cit.* p. 199.
[9] Bogoraz, quoted by Demidoff, *op. cit.* p. 75. Jochelson, *op. cit.* p. 52 *sq.*

effeminate men assist in all the juggleries and the solemn
dance in honour of the *calumet*, or sacred tobacco pipe, for
which the Indians have such a deference that one may call
it " the god of peace and war, and the arbiter of life and
death " ; but they are not permitted either to dance or
sing.   They are called into the councils of the Indians,
and nothing can be decided upon without their advice ;
for because of their extraordinary manner of living they
are looked upon as *manitous*, or supernatural beings, and
persons of consequence.[1]   The Sioux, Sacs, and Fox
Indians give once a year, or oftener if they choose, a feast
to the *Berdashe*, or *I-coo-coo-a*, who is a man dressed in
woman's clothes, as he has been all his life.   " For extraordinary privileges which he is known to possess, he is
driven to the most servile and degrading duties, which he
is not allowed to escape ; and he being the only one of the
tribe submitting to this disgraceful degradation, is looked
upon as ' medicine ' and sacred, and a feast is given to him
annually ; and initiatory to it, a dance by those few young
men of the tribe who can . . . . dance forward and
publicly make their boast (without the denial of the
Berdashe) . . . . Such, and such only, are allowed to
enter the dance and partake of the feast." [2]   Among some
American tribes, however, these effeminate men are said to
be despised, especially by the women.[3]   In ancient Peru,
also, homosexual practices seem to have entered in the
religious cult.   In some particular places, says Cieza de
Leon, boys were kept as priests in the temples, with whom
it was rumoured that the lords joined in company on days
of festivity.   They did not meditate, he adds, the committing of such sin, but only the offering of sacrifice to
the demon.   If the Incas by chance had some knowledge
of such proceedings in the temple, they might have

[1] Marquette, *op. cit.* p. 53 *sq.*
[2] Catlin, *North American Indians*,
ii. 214 *sq.*
[3] ' La Salle's Last Expedition in
North America,' in *Collections of the
New-York Historical Society*, ii. 238
(Illinois).   Perrin du Lac, *Voyage*
*dans les deux Louisianes et chez les
nations sauvages du Missouri*, p. 352.
Bossu, *op. cit.* i. 303 (Chactaws).
Oviedo y Valdés, *loc. cit.* p. 508
(Isthmians).   von Martius, *Von dem
Rechtszustande unter den Ureinwoh-
nern Brasiliens*, p. 28 (Guaycurûs).

ignored them out of religious tolerance.[1] But the Incas themselves were not only free from such practices in their own persons, they would not even permit any one who was guilty of them to remain in the royal houses or palaces. And Cieza heard it related that, if it came to their knowledge that somebody had committed an offence of that kind, they punished it with such a severity that it was known to all.[2] Las Casas tells us that in several of the more remote provinces of Mexico sodomy was tolerated, if not actually permitted, because the people believed that their gods were addicted to it ; and it is not improbable that in earlier times the same was the case in the entire empire.[3] But in a later age severe measures were adopted by legislators in order to suppress the practice. In Mexico people found guilty of it were killed.[4] In Nicaragua it was punished capitally by stoning,[5] and none of the Maya nations was without strict laws against it.[6] Among the Chibchas of Bogota the punishment for it was the infliction of a painful death.[7] However, it should be remembered that the ancient culture nations of America were generally extravagant in their punishments, and that their penal codes in the first place expressed rather the will of their rulers than the feelings of the people at large.[8]

Homosexual practices are said to be taken little notice of even by some uncivilised peoples who are not addicted to them. In the Pelew Islands, where such practices occur only sporadically, they are not punished, although, if I understand Herr Kubary rightly, the persons committing them may be put to shame.[9] The Ossetes of the Caucasus,

[1] Cieza de Leon, *Segunda parte de la Crónica del Perú*, ch. 25, p. 99. See also *Idem, Crónica del Perú [primera parte]*, ch. 64 (*Biblioteca de autores españoles*, xxvi. 416 sq.).
[2] *Idem, Segunda parte de la Crónica del Perú*, ch. 25, p. 98. See also Garcilasso de la Vega, *op. cit.* ii. 132.
[3] Las Casas, quoted by Bancroft, *op. cit.* ii. 467 sq. Cf. *ibid.* ii. 677.
[4] Clavigero, *History of Mexico*, i. 357.
[5] Squier, ' Archæology and Ethno-logy of Nicaragua,' in *Trans. American Ethn. Soc.* iii. pt. i. 128.
[6] Bancroft, *op. cit.* ii. 677.
[7] Piedrahita, *Historia general de las conquistas del nuevo reyno de Granada*, p. 46.
[8] See *supra*, i. 186,195.
[9] Kubary, ' Die Verbrechen und das Strafverfahren auf den Pelau-Inseln,' in *Original-Mittheilungen aus der ethnologischen Abtheilung der königlichen Museen zu Berlin*, i, 84.

among whom pederasty is very rare, do not generally
prosecute persons for committing it, but ignore the act.[1]
The East African Masai do not punish sodomy.[2] But we
also meet with statements of a contrary nature.   In a
Kafir tribe Mr. Warner heard of a case of it—the only
one during a residence of twenty-five years—which was
punished with a fine of some cattle claimed by the chief.[3]
Among the Ondonga pederasts are hated, and the men
who behave like women are detested, most of them being
wizards.[4] The Washambala consider pederasty a grave
moral aberration and subject it to severe punishment.[5]
Among the Waganda homosexual practices, which have
been introduced by the Arabs and are of rare occurrence,
" are intensely abhorred," the stake being the punishment.[6] The Negroes of Accra, who are not addicted to
such practices, are said to detest them.[7] In Nubia
pederasty is held in abhorrence, except by the Kashefs
and their relations, who endeavour to imitate the Mame-
lukes in everything.[8]

Muhammed forbade sodomy,[9] and the general opinion
of his followers is that it should be punished like fornication—for which the punishment is, theoretically, severe
enough [10]—unless the offenders make a public act of penitence.   In order to convict, however, the law requires
that four reliable persons shall swear to have been eye-
witnesses,[11] and this alone would make the law a dead
letter, even if it had the support of popular feelings ; but
such support is certainly wanting.   In Morocco active

---

[1] Kovalewsky, *Coutume contemporaine*, p. 340.
[2] Merker, *Die Masai*, p. 208. The
Masai, however, slaughter at once
any bullock or he-goat which is
noticed to practise unnatural intercourse, for fear lest otherwise
their herds should be visited by a
plague as a divine punishment (*ibid.*
p.159).
[3] Warner, in Maclean, *Compendium
of Kafir Laws*, p. 62.
[4] Rautanen, in Steinmetz, *Rechtsverhältnisse*, p. 333 *sq.*
[5] Lang, *ibid.* p. 232.

[6] Felkin, in *Proceed. Roy. Soc.
Edinburgh*, xiii. 723.
[7] Monrad, *op. cit.* p. 57.
[8] Burckhardt, *Travels in Nubia*, p.
135.
[9] *Koran*, iv. 20.
[10] Sachau,   *Muhammedanisches
Recht nach Schafiitischer Lehre*, pp.
809, 818 :—" Sodomita si *muhṣan*
(that is, a married person in possession of full civic rights) est punitur
lapidatione,   si non est *muhṣan*
punitur et flagellatione et exsilio."
[11] Burton, *Arabian Nights*, x. 224.

pederasty is regarded with almost complete indifference, whilst the passive sodomite, if a grown-up individual, is spoken of with scorn. Dr. Polak says the same of the Persians.[1] In Zanzibar a clear distinction is made between male congenital inverts and male prostitutes ; the latter are looked upon with contempt, whereas the former, as being what they are " by the will of God," are tolerated.[2] The Muhammedans of India and other Asiatic countries regard pederasty, at most, as a mere peccadillo.[3] Among the Hindus it is said to be held in abhorrence,[4] but their sacred books deal with it leniently. According to the ' Laws of Manu,' " a twice-born man who commits an unnatural offence with a male, or has intercourse with a female in a cart drawn by oxen, in water, or in the day-time, shall bathe, dressed in his clothes " ; and all these are reckoned as minor offences.[5]

Chinese law makes little distinction between unnatural and other sexual offences. An unnatural offence is variously considered according to the age of the patient, and whether or not consent was given. If the patient be an adult, or a boy over the age of twelve, and consent, the case is treated as a slightly aggravated form of fornication, both parties being punished with a hundred blows and one month's cangue, whilst ordinary fornication is punished with eighty blows. If the adult or boy over twelve resist, the offence is considered as rape ; and if the boy be under twelve, the offence is rape irrespective of consent or resistance, unless the boy has previously gone astray.[6] But, as a matter of fact, unnatural offences are regarded as less hurtful to the community than ordinary immorality,[7] and pederasty is not looked down upon. " L'opinion publique reste tout à fait indifférente à ce genre de distraction et la

[1] Polak, in *Wiener Medizinische Wochenschrift*, xi. 628 *sq.*
[2] Baumann, in *Verhandl. Berliner Gesellsch. Anthrop.* 1899, p. 669.
[3] Chevers, *op. cit.* p. 708. Burton, *Arabian Nights*, x. 222 *sqq.*
[4] Burton, *Arabian Nights*, x. 237.
[5] *Laws of Manu*, xi. 175. *Cf. Insti-*tutes of Vishnu, liii. 4 ; *Âpastamba*, i. 9. 26. 7 ; *Gautama*, xxv. 7.
[6] Alabaster, *Notes and Commentaries on Chinese Criminal Law*, p. 367 *sqq.* *Ta Tsing Leu Lee*, Appendix, no. xxxii. p. 570.
[7] Alabaster, *op. cit.* p. 369.

morale ne s'en émeut en rien : puisque cela plaît à l'opéra-
teur et que l'opéré est consentant, tout est pour le mieux ;
la loi chinoise n'aime guère à s'occuper des affaires trop
intimes. La pédérastie est même considérée comme une
chose de bon ton, une fantaisie dispendieuse et partout un
plaisir élégant. . . . La pédérastie a une consécration
officielle en Chine. Il existe, en effet, des pédérés pour
l'Empereur." [1] Indeed, the only objection which Dr. Matignon has heard to be raised to pederasty by public opinion
in China is that it has a bad influence on the eyesight.[2]
In Japan there was no law against homosexual intercourse
till the revolution of 1868.[3] In the period of Japanese chivalry it was considered more heroic if a man loved a person
of his own sex than if he loved a woman ; and nowadays
people are heard to say that in those provinces of the country where pederasty is widely spread the men are more
manly and robust than in those where it does not prevail.[4]

The laws of the ancient Scandinavians ignored homosexual practices ; but passive pederasts were much despised
by them. They were identified with cowards and regarded
as sorcerers. The epithets applied to them—*argr*, *ragr*,
blandr, and others—assumed the meaning of " poltroon "
in general, and there are instances of the word *arg* being
used in the sense of " practising witchcraft." This connection between pederasty and sorcery, as a Norwegian
scholar justly points out, helps us to understand Tacitus'
statement that among the ancient Teutons individuals
whom he describes as *corpore infames* were buried alive in
a morass.[5] Considering that drowning was a common
penalty for sorcery, it seems probable that this punishment
was inflicted upon them not, in the first place, on account
of their sexual practices, but in their capacity of wizards.
It is certain that the opprobrium which the pagan Scandinavians attached to homosexual love was chiefly restricted
to him who played the woman's part. In one of the poems

[1] Matignon, in *Archives d'anthropologie criminelle*, xiv. 42, 43, 52.
[2] *Ibid.* p. 44.
[3] Karsch, *op. cit.* p. 99.

[4] Jwaya, in *Jahrbuch für sexuelle
Zwischenstufen*, iv. 266, 270 *sq.*
[5] Tacitus, *Germania*, 12.

the hero even boasts of being the father of offspring borne by another man.[1]

In Greece pederasty in its baser forms was censured, though generally, it seems, with no great severity, and in some states it was legally prohibited.[2] According to an Athenian law, a youth who prostituted himself for money lost his rights as a free citizen and was liable to the punishment of death if he took part in a public feast or entered the *agora*.[3] In Sparta it was necessary that the "listener" should accept the "inspirator" from real affection; he who did so out of pecuniary considerations was punished by the ephors.[4] We are even told that among the Spartans the relations between the lover and his friend were truly innocent, and that if anything unlawful happened both must forsake either their country or their lives.[5] But the universal rule in Greece seems to have been that when decorum was observed in the friendship between a man and a youth, no inquiries were made into the details of the relationship.[6] And this attachment was not only regarded as permissible, but was praised as the highest and purest form of love, as the offspring of the heavenly Aphrodite, as a path leading to virtue, as a weapon against tyranny, as a safeguard of civic liberty, as a source of national greatness and glory. Phaedrus said that he knew no greater blessing to a young man who is beginning life than a virtuous lover, or to the lover than a beloved youth; for the principle which ought to be the guide of men who would lead a noble life cannot be implanted by any other motive so well as by love.[7] The Platonic Pausanias argued that if love of youths is held in ill repute it is so only because it is inimical to tyranny; " the interests of rulers require that their subjects should

---

[1] 'Spuren von Konträrsexualität bei den alten Skandinaviern (Mitteilungen eines norwegischen Gelehrten), in *Jahrbuch für sexuelle Zwischenstufen*, iv. 245, 256 sqq.
[2] Xenophon, *Lacedæmoniorum respublica*, ii. 13. Maximus Tyrius, *Dissertationes*, xxv. 4; xxvi. 9.

[3] Aeschines, *Contra Timarchum*, 21.
[4] Aelian, *Varia historia*, iii. 10. Cf. Plato, *Leges*, viii. 910.
[5] Aelian, *op. cit.* iii. 12. Cf. Maximus Tyrius, *op. cit.* xxvi. 8.
[6] Cf. Symonds, *loc. cit.* p. 92 sqq.
[7] Plato, *Symposium*, p. 178.

be poor in spirit, and that there should be no strong bond
of friendship or society among them, which love, above all
other motives, is likely to inspire."[1] The power of the
Athenian tyrants was broken by the love of Aristogeiton
and the constancy of Harmodius; at Agrigentum in
Sicily the mutual love of Chariton and Melanippus produced a similar result; and the greatness of Thebes was
due to the Sacred Band established by Epaminondas. For
" in the presence of his favourite, a man would choose to
do anything rather than to get the character of a coward."[2]
It was pointed out that the greatest heroes and the most
warlike nations were those who were most addicted to the
love of youths;[3] and it was said that an army consisting
of lovers and their beloved ones, fighting at each other's
side, although a mere handful, would overcome the whole
world.[4]

Herodotus asserts that the love of boys was introduced
from Greece into Persia.[5] Whether his statement be
correct or not, such love could certainly not have been a
habit of the Mazda worshippers.[6] In the Zoroastrian books
" unnatural sin " is treated with a severity to which there
is a parallel only in Hebrewism and Christianity. According to the Vendîdâd, there is no atonement for it.[7] It is
punished with torments in the other world, and is capital
here below.[8] Even he who committed it involuntarily,
by force, is subject to corporal punishment.[9] Indeed, it is
a more heinous sin than the slaying of a righteous man.[10]
" There is no worse sin than this in the good religion, and
it is proper to call those who commit it worthy of death in
reality. If any one comes forth to them, and shall see

[1] Plato, *Symposium*, p. 182.
[2] Hieronymus, the Peripatetic, referred to by Athenaeus, *op. cit.*
xiii. 78, p. 602. See also Maximus
Tyrius, *op. cit.* xxiv. 2.
[3] Plutarch, *Amatorius*, xvii. 14.
[4] Plato, *Symposium*, p. 178.
[5] Herodotus, i. 135.
[6] Ammianus Marcellinus says
(xxiii. 76) that the inhabitants of

Persia were free from pederasty.
But see also Sextus Empiricus,
Pyrrhoniæ hypotyposes, i. 152.
[7] *Vendîdâd*, i. 12; viii. 27.
[8] Darmesteter, in *Sacred Books of
the East*, iv. p. lxxxvi.
[9] *Vendîdâd*, viii. 26.
[10] *Dînâ-î Maînôg-î Khirad*, xxxvi.
1 *sqq.*

them in the act, and is working with an axe, it is requisite for him to cut off the heads or to rip up the bellies of both, and it is no sin for him. But it is not proper to kill any person without the authority of high-priests and kings, except on account of committing or permitting unnatural intercourse." [1]

Nor are unnatural sins allowed to defile the land of the Lord. Whosoever shall commit such abominations, be he Israelite or stranger dwelling among the Israelites, shall be put to death, the souls that do them shall be cut off from their people. By unnatural sins of lust the Canaanites polluted their land, so that God visited their guilt, and the land spued out its inhabitants.[2]

This horror of homosexual practices was shared by Christianity. According to St. Paul, they form the climax of the moral corruption to which God gave over the heathen because of their apostasy from him.[3] Tertullian says that they are banished " not only from the threshold, but from all shelter of the church, because they are not sins, but monstrosities." [4] St. Basil maintains that they deserve the same punishment as murder, idolatry, and witchcraft.[5] According to a decree of the Council of Elvira, those who abuse boys to satisfy their lusts are denied communion even at their last hour.[6] In no other point of morals was the contrast between the teachings of Christianity and the habits and opinions of the world over which it spread more radical than in this. In Rome there was an old law of unknown date, called Lex Scantinia (or Scatinia), which imposed a mulct on him who committed pederasty with a free person ;[7] but this law, of which

---

[1] *Sad Dar*, ix. 2 *sqq.*

[2] *Leviticus*, xviii. 22, 24 *sqq.* ; xx. 13.

[3] *Romans*, i. 26 *sq.*

[4] Tertullian, *De pudicitia*, 4 (Migne, *Patrologiæ cursus*, ii. 987).

[5] St. Basil, quoted by Bingham, *Works*, vi. 432 *sq.*

[6] *Concilium Eliberitanum*, ch. 71 (Labbe-Mansi, *Sacrorum Conciliorum collectio*, ii. 17).

[7] Juvenal, *Satiræ*, ii. 43 *sq.*

Valerius Maximus, *Facta dictaque memorabilia*, vi. 1. 7. Quintilian, *Institutio oratoria*, iv. 2. 69 :— " Decem milia, quae poena stupratori constituta est, dabit." Christ, *Hist. Legis Scatiniæ*, quoted by Döllinger, *op. cit.* ii. 274. Rein, *Criminalrecht der Römer*, p. 865 *sq.* Bingham, *op. cit.* vi. 433 *sqq.* Mommsen, *Römisches Strafrecht*, p. 703 *sq.*

very little is known, had lain dormant for ages, and the
subject of ordinary homosexual intercourse had never
afterwards attracted the attention of the pagan legislators.[1]
But when Christianity became the religion of the Roman
Empire, a veritable crusade was opened against it.   Con-
stantius and Constans made it a capital crime, punishable
with the sword.[2] Valentinian went further still and ordered
that those who were found guilty of it should be burned
alive in the presence of all the people.[3] Justinian, terrified
by certain famines, earthquakes, and pestilences, issued an
edict which again condemned persons guilty of unnatural
offences to the sword, " lest, as the result of these impious
acts, whole cities should perish together with their inhabitants," as we are taught by Holy Scripture that through
such acts cities have perished with the men in them.[4] " A
sentence of death and infamy," says Gibbon, " was often
founded on the slight and suspicious evidence of a child or
a servant, . . . and pederasty became the crime of those
to whom no crime could be imputed." [5]

This attitude towards homosexual practices had a profound and lasting influence on European legislation.
Throughout the Middle Ages and later, Christian law-
givers thought that nothing but a painful death in the
flames could atone for the sinful act.[6] In England Fleta

[1] Mommsen, *op. cit.* p. 704. Rein, *op. cit.* p. 866. The passage in *Digesta*, xlviii. 5. 35. 1, refers to *stuprum* independently of the sex of the victim.

[2] *Codex Theodosianus*, ix. 7. 3. *Codex Justinianus*, ix. 9. 30.

[3] *Codex Theodosianus*, ix. 7. 6.

[4] *Novellæ*, 77. See also *ibid.* 141, and *Institutiones*, iv. 18. 4.

[5] Gibbon, *History of the Decline and Fall of the Roman Empire*, v. 323.

[6] Du Boys, *Histoire du droit criminel de l'Espagne*, pp. 93, 403. Les *Établissements de Saint Louis*, i. 90, vol. ii. 147. Beaumanoir, *Coutumes du Beauvoisis*, xxx. 11, vol. i. 413. Montesquieu, *De l'esprit des lois*, xii. 6 (*Œuvres*, p. 283). Hume, *Commentaries on the Law of Scotland*, ii. 335 ; Pitcairn, *Criminal Trials in Scotland*, ii. 491, n. 2. Clarus, *Practica criminalis*, book v. § Sodomia, 4 (*Opera omnia*, ii. 151). Jarcke, *Handbuch des gemeinen deutschen Strafrechts*, iii. 172 *sqq.* Charles V.'s *Peinliche Gerichtsordnung*, art. 116. Henke, *Geschichte des deutschen peinlichen Rechts*, i. 289. Numa Praetorius, ' Die strafrechtlichen Bestimmungen gegen den gleichgeschlechtlichen Verkehr,' in *Jahrbuch für sexuelle Zwischenstufen*, i. 124 *sqq.* In the beginning of the nineteenth century sodomy was still nominally subject to capital punishment by burning in Bavaria (von Feuerbach, *Kritik des Kleinschrodischen Entwurfs zu einem peinlichen Gesetzbuche für die Chur-Pfalz-Bayrischen Staaten*, ii. 13), and in Spain as late as 1843 (Du Boys, *op. cit.* p. 721).

speaks of the offender being buried alive ;[1] but we are elsewhere told that burning was the due punishment.[2] As unnatural intercourse, however, was a subject for ecclesiastical cognizance, capital punishment could not be inflicted on the criminal unless the Church relinquished him to the secular arm ; and it seems very doubtful whether she did relinquish him. Sir Frederick Pollock and Professor Maitland consider that the statute of 1533, which makes sodomy felony, affords an almost sufficient proof that the temporal courts had not punished it, and that no one had been put to death for it for a very long time past.[3] It was said that the punishment for this crime —which the English law, in its very indictments, treats as a crime not fit to be named [4]—was determined to be capital by " the voice of nature and of reason, and the express law of God " ;[5] and it remained so till 1861,[6] although in practice the extreme punishment was not inflicted.[7] In France persons were actually burned for this crime in the middle and latter part of the eighteenth century.[8] But in this, as in so many other respects, the rationalistic movement of that age brought about a change.[9] To punish sodomy with death, it was said, is atrocious ; when unconnected with violence, the law ought to take no notice of it at all. It does not violate any other person's right, its influence on society is merely indirect, like that of drunkenness and free love ; it is a disgusting vice, but its only proper punishment is contempt.[10] This view was adopted by the French ' Code pénal,' according to which homosexual practices in private, between two consenting adult parties, whether men or women, are absolutely

[1] Fleta, i. 37. 3, p. 84.
[2] Britton, i. 10, vol. i. 42.
[3] Pollock and Maitland, *History of English Law before the Time of Edward I*. ii. 556 *sq.*
[4] Coke, *Third Part of the Institutes of the Laws of England*, p. 58 *sq.* Blackstone, *Commentaries on the Laws of England*, iv. 218.
[5] Blackstone, *op. cit.* iv. 218.
[6] Stephen, *History of the Criminal Law of England*, i. 475.
[7] Blackstone, *op. cit.* iv. 218.
[8] Desmaze, *Pénalités anciennes*, p. 211. Havelock Ellis, *op. cit.* p. 207.
[9] Numa Praetorius, *loc. cit.* p. 121 *sqq.*
[10] Note of the editors of Kehl's edition of Voltaire's ' Prix de la justice et de l'humanité,' in *Œuvres complètes*, v. 437, n. 2.

unpunished. The homosexual act is treated as a crime only when it implies an outrage on public decency, or when there is violence or absence of consent, or when one of the parties is under age or unable to give valid consent.[1] This method of dealing with homosexuality has been followed by the legislators of various European countries,[2] and in those where the law still treats the act in question *per se* as a penal offence, notably in Germany, a propaganda in favour of its alteration is carried on with the support of many men of scientific eminence. This changed attitude of the law towards homosexual intercourse undoubtedly indicates a change of moral opinions. Though it is impossible to measure exactly the degree of moral condemnation, I suppose that few persons nowadays attach to it the same enormity of guilt as did our forefathers. And the question has even been put whether morality has anything at all to do with a sexual act, committed by the mutual consent of two adult individuals, which is productive of no offspring, and which on the whole concerns the welfare of nobody but the parties themselves.[3]

From this review of the moral ideas on the subject, incomplete though it be, it appears that homosexual practices are very frequently subject to some degree of censure, though the degree varies extremely. This censure is no doubt, in the first place, due to that feeling of aversion or disgust which the idea of homosexual intercourse tends to call forth in normally constituted adult individuals whose sexual instincts have developed under normal conditions. I presume that nobody will deny the general prevalence of such a tendency. It corresponds to that instinctive repugnance to sexual connections with women which is so frequently found in congenital inverts ; whilst that particular form of it with which legislators have chiefly busied themselves evokes, in addition, a physical disgust of its own. And in a society where the

---

[1] *Code pénal*, 330 *sqq.* Cf. Chevalier, *L'inversion sexuelle*, p. 431 *sqq.* ; Havelock Ellis, *op. cit.* p. 207 *sq.*
[2] Numa Praetorius, *loc. cit.* pp. 131–133, 143 *sqq.*
[3] See, *e.g.*, Bax, *Ethics of Socialism.* p. 126.

large majority of people are endowed with normal sexual desires their aversion to homosexuality easily develops into moral censure and finds a lasting expression in custom, law, or religious tenets. On the other hand, where special circumstances have given rise to widely spread homosexual practices, there will be no general feeling of disgust even in the adults, and the moral opinion of the society will be modified accordingly. The act may still be condemned, in consequence of a moral doctrine formed under different conditions, or of the vain attempts of legislators to check sexual irregularities, or out of utilitarian considerations ; but such a condemnation would in most people be rather theoretical than genuine. At the same time the baser forms of homosexual love may be strongly disapproved of for the same reasons as the baser forms of intercourse between men and women ; and the passive pederast may be an object of contempt on account of the feminine practices to which he lends himself, as also an object of hatred on account of his reputation for sorcery. We have seen that the effeminate men are frequently believed to be versed in magic ;[1] their abnormalities readily suggest that they are endowed with supernatural power, and they may resort to witchcraft as a substitute for their lack of manliness and physical strength. But the supernatural qualities or skill in magic ascribed to men who behave like women may also, instead of causing hatred, make them honoured or reverenced.

It has been suggested that the popular attitude towards homosexuality was originally an aspect of economics, a question of under- or over-population, and that it was forbidden or allowed accordingly. Dr. Havelock Ellis thinks it probable that there is a certain relationship

[1] See also Bastian, in *Zeitschr. f. Ethnol.* i. 88 *sq.* Speaking of the witches of Fez, Leo Africanus says (*History and Description of Africa,* ii. 458) that " they haue a damnable custome to commit vnlawfull Venerie among themselues." Among the Patagonians, according to Falkner (*Description of Patagonia,* p. 117), the male wizards are chosen for their office when they are children, and " a preference is always shown to those who at that early time of life discover an effeminate disposition." They are obliged, as it were, to leave their sex, and to dress themselves in female apparel.

between the social reaction against homosexuality and
against infanticide :—" Where the one is regarded leniently and favourably, there generally the other is also ;
where the one is stamped out, the other is usually stamped
out."[1] But our defective knowledge of the opinions of
the various savage races concerning homosexuality hardly
warrants such a conclusion ; and if a connection really
does exist between homosexual practices and infanticide it
may be simply due to the numerical disproportion between
the sexes resulting from the destruction of a multitude of
female infants.[2] On the other hand we are acquainted
with several facts which are quite at variance with Dr.
Ellis's suggestion. Among many Hindu castes female
infanticide has for ages been a genuine custom,[3] and yet
pederasty is remarkably rare among the Hindus. The
ancient Arabs were addicted to infanticide,[4] but not to
homosexual love,[5] whereas among modern Arabs the case
is exactly the reverse. And if the early Christians deemed
infanticide and pederasty equally heinous sins, they did so
certainly not because they were anxious that the population should increase ; if this had been their motive they
would hardly have glorified celibacy. It is true that in a
few cases the unproductiveness of homosexual love has
been given by indigenous writers as a reason for its
encouragement or condemnation. It was said that the
Cretan law on the subject had in view to check the growth
of population ; but, like Döllinger,[6] I do not believe that
this assertion touches the real root of the matter. More
importance may be attached to the following passage in
one of the Pahlavi texts :—" He who is wasting seed
makes a practice of causing the death of progeny ; when
the custom is completely continuous, which produces an
evil stoppage of the progress of the race, the creatures
have become annihilated ; and certainly, that action, from
which, when it is universally proceeding, the depopulation

---

[1] Havelock Ellis, *op. cit.* p. 206.
See Additional Notes.
[2] *Cf. supra*, ii. 466 (Tahitians).
[3] *Supra*, i. 407.
[4] *Supra*, i. 406 *sq.*
[5] von Kremer, *Culturgeschichte de Orients*, ii. 129.
[6] Döllinger, *op. cit.* ii. 239.

of the world must arise, has become and furthered the greatest wish of Aharman."[1] I am, however, of opinion that considerations of this kind have generally played only a subordinate, if any, part in the formation of the moral opinions concerning homosexual practices. And it can certainly not be admitted that the severe Jewish law against sodomy was simply due to the fact that the enlargement of the population was a strongly felt social need among the Jews.[2] However much they condemned celibacy, they did not put it on a par with the abominations of Sodom. The excessive sinfulness which was attached to homosexual love by Zoroastrianism, Hebrewism, and Christianity, had quite a special foundation. It cannot be sufficiently accounted for either by utilitarian considerations or instinctive disgust. The abhorrence of incest is generally a much stronger feeling than the aversion to homosexuality. Yet in the very same chapter of Genesis which describes the destruction of Sodom and Gomorrah we read of the incest committed by the daughters of Lot with their father ;[3] and, according to the Roman Catholic doctrine, unnatural intercourse is an even more heinous sin than incest and adultery.[4] The fact is that homosexual practices were intimately associated with the gravest of all sins : unbelief, idolatry, or heresy.

According to Zoroastrianism, unnatural sin had been created by Angra Mainyu.[5] "Aharman, the wicked, miscreated the demons and fiends, and also the remaining corrupted ones, by his own unnatural intercourse."[6] Such intercourse is on a par with Afrâsiyâb, a Turanian king who conquered the Iranians for twelve years;[7] with Dahâk, a king or dynasty who is said to have conquered Yim and reigned for a thousand years ;[8] with Tûr-i Brâdar-vakhsh,

---

[1] *Dâdistân-î Dînîk*, lxxvii. 11.
[2] Havelock Ellis, *op. cit.* p. 206.
[3] *Genesis*, xix. 31 *sqq.*
[4] Thomas Aquinas, *Summa theologica*, ii.-ii. 154. 12. Katz, *Grundriss des kanonischen Strafrechts*, pp. 104, 118, 120. Clarus, *Practica criminalis*, book v. § Sodomia, Additiones, 1 (*Opera omnia*, ii. 152) :—

[5] *Vendîdâd*, i. 12.
[6] *Dînâ-î Maînôg-î Khirad*, viii. 10.
[7] *Sad Dar*, ix. 5. West's note to *Dînâ-î Maînôg-î Khirad*, viii. 29 (Sacred Books of the East, xxiv. 35, n. 4.)
[8] *Sad Dar*, ix. 5. West's note to

a heterodox wizard by whom the best men were put to death.[1] He who commits unnatural sin is " in his whole being a Daêva " ;[2] and a Daêva-worshipper is not a bad Zoroastrian, but a man who does not belong to the Zoroastrian system, a foreigner, a non-Aryan.[3] In the Vendîdâd, after the statement that the voluntary commission of unnatural sin is a trespass for which there is no atonement for ever and ever, the question is put, When is it so ? And the answer given is :—If the sinner be a professor of the religion of Mazda, or one who has been taught in it. If not, his sin is taken from him, in case he makes confession of the religion of Mazda and resolves never to commit again such forbidden deeds.[4] This is to say, the sin is inexpiable if it involves a downright defiance of the true religion, it is forgiven if it is committed in ignorance of it and is followed by submission. From all this it appears that Zoroastrianism stigmatised unnatural intercourse as a practice of infidels, as a sign of unbelief. And I think that certain facts referred to above help us to understand why it did so. Not only have homosexual practices been commonly associated with sorcery, but such an association has formed, and partly still forms, an incident of the shamanistic system prevalent among the Asiatic peoples of Turanian stock, and that it did so already in remote antiquity is made extremely probable by statements which I have just quoted from Zoroastrian texts. To this system Zoroastrianism was naturally furiously opposed, and the " change of sex " therefore appeared to the Mazda worshipper as a devilish abomination.

So also the Hebrews' abhorrence of sodomy was largely due to their hatred of a foreign cult. According to Genesis, unnatural vice was the sin of a people who were not the Lord's people, and the Levitical legislation represents Canaanitish abominations as the chief reason

Dînâ-î Maînôg-î Khirad, viii. 29 (*Sacred Books of the East,* xxiv. 35, n. 3).

[1] *Sad Dar,* ix. 5. West's note to *Dâdistân-î Dînîk,* lxxii. 8 (*Sacred Books of the East,* xviii. 218).

[2] *Vendîdâd,* viii. 32.

[3] Darmesteter, in *Sacred Books of the East,* iv. p. li.

[4] *Vendîdâd,* viii. 27 *sq.*

why the Canaanites were exterminated.[1] Now we know that sodomy entered as an element in their religion. Besides *kedēshōth*, or female prostitutes, there were *kedē-shīm*, or male prostitutes, attached to their temples.[2] The word *kadēsh*, translated " sodomite," properly denotes a man dedicated to a deity ;[3] and it appears that such men were consecrated to the mother of the gods, the famous Dea Syria, whose priests or devotees they were considered to be.[4] The male devotees of this and other goddesses were probably in a position analogous to that occupied by the female devotees of certain gods, who also, as we have seen, have developed into libertines ; and the sodomitic acts committed with these temple prostitutes may, like the connections with priestesses, have had in view to transfer blessings to the worshippers.[5] In Morocco supernatural benefits are expected not only from heterosexual, but also from homosexual intercourse with a holy person.[6] The *kedēshīm* are frequently alluded to in the Old Testament, especially in the period of the monarchy, when rites of foreign origin made their way into both Israel and Judah.[7] And it is natural that the Yahveh worshipper should regard their practices with the utmost horror as forming part of an idolatrous cult.

The Hebrew conception of homosexual love to some extent affected Muhammedanism, and passed into Christianity. The notion that it is a form of sacrilege was here strengthened by the habits of the gentiles. St. Paul found the abominations of Sodom prevalent among nations who had " changed the truth of God into a lie, and worshipped and served the creature more than the

---

[1] *Leviticus*, xx. 23.
[2] *Deuteronomy*, xxiii. 17. Driver, *Commentary on Deuteronomy*, p. 264.
[3] Driver, *op. cit.* p. 264 *sq.* Selbie, Sodomite,' in Hastings, *Dictionary of the Bible*, iv. 559.
[4] St. Jerome, *In Osee*, i. 4. 14 (Migne, *op. cit.* xxv. 851). Cook's note to 1 *Kings*, xiv. 24, in his edition of *The Holy Bible*, ii. 571. See also Lucian, *Lucius*, 38.

[5] Rosenbaum suggests (*Geschichte der Lustseuche im Alterthume*, p. 120) that the eunuch priests connected with the cult of the Ephesian Artemis and the Phrygian worship of Cybele likewise were sodomites.
[6] See Westermarck, *The Moorish Conception of Holiness*, p. 85.
[7] 1 *Kings*, xiv. 24 ; xv. 12 ; xxii. 46. 2 *Kings*, xxiii. 7. *Job*, xxxvi. 14. Driver, *op. cit.* p. 265.

Creator." [1] During the Middle Ages heretics were accused.
of unnatural vice as a matter of course.[2] Indeed, so
closely was sodomy associated with heresy that the same
name was applied to both. In 'La Coutume de
Touraine-Anjou' the word *herite*, which is the ancient
form of *hérétique*,[3] seems to be used in the sense of
" sodomite " ; [4] and the French *bougre* (from the Latin
Bulgarus, Bulgarian), as also its English synonym, was
originally a name given to a sect of heretics who came from
Bulgaria in the eleventh century, and was afterwards
applied to other heretics, but at the same time it became
the regular expression for a person guilty of unnatural intercourse.[5] In mediæval laws sodomy was also repeatedly
mentioned together with heresy, and the punishment was
the same for both.[6] It thus remained a religious offence
of the first order. It was not only a " vitium nefandum
et super omnia detestandum," [7] but it was one of the four
" clamantia peccata," or crying sins,[8] a " crime de
Majestie, vers le Roy celestre." [9] Very naturally, therefore, it has come to be regarded with somewhat greater
leniency by law and public opinion in proportion as they
have emancipated themselves from theological doctrines.
And the fresh light which the scientific study of the sexual
impulse has lately thrown upon the subject of homosexuality must also necessarily influence the moral ideas
relating to it, in so far as no scrutinising judge can fail to
take into account the pressure which a powerful non-
volitional desire exercises upon an agent's will.

[1] *Romans*, i. 25 sqq.
[2] Littré, *Dictionnaire de la langue française*, i. 386, ' Bougre.' Haynes, *Religious Persecution*, p. 54.
[3] Littré, *op. cit.* i. 2010, ' Héré-tique.'
[4] *Les Établissements de Saint Louis*, i. 90, vol. ii. 147. Viollet, in his Introduction to the same work, i. 254.
[5] Littré, *op. cit.* i. 386, ' Bougre.' Murray, *New English Dictionary*, i. 1160, ' Bugger.' Lea, *History of the Inquisition of the Middle Ages*, i. 115, note.
[6] Beaumanoir, *Coutumes du Beau-*

voisis, xxx. 11, vol. i. 413 :—" Qui erre contre le foi, comme en mescreance, de le quele il ne veut venir à voie de verité, ou qui fet sodomiterie, il doit estre ars, et forfet tout le sien en le maniere dessus." Britton, i. 10, vol. i. 42. Montesquieu, *De l'esprit des lois*, xii. 6 (*Œuvres*, p. 283). Du Boys, *Histoire du droit criminel de l'Espagne*, pp. 486, 721.
[7] Clarus, *Practica criminalis*, book v. § Sodomia, 1 (*Opera omnia*, ii.151).
[8] Coke, *Third Part of the Institutes of the Laws of England*, p. 59.
[9] *Mirror*, quoted *ibid.* p. 58.

CHAPTER XLIV

REGARD FOR THE LOWER ANIMALS

MEN's conduct towards the lower animals is frequently a subject of moral valuation.

Totem animals must be treated with deference by those who bear their names, and animals generally regarded as divine must be respected by all; of this more will be said in a subsequent chapter.[1] Among various peoples the members of certain animal species must not be killed, because they are considered to be receptacles for the souls of departed men,[2] or because the species is believed to have originated through a transformation of men into animals.[3] The Dyaks of Borneo have a superstitious dread of killing orang-utans, being of opinion that these apes are men who went to live in the forest and abstain from speaking merely in order to be exempt from paying taxes.[4] The Moors consider it wrong to kill a monkey, because the monkey was once a man whom God changed into his present shape as a punishment for the sin he committed by performing his ablutions with milk; and they would never do harm to a stork, because, as they say, the stork was originally a judge, who passed unjust sentences upon his fellow creatures and therefore became what he is. They also account it a sin to kill a swallow or a pigeon, a white spider or a bee, because they regard them as holy. Other creatures, again, are spared by the Moors because they

---

[1] *Infra*, on Duties to Gods.
[2] *Infra*, p. 516 *sq.*
[3] See Meiners, *Allgemeine Ge-*
schichte der Religionen, i. 213 *sqq.*
[4] Selenka, *Sonnige Welten*, p. 57.

appear uncanny or are suspected of being evil spirits in disguise. It is believed that anybody who kills a raven easily goes mad and that he who kills a toad will get fever or die ; and no Moor would dare to hit a cat or a dog in the dark, since it seems very doubtful what kind of being it really is. Superstitions of this sort are world-wide.

It is a common belief among uncultured peoples that a person who slays an animal is exposed to the vengeance either of its disembodied spirit or of all the other creatures belonging to the same species.[1] Hence, as Sir J. G. Frazer has shown, the savage often makes it a rule to spare the lives of those animals which he has no pressing motive for killing, at least such fierce and dangerous ones as are likely to exact a bloody revenge for the slaughter of any of their kind ; and when, for some reason or other, he overcomes his superstitious scruples and takes the life of the beast, he is anxious to appease the victim and its kindred by testifying his respect for them, or making apologies, or trying to conceal his share in procuring the death of the animal, or promising that its remains will be honourably treated.[2] The Stiêns of Cambodia, for instance, who believe that animals have souls which wander about after death, ask pardon when they have killed one, lest its soul should visit and torment them ; and they also offer it sacrifices proportioned to the strength and size of the animal.[3] When a party of Koriaks have killed a bear or a wolf, they skin the beast, dress one of their family in the skin, and dance round the skin-clad man, saying that it was not they who killed the animal but someone else, by preference a Russian.[4] The Eskimo about Behring Strait maintain that the dead bodies of various animals must be treated very carefully by the hunter who obtains them, so that their shades may not be offended and bring bad luck or even death upon him or his people.[5]

[1] *Supra*, i. 258.
[2] Frazer, *Golden Bough*, ii. 389 *sqq.*
[3] Mouhot, *Travels in the Central Parts of Indo-China*, i. 252.
[4] Bastian, *Der Mensch in der Geschichte*, iii. 26.
[5] Nelson, ' Eskimo about Bering Strait,' in *Ann. Rep. Bur. Ethn.* xviii. 438.

The savage, moreover, desires to keep on good terms with animals which, without being feared, are either eaten or valued for their skins. Hence, when he captures one, he shows such deference for it as may be necessary for inducing its fellows to come and be killed also.[1] Alaskan hunters preserve the bones of sables and beavers out of reach of the dogs for a year and then bury them carefully, lest the spirits which look after these species should consider that " they are regarded with contempt and hence no more should be killed or trapped." [2] The Thompson River Indians of British Columbia said that when a deer was killed its fellows would be well pleased if the hunters butchered the animal nicely and cleanly.[3] The Hurons refrained from throwing fish bones into the fire, lest the souls of the fish should go and warn the other fish not to let themselves be caught, since, if they were, their own bones would also be burned.[4] Some savages respect the bones of the animals which they eat because they believe that the bones, if preserved, will, in the course of time, be reclothed with flesh and the animal thus come to life again.[5]

Besides the creatures which primitive man treats with respect because he dreads their strength and ferocity or on account of the benefits he expects from them, there is yet a third class of animate beings which he sometimes deems it necessary to conciliate, namely, vermin that infest the crops.[6] Among the Saxons of Transylvania, in order to keep sparrows from the corn, the sower begins by throwing the first handful of seed backwards over his head, saying, " That is for you, sparrows." [7] And of the Drâvidian tribes of Mirzapur we are told that, when locusts threaten to eat up the fruits of the earth, the people catch one, decorate its head with a spot of red

[1] Frazer, *op. cit.* ii. 403 *sqq.*
[2] Dall, *Alaska*, p. 89.
[3] Teit, 'Thompson Indians of British Columbia,' in *Memoirs of the American Museum of Natural History*, ' Anthropology,' i. 346.
[4] Sagard, *Le grand voyage du pays des Hurons*, p. 255.
[5] Frazer, *op. cit.* ii. 415 *sqq.*
[6] *Ibid.* ii. 422 *sqq.*
[7] Heinrich, quoted *ibid.* ii. 423.

lead, salaam to it, and let it go ; after which civilities the whole flight immediately departs.[1]

Domestic animals are frequently objects of superstitious reverence.[2] They are expected to reward masters who treat them well, whereas those who harm them are believed to expose themselves to their revenge. Among the Eskimo about Behring Strait dogs are never beaten for biting people, lest the *inua* or shade of the dog should become angry and prevent the wound from healing.[3] Butchers are often regarded as unclean, and the original reason for this was in all probability the idea that they were haunted by the spirits of the animals they had slain. Among the Guanches of the Canary Islands it was unlawful for anybody but professional butchers to kill cattle, and a butcher was forbidden to enter other persons' houses, to touch their property, and to keep company with any one not of his own trade.[4] In Morocco a butcher, like a manslayer, is thought to be haunted by *jnûn* (*jinn*), and it seems that in this case also the notion of haunting *jnûn* has replaced an earlier belief in troublesome ghosts.[5] So, too, the ancient Troglodytes of East Africa, who derived their whole sustenance from their flocks and herds, are said to have looked upon butchers as unclean.[6] In the rural districts of Japan it is believed that a butcher will have a cripple among his descendants.[7]

How far ideas of this sort may account for the great disinclination of many peoples to kill their cattle, it is impossible to say ; but they certainly do not constitute the only motive. We have noticed above that pastoral tribes are unwilling to reduce their herds and agricultural peoples to kill the ploughing ox, because this would imply

[1] Crooke, *Popular Religion and Folk-lore of Northern India*, ii. 303.
[2] See Robertson Smith, *Religion of the Semites*, p. 296 sqq.
[3] Nelson, in *Ann. Rep. Bur. Ethn.* xviii. 435.
[4] Abreu de Galindo, *History of the Discovery and Conquest of the Canary Islands*, p. 71 sq. Bory de St. Vincent, *Essais sur les Isles Fortunées*, p. 103 sq.
[5] *Cf. supra*, i. 378.
[6] Robertson Smith, *op. cit.* p. 296 sq.
[7] Griffis, *Mikado's Empire*, p. 472.

loss of valuable property.[1]   And apart from economic
considerations, we may assume that feelings of genuine
sympathy also induce them to treat their animals with
kindness. The altruistic sentiment has not necessarily
reference to members of the same species only ; of this
we find instances even among animals in confinement
and domesticated animals, which frequently become
attached to individuals of a different species with whom
they live together.[2] And the savage feels himself much
more closely related to the animal world than does his
civilised fellow creature ; indeed, as we have seen, he
habitually obliterates the boundaries between man and
beast and regards all animals as practically on a footing
of equality with himself.[3] Among the pastoral races of
Africa the men delight in attending their cattle, and spend
much time in ornamenting and adorning them ; the
herdsman knows every beast in his herd, calls it by its
name, and affectionately observes all its peculiarities.[4] Of
the Bahima, a cow tribe in Uganda, the Rev. J. Roscoe
tells us that the men form warm attachments for their
cattle ; some of them love the animals like children, pet
and coax them, talk to them, and weep over their
ailments, and should a favourite die their grief is so
extreme that it sometimes leads to suicide.[5] The mythical
founder of the kingdom of Uganda, Kintu, is said to have
been so humane and averse from the sight of blood, that
" even cattle killed for necessary food were slaughtered
at some distance from his dwelling." [6]   But cattle are
not the only dumb creatures that excite tender feelings
in the bosom of a savage. The For tribe of Central
Africa regard it as a characteristic of a good man to be
kind to animals in general, and consider it wicked to be
otherwise.[7] Concerning the Eastern Central Africans Mr.

[1] *Supra*, ii. 331.
[2] See *supra*, i. 112.
[3] *Supra*, i. 258.
[4] Ratzel, *History of Mankind*, ii. 415.
[5] Roscoe,' Bahima,' in *Jour. Anthr. Inst.* xxxvii. 94 *sq.*

[6] Felkin, ' Notes on the Waganda Tribe,' in *Proceed. Roy. Soc. Edinburgh*, xiii. 764.
[7] Felkin, ' Notes on the For Tribe,' in *Proceed. Roy. Soc. Edinburgh*, xiii. 232 *sq.*

not times for eating, since one might then swallow a live thing by mistake ; and he rejects not only meat but even honey, together with various fruits that are supposed to contain worms, not because of his distaste for worms but because of his regard for life.[1] Some towns in Western India in which Jains are found have their beast hospitals, where animals are kept and fed. At Surat there was quite recently an establishment of this sort with a house where a host of noxious and offensive vermin, dense as the sands on the sea-shore, were bred and nurtured ; and at Anjár, in Kutch, about five thousand rats were kept in a certain temple and daily fed with flour, which was procured by a tax on the inhabitants of the town.[2]

According to ' Thâi-Shang,' one of the books of Taouism, a good man will feel kindly towards all creatures, and refrain from hurting even the insect tribes, grass, and trees ; and he is a bad man who " shoots birds and hunts beasts, unearths the burrowing insects and frightens roosting birds, blocks up the dens of animals and overturns nests, hurts the pregnant womb and breaks eggs." [3] In the book called ' Merits and Errors Scrutinised,' which enjoys great popularity in China, it is said to be meritorious to save animals from death—even insects if the number amounts to a hundred,—to relieve a brute that is greatly wearied with work, to purchase and set at liberty animals intended to be slaughtered. On the other hand, to confine birds in a cage, to kill ten insects, to be unsparing of the strength of tired animals, to disturb insects in their holes, to destroy the nests of birds, without great reason to kill and dress animals for food, are all errors of various degrees. And " to be the foremost to encourage the slaughter of animals, or to hinder persons from setting them at liberty," is regarded as an error of the same magnitude as the crime of devising a person's death or of drowning or murdering a child.[4] Kindness

[1] Hopkins, *Religions of India*, p. 288. Barth, *op. cit.* p. 145. Kipling, *op. cit.* p. 10 *sq.*
[2] Burnes, ' Notice of a remarkable Hospital for Animals at Surat,' in *Jour. Roy. Asiatic Soc.* i. 96 *sq.*
[3] *Thâi-Shang*, 3 *sq.*
[4] *Indo-Chinese Gleaner*, iii. 164, 205 *sq.*

to animals is conspicuous in the writings of Confucius and Mencius ;[1] the Master angled but did not use a net, he shot but not at birds perching.[2] Throughout Japan, according to Sir Edward Reed, " the life of animals has always been held more or less sacred. . . ., neither Shintoism nor Buddhism requiring or justifying the taking of the life of any creature for sacrifice." [3]

The regard for the lower animals which is shown by these Eastern religions and their adherents is to some extent due to superstitious ideas, similar to those which we found prevalent among many savages.   Dr. de Groot observes that in China the virtues of benevolence and humanity are extended to animals because these, also, have souls which may work vengeance or bring reward.[4]   The conduct of Orientals towards the brute creation has further been explained by their belief in the transmigration of souls.   But it seems that the connection between their theory of metempsychosis and their rules relating to the treatment of animals is not exclusively, nor even chiefly, one of cause and effect, but rather one of a common origin.   This theory itself may in some measure be regarded as a result of that intimacy which prevails in the East between animals and men.   Buddhism recognises no fundamental distinction between them, only an accidental or phenomenal difference ;[5] and the step is not long from this attitude to the doctrine of metempsychosis.   Captain Forbes maintains that the humanity with which the Burmans treat dumb animals comes " more from the innate good nature and easiness of their dispositions than from any effect over them of this peculiar doctrine " ;[6] and they laugh at the suggestion made by Europeans that Buddhists abstain from taking life because they believe in the transmigration of souls, having never heard of it before.   Their motive, says Mr. Fielding Hall, is compassion and *noblesse oblige*.[7]   But by its punishments

[1] Mencius, i. i. 7.
[2] *Lun Yü*, vii. 26.
[3] Reed, *Japan*, i. 61.
[4] de Groot, *Religious System of China*, (vol. iv. book) ii. 450.

[5] Rhys Davids, *Hibbert Lectures on Buddhism*, p. 214.
[6] Forbes, *British Burma*, p. 321.
[7] Fielding Hall, *op. cit.* p. 237 *sq.*

acts which are, or are believed to be, injurious to the agent, by exposing him to an animal's revenge or otherwise, are prohibited because they are imprudent ; and, as we have often noticed, such prohibitions are apt to assume a moral character. Finally, if a certain mode of conduct is considered to be productive of public harm, as is the case with any act or omission which reduces, or is supposed to reduce, the supply of food or animal clothing, it is naturally looked upon as a wrong against the community.

Similar facts have, among peoples of a higher culture, led to moral rules inculcating regard for animals—rules which have often assumed a definite shape in their laws or religious books.

According to Brahmanism tenderness towards all creatures is a duty incumbent upon the four castes. It is said that " he who injures innoxious beings from a wish to give himself pleasure, never finds happiness, neither living nor dead."[1] If a blow is struck against animals in order to give them pain, the judge shall inflict a fine in proportion to the amount of pain caused, just as if the blow had been struck against a man.[2] The killing of various creatures, including fish and snakes, reduces the offender to a mixed caste ;[3] and, according to 'Vishnu Purana,' fishermen go after death to the same hell as awaits prisoners, incendiaries, and treacherous friends.[4] To kill a cow is a great crime ;[5] whereas he who unhesitatingly abandons life for the sake of a cow is freed even from the guilt of the murder of a Brâhmana, and so is he who saves the life of a cow.[6] Among many of the Hindus the slaughter of a cow excites more horror than the killing of a man, and is punished with great severity, even with death.[7]

In Buddhism, Jainism, and Taouism the respect for animal life is extreme. A disciple of Buddha may not

[1] *Laws of Manu,* v. 45.
[2] *Ibid.* viii. 286.
[3] *Ibid.* xi. 69.
[4] *Vishńu Purâńa,* p. 208 *sq.*
[5] *Institutes of Vishnu,* 1. 16 *sqq.* Gautama, xxii. 18. *Âpastamba,* i. 26.

[1] *Laws of Manu,* xi. 109 *sqq.*
[6] *Laws of Manu,* xi. 80.
[7] Barth, *Religions of India,* p. 264. Kipling, *Beast and Man in India,* p. 118 *sq.* Crooke, *Things Indian,* p. 91.

knowingly deprive any creature of life, not even a worm
or an ant. He may not drink water in which animal life
of any kind whatever is contained, and must not even
pour it out on grass or clay.[1] And the doctrine which
forbids the killing of animate beings is not only professed,
but in a large measure followed, by the great majority of
people in Buddhistic countries. In Siam the tameness of
many living creatures which in Europe fly from the
presence of man is very striking. Instances have been
known in which natives have quitted the service of
Europeans on account of their unwillingness to destroy
reptiles and vermin, and it is a not uncommon practice for
rich Siamese to buy live fish to have the merit of restoring
them to the sea.[2] In Burma, though fish is one of the
staple foods of the people, the fisherman is despised ; not
so much, perhaps, as if he killed other living things, but
he is still an outcast from decent society, and " will have
to suffer great and terrible punishment before he can be
cleansed from the sins that he daily commits." [3] The
Buddhists of Ceylon are more forbearing : they excuse the
fisherman by saying that he does not kill the fish, but only
removes it from the water.[4] In Tibet all dumb
creatures are treated with humanity, and the taking of
animal life is rather strictly prohibited, except in the case
of yaks and sheep needed for food. Owing to the coldness of the climate, flesh forms an essential staple of diet ;
but the butchers are regarded as professional sinners and
are therefore the most despised of all classes in Tibet.
Wild animals and even small birds and fish are seldom or
never killed, on account of the religious penalties attached
to this crime.[5]

The Jain is stricter still in his regard for animal life.
He sweeps the ground before him as he goes, lest animate
things be destroyed ; he walks veiled, lest he inhale a living
organism ; he considers that the evening and night are

[1] Oldenberg, *Buddha*, pp. 290 n.,*
351.
[2] Bowring, *Siam*, i. 107.
[3] Fielding Hall, *The Soul of a*

People, p. 230.
[4] Schmidt, *Ceylon*, p. 316 *sq.*
[5] Waddell, *Buddhism of Tibet*, p.
567 *sq.*

Macdonald writes that if they appear destitute of pity, say, for their fowls in their methods of carrying them, it is because they do not reflect that it gives them pain—" all would admit that it was a cruel thing to pain the fowl " ; and they have fables in their language which show a desire to enter minutely into the feelings of dumb creatures, representing, for instance, fowls as reasoning on their hard fate in being killed for their master's supper.[1] Among the Indians of the province of Quito, according to Juan and Ulloa, the women are so fond of their fowls that they will not sell them, much less kill them with their own hands ; " so that if a stranger, who is obliged to pass the night in one of their cottages, offers ever so much money for a fowl, they refuse to part with it, and he finds himself under a necessity of killing the fowl himself. At this his landlady shrieks, dissolves in tears, and wrings her hands, as if it had been an only son ; till seeing the mischief past remedy she wipes her eyes, and quietly takes what the traveller offers her." [2]   North American Indians, again, are very fond of their hunting dogs. Those on the west side of the Rocky Mountains " appear to have the same affection for them that they have for their children ; and they will discourse with them, as if they were rational beings. They frequently call them their sons or daughters ; and when describing an Indian, they will speak of him as father of a particular dog which belongs to him. When these dogs die, it is not unusual to see their masters or mistresses place them on a pile of wood, and burn them in the same manner as they do the dead bodies of their relations ; and they appear to lament their deaths, by crying and howling, fully as much as if they were their kindred." [3]   So also the natives of Australia often display much affection for their dogs ; Mr. Gason has seen women crying over a dog when bitten by a snake as if it had been one of their own children, and if a puppy has lost its mother the

---

[1] Macdonald, *Africana*, i. 10 *sq.*

[2] Juan and Ulloa. *Voyage to South America*, i. 426 *sq.*

[3] Harmon, *Journal of Voyages in the Interior of North America*, p. 335 *sq.*

women suckle and nurse it.[1] Of the Maoris of New
Zealand we read that their extreme love of offspring " was
also carried out to excess towards the young of brutes—
especially of their dogs, and, afterwards, of cats and pigs
introduced. Hence it was by no means an unusual sight
to see a woman carrying her child at her back, and a pet
dog, or pig, in her bosom." [2] The Chukchi of North-
Eastern Siberia believe that if a person is cruel to brutes
his soul will after his death migrate into some domestic
animal—a dog, a horse, or a reindeer.[3] Even the
miserable Veddahs of Ceylon are said to be indignant at
the needless killing of a beast.[4]

On the other hand we also hear of savages who are
greatly lacking in sympathy for the brute creation.
Darwin says that humanity to the lower animals is apparently unfelt by savages, except towards their pets.[5]
Mr. Atkinson charges the New Caledonians with great
cruelty to animals.[6] The Tasmanians appeared much to
enjoy the tortures of a wounded bird or beast.[7] It is not
to be expected that people whose kindly feelings towards
men hardly extend beyond the borders of their own
communities should be compassionate to wild animals.
They may also appear wantonly cruel because they do not
realise the pain which they inflict. And, like children,
they may enjoy the agony of a suffering beast or bird
because it excites their curiosity.

It is obvious from what has been said above that
already at the savage stage men's conduct towards the
lower animals must in some cases be a matter of moral
concern. For hand in hand with the altruistic sentiment
we always find the feeling of sympathetic resentment
whenever there is an occasion for its outburst. Moreover,

[1] Gason, ' Dieyerie Tribe,' in Woods, Native Tribes of South Australia, p. 259. Fraser, Aborigines of New South Wales, p. 5. Williams, ' Yircla Meening Tribe,' in Curr, The Australian Race, i. 402.
[2] Colenso, Maori Races of New Zealand, p. 43.
[3] Ratzel, op. cit. ii. 231.
[4] Sarasin, Ergebnisse naturwissenschaftlicher Forschungen auf Ceylon, iii. 539.
[5] Darwin, Descent of Man, p. 123.
[6] Atkinson, ' Natives of New Caledonia,' in Folk-lore, xiv. 248.
[7] Davies, quoted by Ling Roth, Tasmanians, p. 66.

streams that issue from the living fountain. We ought
to take care of our dogs and horses not only when they
are young, but when they are old and past service.[1] We
ought not to violate or kill anything whatsoever that has
life, unless it hurt us first.[2] And if we cannot live
unblamably we should at least sin with discretion : when
we kill an animal in order to satisfy our hunger we should
do so with sorrow and pity, without abusing and
tormenting it.[3] Cicero says it is a crime to injure an
animal.[4] And Marcus Aurelius enjoins man to make use
of brutes with a generous and liberal spirit, since he has
reason and they have not.[5]

In the Old Testament we meet with several instances of
kindly feeling towards animals.[6] God watches over and
controls the sustenance of their life. He sends springs
into the valleys which will give drink to every beast
of the field. He gives nests to the birds of the heaven,
which sing among the branches. He causes grass to
grow for the cattle ; and the young lions, roaring after
their prey, seek their food from God.[7] Whilst the Jews,
as Professor Toy observes, found it hard to conceive
of the God of Israel as thinking kindly of its enemies,
they had no such feeling of hostility towards beasts and
birds.[8] But at the same time man is the centre of the
creation, a being set apart from all other sentient
creatures as God's special favourite, for whose sake
everything else was brought into existence. The sun,
the moon, and the stars were placed in the firmament of
the heaven to give light upon the estate of man.[9] For
his sustenance the fruits of the earth were made to grow,
and to him was given dominion over the fish of the sea,

---

[1] Plutarch, *Cato Major*, v. 3 *sq.*
[2] *Idem, Questiones Romanæ*, 75.
[3] *Idem, De carnium esu oratio II.*
i. 3.
[4] Cicero, *De republica*, iii. 11.
[5] Marcus Aurelius, *Commentarii*,
vi. 23.
[6] See Bertholet, *Die Stellung der
Israeliten zu den Fremden*, p. 14.
Various passages, however, which
are often quoted as instances of
tenderness towards animals allow
of another and more natural interpretation. This is especially the
case with the sabbatarian injunctions referring to domestic animals.
[7] *Psalms*, civ. 10–12, 14, 17, 21.
[8] Toy, *Judaism and Christianity*,
p. 81.
[9] *Genesis*, i. 16 *sq.*

and over the fowl of the air, and over every living thing
that moves upon the earth.[1] And when the earth is to be
replenished after the deluge, the same privileges are again
granted to him. The fear of man and the dread of man
shall be upon all living creatures, into his hand are they
all delivered, they shall all be meat for him.[2] And they are
given over to his supreme and irresponsible control
without the slightest injunction of kindness or the
faintest suggestion of any duties towards them. They
are to be regarded by him simply as food.[3]

Among the Hebrews the harshness of this anthropocentric doctrine was somewhat mitigated by the sympathy which a simple pastoral and agricultural people
naturally feels for its domestic animals. In Christianity,
on the other hand, it was further strengthened by the
exclusive importance which was attached to the spiritual
salvation of man. He was now more than ever separated
from the rest of sentient beings. Even his own animal
nature was regarded with contempt, the immortality of
his soul being the only object of religious interest. " It
would seem," says Dr. Arnold, " as if the primitive
Christian, by laying so much stress upon a future life in
contradistinction to this life, and placing the lower creatures
out of the pale of hope, placed them at the same time out
of the pale of sympathy, and thus laid the foundation for
this utter disregard of animals in the light of our fellow-
creatures." [4] St. Paul asks with scorn, " Doth God take
care for oxen ? " [5] No creed in Christendom teaches
kindness to animals as a dogma of religion.[6] In the Middle
Ages various councils of the Church declared hunting
unlawful for the clergy ;[7] but the obvious reason for this
prohibition was its horror of bloodshed,[8] not any consider-

[1] *Genesis*, i. 28.
[2] *Ibid.* ix. 2 *sq.*
[3] *Cf.* Evans, ' Ethical Relations
between Man and Beast,' in *Popular
Science Monthly*, xlv. 637 *sq.*
[4] Arnold, quoted by Evans, in
Popular Science Monthly, xlv. 639.
[5] 1 *Corinthians*, ix. 9.
[6] The Manichæans prohibited all

killing of animals (Baur, *Das Manichäische Religionssystem*, p. 252 *sqq.*);
but Manichæism did not originate
on Christian ground (Harnack,
' Manichæism,' in *Encyclopædia
Britannica*, xv. 485 ; *supra*, ii. 312).
[7] Le Grand d'Aussy, *Histoire de la
vie privée des François*, i. 394 *sq.*
[8] *Supra*, i. 381 *sq.*

be treated with consideration and not be overworked ;[1] and in various Muhammedan countries this law has also been habitually put into practice. The Moslems of India are kind to animals.[2] In his earlier intercourse with the people of Egypt, Mr. Lane noticed much humanity to beasts.[3] Montaigne said that the Turks gave alms to brutes and had hospitals for them ;[4] and Mr. Bosworth Smith is of opinion that beasts of burden and domestic animals are nowhere in Christendom—with the one exception, perhaps, of Norway—treated with such unvarying kindness and consideration as they are in Turkey. " In the East," he adds, " so far as it has not been hardened by the West, there is a real sympathy between man and the domestic animals ; they understand one another." [5]

So also the ancient Greeks were on familiar terms with the animal world. This appears from the frequency with which their poets illustrate human qualities by metaphors drawn from it. And as men were compared with animals, so animals were believed to possess human peculiarities. When a beast was going to be sacrificed it had to give its consent to the act by a nod of the head before it was killed.[6] Animals were held in some measure responsible for their deeds ; they were tried for manslaughter, sentenced, and executed.[7] On the other hand, honours were bestowed upon beasts which had rendered signal services to their masters. The graves of Cimon's mares with which he three times conquered at the Olympic games were still in the days of Plutarch to be seen near his own tomb ;[8] and a certain Xanthippus honoured his dog by burying it on a promontory, since then called " the dog's grave," because when the Athenians were compelled to abandon their city it swam by the side of his galley to Salamis.[9] According to Xenocrates, there were in existence

[1] Sachau, *Muhammedanisches Recht*, pp. 18, 103.
[2] Pool, *Studies in Mohammedanism*, pp. 176, 177, 247. *Cf.* Heber, *Journey through the Upper Provinces of India*, ii. 131.
[3] Lane, *Modern Egyptians*, p. 293.
[4] Montaigne, *Essais*, ii. 11.
[5] Bosworth Smith, *Mohammed and Mohammedanism*, pp. 180, 217.
[6] Schmidt, *Die Ethik der alten Griechen*, ii. 96 *sq.*
[7] *Supra*, i. 254.
[8] Plutarch, *Cato Major*, v. 6.
[9] *Ibid.* v. 7.

at Eleusis three laws which had been made by an ancient legislator, namely :—" Honour your parents ; Sacrifice to the gods from the fruits of the earth ; Injure not animals."[1] At Athens a man was punished for flaying a living ram.[2] The Areopagites once condemned a boy to death because he had picked out the eyes of some quails.[3] As we have noticed before, the life of the ploughing ox was sacred ; [4] and young animals in particular were believed to be under the protection of the gods.[5] An ancient proverb says that " there are Erinyes even for dogs." [6] This seems to indicate that the Greeks, also, were influenced by the common notion that the soul of an animal may take revenge upon him who killed it, the Erinys of the slain animal being originally its persecuting ghost. Among the Pythagoreans, again, the rule that animals which are not obnoxious to the human race should be neither injured nor killed[7] was connected with their theory of metempsychosis ; [8] and in some cases the prohibition of slaying useful animals may be traced to utilitarian motives.[9] But both in Greece and Rome kindness to brutes was also inculcated for their own sake, on purely humanitarian grounds. Porphyry says that, as justice pertains to rational beings and animals have been proved to be possessed of reason, it is necessary that we should act justly towards them.[10] He adds that " he who does not restrict harmless conduct to man alone, but extends it to other animals, most closely approaches to divinity ; and if it were possible to extend it to plants, he would preserve this image in a still greater degree." [11] According to Plutarch kindness and beneficence to creatures of every species flow from the breast of a well-natured man as

[1] Porphyry, *De abstinentia ab esu animalium*, iv. 22.

[2] Plutarch, *De carnium esu oratio I*. vii. 2.

[3] Quintilian, *De institutione oratoria*, v. 9. 13.

[4] *Supra*, ii. 331.

[5] Aeschylus, *Agamemnon*, 48 *sqq.* Xenophon, *Cynegeticus*, v. 14.

[6] Schmidt, *op. cit.* ii. 96.

[7] Jamblichus, *De Pythagorica vita*, 21 (98).

[8] Diogenes Laertius, *Vitæ philosophorum*, viii. 2. 12 (77). Aristotle, *Rhetorica*, i. 13. 2, p. 1373 b. Schmidt, *op. cit.* ii. 94.

[9] Porphyry, *op. cit.* iv. 22. *Supra*, ii. 331.

[10] Porphyry, *op. cit.* iii. 18.

[11] *Ibid.* iii. 28.

and rewards, religion has greatly increased the natural
regard for animal life and welfare, and introduced a new
motive for conduct which originally sprang in the main
from kindly feeling.

In Zoroastrianism we meet with a different attitude
towards the lower animal world. A fundamental distinction is made between the animals of Ormuzd and those of
Ahriman. To kill one of the former is a heinous sin, to
kill one of the latter is a pious deed.[1] Sacred above all
other animals is the dog. The ill-feeding and maltreat-
ment of dogs are prosecuted as criminal, and extreme
penalties are inflicted on those who venture to kill them.[2]
Nay, if there be in the house of a worshipper of Mazda
a mad dog who has no scent, the worshippers of Mazda
" shall attend him to heal him, in the same manner as they
would do for one of the faithful." [3]   In the eyes of the
Parsis, animals are enlisted under the standards of either
Ormuzd or Ahriman according as they are useful or
hurtful to man ; but M. Darmesteter is of opinion that
they originally belonged to the one or the other not on
account of any such qualities, but according as they
chanced to have lent their forms to either the god or the
fiend in the storm tales. " It was not animal psychology,"
he says, " that disguised gods and fiends as dogs, otters,
hedge-hogs, and cocks, or as snakes, tortoises, frogs, and
ants, but the accidents of physical qualities and the caprice
of popular fancy, as both the god and the fiend might be
compared with, and transformed into, any object, the idea
of which was suggested by the uproar of the storm, the
blazing of the lightning, the streaming of the water, or the
hue and shape of the clouds." [4] This hypothesis, however,
seems to attach undue importance to mythical fancies, and
it presupposes an almost unbounded and capricious
allegorism, for which there is apparently little foundation

---

[1] Darmesteter, *Ormazd et Ahri-*
man, p. 283.
   [2] *Vendîdâd,* xiii. *sq.* Geiger,
Civilization of the Eastern Irānians,
ii. 36.

[3] *Vendîdâd,* xiii. 35.
   [4] Darmesteter, in *Sacred Books of*
the East, iv. (1st edit.) p. lxxii. *sq.*
See also *Idem, Ormazd et Ahriman,*
p. 283 *sqq.*

in facts. The suggestion that the animals are referred to either the one or the other category according as they are useful or obnoxious to man, is at all events borne out by a few salient features, although in many details the matter remains obscure.

It appears that among the Zoroastrians, also, the respect for the life of animals is partly due to superstitious ideas about their souls and fear of their revenge. According to the ' Yasts,' " the souls of the wild beasts and of the tame " are objects of worship ;[1] and in one of the Pahlavi texts it is said that people should abstain from unlawfully slaughtering any species of animals, since otherwise, in punishment for such an act, each hair of the animal killed becomes like a sharp dagger, and he who is unlawfully a slaughterer is slain.[2] But here again we may assume the co-operating influence of the feeling of sympathy. Various passages in the Zoroastrian ' Gathas ' which enjoin kindness to domestic animals [3] suggest as their motives not only considerations of utility but genuine tenderness. In a later age Firdausi sang, " Ah ! spare yon emmet rich in hoarded grain : He lives with pleasure, and he dies with pain." [4] And of the modern Persian Dr. Polak says that, " naturally not cruel, he treats animals with more consideration than men." [5] His present religion, too, enjoins kindness to animals as a duty.

According to Muhammedanism, beasts, birds, fish, insects, are all, like man, the slaves of God, the tools of His will. There is no intrinsic distinction between them and the human species, except what accidental diversity God may have been pleased to make.[6] Muhammed said to his followers :—" There is not a beast upon the earth nor a bird that flies with both its wings, but is a nation like to you ; . . . to their Lord shall they be gathered." [7] Muhammedan law prescribes that domestic animals shall

[1] *Yasts*, xiii. 154.
[2] *Shâyast Lâ-Shâyast*, x. 8.
[3] Darmesteter, in *Le Zend-Avesta*, i. p. cvi.
[4] Firdausi, quoted by Jones, 'Tenth Anniversary Discourse,' in *Asiatick*

Researches, iv. 12.
[5] Polak, *Persien*, i. 12.
[6] *Cf.* Palgrave, *Journey through Central and Eastern Arabia*, i. 368.
[7] *Koran*, vi. 38.

ation for the animals. Mr. Mauleverer in Sir Arthur Helps'
'Talk about Animals and their Masters,' says, "Upon a
moderate calculation, I think I have heard, in my time,
1320 sermons ; and I do not recollect that in any one of
them I ever heard the slightest allusion made to the
conduct of men towards animals." [1] Nor is there any such
allusion in most treatises on Ethics which base their
teachings upon distinctly Christian tenets. The kindest
words, I think, which from a Christian point of view have
been said about animals have generally come from
Protestant sectarians, Quakers and Methodists, [2] whereas
Roman Catholic writers—with a few exceptions [3]—when
they deal with the subject at all, chiefly take pains to show
that animals are entirely destitute of rights. Brute beasts,
says Father Rickaby, cannot have any rights for the reason
that they have no understanding and therefore are not
persons. We have no duties of any kind to them, as
neither to stocks and stones ; we only have duties *about*
them. We must not harm them when they are our
neighbour's property, we must not vex and annoy them
for sport, because it disposes him who does so to
inhumanity towards his own species. But there is no
shadow of evil resting on the practice of causing pain
to brutes *in* sport, where the pain is not the sport itself,
but an incidental concomitant of it. Much more in all
that conduces to the sustenance of man may we give pain
to animals, and we are not " bound to any anxious care
to make this pain as little as may be. Brutes are as *things*
in our regard : so far as they are useful to us, they
exist for us, not for themselves ; and we do right in
using them unsparingly for our need and convenience,
though not for our wantonness." [4] According to another

[1] Helps, *Some Talk about Animals and their Masters*, p. 20. *Cf.* Mrs. Jameson, *Common-Place Book of Thoughts*, p. 212.
[2] See Gurney, *Views and Practices of the Society of Friends*, p. 392 sq. n. 8 ; Richmond, ' Sermon on the Sin of Cruelty to the Brute Creation,' in *Methodist Magazine* (London), xxx. 490 *sqq.* ; Chalmers, Cruelty to Animals,' in *Methodist Magazine* (New York), ix. 259 *sqq.*
[3] See de la Roche-Fontenelles, *L'Église et la pitié envers les animaux, passim.*
[4] Rickaby, *Moral Philosophy*, p. 248 *sqq.* See also Addis and Arnold, *Catholic Dictionary*, p. 33 ; Clarke,

modern Catholic writer the infliction of suffering upon an animal is not only justifiable, but a duty, " when it confers a certain, a solid good, however small, on the spiritual nature of man."[1]   Pope Pius IX. refused a request for permission to form in Rome a Society for Prevention of Cruelty to Animals on the professed ground that it was a theological error to suppose that man owes any duty to an animal.[2]

It is not only theological moralists that maintain that animals can have no rights and that abstinence from wanton cruelty is a duty not to the animal but to man. This view has been shared by Kant[3] and by many later philosophers.[4] So also the legal protection of animals has often been vindicated merely on the ground that cruelty to animals might breed cruelty to men or shows a cruel disposition of mind,[5] or that it wounds the sensibilities of other people.[6] In ' Parliamentary History and Review ' for 1825–1826 it is stated that no reason can be assigned for the interference of the legislator in the protection of animals unless their protection be connected, either directly or remotely, with some advantage to man.[7] The Bill for the abolition of bear-baiting and other cruel practices was expressly propounded on the ground that nothing was more conducive to crime than such sports, that they led the lower orders to gambling, that they educated them for thieves, that they gradually trained them up to bloodshed and murder.[8] The criminal code of the German Empire, again, imposes a fine upon any person " who spitefully tortures or cruelly ill-treats beasts,

---

' Cruelty to Animals,' in *The Month and Catholic Review*, xxv. 401 *sqq.* ; Hedley, ' Dr. Mivart on Faith and Science,' in *Dublin Review*, ser. iii. vol. xviii. 418.

[1] Clarke, in *The Month and Catholic Review*, xxv. 406.

[2] Cobbe, *Modern Rack*, p. 6.

[3] Kant, *Metaphysische Anfangungsgründe der Tugendlehre*, § 16 *sq.*, pp. 106, 108.

[4] *E.g.*, Alexander, *Moral Order and*

Progress, p. 281 ; Ritchie, *Natural Rights*, p. 110 *sq.*

[5] Hommel, quoted by von Hippel, *Die Thielquälerei in der Strafgesetzgebung*, p. 110. Tissot, *Le droit pénal*, i. 17. Lasson, *System der Rechtsphilosophie*, p. 548 *sq.*

[6] Lasson, *op. cit.* p. 548. von Hippel, *op. cit.* p. 125.

[7] *Parliamentary History and Review*, 1825–6, p. 761.

[8] *Ibid.* p. 546.

either publicly or in a manner to create scandal "[1]—in other words, he is punished, not because he puts the animal to pain, but because his conduct is offensive to his fellow men.

Indifference to animal suffering has been a characteristic of public opinion in European countries up to quite modern times. Only a little more than a hundred years ago Thomas Young declared in his ' Essay on Humanity to Animals ' that he was sensible of laying himself open to no small portion of ridicule in offering to the public a book on such a subject.[2] Till the end of the eighteenth century and even later cock-fighting was a very general amusement among the English and Scotch, entering into the occupations of both the old and young. Travellers agreed with coachmen that they were to wait a night if there was a cock-fight in any town through which they passed. Schools had their cock-fights; on Shrove Tuesday every youth took to the village schoolroom a cock reared for his special use, and the schoolmaster presided at the conflict.[3] Those who felt that the practice required some excuse found it in the idea that the race was to suffer this annual barbarity by way of punishment for St. Peter's crime;[4] but the number of people who had any scruples about the game cannot have been great considering that even such a strong advocate of humanity to animals as Lawrence had no decided antipathy to it.[5] Other pastimes indulged in were dog-fighting, bull-baiting and badger-baiting; and in the middle of the eighteenth century the bear-garden was described by Lord Kames as one of the chief entertainments of the English, though it was held in abhorrence by the French and " other polite nations," being too savage an amusement to be relished

---

[1] *Strafgesetzbuch*, § 360 (13).
[2] Young, *Essay on Humanity to Animals*, p. 1.
[3] Roberts, *Social History of the People of the Southern Counties of England*, p. 421 *sqq.* Rogers, *Social Life in Scotland*, ii. 340. In 1856, when Roberts wrote his book, cock-

penance was still paid in some English grammar schools to the master as a perquisite on Shrove Tuesday (Roberts, p. 423).
[4] Roberts, *op. cit.* p. 422.
[5] Lawrence, *Philosophical and Practical Treatise on Horses*, ii. 12.

by those of a refined taste.[1] As late as 1824 Sir Robert
(then Mr.) Peel argued strongly against the legal prohibition of bull-baiting.[2]

About two years previously, however, humanity to
animals had, for the first time, become a subject of English
legislation by the Act which prevented cruel and improper
treatment of cattle.[3] This Act was afterwards followed by
others which prohibited bear-baiting, cock-fighting, and
similar pastimes, as also cruelty to domestic animals in
general. In 1876 vivisection for medical or scientific
purposes was subjected to a variety of restrictions, and
since 1900 cases of ill-treatment of wild animals in
captivity may be dealt with under the Wild Animals in
Captivity Protection Act.[4] On the Continent cruelty to
animals was first prohibited by criminal law in Saxony, in
1838,[5] and subsequently in most other European states.
But in the South of Europe there are still countries in
which the law is entirely silent on the subject.[6]

Whatever be the professed motives of legislators for
preventing cruelty to animals, there can be no doubt
that the laws against it are chiefly due to a keener and
more generally felt sympathy with their sufferings. The
actual feelings of men have commonly been somewhat
more tender than the theories of law, philosophy, and
religion. The anthropocentric exclusiveness of Christianity was from ancient times to some extent counterbalanced
by popular sentiments and beliefs. In the folk-tales of
Europe man is not placed in an isolated and unique
position in the universe. He lives in intimate and
friendly intercourse with the animals round him, attributes
to them human qualities, and regards them with mercy.[7]
Tender feelings towards the brute creation are also displayed in many legends of saints.[8] St. Francis of Assisi

---

[1] Kames, *Essays on the Principles of Morality*, p. 7.
[2] Hansard, *Parliamentary Debates*, New Series, x. 491 *sqq.*
[3] *Statutes of Great Britain and Ireland*, lxii. 403 *sqq.*
[4] Stephen, *New Commentaries on the Laws of England*, iv. 213 *sqq.*
[5] von Hippel, *op. cit.* p. 1.
[6] *Ibid.* p. 90 *sq.*
[7] *Supra*, i. 259. Schwarz, *Prähis-torisch-anthropologische Studien*, p. 203.
[8] Lecky, *History of European*

CHAPTER XLV

REGARD FOR THE DEAD

MORALITY takes notice not only of men's conduct towards the living but of their conduct towards the dead. There is a general tendency in the human mind to assume that what has existed still exists and will exist. When a person dies it is difficult for those around him to conceive that he is really dead, and when the cold motionless body bears sad testimony to the change which has taken place, there is a natural inclination to believe that the soul has only changed its abode. In the savage the tendency to assume the continued existence of the soul after death is strongly supported by dreams and visions of his deceased friends. What else could these mean but visits of their souls?

There are, it is true, some savages who are reported to believe in the annihilation of the soul at the moment of death, or to have no notion whatever of a future state.[1] But the accuracy of these statements is hardly beyond suspicion. We sometimes hear that the very people who are said to deny any belief in an after-life are afraid of ghosts.[2] A native of Madagascar will almost in the same

[1] Powers, *Tribes of California*, p. 348 *sq.* (Miwok). Brinton, *Myths of the New World*, p. 233 *sq.* (some Oregon Indians). Lumholtz, *Among Cannibals*, p. 101 (natives of the Herbert River, Northern Queensland). Martin, *Reisen in den Molukken*, p. 155 (Alfura). Worcester, *Philippine Islands*, p. 412 (Mang-

yans). Colquhoun, *Amongst the Shans*, p. 76 (Lethtas). Dalton, *Ethnology of Bengal*, p. 257 (Oráons). Petherick, *Travels in Central Africa*, i. 321 (Nouaer tribes). Du Chaillu, *Explorations in Equatorial Africa*, p. 385.

[2] New, *Life in Eastern Africa*, p. 105.

breath declare that when he dies he ceases altogether to
exist and yet confess the fact that he is in the habit of
praying to his dead ancestors.[1] Of the Masai in Eastern
Africa some writers state that they believe in annihilation,[2]
others that they attribute a future existence to their chiefs,
medicine men, or influential people.[3] The ideas on this
subject are often exceedingly vague, and inconsistencies
are only to be expected.

The disembodied soul is commonly supposed to have the
shape of a small unsubstantial human image, and to be in
its nature a sort of vapour, film, or shadow.[4] It is
believed to have the same bodily wants and to possess the
same mental capacities as its owner possessed during his
lifetime. It is not regarded as invulnerable or immortal—
it may be hurt and killed. It feels hunger and thirst, heat
and cold. It can see and hear and think, it has human
passions and a human will, and it has the power to influence
the living for evil or for good. These notions as regards
the disembodied soul determine the relations between the
living and the dead.

The dead are supposed to have rights very similar to
those they had whilst alive. The soul must not be killed
or injured. The South Australian Dieyerie, for instance,
show great reverence for certain trees, which are believed
to be their fathers transformed ; they will not cut them
down and protest against the settlers doing so.[5] So also
some of the Philippine Islanders maintain that the souls
of their forefathers are in trees, which they therefore
spare.[6] The North American Powhatans refrained from
doing harm to some small wood-birds, which were
supposed to receive the souls of their chiefs.[7] In Lifu,

[1] Ellis, *History of Madagascar*, i.
393.
[2] Thomson, *Through Masai Land*,
p. 259. Hinde, *The Last of the
Masai*, p. 99.
[3] Johnston, *Uganda*, ii. 832.
Hollis, *Masai*, pp. 304, 305, 307.
Elict, *ibid.* p. xx.
[4] Tylor, *Primitive Culture*, i. 429.
[5] Gason, ' Dieyerie Tribe,' in

Woods' *Native Tribes of South
Australia*, p. 280.
[6] Blumentritt, ' Der Ahnencultus
der Malaien des Philippinen-Archipels,' in *Mittheil. d. kais. u. kön.
Geograph. Gesellsch. in Wien*, xxv.
164 *sqq.*
[7] Brinton, *Myths of the New World*,
p. 102.

lessness has been responsible for much needless pain to
which they have been made subject. In spite of some
improvement it is so still ; whilst, at the same time, the
movement advocating greater humanity to animals is
itself not altogether free from inconsistencies and a
certain lack of discrimination.

It has been observed that the Neapolitan would not
act so cruelly as he does to almost all animals
except the cat if he could bring himself to conceive
their capacity for joy and pain.[1] So also we ourselves
should often behave differently if we realised the tortures
we thoughtlessly cause to creatures whose sufferings
escape our notice from want of obvious outward expression. While the practice of whipping young pigs to
death to make them tender, which occurred in England
not much more than a century ago,[2] would nowadays be
regarded with general horror, cruelties inflicted for
gastronomic purposes upon creatures of a lower type are
little thought of. Cray-fish, oysters, and fish in general,
as Mandeville observed, excite hardly any compassion at
all, because " they express themselves unintelligibly to us ;
they are mute, and their inward formation, as well as
outward figure, vastly different from ours." [3] On the
other hand, even passionate sportsmen describe the
hunting of monkeys as repulsive on account of their
resemblance to man ; Rajah Brooke thought it almost
barbarous to kill an orang-utan, unless for the sake of
scientific research.[4] Buddhism itself declares that " he
who takes away the life of a large animal will have greater
demerit than he who takes away the life of a small one. . . .
The crime is not great when an ant is killed ; its magnitude
increases in this progression—a lizard, a guana, a hare, a
deer, a bull, a horse, and an elephant." [5] How little the
feelings which underlie men's opinions concerning conduct

[1] ' Cruelty to Animals in Naples,'
in *Saturday Review*, lix. 854.
[2] *The World*, 1756, nr. 190, p.
1142. Young, *op. cit.* p. 129.
[3] Mandeville, *op. cit.* p. 187.
[4] Brooke, *Ten Years in Saráwak*,
i. 100. *Cf.* Rengger, *Naturgeschichte
der Säugethiere von Paraguay*, p.
26.
[5] Hardy, *Manual of Budhism*, pp.
478, 480.

towards the lower animals are influenced by reflection is
also apparent in the present crusade against vivisection,
when compared with the public indifference to the sufferings inflicted on wild animals in sport. The vivisector who
in cold blood torments his helpless victim in the interest
of science and for the benefit of mankind is called a
coward, and is a much more common object of hatred than
the sportsman who causes agonies to the creature he
pursues for sheer amusement. The pursued animal, it is
argued, has " free chances of escape." [1] This is an excellent
argument—provided we share the North American
Indian's conviction that an animal can never be killed
without its own permission.

At present there is among ourselves no topic of moral
concern which presents a greater variety of opinion than
the question how far the happiness of the lower animals
may be justly sacrificed for the benefit of man. The
extreme views on this subject might, no doubt, be
somewhat modified, on the one hand by a more vivid
representation of animal suffering, on the other hand by
the recognition of certain facts, often overlooked, which
make it unreasonable to regard conduct towards dumb
creatures in exactly the same light as conduct towards
men. It should especially be remembered that the
former have none of those long-protracted anticipations of
future misery or death which we have.[2] If they are
destined to serve as meat they are not aware of it ;
whereas many domestic animals would never have come
into existence, and been able to enjoy what appears a very
happy life, but for the purpose of being used as food.
But though greater intellectual discrimination may
somewhat lessen the divergencies of moral opinion on the
subject, nothing like unanimity can be expected, for the
simple reason that moral judgments are ultimately based
upon emotions, and sympathy with the animal world is
a feeling which varies extremely in different individuals.

[1] Cobbe, *op. cit.* p. 10.
[2] *Cf.* Bentham, *Introduction to the*   *Principles of Morals and Legislation,* p. 311, n.

talked with the birds and called them " brother birds " or
" little sister swallows," and was seen employed in removing worms from the road that they might not be trampled
by travellers.[1] John Moschus speaks of a certain abbot
who early in the morning not only used to give food to
all the dogs in the monastery, but would bring corn to the
ants and to the birds on the roof.[2] In the ' Revelations
of St. Bridget ' we read, " Let a man fear, above all, me,
his God, and so much the gentler will he become towards
my creatures and animals, on whom, on account of me,
their Creator, he ought to have compassion." [3] Many
kind words about animals have come from poets and
thinkers. Montaigne says that he has never been able to
see without affliction an innocent beast, which is without
defence and from which we receive no offence, pursued
and killed.[4] Shakespeare points out that " the poor beetle
that we tread upon, in corporal sufferance finds a pang as
great as when a giant dies." [5] Mandeville thinks that if
it was not for that tyranny which custom usurps over us,
no men of any tolerable good-nature could ever be
reconciled to the killing of so many animals for their
daily food, as long as the bountiful earth so plentifully
provides them with varieties of vegetable dainties.[6]
Towards the end of the eighteenth century Bentham
wrote :—" Men must be permitted to kill animals ; but
they should be forbidden to torment them. Artificial death
may be rendered less painful than natural death by simple
processes, well worth the trouble of being studied, and of
becoming an object of police. Why should the law
refuse its protection to any sensitive being ? A time
will come when humanity will spread its mantle over
everything that breathes. The lot of slaves has begun to

Morals, ii. 168 *sqq.* Joyce, *Social
History of Ancient Ireland*, ii. 517 *sq.*
[1] Sabatier, *Life of St. Francis of
Assisi*, p. 176 *sq.* Digby, *Mores
Catholici*, ii. 291.
[2] Moschus, *Pratum spirituale*, 184
(Migne, *Patrologiæ cursus*, Ser.
Græca, lxxxvii. 3056).

[3] St. Bridget, quoted by Helps,
op. cit. p. 124.
[4] Montaigne, *Essais*, ii. 11.
[5] Shakespeare, *Measure for Measure*, iii. 1.
[6] Mandeville, *Fable of the Bees*, p.
187.

excite pity ; we shall end by softening the lot of the animals which labour for us and supply our wants." [1] Some years later Thomas Young pronounced hunting, shooting, and fishing for sport to be " unlawful, cruel, and sinful." [2] And in the course of the nineteenth century humanity to animals, from being conspicuous in a few individuals only, became the keynote of a movement gradually increasing in strength. Humanitarians, says Mr. Salt, " insist that the difference between human and non-human is one of degree only and not of kind, and that we owe duties, the same in kind though not in degree, to all our sentient fellow-beings." [3] Some people maintain that it is wrong to kill animals for food or in sport ; but the most vigorous attacks concerning the treatment of the brute creation are at present directed against the practice of vivisection. The claim is made that this practice should be, not merely restricted, but entirely prohibited by law. And while the antivivisectionists generally endeavour to deny or minimise the scientific importance of experiments on living animals, their cry for the abolition of such experiments is mainly based on the argument that humanity at large has no right to purchase relief from its own suffering by torturing helpless brutes.

This rapidly increasing sympathy with animal suffering is no doubt to a considerable extent due to the decline of the anthropocentric doctrine and the influence of another theory, which regards man, not as an image of the deity separated from the lower animals by a special act of creation, but as a being generally akin to them, and only representing a higher stage in the scale of mental evolution. Through this doctrine the orthodox contempt for dumb creatures was succeeded by feelings of affinity and kindly interest. But apart from any theory as regards human origins, growing reflection has also taught men to be more considerate in their treatment of animals by producing a more vivid idea of their sufferings. Human thought-

---

[1] Bentham, *Theory of Legislation*, p. 428 *sq.*

[2] Young, *op. cit.* p. 75 *sq.*

[3] Salt, *Animals' Rights*, p. v.

The grave is represented as a place where the deceased finds his desired rest, and if denied proper burial he is believed not only to walk but to suffer. The Iroquois considered that unless the rites of burial were performed, the spirits of the dead had to wander for a time upon the earth in a state of great unhappiness ; hence their extreme solicitude to recover the bodies of their slain in battle.[1] The Abipones regard it as the greatest misfortune for the dead to be left to rot in the open air, and they therefore inter even the smallest bone of a departed friend.[2]   In Ashantee the spirits of those who for some reason or other have been deprived of the customary funeral rites are doomed, in the imagination of the people, to haunt the gloom of the forest, stealing occasionally to their former abodes in rare but lingering visits, troubling and bewitching their neglectful relatives.[3]   The Negroes of Accra believe that happiness in a future life depends not only upon courage, power, and wealth in this world, but also upon a proper burial.[4]   In some Australian tribes the souls of those whose bodies have been left to lie unburied are supposed to have to prowl on the face of the earth and about the place of death, with no gratification but to harm the living ;[5] or there is said to be no future existence for them, as their bodies will be devoured by crows and native dogs.[6]   Among the Bataks of Sumatra nothing is considered to be a greater disgrace to a person than to be denied a grave ; for by not being held worthy of burial he is declared to be spiritually dead.[7]   The Samoans believed that the souls of unburied friends, for instance such as had been drowned or had fallen in war, haunted them everywhere, crying out in a pitiful tone, " Oh, how cold ! Oh, how cold ! "[8]   According to Karen ideas the

[1] Morgan, *League of the Iroquois,* p. 175.
[2] Dobrizhoffer, *Account of the Abipones,* ii. 284.
[3] Bowdich, *Mission to Ashantee,* p. 262 *sq.*
[4] Monrad, *Skildring af Guinea-Kysten,* p. 4.
[5] Oldfield, ' Aborigines of Australia,' in *Trans. Ethn. Soc.* N.S. iii.

228, 236 *sq.*
[6] Chauncy, in Brough Smyth, *Aborigines of Victoria,* ii. 280.
[7] Buning, in *Glimpses of the Eastern Archipelago,* p. 75.
[8] Turner, *Nineteen Years in Polynesia,* p. 233. Hood, *Cruise in H.M.S. " Fawn " in the Western Pacific,* p. 142.

spirits of those who die a natural death and are decently buried go to a beautiful country and renew their earthly life, whereas the ghosts of persons who by accident are left uninterred will wander about the earth, occasionally showing themselves to mankind.[1] Confucius connected the disposal of the dead immediately with the great virtue of submission and devotion to superiors.[2] No act is in China recognised more worthy a virtuous man than that of interring stray bones and covering up exposed coffins,[3] and to bury a person who is without friends is considered to be as great a merit as to save life.[4] It is also held highly important to provide the proper place for a grave ; the Taouists maintain that " if a coffin be interred in an improper spot, the spirit of the dead is made unhappy, and avenges itself by causing sickness and other calamities to the relatives who have not taken sufficient care for its repose." [5] The ancient Chaldeans believed that the spirits of the unburied dead, having neither place of repose nor means of subsistence, wandered through the town and country, occupied with no other thought than that of attacking and robbing the living.[6] In classical antiquity it was the most sacred of duties to give the body its funeral rites,[7] and the Greeks referred the right of sepulture to the gods as its authors.[8]

So also among peoples who practise cremation the dead themselves are considered to be benefited by being burned. The Nâyars of Malabar are of opinion that no time should be lost in setting about the funeral, as the disposal of a corpse either by cremation or burial as soon

---

[1] Cross, quoted by Mac Mahon, *Far Cathay*, p. 202 *sq.* Mason, ' Religion, &c. among the Karens,' in *Jour. Asiatic Soc. Bengal*, xxxiv. pt. ii. 203.

[2] de Groot, *Religious System of China*, (vol. ii. book) i. 659.

[3] Giles, *Strange Stories from a Chinese Studio*, ii. 147, n. 11.

[4] *Indo-Chinese Gleaner*, iii. 161.

[5] Legge, *Religions of China*, p. 200.

[6] Maspero, *Dawn of Civilization*, p. 689. Jeremias, *Die babylonisch-assyrischen Vorstellungen vom Leben nach dem Tode*, p. 54 *sqq.* Halévy, *Mélanges de critique et d'histoire relatifs aux peuples sémitiques*, p. 368.

[7] See Schmidt, *Die Ethik der alten Griechen*, ii. 97 *sqq.* ; Granger, *Worship of the Romans*, p. 37 *sqq.* ; Aust, *Die Religion der Römer*, p. 226 *sq.*

[8] Sophocles, *Antigone*, 454 *sq.* Euripides, *Supplices*, 563.

dead.[1]   Among the Maoris " the least violation of any
portion of the precincts of the dead is accounted the
greatest crime that a human being can commit, and is
visited with the direst revenge of a surviving tribe." [2]
The laws of Athens [3] and Rome [4] and the ancient
Teutonic law-books [5] punished with great severity the
plunder of a corpse or a tomb. In Rome the punishment
was death if the offence was committed by force, otherwise
condemnation to the mines.

Like living men the dead are sensitive to insults and
fond of praise ; hence respect must be shown for their
honour and self-regarding pride. *De mortuis nil nisi bonum;*
οὐ γὰρ ἐσθλὰ κατθανοῦσι κερτομεῖν ἐπ᾽ ἀνδράσιν.[6]   In Greece
custom required that at the funeral meal the virtues of the
deceased should be enumerated and extolled, [7] and calumny
against a dead person was punished by law. [8] The same
was the case in ancient Egypt. [9] In Greenland, after the
interment, the nearest male relative of the dead com-
memorated in a loud plaintive voice all the excellent
qualities of the departed.[10] Among the Iroquois the near
relatives and friends approached the body in turn and
addressed it in a laudatory speech.[11]

The dead also demand obedience and are anxious that
the rules they laid down while alive should be followed by
the survivors. Hence the sacredness which is attached to
a will ; [12] hence also, in a large measure, the rigidity of
ancestral custom. The greatest dread of the natives of
South-Eastern Africa " is to offend their ancestors and the
only way to avoid this is to do everything according to

---

[1] Reid, ' Religious Belief of the Ojibois,' in *Jour. Anthr. Inst.* iii. 112.
[2] Polack, *Manners and Customs of
the New Zealanders*, i. 111 *sq.*
[3] Cicero, *De legibus*, ii. 26. See
also Schmidt, *Die Ethik der alten
Griechen*, ii. 105 *sq.*
[4] *Digesta*, xlvii. 12, ' De sepulchro
violato.'
[5] Wilda, *Das Strafrecht der Germanen*, p. 975 *sqq.*
[6] Archilochus, *Reliquiæ*, 40.
[7] Schmidt, *Die Ethik der alten
Griechen*, ii. 122 *sq.*

[8] Rohde, *Psyche*, p. 224.
[9] Diodorus Siculus, i. 92. 5. Erman, *Life in Ancient Egypt*, p. 322.
[10] Cranz, *History of Greenland*, i.
218.
[11] Morgan, *League of the Iroquois*, p.
175, n. 2.
[12] Ellis, *Polynesian Researches*, iii.
116 (Tahitians). Shortland, *Traditions and Superstitions of the New
Zealanders*, p. 257. Sarbah, *Fanti
Customary Laws*, p. 82. Schmidt,
Die Ethik der alten Griechen, ii.
124 *sq.*

traditional usage." [1] Among the Basutos " the anger of the deified generations could not be more directly provoked than by a departure from the precepts and examples they have left behind them." [2] The Ewe-speaking peoples of the Slave Coast have a proverb which runs :—" Follow the customs of your father. What he did not do, avoid doing, or you will harm yourself." [3] Among the Aleuts the old men always impress upon the native youth the great importance of strictly observing the customs of their forefathers in conducting the chase and other matters, as any neglect in this respect would be sure to bring upon them disaster and punishment.[4] The Kamchadales, says Steller, consider it a sin to do anything which is contrary to the precepts of their ancestors.[5] The Papuans of the Motu district, in New Guinea, believe that when men and women are bad—adulterers, thieves, quarrellers, and the like—the spirits of the dead are angry with them.[6] One of the most powerful sentiments in the mind of a Chinese is his reverence for ancestral custom ; and in a large sense Japan also is still a country governed by the voices that are hushed.[7] The life of the ancient Roman was beset with a society of departed kinsmen whose displeasure he provoked if he varied from the practice handed down from his fathers. The expression *mos majorum*, " the custom of the elders," was used by him as a charm against innovation.[8]

Besides such duties to the dead as are similar in nature to those which men owe to their living fellow men or superiors, there are obligations of a different character arising from the fact of death itself. The funeral, the rites connected with it, and the mourning customs are largely regarded as duties to the dead.

[1] Macdonald, *Light in Africa*, p. 192.
[2] Casalis, *Basutos*, p. 254.
[3] Ellis, *Ewe-speaking Peoples of the Slave Coast*, p. 263.
[4] Elliott, *Alaska and the Seal Islands*, p. 170. Veniaminof, quoted by Petroff, *Report on the Population, &c. of Alaska*, p. 156.
[5] Steller, *Beschreibung von Kamt-schatka*, p. 274.
[6] Chalmers, *Pioneering in New Guinea*, p. 169.
[7] Griffis, *Religions of Japan*, p. 308. Hozumi, *Ancestor-Worship and Japanese Law*, p. 1, &c.
[8] Granger, ' Moral Life of the Early Romans,' in *Internat. Jour. of Ethics*, vii. 287. *Idem, Worship of the Romans*, pp. 65, 66, 138.

when a father was about to die, surrounded by members of his family, he might say what animal he would be, for instance a butterfly or some kind of bird, and that creature would be sacred to his family, who would neither injure nor kill it.[1] The Rejangs of Sumatra imagine that tigers in general contain the spirits of departed men, and " no consideration will prevail on a countryman to catch or to wound one, but in self-defence, or immediately after the act of destroying a friend or relation." [2] Among other peoples monkeys, crocodiles, or snakes, being thought men in metempsychosis, are held sacred and must not be hurt.[3] Some Congo Negroes, again, abstain for a whole year after a death from sweeping the house, lest the dust should injure the delicate substance of the ghost.[4] In China, for seven days after a man's death his widow and children avoid the use of knives and needles, and even of chopsticks, eating their food with their fingers, so as not to wound the ghost.[5] And to this day it remains a German peasants' belief that it is wrong to slam a door, lest one should pinch a soul in it.[6]

But the survivors must not only avoid doing anything which might hurt the soul, they must also positively contribute to its comfort and subsistence. They often provide it with a dwelling, either burying the deceased in his own house, or erecting a tent or hut on his grave. Some Australian natives kindle a fire at a few yards' distance from the tomb, and repeat this until the soul is supposed to have gone somewhere else ;[7] others, again, are in the habit of wrapping the body up in a rug, professedly for the purpose of keeping it warm.[8] In the Saxon district of Voigtland people have been known to

[1] Codrington, quoted by Tylor, Remarks on Totemism,' in *Jour. Anthr. Inst.* xxviii. 147.

[2] Marsden, *History of Sumatra*, p. 292. The same belief prevails among the natives of the Malay Peninsula (Newbold, *British Settlements in the Straits of Malacca*, ii. 192).

[3] Meiners, *Geschichte der Religionen*,

i. 212. Tylor, *Primitive Culture*, ii. 8.

[4] Bastian, *Der Mensch in der Geschichte*, ii. 323.

[5] Gray, *China*, i. 288.

[6] Wuttke, *Der deutsche Volksaberglaube der Gegenwart*, § 609, p. 396 sq.

[7] Roth, *North-West-Central Queensland Aborigines*, p. 165.

[8] Fraser, *Aborigines of New South Wales*, p. 79 sq.

put into the coffin an umbrella and a pair of galoshes.[1] An extremely prevalent custom is to place provisions in or upon the grave, and very commonly feasts are given for the dead.[2] Weapons, implements, and other movables are deposited in the tomb ; domestic animals are buried or slaughtered at the funeral ; [3] and, as we have seen before, even human beings are sacrificed to the dead to serve them as companions or attendants, or to vivify their spirits with their blood, or to gratify their craving for revenge.[4]

The offerings made to the dead may be gifts presented to them by the survivors, but the regular funeral sacrifice consists of the deceased person's own individual property. Among savages the whole, or a large part, of it is often consigned to the grave or destroyed.[5] The right of ownership does not cease with death where the belief prevails that the dead stand in need of earthly chattels. The recognition of this right is also apparent in the severe condemnation of robbery or violation committed at a tomb. Among various North American tribes such an act was regarded as an offence of the first magnitude and provoked cruel revenge.[6] Of the Chippewa Indians it is said that however bad a person may be or however much inclined to steal, the things left at a grave, valuable or not, are never touched, being sacred to the spirit of the

[1] Köhler, *Volksbrauch im Voigtlande,* p. 441.

[2] See Tylor, *op. cit.* ch. xi. *sq.* ; Spencer, *Principles of Sociology,* i. 155 *sqq.,* 257 *sqq.* ; Frazer, *Adonis Attis Osiris,* p. 242 *sqq.*

[3] See Spencer, *op. cit.* i. 184 *sqq.*

[4] *Supra,* i. 472 *sqq.*

[5] Boas, ' Central Eskimo,' in *Ann. Rep. Bur. Ethn.* vi. 580. Murdoch, ' Ethn. Results of the Point Barrow Expedition,' *ibid.* ix. 424 *sq.* (Point Barrow Eskimo). Powell, *ibid.* iii. p. lvii. (North American Indians). Yarrow, ' Mortuary Customs of the North American Indians,' *ibid.* i. 98 (Pimas), 100 (Comanches). McGee, ' Siouan Indians,' *ibid.* xv. 178. Roth, *op. cit.* p. 164 (certain Queensland tribes). Colenso, *Maori Races of New Zealand,* p. 57. Kolff, *Voyages of the Dourga,* p. 166 *sq.* (Arru Islanders). Kloss, *In the Andamans and Nicobars,* p. 304 (Kar Nicobarese). Batchelor, *Ainu and their Folk-Lore,* p. 560 *sq.* Georgi, *Russia,* iv. 152 (Burats). Caillié, *Travels through Central Africa,* i. 164 (Bagos). Burrows, *Land of the Pigmies,* p. 107 (Monbuttu). Decle, *Three Years in Savage Africa,* p. 79 (Barotse). Strabo, xi. 4. 8 (Albanians of the Eastern Caucasus). See also Spencer, *Principles of Sociology,* i. 185 *sq.* ; Post, *Entwicklungsgeschichte des Familienrechts,* p. 295 *sq.* ; *Idem, Grundriss der ethnologischen Jurisprudenz,* ii. 173 *sq.* ; *infra,* p. 514 *sq.*

[6] Sagard, *Voyage du Pays des Hurons,* p. 288. Gibbs, ' Tribes of Western Washington and Northwestern Oregon,' in *Contributions to North American Ethnology,* i. 204.

as possible after death is conducive to the happiness of the spirit of the departed ; they say that " the collection and careful disposal of the ashes of the dead gives peace to his spirit." [1] The Thlinkets maintain that those whose bodies are burned will be warm and comfortable in the other world, whereas others will have to suffer from cold. " Burn my body ! Burn me ! " pleaded a dying Thlinket ; " I fear the cold. Why should I go shivering through all the ages and the distances of the next world ? " [2] The ancient Persians, on the other hand, considered both cremation and burial to be sins for which there was no atonement, and exposed their dead on the summits of mountains, thinking it a great misfortune if neither birds nor beasts devoured their carcases.[3] So also the Samoyedes and Mongols held it to be good for the deceased if his corpse was soon devoured by beasts,[4] and the Kamchadales regarded it as a great blessing to be eaten by a beautiful dog.[5] The East African Masai, who likewise, as a rule, expose their dead to the wild beasts, say that if the corpse is eaten by the hyænas the first night, the deceased must have been a good man, as the hyænas are supposed to act by the command of 'Ng ais, or God.[6]

Certain ceremonies are professedly performed for the purpose of preventing evil spirits from doing harm to the dead.[7] This is sometimes the case with cremation ; we are told that among some Siberian peoples the dead are burned so as to be " effectually removed from the machinations of spirits." [8] The Teleutes believe that the

[1] Fawcett, ' Nâyars of Malabar,' in the Madras Government Museum's *Bulletin*, iii. 245, 251.

[2] Dall, *Alaska*, p. 423. Petroff, *op. cit.* p. 175. McNair Wright, *Among the Alaskans*, p. 333.

[3] *Vendîdâd*, i. 13, 17 ; vi. 45 *sqq.* ; viii. 10. Darmesteter, in *Sacred Books of the East*, iv. p. lxxv. *sqq.* Agathias, *Historiæ*, ii. 22 *sq.* (Migne, *Patrologiæ cursus*, Ser. Graeca, lxxxviii. 1377). Herodotus, i. 140 ; iii. 16.

[4] Preuss, *Die Begräbnisarten der*
Amerikaner und Nordostasiaten, p. 272. Cf. Yarrow, in *Ann. Rep. Bur. Ethn.* i. 103 (Caddoes or Timber Indians).

[5] Steller, *op. cit.* p. 273.

[6] Merker, *Die Masai*, p. 193.

[7] See Frazer, ' Certain Burial Customs as illustrative of the Primitive Theory of the Soul,' in *Jour. Anthr. Inst.* xv. 87 *sq.* ; Hertz, ' La représentation collective de la mort,' in *L'année sociologique*, x., 1905–1906, p. 56 *sq.*

[8] Georgi, *op. cit.* iii. 264.

spirits of the earth do much mischief to the departed ; hence their shamans drive them off at the funeral by striking the air several times with an axe.[1] In Christian countries the passing-bell has likewise been supposed to repel evil spirits.[2]

Fasting after a death is regarded as a dutiful tribute to the dead ; the Chinese say that it is " a means of raising the mind up to the soul, a means to enable the sacrificer to perform in a more perfect way the acts of worship incumbent upon him, by bringing about a closer contact between himself and the soul." [3] The self-mutilations performed by the relatives of the dead are supposed to be pleasing to him as tokens of affliction ; [4] and the same is of course the case with the lamentations at funerals. In some Central Australian tribes the custom of painting the body of a mourner is said to have as its object " to render him or her more conspicuous, and so to allow the spirit to see that it is being properly mourned for." [5] The mourning dress is a sign of regard for the dead. Nay, even the custom of not mentioning his name is looked upon in the same light. Some peoples maintain that to name him would be to disturb his rest,[6] or that he would take it as an indication that his relatives are not properly mourning for him, and would feel it as an insult. [7]

As the duties to the living, so the duties to the dead are greatly influenced by the relationship between the parties. Everywhere the obligation to satisfy the wants of the deceased is incumbent upon those who were nearest to him whilst alive. In the archaic State, as we have seen, it is considered the greatest misfortune which can befall a person to die without descendants, since in such a case there would be nobody to attend to his soul.[8] Confucius

---

[1] Georgi, *op. cit.* iii. 264.

[2] Frazer, in *Jour. Anthr. Inst.* xv. 87.

[3] de Groot, *op. cit.* (vol. ii. book) i. 657.

[4] Dorman, *Origin of Primitive Superstitions*, p. 216 *sqq.*

[5] Spencer and Gillen, *Native Tribes of Central Australia*, p. 511.

[6] Nansen, *Eskimo Life*, p. 233 (Greenlanders). Tout, ' Ethnology of the Stlatlumh of British Columbia,' in *Jour. Anthr. Inst.* xxxv. 138. Georgi, *op. cit.* iii. 27 (Samoyedes).

[7] Spencer and Gillen, *Native Tribes of Central Australia*, p. 498.

[8] *Supra*, ii. 400 *sqq.*

said, " For a man to sacrifice to a spirit which does not belong to him is flattery."[1] The distinction between a tribesman or fellow countryman and a stranger also applies to the dead. In Greenland a stranger without relatives or friends was generally suffered to lie unburied.[2] Among North American Indians it is permitted to scalp warriors of a hostile tribe, whereas " there is no example of an Indian having taken the scalp of a man of his own tribe, or of one belonging to a nation in alliance with his own, and whom he may have killed in a quarrel or a fit of anger " ;[3] and an Indian who would never think of desecrating the grave of a tribesman may have " no such scruple in regard to the graves of another tribe."[4] Yet already from early times we hear of the recognition of certain duties even to strangers and enemies. The Greeks of the post-Homeric age made it a rule to deliver up a slain enemy so that he should receive the proper funeral rites.[5] It was considered a disgraceful act of Lysander not to accord burial to Philocles, the Athenian general at Aegospotami, together with about four thousand prisoners whom he put to the sword ;[6] and the Athenians themselves boasted that their ancestors had with their own hands buried the Persians who had fallen in the battle of Marathon, holding it to be " a sacred and imperative duty to cover with earth a human corpse."[7] According to the Chinese penal code, " destroying, mutilating, or throwing into the water the unenclosed and unburied corpse of a stranger," though a much less serious crime than the same injury inflicted upon the corpse of a relative, is yet an offence punishable with 100 blows, and perpetual banishment to the distance of 3,000 *lee*.[8]

The duties to the dead also vary according to the age,

[1] *Lun Yü*, ii. 24. 1.
[2] Cranz, *op. cit.* i. 218.
[3] Domenech, *Seven Years' Residence in the Great Deserts of North America*, ii. 357.
[4] Dodge, *Our Wild Indians*, p. 162.
[5] Schmidt, *Die Ethik der alten Griechen*, ii. 100 *sqq.* Rohde, *op. cit.* p. 200 *sq.*
[6] Pausanias, ix. 32. 9.
[7] *Ibid.* i. 32. 5 ; ix. 32. 9.
[8] *Ta Tsing Leu Lee*, sec. cclxxvi. p. 295.

sex, and social position of the departed. Among the natives of Australia children and women are interred with but scant ceremony.[1] In the tribes of North-West-Central Queensland nobody paints his body in mourning for a young child.[2] In Eastern Central Africa the spirit of a child which dies when about four or five days of age gets nothing of the attention usually bestowed on the dead.[3] Among the Wadshagga married persons are buried in their huts, whilst the bodies of unmarried ones and especially children are put in some hidden place, where they are left to rot or be devoured by beasts.[4] Some Siberian tribes were formerly accustomed to inhume adults only, whereas the corpses of children were exposed on trees.[5] The natives of Port Jackson, in New South Wales, consigned their young people to the grave, but burned those who had passed middle age.[6] The Kondayamkottai Maravars, a Dravidian tribe of Tinnevelly in Southern India, bury the corpses of unmarried persons, whilst those of married ones are cremated.[7] In some other tribes in India burial is practised in the case of young children only,[8] and this has long been a rule of Brahmanism.[9] Among the Andaman Islanders, again, infants are buried within the encampment, whereas all other dead are carried to some distant and secluded spot in the jungle.[10] We meet with a kindred custom in the neighbourhood of Victoria Nyanza in Central Africa : in Karagwe and Nkole " children are buried in the huts themselves, grown-up people outside, generally in cultivated fields, or in such as are going to be cultivated." [11] The bodies of women are sometimes disposed of in a

[1] Curr, *The Australian Race*, i. 89.

[2] Roth, *op. cit.* p. 164.

[3] Macdonald, *Africana*, i. 59.

[4] Volkens, *Der Kilimandscharo*, p. 253.

[5] Georgi, *op. cit.* iii. 31 (Koibales).

[6] Collins, *English Colony of New South Wales*, i. 601.

[7] Fawcett, 'Kondayamkottai Maravars,' in *Jour. Anthr. Inst.* xxiii. 64.

[8] Thurston, in the Madras Government Museum's *Bulletin*, i. 198 (Kotas). Fawcett, 'Nâyars of Malabar,' *ibid.* iii. 245.

[9] Hopkins, *Religions of India*, p. 273.

[10] Man, 'Aboriginal Inhabitants of the Andaman Islands,' in *Jour. Anthr. Inst.* xii. 144.

[11] Kollmann, *Victoria Nyanza*, p. 63 *sq.*

different way from those of men. Thus among the
Blackfeet Indians the latter were fastened in the branches
of trees so high as to be beyond the reach of wolves, and
then left to waste in the dry winds ; whilst the body
of a woman or child was thrown into the underbush
or jungle, where it soon became the prey of the wild
animals.[1] Among the Tuski (Chukchi), who cremate
or rather boil the bodies of good men, women are not
usually burned, on account of the scarcity of wood.[2]

Class distinctions likewise influence the disposal of the
dead. In some American tribes cremation seems to be
reserved for persons of higher rank.[3] Among the pagans
of Obubura Hill district in Southern Nigeria " the bodies
of ordinary people are buried in the bush, sometimes
being merely thrown on the ground, but those of chiefs
and important men and women are buried in their huts or
in the adjoining verandah." [4] The Masai throw away the
corpses of ordinary persons to be eaten by hyænas, whereas
medicine-men and influential people are buried.[5] The
Nandi do not bury their dead unless they have been very
important persons.[6] Among the Waganda, when a chief
dies, he is buried in a wooden coffin, whilst the bodies of
slaves are thrown into the jungle.[7] Some other African
peoples throw the corpses of slaves into a morass or the
nearest pool of water.[8] The Thlinkets committed them
to the tender mercies of the sea.[9] Among the Maoris a
slave would not be greatly bewailed after death, nor have
his bones ceremonially scraped.[10] The Roman ' Law of the
Twelve Tables ' prohibited the bodies of slaves from being
embalmed.[11] Moral distinctions, also, are noticeable in

[1] Yarrow, *Introduction to the Study of Mortuary Customs among the North American Indians*, p. 67.
[2] Dall, *op. cit.* p. 382.
[3] Preuss, *op. cit.* p. 301.
[4] Partridge, *Cross River Natives*, p. 237.
[5] Hollis, *op. cit.* pp. 304, 305, 307 ; Eliot, *ibid.* p. xx.
[6] Johnston, *Uganda*, ii. 880.
[7] Wilson and Felkin, *Uganda*, i. 188.
[8] Denham and Clapperton, *Travels in Northern and Central Africa*, ii. 64 (natives of Kano). Pogge, *Im Reiche des Muata Jamwo*, p. 243 (Kalunda).
[9] Holmberg, ' Ethnographische Skizzen über die Völker des russischen Amerika,' in *Acta Soc. Scient. Fennicæ*, iv. 323. Dall, *op. cit.* pp. 417, 420.
[10] Colenso, *op. cit.* p. 30.
[11] *Lex Duodecim Tabularum*, x. 6.

the treatment of the dead. In some parts of Central
America the bodies of men of high standing who had
committed a crime were, like those of the common people,
exposed to be devoured by wild beasts.[1] Among the
Tuski the corpses of bad men were simply left to rot.[2]
In Greenland the body of a dead malefactor was dis-
membered, and the separate limbs were thrown apart.[3]
To the same class of facts belong the punishments which
were inflicted upon the corpses of criminals in classical
antiquity and formerly in Christian Europe.[4]

From this survey of facts we shall now pass to a consideration of the causes from which the duties to the dead
have sprung. In the first place, there can be no doubt that
these duties to a considerable extent are based upon the
feeling of sympathetic resentment, in the same way as is the
case with duties to living persons. Death does not entirely
extinguish the affection which was felt for a person whilst
he was alive. The rites and customs connected with a
death are very largely similar to or identical with natural
expressions of grief, and in spite of their ceremonial
character it is impossible to believe that they are altogether
counterfeit. We are told by trustworthy eye-witnesses
that, although the self-inflicted pain and the loud lamentations which form part of a funeral among the Australian
blacks are not to be taken as a measure of the grief actually
felt, this expression of despair " is not all artificial or
professional " ;[5] and Mr. Man believes that among the
Andaman Islanders " in the majority of cases the display
of grief is thoroughly sincere." [6] But the dead also
inspire other feelings than sympathy and sorrow, and the
duties towards them have consequently a complex origin.

The souls of the dead are not generally supposed to
lead a merely passive existence. They are conceived as

[1] Preuss, op. cit. p. 301.
[2] Dall, op. cit. p. 382.
[3] Rink, Tales and Traditions of the Eskimo, p. 64.
[4] Ayrault, Des procez faicts au cadaver, p. 5 sqq. Trummer, Vorträge über Tortur, &c. i. 455 sqq. Supra,

ii. 254.
[5] Fraser, Aborigines of New South Wales, p. 44. Spencer and Gillen, Native Tribes of Central Australia, p. 510 sq.
[6] Man, in Jour. Anthr. Inst. xii. 145.

capable of acting upon the living, of conferring upon
them benefits, or at all events of inflicting upon them
harm. Death has in some respects enhanced their powers.
They know what is going on upon earth, what those
whom they have left behind are doing. Their power
of acting, also, is greater than that which they possessed
when they were tied to the flesh. They are raised to a
higher sphere of influence ; magic properties are ascribed
even to their corpses. Their character may remain on
the whole unchanged, and so, too, their affection for their
surviving friends. Hence they often become guardians of
their descendants. Among the Amazulu the head of each
house is worshipped by his children ; remembering his
kindness to them while he was living, they say, " He will
still treat us in the same way now he is dead." [1] The
Herero invoke the blessings of their deceased friends or
relatives, praying for success against their enemies, an
abundance of cattle, numerous wives, and prosperity in
their undertakings.[2] On the West African Slave Coast
the head of a family, after death, often becomes its protector, and is sometimes regarded as the guardian of a
whole community or village.[3] The Mpongwe teach the
child " to look up to the parent not only as its earthly
protector, but as a friend in the spirit-land." [4] The
Gournditch-mara in Australia believed that " the spirit
of the deceased father or grandfather occasionally visited
the male descendant in dreams, and imparted to him
charms (songs) against disease or against witchcraft." [5]
The Veddah of Ceylon invokes the spirits of his departed
relatives " as sympathetic and kindred, though higher
powers than man, to direct him to a life pleasing to the
gods, through which he may gain their protection or
favour." [6] The Nayadis of Malabar, on certain ceremonial
occasions, offer solemn prayers that the souls of the

[1] Callaway, *Religious System of the
Amazulu*, p. 144 *sq.*
[2] Andersson, *Lake Ngami*, p. 222.
[3] Ellis, *Ewe-speaking Peoples*, p.
104. See also *ibid.* p. 24 (Slave and
Gold Coast natives).

[4] Wilson, *Western Africa*, p. 394.
[5] Fison and Howitt, *Kamilaroi and
Kurnai*, p. 278.
[6] Nevill, ' Vaeddas of Ceylon,' in
Taprobanian, i. 194.

departed may protect them from the ravages of wild beasts and snakes.[1] The Vedic people called upon the aid of their dead :—" O Fathers, may the sky-people grant us life ; may we follow the course of the living." [2] So also the Zoroastrian Fravashis, who corresponded to the Vedic " Fathers," helped their own kindred, borough, town, or country.[3] Aeschylus, in his ' Eumenides,' represents Orestes as saying, " My father will send me aid from the tomb." [4] The Lar Familiaris, the spirit guardian of the Roman family, was undoubtedly the spirit of a deceased ancestor.[5] The old Slavonians believed that the souls of fathers watched over their children and their children's children. In Galicia the people still think that their hearths are haunted by the souls of the dead, who make themselves useful to the family ; and among the Czechs it is a common belief that departed ancestors look after the fields and herds of their descendants and assist them in hunting and fishing.[6]

But the ancestral guardian spirit does not bestow his favours for nothing. He must be properly attended to,[7] and if neglected he easily becomes positively dangerous to his living relatives. The same Africans who invoke the dead in adversity think them " capable of wreaking their vengeance on those who do not liberally minister to their wants and enjoyments." [8] The Chaldeans believed that

---

[1] Iyer, ' Nayādis of Malabar,' in the Madras Government Museum's *Bulletin*, iv. 72.

[2] *Rig-Veda*, x. 57. 5. *Cf.* Hopkins, *op. cit.* p. 143 *sq.*

[3] *Yasts*, xiii. 66 *sqq.* ; &c.

[4] Aeschylus, *Eumenides*, 598.

[5] Jevons, in Plutarch's *Romane Questions*, p. xli. Rohde, *op. cit.* p. 232.

[6] Ralston, *Songs of the Russian People*, pp. 119, 121. For other instances of a similar kind see Shooter, *Kafirs of Natal*, p. 161 ; Arbousset and Daumas, *Tour to the North-East of the Colony of the Cape of Good Hope*, p. 340 (Bechuanas) ; Casalis, *Basutos*, p. 248 ; Wilken, *Het animisme bij de volken van den*

Indischen Archipel, p. 194 *sqq.* ; Nansen, *Eskimo Life*, p. 290 (Greenlanders) ; Jessen, *Afhandling over de Norske Finners og Lappers Hedenske Religion*, p. 27 ; Friis, *Lappisk Mythologi*, p. 115 *sq.* ; von Düben, *Lappland*, p. 249 ; Abercromby, *Pre- and Proto-historic Finns*, i. 178 (Mordvins) ; von Wlislocki, *Volksglaube der Zigeuner*, p. 43 *sqq.* (Gypsies).

[7] Wilken, *op. cit.* p. 194 *sq.* (peoples in the Malay Archipelago). Abercromby, *op. cit.* i. 178 (Mordvins). Jessen, *op. cit.* p. 27 ; Friis, *op. cit.* p. 116 *sq.* (Laplanders).

[8] Rowley, *Religion of the Africans*, p. 90.

the departed who otherwise carefully watched over the welfare of his children, if abandoned and forgotten, avenged himself for their neglect by returning to torment them in their homes, by letting sickness attack them, and by ruining them with his imprecaticns.[1] The Vedic poet prays to the Fathers, " May ye not injure us for whatever impiety we have as men committed." [2] The Fravashis come to the help of those only who treat them well, and are " dreadful unto those who vex them." [3] In Rome, according to Ovid, once upon a time when the great festival of the dead was not observed, and the manes failed to receive the customary gifts, the injured spirits revenged themselves on the living, and the city " became heated by the suburban funeral pyres." [4] So also, according to Slavonic beliefs, the dead " might be induced, if proper respect was not paid to them, to revenge themselves on their forgetful survivors." [5]

Moreover, we must not conclude that wherever the spirits of deceased ancestors are invoked as guardians they are necessarily looked upon as essentially benevolent to their descendants.[6] Concerning the ancient Babylonians and Assyrians Professor Jastrow writes :—" In general the dead were not favorably disposed towards the living, and they were inclined to use what power they had to work evil rather than for good. In this respect they resembled the demons, and it is noticeable that an important class of demons was known by the name *ekimmu*, which is one of the common terms for the shades of the dead."[7] The Greeks were much afraid of their dead, and regarded their " heroes " as extremely irritable, in later times as exclusively malicious.[8] It appears from Ovid's ' Fasti ' that fear was the predominant feeling of the Romans with reference to the spirits of the departed, who were sup-

---

[1] Halévy, *op. cit.* p. 368.
[2] *Rig-Veda*, x. 15. 6.
[3] *Yasts*, xiii. 31, 42, 51, 70, &c.
[4] Ovid, *Fasti*, ii. 549 *sqq.*
[5] Ralston, *op. cit.* p. 335.

[6] *Cf.* Karsten, *Origin of Worship*, p. 122 *sqq.*
[7] Jastrow, *op. cit.* p. 581.
[8] Rohde, *op. cit.* pp. 177 *sqq.*, 225 n. 4. Schmidt, *Die Ethik der alten Griechen*, ii. 130.

posed to wander about by night, causing men to pine away or bewitching them into madness.[1] Even in China, where the souls of the dead are supposed effectually to control the destiny of the living,[2] malevolent rather than benevolent inclinations are ascribed to them by the popular belief, as appears from the fact that the words for " ghost " and " devil " are the same and form a portion of the objectionable epithets applied to foreigners.[3] Generally speaking, my collection of facts has led me to the conclusion that the dead are more commonly regarded as enemies than friends,[4] and that Professor Jevons[5] and Mr. Grant Allen[6] are mistaken in their assertion that, according to early beliefs, the malevolence of the dead is for the most part directed against strangers only, whereas they exercise a fatherly care over the lives and fortunes of their descendants and fellow clansmen.

Thus the Bondeis in East Africa apparently make little difference between a devil and a departed ancestor.[7] Among the Fjort of Loango the good people who have left this life "are generally considered the enemies of mankind."[8] Other Africans maintain that the spirits of the dead hover in the air, "watching the destiny of friends, haunting houses, killing children, injuring cattle, and causing disease and destruction," all being malevolent to the living.[9] Of the Savage Islanders in Polynesia we are told that " no effort of the missionary can avail to break them of their belief in the malevolence of ghosts, even of those who loved them best in life ; the spirits of the dead seem compelled to work ill to the living without their own volition."[10] In Tahiti the spirits of parents and children, sisters and brothers, " seemed to have been regarded as a sort of

[1] Ovid, *Fasti*, v. 429 *sqq.* Granger, *Worship of the Romans*, p. 67.
[2] de Groot, *op. cit.* (vol. v. book) ii. 464.
[3] Dennys, *Folk-Lore of China*, p. 73. See also Legge, *Religions of China*, pp. 13, 201.
[4] Dr. Steinmetz (*Ethnol. Studien zur ersten Entwicklung der Strafe*, i. 283) has arrived at the same conclusion. See also Meiners, *Geschichte der Religionen*, i. 301 *sqq.* ; Karsten, *op. cit.* p. 115 *sqq.*

[5] Jevons, *Introduction to the History of Religion*, p. 53 *sq.*
[6] Grant Allen, *Evolution of the Idea of God*, p. 347 *sq.*
[7] Dale, 'Natives inhabiting the Bondei Country,' in *Jour. Anthr. Inst.* xxv. 233.
[8] Dennett, *Folklore of the Fjort*, p. 11 *sq.*
[9] Burton, *Lake Regions of Central Africa*, ii. 344.
[10] Thomson, *Savage Island*, p. 94.

demons." [1]   Among the Maoris "the nearest and most beloved relatives were supposed to have their natures changed by death, and to become malignant, even towards those they formerly loved." [2]   The natives of Erromanga, in the New Hebrides, maintained that all the spirits of their departed ancestors were evil, and roamed the earth doing harm to men.[3]   In the tribes inhabiting the mouth of the Wanigela River, in New Guinea, all dead ancestors are supposed to be constantly on the watch to deal out sickness or death to anyone who may displease them ; hence the natives are most particular to do nothing that should raise their anger.[4]   Australian natives believe that a deceased person is malevolent for a long time after death, and the more nearly related the more he is feared.[5]   The *anitos*, or ghosts, of the Tagales in the Philippine Islands are likewise perpetually anxious to do harm to their descendants, trying to kill people, especially shortly after death, and being the causes of nearly all diseases.[6]   The Saora of the Madras Presidency only know the existence of the departed souls by the mischief they do, and think that all ills are occasioned either by ancestral spirits or gods.[7]   In the North-Western Provinces of India the *dîwârs*, or *genii loci*, are oftentimes "the spirits of good men, Brahmans, or village heroes, who manage, when they become objects of worship, to be generally considered very malicious devils " ; [8] and the ghosts of all low caste natives are notoriously malignant.[9]   The Tibetans are of opinion that a ghost is always malicious, and that it returns and gives troubles either on account of its malevolence or its desire to see how its former property is being disposed of.[10]   The Finns and other peoples of the same stock believed that the souls of the dead were generally intent to do harm to the living, their nearest relatives included.[11]   Thus, according to Votyak ideas, even a mother may become

[1] Ellis, *Polynesian Researches*, i. 334 *sq.*

[2] Taylor, *Te Ika a Maui*, p. 18. See also *ibid.* pp. 137, 221 ; Polack, *op. cit.* i. 242.

[3] Robertson, *Erromanga*, p. 389.

[4] Guise, ' Tribes inhabiting the Mouth of the Wanigela River,' in *Jour. Anthr. Inst.* xxviii. 216.

[5] Fraser, *Aborigines of New South Wales*, p. 80. Curr, *The Australian Race*, i. 87.

[6] Blumentritt, in *Mittheil. d. kais. u. kön. Geograph. Gesellsch. in Wien*, p. 166 *sqq.* de Mas, *Informe sobre el estado de las Islas Filipinas en* 1842,

' Orijen de los habitantes de la Oceania,' p. 15 ; ' Poblacion,' p. 29. *Cf. ibid.* ' Poblacion,' p. 17 ; Blumentritt, p. 168 (Igorrotes).

[7] Fawcett, *Saoras*, pp. 43, 51.

[8] Elliot, *Races of the North Western Provinces of India*, p. 243.

[9] Crooke, *Popular Religion of Northern India*, i. 269.

[10] Waddell, *Buddhism of Tibet*, p. 498.

[11] Castrén, *Nordiska resor och forskningar*, iii. 121 *sqq.* Waronen, *Vainajainpalvelus muinaisilla Suomalaisilla*, p. 23.

the enemy of her own child from the moment of her death.[1] Among the Ainu of Japan, " if a man is at a loss for the authorship of any particular calamity, which has befallen him, he is very apt to refer it to the ghost of a dead wife, mother, grandmother, or, still more certainly, to that of a dead mother-in-law " ; [2] an Ainu who accompanied Mr. Batchelor would on no account come within twenty-five or thirty yards of the spot where his own mother was burned.[3]   The Koniagas believe that after death every man becomes a devil.[4]   According to ideas prevalent among the Central Eskimo, the dead are at first malevolent spirits who frequently roam around the villages, causing sickness and mischief and killing men by their touch ; but subsequently they are supposed to attain to rest and are no longer feared.[5]   The Tarahumares of Mexico are afraid of their dead ; a mother asks her deceased infant to go away and not to come back, and the weeping widow implores her husband not to carry off, or do harm to, his own sons or daughters.[6]   Mr. Bridges informs us that the Fuegian word for a ghost, cúshpich, is also an adjective signifying " frightful, dreadful, awful." [7]

The belief in the irritable or malevolent character of the dead is easily explained. As Bishop Butler observed, we presume that a thing will remain as it is except when we have some reason to think that it will be altered.[8] And in the case of the souls of departed friends men may have reason to suppose that they undergo a change. Death is commonly regarded as the gravest of all misfortunes ; hence the dead are believed to be exceedingly dissatisfied with their fate. According to primitive ideas a person only dies if he is killed—by magic if not by force,—and such a death naturally tends to make the soul revengeful and ill-tempered. It is envious of the living and is longing for the company of its old friends ; no wonder, then, that it sends them diseases to cause their

---

[1] Buch, ' Die Wotjäken,' in *Acta Soc. Scient. Fennicæ*, xii. 607.

[2] Howard, *Life with Trans-Siberian Savages*, p. 196.

[3] Batchelor, *Ainu of Japan*, p. 220 sq.

[4] Holmberg, in *Acta Soc. Scient. Fennicæ*, iv. 402.

[5] Boas, in *Ann. Rep. Bur. Ethn.*

vi. 591.

[6] Lumholtz, *Unknown Mexico*, i. 380, 382.

[7] Bridges, ' Manners and Customs of the Firelanders,' in *A Voice for South America*, xiii. 211.

[8] Butler, *Analogy of Religion*, i. 1, p. 82.

death. The Basutos maintain that their dead ancestors are continually endeavouring to draw them to themselves, and therefore attribute to them every disease ;[1] and the Tarahumares in Mexico suppose that the dead make their relatives ill from a feeling of loneliness, that they, too, may die and join the departed.[2] But the notion that the disembodied soul is on the whole a malicious being constantly watching for an opportunity to do harm to the living is also, no doubt, intimately connected with the instinctive fear of the dead, which is in its turn the outcome of the fear of death.

We are told, it is true, that many savages meet death with much indifference, or regard it as no great evil, but merely as a change to a life very similar to this.[3] But it is a fact often noticed among ourselves, that a person on the verge of death may resign himself to his fate with the greatest calmness, although he has been afraid to die throughout his life. Moreover, the fear of death may be disguised by thoughtlessness, checked by excitement, or mitigated by dying in company. There are peoples who are conspicuous for their bravery, and yet have a great dread of death.[4] Nobody is entirely free from this feeling, though it varies greatly in strength among different races and in different individuals. In many savages it is so strongly developed, that they cannot bear to hear death mentioned.[5] And inseparably mingled with

[1] Casalis, op. cit. p. 249.
[2] Lumholtz, Unknown Mexico, i. 380.
[3] Turner, ' Ethnology of the Ungava District,' in Ann. Rep. Bur. Ethn. xi. 192 (Hudson Bay Eskimo), 269 sq. (Hudson Bay Indians). de Brebeuf, ' Relation de ce qui s'est passé dans le pays des Hurons,' in Relations des Jésuites, i. 1636, p. 129. Roth, North-West-Central Queensland Aborigines, p. 161. Tregear, ' Niue,' in Jour. Polynesian Soc. ii. 14 (Savage Islanders). Williams and Calvert, Fiji, p. 204 sq. Romilly, From my Verandah in New Guinea, p. 45 (Solomon Islanders). Georgi, op. cit. iii. 266 (Siberian shamans).

Monrad, op. cit. p. 23 (Negroes of Accra). Brinton, Religions of Primitive Peoples, p. 72.
[4] E.g., the Kalmucks (Bergmann, Nomadische Streifereien unter den Kalmüken, ii. 318 sqq.) and the ancient Caribs (Müller, Geschichte der Amerikanischen Urreligionen, p. 215).
[5] Dunbar, ' Pawnee Indians,' in Magazine of American History, viii. 742. Batchelor, Ainu of Japan, p. 203. Bergmann, op. cit. ii. 318. Bosman, Description of the Coast of Guinea, p. 327 (Negroes of Fida). Du Chaillu, Explorations in Equatorial Africa, p. 338. Kropf, Das Volk der Xosa-Kaffern, p. 155. For other instances of savages' great fear of

this fear of death is the fear of the dead. The place in which a death occurs is abandoned,[1] or the hut is destroyed,[2] or the corpse is carried out from it as speedily as possible.[3] The survivors endeavour to frighten away the ghost by firing off guns,[4] or shooting into the grave,[5] or throwing sticks and stones behind themselves after they have interred the corpse.[6] To prevent the return of the ghost the body is buried face downwards,[7] or its limbs are firmly tied,[8] or, in extreme cases, it is fixed in the ground with a stake driven through it.[9] We may assume that these and many other funeral ceremonies are very closely connected with the fear of the pollution of death ; for even when their immediate object is to keep the ghost at

death, see Bridges, in *A Voice for South America*, xiii. 211 (Fuegians) ; Müller, *Geschichte der Amerikanischen Urreligionen*, p. 215 (Caribs) ; Dunbar, in *Magazine of American History*, v. 334 (various North American tribes) ; Brinton, *Myths of the New World*, p. 238 ; Georgi, *op. cit.* ii. 400 (Jakuts) ; Bosman, *op. cit.* p. 130 (Gold Coast natives).

[1] Dorman, *op. cit.* p. 22 (North American Indians). von den Steinen, *Unter den Naturvölkern Zentral-Brasiliens*, p. 502 (Bororó). Hyades and Deniker, *Mission scientifique du Cap Horn*, vii. 379 (Fuegians). Curr, *The Australian Race*, i. 44. Fraser, *Aborigines of New South Wales*, p. 82. Spencer and Gillen, *Native Tribes of Central Australia*, p. 498. Worcester, *Philippine Islands*, p. 496 (Tagbanuas of Busuanga). Bailey, 'Veddahs of Ceylon,' in *Trans. Ethn. Soc.* N. S. ii. 296 ; Deschamps, *Carnet d'un voyageur*, p. 383 (Veddahs). Decle, *op. cit.* p. 79 (Barotse). von Düben, *Lappland*, pp. 241, 249.

[2] Hyades and Deniker, *op. cit.* vii. 379 (Fuegians). Batchelor, *Ainu of Japan*, p. 222 *sq.* Worcester, *op. cit.* p. 108 *sq.* (Tagbanuas of Palawan). Butler, *Travels in Assam*, p. 228. Fawcett, *Saoras*, p. 50 *sq.* Cunningham, *Uganda*, p. 130 (Bavuma).

[3] Howard, *op. cit.* p. 197 (Ainu). Selenka, *Sonnige Welten*, p. 89 (Dyaks). The rapid pace of the

funeral procession among the Bataks (von Brenner, *Besuch bei den Kannibalen Sumatras*, p. 235) probably belongs to the same class of facts.

[4] von Brenner, *op. cit.* p. 235 (Bataks). Fawcett, *Saoras*, p. 46 *sq.*

[5] von Brenner, *op. cit.* p. 235 (Bataks). von Wlislocki, *Volksglaube der Magyaren*, p. 134.

[6] Crooke, *Tribes and Castes of the North-Western Provinces*, i. 45 (Aheriya, in Duâb), 287 (Bhangi, the sweeper tribe of Hindustan). Ralston, *op. cit.* p. 320 (ancient Bohemians).

[7] Dorsey, in *Ann. Rep. Bur. Ethn.* xi. 420 (Omahas). Crooke, *op. cit.* i. 44 (Aheriya, in Duâb).

[8] Zimmer, *Altindisches Leben*, p. 402 (Vedic people). Turner, in *Ann. Rep. Bur. Ethn.* xi. 191 (Hudson Bay Eskimo). Yarrow, *ibid.* i. 98 (Pimas of Arizona). Southey, *History of Brazil*, i. 248 (Tupinambas). Of the trussing and tying of the dead body which is practised in various Australian tribes the blacks themselves say that it is done " to prevent the spirit of the deceased from wandering in the night from its bed, and disturbing the living and doing them harm " (Fraser, *Aborigines of New South Wales*, p. 79 *sq.* ; see also Curr, *The Australian Race*, i. 44, 87).

[9] *Supra*, ii. 256. Hyltén-Cavallius, *Wärend och Wirdarne*, i. 472 (Middle Ages).

a distance, it is likely that they are largely due to dread of its presence for the reason that it is conceived as a seat of deadly contagion.[1] It seems to me that certain anthropologists, in their explanations of funeral ceremonies, have too much accentuated the volitional activity of ghosts. To take an instance. The common custom of carrying the dead body away through some aperture other than the door,[2] has generally been interpreted as a means of preventing the ghost from finding its way back to the old home ; but various facts indicate that it also may have sprung from a desire to keep the ordinary exit free from pollution. According to the Vendîdâd a spirit of death is breathing all along the way which a corpse has passed ; hence no man, no flock, no being whatever that belongs to the world of Ahura Mazda is allowed to go that way until the deadly breath has been blown away to hell.[3] In the capital of Corea there is a small gate in the city-wall known as the " Gate of the Dead," through which alone a dead body can be carried out, and no one is ever allowed to enter through that passage-way.[4] In China even a messenger who delivers tidings of death strictly abstains from passing the threshold of the houses at which he knocks, unless urgently requested by the inmates to walk in.[5] Among the Kwakiutl Indians of British Columbia a mourner, who is regarded as unclean, " must not use the house door, but a separate door is cut for his use " ; girls at puberty, whilst in a state of uncleanness, may leave

---

[1] *Cf. supra*, ii. 303. For the contagion of death see also Crawley, *The Mystic Rose*, p. 95 *sqq.*

[2] Tylor, *Primitive Culture*, ii. 26 *sq.* Frazer, in *Jour. Anthr. Inst.* xv. 69 *sq.* Trumbull, *Threshold Covenant*, p. 23 *sqq.* Liebrecht, *Zur Volkskunde*, pp. 372, 373, 414 *sq.* Lippert, *Christenthum, Volksglaube und Volksbrauch*, p. 391 *sq.* Egede, *Description of Greenland*, p. 152 *sq.* ; Nansen, *Eskimo Life*, p. 245 *sq.* (Greenlanders). Turner, in *Ann. Rep. Bur. Ethn.* xi. 191 (Hudson Bay Eskimo). McNair Wright, *Among the Alaskans*, p. 313. Jochel-son, ' Koryak Religion,' in *Jesup North Pacific Expedition*, vi. 110 *sq.* Georgi, *op. cit.* iii. 26 *sq.* ; Jackson, in *Jour. Anthr. Inst.* xxiv. 406 (Samoyedes). Ramseyer and Kühne, *Four Years in Ashantee*, p. 50. Kålund, ' Skandinavische Verhältnisse,' in Paul, *Grundriss der germanischen Philologie*, ii. pt. ii. 227 (ancient Scandinavians).

[3] *Vendîdâd*, viii. 14 *sqq.* Darmesteter, in *Sacred Books of the East*, iv. p. lxxiv. *sq.*

[4] Trumbull, *op. cit.* p. 24.

[5] de Groot, *op. cit.* (vol. ii. book) i. 644.

and enter their room only through a hole made in the floor ;[1] and men who have polluted themselves by partaking of human flesh are for four months allowed to go out only by the secret door in the rear of the house.[2] Even the water and fire ceremonies performed in connection with a death have been represented as methods of preventing the ghost from attacking the living by placing a physical barrier of water or fire between them.[3] But I see no reason whatever to assume, with Sir J. G. Frazer, that " the conceptions of pollution and purification are merely the fictions of a later age, invented to explain the purpose of a ceremony of which the original intention was forgotten." [4]

It is obvious that the beliefs held as regards the character, activity, and polluting influence of the dead greatly affect the conduct of the survivors. They are

[1] Boas, in *Fifth Report on the North-Western Tribes of Canada*, p. 42 *sqq.*

[2] *Idem*, quoted by Frazer, *Golden Bough*, i. 341 *sq.* Among the Bhuiyâr, a Dravidian tribe in South Mirzapur, each house has two doors, one of which is only used by menstruous women ; and when such a woman has to quit the house " she is obliged to creep out on her hands and knees so as to avoid polluting the house thatch by her touch " (Crooke, *Tribes and Castes of the North-Western Provinces*, ii. 87). Among the Thompson River Indians of British Columbia meat was only taken into the hunting lodge through a hole in the back of the structure, because the common door was used by women and women were regarded as unclean (Teit, ' Thompson Indians,' in *Memoirs of the American Museum of Natural History*, ' Anthropology,' i. 347). In other instances ordinary people are prohibited from using a door through which a sacred person has passed, obviously because contact with his sanctity is looked upon as dangerous. In some of the South Sea Islands, where the first-born, whether male or female, was especially sacred, no one else was allowed to pass by the door through

which he or she entered the paternal dwelling (Gill, *Life in the Southern Isles*, p. 46). " In some parts of the Pacific, the door through which the king or queen passed in opening a temple was shut up, and ever after made sacred " (Turner, *Nineteen Years in Polynesia*, p. 328). Ezekiel (xliv. 2 *sq.*) represents the Lord as saying :—" This gate shall be shut, it shall not be opened, and no man shall enter in by it ; because the Lord, the God of Israel, hath entered in by it, therefore it shall be shut. It is for the prince ; . . . he shall enter by the way of the porch of that gate, and shall go out by the way of the same." Among the Arabs in olden days those who returned from a pilgrimage to Mecca entered their houses not by the door but by a hole made in the back wall (Palmer, in *Sacred Books of the East*, vi. 27, n. 1). This practice was forbidden by Muhammed (*Koran*, ii. 185).

[3] Frazer, in *Jour. Anthr. Inst.* xv. 76 *sqq.*

[4] It should be added, however, that Sir J. G. Frazer's important essay on ' Burial Customs ' was published many years ago and therefore perhaps does not exactly represent the author's present views on the subject.

naturally anxious to gain the favour of the disembodied soul, to avert its ill-will, to keep it at a distance, and to avoid the defilement of death. Self-interest is often a conspicuous motive for acts and omissions which are regarded as duties to the dead, and prudence also has a very large share in their being enjoined as obligatory. This is obviously true of the offerings made to the dead. The Thompson River Indians of British Columbia threw some food on the ground near the grave of the deceased, " that he might not visit the house in search of food, causing sickness to the people." [1] Among the Iroquois, " on the death of a nursing child two pieces of cloth are saturated with the mother's milk and placed in the hands of the dead child so that its spirit may not return to haunt the bereaved mother." [2] The Negroes of Accra, when asked why they slaughtered animals at the tombs of their departed friends, answered that they did so in order to prevent the ghosts from walking.[3] The Monbuttu place some oil and other victuals in the little hut which is erected for the dead in the forest, so that his spirit shall not return to his old home in search of food.[4] For the same reason the Bataks of Sumatra put various things into the graves of their deceased friends, ask the dead to be quiet and not to long for the company of the living, and finish their address with the words, " Here you have still some *sirih* and tobacco, and every year, at harvest time, we shall give you some rice."[5] Among the Chuvashes the son says to his departed father, " We remember you with a feast, here are bread and different kinds of food for you, everything you have before you, do not come to us."[6] It is considered particularly dangerous to keep back and make use of articles which belonged to the dead. The Gypsies burn on the grave all those chattels which the deceased was in the habit of using during his lifetime, " because his soul would other-

[1] Teit, *loc. cit.* p. 329.
[2] Smith, ' Myths of the Iroquois, in *Ann. Rep. Bur. Ethn.* ii. 69.
[3] Monrad, *op. cit.* p. 26.
[4] Burrows, *op. cit.* p. 103.
[5] von Brenner, *op. cit.* p. 234 *sqq.*
[6] Castrén, *op. cit.* iii. 123 *sq.*

wise return to torment his relatives and claim back his property." [1] A Saora gave the following reason for the custom of burning all the belongings of a dead person :— " If we do not burn these things with the body, the Kulba (soul) will come and ask us for them and trouble us." [2] The Kafirs believe that, after his death, " a man's personality haunts his possessions." [3] Among the Brazilian Tupinambas " whoever happened to have any thing which had belonged to the dead produced it, that it might be buried with him, lest he should come and claim it." [4] When a Navaho Indian dies within a house the rafters are pulled down over the remains and the place is usually set on fire ; after that nothing would induce a Navaho to touch a piece of the wood or even approach the immediate vicinity of the place, the shades of the dead being regarded " as inclined to resent any intrusion or the taking of any liberties with them or their belongings." [5] The Greenlanders, as soon as a man is dead, " throw out every thing which has belonged to him ; otherwise they would be polluted, and their lives rendered unfortunate. The house is cleared of all its movables till evening, when the smell of the corpse has passed away." [6]

The fear of the dead has also taught men to abstain from robbing or violating their tombs. The Omahas believe that, if anybody touched an article of food exposed at a grave, " the ghost would snatch away the food and paralyse the mouth of the thief, and twist his face out of shape for the rest of his life ; or else he would be pursued by the ghost, and food would lose its taste, and hunger ever after haunt the offender." [7] The Brazilian Coroados " avoid disturbing the repository of the dead, for fear they should appear to them and torment them." [8]

[1] von Wlislocki, *Volksglaube der Zigeuner*, p. 100.
[2] Fawcett, *op. cit.* p. 47.
[3] Kidd, *The Essential Kafir*, p. 83.
[4] Southey, *op. cit.* i. 248. *Cf.* von den Steinen, *Unter den Naturvölkern Zentral-Brasiliens*, p. 502 (Bororó).
[5] Mindeleff, ' Navaho Houses,' in *Ann. Rep. Bur. Ethn.* xvii. 487.

[6] Cranz, *op. cit.* i. 217.
[7] La Flesche, ' Death and Funeral Customs among the Omahas,' in *Jour. American Folk-Lore*, ii. 11. *Cf.* Reid, in *Jour. Anthr. Inst.* iii. 112 (Chippewas).
[8] von Spix and von Martius, *Travels in Brazil*, ii. 251.

The Maoris suppose that the violation of a burial place would bring disease and death on the criminal.[1] The extreme dislike of the Chinese to disturbing a grave is based on the supposition that the spirit of the person buried will haunt and cause ill-luck or death to the disturber.[2] According to the popular beliefs of the Magyars, he who seizes upon anything belonging to a tomb, even if it were only a flower, will be unhappy for the rest of his life.[3] The Rumanians of Transylvania think that a person who picks a flower which grows on a grave will die in consequence, and that he who smells at such a flower will lose his sense of smell.[4]

The transgression of ancestral custom, as we have already seen, is supposed to be punished by the spirits of the dead ; and the sacredness of a will largely springs from superstitious fear. The South Slavonian belief that, if a son does not fulfil the last will of his father the soul of the father will curse him from the grave,[5] has its counterpart in the denunciatory clause in Anglo-Saxon landbooks, which usually curses all and singular who attack the donee's title.[6]

The custom of praising the dead, again, is mainly flattery, and the lamentations over them are not altogether sincere.[7] By their excessive demonstrations of grief the Andaman Islanders hope to conciliate the spirits of the departed, and to be preserved from many misfortunes which might otherwise befall them.[8] The Central Australian native fears " that, unless a sufficient amount of grief be displayed, he will be harmed by the offended *Ulthana* or spirit of the dead man." [9] The Angmagsa-

---

[1] Polack, *op. cit.* i. 112.
[2] Dennys, *op. cit.* p. 26. de Groot, *op. cit.* (vol. iv. book) ii. 446 *sq.*
[3] von Wlislocki, *Volksglaube der Magyaren*, p. 135. *Cf. Idem, Volksglaube der Zigeuner*, p. 96 *sq.*
[4] Prexl, ' Geburts- und Todtengebräuche der Rumänen in Siebenbürgen,' in *Globus*, lvii. 30.
[5] *Supra*, i. 624.
[6] Pollock and Maitland, *History of*

English Law before the Time of Edward I. ii. 251 *sq.*
[7] See Gibbs, *loc. cit.* p. 205 (tribes of Western Washington and Northwestern Oregon) ; Wied-Neuwied, *Reise nach Brasilien*, ii. 56 (Botocudos).
[8] Man, in *Jour. Anthr. Inst.* xii. 145.
[9] Spencer and Gillen, *Native Tribes of Central Australia*, p. 510.

liks on the East Coast of Greenland say that they cry and groan and perform other mourning rites " in order to prevent the dead from getting angry." [1]   But the loud wailing of mourners may also, like the shouting after a death,[2] be intended to drive away the ghost, or perhaps death itself.

Fear is certainly a very common motive for funeral and mourning rites which have been interpreted as duties to the dead.   This is the case with the various methods of disposing of the corpse.   Thus the custom of leaving it as food for beasts of prey [3] is, in some instances at least, deliberately practised for the purpose of preventing the ghost from walking.   The Herero who accompanied Chapman said of two of their sick comrades who formed part of the company, " You must throw them away, and let the wolves eat them ; then they won't come and bother us." [4]   Cremation, also, has frequently been resorted to as a means of protecting the living from unwelcome visits of the dead, or, as the case may be, of effectually getting rid of the contagion of death.[5]   The Vedic people, while burning the corpses of their dead, cried aloud, " Away, go away, O Death ! injure not our sons and our men." [6]   In Northern India the corpses of all low caste people are either cremated or buried face downwards, in order to prevent the evil spirit from escaping and troubling its neighbours.[7]   The Nâyars of Malabar not only believe that the collection and careful disposal of the ashes of the dead man gives peace to his spirit, but, " what is more import- ant, the pacified spirit will not thereafter injure the living members of the Taravâd (house or family), cause mis-

[1] Holm, ' Ethnologisk Skizze af Angmagsalikerne,' in *Meddelelser om Grønland*, x. 107.

[2] Spencer and Gillen, *op. cit.* p. 506. *Cf.* Robertson Smith, *Religion of the Semites*, p. 432, n. 2.

[3] For this custom see also Murdoch, in *Ann. Rep. Bur. Ethn.* ix. 424 *sq.* (Point Barrow Eskimo) ; Norden- skiöld, *Vegas färd kring Asien och Europa*, ii. 93 (Chukchi) ; Anders-

son, *Notes on Travel in South Africa*, p. 234 (Ovambo).

[4] Chapman, *Travels in the Interior of South Africa*, ii. 282.

[5] *Cf.* Rohde, *op. cit.* p. 28 *sqq.* (ancient Greeks) ; Preuss, *op. cit.* p. 294.

[6] *Rig-Veda*, x. 18. 1.

[7] Crooke, *Popular Religion of Northern India*, i. 269.

carriage to the women, possess the men, as with an evil spirit, and so on."[1] In Tibet a ghost which makes its presence felt in dreams or by causing deliriousness or temporary insanity is disposed of by cremation.[2] In his description of the Savage Islanders, Mr. Thomson tells us of a mother who destroyed her own daughter's grave by fire in order to burn the spirit which was afflicting her.[3] Among the ancient Scandinavians the bodies of persons who were believed to walk after death were dug up from their graves and burned.[4] And exactly the same is done in Albania to this day.[5]

Burial itself has served a similar purpose.[6] According to the Danish traveller Monrad, the Negroes of Accra expressly believe that by covering the body of a dead person with earth they keep the ghost from walking and causing trouble to the survivors ; and he adds that exactly the same superstition prevails in Jutland in Denmark.[7] This belief is also preserved in the Swedish word for committing a corpse to the earth, *jordfästa*, which literally means " to fasten to the earth." In Gothland, in Sweden, there was an old tradition of a man called Takstein who in his lifetime was overbearing and cruel and after his death haunted the living, in consequence of which " a wizard finally earth-fastened him in such a manner that he afterwards lay quiet."[8] But burial has often been supplemented by other precautions against the return of the ghost. Högström says that the Laplanders carefully wrapped up their dead in cloth so as to prevent the soul from slipping away.[9] The practice of placing logs or stones immediately over the corpse may have a similar origin ; in some Queensland tribes, when an individual has been killed by the whole tribe in punishment for some

---

[1] Fawcett, in the Madras Government Museum's *Bulletin*, iii. 251. See also Iyer, ' Nayādis of Malabar,' *ibid*. iv. 71.

[2] Waddell, *op. cit.* p. 498.

[3] Thomson, *Savage Island*, p. 134.

[4] Kålund, *loc. cit.* p. 227.

[5] von Hahn, *Albanesische Studien*, i. 163.

[6] *Cf.* Frazer, in *Jour. Anthr. Inst.* xv. 64 *sq.* ; Preuss, *op. cit.* p. 292 *sq.*

[7] Monrad, *op. cit.* p. 13.

[8] Läffler, *Den gottländska Taksteinar-sägnen*, p. 5.

[9] Högström, *Beskrifning öfver de til Sveriges Krona lydande Lapmarker*, p. 207.

serious crime, boomerangs are substituted for the ordinary
logs, evidently for fear of the ghost.[1]   The Chuvashes,
again, put two stakes across the coffin of a dead man for
the purpose of preventing him from lifting up the cover.[2]
Graves are often provided with mounds, tombstones, or
enclosures in order to keep the dead from walking.[3]   The
Omahas raise no mound over a man who has been killed
by lightning, but bury him face downwards and with the
soles of his feet split, in the belief that he will then go to
the spirit-land without giving further trouble to the
living.[4]   The Savage Islanders pile heavy stones upon the
grave to keep the ghost down.[5]   The Cheremises believe
that the ghosts cannot step over the fence-poles with
which they surround the graves.[6]   When ceremonies like
that of striking the air at a funeral or the ringing of bells
are represented as means of keeping off evil spirits from
the dead, we have reason to suspect that their original
object was to keep off the ghost from the living.   At
Central Australian funerals women beat the air with the
palms of their hands for the express purpose of driving the
spirit away from the old camp which it is supposed to
haunt, and the men beat the air with their spear-throwers.[7]
The Bondeis of East Africa frighten the ghosts by beating
drums.[8]   And at Port Moresby, in New Guinea, when
the church bell was first used, the natives thanked the
missionaries for having driven off numerous bands of
ghosts.[9]

That the mourning fast is essentially a precaution taken
by the survivors, and not a tribute to the dead, is obvious
from what has been said in a previous chapter.[10]   When
mourners mutilate, cut, or beat themselves, the original
object of their doing so seems often to be to ward off the

[1] Roth, *op. cit.* p. 165.
[2] Castrén, *op. cit.* iii. 121.
[3] *Cf.* Frazer, in *Jour. Anthr. Inst.*
xv. 65 *sq.* ; Preuss, *op. cit.* p. 293.
[4] Dorsey, in *Ann. Rep. Bur. Ethn.*
xi. 420.   La Flesche, in *Jour.*
American Folk-Lore, ii. 11.
[5] Thomson, *Savage Island*, p. 52.

[6] Castrén, *op. cit.* iii. 122.
[7] Spencer and Gillen, *Native Tribes*
of Central Australia, p. 506.
[8] Dale, in *Jour. Anthr. Inst.* xxv.
238.
[9] Chalmers and Gill, *Work and*
Adventure in New Guinea, p. 260.
[10] *Supra*, ii. 302 *sqq.*

contagion of death.[1] Among the Bedouins of Morocco women at funerals not only scratch their faces, but also rub the wounds with cow-dung, and cow-dung is regarded as a means of purification. The mourning customs of painting the body and of assuming a special costume have been explained as attempts on the part of the survivors to disguise themselves ; [2] but the latter custom may also have originated in the idea that a mourner is more or less polluted for a certain period and that therefore a dress worn by him then, being a seat of contagion, could not be used afterwards. Egede writes of the Greenlanders, " If they have happened to touch a corpse, they immediately cast away the clothes they have then on ; and for this reason they always put on their old clothes when they go to a burying, in which they agree with the Jews." [3] There can, finally, be no doubt that the widespread prohibition of mentioning the name of a dead person [4] does not in the first instance arise from respect for the departed, but from fear. To name him is to summon him ; the Indians of Washington Territory even change their own names when a relative dies, because " they think the spirits of the dead will come back if they hear the same name called that they were accustomed to hear

---

[1] Cf. Frazer, Golden Bough, i. 302.
[2] Frazer, in Jour. Anthr. Inst. xv. 73. Idem, ' Folk-Lore in the Old Testament,' in Anthropological Essays presented to E. B. Tylor, p. 110.
[3] Egede, op. cit. p. 197.
[4] Tylor, Researches into the Early History of Mankind, p. 144. Nyrop, ' Navnets magt,' in Mindre afhandlinger udgivne af det philologisk-historiske samfund, pp. 147–151, 190 sq. and passim. Frazer, Golden Bough, i. 421 sqq. Clodd, Tom Tit Tot, p. 166 sqq. Nansen, Eskimo Life, p. 230 sq. (Greenlanders). Müller, Geschichte der Amerikanischen Urreligionen, p. 84 (North American Indians). Bourke, ' Medicine-Men of the Apache,' in Ann. Rep. Bur. Ethn. ix. 462. Batchelor, Ainu and their Folk-Lore, p. 242. Georgi, op. cit. iii. 27, 28, 262 sq. (Samoyedes

and shamanistic peoples in Siberia). Jackson, in Jour. Anthr. Inst. xxiv. 406 (Samoyedes). Rivers, Todas, p. 625 sqq. Crooke, Tribes and Castes of the North-Western Provinces, i. 11 (Agariya, a Dravidian tribe). von Wlislocki, Volksglaube der Zigeuner, p. 96 (Gypsies). Yseldijk, in Glimpses of the Eastern Archipelago, p. 42. (Kotting, in the island of Flores). Roth, North-West-Central Queensland Aborigines, p. 164. Spencer and Gillen, Native Tribes of Central Australia, p. 498. Fraser, Aborigines of New South Wales, p. 82. Thornton, in Hill and Thornton, Aborigines of New South Wales, p. 7. Fison and Howitt, op. cit. p. 249 (Kurnai). Curr, Squatting in Victoria, p. 272 (Bangerang). Hinde, op. cit. p. 50 (Masai). Duveyrier, Exploration du Sahara, p. 415

before death." [1] But apart from this, a dead man's name itself is probably felt to be defiling, or at all events produces an uncanny association of thought, which even among ourselves makes many people reluctant to mention it.[2] And to do so may also be a wrong to other persons who would be endangered thereby. Among the Goajiro Indians of Colombia, to mention a dead man before his relatives is a dreadful offence, which is often punished even with death.[3]

By all this I certainly do not mean to assert that the funeral and mourning customs to which I have just referred have exclusively or in every case originated in fear of the dead or of the pollution of death. Burial may also be genuinely intended to protect the body from beasts or birds ; and the same may be the case with mounds, tombstones, and enclosures.[4] Some savages are reported to burn the dead in order to prevent their bodies from falling into the hands of enemies,[5] which might be bad both for the dead and for their friends, as charms might be made from the corpses.[6] Moreover, cremation does away with the slow process of transformation to which a dead body is naturally subject, and this process is regarded not only as a danger to the living but also as painful to the deceased himself.[7] The same object may be achieved by exposing the corpse to wild animals. And we should also remember that the putrefactive process

(Touareg).   Werner, ' Custom of " Hlonipa," ' in *Jour. African Soc.* 1905, April, p. 346 (Zulus).

[1] Swan, *Residence in Washington Territory*, p. 189.

[2] I had much difficulty in inducing my teacher in Shelḥa, a Berber from the Great Atlas Mountains, to tell me the equivalent for " illness " in his own language ; and when he finally did so, he spat immediately afterwards.   Among the Central Australian Arunta the older men will not look at the photograph of a deceased person (Gillen, ' Aborigines of the McDonnell Ranges,' in *Report of the Horn Expedition*, iv. ' Anthropology,' p. 168).

[3] Simons, ' Exploration of the Goajira Peninsula,' in *Proceed. Roy. Geograph. Soc.* N. S. vii. 791.

[4] Cranz, *op. cit.* i. 217 (Greenlanders). Turner, in *Ann. Rep. Bur. Ethn.* xi. 192 (Hudson Bay Eskimo). Yarrow, *ibid.* i. 102 (Wichita Indians). Dunbar, in *Magazine of American History*, viii. 734 (Pawnee Indians). Curr, *The Australian Race*, i. 87.

[5] Hyades and Deniker, *op. cit.* vii. 379 (Fuegians). Preuss, *op. cit.* p. 310 (Seminole Indians of Florida).

[6] Ralph, quoted by Hartland, *Legend of Perseus*, ii. 437 (Haidahs of British Columbia).

[7] See Hertz, *loc. cit.* p. 71.

itself, whether accompanied by any superstitious ideas or not, is a sufficient motive for disposing of the dead body in some way or other—either by burial or cremation or exposure ; and if one method is held objectionable another will be resorted to. Among the Masai the custom of throwing away corpses is said to spring from the notion that to bury them would be to poison the soil ; [1] and the Zoroastrian law enjoining the exposure of the dead was closely connected with the sacredness ascribed to fire and earth and the consequent dread of polluting them.

Again, as for the mutilations and self-inflicted wounds which accompany funerals, I have suggested in a previous chapter that they may be partly practised for the purpose of refreshing the departed soul with human blood ; [2] or, as Dr. Hirn observes, they may be instinctive efforts to procure that relief from overpowering feelings which is afforded by pain and the subsequent exhaustion.[3] The reluctance to name the dead may, in some measure, be traced to a natural unwillingness in his old friends to revive past sorrows.[4] And with reference to the mourning apparel, Dr. de Groot believes—if rightly or wrongly I am not in a position to decide—that, so far as China is concerned, it originated in the custom of sacrificing to the dead the clothes on one's own back. He thinks that this explanation is confirmed by the fact that in the age of Confucius it was customary for the mourners to throw off their clothes as far as decency allowed when the corpse was being dressed.[5]

There are several reasons why practices connected with death which originally sprang from self-regarding motives have come to be enjoined as duties. We have first to remember the various factors mentioned above [6] which tend to make self-regarding conduct a matter of moral concern.

[1] Thomson, *Through Masai Land,* p. 259.
[2] *Supra,* i. 476.
[3] Hirn, *Origins of Art,* p. 66 sq.
[4] Fison and Howitt, *op. cit.* p. 249 (Kurnai). Frazer, *Golden Bough,* i. 422.
[5] de Groot, *op. cit.* (vol. ii. book) i. 475 sq.
[6] *Supra,* ii. 266 sq.

But in this case the transition from the prudential to the obligatory has been much facilitated by the circumstance that all the acts which a person's self-interest induces him to perform or to abstain from have direct reference to another individual, and, indeed, to an individual who is supposed to reward benefits bestowed upon him or at all events to resent injuries and neglect. These punishments and rewards sent by the departed soul are all the more readily recognised to be well deserved, as the claims of the dead are similar in nature to those of the living and are at the same time in some degree supported by sympathetic feelings in the survivors. Nor is it difficult to explain why even such practices as are not originally supposed to comfort the dead have assumed the character of duties towards them. The dead are not only beings whom it is dangerous to offend and useful to please, but they are also very easily duped. No wonder therefore that the living are anxious to put the most amiable interpretation upon their conduct, trying to persuade the ghost, as also one another, that they do what they do for *his* benefit, not for their own. It is better for him to have rest in his grave than to wander about on earth unhappy and homeless. It is better for him to enjoy the heat of the flames than to suffer from the cold of an arctic climate. It is better for him to be eaten by an animal—say, a beautiful dog or a hyæna sent by God —than to lie and rot in the open air. And all the mourning customs, what are they if not tokens of grief ? Moreover, if the corpse is not properly disposed of or any funeral or mourning rite calculated to keep off the ghost is not observed, the dead man will easily do harm to the survivors. And does not this indicate that they have been neglectful of their duties to him ?

The mixture of sympathy and fear which is at the bottom of the duties to the dead accounts for the fact that these duties are rarely extended to strangers. A departed stranger is not generally an object of either pity or fear. He expects attention from his own people only, he haunts his own home. But he may of course be dangerous to

anybody who directly offends him, for instance by inflicting an injury upon his body, or to people who live in the
vicinity of his grave. We are told that the Angami
Nagas bestow as much care on the tombs of foes who have
fallen near their villages as on those of their own warriors.[1]
So also the differences in the treatment of the dead which
depend upon age, sex, and social position are no doubt
closely connected with variations in the feelings of sympathy, respect, or fear,[2] although in many cases we are
unable to explain those differences in detail. Among the
Australian natives women and children are said to be
interred with little ceremony because they are held to be
very inferior to men while alive and consequently are not
much feared after death;[3] and if in Eastern Central
Africa the attention usually bestowed upon the dead is
not extended to children which die when four or five days
old, the reason seems to be that such children are hardly
supposed to possess a soul.[4] We may assume that the
special treatment to which the bodies of criminals are
subject is due not only to indignation but, in some
instances at least, to fear of their ghosts. And we have
noticed above that suicides, murdered persons, and those
struck with lightning are sometimes left unburied because
no one dares to interfere with their bodies, or perhaps in
order to prevent them from mixing with the other dead.[5]

It should finally be noticed that the duties to the
departed become less stringent as time goes on. As Dr.
Hertz has recently shown, the fear of the dead is greatest
as long as the process of decomposition lasts and till the
second funeral is performed, and this ceremony brings
the period of mourning to an end.[6] Moreover, the dead
are gradually less and less thought of, they appear less
frequently in dreams and visions, the affection for them
fades away, and, being forgotten, they are no longer
feared. The Chinese say that ghosts are much more

[1] Prain, ' Angami Nagas,' in *Revue
coloniale internationale*, v. 493.
[2] *Cf.* Hertz, *loc. cit.* pp. 122,
132 *sqq.*

[3] Curr, *The Australian Race*, i. 89.
[4] Macdonald, *Africana*, i. 68.
[5] *Supra*, ii. 238 *sq.*
[6] Hertz, *loc. cit. passim.*

liable to appear very shortly after death than at any other period.[1] The natives of Australia are only afraid of the spirits of men who have lately died.[2] In the course of time savages also become more willing to speak of their dead.[3] But whilst the large bulk of disembodied souls sooner or later lose their individuality and dwindle into insignificance or sink into the limbo of All Souls, it may be that some of them escape this fate, and, instead of being ignored, are raised to the rank of gods.

Progress in intellectual culture has a tendency to affect the notions of death. The change involved in it appears greater. The soul, if still thought to survive the death of the body, is more distinctly separated from it ; it is rid of all sensuous desires, as also of all earthly interests. Duties to the dead which arose from the old ideas may still be maintained, but their meaning is changed.

Thus the funeral sacrifice may be continued as a mark of respect or affection. In Melanesia, for instance, at the death-meals which follow upon funerals or begin before them, and which still form one of the principal institutions of the natives, a piece of food is put aside for the dead. " It is readily denied now," says Dr. Codrington, " that the dead . . . are thought to come and eat the food, which they say is given as a friendly remembrance only, and in the way of associating together those whom death has separated." [4] In many cases the offerings made to the dead have become alms given to the poor, just as has been the case with sacrifices offered to gods ; [5] and this almsgiving is undoubtedly looked upon as a duty to the dead. Among the Omahas goods are collected from the kindred of the dead between the death and the funeral, and when the body has been deposited in the grave they

---

[1] Dennys, op. cit. p. 76.
[2] Curr, The Australian Race, i. 44, 87. Lumholtz, Among Cannibals, p. 279 (Northern Queensland aborigines).
[3] Tout, ' Ethnology of the Stlatlumh of British Columbia,' in Jour.

Anthr. Inst. xxxv. 138. Bourke, ' Medicine-Men of the Apache,' in Ann. Rep. Bur. Ethn. ix. 462. Frazer, Golden Bough, i. 431 sqq.
[4] Codrington, Melanesians, p. 271 sq. Cf. ibid. p. 128.
[5] Supra, i. 565 sqq.

are brought forth and equally divided among the poor
who are assembled on the spot.[1] At a Hindu funeral in
Sindh, on the road to the burning place, the relatives of
the dead throw dry dates into the air over the corpse ;
these are considered as a kind of alms and are left to the
poor.[2] Among some peoples of Malabar, at the *çrâddha*,
or yearly anniversary of a death, not less than three
Brahmins are well fed and presented with money and
cloth ;[3] and according to Brahmanism the *çrâddha* is " a
debt which is transferred from one generation to another,
and on the payment of which depends the happiness of the
dead in the next life." [4] Among Muhammedans alms,
generally consisting of food, are distributed in connection
with a death in order to confer merits upon the deceased.[5]
Thus in Morocco bread or dried fruits are given to the
poor who are assembled at the grave-side on the day of the
funeral, as also on the third and sometimes on the fortieth
day after it, on the tenth day of Muḥarram, and in many
parts of the country on other feast-days as well, when the
graves are visited by relatives of the dead. These alms
are obviously survivals of offerings to the dead themselves. While residing among the Bedouins of Dukkâla,
I was told that if the funeral meal were omitted the dead
man's mouth would be filled with earth ; and it is a
common custom among the Moors that, if a dead person
appears in a dream complaining of hunger or thirst, food
or drink is at once given to some poor people. Among
the Christians, in former days, alms were distributed in
the church when, soon after a death or on the anniversary
of a death, the sacrifice of the mass was offered ; and alms
were also given at funerals and at graves, in the hope that
their merit might be of advantage to the deceased.[6] At
Mykonos, in the Cyclades, on some fixed days after the

[1] La Flesche, in *Jour. American Folk-Lore*, ii. 8 *sqq.*
[2] Burton, *Sindh*, p. 350.
[3] Fawcett, ' Notes on some of the People of Malabar,' in the Madras Government Museum's *Bulletin*, iii. 71.

[4] Barth, *Religions of India*, p. 52.
[5] Garnett, *Women of Turkey*, ii. 496. Lane, *Modern Egyptians*, p. 530. Certeux and Carnoy, *L'Algérie traditionelle*, p. 220.
[6] Uhlhorn, *Die christliche Liebes-thätigkeit*, i. 281.

burial a dish consisting of boiled wheat adorned with sugar plums or other delicacy is put on the tomb, and finally distributed to the poor at the church door ; [1] and in some parts of Russia the people still believe that if the usual alms are not given at a funeral the dead man's soul will reveal itself to his relatives in the form of a moth flying about the flame of a candle.[2] The supposed conferring of merits upon the dead and the prayers on their behalf, so common both in Christianity and Muhammedanism, are the last remains of a series of customs by means of which the living have endeavoured to benefit their departed friends.

But even when the dead are no longer believed to be in need of human care, nay, though death be thought to put an end to existence, there are still duties, if not to the dead, at all events to those who were once alive. A person may be wronged by an act which he can no longer feel. There are rights that are in force not only during his lifetime but after his death. A given promise is not buried with him to whom it was made. A dead man's will is binding. His memory is protected against calumny. These rights have the same foundation as all other rights : the feelings of the person himself and the claims of others that his feelings shall be respected. We have wishes with regard to the future when we live no more. We take an interest in persons and things that survive us. We desire to leave behind a spotless name. And the sympathy felt for us by our fellow men will last when we ourselves are gone.

---

[1] Bent, *Cyclades*, p. 221 *sq.*   [2] Ralston, *op. cit.* p. 117.

CHAPTER XLVI

CANNIBALISM

BEFORE we take leave of the dead we have still to consider the practice of eating them.

Habitual cannibalism, permitted or in some cases enjoined by custom, has been met with in a large number of savage tribes and, as a religious or magical rite, among several peoples of culture. It is, or has been, particularly prevalent in the South Sea Islands, Australia, Central Africa, and South and Central America. But it has also been found among various North American Indians, in certain tribes of the Malay Archipelago, and among a few peoples on the Asiatic continent. And it is proved to have occurred in many parts of Europe.[1]

[1] For the prevalence and extension of cannibalism see Andree, *Die Anthropophagie*, p. 1 *sqq.*; Bergemann, *Die Verbreitung der Anthropophagie*, p. 5 *sqq.*; Steinmetz, *Endokannibalismus*, p. 2 *sqq.*; Schneider, *Die Naturvölker*, i. 121 *sqq.*; Letourneau, *L'évolution de la morale*, p. 82 *sqq.*; Ritson, *Abstinence from Animal Food*, p. 125 *sqq.*; Hartland, *Legend of Perseus*, ii. 279 *sqq.*; Schaafhausen, 'Die Menschenfresserei und das Menschenopfer,' in *Archiv f. Anthropologie*, iv. 248 *sqq.*; Henkenius, 'Verbreitung der Anthropophagie,' in *Deutsche Rundschau f. Geographie u. Statistik*, xv. 348 *sqq.*; de Nadaillac, 'L'Anthropophagie et les sacrifices humains,' in *Revue des Deux Mondes*, lxvi. 406 *sqq.*; *Idem*, in *Bulletins de la Soc. d'Anthrop. de Paris*, 1888, p. 27 *sqq.*; Dorman, *Origin of Primitive Superstitions*, p. 145 *sqq.* (American aborigines); Koch, 'Die Anthropophagie der südamerikanischen Indianer,' in *Internationales Archiv f. Ethnographie*, xii. 84 *sqq.*; Preuss, *Die Begräbnisarten der Amerikaner und Nordostasiaten*, p. 217 *sqq.*; Vos, 'Die Verbreitung der Anthropophagie auf dem asiatischen Festlande,' in *Intern. Archiv f. Ethnogr.* iii. 69 *sqq.*; de Groot, *Religious System of China*, (vol. iv. book) ii. 363 *sqq.*; Hübbe-Schleiden, *Ethiopien*, p. 209 *sqq.*; Matiegka, 'Anthropophagie in der prähistorischen Ansiedlung bei Knovíze und in der prähistorischen Zeit überhaupt,' in *Mittheil. d. Anthrop. Gesellsch. in Wien*, xxvi. 129 *sqq.*; Wood-Martin, *Traces of the Elder Faiths of Ireland*, ii. 286 *sqq.*

Sometimes the whole body is eaten, with the exception of the bones, sometimes only a part of it, as the liver or the heart. Frequently the victim is an enemy or a member of a foreign tribe, but he may also be a relative or fellow tribesman. Among various savages exo- and endo-anthropophagy prevail simultaneously; but many cannibals restrict themselves to eating strangers, slain enemies, or captives taken in war, whereas others eat their own people in preference to strangers, or are exclusively endo-anthropophagous. Thus the Birhors of the Central Provinces of India are said to eat their aged relatives, but to abhor any other form of cannibalism;[1] and in certain Australian tribes it is not the dead bodies of slain enemies that are eaten, but the bodies of friends, the former being left where they fell.[2] Sometimes people feed on the corpses of such kinsmen as have happened to die, sometimes they kill and eat their old folks, sometimes parents eat their children, sometimes criminals are eaten by the other members of their own community. The Australian Dieyerie have a fixed order in which they partake of their dead relatives :—" The mother eats of her children. The children eat of their mother. Brothers-in-law and sisters-in-law eat of each other. Uncles, aunts, nephews, nieces, grandchildren, grandfathers, and grandmothers eat of each other. But the father does not eat of his offspring, or the offspring of the sire."[3] Among some peoples cannibalism is an exclusively masculine custom, the women being forbidden to eat human flesh, except perhaps in quite exceptional circumstances.[4]

---

[1] Dalton, *Ethnology of Bengal*, p. 220 sq.

[2] Palmer, 'Some Australian Tribes,' in *Jour. Anthr. Inst.* xiii. 283; Fraser, *Aborigines of New South Wales*, p. 56; Howitt, *Native Tribes of South-East Australia*, p. 753 (Queensland aborigines). Dawson, *Australian Aborigines*, p. 67 (tribes of Western Victoria).

[3] Gason, 'Dieyerie Tribe,' in Woods, *Native Tribes of South Australia*, p. 274.

[4] Coquilhat, *Sur le Haut-Congo*, p. 274 (Bangala). Torday and Joyce, 'Ethnography of the Ba-Mbala,' in *Jour. Anthr. Inst.* xxxv. 403 sq. Iidem, 'Ethnography of the Ba-Huana,' *ibid.* xxxvi. 279. Reade, *Savage Africa*, p. 158 (West Equatorial Africans). Thomson, *Story of New Zealand*, i. 145; Best, 'Art of War, as conducted by the Maori,' in *Jour. Polynesian Soc.* xi. 71 (some of the Maoris). von Langsdorf, *op. cit.* i. 134 (Nukahivans). Erskine,

The practice of cannibalism may be traced to many different sources. If often springs from scarcity or lack of animal food.[1] In the South Sea Islands, according to Ellis, " the cravings of nature, and the pangs of famine, often led to this unnatural crime." [2] The Nukahivans, who were in the habit of eating their enemies slain in battle, also killed and ate their wives and children in times of scarcity, but not unless forced to it by the utmost necessity.[3] Hunger has been represented as the motive for cannibalism in some North and West Australian tribes, parents sometimes consuming even their own children when food is scarce.[4] The Indians north of Lake Superior often resorted to the eating of human flesh when hard pressed by their enemies or during a famine.[5] Among the Hudson Bay Eskimo " instances are reported where, in times of great scarcity, families have been driven to cannibalism after eating their dogs and the clothing and other articles made of skins."[6]

But whilst among some peoples starvation is the only inducement to cannibalism, there are others who can plead no such motive for their anthropophagous habits. The Fijians, until lately some of the greatest man-eaters on earth, inhabit a country where food of every kind abounds.[7] The Brazilian cannibals generally have a great

Cruise among the Islands of Western Pacific, p. 260 (Fijians). Spencer and Gillen, *Northern Tribes of Central Australia*, p. 548. With reference to the natives of Australia Mr. Curr says (*The Australian Race*, i. 77) that " human flesh seems to have been entirely forbidden to females "; but this certainly does not hold true of all the Australian tribes.

[1] Bergemann, *op. cit.* p. 48. de Nadaillac, in *Bull. Soc. d'Anthr.* 1888, p. 27 *sqq. Idem*, in *Revue des Deux Mondes*, lxvi. 428 *sq.* Steinmetz, *Endokannibalismus*, p. 25 *sqq.* Lippert, *Kulturgeschichte der Menschheit*, ii. 281 *sqq.* Henkenius, *loc. cit.* p. 348 *sq.* Letourneau, *L'évolution de la Morale*, p. 97. Matiegka, *loc. cit.* p. 136. Hübbe-Schleiden,

Ethiopien, p. 216 *sq.* Rochas, *La Nouvelle Calédonie*, p. 304 *sq.*
[2] Ellis, *Polynesian Researches*, i. 359.
[3] von Langsdorf, *op. cit.* i. 144.
[4] Lumholtz, *Among Cannibals*, p. 134. Nisbet, *A Colonial Tramp*, ii. 143. Oldfield, ' Aborigines of Australia,' in *Trans. Ethn. Soc.* N.S. iii. 285. In hard summers the new-born babies were all eaten by the Kaura tribe in the neighbourhood of Adelaide (Howitt, *op. cit.* p. 749).
[5] Warren, in Schoolcraft, *Indian Tribes of the United States*, ii. 146.
[6] Turner, ' Ethnology of the Ungava District,' in *Ann. Rep. Bur. Ethn.* xi. 187.
[7] Williams and Calvert, *Fiji*, p. 182. Erskine, *op. cit.* p. 262.

plenty of game or fish.[1] In Africa cannibalism prevails in many countries which are well supplied with food.[2] Thus the Bangala of the Upper Congo have been known to make frequent warlike expeditions against adjoining tribes seemingly for the sole object of obtaining human flesh to eat, although their land is well provided with a variety of vegetable food and domestic animals, to say nothing of the incredible abundance of fish in its lakes and rivers.[3] Of the cave-cannibals in the Trans-Gariep Country, in South Africa, a traveller remarks with some surprise :—" They were inhabiting a fine agricultural tract of country, which also abounded in game. Notwithstanding this, they were not contented with hunting and feeding upon their enemies, but preyed much upon each other also, for many of their captures were made from amongst the people of their own tribe."[4] Far from being an article of food resorted to in emergency only, human flesh is not seldom sought for as a delicacy.[5] The highest praise which the Fijians could bestow on a dainty was to say that it was " tender as a dead man."[6] In various other islands of the South Seas human flesh is spoken of as a delicious food, far superior to pork.[7] The

[1] von Martius, *Beiträge zur Ethnographie Amerika's*, i. 538. Koch, *loc. cit.* p. 87. de Nadaillac, in *Bull. Soc. d'Anthr.* 1888, p. 30 sq.

[2] Johnston, ' Ethics of Cannibalism,' in *Fortnightly Review*, N.S. xlv. 20 sqq. Hübbe-Schleiden, *Ethiopien*, p. 212. de Nadaillac, in *Bull. Soc. d'Anthr.* 1888, p. 32 sq.

[3] Coquilhat, *op. cit.* pp. 271, 273. Johnston, in *Fortnightly Review*, N.S. xlv. 20.

[4] Layland, quoted by Burton, *Two Trips to Gorilla Land*, i. 216.

[5] Bergemann, *op. cit.* p. 49 sq. von Langsdorf, *op. cit.* i. 141. Hübbe-Schleiden, *Ethiopien*, p. 218. Johnston, in *Fortnightly Review*, N.S. xlv. 20 sqq. (various African peoples). Kingsley, *Travels in West Africa*, p. 330 (Fans). Reade, *op. cit.* p. 158 (West Equatorial Africans). Coquilhat, *op. cit.* p. 271 (Bangala). Torday and Joyce. ' Ba-Mbala,' in *Jour. Anthr. Inst.* xxxv. 404. *Iidem*,

' Ba-Huana,' *ibid.* xxxvi. 279.

[6] Wilkes, *U. S. Exploring Expedition*, iii. 101. *Cf.* Williams and Calvert, *op. cit.* pp. 175, 178, 195.

[7] Romilly, *Western Pacific*, p. 59 (New Irelanders). *Idem, From my Verandah in New Guinea*, p. 65. Brenchley, *Cruise of H.M.S. Curaçoa*, p. 209 ; Turner, *Samoa*, p. 313 (natives of Tana, in the New Hebrides). *Cf. ibid.* p. 344 (New Caledonians) ; Hale, *U. S. Exploring Expedition. Vol. VI. Ethnography and Philology*, p. 39 (Polynesians). The Bataks of Sumatra likewise consider human flesh even better than pork (Junghuhn, *Die Battaländer auf Sumatra*, ii. 160 sq.). For the high appreciation of its taste see also Marco Polo, *Book concerning the Kingdoms and Marvels of the East*, ii. 179 (hill people in Fokien), 209 (Islanders in the Seas of China) ; Schaafhausen, *loc. cit.* p. 247 sq.; Matiegka, *loc. cit.* p. 136, n. 3.

Australian Kurnai said that it tasted better than beef.[1]
In some tribes in Australia a plump child is considered " a
sweet mouthful, and, in the absence of the mother, clubs
in the hands of a few wilful men will soon lay it low." [2]
Of certain natives of Northern Queensland we are told
that the greatest incentive to taking life is their appetite
for human flesh, as they know no greater luxury than the
flesh of a black man.[3]

However, bodily appetites, whether hunger or
gourmandise, are by no means the sole motives for
cannibalism. Very frequently it is described as an act of
revenge.[4] The Typees of the Marquesas Islands,
according to Melville, are cannibals only when they seek
to gratify the passion of revenge upon their foes.[5] The
cannibalism of the Solomon Islanders seems mainly to
have been an expression of the deepest humiliation to
which they could make a person subject.[6] The Samoans
affirmed that, when in some of their wars a body was
occasionally cooked, " it was always some one of the
enemy who had been notorious for provocation or cruelty,
and that eating a part of his body was considered the
climax of hatred and revenge, and was not occasioned by
the mere relish for human flesh." To speak of roasting

[1] Howitt, *op. cit.* p. 752.
[2] Fraser, *Aborigines of New South
Wales.* pp. 3, 57.
[3] Lumholtz, *op. cit.* pp. 101, 271.
[4] Ellis, *Polynesian Researches*, i.
310 (Tahitians). von Langsdorf, *op.
cit.* i. 149 (Nukahivans). Forster,
Voyage round the World, ii. 315
(natives of Tana and generally).
Powell, *Wanderings in a Wild
Country*, p. 248 (natives of New
Britain and New Ireland). Howitt,
Natives of South-East Australia, pp.
247, 751. Marsden, *History of
Sumatra*, p. 391 ; Buning, in
Glimpses of the Eastern Archipelago,
p. 74 *sq.* ; Junghuhn. *op. cit.* ii. 156,
160 (Bataks). de Groot, *op. cit.* (vol.
iv. book) ii. 369 *sqq.* (ancient Chinese). Schneider, *Die Religion der
afrikanischen Naturvölker*, p. 208 *sq.*
(Negroes). Burton, *Two Trips to
Gorilla Land*, i. 216 (natives of

Bonny and New Calabar). Müller,
*Geschichte der Amerikanischen Urre-
ligionen*, p. 145 *sq.* Carver, *Travels
through the Interior Parts of North
America*, p. 303 *sq.* (Naudowessies).
Keating, *Expedition to the Source of
St. Peter's River*, i. 104 (Potawatomis). Koch, *loc. cit.* pp. 87, 89 *sqq.*
(South American tribes). von Humboldt, *Travels to the Equinoctial
Regions of the New Continent*, v.
421 (Indians of Guyana). Wied-
Neuwied, *Reise nach Brasilien*, ii. 50
(Botocudos and some other Brazilian
tribes). Lomonaco, ' Sulle razze indigene del Brasile,' in *Archivio per
l'antropologia e la etnologia*, xix. 58
(Tupis). Andree, *op. cit.* p. 102 *sq.*
and *passim*.
[5] Melville, *Typee*, p. 181.
[6] Parkinson, *Zur Ethnographie der
nordwestlichen Salomo Inseln*, p. 14.

him is the very worst language that can be addressed to a Samoan, and if applied to a chief of importance, he may raise war to avenge the insult.[1] Among the Maoris human flesh was frequently eaten from motives of revenge and hatred, to cast disgrace on the person eaten, and to strike terror. " It was such a disgrace for a New Zealander to have his body eaten, that if crews of Englishmen and New Zealanders, all friends, were dying of starvation in separate ships, the English might resort to cannibalism, but the New Zealanders never would." [2] Even in Fiji, where cannibalism was largely indulged in for the mere pleasure of eating human flesh as food, revenge is said to have been the chief motive for it.[3] Thus, " in any transaction where the national honour had to be avenged, it was incumbent upon the king and principal chiefs—in fact, a duty they owed to their exalted station—to avenge the insult offered to the country by eating the perpetrators of it." [4]

The practice of eating criminals, which is quite a common form of cannibalism, seems to be largely due to revenge or indignation.[5] In Lepers' Island, in the New Hebrides, the victims of it were not generally enemies who had been killed in fighting, but " it was a murderer or particularly detested enemy who was eaten, in anger and to treat him ill." [6] Among the Bataks of Sumatra offenders condemned for certain capital crimes, such as atrocious murder, treason, and adultery, were usually eaten by the injured persons and their friends with all the signs of angry passion.[7] But this form of cannibalism may also have another foundation.[8] If for any reason there is a desire to eat human flesh, an unsympathetic being like a criminal is apt to be chosen as a victim.

[1] Turner, *Nineteen Years in Polynesia*, p. 194. *Cf.* Pritchard, *Polynesian Reminiscences*, p. 125 *sq.*

[2] Thomson, *Story of New Zealand*, i. 141 *sqq.* Yate, *Account of New Zealand*, p. 129. Dieffenbach, *Travels in New Zealand*, ii. 128. Taylor, *Te Ika a Maui*, p. 353. Best, in *Jour. Polynesian Soc.* xi. 71 *sq.*

[3] Wilkes, *op. cit.* iii. 101. Williams and Calvert, *op. cit.* p. 178.

[4] Seemann, *Viti*, p. 181.

[5] *Cf.* Matiegka, *loc. cit.* p. 137.

[6] Codrington, *Melanesians*, p. 344.

[7] Marsden, *op. cit.* p. 391. Junghuhn, *op. cit.* ii. 156 *sq.*

[8] See Steinmetz, *op. cit.* p. 55 *sq.*

It is said that some of the Line Islanders in the South Seas began their cannibalism by eating thieves and slaves.[1] In Melanesia, where human sacrifices were combined with the eating of bits of the victim, " advantage was taken of a crime, or imputed crime, to take a life and offer the man to some *tindalo*." [2]

It has been questioned whether cannibalism can be a direct expression of hatred ; [3] but for no good reason. To eat a person is, according to primitive ideas, to annihilate him as an individual,[4] and we can readily imagine the triumphant feelings of a savage who has his enemy between his jaws. The Fijian eats in revenge even the vermin which bite him, and when a thorn pricks him he picks it out of his flesh and eats it.[5] The Cochin-Chinese express their deepest hatred of a person by saying, " I wish I could eat his liver or his flesh." [6] Other people want to " drink the blood " of their enemies.

The idea that a person is annihilated or loses his individuality by being eaten has led to cannibalism not only in revenge but as an act of protection, as a method of making a dangerous individual harmless after death.[7] Among the Botocudos warriors devoured the bodies of their fallen enemies in the belief that they would thus be safe from the revengeful hatred of the dead.[8] In Ashantee " several of the hearts of the enemy are cut out by the fetish men who follow the army, and the blood and small pieces being mixed (with much ceremony and incantation) with various consecrated herbs, all those who have never killed an enemy before eat a portion, for it is believed that if they did not, their vigour and courage would be secretly wasted by the haunting spirit of the

---

[1] Tutuila, 'Line Islanders,' in *Jour. Polynesian Soc.* i. 270.
[2] Codrington, *op. cit.* p. 135.
[3] Steinmetz, *op. cit.* p. 33.
[4] Dieffenbach, *op. cit.* ii. 118 (Maoris). Johnston, in *Fortnightly Review*, N. S. xlv. 27 (Negroes of the Niger Delta). Koch, *loc. cit.* pp. 87, 109. Lippert, *Der Seelencult*, p. 69. *Idem, Kulturgeschichte der Mensch-* *heit*, ii. 282 *sq.*
[5] Pritchard, *op. cit.* p. 371.
[6] von Langsdorf, *op. cit.* i. 148.
[7] *Cf.* Lippert, *Kulturgeschichte der Menschheit*, ii. 282 ; Koch, *loc. cit.* pp. 87, 109.
[8] Featherman, *Social History of Mankind*, ' Chiapo- and Guarano-Maranonians,' p. 355.

deceased." [1] In Greenland " a slain man is said to have the power to avenge himself upon the murderer by ' rushing into him,' which can only be prevented by eating a piece of his liver." [2] Many cannibals are in the habit of consuming that part of a slain enemy which is supposed to contain his soul or courage or strength, and one reason for this practice may be the wish to render him incapable of doing further harm. Queensland natives eat the kidneys of the persons whom they have killed, believing that " the kidneys are the centre of life." [3] Among the Maoris a chief was often satisfied with the left eye of his enemy, which they considered to be the seat of the soul ; or they drank the blood from a corresponding belief ; [4] or in the case of a blood feud the heart of the enemy, representing the vital essence of him, was eaten " to fix or make firm the victory and the courage of the victor." [5] Other peoples likewise eat the hearts or suck the brains of their foes.

Moreover, by eating the supposed seat of a certain quality in his enemy the cannibal thinks not only that he deprives his victim of that quality, but also that he incorporates it with his own system. [6] In many cases this is the chief or the only reason for the practice of cannibalism. The Shoshone Indians supposed that they became animated by the heroic spirit of a fallen foe if they partook of his flesh. [7] Among the Hurons, if an enemy had shown courage, his heart, roasted and cut into small pieces,

[1] Bowdich, *Mission to Ashantee,* p. 300.
[2] Rink, *Tales and Traditions of the Eskimo,* p. 45.
[3] Lumholtz, *op. cit.* p. 272.
[4] Dieffenbach, *op. cit.* ii. 128 *sq.*
[5] Best, in *Jour. Polynesian Soc.* xii. 83, 147.
[6] Blumentritt, ' Der Ahnencultus der Malaien des Philippinen-Archipels,' in *Mittheil. d. kais. u. könig. Geograph. Gesellsch. in Wien,* xxv. 154 (Italones). Lewin, *Wild Races of South-Eastern India,* p. 269 (Kukis). de Groot, *op. cit.* (vol. iv. book) ii. 373 *sqq.* (ancient

Chinese). Schneider *Die Religion der afrikanischen Naturvölker,* p. 209 *sq.* (Negroes). Dorman, *op. cit.* p. 145 *sq.* (North American Indians). Keating, *op. cit.* i. 104 (Potawatomis). Koch, *loc. cit.* pp. 87, 89 *sqq.,* 109 (South American Indians). Andree, *op. cit.* p. 101 *sq.* and *passim.* Lippert, *Der Seelencult,* p. 70 *sqq. Idem, Kulturgeschichte,* ii. 282. Trumbull, *Blood Covenant,* p. 128 *sqq.* Frazer, *Golden Bough,* ii. 357 *sqq.* Gomme, *Ethnology in Folklore,* p. 151 *sqq.* Crawley, *Mystic Rose,* p. 101 *sqq.*
[7] Featherman, *op. cit.* ' Aoneo-Maranonians,' p. 206.

was given to the young men and boys to eat.[1] The Ewe-speaking peoples of the Slave Coast used to eat the hearts of foes remarkable for sagacity, holding that the heart is the seat of the intellect as well as of courage.[2] Among the Kimbunda of South-Western Africa, when a new king succeeds to the throne, a brave prisoner of war is killed in order that the king and nobles may eat his flesh, and so acquire his strength and courage.[3] The idea of transference very largely underlies Australian cannibalism.[4] In some tribes enemies are consumed with a view to acquiring some part of their qualities and courage.[5] The Dieyerie devour the fatty portions of their foes because they think it will impart strength to them.[6] And similar motives are often given for the practice of eating relatives or friends. When a man is killed in one of the ceremonial fights in the tribes about Maryborough, in Queensland, his friends skin and eat him in the hope that his virtues as a warrior may go into those who partake of him.[7] Among the natives of the River Darling, in New South Wales, a piece of flesh is cut from the dead body and taken to the camp, and after being sun-dried is cut up into small pieces, which are distributed among the relatives and friends of the deceased. Some of them use the piece in making a charm, or throw it into the river to bring a flood and fish, but others suck it to get strength and courage.[8] In certain Central Australian tribes, when a party starts on an avenging expedition, every man of it drinks some blood and also has some spurted over his body, so as to make him lithe and active ; the elder men

[1] Parkman, *Jesuits in North America*, p. xxxix.
[2] Ellis, *Ewe-speaking Peoples of the Slave Coast*, p. 100.
[3] Magyar, *Reisen in Süd-Afrika*, p. 273.
[4] Fraser, *Aborigines of New South Wales*, pp. 56, 81. Brough Smyth, *Aborigines of Victoria*, i. p. xxxviii. Howitt, 'Australian Medicine Men,' in *Jour. Anthr. Inst.* xvi. 30. Langloh Parker, *Euahlayi Tribe*, p. 38. Gason, 'Dieyerie Tribe,' in Curr,

op. cit. ii. 52.
[5] Howitt, *Native Tribes of South-East Australia*, p. 752.
[6] Gason, in *Jour. Anthr. Inst.* xxiv. 172.
[7] Howitt, *op. cit.* p. 753. McDonald, 'Mode of Preparing the Dead among the Natives of the Upper Mary River, Queensland,' in *Jour. Anthr. Inst.* ii. 179.
[8] Bonney, 'Aborigines of the River Darling,' in *Jour. Anthr. Inst.* xiii. 135.

indicate from whom the blood is to be drawn, and the persons thus selected must not decline.[1] In certain South Australian tribes cannibalism is only practised by old men and women, who eat a baby in order to get the youngster's strength.[2] Among other natives of the same continent, as we have noticed above, a mother used to kill and eat her first child, as this was believed to strengthen her for later births.[3] And in various Australian tribes it is, or has been, the custom when a child is weak or sickly to kill its infant brother or sister and feed it with the flesh to make it strong.[4] Many of the Brazilian Indians are in the habit of burning the bones of their departed relatives, and mix the ashes with a drink of which they partake for the purpose of absorbing their spirits or virtues.[5] Dr. Couto de Magalhães was informed that the savage Chavantes " eat their children who die, in the hope of gathering again to their body the soul of the child."[6]

The belief in the principle of transference has also led to cannibalism in connection with human sacrifice and to the eating of man-gods. At Florida, in the Solomon Islands, human flesh was eaten in sacrifice only.[7] In Hawaii, " après le sacrifice, le peuple, qui d'ailleurs ne fut jamais anthropophage, pratiquait une sorte de communion en mangeant certaines parties de la victime."[8] In West Equatorial Africa, according to Mr. Winwood Reade, there are two kinds of cannibalism—the one is simply an

---

[1] Spencer and Gillen, *Native Tribes of Central Australia*, p. 461.
[2] Crauford, in *Jour. Anthr. Inst.* xxiv. 182.
[3] *Supra*, i. 458.
[4] Howitt, *Native Tribes of South-East Australia*, p. 749 *sq.* (all the tribes of the Wotjo nation, and the Tatathi and other tribes on the Murray River frontage). Stanbridge, 'Tribes in the Central Part of Victoria,' in *Trans. Ethn. Soc. London*, N.S. i. 289. Spencer and Gillen, *Native Tribes of Central Australia*, pp. 52, 475 (Luritcha tribe).
[5] Wallace, *Travels on the Amazon*, p. 498 (Tariánas, Tucános, and some other tribes of the Uaupés). Cou-

dreau, *La France équinoxiale*, ii. 173 (Cobbéos, of the Uaupés). Monteiro, quoted by von Spix and von Martius, *Reise in Brasilien*, iii. 1207, n. * (Jumánas). Koch, *loc. cit.* p. 83 *sq.* Dorman, *op. cit.* p. 151.
[6] Couto de Magalhães, *Trabalho preparatorio para aproveitamento do selvagem e do solo por elle occupado no Brazil—O selvagem*, p. 132. *Cf.* de Castelnau, *Expédition dans les parties centrales de l'Amérique du Sud*, iv. 382 (Camacas).
[7] Codrington, *op. cit.* p. 343. See also Geiseler, *Die Oster-Insel*, p. 30 *sq.* (Easter Islanders).
[8] Remy, *Ka Mooolelo Hawaii*, p. xl.

act of *gourmandise*, the other is sacrificial and is
performed by the priests, whose office it is to eat a
portion of the victims, whether men, goats, or fowls.[1]
And this sacrificial cannibalism is not restricted to the
priests. In British Nigeria " no great human sacrifice
offered for the purpose of appeasing the gods and
averting sickness or misfortune is considered to be
complete unless either the priests or the people eat the
bodies of the victims " ;[2] and among the Aro people in
Southern Nigeria the human victims offered to the god
were eaten by all the people, the flesh being distributed
throughout their country.[3] The inhabitants of the
province of Caranque, in ancient Peru, likewise consumed
the flesh of those whom they sacrificed to their gods.[4]
The Aztecs ate parts of the human bodies whose blood
had been poured out on the altar of sacrifice,[5] and so did
the Mayas.[6] In Nicaragua the high-priests received the
heart, the king the feet and hands, he who captured the
victim took the thighs, the entrails were given to the
trumpeters, and the rest was divided among the people.[7]
In ancient India it was a prevalent opinion that he who
offered a human victim in sacrifice should partake of its
flesh ; though, in opposition to this view, it was also said
that a man cannot be allowed, much less required, to eat
human flesh.[8] The sacrificial form of cannibalism
obviously springs from the idea that a victim offered to a
supernatural being participates in his sanctity[9] and from
the wish of the worshipper to transfer to himself something of its benign virtue. So also the divine qualities of
a man-god are supposed to be assimilated by the person

[1] Reade, *op. cit.* p. 158. See also
Schneider, *Die Religion der afrikanischen Naturvölker*, p. 209 *sq.*
[2] Mockler-Ferryman, *British Nigeria*, p. 261.
[3] Partridge, *Cross River Natives*,
p. 59.
[4] Ranking, *Researches on the Conquest of Peru*, p. 89.
[5] Prescott, *History of the Conquest
of Mexico*, p. 41. Réville, *Hibbert

Lectures on the Religions of Mexico
and Peru*, p. 89. Bancroft, *Native
Races of the Pacific States*, ii. 176 ;
iii. 443 *sq.*
[6] Bancroft, *op. cit.* ii. 725.
[7] *Ibid.* ii. 725.
[8] Weber, ' Ueber Menschenopfer
bei den Indern der vedischen Zeit,'
in *Indische Streifen*, i. 72 *sq.*
[9] See *supra*, i. 445 *sq.*

who eats his flesh or drinks his blood.[1] This was the idea of the early Christians concerning the Eucharist. In the holy food they assumed a real bestowal of heavenly gifts, a bodily self-communication of Christ, a miraculous implanting of divine life. The partaking of the consecrated elements had no special relation to the forgiveness of sins ; but it strengthened faith and knowledge, and, especially, it was the guarantee of eternal life, because the body of Christ was eternal. The holy food was described as the " medicine of immortality." [2]

In various other instances human flesh or blood is supposed to have a supernatural or medicinal effect upon him who partakes of it. The Banks' Islanders in Melanesia believe that a man or woman may obtain a power like that of Vampires by stealing and eating a morsel of a corpse ; the ghost of the dead man would then " join in a close friendship with the person who had eaten, and would gratify him by afflicting any one against whom his ghostly power might be directed." [3] Australian sorcerers are said to acquire their magic influence by eating human flesh.[4] The Egyptian natives who accompanied Baker on one of his expeditions imagined that the rite of consuming an enemy's liver would give a fatal direction to a random bullet.[5] Among the aborigines of Tasmania a man's blood was often administered as a healing draught.[6] In China the heart, the liver, the gall, and the blood of executed criminals are used for life-strengthening purposes ;[7] thus at Peking, when a person has been executed by the sword, certain large pith balls are steeped in the blood and, under the name of " blood-bread," sold as a medicine for consumption.[8] Tertullian speaks of those " who at the gladiatorial shows, for the cure of epilepsy,

[1] See Frazer, *Golden Bough*, ii. 352, 353, 366.
[2] Harnack, *History of Dogma*, i. 211 ; ii. 144 *sqq.* ; iv. 286, 291, 294, 296, 297, 299 *sq.*
[3] Codrington, *op. cit.* p. 221 *sq.*
[4] Eyre, *Expeditions of Discovery into Central Australia*, ii. 255.
[5] Baker, *Ismailïa*, p. 393.
[6] Bonwick, *Daily Life and Origin of the Tasmanians*, p. 89.
[7] de Groot, *op. cit.* (vol. iv. book) ii. 377.
[8] Rennie, quoted by Yule, in his translation of Marco Polo, i. 275, n. 7.

quaff with greedy thirst the blood of criminals slain
in the arena, as it flows fresh from the wound."[1]   So
also in Christian Europe the blood of criminals has been
drunk as a remedy against epilepsy, fever, and other
diseases.[2]   In these cases the ascription of a healing effect
to the blood of the dead may perhaps have been derived
from a belief in the transference of some quality which
they possessed in their lifetime ; the blood or life of a
sound and strong individual might impart health to the
sickly. But the mystery of death would also give to the
corpse a miraculous power of its own, especially when combined with the horror or awe inspired by an executed felon.

In other instances, again, the belief in the wonderful
effects of cannibal practices may have originated in the
notion that, if a person or the essential part of him is eaten,
he ceases to exist even as a spirit, or at all events loses
his power of doing mischief. Among the Indians of
British Guiana, when a man is pointed out as the secret
murderer of a relative who has died, the avenger will
shoot him through the back ; and if he happens to fall
dead to the ground, his corpse is dragged aside and buried
in a shallow grave. The third night the avenger goes
to the grave and presses a pointed stick through the
corpse ; and if on withdrawing the stick he finds blood on
the end of it, he tastes the blood in order to ward off any
evil effects that might follow from the murder, returning
home appeased and apparently at ease. But if it happens
that the wounded individual is able to escape, he charges
his relatives to bury him after his death in some place
where he cannot be found. This is to punish the
murderer for his deed, " inasmuch as the belief prevails
that if he taste not the blood he must perish by
madness."[3]   In Prussia it was a popular superstition that

[1] Tertullian, *Apologeticus*, 9 (Migne,
Patrologiæ cursus, i. 321 *sqq.*).

[2] Strack, *Der Blutaberglaube in der
Menschheit*, p. 27 *sqq.* Wuttke, *Der
deutsche Volksaberglaube der Gegenwart*, § 189 *sqq.*, p. 137 *sq.* Jahn,
' Ueber den Zauber mit Menschenblut,' in *Verhandl. d. Berliner*

Gesellsch. f. Anthrop. 1888, p. 134
sqq. Havelock Ellis, *The Criminal*, p.
284. Peacock, ' Executed Criminals
and Folk-Medicine,' in *Folk-Lore*,
vii. 270 *sq.*

[3] Bernau, *Missionary Labours in
British Guiana*, p. 57 *sq.*

if a murderer cut off, roasted, and ate a piece of his victim's body, he would never after think of his deed.[1] But by eating a part of the corpse a homicide may also protect himself against the vengeance of the survivors, presumably because he has now absorbed their relative into his own system.[2] The natives of New Britain eat their enemies and fix the leg and arm bones of the victims at the butt end of their spears, believing that this not only gives them the strength of the man whose bones they carry but also makes them invulnerable by his relatives.[3] The Botocudos thought that by devouring their fallen enemies they both protected themselves from the hatred of the dead and at the same time prevented the arrows of the hostile tribe from hitting them.[4] In Greenland the relatives of a murdered person, when highly enraged, will cut to pieces the body of the murderer and devour part of the heart or liver, " thinking thereby to disarm his relatives of all courage to attack them." [5] In the South of Italy there is a popular belief that a murderer will not be able to escape unless he taste or bedaub himself with his victim's blood.[6] Sometimes, we are told, cannibalism is even supposed to have a positively injurious effect upon the victim's relatives, in accordance, as it seems, with the principle of sympathetic magic. Among the Chukchi, in the case of revenge for blood, the slayers eat a little bit of the enemy's heart or liver, supposing that they in this way cause the hearts of his kinsfolk to sicken.[7]

Human flesh or blood is not only believed to impart certain qualities or beneficial magic energy to him who partakes of it, but also serves as a means of transferring conditional curses from one person to another. This I take to be the explanation of cannibalism as a covenant rite ; in a previous chapter I have tried to show that the

[1] von Tettau and Temme, *Die Volkssagen Ostpreussens*, p. 267.
[2] *Cf.* Hartland, *op. cit.* ii. 245 *sq.*
[3] Powell, *Wanderings in a Wild Country*, p. 92.
[4] Castelnau, *Expédition dans les parties centrales de l'Amérique du Sud*, iv. 382.
[5] Cranz, *History of Greenland*, i. 178.
[6] Pasquarelli, quoted by Hartland, *op. cit.* ii. 246.
[7] Ratzel, *History of Mankind*, ii. 212.

main principle underlying the blood-covenant is the idea
that the transference of blood conveys to the person who
drinks it, or is inoculated with it, a conditional curse
which will injure or destroy him should he break his
promise.[1] The drinking of human blood, or of wine,
mixed with such blood, has been a form of covenant
among various ancient and mediæval peoples, as well as
among certain savages.[2] In some South Slavonic districts
compacts between different clans are even now made by
their representatives sucking blood from each other's
right hands and swearing fidelity till the grave.[3] In certain
parts of Africa, again, the partaking of human flesh, generally prepared in a kind of paste mixed with condiments
and kept in a quaintly-carved wooden box and eaten with
round spoons of human bone, constitutes a bond of union
between strangers who are suspicious of one another or
between former enemies, or accompanies the making of
a solemn declaration or the taking of an oath.[4] Among
the Bambala, a Bantu tribe in the Kasai, south of the
River Congo, cannibalism accompanies the ceremony by
which a kind of alliance is established between chiefs of
the same region. The most powerful chief will invite
the other chiefs of the neighbourhood to a meeting held
on his territory, in order to make a compact against
bloodshed. " A slave is fattened for the occasion and
killed by the host, and the invited chiefs and their followers partake of the flesh. Participation in this banquet
is taken as a pledge to prevent murder. Supposing that
a chief, after attending an assembly of this kind, kills a
slave, every village which took part in the bond has the
right to claim compensation, and the murderer is sure to
be completely ruined." [5]

For the practice of eating relatives or friends, finally,
some special reasons are given besides those already men-

---

[1] *Supra*, ii. 208.
[2] Strack, *op. cit.* p. 9 *sqq.* Rühs,
*Handbuch der Geschichte des Mittel-
alters*, p. 323. *Supra*, ii. 207 *sqq.*
[3] Krauss, 'Sühnung der Blutrache
im Herzögischen,' in *Am Ur-Quell*,

N.F. i. 196.
[4] Johnston, in *Fortnightly Review*,
N.S. xlv. 28.
[5] Torday and Joyce, in *Jour.
Anthr. Inst.* xxxv. 404, 409.

tioned. It is represented as a mark of affection or respect for the dead,[1] as an act which benefits not only the person who eats but also him who is eaten. The reason which the Australian Dieyerie assign for their endo-anthro-pophagy is, that should they not eat their relatives they would be perpetually crying and become a nuisance to the camp.[2] The natives of the Boulia district, Queensland, among whom children that die suddenly are partly eaten by the parents and their blood brothers and sisters, say that " putting them along hole " would make them think too much about their beloved little ones.[3] In the Turrbal tribe in Southern Queensland a man who happened to be killed in one of the ceremonial combats which followed the initiation rites was eaten by those members of the tribe who were present ; and the motive stated is that they ate him because " they knew him and were fond of him, and they now knew where he was, and his flesh would not stink." [4] The Bataks of Sumatra declared that they fre-quently ate their own relatives when aged and infirm, " not so much to gratify their appetite, as to perform a pious ceremony." [5] Among the Samoyedes old and decrepit persons who were no longer able to work let their children kill and eat them in the hope that they thereby might fare better after death.[6] The Indian of Hayti " would think he was wanting to the memory of a relation, if he had not thrown into his drink a small portion of the body of the deceased, after having dried it . . . and reduced it to powder." [7] Among the Botocudos old men who were unable to keep up in the march were at their own request eaten up by their sons so that their

---

[1] Dawson, *op. cit.* p. 67 (tribes of Western Victoria). McDonald, in *Jour. Anthr. Inst.* ii. 179 (natives of the Upper Mary River, Queensland). Featherman, *op. cit.* ' Oceano-Melane-sians,' p. 243 (Hawaiians). Southey, *History of Brazil*, i. 379 (Tapuyas). Marcgravius de Liebstad, *Historia rerum naturalium Brasiliæ*, viii. 12, p. 282 (ancient Tupis).

[2] Gason, in *Jour. Anthr. Inst.*

xxiv. 172. *Idem*, in Woods, *op. cit.* p. 274.

[3] Roth, *North-West-Central Queens-land Aborigines*, p. 166.

[4] Howitt, *op. cit.* p. 753.

[5] Leyden, ' Languages and Litera-ture of the Indo-Chinese Nations,' in *Asiatick Researches*, x. 202.

[6] Preuss, *op. cit.* p. 218.

[7] Bembo, quoted by von Hum-boldt, *op. cit.* v. 248.

enemies should be prevented from digging up and injuring their bodies;[1] whilst mothers not infrequently
consumed their dead children out of love.[2] The
Mayorunas considered it more desirable for the departed to be eaten by relatives than by worms;[3] and
the Cocomas, a tribe of the Marañon and Lower Huallaga,
said it was better to be inside a friend than to be swal-
lowed up by the cold earth.[4] It is impossible to decide
how far these statements represent original motives for
the custom of eating dead relatives. They may be later
interpretations of a habit which in the first place sprang
from selfishness rather than love.

The cannibalism of modern savages has often been
represented as the survival of an ancient practice which
was once universal in the human race.[5] The advocates
of this theory, however, have not generally made any
serious attempts to prove it. I have in another place put
the question how ethnographical facts can give us information regarding the early history of mankind, and
my answer was :—We have first to find out the causes of
the social phenomena ; we may then from the prevalence
of the causes infer the prevalence of the phenomena
themselves, if the former must be assumed to have
operated without being checked by other causes.[6] This
seems a very obvious method ; but, so far as I know,
Dr. Steinmetz is the only one who has strictly applied
it to the question of cannibalism. He has arrived at the
conclusion that primitive man most probably was in the
habit of eating the bodies of his dead kinsmen as also of
slain enemies. His argument is briefly as follows :—

---

[1] Voss, in *Verhandl. Berliner Gesellsch. Anthr.* 1891, p. 26.
[2] Waitz, *Anthropologie der Naturvölker*, iii. 446.
[3] von Schütz-Holzhausen, *Der
Amazonas*, p. 209.
[4] Markham, 'List of the Tribes in
the Valley of the Amazon,' in *Jour.
Anthr. Inst.* xxiv. 253.
[5] Andree, *op. cit.* p. 98 *sq.* Lippert,
Kulturgeschichte der Menschheit, ii.

279. Schurtz, *Speiseverbote*, p. 25.
Réville, *Hibbert Lectures on the
Religions of Mexico and Peru*, p. 87.
Johnston, in *Fortnightly Review*, N.S.
xlv. 28. M. Letourneau (*L'évolution
de la morale*, p. 76) calls cannibalism " le péché originel de toutes
les races humaines."
[6] Westermarck, *History of Human
Marriage*, p. 3 *sq.*

The chief impulse of primitive man was his desire for food. He fed not only on fruits and vegetables, but on flesh. His taste for animal food was not limited by any sufficient esthetic horror of human corpses. Nor was he kept back from eating them by fear of exposing himself to the revenge of the disembodied soul of his victim, nor by any fantastic sympathy for the dead body. Consequently, he was an habitual cannibal.[1] If I cannot accept Dr. Steinmetz's conclusion it is certainly not because I find fault with his method, but because I consider his chief premise exceedingly doubtful.

It is quite likely that early man preferred cannibalism to death from starvation, and that he occasionally practised it from the same motive as has induced many shipwrecked men even among civilised peoples to have recourse to the bodies of their comrades in order to save their lives. But we are here concerned with habitual cannibalism only. Although I consider it highly probable that man was originally in the main frugivorous, there can be no doubt that he has from very early times fed largely on animal food. We may further take for granted that he has habitually eaten the flesh of whatever animals he could get for which he had a taste and from the eating of which no superstitious or sentimental motive held him back. But that he at first had no aversion to human flesh seems to me a very precarious assumption.

A large number of savage tribes have never been known to be addicted to cannibalism, but are, on the contrary, said to feel the greatest dislike of it. In times of scarcity the Eskimo will eat their clothing sooner than touch human flesh. The Fuegians have been reported to devour their old women in cases of extreme distress;[2] but Mr. Bridges, who has spent most part of his life among them, emphatically affirms that cannibalism is unknown amongst the natives of Cape Horn and that

---

[1] Steinmetz, *Endokannibalismus*, p. 34 *sqq.*

[2] Darwin, *Journal of Researches*, p. 214. King and Fitzroy, *Voyages of the "Adventure" and "Beagle,"* ii. 183, 189.

they abhor it.[1] Concerning the natives of South
Andaman Mr. Man observes :—" Not a trace could be
discovered of the existence of such a practice in their
midst, even in far-off times. . . . They express the
greatest horror of the custom, and indignantly deny that
it ever held a place among their institutions."[2] We meet
with similar statements with reference to many African
tribes. The editor of Livingstone's ' Last Journals ' says
that it was common on the River Shiré to hear Manganja
and Ajawa people speak of tribes far away to the north
who eat human bodies, and that on every occasion the
fact was related with the utmost abhorrence and disgust.[3]
Amongst the Dinka the accounts of the cannibalism of
the Niam-Niam excites as much horror as amongst
ourselves.[4] The Bakongo " shudder with repugnance at
the mere mention of eating human flesh."[5] Among
the Bayaka, in the Congo Free State, " cannibalism is
never found, and is regarded as something quite abhor-
rent."[6] No intermarriage takes place between the Fans
and their non-cannibal neighbours, as " their peculiar
practices are held in too great abhorrence."[7] According
to Burton, cannibalism " is execrated by the Efiks of Old
Calabar, who punish any attempts of the kind with
extreme severity."[8] Even amongst the South Sea
Islanders there are tribes which have been known to view
cannibalism with great repugnance.[9]

It is true that the information which a traveller visiting
a savage tribe receives as regards its attitude towards

[1] Bridges, 'Manners and Customs of
the Firelanders,' in A Voice for South
America, xiii. 207. Idem, quoted
by Hyades and Deniker, Mission
scientifique du Cap Horn, vii. 259.
[2] Man, 'Aboriginal Inhabitants of
the Andaman Islands,' in Jour.
Anthr. Inst. xii. 113.
[3] Livingstone, Last Journals, ii. 39.
[4] Schweinfurth, Heart of Africa, i.
158.
[5] Ward, Five Years with the Congo
Cannibals, p. 37.
[6] Torday and Joyce, 'Ethnography
of the Ba-Yaka,' in Jour. Anthr.

Inst. xxxvi. 42.
[7] Du Chaillu, Explorations in
Equatorial Africa, p. 97.
[8] Burton, Two Trips to Gorilla
Land, i. 216 sq.
[9] Nisbet, op. cit. ii. 136. Turner,
Samoa, p. 305 (Savage Islanders).
Angas, Polynesia, p. 385 (natives of
Bornabi, in the Caroline Islands).
Powell, Wanderings in a Wild
Country, p. 247 (some of the tribes
in New Guinea). Calder, ' Native
Tribes of Tasmania,' in Jour. Anthr.
Inst. iii. 23 ; Ling Roth, Aborigines
of Tasmania, p. 111.

cannibalism is often apt to be misleading. There is nothing as to which many savages are so reticent or the practice of which they will deny so readily as cannibalism, though at the same time they are much inclined to accuse other peoples of it.[1] The reason why they are so anxious to conceal its prevalence among themselves is of course their knowledge of the detestation in which it is held by the visiting stranger ; but not infrequently they really seem to feel that it is something to be ashamed of. It has been said of some Australian natives that, " unlike many other offences with which they are justly charged, . . . this one in general they knew to be wrong," their behaviour when they were questioned on the subject showing that " they erred knowingly and wilfully." [2] At all events the reproaches of the whites have been taken to heart with remarkable readiness. Even among peoples who have been extremely addicted to it, cannibalism has disappeared with a rapidity to which, I think, there is hardly any parallel in the history of morals. Erskine wrote in the middle of the last century :—" Our experience in New Zealand has proved that this unnatural propensity can be eradicated from the habits of a whole savage nation, in the course of a single generation. I have heard it asserted that there did not exist in 1845 many New Zealand males of twenty years of age who had not, in their childhood, tasted of human flesh ; yet it is perfectly well known that at the present time the occurrence of a single case of cannibalism, in any part of those islands, would attract as much notice as in any country of Europe ; and that, when a native can be induced to talk on the subject, his information is given reluctantly, and with an unmistakable consciousness of degradation, and a feeling of shame that he and his

---

[1] Curr, *The Australian Race*, i. 77 ; Brough Smyth, *Aborigines of Victoria*, i. p. xxxvii. *sq.* ; Fraser, *Aborigines of New South Wales*, p. 56. Romilly, *Western Pacific*, p. 59 *sqq. Idem, From my Verandah in New Guinea*, p. 68. Powell, *op. cit.* pp. 52, 59 (natives of the Duke of York Group). Erskine, *op. cit.* p. 190 *sq.* (Fijians). Melville, *op. cit.* p. 341 (Polynesians). Reade, *op. cit.* p. 159 ; Kingsley, *Travels in West Africa*, p. 330 (Fans). At the same time there are many cannibals who make no attempts to conceal the practice.

[2] Brough Smyth, *op. cit.* i. p. xxxviii.

countrymen should ever have been liable to such a reproach."[1] Of the Bataks it was said some time ago that the rising generation began to refrain from cannibalism, and that those of them who had submitted to European rule thought with horror of the wild times when they or their ancestors were addicted to it.[2] Cieza de Leon remarks with some astonishment that, as soon as the Peruvian Incas began to put a stop to this practice among all the peoples with whom they came in contact, it was in a short time forgotten throughout their empire even by those who had previously held it in high estimation.[3] Moreover, the extinction of cannibalism has not always been due to the intervention of superior races.[4]

Even among peoples very notorious for cannibalism there are individuals who abhor the practice. Dr. Schweinfurth asserts that some of the Niam-Niam " turn with such aversion from any consumption of human flesh that they would peremptorily refuse to eat out of the same dish with any one who was a cannibal."[5] With reference to Fijian cannibalism Dr. Seemann observes :—
" It would be a mistake to suppose that all Fijians, not converted to Christianity, are cannibals. There were whole towns, as for instance Nakelo, on the Rewa river, which made a bold stand against this practice, declaring that it was *tabu*, forbidden to them by their gods, to indulge in it. The common people throughout the group, as well as women of all classes, were by custom debarred from it. Cannibalism was thus restricted to the chiefs and gentry, and again amongst them there is a number . . . who never eat human flesh, nor go near the biers when any dead bodies have been brought in, and who abominate the practice as much as any white man does."[6]

[1] Erskine, *op. cit.* p. 275 *sq.*
[2] Buning, in *Glimpses of the Eastern Archipelago*, p. 74.
[3] Cieza de Leon, *Segunda parte de la Crónica del Perú*, ch. 25, p. 100.
[4] Waitz-Gerland, *Anthropologie der Naturvölker*, vi. 158 *sqq.* (Polynesians). Casalis, *Basutos*, p. 303.

Ribot, *Psychology of the Emotions*, p. 295 *sq.* Schurtz, *Speiseverbote*, p. 26. *Cf.* Spencer and Gillen, *Native Tribes of Central Australia*, p. 324.
[5] Schweinfurth, *op. cit.* ii. 18 *sq.*
[6] Seemann, *Viti*, p. 179 *sq.* *Cf.* Williams and Calvert, *op. cit.* p. 179.

It should also be remembered that many cannibals eat human flesh not as ordinary food, but only in special circumstances, and that their cannibalism is often restricted to the devouring of some small part of the victim's body.

The dislike of cannibalism may be a complex feeling. In many instances sympathy for the dead is undoubtedly one of its ingredients. It is true that endo-anthropophagy is frequently described as a mark of affection, but on the other hand there are many cannibals who never eat their dead friends though they eat strangers or foes. Some cannibals exchange their own dead for those of another tribe so as to avoid feeding on their kinsmen ; [1] the natives of Tana, in the New Hebrides, are said to do so " when they happen to have a particular regard for the deceased." [2] But neither affection nor regard can be the reason why savages abstain from eating their enemies. I think that aversion to cannibalism is most likely, in the first instance, an instinctive feeling akin to those feelings which regulate the diet of the various animal species. Although our knowledge of their habits in this respect is defective, there can be little doubt that carnivorous animals as a rule refuse to eat members of their own species ; and this reluctance is easy to understand considering its race-preserving tendency.

Moreover, the eating of human flesh is regarded with some degree of superstitious dread. This is not seldom the case even among peoples who are themselves cannibals. In Lepers' Island, in the New Hebrides, where cannibalism still prevails, the natives say that " to eat human flesh is a dreadful thing," and that a man-eater is a person who is afraid of nothing ; hence " men will buy flesh when some one has been killed, that they may get the name of valiant men by eating it." [3] In those parts of Fiji where cannibalism was a national institution, only the select few, the taboo-class, the priests, chiefs, and higher orders, were deemed fit to indulge in it ; and

---

[1] Arbousset and Daumas, *Exploratory Tour to the Cape of Good Hope*, p. 123. Steinmetz, *Endokannibalismus*, pp. 22, 47.

[2] Brenchley, *op. cit.* p. 209.

[3] Codrington, *op. cit.* p. 344.

whilst every other kind of food was eaten with the
fingers, human flesh was eaten with forks, which were
handed down as heirlooms from generation to generation,
and with which the natives would not part even for a
handsome equivalent.[1] The Fijians of Nakelo, again,
who did not practise cannibalism, attributed to it those
fearful skin diseases with which children are so often
visited in Fiji.[2] The New Caledonians, who are exo-
anthropophagous, believe that if a man eats a tribes-
fellow he will break out into sores and die.[3] Among the
Maoris no men but sacred chiefs could partake of
human flesh without becoming *tapu*, in which state they
could not return to their usual occupations without
having the *tapu* removed from their bodies.[4] So also among
the Kwakiutl Indians of British Columbia a man who has
eaten human flesh as a ceremonial rite is for a long time
afterwards subject to a variety of restrictions, being considered unclean. For sixteen days he must not eat any
warm food. For four months he is not allowed to blow
hot food in order to cool it. For the same period he
uses a spoon, dish, and kettle of his own, which are
thrown away after the lapse of the prescribed time. He
must stay alone in his bedroom, and is not allowed to go
out of the house door but must use the secret door in the
rear of the house. And for a whole year he must not
touch his wife, nor is he allowed to gamble or to work.[5]
Among the West African Fans, before a cannibal meal,
the corpse is carried to a hut built on the outskirts of the
settlement. There " it is eaten secretly by the warriors,
women and children not being allowed to be present, or
even to look upon man's flesh ; and the cooking pots
used for the banquet must all be broken. A joint of
' black brother ' is never seen in the villages." [6] So also

[1] Seemann, *Viti*, pp. 179, 181 *sq.*
[2] *Ibid.* p. 179 *sq.*
[3] Atkinson, ' Natives of New Caledonia,' in *Folk-Lore*, xiv. 253.
[4] Thomson, *op. cit.* i. 147 *sq.*
[5] Boas, ' Social Organization of the
Kwakiutl Indians,' in *Report of the*

U.S. National Museum, 1895, p. 537
sq. Cf. Woldt, *Kaptein Jacobsens
Reiser til Nordamerikas Nordvestkyst*,
p. 44 *sqq.* ; Mayne, *Four Years in
British Columbia*, p. 256 *sq.*
[6] Burton, *Two Trips to Gorilla
Land*, i. 212.

among the Bambala, south of the River Congo, vessels in which human flesh has been cooked are broken and the pieces thrown away.[1] In Eastern Central Africa the person who eats a human being is believed to run a great risk; Mr. Macdonald knew a headman whose success in war was attributed to the fact that he had eaten the whole body of a strong young man, but it was supposed that if he had not been protected by powerful charms, such cannibalism might have been dangerous to him.[2]

One reason for this superstitious dread of cannibalism is undoubtedly fear of the dead man's spirit, which is then supposed not to be annihilated by the act, but to become a danger to him who partakes of the corpse. The Fijian cannibals avowed " that they were always frightened at night lest the spirit of the man they had eaten should haunt them." [3] In the Luritcha tribe in Central Australia care is invariably taken to destroy the bones of those enemies who have been eaten, " as the natives believe that unless this is done the victims will arise from the coming together of the bones, and will follow and harm those who have killed and eaten them." [4] And among the Kwakiutl Indians the taboos imposed upon a cannibal are more obligatory when he has devoured a corpse than when he has contented himself with taking bites out of a living man.[5] But it may also be that the superstitious fear of cannibalism is to some extent an outcome of the natural reluctance to partake of human flesh, just as the aversion to eating certain animals may give rise to the idea that their meat is unwholesome food,[6] and as the supernatural dangers attributed to incest spring from the instinctive horror of it.[7]

The fact that so many peoples partake or are known to have partaken of human flesh without repugnance, or even with the greatest eagerness, by no means proves

[1] Torday and Joyce, in *Jour. Anthr. Inst.* xxxv. 404.

[2] Macdonald, *Africana*, i. 170.

[3] Pritchard, *op. cit.* p. 372.

[4] Spencer and Gillen, *Native Tribes of Central Australia*, p. 475.

[5] Boas, *loc. cit.* p. 537 *sq.* Cf. Frazer, *Golden Bough*, i. 342.

[6] *Supra*, ii. 332.

[7] *Supra*, ii. 375 *sq.*

that there was no original aversion to it in the human race. It is easy to imagine that the feeling of reluctance may have been overcome by other motives, such as hunger, revenge, the desire to acquire another person's courage or strength, the hope of making an enemy harmless, or of gaining supernatural benefits. And everybody knows that men and even many animals, when once induced to taste a certain food which they have previously avoided, often conceive a great liking for it. There is evidence that this also applies to cannibalism. In 1200 Egypt was afflicted with a terrible famine, in consequence of which the poor fed even upon human corpses and fell to devouring children. An eyewitness, the Arabian physician 'Abd-Allatif, writes that, when the poor began to eat human flesh, the wonder and horror excited were such, that these crimes were in every mouth, and people were never weary of the extraordinary topic. But by degrees custom operated, and produced even a taste for such detestable repasts. Many men made children their ordinary food, eating them from pure gluttony and laying up stores of their flesh. Various modes of cooking and seasoning this kind of food were invented ; and the practice soon spread through the provinces, so that there was not a single district in which cannibalism became not common. By this time it caused no longer either surprise or horror, and the matter was discussed with indifference. Diverse rich people, who could have procured other food, seemed to become infatuated, and practised cannibalism as a luxury, using murderers as their purveyors and inviting their friends to dinner, without taking too much trouble to conceal the truth.[1] There is a similar story from Polynesia. Cannibalism, we are told, was introduced into Futuna by king Veliteki in consequence of a great tempest which brought on a disastrous famine ; but in time it became a dreadful scourge, which threatened to depopulate the island. The desire to eat human flesh arrived at such a point that wars no longer sufficed to

---

[1] 'Abd-Allatif, *Relation de l'Égypte*, p. 360 *sqq.*

furnish victims in sufficient numbers, hence the people took to hunting down members of their own tribes.[1] It has been suggested that in other islands of the South Seas cannibalism likewise arose in times of great famine, and that the inhabitants, becoming used to it, acquired a taste for human flesh.[2] In Western Equatorial Africa, again, gastronomic cannibalism has been supposed to be a practical extension of the sacrificial ceremony, neither the women nor the young men being allowed to touch the dainty.[3] That such a practice may easily grow up when the beginning has been made, is well illustrated by the words of a cannibal chief who declared that he who has once indulged in a repast of human flesh will find it very difficult to abstain from it in the future.[4]

The question whether early man was in the habit of eating human flesh may thus, I think, be resolved into the question whether his natural shrinking from it may be assumed to have been subdued by any of those factors which in certain circumstances have induced men to become habitual cannibals. For such an assumption I find no sufficient grounds. On the contrary, I maintain that it is made highly improbable by the fact that cannibalism is much less prevalent among the lowest savages than among races somewhat more advanced in culture.[5] In America, instead of being confined to savage peoples, it was practised " to a greater extent and with more horrible rites among the most civilised. Its religious inception," Mr. Dorman adds, " was the cause of this." [6] Humboldt observed long ago : — " The nations who hold it a point of honour to devour their prisoners are not always the rudest and most ferocious . . . . The Cabres, the Guipunavis, and the Caribees, have

[1] Percy Smith, ' Futuna,' in *Jour. Polynesian Soc.* i. 37.

[2] Macdonald, *Oceania*, p. 196 *sq.* Powell, *Wanderings in a Wild Country*, p. 248.

[3] Reade, *op. cit.* p. 158.

[4] Powell, *op. cit.* p. 248.

[5] See Peschel, *Races of Man*, p. 162 *sq.*; Schneider, *Die Naturvölker*, i. 186 ; Bergemann, *op. cit.* p. 53 ; Ratzel, *op. cit.* ii. 352 ; Sutherland, *Origin and Growth of the Moral Instinct*, i. 372.

[6] Dorman, *op. cit.* p. 152.

XLVI CANNIBALISM 579

always been more powerful and more civilised than the
other hordes of the Oroonoko ; and yet the former are
as much addicted to anthropophagy, as the last are
repugnant to it."[1] In Brazil, Martius found the
cannibalism of the Central Tupis to form a strange
contrast to their relatively high state of culture.[2]
Cannibals like the Fijians and Maoris were on the verge of
semi-civilisation, and the Bataks of Sumatra were already
in early times so advanced as to frame an alphabet of
their own, though after the Indian model. Among the
African Niam-Niam and Monbuttu a great predilection
for human flesh coexists with a remarkable degree of
culture ; whereas in the dwarf tribes of Central Africa,
which are of a very low type, Mr. Burrows never heard
of a single case of cannibalism.[3]

It would be very instructive to follow the history of
cannibalism among those peoples who are, or have lately
béen, addicted to it, if we were able to do so ; but the
subject is mostly obscure. The most common change
which we have had an opportunity to notice is the decline
and final disappearance of the practice under European
influence ; but we must not assume that every change
has been in the direction towards extinction. Among the
East African Wadoe and Wabembe cannibalism is,
according to their own account, of modern origin.[4] Mr.
Torday informs me that among some of the Congo
natives it is spreading in the present day. In the Solomon
Islands it has recently extended itself ; it is asserted by
the elder natives of Florida that man's flesh was formerly
never eaten except in sacrifice, and that human sacrifice is
an innovation introduced from further west.[5] Erskine
maintains that in Fiji cannibalism, though a very ancient
custom, did not prevail in earlier times to the same extent
as it did more recently ; [6] and Mr. Fornander has arrived

[1] von Humboldt, *op. cit.* v. 424 *sq.*
[2] von Martius, *op. cit.* i. 199 *sq.*
[3] Burrows, *Land of the Pigmies,*
p. 149.

[4] Burton, *Two Trips to Gorilla
Land,* i. 214.
[5] Codrington, *op. cit.* p. 343.
[6] Erskine, *op. cit.* p. 272.

at the conclusion that among the Polynesians this practice was not an original heirloom brought with them from their primitive homes in the Far West, but was adopted subsequently by a few of the tribes under conditions and circumstances now unknown.[1] For various reasons, then, it is an illegitimate supposition to regard the cannibalism of modern savages as a survival from the first infancy of mankind, or, more generally, from a stage through which the whole human race has passed.

As for the moral opinions about cannibalism, we may assume that peoples who abstain from it also generally disapprove of it, or would do so if they were aware of its being practised. Aversion, as we have often noticed, leads to moral indignation, especially where the moral judgment is little influenced by reflection. Another source of the condemnation of cannibalism may be sympathetic resentment resulting from the idea that the dead is annihilated or otherwise injured by the act, or from the feeling that it is an insult to him to use his body as an article of food ; but this could certainly not be the origin of savages' disapproval of eating their foes. Among civilised races, as well as among non-anthropophagous savages, horror or disgust is undoubtedly the chief reason why cannibalism is condemned as wrong. This emotion is often so intense that the same people whose moral feelings are little affected by a conquest, with all its horrors, made for the purpose of gain, shudder at the stories of wars waged by famished savages for the purpose of procuring human flesh for food. On the other hand, where the natural aversion to such food is for some reason or other overcome, the disapproval of cannibalism is in consequence no longer felt. But an attitude of moral indifference towards this practice has also been advocated on a totally different ground, by persons whose moral emotions are too much tempered by thought to allow them to pronounce an act as wrong simply because it creates in them

---

[1] Fornander, *Account of the Polynesian Race*, i. 132.

disgust. Thus, Montaigne argued that it is more barbarous
to torture a man to death under colour of piety and
religion than to roast and eat him after he is dead.[1]   And
he quotes with apparent agreement the opinion of some
Stoic philosophers that there is no harm in feeding upon
human carcases to avoid starvation.[2]

[1] Montaigne, *Essais*, i. 30.

[2] Diogenes Laertius, *Vitæ philoso-*   *phorum*, vii. 1. 64 (121) ; vii. 7. 12   (188).   Zeller, *Stoics*, p. 307.

CHAPTER XLVII

THE BELIEF IN SUPERNATURAL BEINGS

WE now come to the last of those six groups of moral ideas into which we have divided our subject—ideas concerning conduct towards beings, real or imaginary, that are regarded as supernatural. But before we enter upon a discussion of human behaviour in relation to such beings, it is necessary to say some words about man's belief in their existence and the general qualities attributed to them.

Men distinguish between two classes of phenomena— " natural " and " supernatural," [1] between phenomena which they are familiar with and, in consequence, ascribe to " natural causes," and other phenomena which seem to them unfamiliar, mysterious, and are therefore supposed to spring from causes of a " supernatural " character. We meet with this distinction at the lowest stages of culture known to us, as well as at higher stages. It may be that in the mind of a savage the natural and supernatural are often confused, and that no definite limit can be drawn between the phenomena which he refers to the one class and those which he refers to the other ; but he certainly sees a difference between events of everyday occurrence or ordinary objects of nature and other events or objects which fill him with mysterious awe. The germ of such a

---

[1] I do not share the objections raised by various writers to the term " supernatural." It has the sanction of common usage; and I consider it preferable to the word " super-human," when applied to inanimate things or animals which are objects of worship.

distinction is found even in the lower animal world. The horse fears the whip but it does not make him shy ; on the other hand, he may shy when he sees an umbrella opened before him or a paper moving on the ground. The whip is well known to the horse, whereas the moving paper or umbrella is strange and uncanny. Dogs and cats are alarmed by an unusual noise or appearance, and remain uneasy till they have by examination satisfied themselves of the nature of its cause.[1] Professor Romanes frightened a dog by attaching a fine thread to a bone and surreptitiously drawing it from the animal, giving to the bone the appearance of self-movement ; and the same dog was frightened by soap-bubbles.[2] Even a lion is scared by an unexpected noise or the sight of an unfamiliar object ; a horse, the lion's favourite prey, has been known to wander for days in the vicinity of a troop of these animals and be left unmolested simply because it was blanketed and knee-haltered.[3] And we are told of a tiger which stood trembling and roaring in an ecstasy of fear when a mouse tied by a string to a stick had been inserted into its cage.[4] Little children are apt to be terrified by the strange and irregular behaviour of a feather as it glides along the floor or lifts itself into the air.[5]

But the primitive mind not only distinguishes between the natural and the supernatural, it makes, practically, yet a further distinction. The supernatural, like the natural, may be looked upon in the light of mechanical energy, which discharges itself without the aid of any volitional activity. This is, for instance, the case with the supernatural force inherent in a tabooed object ; mere contact with such an object communicates the taboo infection. So also the baneful energy in a curse is originally conceived as a kind of supernatural miasma, which injures or destroys anybody to whom it cleaves ; in fact, to

[1] Morgan, *Animal Life and Intelligence*, p. 339.
[2] Romanes, *Animal Intelligence*, p. 455 *sq.*
[3] Gillmore, quoted by King, *The Supernatural*, p. 80.
[4] Basil Hall, quoted *ibid.* p. 81. See also *ibid.* p. 78 *sqq.* ; Vignioli, *Myth and Science*, p. 58 *sqq.*
[5] Sully, *Studies of Childhood*, p. 205 *sq.*

taboo a certain thing commonly consists in charging it with a curse. On the other hand, supernatural qualities may also be attributed to the mental constitution of animate beings, especially to their will. Such an attribution makes them supernatural beings, as distinct from any ordinary individuals who, without being endowed with special miraculous gifts, may make use of supernatural mechanical energy in magical practices. This distinction is in many cases vague ; a wizard may be looked upon as a god and a god as a wizard. But it is nevertheless essential, and is at the bottom of the difference between religion and magic. Religion may be defined as a belief in and a regardful [1] attitude towards a supernatural being on whom man feels himself dependent and to whose will he makes an appeal in his worship. Supernatural mechanical power, on the other hand, is applied in magic. He who performs a purely magical act utilises such power without making any appeal at all to the will of a supernatural being. [2]

This, I think, is what we generally understand by religion and magic. But in the Latin word *religio* there seems to be no indication of such a distinction. *Religio* is probably related to *religare*, which means " to tie." It is commonly assumed that the relationship between these words implies that in religion man was supposed to be tied by his god. But I venture to believe that the connection between them allows of another and more natural interpretation—that it was not the man who was tied by the god, but the god who was tied by the man. This interpretation was suggested to me by certain ideas and practices prevalent in Morocco. The Moors are in the habit of tying rags to objects belonging to a *siyid*, that is, a place where a saint has, or is supposed to have, his grave, or where such a person is said to have sat or camped. In very many cases, at least, this tying of rags is *'âr* upon the

---

[1] Though somewhat indefinite, the epithet " regardful " seems a necessary attribute of a religious act. We do not call it religion when a savage flogs his fetish to make it submissive.

[2] See *infra*, Additional Notes.

saint, and *l-'âr* implies the transference of a conditional curse.[1] Thus, in the Great Atlas Mountains I found a large number of rags tied to a pole which was stuck in a cairn dedicated to the great saint Mûlai 'Abd-ŭl-Ḳâder, and when I asked for an explanation the answer was that petitioners generally fasten a strip of their clothes to the pole muttering some words like these :—" O saint, behold ! I promised thee an offering, and I will not release (literally ' open ') thee until thou attendest to my business." If the petitioner's wish is fulfilled he goes back to the place, offers the sacrifice which he promised, and unties the knot which he made. A Berber servant of mine from Aglu in Sûs told me that once when in prison he invoked Lälla Räḥma Yusf, a great female saint whose tomb is in a neighbouring district, and tied his turban, saying, " I am tying thee, Lälla Räḥma Yusf, and I am not going to open the knot till thou hast helped me." Or a person in distress will go to her grave and knot the leaves of some palmetto growing in its vicinity, with the words, " I tied thee here, O saint, and I shall not release thee unless thou releasest me from the toils in which I am at present." All this is what we should call magic, but the Romans would probably have called it *religio*. They were much more addicted to magic than to true religion ; they wanted to compel the gods rather than to be compelled by them. Their *religio* was probably nearly akin to the Greek κατάδεσμος, which meant not only an ordinary tie, but also a magic tie or knot or a bewitching thereby.[2] Plato speaks of persons who with magical arts and incantations bound the gods, as they said, to execute their will.[3] That *religio*, however, from having originally a magical signifi-

---

[1] See Westermarck, '*L-'âr*, or the Transference of Conditional Curses in Morocco,' in *Anthropological Essays presented to E. B. Tylor*, p. 361 *sqq.*

[2] I am indebted to my friend Mr. R. R. Marett for drawing my attention to this meaning of the word κατάδεσμος. So also the verb καταδέω means not only "to tie" but "to bind by magic knots " (Athenaeus, *Deipnosophistæ*, xv. 9, p. 670 ; Dio Cassius, *Historia Romana*, l. 5), and κατάδεσις is used to denote "a binding by magic knots " (Plato, *Leges*, xi. 933). See Liddell-Scott, *Greek-English Lexicon*, p. 754; Harrison, *Prolegomena to the Study of Greek Religion*, p. 138 *sqq.*

[3] Plato, *Respublica*, ii. 364.

cance, has come to be used in the sense which we attribute
to the term " religion," is not difficult to explain.   Men
make use of magic not only in relation to their fellow
men, but in relation to their gods. Magical and religious
elements are often almost inseparably intermingled in one
and the same act ; and, as we shall soon see, the magical
means of constraining a god are often externally very
similar to the chief forms of religious worship, prayer
and sacrifice.

That mystery is the essential characteristic of supernatural beings is proved by innumerable facts. It is
testified by language. The most prominent belief
in the religion of the North American Indians was
their theory of *manitou*, that is, of " a spiritual and
mysterious power thought to reside in some material
form." The word is Algonkin, but all the tribes had
some equivalent for it.[1] Thus the Dacotahs express the
essential attribute of their deities by the term *wakan*,
which signifies anything which they cannot comprehend,
" whatever is wonderful, mysterious, superhuman, or
supernatural." [2] The Navaho word *digï'n* likewise means
" sacred, divine, mysterious, or holy " ; [3] and so does
the Hidatsa term *mahopa*.[4] In Fiji " the native word
expressive of divinity is *kalou*, which, while used to denote
the people's highest notion of a god, is also constantly
heard as a qualification of anything great or marvellous." [5]
The Maoris of New Zealand applied the word *atua*,
which is generally translated as " god," not only to spirits
of every description, but to various phenomena not understood, such as menstruation and foreign marvels, a compass
for instance, or a barometer.[6] The natives of Madagascar,

[1] Dorman, *Origin of Primitive Super-
stitions*, p. 226.   Parkman, *Jesuits
in North America*, p. lxxix. Brinton,
Religions of Primitive Peoples, p. 102.
Hoffman, ' Menomini Indians,' in
Ann. Rep. Bur. Ethn. xiv. 39, n. 1.

[2] Schoolcraft, *Archives of Abori-
ginal Knowledge*, iv. 642. Dorsey,
' Siouan Cults,' in *Ann. Rep. Bur.
Ethn.* xi. 366.   McGee, ' Siouan
Indians,' *ibid.* xv. 182 *sq.*

[3] Matthews, *Navaho Legends*, p. 37.
[4] *Idem, Hidatsa Indians*, p. 47 *sq.*
[5] Williams and Calvert, *Fiji*, p. 183.
[6] Best, ' Lore of the Whare-Kohanga,' in *Jour. Polynesian Soc.* xiv.
210. Dieffenbach, *Travels in New
Zealand*, ii. 116, 118. The word *tupua*
(or *tipua*) is used in a very similar
way (Tregear, *Maori-Polynesian
Comparative Dictionary*, p. 557).

says Ellis, designate by the term *ndriamanitra*, or god, everything that exceeds the capacity of their understanding. " Whatever is new and useful and extraordinary, is called god. . . . Rice, money, thunder and lightning, and earthquakes, are all called god. . . . *Taratasy*, or book, they call god, from its wonderful capacity of speaking by merely looking at it." [1] The Monbuttu use the word *kilima* for anything they do not understand— the thunder, a shadow, the reflection in water, as well as the supreme being in which they vaguely believe.[2] The Masai conception of the deity (*ngǎi*), says Dr. Thomson, " seems to be marvellously vague. I was Ngǎi. My language was Ngǎi. Ngǎi was in the steaming holes. . . . In fact, whatever struck them as strange or incomprehensible, that they at once assumed had some connection with Ngǎi." [3] Mr. and Mrs. Hinde use " the Unknown " as their equivalent of the word *ngǎi*.[4]

The testimony of language is corroborated by kindred facts referring to the nature of those objects which are most commonly worshipped.[5] Among all the American tribes, says Mr. Dorman, " any remarkable features in natural scenery or dangerous places became objects of superstitious dread and veneration, because they were supposed to be abodes of gods." [6] A great cataract, a difficult and dangerous ford in a river, a spring bubbling up from the ground, a volcano, a high mountain, an isolated rock, a curious or unusually large tree, the bones of the mastodon or of some other immense animal—all were looked upon by the Indians with superstitious respect

[1] Ellis, *History of Madagascar*, i. 390 *sqq.*
[2] Burrows, *Land of the Pigmies*, p. 100.
[3] Thomson, *Through Masai Land*, p. 260.
[4] Hinde, *Last of the Masai*, p. 99.
[5] See, besides the instances referred to below, Karsten, *Origin of Worship*, p. 14 *sqq.*; von Brenner, *Besuch bei den Kannibalen Sumatras*, p. 220 (Bataks) ; *Mitteil. d. Geograph. Gesellsch. zu Jena*, iii. 14 (Bannavs,

between Siam and Annam). In Lord Kames's *Essays on the Principles of Morality and Religion* there is (p. 309 *sqq.*) an interesting discussion on the dread of unknown objects.
[6] Dorman, *op. cit.* p. 300. See also Müller, *Geschichte der Amerikanischen Urreligionen*, i. 52 ; Harmon, *Voyages and Travels in the Interior of North America*, p. 363 *sq.*; Smith, ' Myths of the Iroquois,' in *Ann. Rep. Bur. Ethn.* ii. 51.

or were propitiated by offerings.[1] In Fiji " every object
that is specially fearful, or vicious, or injurious, or novel,"
is eligible for admission to the native Pantheon.[2] It is
said that when the Aëtas of the Philippines saw the first
locomotive passing through their country " they all fell
upon their knees in abject terror, worshipping the strange
monster as some new and powerful deity." [3] Of the
shamanistic peoples in Siberia Georgi writes, " All the
celestial bodies, and all terrestrial objects of a considerable
magnitude, all the phenomena of nature that can do good
or harm, every appearance capable of conveying terror
into a weak and superstitious mind, are so many gods to
whom they direct a particular adoration." [4] Among the
Samoyedes " a curiously twisted tree, a stone with an
uncommon shape would receive, and in some quarters
still receives, not only veneration but actual ceremonial
worship." [5] Castrén states that the Ostyaks worshipped no
other objects of nature but such as were very unusual and
peculiar either in shape or quality.[6] The Lapps made
offerings not only to large and strange-looking objects,
but to places which were difficult to pass, or where some
accident had occurred, or where they had been either
exceptionally unlucky or exceptionally lucky in fishing or
the chase.[7] The Ainu of Japan deify all objects and
phenomena which seem to them extraordinary or dreadful.[8] In China " a steep mountain, or any mountain at all
remarkable, is supposed to have a special local spirit, who
acts as guardian." [9] The average middle-class Hindu,
according to Sir Alfred Lyall, worships stocks or stones
which are unusual or grotesque in size, shape, or position ;
or inanimate things which are gifted with mysterious

[1] Dorman, op. cit. pp. 279, 290, 291,
302, 303, 308, 313–315, 319. Chamberlain, in Jour. American Folk-
Lore, i. 157 (Mississagua Indians).
Georgi, Russia, iii. 237 sq. (Aleuts.)
[2] Williams and Calvert, op. cit. p.
183.
[3] Lala, Philippine Islands, p. 96.
[4] Georgi, op. cit. iii. 256.
[5] Jackson, in Jour. Anthr. Inst.
xxiv. 398. Cf. Castrén, Nordiska

resor och forskningar, iii. 230.
[6] Castrén, op. cit. iii. 227.
[7] Ibid. iii. 210. Högström, Beskrifning öfver de til Sveriges Krona
lydande Lapmarker, p. 182. Leem,
Beskrivelse over Finmarkens Lapper,
p. 442 sq. Friis, Lappisk Mythologi,
p. 133 sq.
[8] Sugamata, quoted in L'Anthropologie, x. 98.
[9] Edkins, Religion in China, p. 221.

motion; or animals which he fears; or visible things, animate or inanimate, which are directly or indirectly useful and profitable or which possess any incomprehensible function or property.[1] From all parts of Africa we hear of similar cults.[2] The Negroes of Sierra Leone dedicate to their spirits places which " inspire the spectator with awe, or are remarkable for their appearance, as immensely large trees rendered venerable by age, rocks appearing in the midst of rivers, and having something peculiar in their form, in short, whatever appears to them strange or uncommon." [3] When Tshi-speaking natives of the Gold Coast take up their abode near any remarkable natural feature or object, they worship and seek to propitiate its indwelling spirit; whereas they do not worship any of the heavenly bodies, the regularity of whose appearance makes little impression upon their minds.[4] Throughout East Africa the people seem to attach religious sanctity to anything of extraordinary size; in the island of Zanzibar, where the hills are low, they reverence the baobab tree, which is the largest growing there, and in all parts of the country where hills are not found they worship some great stone or tall tree.[5] In Morocco places of striking appearance are generally supposed to be haunted by jnûn (jinn) or are associated with some dead saint.[6] As I have elsewhere tried to show, the Arabic jinn were probably " beings invented to explain what seems to fall outside the ordinary pale of nature, the wonderful and unexpected, the superstitious imaginations of men who fear" ;[7] and the saint was in many cases only the successor of the jinn. Indeed, the superstitious dread of unusual objects is not altogether dead even among our-

[1] Lyall, Asiatic Studies, p. 7.
[2] Wilson, Western Africa, p. 388 (Mpongwe). Mockler - Ferryman, British Nigeria, p. 255. Fritsch, Die Eingeborenen Süd-Afrika's, p. 340 (Hottentots).
[3] Winterbottom, Native Africans of Sierra Leone, i. 223.
[4] Ellis, Yoruba-speaking Peoples of the Slave Coast, p. 282. Idem, Tshi-speaking Peoples of the Gold Coast, p. 21.
[5] Chanler, Through Jungle and Desert, p. 188.
[6] See Westermarck, The Moorish Conception of Holiness (Baraka), passim.
[7] Idem, ' Nature of the Arab Ğinn,' in Jour. Anthr. Inst. xxix. 268.

selves. It survives in England to this day in the habit of
ascribing grotesque and striking landmarks or puzzling
antiquities to the Devil, who became the residuary legatee
of obsolete pagan superstitions in Christian countries.[1]

The common prevalence of animal worship is no doubt
due to the mysteriousness of the animal world ; the most
uncanny of all creatures, the serpent, is also the one most
generally worshipped. Throughout India we meet with
the veneration of animals which by their appearance or
habits startle human beings.[2] In the Indian tribes of
North America animals of an unusual size were objects of
some kind of adoration.[3] In certain parts of Africa a cock
crowing in the evening or a crane alighting on a house-top
is regarded as supernatural.[4] White men have often
been taken for spirits by red, yellow, or black savages,
when seen by them for the first time.[5] Religious veneration is among various races bestowed on persons suffering
from some abnormality, such as deformity, albinoism, or
madness.[6] Some South American Indians " regard as
divinities all phenomenal children, principally such as are
born with a larger number of fingers or toes than is
natural."[7] The Hindus venerate persons remarkable for
any extraordinary qualities—great valour, virtue, or even
vice.[8] By performing miracles men directly prove that
they are supernatural beings. The Muhammedan saints,
like the Christian in olden days, are believed to perform all
kinds of wonders, such as flying in the air, passing unhurt

[1] Lyall, op. cit. p. 9.
[2] Ibid. p. 13.
[3] Dorman, op. cit. p. 258. Harmon, op. cit. p. 364.
[4] Macdonald, Religion and Myth, p. 39.
[5] Avebury, Origin of Civilisation, pp. 272, 273, 375. Goblet d'Alviella, Hibbert Lectures on the Origin and Growth of the Conception of God, p. 67. Schultze, Fetischismus, p. 224. In Australia and elsewhere white people were taken for ghosts by the natives (Fison and Howitt, Kamilaroi and Kurnai, p. 248; Brough Smyth, Aborigines of Victoria, ii. 269 sq.; Tylor, Primitive Culture, ii. 5 sq.;

Spencer, Principles of Sociology, i. 170 sq.).
[6] Schultze, op. cit. p. 222. Supra, i. 270 sq. "Among many savage or barbarous peoples of the world albinos have been reserved for the priestly office" (Bourke, 'Medicine-Men of the Apache,' in Ann. Rep. Bur. Ethn. ix. 460).
[7] Guinnard, Three Years' Slavery among the Patagonians, p. 144.
[8] Monier - Williams, Brāhmanism and Hindūism, p. 350. For criminal-worship in Sicily, see Peacock, 'Executed Criminals and Folk-Medicine,' in Folk-Lore, vii. 275.

through fire, walking upon water, transporting themselves in a moment of time to immense distances, or supporting themselves and others with food in desert places.[1] When Muhammed first claimed to be the Prophet of Allah, he was urged to give proof of his calling by working some miracle ; and though he uniformly denied that he possessed such power, it was nevertheless ascribed to him even by his contemporaries.[2]

The dead are objects of worship much more commonly than are the living. Whilst the human individual consisting of body and soul is as a rule well-known, the disembodied soul, seen only in dreams or visions, is a mysterious being which inspires the survivors with awe. Mr. Spencer and Mr. Grant Allen even regard the worship of the dead as " the root of every religion." [3] But this is to carry the ghost theory to an extreme for which there is no justification in facts. The spirits of the dead are worshipped because they are held capable of influencing, in a mysterious manner, the welfare of the living ; but there is no reason to assume that they were originally conceived as the only supernatural agents existing. We have noticed that even the lower animals show signs of the same feeling as underlies the belief in supernatural beings ; and we can hardly suppose that they are believers in ghosts.

On account of their wonderful effects medicines, intoxicants, and stimulants, are frequently objects of veneration. Most of the plants for which the American Indians had superstitious feelings were such as have medical qualities ; [4] tobacco was generally held sacred by them,[5] and so was cocoa in Peru.[6] The Vedic deification

[1] Lane, *Arabian Society in the Middle Ages*, p. 49. Westermarck, ' Sul culto dei santi nel Marocco,' in *Actes du XII. Congrès International des Orientalistes*, iii. 153 sqq. Idem, *The Moorish Conception of Holiness*, p. 77 sqq.

[2] Muir, *Life of Mahomet*, i. p. lxv. sq. Bosworth Smith, *Mohammed and Mohammedanism*, p. 19. Sell, *Faith of Islám*, p. 218.

[3] Spencer, *Principles of Sociology*, i. 411. Grant Allen, *The Evolution of the Idea of God*, pp. 91, 433, 438, &c.

[4] Dorman, *op. cit.* p. 298 sq. Dorsey, ' Siouan Cults,' in *Ann. Rep. Bur. Ethn.* xi. 428.

[5] Mooney, ' Myths of the Cherokee,' in *Ann. Rep. Bur. Ethn.* xix. 439. Dorman, *op. cit.* p. 295.

[6] Dorman, *op. cit.* p. 295.

of the drink *soma* was due to its exhilarating and invigorating effects.[1]

Among all the phenomena of nature none is more wonderful, impressive, awe-inspiring than thunder, and none seems more generally to have given rise to religious veneration. But with growing reflection man finds a mystery even in events of daily occurrence. The Vedic poet, when he sees the sun moving freely through the heavens, asks how it comes that it does not fall downward, although "unpropped beneath, not fastened firm, and downward turned"; [2] and it seems to him a miracle that the sparkling waters of all rivers flow into one ocean without ever filling it.[3] "Verily," says the Koran, "in the creation of the heavens and the earth, and in the succession of night and day, are signs to those possessed of minds." [4]

The attribution of miraculous power to a certain object or being may be due to direct experience of some effect produced by it, as in the case of a medical plant, or a poisonous snake, or a miracle-working spring, or a Christian or Muhammedan saint. Or it may be based on the inference that objects with a strange and mysterious appearance also possess strange and mysterious powers. This inference, too, is in a way supported by facts. The unusual appearance of the object makes an impression on the person who sees it, and predisposes him to the belief that the object is endowed with secret powers. If then anything unusual actually happens in its neighbourhood or shortly after it has been seen, the strange event is attributed to the influence of the strange object. Thus a Siberian tribe came to regard the camel as the small-pox demon because, just when the animal had appeared among them for the first time with a passing caravan, the small-pox broke out.[5] Of the British Guiana Indian we are

[1] Whitney, ' Vedic Researches in Germany,' in *Jour. American Oriental Soc.* iii. 299. Macdonell, *Vedic Mythology*, p. 108.
[2] *Rig-Veda*, iv. 13. 5.
[3] *Ibid.* v. 85. 6.
[4] *Koran*, iii. 87.
[5] Tiele, *Elements of the Science of Religion*, i. 70.

told by Sir E. F. Im Thurn that if his eye falls upon a rock in any way abnormal or curious, and if shortly after any evil happens to him, he regards rock and evil as cause and effect, and perceives a spirit in the rock.[1] With the lapse of time the data of experience readily increase. If a certain object has gained the reputation of being supernatural, it is looked upon as the cause of all kinds of unusual events which may possibly be associated with it. When I visited the large cave Imi-ntakḳándut in the Great Atlas Mountains, the interior of which is said to contain a whole spirit city, my horse happened to stumble on my way back to my camp, and fell upon one of my servants who was carrying a gun. The gun was broken and the man became lame for some days. I was told that the accident was caused by the cave spirits, because they were displeased at my visit. When the following day I again passed the cave with my little caravan, heavy rain began to fall ; and now the rain was attributed to the ill-temper of the spirits.

Startling events are ascribed to the activity not only of visible, but of invisible supernatural agents. Thus sudden or strange diseases are, at the lower stages of civilisation, commonly supposed to be occasioned by a supernatural being, which has taken up its abode in the sick person's body, or otherwise sent the disease.[2] Among the Maoris, for instance, " each disease was supposed to be occasioned by a different god, who resided in the part affected." [3] The Australian Kurnai maintain that phthisis, pneumonia, bowel complaints, and insanity are produced by an evil spirit, " who is like the wind." [4] According to Moorish beliefs convulsions, epileptic or paralytic fits, rheumatic or neuralgic pains, and certain rare and violent epidemics, like the cholera, are caused by spirits, which either strike their victim, or enter his body, or sometimes, in the case of an epidemic, shoot at the

---

[1] Im Thurn, *Indians of Guiana*, p. 354.
[2] Tylor, *Primitive Culture*, ii. 146 sqq. Schneider, *Die Naturvölker*, i. 217. Bartels, *Die Medicin der Naturvölker*, p. 27 sqq. Höfler, ' Krank-heits-Dämonen,' in *Archiv für Religionswissenschaft*, ii. 86 sqq. Karsten, *op. cit.* p. 27 sqq.
[3] Taylor, *Te Ika a Maui*, p. 137.
[4] Fison and Howitt, *op. cit.* p. 250.

people with poisonous arrows. Indeed, unexpected events of every kind are readily ascribed to supernatural influence, in Morocco and elsewhere. Among the North American Indians " the storms and tempests were generally thought to be produced by aerial spirits from hostile lands."[1] Among the Hudson Bay Indians " everything not understood is attributed to the working of one of the numerous spirits."[2] " Dans toute l'Afrique," says M. Duveyrier in his description of the Touareg, " il n'y a pas un individu, éclairé ou ignare, instruit ou illettré, qui n'attribue aux génies tout ce qui arrive d'extraordinaire sur la terre."[3] Of the South African natives Livingstone writes, " Everything not to be accounted for by common causes, whether of good or evil, is ascribed to the Deity."[4] With the progress of science the chain of natural causes is extended, and, as Livy puts it, it is left to superstition alone to see the interference of the deity in trifling matters. Among ourselves the ordinary truths of science are so generally recognised that in this domain God is seldom supposed to interfere. On the other hand, with regard to social events, the causes of which are often hidden, the idea of Providence is still constantly needed to fill up the gap of human ignorance.

Man's belief in supernatural agents, then, is an attempt to explain strange and mysterious phenomena which suggest a volitional cause.[5] The assumed cause is the will of a supernatural being. Such beings are thus, in the first place, conceived as volitional. But a being which has a will must have a mind, with emotions, desires, and a certain amount of intelligence. Neither the savage nor ourselves can imagine a volitional being

---

[1] Dorman, op. cit. p. 350.

[2] Turner, 'Ethnology of the Ungava District,' in Ann. Rep. Bur. Ethn. xi. 272.

[3] Duveyrier, Exploration du Sahara, p. 418. See also Schneider, Religion der afrikanischen Naturvölker, p. 103.

[4] Livingstone, Expedition to the Zambesi, p. 521 sq.

[5] Already Hobbes (Leviathan, i. 12, p. 79) traced, in part, the origin of religion to the fact that when man cannot assure himself of the true causes of things, he supposes causes of them. See also Meiners, Geschichte der Religionen, i. 16.

which has nothing but a will.   If an object of nature, therefore, is looked upon as a supernatural agent, mentality and life are at the same time attributed to it as a matter of course. This I take to be the real origin of animism. It is not correct to say that " as the objects of the visible world are conceived as animated, volitional, and emotional, they may be deemed the originators of those misfortunes of which the true cause is unknown." [1] This is to reverse the actual order of ideas. Inanimate things are conceived as volitional, emotional, and animate, *because* they are deemed the originators of startling events. The savage does not speculate upon the nature of things unless he has an interest in doing so. He is not generally inquisitive as to causes.[2] The natives of West Australia, says Eyre, " are not naturally a reasoning people, and by no means given to the investigation of causes or their effects." [3] In matters not concerning the common wants of life the mind of the Brazilian Indian is a blank.[4] When Mungo Park asked some negroes, what became of the sun during the night ? they considered his question a very childish one ; " they had never indulged a conjecture, nor formed any hypothesis, about the matter." [5] I often found the Beduins of Morocco extremely curious, but their curiosity consisted in the question, What ? rather than in the question, Why ?

Whilst belief in supernatural agents endowed with a will made the savage an animist, the idea that a mind presupposes a body, when thought out, led to anthropomorphism. Impossible as it is to imagine a will without a mind, it is hardly less impossible to imagine a mind without a body. The immaterial soul is an abstraction to which has been attributed a metaphysical reality, but of which no clear conception can be formed. As Hobbes observed, the opinion that spirits are incorporeal or immaterial, " could

[1] Peschel, *Races of Man*, p. 245.
[2] *Cf.* Spencer, *Principles of Sociology*, i. 86 *sq.* ; Karsten, *op. cit.* p. 43 *sq.*
[3] Eyre, *Expeditions of Discovery* into *Central Australia*, ii. 355.
[4] Bates, *The Naturalist on the River Amazons*, ii. 163.
[5] Mungo Park, *Travels in the Interior of Africa*, i. 413.

never enter into the mind of any man by nature ; because, though men may put together words . . . . as *Spirit* and *Incorporeall* ; yet they can never have the imagination of anything answering to them." [1] Descartes himself frankly confessed, "What the soul itself was I either did not stay to consider, or, if I did, I imagined that it was something extremely rare and subtile, like wind, or flame, or ether, spread through my grosser parts." [2] The supernatural agents were consequently of necessity considered to possess a more or less material constitution. The disembodied human soul which the savage saw in dreams or visions, in the shadow or the reflection, was only the least material being which he could imagine ; and when raised to the dignity of an ancestor-god, it by no means lost its materiality, but, on the contrary, tended to acquire a more substantial body.

Of a grosser substantiality and very unlike the human shape are the inanimate objects of nature which receive divine veneration. It has been said of savages that they do not worship the thing itself, only the spirit dwelling in it. But such a distinction cannot be primitive. The natural object is worshipped because it is believed to possess supernatural power, but it is nevertheless the object itself that is worshipped.[3] Castrén, who combined great personal experience with unusual acuteness of judgment, states that the Samoyedes do not know of any spirits attached to objects of nature, but worship the objects as such ; " in other words, they do not separate the spirit from the matter, but adore the thing in its totality as a divine being." [4] Of the deification of the Nerbudda river Sir. W. H. Sleeman likewise observes, " As in the case of the Ganges, it is the river itself to whom they address themselves, and not to any deity residing in it, or presiding over it—the stream itself is the deity which fills their imaginations, and receives their

---

[1] Hobbes, *op. cit.* i. 12, p. 80.
[2] Descartes, *Meditationes*, 2, p. 10.
[3] *Cf.* Tiele, *Max Müller und Fritz Schultze über ein Problem der Religionswissenschaft*, p. 35 ; Parkman, *op. cit.* p. lxvii. (North American Indians).
[4] Castrén, *op. cit.* iii. 192. *Cf. ibid.* iii. 161, 200 *sq.*

homage." [1] The animist who endows an inanimate object
with a soul regards the visible thing itself as its body. [2]
How a being with such a body, like a tree or a stone,
can hear the words of men, can see their doings, and can
partake of the food they offer, might be difficult to
explain—if it had to be explained. But, as I have said,
the inquisitiveness of savage curiosity does not go to the
roots of things, and religion is in its essence mystery.

However, in proportion as a supernatural being comes
more and more to occupy the thoughts of its worshippers
and to stir their imagination, a more distinct personality
is attributed to it ; and at length neither the ethereal or
vaporous materiality of a departed human soul, nor the
crude substantiality of an inanimate object is considered a
satisfactory body for such a being. It is humanised also
with regard to its essential shape. The Koriaks of
Siberia believe " that objects and phenomena of nature
conceal an anthropomorphic substance underneath their
outer forms " ; but they also show the first signs of a belief
in spiritual owners or masters ruling over certain classes
of things or over large objects. [3] The supernatural being
which is originally embodied in a natural phenomenon is
gradually placed behind it. In the Vedic hymns we may
study this anthropomorphism as a process in growth.
The true gods of the Veda are almost without exception
the deified representatives of the phenomena or forces of
nature, [4] which are personified, though in varying degrees.
When the name of the god is the same as that of his natural
basis, the personification has not yet advanced beyond the
rudimentary stage ; names like Dyaus (" heaven "), Pṛthivī
(" earth "), Sūrya (" sun "), Uṣas (" dawn "), represent
the double character of natural phenomena and of the
personalities presiding over them. Speaking of the
nature of the gods, the ancient Vedic interpreter Yāska
remarks that " what is seen of the gods is certainly not

[1] Sleeman, *Rambles and Recollections of an Indian Official*, i. 20.
[2] Castrén, *op. cit.* iii. 164 *sq.*
[3] Jochelson, ' Koryak Religion and

Myth,' in *Jesup North Pacific Expedition*, vi. 115, 118.
[4] Oldenberg, *Religion des Veda*, p.
591 *sqq.*

anthropomorphic, for example the sun, the earth, and so forth."[1] Again, when the name of the god is different from that of the physical substance he is supposed to inhabit, the anthropomorphism is more developed, though never very distinct. The Vedic people always recognised behind its gods the natural forces of which they were the expression, and their physical appearance often only represents aspects of their natural bases figuratively described to illustrate their activities. The sun is spoken of as the eye with which Varuna observes mankind ;[2] or it is said that the all-seeing sun, rising from his abode, goes to the dwellings of Mitra and Varuna to report the deeds of men.[3] Even to this day the Hindu, to whatever sect he may belong, does homage to the rising sun every morning of his life by repeating a text of the Veda.[4] The god does not very readily change his old solid body for another which, though more respectable, has the disadvantage of being invisible. The simple unreflecting mind finds it easier to worship a material thing which may be seen, than a hidden god, however perfect in shape. To the common Japanese the sun is still the god to whom he prays morning and evening.[5] Whilst Chinese scholars declare that the sacrifice offered to Heaven " is assuredly not addressed to the material and sensible heaven, which our eyes see, but to the Master of heaven, earth, and all things,"[6] the people are less metaphysical ; and the Russian peasant to this day makes an appeal to the Svarog of the old religion when crying, " Dost thou hear, O Sky ? dost thou see, O Sky ? "[7] That the worship of animals survives at comparatively late stages of civilisation is probably due to the double advantage of their bodies being both visible and animate.

[1] *Nirukta*, vii. 4, quoted by Hopkins, *Religions of India*, p. 209.
[2] *Rig-Veda*, i. 50. 6. Hopkins, *op. cit.* p. 67. *Cf. Rig-Veda*, i. 25. 10 *sq.* ; i. 136. 2.
[3] *Rig-Veda*, vii. 60. 1 *sq.* See Macdonell, *op. cit.* pp. 2, 15, 17, 23 ; Muir, *Original Sanskrit Texts*, v. 6 ; Barth, *Religions of India*, p. 178 ;

Oldenberg, *Religion des Veda*, p. 591 *sqq.*
[4] Monier - Williams, *Brāhmanism and Hindūism*, p. 342.
[5] Griffis, *Religions of Japan*, p. 87.
[6] Legge, *Notions of the Chinese concerning God and Spirits*, p. 38.
[7] Ralston, *Songs of the Russian People*, p. 362.

But though man created his gods in his own image and likeness, endowing them with a mind and a body modelled after his own, he never lost sight of the difference between him and them. He always ascribed to them a superior power of action; otherwise they would have been no gods at all. In many cases, at least, he also attributed to them a superior knowledge. The Bechuanas maintain that their gods are much wiser than they are themselves.[1] In the admonitions of an Aztek mother to her daughter reference is made to a god who " sees every secret fault." [2] The gods of the Greeks and Romans were possessed of superhuman wisdom,[3] and so was Yahveh. It is true that the anthropomorphic god acquires knowledge of the affairs of men through his senses. When hearing the cry of Sodom and Gomorrah, Yahveh said, " I will go down now, and see whether they have done altogether according to the cry of it, which is come unto me; and if not, I will know." [4] But the senses of a god are generally superior to those of a man. " A god," says Orestes, " can hear even from a distance." [5] Varuna has an all-seeing eye, and the Zoroastrian Mithra has a thousand ears and ten thousand eyes.[6] In other respects, also, the bodies of gods excel the bodies of men. Sometimes they are more beautiful, sometimes they have a gigantic shape. When Ares is felled to the ground by the stone flung by Athene, his body covers seven roods of land.[7] When Here takes a solemn oath, she grasps the earth with one hand and the sea with the other.[8] In three steps Poseidon goes an immense distance; [9] in three paces Vishnu traverses earth, air, and sky.[10]

However, the tendency to make gods more and more

---

[1] Arbousset and Daumas, *Exploratory Tour to the North-East of the Colony of the Cape of Good Hope*, p. 341.

[2] Sahagun, *Historia general de las cosas de Nueva España*, vi. 19, vol. ii. 131.

[3] *Cf.* Westcott, *Essays in the History of Religious Thought*, p. 101.

[4] *Genesis*, xviii. 20 *sq.*

[5] Aeschylus, *Eumenides*, 297.

[6] *Yasts*, x. 7.

[7] *Iliad*, xxi. 407.

[8] *Ibid.* xiv. 272 *sq.*

[9] *Ibid.* xiii. 20.

[10] Grimm, *Teutonic Mythology*, i. 325.

perfect—of which I shall say more in a following chapter
—gradually led to the notion that materiality is a quality
which is not becoming to a god ; hence men endeavoured,
to the best of their ability, to grasp the idea of a
purely spiritual being, endowed with a will and even
with human emotions, but without a material body.
Like Xenophanes in Greece, the Inca Yupangui in Peru
protested against the prevailing anthropomorphism,
declaring that purely spiritual service was befitting the
almighty creator, not tributes or sacrifices.[1] In the
Bible we notice a successive transformation of the nature
of the deity, from crude sensuousness to pure spirituality.
According to the oldest traditions, Yahveh works and
rests, he plants the garden of Eden, he walks in it in
the cool of the day, and Adam and Eve hear his
voice. In a great part of the Old Testament he is
expressly bound by conditions of time and space. He
is attached in an especial manner to the Jerusalem
temple or some other shrine, and his favour is gained
by definite modes of sacrifice. At the time of the
Prophets the cruder anthropomorphisms of the earlier
religion have been overcome ; Yahveh is no longer seen
in person, and by a prophet like Isaiah his residence
in Zion is almost wholly dematerialised. Yet, as
Professor Robertson Smith observes, not even Isaiah
has risen to the full height of the New Testament
conception that God, who is spirit and who is to be
worshipped spiritually, makes no distinction of spot
with regard to worship, and is equally near to receive
men's prayers in every place.[2] Moslem theologians take
pains to point out that God neither is begotten nor
begets, and that he is without figure, form, colour, and
parts. He hears all sounds, whether low or loud ; but
he hears without an ear. He sees all things, even the
steps of a black ant on a black stone in a dark night ;

[1] Brinton, *American Hero-Myths*, p. 236.
[2] Goblet d'Alviella, *op. cit.* p. 216. Toy, *Judaism and Christianity*, p. 87.

Montefiore, *op. cit.* p. 424. Robertson Smith, *Religion of the Semites*, p. 117.

but he has no eyes, as men have. He speaks ; but not
with a tongue, as men do.[1] He is endowed with knowledge, feelings, and a will.[2] Thus the dematerialised god
still retains a mental constitution modelled upon the
human soul, with all its bodily desires and imperfections
removed, with its higher qualities indefinitely increased,
and, above all, endowed with a supernatural power of
action.

In following chapters we shall see how the moral
ideas of men have been influenced by the attributes they
ascribe to supernatural beings.

[1] Risálah-i-Berkevi, quoted by Sell,   [2] Sell, *op. cit.* p. 185.
op. cit. p. 166 *sq.*

CHAPTER XLVIII

DUTIES TO GODS

MEN not only believe in the existence of supernatural beings, but enter into frequent relations with them. In every religion we may distinguish between two elements : a belief, and a regardful attitude towards the object of this belief. At the same time the assumption that supernatural beings exist is not necessarily connected with religious veneration of them. Relations may be established with some of them to the exclusion of others. If the relations between man and a certain supernatural being are of a more or less permanent character, the latter is generally called his god.

As man attributes to his gods a variety of human qualities, his conduct towards them is in many respects determined by considerations similar to those which regulate his conduct towards his fellow men. He endows them with rights quite after human fashion, and imposes on himself corresponding duties.

Gods have the rights to life and bodily integrity. They are not necessarily either invulnerable or immortal.[1] According to ancient Egyptian beliefs, the life of a god is indeed longer than that of a man, but death puts an end to the one as well as to the other.[2] The Vedic gods were mortal at first ; immortality was only bestowed upon them by Savitr or by Agni, or they obtained it by drink-

---

[1] See Frazer, *Golden Bough*, ii. 1 *sqq.*
[2] Wiedemann, *Religion of the Ancient Egyptians*, p. 173. *Cf.* Maspero, *Dawn of Civilization*, p. 111 ; Erman, *Life in Ancient Egypt*, p. 265.

ing *soma*, or by practising continence and austerity, or by
the performance of certain ceremonies.[1]   Nor were the
Greek gods eternal by nature ; they secured immortality
by feasting on nectar and ambrosia.[2]   The Scandinavian
gods had in Idun's apples a means of preserving perpetual
freshness and youth ; but for all that they were subject
to the encroachments of age, and their death is spoken of
without disguise.[3]

Though liable to death, the invisible anthropomorphic
gods generally run little risk of being killed by men.
But the case is different with such supernatural beings
as live on earth in a visible and destructible shape.
They may be, and occasionally are, slain by human hands,
although in this case killing hardly means absolute
destruction, the soul surviving the death of the body.
But to kill such a being is in ordinary circumstances
looked upon as a dangerous act.   We have noticed above
that people are often reluctant to slay animals of certain
species for fear lest either the disembodied spirit of the
slain animal or others of its kind should avenge the injury;[4]
and the danger is naturally increased when the victim and
its whole species are regarded as divine.   Savages as a
rule avoid killing animals of their own totem, and various
statements imply that the act is disapproved of.[5]

It has been suggested that this regard for the life of a
totemic animal is due to the notion that a man is akin to
his totem.[6]   But the various taboos imposed upon him
with reference to it, and the nature of the penalties
incurred by the taboo-breaker,[7] indicate that the relation
between a human individual and the animal members of
his totem are after all somewhat different from that
between cousins.   It seems that the totemic animal is in

[1] Macdonell, *Vedic Mythology*, p.
17.   Oldenberg, *Religion des Veda*,
p. 176.
[2] *Iliad*, v. 339 *sqq*. *Odyssey*, v. 199.
Cf. Grimm, *Teutonic Mythology*, i.
317 *sq*.
[3] Grimm, *op. cit.* i. 318 *sqq*.
[4] *Supra*, ii. 491.
[5] See Frazer, *Totemism*, p. 7 *sqq*.;

Idem, *Totemism and Exogamy*, iv.
6 *sq*.
[6] Robertson Smith, *Religion of the
Semites*, p. 285.   *Cf.* Frazer, *Totemism*, p. 7.
[7] See Frazer, *Totemism*, p. 11 *sqq*.;
Spencer and Gillen, *Northern Tribes
of Central Australia*, pp. 322, 324 *sq*.

the first place looked upon as a supernatural being, and
that a person's attitude towards it depends on the degree
of dread or veneration which he feels for it. Such sacred
animals as are not conceived to be of one stock with their
devotees are equally tabooed ; in ancient Egypt, we are
told, offences against holy animals were punished even
with death.[1] On the other hand, so little respect is not
seldom felt for the totem that it is treated in a way to
which there is no parallel in the treatment of human
relatives. Speaking of the native tribes of Central
Australia, Messrs. Spencer and Gillen observe, " That the
totemic animal or plant is not regarded exactly as a close
relative, whom it would be wrong to kill, or to assist anyone else to kill, is very evident ; on the contrary, the
members of one totem not only, as it were, give their
permission to those who are not of the totem to kill and
eat the totemic animal or plant, but . . . they will
actually help in the destruction of their totems." [2] The
South Australian Narrinyeri kill their totemic animals
if they are good for food.[3] A Bechuana will kill his
totem if it be a hurtful animal, for instance a lion ; the
slayer then only makes an apology to the beast and goes
through a form of purification for the sacrilege.[4] Among
the Menomini Indians a man belonging to the Bear clan
may kill a bear, although he must first address himself
to his victim and apologise for depriving it of life.[5]
The Indian tribes in the South-Eastern States had no
respect for their totems and would kill them when they
got the chance.[6] Among the Thlinkets a Wolf man will
hunt wolves without hesitation, although he calls them
his relatives when praying them not to hurt him.[7]

In certain cases divine animals are killed as a religious

[1] Wiedemann, *Herodots zweites Buch*, p. 279.

[2] Spencer and Gillen, *Native Tribes of Central Australia*, p. 207.

[3] Taplin, ' Narrinyeri,' in Woods, *Native Tribes of South Australia*, p. 63.

[4] Casalis, *Basutos*, p. 211.

[5] Hoffman, ' Menomini Indians,' in *Ann. Rep. Bur. Ethn.* xiv. 44.

[6] Adair, *History of the American Indians*, p. 16.

[7] Boas, in *Fifth Report on the North-Western Tribes of Canada*, p. 23. For some other instances see Frazer, *Totemism*, p. 19.

or magical ceremony. Several instances of this have been
pointed out by Sir J. G. Frazer.[1] Sometimes, when the
revered animal is habitually spared, it is nevertheless killed
on rare and solemn occasions. In other cases, when the
revered animal is habitually killed, there is a special
annual atonement, at which a select individual of the
species is slain with extraordinary marks of respect and
devotion. Frazer has offered ingenious explanations
of both customs. As regards the former one he
argues that the savage apparently thinks that a species
left to itself will grow old and die like an individual, and
that the only means he can think of to avert the catastrophe is to kill a member of the species in whose veins
the tide of life is still running strong and has not yet
stagnated among the fens of old age ; " the life thus diverted from one channel will flow, he fancies, more freshly
and freely in a new one." [2] The latter custom, again, is
explained by Frazer as a kind of atonement ; by
showing marked deference to a few chosen individuals of a
species the savage thinks himself entitled to exterminate
with impunity all the remainder upon which he can lay
hands.[3] These explanations, as Frazer himself is the
first to admit, are only hypothetical, but, so far as
I know, they are the only ones yet offered. However,
it is worth noticing that certain acts accompanying the
slaughter of divine animals sometimes clearly indicate a
desire in the worshippers to transfer to themselves supernatural benefits—as when they eat the flesh of the animal,
or sprinkle themselves with its blood, or by other means
place themselves in contact with it ; and it may be that in
such cases the animal is killed for the express purpose of
communicating to the people the sanctity, or beneficial
magic energy, with which it is endowed. The Madi or
Moru tribe of Central Africa furnish an instructive
example. Once a year, as it seems, a very choice lamb is
killed by a man belonging to a kind of priestly order, who

---

[1] Frazer, *Golden Bough,* ii. 366   [2] *Ibid.* ii. 368.
sqq.   [3] *Ibid.* ii. 435.

sprinkles some of the blood four times over the assembled people and then smears each individual with the same fluid. But this ceremony is also observed on a small scale at other times—if a family is in any great trouble, through illness or bereavement, their friends and neighbours come together and a lamb is killed with a view to averting further evil.[1] Among the Arunta and some other tribes in Central Australia, as we have noticed above, at the time of Intichiuma, totemic animals are killed with the object of being eaten. But here the sacramental meal is a magical ceremony intended to multiply the species, so as to increase the food supply for other totemic groups ; the fundamental idea being that the members of each totemic group are responsible for providing other individuals with a supply of their totem.[2]

Frazer has also called attention to various instances in which a man-god or divine king is put to death by his worshippers, and has suggested the following explanation of this custom :—Primitive people sometimes believe that their own safety and even that of the world is bound up with the life of one of these god-men or human incarnations of the divinity. They therefore take the utmost care of his life, out of a regard for their own. But no amount of care and precaution will prevent the divine king from growing old and feeble and at last dying. And in order to avert the catastrophes which may be expected from the enfeeblement of his powers and their final extinction in death, they kill him as soon as he shows symptoms of weakness, and his soul is transferred to a vigorous successor before it has been seriously impaired by the threatened decay. But some peoples appear to have thought it unsafe to wait for even the slightest symptom of decay and have preferred to kill the divine king while he is still in the full vigour of life. Accordingly, they have fixed a term beyond which he

[1] Felkin, ' Madi or Moru Tribe of Central Africa,' in *Proceed. Roy. Soc. Edinburgh*, xii. 336 *sq.*
[2] *Supra*, ii. 210 *sq.* Spencer and Gillen, *Native Tribes of Central Australia*, ch. vi. Iidem, *Northern Tribes of Central Australia*, ch. ix. *sq.*

may not reign, and at the close of which he must die, the term fixed upon being short enough to exclude the probability of his degenerating physically in the interval. Thus it appears that in some places the people could not trust the king to remain in full bodily and mental vigour for more than a year; whilst in Ngoio, a province of the ancient kingdom of Congo, the rule obtains that the chief who assumes the cap of sovereignty one day shall be put to death on the next.[1]

Every reader of *The Golden Bough* must admire the ingenuity, skill, and learning with which its author has worked out his theory, even though he may fail to find the argument in every point convincing. It is obvious that the supernatural power of divine kings is frequently supposed to be influenced by the condition of their bodies. In some cases it is also obvious that they are killed on account of some illness, corporal defect, or symptom of old age, and that the ultimate reason for this lies in the supposed connection between physical deterioration and waning divinity. But, as Frazer himself observes, in the chain of his evidence a link is wanting: he can produce no direct proof of the idea that the soul of the slain man-god is transmitted to his royal successor.[2] In the absence of such evidence I venture to suggest a somewhat different explanation, which seems to me more in accordance with known facts—to wit, that the new king is supposed to inherit, not the predecessor's soul, but his divinity or holiness, which is looked upon in the light of a mysterious entity, temporarily seated in the ruling sovereign, but separable from him and transferable to another individual.

This modification of Frazer's theory is suggested by certain beliefs prevalent among the Moors. The Sultan of Morocco, who is regarded by the people as "the vicegerent of God," appoints before his death some member of his family—by preference one of his sons—as his successor, and this implies that his *baraka*, or holiness, will

---

[1] Frazer, *Golden Bough*, ii. 5 *sqq.*   [2] *Ibid.* ii. 56.

be transferred to the new sovereign. But his holiness may also be appropriated by a pretender during his lifetime, which proves that it is regarded as something quite distinct from his soul. Thus the people told me that the pretender Buḥamâra had come into possession of the Sultan's *baraka*, and that he would subsequently hand it over to one of the Sultan's brothers, who was then denied his liberty. Like the sultans of Morocco, the divine Kafir kings of Sofala, who were put to death if afflicted with some disease, nominated their successors.[1]   In ancient Bengal, again, whoever killed the king and succeeded in placing himself on the royal throne, was immediately acknowledged as king ; the people said, " We are faithful to the throne, whoever fills the throne we are obedient and true to it." [2]   In the kingdom of Passier, on the northern coast of Sumatra, whose sacred monarch was not allowed by his subjects to live long, " the man who struck the fatal blow was of the royal lineage, and as soon as he had done the deed of blood and seated himself on the throne he was regarded as the legitimate king, provided that he contrived to maintain his seat peaceably for a single day." [3]   In these cases, it seems, the sanctity was considered to be inherent in the throne and to be partly communicated to persons who came into close contact with it.[4]

Now, as we have noticed before, holiness is generally held to be exceedingly susceptible to any polluting influence,[5] and this would naturally suggest the idea that, in order to remain unimpaired, it has to be removed from a body which is defiled by disease or blemish. Such an idea may be supposed to underlie those cases in which

[1] Frazer, *Golden Bough*, ii. 10.
[2] *Ibid.* ii. 16.
[3] *Ibid.* ii. 16.
[4] Since the above was written, Sir J. G. Frazer himself has kindly drawn my attention to some statements in his *Lectures on the Early History of the Kingship* (p. 121 *sqq.*) from which it appears that in some parts of the Malay region the regalia are regarded as wonder-working talismans or fetishes, the possession of which carries with it the right to the throne. Among the Yorubas of West Africa, a miraculous virtue seems to be attributed to the royal crown, and the king sometimes sacrifices sheep to it (*ibid.* p. 124, n. 1). See *infra*, Additional Notes.
[5] See especially *supra*, ii. 294–296, 352, 353, 415 *sqq.*

even the slightest bodily defect is a sufficient motive for putting the divine king to death. It is of the greatest importance for the community that the holiness on which its welfare depends should not be attached to an individual whose organism is no longer a fit receptacle for it, and who is consequently unable to fulfil the duties incumbent upon a divine monarch ; and it may be thought that the only way of removing the holiness from him is to kill him. The same explanation would seem to apply to the killing of kings or magicians who have actually proved incapable of bringing about the benefits expected from them, such as rain or good crops,[1] although in these instances the murderous act may also be a precaution against the revenge they might otherwise take for being deposed, or it may be a punishment for their failure,[2] or have the character of a sacrifice to a god.[3] Moreover, the disease, weakness, or physical deterioration of the king might cause his death ; and, owing to the extremely polluting effect ascribed to natural death, this would be the greatest catastrophe which could happen to the holiness seated in him. The people of Congo believed that if their pontiff, the Chitomé, were to die a natural death, the world would perish, and the earth, which he alone sustained by his power and merit, would immediately be annihilated ; hence, when he fell ill and seemed likely to die, the man who was destined to be his successor entered the pontiff's house with a rope or a club and strangled or clubbed him to death.[4] Similar motives may also have induced people to kill their divine king after a certain period, as everybody is sooner or later liable to fall ill or grow weak and die. But I can also imagine another possible reason for this custom. Supernatural

---

[1] Frazer, *Golden Bough*, i. 158 *sq.* Landtman, *Origin of Priesthood*, p. 144 *sqq.*

[2] Landtman, *op. cit.* p. 144. Divine animals are sometimes treated in a similar way. In ancient Egypt, if the sacred beasts could not, or would not, help in emergency, they were beaten ; and if this measure failed to prove efficacious, then the creatures were punished with death (Wiedemann, *Religion of the Ancient Egyptians*, p. 178 ; *Idem, Herodots zweites Buch*, p. 428 *sq.*).

[3] *Supra*, i. 443.

[4] Frazer, *Golden Bough*, ii. 8.

energy is sometimes considered so sensitive to external influences that it appears to wear away almost by itself in the course of time. I have heard from Arabs in Morocco that a pretender's holiness usually lasts only for half a year. And it may be that some of the divine kings mentioned by Frazer were exposed to a similar fatality and therefore had to be slain in time.

As the right to life, generally granted to gods, is thus in certain circumstances abrogated for the benefit of their worshippers, so their right to bodily integrity may be suspended if their behaviour does not answer the expectations of their devotees. Men punish their gods as they punish their fellow men. Among the Amazulu, when it thunders or, as they say, " the heaven is coming badly," the doctors go out and scold it ; " they take a stick and say they are going to beat the lightning of heaven."[1] The negro cudgels his fetish unmercifully to make it submissive.[2] The Samoyede flogs his idol or throws it away if he does not succeed in his doings.[3] The idols of the Typees, in the Marquesas Islands, " received more hard knocks than supplications."[4] When his guardian spirit proves stubborn, the Hudson Bay Eskimo deprives it of food, or strips it of its garments.[5]

In normal circumstances men regard it as a duty, not only to refrain from killing or injuring their gods, but positively to promote their existence and comfort. According to early beliefs, supernatural beings are subject to human needs. The gods of the heathen Siberians laboured for their subsistence, engaged in hunting and fishing, and laid up provisions of roots against times of dearth.[6] When the heavens appear checkered with white clouds on a blue surface, the Maoris of New Zealand say that the god is planting his potatoes and

[1] Callaway, *Religious System of the Amazulu*, p. 404.
[2] Bastian, *Afrikanische Reisen*, p. 61.
[3] von Struve, in *Ausland*, 1880 p. 795.
[4] Melville, *Typee*, p. 261.
[5] Turner, ' Ethnology of the Ungava District,' in *Ann. Rep. Bur. Ethn.* xi. 194.
[6] Georgi, *Russia*, iii. 259.

other divine edibles.¹ The Fijian gods are described as
enormous eaters.² The Vedic gods wore clothes, were
great drunkards, and suffered from constant hunger ; ³ I
need only refer to the numerous passages in the Rig-
Veda where mention is made of the appetite or thirst of
Indra and the pleasure he has in filling his belly.⁴ An
Egyptian god cannot be conceived without his house in
which he lives, in which his festivals are solemnised, and
which he never leaves except on professional days. His
dwelling has to be cleaned, and he is assisted at his toilet
by his attendants ; the priest has to dress and serve his
god, and places every day on his table offerings of food
and drink.⁵ So also the Chaldean gods had to be
nourished, clothed, and amused ; and the stone or
wooden statues erected to them in the sanctuaries
furnished them with bodies which they animated with
their breath.⁶

The idea that supernatural beings have human
appetites and human wants leads to the practice of
sacrifice. Whatever means they may have of earning
their livelihood, they are certainly not indifferent to
gifts offered by men. If such offerings fail them
they may even suffer want and become feeble and
powerless. The Egyptian gods, says M. Maspero,
" were dependent upon the gifts of mortals, and the
resources of each individual deity, and consequently his
power, depended on the wealth and number of his
worshippers."⁷ We meet with the same idea at every
step in the Vedic hymns.⁸ Should sacrifices cease for an
instant to be offered, the gods would cease to send rain,

¹ Polack, *Manners and Customs of
the New Zealanders*, i. 244.
² Williams and Calvert, *Fiji*, pp.
184, 195.
³ Oldenberg, *Religion des Veda*, pp.
304, 366 *sqq.* Barth, *Religions of
India*, p. 36, n. 2.
⁴ *Rig-Veda*, ii. 11. 11 ; viii. 4. 10 ;
viii. 17. 4 ; viii. 78. 7 ; x. 86. 13 *sqq.*
⁵ Erman, *op. cit.* pp. 273, 275,
279. Maspero, *op. cit.* p. 110.
⁶ Ball, 'Glimpses of Babylonian

Religion,' in *Proceed. Soc. Biblical
Archæology*, xiv. 153 *sqq.* Maspero,
op. cit. p. 679.
⁷ Maspero, *op. cit.* p. 302. *Cf.*
Wiedemann, *Ancient Egyptian Doctrine of the Immortality of the Soul*,
p. 19.
⁸ *Rig-Veda*, ii. 15. 2 ; x. 52. 5 *sq.* ;
x. 121. 7. *Cf. Atharva-Veda*, xi. 7. 14
sq. ; Hopkins, *Religions of India*, p.
149 ; Kaegi, *Rigveda*, p. 31 ; Darmesteter, *Ormazd et Ahriman*, p. 329.

to bring back at the appointed hour Aurora and the sun, to raise and ripen harvests—not only because they would be unwilling, but because they would be unable to do so.[1] It was by sacrifice that the gods delivered the world from chaos, and it is by sacrifice that man prevents it from lapsing back into the same state;[2] in the 'Laws of Manu' it is said that sacrifices support "both the movable and the immovable creation."[3] The Zoroastrian books likewise represent the sacrifice as an act of assistance to the gods, by which they become victorious in their combats with the demons.[4] When not strengthened by offerings they fly helpless before their foes. Overcome by the demon Apaosha, the bright and glorious Tistrya cries out in distress :— "Woe is me, O Ahura Mazda! . . . Men do not worship me with a sacrifice in which I am invoked by my own name. . . . If men had worshipped me with a sacrifice in which I had been invoked by my own name, as they worship the other Yazatas with sacrifices in which they are invoked by their own names, I should have taken to me the strength of ten horses, the strength of ten camels, the strength of ten bulls, the strength of ten mountains, the strength of ten rivers."[5]

Men are induced by various motives to offer sacrificial gifts to supernatural beings. In early religion the most common motive is undoubtedly a desire to avert evils ; and we have reason to believe that such a desire was the first source of religious worship. In spite of recent assertions to the contrary, the old saying holds true that religion was born of fear. Those who maintain that the savage is little susceptible to this emotion,[6] and that he for the most part takes his gods joyously,[7] show ignorance

---

[1] Barth, *op. cit.* p. 36.
[2] *Rig-Veda*, x. 130. Barth, *op. cit.* p. 37.
[3] *Laws of Manu*, iii. 75 *sqq.*
[4] See Darmesteter, *Ormazd et Ahriman*, p. 327 ; *Idem*, in *Sacred Books of the East* (1st edit.), iv. p. lxviii.
[5] *Yašts*, viii. 23 *sq.*
[6] Gruppe, *Die griechischen Culte und Mythen*, p. 244 *sq.*
[7] Grant Allen, *Evolution of the Idea of God*, p. 347.

of facts. One of his characteristics is great nervous susceptibility,[1] and he lives in constant apprehension of danger from supernatural powers. We are told of the Samoyedes that a sudden blow on the outside of a tent will sometimes throw the occupants into spasms. " The Indian," says Parkman, " lived in perpetual fear. The turning of a leaf, the crawling of an insect, the cry of a bird, the creaking of a bough, might be to him the mystic signal of weal or woe." [2] From all quarters of the uncivilised world we hear that terror or fear is the predominant element in the religious sentiment, that savages are more inclined to ascribe evil than good to the influence of supernatural agents, that their sacrifices and other acts of worship more frequently have in view to avert misfortunes than to procure positive benefits, or that, even though benevolent deities are believed in, much more attention is paid to malignant ones.[3] And even among peoples who have passed beyond the stage of

---

[1] See Brinton, *Religions of Primitive Peoples*, p. 14.

[2] Parkman, *Jesuits in North America*, p. lxxxiv.

[3] Dorman, *Origin of Primitive Superstitions*, p. 391 (American Indians generally). Müller, *Geschichte der Amerikanischen Urreligionen*, pp. 84, 171, 214, 260. von Spix and von Martius, *Travels in Brazil*, ii. 243 (Coroados). Brett, *Indian Tribes of Guiana*, p. 361 *sq.* ; Im Thurn, *Among the Indians of Guiana*, p. 367 *sq.* Dunbar, ' Pawnee Indians,' in *Magazine of American History*, viii. 736. McGee, ' Siouan Indians,' in *Ann. Rep. Bur. Ethn.* xv. 184. Murdoch, ' Ethn. Results of the Point Barrow Expedition,' *ibid.* ix. 432 (Point Barrow Eskimo). Ross, ' Eastern Tinneh,' in *Smithsonian Report*, 1866, p. 306. Radloff, *Schamanenthum*, p. 15 (Turkish tribes of the Altai). Fawcett, *Saoras*, p. 57. Campbell, *Wild Tribes of Khondistan*, p. 163 *sq.* Hunter, *Annals of Rural Bengal*, i. 181 *sq.* (Santals). Mouhot, *Travels in the Central Parts of Indo-China*, ii. 29 (Bannavs of Cambodia). Man, ' Aboriginal Inhabitants of the Andaman Islands,' in *Jour. Anthr. Inst.* xii. 157. Wilken, *Het animisme bij de volken van den Indischen Archipel*, p. 207 *sq.* St. John, *Life in the Forests of the Far East*, i. 69, 70, 178 ; Low, *Sarawak*, p. 253 ; Selenka, *Sonnige Welten*, p. 111 (Dyaks). von Brenner, *Besuch bei den Kannibalen Sumatras*, p. 216. Kubary, ' Die Palau-Inseln,' in *Jour. des Museum Godeffroy*, iv. 44 (Pelew Islanders). Williams and Calvert, *Fiji*, p. 189. Percy Smith, ' Uea,' in *Jour. Polynesian Soc.* i. 114. Turner, *Samoa*, p. 21. Ellis, *Polynesian Researches*, i. 336 (Tahitians). Taylor, *Te Ika a Maui*, pp. 104, 148 ; Yate, *Account of New Zealand*, p. 141 ; Polack, *op. cit.* i. 244 (Maoris). Fritsch, *Die Eingeborenen Süd-Afrika's*, pp. 338, 339, 341 (Hottentots). Decle, *Three Years in Savage Africa*, p. 153 (Matabele). Livingstone, *Missionary Travels*, p. 435 (peoples inhabiting the country north of the Zambesi). Monrad, *Skildring af Guinea-Kysten*, p. 2 (Negroes of Accra). See also Karsten, *Origin of Worship*, p. 44 *sqq.* ; *infra*, p. 665 *sqq.*

savagery fear still remains a prominent factor in their religion. The great bulk of Homeric cult-operations lay in propitiatory rites in avoidance of evil.[1] " No one," says Sir Monier-Williams, " who has ever been brought into close contact with the Hindūs in their own country can doubt the fact that the worship of at least ninety per cent. of the people of India in the present day is a worship of fear." [2] In one of the Pahlavi texts we read that " he is not to be considered as faithful who has no fear of the sacred beings." [3] The Egyptian Amon Râ, who is praised as " the beautiful and beloved god, who giveth life by all manner of warmth, by all manner of fair cattle," is at the same time styled " Lord of fear, great one of terror." [4] The Psalmist says that " the fear of the Lord is the beginning of wisdom," [5] and, as Nöldeke points out, " the fear of God " was used in its literal sense.[6] Although the Koran has much to tell about the loving kindness of God, the god of Islam evokes much more fear than love. Faith is said by Muhammedan theologians to " stand midway between hope and fear." [7]

Hope, indeed, forms an element in every religion, even the lowest. The assumed authors of painful or alarming events became objects of worship because they were conceived, not as mechanical causes, but as personal agencies which might be influenced by the regardful attitude of the worshipper. The savage is not so irrational as to make offerings to beings from whom he expects no benefits in return. And in proportion as the deities grew more benignant and their sphere of action was extended, their worshippers became more confident, expecting from them not only mercy but positive assistance.

We may suppose that already at an early stage of

[1] Cf. Keller, Homeric Society, p. 115 sq.

[2] Monier - Williams, Brāhmanism and Hindūism, p. 230.

[3] Dînâ-î Maînôg-î Khirad, xxxix. 33

[4] Wiedemann, Religion of the Ancient Egyptians, p. 111 sq.

[5] Psalms, cxi. 10.

[6] Nöldeke, in Archiv für Religionswissenschaft, i. 362.

[7] Sell, Faith of Islâm, p. 165.

culture man, occasionally, was struck by some unexpected
fortunate event and ascribed it to the influence of a
friendly spirit with which he was anxious to keep on
amicable terms.. Among the Tshi-speaking peoples of
the Gold Coast worship is the result not only of fear,
but also of the hope of obtaining some direct advantage
or protection.[1] The pagans of Siberia accompanied their
sacrifices with words like these :—" Behold what I bring
you to eat ; bring me then in return children, cattle, and
a long life." [2] The Point Barrow Eskimo, when he arrives at a river, throws into the air a small piece of tobacco,
crying out, " Spirits, spirits, I give you tobacco, give me
plenty of fish ! " [3]   Of the Sia Indians (Pueblos) Mrs.
Stevenson writes that their religion is not mainly one of
propitiation, but rather of supplication for favours and
payment for the same—they " do the will of and thereby
please the beings to whom they pray." [4] We even hear
of savages making thank-offerings to their gods. In Fiji,
after successful fishing for turtle, or remarkable deliverance
from danger in war or at sea, or recovery from sickness,
a kind of thank-offering was sometimes presented to the
deities.[5] When certain natives of Eastern Central Africa,
after they have prayed for a successful hunting expedition,
return home laden with venison or ivory, they know that
they are indebted to " their old relative " for their good
fortune, and give him a thank-offering.[6] We are told that
in Northern Guinea, when a person has been repeatedly
fortunate through the agency of a fetish, " he contracts a
feeling of attachment and gratitude to it." [7] Yet we have
reason to suspect that the gratitude of the sacrificer is com-

---

[1] Ellis, *Tshi-speaking Peoples of the Gold Coast*, p. 17. Cf. *Idem, Yoruba-speaking Peoples of the Slave Coast*, p. 277.
[2] Georgi, *Russia*, iii. 284.
[3] Murdoch, in *Ann. Rep. Bur. Ethn.* ix. 433.
[4] Stevenson, ' Sia,' in *Ann. Rep. Bur. Ethn.* xi. 67.
[5] Williams and Calvert, *op. cit.* p. 195.

[6] Macdonald, *Africana*, i. 61. For other instances of thank-offerings see Shooter, *Kafirs of Natal*, p. 165 ; Smith, ' Myths of the Iroquois,' in *Ann. Rep. Bur. Ethn.* ii. 51 . Jochelson, ' Koryak Religion and Myth,' in *Jesup North Pacific Expedition*, vi. 25, 92. Leem, *Beskrivelse over Finmarkens Lapper*, p. 431 (Lapps).
[7] Wilson, *Western Africa*, p. 212.

monly of the kind which La Rochefoucauld defined as " a
secret desire to receive greater benefits in the future." [1]
Sometimes the thank-offering, if it may be called so, is expressly preceded by a vow. Among the Kansas the warrior,
when going to war says, facing the East, " I wish to pass
along the road to the foe ! O Wakanda ! I promise
you a blanket if I succeed " ; and turning to the West,
" O Wakanda ! I promise you a feast if I succeed." [2]
Even in religions of a higher type the offering of sacrificial
gifts is mainly a sort of bargain with the god to whom
they are offered. In the Vedic hymns the gods are
addressed by phrases like these, " If you give me this, I
shall give you that," or, " As you have given me this, I
shall give you that." [3] The singer naïvely confesses,
" I looked forth in spirit, seeking good, O Indra and
Agni, to relations and kinsmen ; but I have no other
helper than you ; therefore I have made you a powerful
song." [4] The Greeks expressed the idea connected with
their sacrifices in the proverbial saying, δῶρα θεοὺς
πείθει. [5] The ancient Hebrew view on the subject is
illustrated by the vow of Jacob :—" If God will be with
me, and will keep me in this way that I go, and will give
me bread to eat, and raiment to put on, so that I come
again to my father's house in peace ; then shall the Lord
be my God : And this stone, which I have set for a
pillar, shall be God's house : and of all that thou shalt
give me I will surely give the tenth unto thee." [6]

In many cases the sacrificial victims are intended to
serve as substitutes for other individuals, whose lives are
in danger. We have previously noticed that the practice
of human sacrifice is mainly based on the idea of substitution. [7] We have also seen that a growing reluctance to
this practice often led to the offering of animals instead of

[1] La Rochefoucauld, *Maximes*, 298.
[2] Dorsey, ' Mourning and War
Customs of the Kansas,' in *American Naturalist*, xix. 678.
[3] Müller, *Physical Religion*, p. 100.
Oldenberg, *Religion des Veda*, pp.

302–326, 430 *sqq.*
[4] *Rig-Veda*, i. 109. 1. *Cf. ibid.* i.
71. 7.
[5] Plato, *Respublica*, iii. 390.
[6] *Genesis*, xxviii. 20 *sqq.*
[7] *Supra*, ch. xix.

men.[1] But we have no right to assume that the sacrifice
of an animal for the purpose of saving the life of a man
is in every case a later modification of a previous human
sacrifice. The idea that spirits which threaten the lives
of men are appeased by other than human blood may in
some instances be primary though in others it is derivative.
The Moors invariably sacrifice an animal at the foundation
of a new building ; and though this is said to be '*ár* upon
the spirit owners of the place some idea of substitution
seems also to be connected with the act, as they maintain
that if no animal were killed the inmates of the house
would die or remain childless. A similar practice prevails
in Syria, where the people believe that " every house
must have its death, either man, woman, child, or
animal." [2] Among the Jews it is or has been the custom
for the master of each house to kill a cock on the eve
of the fast of atonement. Before doing so he strikes
his head with the cock three times, saying at each stroke,
" Let this cock be a commutation for me, let him be
substituted for me " ; and when he strangles his victim
by compressing the neck with his hand, he at the same
time reflects that he himself deserves to be strangled.[3]
These customs can certainly not be regarded as survivals
of an earlier practice of killing a human being. Moreover an animal is sometimes sacrificed for the purpose of
saving the lives of other animals. Thus in a place in
Scotland, in 1767, a young heifer was offered in the
holy fire during a cattle-plague.[4] And in Great Benin,
in West Africa, on the anniversary of the death of Adolo,
king Overami's father, not only twelve men, but twelve
cows, twelve goats, twelve sheep, and twelve fowls were
offered, and Overami, addressing his father, asked him to
look after the " cows, goats, and fowls, and everything in
the farms," as well as the people.[5] Sacrifices which are

---

[1] *Supra*, i. 469 *sq.*
[2] Curtiss, *Primitive Semitic Reli-*
gion To-day, p. 224 *sq.*
[3] Allen, *Modern Judaism*, p. 406.
[4] Grimm, *Teutonic Mythology*, ii.

608.
[5] Moor and Roupell, quoted by
Read and Dalton, *Antiquities from
the City of Benin*, p. 6, and by Ling
Roth, *Great Benin*, p. 70 *sq.*

substitutional in character may or may not be intended to satisfy the material needs of supernatural beings. In some cases, as we have seen, their object is to appease a resentful god by the mere death of the victim.[1]

We have further noticed that, in the case of human sacrifice, the victim is occasionally regarded as a messenger between the worshippers and their god even though the primary object of the rite be a different one.[2] The same is sometimes true of other offerings as well.[3] The Iroquois' sacrifice of the white dog [4] was, according to Mr. Morgan, intended " to send up the spirit of the dog as a messenger to the Great Spirit, to announce their continued fidelity to his service, and, also, to convey to him their united thanks for the blessings of the year " ; and in their thanksgiving addresses they were in the habit of throwing leaves of tobacco into the fire from time to time that their words might ascend to the dwelling of the Great Spirit in the smoke of their offerings.[5] The Huichols of Mexico often use the arrows which they sacrifice to their gods as carriers of special prayers.[6]

Not only are sacrifices used as bearers of prayers, but they are also frequently offered for the purpose of transferring curses. In Morocco every *siyid* [7] of any importance is constantly visited by persons who desire to invoke the saint to whom it is dedicated with a view to being cured of some illness, or being blessed with children, or getting a suitable husband or wife, or receiving help against an enemy, or deriving some other benefit from the saint. To secure his assistance the visitor makes '*âr* upon him ; and the Moorish '*âr*, of which I have spoken above,[8] implies the transference of a conditional curse, whether it be made upon an ordinary man or a saint, living or dead. The '*âr* put upon a saint may consist in throwing stones upon a cairn connected with his sanctuary, or making a pile of

---

[1] *Supra*, i. 438 *sqq.*
[2] *Supra*, i. 465 *sq.*
[3] *Cf.* Hubert and Mauss, ' Essai sur la nature et la fonction du sacrifice,' in *L'année sociologique*, ii. 106, n. i.
[4] See *supra*, i. 53, 64.
[5] Morgan, *League of the Iroquois*, p. 216 *sqq.*
[6] Lumholtz, *Unknown Mexico*, ii. 205.
[7] For the meaning of this word see *supra*, ii. 584.
[8] *Supra*, i. 586 *sq.* ; ii. 584 *sq.*

stones to him, or tying a piece of cloth at the *styid*, or knotting the leaves of some palmetto or the stalks of white broom growing in its vicinity, or offering an animal sacrifice to the saint.[1] This making of *'âr* is accompanied by a promise to reward the saint if he grants the request ; but the sacrifice offered in fulfilment of such a promise (*l-wâ 'da*) is totally distinct from that offered as *'âr*. It is a genuine gift, whereas the *'âr*-sacrifice is a means of constraining the saint. When an animal is killed as *'âr* the usual phrase *bismillâh*, " In the name of God," is not used, and the animal may not be eaten, except by poor people.[2] On the other hand, the animal which is sacrificed as *wâ'da* is always killed " in the name of God," and is offered for the very purpose of being eaten by the saint's earthly representatives. Nothing can better show than the Moorish distinction between *l-'âr* and *l-wâ'da* how futile it would be to try to explain every kind of sacrifice by one and the same principle. The distinction between them is fundamental : the former is a threat, the latter is a promised reward.[3] But at the same time it is not improbable that the idea of transferring curses to a supernatural being by means of a sacrifice was originally suggested by the previous existence of sacrifice as a religious act, combined with the ascription of mysterious propensities to blood, and especially to sacrificial blood, which, according to primitive ideas, made it a most efficient conductor of curses.

[1] Westermarck, ' *L-'âr*, or the Transference of Conditional Curses in Morocco,' in *Anthropological Essays presented to E. B. Tylor*, p. 368 *sqq*. Idem, *The Moorish Conception of Holiness (Baraka)*, p. 90 *sqq*.

[2] However, if the *styid* has a *mķâddem*, or regular attendant, the petitioner often hands the animal over to him alive, so that he may himself kill it " in the name of God," and thus make it eatable. Then the descendants of the saint, if he has any, and the *mķâddem* himself, have no hesitation in eating the animal, *bismillâh* being a holy word which removes the curse or evil energy inherent in *l-'âr*.

[3] When I have asked how it is that a saint, although invoked with *l-'âr*, does not always grant the request made to him, the answer has been that the saint does all that he can, but that he is not all-powerful and the failure is due to the fact that God does not listen to his prayer. But it also occurs that a person who has in vain made *'âr* upon a saint goes to another *styid* to complain of him. There is a general belief that saints do not help unless *'âr* is made on them—an idea which is not very flattering to their character.

There are obvious indications that the '*âr*-sacrifice of the Moors is not unique of its kind, but has its counterpart among certain other peoples. In ancient religions sacrifice is often supposed to exercise a constraining influence on the god to whom it is offered. We meet with this idea in Zoroastrianism,[1] in many of the Vedic hymns,[2] and especially in Brahmanism. " Here," says Barth, " the rites of religion are the real deities, or at any rate they constitute together a sort of independent and superior power, before which the divine personalities disappear, and which almost holds the place allotted to destiny in other systems. The ancient belief, which is already prominent in the Hymns, that sacrifice conditionates the regular course of things, is met with here in the rank of a commonplace, and is at times accompanied with incredible details."[3] Now, there can be little doubt that this ascription of a magic power to the sacrifice, by means of which it could control the actions of the gods, was due to the idea that it served as a conductor of imprecations ; for it was invariably accompanied by a formula which was considered to possess irresistible force. In the invocation lies the hidden energy which gives the efficacy to the sacrifice ; without Brahmanaspati, the lord of prayer, sacrifice does not succeed.[4] The Greeks actually offered anathemata, or curses, to their gods.[5] The ancient Arabs, again, after killing the sacrificial animal, threw its hair on a holy tree as a curse.[6] But so little has the true import of such sacrifices been understood even by eminent scholars, that they have been represented as votive offerings or gifts to the deity.[7]

Considering that the idea of sacrifice being a conductor of imprecations has hitherto almost entirely escaped the notice of students of early religion, it is impossible to say

[1] Darmesteter, *Ormazd et Ahriman*, p. 330.
[2] *Rig-Veda*, iii. 45. 1 ; iv. 15. 5 ; vi. 51. 8 ; viii. 2. 6. Oldenberg, *Religion des Veda*, p. 311 *sq.*
[3] Barth, *Religions of India*, p. 47 *sq.*
[4] *Rig-Veda*, i. 18. 7.
[5] Rouse, *Greek Votive Offerings*, p. 337 *sqq.*
[6] Wellhausen, *Reste arabischen Heidentums*, p. 124.
[7] Rouse, *op. cit.* p. 337. Wellhausen, *op. cit.* p. 124.

how widely it prevails and whether it also occurs in the
savage world. We know that the practice of cursing a
god not only was familiar to the ancient nations of culture,
including the Egyptians,[1] Hebrews, and other Semites,[2]
but is common among peoples like the South African
Bechuanas[3] and the Nagas of India.[4] And that the
shedding of blood is frequently applied as a means of
transferring curses is suggested by various cases in which,
however, the object of the imprecation is not a god but a
man. We have previously noticed the reception sacrifices
offered to visiting strangers, presumably for the purpose of
transmitting to them conditional curses ;[5] and a very
similar idea seems to underlie certain cases of oath-taking.
Sometimes the oath is taken in connection with a sacrifice
made to a god, and then the sanctity of the sacrificial
animal naturally increases the efficacy of the self-imprecation. In other instances the oath is taken on the blood of
an animal which is killed for the purpose, apparently
without being sacrificed to a god. But in either case, I
believe, the blood of the animal is thought not only to add
supernatural energy to the oath, but to transfer, as it were,
the self-imprecation to the very person who pronounces it.
The Mrús, a Chittagong hill tribe, " will swear by one of
their gods, to whom, at the same time, a sacrifice must be
offered." [6] Among the ancient Norsemen both the
accused and the accuser grasped the holy ring kept for
that purpose on the altar, stained with the blood of a
sacrificial bull, and made oath by invoking Freyr, Niordr,
and the almighty among the Asas.[7] At Athens a person
who charged another with murder made an oath with
imprecations upon himself and his family and his house,
standing upon the entrails of a boar, a ram, and a bull,

---

[1] *Book of the Dead*, ch. 125.
[2] *Exodus*, xxii. 28. 1 *Samuel*, xvii.
43. *Isaiah*, viii. 21.
[3] Chapman, *Travels in the Interior
of South Africa*, i. 45 *sq.*
[4] Woodthorpe, ' Wild Tribes inhabiting the so-called Naga Hills,'
in *Jour. Anthr. Inst.* xi. 70.
[5] *Supra*, i. 590 *sq.*

[6] Lewin, *Wild Races of South-
Eastern India*, p. 233. *Cf. ibid.* p.
244 (Pankhos and Bunjogees).
[7] *Landnámabók*, iv. 7 (*Islendinga
Sögur*, i. 258). Lea, *Superstition and
Force*, p. 27. Keyser, *Efterladte
Skrifter*, ii. pt. i. 388. Gummere,
Germanic Origins, p. 301.

which had been sacrificed by special persons on the appointed days.[1] Tyndareus " sacrificed a horse and swore the suitors of Helen, making them stand on the pieces of the horse," the oath being to defend Helen and him who might be chosen to marry her if ever they should be wronged.[2] One of the three binding forms of oath prevalent among the Sânsiya in India is to " kill a cock and pouring its blood on the ground swear over it." [3] When the Annamese swear by heaven and earth, they often kill a buffalo or he-goat and drink its blood.[4] Among the ancient Arabs comrades in arms swore fidelity to each other by dipping their hands in the blood of a camel killed for the purpose.[5]

The last mentioned case, which implies shedding of blood as a means of sealing a compact, leads us to a special class of sacrifices offered to gods, namely, the covenant sacrifice, known to us from Semitic antiquity. The Hebrews, as Professor Robertson Smith observes,[6] thought of the national religion as constituted by a formal covenant sacrifice at Mount Sinai, where half of the blood of the sacrificed oxen was sprinkled on the altar and the other half on the people,[7] or even by a still earlier covenant rite in which the parties were Yahve and Abraham ;[8] and the idea of sacrifice establishing a covenant between God and man is also apparent in the Psalms.[9] In various cases recorded in the Old Testament sacrifice is accompanied by a sacrificial meal ;[10] " the god and his worshippers are wont to eat and drink together, and by this token their fellowship is declared

---

[1] Demosthenes, *Oratio (xxiii.) contra Aristocratem*, 67 *sq.*, p. 642.
[2] Pausanias, iii. 20. 9. For Homeric oath sacrifices see *Iliad*, iii. 260 *sqq.* ; xix. 250 *sqq.* ; Keller, *Homeric Society*, p. 176 *sqq.*
[3] Crooke, *Tribes and Castes of the North-Western Provinces*, iv. 281.
[4] Kohler, *Rechtsvergleichende Studien*, p. 208.
[5] Wellhausen, *Reste arabischen Heidentums*, p. 128.

[6] Robertson Smith, *Religion of the Semites*, p. 318 *sq.*
[7] *Exodus*, xxiv. 4 *sqq.*
[8] *Genesis*, xv. 8 *sqq.*
[9] *Psalms*, l. 5.
[10] *Genesis*, xxxi. 54. *Exodus*, xxiv. 11. 1 *Samuel*, xi. 15. Wellhausen says (*Prolegomena to the History of Israel*, p. 71) that, according to the practice of the older period, a meal was nearly always connected with a sacrifice.

and sealed." [1] Robertson Smith and his followers have
represented this as an act of communion, as a sacrament
in which the whole kin—the god with his clansmen—
unite, and in partaking of which each member renews his
union with the god and with the rest of the clan. At
first, we are told, the god—that is, the totem god—himself was eaten, whilst at a later stage the practice of
eating the god was superseded by the practice of eating
with the god. Communion still remains the core of
sacrifice ; and it is said that only subsequently the practice of offering gifts to the deity develops out of the
sacrificial union between the worshippers and their god.[2]
But I venture to think that the whole of this theory is
based upon a misunderstanding of the Semitic evidence,
and that existing beliefs in Morocco throw new light upon
the covenant sacrifice.

The Moorish covenant (*l-'ahd*) is closely connected with
the Moorish *'âr*. Whilst *l-'âr* is one-sided, *l-'ahd* is
mutual, both parties transferring conditional curses to
one another. And here again the transference requires a
material conductor. Among the Arabs of the plains and
the Berbers of Central Morocco chiefs, in times of rebellion, exchange their cloaks or turbans, and it is believed
that if any of them should break the covenant he would
be punished with some grave misfortune. Among the
Ulád Bu 'Azîz, in the province of Dukkâla, it is a
common custom for persons who wish to be reconciled
after a quarrel to go to a holy man and in his presence
join their right hands so that the fingers of the one go
between the fingers of the other, after which the saint
throws his· cloak over the united hands, saying, " This is
'ahd between you." Or they may in a similar manner
join their hands at a saint's tomb over the head of the
box under which the saint is buried, or they may perform
the same ceremony simply in the presence of some
friends. In either case the joining of hands is usually

[1] Robertson Smith, *op. cit.* p. 271.   *Introduction to the History of*
[2] *Ibid*. lec. ix. *sqq.* Hartland,   *Religion*, p. 225.
Legend of Perseus, ii. 236. Jevons,

accompanied by a common meal, and frequently the hands are joined over the dish after eating. If a person who has thus made a compact with another is afterwards guilty of a breach of faith, it is said that " God and the food will repay him " ; in other words, the conditional curse embodied in the food which he ate will be realised. All over Morocco the usual method of sealing a compact of friendship is by eating together, especially at the tomb of some saint. As we have noticed above,[1] the sacredness of the place adds to the efficacy of the imprecation, but its vehicle, the real punisher, is the eaten food, because it contains a conditional curse.

The '*ahd* of the Moors helps us to understand the covenant sacrifice of the ancient Semites. The only difference between them is that the former is a method of establishing a compact between men and men, whilst the latter established a compact between men and their god. The idea of a mutual transference of conditional curses undoubtedly underlies both. It should be noticed that in the Old Testament also, as among the Moors, we meet with human covenants made by the parties eating together.[2] Thus the Israelites entered into alliance with the Gibeonites by taking of their victuals, without consulting Yahve, and the meal was expressly followed by an oath.[3] In other instances, again, the common dish consisted of sacrificial food, either because the sacredness of such food was supposed to make the conditional curse embodied in it more efficacious, or because the deity was included as a third party to the covenant.

Whilst in some cases the object of a sacrifice is to transfer conditional curses either to the god to whom it is made, or to both the god and the worshipper, the victim or article offered may in other instances be used as a vehicle for transferring benign virtue to him who offered it or to other persons. As we have noticed

---

[1] *Supra*, i. 587.
[2] *Genesis*, xxvi. 30 ; xxxi. 46. 2 *Samuel*, iii. 20 *sq.* Robertson Smith,
op. cit. p. 271. Nowack, *Lehrbuch der hebräischen Archäologie*, i. 359.
[3] *Joshua*, ix. 14 *sq.*

above, a sacrifice is very frequently believed to be
endowed with beneficial magic energy in consequence of
its contact or communion with the supernatural being
to which it is offered, and this energy is then supposed
to have a salutary effect upon the person who comes in
touch with it. I have said before that in Morocco magic
virtue is ascribed to various parts of the sheep which is
sacrificed at the " Great Feast," and that every offering
to a holy person, especially a dead saint, is considered
to participate to some extent in his sanctity.[1] The Vedic
people regarded sacrificial food as a kind of medicine.[2]
The Siberian Kachinzes blessed their huts with sacrificial
milk.[3] The Lapps strewed the ashes of their burnt-
offerings upon their heads.[4] It is quite possible that in
some instances a desire to receive the benefit of the
supernatural energy with which the sacrifice is endowed
is by itself a sufficient motive for offering it to a god.

As is the case with other rites, sacrifices also have a
strong tendency to survive the ideas from which they
sprang. Thus when the materialistic conception of the
nature of gods faded away, offerings continued to be
made to them, though their meaning was changed. As
Sir E. B. Tylor observes, " the idea of practical accept-
ableness of the food or valuables presented to the deity,
begins early to shade into the sentiment of divine gratification or propitiation by a reverent offering, though in
itself of not much account to so mighty a divine
personage." [5] Sacrifice then becomes mainly, or exclusively, a symbol of humility and reverence. Even in the
Rig-Veda, in spite of its crude materialism, we meet with
indications of the idea that the value of a sacrifice lies in
the feelings of the worshipper ; if unable to offer an ox or
cow, the singer hopes that a small gift from the heart, a
fagot, a libation, a bundle of grass, offered with reverence,

---

[1] *Supra*, i. 445 *sq.* See also Westermarck, ' The Popular Ritual of the
Great Feast in Morocco,' in *Folk-
Lore*, xxii. 145 *sqq.* ; Hubert and
Mauss, *loc. cit.* p. 133.
[2] Oldenberg, *Die Religion des Veda*,
p. 328 *sqq.*
[3] Georgi, *op. cit.* iii. 275.
[4] von Düben, *Lappland och Lapparne*, p. 258.
[5] Tylor, *Primitive Culture*, ii. 394.

will be more acceptable to the god than butter or honey.[1] In Greece, though the sacrificial ritual remained unchanged till the end of paganism, we frequently come upon the advanced reflection that righteousness is the best sacrifice, that the poor man's slight offering avails more with the deity than hecatombs of oxen.[2] According to Porphyry, the gods have no need of banquets and magnificent sacrifices, but we should with the greatest alacrity make a moderate oblation to them of our own property, as " the honours which we pay to the gods should be accompanied by the same promptitude as that with which we give the first seat to worthy men."[3] It is said in the Talmud that " he who offers humility unto God and man, shall be rewarded with a reward as if he had offered all the sacrifices in the world."[4]

I have here spoken of the *practice* of sacrifice and the ideas on which it is based. But sacrifice has also a moral value attached to it. Though no doubt in many cases optional, it is under various circumstances regarded as a stringent duty. This is particularly the case with the offerings regularly made by the community at large on special occasions fixed by custom.

As supernatural beings have material needs like men, they also possess property like men, and this must not be interfered with. The Fjort of West Africa believe that the spirits of the rivers kill those who drink their waters and sometimes punish those who fish in them for greediness, by making them deaf and dumb.[5] When their chief god " played " by thundering, the Amazulu said to him who was frightened, " Why do you start, because the lord plays ? What have you taken which belongs to him ? "[6] The Fijians speak of a deluge

[1] *Rig-Veda*, viii. 19. 5. Kaegi, *op. cit.* p. 30.

[2] Farnell, *Cults of the Greek States,* i. 101. Schmidt, *Die Ethik der alten Griechen,* ii. 43. Westcott, *Essays in the History of Religious Thought,* p. 116.

[3] Porphyry, *De abstinentia ab esu animalium,* ii. 60.

[4] Deutsch, *Literary Remains,* p. 55.

[5] Dennett, *Folklore of the Fjort,* p. 5 *sq.*

[6] Callaway, *Religious System of the Amazulu,* p. 57.

the cause of which was the killing of a favourite bird
belonging to the god Ndengei by two mischievous lads,
his grandsons.[1] In Efate, of the New Hebrides, to steal
cocoanuts which are consecrated to the worship of the
gods at some forthcoming festival " would be regarded
as a much greater offence than common stealing." [2] So,
too, the pillaging of a temple has commonly been looked
upon as the worst kind of robbery.[3] Among the
Hebrews any trespass upon ground which was hallowed
by the localised presence of Yahveh was visited with
extreme punishment.[4] In Arabia people were forbidden
to cut fodder, fell trees, or hunt game within the
precincts of a sacred place.[5] The Moors believe that a
person would incur a very great risk indeed by cutting the
branch of a tree or shooting a bird in the *horm* of a *siyid*,
or dead saint. The *horm* is the homestead and domain
of the saint, and he is the owner of everything within its
borders. But the offence is not exclusively one against
property, and it may be doubted whether originally any
clear idea of ownership at all was connected with it.
In a holy place all objects are endowed with supernatural
energy, and may therefore themselves, as it were, avenge
injuries committed against them. This is true of the
horm of a saint, as well as of any other sanctuary, all his
belongings being considered to partake of his sanctity.
But, as a matter of fact, the so-called tomb of a saint is
frequently a place which was at first regarded as holy by
itself, on account of its natural appearance, and was only
afterwards traditionally associated with a holy person,
when the need was felt of giving an anthropomorphous
interpretation of its holiness.[6] According to early ideas a

---

[1] Williams and Calvert, *op. cit.* p.
212.

[2] Macdonald, *Oceania*, p. 208.

[3] Schmidt, *Ethik der alten Griechen*,
ii. 19 *sq.* Cicero, *De legibus*, ii. 9,
16 ; Mommsen, *Römisches Strafrecht*, p. 458. Wilda, *Strafrecht der
Germanen*, p. 950 ; Dahn, *Bausteine*,
ii. 106 (Teutons). Du Boys, *Histoire
du droit criminel des peuples mo-*

dernes, ii. 605 *sq.* Filangieri, *La
scienza della legislazione*, iv. 205
(laws of Christian countries).

[4] Montefiore, *Hibbert Lectures on
the Religion of the Ancient Hebrews*,
p. 38.

[5] Wellhausen, *Reste arabischen Heidentums*, p. 106.

[6] Westermarck, ' Sul culto dei
santi nel Marocco,' in *Actes du XII.*

sacred object cannot with impunity be appropriated for ordinary purposes ;[1] but, on the other hand, visitors are allowed to take a handful of earth from the tomb of the saint or in certain cases to cut a small piece of wood from some tree growing in his *ḥorm*, to be used as a charm.[2] It also deserves notice that the saint protects not only his own property, but any goods left in his care ; hence the country Arabs of Morocco often have their granaries in the *ḥorŭmat* of saints.

Moreover, anybody who takes refuge at a *siyid* is for the moment safe. The right of sanctuary is regarded as very sacred in Morocco, especially in those parts of the country where the Sultan's government has no power. To violate it is an outrage which the saint is sure to punish. I saw a madman whose insanity was attributed to the fact that he once had forcibly removed a fugitive from a saint's tomb ; and of a late Grand-Vizier it is said that he was killed by two powerful saints of Dukkâla, on whose refugees he had laid violent hands. Even the descendants of the saint or his manager (*mḳâddem*) can only by persuasion and by promising to mediate between the suppliant and his pursuer induce the former to leave the place.[3] As is well known, this is not a custom restricted to Morocco. Among many peoples, at different stages of civilisation, sacred places give shelter to refugees.[4]

Among the Central Australian Arunta there is in each local totem centre a spot called *ertnatulunga*, in the immediate neighbourhood of which everything is sacred and must on no account be hurt. The plants growing there are never interfered with in any way ; animals which come there are safe

Congrès International des Orientalistes, iii. 175. *Cf.* Goldziher, *Muhammedanische Studien,* ii. 344 *sqq.*
[1] See Robertson Smith, *op. cit.* lec. iv. and Additional Note B.
[2] Westermarck, in *Actes du XII. Congrès des Orientalistes,* iii. 167 *sq.*
[3] See Westermarck, *The Moorish Conception of Holiness,* p. 116 *sqq.*

[4] See Andree, ' Die Asyle,' in *Globus,* xxxviii. 301 *sq.* ; Frazer, ' Origin of Totemism,' in *Fortnightly Review,* N. S. lxv. 650 *sqq.* ; Hellwig, *Das Asylrecht der Naturvölker, passim;* Bulmerincq, *Das Asylrecht, passim;* Fuld, ' Das Asylrecht im Alterthum und Mittelalter,' in *Zeitschr. f. vergl. Rechtswiss.* vii. p. 103 *sqq.*

from the spear of the hunter; and a man who was being pursued by others would not be touched so long as he remained at this spot.[1]   In Upolu, one of the Samoan Islands, a certain god, Vave, had his residence in an old tree, which served as an asylum for murderers and other great offenders; if that tree was reached by the criminal he was safe, and the avenger could pursue no farther, but had to wait for investigation and trial.[2]   In the island of Hawaii there were two *puhonuas*, or cities of refuge, which afforded an inviolable sanctuary even to the vilest criminal who entered their precincts, and during war offered safe retreat to all the non-combatants of the neighbouring districts who flocked into them, as well as to the vanquished. As soon as the fugitive had entered, he repaired to the presence of the idol and made a short ejaculatory address, expressive of his obligations to him in reaching the place with security.   The priests and their adherents would immediately put to death anyone who should have the temerity to follow or molest those who were once within the pale of the *pahu tabu*, and, as they put it, under the shade or protection of the spirit of Keave, the tutelary deity of the place.   After a short period, probably not more than two or three days, the refugee was permitted to return unmolested to his home, the divine protection being supposed still to abide with him.[3]   In Tahiti the *morais*, or holy places, likewise gave shelter to criminals of every kind.[4]   At Maiva, in the South-Eastern part of New Guinea, "should a man be pursued by an enemy and take refuge in the *dubu* [or temple], he is perfectly safe inside.   Any one smiting another inside the *dubu* would have his arms and legs shrivelled up, and he could do nothing but wish to die."[5]

In many North American tribes certain sacred places or whole villages served as asylums, in which those who were pursued by the tribe or even an enemy were safe as soon as they had obtained admission.[6]   Among the Acagchemem Indians, in the valley and neighbourhood of San Juan Capistrano in California, a criminal who had fled to a *vanquech*, or place of worship, was secure not only as long as he remained there, but

[1] Spencer and Gillen, *Native Tribes of Central Australia*, p. 133 *sqq.*
[2] Turner, *Samoa*, p. 64 *sq.*
[3] Ellis, *Tour through Hawaii*, p. 155 *sqq.*   Jarves, *History of the Hawaiian Islands*, p. 28 *sq.*
[4] Turnbull, *Voyage round the World*, p. 366. Wilson, *Missionary Voyage to the Southern Pacific Ocean*, p. 351.
[5] Chalmers and Gill, *Work and Adventure in New Guinea*, p. 186.
[6] Adair, *History of the American Indians*, pp. 158, 159, 416. Bradbury, *Travels in the Interior of America*, p. 165 *sq.* (Aricaras of the Missouri). Bourke, 'Medicine-Men of the Apache,' in *Ann. Rep. Bur. Ethn.* ix. 453.   Kohl, *Kitchi-Gami*, p. 271 (Chippewas).

also after he had left the sanctuary. It was not even lawful to
mention his crime, but all that the avenger could do to him was
to point at him and deride him, saying, "Lo, a coward, who
has been forced to flee to Chinigchinich!" This flight, however, turned the punishment from the head of the criminal upon
that of some of his relatives.[1]

The South-Central African Barotse have a city of refuge.
"Anyone incurring the king's wrath, or committing a crime,
may find safety by fleeing to this town. The man in charge
of it is expected to plead for him before the chief, and he can
then return to his house in peace."[2] Among the same people
the tombs of chiefs are sanctuaries or places of refuge,[3] and this
is also the case among the Kafirs.[4] So, too, in the monarchical
states of the Gallas homicides enjoy a legal right of asylum if
they have succeeded in taking refuge in a hut near the burial-
place of the king.[5] Among the Ovambo in South-Western
Africa the village of a great chief is abandoned at his death,
except by the members of a certain family, who remain there to
prevent it from falling into utter decay. Condemned criminals
who contrive to escape to one of these deserted villages are safe,
at least for a time ; for not even the chief himself may pursue a
fugitive into the sacred place.[6] In Congo Français there are
several sanctuaries :—"The great one in the Calabar district is
at Omon. Thither mothers of twins, widows, thieves, and
slaves fly, and if they reach it are safe."[7] In Ashantee a slave
who flies to a temple and dashes himself against the fetish cannot
easily be brought back to his master.[8] Among the Negroes of
Accra criminals used to "seat themselves upon the fetish," that
is, place themselves under its protection ; but murderers who
sought refuge with the fetish were always liable to be delivered
up to their pursuers.[9] A traveller in the seventeenth century
tells us that in Fetu, on the Gold Coast, a criminal who
deserved death was pardoned by taking refuge in the hut of the
high-priest.[10] Among the Krumen of the Grain Coast the
house of the high-priest (*bodio*) "is a sanctum to which culprits

[1] Bancroft, *Native Races of the
Pacific States*, iii. 167. Boscana, in
[Robinson,] *Life in California*, p.
262 *sq.*
[2] Arnot, *Garenganze*, p. 77.
[3] Decle, *Three Years in Savage
Africa*, p. 75.
[4] Rehme, ' Das Recht der Amaxosa,' in *Zeitschr. f. vergl. Rechtswiss.*
x. 51.
[5] Paulitschke, *Ethnographie Nord-*

*ost-Afrikas, Die geistige Cultur der
Danâkil, &c.* p. 157.
[6] Schinz, *Deutsch-Südwest-Afrika*,
p. 312.
[7] Kingsley, *Travels in West Africa*,
p. 466.
[8] Bowdich, *Mission to Ashantee*, p.
265. *Cf.* Monrad, *op. cit.* p. 42.
[9] Monrad, *op. cit.* p. 89.
[10] Müller, *Die Africanische Landschafft Fetu*, p. 75.

may betake themselves without the danger of being removed by anyone except by the *bodio* himself."[1] In Usambara a murderer cannot be arrested at any of the four places where the great wizards of the country reside.[2]

In other Muhammedan countries besides Morocco the tombs of saints, as also the mosques, are or have been places of refuge.[3] In Persia the great number of such asylums proved so injurious to public safety, that about the middle of the nineteenth century only three mosques were left which were recognised by the government as affording protection to criminals of every description.[4] Among the Hebrews the right of asylum originally belonged to all altars,[5] but on the abolition of the local altars it was limited to certain cities of refuge.[6] According to the Old Testament manslayers could find shelter there only in the case of involuntary homicide ; but this was undoubtedly a narrowing of the ancient custom. Many heathen sanctuaries of the Phœnicians and Syrians retained even in Roman times what seems to have been an unlimited right of asylum ;[7] and at certain Arabian shrines the god likewise gave shelter to all fugitives without distinction, and even stray or stolen cattle that reached the holy ground could not be reclaimed by their owners.[8]

On the Coast of Malabar a certain temple situated to the south-east of Calicut affords protection to thieves and adulterous women belonging to the Brahmin caste, but this privilege is reckoned among the sixty-four *anatcharams*, or "abuses," which were introduced by Brahmanism.[9] Among the Káfirs of the Hindu-Kush there are several "cities of refuge," the largest being the village of Mergrom, which is almost entirely peopled by *chiles*, or descendants of persons who have slain some fellow tribesman.[10] In the Caucasus holy groves offer refuge to criminals, as also to animals, which cannot be shot there.[11]

In Greece many sanctuaries possessed the right of asylum down to the end of paganism, and any violation of this right

[1] Wilson, *Western Africa*, p. 129.
[2] Krapf, *Reisen in Ost-Afrika*, ii. 132.
[3] Goldziher, *Muhammedanische Studien*, i. 237 *sq.* Quatremère, 'Mémoire sur les asiles chez les Arabes,' in *Mémoires de l'Institut de France, Académie des Inscriptions et Belles-Lettres*, xv. pt. ii. 313 *sq.*
[4] Polak, *Persien*, ii. 83 *sqq.* Brugsch, *Im Lande der Sonne*, p. 246.
[5] *Exodus*, xxi. 13 *sq.* Cf. Robert-son Smith, *Religion of the Semites*, p. 148, n. 1.
[6] *Numbers*, xxxv. 11 *sqq.* *Deuteronomy*, iv. 41 *sqq.* ; xix. 2 *sqq.*
[7] Robertson Smith, *op. cit.* p. 148.
[8] *Ibid.* p. 148 *sq.*
[9] Graul, *Reise nach Ostindien*, iii. 332, 335.
[10] Scott Robertson, *Káfirs of the Hindu-Kush*, p. 441.
[11] Hahn, *Kaukasische Reisen*, p. 122.

was supposed to be severely punished by the deity.[1] According
to an old tradition, Romulus established a sanctuary, dedicated
to some unknown god or spirit, on the slope of the Capitoline
Hill, proclaiming that all who resorted to it, whether bond or
free, should be safe.[2] This tradition, and also some other statements made by Latin writers,[3] seem to indicate that from
ancient times certain sacred places in Rome gave shelter to
refugees ; but it was only in a comparatively late period of
Roman history that the right of sanctuary, under Greek influence, became a recognised institution of some importance.[4]
This right was expressly conferred upon the temple which in
the year 42 B.C. was built in honour of Cæsar ;[5] and other
imperial temples, as also the statues of emperors, laid claim to
the same privilege.[6] When Christianity became the religion of
the State a similar claim was made by the churches ; but a legal
right of asylum was only granted to them by Honorius in the
West and Theodosius in the East.[7] Subsequently it was
restricted by Justinian, who decreed that all manslayers,
adulterers, and kidnappers of women who fled to a church
should be taken out of it.[8]

The right of sanctuary existed among the pagan Slavs, or
some of them,[9] and probably also among the ancient Teutons.[10]
After their conversion to Christianity the privilege of asylum
within the church was recognised in most of their codes. In
the Middle Ages and later, persons who fled to a church or to
certain boundaries surrounding it were, for a time at least, safe
from all persecution, it being considered treason against God, an
offence beyond compensation, to force even the most flagrant
criminal from His altar. The ordinary of the sacred place, or

---

[1] Tacitus, *Annales*, iii. 60 *sqq.*
Farnell, *op. cit.* i. 73. Westcott, *op.
cit.* p. 115. Schmidt, *Die Ethik der
alten Griechen*, ii. 285. Bulmerincq,
op. cit. p. 35 *sqq.* Fuld, *loc. cit.* p.
118 *sqq.*
[2] Dionysius of Halicarnassus, *Antiquitates Romanæ*, ii. 15. Livy, i. 8.
5 *sq.* Plutarch, *Romulus*, ix. 5.
Strabo, v. 3. 2, p. 230.
[3] Valerius Maximus, *Facta dictaque
memorabilia*, viii. 9. 1. Dionysius of
Halicarnassus, *Antiquitates Romanæ*,
vi. 45. Cicero, *De lege agraria oratio
secunda*, 14 (36). See also Hartung,
Die Religion der Römer, ii. 58 *sq.*
[4] See Tacitus, *Annales*, iii. 36 ;
Plautus, *Rudens*, 723 ; Dio Cassius,
Historia Romana, xlvii. 19 ; Bul-

merincq, *op. cit.* p. 58 *sqq.* ; Mommsen, *Römisches Strafrecht*, p. 458 *sq.*
[5] Dio Cassius, xlvii. 19.
[6] Tacitus, *Annales*, iv. 67. Suetonius, *Tiberius*, 53. Mommsen, *op.
cit.* p. 460.
[7] Mommsen, *op. cit.* p. 461 *sq.*
[8] *Novellæ*, xvii. 7.
[9] Helmold, *Chronik der Slaven*, i.
83, p. 170.
[10] Wilda, *Das Strafrecht der Germanen*, p. 248 *sq.* Stemann, *Den
danske Retshistorie indtil Christian
V.'s Lov*, p. 578. Brunner, *Deutsche
Rechtsgeschichte*, ii. 610. Fuld, *loc.
cit.* p. 138 *sq.* Frauenstädt, *Blutrache und Todtschlagsühne im
Deutschen Mittelalter*, p. 51.

his official, was the only one who could try to induce him to leave it, but if he failed, the utmost that could be done was to deny the refugee victuals so that he might go forth voluntarily.[1] In the 'Lex Baiuwariorum' it is asserted in the strongest terms that there is no crime which may not be pardoned from the fear of God and reverence for the saints.[2] But the right of sanctuary was gradually subjected to various restrictions both by secular legislation and by the Church.[3] Innocentius III. enjoined that refuge should not be given to a highway robber or to anybody who devastated cultivated fields at night ;[4] and according to Beaumanoir's 'Coutumes du Beauvoisis,' dating from the thirteenth century, it was also denied to persons guilty of sacrilege or arson.[5] The Parliament of Scotland enacted that whoever took the protection of the Church for homicide should be required to come out and undergo an assize, that it might be found whether it was committed of "forethought felony" or in "chaudemelle" ; and only in the latter case was he to be restored to the sanctuary, the sheriff being directed to give him security to that effect before requiring him to leave it.[6] In England, in the reign of Henry VIII., there were certain places which were allowed to be "places of tuition and privilege," in addition to churches and their precincts. They were in fact cities of permanent refuge for persons who should, according to ancient usage, have abjured the realm, after they had fled in the ordinary way to a church. There was a governor in each of these privileged places, charged with the duty of mustering every day his men, who were not to exceed twenty in each town and who had to wear a badge whenever they appeared out of doors. But when these regulations were made, the protection of sanctuary was taken away from persons guilty of murder, rape, burglary, highway robbery, or arson. The law of sanctuary was then left unchanged till the reign of James I., when, in theory, the privilege in question was altogether denied to criminals.[7] Yet

---

[1] Milman, *History of Latin Christianity*, ii. 59. Bulmerincq, *op. cit.* p. 73 *sqq.* Fuld, *loc. cit.* p. 136 *sqq.* Bracton, *De legibus et consuetudinibus Angliæ*, fol. 136 b, vol. ii. 392 *sq.* Réville, 'L'abjuratio regni,' in *Revue historique*, l. 14 *sqq.* Pollock and Maitland, *History of English Law before the Time of Edward I.* ii. 590 *sq.* Innes, *Scotland in the Middle Ages*, p. 195 *sq*

[2] *Lex Baiuwariorum*, i. 7.

[3] Brunner, *op. cit.* ii. 611 *sq.* Bulmerincq, *op. cit.* p. 91 *sqq.* Fuld, *loc. cit.* p. 140 *sq.*

[4] Gregory IX. *Decretales*, iii. 49. 6.

[5] Beaumanoir, *Coutumes du Beauvoisis*, xi. 15 *sqq.*, vol. i. 164 *sq.*

[6] Innes, *op. cit.* p. 198.

[7] Pike, *History of Crime in England*, ii. 253. Blackstone, *Commentaries on the Laws of England*, iv. 347, n. a.

as a matter of fact, asylums continued to exist in England so late as the reign of George I., when that of St. Peter's at Westminster was demolished.[1] In the legislation of Sweden the last reference to the privilege of sanctuary is found in an enactment of 1528.[2] In France it was abolished by an *ordonnance* of 1539.[3] In Spain it existed even in the nineteenth century.[4] Not long ago the most important churches in Abyssinia,[5] the monastery of Affaf Woira in the same country,[6] and the quarter in Gondar where the head of the Abyssinian clergy has his residence,[7] were reported to be asylums for criminals. And the same is the case with the old Christian churches among the Suanetians of the Caucasus.[8]

The right of sanctuary has been ascribed to various causes. Obviously erroneous is the suggestion that places of refuge were established with a view to protecting unintentional offenders from punishment or revenge.[9] The restriction of the privilege of sanctuary to cases of accidental injuries is not at all general, and where it occurs it is undoubtedly an innovation due to moral or social considerations. Very frequently this privilege has been attributed to a desire to give time for the first heat of resentment to pass over before the injured party could seek redress.[10] But although I admit that such a desire may have helped to preserve the right of asylum where it has once come into existence, I do not believe that it could account for the origin of this right. We should remember that the privilege of sanctuary not only affords

---

[1] Jusserand, *English Wayfaring Life in the Middle Ages*, p. 166.
[2] Nordström, *Bidrag till den svenska samhälls-författningens historia*, ii. 405.
[3] Du Boys, *Histoire du droit criminel des peuples modernes*, ii. 246.
[4] *Idem, Histoire du droit criminel de l'Espagne*, p. 227 sq.
[5] Hellwig, *op. cit.* p. 52.
[6] Harris, *Highlands of Æthiopia*, ii. 93.
[7] Rüppell, *Reise in Abyssinien*, ii. 74, 81. von Heuglin, *Reise nach Abessinien*, p. 213.
[8] von Haxthausen, *Transcaucasia*, p. 160, n.*
[9] Hegel, *Grundlinien der Philosophie des Rechts*, § 117, p. 108. Powell, ' Outlines of Sociology,' in *Saturday Lectures*, p. 82.
[10] Meiners, *Geschichte der Menschheit*, p. 189. Nordström, *op. cit.* ii. 401. Pardessus, *Loi Salique*, p. 656. Bulmerincq, *op. cit.* pp. 34, 47. Fuld, *loc. cit.* pp. 102, 118, 119, 294 sqq. Kohler, *Shakespeare vor dem Forum der Jurisprudenz*, p. 185. Quatremère, *loc. cit.* p. 314. Mr. Mallery (*Israelite and Indian*, p. 33 sq.), also, thinks that the original object of the right of sanctuary was to restrict vengeance and maintain peace, and that this right only subsequently appeared as a prerogative of religion.

temporary protection to the refugee, but in many cases altogether exempts him from punishment or retaliation, and that shelter is given even to animals which have fled to a sacred place. And, if the theory referred to were correct, how could we explain the fact that the right of asylum is particularly attached to sanctuaries ?

It has been said that the right of sanctuary bears testimony to the power of certain places to transmit their virtues to those who entered them.[1] But we have no evidence that the fugitive is supposed to partake of the sanctity of the place which shelters him. In Morocco persons who are permanently attached to mosques or the shrines of saints are generally regarded as more or less holy, but this is never the case with casual visitors or suppliants ; hence it is hardly for fear of the refugee that his pursuer refrains from laying hands on him. Professor Robertson Smith has stated part of the truth in saying that " the assertion of a man's undoubted rights as against a fugitive at the sanctuary is regarded as an encroachment on its holiness." [2] There is an almost instinctive fear not only of shedding blood,[3] but of disturbing the peace in a holy place ; and if it is improper to commit any act of violence in the house of another man,[4] it is naturally considered equally offensive, and also infinitely more dangerous, to do so in the homestead of a supernatural being. In the Tonga Islands, for instance, " it is for-

[1] Granger, *Worship of the Romans*, p. 223 *sq.*

[2] Robertson Smith, *Religion of the Semites*, p. 148.

[3] *Supra*, i. 380.

[4] Among the Barea and Kunáma in Eastern Africa a murderer who finds time to flee into another person's house cannot be seized, and it is considered a point of honour for the community to help him to escape abroad (Munzinger, *Ostafrikanische Studien*, p. 503). In the Pelew Islands " no enemy may be killed in a house, especially in the presence of the host " (Kubary, ' Die Palau-Inseln in der Südsee,' in *Jour. d. Museum Godeffroy*, iv. 25). In Europe the privilege of asylum went hand in hand with the sanctity of the homestead (Wilda, *op. cit.* pp. 242, 243, 538, 543 ; Nordström, *op. cit.* ii. 435 ; Fuld, *loc. cit.* p. 152 ; Frauenstädt, *op. cit.* p. 63 *sqq.*); and the breach of a man's peace was proportionate to his rank. Whilst every man was entitled to peace in his own house, the great man's peace was of more importance than the common man's, the king's peace of more importance than the baron's, and in the spiritual order the peace of the Church commanded yet greater reverence (Pollock, ' The King's Peace,' in *Law Quarterly Review*, i. 40 *sq.*).

bidden to quarrel or fight upon consecrated ground."[1]
But this is only one aspect of the matter ; another, equally
important, still calls for an explanation. Why should
the gods or saints themselves be so anxious to protect
criminals who have sought refuge in their sanctuaries ?
Why do they not deliver them up to justice through
their earthly representatives ?

The answer lies in certain ideas which refer to human
as well as divine protectors of refugees. The god or
saint is in exactly the same position as a man to whose
house a person has fled for shelter. Among various
peoples the domicile of the chief or king is an asylum for
criminals ;[2] nobody dares to attack a man who is sheltered
by so mighty a personage, and from what has been said
above, in connection with the rules of hospitality, it is
also evident why the chief or king feels himself compelled
to protect him. By being in close contact with his host,
the suppliant is able to transfer to him a dangerous curse.
Sometimes a criminal can in a similar way be a danger to
the king even from a distance, or by meeting him, and
must in consequence be pardoned. In Madagascar an
offender escaped punishment if he could obtain sight of
the sovereign, whether before or after conviction ; hence
criminals at work on the highroad were ordered to
withdraw when the sovereign was known to be coming
by.[3] Among the Bambaras " une fois la sentence
prononcée, si le condamné parvient à cracher sur un

---

[1] Mariner, *Natives of the Tonga Islands*, ii. 232. *Cf. ibid*. i. 227.

[2] Harmon, *Voyages and Travels in the Interior of North America*, p. 297 (Tacullies). Lewin, *Hill Tracts of Chittagong*, p. 100 (Kukis). Jung-huhn, *Die Battaländer auf Sumatra*, ii. 329 (Macassars and Bugis of Celebes). Tromp, ' Uit de Salasila van Koetei,' in *Bijdragen tot de taal-land- en volkenkunde van Neder-landsch-Indië*, xxxvii. 84 (natives of Koetei, a district of Borneo). Jung, quoted by Kohler, ' Recht der Marschallinsulaner,' in *Zeitschr. f. vergl. Rechtswiss.* xiv. 447 (natives of

Nauru in the Marshall Group).
Turner, *Nineteen Years in Poly-nesia*, p. 334 (Samoans). Rautanen, in Steinmetz, *Rechtsverhältnisse*, p. 342 (Ondonga). Schinz, *op. cit.* p. 312 (Ovambo). Rehme, ' Das Recht der Amaxosa,' in *Zeitschr. f. vergl. Rechtswiss.* x. 50. Merker, quoted by Kohler, ' Banturecht in Ost-afrika,' *ibid.* xv. 55 (Wadshagga). Merker, *Die Masai*, p. 206. Among the Barotse the residences of the Queen and the Prime Minister are places of refuge (Decle, *op. cit.* p. 75).

[3] Ellis, *History of Madagascar*, i. 376.

prince, non-seulement sa personne est sacrée, mais elle est nourrie, logée, etc., par le grand seigneur qui a eu l'imprudence de se tenir à portée de cet étrange projectile." [1] In Usambara even a murderer is safe as soon as he has touched the person of the king.[2] Among the Marutse and neighbouring tribes a person who is accused of any crime receives pardon if he lays a *cupa*— the fossilised base of a conical shell, which is the most highly valued of all their instruments—at the feet of his chief ; and a miscreant likewise escapes punishment if he reaches and throws himself on the king's drums.[3] On the Slave Coast " criminals who are doomed to death are always gagged, because if a man should speak to the king he must be pardoned." [4] In Ashantee, if an offender should succeed in swearing on the king's life, he must be pardoned, because such an oath is believed to involve danger to the king ; hence knives are driven through the cheeks from opposite sides, over the tongue, to prevent him from speaking.[5] So also among the Romans, according to an old Jewish writer, a person condemned to death was gagged to prevent him from cursing the king.[6] Fear of the curses pronounced by a dissatisfied refugee likewise, in all probability, underlay certain other customs which prevailed in Rome. A servant or slave who came and fell down at the feet of Jupiter's high-priest, taking hold of his knees, was for that day freed from the whip ; and if a prisoner with irons and bolts at his feet succeeded in approaching the high-priest in his house, he was let loose and his fetters were thrown into the road, not through the door, but from the roof.[7] Moreover, if a criminal who had been sentenced to death accidentally met a Vestal virgin on his way to the place of execution, his

[1] Raffenel, *Nouveau voyage dans le pays des nègres*, i. 385.

[2] Krapf, *Reisen in Ost-Afrika*, ii. 132, n.* See also Schinz, *op. cit.* p. 312 (Ovambo).

[3] Gibbons, *Exploration in Central Africa*, p. 129. I am indebted to Mr. N. W. Thomas for drawing my attention to this statement.

[4] Ellis, *Ewe-speaking Peoples of the Slave Coast*, p. 224.

[5] *Ibid.* p. 224.

[6] Quoted by Levias, ' Cursing,' in *Jewish Encyclopedia*, iv. 390.

[7] Plutarch, *Questiones Romanæ*, III. Aulus Gellius, *Noctes Atticæ*, x. 15. 8, 10.

life was saved.[1] So sensitive to imprecations were both
Jupiter's high-priest and the priestesses of Vesta, that the
Praetor was never allowed to compel them to take an
oath.[2] Now, as a refugee may by his curse force a king or a
priest or any other man with whom he establishes some
kind of contact to protect him, so he may in a similar
manner constrain a god or saint as soon as he has entered
his sanctuary. According to the Moorish expression he is
then in the 'âr of the saint, and the saint is bound to protect him, just as a host is bound to protect his guest. It is
not only men that have to fear the curses of dissatisfied
refugees. Let us once more remember the words
which Aeschylus puts into the mouth of Apollo, when
he declares his intention to assist his suppliant, Orestes :—
" Terrible both among men *and gods* is the wrath of a
refugee, when one abandons him with intent." [3]

[1] Plutarch, *Numa*, x. 5.   [3] Aeschylus, *Eumenides*, 232 *sqq.*
[2] Aulus Gellius, *op. cit.* x. 15. 31.

CHAPTER XLIX

DUTIES TO GODS (*concluded*)

SUPERNATURAL beings are widely believed to have a feeling of their worth and dignity. They are sensitive to insults and disrespect, they demand submissiveness and homage.

" The gods of the Gold Coast," says Major Ellis, " are jealous gods, jealous of their dignity, jealous of the adulation and offerings paid to them ; and there is nothing they resent so much as any slight, whether intentional or accidental, which may be offered them. . . . There is nothing that offends them so deeply as to ignore them, or question their power, or laugh at them." [1] The wrath of Yahveh burst forth with vehemence whenever his honour or sanctity was in the least violated, however unintentionally.[2] Many peoples consider it insulting and dangerous merely to point at one of the celestial bodies ; [3] and among the North American Indians it is a widespread belief that, if anybody points at the rainbow, the finger will wither or become misshapen.[4]

Nor is it to supernatural danger only that a person exposes himself by irreverence to a god, but in many cases he is also punished by his fellow men. On the Slave Coast insults to a god " are always resented and punished by the

[1] Ellis, *Tshi-speaking Peoples of the Gold Coast*, p. 11.
[2] *Cf.* Montefiore, *Hibbert Lectures on the Religion of the Ancient Hebrews*, pp. 38, 102.
[3] Liebrecht, *Zur Volkskunde*, p. 341. Dorman, *Origin of Primitive Superstitions*, p. 344 (Chippewas). Wuttke, *Der deutsche Volksaberglaube der Gegenwart*, § 11, p. 13 *sq.*
[4] Mooney, ' Myths of the Cherokee,' in *Ann. Rep. Bur. Ethn.* xix. 257, 442.

priests and worshippers of that god, it being their duty to guard his honour."[1] Among the ancient Peruvians[2] and Hebrews,[3] as also among Christian nations up to comparatively recent times, blasphemy was a capital offence. In England, in the reign of Henry VIII., a boy of fifteen was burned because he had spoken, much after the fashion of a parrot, some idle words affecting the sacrament of the altar, which he had chanced to hear but of which he could not have understood the meaning.[4] According to Muhammedan law a person guilty of blasphemy is to be put to death without delay, even though he profess himself repentant, as adequate repentance for such a sin is deemed impossible.[5] These and similar laws are rooted in the idea that the god is personally offended by the insult. It was the Lord himself who made the law that he who blasphemed His name should be stoned to death by all the congregation.[6] " Blasphemy," says Thomas Aquinas, " as being an offence directly against God, outweighs murder, which is an offence against our neighbour . . . . The blasphemer intends to wound the honour of God."[7] That blasphemy is, or should be, punished not as a sin against the deity but as an offence against the religious feelings of men, is an idea of quite modern origin.

In many cases it is considered offensive to a supernatural being merely to mention his name. Sometimes the name is tabooed on certain occasions only or in ordinary conversation, sometimes it is not to be pronounced at all.

In Morocco the *jnûn* (*jinn*) must not be referred to by name in the afternoon and evening after the '*âsar*. If speaking of them at all, the people then make use of some circumlocution; the Berbers of Southern Morocco call them *wîd-iâdnin*, " those others," or *wîd-urḍ-hĕr'nin*, " those unseen," or *wîd-tntl-tîsnt*, " those who shun salt." The Greenlanders dare not pronounce the name of a glacier

---

[1] Ellis, *Ewe-speaking Peoples of the Slave Coast*, p. 81.
[2] Prescott, *History of the Conquest of Peru*, i. 42.
[3] *Leviticus*, xxiv. 14 *sqq.*
[4] Pike, *History of Crime in Eng-*land, ii. 56.
[5] Lane, *Manners and Customs of the Modern Egyptians*, p. 123.
[6] *Leviticus*, xxiv. 16.
[7] Thomas Aquinas, *Summa theologica*, ii.–ii. 13.3.1.

as they row past it, for fear lest it should be offended and throw off an iceberg.[1] Some North American Indians believe that if, when travelling, they mention the names of rocks or islands or rivers, they will have much rain or be wrecked or be devoured by some monster in the river.[2] The Omahas, again, " are very careful not to use names which they regard as sacred on ordinary occasions ; and no one dares to sing sacred songs except the chiefs and old men at the proper times." [3] Some other Indians considered it a profanation to mention the name of their highest divinity.[4] Among certain Australian natives the elders of the tribe impart to the youth, on his initiation, the name of the god Tharamŭlŭn ; but there is such a disinclination to pronounce his name that, in speaking of him, they generally use elliptical expressions, such as " He," " the man," or " the name I told you of," and the women only know him by the name of Papang (father).[5] The Marutse and allied tribes along the Zambesi shrink from mentioning the real name of their chief god Nyambe and therefore substitute for it the word *molemo*, which has a very comprehensive meaning, denoting, besides God, all kinds of good and evil spirits, medicines, poisons, and amulets.[6] According to Cicero, there was a god, a son of Nilus, whose name the Egyptians considered it a crime to pronounce ; [7] and Herodotus is unwilling to mention the name of Osiris on two occasions when he is speaking of him.[8] The divine name of Indra was secret, the real name of Agni was unknown.[9] The gods of Brahmanism have mystic names, which nobody dares to speak.[10] The real name of Confucius is so sacred that it is a statutable offence in China to

[1] Nansen, *Eskimo Life*, p. 233.
[2] Nyrop, ' Navnets magt,' in *Mindre Afhandlinger udgivne af det philologisk-historiske Samfund*, 1887, p. 28.
[3] Dorsey, ' Omaha Sociology,' in *Ann. Rep. Bur. Ethn.* iii. 370.
[4] Adair, *History of the American Indians*, p. 54.
[5] Howitt, ' Some Australian Beliefs,' in *Jour. Anthr. Inst.* xiii. 192.

See also *Idem, Native Tribes of South-East Australia*, pp. 489, 495.
[6] Holub, *Seven Years in South Africa*, ii. 301.
[7] Cicero, *De natura deorum*, iii. 22 (56).
[8] Herodotus, ii. 132, 171.
[9] Hopkins, *Religions of India*, pp. 93, 111.
[10] *Ibid.* p. 184.

pronounce it ; and the name of the supreme god of the Chinese is equally tabooed. " *Tien*," they say, " means properly only the material heaven, but it also means Shang-Te (supreme ruler, God) ; for, as it is not lawful to use his name lightly, we name him by his residence, which is in *tien*."[1] The " great name " of Allah is a secret name, known only to prophets, and possibly to some great saints.[2] Yahveh said, " Thou shalt not take the name of the Lord thy God in vain ; for the Lord will not hold him guiltless that taketh his name in vain " ;[3] and orthodox Jews avoid mentioning the word Yahveh altogether.[4] Among Christian nations, as Professor Nyrop observes, there is a common disinclination to use the word " God " or its equivalents in everyday speech. The English say *good* instead of *God* (" good gracious," " my goodness," " thank goodness ") ; the Germans, *Potz* instead of *Gotts* (" Potz Welt," " Potz Wetter," " Potz Blitz ") ; the French, *bleu* instead of *Dieu* (" corbleu," " morbleu," " sambleu ") ; the Spaniards, *brios* or *diez* instead of *Dios* (" voto á brios," " juro á brios," " par diez ").[5]

These taboos have sprung from fear. There is, first, something uncanny in mentioning the name of a supernatural being, even apart from any definite ideas connected with the act. But to do so is also supposed to summon him or to attract his attention, and this may be considered dangerous, especially if he is looked upon as malevolent or irritable, as is generally the case with the Moorish *jnûn*. The uncanny feeling or the notion of danger readily leads to the belief that the supernatural being feels offended if his name is pronounced ; we have noticed a similar association of thought in connection with the names of the dead. But a god may also have good reason for wishing that his name should not be used lightly or taken in vain. Accord-

---

[1] Friend, ' Euphemism and Tabu in China,' in *Folk-Lore Record*, iv. 76. Cf. Edkins, *Religion in China*, p. 72.
[2] Sell, *Faith of Islám*, p. 185. Lane, *Modern Egyptians*, p. 273.

[3] *Exodus*, xx. 7.
[4] Herzog-Plitt, *Real-Encyklopädie für protestantische Theologie*, vi. 501 *sq.*
[5] Nyrop, *loc. cit.* p. 155 *sqq.*

ing to primitive ideas a person's name is a part of his personality, hence the holiness of a god may be polluted by his name being mentioned in profane conversation. Moreover, it may be of great importance for him to prevent his name from being divulged, as magic may be wrought on a person through his name just as easily as through any part of his body. In early civilisation there is a common tendency to keep the real name of a human individual secret so that sorcerers may not make an evil use of it ;[1] and it is similarly believed that gods must conceal their true names lest other gods or men should be able to conjure with them.[2] The great Egyptian god Râ declared that the name which his father and mother had given him remained hidden in his body since his birth, so that no magician might have magic power over him.[3] The list of divine names possessed by the Roman pontiffs in their *indigitamenta* was a magical instrument which laid at their mercy all the forces of the spirit world ;[4] and we are told that the Romans kept the name of their tutelary god secret in order to prevent their enemies from drawing him away by pronouncing it.[5] There is a Muhammedan tradition that whosoever calls upon Allah by his " great name " will obtain all his desires, being able merely by mentioning it to raise the dead to life, to kill the living, in fact to perform any miracle he pleases.[6]

One of the greatest insults which can be offered a god is to deny his existence. Plutarch was astonished at people's saying that atheism is impiety, while at the same time they attribute to gods all kinds of less creditable qualities. " I for my part," he adds, " would much rather have men to say of me that there never was a

---

[1] Tylor, *Early History of Mankind*, p. 139 *sqq.* Andree, *Ethnographische Parallelen*, p. 179 *sqq.* Frazer, *Golden Bough*, i. 403 *sqq.* Clodd, *Tom Tit Tot*, pp. 53–55, 81 *sqq.* Haddon, *Magic and Fetishism*, p. 22 *sq.*
[2] Tylor, *op. cit.* p. 124 *sq.* Frazer, *op. cit.* i. 443. Clodd, *op. cit.* p. 173. Haddon, *op. cit.* p. 23 *sqq.*

[3] Frazer, *op. cit.* i. 444.
[4] Granger, *Worship of the Romans*, pp. 212, 277. *Cf.* Jevons, in Plutarch's *Romane Questions*, p. lvii.
[5] Plutarch, *Questiones Romanæ*, 61. Pliny, *Historia naturalis*, xxviii. 4. Macrobius, *Saturnalia*, iii. 9.
[6] Sell, *op. cit.* p. 185. Lane, *Modern Egyptians*, p. 273.

Plutarch at all, nor is now, than to say that Plutarch is a man inconstant, fickle, easily moved to anger, revengeful for trifling provocations, vexed at small things." [1] But Plutarch seems to have forgotten that a person is always most sensitive on his weak points, and that the weakest point in a god is his existence. Religious intolerance is in a large measure the result of that feeling of uncertainty which can hardly be eradicated even by the strongest will to believe. It is a means of self-persuasion in a case where such persuasion is sorely needed. Moreover, a god who is not believed to exist can be no object of worship, and to be worshipped is commonly held to be the chief ambition of a god. But atheism is a sin of civilisation. Uncultured people are ready to believe that all supernatural beings they hear of also exist.

Some gods are extremely ungenerous towards all those who do not recognise them, and only them, as *their* gods. To believe in Ahura Mazda was the first duty which Zoroastrianism required of a man ; it was Angra Mainyu, the evil spirit, that had countercreated the sin of unbelief.[2] Doubt destroyed even the effects of good actions ; [3] indeed, only the true believer was to be regarded as a man.[4] The faithful were summoned to a war to the death against the opposing spirits, the Daevas, and their followers.[5] And to judge from ancient writers, the Persians, when they came into contact with nations of another religion, also carried into practice the intolerant spirit of their own.[6] Yahveh said :—" Thou shalt have no other gods before me. . . . Thou shalt not bow down thyself to them, nor serve them : for I the Lord thy God am a jealous God."[7] In the pre-prophetic period the existence of other gods was recognised,[8] but they were not

---

[1] Plutarch, *De superstitione*, 10.

[2] *Vendîdâd*, i. 8. 16.

[3] Darmesteter, *Ormazd et Ahriman*, p. 330, n. 4.

[4] *Dînâ-î Maînôg-î Khirad*, xlii. 6 *sqq.*

[5] See Darmesteter, in *Sacred Books of the East*, iv. p. lii. ; Spiegel, *Erânische Alterthumskunde*, iii. 692.

[6] Spiegel, *op. cit.* iii. 708.

[7] *Exodus*, xx. 3, 5.

[8] Kuenen, *Hibbert Lectures on National Religions and Universal Religions*, p. 119. Baudissin, *Studien zur semitischen Religionsgeschichte*, i. 49 *sqq.*

to be worshipped by Yahveh's people. Nor was any mercy to be shown to their followers, for Yahveh was " a man of war." [1] The God of Christianity inherited his jealousy. In the name of Christ wars were waged, not, it is true, for the purpose of exterminating unbelievers, but with a view to converting them to a faith which alone could save their souls from eternal perdition. So far as the aim of the persecution is concerned we can thus notice a distinct progress in humanity. But whilst the punishment which Yahveh inflicted upon the devotees of other gods was merely temporal and restricted to a comparatively small number of people—he took notice of such foreign nations only which came within his sphere of interests,—Christianity was a proselytising religion on a large scale, anxious to save but equally ready to condemn to everlasting torments all those who refused to accept it, nay even the milliards of men who had never heard of it. In this point Christianity was even more intolerant than the Koran itself, which does not absolutely confine salvation to the believers in Allah and his Prophet, but leaves some hope of it to Jews, Christians, and Sabæans, though all other infidels are hopelessly lost.[2]

That Muhammedanism has in course of time become the most fanatical of existing religions is due to political rather than religious causes. For a thousand years the Christian and Muhammedan world were engaged in a deadly contest, in which the former came off victorious. Most nations confessing Islam have either lost their independence or are on the verge of losing it. The memory of past defeats and cruelties, the present state of subjection or national weakness, the fear of the future—are all factors which must be taken into account when we judge of Moslem fanaticism. In its younger days Islam was undoubtedly, not only in theory but in practice, less intolerant than its great rival, Christian subjects of Muhammedan rulers being on the whole treated with

[1] *Exodus*, xv. 3.　　[2] *Koran*, v. 73.

consideration.[1] Earlier travellers in Arabia also speak favourably of the tolerance of its inhabitants. Niebuhr was able to write :—" I never saw that the Arabs have any hatred for those of a different religion. They, however, regard them with much the same contempt with which Christians look upon the Jews in Europe . . . . The Mahometans in India appear to be even more tolerant than those of Arabia . . . . The Mussulmans in general do not persecute men of other religions, when they have nothing to fear from them, unless in the case of an intercourse of gallantry with a Mahometan woman." [2] In China the Muhammedans live amicably with the infidel, regarding their Buddhist neighbours " with a kindly feeling which it would be hard to find in a mixed community of Catholics and Evangelicals." [3] Muhammedanism looks upon the founder of Christianity with profound reverence, as one of the apostles of God, as the only man without sin. Christian writers, on the other hand, till the middle of the eighteenth century universally treated Muhammed as a false prophet and rank impostor. Luther called him " a devil, and a first-born child of Satan," whilst Melanchthon was inclined to see in him both Gog and Magog.[4]

Equal in enormity with the sin of not believing in a certain god is sometimes the sin of having a false belief about him. It seems strange that a god should be so easily offended as to punish with the utmost severity those who hold erroneous notions regarding some attribute of his which in no way affects his honour or glory, or regarding some detail of ritual. Thomas Aquinas himself admits that the heretic *intends* to take the word of Christ, although he fails " in the election of articles whereon to take that word." But it is in this election that his sin consists.

[1] See von Kremer, *Culturgeschichte des Orients*, ii. 166 *sq.*

[2] Niebuhr, *Travels through Arabia*, ii. 192, 189 *sq.* Cf. d'Arvieux, *Travels in Arabia the Desart*, p. 123 ; Wallin, *Notes taken during a Journey through Northern Arabia*, p. 21.

[3] Lane-Poole, *Studies in a Mosque*, p. 298 *sq.*

[4] [Deutsch,] ' Islam,' in *Quarterly Review*, cxxvii. 295 *sq.* Bosworth Smith, *Mohammed and Mohammedanism*, pp. 67, 69. Pool, *Studies in Mohammedanism*, p. 406.

Instead of choosing those articles which are truly taught by Christ, he chooses those which his own mind suggests to him. Thus he perverts the doctrines of Christ, and in consequence deserves not only to be separated from the Church by excommunication, but to be banished from the world by death.[1] Moreover, the heretic is an apostate, a traitor who may be forced to pay the vow which he has once taken.[2] The extreme rigour of this sophistical argumentation can only be understood in connection with its historical surroundings. It presupposes a Church which not only regards itself as the sole possessor of divine truth, but whose cohesion and power depend upon a strict adherence to its doctrines.[3] Nor was it a religious motive only that induced Christian sovereigns to persecute heretics. Certain heresies, as Manichæism and Donatism, were expressly declared to affect the common welfare ; [4] and the Frankish kings treated heretics not only as rebels against the Church, but as traitors to the State, as confederates of hostile Visigoths or Burgundians or Lombards.[5]

Whilst intolerance is a characteristic of all monotheistic religions which attribute human passions and emotions to their godhead, polytheism is by nature tolerant. A god who is always used to share with other gods the worship of his believers cannot be a very jealous god. The pious Hennepin was struck by the fact that Red Indians were " incapable of taking away any person's life out of hatred to his religion." [6] Among the natives of the African Gold and Slave Coasts, though a man must show outward respect for the gods so as not to provoke calamities, he may worship many gods or none, just as he pleases. " There is perfect liberty of thought in matters of religion. . . . At this stage, man tolerates any form of religion that tolerates others ; and as he thinks it perfectly

---

[1] Thomas Aquinas, *op. cit.* ii.–ii. 11. 1, 3.
[2] *Ibid.* ii.–ii. 10. 8.
[3] *Cf.* Ritchie, *Natural Rights*, p. 183.

[4] Milman, *History of Latin Christianity*, ii. 33.
[5] *Ibid.* ii. 61.
[6] Hennepin, *New Discovery of a Vast Country in America*, ii. 70.

natural that different people should worship different gods, he does not attempt to force his own personal opinions upon anyone, or to establish conformity of ideas."[1]   On the Slave Coast even a sacrilege committed by a European is usually regarded with indifference, as the gods of a country are supposed to be concerned about the actions of the people of that country only.[2]   " The characteristics of Natural Religion," says Sir Alfred Lyall, " the conditions of its existence as we see it in India, are complete liberty and material tolerance ; there is no monopoly either of divine powers or even of sacerdotal privilege."[3]   In China the hatred of foreigners has not its root in religion. The Catholics residing there were left undisturbed until they began to meddle with the civil and social institutions of the country ;[4] and the difficulty in persuading the Chinese to embrace Christianity is said by a missionary to be due to their notion that one religion is as good as another provided that it has a good moral code.[5]   Among the early Greeks and Romans it was a principle that the religion of the State should be the religion of the people, as its welfare was supposed to depend upon a strict observance of the established cult ; but the gods cared for external worship rather than for the beliefs of their worshippers, and evidently took little notice even of expressed opinions. Philosophers openly despised the very rites which they both defended and practised ; and religion was more a pretext than a real motive for the persecutions of men like Anaxagoras, Protagoras, Socrates, and Aristotle.[6]   So also the measures by which the Romans in earlier times repressed the introduction of new religions were largely suggested by worldly considerations ; " they grew out of that intense national spirit which sacrificed every

[1] Ellis, *Yoruba-speaking Peoples of the Slave Coast*, p. 295.   See also *Idem, Ewe - speaking Peoples of the Slave Coast*, p. 81 ; Monrad, *Skildring af Guinea-Kysten*, p. 28 ; Kubary, ' Die Verbrechen und das Strafverfahren auf den Pelau-Inseln,' in *Original-Mittheil. aus d. ethnol. Abtheil. d. königl. Museen zu Berlin*, i. 90.

[2] Ellis, *Ewe-speaking Peoples*, p. 81.
[3] Lyall, *Natural Religion in India*, p. 52.
[4] Davis, *China*, ii. 7.   *Cf.* Edkins, *op. cit.* p. 178.
[5] Edkins, *op. cit.* p. 75.
[6] See Schmidt, *Die Ethik der alten Griechen*, ii. 24 *sqq.*

other interest to the State, and resisted every form of
innovation, whether secular or religious, that could impair
the unity of the national type, and dissolve the discipline
which the predominance of the military spirit and the
stern government of the Republic had formed." [1] It has
also been sufficiently proved that the persecutions of the
Christians during the pagan Empire sprang from motives
quite different from religious intolerance. Liberty of
worship was a general principle of the Imperial rule. That
it was denied the Christians was due to their own aggressiveness, as also to political suspicion. They grossly
insulted the pagan cult, denouncing it as the worship of
demons, and every calamity which fell upon the Empire was
in consequence regarded by the populace as the righteous
vengeance of the offended gods. Their proselytism
disturbed the peace of families and towns. Their secret
meetings aroused suspicion of political danger ; and this
suspicion was increased by the doctrines they professed.
They considered the Roman Empire a manifestation of
Antichrist, they looked forward with longing to its destruction, and many of them refused to take part in its defence.
The greatest and best among the pagans spoke of the
Christians as " enemies," or " haters of the human race." [2]

The same difference in toleration between monotheistic
and polytheistic religions shows itself in their different
attitudes towards witchcraft. A monotheistic religion is
not necessarily averse from magic ; its god may be supposed
to have created magical as well as natural energy, and
also to have given mankind permission to utilise it in a
proper manner. Both Christianity in its earlier phases and
Muhammedanism are full of magical practices expressly
sanctioned by their theology—for instance, the use made
of sacred words and of the relics of saints. But besides
this sort of magic there is another kind—witchcraft, in the
narrow sense of the term,—which is ascribed to the

[1] Lecky, *History of European
Morals,* i. 403. *Cf.* Dio Cassius,
Historia Romana, lii. 36.
[2] Lecky, *op. cit.* i. 408 *sqq.* Ramsay, *The Church in the Roman
Empire,* p. 346 *sqq.* See also *supra,*
i. 345 *sq.* ; ii. 178 *sq.*

assistance of exorcised spirits, regarded not as the willing
agents but as the adversaries of God ; and this practice is
naturally looked upon as highly offensive to His feelings.
In Christianity witchcraft was esteemed the most horrible
form of impiety.[1] The religious law of the Hebrews—
which generally prohibited all practices that savoured of
idolatry, such as soothsaying and oracles—punished
witches and wizards with death.[2] Islam disapproves of all
magic which is practised with the assistance of evil spirits, or
jinn, although such magic is very prevalent and popularly
tolerated in Muhammedan countries.[3] Among polytheistic peoples, again, witchcraft is certainly in many cases
treated with great severity ; a large number of uncivilised
races punish it with death,[4] and among some of them it is
the only offence which is capital.[5] But then witchcraft is
punished because it is considered destructive to human life
or welfare.[6] " In Africa," says Mr. Rowley, " there is
what is regarded as lawful as well as unlawful witchcraft,
the lawful being practised professedly for the welfare of
mankind, and in opposition to the unlawful, which is resorted to for man's injury." But " the purposes of witch-

[1] Lea, History of the Inquisition,
iii. 422, 453. Pollock and Maitland,
History of English Law before the
Time of Edward I. ii. 552 sqq. Milman, op. cit. ix. 69. Lecky, Rise and
Influence of Rationalism in Europe,
i. 26. Keary, Outlines of Primitive
Belief among the Indo-European
Races, p. 511 sqq. Rogers, Social Life
in Scotland, iii. 265, 268. Ralston,
Songs of the Russian People, pp. 386,
416 sq.
[2] Exodus, xxii. 18. Leviticus, xix.
26, 31 ; xx. 6, 27. Deuteronomy,
xviii. 10 sqq.
[3] Polak, Persien, i. 348. Lane,
Modern Egyptians, i. 333.
[4] Supra, i. 189 sq. Cruickshank,
Eighteen Years on the Gold Coast, ii.
179. Bowdich, Mission to Ashantee,
p. 260. Johnston, British Central
Africa, p. 403 (Bakongo). Cunningham, Uganda, pp. 35 (Banyoro), 140
(Bavuma), 305 (Basukuma), Arnot,
Garenganze, p. 75. Decle, Three
Years in Savage Africa, p. 76 (Ba-

rotse). Casalis, Basutos, p. 229.
Kidd, The Essential Kafir, p. 148 sq.
Sibree, The Great African Island, p.
292 (Malagasy). Swettenham, Malay
Sketches, p. 196 (Malays of Perak).
Dalton, Ethnology of Bengal, p. 257
(Oraons). Egede, Description of
Greenland, p. 123 sq. Krause, Die
Tlinkit-Indianer, p. 293 sq. Jones,
quoted by Kohler, ' Die Rechte der
Urvölker Nordamerikas,' in Zeitschr.
f. vergl. Rechtswiss. xii. 412 (Chippe-
was). Morgan, League of the Iro-
quois, p. 330 ; Seaver, Life of Mrs.
Jemison, p. 167 (Iroquois). Powell,
' Wyandot Government,' in Ann.
Rep. Bur. Ethn. i. 67. Stevenson,
' Sia,' ibid. xi. 19. Lumholtz, Un-
known Mexico, i. 325 (Tarahumares). Forbes, ' Aymara Indians
of Bolivia and Peru,' in Jour. Ethn.
Soc. N. S. ii. 236, n.*
[5] Supra. i. 189.
[6] Cf. Dorsey, 'Omaha Sociology,'
in Ann. Rep. Bur. Ethn. iii. 364.

craft are now generally wicked ; its processes generally
involve moral guilt ; the spirits invoked are, for the most
part, avowedly evil and maleficent." [1] Among the Gaika
tribe of the Kafirs " witchcraft is supposed to be an
influence for evil, possessed by one individual over another,
or others." [2] Among the Bondeis " the meaning of
witchcraft is simply murder." [3] That witchcraft, as a
malicious practice, must be a grave and at the same time
frequent offence among savages, is obvious from the
common belief that death, disease, and misfortunes of
every description are caused by it. From a similar point of
view it is condemned by polytheistic nations of a higher
type. Among the Aztecs of ancient Mexico anybody who
employed sorcery or incantations for the purpose of doing
harm to the community or to individuals was sacrificed to
the gods. [4] The Chinese Penal Code punishes with death
those who have been convicted of writing and editing
books of sorcery, or of employing spells and incantations,
" in order to agitate and influence the minds of the
people." [5] But, according to Mr. Dennys, the hatred of
witches and wizards cherished in the West does not seem
to exist in China ; " those reputed to possess magic
powers are regarded with dread, but it is rare to hear of
any of them coming to untimely end by mob violence." [6]
The Laws of Ḥammurabi, the ancient Babylonian legislator, enjoin that "if a man weave a spell and put a ban upon
a man, and has not justified himself, he that wove the spell
upon him shall be put to death." [7] It is said in ' Vishnu
Purâna ' that he who practises magical rites " for the harm
of others " is punished in the hell called Krimîsa. [8] Among
the ancient Teutons not every kind of magic but only
such as was considered of injurious nature was criminal. [9]

---

[1] Rowley, *Religion of the Africans*,
p. 125 *sq.* See also Kidd, *The
Essential Kafir*, p. 148.
[2] Maclean, *Compendium of Kafir
Laws*, p. 123.
[3] Dale, in *Jour. Anthr. Inst.* xxv.
223.
[4] Bancroft, *Native Races of the*

Pacific States, ii. 462.
[5] *Ta Tsing Leu Lee*, sec. cclvi. p.
273.
[6] Dennys, *Folk-Lore of China*, p. 80.
[7] *Laws of Ḥammurabi*, 1.
[8] *Vishńu Purâńa*, p. 208.
[9] Brunner, *Deutsche Rechtsgeschichte*, ii. 678.

In Rome, also, what was deemed harmless magic was left undisturbed, whereas, according to the ' Law of the Twelve Tables,' " he who affects another by magical arts or with poisonous drugs " is to be put to death ; [1] and during the Empire persons were severely persecuted for political astrology or divination practised with a view to discovering the successors to the throne.[2] Plato writes in his ' Laws ' :—" He who seems to be the sort of man who injures others by magic knots or enchantments or incantations or any of the like practices, if he be a prophet or divine, let him die ; and, if not being a prophet, he be convicted of witchcraft, as in the previous case, let the court fix what he ought to pay or suffer." [3] As Mr. Lecky justly remarks, both in Greece and Rome the measures taken against witchcraft seem to have been almost entirely free from religious fanaticism, the magician being punished because he injured man and not because he offended God.[4] Sometimes we find even among a polytheistic people that sorcery is particularly opposed by its priesthood ; [5] but the reason for this is no doubt hatred of rivals rather than religious zeal. Miss Kingsley, however, does not think that the dislike of witchcraft in West Africa at large has originally anything to do with the priesthood.[6]

The religious intolerance which has accompanied the rise of monotheism is, as we have just observed, the result of the nature attributed to its godhead. But the evolution of religion does not end with the triumph of a jealous and irritable heavenly despot. There is a later stage where men believe in a god or supernatural power which is absolutely free from all human weakness, and in such a religion intolerance has no place. It has been said that the tolerant spirit of Buddhism[7] is due to religious

[1] *Lex Duodecim Tabularum,* viii. 25.
[2] Lecky, *History of European Morals,* i. 420.
[3] Plato, *Leges,* xi. 933.
[4] Lecky, *Rationalism in Europe,* i. 18.
[5] Kingsley, *West African Studies,* p. 137. Rink, *Greenland,* p. 201.
[6] Kingsley, *West African Studies,*

p. 135 *sq.*
[7] Hardy, *Eastern Monachism,* p. 412. Monier-Williams, *Buddhism,* p. 126. Waddell, *Buddhism of Tibet,* p. 568. Edkins, *Religion in China,* p. 127. Gutzlaff, *Sketch of Chinese History,* i. 70. Forbes, *British Burma,* p. 322 *sq.*

indifference,[1] but the original cause of it seems to be the absence of a personal god ; and the increasing tolerance of modern Christianity is undoubtedly connected with the more ethical view it takes of the Deity when compared with the opinions of earlier ages. It should be remembered, however, that religious toleration does not mean passive indifference with regard to dissenting religious ideas. The tolerant man may be a great propagandist. He may do his utmost to eradicate, by means of persuasion, what he considers to be a false belief. He may even resort to stronger measures against those who do mischief in the name of their religion. But he does not persecute anybody for the sake of his faith ; nor does he believe in an intolerant and persecuting god.

Supernatural beings, according to the belief of many races, desire to be worshipped not only because they depend upon human care for their subsistence or comfort, but because worship is an act of homage. We have seen that sacrifice, after losing its original significance, still survives as a reverent offering. So also prayer is frequently a tribute to the self-regarding pride of the god to whom it is addressed. A supplication is an act of humility, more or less flattering to the person appealed to and especially gratifying where, as in the case of a god, the granting of the request entails no deprivation or loss, but on the contrary is rewarded by the worshipper. Moreover, the request is very commonly accompanied by reverential epithets or words of eulogy ; and praise, nay even flattery, is just as pleasant to superhuman as to human ears. Gods are addressed as great or mighty, as lords or kings, as fathers or grandfathers.[2] A prayer of the ancient Peruvians began with the following words :—" O conquering Viracocha ! Ever present Viracocha ! Thou art in the ends of the earth without equal ! "[3]

[1] Forbes, *op. cit.* p. 322. *Cf.* Kuenen, *Hibbert Lectures on National Religions and Universal Religions,* p. 290.
[2] See Brinton, *Religions of Primi-tive Peoples,* p. 105.
[3] de Molina, ' Fables and Rites of the Yncas,' in *Narratives of the Rites and Laws of the Yncas,* p. 33.

The ancient Egyptians flattered their gods,[1] the Vedic and Zoroastrian hymns are full of praise. Muhammedans invoke Allah by sentences such as, "God is great," "God is merciful," "God is he who seeth and heareth." Words of praise, as well as words of thanks, addressed to a god, may certainly be the expressions of unreflecting admiration or gratitude, free from all thought of pleasing him ; but where laudation is demanded by the god as a price for good services, it is simply a tribute to his vanity. There is a Chinese story which amusingly illustrates this little weakness of so many gods :—At the hottest season of the year there was a heavy fall of snow at Soochow. The people, in their consternation, went to the temple of the Great Prince to pray. Then the spirit moved one of them to say, "You now address me as Your Honour. Make it Your Excellency, and, though I am but a lesser deity, it may be well worth your while to do so." Thereupon the people began to use the latter term, and the snow stopped at once.[2] The Hindus say that by praise a person may obtain from the gods whatever he desires.[3]

We have different means of gratifying a person's self-regarding pride : one is to praise him, another is to humiliate ourselves. Both have been adopted by men with reference to their gods. Besides hymns of praise there are hymns of penitence, the object of which is largely to appease the angry feelings of offended gods. Prayers for remission of sins form a whole literature among peoples like that of the Vedic age, the Chaldeans,[4] and the Hebrews, who commonly regarded calamities to which men were subject not as the result of an inexorable fate nor as the machinations of evil spirits, but as divine punishments. According to early ideas, as we have seen, sin is a substance charged with injurious

[1] Amélineau *L'évolution des idées morales dans l'Égypte ancienne*, p. 214.

[2] Giles, *Strange Stories from a Chinese Studio*, ii. 294.

[3] Ward, *View of the History, Literature, and Religion of the Hindoos*, ii. 69.

[4] Zimmern, *Babylonische Busspsalmen*, *passim.* Mürdter-Delitzsch, *Geschichte Babyloniens und Assyriens*, p. 38 *sq.* Delitzsch, *Wo lag das Paradies ?* p. 86. Hommel, *Die semitischen Völker und Sprachen*, p. 315 *sqq.* Meyer, *Geschichte des Alterthums*, i. 178.

energy, from which the infected person tries to rid himself by mechanical means.[1] But at the same time the effect of sin is conceived as a divine punishment, and this suggests atonement. In the Rig-Veda we not only hear of the removal of sins by magical operations, but the gods are requested to free the sufferer from his sin.[2]

Gods are fond of prayers not only as expressions of humility or repentance but for other reasons as well. In early religion a prayer is commonly connected with an offering, since the god is not supposed to bestow his favours gratuitously.[3] By the call contained in it he is invited to partake of the offering, or his attention is drawn to it.[4] " Compassionate father ! " says the Tanna priest when he offers first-fruits to a deified ancestor ; " here is some food for you, eat it, and be kind to us on account of it ! " [5] In one of the Pahlavi texts it is said that when the guardian spirits of the righteous are invited they accept the sacrifice, whereas if they are not invited " they go up the height of a spear and will remain." [6] Throughout the Yasts we hear of the claims of deities to be worshipped with sacrifices in which they are invoked by their own names and with the proper words.[7] Mithra complains, " If men would worship me with a sacrifice in which I were invoked by my own name, as they worship the other Yazatas with sacrifices in which they are invoked by their own names, then I would come to the faithful at the appointed time."[8]

---

[1] *Supra*, i. 52 *sqq.*
[2] See Oldenberg, *Die Religion des Veda*, pp. 292, 296, 317 *sq.*
[3] Tylor, *Primitive Culture*, ii. 364 *sqq.* Georgi, *Russia*, iii. 272 (shamanistic peoples of Siberia). Maspero, *Études de mythologie et d'archéologie égyptiennes*, i. 163 ; *Idem, Dawn of Civilization*, p. 124, n. 5 (ancient Egyptians). Darmesteter, in *Sacred Books of the East*, iv. (1st ed.) p. lxix. (Zoroastrians). Oldenberg, *op. cit.* p. 430 *sqq* ; Barth, *Religions of India*, p. 34 (Vedic people). Donaldson, 'Expiatory and Substitutionary Sacrifices of the Greeks,' in *Trans.*

Roy. Soc. Edinburgh, xxvii. 430. Grimm, *Teutonic Mythology*, i. 29. Among the Kafirs of Natal " a soldier wounded in battle would only pray if his hurt were slight ; but if it were serious, he would vow a sacrifice on his return, naming perhaps the particular beast " (Shooter, *Kafirs of Natal*, p. 164).
[4] *Cf.* Brinton, *Religions of Primitive Peoples*, p. 104.
[5] Turner, *Nineteen Years in Polynesia*, p. 88.
[6] *Shâyast Lâ-Shâyast*, ix. 12.
[7] *Yasts*, viii. 23 *sqq.* ; x. 30.
[8] *Ibid.* x. 55. *Cf. ibid.* x. 74.

According to Vedic and Zoroastrian texts the gods were purified, strengthened, and encouraged not only by offerings but by prayers, although it is difficult in this respect to distinguish between two elements in one and the same rite which are so closely interwoven with each other.[1] By his invocations man assists the gods in their combats with evil demons, he sends his prayer between the earth and the heavens there to smite the fiends.[2] In a Vedic hymn the people are exhorted to " sing to Indra a song very destructive to the demons." [3] By pronouncing the praise of Asha, Zarathustra brings the Daevas to naught ; [4] by mentioning the name of Ahura Mazda their malice is most effectually destroyed.[5] Thus prayer may be a religious duty also on account of the magic efficacy ascribed to it, and the same is the case with incantations directed against evil spirits.

In earlier chapters we have often noticed how curses gradually develop into genuine prayers, and *vice versa* may a prayer develop into a curse or spell. Dr. Rivers observes that the formulæ used in Toda magic have the form of prayers.[6] So also Assyrian incantations are often dressed in the robe of supplication, and end with the formula, " Do so and so, and I shall gladden thine heart and worship thee in humility." [7] Vedic texts which were not originally meant as charms became so afterwards. Incantations are comparatively rare in the Rig-Veda, and seem even to be looked upon as objectionable, but towards the end of the Vedic period the reign of Brahma, the power of prayer, as the supreme god in the Indian Pantheon began to dawn.[8]

[1] See Bergaigne, *La religion védique*, ii. 237, 250, 273 *sqq.* ; Zimmer, *Altindisches Leben*, p. 337 *sqq.*; Oldenberg, *Religion des Veda*, p. 437; Macdonell, *Vedic Mythology*, p. 60 ; Meyer, *Geschichte des Alterthums*, i. 534 *sq.* (Zoroastrianism).

[2] *Yasna*, xxviii. 7. *Yasts*, iii. 5. *Vendîdâd*, xix. 1, 2, 8 *sqq.* Darmesteter, *Ormazd et Ahriman*, pp. 101, 119, 131, 193. *Idem*, in *Sacred Books of the East*, iv. (1st ed.) p. lxix.

[3] *Rig-Veda*, viii. 78. 1.

[4] *Yasts*, xiii. 89. *Cf. ibid.* xiii. 90.

[5] *Ibid.* i. 3, 4, 10, 11, 19.

[6] Rivers, *Todas*, pp. 450, 453.

[7] Tallqvist, ' Die assyrische Beschwörungsserie Maqlû,' in *Acta Soc. Scient. Fennicæ*, xx. 22.

[8] Oldenberg, *op. cit.* p. 311 *sqq.* Hopkins, *op. cit.* p. 149. Roth, ' Brahma und die Brahmanen,' in *Zeitschr. d. Deutschen Morgenländischen Gesellsch.* i. 67, 71. Darmesteter, *Essais orientaux*, p. 132.

Brahma is a force by which the gods act, by which they
are born, and by which the world has been formed ;[1]
but it is also the prayer which ascends from the altar to
heaven and by means of which man wrests from the gods
the boon he demands [2]—" the prayer governs them." [3]
This omnipresent force is personified in Brahmaṇaspati, the
lord of prayer, who resides in the highest heaven but of
whom not only every separate god but the priest himself
becomes a manifestation at the moment he pronounces the
mantras or sacred texts.[4] It is a current saying in India
that the whole universe is subject to the gods, that the
gods are subject to the mantras, that the mantras are
subject to the Brahmans, and that therefore the Brahmans
are the real gods.[5] In Zoroastrianism prayers are not made
efficacious by devotion and fervency, but to the words
themselves belongs a mysterious power and the mere
recitation of them, if correct and faultless, brings that
power into action ; [6] in the Yasts prayer is regarded as a
goddess, as the daughter of Ahura Mazda.[7] In ancient
Egypt, M. Maspero observes, " la prière n'était pas comme
chez nous une pétition que l'homme présente au dieu, et
que le dieu est libre d'accepter ou de refuser à son gré :
c'était une formule dont les terms ont une valeur impéra-
tive, et dont l'énonciation exacte oblige le dieu à concéder
ce qu'on lui demande."[8] Greek literature supplies other
instances of men conjuring their gods by incantations ;[9]
the word ἀρά means both prayer and curse.[10] And " in the
Roman, as in the majority of the old Italian cults, prayer
is a magic formula, producing its effect by its own inherent
quality." [11]

[1] *Atharva-Veda*, xi. 5. 5. Barth, *op. cit.* p. 38.
[2] Roth, *loc. cit.* p. 66 *sqq.* Barth, *op. cit.* p. 38. Darmesteter, *Ormazd et Ahriman*, p. 101.
[3] *Rig-Veda*, vi. 51. 8.
[4] Barth, *op. cit.* p. 15 *sq.* Roth, *loc. cit.* p. 71.
[5] Monier - Williams, *Brāhmanism and Hindūism*, p. 201 *sq.*
[6] See Geiger, *Civilization of the Eastern Irānians*, i. 71.
[7] *Yasts*, xiii. 92 ; xvii. 16.
[8] Maspero, *Études de mythologie et d'archéologie égyptiennes*, i. 163.
[9] See Usener, *Götternamen*, p. 335*sq.*
[10] *Cf.* von Lasaulx, *Der Fluch bei Griechen und Römern*, p. 6. So also the Manx word *gwee* means both prayer and curse (Rhys, *Celtic Folklore*, i. 349).
[11] Renan, *Hibbert Lectures on the Influence of the Institutions, &c. of Rome on Christianity*, p. 10 *sq.* *Cf.*

Whilst an ordinary curse readily develops into a prayer when the name of a god is brought in for the purpose of giving magic efficacy to the curse, a prayer may contrariwise assume a magic character by being addressed to a god —just as a sacrifice becomes endowed with magic energy in consequence of its contact or communion with the supernatural being to which it is offered; and the constraining force in the prayer or sacrifice may then be directed even against the god himself. But there can be little doubt that the extreme importance which the magic element in the cult attained among the nations of ancient civilisation was chiefly due to the prevalence of a powerful priesthood or class of persons well versed in sacred texts. A successful incantation presupposes a certain knowledge in him who utters it. The words of the formulæ are fixed and may not suffer the slightest modification under penalty of losing their potency. Right intonation is equally important.[1] The Brâhmanic mantras " must be pronounced according to certain mystic forms and with absolute accuracy, or their efficacy is destroyed " ; nay, if in the repetition of a mantra the slightest mistake is made, either by omission of a syllable or defective pronunciation, the calamity which it was intended to bring down on an enemy will inevitably recoil on the head of the repeater.[2] The potency of the incantation largely lies in the voice, which is the magical instrument *par excellence*.[3] A Buddhist priest who was asked what advantage he could expect to derive from merely repeating a number of words with the sense of which he was entirely unacquainted, gave the answer that the advantage of often repeating the sounds was incalculable, infinite ;[4] and a Muhammedan writer argues that prayers which are offered in any other language than

Jevons, in Plutarch's *Romane Questions*, p. xxviii. ; Granger, *Worship of the Romans*, p. 158.
[1] Maspero, *Études*, i. 109 ; *Idem, Dawn of Civilization*, pp. 146, 213 (ancient Egyptians). Sayce, *Hibbert Lectures on the Religion of the Ancient Babylonians*, p. 319. Darmesteter, *Ormazd et Ahriman*, p. 9. Sell,

Faith of Islám, pp. 53, 79, 334, 341.
[2] Monier-Williams, *Brâhmanism and Hindüism*, p. 199.
[3] *Yasts*, iv. 5. Maspero, *Études*, ii. 373 *sq.* ; *Idem, Dawn of Civilization*, p. 146 (ancient Egyptians). Sell, *op. cit.* p. 318 (Muhammedans).
[4] *Indo-Chinese Gleaner*, iii. 145.

Arabic are profane and useless, because " the sounds of
this language "—whether understood or not—" illuminate
the darkness of men " and " purify the hearts of the
faithful." [1] Ideas of this sort are of course most strongly
advocated by those who derive the greatest profit from
them—priests or scribes. And it is easy to understand
that with their increasing influence among a superstitious
and credulous people the magic significance which is so
readily ascribed to a religious act also has a tendency to
grow in importance.

Among all sins there is none which gods resent more
severely than disobedience to their commandments. Mr.
Macdonald says of the Efatese, in the New Hebrides, that
no people under the sun is more obedient to what they
regard as divine mandates than these savages, who believe
that an offence against a spiritual being means calamity
and death.[2] The Chaldeans had a lively sense of the
risks entailed upon the sinner by disobedience to the gods.[3]
According to the Bible disobedience was the first sin
committed by man, and death was introduced into the
world as its punishment. " Rebellion is as the sin of
witchcraft, and stubbornness is as iniquity and idolatry."[4]
On the history of morals this demand of obedience has
exercised considerable influence. It gives emphasis to
moral rules which are looked upon as divine injunctions,
and it helps to preserve such rules after the conditions
from which they sprang have ceased to exist. The fact
that they have become meaningless does not render them
less binding ; on the contrary, the mystery surrounding
them often increases their sanctity. The commandments
of a god must be obeyed independently of their contents,
simply because disobedience to him is a sin. Acts totally
different in character, crimes of the worst description and

---

[1] *Indo-Chinese Gleaner*, iii. 146.
[2] Macdonald, *Oceania*, p. 201.
[3] Maspero, *Dawn of Civilization*, p.
682. Delitzsch, *Wo lag das Paradies?*
p. 86.
[4] 1 *Samuel*, xv. 23. Schultz, *Old*

Testament Theology, ii. 286. For
other instances see *Rig-Veda*, vii. 89.
5 ; Geiger, *Civilization of the Eastern
Iranians*, i. p. li. ; Schmidt, *Die
Ethik der alten Griechen*, ii. 51 *sq.*

practices by themselves perfectly harmless, are grouped together as almost equally offensive to the deity because they have been forbidden by him.[1] And moral progress is hampered by a number of precepts which, though rooted in obsolete superstitions or antiquated ideas about right and wrong, have an obstinate tendency to persist on account of their supposed divine origin.[2]

Duties to gods are in the first place based on prudential considerations. Supernatural beings, even when on the whole of a benevolent disposition, are no less resentful than men, and, owing to their superhuman power, much more dangerous. On the other hand, they may also bestow wonderful benefits upon those who please them. The general rule that prudence readily assumes a moral value holds particularly true of religious matters, where great individual interests are at stake. Waterland says in his Sermon on Self-love :—" The wisest course for any man to take is to secure an interest in the life to come. . . . He may love himself, in this instance, as highly and as tenderly as he pleases. There can be no excess of fondness, or self-indulgence, in respect of eternal happiness. This is loving himself in the best manner, and to the best purposes. All virtue and piety are thus resolvable into a principle of self-love. . . . It is with reference to ourselves, and for our own sakes, that we love even God himself." [3]

At the same time it may be not only in people's own interests, but in the interests of their fellow men as well, for them to be on friendly terms with supernatural beings. These beings often visit the iniquity of fathers or forefathers upon children or descendants, or punish the community for the sins of one of its members ; [4] and, on the other hand, they reward the whole family or group for the virtues of a single individual.[5] So also, when the

---

[1] *Cf. supra*, i. 193 *sqq.*
[2] *Cf.* Pollock, *Essays on Jurisprudence and Ethics*, p. 306 *sq.*
[3] Waterland, 'On Self-Love,' in *The English Preacher*, i. 101 *sq. Cf.* Paley's definition of virtue in his *Principles of Moral and Political Philosophy*, i. 7 (*Complete Works*, ii. 38; *supra*, i. 300).
[4] *Supra*, i. 48 *sqq.*
[5] *Supra*, i. 96 *sqq.*

members of a community join in common acts of worship, each worshipper promotes not only his own welfare, but the welfare of his people. In early religion it is of the utmost importance for the tribe or nation that the established cult should be strictly observed. This is a fact which cannot be too much emphasised when we have to explain how conduct which is pleasing to a god has come to be regarded as a moral duty; for, if the latest stages of religious development be excepted, the relations between men and their gods are communal rather than individual in character. Ahura Mazda said, " If men sacrifice unto Verethraghna, made by Ahura, if the due sacrifice and prayer is offered unto him just as it ought to be performed in the perfection of holiness, never will a hostile horde enter the Aryan countries, nor any plague, nor leprosy, nor venomous plants, nor the chariot of a foe, nor the uplifted spear of a foe! " [1] Thus the duties to gods are at the same time social duties of the first order, owing to the intensely social character of religious relationships.

Another circumstance which has contributed to the moral condemnation of offences against gods is that people are anxious to punish such offences in order to prevent the divine wrath from turning against themselves; [2] for punishment, as we have seen, easily leads to moral disapproval. But although prudential considerations of some kind or other be the chief cause of the obligatory character attached to men's conduct towards their gods, they are not the only cause. We must also remember that gods are regarded with genuine reverence by their worshippers; and where this is the case offences against religion naturally excite sympathetic resentment in the latter, whilst great piety calls forth sympathetic approval and is praised as a virtue.

I have here spoken of duties which men consider they owe to their gods, not of duties to supernatural beings in general. This distinction, though not always easy to

---

[1] *Yasts*, xiv. 48.　　　　[2] *Supra*, i. 194.

follow in detail, is yet of vital importance. People may no doubt be afraid to offend and even anxious to please other spirits besides their gods, but religious duties chiefly arise where there are established relationships between men and supernatural beings ; indeed, it may even be a duty to refrain from worshipping or actually to persecute other spirits, as is the case in monotheistic religions. Men depend for their welfare on their gods more than on any other members of the spiritual world. They select as their gods those supernatural beings from whom they think they have most to fear or most to hope. Hence it is generally in the relations to them only that those factors, prudential and reverential, are to be found which lead to the establishment of religious duties.

CHAPTER L

GODS AS GUARDIANS OF MORALITY

As men are concerned about the conduct of their fellow men towards their gods, so gods are in many cases concerned about men's conduct towards one another—disapproving of vice and punishing the wicked, approving of virtue and rewarding the good. But this is by no means a universal characteristic of gods. It is a quality attributed to certain deities only and, as it seems, in most instances slowly acquired.

We are told by competent observers that the supernatural beings of savage belief frequently display the utmost indifference to all questions of worldly morality. According to Messrs. Spencer and Gillen, the Central Australian natives, though they assume the existence of both friendly and mischievous spirits, " have not the vaguest idea of a personal individual other than an actual living member of the tribe who approves or disapproves of their conduct, so far as anything like what we call morality is concerned." [1] The Society Islanders maintained that " the only crimes that were visited by the displeasure of their deities were the neglect of some rite or ceremony." [2] The religious belief of the Gonds of Central India is said to be wholly unconnected with any idea of morality ; a moral deity demanding righteous conduct from his creatures, our informant adds, is a religious

---

[1] Spencer and Gillen, *Northern Tribes of Central Australia*, p. 491.

[2] Ellis, *Polynesian Researches*, i. 397.

conception far beyond the present capacity either of the Indian savage or the ordinary Hindu.[1] Of the Ewe-, Yoruba-, and Tshi-speaking peoples of the West African Slave and Gold Coasts Major Ellis writes :—" Religion, at the stage of growth in which we find it among these three groups of tribes, has no connection with morals, or the relations of men to one another. It consists solely of ceremonial worship, and the gods are only offended when some rite or ceremony has been neglected or omitted. . . . Murder, theft, and all offences against the person or against property, are matters in which the gods have no immediate concern, and in which they take no interest, except in the case when, bribed by a valuable offering, they take up the quarrel in the interests of some faithful worshipper."[2] So also among the Bambala, a Bantu tribe in the Kasai, south of the River Congo, " there is no belief that the gods or spirits punish wrong-doing by afflicting the criminal or his family, nor are the acts of a man supposed to affect his condition after death."[3] The Indians of Guiana, says Sir E. F. Im Thurn, observe an admirable code of morality, which exists side by side with a simple animistic form of religion, but the two have absolutely no connection with one another.[4] With reference to the Tarahumares of Mexico Dr. Lumholtz states that the only wrong towards the gods of which an Indian may consider himself guilty is that he does not dance enough. " For this offence he asks pardon. Whatever bad thoughts or actions toward man he may have on his conscience are settled between himself and the person offended."[5] " In the primitive Indian's conception of a god," Mr. Parkman observes, " the idea of moral good

---

[1] Forsyth, *Highlands of Central India*, p. 145. See also Hodgson, *Miscellaneous Essays*, i. 124 (Bódo and Dhimáls) ; Caldwell, *Tinnevelly Shanars*, p. 36; Lyall, *Asiatic Studies*, p. 45 ; Radloff, *Das Schamanenthum*, p. 13 (Turkish tribes of the Altai).

[2] Ellis, *Yoruba-speaking Peoples of the Slave Coast*, p. 293. *Idem, Tshi-speaking Peoples of the Gold Coast*,

p. 10. The Ewe god Mawu is represented as an exception to this rule (*infra*, p. 686).

[3] Torday and Joyce, ' Ethnography of the Ba-Mbala,' in *Jour. Anthr. Inst.* xxxv. 415.

[4] Im Thurn, *Indians of Guiana*, p. 342.

[5] Lumholtz, *Unknown Mexico*, i. 332.

has no part. His deity does not dispense justice for this world or the next." [1]

That many savage gods are so thoroughly selfish as to care about nothing else than what concerns their own interests, may also be inferred from the character attributed to them. We have seen that the altruistic sentiment is the chief source from which moral emotions spring, and of the gods of various uncivilised peoples we hear not only that they are totally destitute of benevolent feelings, but that they are of a malicious nature and mostly intent on doing harm to mankind.[2]

The Maoris of New Zealand regarded their deities as the causes of pain, misery, and death, as mighty enemies from whom nobody ever thought of getting any aid or good, but who were to be rendered harmless by means of charms or spells or by sacrifices offered to appease their wrath.[3] The Tahitians "supposed their gods were powerful spiritual beings, in some degree acquainted with the events of this world, and generally governing its affairs ; never exercising any thing like benevolence towards even their most devoted followers, but requiring homage and obedience, with constant offerings ; denouncing their anger, and dispensing destruction on all who either refused or hesitated to comply." [4] The Fijians "formed no idea of any voluntary kindness on the part of their gods, except the planting of wild yams, and the wrecking of strange canoes and foreign vessels on their coast " ;[5] and that some of these beings were conceived as positively wicked is indicated by the names given them—" the adulterer," " the rioter," " the murderer," and so forth.[6] The people of Aneiteum, in the New Hebrides, maintained that " earth and air and ocean were filled with natmasses, spiritual beings, but all malignant, who ruled over everything that affected the human race. . . . Their deities, like themselves, were

[1] Parkman, *Jesuits in North America*, p. lxxviii. See also Eastman, *Dacotah*, p. xx. ; Schoolcraft, *Indian Tribes of the United States*, ii. 195 (Dacotahs).

[2] See Meiners, *Geschichte der Religionen*, i. 405 ; Tylor, *Primitive Culture*, ii. 329 ; Avebury, *Origin of Civilisation*, p. 232 *sqq.* ; Roskoff, *Geschichte des Teufels*, i. 20 *sq.* ;

Frazer, *Golden Bough*, iii. 40 *sqq.* ; Karsten, *Origin of Worship*, p. 46 *sqq.*

[3] Taylor, *Te Ika a Maui*, pp. 104, 148. Colenso, *Maori Races of New Zealand*, p. 62. *Cf.* Dieffenbach, *Travels in New Zealand*, ii. 118.

[4] Ellis, *Polynesian Researches*, i. 336.

[5] Williams and Calvert, *Fiji*, p. 195.

[6] *Ibid.* p. 185.

all selfish and malignant; they breathed no spirit of benevolence."[1]

The Santal of India believes in no god from whose benignity he may expect favour, but in "a multitude of demons and evil spirits, whose spite he endeavours by supplications to avert." Even his family god "represents the secret principle of evil, which no bolts can shut out, and which dwells in unseen but eternally malignant presence beside every hearth."[2] The Kamchadales do not seem to have hoped for anything good from their deities ; Kutka himself, the creator of the universe and the greatest of the gods, was once caught in adultery and castrated.[3]

According to the beliefs of the Koksoagmyut, or Hudson Bay Eskimo, all the minor spirits are under the control of the great spirit whose name is Tung ak, and this being " is nothing more or less than death, which ever seeks to torment and harass the lives of people that their spirits may go to dwell with him."[4] Nay, even the special guardian spirit by which each person is supposed to be attended is malignant in character and ever ready to seize upon the least occasion to work harm upon the individual whom it accompanies ; its good offices can be obtained by propitiation only.[5] Among the Nenenot, or Indians of Hudson Bay, " the rule seems to be that all spirits are by nature bad, and must be propitiated to secure their favour."[6] Of various Brazilian tribes we are likewise told that they do not believe in the existence of any benevolent spirits. Thus the Coroado Indian acknowledges only an evil principle, which sometimes meets him in the form of a lizard or a crocodile or an ounce or a man with the feet of a stag, sometimes transforms itself into a swamp, and leads him astray, vexes him, brings him into difficulty and danger, and even kills him.[7] The Mundrucus of the Cuparí have no notion of a good supreme being, but believe in an evil spirit, regarded merely as a kind of hobgoblin, who is at the bottom of all their little failures and gives them troubles in fishing, hunting, and so forth.[8] The Uaupés, says Mr. Wallace, "appear to have no definite idea of a God. . . . They have much more definite ideas of a bad spirit, ' Jurupari,' or Devil, whom they fear and

---

[1] Inglis, In the New Hebrides, pp. 30, 32.

[2] Hunter, Annals of Rural Bengal, i. 181 sq.

[3] Klemm, Cultur-Geschichte der Menschheit, ii. 318 sq. Steller, Beschreibung von Kamtschatka, p. 264.

[4] Turner, ' Ethnology of the Un-gava District,' in Ann. Rep. Bur. Ethn. xi. 272.

[5] Ibid. p. 194.

[6] Ibid. p. 193 sq.

[7] von Spix and von Martius, Travels in Brazil, ii. 243.

[8] Bates, The Naturalist on the River Amazons, ii. 137.

endeavour through their *pagés* [or medicine men] to propitiate. When it thunders, they say the ' Juruparí ' is angry, and their idea of natural death is that the ' Juruparí ' kills them." [1]

In Eastern Africa, according to Burton, " the sentiment generally elicited by a discourse upon the subject of the existence of a Deity is a desire to see him, in order to revenge upon him the deaths of relatives, friends, and cattle." [2] The only quality of a moral character which the Wanika are said to ascribe to the supreme being, Mulungu, is that of vindictiveness and cruelty.[3] To the Matabele the idea of a benevolent deity is utterly foreign, but they have a vague notion of a number of evil spirits always ready to do harm, and the chief among these are the spirits of their ancestors.[4] All the good the Bechuanas enjoy they ascribe to rainmakers, but " all the evil that comes they attri- bute to a supernatural being " ; [5] of their principal god, Morimo, Mr. Moffat never once, in the course of twenty-five years spent in missionary labour, heard that he did good or was capable of doing so.[6] Among various other African peoples, travellers assure us, supernatural beings are supposed to exercise a potent influence for evil rather than for good, or beneficent spirits are, at any rate, almost unknown.[7] On the Gold Coast, according to Major Ellis, the majority of spirits are malignant, and every misfortune is ascribed to their action. " I believe," he adds, " that originally all were conceived as malignant, and that the indifference, or the beneficence (when propitiated by sacrifice and flattery), which are now believed to be characteristics of some of these beings, are later modifications of the original idea." [8]

Of many savages it is reported that they have notions of good, as well as of evil spirits, but that they chiefly or exclusively worship the evil ones, since the others are supposed to be so good that they require no offerings or homage.[9] But adoration of supernatural beings which are

[1] Wallace, *Travels on the Amazon*, p. 500.
[2] Burton, *Lake Regions of Central Africa*, ii. 348.
[3] New, *Life, Wanderings, and Labours in Eastern Africa*, p. 103 sq.
[4] Decle, *Three Years in Savage Africa*, p. 153.
[5] Campbell, *Second Journey in the Interior of South Africa*, ii. 204.
[6] Moffat, *Missionary Labours in Southern Africa* (ed. 1842), p. 262.
[7] Rowley, *Religion of the Africans*, p. 55. Kingsley, *Travels in West Africa*, p. 443. Mockler-Ferryman, *British Nigeria*, p. 255 sq.
[8] Ellis, *Tshi-speaking Peoples*, pp. 12, 18, 20. *Cf.* Cruickshank, *Eigh- teen Years on the Gold Coast*, ii. 134.
[9] Wilken, *Het Animisme bij de vol- ken van den Indischen Archipel*, p. 207 sq. Perham, ' Sea Dyak Religion,' in *Jour. Straits Branch Roy. Asiatic Soc.* no. 10, p. 220 ; St. John, *Life in*

considered at least occasionally beneficent is also very prevalent among uncivilised peoples.[1] The gods of the pagan Lapps were all good, although they took revenge upon those who offended them.[2] Among the Navaho Indians of New Mexico " the gods who are supposed to love and help men the most receive the greatest honour " ; whereas the evil spirits are not worshipped except, rumour says, by the witches.[3] The belief in guardian or tutelary spirits of tribes, clans, villages, families, or individuals, is extremely widespread.[4] These spirits may be exacting enough—they are often greatly feared by their own worshippers, and sometimes described as distinctly malig-

the Forests of the Far East, i. 69 sq. (Sea Dyaks). Blumentritt, ' Der Ahnencultus und die religiösen Anschauungen der Malaien des Philippinen-Archipels,' in Mittheil. d. kais. u. kön. Geograph. Gesellsch. in Wien, xxv. 166 sqq. Prain, ' Angami Nagas,' in Revue coloniale internationale, v. 489. Forsyth, op. cit. pp. 141, 143 (Gonds). Hooker, Himalayan Journals, i. 126 (Lepchas). Robertson, History of America, i. 383 ; Müller, Geschichte der Amerikanischen Urreligionen, pp. 150, 151, 232, 260 ; Dorman, Origin of Primitive Superstition, p. 30 (American Indians). Sproat, Scenes and Studies of Savage Life, p. 212 (Ahts). Falkner, Description of Patagonia, p. 116 ; Prichard, Through the Heart of Patagonia, p. 97.

[1] See supra, ii. 615 sq.
[2] von Düben, Lappland, pp. 227, 285. Friis, Lappisk Mythologi, p. 106. Jessen, Norske Finners og Lappers Hedenske Religion, p. 33.
[3] Matthews, Navaho Legends, p. 40. See also ibid. p. 33.
[4] Ellis, Tshi-speaking Peoples of the Gold Coast, pp. 17, 18, 77, 92. Idem, Ewe-speaking Peoples of the Slave Coast, p. 75. Wilson, Western Africa, p. 387 (Mpongwe). Tuckey, River Zaire, p. 375. Ellis, History of Madagascar, i. 395 sq. Ratzel, History of Mankind, i. 321 (various South Sea Islanders). Turner, Samoa, p. 17 sq. Williams and Calvert, Fiji, p. 185 sq. Inglis, op. cit. p. 30 (people of Aneiteum). Christian, Caroline Islands, p. 75. Wilken, Het Animisme, pp. 231

sqq. (Minahassers, Macassars, and Bugis of Celebes), 243 (Javanese). Selenka, Sonnige Welten, p. 103 sq. (Dyaks). Forbes, Insulinde, p. 203 (natives of Tenimber). von Brenner, Besuch bei den Kannibalen Sumatras, p. 221 (Bataks). Mason, ' Religion, &c. among the Karens,' in Jour. Asiatic Soc. Bengal, xxxiv. 196. Hunter, Annals of Rural Bengal, i. 182, 186 sq. (Santals). Hodgson, Miscellaneous Essays, i. 128 (Bódo and Dhimáls). Bailey, ' Veddahs of Ceylon,' in Trans. Ethn. Soc. N.S. ii. 301; Nevill, ' Vaeddas of Ceylon,' in Taprobanian, i. 194. Schmidt, Ceylon, p. 291 sq. (Tamils). Bergmann, Nomadische Streifereien unter den Kalmüken, iii. 182 sq. Abercromby, Pre- and Protohistoric Finns, i. 160 (Ostiaks). Buch, ' Die Wotjäken,' in Acta Soc. Scient. Fennicæ, xii. 595 sq. Castrén, Nordiska resor och forskningar, iii. 106, 107, 174 sq. (Finnish tribes). Boas, ' Central Eskimo,' in Ann. Rep. Bur. Ethn. vi. 591. Turner, ibid. xi. 193 sq. (Hudson Bay Eskimo), 272 (Hudson Bay Indians). Hoffman, ' Menomini Indians,' ibid. xiv. 65. McGee, ' Siouan Indians,' ibid. xv. 179 ; Parkman, op. cit. p. lxx ; Dorman, op. cit. p. 227 (North American Indians). Müller, Geschichte der Amerikanischen Urreligionen, pp. 72 (North American Indians), 171 (Indians of the Great Antilles). Couto de Magalhães, Trabalho preparatorio para aproveitamento do selvagem no Brazil —O selvagem, p. 128 sqq. Tylor, op. cit. ii. 199 sqq.

nant by nature; [1] but their general function is nevertheless to afford assistance to the person or persons with
whom they are associated. At the same time it should be
noticed that the goodness of many savage gods only
consists in their readiness to help those who please them
by offerings or adoration; and in no case does their
benevolence prove that they take an active interest in
morality at large. A friendly supernatural being is not
necessarily a guardian of men's behaviour towards their
fellow men. In Morocco the patron saint of a town,
village, or tribe is not in the least concerned about any
kind of conduct which has not immediate reference to
himself. [2] It is believed that even the robber may, by
invoking a dead saint, secure his assistance in an unlawful
enterprise.

On the other hand, instances are not wanting in which
savage gods are supposed to punish the transgression of
rules relating to worldly morality. Occasionally, as we
have noticed above, such gods are represented as avengers
of some special kind of wrong-doing—murder, [3] theft, [4]
niggardliness, [5] want of hospitality, [6] or lying. [7] Of certain
Negro tribes we are told that, " when a man is about to
commit a crime, or do that which his conscience tells him
he ought not to do, he lays aside his fetiche, and covers
up his deity, that he may not be privy to the deed." [8]
The Tonga Islanders " firmly believe that the gods
approve of virtue, and are displeased with vice; that
every man has his tutelar deity, who will protect him as
long as he conducts himself as he ought to do; but, if
he does not, will leave him to the approaches of misfortune, disease, and death. . . . All rewards for virtue or
punishments for vice happen to men in this world only,

---

[1] Schmidt, Ceylon, p. 291 sq. (Tamils). Turner, in Ann. Rep. Bur.
Ethn. xi. 193 sq. (Hudson Bay Eskimo), 272 (Hudson Bay Indians).
McGee, ibid. xv. 179 ; Müller, op. cit.
p. 72 (North American Indians).
  [2] For a singular exception to this
rule see supra, ii. 67 sq.

[3] Supra, i. 378 sq.
[4] Supra, ii. 59 sq.
[5] Supra, i. 561 sq.
[6] Supra, i. 578.
[7] Supra, ii. 114 sq.
[8] Tuckey, op. cit. p. 377.   Cf.
Monrad, Skildring af Guinea-Kysten,
p. 27, n.*

and come immediately from the gods."[1] The Ainu of Japan are heard to say, " We could not go contrary to the customs of our ancestors without bringing down upon us the wrath of the gods."[2] And of various savages we are told that they believe in the existence of a supreme being who is a moral lawgiver or judge.

In Australia, especially in New South Wales and Victoria but also in other parts of the continent, many of the native tribes have the notion of an " All-father," called Baiame, Daramulun, Mungan-ngalla, Bunjil, Nurelli, Nurundere, or by some other name.[3] He is represented as an anthropomorphic, supernatural being and as the father of the race or the maker of everything, who at one time dwelt on the earth but afterwards ascended to a land beyond the sky, where he still remains. He is of a kindly disposition, and requires no worship ; in a very few cases only we meet with some faint traces of a cult offered him.[4]

[1] Mariner, *Natives of the Tonga Islands*, ii. 149, 107.

[2] Batchelor, *Ainu of Japan*, p. 243 sq.

[3] Henderson, *Colonies of New South Wales*, p. 147. de Strzelecki, *New South Wales*, p. 339. Manning, ' Aborigines of New Holland,' in *Jour. and Proceed. Roy. Soc. N.S. Wales*, xvi. 157 sqq. Ridley, *Kámilarói*, p. 135 sqq. Cameron, ' Some Tribes of New South Wales,' in *Jour. Anthr. Inst.* xiv. 364 sq. Langloh Parker, *Euahlayi Tribe*, p. 4 sqq. Threlkeld, *An Australian Language as spoken by the Awabakal*, p. 47. Mathews, *Aboriginal Tribes of New South Wales and Victoria*, p. 138 sqq. Mathew, *Eaglehawk and Crow*, p. 146 sqq. Fountain and Ward, *Rambles of an Australian Naturalist*, p. 296. *Missions-Blatt aus der Brüdergemeine*, xvi. 101,143 ; Parker, *Aborigines of Australia*, p. 24 ; Dawson, *Australian Aborigines*, p. 49 (tribes in Victoria). Brough Smyth, *Aborigines of Victoria*, i. 423 sqq. Taplin, ' Narrinyeri,' in Woods, *Native Tribes of South Australia*, p. 55 sqq. Howitt, *Native Tribes of South-East Australia*, p. 489 sqq. Spencer and Gillen, *Northern Tribes of Central Australia*, p. 498 sq. (Kaitish). Strehlow, quoted by Thomas, ' Religious Ideas of the Arunta,' in *Folk-Lore*, xvi. 429 sq. *Idem*, quoted by von Leonhardi, ' Religiöse und totemistische Vorstellungen der Aranda und Loritja in Zentralaustralien,' in *Globus*, xci. 286 sq. Curr, *The Australian Race*, i. 253 (Larrakia) ; ii. 465, 475 (some Cape River natives). Lang, *Cooksland*, p. 459 sq. ; *Idem, Queensland*, p. 379 sq. Roth, *Ethnol. Studies among the North-West-Central Queensland Aborigines*, pp. 16, 153, 158. Salvado, *Mémoires historiques sur l'Australie*, p. 258 (natives of West Australia).

[4] When the natives of Cooksland, in North-Eastern Australia, rob a wild bees' hive they generally leave a little of the honey for Buddai, the supernatural ancestor of their race (Lang, *Cooksland*, p. 460 ; *Idem, Queensland*, p. 380). Mrs. Langloh Parker (*op. cit.* pp. 8, 9, 79, 89) was told that in the Euahlayi tribe prayers are addressed to Byamee at funerals for the souls of the dead, and that at some initiatory rites the oldest medicine-man present addresses a prayer to him asking him to give the people long life as they have kept his law ; but they do not profess to pray or to have prayed to Byamee on any other occasions (*cf.* Manning, *loc. cit.* p. 164). The natives inhabiting the neighbourhood of Lake Boga in

He is frequently believed to have instituted the initiation ceremonies,[1] and to have given the people their laws.[2] Thus
Nurundere is said to have taught the Narrinyeri all the rites and
ceremonies whether connected with life or death ; on inquiry
why they adhere to any custom, the reply is that Nurundere
commanded it.[3] At the *boorah*, or initiation, of the Euahlayi
tribe, Byamee is proclaimed as " Father of All, whose laws the
tribes are now obeying " ; and in one of their myths he is
described as the original source of all the totems and of the law
that persons of the same totem may not intermarry.[4] Bunjil
taught the Kulin the arts of life, and told them to divide themselves into two intermarrying classes so as to prevent marriages
between kindred.[5] Daramulun instructed the Yuin what to
do and gave them laws which the old people have handed down
from father to son to the present time.[6] And in several instances
the Australian " All-father " is represented as a guardian of
morality who punishes the wicked and rewards the good.
Bunjil " very frequently sent his sons to destroy bad men and
bad women . . . who had killed and eaten blacks."[7]
Daramulun, or Tharamulun, who from his residence in the sky
watches the actions of men, " is very angry when they do things
that they ought not to do, as when they eat forbidden food."[8]
The natives of the Herbert River, in Queensland, believe that
anybody who takes a wife from the prohibited sub-class, or who
does not wear the morning necklace for the prescribed period,
or who eats forbidden food, will sooner or later die in consequence, since his behaviour is offensive to Kohin, a
supernatural being who is supposed to have his dwelling in the
Milky Way but to roam about at night on earth as a
gigantic warrior killing those whom he meets.[9] Most
commonly, however, the retribution is said to come after death.

Victoria have to placate Pei-a-mei
by dances (*Missions-Blatt aus der
Brüdergemeine*, xvi. 143). Of the
South-Eastern Australian Daramulun Mr. Howitt says (*op. cit.* p. 507
sq.) that, although there is no worship of him, " the dances round the
figure of clay and the invocating of
his name by the medicine-men certainly might have led up to it."
[1] Manning, *loc. cit.* p. 165 ; Ridley,
op. cit. pp. 141, 155 ; Langloh Parker, *op. cit.* p. 7 (Boyma, Baiame,
Byamee). Howitt, *op. cit.* p. 495
(Daramulun). M'Kinlay, quoted *ibid.*
p. 496. Mr. Threlkeld says (*op. cit.*

p. 47) that Koin, an imaginary male
being who has the appearance of a
black, is supposed to precede the
coming of the natives from distant
parts when they assemble to celebrate certain of their ceremonies.
[2] Howitt, *op. cit.* p. 489 (Nurelli of
the Wiimbaio). M'Kinlay, quoted
ibid. p. 496.
[3] Taplin, in Woods, *op. cit.* p. 55.
[4] Langloh Parker, *op. cit.* p. 7 *sq.*
[5] Howitt, *op. cit.* p. 491.
[6] *Ibid.* p. 495.
[7] Brough Smyth, *op. cit.* i. 423.
[8] Howitt, *op. cit.* p. 495.
[9] *Ibid.* p. 499.

The tribes about Maryborough, in Queensland, maintain that the ghosts of those who are good or those who have a high degree of excellence in any particular line—fishing, hunting, fighting, dancing, and so forth—are directed by Birral to an island in the Far North, where he resides.[1] Among the Cape River tribes, "when a Blackfellow dies whose actions during life have been what they hold to be good, he is said to ascend to Boorala (*i.e.*, to the Creator, literally 'good'), where he lives much as he did on earth, less the usual terrestrial discomforts"; whereas to the man who has led a bad life death is thought to be simple annihilation.[2] The Kulin said that when they die they will be subjected to a sort of trial by Binbeal, "the good being rewarded in a better land, the bad driven away, but where they seemed to have no idea."[3] According to another account, again, Binbeal, after he has subjected the spirits of the deceased to an ordeal of fire to try whether they are good or bad, liberates the good at once, whereas the bad are confined and punished.[4] The Illawarra, who lived from thirty to a hundred miles south of Sidney, believed that when people die they are brought up to a large tree where Mirirul, the supreme ruler, examines and judges them. The good he takes up to the sky, the bad he sends to another place to be punished. The women said to their children when they were naughty, "Mirirul will not allow it."[5] Among the Wathiwathi, in New South Wales, the belief prevails that if the spirit of a bad man escapes the traps which are set for it on its course in the sky, it is sure to fall into the hell of fire. The good spirit, on the other hand, is received by two old women who take care of it till it becomes accustomed to its new abode; and after a time the great God, Tha-tha-puli, comes with a host of spirits to see the newcomer and try his strength.[6] According to a report written by Archdeacon Günther in 1839, Baiame is supposed to like the blacks who are good; and "there is also an idea entertained by the more thoughtful that good natives will go to Baiame when they die."[7] Later authorities state that Baiame is believed not only to reward the good after death, but also to punish the wicked—that is, persons who tell lies or kill men by striking them secretly or who are unkind towards the old and sick or, generally, who break his laws.[8] A very elaborate

[1] Howitt, *op. cit.* p. 498.
[2] Curr, *op. cit.* ii. 475.
[3] Parker, *Aborigines of Australia*, p. 24.
[4] Ridley, *op. cit.* p. 137.
[5] *Ibid.* p. 137.

[6] Cameron, in *Jour. Anthr. Inst.* xiv. 364 *sq.*
[7] Günther, quoted by Thomas, in *Man*, 1905, p. 51.
[8] Ridley, *op. cit.* pp. 135, 136, 140. Langloh Parker, *op. cit.* p. 70.

theory of retribution is communicated by Mr. Manning, whose notes date from 1844 or 1845. Boyma (Baiame) is said to be seated far away in the north-east on an immense throne made of transparent crystal and standing in a great lake. He has a son, Grogoragally, equal with him in omniscience, who acts as mediator for the souls to the Great God. His office is to watch over the actions of mankind and to bring to life the dead to appear before the judgment-seat of his Father, who alone pronounces the judgment of eternal happiness in heaven or eternal misery in a hell of everlasting fire. Women and boys dying before the initiation, however, do not go to heaven ; the men have a vague idea that another world is reserved for them. There is also a third person, half human, half divine, called Moodgeegally, who makes Boyma's will known to mankind and is the avowed enemy of all wicked people, transmitting their misdeeds to Grogoragally.[1]

It seems probable that these statements represent a mixture of Christian ideas and genuine aboriginal beliefs. There is reason to believe that the Australian notion of an " All-father " is not in the first instance due to missionary influence ; [2] we have records of it from a comparatively early date, it is spread over a wide area, it has been found among natives who live in a state of great isolation, and the multitude of different names by which the " All-father " is called in different tribes does not suggest a recent origin from a common source. He may very well be a mythical ancestor. Mr. Howitt observes that the master in the sky-country represents the Australian idea of a headman—"a man who is skilful in the use of weapons of offence and defence, all-powerful in magic, but generous and liberal to his people, who does no injury or violence to any one, yet treats with severity any breaches of custom or morality." [3] But he may also be a personification of supernatural force in general, or a being who has been invented to account for all kinds of marvellous phenomena. The word *altjira*, by which the Arunta call their great god, is apparently not a proper name ; according to Kempe, it is applied to five gods, whose names he gives, as also to the sun, moon, and remarkable things generally.[4] And Mulkari, who figures in the beliefs of some Queensland tribes, is described not only as "a benevolent, omnipresent, supernatural being," but as "anything incomprehensible," as

[1] Manning, *loc. cit.* p. 159 *sqq.*
[2] See especially Howitt, *op. cit.* p. 504 *sqq.* ; Lang, *Magic and Religion*, p. 25 *sqq.* ; Thomas, in *Man*, p. 50

sqq. ; von Leonhardi, in *Globus*, xci. 287.
[3] Howitt, *op. cit.* p. 507. See also *ibid.* p. 501.
[4] Thomas, in *Folk-Lore*, xvi. 431.

the supernatural power who makes everything which the blacks cannot otherwise account for.[1] On the other hand, it is hardly possible to doubt that in various instances Christian conceptions have been infused into the aboriginal belief either by the natives themselves or by our informants.[2] Biblical traits are conspicuous in some of the legends. Bishop Salvado tells us that, according to West Australian beliefs, the Creator, Motogon, "employa ces paroles : 'Terre, parais dehors' : et il souffla, et la terre fut créée. 'Eau, parais dehors' ; et il souffla, et l'eau fut créée." [3] The believers in Nourelle give the following account of the origin of death :—The first created man and woman were told not to go near a certain tree in which a bat was living, as the bat was not to be disturbed. But one day the woman, while gathering firewood, went near the forbidden tree ; the bat flew away and after that came death.[4] And the same natives also believe that Nourelle created a great serpent, to which he gave power over all created things.[5] So also the doctrine of a hell with everlasting fire has almost certainly a foreign origin ; and in some other points the genuineness of the Australian theories of retribution is at least open to doubt, even though the function of a judge cannot be regarded as incompatible with the notion of a mythical headman in the sky. Messrs. Spencer and Gillen observe that it would be a very easy matter indeed to form, as the result of a general statement such as might be made by any individual native in reply to a question, a perfectly wrong impression with regard to the native's idea as to the existence of anything like a supreme being inculcating moral rules.[6] Of the Central Australian aborigines they say :— "Any such idea as that of a future life of happiness or the reverse, as a reward for meritorious or as a punishment for blameworthy conduct, is quite foreign to them. . . . We know of no tribe in which there is a belief of any kind in a supreme being who rewards or punishes the individual according to his moral behaviour, using the word moral in the native sense." [7] So far as the Arunta are concerned, this statement is confirmed by Mr. Strehlow. He writes that their god Altjira, who lives in the sky and shows himself to man in the lightning, is a

---

[1] Roth, *op. cit.* pp. 36, 153.

[2] Mr. J. D. Lang (*Queensland*, p. 379 *sq.* ; *Cooksland*, p. 459 *sq.*) even suspects Asiatic influence in the case of Buddai, or Budjah, the mythical ancestor of certain Queensland aborigines. Not only does his name remind of Buddha, but a story told of him is remarkably similar to an Eastern legend.

[3] Salvado, *op. cit.* p. 258.

[4] Brough Smyth, *op. cit.* i. 428.

[5] *Ibid.* i. 423.

[6] Spencer and Gillen, *Northern Tribes of Central Australia*, p. 492 *sqq.*

[7] *Ibid.* p. 491.

good god who never inflicts any punishments on human beings.[1]

From various Polynesian and Melanesian islands we hear of a supreme being—called Io by the Maoris,[2] Tangaroa by the Samoans,[3] Taaroa by the Society Islanders,[4] and so forth [5]—who has made everything, but who is too remote and indistinct to be an object of worship and takes no interest in the morals of men. In some instances at least he seems to be a very shadowy deification of the forces of nature. Thus Io is described as "the great originator, the All-Father, who pervades space, has no residence, and cannot be localised"; and the conception of Tangaroa is equally abstract.[6] Mr. Guppy learned that the natives of Treasury Island and the Shortlands, in the Solomon Group, believe in a Good Spirit who lives in a pleasant land, whither all men who have led good lives go after death; whereas all bad people are transported to the crater of Bagana, the burning volcano of Bougainville, which is the home of the Evil Spirit and his companion spirits.[7] But this belief savours too much of a Christian hell to be accepted as genuine without further evidence.

The Sea Dyaks of Borneo have a great good god called Batara, or Petara, who created the world and rules over it, and is the cause of every blessing. He is not susceptible to human influence, and therefore receives no worship. But he approves of industry, honesty, purity of speech, and skill in word and work. He punishes theft, injustice, disrespect for old persons, and adultery; and immorality among the unmarried is supposed to bring a plague of rain upon the earth as a punishment inflicted by Petara. In general, says Mr. Perham, he is against man's sin; but over and above moral offences many sins have been invented which are simply the infringement of *pemate*, or *tabu*.[8] Like many other great gods of savages, Petara is lacking in individuality. He is at all events not now supposed to be one supreme god, but the general belief is that there are many Petaras —in fact as many Petaras as men. Each man, the people say, has his own peculiar Petara, his own tutelary deity, and if a

[1] Strehlow, quoted by Thomas, in *Folk-Lore*, xvi. 429 *sq. Idem*, quoted by von Leonhardi, in *Globus*, xci. 287.
[2] Gudgeon, 'Maori Religion,' in *Jour. Polynesian Soc.* xiv. 108 *sq.*
[3] *Ibid.* p. 108 *sq.*
[4] Ellis, *Polynesian Researches*, i. 323 *sqq.*
[5] Tylor, *op. cit.* ii. 344 *sqq.* Hoffmann, *La notion de l'Être suprême*

chez les peuples non civilisés, p. 70 *sqq.*
[6] Gudgeon, in *Jour. Polynesian Soc.* xiv. 108.
[7] Guppy, *Solomon Islands*, p. 53.
[8] Perham, 'Petara,' in *Jour. Straits Branch Roy. Asiatic Soc.* no. 8, p. 149 *sq.* St. John, *Life in the Forests of the Far East*, i. 69 *sq.* Selenka, *op. cit.* p. 97 *sqq.*

person is miserable it is because his Petara is miserable.[1] This account, however, loses much of its interest when we find that the name Batara or Petara has obviously been borrowed from Sanscrit, where the word *bhaṭṭâra* means "lord" or "master."[2] The great gods of some other peoples in the Malay Archipelago, again, have names which are derived from Arabic—Lahatala, Latala, or Hatalla, from *Allah taʿâla*. Hence when the Alfura of Bura are heard to say that their highest god, Opo-geba-snulat or Lahatala, writes down in a book the actions of men so as to be able to reward the virtuous and punish the wicked as they deserve, there is every reason to think of influence from Muhammedanism.[3]

The Andaman Islanders are reported to believe in a supreme being, Pūluga, who was never born and is immortal, who has created the world and all its objects, who is omniscient when it is day, knowing even the thoughts of their hearts. Whilst pitiful to those in distress, he is angered by the commission of certain sins—falsehood, theft, grave assault, murder, adultery, and burning wax. He is the judge from whom each soul receives its sentence after death. The "spirits" of the departed are sent by him to a place comprising the whole area under the earth, to await the resurrection. The "souls" of the departed, again, pass either into paradise or to another place which might be described as purgatory, a place of punishment for those who have been guilty of heinous sins, such as murder. At the resurrection the soul (from which evil emanates) and the spirit (from which all good emanates) will be reunited and will henceforth live permanently on the new earth, since the souls of the wicked will then have been reformed by the punishments inflicted on them during their residence in the "purgatory."[4] Mr. Man, who has given us this account, thinks it is extremely improbable that the legends about Pūluga, about the powers of good and evil, and about a world beyond the grave, are the result of the teaching of missionaries or others.[5] But his assumption that they are indigenous seems hardly justified by the very scanty knowledge we possess of the past history of these islanders. Considering their low state of culture, the metaphysical subtlety in some of the notions recorded by Mr. Man would certainly be more astonishing if India were not so near.

[1] Perham, in *Jour. Straits Branch Roy. Asiatic Soc.* no. 8, p. 134 *sq.*
[2] *Ibid.* p. 133. Wilken, *Het Animisme*, p. 162.
[3] Wilken, *op. cit.* pp. 162, 240 *sq.*
[4] Man, 'Aboriginal Inhabitants of the Andaman Islands,' in *Jour. Anthr. Inst.* xii. 112, 157, 158, 161 *sq.*
[5] *Ibid.* p. 156.

Among the Karens of Burma the belief is held that Hades has a king or judge who stands at the door to admit or reject those who apply for admission into his kingdom. He decides the future of each. Those who have performed meritorious works are sent to the regions of happiness above ; those who have done wickedness, such as striking father or mother, are delivered over to the king of hell who is in waiting ; whilst those who have neither performed deeds of merit nor are guilty of great crimes are allotted a place in Hades.[1] At the same time the Karens' ideas of a future state are described as confused, indefinite, and contradictory. Mr. Mason writes :—"They seem to be a melee of different systems. That which appears to me indigenous Karen . . . represents the future world as a counterpart of this, located under the earth, where the inhabitants are employed precisely as they are here." [2] The Pahárias of the Rájmahal Hills believe that the souls of those who have been disobedient to the commands of Bedo Gosain will be condemned either to inhabit some portion of the vegetable kingdom for a certain number of years, or to be cast into a pit of fire, where the offender will suffer eternal punishment or be regenerated in the shape of a dog or a cat. Those who have led a good life, on the other hand, will be rewarded, first by enjoying a short but happy residence with Bedo Gosain in heaven, and subsequently by being born a second time on earth of women and being exalted to posts of great honour, as also by possessing an abundance of worldly goods.[3] In these notions our chief informant, Lieutenant Shaw, sees traces of Hinduism.[4] Lack of detailed information makes it impossible to decide whether the belief in a creator and heavenly judge which has been found in some other uncivilised tribes in India might be traced to a similar influence. The Munda Kols in Central Bengal maintain that the good and almighty Singbonga, who lives in the sky and is connected with the sun, has made everything. Being so far away he occupies himself very little with earthly matters, and is only in exceptional cases an object of worship ; but he sees everything which happens, and is said to punish theft and insincerity.[5] So also the Kukis recognise a benevolent and all-powerful god

---

[1] Mason, in *Jour. Asiatic Soc. Bengal*, xxxiv. 196.

[2] *Ibid.* p. 195.

[3] Shaw, 'Inhabitants of the Hills near Rájamahall,' in *Asiatick Researches*, iv. 48 *sqq.* Sherwill, ' Tour through the Rájmahal Hills,' in *Jour. Asiatic Soc. Bengal*, xx. 556.

[4] Shaw, in *Asiatick Researches*, iv. 46.

[5] Jellinghaus, ' Sagen, Sitten und Gebräuche der Munda-Kolhs in Chota Nagpore,' in *Zeitschr. f. Ethnologie*, iii. 330 *sq*

and creator, called Puthén, who is the judge of all mortals and awards punishments to the wicked both in this world and in the next.[1]

The Ainu of Japan believe in a great god or creator who bestows blessings upon the good and visits the bad with disease, unless they repent. They also say that good people go after death to the " island of the Great Spirit," or to the " kingdom of God," to lead a happy life ; whereas bad people go to the " bad island," or to the " wet underground world," in which they suffer discomfort or, according to some, are burned in everlasting fires.[2] Of the pagan Samoyedes we are told that they regard the great Num as the creator of the universe, as an all-powerful and omniscient being, who protects the innocent, rewards the virtuous, and punishes the wicked.[3] But the primitive Num, who was simply the sky, was too far removed from the nomads who wandered across the frozen plain, to interfere to prevent catastrophe or accomplish their well-being ; and in the provident actions and overseeing which some of the Samoyedes now ascribe to him, " we can clearly enough trace the influence of the missionary and the suggestion of the Christian faith." [4]

Dr. Rink asserts that the Greenlanders considered Tornarsuk as the supreme being on whom they were dependent for any supernatural aid, and in whose abodes in the depth of the earth all such persons as had striven and suffered for the benefit of their fellow men should find a happy existence after death.[5] Dr. Nansen, however, is of opinion that Tornarsuk owes a great deal to missionary influence.[6] That he was not so superior a being as is commonly stated is evident from Captain Holm's description of the Angmagsaliks in Eastern Greenland, where he is represented as a monster living in the sea, of about the same length as a big seal, but thicker.[7] And to judge from Egede's description dating from the earlier part of the eighteenth century, Tornarsuk's notions of justice, if he had any, must in olden times have been very limited, as he took to his subterranean paradise only women that died in labour and men that perished at sea.[8]

[1] Stewart, ' Northern Cachar,' in *Jour. Asiatic Soc. Bengal*, xxiv. 628.
[2] von Siebold, *Die Aino auf der Insel Yesso*, p. 24. Batchelor, *Ainu of Japan*, pp. 199, 235 *sqq.* Howard, *Life with Trans-Siberian Savages*, p. 193.
[3] Castrén, *op. cit.* iii. 14.
[4] Jackson, in *Jour. Anthr. Inst.* xxiv. 398. See also Castrén, *op. cit.* iii. 14–16, 182 *sqq.*
[5] Rink, *Greenland*, p. 141.
[6] Nansen, *Eskimo Life*, p. 242.
[7] Holm, ' Ethnologisk Skizze af Angmagsalikerne,' in *Meddelelser om Grönland*, x. 115.
[8] Egede, *Description of Greenland*, p. 197.

The " Great Spirit " so often referred to in accounts of North American Indians, is described as a being too elevated and remote to take much interest in the destinies and actions of men and too benevolent by nature to require propitiation or worship. Schoolcraft asserts that in their oral traditions there is no attempt " to make ·man accountable to him, here or hereafter, for aberrations from virtue, good will, truth, or any form of moral right. With benevolence and pity as prime attributes the Great Transcendental Spirit of the Indian does not take upon himself a righteous administration of the world's affairs, but, on the contrary, leaves it to be filled, and its affairs, in reality, governed, by demons and fiends in human form." [1] Yet there are instances in which he is represented in a different light. The most essential moral precepts of the Iroquois " were taught as the will of the Great Spirit, and obedience to their requirements as acceptable in his sight " ; [2] but whilst highly gratified with their virtues, he detested their vices, and punished them for their bad conduct not only in this world but in a future state of existence.[3] The Potawatomis considered that rape was visited by the anger of the Great Spirit.[4] Ti-ra'-wa, the supreme being of the Pawnees, applauds valour, abhors theft, and punishes the wicked by annihilation, whilst the good dwell with him in his heavenly home.[5] The Indians of Alabama told Bossu that those who behave themselves foolishly and disregard the supreme being will after death go to a barren land full of thorns and briars, with no hunting and no wives, whereas those who neither rob nor kill nor take other men's wives will occupy a very fertile country and live there a happy life.[6] Keating states that, according to the beliefs of the Dacotahs, men go to the residence of the Great Spirit if they have been good and peaceable, or if they died by the hand of their enemy, but that their souls are doomed to the residence of the Evil Spirit if they perish in a broil with their own countrymen.[7] This statement, however, is not supported by other authorities. Prescott writes of the same Indians :—" They have very little notion of punishment for crime hereafter in eternity : indeed, they know very little about whether the Great Spirit has anything to do with their affairs, present or future." [8]

[1] Schoolcraft, op. cit. i. 35.
[2] Morgan, League of the Iroquois, p. 172.
[3] Seaver, Narrative of the Life of Mrs. Jemison, p. 155.
[4] Keating, Expedition to the Source of St. Peter's River, i. 127.
[5] Grinnell, Pawnee Hero Stories, p. 355. Lang, Making of Religion, p. 257.
[6] Bossu, Travels through Louisiana, i. 256 sq.
[7] Keating, op. cit. i. 393 sq.
[8] Schoolcraft, op. cit. ii. 195. Cf. ibid. iii. 229.

And among the Omaha and Ponka, who are branches of the same people, the old men used to say to their fellow tribesmen, "If you are good, you will go to the good ghosts ; if you are bad you will go to the bad ghosts." But nothing was ever said of going to dwell with Wakanda, or with demons.[1] As regards the origin of the North American notion of the Great Spirit different opinions have been expressed. On the one hand we are told that it is essentially only " the Indian's conception of the white man's god," which belongs not to the untutored but to the tutored mind of the savage.[2] On the other hand it is argued that the belief in the Great Spirit must be a native product, since it is reported to have occurred already before the arrival of the earliest Jesuit missionaries.[3] Unfortunately, however, we cannot be sure that our informants have accurately interpreted the beliefs of the Indians. Mr. Dorsey has pointed out that a fruitful source of error has been a misunderstanding of their terms and phrases.[4] The Dacotah word *wakanda*, which has been rendered into " Great Spirit," simply means " mystery," or " mysterious," and signifies rather a quality than a definite entity. Among many tribes the sun is wakanda, among the same tribes the moon is wakanda, and so are thunder, lightning, the stars, the winds, as also various animals, trees, and inanimate objects or places of a striking character ; even a man, especially a medicine-man, may be considered wakanda.[5] So, too, the Menomini term *mashä' ma' nidō*, or " great unknown," is not to be understood as implying a belief in one supreme being ; there are several manidos, each supreme in his own realm, as well as many lesser mysteries, or deities, or spirits.[6] Mr. Dorsey also observes that in many cases Indians have been quick to adopt the phrases of civilisation in communicating with white people, whilst in speaking to one another they use their own terms.[7] At the same time it seems to me that if the notion of a Great Spirit had altogether a Christian origin we might expect to find an idea of moral retribution more commonly associated with it than the

[1] Dorsey, ' Siouan Cults,' in *Ann. Rep. Bur. Ethn.* xi. 419.

[2] Smith, ' Myths of the Iroquois,' in *Ann. Rep. Bur. Ethn.* ii. 112. Tylor, ' Limits of Savage Religion,' in *Jour. Anthr. Inst.* xxi. 284. Boyle, ' Paganism of the Civilised Iroquois,' *ibid.* xxx. 266.

[3] Lang, *Making of Religion*, p. 251 *sqq. Idem, Magic and Religion*, p. 19 *sqq.* Hoffmann, *op. cit.* p. 86 *sq.*

[4] Dorsey, in *Ann. Rep. Bur. Ethn.* xi. 365 *sq.*

[5] *Ibid.* p. 366. McGee, in *Ann. Rep. Bur. Ethn.* xv. 181 *sqq. Cf.* James, *Expedition to the Rocky Mountains*, i. 268 ; Tylor, *op. cit.* ii. 343.

[6] Hoffman, ' Menomini Indians,' in *Ann. Rep. Bur. Ethn.* xiv. 39, n. 1. *Cf.* Parkman, *Jesuits in North America*, p. lxxix.

[7] Dorsey, in *Ann. Rep. Bur. Ethn.* xi. 365. See also Smith, *ibid.* ii. 112.

statements imply. It may be that among the North American Indians also, as among some other peoples, a vague conception of something like a supreme being has arisen through a personification of the mysteries in nature.[1] But if this be the case the interest which the Great Spirit in rare instances takes in human conduct may all the same be due to missionary influence. It is certainly not an original characteristic of his nature. Among the Iroquois and Pawnees, who attribute to their great god the function of a moral judge, he also receives offerings—[2] a circumstance which indicates that he cannot be regarded as a typical representative of his class.

In South America, too, several tribes have been found to believe in a benevolent Great Spirit, who is indifferent to men's behaviour and is not worshipped by them.[3] Of the Passés, however, we are told by a Portuguese official who travelled in Brazil in 1774–75 that they have the idea of a creator who rewards good people by allowing their souls to stay with him and punishes the wicked by turning their souls into evil spirits.[4] But according to Mr. Bates "these notions are so far in advance of the ideas of all other tribes of Indians . . . that we must suppose them to have been derived by the docile Passés from some early missionary or traveller."[5] Of the Fuegians, again, Admiral Fitzroy writes:—"A great black man is supposed to be always wandering about the woods and mountains, who is certain of knowing every word and every action; who cannot be escaped, and who influences the weather according to men's conduct." Of this influence our informant gives the following instance. A native related a story of his brother who once killed a man—one of those very wild men who wander about in the woods supporting themselves by theft—because he stole from him a bird. Afterwards he was very sorry for what he had done, particularly when it began to blow hard. In telling the story, the brother said:—"Rain come down—snow come down—hail come down—wind blow—blow—very much blow. Very bad to kill man. Big man in woods no like it, he very angry." The same native also reproached the surgeon

---

[1] The Great Spirit is represented by Schoolcraft (*op. cit.* i. 15) as a "Soul of the Universe which inhabits and animates every thing," and is supposed to exist under every possible form in the world, animate and inanimate. Of Ti-ra'-wa it is said that he "is in and of everything" (*supra*, i. 448).

[2] Seaver, *op. cit.* p. 155. *Supra* i. 448.

[3] Bernau, *Missionary Labours in British Guiana*, p. 49. Hoffmann, *op. cit.* p. 90 *sqq.*

[4] Ribeiro de Sampaio, *Diario da viagem*, p. 79.

[5] Bates, *The Naturalist on the River Amazons*, ii. 244. *Cf. ibid.* ii. 162; Dobrizhoffer, *Account of the Abipones*, ii. 57 *sq.*; Müller, *Geschichte der Amerikanischen Urreligionen*, p. 289.

of the Beagle for shooting some young ducks with the old bird :—
" Very bad to shoot little duck—come wind—come rain—blow
—very much blow." [1]   In the latter case, however, no mention
was made of the black man in the woods.   From Admiral
Fitzroy's account Mr. Andrew Lang draws the conclusion that the
Fuegians have evolved the idea of a high deity, an ethical judge,
who "makes for righteousness," who searches the heart, who almost
literally "marks the sparrow's fall," and whose morality is
so much above the ordinary savage standard that he regards the
slaying of a stranger and an enemy, caught redhanded in
robbery, as a sin.[2]   This statement may serve as a specimen
of the spirit in which its author deals with the subject of supreme
beings in savage beliefs.   There is after all some difference
between a high moral god and a mythical weather doctor who
lives in the woods and sends bad weather if a wild man, who
also lives in the woods, is killed.   Mr. Bridges, our most trustworthy authority on the Fuegians, says nothing of the black
man, but states that nearly all the old men among the Fuegians
are medicine-men, and that these wizards make frequent incantations in which they seem to address themselves to a mysterious
being called Aïapakal.   And they also believe in another spirit,
named Hoakils, from whom they pretend to obtain a supernatural power over life and death.[3]

The South African Bushmans, another very backward people,
are likewise represented by Mr. Lang and M. Hoffmann as believers in a supreme being.[4]   A native said to Mr. Orpen that
Cagn made all things, and that the people prayed to him :—
" O Cagn ! O Cagn ! are we not your children, do you not see
our hunger ? Give us food."   And he gave them what they asked
for both hands full.   But although he was at first very good
and nice, he afterwards "got spoilt through fighting so many
things." [5]   However, according to another statement, made by
a person who from childhood had much intercourse with Bushmans and knew their language, they did not believe in a God or
the great father of men, but in a devil who made everything
with his left hand.[6]   The Hottentots spoke of Tsui-goab as
" the giver of all blessings, the Father on high, All-father, the

---

[1] King and Fitzroy, *Voyages of the
" Adventure " and " Beagle,"* ii. 180.
[2] Lang, *Making of Religion*, pp.
188, 198.   The same description of
the Fuegian black man is repeated
by M. Hoffmann (*op. cit.* p. 40).
[3] Bridges, quoted by Hyades and
Deniker, *Mission scientifique du Cap*

Horn, vii. 256.
[4] Lang, *Making of Religion*, p. 210.
Hoffmann, *op. cit.* p. 40 *sq.*
[5] Orpen, ' Glimpse into the Mythology of the Maluti Bushmen,' in *The
Cape Monthly Magazine*, N.S. ix. 2.
[6] Campbell, *Second Journey in the
Interior of South Africa*, i. 29.

avenger, who fought daily the battle for his people." They thus identified him with the ancestor of the tribe, but Tsui-goab was also the name by which they called the Infinite.[1] Among the pagans of Africa there is, in fact, a very wide-spread belief in a benevolent supreme deity, a creator or maker of things, who lives in or above the sky, who generally takes no concern whatever in the affairs of mankind, who mostly receives no worship, and is, as a rule, totally in-different to good or evil.[2] In some rare instances only he is described as a judge of human conduct. Thus some of the Bechuanas believe that a being who is vaguely called by the name of Lord and Master of things, Mongalinto, punishes thieves by striking them with the lightning.[3] According to an old writer, Father Santos, the natives of Sofala in South-Eastern Africa acknowledge a god, called Molungo, "who both in this and the world to come they fancy measures retribution for the good and evil done in this." They believe in the existence of twenty-seven paradises, where everyone enjoys a pleasure pro-portionate to the merits of his life ; while those who have passed their lives in wickedness are supposed to be condemned to a privation from the sight of the holy presence of Molungo, and to suffer torments in one of the thirteen hells they assume to exist, each according to the evil he has done.[4] The Baluba, a Bantu people of Equatorial Africa, have the notion of a creator, named Fidi-Mukullu, who punishes the souls of the wicked before they are reborn on earth, whereas the good return to life again, in the shape of chiefs or other important persons, immediately after they have died.[5] The Awemba,

[1] Hahn, *The Supreme Being of the Khoi-Khoi*, pp. 122, 126 *sq.*

[2] Livingstone, *Missionary Travels,* p. 641 (tribes of the Zambesi). Rat-tray, *Stories and Songs in Chinyanja,* p. 198 (natives of Central Angoni-land). Stigand, ' Natives of Nyassa-land,' in *Jour. Roy. Anthr. Inst.* xxxvii. 130. Roscoe, ' Bahima,' *ibid.* xxxvii. 108 *sq.* Wilson and Felkin, *Uganda,* i. 206. Beltrame, *Il Fiume Bianco e i Dénka,* pp. 191, 192, 276 *sq.* Kingsley, ' Fetish View of the Human Soul,' in *Folk-Lore,* viii. 142 *sq.* ; *Idem, Travels in West Africa,* pp. 442, 508. Parkinson, ' Asaba People of the Niger,' in *Jour. Anthr. Inst.* xxxvi. 312. Bosman, *Descrip-tion of the Coast of Guinea,* pp. 121 *sq.* (Gold Coast natives), 348 (Slave Coast natives). Cruickshank, *Eigh-teen Years on the Gold Coast,* ii. 126 *sq.* Ellis *Tshi-speaking Peoples of the Gold Coast,* p. 26 *sqq. Idem, Ewe-speaking Peoples of the Slave Coast,* p. 33 *sq.* Winterbottom, *Native Afri-cans in the Neighbourhood of Sierra Leone,* i. 222. Wilson, *Western Africa,* p. 209 (natives of Northern Guinea). Rowley, *Religion of the Africans,* pp. 15, 16, 54. Tylor, *op. cit.* ii. 347 *sqq.* Lang, *Making of Religion,* p. 230 *sqq.* Hoffmann, *op. cit.* p. 45 *sqq.*

[3] Arbousset and Daumas, *Explora-tory Tour to the North-East of the Colony of Good Hope,* p. 322 *sq.*

[4] Santos, ' History of Eastern Ethiopia,' in Pinkerton, *Collection of Voyages and Travels,* xvi. 687.

[5] Wissmann, Wolf, &c., *Im Innern Afrikas,* p. 158. Wissmann, *Quer durch Afrika,* p. 379.

another Bantu people, who inhabit the stretch of country lying between Lake Tanganyika and Lake Bangweolo, acknowledge a supreme being, Leza, who " is the Judge of the dead, and condemns thieves, adulterers and murderers to the state of Vibanda, or Viwa (evil spirits), exalting the good to the rank of *mipashi*, or benevolent spirits." [1]   Other natives in the neighbourhood of Lake Tanganyika recognise a creator called Kabesa, who lives in the sky and admits to his abode the souls of good people after death, but turns away the souls of the wicked.[2] The Akikuyu of British East Africa recognise three gods all of whom are called Ngai.   One of them, however, is considered the supreme deity.   "If a man is good this Ngai can give him much property.   If he does wrong the same power can strike him down with disease and cause his livestock to dwindle away. . . . The sudden death of a man, for instance by lightning, is ascribed to some evil act of his life being punished by Ngai."[3] Proyart tells us that the Negroes of Loango believed in a supreme being, Zambi, who had created all that is good in the world, who was himself good and loved justice in others, and who severely punished fraud and perjury.[4]   It is of course impossible to say exactly how far the statements referring to African supreme beings represent unadulterated native beliefs. In criticising Kolb's account of the supreme and perfect god of the Hottentots, Bishop Callaway observes, "Nothing is more easy than to enquire of heathen savages the character of their creed, and during the conversation to impart to them . . . ideas which they never heard before, and presently to have these come back again as articles of their own original faith, when in reality they are but the echoes of one's own thoughts."[5]   With reference to the West African native Miss Kingsley likewise remarks that he has a wonderful power of assimilating foreign forms of belief, and that when he once has got hold of a new idea it remains in his mind long after the missionaries who put it there have passed away.[6]   And besides the teaching of missionaries there are in Africa several factors which for centuries have tended to introduce foreign conceptions, namely, intercourse with European settlers, the operations of the slave trade, and the influence of Muhammedanism.[7]   But at the same

[1] Sheane, ' Awemba Religion,' in *Jour. Anthr. Inst.* xxxvi. 150 *sq.*
[2] Schneider, *Die Religion der afrikanischen Naturvölker*, p. 84.
[3] Tate, ' Kikuyu Tribe,' in *Jour. Anthr. Inst.* xxxiv. 263.
[4] Proyart, ' History of Loango,' in Pinkerton, *Collection of Voyages and Travels*, xvi. 594.
[5] Callaway, *Religious System of the Amazulu*, p. 105 *sq.*
[6] Kingsley, in *Folk-Lore*, viii. 150.
[7] *Cf.* Rowley, *Religion of the Africans*, pp. 28, 90 ; Wilson, *Western*

time it seems exceedingly probable that the African belief in a supreme being has a native substratum. In many cases he is apparently the heaven god ;[1] but he may also be a mythical ancestor, as the Hottentot god Tsui-goab and the Zulu god Unkulunkulu ; or a personification of the supernatural, as is suggested by such names as the Masai Ngǎi, the Monbuttu Kilima, and the Malagasy Andriamanitra ;[2] or the assumed cause of anything which particularly fills the savage mind with wonder or awe. Among the natives of Northern Guinea, according to Mr. Wilson, " every thing which transpires in the natural world beyond the power of man, or of spirits, who are supposed to occupy a place somewhat higher than man, is at once and spontaneously ascribed to the agency of God."[3] Nay, for reasons which will be stated immediately, I am even of opinion that the function of a moral judge, occasionally attributed to the great god of African pagans, has in some instances an independent origin.

Generally speaking, then, it seems that the All-father, supreme being, or high god of savage belief may be traced to several different sources. When not a " loan-god " of foreign extraction, he may be a mythical ancestor or headman ; or a deification of the sky or some large and remote object of nature, like the sun ; or a personification or personified cause of the mysteries or forces of nature. The argument that the belief in such a being is " irreducible " because it prevails among savages who worship neither ancestors nor nature,[4] can carry no weight in consideration of the fact that he himself, as a general rule, is no object of worship. In various instances we have reason to suppose that even though the notion of a supreme being is fundamentally of native origin, foreign conceptions have been engrafted upon it ; and to these belongs in particular the idea of a heavenly judge who in the after-life punishes the wicked and rewards the good. But we are not entitled to assume that the idea of moral retribution as a function of the great god has in every case been adopted

---

Africa, p. 229 *sq.* ; Cruickshank, *op. cit.* ii. 126.

[1] See Tylor, *op. cit.* ii. 347 *sqq.*

[2] See *supra*, ii. 586 *sq.*

[3] Wilson, *op. cit.* p. 209. See also

Livingstone, *Expedition to the Zambesi*, p. 521 *sq.*, quoted *supra*, ii. 594.

[4] Lang, *Magic and Religion*, p. 42. Hoffmann, *op. cit.* pp. 122, 126, 131.

from people of a higher culture. A mythical ancestor or
headman may of his own accord approve of virtue and disapprove of vice ; and, besides, justice readily becomes the
attribute of a god who is habitually appealed to in curses or
oaths. That the supreme being of savages is thus invoked,
is in some cases directly stated by our authorities. In
making solemn treatises, the Hurons called on Oki, the
heaven god.[1] The Negroes of Loango, who believed that
Zambi, the supreme being, punished fraud and perjury,
took his name in testimony of the truth.[2] Among the
Awemba the supreme god Leza, who is believed to reward
the good and to punish thieves, adulterers, and murderers,
is invoked both in blessings and curses, the injured man
praying that Leza will send a lion to devour the evildoer.[3]
In the Ewe-speaking Ho tribe on the Slave Coast the great
god Mawu, who is said to inflict punishment on the
wicked, is frequently appealed to in law-cases, by the judge
as well as by the plaintiff and the accused.[4] In Northern
Guinea the name of the supreme being is solemnly called
on three times at the ratification of an important treaty, or
when a person is condemned to undergo the " red-water
ordeal."[5] Of the Mpongwe we are told that " when a
covenant is about to be formed among the different
tribes, Mwetyi [the supreme being] is always invoked as
a witness, and is commissioned with the duty of visiting
vengeance upon the party who shall violate the engagement. Without this their national treaties would have
little or no force. When a law is passed which the people
wish to be especially binding, they invoke the vengeance
of Mwetyi upon every transgressor, and this, as a general
thing, is ample guarantee for its observance."[6] Among
the East African Wakamba, when the supposed criminal
is to undergo the ordeal of the hatchet, a magician makes
him repeat the following words :—" If I have stolen the
property of so and so, or committed this crime, let

---

[1] Tylor, *op. cit.* ii. 342.
[2] Proyart, *loc. cit.* p. 594.
[3] Sheane, in *Jour. Anthr. Inst.*
xxxvi. 151.

[4] Spieth, *Die Ewe-Stämme*, p. 415.
[5] Wilson, *Western Africa*, p. 210.
[6] *Ibid.* p. 392.

Mulungu respond for me ; but if I have not stolen, nor done this wickedness, may he save me." The magician then passes the red-hot iron four times over the flat hand of the accused ; and the people believe that if he is guilty, his hand will be burned, but that, if innocent, he will suffer no injury.[1] Among the Masai a person who is accused of cattle-lifting and on that account subjected to the ordeal of drinking a mixture of blood and milk, has first to swear, " O God, I drink this blood, if I have stolen the cattle this blood will kill me." Should he not die within a fortnight he is considered innocent.[2] The Madi of Central Africa have various means of trial by ordeal, through which it is believed that the guilt of a suspected individual can be detected ; and " before any of these trials the men look up and solemnly invoke some invisible being to punish him if guilty, or help him if innocent." [3] Of the natives of the Zambesi, all of whom have an idea of a supreme being, Livingstone states that, when undergoing an ordeal, " they hold up their hands to the Ruler of Heaven, as if appealing to him to assert their innocence." [4]

It has often been said that the oath and ordeal involve a belief in the gods as vindicators of truth and justice, that they are " appeals to the moral nature of the Divinity." [5] If this were true, moral retribution would certainly be an exceedingly common function of savage gods. But, as we have noticed before,[6] the efficacy ascribed to an oath is originally of a magic character, and if it contains an appeal to a god he is, according to primitive notions, a mere tool in the hand of the person invoking him. So also the ordeal is essentially a magical ceremony. In many cases at least, it contains a curse or an oath which has reference to the guilt or innocence of a suspected person, and the

[1] Krapf, *Travels in Eastern Africa,* p. 173.
[2] Merker, *Die Masai,* p. 211.
[3] Felkin, ' Notes on the Madi,' in *Proceed. Roy. Soc. Edinburgh,* xii. 334.
[4] Livingstone, *Missionary Travels,* p. 641 *sq.*
[5] Tiele, *Elements of the Science of* *Religion,* i. 86. Réville, *Les religions des peuples non-civilisés,* i. 103. Brinton, *Religions of Primitive Peoples,* p. 225. Schneider, *Religion der afrikanischen Naturvölker,* p. 255. Hodgson, *Miscellaneous Essays,* i. 126. Dahn, *Bausteine,* ii. 21, 24. Gummere, *Germanic Origins,* p. 183.
[6] *Supra,* ii. 118 *sqq.*

proper object of the ordeal is then to give reality to the imprecation for the purpose of establishing the validity or invalidity of the suspicion.

Thus in West Africa the common ordeal which consists in drinking a certain draught or "eating the fetish" is regularly accompanied by an oath or a curse.[1] In the Calabar the accused person, before swallowing the ju-ju drink *mbiam*, which is made of filth and blood, recites an oath beginning with the words, "If I have been guilty of this crime," and ending with the words, "Then, Mbiam, Thou deal with me ! " And whenever this ordeal is used the greatest care is taken that the oath shall be recited in full.[2] Of the Negroes of the Gold Coast Bosman states that " if any person is suspected of thievery, and the indictment is not clearly made out, he is obliged to clear himself by drinking the oath-draught, and to use the imprecation, that the Fetiche may kill him if he be guilty of thievery."[3] In Ashantee, " when any one denies a theft, an aggry bead is placed in a small vessel, with some water, the person holding it puts his right foot against the right foot of the accused, who invokes the power of the bead to kill him if he is guilty, and then takes it into his mouth with a little of the water."[4] Among the Negroes of Northern Guinea, in the case of the " red-water ordeal," the accused " invokes the name of God three times, and imprecates his wrath in case he is guilty of the particular crime laid to his charge." He then steps forward and drinks freely of the " red water "—that is, a decoction made from the inner bark of a tree of the mimosa family. If it nauseates and makes him vomit freely, he is at once pronounced innocent, whereas, if it causes vertigo and he loses self-control, it is regarded as evidence of guilt.[5] According to an old account, the Negroes of Sierra Leone have a " water of cursing," boiled of barks and herbs. The witch-doctor puts his divining-staff into the pot and drops or presses the water out of it upon the arm or leg of the suspected person, muttering over it these words :—" Is he guilty of this, or hath he done this or that ; if yea, then let it scald or burn him, till the very skin come off." If the person remains unhurt they hold him innocent, and proceed to

---

[1] See, besides the references below, Monrad, *Skildring af Guinea-Kysten*, p. 35 *sq.* (Negroes of Accra) ; Beecham, *Ashantee*, p. 215 *sqq.* ; Ratzel, *op. cit.* iii. 130.

[2] Kingsley, *Travels in West Africa*,

p. 465.

[3] Bosman, *op. cit.* p. 125.

[4] Bowdich, *Mission to Ashantee*, p. 267.

[5] Wilson, *Western Africa*, p. 225 *sq.*

the trial of another, till the guilty is discovered.[1] Among the Wadshagga of Eastern Africa the medicine-man gives to the accused a poisonous draught with the words, " If you fall down, you have committed the crime and told a lie, if you remain standing we recognise that you have spoken the truth." [2]

Among the Hawaiians, in the ordeal called *wai haalulu*," prayer was offered by the priest " while a large dish of water was placed before the culprit, who was required to hold his hands over the fluid ; and if it shook, his fate was sealed.[3] Among the Tinguianes in the district of El Abra in Luzon, if a man is accused of a crime and denies it, the headman of the village, who is also the judge, causes a handful of straw to be burned in his presence. The accused then holds up an earthern pot and says, " May my belly be changed to a pot like this if I am guilty of the crime of which I am accused." If he remains unchanged in body, the judge declares him innocent.[4] The following ordeal is in use among the Tunguses of Siberia. A fire is made and a scaffold erected near the hut of the accused. A dog's throat is then cut and the blood received in a vessel. The body is put on the wood of the fire, but in such a position that it does not burn. The accused passes over the fire, and drinks two mouthfuls of the blood, the rest whereof is thrown into the fire ; and the body of the dog is placed on the scaffold. Then the accused says :—" As the dog's blood burns in the fire, so may what I have drunk burn in my body ; and as the dog put on the scaffold will be consumed, so may I be consumed at the same time if I be guilty." [5]

The "trial of jealousy" mentioned in the Old Testament involved a curse pronounced by the priest to the effect that the holy water which the woman suspected of adultery had to drink should cause her belly to swell and her thigh to rot.[6] In India the ordeal was expressly regarded as a form of the oath, the same word, *sapatha*, being used to denote both.[7] We have seen above that in the Middle Ages every judicial combat was necessarily preceded by an oath, which essentially decided the issue of the fight and the question of guilt.[8] So also at the moment when the hot iron was raised and the accused took

---

[1] Dapper, *Africa*, p. 405.
[2] Volkens, *Der Kilimandscharo*, p. 249.
[3] Jarves, *History of the Hawaiian Islands*, p. 20.
[4] Lala, *Philippine Islands*, p. 100.
[5] Hartland, *Legend of Perseus*, ii. 85 *sq.*

[6] *Numbers*, v. 20 *sqq.*
[7] Jolly, ' Beiträge zur indischen Rechtsgeschichte,' in *Zeitschr. d. Deutschen Morgenländischen Gesellsch.* xliv. 346. Oldenberg, *Die Religion des Veda*, p. 510, n. 1. See also Patetta, *Le ordalie*, p. 14.
[8] *Supra*, i. 505.

it into his hand, the Deity was invoked to manifest the truth.[1]
The ordeal of the Eucharist involved the following formula recited
by the victim :—" Et si aliter est quam dixi et juravi, tunc hoc
Domini nostri Jesu Christi corpus non pertranseat gutur meum,
sed hæreat in faucibus meis, strangulet me suffocet me ac inter-
ficiat me statim in momento." [2]

To the list of ordeals which contain an oath or a curse
as their governing element many other instances might
probably be added in which no imprecation has been
expressly mentioned by our authorities in their short
descriptions of the ceremonies. This is all the more
likely to be the case as magical practices often imply imprecations which are not formally expressed.[3] But there
may also be ordeals which have a different origin. Thus
the custom of swimming witches seems to have arisen
from the notion that everything unholy is repelled by
water and unable to sink into its depths ; [4] and the ordeal
of touching the corpse of a murdered person no doubt
originated in the belief that the soul of such a person
lingered about the body until appeased by the shedding
of the murderer's blood and that " by the murderer's
approach, and especially by his polluted touch, the soul
was excited to an instant manifestation of its indignation,
by appearing in the form in which it was supposed to
subsist, *viz.* in that of blood." [5] However, even though
all ordeals have not the same foundation, it seems highly
improbable that any people, in the first instance, resorted
to this method of discovering innocence and guilt from a
belief in a god who is by his nature a guardian of truth
and justice.

Nor must we make any inference as to the moral
character of gods from the mere prevalence of a belief in

[1] Beames, in his *Translation of Glanville*, p. 351 *sq.*

[2] Dahn, *op. cit.* ii. 16.

[3] See, for instance, Westermarck, 'L-'âr, or the Transference of Conditional Curses in Morocco,' in *Anthropological Essays presented to E. B. Tylor*, p. 361 *sqq.*

[4] Binsfeldius, *Tractatus de confes-*
sionibus maleficorum et sagarum, p. 315. In the North-East of Scotland
it was believed that, if a person com-
mitted suicide by drowning, the
body did not sink, but floated on the
surface (Gregor, *Folk-Lore of the North-East of Scotland*, p. 208).

[5] Pitcairn, *Criminal Trials in Scotland*, iii. 187.

a future world where men are in some way or other
punished or rewarded for their conduct during their life.
Such a belief is said to be fairly common among uncivilised races;[1] and, although in several cases it is
undoubtedly due to Christian or other foreign influence,[2]
I agree with Dr. Steinmetz that we are not entitled to

[1] Thomson, *Savage Island*, p. 94.
Percy Smith, ' Futuna,' in *Jour.
Polynesian Soc.* i. 39. Seemann, *Viti*,
p. 400 ; Williams and Calvert, *Fiji*,
p. 208. Codrington, *Melanesians*, p.
274 *sq.* (Banks' Islanders). Inglis,
New Hebrides, p. 31 ; Turner, *Samoa*,
p. 326 (people of Aneiteum). Campbell, *A Year in the New Hebrides*, p.
169 (people of Tana). Schwaner,
Borneo, i. 183 (natives of the Barito
district). Selenka, *op cit.* pp. 88, 94,
112 (Dyaks). von Brenner, *op. cit.* p.
240 (Bataks of Sumatra). de Mas,
*Informe sobre el estado de las Islas
Filipinas*, ' Orijen, &c.' p. 14. Best,
' Prehistoric Civilisation in the Philippines,' in *Jour. Polynesian Soc.* i.
200 (Tagalo-Bisaya tribes). Worcester, *Philippine Islands*, p. 110 (Tagbanuas of Palawan). Smeaton, *Loyal
Karens of Burma*, p. 186 *sq.* Ander-
son, *Mandalay to Momien*, p. 146
(Kakhyens). Lewin, *Wild Races of
South-Eastern India*, p. 243 *sq.*
(Pankhos and Bunjogees). Hunter,
Rural Bengal, i. 210 (Santals). Ma-
crae, ' Account of the Kookies,' in
Asiatick Researches, vii. 195 ; Butler,
Travels in Assam, p. 88 (Kukis).
Stewart, ' Notes on Northern Ca-
char,' in *Jour. Asiatic Soc. Bengal*,
xxiv. 620 (Old Kukis), 632 (Nagas).
Macpherson, *Memorials of Service in
India*, p. 92 *sqq.* (Kandhs). Thur-
ston,' Todas of the Nilgiris,' in the
Madras Government Museum's *Bul-
letin*, i. 166 *sq.* Breeks, *Tribes and
Monuments of the Nīlagiris*, p. 28
(Todas and Badagas). Radloff, *op.
cit.* p. 11 *sq.* (Turkish tribes of the
Altai). Georgi, *Russia*, i. 106 (Chu-
vashes). Cranz, *History of Greenland*,
i. 186. Hall, *Arctic Researches among
the Esquimaux*, p. 571 *sq.* Lyon,
Private Journal, p. 372 *sqq.* (Eskimo
of Igloolik). Boas, ' Central Eskimo,'
in *Ann. Rep. Bur. Ethn.* vi. 590.
Nelson, ' Eskimo about Bering
Strait,' *ibid.* xviii. 423. Douglas,

quoted by Petroff, *Report on Alaska,*
p. 177 (Thlinkets). Harrison, ' Religion and Family among the Haidas,'
in *Jour. Anthr. Inst.* xxi. 17 *sqq.*
Duncan, quoted by Mayne, *Four
Years in British Columbia*, p. 293 *sq.*
(Coast Indians of British Columbia).
Mackenzie, *Voyages to the Frozen and
Pacific Oceans*, p. cxix. (Chippewyans). Morgan, *League of the Iroquois*,
p. 168 *sqq.* Harmon, *Journal of Voyages in the Interior of North America*,
p. 364 *sq.* (Indians on the East side
of the Rocky Mountains). Keating,
op. cit. i. 110 *sq.* (Potawatomis) ; ii.
158 *sq.* (Chippewas). Say, quoted by
Dorsey, ' Siouan Cults,' in *Ann. Rep.
Bur. Ethn.* xi. 422 (Kansas). Stevenson, ' Sia,' *ibid.* xi. 145 *sq.* Bartram,
in *Trans. American Ethn. Soc.* iii. pt.
i. 27 (Creek and Cherokee Indians).
Powers, *Tribes of California*, pp. 34,
58, 59, 91, 110, 144, 155, 161. Buchanan, *North American Indians*, p.
235 *sqq.* ; Heriot, *Travels through the
Canadas*, pp. 362, 536 ; Catlin, *North
American Indians*, i. 156, and ii. 243;
Domenech, *Great Deserts of North
America*, ii. 380 (various Indian
tribes of North America). von Martius, *Beiträge zur Ethnographie
Amerika's*, i. 247 (Guatós). von den
Steinen, *Unter den Naturvölkern Zentral-Brasiliens*, p. 435 (Paressí). de
Azara, *Voyages dans l'Amérique méridionale*, ii. 138 (Payaguás). Bosman, *op. cit.* p. 424 (people of Benin).
Wilson, *Western Africa*, p. 217
(Negroes of Northern Guinea).
Reade, *Savage Africa*, p. 539 (Ibos).
Mungo Park, *Travels in the Interior
of Africa*, p. 250 (Mandingoes). Tylor, *op. cit.* ii. 83 *sqq.* Marillier, *La
survivance de l'âme et l'idée de justice
chez les peuples non civilisés*, p. 33
sqq. Steinmetz, *Ethnologische Studien
zur ersten Entwicklung der Strafe*, ii.
368 *sqq.*

[2] *Cf.* Tylor, *op. cit.* ii. 84, 91 *sqq.* ;
Marillier, *loc. cit.* p. 32 *sq.*

assume that it is so in all.[1] It seems that the savage mind
may by itself, in various ways, come to the idea of some
kind of moral retribution after death.   First, the condition of the dead man is often supposed to depend upon
the attentions bestowed on him by the survivors.
Mr. Turner was told that, in the belief of the St. Augustine Islanders in Polynesia, the souls of the departed " if
good " went to a land of brightness and clear weather in
the heavens, but " if bad " were sent to mud and darkness ; and the answer to his next question informed him
that in this case " goodness " meant that the friends of the
deceased had given him a good funeral feast, and that
" badness " meant that his stingy friends had provided
nothing at all.[2]   Although Mr. Turner sees no moral distinction in these terms, there may be one nevertheless.
Speaking of the Efatese, in the New Hebrides, Mr.
Macdonald observes :—" A man's condition in the future
would be, to some extent, happy or miserable according to
his life here. Supposing he were a worthless fellow, very
scanty worship would be rendered to him at his death and
few animals slain to accompany him to the spirit world ;
and thus he would occupy an inferior position there corresponding to his social worthlessness here. This belief,"
our informant adds, " has undoubtedly great influence in
making men strive to live so as to obtain the good
opinion of their fellows, and leave an honourable memory
behind them at death."[3]   The Bushmans, who maintain
that the dead will ultimately go to a land abounding in
excellent food, put a spear by the side of a departed
friend in order that, when he arises, he may have something to defend himself with and procure a living ; but, if
they hate the person, they deposit no spear, so that on
his resurrection he may either be murdered or starved.[4]
The dead may also have to suffer from the curses of
those whom they injured while alive. At Motlav, in the

---

[1] Steinmetz, *Studien*, ii. 366 *sqq.*
Idem, ' Continuität oder Lohn und
Strafe im Jenseits der Wilden,' in
Archiv f. Anthropologie, xxiv. 577 *sqq.*

[2] Turner, *Samoa*, p. 292 *sq.*
[3] Macdonald, *Oceania*, p. 209.
[4] Campbell, *Second Journey in the
Interior of South Africa*, i. 29.

Banks' Islands, relatives "watch the grave of a man whose life was bad, lest some man wronged by him should come at night and beat with a stone upon the grave, cursing him."[1] At Gaua, in the same group, "when a great man died his friends would not make it known, lest those whom he had oppressed should come and spit at him after his death, or *govgov* him, stand bickering at him with crooked fingers and drawing in the lips, by way of curse."[2] The Maoris were careful to prevent the bones of their dead relatives from falling into the hands of their enemies, "who would dreadfully desecrate and ill-use them, with many bitter jeers and curses."[3] A person may, moreover, himself during his lifetime directly provide for his comfort in the life to come, and if the act by which he does so is apt to call forth approval its result is easily interpreted as its reward. Thus the Kukis of India believe that all enemies whom a person has killed will in his future abode be in attendance on him as slaves;[4] and this belief probably accounts for their opinion that nothing more certainly ensures future happiness than destroying a number of enemies.[5] We have further to notice the common idea that a person's character after his death remains more or less as it was during his life. Hence the souls of bad people are supposed to reappear in the shape of obnoxious animals[6] or become evil spirits,[7] and this may lead to the notion that they have to do so as a punishment for their wickedness.[8] And as the revengeful feelings of men likewise are believed to last beyond death, offenders may in the

[1] Codrington, *op. cit.* p. 269.

[2] *Ibid.* p. 269.

[3] Colenso, *Maori Races*, p. 28.

[4] Dalton, *Ethnology of Bengal*, p. 46.

[5] Macrae, 'Account of the Kookies,' in *Asiatick Researches*, vii. 195.

[6] Hill and Thornton, *Aborigines of New South Wales*, p. 4. Ratzel, *op. cit.* i. 317 (Solomon Islanders). Junghuhn, *Die Battaländer auf Sumatra*, ii. 338 (natives of Bali and Lombok). Cross, quoted by Mac Mahon, *Far Cathay and Farther India*, p. 203

(Karens). Waitz, *Anthropologie der Naturvölker*, ii. 419 (Maravi). Southey, *History of Brazil*, iii. 392 (Guaycurus). Powers, *Tribes of California*, pp. 144 (Tatu), 155 (Kato Pomo).

[7] Bailey, 'Wild Tribes of the Veddahs,' in *Trans. Ethn. Soc.* N.S. ii. 302, n. ‡ (Sinhalese). von den Steinen, *Unter den Naturvölkern Zentral-Brasiliens*, p. 349 (Bakaïrí).

[8] See Steinmetz, *Studien*, ii. 376; *Idem*, in *Archiv für Anthropologie*, xxiv. 603 *sq.*

other world have to suffer from the hands of those whom they injured in this.[1] Some of the Nagas of Central India maintain that " a murdered man's soul receives that of his murderer in the spirit world and makes him his slave." [2] The Chippewas think that in the land of the dead " the souls of bad men are haunted by the phantoms of the persons or things they have injured." [3] In Aurora, in the New Hebrides, the belief prevails that the ghosts of those whom a man has wronged in this world take a full revenge upon him after death.[4] According to the Banks' Islanders, if a person has killed a good man without cause, the good man's ghost withstands his murderer, when the latter after death wants to enter into Panoi, the good place ; but if one man has killed another in fair fight he will not be withstood by the person whom he slew.[5] And not only the offended party but the other dead as well may, from dislike or fear, be anxious to refuse the souls of bad people admittance to their company. In the belief of the Pentecost Islanders, when the soul of a murdered man comes to the land of ghosts with the instrument of death upon him, he tells who killed him, and when the murderer arrives the ghostly people will not receive him, but he has to stay apart with other murderers.[6] The Iroquois allot separate villages even to the souls of those who have died in war and of those who have committed suicide, because the other dead are afraid of their presence.[7] Among the Negroes of Northern Guinea, according to Mr. Wilson, " the only idea of a future state of retribution is implied in the use of a separate burial-place for those who have died ' by the red-water ordeal ' or who have been guilty of grossly wicked deeds " ;[8] and if a person's body is buried apart, his soul will naturally remain equally isolated.[9] That the frequent idea of the bad being separ-

---

[1] Cf. Marillier, loc cit. p. 44 sq.
[2] Fytche, Burma, i. 354.
[3] Keating, op. cit. ii. 158 sq.
[4] Codrington, op. cit. p. 279 sq.
[5] Ibid. p. 274.
[6] Ibid. p. 288.
[7] Brebeuf, ' Relation de ce qui s'est

passé dans le pays des Hurons,' in Relations des Jésuites, 1636, p. 104 sq. Hewitt, ' The Iroquoian Concept of the Soul,' in Jour. of American Folk-Lore, viii. 109.
[8] Wilson, Western Africa, p. 210.
[9] See supra, ii. 236 sqq.

ated from the good after death is largely due to the assumed unwillingness of the latter to associate with dangerous or disreputable souls, seems probable from the fact
that, in the beliefs of the lower races, paradise generally
plays a much more prominent part than hell, the lot of the
wicked being to suffer want rather than to be subjected to
torments.[1] But, finally, it must also be remembered that
the other world is a creation of men's fancy, and may therefore be formed in accordance with their hopes and wishes.
Beyond the gloom of death they imagine a paradise where
life is much happier than here on earth.[2] Why, then,
might not their moral feelings, only too often ungratified
in the reality of the present, occasionally seek satisfaction
in the dreams of the future ?

The belief in a moral retribution after death may thus
originate in various ways, quite independently of any
notion of a god who acts as a judge of human conduct.
When such a belief is said to prevail among a savage people
it is by no means the rule that the rewards or punishments
are associated with the activity of a divine being. And
when, as is sometimes the case, the fate of the dead is supposed to depend upon the will of a high god, the notions
held about the other world, and especially about the place
reserved for the wicked, in several instances suggest influence from a more advanced religion. But on the other
hand it is not an idea which seems incompatible with
genuine savage thought that, in cases where the souls of
men are believed to go to live with gods, the latter select
their companions and, like the human inhabitants of the
other world, refuse admittance to undesirable individuals.
Religious ideas have no doubt already at the savage

---

[1] This is especially the case among
the Indians of North America (cf.
Brinton, *Myths of the New World*, p.
242 *sq.*; Dorman, *op. cit.* p. 33 ;
Steinmetz, in *Archiv f. Anthrop.*
xxiv. 591). See also Codrington, *op.
cit.* p. 274 *sq.* (Banks' Islanders).

[2] Dove, ' Aborigines of Tasmania,'
in *Tasmanian Jour. Natural Science,*
i. 253. Polack, *Manners and Customs*
of the New Zealanders, i. 254 ; Dieffenbach, *Travels in New Zealand,* ii.
118. Percy Smith, ' Futuna,' in *Jour.
Polynesian Soc.* i. 39. Batchelor,
Ainu of Japan, p. 225. Steller, *op.
cit.* p. 269 (Kamchadales). Cranz, *op.
cit.* i. 186 (Greenlanders). Robertson,
History of America, ii. 202. Arbousset and Daumas, *op. cit.* p. 343
(Bechuanas).

stage begun to influence the moral consciousness even in points which have no direct bearing upon the personal interests of gods ; but this influence is not known to have been so great as it has often been represented to be. I can find no solid foundation for the statements made by recent writers, that " the historical beginning of all morality is to be found in religion " ; [1] that even in the earliest period of human history " religion and morality are necessary correlates of each other " ; [2] that " all moral commandments originally have the character of religious commandments " ; [3] that in ancient society " all morality—as morality was then understood—was consecrated and enforced by religious motives and sanctions " ; [4] that the clan-god was the guardian of the tribal morality.[5] From various facts stated in this and earlier chapters I have been led to the conclusion that among uncivilised races the moral ideas relating to men's conduct towards one another have been much more influenced by the belief in magic forces which may be utilised by man, than by the belief in the free activity of gods.

[1] Pfleiderer, *Philosophy and Development of Religion*, iv. 230.
[2] Caird, *Evolution of Religion*, i. 237.
[3] Wundt, *Ethik*, p. 99

[4] Robertson Smith, *Religion of the Semites*, p. 267. *Cf. ibid.* p. 53.
[5] Jevons, *Introduction to the History of Religion*, pp. 112, 177.

CHAPTER LI

GODS AS GUARDIANS OF MORALITY (*continued*)

FROM the gods of savage races we shall now pass to consider the attitudes of more civilised gods towards matters of worldly morality.

The deities of ancient Mexico were generally clothed with terror, and delighted in vengeance and human sacrifices. But there was also the god Quetzalcoatl, generous of gifts, mild and gentle, and so averse from such sacrifices that he shut his ears with both hands when they were mentioned.[1] The god Tezcatlipoca, again, was looked upon as the austere guardian of law and morals ; but, as Sir E. B. Tylor observes, the remarkable Aztec formulas collected by Sahagun, in which this deity is so prominent a figure, show traces of Christian admixture in their material, as well as of Christian influence in their style.[2] It seems that the Mexicans had reached no fixed or systematic conclusions as to the relation of the moral to the religious life.[3] They held that departed souls attained different degrees of felicity or of wretchedness according to their different modes of death. Warriors who died on the battle-field or in the hands of the enemy's priests, and merchants who died on their journey, went to the house of the sun ; those who were killed by lightning, who were drowned,

[1] Brinton, *Myths of the New World,* p. 294 *sq.* Bancroft, *Native Races of the Pacific States,* iii. 259.
[2] Tylor, *Primitive Culture,* ii. 344.
[3] Réville, *Hibbert Lectures on the Native Religions of Mexico and Peru,* p. 104 *sq.*

or who died from some incurable disease went to a terrestrial paradise ; and those who died of·old age or any ordinary disease went to a land of darkness and desolation, where they after a time sunk in a sleep which knew no waking.[1]

Among the ancient Peruvians morality obtained a religious sanction through the divinity ascribed to their rulers. " They considered every mere order of the king to be a divine decree," says Garcilasso de la Vega ; " how much more would they venerate the special laws instituted for the common good. They said that the sun had ordered these laws to be made, and had revealed them to his child the Ynca ; and hence a man who broke them was held to be guilty of sacrilege." [2] According to the beliefs of the higher classes the Incas were after death transported to the mansion of the Sun, their father, where they still lived together as his family. The nobles would either follow them there or would live beneath the earth under the sceptre of Supay, the god of the dead. There was no idea of positive suffering inflicted on the wicked under his direction, but the subterranean abode was gloomy and dismal. Exceptional considerations of birth, rank, or valour in war determined the passage of chosen souls to heaven, where their lot would be far happier than that of the souls who remained in the regions below. The common people, on the other hand, thought of the future life as a continuation, pure and simple, of the present existence.[3]

The great gods of ancient Egypt were mostly conceived as friendly beings.[4] Amon Râ, " the king of the gods," was, in his character of the sun god, the creator, preserver, and supporter of all living things. He it is who makes pasture for the herds and fruit trees for men, on his account the Nile comes and mankind lives. He is verily

---

[1] Bancroft, op. cit. iii. 532 sqq. Clavigero, History of Mexico, i. 242 sq.

[2] Garcilasso de la Vega, Royal Commentaries of the Yncas, i. 148.

[3] Réville, op. cit. p. 236 sqq.

[4] On Egyptian gods as guardians of morality see, generally, Gardiner, ' Egyptian Ethics and Morality,' in Hastings, Encyclopædia of Religion and Ethics, v. 479 sq.

of kindly heart : " when men call to him he delivers the
fearful from the insolent." He is " the vizier of the
poor, who takes no bribes," and who does not corrupt
witnesses ; and to him officials pray for promotion.[1]
Thoth, the moon god, was also the god of all wisdom
and learning, who gave men " speech and writing," who
discovered the written characters, and by his arithmetic
enabled gods and men to keep account of their possessions.[2] Osiris ruled over the whole of Egypt as
king, and instructed its inhabitants in all that was good—
in agriculture as well as in the true religion—and gave
them laws.[3] After a long and blessed reign, however,
he fell a prey to the machinations of his brother Set, and,
having been slain, was constrained to descend into the
Underworld, where he evermore lived and reigned as
judge and king of the dead. But the wicked god Set
was also an object of worship ; for he was strong and
mighty, a terror to gods and men, and kings were
anxious to secure his favour.[4] We have noticed above
that certain Egyptian gods were believed to be guardians
of truth ; [5] and closely connected with this function was
their love of justice. Thoth, who was called to witness
by him who wished to give assurance of his honesty and
good faith,[6] was styled " the judge in heaven " ; [7] while
his wife Maā, or Maat, was the goddess of both truth
and justice, and her priests were the supreme judges.[8]
But it seems that the Egyptian gods after all chiefly took
notice of such acts as concerned their own wellbeing.

[1] Erman, *Handbook of Egyptian Religion*, pp. 58-60, 83. Wiedemann, *Religion of the Ancient Egyptians*, p. 114.

[2] Erman, *op. cit.* p. 11. Maspero, *Dawn of Civilization*, p. 220.

[3] Erman, *op. cit.* p. 32. *Idem, Life in Ancient Egypt*, p. 270. Maspero, *op. cit.* p. 174. Plutarch, *De Iside et Osiride*, 13. Diodorus Siculus, *Bibliotheca historica*, i. 14, 15, 25. Kaibel, *Epigrammata Græca*, p. xxi.

[4] It is probable that Set originally was the divine protector of the kings of Upper Egypt, while Osiris' son Horus, who defeated him, was the protector of the kings of Lower Egypt (Erman, *Egyptian Religion*, p. 19 *sq.*).

[5] *Supra*, ii. 115.

[6] *Supra*, ii. 121.

[7] Erman, *Egyptian Religion*, p. 11.

[8] *Supra*, ii. 115. Wiedemann, *op. cit.* p. 142. Amélineau, *L'évolution des idées morales dans l'Égypte ancienne*, pp. 182, 187. Erman, *Egyptian Religion*, p. 21.

This is true even of Osiris, " the great god, the lord of justice," [1] in whose presence the judgment of the dead was given which decided upon their admission into his kingdom. In thousands upon thousands of funerary inscriptions we read words like these :—" May a royal offering be given to Osiris, that he may grant all manner of good things, food and drink to the soul of the deceased." [2] And whilst the living paid him his dues in sacrifices repeated from year to year at regular intervals, the dead were not allowed to receive directly the sepulchral meals or offerings of kindred on feast-days, but all that was addressed to them must first pass through the hands of the god.[3] In the " Negative Confession," which the worshippers of Osiris taught to their dead, great importance was attached to religious offences, such as to snare the birds of the gods, to catch the fish in their lakes, to injure the herds in the temple domains, to diminish the food in the temples, to revile the god. At the same time the list of offences which excluded the dead from Osiris' kingdom contained very many of a social character—murder, oppression, stealing, robbing minors, fraud, lying, slander, reviling, adultery.[4] But the meaning of this seems to have been not so much that the god was animated by a righteous desire to punish the wicked and reward the good, as, rather, that he did not like to have any rascals among his vassals. As to the fate of the non-justified dead very little is said, and the punishment devised for them seems to have been a comparatively modern invention.[5] Nay, the virtuous dead themselves depended for their welfare

---

[1] Erman, *Egyptian Religion*, p. 101.
[2] Wiedemann, *op. cit.* p. 217.
[3] Maspero, *op. cit.* p. 117.
[4] Erman, *Egyptian Religion*, p. 103 *sqq.*
[5] Wiedemann, *op. cit.* p. 95 *sq.* *Idem, Egyptian Doctrine of the Immortality of the Soul*, p. 55. Erman, *Egyptian Religion*, p. 105. In the Pyramid texts we read that, if among the deceased there is one of whom it can be said, " There is no

evil which he hath done," the saying penetrates to the sun god, and he receives him kindly in heaven. The deceased also profits with regard to his reception there if he has never spoken evil of the king nor slighted the gods. But, as a rule, it is rather bodily cleanliness which the gods demand of their new companion in heaven, and they themselves help to purify him (Erman, p. 94).

upon their knowledge of magic words and formulas,
upon amulets laid in their tombs, and upon the offerings
made to them by their kindred. Ignorant souls, or
those ill prepared for the struggle, were overcome by
hunger and thirst, were attacked by demons and
poisonous animals in traversing the regions of the
Underworld, and, when in Osiris' kingdom, had to work
and till the land and earn their own living if the offerings
ceased.[1] The Book of the Dead is itself essentially
a collection of spells intended to secure to the dead
victory over evil demons and protection from
the gods; and the "Negative Confession" is a
later addition, which shows that originally the conduct
of earthly life was not considered at all.[2] So also in
the book of Am Dûat the whole doctrine of a future
life is based upon a belief in the power of magic, with
the single exception that nobody can look forward to
possessing fields in Dûat who in life has been an enemy
of the god Râ.[3]

The religion of the Chaldeans was a religion of dread.
Everywhere they felt themselves surrounded by hostile
demons; feared above all were the seven evil spirits, who
were everywhere and yet invisible, who slipped through
bolts and doorposts and sockets, and who had power even
to bewitch the gods.[4] In their incessant warfare against
these fiends men were assisted by the more propitious
among the deities: by Marduk, the "merciful" god, the
god of the youthful sun of spring and early morning;[5]

[1] Erman, *Life in Ancient Egypt*, p. 315 sqq. Idem, *Egyptian Religion*, p. 99 sq. Maspero, *op. cit.* p. 185 sq. Idem, *Études de mythologie et d'archéologie égyptiennes*, i. 347. Wiedemann, *Religion of the Ancient Egyptians*, pp. 279, 296. Idem, *Egyptian Doctrine of the Immortality of the Soul*, p. 60 sq.
[2] Maspero, *Études*, i. 348. Amélineau, *op. cit.* p. 243. Renouf, in *Book of the Dead*, p. 220. Erman, *Egyptian Religion*, p. 101.
[3] Wiedemann, *Religion of the Ancient Egyptians*, p. 94 sq. Maspero, *Études*, ii. 163.
[4] Jastrow, *Religion of Babylonia and Assyria*, p. 260 sqq. Smith, *Chaldean Account of Genesis*, pp. 87, 88, 106 sq. Idem, *Chaldäische Genesis*, edited by Delitzsch, pp. 83, 306 sq.
[5] Mürdter-Delitzsch, *Geschichte Babyloniens und Assyriens*, p. 31. Sayce, *Hibbert Lectures on the Religion of the Ancient Babylonians*, p. 98. King, *Babylonian Magic and Sorcery*, p. 52 sqq. Jensen, *Die Kosmologie der Babylonier*, pp. 87, 88, 249 sq. Schrader-Zimmern, *Die Keilinschriften und das Alte Testament*, p. 372 sq.

by Ea, the " good " god, the god of the waters of the deep and the source of wisdom ;[1] by Gibil-Nusku, the lord of fire, who put to flight the demons of night when the fire was kindled on the household hearth, and who in the flame carried to the other gods the sacrifices offered them;[2] as also by the tutelary deities of each individual, household, and city.[3] The gods were on the whole favourably disposed towards man. But they helped only those who piously observed the prescribed rites, who recited the conventional prayers and offered them sacrifices ; on such persons they bestowed a happy old age and a numerous posterity. On the other hand, he who did not fear his god would be cut down like a reed ; and by neglecting the slightest ceremonial detail the king excited the anger of the deities against himself and his subjects.[4] During the whole of their lives the Chaldeans were haunted by the dread of offending their gods, and they continually implored pardon for their sins.[5] But the sinner became conscious of his guilt only as a conclusion drawn from the fact that he was suffering from some misfortune, which he interpreted as a punishment sent by an offended god. It mattered little what had called forth the wrath of the god or whether the deity was acting in accordance with just ideas ;[6] and in none of the penitential psalms known to us is there any indication that the notion of sin comprised offences against fellow men. It is true that in the incantation series ' Shurpu ' not only offences against gods and ceremonial transgressions, but a large number of wrongs of a social character, are included in the list of possible causes of the suffering which the incantation is intended to remove. On behalf of the afflicted individual the exorciser asks :—" Has he sinned against a god, Is his

---

[1] Hommel, *Die semitischen Völker und Sprachen*, i. 374 *sqq.* Mürdter-Delitzsch, *op. cit.* p. 27. Sayce, *op. cit.* pp. 131, 140.

[2] Tallqvist, ' Die assyrische Beschwörungsserie Maqlû,' in *Acta Soc. Scient. Fennicæ*, xx. 25, 28 *sq.*

[3] Mürdter-Delitzsch, *op. cit.* p. 37 *sq.* Maspero, *Dawn of Civilization*, pp. 643, 674, 682 *sq.*

[4] Jeremias, *Die babylonisch-assyrischen Vorstellungen vom Leben nach dem Tode*, p. 46 *sq.* Maspero, *Dawn of Civilization*, pp. 697, 705.

[5] See Zimmern, *Babylonische Busspsalmen, passim.*

[6] *Cf.* Jastrow, *op. cit.* p. 313 *sqq.*

guilt against a goddess, Is it a wrongful deed against his master, Hatred towards his elder brother, Has he despised father or mother, Insulted his elder sister, Has he given too little,[1] Has he withheld too much, 'For ' no ' said ' yes,' For ' yes ' said ' no ' ? . . . Has he fixed a false boundary, Not fixed a just boundary, Has he removed a boundary, a limit, or a territory, Has he possessed himself of his neighbour's house, Has he approached his neighbour's wife, Has he shed the blood of his neighbour, Robbed his neighbour's dress ? " and so forth.[2] But I fail to see any legitimate ground for the conclusion which Schrader and Zimmern have drawn from these passages, to wit, that the gods were believed to be angry with persons guilty of any of the offences enumerated.[3] It seems to me quite obvious that the evils which were hypothetically associated with injuries inflicted upon fellow men were ascribed, not to the avenging activity of a god, but to the curses of the injured party. The gods are expressly invoked to relieve the unhappy individual from the curses under which he is suffering, whether he has been cursed by his father, mother, elder brother, elder sister, friend, master, king, or god, or has approached an accursed person, or slept in such a person's bed, or sat on his chair, or eaten from his dish or drunk from his cup.[4] In these incantations there is no plea for forgiveness ; the possible causes for the suffering are enumerated simply because the mention of the real cause is supposed to go a long way towards expelling the evil.[5] Some of the gods, however, are invoked as judges. This is frequently the case with Shamash, the sun god, " the supreme judge of heaven and earth," who, seated on a throne in the chamber of judgment, receives the supplications of men.[6] Of the moon god Sin it is said in a hymn

---

[1] In mercantile transactions (Jastrow, *op. cit.* p. 291, n. 2).

[2] Zimmern, *Beiträge zur Kenntnis der babylonischen Religion,* ' Die Beschwörungstafeln Surpu,' p. 3 *sqq.*

[3] *Idem,* in Schrader, *Die Keilinschriften und das Alte Testament,* p. 612.

[4] Zimmern, *Die Beschwörungstafeln*

Šurpu, ii. 89–93, 99–104, pp. 7, 23

[5] See Jastrow, *op. cit.* p. 292.

[6] Tallqvist, Maqlû, ii. 94. Zimmern, Surpu, ii. 130, p. 9. *Idem, Babylonische Hymnen und Gebete,* p. 13. Mürdter-Delitzsch, *op. cit.* p. 28. Schrader-Zimmern, *op. cit.* p. 368. Jastrow, *op. cit.* pp 71, 120, 209 *sqq.*

dedicated to him that his " word produces truth and justice, so that men speak the truth."¹ And the lord of fire
is addressed as a judge, who burns the evildoers and annihi-
lates the bad,² and is exhorted by the conjurer to help him
to his right ; ³ but this probably means little more than the
invocation, " Eat my enemies, destroy those who have
done harm to me." ⁴ Of a moral retribution after death
there is no trace in the Chaldean religion. Those who
have obtained the goodwill of the gods receive their reward in this world, by a life of happiness and of good
health, but the moment that death ensues the control of
the gods comes to an end. All mankind, kings and subjects,
virtuous and wicked, go to Aralû, the gloomy subterranean
realm presided over by Allatu and her consort Nergal,
where the dead are doomed to everlasting sojourn or imprisonment in a state of joyless inactivity. A kind of judgment is spoken of, but nothing indicates that it is based on
moral considerations.⁵ According to the Gilgamesh epic,
however, the fortunes awaiting those who die are not all
alike. Those who fall in battle seem to enjoy special privileges, provided that they are properly buried and there is
someone to make them comfortable in their last hour and
to look after them when dead. But he whose corpse remains
in the field has no rest in the earth, and he whose spirit is
not cared for by any one is consumed by gnawing hunger.⁶

In a still higher degree than the Chaldean religion Zoroastrianism represents an incessant struggle against evil
spirits. Here everything in heaven and on earth is engaged
in the conflict ; it is a war between two mighty sovereigns,
Ahura Mazda and Angra Mainyu, and their respective
forces.⁷ Whatever works for the good of man comes from

---

¹ Zimmern, *Babylonische Hymnen und Gebete*, p. 12.
² Tallqvist, *Maqlû*, i. 95 ; ii. 70, 89, 116, 130, 131, 184.
³ *Ibid*. i. 114.
⁴ *Ibid*. i. 116 ; ii. 120.
⁵ Jeremias, *op. cit. passim.* Schrader-Zimmern, *op. cit.* p. 636 *sq.* Jastrow, *op. cit.* p. 565 *sqq.* Jensen, *op. cit.* p. 217 *sqq.*
⁶ Haupt, ' Die zwölfte Tafel des babylonischen Nimrod-Epos,' in *Beiträge zur Assyriologie,* i. 69 *sq.* Jensen, ' Das Gilgamis(Nimrod)-Epos,' xii. 6, in *Assyrisch-Babylonische Mythen und Epen,* p. 265.
⁷ According to the *Vendîdâd* (i. 3 *sqq.*) Angra Mainyu constantly countercreated the creations of Ahura Mazda. But this idea is not yet to be found in the Gathas, where the wickedness of Ako Mainyu is only

and strives for Ahura Mazda, whatever works for the harm
of man comes from and strives for Angra Mainyu. There
can be no doubt that the powers of goodness will absolutely
triumph in the end ; but though Angra Mainyu and his
band have been defeated, the battle is still raging. Ahura
Mazda, being the originator of everything good in the
world, is also the founder of the order of the universe, " the
creator of the righteous order." [1] In the Vendîdâd he is
asked about the rules of life, and he is pleased to answer ; [2]
M. Darmesteter observes that the Avesta and the Penta-
teuch are the only two religious books known in which
legislation descends from the heavens to the earth in a
series of conversations between the lawgiver and his god.[3]
The sacred law of Zoroastrianism enjoins charity [4] and
industry,[5] it condemns the murder of a believer,[6] abortion, [7]
theft,[8] non-payment of debts,[9] and, with special emphasis,
falsehood and breach of faith,[10] and unnatural intercourse.[11] But the "good thoughts, words, and deeds" most
urgently insisted upon are orthodoxy, prayer, and sacrifice ; whilst the greatest sins are apostasy, transgressions of
the rules of ceremonial cleanliness, and offences against
sacred beings. It is less criminal to kill a man than to serve
bad food to a shepherd's dog ; for the manslayer gets off
with ninety stripes, whereas the bad master will receive
two hundred.[12] And the killing of a water dog is punished
with ten thousand stripes.[13] Offenders will be liable to
penalties not only here below, but in the next world as
well, where Ahura Mazda, " the discerning arbiter," [14]
establishes " evil for the evil, and happy blessings for the
good." [15] The views accepted in regard to the future life,

---

represented as an attempt to destroy
the good creation (see Lehmann,
Zarathustra, ii. 75, 165).

[1] *Yasna*, xxxi. 7.   Darmesteter,
Ormazd et Ahriman, pp. 19, 24, 88,
&c.

[2] *Vendîdâd*, xviii. 13 *sqq.*

[3] Darmesteter, in *Sacred Books of
the East*, iv. (2nd edit.) p. lviii.

[4] *Supra*, i. 551.

[5] *Supra*, ii. 275.

[6] *Vendîdâd*, iii. 41 ; v. 14.

[7] *Ibid.* xv. 9 *sqq.*

[8] *Supra*, ii. 60.   *Yasna*, xi. 3.

[9] *Vendîdâd*, iv. 1.

[10] *Supra*, ii. 93

[11] *Supra*, ii. 479 *sq.*

[12] *Vendîdâd*, iv. 40 ; xiii. 24 ; xv. 3.

[13] *Ibid.* xiv. 1 *sq.*

[14] *Yasna*, xxix. 4.

[15] *Ibid.* xliii. 5.

whilst incomplete in the Gathas, are expanded in the Younger Avesta, and fully given in the Pahlavi books.[1] The man who has lived for Ahura Mazda will have a seat near him in heaven, and there he remains undecaying and immortal, unalarmed and undistressed, full of glory and delight ; whereas the wicked soul will be tormented in the darkness of hell, " the dwelling of the demons." [2] The good deeds of the virtuous and the bad deeds of the wicked, in the form of maidens, come to meet them on their roads to paradise or hell.[3] But the fate of the dead is not merely influenced by their conduct towards their fellow men while alive. It is said that " he who wishes to seize the heavenly reward, will seize it by giving gifts to him who holds up the Law." [4] And the soul of him who recites the prayer Ahuna Vairya in the manner prescribed crosses over the bridge which separates this world from the next, and reaches the highest paradise.[5]

In Vedic religion we likewise meet with a conflict between gods and demons, but the struggle is too unequal to result in anything like the Zoroastrian dualism.[6] Various misfortunes are attributed to the ill-will of evil spirits, but their power is comparatively slight, and the greater demons, like Vṛtra, are represented as defeated or destroyed by the gods.[7] On the other hand there is among the great gods themselves one who has a distinctly malevolent character, namely Rudra, a god of storm,[8] " terrible like a wild beast " ; [9] but though the hymns

---

[1] Cf. Jackson, Avesta Grammar, i. p. xxviii.

[2] Vendîdâd, xix. 28 sqq. Yasts, xxii. Bundahis, ch. xxx. Dînâ-î Maînôg-î Khirad, ii. 123 sqq. ch. vii. Ardâ Vîrâf, ch. xvii. Cf. Geiger, Civilization of the Eastern Irānians, i. 101.

[3] Dînâ-î Maînôg-î Khirad, ii. 125, 167 sqq.

[4] Yasts, xxiv. 30.

[5] Geiger, op. cit. i. 73. See also Yasts, xii. 335 ; xxiv. 39, 47 sq. ;

Darmesteter, Ormazd et Ahriman, p. 28.

[6] Cf. Barth, Religions of India, p. 13.

[7] Oldenberg, Die Religion des Veda, p. 281. Macdonell, Vedic Mythology, p. 18.

[8] Muir, Original Sanskrit Texts, v. 147. Barth, op. cit. p. 14. Macdonell, op. cit. p. 77.

[9] Oldenberg, op. cit. pp. 63, 281, 284.   Macdonell, op. cit. p. 18. Bergaigne, La religion védique, iii. 152 sqq.

addressed to him chiefly express fear of his dreadful shafts
and deprecations of his wrath, he is also sometimes
supplicated to confer blessings upon man and beast.[1]
With this exception the great gods are all beneficent
beings,[2] though of course liable to punish those who
offend them.   Varuna has established heaven and earth,[3]
has made the celestial bodies to shine[4] and the rivers
to flow.[5]   He rules over nature by laws which are fixed
and immutable, and which must be followed by the gods
themselves.[6] He sees and knows everything, because
he is the infinite light and the sun is his eye ;[7] and in
connection with Mithra he is said to dispel and punish
falsehood.[8] Varuna has even been represented as " the
supreme moral ruler," but it seems to me that scholars
have generally credited him with a somewhat more comprehensive sense of justice than the hymns imply.[9] Every
hymn to Varuna contains a prayer for forgiveness, but
there is no indication that the sins which excite his wrath
include ordinary moral wrongdoing.   That sin and moral
guilt are not identical conceptions in the Rig-Veda is fairly
obvious from the fact that forgiveness of sin is also sought
from Indra,[10] whose favour is only won by those who
contribute to his wellbeing or who destroy persons
neglectful of his worship.[11] The Vedic religion is pre-eminently ritualistic.   The pious man *par préférence* is he who
makes the *soma* flow in abundance and whose hands are
always full of butter, the reprobate man is he who is
penurious towards the gods ;[12] and just like the other gods,

[1] Macdonell, *op. cit.* p. 75 *sq.*
[2] Oldenberg, *op. cit.* pp. 60, 281.
Macdonell, *op. cit.* p. 18.
[3] *Rig-Veda*, viii. 42. 1.
[4] *Ibid.* i. 24. 10 ; vii. 87. 5.
[5] *Ibid.* ii. 28. 4.
[6] *Ibid.* viii. 41. 7. Macdonell, *op. cit.* p. 26. Bohnenberger, *Der altindische Gott Varuṇa*, p. 38 *sqq.*
[7] *Supra*, ii. 598. Darmesteter, *Essais orientaux*, p. 126.
[8] Macdonell, *op. cit.* p. 26.
[9] Macdonell, *op. cit.* pp. 20, 26. Whitney, ' On the main Results of

the later Vedic Researches in Germany,' in *Jour. American Oriental Soc.* iii. 326. Roth, ' On the Morality of the Veda,' *ibid.* iii. 340 *sq.* Bergaigne, *op. cit.* iii. 156. Darmesteter, *Essais orientaux*, p. 111. Bohnenberger, *op. cit.* p. 49 *sqq.*
[10] Oldenberg, *op. cit.* p. 299.
[11] *Ibid.* pp. 282, 283, 300.
[12] *Rig-Veda*, viii. 31.   See Barth, *op. cit.* p. 34 ; Kaegi, *Rigveda*, p. 29 ; Muir, *op. cit.* v. 20 ; Macdonell, *op. cit.* p. 18.

Varuna visits with disease those who neglect him,[1] and is appeased by sacrifices and prayers.[2] After death the souls of those who have practised rigorous penance,[3] of those who have risked their lives in battle,[4] and above all of those who have bestowed liberal sacrificial gifts,[5] go with the smoke arising from the funeral pile to the heavenly world, where the Fathers dwell with Yama—the first man who died [6]—and Varuna, the two kings who reign in bliss.[7] There they enjoy an endless felicity among the gods, clothed in glorious bodies and drinking the celestial *soma*, which renders them immortal.[8] Yet there are different degrees of happiness in this heavenly mansion. The performance of rites in honour of the manes causes the souls to ascend from a lower to a higher state ; indeed, if no such offerings are made they do not go to heaven at all.[9] Another source of happiness for the dead is their own pious conduct during their lifetime ; for in the abode of bliss they are united with what they have sacrificed and given, especially reaping the reward of their gifts to priests.[10] Unworthy souls, on the other hand, are kept out of this abode by Yama's dogs, which guard the road to his kingdom.[11] As to the destiny in store for those who are not admitted to heaven, the hymns have little to tell. Zimmer and others erroneously argue that a race who believe in future rewards for the good must logically believe in future punishments for the wicked.[12] So far as I can see, all the traces of such a belief which are to be found in the Vedic literature are requests made to gods,

[1] *Rig-Veda*, i. 122. 9.
[2] *Ibid.* i. 24. 14.
[3] *Ibid.* x. 154. 2.
[4] *Ibid.* x. 154. 3.
[5] *Ibid.* i. 125. 5 *sq.* ; x. 107. 2 ; x. 154. 3. Muir, *op. cit.* v. 285. Oldenberg, *op. cit.* p. 536. Macdonell, *op. cit.* p. 167.
[6] Muir, *op. cit.* v. 301.
[7] *Rig-Veda*, x. 14. 7 *sq.* Barth, *op. cit.* p. 22 *sq.* Macdonell, *op. cit.* p. 165 *sqq.*
[8] Zimmer, *Altindisches Leben*, p. 410 *sqq.* Barth, *op. cit.* p. 23. Macdonell, *op. cit.* p. 167 *sq.*

[9] Hopkins, *Religions of India*, p. 155. Oldenberg, *op. cit.* p. 535.
[10] *Rig-Veda*, x. 14. 8 ; x. 154. 3. Oldenberg, *op. cit.* p. 535. Macdonell, *op. cit.* p. 168.
[11] *Rig-Veda*, x. 14. 10 *sqq.* Cf. Zimmer, *op. cit.* p. 421 ; Hopkins, *op. cit.* p. 147.
[12] Zimmer, *op. cit.* p. 418. Scherman, *Indische Visionslitteratur*, p. 123. *Idem*, ' Eine Art visionärer Höllenschilderung aus dem indischen Mittelalter,' in *Romanische Forschungen*, v. 569. Oldenberg, *op. cit.* p. 537.

or simply curses, to the effect that evil-doers may be thrown into deep and dismal pits under the earth.[1] They do not imply that gods of their own accord punish wicked people after death.

In post-Vedic times ritualism grew more important still. Sometimes the gods are represented as beings indifferent to every moral distinction, and the most indelicate stories are unscrupulously related of them.[2] In the Taittirîya Samhitâ of the Yajur Veda we are told that if anybody wishes to injure another, he need only say to Sûrya, one of the most important among the solar deities,[3] " Smite such a one, and I will give you an offering," and Sûrya, to get the offering, will smite him.[4] Çiva, who is connected with the Vedic god Rudra, is in the Mahabharata clothed in terrible " forms," being armed with the trident and wearing a necklace of skulls ; he exacts a bloody cultus, and is the chief of the mischievous spirits and vampires that frequent places of execution and burial grounds.[5] Vishnu, the other great god of Hinduism, though less fierce than Çiva, is nevertheless, on one side of his character, an inexorable god ;[6] and Krishna, as accepted by Vishnuism, is a crafty hero of a singularly doubtful moral character.[7] In Brahmanism religion is largely replaced by magic, the rites themselves are raised to the rank of divinities, the priests become the gods of gods.[8] And the point of view from which these man-gods look upon human conduct is expressed in the Satapatha Brâhmana, where it is said that fees paid to priests are like sacrifices offered to other gods—those who gratify them are placed in a state of bliss.[9] Ritual observances are essential for a man's wellbeing both in this life and in the life to come, where paradise, hell, or transmigration

[1] Rig-Veda, iv. 5. 5 ; vii. 104. 3, 11, 17. Atharva-Veda, v. 19. 3, 12 sqq. ; xii. 4. 3, 36.
[2] Barth, op. cit. p. 46 sq. Macdonell, op. cit. p. 76.
[3] Barth, op. cit. p. 20.
[4] Taittirîya Samhitâ, vi. 4 sqq., quoted by Goblet d'Alviella, Hibbert

Lectures on the Origin and Growth of the Conception of God, p. 85.
[5] Barth, op. cit. pp. 159, 164.
[6] Ibid. p. 174.
[7] Ibid. p. 172.
[8] Supra, ii. 657.
[9] Satapatha Brâhmana, ii. 2. 2. 6.

awaits the dead. In the Brâhmanas immortality, or at
least longevity, is promised to those who rightly understand and practise the rites of sacrifice, whilst those who
are deficient in this respect depart before their natural
term of life to the next world, where they are weighed in
a balance and receive good or evil according to their
deeds.[1] To repeat sacred texts a certain number of times
is also laid down as a condition of salvation,[2] and the
doctrine is gradually developed that a single invocation
of the divine name cancels a whole life of iniquity and
crime. Hence the importance attached—as early as the
Bhagavad Gîtâ—to the last thought before death, and the
idea of attaining complete possession of this thought by
an act of suicide.[3] According to the Purânas it is
sufficient even in the case of the vilest criminal, when at
the point of death, to pronounce by chance some syllables
of the names Vishnu or Çiva in order to obtain salvation ;[4]
and in the preface to the Prem Sâgar, which displays the
religion of the Hindus at the present day, it is said that
those who even ignorantly sing the praises of the greatness
of Krishn Chand are rewarded with final beatitude, just
as a person would acquire eternal life by partaking of the
drink of immortality though he did not know what he
was drinking.[5] On the other hand, " according to the
Hindu Scriptures, whatever a man's life may have been,
if he do not die near some holy stream, if his body is not
burned on its banks, or at any rate near some water as a
representative of the stream ; or where this is impracticable,
if some portion of his body be not thrown into it—his
spirit must wander in misery, unable to obtain the bliss
for which he has done and suffered so much in life."[6] At
the same time we also find a great variety of social duties

[1] Weber, ' Eine Legende des Çata-patha-Brâhmaṇa über die strafende Vergeltung nach dem Tode,' in Zeitschr. d. Deutschen Morgenländischen Gesellsch. ix. 238 sq. See also Macdonell, op. cit. p. 168 ; Hopkins, op. cit. pp. 190, 193 ; Vishṅu Purâṅa, p. 44.
[2] Aitareya Brahmanam, ii. 17.
[3] Bhagavad Gîtâ, ch. 8. Barth, op. cit. p. 228.
[4] Barth, op. cit. p. 228.
[5] Prem Sâgar, p. 56. Cf. Wilson, in Vishṅu Purâṅa, p. 210, n. 13 ; Idem, ' Religious Sects of the Hindus,' in Asiatic Researches, xvi. 115.
[6] Wilkins, Modern Hinduism, p. 439 sq.

inculcated in the sacred books of India—humanity even to
enemies [1] and slaves,[2] filial piety,[3] charity,[4] hospitality,[5]
veracity ; [6] and in the Sûtras the doctrine appears that in
order to obtain the chief fruit of sacrifice it is necessary to
practise the moral virtues in addition to the rite.[7] But
this doctrine is singularly free from any reference to the
justice of gods. In the Upanishads and Buddhistic books
it is distinctly formulated in the idea of *karma*, according
to which each act of the soul, good or bad, inevitably and
naturally works out its full effect to the sweet or bitter
end without the intervention of any deity to apportion
the reward or punishment.[8]

Buddha did not base his system on any belief in gods,
hence there is no place in it for a ritual nor for sin
in the sense of offending a supernatural being. He
that is pure in heart is the true priest, not he that knows
the Vedas ; the Vedas are nothing, the priests are of no
account, save as they be morally of repute.[9] If the
genuine Buddhist can be said to worship any higher
power, it is the moral order which never fails to assert
itself in the law of cause and effect. But Buddha's
followers were less metaphysical, and " the clouds
returned after the rain." The old gods of Brahmanism
came back, Buddha himself was deified as an omniscient
and everlasting god, and Buddhism incorporated most
of the local deities and demons of those nations it
sought to convert.[10] From being originally a metaphysical
and ethical doctrine, it was thus transformed into a
religion full of ritualism, and, it should be added,
profusely mixed with magic. In Lamaism, especially,

[1] *Supra*, i. 342.
[2] *Supra*, i. 689.
[3] *Supra*, i. 612.
[4] *Supra*, i. 550 *sq*.
[5] *Supra*, i. 578 *sq*.
[6] *Supra*, ii. 91.
[7] Barth, *op. cit.* p. 49. See, *e.g.*,
Âpastamba, i. 7. 20. 1 *sqq.* ; i. 8.
23. 6.
[8] Barth, *op. cit.* pp. 77, 78, 115 *sq.*
Müller, *Anthropological Religion*, p.

301. *Dhammapada*, i. 1 *sq.* Rhys
Davids, *Hibbert Lectures on the History of Buddhism*, p. 85. Oldenberg,
Buddha, p. 289. Hopkins, *op. cit.*
p. 319 *sq.*
[9] Hopkins, *op. cit.* p. 319.
[10] Waddell, *Buddhism in Tibet*, pp.
126, 325 *sq.* Griffis, *Religions of
Japan*, pp. 187, 207. Davis, *China*,
ii. 51.

ritual is elevated to the front rank of importance ; we find there pompous services closely resembling those of the Church of Rome, litanies and chants, offerings and sacrifice.[1] And the muttering of certain mystic formulas and short prayers is alleged to be far more efficacious than mere moral virtue as a means of gaining the glorious heaven of eternal bliss, the paradise of the fabulous Buddha of boundless light.[2] So also in China the teachers of Buddhism " were by no means rigorous in enforcing the obligations of men to morality. To expiate sins, offerings to the idols and to the priests were sufficient. A temple built in honour of Fŏ, and richly endowed, would suffice to blot out every stain of guilt, and serve as a portal to the blessed mansions of Buddha." [3]

In the national religion of China the heaven god, Shang-te, is the supreme being, the creator and sovereign ruler of the universe, whose power knows no bounds, and whose sight equally comprehends the past, the present, and the future, penetrating even to the remotest recesses of the heart.[4] He is the author and upholder not only of the physical but of the moral order of the world, watching over the conduct of men, rewarding the good, and punishing the wicked.[5] Sometimes he appears to array himself in terrors, as in the case of public calamities and the irregularity of the seasons ; but these are only salutary warnings intended to call men to repentance.[6] The cult which is offered Shang-te is frigid and ceremonial. The rules of ceremony have their origin in heaven, and the movement of them

[1] Waddell, op. cit. 421, 476.
[2] Ibid. pp. 142, 148, 573.
[3] Gutzlaff, quoted by Davis, op. cit. ii. 51. Cf. Edkins, Religion in China, p. 150.
[4] Legge, Notions of the Chinese concerning God, pp. 33, 34, 100 sq. Idem, Chinese Classics, i. 98. Staunton, Inquiry into the proper Mode of rendering the Word " God " in translating the Sacred Scriptures into the Chinese Language, p. 8 sq. Douglas, Confucianism and Taouism, pp.

77, 82.
[5] Doolittle, Social Life of the Chinese, ii. 272. Legge, Chinese Classics, i. 98 ; iii. 46. Smith, Proverbs of the Chinese, p. 40. Boone, Essay on the proper rendering of the Words Elohim and Θεός into the Chinese Language, p. 55. Indo-Chinese Gleaner, i. 162. Davis, op. cit. ii. 26, 34. Douglas, op. cit. pp. 77, 78, 83.
[6] Staunton, op. cit. p. 9. Legge, Chinese Classics, iii. 46 sq.

reaches to earth ; their abandonment leads to " the ruin of states, the destruction of families, and the perishing of individuals." [1]   The Chinese are inclined to place ritualism on an equality with social morality. Confucius himself humbly submitted to the rules of ceremony, although he denounced hypocrisy.   But to him morality was infinitely more important than religion. He altogether avoided the personal term God, and made only use of the abstract term Heaven.   He admitted that spiritual beings exist, and even sacrificed to them,[2] but when questioned about matters relating to religion he was systematically silent.[3]   Religious duties occupy a very insignificant place in his system.   " To give one's self earnestly to the duties due to men, and, while respecting spiritual beings, to keep aloof from them, may be called wisdom." [4]   Prayer is unnecessary because Heaven does not actively interfere with the soul of man ; it has endowed him at his birth with goodness, which, if he will, may become his nature, and the reward or punishment is only the natural or providential result of his conduct.[5]   Of punishments in a future life Confucius says nothing, though he maintains that there are rewards and dignity for the good after death.[6]   The belief of the Chinese in *post mortem* punishments comes from Buddhism. [7]

The gods of ancient Greece were on the whole beneficent beings, who conferred blessings upon those who secured their goodwill.   Zeus protects the life of the family, city, and nation ; he is a god of victory and victorious peace, who gathers the hosts against Troy, and saves Greece from Persia ; he brings the ships to land ; he is " the warder off of evil." [8]   But neither he nor the other gods bestow their

---

[1] *Lî Kî*, vii. 4. 5 *sq.*
[2] *Lun Yü*, iii. 12. I ; x. 8. 10.
[3] *Ibid.* vii. 20.   *Cf.* Réville, *La religion chinoise*, p. 326.
[4] *Lun Yü*, vi. 20.
[5] Douglas, *op. cit.* p. 78. Legge, *Religions of China*, p. 300. Réville, *op. cit.* p. 645.
[6] Legge, *Religions of China*, pp.

115, 299 *sq.* Réville, *op. cit.* p. 345.
[7] *Indo-Chinese Gleaner*, iii. 288. Edkins, *op. cit.* pp. 83, 87 *sqq.* Smith, *Proverbs of the Chinese*, p. 227.
[8] Farnell, *Cults of the Greek States*, i. 59–61, 83, 107. Vischer, *Kleine Schriften*, ii. 352 *sq.* Preller, *Griechische Mythologie*, i. 146 *sqq.*

favours for nothing ; Xenophon says that they assist with
good advice those who worship them regularly,[1] but take
revenge on those who neglect them.[2] They punish severely
even offences committed against them accidentally,[3] and
not infrequently they display actual malevolence towards
men by seducing them into sin [4] or inflicting harm upon
them out of sheer envy.[5] In other respects, also, they are by
no means models of morality ; but this does not prevent
them from acting as administrators of justice any more
than, among men, a judge is supposed to lose all regard for
justice because he himself transgresses the rules of morality
in some particular of private life.[6] " For great crimes,"
says Herodotus, " great punishments at the hands of the
gods are in store."[7] Dike, or Justice, the terrible virgin
" who breathes against her enemies a destructive wrath,"[8]
is represented sometimes as the daughter, sometimes as the
companion of the all-seeing Zeus ; [9] and, as Welcker observes, Zeus was not only a god among other gods, but also
the deity solely and abstractedly.[10] We have noticed above
that from ancient times the murder of a kinsman was an
offence against Zeus and under the ban of the Erinyes, and
that later on all bloodshed, if the victim had any rights at
all within the city, became a sin which needed purification.[11]
Zeus protected guests and suppliants,[12] he punished children who reproached their aged parents,[13] he was a guardian of the family property,[14] he protected boundaries,[15] he
was no friend of falsehood,[16] he punished perjury.[17] According to earlier beliefs retribution was exclusively restricted

[1] Xenophon, *Hipparchicus*, ix. 9.
Idem, Cyropædia, i. 6. 46.
[2] *Idem, Anabasis*, v. 3. 13 ; vii.
8. 4.
[3] Nägelsbach, *Die nachhomerische
Theologie des griechischen Volksglaubens*, p. 331 *sqq.*
[4] Schmidt, *Die Ethik der alten
Griechen*, i. 231 *sqq.*
[5] *Ibid.* i. 79 *sqq.*
[6] *Cf.* Nägelsbach, *Homerische Theologie*, pp. 288, 317 *sqq.* ; Schmidt, *op.
cit.* i. 48 *sqq.* ; Maury, *Histoire des
religions de la Grèce antique*, i. 342 ;
Gladstone, *Studies on Homer*, ii. 384.

[7] Herodotus, ii. 120.
[8] Aeschylus, *Choephoræ*, 949 *sqq.*
[9] *Ibid.* 949. Hesiod, *Opera et dies*,
256 (254). Usener, *Götternamen*, p.
197. Farnell, *op. cit.* i. 71, Darmesteter, *Essais orientaux*, p. 106 *sq.*
[10] Welcker, *Griechische Götterlehre*,
i. 181.
[11] *Supra*, i. 379.
[12] *Supra*, i. 579, 585.
[13] *Supra*, i. 624.
[14] *Supra*, ii. 60.
[15] *Supra*, ii. 61.
[16] *Supra*, ii. 116.
[17] *Supra*, ii. 121.

to this earthly existence, and if the guilty person himself
escaped the punishment for his deed it fell on some of his
descendants.[1] The transference of Menelaus to the Elysian
plain, spoken of in the Odyssey,[2] was not a reward for his
virtue—indeed, he was not particularly conspicuous for any
of the Homeric virtues—but a privilege resulting from his
being married to Zeus' daughter Helena ; [3] and if the perjurer was tortured in Hades [4] the simple reason was that he
had called down upon himself such torture in his oath.[5] In
later times we meet with the doctrine of retribution after
death, not only in the speculations of isolated philosophers,
but as a popular belief ; [6] but this belief seems to have been
quite unconnected with any notion of Olympian justice.[7]
The souls in the world beyond the grave are sentenced by
special judges ; [8] Aeschylus expressly says that it is another
Zeus that administers justice there.[9] For him Hades with
the powers by which it is governed exists only as a place
where the guilty are punished, whereas for the virtuous he
has no word of true hope ; [10] and other writers also have
much more to tell about future punishments than about
future rewards.[11] Particularly prominent among the offences
which are punished in Hades are, besides perjury,[12] injuries
to parents [13] and guests,[14] that is, offences which in this
world are visited with the most powerful curses.[15] According to Aeschylus, the retribution which the Erinyes—personifications of curses—have begun on earth is completed
in the nether world, and according to Pythagoras unpurified
souls are kept chained there by the Erinyes without any hope
of escape.[16] We are, moreover, told that painters used to represent allegorical figures of curses in connection with their

[1] Supra, i. 49 sq.
[2] Odyssey, iv. 561 sqq.
[3] Cf. Rohde, Psyche, p. 74.
[4] Iliad, iii. 278 sq. ; xix. 259 sq.
[5] Cf. Rohde, op. cit. p. 60.
[6] Schmidt, op. cit. i. 99 sqq. Nägelsbach, Nachhomerische Theologie, p.
35 sq.
[7] Cf. Schmidt, op. cit. i. 104.
[8] Ibid. i. 101.
[9] Aeschylus, Supplices, 230 sq.
[10] Cf. Westcott, Essays in the His-

tory of Religious Thought, p. 87.
[11] Schmidt, op. cit. i. 101 sq.
[12] Aristophanes, Ranæ, 150, 275.
[13] Aeschylus, Eumenides, 175, 267
sqq., 335 sqq. Pausanias, x. 28. 4 sq.
Aristophanes, Ranæ, 147–150, 274.
[14] Aeschylus, Eumenides, 269 sq.
Aristophanes, Ranæ, 147 sq.
[15] See supra, i. 584 sqq., 621 sqq.
[16] Diogenes Laertius, De vitis philosophorum, viii. 1. 31.

images of wicked dead.[1] From all these facts I conclude that the notion of punishments in Hades did not arise from a belief in the justice of gods, but from the idea that the efficacy of a curse may extend beyond the grave—an idea which we have already met with both in Vedic texts and among certain savages, and of which the supposed punishment of perjury in Hades is only a particular instance.[2] As for the gods it should be added that the vulgar opinion of their character was not shared by all. Euripides affirms that the legends about them which tend to confuse human ideas as to right and wrong are not literally true.[3] " I think," he says, " that none of the gods is bad " ; [4] " if the gods do aught that is base, they are not gods." [5] Plato opposes the popular views that the deity induces men to commit crimes,[6] that he is capable of feeling envy,[7] and that evil-doers may avert divine punishments by sacrifices offered to the gods as bribes.[8] God is good, he is never the author of evil to any one, and if the wicked are miserable the reason is that they require to be punished and are benefited by receiving punishment from God.[9] Plutarch likewise asserts in the strongest terms that God is perfectly good and least of all wanting in justice and love, " the most beautiful of virtues and the best befitting the Godhead." [10]

The gods of the Romans were on the whole unsympathetic and lifeless beings, some of them even actually pernicious, as the god of Fever, who had a temple on the Palatine hill, and the god of Ill-Fortune, who had an altar on the Esquiline hill.[11] The relations between the gods

---

[1] Demosthenes (?), *Contra Aristogitonem oratio I.* 52.

[2] The Arabs of the Ulád Bu 'Azîz in Southern Morocco maintain that there are three classes of persons who are infallibly doomed to hell, namely, those who have been cursed by their parents, those who have been guilty of unlawful homicide, and those who have burned corn. They say that every grain curses him who burns it.

[3] *Cf.* Westcott, *op. cit.* p. 104.

[4] Euripides, *Iphigenia in Tauris,* 391.

[5] *Idem, Bellerophon,* 17 (*Fragmenta,* 300).

[6] Plato, *Respublica,* ii. 379 *sq.*

[7] *Idem, Phædrus,* p. 247. *Idem, Timæus,* p. 29.

[8] *Idem, Respublica,* ii. 364 *sqq. Idem, Leges,* x. 905 *sqq.* ; xii. 948.

[9] *Idem, Respublica,* ii. 379 *sq. Cf.* Aeschylus, *Agamemnon,* 176 *sqq.*

[10] Plutarch, *De defectu oraculorum,* 24. See also *Idem, De adulatore et amico,* 22.

[11] Cicero, *De natura deorum,* iii. 25.

and their worshippers were cold, ceremonial, legal. The chief thing was not to break " the peace of the gods," or, when it was broken, to restore it.[1] They were rendered propitious by " sanctity " and " piety."[2] But sanctity was defined as " the knowledge of how we ought to worship them," and piety was only " justice towards the gods," the return for benefits received ; Cicero asks, " What piety is due to a being from whom you receive nothing ? "[3] The divine law, *fas*, was distinguished from the human law, *jus*. To the former belonged not only the religious rites but the duties to the dead, as also the duties to certain living individuals.[4] Offences against parents were avenged by the *divi parentum* ;[5] the duty of hospitality was enforced by the *dii hospitales* and Jupiter;[6] boundaries were protected by Jupiter Terminalis and Terminus ;[7] and Jupiter, Dius Fidius, and Fides, were the guardians of sworn faith.[8]

The god of Israel was a powerful protector of his chosen people, but he was a severe master who inspired more fear than love. In the pre-prophetic period at least, he was no model of goodness. He had unaccountable moods, his wrath often resembled " rather the insensate violence of angered nature, than the reasonable indignation of a moralised personality "[9]—as appears, for instance, from the suggestion of David that Saul's undeserved enmity might be due to the incitement of God.[10] At the same time his severity was also a guardian of human relationships. It turned against children who were disrespectful to their parents, against murderers, adulterers, thieves, false witnesses—indeed, the whole criminal law was a revelation of the Lord. He was moreover a protector of

---

[1] Leist, *Græco-italische Rechtsge-schichte*, p. 219 *sqq.* Granger, *Wor-ship of the Romans*, p. 217.
[2] Cicero, *De officiis*, ii. 3.
[3] *Idem, De natura deorum*, i. 41.
[4] On the distinction between *fas* and *jus* see von Jhering, *Geist des römischen Rechts*, i. 258.
[5] *Supra*, i. 624.

[6] *Supra*, i. 580.
[7] *Supra*, ii. 61.
[8] *Supra*, ii. 96, 121 *sq.* Wissowa, *Religion und Kultus der Römer*, pp. 48, 103, 104, 123 *sq.*
[9] Montefiore, *Hibbert Lectures on the Religion of the Ancient Hebrews*, p. 38.
[10] 1 Samuel, xxvi. 19.

the poor and needy,[1] and a preserver of strangers.[2] But
offences against God were, in the Ten Commandments,
mentioned before offences against man ; religious rites
were put on the same level with the rules of social
morality ; neglect of circumcision, or disregard of the
precepts of ceremonial cleanliness, or sabbath-breaking,
was punished with the same severity as the greatest
crimes.[3] " To the ordinary man," says Wellhausen, " it
was not moral but liturgical acts that seemed to be truly
religious." [4] A different opinion, however, was expressed
by the Prophets. They opposed the vice of the heart to
the outward service of the ritual.[5] God was said by them
to desire not sacrifice but mercy,[6] and to hate the hypo-
critical service of Israel with its feast-days and solemn
assemblies ;[7] and the true fast was declared to consist in
moral welldoing.[8] To them righteousness was the fundamental virtue of Yahveh, and if he punished Israel his
anger was no longer a merely fitful outburst, unrelated to
Israel's own wrongdoing, but an essential element of his
righteousness.[9] However, as M. Halévy observes, the
truly national conceptions of the Hebrews were not those
which the Prophets maintained, but those which they
opposed.[10] The importance of ritual was more than ever
emphasised in the post-prophetic priestly code.

The opposition against ritualism which was started by
the Prophets reached its height in Christ. Men are defiled
not by external uncleanness, but by evil thoughts and evil
deeds.[11] " It is lawful to do well on the sabbath days." [12]
Those whose righteousness does not exceed that of the
scribes and Pharisees shall not enter into the kingdom of
heaven.[13] The first and great commandment is that which

---

[1] *Supra*, i. 552, 565.
[2] *Supra*, i. 580.
[3] Montefiore, *op. cit.* pp. 327, 470.
Kuenen, *Religion of Israel*, ii. 276.
[4] Wellhausen, *Prolegomena to the History of Israel*, p. 468.
[5] *Cf.* Caird, *Evolution of Religion*, ii. 119.
[6] *Hosea*, vi. 6.
[7] *Amos*, v. 21 *sqq.*

[8] *Isaiah*, lviii. 6 *sqq.*
[9] *Cf.* Montefiore, *op. cit.* p. 122 *sq.*
[10] Halévy, *Mélanges de critique et d'histoire relatifs aux peuples sémitiques*, p. 371.
[11] *St. Matthew*, xv. 19 *sq. St. Mark*, vii. 6 *sqq.*
[12] *St. Matthew*, xii. 12.
[13] *Ibid.* v. 20.

enjoins love to God, but the second, according to which a man shall love his neighbour as himself, " is like unto it." [1] At the same time there are in the New Testament passages in which God's judgment of men seems to be represented as determined by theological dogma.[2] The only sin which can never be forgiven either in this world or in the world to come, is blasphemy against the Holy Ghost ; [3] and the belief in Jesus is laid down as indispensable for salvation.[4] According to St. Paul, a man is justified by faith alone, without the deeds of the law.[5] This doctrine, which makes man's salvation dependent upon his acceptance of the Messiahship of Jesus, has had a lasting influence upon Christian theology, and has, together with certain other dogmas, led to that singular discrepancy between the notions of divine and human justice which has up to the present day characterised the chief branches of the Christian Church.

Some of the early Fathers maintained that the interference and suffering of Christ, in itself, unconditionally saved all souls and emptied hell for ever; [6] but this theory never became popular. According to St. Augustine and, subsequently, Calvinian theology, the benefits of the atonement are limited to those whom God, of his sovereign pleasure, has from eternity arbitrarily elected, the effect of faith and conversion being not to save the soul, but simply to convince the soul that it is saved. A third theory— that of Pelagius, Armenius, and Luther—attributes to the sufferings of Christ a conditional efficacy, depending upon personal faith in his vicarious atonement, whereas those who for some reason or other do not possess such faith are excluded from salvation. A fourth doctrine, which early began to be constructed by the Fathers and was adopted by the Roman Catholic and the consistent portion of the Episcopalian Church, declares that by Christ's vicarious

---

[1] *St. Matthew*, xxii. 37 *sqq.*
[2] Toy, *Judaism and Christianity*, p. 82 *sq.*
[3] *St. Matthew*, xii. 31 *sq.* St. *Mark*, iii. 28 *sq.*
[4] *St. Mark*, xvi. 16. *St. John*, iii.

18, 36 ; viii. 24.
[5] *Romans*, iii. 28.
[6] Alger, *History of the Doctrine of a Future Life*, pp. 550–552, 563. Farrar, *Mercy and Judgment*, p. 58 *sq.*

suffering power is given to the Church, a priestly hierarchy, to save those who confess her authority and observe
her rites, whilst all others are lost. Certain sectarians, like
the Unitarians, or those " liberal Christians " who do not
feel themselves tied by the dogmas of any special creed,
are the only ones among whom we meet with the opinion
that a free soul, who by the immutable laws which the
Creator has established may choose between good and evil,
is saved or lost just so far and so long as it partakes of
either the former or the latter.[1]

According to the leading doctrines of Christianity, then,
the fates of men beyond the grave are determined by quite
other circumstances than what the moral consciousness by
itself recognises as virtue or vice. They are all doomed to
death and hell in consequence of Adam's sin, and their
salvation, if not absolutely predestined, can only be effected
by sincere faith in the atonement of Christ or by valid
reception of sacramental grace at the hands of a priest.
Persons who on intellectual or moral grounds are unable
to accept the dogma of atonement or to acknowledge the
authority of an exacting hierarchy, are subject to the most
awful penalties for a sin committed by their earliest
ancestor, and so are the countless millions of heathen who
never even had an opportunity to embrace the Christian
religion. Luther was considered to have shown an
exceptional boldness when he expressed the hope that " our
dear God would be merciful to Cicero, and to others like
him." [2]   In the Westminster Confession of Faith the
Divines declared the opinion that men not professing
Christianity may be saved to be " very pernicious, and to
be detested " ; [3] and in their Larger Catechism they expressly said that " they who, having never heard the gospel,
know not Jesus Christ, and believe not in him, cannot
be saved, be they never so diligent to frame their lives
according to the light of nature, or the laws of that religion
which they profess." [4]   This doctrine has had many

---

[1] Alger, op. cit. p. 553 sqq.
[2] Farrar, op. cit. p. 146.
[3] Confession of Faith, x. 4.

[4] Larger Catechism, Answer to
Question 60.

adherents up to the present time,[1] although a more liberal view in favour of virtuous heathen has obviously been gaining ground.[2] Even in the case of Christians errors in belief on such subjects as church government, the Trinity, transubstantiation, original sin, and predestination, have been declared to expose the guilty to eternal damnation.[3] In the seventeenth century it was a common theme of certain Roman Catholic writers that " Protestancy unrepented destroys salvation," [4] while the Protestants on their part taxed Du Moulin with culpable laxity for admitting that some Roman Catholics might escape the torments of hell.[5] Nathanael Emmons, the sage of Franklin, tells us that " it is absolutely necessary to approve of the doctrine of reprobation in order to be saved." [6]

Besides the heathen there is another large class of people whom Christian theology has condemned to hell for no fault of theirs, namely, infants who have died unbaptised. From a very early age the water of baptism was believed by the Christians to possess a magic power to wipe away sin,[7] and since the days of St. Augustine it was deemed so indispensable for salvation that any child dying without " the bath of regeneration " was regarded as lost for ever.[8] St. Augustine admitted that the punishment of such children was of the mildest sort,[9] but other writers were more severe ; St. Fulgentius condemned to " everlasting punishment in eternal fire " even infants who died in their mother's womb.[10] However,

---

[1] Farrar, *op. cit.* p. 146 *sq.*

[2] Prentiss, ' Infant Salvation,' in *Presbyterian Review,* iv. 576. For earlier instances of this opinion see Abbot, ' Literature of the Doctrine of a Future Life,' forming an Appendix to Alger's *History of the Doctrine of a Future Life,* pp. 859, 863, 865.

[3] Abbot, *loc. cit.* p. 863.

[4] Wilson, *Charity Mistaken, with the Want whereof Catholickes are unjustly charged, for affirming . . . that Protestancy unrepented destroys Salvation.*

[5] Abbot, *loc. cit.* p. 860.

[6] Emmons, *Works,* iv. 336.

[7] Tertullian, *De baptismo,* 1 *sqq.* (Migne, *Patrologiæ cursus,* i. 1197 *sqq.*). Harnack, *History of Dogma,* i. 206 *sq.* ; ii. 227. Stanley, *Christian Institutions,* p. 16. Lewis, *Paganism surviving in Christianity,* pp. 72, 73, 129, 144 *sq.*

[8] Bingham, *Works,* iii. 488 *sqq.* Prentiss, *loc. cit.* p. 549.

[9] St. Augustine, *De peccatorum meritis et remissione,* i. 16 (Migne, *op. cit.* xliv. 16).

[10] St. Fulgentius, *De fide,* 27 (Migne, *op. cit.* lxv. 701).

the notion that unbaptised children will be tormented, gradually gave way to a more humane opinion. In the middle of the twelfth century Peter Lombard determined that the proper punishment of original sin, when no actual sin is added to it, is " the punishment of loss," that is, loss of heaven and the sight of God, but not " the punishment of sense," that is, positive torment. This doctrine was confirmed by Innocentius III. and shared by the large majority of the schoolmen, who assumed the existence of a place called *limbus*, or *infernus puerorum*, where unbaptised infants will dwell without being subject to torture.[1] But the older view was again set up by the Protestants, who generally maintained that the due punishment of original sin is, in strictness, damnation in hell, although many of them were inclined to think that if a child dies by misfortune before it is baptised the parents' sincere intention of baptising it, together with their prayers, will be accepted with God for the deed.[2] In the Confession of Augsburg the Anabaptistic doctrine is emphatically condemned ;[3] and although Zwingli rejected the dogma that infants dying without baptism are lost, and Calvin, in harmony with his theory of election, refused to tie the salvation of infants to an outward rite, the necessity of baptism as the ordinary channel of receiving grace appears to have been a general belief in the Reformed churches throughout the sixteenth and seventeenth centuries.[4] The damnation of infants was in fact an acknowledged doctrine of Calvinism,[5] though an exception was made for the children of pious parents.[6] But in the latter part of the eighteenth century Toplady, who was a vehement Calvinist, avowed

---

[1] Wall, *History of Infant-Baptism,* i. 460 *sq.*

[2] *Ibid.* i. 462, 468. Luther and his followers, however, speak more doubtfully about the efficacy of the parents' unrealised intention, and lay much stress on actual baptism (*ibid.* i. 469).

[3] *Augsburg Confession,* i. 9.

[4] Prentiss, *loc. cit.* p. 550.

[5] Calvin, *Institutio Christianæ religionis,* iv. 15. 10, vol. ii. 371. Norton, *Tracts concerning Christianity,* p. 179 *sqq.*

[6] Calvin, *op. cit.* iv. 16. 9, vol. ii. 383 *sq.* Wall, *op. cit.* i. 469. Anderson, ' Introductory Essay,' to Logan's *Words of Comfort for Parents bereaved of Little Children,* p. xxi.

his belief in the universal salvation of all departed infants, whether baptised or unbaptised.[1] And a hundred years later Dr. Hodge thought he was justified in stating that the common opinion of evangelical Protestants was that " all who die in infancy are saved." [2] The accuracy of this statement, however, seems somewhat doubtful. In 1883 Mr. Prentiss wrote of the doctrine of infant salvation independently of baptism :—" My own impression is that, had it been taught as unequivocally in the Presbyterian Church even a third of a century ago, by a theologian less eminent than Dr. Hodge for orthodoxy, piety, and weight of character, it would have called forth an immediate protest from some of the more conservative, old-fashioned Calvinists." [3]

In order fully to realise the true import of the dogma of damnation it is necessary to consider the punishment in store for the condemned. The immense bulk of the Christians have always regarded hell and its agonies as material facts.[4] Origen, who was a Platonist and an heretic on many points, was severely censured for saying that the fire of hell was inward and of the conscience rather than outward and of the body ; [5] and in the later Middle Ages Scotus Erigena showed unusual audacity in questioning the locality of hell and the material tortures of the condemned.[6] The punishment is burning —a penalty which even in the most barbaric codes is reserved for the very gravest crimes ; and some great divines, like Jeremy Taylor and Jonathan Edwards, have been anxious to point out that the fire of hell is infinitely more painful than any fire on earth, being " fierce enough to melt the very rocks and elements." [7] This awful punishment also exceeds in dreadfulness anything which even the most vivid imagination can conceive, because it will last not for a passing moment,

[1] Toplady, *Works*, p. 645 *sq.*
[2] Hodge, *Systematic Theology*, i. 26 *sq.*
[3] Prentiss, *loc. cit.* p. 559. See also Anderson, *loc cit.* p. xxiii.
[4] Alger, *op. cit.* p. 516.
[5] *Ibid.* p. 516.
[6] Milman, *History of Latin Christianity*, ix. 88, n.k.
[7] Alger, *op. cit.* p. 516 *sq.*

nor for a year or a hundred, thousand, million, or milliard years, but for ever and ever. In case any doubt should arise as regards the physical capacity of the damned to withstand the heat, we are assured by some modern theologians that their bodies will be annealed like glass or asbestos-like or of the nature of salamanders.[1] This, then, is the future state of the large majority of men, quite independently of any fault of their own, or of the degree of their " guilt." [2] It would seem that even the felicity of the few who are saved must be seriously impaired by their contemplation of this endless and undescribable misery, but we are told that the case is just the reverse. They become as merciless as their god. Thomas Aquinas says that a perfect sight of the punishment of the damned is granted to them that they " may enjoy their beatitude and the grace of God more richly." [3] And the Puritans, especially, have revelled in the idea that " the sight of hell torments will exalt the happiness of the saints for ever," as a sense of the opposite misery always increases the relish of any pleasure.[4]

In the present times there is a distinct tendency among Christian theologians to humanise somewhat the doctrines of the future life.[5] But if Christianity is to be judged from the dogmas which almost from its beginning until quite recent times have been recognised by the immense majority of its adherents, it must be admitted that its

[1] Alger, op. cit. pp. 518, 520. Cf. St. Augustine, De Civitate Dei, xxi. 2 sqq.

[2] For the numbers of souls supposed to be lost see Alger, op. cit. p. 530 sqq. St. Chrysostom (In Acta Apostolorum Homil. XXIV. 4 [Migne, op. cit. Ser. Graeca, lx. 189]) doubted whether out of the many thousands of souls constituting the Christian population of Antioch in his day one hundred would be saved. And at the end of the seventeenth century a History Professor at Oxford published a book to prove "that not one in a hundred thousand (nay probably not one in a million) from Adam down to our times, shall be saved " (Du-Moulin, Moral Reflections upon the Number of the Elect, title page).

[3] Thomas Aquinas, Summa theologica, iii. Supplementum, qu. xciv. I. 2 (Migne, op. cit. Ser. Secunda, iv. 1393).

[4] Jonathan Edwards, Works, vii. 480. Alger, op. cit. p. 541.

[5] Thus the doctrine of endless torments is opposed by a considerable number of theologians (Alger, op. cit. p. 546), and, " if held, is not practically taught by the vast majority of the English clergy " (Stanley, op. cit. p. 94).

conception of a heavenly Father and Judge has been
utterly inconsistent with all ordinary notions of goodness
and justice. Calvin himself avowed that the decree
according to which the fall of Adam involved, without
remedy, in eternal death so many nations together with
their infant children, was a " horrible " one. " But,"
he adds, " no one can deny that God foreknew the future
final fate of man before he created him, and that he did
foreknow it because it was appointed by his own decree." [1]

Like Christianity, Muhammedanism adorns its godhead
with the highest moral attributes and at the same time
ascribes to him decrees and actions which flatly contradict
even the most elementary notions of human justice. The
god of Islam is addressed as the compassionate and merciful ; but his love is restricted to " those who fear," [2] and
his mercy can only be gained by that submissiveness or
self-surrender which is indicated by the very name of
Islam. He demands a righteous life, he punishes the
wrongdoer and rewards the charitable.[3] Through his
Prophet he has revealed to mankind both the rules of
morality and the elements of a social system containing
minute regulations for a man's conduct in various circumstances of life, with due rewards or penalties according to
his fulfilment of these regulations.[4] The whole constitution of the State has on it a divine stamp ; as an Arab
proverb says, " country and religion are twins." [5] But
foremost among duties is to believe in God and his
Prophet. " God," it is said, " does not pardon polytheism
and infidelity, but He can, if He willeth, pardon other
crimes." [6] And the " pillars of religion " are the five duties
of reciting the Kalimah or creed, of performing the five
stated daily prayers, of fasting—especially in the month of
Ramaḍân,—of giving the legal alms, and of making the
pilgrimage to Mecca.[7] These duties are based on clear

[1] Calvin, *op. cit.* iii. 23. 7, vol. ii.
151.
[2] *Koran*, iii. 70.
[3] *Supra*, i. 553.
[4] *Cf.* Muir, *Life of Mahomet*, iii.

295 *sq.* ; Lane-Poole, *Studies in a Mosque*, p. 101.
[5] Sell, *Faith of Islám*, pp. 19, 39.
[6] *Ibid.* p. 241.
[7] *Ibid.* p. 251.

sentences of the Koran, but the traditions have raised the most trivial ceremonial observances into duties of the greatest importance. It is true that hypocrisy and formalism without devotion were strongly condemned by Muhammed. " Righteousness," he said, " is not that ye turn your faces towards the East or the West, but righteousness is, one who believes in God, and the last day, and the angels, and the Book, and the prophets, and who gives wealth for His love to kindred, and orphans, and the poor, and the son of the road, and beggars, and those in captivity ; and who is steadfast in prayer, and gives alms ; and those who are sure of their covenant when they make a covenant ; and the patient in poverty, and distress, and in time of violence ; these are they who are true, and these are those who fear." [1] Yet in Muhammedanism, as in other ritualistic religions, the chief importance is practically attached to the punctual performance of outward ceremonies, and the virtue of prayer is made dependent upon an ablution.[2] In the future life the felicity or suffering of each person will be proportionate to his merits or demerits,[3] but the admittance into paradise depends in the first place on faith. " Those who believe, and act righteously, and are steadfast in prayer, and give alms, theirs is their hire with their Lord." [4] Those who have acknowledged the faith of Islam and yet acted wickedly will be punished in hell for a certain period, but will finally enter paradise.[5] As regards the future state of certain infidels the Koran contains contradictory statements. In one place it is said, " Verily, whether it be of those who believe, or those who are Jews or Christians or Sabaeans, whosoever believe in God and

[1] *Koran*, ii. 172.
[2] *Cf*. Polak, *Persien*, i. 9 ; Wallin, *Reseanteckningar från Orienten*, iv. 284 *sq.* ; Sell, *op. cit.* p. 256.
[3] Lane, *Manners and Customs of the Modern Egyptians*, i. 95 *sq.* Sell, *op. cit.* p. 231. Lane-Poole, *Studies in a Mosque*, p. 319.
[4] *Koran*, ii. 277.
[5] Lane, *op. cit.* i. 95. Sell, *op. cit.* p. 228. The Mu'tazilas, however,

teach that the Muslim who enters hell will remain there for ever. They maintain that the person who, having committed great sins, dies unrepentant, though not an infidel, ceases to be a believer, and hence suffers as the infidels do, though the punishment is lighter than that which an infidel receives (Sell, *op. cit.* pp. 229, 241).

the last day and act aright, they have their reward
at their Lord's hand, and there is no fear for them,
nor shall they grieve." [1]   But this passage is considered
to have been abrogated by another where it is stated
that whoso desires any other religion than Islam shall
in the next world be among the lost. [2] The punishments
inflicted upon unbelievers are no less horrible than the
torments of the Christian hell.   Yet in one point the
Muhammedan doctrine of the future life is more merciful
than the dogmas of Christianity.   The children of
believers will all go to paradise, and the children of
unbelievers are generally supposed to escape hell.   Some
think they will be in A'ráf, a place situated between
heaven and hell ; whilst others maintain that they will be
servants to the true believers in paradise. [3]

The formalism of Muhammedan orthodoxy has from
time to time called forth protests from minds with deeper
aspirations.   The earlier Muhammedan mystics sought
to impart life to the rigid ritual ; [4] and in the nineteenth
century Bábíism revolted against orthodox Islam,
opposing bigotry and enjoining friendly intercourse with
persons of all religions. [5] At present there are some
liberal Muhammedans who set aside the scholastic
tradition, maintain the right of private interpretation
of the Koran, and warmly uphold the adaptability of
Islam to the most advanced ideas of civilisation. [6] To
them Muhammed's mission was chiefly that of a moral
reformer.   " In Islam," says Syed Ameer Ali, " the
service of man and the good of humanity constitute
pre-eminently the service and worship of God." [7]

In the next chapter I shall try to explain the chief
facts now set forth relating to gods as guardians of
wordly morality.

[1] *Koran*, ii. 59.
[2] *Ibid.* iii. 79. Sell, *op. cit.* p.
359 *sq.*
[3] Sell, *op. cit.* p. 204 *sq.*
[4] *Ibid.* p. 110.
[5] *Ibid.* p. 136 *sqq.*
[6] Ameer Ali, *Life and Teachings of*
Mohammed, passim. Idem, Ethics of
Islâm, passim. Cf. Lane-Poole,
Studies in a Mosque, p. 324 ; Sell,
op. cit. p. 198 *sq.*
[7] Ameer Ali, *Ethics of Islâm,* p.
3 *sq. Idem, Life and Teachings of*
Mohammed, p. 274.

CHAPTER LII

GODS AS GUARDIANS OF MORALITY (*concluded*)

WE have seen that the gods of uncivilised races are to a very large extent of a malevolent character, that they as a rule take little interest in any kind of human conduct which does not affect their own welfare, and that, if they show any signs of moral feelings, they may be guardians either of tribal customs in general or only of some special branch of morality. Among peoples of a higher culture, again, the gods are on the whole benevolent to mankind, when duly propitiated. They by preference resent offences committed against themselves personally ; but they also avenge social wrongs of various kinds, they are superintendents of human justice, and are even represented as the originators and sustainers of the whole moral order of the world. The gods have thus experienced a gradual change for the better ; until at last they are described as ideals of moral perfection, even though, when more closely scrutinised, their goodness and notions of justice are found to differ materially from what is deemed good and just in the case of men.

The malevolence of savage gods is in accordance with the theory that religion is born of fear. The assumed originators of misfortunes were naturally regarded as enemies to be propitiated, whilst fortunate events, if attracting sufficient attention and appearing sufficiently marvellous to suggest a supernatural cause, were commonly ascribed to beings who were too good to require

worship. But growing reflection has a tendency to attribute more amiable qualities to the gods. The religious
consciousness of men becomes less exclusively occupied
with the hurts they suffer, and comes more and more to
reflect upon the benefits they enjoy. The activity of a
god which displays itself in a certain phenomenon, or
group of phenomena, appears to them on some occasions
as a source of evil, but on other occasions as a source of
good ; hence the god is regarded as partly malevolent,
partly benevolent, and in all circumstances as a being
who must not be neglected. Moreover, a god who is by
nature harmless or good may by proper worship be
induced to assist man in his struggle against evil spirits.[1]
This protective function of gods becomes particularly
important when the god is more or less disassociated from
the natural phenomenon in which he originally manifested
himself. Nothing, indeed, seems to have contributed
more towards the improvement of nature gods than the
expansion of their sphere of activity. When supernatural
beings can exert their power in the various departments of
life, men naturally choose for their gods those among them
who with great power combine the greatest benevolence.
Men have selected their gods according to their usefulness.
Among the Maoris " a mere trifle, or natural casualty,
will induce a native (or a whole tribe) to change his
Atua." [2] The negro, when disappointed in some of
his speculations, or overtaken by some sad calamity,
throws away his fetish, and selects a new one.[3] Wher
hard-pressed, the Samoyede, after invoking his own
deities in vain, addresses himself to the Russian god,
promising to become his worshipper if he relieves him
from his distress ; and in most cases he is said to be
faithful to his promise, though he may still try to keep
on good terms with his former gods by occasionally

[1] von Rosenberg, *Der malayische Archipel*, p. 162 (Niase). Howard, *Life with Trans-Siberian Savages*, p. 192 (Ainu). Georgi, *Russia*, iii. 273 *sq.* (shamanistic peoples of Siberia). Buch, ' Die Wotjäken,' in *Acta Soc. Scient. Fennicæ*, xii. 633. *Supra*, ii. 701, 702, 704 *sq.*

[2] Polack, *Manners and Customs of the New Zealanders*, i. 233.

[3] Wilson, *Western Africa*, p. 212.

offering them a sacrifice in secret.[1] North American Indians attribute all their good or bad luck to their Manitou, and " if the Manitou has not been favourable to them, they quit him without any ceremony, and take another." [2] Among many of the ancient Indians of Central America there was a regular and systematical selection of gods. Father Blas Valera says that their gods had annual rotations and were changed each year in accordance with the superstitions of the people. " The old gods were forsaken as infamous, or because they had been of no use, and other gods and demons were elected. . . . Sons when they inherited, either accepted or repudiated the gods of their fathers, for they were not allowed to hold their pre-eminence against the will of the heir. Old men worshipped other greater deities, but they likewise dethroned them, and set up others in their places when the year was over, or the age of the world, as the Indians had it. Such were the gods which all the nations of Mexico, Chiapa, and Guatemala worshipped, as well as those of Vera Paz, and many other Indians. They thought that the gods selected by themselves were the greatest and most powerful of all the gods." [3] These are crude instances of a process which in some form or other must have been an important motive force in religious evolution by making the gods better suited to meet the wants of their believers.

But men not only select as their gods such supernatural beings as may be most useful to them in their struggle for life, they also magnify their good qualities in worshipping them. Praise and exaggerating eulogy are common in the mouth of a devout worshipper. In ancient Egypt the god of each petty state was within it held to be the ruler of the gods, the creator of the world, and the giver of all good things.[4] So also in Chaldea the god of

---

[1] Ahlqvist, ' Unter Wogulen und Ostjaken,' in *Acta Soc. Scient. Fennicæ*, xiv. 240.

[2] Bossu. *Travels through Louisiana*, p. 103. Frazer, *Totemism*, p. 55.

[3] Blas Valera, quoted by Garcilasso de la Vega, *First Part of the Royal Commentaries of the Yncas*, i. 124 *sq.*

[4] Wiedemann, *Religion of the Ancient Egyptians*, p. 11.

a town was addressed by its inhabitants with the most
exalted epithets, as the master or king of all the gods.[1]
The Vedic poets were engrossed in the praise of the
particular deity they happened to be invoking, exaggerating his attributes to the point of inconsistency.[2] " Every
virtue, every excellence," says Hume, " must be ascribed
to the divinity, and no exaggeration will be deemed
sufficient to reach those perfections with which he is
endowed." [3] The tendency of the worshipper to extol his
god beyond all measure is largely due to the idea that the
god is fond of praise,[4] but it may also be rooted in a sincere
will to believe or in genuine admiration. That nations of
a higher culture have especially a strong faith in the power
and benevolence of their gods is easy to understand when
we consider that these are exactly the peoples who have
been most successful in their national endeavours.[5] As the
Greeks attributed their victory over the Persians to the
assistance of Zeus,[6] so the Romans maintained that the
grandeur of their city was the work of the gods whom they
had propitiated by sacrifices.[7]

The benevolence of a god, however, does not imply
that he acts as a moral judge. A friendly god is not generally supposed to bestow his favours gratuitously ; it is
hardly probable, then, that he should meddle with matters
of social morality out of sheer kindliness and of his own
accord. But by an invocation he may be induced to reward
virtue and punish vice. We have often noticed how closely
the retributive activity of gods is connected with the
blessings and curses of men. In order to give efficacy to
their good or evil wishes men appeal to some god, or simply
bring in his name when they pronounce a blessing or a
curse ; and if this is regularly done in connection with
some particular kind of conduct, the idea may grow up
that the god rewards or punishes it even independently of

---

[1] Mürdter - Delitzsch, *Geschichte Babyloniens und Assyriens*, p. 24.
[2] Macdonell, *Vedic Mythology*, p. 16 *sq*. Barth, *Religions of India*, p. 26. Hopkins, *Religions of India*, p. 139.
[3] Hume, *Philosophical Works*, iv. 353.
[4] See *supra*, ii. 653 *sq*.
[5] *Cf*. Oldenberg, *Die Religion des Veda*, p. 281 ; Macdonell, *op. cit*. p. 18.
[6] *Supra*, ii. 713.
[7] Cicero, *De natura deorum*, iii. 2.

any human invocation. Moreover, powerful curses, as
those uttered by parents or strangers, may be personified as
supernatural beings, like the Greek Erinyes ; or the magic
energy inherent in a blessing or a curse may become an
attribute of the chief god, owing to the tendency of such
a god to attract supernatural forces which are in harmony
with his general nature.[1] So also, the notion of a persecuting ghost may be changed into the notion of an avenging god.[2] Various departments of social morality have
thus come to be placed under the supervision of gods :—
the rights of life [3] and property,[4] charity [5] and hospitality,[6]
the submissiveness of children,[7] truthspeaking and fidelity
to a given promise.[8] That gods are so frequently looked
upon as guardians of truth and good faith is, as we have
seen, mainly a result of the common practice of confirming
a statement or promise by an oath ; and where the oath is
an essential element in the judicial proceedings, as was the
case in the archaic State,[9] the consequence is that the
guardianship of gods is extended to the whole sphere of
justice. Truth and justice are repeatedly mentioned hand
in hand as matters of divine concern. We have seen how
frequently the same gods as are appealed to in oaths or
ordeals are described as judges of human conduct.[10] " En
Égypte," says M. Amélineau, " la vérité et la justice
n'avaient qu'un seul et même nom, *Mât*, qui veut aussi
bien dire vérité que justice, et justice que vérité." [11] Zeus
presided over assemblies and trials ; [12] according to a law of
Solon, the judges of Athens had to swear by him.[13] And
the Erinyes, the personifications of oaths and curses, are
sometimes represented by poets and philosophers as
guardians of right in general.[14]

[1] See *supra*, ii. 68.
[2] *Supra*, i. 378 *sq.*
[3] *Supra*, i. 379 *sqq.*
[4] *Supra*, ii. 59 *sqq.*
[5] *Supra*, i. 561 *sqq.*
[6] *Supra*, i. 578 *sqq.*
[7] *Supra*, i. 621 *sqq.*
[8] *Supra*, ii. 114 *sqq.*
[9] Leist, *Græco-italische Rechtsge-schichte*, p. 228.

[10] *Supra*, ii. 115, 116, 121, 122, 686, 687, 699.
[11] Amélineau, *L'évolution des idées morales dans l'Égypte ancienne*, p. 187. See also *supra*, ii. 115, 699.
[12] Farnell, *Cults of the Greek States*, i. 58.
[13] Pollux, *Onomasticum*, viii. 12. 142.
[14] Rohde, *Psyche*, p. 246.

It has been said that when men ascribe to their gods a mental constitution similar to their own they also *eo ipso* consider them to approve of virtue and disapprove of vice.[1] But this conclusion is certainly not true in general. Malevolent gods cannot be supposed to feel emotions which essentially presuppose altruistic sentiments ; and, as we have just noticed, an invocation is frequently required to induce benevolent gods to interfere with the worldly affairs of men.   Moreover, where the system of private retaliation prevails, not even the extension of human analogies to the world of supernatural beings would lead to the idea of a god who of his own accord punishes social wrongs.   But it is quite probable that such analogies have in some cases made gods guardians of morality at large, especially ancestor gods who may readily be supposed not only to preserve their old feelings with regard to virtue and vice but also to take a more active interest in the morals of the living, and who are notoriously opposed to any deviation from ancient custom.[2]   I also admit that the conception of a great or supreme god may perhaps, independently of his origin, involve retributive justice as a natural consequence of his power and benevolence towards his people.   Yet it is obvious that even a god like Zeus was more influenced by the invocation of a suppliant than by his sense of justice.   Dr. Farnell points out that the epithets which designate him as the god to whom those stricken with guilt can appeal are far more in vogue in actual Greek cult than those which attribute to him the function of vengeance and retribution.[3]   Hermes was addressed by thieves as their patron.[4]   According to the Talmud " the thief invokes God while he breaks into the house." [5]   And the Italian bandit begs the Virgin herself to bless his endeavours.

At the same time we must again remember that men

---

[1] Adam Smith, *Theory of Moral Sentiments*, p. 232 *sq.* Darwin, *Descent of Man*, p. 95. Tiele, *Elements of the Science of Religion*, i. 92 *sq.*
[2] See *supra*, ii. 519 *sq.* Cf. Tylor, *Anthropology*, p. 369 ; Macdonald, *Religion and Myth*, p. 229.
[3] Farnell, *op. cit.* i. 66 *sq.*
[4] Schmidt, *Die Ethik der alten Griechen*, i. 136.
[5] Deutsch, *Literary Remains*, p. 57.

ascribe to their gods not only ordinary human qualities but excellences of various kinds, and among these may also be a strong desire to punish wickedness and to reward virtue. The gods of monotheistic religions in particular have such a multitude of the most elevated attributes that it would be highly astonishing if they had remained unconcerned about the morals of mankind. If flattery and admiration make the deity all-wise, all-powerful, all-good, they also make him the supreme judge of human conduct. And there is yet another reason for investing him with the moral government of the world. The claims of justice are not fully satisfied on this earth, where it only too often happens that virtue is left unrewarded and vice escapes unpunished, that right succumbs and wrong triumphs ; hence persons with deep moral feelings and a religious or philosophical bent of mind are apt to look for a future adjustment through the intervention of the deity, who alone can repair the evils and injustices of the present. This demand of final retribution is sometimes so strongly developed that it even leads to the belief in a deity when no other proof of his existence is found convincing. Kant maintained that we must postulate a future life in which everybody's happiness is proportionate to his virtue, and that such a postulate involves the belief in a God of infinite power, wisdom, and goodness who governs the moral as well as the physical world. Not even Voltaire could rid himself of the notion of a rewarding and avenging deity, whom, if he did not exist, " it would be necessary to invent."

The belief in a god who acts as a guardian of wordly morality undoubtedly gives emphasis to its rules. To the social and legal sanctions a new one is added, which derives particular strength from the supernatural power and knowledge of the deity. The divine avenger can punish those who are beyond the reach of human justice and those whose secret wrongs even escape the censure of their fellow men. But on the other hand there are also certain circumstances which considerably detract from the

influence of the religious sanction when compared with
other sanctions of morality. The supposed punishments
and rewards of the future life have the disadvantage of being
conceived as very remote ; and fear and hope decrease in
inverse ratio to the distance of their objects. Men commonly live in the happy illusion that death is far off, even
though it in reality is very near, hence also the retribution
after death appears distant and unreal and is comparatively
little thought of by the majority of people who believe in
it. Moreover, there seems always to be time left for
penance and repentance. Manzoni himself admitted, in his
defence of Roman Catholicism, that many people think it
an easy matter to procure that feeling of contrition by
which, according to the doctrine of the Church, sins may
be cancelled, and therefore encourage themselves in the
commission of crime through the facility of pardon. The
frequent assumption that the moral law would hardly
command obedience without the belief in retribution
beyond the grave is contradicted by an overwhelming
array of facts. We hear from trustworthy witnesses that
unadulterated savages follow their own rules of morality
no less strictly, or perhaps more strictly, than civilised
people follow theirs. Nay, it is a common experience
that contact with a higher civilisation exercises a deterior-
ating influence upon the conduct of uncultured races,
although we may be sure that Christian missionaries do not
fail to impart the doctrine of hell to their savage converts.

It has also been noticed that a high degree of religious
devotion is frequently accompanied by great laxity of
morals. Of the Bedouins Mr. Blunt writes that, with
one or two exceptions, " the practice of religion may be
taken as the sure index of low morality in a tribe." [1]
Wallin, who had an intimate and extensive knowledge of
Muhammedan peoples, often found that those Muslims
who attended to their prayers most regularly were the
greatest scoundrels.[2] " One of the most remarkable traits

[1] Mr. Blunt, in Lady Anne Blunt's
Bedouin Tribes of the Euphrates, ii.
217.

[2] Wallin, *Reseanteckningar rån
Orienten*, iii. 166.

in the character of the Copts," says Lane, " is their
bigotry " ; and at the same time they are represented as
" deceitful, faithless, and abandoned to the pursuit of
worldly gain, and to indulgence in sensual pleasure." [1]
Among two hundred Italian murderers Ferri did not find
one who was irreligious ; and Naples, which has the worst
record of any European city for crimes against the person,
is also the most religious city in Europe.[2] On the other
hand, according to Dr. Havelock Ellis, "it seems extremely
rare to find intelligently irreligious men in prison " ; [3]
and Laing, who himself was anything but sceptical,
observed that there was no country in Europe where there
was so much morality and so little religion as Switzerland.[4] Most religions contain an element which constitutes a real peril to the morality of their votaries. They
have introduced a new kind of duties—duties towards
gods ;—and, as we have noticed above, even where religion
has entered into close union with worldly morality, much
greater importance has been attached to ceremonies or
worship or the niceties of belief than to good behaviour
towards fellow men. People think that they may
make up for lack of the latter by orthodoxy or pious
performances. A Christian bishop of the seventh
century, who was canonised by the Church of Rome,
described a good Christian as a man " who comes
frequently to church ; who presents the oblation which is
offered to God upon the altar ; who doth not taste of the
fruits of his own industry until he has consecrated a part
of them to God ; who, when the holy festivals approach,
lives chastely even with his own wife during several days,
that with a safe conscience he may draw near the altar of
God ; and who, in the last place, can repeat the Creed and
the Lord's Prayer." [5] A scrupulous observance of external
ceremonies—that is all which in this description is required

---

[1] Lane, *Manners and Customs of the Modern Egyptians*, p. 551.
[2] Havelock Ellis, *The Criminal*, p. 156.
[3] *Ibid.* p. 159.
[4] Laing, *Notes of a Traveller*, pp. 323, 324, 333.
[5] Robertson, *History of the Reign of the Emperor Charles V*. i. 282 *sq.*

of a good Christian. And since then popular ideas on the subject have undergone but little change. Smollett observes in his 'Travels into Italy' that it is held more infamous to transgress the slightest ceremonial institution of the Church of Rome than to transgress any moral duty ; that a murderer or adulterer will be easily absolved by the Church, and even maintain his character in society ; but that a man who eats a pigeon on a Saturday is abhorred as a monster of reprobation.[1] In the nineteenth century Simonde de Sismondi could write :—" Plus chaque homme vicieux a été régulier à observer les commandemens de l'Eglise, plus il se sent dans son cœur dispensé de l'observation de cette morale céleste, à laquelle il faudroit sacrifier ses penchans dépravés." [2] And how many a Protestant does not imagine that by going to church on Sundays he can sin more freely on the six days between.

It should also be remembered that the religious sanction of moral rules only too often leads to an external observance of these rules from purely selfish motives. Christianity itself has, essentially, been regarded as a means of gaining a blessed hereafter. As for its influence upon the moral life of its adherents I agree with Professor Hobhouse that its chief strength lies not in its abstract doctrines but in the simple personal following of Christ.[3] In moral education example plays a more important part than precept. But even in this respect Christianity has unfortunately little reason to boast of its achievements.

[1] Smollett, quoted by Kames, *Sketches of the History of Man*, iv. 380.
[2] Simonde de Sismondi, *Histoire des républiques italiennes du moyen-âge*, xvi. 419.
[3] Hobhouse, *Morals in Evolution*, ii. 159.

CHAPTER LIII

CONCLUSION

We have completed our task. Only a few words will be added to emphasise the leading features of our theory of the moral consciousness and to point out some general conclusions which may be drawn as regards its evolution.

Our study of the origin and development of the moral ideas was divided into three main sections. As moral ideas are expressed in moral judgments, we had to examine the general nature of both the predicates and the subjects of such judgments, as well as the moral valuation of the chief branches of conduct with which the moral consciousness of mankind concerns itself. And in each case our aim was not only to describe or analyse but also to explain the phenomena which came under our observation.

The theory was laid down that the moral concepts, which form the predicates of moral judgments, are ultimately based on moral emotions, that they are essentially generalisations of tendencies in certain phenomena to call forth either indignation or approval. It was therefore necessary for us to investigate the nature and origin of these emotions, and subsequently to consider their relations to the various moral concepts.

We found that the moral emotions belong to a wider class of emotions, which may be described as retributive; that moral disapproval is a kind of resentment, akin to anger and revenge, and that moral approval is a kind of retributive kindly emotion, akin to gratitude. At the same time they differ from kindred non-moral emotions by their disinterestedness, apparent impartiality, and flavour of generality. As for the origin of the retributive emotions, we may assume that they have been acquired by means of natural selection in the struggle for existence ; both resentment and retributive kindly emotion are states of mind which have a tendency to promote the interests of the individuals who feel them. This explanation also applies to the moral emotions in so far as they are retributive : it accounts for the hostile attitude of moral disapproval towards the cause of pain, and for the friendly attitude of moral approval towards the cause of pleasure. Our retributive emotions are always reactions against pain or pleasure felt by ourselves ; this holds true of the moral emotions as well as of revenge and gratitude. But how shall we explain those elements in the moral emotions by which they are distinguished from other, non-moral retributive emotions ? First, why should we, quite disinterestedly, feel pain evoking indignation because our neighbour is hurt, and pleasure calling forth approval because he is benefited ?

We noticed that sympathy aided by the altruistic sentiment—sympathy in the common sense of the word—tends to produce disinterested retributive emotions. In all animal species which possess the altruistic sentiment in some form or other we may be sure to find sympathetic resentment as its accompaniment. And this sentiment may also give rise to disinterested retributive kindly emotion, even though it is more readily moved by the sight of pain than by the sight of pleasure and though sympathetic retributive kindliness has a powerful rival in the feeling of envy. Moreover, sympathetic retributive emotions may not only be reactions against sympathetic pain or pleasure, but may also be directly produced by the cognition of the signs of resentment or of the signs of retributive kindliness. Punishments and rewards tend to reproduce the emotions from which they sprang, and language communicates retributive emotions by terms of condemnation and by terms of praise. Finally, there are cases of disinterested retributive emotions into which sympathy does not enter at all— sentimental antipathies and likings quite disinterested in character.

There are thus various ways in which disinterested retributive emotions may originate. But how shall we explain the fact that disinterestedness together with apparent impartiality and the flavour of generality have become characteristics by which the so-called moral emotions are distinguished from other retributive emotions ? To this question the following answer was given :—Society is the birthplace of the moral consciousness. The first moral judgments expressed not the private emotions of isolated individuals but emotions which were felt by the community at large. Public indignation is the prototype of moral disapproval and public approval the prototype of moral approbation. And these public emotions are characterised by generality, individual disinterestedness, and apparent impartiality.

The moral emotions give rise to a variety of moral concepts, which are in different ways connected with the emotions from which they were derived. Thus moral disapproval is at the bottom of the concepts bad, vice, and wrong, ought and duty, right and rights, justice and injustice ; whilst moral approval has led to the concepts good, virtue, and merit. It has, in particular, been of fundamental importance for the whole of our investigation to recognise the true contents of the notions of ought and duty. If these concepts were unanalysable, as they have often been represented to be, any attempt to explain the origin and development of the moral ideas would, in my opinion, be a hopeless failure.

From the predicates of moral judgments we proceeded to consider their subjects. Generally speaking, such judgments are passed on conduct or character, and allowance is made for the various elements of which conduct and character are composed in proportion as the moral judgment is scrutinising and enlightened. It is only owing to ignorance or lack of due reflection if, as is often the case, moral estimates are influenced by external events which are entirely independent of the agent's will ; if individuals who are incapable of recognising any act of theirs as right or wrong are treated as responsible beings ; if motives are completely or partially disregarded ; if little cognisance is taken of forbearances in comparison with acts ; if want of foresight or want of self-restraint is overlooked when the effect produced by it is sufficiently remote. We were also able to explain *why* moral judgments are passed on conduct and character. This is due to the facts that moral judgments spring from moral emotions ; that the moral emotions are retributive emotions ; that a retributive emotion is a reactive attitude of mind, either kindly or hostile, towards a living being (or something looked upon in the light of a living being), regarded as a cause of pleasure or as a cause of pain ; and that a living being is regarded as a true cause of pleasure or pain only in so far as this feeling is assumed to be caused by its will. It is a circumstance of the greatest importance that not only moral emotions but non-moral retributive emotions are felt with reference to phenomena exactly similar in their general nature to those on which moral judgments are passed. How could we account for this remarkable coincidence unless the moral judgments were based on emotions and the moral emotions were retributive emotions akin to gratitude and revenge ?

Our theory as to the nature of the moral concepts and emotions is further supported by another and very comprehensive set of facts. In our discussion of the particular modes of conduct which are subject to moral valuation and of the judgments passed on them by different peoples and in different ages, this theory has constantly been called in to explain the data before us. It is noteworthy that the very acts, forbearances, and omissions which are condemned as wrong are also apt to call forth anger and revenge, and that the acts and forbearances which are praised as morally good are apt to call forth gratitude. This coincidence, again, undoubtedly bears testimony both to the emotional basis of the moral concepts and to the retributive character of the moral emotions. Thus the conclusions arrived at in the first section of the work, while helping to explain the facts mentioned in the two other sections, are at the same time greatly strengthened by these facts. Any attempt to discover the nature and origin of the moral consciousness must necessarily take into account the moral ideas of mankind at large. And though painfully conscious of the incompleteness of the present treatise, I think I may confidently ask, with reference to its fundamental thesis, whether any other theory of the moral consciousness has ever been subjected to an equally comprehensive test.

The general uniformity of human nature accounts for the great similarities which characterise the moral ideas of mankind. But at the same time these ideas also present radical differences. A mode of conduct which among one people is condemned as wrong is among another people viewed with indifference or regarded as praiseworthy or enjoined as a duty. One reason for these variations lies in different external conditions. Hardships of life may lead to the killing of infants or abandoning of aged parents or eating of human bodies ; and necessity and the force of habit may deprive these actions of the stigma which would otherwise be attached to them. Economic conditions have influenced moral ideas relating, for instance, to slavery, labour, and cleanliness ; whilst the form of marriage and the opinions concerning it have been largely determined by such a factor as the numerical proportion between the sexes. But the most common differences of moral estimates have undoubtedly a psychical origin.

When we examine the moral rules of uncivilised races we find that they in a very large measure resemble those prevalent among nations of culture. In every savage community homicide is prohibited by custom, and so is theft. Savages also regard charity as a duty and praise generosity as a virtue—indeed, their customs concerning mutual aid are often much more stringent than our own ; and many uncivilised peoples are conspicuous for their aversion to telling lies. But at the same time there is a considerable difference between the regard for life, property, truth, and the general wellbeing of a neighbour, which displays itself in primitive rules of morality and that which is found among ourselves. Savages' prohibitions of murder, theft, and deceit, as also their injunctions of charity and kind behaviour, have, broadly speaking, reference only to members of the same community or tribe. They carefully distinguish between an act of homicide committed among their own people and one where the victim is a stranger ; whilst the former is in ordinary circumstances disapproved of, the latter is in most cases allowed and often considered worthy of praise. And the same thing holds true of theft and lying and other injuries. Apart from the privileges which are granted to guests, and which are always of very short duration, a stranger is in early society devoid of all rights. This is the case not only among savages but among nations of archaic culture as well. When we from the lower races pass to peoples more advanced in civilisation we find that the social unit has grown larger, that the nation has taken the place of the tribe, and that the circle of persons within which the infliction of injuries is prohibited has extended accordingly. But the old distinction between offences against compatriots and harm done to foreigners remains. Nay, it survives to some extent even among ourselves, as appears from the prevailing attitude towards war and the readiness with which wars are waged. But although the difference between a fellow countryman and a foreigner has not ceased to affect the moral feelings of men even in the midst of modern civilisation, its influence has certainly been decreasing. The doctrine has been set forth, and has been gradually gaining ground, that our duties towards our fellow men are universal duties, not restricted by the limits of country or race. Those who recognise the emotional origin of the rules of duty find no difficulty in explaining all these facts. The expansion of the commandments relating to neighbours coincides with the expansion of the altruistic sentiment. And the cause of this coincidence at once becomes clear when we consider that such commandments mainly spring from the emotion of sympathetic resentment, and that sympathetic resentment is rooted in the altruistic sentiment.

Besides the extension of duties towards neighbours so as to embrace wider and wider circles of men, there is another point in which the moral ideas of mankind have undergone an important change on the upward path from savagery and barbarism to civilisation. They have become more enlightened. Though moral ideas are based upon emotions, though all moral concepts are essentially generalisations of tendencies in certain phenomena to call forth moral approval or disapproval, the influence of intellectual considerations upon moral judgments is naturally very great. All higher emotions are determined by cognitions —sensations or ideas ; they therefore vary according as the cognitions vary, and the nature of a cognition may very largely depend upon reflection or insight. If a person tells us an untruth we are apt to feel indignant ; but if, on due reflection, we find that his motive was benevolent, for instance a desire to save the life of the person to whom the untruth was told, our indignation ceases, and may even be succeeded by approval. The change of cognitions, or ideas, has thus produced a change of emotions. Now, the evolution of the moral consciousness partly consists in its development from the unreflecting to the reflecting stage, from the unenlightened to the enlightened. This appears from the decreasing influence of external events upon moral judgments and from the growing discrimination with reference to motives, negligence, and other factors in conduct which are carefully considered by a scrupulous judge. More penetrating reflection has also reduced the part played by disinterested likes and dislikes in the formation of moral ideas. When we clearly realise that a certain act is productive of no real harm but is condemned simply because it causes aversion or disgust, we can hardly look upon it as a proper object of moral censure—unless, indeed, its commission is considered to imply a blamable disregard for other persons' sensibilities. Deliberate resentment, whether moral or non-moral, is too much concerned with the will of the agent to be felt towards a person who obviously neither intends to offend anybody nor is guilty of culpable oversight. Nay, even when the agent knows that his behaviour is repulsive to others, he may be considered justified in acting as he does. Some degree of reflection easily leads to the notion that senti-mental antipathies are no sufficient ground for interfering with other individuals' liberty of action either by punish-ing them or by subjecting them to moral censure, provided of course that they do not in an indelicate manner shock their neighbours' feelings. Hence many persons have recourse to utilitarian pretexts to support moral opinions or legal enactments which have originated in mere aver-sions ; thus making futile attempts to reconcile old ideas with the requirements of a moral consciousness which is duly influenced by reflection.

In innumerable cases the variations of moral estimates are due to differences of beliefs. Almost every chapter of this work has borne witness to the enormous influence which the belief in supernatural forces or beings or in a future state has exercised upon the moral ideas of man-kind, and has at the same time shown how exceedingly varied this influence has been. Religion, or superstition (as the case may be), has on the one hand stigmatised murder and suicide, on the other hand it has commended human sacrifice and certain cases of voluntary self-destruc-tion. It has inculcated humanity and charity, but has also led to cruel persecutions of persons embracing another creed. It has emphasised the duty of truthspeaking, and has itself been a cause of pious fraud. It has promoted both cleanly habits and filthiness. It has enjoined labour and abstinence from labour, sobriety and drunkenness, marriage and celibacy, chastity and temple prostitution. It has introduced a great variety of new duties and virtues, quite different from those which are recognised by the moral consciousness when left to itself, but nevertheless in many cases considered more important than any other duties or virtues. It seems that the moral ideas of uncivilised men are more affected by magic than by religion, and that the religious influence has reached its greatest extension at certain stages of culture which, though comparatively advanced, do not include the highest stage. Increasing knowledge lessens the sphere of the supernatural, and the ascription of a perfectly ethical character to the godhead does away with moral estimates which have sprung from less elevated religious conceptions.

I have here pointed out only the most general changes to which the moral ideas have been subject in the course of progressive civilisation; the details have been dealt with each in their separate place. There can be no doubt that changes also will take place in the future, and that similar causes will produce similar effects. We have every reason to believe that the altruistic sentiment will continue to expand, and that those moral commandments which are based on it will undergo a corresponding expansion; that the influence of reflection upon moral judgments will steadily increase; that the influence of sentimental antipathies and likings will diminish; and that in its relation to morality religion will be increasingly restricted to emphasising ordinary moral rules, and less preoccupied with inculcating special duties to the deity.

ADDITIONAL NOTES TO VOL. II

P. 287, *n.* 6.—The connection between the Hebrew Sabbath and the moon has been fully discussed by Professor Webster in his recent book, *Rest Days*, ch. viii.

P. 377, *n.* 1.—In his book, *Totemism and Exogamy*, Sir J. G. Frazer has definitely separated exogamy from totemism and thereby, it is to be hoped, saved us from further speculations about the totemic origin of the exogamous rules. Like myself, Frazer thinks (iv. 105 *sqq.*) that these rules have sprung from an aversion to the marriages of near kin. But whilst my own belief is that the aversion to such marriages through an association of ideas led to the prohibitions of marriage between members of the same clan on account of the notion of intimacy connected with a common descent and a common name, Frazer is of opinion that exogamy was deliberately instituted for the purpose of preventing the sexual unions of near kin. To me it seems almost inconceivable that the extensive, cumbersome, and sometimes very complicated institution of exogamy should have been invented simply as a precaution against unions between the nearest relatives.

Granting the prevalence of an aversion to the marriages of near kin, Frazer is confronted with the question how it has originated. His answer is, " We do not know and it is difficult even to guess." Yet he makes a cautious attempt to solve the riddle. He observes (iv. 156 *sqq.*) that the great severity with which incest is generally punished by savages seems to show that they believe it to be a crime which endangers the whole community. It may have been thought to render the women of the tribe sterile and to prevent animals and plants from multiplying ; such beliefs, Frazer remarks, appear in point of fact to have been held by many races in different parts of the world. But he admits himself that all the peoples who are known to hold them seem to be agricultural, and that incest is in particular supposed to have a sterilising effect on the crops. It is indeed a poor argument to conjecture that a careful search among the most primitive exogamous peoples now surviving, especially among the Australian aborigines, might still reveal the existence of a belief in the sterilising or injurious effects of incest " upon women generally and particularly upon edible animals and plants." It may also be asked if it really is reasonable to presume that an aversion which had originated in the superstition mentioned could have remained unimpaired among all the civilised nations of the world. Moreover, if this superstition were the root of the aversion to incest, we should still have to explain the origin of the superstition itself, and this Frazer has not even attempted to do. If, on the other hand, the abhorrence of incest has originated in the way I have suggested, the superstition which he is inclined to regard as the cause of that feeling is a very natural result of it or of the prohibition to which it gave rise. That this is the case is all the more probable because the same injurious effects as are attributed to incest are supposed to result from other sexual irregularities as well, such as adultery and fornication (*cf. supra*, ii. 417).

Sir J. G. Frazer also subjects my theory to a detailed criticism (iv. 96 *sqq.*). He admits that there seems to be some ground for believing in the existence of " a natural aversion to, or at least a want of inclination for, sexual intercourse between persons who have been brought up closely together from early youth " ; but he finds it difficult to understand how this could have been changed into an aversion to sexual intercourse with persons near of kin, and maintains that, till I explain this satisfactorily, the chain of reasoning by which I support my theory breaks down entirely at the crucial point. For my own part I think that the transition which Frazer finds so difficult to understand is not only possible and natural, but well-nigh proved by an exactly analogous case of equally world-wide occurrence and of still greater social importance, namely, the process which has led to the association of all kinds of social rights and duties with kinship. As I have pointed out above (ch. xxxiv.), the maternal and paternal sentiments, which largely are at the bottom of parental duties and rights, cannot in their simplest forms be based on a knowledge of blood relationship, but respond to stimuli derived from other circumstances, notably the proximity of the helpless young, that is, the external relationship in which the offspring from the beginning stand to the parents. Nor is the so-called filial love in the first instance rooted in considerations of kinship ; it is essentially retributive, the agreeable feeling produced by benefits received making the individual look with pleasure and kindliness upon the giver. Here again the affection is ultimately due to close living together, and is further strengthened by it, as appears from the cooling effect of long separation of children from their parents. So also fraternal love and the duties and rights which have sprung from it depend in the first place on other circumstances than the idea of a common blood ; and the same may be said of the tie which binds together relatives more remotely allied. Its social force is ultimately derived from near relatives' habit of living together. " Men became gregarious by remaining in the circle where they were born ; if, instead of keeping together with their kindred, they had preferred to isolate themselves or to unite with strangers, there would certainly be no blood-bond at all. The mutual attachment and the social rights and duties which resulted from this gregarious condition were associated with the relation in which members of the group stood to one another—the relation of kinship as expressed by a common name—and these associations might last even after the local tie was broken," being kept up by the common name (supra, ii. 203).

Here we have an immense group of facts which, though ultimately depending upon close living together, have been interpreted in terms of kinship. Why, then, could not the same have been the case with the aversion to incest and the prohibitory rules resulting from it ? They really present a most striking analogy to the instances just mentioned. They have been associated with kinship because near relatives normally live together. They have come to include relatives more remotely allied who do not live together, owing to an association of ideas, especially through the influence of a common name ; clan exogamy has its counterpart, for instance, in the blood feud as a duty incumbent on the whole clan. But there are also cases in which marriages between unrelated persons who have been brought up together in the same family, or who belong to the same local group, are held blamable or are actually prohibited ; and so there are, even in early society, social rights and duties which are associated not with a common descent but with close living together. Frazer asks : " If the root of the whole matter is a horror of marriage between persons who have always lived with each other, how comes it that at the present day that horror has been weakened into a mere general preference for marriage with persons whose attractions have not been blunted by long familiarity ? . . . Why should the marriage of a brother with a sister, or of a mother with a son, excite the deepest detestation, . . . while the origin of it all, the marriage between housemates, should excite at most a mild surprise too slight probably to suggest even a subject for a farce, and should be as legitimate in the eye of the law among all civilised nations as any other marriage ? " For my own part, I believe that marriage between a man and his foster-daughter or between a foster-brother and a foster-sister, in case the social relations between them have been exactly similar to those of blood-relatives of corresponding degrees, would cause more than a mild surprise, and appear unnatural and objectionable. As I have said above (ii. 375), I do not deny that unions between the nearest blood-relatives inspire a horror of their own, but it seems quite natural that they should do so considering that from earliest times the aversion to sexual intercourse between persons living closely together has been expressed in prohibitions against unions between kindred. Nor can it be a matter of surprise that the prohibitory rules so commonly refer to marriages of kindred alone. Law only takes into account general and well-defined cases, and hence relationships of some kind or other between persons who are nearly always kindred are defined in terms of blood-relationship. This is true not only of the prohibitions of incest, but of many duties and rights inside the family circle.

Sir J. G. Frazer raises another objection to my theory. He argues that, if exogamy resulted from a natural instinct, there would be no need to reinforce that instinct by legal pains and penalties ; the law only forbids men to do what their instincts incline them to do, and hence we may always safely assume that crimes forbidden by law are crimes which many men have a natural propensity to commit. I must confess that this argument greatly surprises me. Of course, where there is no transgression there is no law. But Frazer cannot be ignorant of the variability of instincts and of the great variability of the sexual instinct ; nor should he forget that there are circumstances in which a natural sentiment may be blunted and overcome. Would he maintain that there can be no deep natural aversion to bestiality because bestiality is forbidden by law, and that the exceptional severity with which parricide is treated by many law books proves that a large number of men have a natural propensity to kill their parents ? The law expresses the feelings of the majority and punishes acts that shock them.

Sir J. G. Frazer accuses me of having extended Darwin's methods to subjects which only partially admit of such treatment, because my theory of the origin of exogamy attempts to explain the growth of a human institution " too exclusively from physical and biological causes without taking into account the factors of intelligence, deliberation, and will." This, he adds, is " not science, but a bastard imitation of it." What have I done to incur so severe an accusation ? I have suggested that the instinctive aversion to sexual intercourse between persons who have been living very closely together from early youth may be the result of natural selection. I am inclined to think—and so is Frazer—that consanguineous marriages are in some way or other detrimental to the species. This fact would lead to the development of a sentiment which would be powerful enough, as a rule, to prevent injurious unions—a sentiment which would not, of course, show itself as an innate aversion to sexual connections with near relatives as such, but as an aversion on the part of individuals to union with others with whom they lived closely together from early childhood. These, as a matter of fact, would be blood-relations, and the result would consequently be the survival of the fittest. All that I have done, then, is to appeal to natural selection to explain the origin of a primeval instinctive sentiment ; and I can never believe that this is to transgress the legitimate boundaries of Darwinism.

Sir J. G. Frazer himself thinks that " we may safely conclude that infertility is an inevitable consequence of inbreeding continued through many generations in the same place and under the same conditions," and in support of this view he quotes the valuable opinions of Mr. Walter Heape and Mr. F. H. A. Marshall. He thus finds that the principles of exogamy present " a curious resemblance " to the principles of scientific breeding, but he rightly assumes that this analogy cannot be due to any exact knowledge or farseeing care on the part of its savage founders. How then shall we explain this analogy ? Frazer's answer is that " it must be an accidental result of a superstition, an unconscious mimicry of science." In prohibiting incest the poor savages " blindly obeyed the impulse of the great evolutionary forces which in the physical world are constantly educing higher out of lower forms of existence and in the moral world civilisation out of savagery. If that is so, exogamy has been an instrument in the hands of that unknown power, the masked wizard of history, who by some mysterious process, some subtle alchemy, so often transmutes in the crucible of suffering the dross of folly and evil into the fine gold of wisdom and good." I hope it will not be considered uncalled-for impertinence on my part to ask if this reasoning is a specimen of what Frazer regards as science proper in contradistinction to my own " bastard imitation of it " ?

In any attempt to explain the origin of exogamy there are, in my opinion, three parallel groups of facts of general occurrence which necessarily must be taken into consideration :—Firstly, the prohibitions of incest and rules of exogamy themselves ; secondly, the aversion to sexual intercourse between persons living together from early youth ; thirdly, the injurious consequences of inbreeding. As for the facts of the first group, Frazer and I agree that they all have the same root, exogamy being in some way or other derived from an aversion to the marriages of near kin. As for the facts of the second group, Frazer at all events admits that "there seems to be some ground " for believing in them. As for the facts of the third group, there is complete agreement between us. I ask : Is it reasonable to think that there is no causal connection between these three groups of facts ? Is it right to ignore the second group altogether, as does Frazer, and to look upon the coincidence of the first and the third as accidental ? I gratefully acknowledge that Frazer's chapter on the Origin of Exogamy has only strengthened my belief in my own theory.

Other objections to my theory have recently been made by Messrs. Hose and McDougall in their work on *The Pagan Tribes of Borneo*, vol. ii., p. 197, note. They observe that intercourse between a youth and his sister-by-adoption is not regarded as incest in these tribes, and that they know at least one instance of marriage between two young Kenyahs brought up together as adopted brother and sister. " This occurrence of incest between couples brought up in the same household," they say, " is, of course, difficult to reconcile with Professor Westermarck's well-known theory of the ground of the almost universal feeling against incest, namely, that it depends upon sexual aversion or indifference engendered by close proximity during childhood." They moreover maintain that "the occurrence of incest between brothers and sisters, and the strong feeling of the Sea Dyaks against incest between nephew and aunt (who often are members of distinct communities)," are facts which are fatal to this theory.

In my attempt to explain the rules against incest I certainly did not overlook the fact that these rules very frequently have reference to persons who are, or may be, members of different communities, and I found no difficulty in accounting for it (see *supra*, ii. 369 ; *History of Human Marriage*, p. 330 *sq.*). Curiously enough Messrs. Hose and McDougall's own attempt to solve the problem is, if I understand them rightly, based on the supposition that the prohibitions of intermarriage originally referred to persons who belonged to the same community. They write :—" If we accept some such view of the constitution of primitive society as has been suggested by Messrs. Atkinson and Lang (*Primal Law*), namely, that the social group consisted of a single patriarch and a group of wives and daughters, over all of whom he exercised unrestricted power or rights ; we shall see that the first step towards the constitution of a higher form of society must have been the strict limitation of his rights over certain of the women, in order that younger males might be incorporated in the society and enjoy the undisputed possession of them. The patriarch, having accepted this limitation of his rights over his daughters for the sake of the greater security and strength of the band given by the inclusion of a certain number of young males, would enforce all the more strictly upon them his prohibition against any tampering with the females of the senior generation. Thus very strict prohibitions and severe penalties against the consorting of the patriarch with the younger generation of females, *i.e.* his daughters, and against intercourse between the young males admitted to membership of the group and the wives of the patriarch, would be the essential conditions of advance of social organisation. The enforcement of these penalties would engender a traditional sentiment against such unions, and these would be the unions primitively regarded as incestuous. The persistency of the tendency of the patriarch's jealousy to drive his sons out of the family group as they attained puberty would render the extension of this sentiment to brother-and-sister unions easy and almost inevitable. For the young male admitted to the group would be one who came with a price in his hand to offer in return for the bride he sought. Such a price could only be exacted by the patriarch on the condition that he maintained an absolute prohibition on sexual relations between his offspring so long as the young sons remained under his roof." I should like to know how Messrs. Hose and McDougall, on the basis of this theory, would explain " the strong feeling of the Sea Dyaks against incest between nephew and aunt (who often are members of distinct communities)," and, generally speaking, the rules prohibiting the intermarriage of persons belonging to different local groups. For the rest, I must confess that the assumptions on which their whole theory rests seem to me extremely arbitrary. Brothers are prohibited from marrying their sisters because the old patriarch drove away his grown-up sons out of jealousy ; but his jealousy was not strong enough to prevent other young males from joining the band. ˙On the contrary, he allowed them to be incorporated in it, because they added to its strength ; nay, he gave them his own daughters in marriage, and refrained henceforth himself from intercourse with these young women so rigorously that ever since a father has been prohibited from marrying his daughter. But the young men had to pay a price for their wives. It may be asked : Why did not the old patriarch accept a˙price from his own sons or let them work for him, instead of mercilessly turning them out of their old home, although they would have been just as good protectors of it as anybody else ? And why did he give the young men his *daughters* ? He might have kept the young women for himself and let the young men have the old ones. This is what is done by the old men in Australia, where the young girls are, as a rule, allotted to old men, and the boys, whenever they are allowed to marry, get old *lubras* as wives (Malinowski, *The Family among the Australian Aborigines*, p. 259 *sqq.*). Yet, in spite of this custom, there is no country where incest has been more strictly prohibited than in Australia.

Messrs. Hose and McDougall maintain that the occurrence of incest between brothers and sisters and the feeling of the Sea Dyaks against incest between nephew and aunt are facts which seem " to point strongly to the view that the sentiment has a purely conventional or customary source." I ask : Is it reasonable to suppose that, if this were the case, the feeling against sexual intercourse between the nearest relatives could have so long survived the conditions from which it sprang without showing any signs of decay ? As I have pointed out above, the prohibited degrees are very differently defined in the customs or laws of different peoples, generally being more numerous among peoples unaffected by modern civilisation than they are in more advanced communities ; and it appears that the extent to which relatives are prohibited from intermarrying is closely connected with the intimacy of their social relations. Whilst among ourselves cousins are allowed to intermarry, there is still a strong sentiment against intercourse between parents and children and between brothers and sisters, who in normal cases belong to the same family circle. Why should the feeling against incest have survived in this case but not in others, if it had a purely conventional origin ? And how could any law based on convention alone account for the normal absence of erotic feelings in the relation between parents and children and brothers and sisters ? It is true that cases of intercourse between the nearest relatives do occur, but they are certainly quite exceptional. Messrs. Hose and McDougall say themselves (p. 198) that " incest of any form is very infrequent " among the tribes of Borneo, and they seem to know of only one instance of marriage between young Kenyahs brought up together as adopted brother and sister, although such marriages are allowed. To maintain that cases of this kind are fatal to my theory seems to me as illogical as it would be to assume that the occurrence of a *horror feminæ* in many men disproves the general prevalence of a feeling of love between the sexes.

P. 396, *n.* 1.—In his recent work, *The Family among the Australian Aborigines*, Dr. Malinowski has come to the same conclusion. He observes that the individual family plays a foremost part in the social life of those aborigines ; it has a very firm basis in their customs and ideas, and " by no means bears the features of anything like recent innovation, or a subordinate form subservient to the idea of group marriage." The Australian husband had generally a definite sexual " over-right " over his wife, which secured to him the privilege of disposing of her, or at least of exercising a certain control over her conduct in sexual matters, even though this " over-right " did not, as a rule, amount to an exclusive right. There were customs like wife-lending, exchange of wives, ceremonial defloration of girls by old men, the different forms of licence practised at large tribal gatherings, and especially the *Pirrauru* relationship found in several of the southern central tribes. But all this does not constitute group *marriage*, the complete content of which does not consist in sexual relations alone. Dr. Malinowski emphasises the fact that marriage cannot be detached from family life ; " it is defined in all its aspects by the problems of the economic unity of the family, of the bonds created by common life in one wurley, through the common rearing of, and affection towards, the offspring." In nearly all these respects even the *Pirrauru* relationship essentially differs from marriage, and cannot, therefore, seriously encroach upon the individual family. Nor can we regard this relationship as a survival of previous group marriage. Dr. Malinowski also points out (p. 89 *sq.*) how highly objectionable it is that " our best informants (especially Howitt and Spencer and Gillen) describe the facts of sexual life of to-day in terms of their hypothetical assumptions."

P. 419, *n.* 5.—For Moorish beliefs relating to contact between sexual uncleanness and holiness see my essays, *The Moorish Conception of Holiness (Baraka)*, p. 123 *sqq.*, and *Ceremonies and Beliefs connected with Agriculture, certain Dates of the Solar Year, and the Weather in Morocco*, pp. 17, 22, 23, 28, 46, 47, 54.

P. 463, *n.* 8.—During the years that have passed since the first edition of this book was issued, the study of homosexuality has been carried on with remarkable activity. The following books are exclusively devoted to this subject :—*Das gleichgeschlechtliche Leben der Naturvölker*, by F. Karsch-Haack (1911), *Intermediate Types among Primitive Folk*, by Edward Carpenter (1914), and *Die Homosexualität des Mannes und des Weibes*, by Magnus Hirschfeld (1914). Carpenter's book chiefly deals with the invert in early religion and in warfare. Hirschfeld's work is a veritable encyclopædia of homosexuality—according to Dr. Havelock Ellis, " not only the largest but the most precise, detailed, and comprehensive—even the most condensed—work which has yet appeared on the subject." In 1915 Dr. Havelock Ellis issued a third, revised and enlarged, edition of his *Sexual Inversion*.

P. 485, *n.* 1.—This passage and, generally, the suggestion that there is a certain relationship between the social reaction against homosexuality and against infanticide, have been excluded from the last edition of Dr. Havelock Ellis's book.

P. 584, *n.* 1.—There is hardly any subject which during the last four or five years has been more eagerly discussed by students of social anthropology than the relation between religion and magic. It has been dealt with, *e.g.*, by Sir J. G. Frazer in *The Magic Art*, by Professor Durkheim in *Les formes élémentaires de la vie religieuse*, by Dr. Marett in *The Threshold of Religion* and other writings, by Dr. Irving King in *The Development of Religion*, by Professor Leuba in *A Psychological Study of Religion*, by Mr. Sidney Hartland in *Ritual and Belief*, and by the present Archbishop of Sweden, Nathan Söderblom, in his book *Gudstrons uppkomst*. According to the French school of sociologists, religion is social in its aims and magic antisocial ; and this distinction has lately been accepted by Dr. Marett, who writes (*Anthropology*, p. 209 *sq.*) : " Magic I take to include all bad ways, and religion all good ways, of dealing with the supernormal—bad and good, of course, not as we may happen to judge them, but as the society concerned judges them." But this use of the terms is neither in agreement with traditional usage nor, in my opinion, suitable for the purpose of scientific classification. Besides black magic, or witchcraft, there is also white magic ; even a medieval theologian like Albertus Magnus asserts that " magical science is not evil, since through knowledge of it evil can be avoided and good attained." The French distinction between magic and religion implies that a prayer to a god for the destruction of an enemy must be classified as religion if it is offered in a cause which is considered just by the community, but as magic if it is disapproved of. If a man makes a girl drink a love-potion in order to gain her favour, it is religion if their union is desirable from the society's point of view, but if he gives the same drink to another man's wife it is magic. The best part of what has been hitherto called imitative or homœopathic magic no longer remains magic at all ; if water is poured out for the purpose of producing rain it is homœopathic magic only in case rain is not wanted by the community, but if it is done during a drought it is religion. Thus the very same practices are qualified as religious or magical according as they have social or antisocial ends ; and, as Mr. Hartland rightly asks (*Ritual and Belief*, p. 76) : " How shall we define these ends ? "

It should be added, however, that the definition of religion which I have given in the text has reference only to religion in the abstract, not to the various religions. In the popular sense of the word, *a* religion may include many practices which are what I have called magical. As I have said above (p. 649), " both Christianity in its earlier phases and Muhammedanism are full of magical practices expressly sanctioned by their theology." Although the magical and the strictly religious attitude differ from each other, they are not irreconcilable, and may therefore very well form parts of one and the same religion ; there is no such thing as *a* magic being opposed to a religion. By a religion is generally understood a system of beliefs and rules of behaviour which have reference to men's relations to one or several supernatural beings whom they call their god or gods, that is, supernatural beings who are the objects of a regular cult and between whom and their worshippers there are established and permanent relationships. If it be admitted that the word religion may be thus legitimately used in two different senses, I think there is little ground left for further controversy on the subject. After all, sociologists may more profitably occupy their time than by continuous quarrelling about the meaning of terms.

P. 608, *n.* 4.—In *The Dying God*, p. 204, *n.* 1, Sir J. G. Frazer writes : " There is a good deal to be said in favour of Dr. Westermarck's theory, which is supported in particular by the sanctity attributed to the regalia. But on the whole I see no sufficient reason to abandon the view adopted in the text, and I am confirmed in it by the Shilluk evidence, which was unknown to Dr. Westermarck when he propounded his theory."

According to Professor C. G. Seligman—to whom Frazer is indebted for detailed information on the subject (*op. cit.* p. 17 *sqq.*)—it is a fundamental article of the Shilluk creed that the spirit of Nyakang, the divine or semi-divine hero who settled the Shilluk in their present territory and founded the dynasty of their kings, is incarnate in the reigning king, who is accordingly himself invested to some extent with the character of a divinity. But while the Shilluk hold their kings in high, indeed religious, reverence and take every precaution against their accidental death, nevertheless they cherish the conviction that the king must not be allowed to become ill or senile, lest with his diminishing vigour the cattle should sicken and fail to bear their increase, the crops should rot in the fields, and man, stricken with disease, should die in ever-increasing numbers. To prevent these calamities it used to be the regular custom with the Shilluk to put the king to death whenever he showed signs of ill-health or failing strength. Nay, from Dr. Seligman's enquiries it appears that even while the king was yet in the prime of health and strength he might at any time be attacked by a rival and have to defend his crown in a combat to the death. According to the common Shilluk tradition any son of a king had the right thus to fight the king in possession and, if he succeeded in killing him, to reign in his stead. Now " an important part of the solemnities attending the accession of a Shilluk king appears to be intended to convey to the new monarch the divine spirit of Nyakang, which has been transmitted from the founder of the dynasty to all his successors on the throne. For this purpose a sacred four-legged stool and a mysterious object which bears the name of Nyakang himself are brought with much solemnity from the shrine of Nyakang at Akurwa to the small village of Kwom near Fashoda, where the king elect and the chiefs await their arrival. The thing called Nyakang is said to be of cylindrical shape, some two or three feet long by six inches broad. The chief of Akurwa informed Dr. Seligman that the object in question is a rude wooden figure of a man, which was fashioned long ago at the command of Nyakang in person. We may suppose that it represents the divine king himself and that it is, or was formerly, supposed to house his spirit, though the chief of Akurwa denied to Dr. Seligman that it does so now. . . . The image of Nyakang is placed on the stool ; the king elect holds one leg of the stool and an important chief holds another. . . . A bullock is killed and its flesh eaten by the men of certain families called *ororo*, who are said to be descended from the third of the Shilluk kings. Then the Akurwa men carry the image of Nyakang into the shrine, and the *ororo* men place the king elect on the sacred stool, where he remains seated for some time, apparently till sunset. When he rises, the Akurwa men carry the stool back into the shrine, and the king is escorted to three new huts, where he stays in seclusion for three days. On the fourth night he is conducted quietly, almost stealthily, to his royal residence at Fashoda, and next day he shows himself publicly to his subjects."

As regards this so-called evidence it should, first, be noticed that it is only Dr. Seligman's own conjecture that the mysterious object called Nyakang is or has been supposed to contain the spirit of the holy founder of the dynasty, and that this conjecture is expressly said to be opposed to the present beliefs of the natives. On the other hand it is obvious that the object in question is regarded as a holy object, and that its holiness, or a particle of it, is supposed to be transmitted to the new king through material contact—an idea which well agrees with my own theory. But even if the Shilluk had once believed that their king was a reincarnation of the spirit of Nyakang, that belief could hardly be regarded as a direct proof of the idea that the soul of the slain man-god is transmitted to his royal successor. The Shilluk believe that Nyakang, unlike his royal descendants of more recent times, did not die but simply disappeared.

AUTHORITIES QUOTED [1]

A Voice for South America. London.

Aas (Einar), *Sjaeleliv og intelligens hos dyr.* Kristiania, 1893.

Abbot (Ezra), ' Literature of the Doctrine of a Future Life ' ; in Alger, *A Critical History of the Doctrine of a Future Life.* Philadelphia, 1864.

'Abd-Allatif, *Relation de l'Égypte.* Trans. by S. de Sacy. Paris, 1810.

'Abd-es-Salâm Shabeeny, *An Account of Timbuctoo and Housa.* Ed. by J. G. Jackson. London, 1820.

Abegg (J. F. H.), *Die verschiedenen Strafrechtstheorieen.* Neustadt a.d.O., 1835.

Abel (Charles W.), *Savage Life in New Guinea.* London, [1901].

Abercromby (John), *The Pre- and Proto-Historic Finns.* 2 vols. London, 1898.

Abreu de Galindo (Juan de), *The History of the Discovery and Conquest of the Canary Islands.* Trans. London, 1764.

Academy (The). London.

Achelis (Th.), ' Animal Worship ' ; in *The Open Court,* vol. xi. Chicago, 1897.

—— *Moderne Völkerkunde.* Stuttgart, 1896.

Achery (L. d'), *Spicilegium sive collectio veterum aliquot scriptorum qui in Galliæ bibliothecis delituerant.* 3 vols. Parisiis, 1723.

Acosta (Joseph de), *The Natural and Moral History of the Indies.* Trans. ed. by C. R. Markham. 2 vols. London, 1880.

Acta Societatis Scientiarum Fennicæ. Helsingfors.

Adair (James), *The History of the American Indians.* London, 1775.

Adalbero, ' Carmen ad Rotbertum regem Francorum ' ; in Bouquet, *Recueil des historiens des Gaules et de la France,* vol. x. Paris, 1760.

Adam of Bremen, ' Gesta Hammaburgensis ecclesiæ pontificum ' ; in Migne, *Patrologiæ cursus completus,* vol. cxlvi. Parisiis, 1853.

Adams (John), *Sketches taken during Ten Voyages to Africa, Between the Years 1786 and 1800.* London, [1825].

Addis (W. E.) and Arnold (Thomas), *A Catholic Dictionary.* London, 1903.

Addosio (Carlo d'), *Bestie delinquenti.* Napoli, 1892.

Aelian, *De natura animalium, Varia historia, &c.* Ed. by R. Hercher. Parisiis, 1858.

Aeschines, ' Orationes ' ; in *Oratores Attici,* ed. by C. Müller, vol. ii. Parisiis, 1858.

Aeschylus, *Tragœdiæ et fragmenta.* Ed. by E. A. J. Ahrens. Parisiis, 1842.

Aethelbirht (*King*), ' The Laws of ' ; in *Ancient Laws and Institutes of England.* London, 1840.

[1] Of articles in periodicals only some of the more important have been included in this list.

Aethelstan (*King*), 'The Laws of'; in *Ancient Laws and Institutes of England.* London, 1840.

Afzelius (A. A.), *Swenska Folkets Sago-Häfder.* 11 vols. Stockholm, 1839–70.

Agathias, 'Historiarum libri quinque'; in Migne, *Patrologiæ cursus*, Ser. Graeca, vol. lxxxviii. Parisiis, 1860.

Ahlqvist (A.), 'Unter Wogulen und Ostjaken'; in *Acta Societatis Scientiarum Fennicæ*, vol. xiv. Helsingfors, 1885.

Ahrens (Heinrich), *Naturrecht.* 2 vols. Wien, 1870–71.

Aitareya Brahmanam of the Rigveda (*The*). Ed. and trans. by M. Haug. 2 vols. Bombay, 1863.

Alabaster (Chal.), 'The Law of Inheritance'; in *The China Review*, vol. v. Hongkong, 1876–77.

Alabaster (Ernest), *Notes and Commentaries on Chinese Criminal Law.* London, 1899.

Alabaster (Henry), *The Wheel of the Law.* London, 1871.

Alagona (Petrus), *Compendium manualis D. Navarri.* Lugduni, 1603.

Alard (Paul), *Condition et droits des enfants naturels.* Paris, 1896.

Albericus, *Visio.* Ed. by Catello de Vivo. Ariano, 1899.

Alberti (L.), *De Kaffers aan de Zuidkust van Afrika.* Amsterdam, 1810.

Alden (T. J. Fox) and Hoesen (J. A. van), *A Digest of the Laws of Mississippi.* New York, 1839.

Alexander (S.), *Moral Order and Progress.* London, 1896.

Alfonso de' Liguori, *Theologia moralis.* 3 vols. Bassani, 1822.

Alfred (*King*), 'The Laws of'; in *Ancient Laws and Institutes of England.* London, 1840.

Alger (W. R.), *A Critical History of the Doctrine of a Future Life.* Philadelphia, 1864.

Alienist and Neurologist (*The*). St. Louis.

Allard (Paul), *Les esclaves chrétiens depuis les premiers temps de l'Église jusqu'à la fin de la domination romaine en Occident.* Paris, 1876.

Allardt (Anders), *Nyländska folkseder och bruk.* (*Nyland*, vol. iv.) Helsingfors, 1889.

Allen (Grant), *The Evolution of the Idea of God.* London, 1897.

Allen (John), *Modern Judaism.* London, 1830.

Allen (W.) and Thomson (T. R. H.), *A Narrative of the Expedition sent by Her Majesty's Government to the River Niger, in* 1841. 2 vols. London, 1848.

Am Ur-Quell. Monatsschrift für Volkskunde. Ed. by F. S. Krauss. Lunden.

Amadori-Virgilj (Giovanni), *L'Istituto famigliare nelle Società primordiali.* Bari, 1903.

Ambrose (*Saint*), *Opera omnia.* (Migne, *Patrologiæ cursus*, vols. xiv.-xvii.) Parisiis, 1845.

Ameer Ali (Syed), *The Ethics of Islâm.* Calcutta, 1893.

——— *The Life and Teachings of Mohammed or the Spirit of Islâm.* London, 1891.

Amélineau (E.), *Essai sur l'évolution historique et philosophique des idées morales dans l'Égypte ancienne.* Paris, 1895.

American Anthropologist (*The*). Washington.

American Antiquarian and Oriental Journal (*The*). Chicago.

American Journal of Psychology (*The*). Worcester.

American Journal of Theology (*The*). Chicago.

American Naturalist (*The*). Philadelphia.

Amira (Karl von), *Nordgermanisches Obligationenrecht.* 2 vols. Leipzig, 1882–95.
—— ' Recht ' ; in Paul, *Grundriss der germanischen Philologie*, vol. ii. Strassburg, 1893.
—— *Thierstrafen und Thierprocesse.* Innsbruck, 1891.
Ammianus Marcellinus. See Marcellinus (A.).
Amos (Andrew), *Ruins of Time exemplified in Sir Matthew Hale's History of the Pleas of the Crown.* London, 1856.
' Ancien Coutumier de Bourgogne,' ed. by A.-J. Marnier ; in *Revue historique de droit français et étranger*, vol. iii. Paris, 1857.
Ancient Laws and Institutes of England. London, 1840.
Ancient Laws and Institutes of Ireland. 4 vols. Dublin & London, 1865–79.
Ancient Laws and Institutes of Wales. London, 1841.
Ancient Sea-Laws of Oleron, Wisby, and the Hanse-Towns (The). Trans. London, 1686.
Ancona (A. d'), *Origini del teatro italiano.* 2 vols. Torino, 1891.
Anderson (John), *Mandalay to Momien.* London, 1876.
Anderson (John W.), *Notes of Travel in Fiji and New Caledonia.* London, 1880.
Andersson (C. J.), *Lake Ngami.* London, 1856.
—— *Notes on Travel in South Africa.* London, 1875.
André (Tony), *L'esclavage chez les anciens Hébreux.* Paris, 1892.
Andree (Richard), *Die Anthropophagie.* Leipzig, 1887.
—— ' Ethnographische Bemerkungen zu einigen Rechtsgebräuchen. I. Jagdrecht. II. Die Asyle ' ; in *Globus*, vol. xxxviii. Braunschweig, 1880.
—— *Ethnographische Parallelen und Vergleiche.* 2 vols. Stuttgart, 1878–89.
—— *Zur Volkskunde der Juden.* Bielefeld & Leipzig, 1881.
Andrews (William), *Old-Time Punishments.* Hull & London, 1890.
Angas (G. F.), *Polynesia.* London, [1866].
—— *Savage Life and Scenes in Australia and New Zealand.* London, 1850.
Annales du Musée Guimet. Paris.
Année sociologique (L'). Ed. by É. Durkheim. Paris.
Annual Reports of the Board of Regents of the Smithsonian Institution. Washington.
Annual Reports of the Bureau of Ethnology. Washington.
Anrich (G.), *Das antike Mysterienwesen in seinem Einfluss auf das Christentum.* Göttingen, 1894.
Antananarivo Annual and Madagascar Magazine. Antananarivo.
Ante-Nicene Christian Library. Ed. by A. Roberts and J. Donaldson. 24 vols. Edinburgh, 1867–72.
Anthropological Essays presented to E. B. Tylor. Oxford, 1907.
Anthropologie (L'). Paris.
Antiquary (The). London.
' Anugîtâ (The),' trans. by K. T. Telang ; in *The Sacred Books of the East*, vol. viii. Oxford, 1898.
' Âpastamba,' trans. by G. Bühler ; in *The Sacred Books of the East*, vol. ii. Oxford, 1897.
Apocryphal Books (The). Trans. London, 1880.
Apollodorus Atheniensis, *Bibliotheca.* Lipsiae, 1854.
Apollonius Rhodius, *Argonautica.* Ed. by F. S. Lehrs. Parisiis, 1840.

Apuleius (L.), *Opera omnia.* 7 vols. Londini, 1825.
Arbois de Jubainville (H. d'), ' Des attributions judiciaires de l'autorité publique chez les Celtes ' ; in *Revue Celtique,* vol. vii. Paris, 1886.
—— *La civilisation des Celtes et celle de l'épopée Homérique.* Paris, 1899.
Arbousset (T.) and Daumas (F.), *Narrative of an Exploratory Tour to the North-East of the Colony of the Cape of Good Hope.* Trans. London, 1852.
Archilochus, *Reliquiæ.* Ed. by I. Liebel. Lipsiae, 1818.
Archiv für Anthropologie. Braunschweig.
—— *für Religionswissenschaft.* Leipzig.
—— *für wissenschaftliche Kunde von Russland.* Ed. by A. Erman. Berlin.
Archives d'anthropologie criminelle. Paris.
Archives de Neurologie. Paris.
Archivio per l'antropologia e la etnologia. Firenze.
Archivio per lo studio delle tradizioni popolari. Palermo.
Arda Viraf. Ed. and trans. by M. Haug and E. W. West. Bombay & London, 1872.
Argentré (Bertrand d'), *L'histoire de Bretaigne.* Paris, 1618.
Aristophanes, *Comœdiæ.* Parisiis, 1838.
Aristotle, *De republica Atheniensium.* Ed. by J. E. Sandys. London, 1893.
—— The same work. Trans. by E. Poste. London, 1891.
—— *Opera omnia.* 5 vols. Parisiis, 1848–74.
—— *Politica and Œconomica.* 2 vols. Oxonii, 1810.
—— *The Politics.* Trans. by B. Jowett. 2 vols. Oxford, 1885.
Armstrong (Alex.), *A Personal Narrative of the Discovery of the North-West Passage.* London, 1857.
Arnesen (John), *Historisk Indledning til den gamle og nye Islandske Rætter-gang.* Kiöbenhavn, 1762.
Arnobius, ' Disputationum adversus gentes libri septem ' ; in Migne, *Patrologiæ cursus,* vol. v. Parisiis, 1844.
Arnold (Thomas), *Fragment on the Church.* London, 1845.
Arnold (Wilhelm), *Deutsche Urzeit.* Gotha, 1879.
Arnot (Fred.), *Garenganze ; or, Seven Years' Pioneer Mission Work in Central Africa.* London, [1889].
Arrian, *Anabasis et Indica.* Ed. by Fr. Dübner. Parisiis, 1846.
Arvieux (*Chevalier* d'), *Travels in Arabia the Desart.* Trans. London, 1718.
Ashe (R. P.), *Two Kings of Uganda.* London, 1889.
Asiatic(k) Researches. Calcutta.
Atharva-Veda, Hymns of the. Trans. by M. Bloomfield. (*The Sacred Books of the East,* vol. xlii.). Oxford, 1897.
Athenaeus, *Dipnosophistarum libri quindecim.* Ed. by G. Kaibel. 3 vols. Lipsiae, 1887–90.
Athenagoras, ' Legatio pro Christianis ' ; in Migne, *Patrologiæ cursus,* Ser. Graeca, vol. vi. Parisiis, 1857.
Atkinson (E. T.), ' Notes on the History of Religion in the Himálaya of the N.W. Provinces ' ; in *Journal of the Asiatic Society of Bengal,* vol. liii. pt. i. Calcutta, 1884.
Atkinson (J. C.), *Forty Years in a Moorland Parish.* London, 1891.
Atkinson (J. J.), ' The Natives of New Caledonia ' ; in *Folk-Lore,* vol. xiv. London, 1903.
—— *Primal Law.* London, 1903.
Augustana Confessio. Lipsiae, 1730.

Augustine (*Saint*), *Opera omnia.* 16 vols. (Migne, *Patrologiæ cursus*, vols. xxxii.–xlvii.) Parisiis, 1845–49.

Aurelius Victor (Sextus), *Libri de Romanæ gentis origine, Viris illustribus, Imperatoribus, Epitome.* Lipsiae & Francofurti, 1704.

Ausland (Das). Stuttgart & Augsburg.

Aust (Emil), *Die Religion der Römer.* Münster i. W., 1899.

Austin (John), *Lectures on Jurisprudence.* 2 vols. London, 1873.

Avebury (*Lord*), *The Origin of Civilisation.* London, 1902.

Ayala (Balthazar), *De jure et officiis bellicis et disciplina militari, libri III.* Duaci, 1582.

Ayrault (Pierre), *Des procez faicts au cadaver, aux cendres, a la mémoire, aux bestes brutes, &c.* Angers, 1591.

Azara (F. de), *Voyages dans l'Amérique méridionale.* 4 vols. Paris, 1809.

Baarda (M. J. van), ' Fabelen, verhalen en overleveringen der Galelareezen' ; in *Bijdragen tot de Taal-, Land- en Volkenkunde van Nederlandsch-Indië*, vol. xlv. (ser. vi. vol. i.). 's-Gravenhage, 1895.

Babington (Churchill), *The Influence of Christianity in promoting the Abolition of Slavery in Europe.* Cambridge, 1846.

Bachofen (J. J.), *Das Mutterrecht.* Stuttgart, 1861.

Bacon (*Lord*), *Works.* Ed. by J. Spedding, R. L. Ellis, and D. D. Heath. 14 vols. London, 1857–74.

Baden-Powell (B. H.), *The Indian Village Community.* London, 1896.

Bagehot (Walter), *Physics and Politics.* London, 1873.

Bailey (John), ' An Account of the Wild Tribes of the Veddahs of Ceylon ' ; in *Trans. Ethn. Soc.* new ser. vol. ii. London, 1863.

Bain (Alex.), *The Emotions and the Will.* London, 1880.

Baker (*Sir* S. W.), *The Albert N'yanza.* 2 vols. London, 1866.

—— *Ismailia.* London, 1879.

—— *The Nile Tributaries of Abyssinia.* London, 1871.

Baldwin (J. M.), *Social and Ethical Interpretations in Mental Development.* New York, 1897.

Balfour (A. J.), *The Foundations of Belief.* London, 1895.

Balfour (Edward), *The Cyclopædia of India, and Eastern and Southern Asia.* 3 vols. London, 1885.

Ball (C. J.), ' Glimpses of Babylonian Religion ' ; in *Proceed. Soc. Biblical Archæology*, vol. xiv. London, 1892.

Ball (J. Dyer), *Things Chinese.* London, 1900.

Ball (W. McK.) and Roane (S. C.), *Revised Statutes of the State of Arkansas.* Boston, 1838.

Balmes (*Don* Jaime), *El Protestantismo comparado con el Catolicismo en sus relaciones con la civilizacion Europea.* 4 vols. Barcelona, 1844–45.

Baluze (Stephen), *Capitularia Regum Francorum.* 2 vols. Parisiis, 1677.

Bancroft (H. H.), *The Native Races of the Pacific States of North America.* 5 vols. New York, 1875–76.

Bar (L. von), *Die Grundlagen des Strafrechts.* Leipzig, 1869.

Barbeyrac (Jean), *Traité de la morale des Pères de l'Église.* Amsterdam, 1728.

Baring-Gould (S.), *The Origin and Development of Religious Belief.* 2 vols. London, 1892.

—— *Strange Survivals.* London, 1892.

Barnes (Albert), *The Church and Slavery*. Philadelphia, 1857.

Baronius (C.), *Annales Ecclesiastici*. 38 vols. Lucae, 1738–59.

Barrington (George), *The History of New South Wales*. London, 1810.

Barrow (John), *An Account of Travels into the Interior of Southern Africa, in the Years* 1797 *and* 1798. 2 vols. London, 1801–04.

Bartels (Max), *Die Medicin der Naturvölker*. Leipzig, 1893.

Barth (A.), *The Religions of India*. Trans. London, 1882.

Barth (Heinrich), *Reisen und Entdeckungen in Nord- und Central-Afrika*. 5 vols. Gotha, 1857–58.

Bartholinus (Thomas), *Antiquitates Danicæ*. Hafniae, 1690.

Bartram (William), ' Observations on the Creek and Cherokee Indians ' ; in *Trans. American Ethn. Soc.* vol. iii. pt. i. New York, 1853.

Basil (*Saint*), *Opera.* 4 vols. (Migne, *Patrologiæ cursus*, Ser. Graeca, vols. xxix.–xxxii.) Parisiis, 1857.

Bastian (A.), *Afrikanische Reisen. Ein Besuch in San Salvador.* Bremen, 1859.

—— *Allerlei aus Volks- und Menschenkunde.* 2 vols. Berlin, 1888.

—— *Die deutsche Expedition an der Loango-Küste.* 2 vols. Jena, 1874–75.

—— *Der Mensch in der Geschichte.* 3 vols. Leipzig, 1860.

Batchelor (John), *The Ainu and their Folk-Lore.* London, 1901.

—— *The Ainu of Japan.* London, 1892.

—— ' Notes on the Ainu ' ; in *Trans. Asiatic Soc. Japan*, vol. x. Yokohama, 1882.

Bates (H. W.), *The Naturalist on the River Amazons.* 2 vols. London, 1863.

' Baudhâyana,' trans. by G. Bühler ; in *The Sacred Books of the East*, vol. xiv. Oxford, 1882.

Baudissin (W. W.), *Studien zur semitischen Religionsgeschichte.* 2 vols. Leipzig, 1876–78.

Baumann (Oscar), ' Conträre Sexual-Erscheinungen bei der Neger-Bevölkerung Zanzibars ' ; in *Verhandl. der Berliner Gesellsch. für Anthropologie*, 1899.

—— *Durch Massailand zur Nilquelle.* Berlin, 1894.

—— *Usambara.* Berlin, 1891.

Baur (F. Chr.), *Das Manichäische Religionssystem.* Tübingen, 1831.

Bax (E. B.), *The Ethics of Socialism.* London, 1893.

Bayle (P.), *Dictionnaire historique et critique.* 16 vols. Paris, 1820.

Baynes (Herbert), *The Idea of God and the Moral Sense in the Light of Language.* London, 1895.

Beardmore (E.), ' The Natives of Mowat, Daudai, New Guinea ' ; in *Jour. Anthr. Inst.* vol. xix. London, 1890.

Beauchamp (W. M.), ' The Iroquois White Dog Feast ' ; in *The American Antiquarian and Oriental Journal*, vol. vii. Chicago, 1885.

Beaumanoir (Philippe de), *Les coutumes du Beauvoisis.* 2 vols. Paris, 1842.

Beccaria Bonesana (Cesare), *Opere.* 2 vols. Milano, 1821–22.

Becker (W. A.), *Charikles.* Ed. by H. Göll. 3 vols. Berlin, 1877–78.

Beecham (John), *Ashantee and the Gold Coast.* London, 1841.

Beechey (F. W.), *Narrative of a Voyage to the Pacific and Behring's Strait.* 2 vols. London, 1831.

Beltrame (A. G.), *Il Fiume Bianco e i Dénka.* Verona, 1881.

—— *Il Sènnaar e lo Sciangàllah.* 2 vols. Verona & Padova, 1879.

Benedict (*Saint*), *Regula monachorum.* Ed. by E. Woelfflin. Lipsiae, 1895.

Benny (Ph. Berger), *The Criminal Code of the Jews according to the Talmud Massecheth Synhedrin*. London, 1880.

Bent (J. Theodore), *The Cyclades*. London, 1885.

Bentham (Jeremy), *Deontology*. Ed. by J. Bowring. 2 vols. London & Edinburgh, 1834.

—— *An Introduction to the Principles of Morals and Legislation*. Oxford, 1879.

—— *The Rationale of Punishment*. London, 1830.

—— *Theory of Legislation*. Trans. from the French of E. Dumont. London, 1882.

—— *The Works of*. 11 vols. Edinburgh, 1838–43.

' Berakhoth ' ; in *Le Talmud de Jérusalem*, trans. by M. Schwab, vol. i. Paris, 1871.

Bergaigne (Abel), *La religion védique*. 3 vols. Paris, 1878–83.

Bergemann (P.), *Die Verbreitung der Anthropophagie über die Erde*. Bunzlau, 1893.

Bergmann (B.), *Nomadische Streifereien unter den Kalmüken*. 4 vols. Riga, 1804–05.

Bernard (*Saint*), *Opera omnia*. 2 vols. Parisiis, 1719.

Bernard (Montague), ' The Growth of Laws and Usages of War ' ; in *Oxford Essays*, 1856. London, [1856].

Bernau (J. H.), *Missionary Labours in British Guiana*. London, 1847.

Berner (A. F.), *Lehrbuch des Deutschen Strafrechtes*. Leipzig, 1881.

Bertholet (Alfred), *Die Stellung der Israeliten und der Juden zu den Fremden*. Freiburg i.B. & Leipzig, 1896.

Best (Elsdon), ' The Lore of the Whare-Kohanga ' ; in *Jour. Polynesian Soc.* vol. xiv. Wellington, 1905.

—— ' Notes on the Art of War, as conducted by the Maori of New Zealand '; in *Jour. Polynesian Soc.* vol. xi. Wellington, 1902.

—— ' Pre-historic Civilisation in the Philippines ' ; in *Jour. Polynesian Soc.* vol. i. Wellington, 1892.

—— ' Tuhoe Land ' ; in *Trans. and Proceed. New Zealand Institute*, vol. xxx., 1897. Wellington, 1898.

Bethune-Baker (J. F.), *The Influence of Christianity on War*. Cambridge, 1888.

' Bhagavadgîtâ (The),' trans. by K. T. Telang ; in *The Sacred Books of the East*, vol. viii. Oxford, 1898.

Bible (*The Holy*). Appointed to be read in Churches.

Bickmore (A. S.), *Travels in the East Indian Archipelago*. London, 1868.

Biener (F. A.), *Das englische Geschwornengericht*. 2 vols. Leipzig, 1852.

Bijdragen tot de Taal-, Land- en Volkenkunde van Nederlandsch-Indië. 's-Gravenhage.

Bindemann (C.), *Der heilige Augustinus*. 2 vols. Berlin, 1844–55.

Binding (Karl), *Die Normen und ihre Übertretung*. 2 vols. Leipzig, 1872–77.

Bingham (J.), *Works*. Ed. by R. Bingham. 10 vols. Oxford, 1855.

Binsfeldius (P.), *Tractatus de confessionibus maleficorum et sagarum recognitus*. Augustae Trevirorum, 1591.

Biot (Édouard), *De l'abolition de l'esclavage ancien en Occident*. Paris, 1840.

—— ' Mémoire sur la condition des esclaves et des serviteurs gagés en Chine ' ; in *Journal Asiatique*, ser. iii. vol. iii. Paris, 1837.

Bird (Isabella L.), *Unbeaten Tracks in Japan*. 2 vols. London, 1880.

Birney (J. G.), *Letter to the Churches* [on the subject of Slavery]. *S.l.*, 1834.

—— *Second Letter* [on the same subject]. *S.l.*, [1834 ?].

Bishop (J. P.), *Commentaries on the Criminal Law.* 2 vols. Boston, 1877.

Black (J. S.), ' Fasting ' ; in *Encyclopædia Britannica*, vol. ix. Edinburgh, 1879.

Blackstone (William), *The Commentaries on the Laws of England.* Adapted to the present State of the Law, by R. M. Kerr. 4 vols. London, 1876.

Blakey (Robert), *The Temporal Benefits of Christianity.* London, 1849.

Bledsoe (A. T.), *An Essay on Liberty and Slavery.* Philadelphia, 1857.

Block (Maurice), *Dictionnaire général de la politique.* 2 vols. Paris, 1873–74.

Blümner (Heinrich), *Ueber die Idee des Schicksals in den Tragödien des Aischylos.* Leipzig, 1814.

Blümner (Hugo), *The Home Life of the Ancient Greeks.* Trans. London, 1893.

Blumentritt (Ferd.), ' Der Ahnencultus und die religiösen Anschauungen der Malaien des Philippinen-Archipels ' ; in *Mittheilungen der kais. und kön. Geographischen Gesellschaft in Wien*, vol. xxv. Wien, 1882.

—— ' Die Sitten und Bräuche der alten Tagalen ' ; in *Zeitschr. f. Ethnol.* vol. xxv. Berlin, 1893.

—— *Versuch einer Ethnographie der Philippinen.* Gotha, 1882.

Blunt (*Lady* Anne), *Bedouin Tribes of the Euphrates.* 2 vols. London, 1879.

Bluntschli (J. C.), *Le droit international codifié.* Trans. Paris, 1886.

Boas (Franz), ' The Central Eskimo ' ; in *Ann. Rep. Bur. Ethn.* vi., 1884–85. Washington, 1888.

—— ' First General Report on the Indians of British Columbia ' ; in *Fifth Report on the North-Western Tribes of Canada.* (Reprinted from the Report of the British Association for 1889.) London.

—— ' The Social Organization and the Secret Societies of the Kwakiutl Indians ' ; in *Annual Report of the Board of Regents of the Smithsonian Institution*, 1895. Washington, 1897.

Bock (Carl), *The Head-Hunters of Borneo.* London, 1881.

Bodenschatz (J. Chr. G.), *Kirchliche Verfassung der heutigen Juden.* 4 vols. Erlang, 1748–49.

Bodin (Jean), *De republica.* Ursellis, 1601.

Boeckh (A.), *Gesammelte kleine Schriften.* 7 vols. Leipzig, 1858–72.

Bogle (George), *Narrative of the Mission of, to Tibet, &c.* Ed. by C. R. Markham. London, 1876.

Bohnenberger (K.), *Der altindische Gott Varuṇa.* Tübingen, 1893.

Boissier (Gaston), *La religion romaine d'Auguste aux Antonins.* 2 vols. Paris, 1874.

Boller (H. A.), *Among the Indians.* Philadelphia, 1868.

Bonaventura (*Saint*), *Opera.* 13 vols. Venetiis, 1751–56.

Bonet (Honoré), *L'arbre des batailles.* Ed. by E. Nys. Bruxelles & Leipzig, 1883.

Bonfanti (M.), ' L'incivilimento dei negri nell' Africa intertropicale ' ; in *Archivio per l'antropologia e la etnologia*, vol. xv. Firenze, 1885.

Bonney (F.), ' On some Customs of the Aborigines of the River Darling ' ; in *Jour. Anthr. Inst.* vol. xiii. London, 1884.

Bonwick (James), *Daily Life and Origin of the Tasmanians.* London, 1870.

Book of the Dead. Trans. by Sir P. le Page Renouf. (Reprinted from the *Proceed. Soc. Biblical Archæology*, vols. xiv.–xix.) London, 1892–97.

Book of the Ordre of Chyualry or Knyghthode (The). Trans. by W. Caxton. [Westminster, 1484 ?]

Boone (W. J.), *An Essay, on the proper Rendering of the Words Elohim and Θεος into the Chinese Language.* Canton, 1848.

Bory de St. Vincent (J. B. G. M.), *Essais sur les Isles Fortunées.* Paris, 1803.

Bose (Shib Chunder), *The Hindoos as they are.* London & Calcutta, 1881.

Bosman (William), *A New and Accurate Description of the Coast of Guinea.* Trans. London, 1721.

Bosquett (A.), *Treatise on Duelling.* London, *s.d.*

Bossu (—), *Travels through that Part of North America formerly called Louisiana.* Trans. 2 vols. London, 1771.

Boston Journal of Natural History. Boston.

Boston Review (The). Devoted to Theology and Literature. Boston.

Bouche (P.), *Sept ans en Afrique occidentale. La Côte des Esclaves et Le Dahomey.* Paris, 1885.

Boulainvilliers (*Count* de), *Histoire de l'ancien gouvernement de la France.* 3 vols. La Haye & Amsterdam, 1727.

Bouquet (Martin) and others, *Recueil des Historiens des Gaules et de la France.* 24 vols. Paris, 1738–1904.

Bourke (J. G.), ' The Medicine-Men of the Apache ' ; in *Ann. Rep. Bur. Ethn.* vol. ix. Washington, 1892.

—— *The Snake-Dance of the Moquis of Arizona.* London, 1884.

Bourquelot (Félix), ' Recherches sur les opinions et la législation en matière de mort volontaire pendant le moyen âge ' ; in *Bibliothèque de l'École des Chartes,* vols. iii.–iv. Paris, 1841–43.

Bouvier (J.-B.), *Institutiones philosophicæ.* Parisiis, 1844.

Bove (Giacomo), *Patagonia. Terra del Fuoco. Mari Australi.* Genova, 1883.

Bowdich (T. E.), *Mission from Cape Coast Castle to Ashantee.* London, 1819.

Bowring (*Sir* John), *The Kingdom and People of Siam.* 2 vols. London, 1857.

—— *A Visit to the Philippine Islands.* London, 1859.

Boyle (D.), ' On the Paganism of the Civilised Iroquois of Ontario ' ; in *Jour. Anthr. Inst.* vol. xxx. London, 1900.

Boyle (Fred.), *Adventures among the Dyaks of Borneo.* London, 1865.

Brace (C. Loring), *Gesta Christi.* London, 1890.

Bracton (Henricus de), *De Legibus et Consuetudinibus Angliæ.* Ed. by Sir Travers Twiss. 2 vols. London, 1878–79.

Bradbury (John), *Travels in the Interior of America, in the Years* 1809–1811. Liverpool, 1817.

Bradley (F. H.), *Ethical Studies.* London, 1876.

Bradley-Birt (F. B.), *Chota Nagpore.* London, 1903.

Brainne (Ch.), *La Nouvelle-Calédonie.* Paris, 1854.

Brandt (A. J. H. W.), *Die Mandäische Religion.* Leipzig, 1889.

—— *Mandäische Schriften übersetzt und erläutert.* Göttingen, 1893.

Brebeuf (Jean de), ' Relation de ce qui s'est passé dans le pays des Hurons, en l'année 1636 ' ; in *Relations des Jésuites,* vol. i. Québec, 1858.

Breeks (J. Wilkinson), *An Account of the Primitive Tribes of the Nīlagiris.* London, 1873.

Brehm (A. E.), *From North Pole to Equator.* Trans. London, 1896.

—— *Thierleben.* 10 vols. Leipzig, 1877–80.

Brenchley (J. L.), *Jottings during the Cruise of H.M.S. Curaçoa among the South Sea Islands in* 1865. London, 1873.

Brenner (J. von), *Besuch bei den Kannibalen Sumatras.* Würzburg, 1894.

Breton (W. H.), *Excursions in New South Wales, &c.* London, 1833.

Brett (W. H.), *The Indian Tribes of Guiana*. London, 1868.

Brevard (Joseph), *An Alphabetical Digest of the Public Statute Law of South Carolina*. 3 vols. Charleston (S. C.), 1814.

Bridel (Louis), *Le droit des femmes et le mariage*. Paris, 1893.

Bridges (Thomas), [Letter referring to the Fuegians,] in *The South American Missionary Magazine*, vol. xiii. London, 1879.

—— ' Manners and Customs of the Firelanders ' ; in *A Voice for South America*, vol. xiii. London, 1866.

' Brihaspati,' trans. by J. Jolly ; in *The Sacred Books of the East*, vol. xxxiii· Oxford, 1889.

Brinton (D. G.), *American Hero-Myths*. Philadelphia, 1882.

—— *The Myths of the New World*. New York, 1868.

—— *Religions of Primitive Peoples*. New York & London, 1899.

Brissonius (B.), *De regio Persarum principatu*. Argentorati, 1710.

Britton, [On the Laws of England]. Ed. and trans. by F. M. Nichols. 2 vols. Oxford, 1865.

Brooke (Charles), *Ten Years in Saráwak*. 2 vols. London, 1866.

Brown (Thomas), *Lectures on the Philosophy of the Human Mind*. Edinburgh, 1834.

Browne (E. H.), *An Exposition of the Thirty-Nine Articles*. London, 1887.

Browne (*Sir* Thomas), *Christian Morals*. Cambridge, 1716.

Bruce (James), *Travels to discover the Source of the Nile*. 8 vols. Edinburgh, 1805.

Brugsch (Heinrich), *Die Ægyptologie*. Leipzig, 1891.

—— *A History of Egypt under the Pharaohs*. Trans. 2 vols. London, 1881.

—— *Im Lande der Sonne*. Berlin, 1886.

Brunner (Heinrich), *Deutsche Rechtsgeschichte*. 2 vols. Leipzig, 1887–92.

—— *Forschungen zur Geschichte des deutschen und französischen Rechtes*. Stuttgart, 1894.

Bruns (C. G.), *Fontes juris romani antiqui*. Ed. by Th. Mommsen and O. Gradenwitz. Friburgi i. B. & Lipsiae, 1893.

Brunus (Conradus), *De Legationibus libri quinque*. Moguntiae, 1548.

Brussel (N.), *Nouvel examen de l'usage général des fiefs en France, pendant les onzième, douzième, treizième et quatorzième siècles*. 2 vols. Paris, 1750.

Bry (Theodor de), *Narrative of Le Moyne, an Artist who accompanied the French Expedition to Florida under Laudonnière*, 1564. Trans. Boston, 1875.

Bryce (James), *Studies in History and Jurisprudence*. 2 vols. Oxford, 1901.

Buch (M.), ' Die Wotjäken ' ; in *Acta Soc. Scientiarum Fennicæ*, vol. xii. Helsingfors, 1883.

Buchanan (James), *Sketches of the History, Manners, and Customs of the North American Indians*. London, 1824.

Buchner (Max), *Kamerun*. Leipzig, 1887.

Buckle (H. T.), *History of Civilization in England*. 3 vols. London, 1894.

—— *Miscellaneous and Posthumous Works*. 3 vols. London, 1872.

Bücher (Karl), *Die Entstehung der Volkswirtschaft*. Tübingen, 1904.

Bühler (J. G.), *Grundriss der indo-arischen Philologie und Altertumskunde*. Ed. by J. G. B. Strassburg, 1896, &c.

Bulletins de la Société d'Anthropologie de Paris.

Bulmerincq (A.), *Das Asylrecht und die Auslieferung flüchtiger Verbrecher*. Dorpat, 1853.

'Bundahis (The),' trans. by E. W. West ; in *The Sacred Books of the East,* vol. v. Oxford, 1880.

Bunsen (C. C. J.), *Analecta Ante-Nicæna.* 3 vols. London, 1854.

—— *Christianity and Mankind.* 7 vols. London, 1854.

—— *De jure hereditario Atheniensium.* Gottingae, 1813.

Buonafede (A.), *Istoria critica e filosofica del suicidio.* Venezia, 1788.

Burchell (W. J.), *Travels in the Interior of Southern Africa.* 2 vols. London, 1822–24.

Burckhardt (J. L.), *Arabic Proverbs.* London, 1830.

——*.Notes on the Bedouins and Wahábys.* London, 1830.

—— *Travels in Arabia.* 2 vols. London, 1829.

—— *Travels in Nubia.* London, 1822.

Buret (F.), *La syphilis aujourd'hui et chez les anciens.* Paris, 1890.

—— *Syphilis in the Middle Ages and in Modern Times.* Trans. Philadelphia, 1895.

Burns (Robert), 'The Kayans of the North-West of Borneo'; in *The Journal of the Indian Archipelago and Eastern Asia,* vol. iii. Singapore, 1849.

Burrows (Guy), *The Land of the Pigmies.* London, 1898.

Burton (R. F.), *Abeokuta and the Camaroons Mountains.* 2 vols. London, 1863.

—— *The Book of the Thousand Nights and a Night.* 10 vols. London, 1885–86. (Quoted in ch. xliii.)

—— The same work. 12 vols. London, 1894.

—— *The City of the Saints.* London, 1861.

—— *First Footsteps in East Africa.* London, 1856.

—— *The Highlands of the Brazil.* 2 vols. London, 1869.

—— *The Lake Regions of Central Africa.* 2 vols. London, 1860.

—— *A Mission to Gelele, King of Dahome.* 2 vols. London, 1864.

—— *Personal Narrative of a Pilgrimage to Al-Madinah & Meccah.* 2 vols. London, 1898.

—— *Sind Revisited.* 2 vols. London, 1877.

—— *Sindh.* London, 1851.

—— *Two Trips to Gorilla Land and the Cataracts of the Congo.* 2 vols. London, 1876.

—— *Wit and Wisdom from West Africa.* London, 1865.

—— *Zanzibar.* 2 vols. London, 1872.

—— and Drake (Ch. F. Tyrwhitt), *Unexplored Syria.* 2 vols. London, 1872.

Butler (John), *Travels and Adventures in the Province of Assam.* London, 1855.

Butler (Joseph), *The Analogy of Religion, Dissertations, and Sermons.* London, 1893.

Buxtorf (J.), *Synagoga Judaica.* Basileæ, 1680.

Bynkershoek (C. van), *Observationum Juris Romani libri quatuor.* Lugduni Batavorum, 1710.

—— *Quæstionum juris publici libri duo.* Lugduni Batavorum, 1737.

Caesar (C. J.), *Opera omnia.* 5 vols. London, 1819.

Caillié (Réné), *Travels through Central Africa to Timbuctoo.* 2 vols. London, 1830.

Caird (Edward), *The Evolution of Religion.* 2 vols. Glasgow, 1894.

Caland (W.), *Die Altindischen Todten- und Bestattungsgebräuche.* Amsterdam, 1896.

Calcutta Review (The). Calcutta.

Caldwell (R.), *The Tinnevelly Shanars.* Madras, 1849.

Callaway (Henry), *The Religious System of the Amazulu.* Natal, 1868–70.

Calvert (A. F.), *The Aborigines of Western Australia.* London, 1894.

Calvin (J.), *Institutio Christianæ religionis.* 2 vols. Berolini, 1834–35.

Cameron (A. L. P.), ' Notes on some Tribes of New South Wales ' ; in *Jour. Anthr. Inst.* vol. xiv. London, 1885.

Campbell (F. A.), *A Year in the New Hebrides, Loyalty Islands, and New Caledonia.* Geelong & Melbourne, [1873].

Campbell (John), *A Personal Narrative of Thirteen Years' Service amongst the Wild Tribes of Khondistan.* London, 1864.

Campbell (John), *Travels in South Africa.* London, 1815.

—— *Travels in South Africa, being a Narrative of a Second Journey in the Interior of that Country.* 2 vols. London, 1822.

Candelier (H.), *Rio-Hacha et les Indiens Goajires.* Paris, 1893.

Canons and Decrees of the Council of Trent (The). Trans. by J. Waterworth. London, 1848.

' Canons enacted under King Edgar ' ; in *Ancient Laws and Institutes of England.* London, 1840.

Cape Monthly Magazine (The). Cape Town.

' Capitularium Caroli Magni et Ludovici Pii libri VII.' ; in Georgisch, *Corpus juris Germanici antiqui.* Halae Magdeburgicae, 1738.

Cardi (Le Comte C. N. de), ' Ju-Ju Laws and Customs in the Niger Delta ' ; in *Jour. Anthr. Inst.* vol. xxix. London, 1899.

Carmichael (Alexander), *Carmina Gadelica.* 2 vols. Edinburgh, 1900.

Carpenter (Edward), *Intermediate Types among Primitive Folk.* London, 1914.

Carrington (F. A.) and Payne (J.), *Reports of Cases argued and ruled at Nisi Prius, in the Courts of King's Bench, Common Pleas, & Exchequer.* 9 vols. London, 1825–41.

Caruthers (R. L.) and Nicholson (A. O. P.), *A Compilation of the Statutes of Tennessee.* Nashville (Tenn.), 1836.

Carver (J.), *Travels through the Interior Parts of North America.* London, 1781.

Casalis (E.), *The Basutos* London, 1861.

Casati (G.), *Ten Years in Eꝗuatoria.* Trans. 2 vols. London, 1891.

Castelnau (F. de), *Expédition dans les parties centrales de l'Amérique du Sud.* 7 vols. Paris, 1850–59.

Castrén (M. A.), *Nordiska resor och forskningar.* 5 vols. Helsingfors, 1852–58.

Catechism of the Council of Trent (The). Trans. by Th. A. Buckley. London, 1852.

Catlin (George), *Illustrations of the Manners, Customs, and Condition of the North American Indians.* 2 vols. London, 1876.

Catullus (C. V.), *Opera omnia.* 2 vols. Londini, 1822.

Cauvet (J.), ' De l'organisation de la famille à Athènes ' ; in *Revue de législation et de jurisprudence,* vol. xxiv. Paris, 1845.

Celtic Magazine (The). Inverness.

Certeux (A.) and Carnoy (E. H.), *L'Algérie traditionnelle.* Paris & Alger, 1884.

Chaikin (A.), *Apologie des Juifs*. Paris, 1887.
Chalmers (—), ' Cruelty to Animals ' ; in *The Methodist Magazine*, vol. ix. New York, 1826.
Chalmers (James), *Pioneer Life and Work in New Guinea* 1877–1894. London, 1895.
—— *Pioneering in New Guinea*. London, 1887.
—— and Gill (W. W.), *Work and Adventure in New Guinea*. London, 1885.
Chalmers (John), ' Chinese Natural Theology ' ; in *The China Review*, vol. v. Hongkong, 1876–77.
Chamberlain (A. F.), *The Child and Childhood in Folk-Thought*. New York, 1896.
Chamberlain (B. H.), *Things Japanese*. London, 1902.
Chambers (R.), *The Book of Days*. 2 vols. London & Edinburgh, [1862–64].
Chambers's Edinburgh Journal. Edinburgh & London.
Chanler (W. A.), *Through Jungle and Desert*. London & New York, 1896.
Chapelain (J.), *De la lecture des vieux romans*. Ed. by A. Feillet. Paris, 1870.
Chapman (J.),*Travels in the Interior of South Africa*. 2 vols. London, 1868.
Charlemagne, *Opera omnia*. 2 vols. (Migne, *Patrologiæ cursus*, vols. xcvii.–xcviii.) Parisiis, 1851.
Charles V. (*Emperor*), *Die Peinliche Gerichtsordnung*. Ed. by H. Zoepfl. Heidelberg, 1842.
Charlevoix (P. F. X. de), *The History of Paraguay*. Trans. 2 vols. London, 1769.
—— *A Voyage to North-America*. Trans. 2 vols. Dublin, 1766.
Chassebœuf de Volney (C. F.), *Travels through Syria and Egypt, in the Years 1783–1785*. Trans. 2 vols. London, 1788.
Chauveau (A.) and Hélie (F.), *Théorie du Code pénal*. 8 vols. Paris, 1852.
Chavanne (J.), *Die Sahara*. Wien, &c., 1879.
Cherry (R. R.), *Lectures on the Growth of Criminal Law in Ancient Communities*. London, 1890.
Chevalier (J.), *L'inversion sexuelle*. Lyon & Paris, 1893.
Chevers (Norman), *A Manual of Medical Jurisprudence for India*. Calcutta, 1870.
Cheyne (T. K.) and Black (J. S.), *Encyclopædia Biblica*. 4 vols. London, 1899–1903.
Childers (R. C.), *A Dictionary of the Pali Language*. London, 1875.
China Review (The). Hongkong.
Chinese Repository (The). Canton.
Chitty (Joseph), *A Treatise on the Laws of Commerce and Manufactures*. 4 vols. London, 1820–24.
Chlotar II. (*King*), ' Edictum de Synodo Parisiensi ' ; in Migne, *Patrologiæ cursus*, vol. lxxx. Paris, 1850.
Christian (F. W.), *The Caroline Islands*. London, 1899.
Christian Review (The). Rochester (N.Y.).
Chrysostom (*Saint* J.), *Opera omnia*. (Migne, *Patrologiæ cursus*, Ser. Graeca, vols. xlvii.–lxiv.) Parisiis, 1858–60.
' Chung Yung ' ; in Legge, *The Chinese Classics*, vol. i. Oxford, 1893.
Church Missionary Intelligencer (The). London.
Churchill (Ch. H.), *Mount Lebanon*. 3 vols. London, 1853.
Chwolsohn (D.), *Die Ssabier und der Ssabismus*. 2 vols. St. Petersburg, 1856.
Cibrario (Luigi), *Della economia politica del medio eve*. 2 vols. Torino, 1861.
—— *Della schiavitù e del servaggio*. 2 vols. Milano, 1868.

Cicero (M. Tullius), *Opera*. 17 vols. Londini, 1830.

Cieza de Leon (P. de), ' La Crónica del Perú [parte primera] ' ; in *Biblioteca de autores españoles*, vol. xxvi. Madrid, 1853.

—— *Segunda parte de la Crónica del Perú*. Madrid, 1880.

Clark (C.) and Finnelly (W.), *Reports of Cases decided in the House of Lords, on Appeals and Writs of Error*. London, 1835–47.

Clark (E. C.), *An Analysis of Criminal Liability*. Cambridge, 1880.

Clarke (R. F.), ' On Cruelty to Animals in its Moral Aspect ' ; in *The Month and Catholic Review*, vol. xxv. London, 1875.

Clarke (Samuel), *A Discourse concerning the Being and Attributes of God, the Obligations of Natural Religion, and the Truth and Certainty of the Christian Revelation*. London, 1738.

Clarkson (Thomas), *An Essay on the Slavery and Commerce of the Human Species*. London, 1788.

Clarus (Julius), *Opera omnia*. 2 vols. Genevae, 1739.

Clavigero (F. S.), *The History of Mexico*. Trans. 2 vols. London, 1807.

Clay (C. C.), *A Digest of the Laws of the State of Alabama*. Tuskaloosa, 1843.

Clay (W. Lowe), *The Prison Chaplain*. Cambridge, 1861.

Cleffelius (J. Chr.), *Antiquitates Germanorum potissimum septentrionalium*. Francofurti & Lipsiae, 1733.

Clement of Alexandria, *Opera omnia*. (Migne, *Patrologiæ cursus*, Ser. Graeca, vols. viii.–ix.) Parisiis, 1857.

Clement I. of Rome (*Saint*), *Opera omnia*. (Migne, *Patrologiæ cursus*, Ser. Graeca, vols. i.–ii.) Parisiis, 1857.

Cleveland (A. R.), *Woman under the English Law*. London, 1896.

Clifford (W. K.), *Lectures and Essays*. Ed. by Leslie Stephen and Frederick Pollock. London, 1886.

Clodd (Edward), *Tom Tit Tot*. London, 1898.

Cnut (*King*), ' The Laws of ' ; in *Ancient Laws and Institutes of England*. London, 1840.

Cobb (Th. R. R.), *An Inquiry into the Law of Negro Slavery in the United States of America*. Philadelphia & Savannah, 1858.

Cobbe (Frances P.), *The Modern Rack. Papers on Vivisection*. London, 1889.

Cochin (A.), *L'abolition de l'esclavage*. 2 vols. Paris, 1861.

Code Civil. Ed. by G. Griolet and Ch. Vergé. Paris, 1907.

Code Napoléon. Paris, 1853.

Code Noir (*Le*). Paris, 1767.

Code of Virginia (*The*). 2 vols. Richmond, 1849.

Code Pénal. 2 vols. Paris, 1810.

Codex Justinianus. See Justinian.

Codex Theodosianus. Ed. by G. Haenel. Bonnae, 1842.

Codice Penale per il Regno d'Italia (*Il*). Ed. by G. Crivellari. Torino, 1889.

Codigo Penal dos Estados Unidos do Brazil. Ed. by M. G. d'Alencastro Autran. Rio de Janeiro, 1892.

Código Penal reformado. Madrid, 1870.

Codrington (R. H.), *The Melanesians*. Oxford, 1891.

Cohn (L.), *Zur Lehre vom versuchten und unvollendeten Verbrechen*. Breslau, 1880.

Coke (Edward), *The Third Part of the Institutes of the Laws of England*. London, 1680.

Cole (H.), ' Notes on the Wagogo of German East Africa ' ; in *Jour. Anthr. Inst.* vol. xxxii. London, 1902.

Colebrooke (T. E.), *Miscellaneous Essays.* 3 vols. London, 1873.

Colenso (William), *On the Maori Races of New Zealand. S. l.*, [1865].

Collins (David), *An Account of the English Colony in New South Wales.* 2 vols. London, 1798–1802.

Colquhoun (A. R.), *Amongst the Shans.* London, 1885.

Compayré (G.), *L'évolution intellectuelle et morale de l'enfant.* Paris, 1893.

Comte (Auguste), *Cours de philosophie positive.* 6 vols. Paris, 1830–42.

Conférence de Bruxelles. La Haye, 1890.

Conférence internationale de la paix. La Haye 18 Mai–29 Juillet 1899. 4 parts. La Haye, 1899.

Confession of Faith (The), together with The Larger and Shorter Catechisms, composed by the Assembly of Divines at Westminster. London, 1717.

Connolly (R. M.), ' Social Life in Fanti-land ' ; in *Jour. Anthr. Inst.* vol. xxvi. London, 1897.

Constant (Benjamin), *De la religion.* 6 vols. Paris, 1824–32.

' Constitutiones Apostolicae ' ; in Bunsen, *Christianity and Mankind,* vol. vi. London, 1854.

Constitutiones Neapolitanæ sive Siculæ. See Frederick II.

Contemporary Review (The). London.

Convention signed at Geneva, August 22, 1864, for the Amelioration of the Condition of the Wounded in Armies in the Field. (Appendix No. VI. in Lorimer, *The Institutes of the Law of Nations,* vol. ii.) Edinburgh, 1884.

Cook (F. C.), *The Holy Bible,* ed. by F. C. C. 10 vols. London, 1871–81.

Cook (James), *A Journal of a Voyage round the World . . . in the Years* 1768–71. London, 1771.

—— *A Voyage to the Pacific Ocean . . . in the Years* 1776–80. 3 vols. London, 1875.

Cooke (G. Wingrove), *China.* London, 1858.

Cooper (T. T.), *The Mishmee Hills.* London, 1873.

Coquilhat (C.), *Sur le Haut-Congo.* Paris, 1888.

Coreal (F.), *Voyages aux Indes Occidentales.* Trans. 3 vols. Amsterdam, 1722.

Cosmos. Ed. by G. Cora. Torino.

Coudreau (H. A.), *La France équinoxiale.* 2 vols. Paris, 1887.

Couto de Magalhães (J. V.), *Trabalho preparatorio para aproveitamento do selvagem e do solo por elle occupado no Brazil. O selvagem.* Rio de Janeiro, 1876.

Couty (Louis), *L'esclavage au Brésil.* Paris, 1881.

Covarruvias a Leyva (D. de), *Opera omnia.* 2 vols. Antverpiæ, 1638.

Coxe (William), *Account of the Russian Discoveries between Asia and America.* London, 1804.

Cranz (David), *The History of Greenland.* Trans. 2 vols. London, 1820.

Crawfurd (John), *History of the Indian Archipelago.* 3 vols. Edinburgh, 1820.

Crawley (Ernest), *The Mystic Rose.* London, 1902.

Crell (J.), *Ethica Christiana.* Selenoburgi, [1663 ?].

Cremony (J. C.), *Life among the Apaches.* San Francisco, 1868.

Crooke (W.), *The North-Western Provinces of India.* London, 1897.

—— *The Popular Religion and Folk-Lore of Northern India.* 2 vols. Westminster, 1896.

—— *Things Indian.* London, 1906.

—— *The Tribes and Castes of the North-Western Provinces and Oudh.* 4 vols. Calcutta, 1896.

VOL. II 3 D

Crowther (S.) and Taylor (J. C.), *The Gospel on the Banks of the Niger*. London, 1859.

Crozals (J. de), *Histoire de la civilisation*. 2 vols. Paris, 1887.

Crozet (—), *Voyage to Tasmania, &c. in the Years* 1771–2. Trans. London, 1891.

' Cruelty to Animals in Naples ' ; in *The Saturday Review*, vol. lix. London, 1885.

Cruickshank (B.), *Eighteen Years on the Gold Coast of Africa*. 2 vols. London, 1853.

Cumming (C. F. Gordon), *In the Himalayas and on the Indian Plains*. London, 1884.

Cunningham (J. F.), *Uganda and its Peoples*. London, 1905.

Cunow (H.), *Die Verwandtschafts-Organisationen der Australneger*. Stuttgart, 1894.

Curr (E. M.), *The Australian Race*. 4 vols. Melbourne & London, 1886–87.

—— *Recollections of Squatting in Victoria*. Melbourne, &c., 1883.

Curtiss (S. I.), *Primitive Semitic Religion To-day*. London, 1902.

Curtius Rufus (Quintus), *De gestis Alexandri Magni*. Ed. by E. Foss. Lipsiae, 1862.

Cusack (M. F.), *A History of the Irish Nation*. London, 1876.

Cyprian (*Saint*), *Opera omnia*. (Migne, *Patrologiæ cursus*, vol. iv.) Parisiis, 1844.

' Dâdistân-î Dînîk (The),' trans. by E. W. West ; in *The Sacred Books of the East*, vol. xviii. Oxford, 1882.

Dahn (Felix), *Bausteine*. Berlin, 1879, &c.

Dalager (Lars), *Grønlandske Relationer*. Kiøbenhavn, *s.d.*

Dale (G.), ' An Account of the Principal Customs and Habits of the Natives inhabiting the Bondei Country ' ; in *Jour. Anthr. Inst.* vol. xxv. London, 1896.

Dall (W. H.), *Alaska and its Resources*. London, 1870.

Dalton (E. T.), *Descriptive Ethnology of Bengal*. Calcutta, 1872.

Damhouder (J. de), *Praxis rerum criminalium*. Antverpiæ, 1570.

Dandini (J.), ' A Voyage to Mount Libanus ' ; in Pinkerton, *Collection of Voyages and Travels*, vol. x. London, 1811.

Dapper (O.), *Africa*. Trans. London, 1670.

Dareste (R.), *Études d'histoire du droit*. Paris, 1889.

—— *Nouvelles Études d'histoire du droit*. Paris, 1902.

Dargun (L.), *Mutterrecht und Vaterrecht*. Leipzig, 1892.

—— 'Ursprung und Entwicklungs-Geschichte des Eigenthums' ; in *Zeitschr. f. vergleichende Rechtswiss.* vol. v. Stuttgart, 1884.

Darmesteter (James), *Essais orientaux*. Paris, 1883.

—— ' Introduction to the Vendîdâd ' ; in *The Sacred Books of the East*, vol. iv. Oxford, 1880.

—— *Ormazd et Ahriman*. Paris, 1877.

Darwin (Charles), ' Biographical Sketch of an Infant ' ; in *Mind*, vol. ii. London, 1877.

—— *The Descent of Man*. London, 1890.

—— *Journal of Researches into the Geology and Natural History of the Various Countries visited by H.M.S. Beagle*. London, 1839.

Daumas (E.), *La vie arabe et la société musulmane*. Paris, 1869.

Dautremer (J.), ' The Vendetta or Legal Revenge in Japan ' ; in *Trans. Asiatic Soc. Japan*, vol. xiii. Yokohama, 1885.

Davids (T. W. Rhys), *Hibbert Lectures on the Origin and Growth of Religion as illustrated by some Points in the History of Indian Buddhism*. London, 1881.

Davis (*Sir* John Francis), *China*. 2 vols. London, 1857.

Davis (W. W. H.), *El Gringo*. New York, 1857.

Dawson (James), *Australian Aborigines*. Melbourne, &c., 1881.

Decle (Lionel), *Three Years in Savage Africa*. London, 1898.

Decrusy (—) and others, *Recueil général des Anciennes Lois Françaises*. 29 vols. Paris, 1822–33.

Delécluze (E. J.), *Roland ou la Chevalerie*. 2 vols. Paris, 1845.

Delepierre (J. O.), *L'enfer décrit par ceux qui l'ont vu*. 2 pts. London, [1864–65].

Delitzsch (Friedrich), *Wo lag das Paradies ?* Leipzig, 1881.

Demangeat (Charles), *Histoire de la condition civile des étrangers en France dans l'ancien et dans le nouveau droit*. Paris, 1844.

Demidoff (E.), *A Shooting Trip to Kamchatka*. London, 1904.

Demosthenes, *Opera*. Ed. by J. T. Vœmelius. Parisiis, 1843.

Denham (Dixon) and Clapperton (Hugh), *Narrative of Travels and Discoveries in Northern and Central Africa*. London, 1826.

Denis (J.), *Histoire des théories et des idées morales dans l'antiquité*. 2 vols. Paris, 1856.

Denkschriften der kaiserlichen Akademie der Wissenschaften. Wien.

Dennett (R. E.), ' Laws and Customs of the Fjort or Bavili Family ' ; in *Jour. African Soc.* vol. i. London, 1902.

—— *Notes on the Folklore of the Fjort (French Congo)*. London, 1898.

Dennys (N. B.), *The Folk-Lore of China*. London, 1876.

Descartes (René), *Meditationes de prima philosophia*. Amstelodami, 1678.

Deschamps (É.), *Carnet d'un voyageur—Au pays des Veddas*. Paris, 1892.

Desmaze (Charles), *Les pénalités anciennes*. Paris, 1866.

Dessoir (Max), ' Zur Psychologie der Vita sexualis ' ; in *Allgemeine Zeitschrift für Psychiatrie und psychisch-gerichtliche Medicin*, vol. l. Berlin, 1893–94.

Deutsch (E.), ' Islam ' ; in *The Quarterly Review*, vol. cxxvii. London, 1869.

—— *Literary Remains*. London, 1874.

Deutsche Rundschau für Geographie und Statistik. Wien, &c.

Dewey (John), *The Study of Ethics*. Ann Arbor (Mich.), 1897.

Dhammapada (The). Trans. by F. Max Müller. (*The Sacred Books of the East*, vol. x.) Oxford, 1898.

Diaz del Castillo (Bernal), ' Verdadera historia de los sucesos de la conquista de la Nueva-España ' ; in *Biblioteca de autores españoles*, vol. xxvi. Madrid, 1853.

Dickinson (G. Lowes), *The Greek View of Life*. London, 1896.

Diderot (Denis), *Œuvres*. 7 vols. Paris, 1818–19.

Dieffenbach (E.), *Travels in New Zealand*. 2 vols. London, 1843.

Diels (Hermann), ' Ein orphischer Demeterhymnus ' ; in *Festschrift Theodor Gomperz dargebracht*. Wien, 1902.

Digby (K. H.), *Mores Catholici*. 3 vols. London, 1845–47.

Digesta. See Justinian.

'Dimetian Code (The) ' ; in *Ancient Laws and Institutes of Wales*. London, 1841.

Dimitroff (Z.), *Die Geringschätzung des menschlichen Lebens und ihre Ursachen bei den Naturvölkern*. Leipzig-Reudnitz, 1891.

'Dînâ-î Maînôg-î Khirad,' trans. by E. W. West ; in *The Sacred Books of the East*, vol. xxiv. Oxford, 1885.

Dio Cassius, *Historia Romana*. 4 vols. Lipsiae, 1863–64.

Dio Chrysostom, *Opera Græca*. 2 vols. Brunsvigae, 1844.

Diodorus Siculus, *Bibliotheca historica*. Ed. by C. Müllerus. 2 vols. Parisiis, 1842–44.

Diogenes Laertius, *De clarorum philosophorum vitis libri decem*. Ed. by C. G. Cobet. Parisiis, 1850.

Dionysius of Halicarnassus, *Antiquitatum Romanarum quæ supersunt*. Parisiis, 1886.

Dirksen (H. E.), *Civilistische Abhandlungen*. 2 vols. Berlin, 1820.

Dithmar of Merseburg, ' Chronicon ' ; in Pertz, *Monumenta Germaniæ historica*, vol. v. Hannoverae, 1839.

Dixon (W. H.), *New America*. Eighth edit. London, *s.d.*

Dobell (Peter), *Travels in Kamtschatka and Siberia*. 2 vols. London, 1830.

Dobrizhoffer (M.), *An Account of the Abipones*. Trans. 3 vols. London, 1822.

Dodge (R. Irving), *Our Wild Indians*. Hartford, 1882.

Döllinger (J. J. I.), *The Gentile and the Jew in the Courts of the Temple of Christ*. Trans. 2 vols. London, 1862.

Domenech (E.), *Seven Years' Residence in the Great Deserts of North America*. 2 vols. London, 1860.

Donaldson (James), ' On the Expiatory and Substitutionary Sacrifices of the Greeks ' ; in *Trans. Roy. Soc. Edinburgh*, vol. xxvii. Edinburgh, 1876.

—— ' The Position of Women among the Early Christians ' ; in *The Contemporary Review*, vol. lvi. London, 1889.

Donne (John), *Biathanatos*. London, 1648.

Doolittle (J.), *Social Life of the Chinese*. 2 vols. New York, 1867.

Dorman (R. M.), *The Origin of Primitive Superstitions*. Philadelphia, 1881.

Dorner (I. A.), *A System of Christian Doctrine*. Trans. 4 vols. Edinburgh, 1880–82.

Dorsey (J. Owen), ' Mourning and War Customs of the Kansas ' ; in *The American Naturalist*, vol. xix. Philadelphia, 1885.

—— ' Omaha Sociology ' ; in *Ann. Rep. Bur. Ethn.* vol. iii. Washington, 1884.

—— ' Siouan Folk-Lore ' ; in *The American Antiquarian*, vol. vii. Chicago, 1885.

—— ' Siouan Sociology ' ; in *Ann. Rep. Bur. Ethn.* vol. xv. Washington, 1897.

—— ' A Study of Siouan Cults ' ; in *Ann. Rep. Bur. Ethn.* vol. xi. Washington, 1894.

Doughty (C. M.), *Travels in Arabia Deserta*. 2 vols. Cambridge, 1888.

Douglas (R. K.), *Confucianism and Taouism*. London, 1889.

—— *Society in China*. London, 1894.

Dove (T.), ' Moral and Social Characteristics of the Aborigines of Tasmania ' ; in *The Tasmanian Journal of Natural Science, &c.* vol. i. Hobart Town, 1842.

Dreyer (I. C. H.), *Specimen juris publici Lubecensis*. Lubecae, 1761.

Driver (S. R.), *A Critical and Exegetical Commentary on Deuteronomy.* Edinburgh, 1895.

Drury (Rob.), *Journal during Fifteen Years' Captivity on the Island of Madagascar.* London, 1890.

Dublin Review (The). London.

Dubois (Félix), *Timbuctoo.* Trans. London, 1897.

Dubois (J. A.), *Description of the Character, Manners, and Customs of the People of India.* Trans. London, 1817.

Du Boys (Albert), *Histoire du droit criminel de l'Espagne.* Paris, 1870.

—— *Histoire du droit criminel des peuples modernes.* 3 vols. Paris, 1854–60.

Du Cange (C. Dufresne), ' Dissertations ou Réflexions sur l'histoire de S. Louys, du Sire de Joinville ' ; in Petitot, *Collection des Mémoires relatifs à l'histoire de France,* vol. iii. Paris, 1824.

—— *Glossarium ad scriptores mediæ et infimæ Latinitatis.* 6 vols. Parisiis, 1733–36.

Du Chaillu (P. B.), *Explorations and Adventures in Equatorial Africa.* London, 1861.

—— *A Journey to Ashango-Land.* London, 1867.

Duchesne (L.), *Christian Worship.* Trans. London, 1904.

Düben (G. von), *Om Lappland och Lapparne.* Stockholm, 1873.

Dümmler (Ernst), *Geschichte des Ostfränkischen Reichs.* 3 vols. Berlin, Leipzig, 1862–88.

Dufour (Pierre), *Histoire de la Prostitution.* 6 vols. Bruxelles, 1851–54.

Dumont (J.), *Corps universel diplomatique du droit des gens.* 8 vols. Amsterdam, 1726–31.

Dumont d'Urville (J. S. C.), *Voyage pittoresque autour du monde.* 2 vols. Paris, 1834–35.

Du-Moulin (Lewis), *Moral Reflections upon the Number of the Elect.* London, 1680.

Dunbar (J. B.), ' The Pawnee Indians ' ; in *The Magazine of American History,* vols. iv., v., viii. New York & Chicago, 1880, 1882.

Dunham (S. A.), *A History of the Germanic Empire.* 3 vols. London, 1834–35.

Durkheim (Émile), *De la division du travail social.* Paris, 1893.

—— ' Deux lois de l'évolution pénale ' ; in *L'année sociologique,* vol. iv., 1899–1900. Paris, 1901.

—— *Les formes élémentaires de la vie religieuse.* Paris, 1912.

—— ' La prohibition de l'inceste et ses origines ' ; in *L'année sociologique,* vol. i., 1896–97. Paris, 1898.

—— *Le suicide.* Paris, 1897.

Du Tertre (J. B.), *Histoire générale des Antilles.* 4 vols. Paris, 1667–71.

Duveyrier (Henri), *Exploration du Sahara.* Paris, 1864.

Dyer (T. F. Thiselton), *The Ghost World.* London, 1893.

Dymond (J.), *Essays on the Principles of Morality.* London, 1851.

Earl (G. W.), *Papuans.* London, 1853.

Eastman (Mary), *Dacotah.* New York, 1849.

Eclectic Magazine of Foreign Literature, Science, and Art (The). New York.

Edda Snorra Sturlusonar. See Snorri Sturluson.

Eden (*Sir* F. M.), *The State of the Poor ; or, an History of the Labouring Classes in England.* 3 vols. London, 1797.

Edinburgh Review (The). London.

Edkins (J.), *Religion in China.* London, 1878.

Edmund (*King*), ' The Laws of ' ; in *Ancient Laws and Institutes of England.* London, 1840.

Edward the Confessor (*King*), ' Leges ' ; in *Ancient Laws and Institutes of England.* London, 1840.

Edwards (Bryan), *The History of the British West Indies.* 5 vols. London, 1819.

Edwards (Jonathan), *Works.* 8 vols. London, 1817.

Egede (Hans), *A Description of Greenland.* Trans. London, 1845.

Eicken (H. von), *Geschichte und System der mittelalterlichen Weltanschauung.* Stuttgart, 1887.

Ellinger (G.), *Das Verhältniss der öffentlichen Meinung zu Wahrheit und Lüge im 10. 11. und 12. Jahrhundert.* Sondershausen, 1884.

Elliot (*Sir* Henry M.), *Memoirs on the History, Folk-Lore, and Distribution of the Races of the North Western Provinces of India.* 2 vols. London, 1869.

Elliot (*Sir* W.), ' On the Characteristics of the Population of Central and Southern India ' ; in *Jour. Ethn. Soc. London,* new ser. vol. i. London, 1869.

Elliott (Henry W.), *Our Arctic Province Alaska and the Seal Islands.* New York, 1886.

—— ' Report on the Seal Islands of Alaska ' ; in *Tenth Census of the United States.* Washington, 1884.

Ellis (A. B.), *The Ewe-speaking Peoples of the Slave Coast of West Africa.* London, 1890.

—— *The Land of Fetish.* London, 1883.

—— *The Tshi-speaking Peoples of the Gold Coast of West Africa.* London, 1887.

—— *The Yoruba-speaking Peoples of the Slave Coast of West Africa.* London, 1894.

Ellis (Havelock), *The Criminal.* London, 1895.

—— *Man and Woman.* London, 1904.

—— *Studies in the Psychology of Sex.* 5 vols. Philadelphia, 1901–06. (The third edition of vol. i., ' Sexual Inversion,' published in 1915, referred to in the Additional Notes.)

—— *Ursprung und Entwicklung der Prostitution.* (Reprinted from *Mutterschutz,* vol. iii.) *S. l. & d.*

—— and Symonds (J. A.), *Das konträre Geschlechtsgefühl.* Trans. Leipzig, 1896.

Ellis (W. Gilmore), ' The Amok of the Malays ' ; in *The Journal of Mental Science,* vol. xxxix. London, 1893.

Ellis (William), *History of Madagascar.* 2 vols. London, 1838.

—— *Narrative of a Tour through Hawaii.* London, 1827.

—— *Polynesian Researches.* 2 vols. London, 1829.

—— The same work. 4 vols. London, 1859. (This edition referred to, if not indicated otherwise.)

Elphinstone (Mountstuart), *An Account of the Kingdom of Caubul.* 2 vols. London, 1839.

—— *The History of India.* 2 vols. London, 1843.

—— The same work. Ed. by E. B. Cowell. London, 1866.

Elton (Ch. I.), *Origins of English History.* London, 1890.

Elton (F.), ' Notes on Natives of the Solomon Islands ' ; in *Jour. Anthr Inst.* vol. xvii. London, 1888.

Emin Pasha in Central Africa. Trans. London, 1888.

Emmons (Nathanael), *Works.* Ed. by J. Ide. 6 vols. Boston, 1842.

Encyclopædia Britannica. Ninth edition. Edinburgh, 1875, &c.

Encyclopédie Méthodique. 167 vols. Paris, 1782–1832.

Epictetus, *Dissertationum libri IV, Enchiridion et Fragmenta.* 5 vols. Lipsiae, 1799–1800.

Erasmus (Desiderius), *Adagiorum chiliades quatuor.* Coloniae Allobrogum, 1612.

Erman (Adolf), *A Handbook of Egyptian Religion.* Trans. London, 1907.

—— *Life in Ancient Egypt.* Trans. London, 1894.

Erman (G. A.), *Reise um die Erde.* 3 vols. Berlin, 1833–48.

Erskine (J. E.), *Journal of a Cruise among the Islands of the Western Pacific.* London, 1853.

Erskine of Carnock (John), *Principles of the Law of Scotland.* Ed. by J. Rankine. Edinburgh, 1890.

Escayrac de Lauture (—d'), *Die afrikanische Wüste.* Trans. Leipzig, 1867.

Eschwege (L. W. von), *Brasilien.* 2 vols. Braunschweig, 1830.

Esmein (A.), *Cours élémentaire d'histoire du droit français.* Paris, 1898.

—— *Histoire de la procédure criminelle en France.* Paris, 1882.

Esquirol (E.), *Des maladies mentales.* 2 vols. Paris, 1838.

Ethelred (*King*), ' The Laws of ' ; in *Ancient Laws and Institutes of England.* London, 1840.

Euripides, *Fabulæ.* Ed. by T. Fix. Parisiis, 1843.

—— *Fragmenta.* Ed. by F. G. Wagner. Parisiis, 1846.

Eusebius, *Opera.* 6 vols. (Migne, *Patrologiæ cursus,* Ser. Graeca, vols. xix–xxiv.) Parisiis, 1857.

Evans (E. P.), ' Ethical Relations between Man and Beast ' ; in *The Popular Science Monthly,* vol. xlv. New York, 1894.

Ewald (G. H. A. von), *The Antiquities of Israel.* Trans. London, 1876.

Ewers (J. Ph. G.), *Das älteste Recht der Russen.* Dorpat & Hamburg, 1826.

Eyre (E. J.), *Journals of Expeditions of Discovery into Central Australia.* 2 vols. London, 1845.

Faber (Ernst), *A Systematical Digest of the Doctrines of Confucius.* Hong-kong, 1875.

Fabrice (H. von), *Die Lehre von der Kindsabtreibung und vom Kindsmord.* Erlangen, 1868.

Falkner (Thomas), *A Description of Patagonia.* Hereford, 1774.

Farnell (L. R.), *The Cults of the Greek States.* Oxford, 1896, &c. *In progress.*

—— ' Sociological Hypotheses concerning the Position of Women in Ancient Religion ' ; in *Archiv für Religionswissenschaft,* vol. vii. Leipzig, 1904.

Farrar (F. W.), *Mercy and Judgment.* London, 1881.

Farrer (J. A.), *Military Manners and Customs.* London, 1885.

—— *Paganism and Christianity.* London & Edinburgh, 1891.

—— *Primitive Manners and Customs,* London, 1879.

Favyn (André), *The Theater of Honour and Knight-Hood.* Trans. London, 1623.

Fawcett (F.), ' The Nâyars of Malabar ' ; in the Madras Government Museum's *Bulletin,* vol. iii. Madras, 1901.

—— *On the Saoras.* (Reprinted from *The Journal of the Anthropological Society of Bombay,* vol. i.) Bombay, 1888.

Featherman (A.), *Social History of the Races of Mankind*. 7 vols. London, 1881–91.

Felkin (R. W.), ' Notes on the For Tribe of Central Africa ' ; in *Proceed. Roy. Soc. Edinburgh*, vol. xiii. Edinburgh, 1886.

—— ' Notes on the Madi or Moru Tribe of Central Africa ' ; in *Proceed. Roy. Soc. Edinburgh*, vol. xii. Edinburgh, 1884.

—— ' Notes on the Waganda Tribe of Central Africa ' ; in *Proceed. Roy. Soc. Edinburgh*, vol. xiii. Edinburgh, 1886.

Ferrero (G.), ' Les formes primitives du travail ' ; in *Revue scientifique*, ser. iv. vol. v. Paris, 1896.

Ferri (Enrico), *Criminal Sociology*. London, 1895.

Festus (S. Pompejus), *De verborum significatione quæ supersunt*. Ed. by C. O. Muellerus. Lipsiae, 1839.

Feuerbach (P. J. A. von), *Aktenmässige Darstellung merkwürdiger Verbrechen*. 2 vols. Giessen, 1828–29.

—— *Caspar Hauser*. Trans. London, 1834.

—— *Kritik des Kleinschrodischen Entwurfs zu einem peinlichen Gesetzbuche für die Chur-Pfalz-Bayrischen Staaten*. 2 vols. Giesen, 1804.

—— *Lehrbuch des gemeinen in Deutschland gültigen Peinlichen Rechts*. Ed. by C. J. A. Mittermaier. Giessen, 1847.

—— *Ueber die Strafe als Sicherungsmittel vor künftigen Beleidigungen des Verbrechers*. Chemnitz, 1800.

—— *Ueber die Unterdrückung und Wiederbefreiung Europens*. [München & Leipzig], 1813.

Feyfer (D. de), *Verhandeling over den Kindermoord*. Utrecht, 1866.

Fichte (J. G.), *Reden an die deutsche Nation*. Leipzig, 1824.

—— *The Science of Ethics*. Trans. London, 1897.

—— *Das System der Sittenlehre*. Jena & Leipzig, 1798.

—— *Ueber den Begriff des wahrhaften Krieges in Bezug auf den Krieg im Jahre* 1813. Tübingen, 1815.

Fielding Hall (H.), *The Soul of a People*. `London, 1902.

Filangieri (Gaetano), *La scienza della legislazione*. 6 vols. Milano, 1822.

Finck (H. T.), *Primitive Love and Love-Stories*. New York, 1899.

Finger (A.), *Compendium des Oesterreichischen Rechtes—Das Strafrecht*. 2 vols. Berlin, 1894–95.

Finsch (Otto), *Neu-Guinea*. Bremen, 1865.

Fischer (Chr. A.), *Bergreisen*. 2 vols. Leipzig, 1804–05.

Fischer (J.), ' Notes sur l'intelligence des singes ' ; in *Revue scientifique*, vol. xxxiii. (ser. iii. vol. vii.). Paris, 1884.

Fisher (*Captain*), ' Memoir of Sylhet, Kachar, &c.' ; in *Jour. Asiatic Soc. Bengal*, vol. ix. pt. ii. Calcutta, 1840.

Fiske (John), *Outlines of Cosmic Philosophy*. 2 vols. London, 1874.

Fison (L.) and Howitt (A. W.), *Kamilaroi and Kurnai*. Melbourne & Sydney, 1880.

Flacourt (É. de), *Histoire de la grande isle Madagascar*. Paris, 1661.

Fleming (William), *A Manual of Moral Philosophy*. London, 1867.

Fleta, seu Commentarius Juris Anglicani. London, 1735.

Fleury (C.), *An Historical Account of the Manners and Behaviour of the Christians*. Trans. London, 1698.

Flügel (G.), *Mani*. Leipzig, 1862.

Folk-Lore. London.

Folk-Lore Journal (The). London.

Folk-Lore Record (The). London.

Fonseca (L. A. da), *A escravidão, o clero e o abolicionismo.* Bahia, 1887.

Forbes (Anna), *Insulinde.* Edinburgh & London, 1887.

Forbes (C. J. F. S.), *British Burma and its People.* London, 1878.

Forbes (David), ' On the Aymara Indians of Bolivia and Peru ' ; in *Jour. Ethn. Soc. London,* new ser. vol. ii. London, 1870.

Forbes (F. E.), *Dahomey and the Dahomans.* 2 vols. London, 1851.

Forbes (H. O.), *A Naturalist's Wanderings in the Eastern Archipelago.* London, 1885.

Foreman (John), *The Philippine Islands.* London, 1890.

Fornander (Abraham), *An Account of the Polynesian Race.* 3 vols. London, 1878–85.

Forsman (J.), *Bidrag till läran om skadestånd i brottmål enligt finsk rätt.* Helsingfors, 1893.

Forster (G.), *A Voyage round the World.* 2 vols. London, 1777.

Forsyth (J.), *The Highlands of Central India.* London, 1871.

Fortnightly Review (The). London.

Foster (Michael), *A Report of . . . Crown Cases.* London, 1776.

Foucart (P.), *Des associations religieuses chez les Grecs.* Paris, 1873.

Fountain (P.) and Ward (Thomas), *Rambles of an Australian Naturalist.* London, 1907.

Fowler (Thomas), *Progressive Morality.* London, 1895.

—— See Wilson (J. M.) and Fowler.

Fowler (W. Warde), *The Roman Festivals of the Period of the Republic.* London, 1899.

Franciscus a Victoria, *Relectiones Theologicæ.* Lugduni, 1587.

François (H. von), *Nama und Damara Deutsch-Süd-West-Afrika.* Magdeburg, [1896].

Frank (J. P.), *System einer vollständigen medicinischen Polizey.* 9 vols. Mannheim, &c., 1784–1827.

Frankel (Z.), *Grundlinien des mosaisch-talmudischen Eherechts.* Leipzig, 1860.

Franklin (B.), *Works.* Ed. by J. Sparks. 10 vols. Boston, 1836–40.

Franklin (John), *Narrative of a Journey to the Shores of the Polar Sea.* London, 1823.

Fraser (J. B.), *Journal of a Tour through Part of the Snowy Range of the Himálá Mountains.* London, 1820.

Fraser (John), *The Aborigines of New South Wales.* Sydney, 1892.

Frauenstädt (Paul), *Blutrache und Todtschlagsühne im Deutschen Mittelalter.* Leipzig, 1881.

Frazer (Sir J. G.), *Adonis Attis Osiris.* London, 1906.

—— ' Certain Burial Customs as illustrative of the Primitive Theory of the Soul ' ; in *Jour. Anthr. Inst.* vol. xv. London, 1886.

—— *The Dying God.* London, 1911.

—— ' Folk-Lore in the Old Testament ' ; in *Anthropological Essays presented to E. B. Tylor.* Oxford, 1907.

—— *The Golden Bough.* 3 vols. London, 1900.

—— *Lectures on the Early History of the Kingship.* London, 1905.

—— *The Magic Art.* 2 vols. London, 1911.

—— ' The Origin of Totemism ' ; in *The Fortnightly Review,* new ser. vol. lxv. London, 1899.

—— *Pausanias's Description of Greece.* 6 vols. London, 1898.

Frazer (*Sir* J. G.), *Totemism*. Edinburgh, 1887.

—— *Totemism and Exogamy*. 4 vols. London, 1910.

Frederick II. (*Emperor*), 'Constitutiones Neapolitanæ sive Siculæ'; in Lindenbrog, *Codex legum antiquarum*. Francofurti, 1613.

Freeman (E. A.), *Comparative Politics*. London, 1896.

—— *The Reign of William Rufus*. 2 vols. Oxford, 1882.

Freytag (G. W.), *Arabum Proverbia*. 3 vols. Bonnae ad Rhenum, 1838–43.

Friedländer (L.), *Darstellungen aus der Sittengeschichte Roms*. 2 vols. Leipzig, 1901.

Friedrichs (Karl), ' Einzeluntersuchungen zur vergleichenden Rechtswissenschaft '; in *Zeitschr. f. vergleichende Rechtswiss*. vol. x. Stuttgart, 1892.

—— ' Mensch und Person '; in *Das Ausland*, vol. lxiv. Stuttgart, 1891.

Fries (J. F.), *Neue oder anthropologische Kritik der Vernunft*. 3 vols. Heidelberg, 1828–31.

Friis (J. A.), *Lappisk Mythologi*. Christiania, 1871.

Fritsch (Gustav), *Drei Jahre in Süd-Afrika*. Breslau, 1868.

—— *Die Eingeborenen Süd-Afrika's*. Breslau, 1872.

Fryer (G. E.), *The Khyeng People of the Sandoway District, Arakan*. (Reprinted from *Jour. Asiatic Soc. Bengal*.) Calcutta, 1875.

Fryer (John), *A New Account of East-India and Persia*. London, 1698.

Fuld (L.), ' Das Asylrecht im Alterthum und Mittelalter '; in *Zeitschr. f. vergleichende Rechtswiss*. vol. vii. Stuttgart, 1887.

Fulgentius (*Saint*), ' De fide '; in Migne, *Patrologiæ cursus*, vol. lxv. Parisiis, 1847.

Funk (——), ' Die Entwicklung des Osterfastens '; in *Theologische Quartalschrift*, vol. lxxv. Tübingen, 1893.

Furness (W. H.), *The Home-Life of Borneo Head-Hunters*. Philadelphia, 1902.

Fustel de Coulanges (N. D.), *La Cité antique*. Paris, 1864. (Quoted in vol. ii.)

—— The same work. Paris, 1866. (Quoted in vol. i.)

Fytche (A.), *Burma Past and Present*. 2 vols. London, 1878.

Gadelius (Bror), *Om tvångstankar*. Lund, 1896.

Gage (Matilda J.), *Woman, Church and State*. Chicago, 1893.

Gaidoz (H.), ' Le suicide '; in *Mélusine*, vol. iv. Paris, 1888–89.

Gaius, *Institutionum juris civilis commentarii quattuor*. Ed. and trans. by E. Poste. Oxford, 1890.

Galton (Francis), ' Eugenics '; in *Sociological Papers*, vols. i.–ii., 1904–05. London, 1905–06.

—— *Inquiries into Human Faculty and its Development*. London, 1883.

Gans (E.), *Das Erbrecht in weltgeschichtlicher Entwickelung*. 4 vols. Berlin, &c., 1824–35.

Garcilasso de la Vega, *First Part of the Royal Commentaries of the Yncas*. Trans. ed. by C. R. Markham. 2 vols. London, 1869–71.

Gardiner (A. H.), ' Egyptian Ethics and Morality '; in Hastings, *Encyclopædia of Religion and Ethics*, vol. v. Edinburgh, 1912.

Garnett (Lucy M. J.), *The Women of Turkey and their Folk-Lore*. 2 vols. 1890–91.

Garofalo (R.), *La Criminologie*. Paris, 1890.

Garraud (R.), *Traité théorique et pratique du droit pénal Français*. 6 vols. Paris, 1898–1902.

Gason (S.), ' The Manners and Customs of the Dieyerie Tribe ' ; in Woods, *The Native Tribes of South Australia.* Adelaide, 1879.

Gass (W.), *Geschichte der christlichen Ethik.* 3 vols. Berlin, 1881–87.

' Gautama,' trans. by G. Bühler ; in *The Sacred Books of the East,* vol. ii. Oxford, 1897.

Gautier (Léon), *La Chevalerie.* Paris, 1884.

Geiger (K. A.), *Der Selbstmord im klassischen Altertum.* Augsburg, 1888.

Geiger (W.), *Civilization of the Eastern Irānians in Ancient Times.* Trans. 2 vols. London, 1885–86.

Geiseler (—), *Die Oster-Insel.* Berlin, 1883.

Gelli (J.), *Il duello.* Firenze, 1886.

Gellius (Aulus), *Noctes Atticæ.* Ed. by A. Lion. 2 vols. Gottingae, 1824.

Gennep (A. van), *Les rites de passage.* Paris, 1911.

—— *Tabou et totémisme à Madagascar.* Paris, 1904.

Geographical Journal (The). London.

Georgi (J. G.), *Russia.* Trans. 4 vols. London, 1780–83.

Georgisch (P.), *Corpus juris Germanici antiqui.* Halae Magdeburgicae, 1738.

Gerhohus, ' De aedificio Dei ' ; in Migne, *Patrologiæ cursus,* vol. cxciv. Parisiis, 1855.

Geusius (J.), *Victimæ Humanæ.* 2 vols. Groningae, 1675.

Geyer (A.), *Die Lehre von der Nothwehr.* Jena, 1857.

Ghani (M. A.), ' Social Life and Morality in India ' ; in *Internat. Jour. of Ethics,* vol. vii. London, 1897.

Ghillany (F. W.), *Die Menschenopfer der alten Hebräer.* Nürnberg, 1842.

Gibb (John), ' The Christian Church and War ' ; in *The British Quarterly Review,* vol. lxxiii. London, 1881.

Gibbon (Edward), *The History of the Decline and Fall of the Roman Empire.* Ed. by W. Smith. 8 vols. London, 1854–55.

Gibbons (A. S. H.), *Exploration and Hunting in Central Africa.* London, 1898.

Gibbs (George), ' Tribes of Western Washington and Northwestern Oregon' ; in *U.S. Geographical and Geological Survey of the Rocky Mountain Region :—Contributions to North American Ethnology,* vol. i. Washington, 1877.

Giddings (F. H.), *The Principles of Sociology.* New York, 1896.

Gide (Paul), *Étude sur la condition privée de la femme.* Ed. by A. Esmein. Paris, 1885.

Gieseler (J. C. L.), *Text-Book of Ecclesiastical History.* Trans. 3 vols. Philadelphia, 1836.

Giles (H. A.), *Strange Stories from a Chinese Studio.* 2 vols. London, 1880.

Gill (W. W.), *Life in the Southern Isles.* London, 1876.

—— *Myths and Songs from the South Pacific.* London, 1876.

Gillen (F. J.), ' Notes on Some Manners and Customs of the Aborigines of the McDonnell Ranges belonging to the Arunta Tribe ' ; in *Report on the Work of the Horn Scientific Expedition to Central Australia,* pt. iv. London & Melbourne, 1896.

Gilmour (James), *Among the Mongols.* London, [1892].

Ginoulhiac (Ch.), *Histoire du régime dotal.* Paris, 1842.

Ginsburg (Ch. D.), *The Essenes.* London, 1864.

Girard (F.), *Manuel élémentaire de droit romain.* Paris, 1901.

Girard de Rialle (J.), *La mythologie comparée.* Paris, 1878.

Gisborne (William), *The Colony of New Zealand.* London, 1888.

AUTHORITIES QUOTED

Gizycki (G. von), *An Introduction to the Study of Ethics.* Adapted from the German by Stanton Coit. London, 1891.

Glaber (R.), ' Historiarum sui temporis libri quinque ' ; in Bouquet, *Recueil des Historiens des Gaules et de la France,* vol. x. Paris, 1760.

Gladstone (W. E.), *Studies on Homer and the Homeric Age.* 3 vols. Oxford, 1858.

Glanvilla (R. de), *Tractatus de Legibus et Consuetudinibus Regni Angliæ.* Londini, [1555 ?].

—— The same work. Trans. by John Beames. London, 1812.

Glasson (Ernest), *Le mariage civil et le divorce.* Paris, 1880.

Glimpses of the Eastern Archipelago. Trans. Singapore, 1894.

Globus. Illustrirte Zeitschrift für Länder- und Völkerkunde. Braunschweig,&c.

Gobineau (A. de), *The Moral and Intellectual Diversity of Races.* Trans. Philadelphia, 1856.

Goblet d'Alviella (Eugène), *Hibbert Lectures on the Origin and Growth of the Conception of God.* London, 1892.

Godwin (William), *Enquiry concerning Political Justice.* 2 vols. London, 1796.

Goehlert (V.), ' Die geschlechtsverschiedenheit der Kinder in den Ehen ' ; in *Zeitschr. f. Ethnol.* vol. xiii. Berlin, 1881.

Göpfert (F. A.), *Moraltheologie.* Vol. i. Paderborn, 1899.

Goesius (W.), *Rei agrariæ auctores legesque variæ.* Amstelredami, 1674.

Götte (W.), *Das Delphische Orakel.* Leipzig, 1839.

Göttinger Studien. Göttingen.

Göttingische gelehrte Anzeigen. Göttingen.

Goiten (E.), *Das Vergeltungsprincip im biblischen und talmudischen Strafrecht.* Frankfurt a.M., 1893.

Goldast (M.), *Collectio consuetudinum et legum imperialium.* Francofordiae ad Moenum, 1613.

Goldziher (Ignaz), *Abhandlungen zur arabischen Philologie.* 2 vols. Leiden, 1896–99.

—— *Muhammedanische Studien.* 2 vols. Halle a.S., 1889–90.

Gomara (F. Lopez de), ' Primera parte de la historia general de las Indias ' ; in *Biblioteca de autores españoles,* vol. xxii. Madrid, 1852.

Gomme (G. L.), *Ethnology in Folklore.* London, 1892.

—— ' Some Traditions and Superstitions connected with Buildings ' ; in *The Antiquary,* vol. iii. London, 1881.

Goodell (William), *The American Slave Code in Theory and Practice.* New York, 1853.

—— *Slavery and Anti-Slavery.* New York, 1852.

Goos (C.), *Forelæsninger over den almindelige Retslære.* 2 vols. Kjøbenhavn, 1889–94.

Gopčević (S.), *Oberalbanien und seine Liga.* Leipzig, 1881.

' Gospel of the Nativity of Mary (The) ' ; in *Ante-Nicene Christian Library,* vol. xvi. Edinburgh, 1870.

' Gospel of Pseudo-Matthew (The) ' ; in *Ante-Nicene Christian Library,* vol. xvi. Edinburgh, 1870.

Gotlands-Lagen. Ed. by C. J. Schlyter. (*Corpus Juris Sueo-Gotorum Antiqui,* vol. vii.) Lund, 1852.

Gråberg di Hemsö (J.), *Specchio geografico, e statistico dell' impero di Marocco.* Genova, 1834.

Grágás, Hin forna lögbók Íslendínga. 2 vols. Havniae, 1829.

Grange (——), ' Extracts from the Journal of an Expedition into the Naga Hills '; in *Jour. Asiatic Soc. Bengal*, vol. ix. pt. ii. Calcutta, 1840.

Granger (F. S.), ' The Moral Life of the Early Romans '; in *Internat. Jour. of Ethics*, vol. vii. London, 1897.

—— *The Worship of the Romans.* London, 1895.

Granville (R. K.) and Roth (F. N.), ' Notes on the Jekris '; in *Jour. Anthr. Inst.* vol. xxviii. London, 1899.

Gratian, *Decretum.* (Migne, *Patrologiæ cursus*, vol. clxxxvii.) Parisiis, 1855.

Graul (K.), *Reise nach Ostindien.* 5 vols. Leipzig, 1854–56.

Gray (J. H.), *China.* 2 vols. London, 1878.

Green (J. R.), *History of the English People.* 4 vols. London, 1879–81.

Greenwood (Thomas), *The First Book of the History of the Germans.* London, 1836.

Gregor (Walter), *Notes on the Folk-lore of the North-East of Scotland.* London, 1881.

Gregorovius (Ferdinand), *Wanderings in Corsica.* Trans. 2 vols. London, 1855.

Gregory I. (*Saint*), surnamed *the Great, Opera omnia.* 5 vols. (Migne, *Patrologiæ cursus*, vols. lxxv.–lxxix.) Parisiis, 1849.

Gregory III., ' Judicia congrua poenitentibus '; in Labbe-Mansi, *Sacrorum Conciliorum collectio*, vol. xii. Florentiæ, 1766.

Gregory IX., ' Decretales '; in *Corpus juris canonici*, ed. by A. Friedberg, vol. ii. Lipsiæ, 1881.

Gregory Nazianzen (*Saint*), *Opera omnia.* 4 vols. (Migne, *Patrologiæ cursus*, Ser. Græca, vols. xxxv.–xxxviii.) Parisiis, 1857–58.

Gregory of Tours (*Saint*), *Opera omnia.* (Migne, *Patrologiæ cursus*, vol. lxxi.) Parisiis, 1849.

Grey (George), *Journals of Two Expeditions of Discovery in North-West and Western Australia.* 2 vols. London, 1841.

—— *Polynesian Mythology.* Auckland, 1885.

Grierson (G. A.), *Bihār Peasant Life.* Calcutta, 1885.

Griesinger (W.), *Mental Pathology and Therapeutics.* Trans. London, 1867.

Griffis (W. E.), *Corea.* London, 1882.

—— *The Mikado's Empire.* New York, 1883.

—— *The Religions of Japan.* London, 1895.

Griffith (William), ' Journal of a Visit to the Mishmee Hills in Assam '; in *Jour. Asiatic Soc. Bengal*, vol. vi. Calcutta, 1837.

Grimm (Jacob), *Deutsche Rechtsalterthümer.* Ed. by A. Heusler and R. Hübner. 2 vols. Leipzig, 1899.

—— *Kinder- und Hausmärchen. Grosse Ausgabe.* Berlin, 1870.

—— *Kleinere Schriften.* 8 vols. Berlin, 1864–90.

—— *Reinhart Fuchs.* Berlin, 1834.

—— *Teutonic Mythology.* Trans. 4 vols. London, 1882–88.

Grinnell (G. B.), *Pawnee Hero Stories and Folk-Tales.* New York, 1889.

—— *The Story of the Indian.* London, 1896.

Gronovius (J.), *Thesaurus Græcarum antiquitatum.* 12 vols. Lugduni Batavorum, 1697–1702.

Groot (J. J. M. de), *The Religious System of China.* Leyden, 1892, &c. *In progress.*

Grosse (Ernst), *Die Formen der Familie und die Formen der Wirthschaft.* Freiburg i.B. & Leipzig, 1896.

Grote (John), *A Treatise on the Moral Ideals*. Ed. by J. B. Mayor. Cambridge, 1876.

Grotius (Hugo), *De jure belli et pacis libri tres*. With a trans. by W. Whewell. 3 vols. Cambridge, 1853.

Gruppe (Otto), *Die griechischen Culte und Mythen*. Vol. i. Leipzig, 1887.

Guazzini (S.), *Tractatus ad defensam inquisitorum, carceratorum reorum, & condemnatorum super quocunque crimine*. Venetiis, 1639.

Gudgeon (W. E.), ' Maori Religion '; in *Jour. Polynesian Soc.* vol. xiv. Wellington, 1905.

Gudmundsson (V.) and Kålund (Kr.), ' Sitte. Skandinavische Verhältnisse '; in Paul, *Grundriss der germanischen Philologie*, vol. iii. Strassburg, 1900.

Günther (L.), *Die Idee der Wiedervergeltung in der Geschichte und Philosophie des Strafrechts*. 3 vols. Erlangen, 1889–95.

Guérard (B. E. C.), *Collection des Cartulaires de France. Tomes I–II. Cartulaire de l'Abbaye de Saint-Père de Chartres*. 2 vols. Paris, 1840.

Guibal (Georges), *Histoire du sentiment national en France pendant la guerre de Cent ans*. Paris, 1875.

Guibertus de Novigento, ' Monodiarum sive de vita sua libri tres '; in Bouquet, *Recueil des Historiens des Gaules et de la France*, vol. xii. Paris, 1781.

Guinnard (A.), *Three Years' Slavery among the Patagonians*. Trans. London, 1871.

Gumilla (J.), *El Orinoco ilustrado*. 2 vols. Madrid, 1745.

Gummere (F. B.), *Germanic Origins*. London, 1892.

Guppy (H. B.), *The Solomon Islands*. London, 1887.

Gurney (J. J.), *Observations on the Distinguishing Views and Practices of the Society of Friends*. London, 1834.

Gutzlaff (Charles), *A Sketch of Chinese History*. 2 vols. London, 1834.

Guyau (J. M.), *Esquisse d'une morale sans obligation ni sanction*. Paris, 1885.

' Gwentian Code (The) '; in *Ancient Laws and Institutes of Wales*. London, 1841.

Haberland (C.), ' Der Kindermord als Volkssitte '; in *Globus*, vol. xxxvii. Braunschweig, 1880.

—— ' Ueber Gebräuche und Aberglauben beim Essen '; in *Zeitschr. f. Völkerpsychologie und Sprachwissenschaft*, vols. xvii.–xviii. Leipzig, 1887–88.

Haddon (A. C.), ' The Ethnography of the Western Tribe of Torres Straits '; in *Jour. Anthr. Inst.* vol. xix. London, 1890.

—— *Head-Hunters*. London, 1901.

—— *Magic and Fetishism*. London, 1906.

—— in *Reports of the Cambridge Anthropological Expedition to Torres Straits*, vol. v. Cambridge, 1904.

Haeckel (Ernst), *A Visit to Ceylon*. Trans. London, 1883.

Hagen (B.), *Unter den Papua's*. Wiesbaden, 1899.

Hagman (Lucina), ' Från samskolan '; in *Humanitas*, vol. ii. Helsingfors, 1897.

Hahn (C.), *Kaukasische Reisen und Studien*. Leipzig, 1896.

Hahn (J. G. von), *Albanesische Studien*. 3 vols. Jena, 1854.

Hahn (Theophilus), *Tsuni-Goam. The Supreme Being of the Khoi-Khoi*. London, 1881.

Hale (Horatio), ' The Iroquois Sacrifice of the White Dog ' ; in *The American Antiquarian and Oriental Journal*, vol. vii. Chicago, 1885.

—— *U.S. Exploring Expedition under the Command of Ch. Wilkes. Vol. VI. Ethnography and Philology.* Philadelphia, 1846.

Hale (Matthew), *The History of the Pleas of the Crown.* 2 vols. London, 1800.

Halévy (J.), *Mélanges de critique et d'histoire relatifs aux peuples sémitiques.* Paris, 1883.

Hall (C. F.), *Arctic Researches and Life among the Esquimaux.* New York, 1865.

Hall (G. Stanley), ' Children's Lies ' ; in *The American Journal of Psychology*, vol. iii. Worcester, 1890–91.

—— ' A Study of Anger ' ; in *The American Journal of Psychology*, vol. x. Worcester, 1898–99.

Hall (W. E.), *A Treatise on International Law.* Oxford, 1890. (Referred to in vol. i.)

—— The same work. Ed. by J. B. Atlay. Oxford, 1904. (Referred to in vol. ii.)

Hallam (Henry), *View of the State of Europe during the Middle Ages.* 3 vols. London, 1837. (Referred to in ch. xxvii.)

—— The same work. 3 vols. London, 1860.

Halleck (H. W.), *International Law.* Ed. by Sir Sherston Baker. 2 vols. London, 1893.

Hamilton (Augustus), *Maori Art.* Wellington, 1896–1901.

Hamilton (William), *Lectures on Metaphysics and Logic.* 2 vols. Edinburgh & London, 1877.

Hamilton (William J.), *Researches in Asia Minor, Pontus, and Armenia.* 2 vols. London, 1842.

Hammurabi (*King of Babylon*), *The Code of Laws promulgated by.* Trans. by C. H. W. Johns. Edinburgh, 1903.

Hanoteau (A.) and Letourneux (A.), *La Kabylie et les coutumes Kabyles.* 3 vols. Paris, 1872–73.

Hansard (T. C.), *The Parliamentary Debates from 1803 to the Present Time.* London, 1812, &c.

Hardeland (A.), *Dajacksch-deutsches Wörterbuch.* Amsterdam, 1859.

Hardisty (W. L.), ' The Loucheux Indians ' ; in *Smithsonian Report*, 1866. Washington, 1867.

Hardman (E. T.), ' Notes on some Habits and Customs of the Natives of the Kimberley District, Western Australia ' ; in *Proceed. Roy. Irish Academy*, ser. iii. vol. i. Dublin, 1889–91.

Hardy (R. Spence), *Eastern Monachism.* London, 1850.

—— *A Manual of Budhism, in its Modern Development.* London, 1880.

Harkness (H.), *A Description of a Singular Aboriginal Race inhabiting the Neilgherry Hills.* London, 1832.

Harmon (D. W.), *A Journal of Voyages and Travels in the Interior of North America.* Andover, 1820.

Harnack (A.), *History of Dogma.* Trans. 7 vols. London, 1894–99.

—— ' Manichaeism ' ; in *Encyclopædia Britannica*, vol. xv. Edinburgh, 1883.

Harris (S.), ' The Christian Doctrine of Labor ' ; in *The New Englander*, vol. xxiv. New Haven, 1865.

Harris (S. F.), *Principles of the Criminal Law.* London, 1899.

Harris (Thomas) and Johnson (R.), *Reports of Cases argued and determined in the General Court and Court of Appeals of the State of Maryland, from 1800 to 1805, inclusive.* 4 vols. Annapolis, 1821–27.

Harris (W. Cornwallis), *The Highlands of Æthiopia.* 3 vols. London, 1844.

Harrison (Ch.), ' Religion and Family among the Haidas ' ; in *Jour. Anthr. Inst.* vol. xxi. London, 1892.

Harrison (Jane Ellen), *Prolegomena to the Study of Greek Religion.* Cambridge, 1903.

Hartknoch (Christ.), *Alt- und Neues Preussen.* 2 vols. Franckfurt & Leipzig, 1684.

Hartland (E. Sidney), ' Concerning the Rite at the Temple of Mylitta ' ; in *Anthropological Essays presented to E. B. Tylor.* Oxford, 1907.

—— *The Legend of Perseus.* 3 vols. London, 1894–96.

—— *Ritual and Belief.* London, 1914.

Hartley (David), *Observations on Man.* 2 vols. London, 1810.

—— *Theory of the Human Mind, on the Principle of the Association of Ideas ; with Essays relating to the Subject of it. By Joseph Priestley.* London, 1790.

Hartmann (R.), *Die menschenähnlichen Affen.* Leipzig, 1883.

Hartshorne (B. F.), ' The Weddas ' ; in *The Indian Antiquary,* vol. viii. Bombay, 1879.

Hartung (J. A.), *Die Religion der Römer.* 2 vols. Erlangen, 1836.

Harvard Law Review. Cambridge (Mass.).

Hastings (J.), *A Dictionary of the Bible.* 5 vols. Edinburgh, 1899–1904.

—— *Encyclopædia of Religion and Ethics.* Edinburgh, 1908, &c. *In progress.*

Haug (B.), *Die Alterthümmer der Christen.* Stuttgart, 1785.

Haupt (Paul), ' Die zwölfte Tafel des babylonischen Nimrod-Epos ' ; in *Beiträge zur Assyriologie,* vol. i. Leipzig, 1889.

Hawtrey (S. H. C.), ' The Lengua Indians of the Paraguayan Chaco ' ; in *Jour. Anthr. Inst.* vol. xxxi. London, 1901.

Haxthausen (A. von), *The Russian Empire.* Trans. 2 vols. London, 1856.

—— *Transcaucasia.* Trans. London, 1854.

Haynes (E. S. P.), *Religious Persecution.* London, 1904.

Haywood (John) and Cobbs (R. L.), *The Statute Laws of the State of Tennessee.* 2 vols. Knoxville, 1831.

Hearn (W. E.), *The Aryan Household.* London & Melbourne, 1879.

Hearne (S.), *A Journey from Prince of Wales's Fort to the Northern Ocean.* Dublin, 1796.

Heber (R.), *Narrative of a Journey through the Upper Provinces of India.* 2 vols. London, 1828.

Hedley (J. C.), ' Dr. Mivart on Faith and Science ' ; in *The Dublin Review,* ser. iii. vol. xviii. London, 1887.

Hefele (C. J.), *Beiträge zur Kirchengeschichte, Archäologie und Liturgik.* 2 vols. Tübingen, 1864.

—— *A History of the Councils of the Church.* Trans. 5 vols. Edinburgh, 1871–96.

Heffter (A. W.), *Das Europäische Völkerrecht der Gegenwart.* Ed. by F. H. Geffken. Berlin, 1882.

Hegel (G. W. F.),¸*Grundlinien der Philosophie des Rechts.* Ed. by G. J. P. J. Bolland. Leiden, 1902.

—— *Philosophy of Right.* Trans. by S. W. Dyde. London, 1896.

Hehn (V.), *The Wanderings of Plants and Animals from their First Home.* Ed. by J. S. Stallybrass. London, 1888.

Hellwald (F. von), *Die menschliche Familie.* Leipzig, 1889.

Hellwig (A.), *Das Asylrecht der Naturvölker.* Berlin, 1903.

Helmold (—), *Chronik der Slaven.* Trans. Berlin, 1852.

Helps (*Sir* Arthur), *Some Talk about Animals and their Masters.* London, 1883.

—— *The Spanish Conquest in America.* 4 vols. London, 1855–61.

Helvetius (C. A.), *De l'Homme, de ses facultés intellectuelles et de son éducation.* 2 vols. London, 1773.

Henault (Ch. J. F.), *Nouvel abregé chronologique de l'histoire de France.* Paris, 1752.

Henderson (John), *Observations on the Colonies of N.S. Wales and Van Diemen's Land.* Calcutta, 1832.

Henke (A.), *Lehrbuch der gerichtlichen Medicin.* Ed. by C. Bergmann. Berlin, 1859.

Henke (E.), *Grundriss einer Geschichte des deutschen peinlichen Rechts und der peinlichen Rechtswissenschaft.* 2 vols. Sulzbach, 1809.

Henkenius (H.), ' Entstehung und Verbreitung der Anthropophagie ' ; in *Deutsche Rundschau für Geographie und Statistik,* vol. xv. Wien, &c., 1893.

Hennepin (Louis), *Description de la Louisiane.* Paris, 1683.

—— *A New Discovery of a Vast Country in America, . . . between New France and New Mexico.* Trans. 2 vols. London, 1698.

—— *Nouvelle Découverte d'un très Grand Pays situé dans l'Amerique, entre Le Nouveau Mexique, et La Mer Glaciale.* Utrecht, 1697.

Henry I. (*King*), ' Leges ' ; in *Ancient Laws and Institutes of England.* London, 1840.

Hepp (F. C. Th.), *Die Zurechnung auf dem Gebiete des Civilrechts insbesondere die Lehre von den Unglücksfällen.* Tübingen, 1838.

Heriot (George), *Travels through the Canadas.* London, 1807.

Hermann (C. F.), *Disputatio de terminis eorumque religione apud Græcos.* Gottingae, 1846.

—— *Lehrbuch der gottesdienstlichen Alterthümer der Griechen.* Ed. by K. B. Stark. Heidelberg, 1858.

—— *Lehrbuch der Griechischen Privatalterthümer.* Ed. by H. Blümner. Freiburg i.B. & Tübingen, 1882.

—— *Lehrbuch der Griechischen Rechtsalterthümer.* Ed. by Th. Thalheim. (*Lehrbuch der Griechischen Antiquitäten,* vol. ii. pt. i.) Freiburg i.B. & Tübingen, 1884.

Hernsheim (Franz), *Beitrag zur Sprache der Marshall-Inseln.* Leipzig, 1880.

Herodotus, *Historiarum libri IX.* Ed. by G. Dindorfius. Parisiis, 1844.

—— The same work. English version, ed. by G. Rawlinson, Col. Rawlinson, and Sir J. G. Wilkinson. 4 vols. London, 1875.

Herrera (Antonio de), *The General History of the West Indies.* Trans. 6 vols. London, 1825–26.

Hershon (P. I.), *Treasures of the Talmud.* London, 1882.

Hertz (E.), *Voltaire und die französische Strafrechtspflege im achtzehnten Jahrhundert.* Stuttgart, 1887.

Hertz (R.), ' Contribution à une étude sur la représentation collective de la mort ' ; in *L'année sociologique,* vol. x., 1905–06. Paris, 1907.

Herzog (J. J.), *Realencyclopädie für protestantische Theologie.* Ed. by A. Hauck. Leipzig, 1896, &c. *In progress.*

Herzog (J. J.), and Plitt (G. L.), *Realencyclopädie für protestantische Theologie.* 18 vols. Leipzig, 1877–88.

Herzog (R.), *Rücktritt vom Versuch und thätige Reue.* Würzburg, 1889.

Hesiod, *Carmina.* Ed. by F. S. Lehrs. Parisiis, 1840.

Hessey (J. A.), *Sunday.* London, 1889.

Hettner (H.), *Geschichte der französischen Literatur im achtzehnten Jahrhundert.* Braunschweig, 1894.

Hetzel (H.), *Die Todesstrafe in ihrer kulturgeschichtlichen Entwicklung.* Berlin, 1870.

Heuglin (M. Th. von), *Reise nach Abessinien.* Jena, 1868.

Hewitt (J. N. B.), ' The Iroquoian Concept of the Soul ' ; in *Jour. of American Folk-Lore,* vol. viii. Boston & New York, 1895.

Hickson (S. J.), *A Naturalist in North Celebes.* London, 1889.

Hilary (*Saint*), *Opera omnia.* 2 vols. (Migne, *Patrologiæ cursus,* vol. ix.–x.) Parisiis, 1844–45.

Hildebrand (R.), *Recht und Sitte auf den verschiedenen wirtschaftlichen Kulturstufen.* Vol. i. Jena, 1896.

Hildebrandt (J. M.), ' Ethnographische Notizen über Wakámba und ihre Nachbaren ' ; in *Zeitschr. f. Ethnologie,* vol. x. Berlin, 1878.

Hilhouse (William), *Indan Notices.* *S.l.,* 1825.

Hill (Richard) and Thornton (George), *Notes on the Aborigines of New South Wales.* Sydney, 1892.

Hillebrandt (Alfred), ' Eine Miscelle aus dem Vedaritual ' ; in *Zeitschr. der Deutschen Morgenländischen Gesellschaft,* vol. xl. Leipzig, 1886.

Hinde (S. L. and Mrs. Hildegarde), *The Last of the Masai.* London, 1901.

Hippel (Robert von), *Die Thielquälerei in der Strafgesetzgebung.* Berlin, 1891.

Hirn (Yrjö), *The Origins of Art.* London, 1900.

Hirschfeld (H.), ' Remarks on the Etymology of Šabbāth ' ; in *Jour. Roy. Asiatic Soc.* London, 1896.

Hirschfeld (Magnus), *Die Homosexualität des Mannes und des Weibes.* Berlin, 1914.

Hislop (S.), *Papers relating to the Aboriginal Tribes of the Central Provinces.* Ed. by R. Temple. *S.l.,* 1866.

Hitopadesa. Trans. by F. Pincott. London, 1880.

Hlothhære and Eadric (*Kings*), ' The Laws of ' ; in *Ancient Laws and Institutes of England.* London, 1840.

Hobbes (Thomas), *Leviathan.* Oxford, 1881.

Hobhouse (L. T.), *Morals in Evolution.* 2 vols. London, 1906.

Hodge (Charles), *Systematic Theology.* 3 vols. London & Edinburgh, 1871–73.

Hodgson (B. H.), *Miscellaneous Essays relating to Indian Subjects.* 2 vols. London, 1880.

Hodgson (C. P.), *Reminiscences of Australia.* London, 1846.

Hodson (T. C.), ' The " Genna " amongst the Tribes of Assam ' ; in *Jour. Anthr. Inst.* vol. xxxvi. London, 1906.

Høffding (H.), *Etik.* København, 1897.

Höfler (M.), ' Krankheits-Dämonen ' ; in *Archiv f. Religionswiss.* vol. ii. Freiburg i.B., 1899.

Högström (M. P.), *Beskrifning öfver de til Sveriges Krona lydande Lap marker.* Stockholm, [1745 ?].

Hoffman (W. J.), ' The Menomini Indians ' ; in *Ann. Rep. Bur. Ethn.* vol. xiv. Washington, 1896.

Hoffmann (René), *La notion de l'Être suprême chez les peuples non civilisés.* Genève, 1907.

Holbach (P. H. D. d'), *Système de la nature.* Ed. by D. Diderot. 2 vols. Paris, 1821.

Holden (W. C.), *The Past and Future of the Kaffir Races.* London, [1866].

Holinshed (R.), *Chronicles of England, Scotland, and Ireland.* 6 vols. London, 1807–08.

Holland (F. M.), *The Reign of the Stoics.* New York, *s.d.*

Holland (Thomas A.), *A Time of War.* Brighton, 1855.

Hollis (A. C.), *The Masai.* Oxford, 1905.

Holm (G.), ' Ethnologisk Skizze af Angmagsalikerne ' ; in *Meddelelser om Grönland,* vol. x. Kjøbenhavn, 1888.

Holmberg (H. J.), ' Ethnographische Skizzen über die Völker des russischen Amerika ' ; in *Acta Soc. Scientiarum Fennicæ,* vol. iv. Helsingfors, 1856.

Holmes (O. W.), *The Common Law.* London, 1882.

Holst (H. von), *The Constitutional and Political History of the United States.* Trans. 5 vols. Chicago, 1876–89.

Holtzendorff (F. von), *Encyclopädie der Rechtswissenschaft.* 2 vols. Leipzig, 1873–76.

Holtzmann (Adolf), *Deutsche Mythologie.* Ed. by A. Holder. Leipzig, 1874.

Holub (E.), ' Central South African Tribes ' ; in *Jour. Anthr. Inst.* vol. x. London, 1881.

—— ' Die Ma-Atabele ' ; in *Zeitschr. f. Ethnol.* vol. xxv. Berlin, 1893.

—— *Seven Years in South Africa.* Trans. 2 vols. London, 1881.

Holzman (M.), ' Sünde und Sühne in den Rigvedahymnen und den Psalmen'; in *Zeitschr. f. Völkerpsychologie und Sprachwissenschaft,* vol. xv. Berlin, 1884.

Home and Foreign Review (The). London.

Homer, *Carmina.* Parisiis, 1838.

Hommel (Fritz), *Die Semitischen Völker und Sprachen.* Leipzig, 1881–83.

Honoré de Sainte Marie, *Dissertations historiques et critiques sur la chevalerie.* Paris, 1718.

Hood (T. H.), *Notes of a Cruise in H.M.S. " Fawn " in the Western Pacific.* Edinburgh, 1863.

Hooker (J. D.), *Himalayan Journals.* 2 vols. London, 1855.

Hooker (Richard), *The Ecclesiastical Polity and other Works.* 3 vols London, 1830.

Hooper (W. H.), *Ten Months among the Tents of the Tuski.* London, 1853.

Hopkins (E. W.), *The Religions of India.* London, 1896.

Horatius Flaccus (Q.), *Opera omnia.* 4 vols. Londini, 1825.

Horwicz (Adolf), *Psychologische Analysen auf physiologischer Grundlage.* 2 vols. Halle & Magdeburg, 1872–78.

Hose (Charles), ' A Journey up the Baram River to Mount Dulit and the Highlands of Borneo ' ; in *The Geographical Journal,* vol. i. London, 1893.

—— and McDougall (W.), *The Pagan Tribes of Borneo.* 2 vols. London, 1912.

—— and McDougall, ' The Relations between Men and Animals in Sarawak ' ; in *Jour. Anthr. Inst.* vol. xxxi. London, 1901.

Hourst (——), *Sur le Niger et au pays des Touaregs.* Paris, 1898.

Howard (B. Douglas), *Life with Trans-Siberian Savages.* London, 1893.

Howard (G. E.), *A History of Matrimonial Institutions.* 3 vols. Chicago & London, 1904.

Howell (T. B. and T. J.). See *State Trials.*

Howitt (A. W.), ' Australian Group Relations '; in *Smithsonian Report,* 1883. Washington, 1885.

—— *The Native Tribes of South-East Australia.* London, 1904.

—— ' The Native Tribes of South-East Australia '; in *Folk-Lore,* vol. xvii. London, 1906.

—— ' On Australian Medicine Men '; in *Jour. Anthr. Inst.* vol. xvi. London, 1887.

—— ' On some Australian Beliefs '; in *Jour. Anthr. Inst.* vol. xiii. London, 1884.

—— ' On some Australian Ceremonies of Initiation '; in *Jour. Anthr. Inst.* vol. xiii. London, 1884.

Hozumi (Nobushige), *Ancestor-Worship and Japanese Law.* Tokyo, Osaka & Kyoto, 1913.

' Hsiâo King (The),' trans. by J. Legge ; in *The Sacred Books of the East,* vol. iii. Oxford, 1879.

Hubert (H.) and Mauss (Marcel), ' Essai sur la nature et la fonction du sacrifice '; in *L'année sociologique,* vol. ii., 1897–98. Paris, 1899.

Huc (E. R.), *The Chinese Empire.* Trans. London, 1859.

—— *Travels in Tartary, Thibet, and China.* Trans. 2 vols. London, *s.d.*

Hübbe-Schleiden (W.), *Ethiopien. Studien über West-Afrika.* Hamburg, 1879.

Hüllmann (K. D.), *Stædtewesen des Mittelalters.* 4 vols. Bonn, 1826–29.

Humboldt (A. von), *Personal Narrative of Travels to the Equinoctial Regions of the New Continent.* Trans. 7 vols. London, 1814–29.

Hume (*Baron* David), *Commentaries on the Law of Scotland, respecting the Description and Punishment of Crimes.* 2 vols. Edinburgh, 1797.

Hume (David), *Philosophical Works.* Ed. by T. H. Green and T. H. Grose. 4 vols. London, 1874–75.

Hunt (A. E.), ' Ethnographical Notes on the Murray Islands '; in *Jour. Anthr. Inst.* vol. xxviii. London, 1899.

Hunter (W. A.), *A Systematical and Historical Exposition of Roman Law.* London, 1885.

Hunter (W. W.), *The Annals of Rural Bengal.* 3 vols. London, 1868–72.

Hutcheson (Francis), *An Essay on the Nature and Conduct of the Passions and Affections. With Illustrations on the Moral Sense.* London, 1730.

—— *An Inquiry into the Original of our Ideas of Beauty and Virtue ; In Two Treatises . . . II. Concerning Moral Good and Evil.* London, 1738.

—— *A System of Moral Philosophy.* 2 vols. London, 1755.

Hyades (P.) and Deniker (J.), *Mission scientifique du Cap Horn,* 1882–1883. *Tome VII. Anthropologie, Ethnographie.* Paris, 1891.

Hyltén-Cavallius (G. O.), *Wärend och Wirdarne.* 2 vols. Stockholm, 1863–68.

Ignatius (*Saint*), ' Epistolae '; in Migne, *Patrologiæ cursus,* Ser. Graeca, vol. v. Parisiis, 1857.

Im Thurn (E. F.), *Among the Indians of Guiana.* London, 1883.

Immerwahr (Walter), *Die Kulte und Mythen Arkadiens.* Vol. i. Leipzig, 1891.

Indian Antiquary (The), a Journal of Oriental Research. Bombay.

Indo-Chinese Gleaner (The). 3 vols. Malacca, 1818–21.

Ine (*King*), ' The Laws of '; in *Ancient Laws and Institutes of England.* London, 1840.

Inge (W. R.), *Society in Rome under the Cæsars.* London, 1888.

Inglis (John), *In the New Hebrides.* London, 1887.

Ingram (J. K.), *A History of Slavery and Serfdom.* London, 1895.

Innes (Cosmo), *Scotland in the Middle Ages.* Edinburgh, 1860.

Institutes of Vishnu (The). Trans. by J. Jolly (*The Sacred Books of the East,* vol. vii.) Oxford, 1880.

Institutiones. See Justinian.

Instructions for the Government of Armies of the United States in the Field. (Appendix No. 1 in Lorimer, *The Institutes of the Law of Nations,* vol. ii.) Edinburgh, 1884.

International Journal of Ethics. London & Philadelphia.

Internationales Archiv für Ethnographie. Ed. by J. D. E. Schmeltz. Leiden.

Irenaeus (*Saint*), *Contra hæreses libri quinque.* (Migne, *Patrologiæ cursus,* Ser. Graeca, vol. vii.) Parisiis, 1857.

Isaeus, ' Orationes ' ; in *Oratores Attici,* ed. by C. Müller, vol. i. Parisiis,1847.

Isambert (F. A.) and others, *Recueil général des Anciennes Lois Françaises.* 29 vols. Paris, 1822–33.

Isocrates, *Orationes.* Ed. J. G. Baiter. Parisiis, 1846.

Itard (E. M.), *An Historical Account of the Discovery and Education of a Savage Man.* Trans. London, 1802.

Ives (George), *The Classification of Crimes.* [London], 1904.

Iyer (S. A.), ' Nayādis of Malabar ' ; in the Madras Government Museum's *Bulletin,* vol. iv. Madras, 1901.

Jackson (A. V. W.), *An Avesta Grammar.* Part i. Stuttgart, 1892.

Jackson (J. G.), *An Account of Timbuctoo and Housa.* See 'Abd-es-Salâm Shabeeny.

Jacob (Georg), *Das Leben der vorislâmischen Beduinen.* Berlin, 1895.

Jacob (K. G.), ' Der muslimische Fastenmonat Ramaḍân ' ; in *VI. Jahresbericht der Geographischen Gesellschaft zu Greifswald,* vol. i. 1893–1896. Greifswald, 1896.

Jacob (William), *An Historical Inquiry into the Production and Consumption of the Precious Metals.* 2 vols. London, 1831.

Jacobs (Joseph), *Studies in Biblical Archæology.* London, 1894.

Jacobs (Julius), *Eenigen Tijd onder de Baliërs.* Batavia, 1883.

Jähns (Max), *Ueber Krieg, Frieden und Kultur.* Berlin, 1893.

Jaffur Shurreef, *Qanoon-e-Islam, or the Customs of the Mussulmans of India.* Trans. by G. A. Herklots. Madras, 1863.

Jagor (F.), *Travels in the Philippines.* [Trans.] London, 1875.

Jahrbuch für sexuelle Zwischenstufen mit besonderer Berücksichtigung der Homosexualität. Ed. by M. Hirschfeld. Leipzig.

Jamblichus, *De mysteriis liber.* Ed. by A. Parthey. Berolini, 1857.
—— *De Pythagorica vita liber.* Ed. by A. Westermann. Parisiis, 1850.

James (Edwin), *Account of an Expedition from Pittsburgh to the Rocky Mountains, performed in the Years 1819 and '20, under the Command of S. H. Long.* 2 vols. Philadelphia, 1823.

James (William), *The Principles of Psychology.* 2 vols. London, 1891.

Jameson (*Mrs.*), *A Common-Place Book of Thoughts, Memories, and Fancies.* London, 1877.

Jamieson (G.), ' Marriage Laws ' ; in *The China Review,* vol. x. Hongkong, 1881–82.

Janka (Karl), *Der strafrechtliche Notstand.* Erlangen, 1878.

Jarcke (C. E.), *Handbuch des gemeinen deutschen Strafrechts.* 3 vols. Berlin, 1827–30.

Jarves (J. J.), *History of the Hawaiian Islands.* Honolulu, 1872.

Jastrow (Morris), 'The Original Character of the Hebrew Sabbath'; in *The American Journal of Theology,* vol. ii. Chicago, 1898.

—— *The Religion of Babylonia and Assyria.* Boston, 1898.

Jātaka Tales, Buddhist Birth Stories. Trans. by T. W. Rhys Davids. London, 1880.

Jellinghaus (Th.), 'Sagen, Sitten und Gebräuche der Munda-Kolhs in Chota Nagpore'; in *Zeitschr. f. Ethnol.* vol. iii. Berlin, 1871.

Jensen (P.), *Assyrisch-Babylonische Mythen und Epen.* Berlin, 1900.

—— *Die Kosmologie der Babylonier.* Strassburg, 1890.

Jeremias (A.), *Die babylonisch-assyrischen Vorstellungen vom Leben nach dem Tode.* Leipzig, 1887.

—— *Izdubar-Nimrod. Eine altbabylonische Heldensage.* Leipzig, 1891.

Jerez (Francisco de), 'Verdadera relacion de la conquista del Perú y provincia del Cuzco'; in *Biblioteca de autores españoles,* vol. xxvi. Madrid, 1853.

Jerome (*Saint*), *Opera omnia.* 11 vols. (Migne, *Patrologiæ cursus,* vols. xxii.–xxx.) Parisiis, 1845–46.

Jessen (E. J.), *Afhandling om de Norske Finners og Lappers Hedenske Religion.* København, 1767.

Jevons (F. B.), *An Introduction to the History of Religion.* London, 1896.

Jewish Encyclopedia (The). 12 vols. New York & London, 1901–06.

Jhering (R. von), *Geist des römischen Rechts.* 3 vols. Leipzig, 1852–78.

—— *Das Schuldmoment im römischen Privatrecht.* Giessen, 1867.

—— *Der Zweck im Recht.* 2 vols. Leipzig, 1877–83.

Jochelson (W.), *The Koryak Religion and Myth.* (*The Jesup North Pacific Expedition,* vol. vi. pt. i.) Leiden & New York, 1905.

Jodl (F.), *Lehrbuch der Psychologie.* Stuttgart, 1896.

Johnston (*Sir* H. H.), *British Central Africa.* London, 1897.

—— 'The Ethics of Cannibalism'; in *The Fortnightly Review,* new ser. vol. xlv. London, 1889.

—— *The Kilima-njaro Expedition.* London, 1886.

—— *The River Congo.* London, 1884.

—— *The Uganda Protectorate.* 2 vols. London, 1902.

Johnstone (J. C.), *Maoria.* London, 1874.

Joinville (——), 'On the Religion and Manners of the People of Ceylon'; in *Asiatick Researches,* vol. vii. Calcutta, 1801.

Jolly (J.), 'Beiträge zur indischen Rechtsgeschichte'; in *Zeitschr. der Deutschen Morgenländischen Gesellsch.* vol. xliv. Leipzig, 1890.

—— 'Recht und Sitte'; in Bühler, *Grundriss der indo-arischen Philologie,* vol. ii. Strassburg, 1896.

Jones (*Sir* William), 'The Tenth Anniversary Discourse'; in *Asiatick Researches,* vol. iv. Calcutta, 1795.

Jordanes, *Romana et Getica.* Ed. by Th. Mommsen. Berolini, 1882.

Josephus, *Opera.* Ed. by G. Dindorfius. 2 vols. Parisiis, 1845–47.

Joubert (J.), *Pensées, essais et maximes.* 2 vols. Paris, 1842.

Jourdan (A. J. L.) and others, *Recueil général des Anciennes Lois Françaises.* 29 vols. Paris, 1822–33.

Journal and Proceedings of the Royal Society of New South Wales. Sydney & London.

Journal Asiatique. Paris.
—— *des Museum Godeffroy.* Hamburg.
—— *of the African Society.* London.
—— *of American Folk-Lore (The).* Boston & New York.
—— *of the American Oriental Society.* New York.
—— *of the (Royal) Anthropological Institute of Great Britain and Ireland (The).* London.
—— *of the Asiatic Society of Bengal.* Calcutta.
—— *of the Ceylon Branch of the Royal Asiatic Society.* Colombo.
—— *of the Ethnological Society of London.*
—— *of the Indian Archipelago and Eastern Asia.* Singapore.
—— *of the Polynesian Society.* Wellington.
—— *of the Royal Asiatic Society.* London.
—— *of the Royal Geographical Society of London.*
—— *of the Straits Branch of the Royal Asiatic Society.* Singapore.
Jousse (D.), *Traité de la justice criminelle de France.* 4 vols. Paris, 1771.
Jouuencel (Le), [A Romance commenced by J. de Soreuil, and completed by J. Tibergeau, M. Morin, and N. Riolai.] Paris, 1493.
Joyce (P. W.), *A Social History of Ancient Ireland.* 2 vols. London, 1903.
Juan (G.) and Ulloa (A. de), *A Voyage to South America.* Trans. 2 vols. London, 1760.
Jung (C. E.), ' Aus dem Seelenleben der Australier ' ; in *Mittheilungen des Vereins für Erdkunde zu Leipzig,* 1877.
—— ' Die Mündungsgegend des Murray und ihre Bewohner ' ; in *Mittheilungen des Vereins für Erdkunde zu Halle a/S,* 1877.
Junghuhn (Franz), *Die Battaländer auf Sumatra.* Trans. 2 vols. Berlin, 1847.
Junker (Wilhelm), *Travels in Africa during the Years 1882–86.* Trans. London, 1892.
Junod (H. A.), *Les Ba-Ronga.* Neuchatel, 1898.
Jusserand (J. J.), *English Wayfaring Life in the Middle Ages.* Trans. London, 1892.
Justi (Ferd.), ' Die Weltgeschichte des Tabari ' ; in *Das Ausland,* vol. xlviii. Stuttgart, 1875.
Justin Martyr, ' Apologia prima pro Christianis ' ; in Migne, *Patrologiæ cursus,* Ser. Graeca, vol. vi. Parisiis, 1857.
Justinian (*Emperor*), *Codex Justinianus.* Ed. by P. Krueger. (*Corpus juris civilis,* vol. ii.) Berolini, 1888.
—— ' Digesta,' ed. by Th. Mommsen ; in *Corpus juris civilis,* vol. i. Berolini, 1889.
—— ' Institutiones,' ed. by P. Krueger ; in *Corpus juris civilis,* vol. i. Berolini, 1889.
—— *Novellæ.* Ed. by R. Schoell and G. Kroll. (*Corpus juris civilis,* vol. iii.) Berolini, 1895.
Juvenalis (D. J.), *Opera omnia.* 3 vols. Londini, 1820.
Jydske Lovbog (Den). Ed. by P. K. Ancher. Kiøbenhavn, 1783.

Kaegi (Adolf), *The Rigveda : the Oldest Literature of the Indians.* Trans. Boston, 1886.
Kaibel (G.), *Epigrammata Græca.* Berolini, 1878.
Kålund (Kr.), ' Skandinavische Verhältnisse ' ; in Paul, *Grundriss der germanischen Philologie,* vol. ii. Strassburg, 1893.

Kames (*Lord*), *Essays on the Principles of Morality and Natural Religion.* Edinburgh, 1751.

—— *Sketches of the History of Man.* 4 vols. Edinburgh, 1788.

Kane (E. K.), *Arctic Explorations.* 2 vols. Philadelphia, 1856.

Kant (I.), *Metaphysische Anfangungsgründe der Tugendlehre.* Königsberg, 1803.

—— *Sämmtliche Werke.* Ed. by G. Hartenstein. 8 vols. Leipzig, 1867–68.

—— *Zum ewigen Frieden.* Königsberg, 1795.

Karsch-Haack (F.), *Das gleichgeschlechtliche Leben der Naturvölker.* München, 1911.

—— *Das gleichgeschlechtliche Leben der Ostasiaten.* München, 1906.

—— ' Päderastie und Tribadie bei den Tieren ' ; in *Jahrbuch f. sexuelle Zwischenstufen*, vol. ii. Leipzig, 1900.

—— ' Uranismus oder Päderastie und Tribadie bei den Naturvölkern ' ; in *Jahrbuch f. sexuelle Zwischenstufen*, vol. iii. Leipzig, 1901.

Karsten (R.), *The Origin of Worship.* Wasa, 1905.

—— *Studies in Primitive Greek Religion.* (*Öfversigt af Finska Vetenskaps-Societetens Förhandlingar*, vol. xlix., 1906–07, no. 1.) Helsingfors, 1907.

Kate (H. F. C. ten), *Reizen en onderzoekingen in Noord-Amerika.* Leiden, 1885.

Katscher (L.), *Bilder aus dem chinesischen Leben.* Leipzig & Heidelberg, 1881.

Katz (Albert), *Der wahre Talmudjude.* Berlin, 1893.

Katz (Edwin), *Ein Grundriss des kanonischen Strafrechts.* Berlin & Leipzig, 1881.

Kaufmann (Georg), *Deutsche Geschichte.* 2 vols. Leipzig, 1880–81.

Kearns (J. F.), *The Tribes of South India.* [London, 1865.]

Keary (Ch. F.), *Outlines of Primitive Belief among the Indo-European Races.* London, 1882.

Keate (George), *An Account of the Pelew Islands.* London, 1788.

Keating (W. H.), *Narrative of an Expedition to the Source of St. Peter's River.* 2 vols. Philadelphia, 1824.

Keil (C. F.), *Manual of Biblical Archæology.* Trans. 2 vols. Edinburgh, 1887–88.

Keller (A. G.), *Homeric Society.* New York, &c., 1902.

Kemble (J. M.), *The Saxons in England.* Ed. by W. De Gray Birch. 2 vols. London, 1876.

Kenny (C. S.), *Outlines of Criminal Law.* Cambridge, 1902.

Kern (H.), *Der Buddhismus und seine Geschichte in Indien.* Trans. 2 vols. Leipzig, 1882–84.

—— *Manual of Indian Buddhism.* Strassburg, 1896.

Kessler (K.), ' Mani, Manichäer ' ; in Herzog-Hauck, *Realencyclopädie f. Protestantische Theologie und Kirche*, vol. xii. Leipzig, 1903.

Keyser (J. R.), *Efterladte Skrifter.* 2 vols. Christiania, 1865–67.

Kidd (Benjamin), *Social Evolution.* London, 1894.

Kidd (Dudley), *The Essential Kafir.* London, 1904.

King (Irving), *The Development of Religion.* New York, 1910.

King (J. H.), *The Supernatural.* 2 vols. London, 1892.

King (L. W.), *Babylonian Magic and Sorcery.* London, 1896.

King (P. P.) and Fitzroy (R.), *Narrative of the Voyages of the "Adventure" and " Beagle."* 3 vols. London, 1839.

King (Richard), ' On the Intellectual Character of the Esquimaux ' ; in *Jour. Ethn. Soc. London*, vol. i. London, 1848.

Kingsley (Mary H.), ' The Fetish View of the Human Soul ' ; in *Folk-Lore*, vol. viii. London, 1897.

—— *Travels in West Africa.* London, 1897.

—— *West African Studies.* London, 1901.

Kipling (J. Lockwood), *Beast and Man in India.* London, 1891.

Kirke (Henry), *Twenty-five Years in British Guiana.* London, 1898.

Kittlitz (F. H. von), *Denkwürdigkeiten einer Reise nach dem russischen Amerika, nach Mikronesien und durch Kamtschatka.* 2 vols. Gotha, 1858.

Klemm (G.), *Allgemeine Cultur-Geschichte der Menschheit.* 10 vols. Leipzig, 1843–52.

Klenze (—), ' Die Cognaten und Affinen nach Römischem Rechte in Vergleichung mit andern verwandten Rechten ' ; in *Zeitschr. f. geschichtliche Rechtswiss.* ed. by F. C. von Savigny and others, vol. vi. Berlin & Stettin, 1828.

Kloss (C. B.), *In the Andamans and Nicobars.* London, 1903.

Klugmann (N.), *Die Frau im Talmud.* Wien, 1898.

Klunzinger (C. B.), *Upper Egypt.* Trans. London, 1878.

Knox (William), *Three Tracts respecting the Conversion and Instruction of the Free Indians and Negroe Slaves in the Colonies.* London, 1789.

Kobelt (W.), *Reiseerinnerungen aus Algerien und Tunis.* Frankfurt a. M., 1885.

Koch (Theodor), ' Die Anthropophagie der südamerikanischen Indianer ' ; in *Internationales Archiv f. Ethnographie*, vol. xii. Leiden, 1899.

Köhler (J. A. E.), *Volksbrauch, Aberglauben, &c. im Voigtlande.* Leipzig, 1867.

Koenigswarter (L. J.), *Études historiques sur le développement de la société humaine.* Paris, 1850.

—— *Histoire de l'organisation de la famille en France.* Paris, 1851.

Kohl (J. G.), *Kitchi-Gami. Wanderings round Lake Superior.* Trans. London, 1860.

—— *Reise nach Istrien, Dalmatien und Montenegro.* 2 vols. Dresden, 1851.

Kohler (J.), *Altindisches Prozessrecht.* Stuttgart, 1891.

—— ' Das Banturecht in Ostafrika ' ; in *Zeitschr. f. vergleichende Rechtswiss.* vol. xv. Stuttgart, 1901.

—— ' Indisches Ehe- und Familienrecht ' ; in *Zeitschr. f. vergleichende Rechtswiss.* vol. iii. Stuttgart, 1882.

—— ' Das Recht der Herero ' ; in *Zeitschr. f. vergleichende Rechtswiss.* vol. xiv. Stuttgart, 1900.

—— ' Das Recht der Hottentotten ' ; in *Zeitschr. f. vergleichende Rechtswiss.* vol. xv. Stuttgart, 1901.

—— ' Das Recht der Marschallinsulaner ' ; in *Zeitschr. f. vergleichende Rechtswiss.* vol. xiv. Stuttgart, 1900.

—— ' Das Recht der Papuas ' ; in *Zeitschr. f. vergleichende Rechtswiss.* vol. xiv. Stuttgart, 1900.

—— ' Die Rechte der Urvölker Nordamerikas ' ; in *Zeitschr. f. vergleichende Rechtswiss.* vol. xii. Stuttgart, 1897.

—— *Rechtsvergleichende Studien über islamitisches Recht, &c.* Berlin, 1889.

—— *Shakespeare vor dem Forum der Jurisprudenz.* Würzburg, 1883.— *Nachwort.* Würzburg, 1884.

Kohler (J.) and Peiser (F. E.), *Aus dem Babylonischen Rechtsleben.* 4 vols. Leipzig, 1890–98.

Kolben (Peter), *The Present State of the Cape of Good-Hope.* Trans. 2 vols. London, 1731.

Kolff (D. H.), *Voyage of the Dutch Brig of War Dourga, through the Southern Parts of the Moluccan Archipelago, &c.* London, 1840.

Kollmann (Paul), *The Victoria Nyanza.* Trans. London, 1899.

Koppenfels (H. von), ' Meine Jagden auf Gorillas ' ; in *Die Gartenlaube,* 1877. Leipzig.

Korân (The). Trans. by J. M. Rodwell. London, 1876.

—— See *Qur'ân (The).*

Kosmos. Leipzig.

Kotzebue (O. von), *A Voyage of Discovery into the South Sea and Behring's Straits.* Trans. 3 vols. London, 1821.

Kovalewsky (Maxime), *Coutume contemporaine et loi ancienne.* Paris, 1893.

—— *Modern Customs and Ancient Laws of Russia.* London, 1891.

—— ' Les origines du devoir ' ; in *Revue internationale de sociologie,* vol. ii. Paris, 1894.

—— *Tableau des origines et de l'évolution de la famille et de la propriété.* Stockholm, 1890.

Krafft-Ebing (R. von), *Lehrbuch der Gerichtlichen Psychopatologie.* Stuttgart, 1900.

—— *Psychopathia sexualis.* Stuttgart, 1903.

Krapf (J. L.), *Reisen in Ost-Afrika.* 2 vols. Kornthal & Stuttgart, 1858.

—— *Travels, Researches, and Missionary Labours, during an Eighteen Years' Residence in Eastern Africa.* London, 1860.

Krasheninnikoff (S. P.), *The History of Kamschatka, and the Kurilski Islands.* Trans. Glocester, 1764.

Krause (Aurel), *Die Tlinkit-Indianer.* Jena, 1885.

Krause (Ernst), ' Die Ablösung der Menschenopfer ' ; in *Kosmos,* vol. iii. Leipzig, 1878.

Krauss (F. S.), ' Das Bauopfer bei den Südslaven ' ; in *Mittheilungen der Anthropologischen Gesellschaft in Wien,* vol. xvii. Wien, 1887.

—— *Sitte und Brauch der Südslaven.* Wien, 1885.

Kremer (Alfred von), *Culturgeschichte des Orients unter den Chalifen.* 2 vols. Wien, 1875–77.

—— *Studien zur vergleichenden Culturgeschichte.* 2 parts. (Reprinted from *Sitzungsberichte der Kais. Akademie der Wissenschaften in Wien, Philosophisch-historische Classe,* vol. cxx.) Wien, 1889–90.

Kropf (A.), *Das Volk der Xosa-Kaffern im östlichen Südafrika.* Berlin, 1889.

Kropotkin (P.), *Mutual Aid.* London, 1902.

Kubary (J.), ' Die Bewohner der Mortlock Inseln ' ; in *Mittheilungen der Geographischen Gesellschaft in Hamburg,* 1878–79.

—— ' Die Ebongruppe im Marshall's Archipel ' ; in *Journal des Museum Godeffroy,* pt. i. Hamburg, 1873.

—— *Ethnographische Beiträge zur Kenntniss der Karolinischen Inselgruppe. Heft I.* : *Die socialen Einrichtungen der Pelauer.* Berlin, 1885.

—— ' Die Palau-Inseln in der Südsee ' ; in *Journal des Museum Godeffroy,* pt. iv. Hamburg, 1873.

—— ' Die Religion der Pelauer ' ; in Bastian, *Allerlei aus Volks- und Menschenkunde,* vol. i. Berlin, 1888.

Kubary (J.), ' Die Verbrechen und das Strafverfahren auf den Pelau-Inseln ' ; in *Original-Mittheilungen aus der ethnologischen Abtheilung der königlichen Museen zu Berlin*, vol. i. Berlin, 1886.

Kükenthal (W.), *Ergebnisse einer zoologischen Forschungsreise in den Molukken und Borneo. Erster Teil : Reisebericht.* Frankfurt a. M., 1896.

Kuenen (A.), *Hibbert Lectures on National Religions and Universal Religions.* London, 1882.

—— *The Religion of Israel.* Trans. 3 vols. London, 1874–75.

Labat (J. B.), *Relation historique de l'Éthiopie occidentale.* 5 vols. Paris, 1732.

Labbe (Ph.), *Sacrorum Conciliorum collectio.* Ed. by J. D. Mansi. 31 vols. Florentiae, Venetiis, 1759–98.

Labillardière (J. J. Houtou de), *An Account of a Voyage in Search of La Pérouse in the Years* 1791–93. Trans. 2 vols. London, 1800.

Laboulaye (E.), *Recherches sur la condition civile et politique des femmes.* Paris, 1843.

Lactantius (L. C. F.), *Opera omnia.* 2 vols. (Migne, *Patrologiæ cursus*, vols. vi.–vii.) Parisiis, 1844.

Läffler (L. F.), *Den gottländska Taksteinar-sägnen. (Bidrag till kännedom om de svenska landsmålen ock svenskt folkliv,* vol. xix. art. 6.) Stockholm, 1903.

—— ' Om den fornsvenska hednalagen ' ; in *Kongl. Vitterhets Historie och Antiquitets Akademiens Månadsbad,* vol. viii. Stockholm, 1879.

Lafitau (J. F.), *Moeurs des sauvages ameriquains.* 2 vols. Paris, 1724.

La Flesche (F.), ' Death and Funeral Customs among the Omahas ' ; in *The Journal of American Folk-Lore,* vol. ii. Boston & New York, 1889.

Lagerborg (Rolf), ' La nature de la morale ' ; in *Revue internationale de sociologie,* vol. xi. Paris, 1903.

Lago (V.), *Memorie sulla Dalmazia.* 3 vols. Venezia, 1869–71.

Lahontan (J. de), *Mémoires de l'Amérique septentrionale.* La Haye, 1703.

Laing (A. Gordon), *Travels in the Timannee, Kooranko, and Soolima Countries in Western Africa.* London, 1825.

Laing (Samuel), *Notes of a Traveller, on the Social and Political State of France, Prussia, Switzerland, Italy, &c.* London, 1842.

Laistner (L.), *Das Recht in der Strafe.* München, 1872.

Lala (R. Reyes), *The Philippine Islands.* New York, 1899.

Lallemand (Léon), *Histoire des enfants abandonnés et délaissés.* Paris, 1885.

Lancelot du Lac. 3 vols. Paris, 1520.

Landa (Diego de), *Relacion de las cosas de Yucatan.* Paris, 1864.

' Landnámabók ' ; in *Íslendínga sögur, udgivne af Det Kongelige Nordiske Oldskrift-Selskab,* vol. i. Kjøbenhavn, 1843.

Landor (A. H. Savage), *Alone with the Hairy Ainu.* London, 1893.

Landtman (G.), *The Origin of Priesthood.* Ekenaes, 1905.

Lane (E. W.), *An Account of the Manners and Customs of the Modern Egyptians.* 2 vols. London, 1871.

—— The same work. London, 1896.

—— *Arabian Society in the Middle Ages.* Ed. by Stanley Lane-Poole. London, 1883.

Lane-Poole (Stanley), *The Speeches and Table-Talk of the Prophet Mohammad.* London, 1882.

—— *Studies in a Mosque.* London, 1893.

Lanessan (J.-L. de), *La morale des philosophes chinois.* Paris, 1896.

Lang (Andrew), *Magic and Religion*. London, 1901.
—— *The Making of Religion*. London, 1898.
—— *Social Origins*. London, 1903.
Lang (J. D.), *Cooksland in North-Eastern Australia*. London, 1847.
—— *Queensland*. London, 1861.
Langkavel (B.), ' Pferde und Naturvölker ' ; in *Internationales Archiv für Ethnographie*, vol. i. Leiden, 1888.
Langsdorf (G. H. von), *Voyages and Travels in various Parts of the World, during the Years*, 1803–1807. 2 vols. London, 1813–14.
La Nouë (François de), *Discours politiques et militaires*. Basle, 1587.
La Pérouse (J. F. G. de), *A Voyage round the World, in the Years* 1785–88. Trans. 3 vols. London, 1799.
Lappenberg (J. M.), *A History of England under the Anglo-Saxon Kings*. Trans. 2 vols. London, 1881.
Larger Catechism (The), agreed upon by the Assembly of Divines at Westminster. Ed. by H. Cooke. Belfast, 1833.
La Roche-Fontenilles (L. A. M. de), *L'Église et la pitié envers les animaux*. Paris, &c., 1903.
La Rochefoucauld (F. de), *Les maximes*. Paris, 1881.
La Salle (R. R. de), ' An Account of Monsieur de la Salle's Last Expedition and Discoveries in North America ' ; in *Collections of the New-York Historical Society, for the Year* 1814, vol. ii. New-York, 1814.
Lasaulx (Ernst von), *Der Eid bei den Römern*. Würzburg, 1844.
—— *Der Fluch bei Griechen und Römern*. Würzburg, 1843.
—— *Die Sühnopfer der Griechen und Römer.* Würzburg, 1841.
Lasch (Richard), ' Die Behandlung der Leiche des Selbstmörders ' ; in *Globus*, vol. lxxvi. Braunschweig, 1899.
—— ' Besitzen die Naturvölker ein persönliches Ehrgefühl ? ' in *Zeitschr. f. Socialwissensch*. vol. iii. Berlin, 1900.
—— ' Rache als Selbstmordmotiv ' ; in *Globus*, vol. lxxiv. Braunschweig, 1898.
—— ' Religiöser Selbstmord und seine Beziehung zum Menschenopfer ' ; in *Globus*, vol. lxxv. Braunschweig, 1899.
—— ' Der Selbstmord aus erotischen Motiven bei den primitiven Völkern ' ; in *Zeitschr. f. Socialwissensch*. vol. ii. Berlin, 1899.
Lasson (Adolf), *System der Rechtsphilosophie*. Berlin & Leipzig, 1882.
Latham (R. G.), *Descriptive Ethnology*. 2 vols. London, 1859.
Laurent (François), *Études sur l'histoire de l'Humanité*. 18 vols. Paris, 1865–80.
Laurie (S. S.), *Ethica*. London, 1891.
Laurière (E. de), *Glossaire du droit françois*. Niort, 1882.
Laveleye (É. de), *De la propriété et de ses formes primitives*. Paris, 1874.
—— *Das Ureigenthum* Ed. by K. Bücher. Leipzig, 1879.
Law Quarterly Review (The). Ed. by Sir F. Pollock. London.
Law Reports, Cases determined in the Queen's Bench Division. London, 1876, &c.
Lawrence (John), *A Philosophical and Practical Treatise on Horses, and on the Moral Duties of Man towards the Brute Creation*. 2 vols. London, 1796–98.
Lawrence (T. J.), *Essays on some disputed Questions in Modern International Law*. Cambridge, 1885.

Laws of Manu (The). Trans. by G. Bühler. (*The Sacred Books of the East*, vol. xxv.) Oxford, 1886.

Layard (A. H.), *Discoveries in the Ruins of Nineveh and Babylon*. London, 1853.

Lea (H. C.), *An Historical Sketch of Sacerdotal Celibacy in the Christian Church*. Boston, 1884.

—— *A History of the Inquisition of the Middle Ages*. 3 vols. London, 1888.

—— *Superstition and Force*. Philadelphia, 1892.

Le Blant (E.), *Inscriptions chrétiennes de la Gaule antérieures au VIII. siècle*. 2 vols. Paris, 1856–65.

Le Bon (Gustave), *La civilisation des Arabes*. Paris, 1884.

Lecky (W. E. H.), *Democracy and Liberty*. 2 vols. London, 1899.

—— *History of European Morals from Augustus to Charlemagne*. 2 vols. London, 1890.

—— *History of the Rise and Influence of the Spirit of Rationalism in Europe*. 2 vols. London, 1893.

Leem (Knud), *Beskrivelse over Finmarkens Lapper*. Kjöbenhavn, 1767.

Leffler (L. F.). See Läffler.

' Leges Burgundionum ' ; in Pertz, *Monumenta Germaniæ historica*, Leges, vol. iii. Hannoverae, 1863.

Legge (James), *The Chinese Classics*. 2 vols. Oxford, 1893–95.

—— *The Notions of the Chinese concerning God and Spirits*. Hongkong, 1852.

—— *The Religions of China*. London, 1880.

Legis Duodecim Tabularum reliquiæ. Ed. by R. Schoell. Lipsiae, 1866.

Legoyt (A.), *Le suicide ancien et moderne*. Paris, 1881.

Legrand (Louis), *L'idée de patrie*. Paris, 1897.

Le Grand d'Aussy (P. J. B.), *Histoire de la vie privée des François*. Ed. by J. B. B. de Roquefort. 3 vols. Paris, 1815.

Leguével de Lacombe (B. F.), *Voyage à Madagascar et aux Iles Comores*. 2 vols. Paris, 1840.

Lehmann (Alfr.), *Hovedlovene for det menneskelige Følelseliv*. København, 1892.

Lehmann (E.), *Zarathustra*. 2 vols. København, 1899–1902.

Leibnitz (G. W.), *Essais de Theodicée sur la bonté de Dieu, la liberté de l'homme, et l'origine du mal*. Amsterdam, 1712.

Leist (B. W.), *Alt-arisches Jus Civile*. 2 vols. Jena, 1892–96.

—— *Alt-arisches Jus Gentium*. Jena, 1889.

—— *Græco-italische Rechtsgeschichte*. Jena, 1884.

Le Mesurier (C. J. R.), ' The Veddás of Ceylon ' ; in *Jour. Roy. Asiatic Soc. Ceylon Branch*, vol. ix. Colombo, 1887.

Leo Africanus, *The History and Description of Africa*. Trans. ed. by R. Brown. 3 vols. London, 1896.

Leo I. (*Saint*), surnamed *the Great, Opera omnia*. 3 vols. (Migne, *Patrologiæ cursus*, vols. liv.–lvi.) Parisiis, 1846.

Leonhardi (M. von), ' Über einige religiöse und totemistische Vorstellungen der Aranda und Loritja in Zentralaustralien ' ; in *Globus*, vol. xci. Braunschweig, 1907.

Lepsius (Richard), *Letters from Egypt, Ethiopia, and the Peninsula of Sinai*. Trans. London, 1853.

Leslie (David), *Among the Zulus and Amatongas*. Edinburgh, 1875.

Letourneau (Ch.), *L'évolution de la morale.* Paris, 1887.

—— *L'évolution religieuse dans les diverses races humaines.* Paris, 1892.

Leuba (J. H.), *A Psychological Study of Religion.* New York, 1912.

Le Vaillant (François), *Travels from the Cape of Good-Hope, into the Interior Parts of Africa.* Trans. 2 vols. London, 1790.

Levy (Jacob), *Neuhebräisches und Chaldäisches Wörterbuch über die Talmudim.* 4 vols. Leipzig, 1876–89.

Lewin (T. H.), *The Hill Tracts of Chittagong.* Calcutta, 1869.

—— *Wild Races of South-Eastern India.* London, 1870.

Lewis (A. H.), *A Critical History of Sunday Legislation.* New York, 1888.

—— *Paganism surviving in Christianity.* London, 1892.

Lewis (M.) and Clarke (W.), *Travels to the Source of the Missouri River, &c.* London, 1814.

'Lex Baiuwariorum'; in Pertz, *Monumenta Germaniæ historica*, Leges, vol. iii. Hannoverae, 1863.

Lex Duodecim Tabularum. See *Legis, &c.*

Lex Frisionum. Ed. by E. T. Gaupp. Vratislaviae, 1832.

'Lex Ripuariorum'; in Georgisch, *Corpus juris Germanici antiqui.* Halae Magdeburgicae, 1738.

Lex Salica : The Ten Texts with the Glosses, and the Lex Emendata. Ed. by J. H. Hessels. London, 1880.

'Lex Saxonum'; in Pertz, *Monumenta Germaniæ historica*, Leges, vol. v. Hannoverae, 1875–89.

'Lex Wisigothorum'; in Georgisch, *Corpus juris Germanici antiqui.* Halae Magdeburgicae, 1738.

Leyden (J.), 'On the Languages and Literature of the Indo-Chinese Nations'; in *Asiatic Researches*, vol. x. Calcutta, 1811.

Lî Kî (The). Trans. by J. Legge. 2 vols. (*The Sacred Books of the East,* vols. xxvii.–xxviii.) Oxford, 1885.

Lichtenberg (G. Chr.), *Vermischte Schriften.* 9 vols. Göttingen, 1800–06.

Lichtenstein (H.), *Travels in Southern Africa.* Trans. 2 vols. London, 1812–15.

Lichtschein (L.), *Die Ehe nach mosaich-talmudischer Auffassung.* Leipzig, 1879.

Liddell (H. G.) and Scott (R.), *A Greek-English Lexicon.* Oxford, 1897.

Liebich (R.), *Die Zigeuner.* Leipzig, 1863.

Liebrecht (Felix), *Zur Volkskunde.* Heilbronn, 1879.

Lilly (W. S.), *On Right and Wrong.* London, 1891.

Lindenbrog (F.), *Codex legum antiquarum.* Francofurti, 1613.

Lippert (Julius), *Christenthum, Volksglaube und Volksbrauch.* Berlin, 1882.

—— *Kulturgeschichte der Menschheit.* 2 vols. Stuttgart, 1886–87.

—— *Die Religionen der europäischen Culturvölker.* Berlin, 1881.

—— *Der Seelencult in seinen Beziehungen zur althebräischen Religion.* Berlin, 1881.

Lisiansky (U.), *A Voyage round the World.* London, 1814.

Lisle (E.), *Du suicide.* Paris, 1856.

Liszt (Franz von), *La législation pénale comparée. Publiée par l'Union internationale de droit pénal.* 1er volume : Le droit criminel des états européens. Berlin, 1894.

—— *Lehrbuch des deutschen Strafrechts.* Berlin, 1891.

Little (H. W.), *Madagascar.* Edinburgh & London, 1884.

Littré (É.), *Dictionnaire de la langue française.* 2 vols. Paris, 1863–72.

—— *Études sur les Barbares et le Moyen Age.* Paris, 1867.

Livingstone (D.), *The Last Journals of, in Central Africa.* Ed. by H. Waller. 2 vols. London, 1874.

—— *Missionary Travels and Researches in South Africa.* London, 1857.

—— and Livingstone (Charles), *Narrative of an Expedition to the Zambesi and its Tributaries.* London, 1865.

Livy (T.), *Historiarum libri qui supersunt.* 25 vols. Londini, 1828.

Lobo (J.), *A Voyage to Abyssinia.* Trans. London, 1887.

Locke (John), *Philosophical Works.* London, 1843.

—— *Two Treatises of Government.* London, 1713.

Locqueneuille (Scarsez de), *L'esclavage, ses promoteurs et ses adversaires.* Liège, 1890.

Löw (Leopold) *Gesammelte Schriften.* 4 vols. Szegedin, 1889–98.

Logan (James), *The Scottish Gaël.* Ed. by Alex. Stewart. 2 vols. Inverness [1876].

Logan (William), *Words of Comfort for Parents bereaved of Little Children.* London, 1861.

Loir (A.), ' L'esclavage en Tunisie ' ; in *Revue scientifique*, ser. iv. vol. xii. Paris, 1899.

Lomonaco (A.), ' Sulle razze indigene del Brasile ' ; in *Archivio per l'antropologia e la etnologia*, vol. xix. Firenze, 1889.

Lopez Cogolludo (Diego), *Historia de Yucathan.* Madrid, 1688.

Lorimer (James), *The Institutes of the Law of Nations.* 2 vols. Edinburgh, 1883–84.

Loskiel (G. H.), *History of the Mission of the United Brethren among the Indians in North America.* Trans. 3 vols. London, 1794.

Lovisato (Domenico), ' Appunti etnografici con accenni geologici sulla Terra del Fuoco ' ; in *Cosmos*, ed. by Guido Cora, vol. viii. Torino, 1884–85.

Low (Hugh), *Sarawak.* London, 1848.

Loysel (Antoine), *Institutes coutumières.* Ed. by M. Dupin and Éd. Laboulaye. 2 vols. Paris, 1846.

Lubbock (*Sir* John). See Avebury (*Lord*).

Lucian, *Opera.* Parisiis, 1867.

Ludwig (G.), *Tertullian's Ethik.* Leipzig, 1885.

Lumholtz (Carl), *Among Cannibals.* London, 1889.

—— *Unknown Mexico.* 2 vols. London, 1903.

' Lun Yü ' ; in Legge, *The Chinese Classics*, vol. i. Oxford, 1893.

Lyall (A. C.), *Asiatic Studies.* London, 1882.

Lycurgus, *Oratio in Leocratem.* Ed. by F. Blass. Lipsiae, 1899.

—— The same work. Ed. and trans. by E. Jenicke. Leipzig, 1856.

Lyon (G. F.), *The Private Journal during the Voyage of Discovery under Captain Parry.* London, 1824.

Lyttelton (George), *The History of the Life of King Henry the Second.* 4 vols. London, 1767–71.

Mabille (Paul), *La guerre.* Paris, 1884.

MacCauley (Clay), ' The Seminole Indians of Florida ' ; in *Ann. Rep. Bur. Ethn.* vol. v. 1887.

McCord (D. J.), *The Statutes at large of South Carolina.* 10 vols. Columbia (S. C.), 1836–41.

McCoy (Isaac), *History of Baptist Indian Missions.* Washington, 1840.

McCurdy (J. F.), ' The Moral Evolution of the Old Testament ' ; in *The American Journal of Theology*, vol. i. Chicago, 1897.

Macdonald (D.), *Oceania.* Melbourne & London, 1889.

Macdonald (Duff), *Africana.* 2 vols. London, 1882.

Macdonald (James), ' East Central African Customs ' ; in *Jour. Anthr. Inst.* vol. xxii. London, 1893.

—— *Light in Africa.* London, 1890.

—— *Religion and Myth.* London, 1893.

Macdonell (A. A.), *Vedic Mythology.* Strassburg, 1897.

Macfie (M.), *Vancouver Island and British Columbia.* London, 1865.

McGee (W. J.), ' The Seri Indians ' ; in *Ann. Rep. Bur. Ethn.* vol. xvii. pt. i. Washington, 1898.

—— ' The Siouan Indians ' ; in *Ann. Rep. Bur. Ethn.* vol. xv. Washington, 1897.

Macgillivray (John), *Narrative of the Voyage of H.M.S. Rattlesnake.* 2 vols. London, 1852.

MacGregor (William), ' Lagos, Abeokuta, and the Alake ' ; in *Jour. African Soc.* nr. xii. London, 1904.

Machiavelli (Niccolò), *Opere.* 10 vols. Milano, 1804-05.

Macieiowski (W. A.), *Slavische Rechtsgeschichte.* Trans. 4 vols. Stuttgart & Leipzig, 1835-39.

Mackenzie (Alex.), *Voyages from Montreal to the Frozen and Pacific Oceans* London, 1801.

Mackenzie (John S.), *A Manual of Ethics.* London, 1900.

Mackenzie (Thomas), *Studies in Roman Law.* Ed. by John Kirkpatrick. Edinburgh, 1886.

Mackintosh (John), *The History of Civilisation in Scotland.* 4 vols. Aberdeen, 1878-92.

Maclean (John), *A Compendium of Kafir Laws and Customs.* Mount Coke, 1858.

McLennan (J. F.), ' The Levirate and Polyandry ' ; in *The Fortnightly Review*, new ser. vol. xxi. London, 1877.

—— *Studies in Ancient History.* London, 1886.

M'Leod (John), *A Voyage to Africa, with some Account of the Manners and Customs of the Dahomian People.* London, 1820.

MacMahon (A. R.), *Far Cathay and Farther India.* London, 1893.

Macmillan (Michael), *The Promotion of General Happiness.* London, 1890.

McNair (F.), *Perak and the Malays.* London, 1878.

Macpherson (S. C.), ' An Account of the Religious Opinions and Observances of the Khonds ' ; in *Jour. Roy. Asiatic Soc.* vol. vii. London, 1843.

—— *Memorials of Service in India.* London, 1865.

Macrae (John), ' Account of the Kookies ' ; in *Asiatick Researches*, vol. vii. Calcutta, 1831.

Mac Ritchie (David), *The Aïnos.* Leiden, 1892.

Macrobius (A. T.), *Opera.* Ed. by L. Janus. 2 vols. Quedlinburgi & Lipsiae, 1845-52.

Madras Government Museum's *Bulletins.* Madras.

Magalhanes de Gandavo (Pero de), *Histoire de la Province de Sancta-Crux.* Trans. Paris, 1837.

Magazine of American History (The). New York & Chicago.

Magyar (L.), *Reisin in Süd-Afrika.* Pest & Leipzig, 1859.

Mahabharata of Krishna-Dwaipayana Vyasa. Trans. by P. Chandra Roy. 18 vols. Calcutta, 1883–96.

Mahaffy (J. P.), *Social Life in Greece from Homer to Menander.* London, 1874.

Maine (*Sir* H. Sumner), *Ancient Law.* London, 1885.

—— *Dissertations on Early Law and Custom.* London, 1891.

—— *Lectures on the Early History of Institutions.* London, 1875.

—— *The Whewell Lectures. International Law.* London, 1888.

Maitland (S. R.), *The Dark Ages.* London, 1844.

Makarewicz (J.), *Évolution de la peine. S. l. & d.*

' Makkoth ' ; in *Le Talmud de Jérusalem,* trans. by M. Schwab, vol. xi. Paris, 1889.

Malalas (J.), ' Chronographia ' ; in Migne, *Patrologiæ cursus,* Ser. Graeca, vol. xcvii. Parisiis, 1860.

Malcolm (*Sir* John), *A Memoir of Central India.* 2 vols. London, 1823.

—— *Sketch of the Sikhs.* London, 1812.

Malinowski (B.), *The Family among the Australian Aborigines.* London, 1913.

Mallat (J.), *Les Philippines.* 2 vols. Paris, 1846.

Mallery (Garrick), *Israelite and Indian.* New York, 1889.

—— ' Manners and Meals ' ; in *The American Anthropologist,* vol. i. Washington, 1888.

Mallet (P. H.), *Northern Antiquities.* Trans. London, 1847.

Malloch (M. M.), ' How the Church dealt with Slavery ' ; in *The Month,* vol. xxvii. London, 1876.

Malone (R. E.), *Three Years' Cruise in the Australian Colonies.* London, 1854.

Man. A Monthly Record of Anthropological Science. London.

Man (E. G.), *Sonthalia and the Sonthals.* London, [1867].

Man (E. H.), ' On the Aboriginal Inhabitants of the Andaman Islands ' ; in *Jour. Anthr. Inst.* vol. xii. London, 1885.

Manaccine (Marie), *Le surmenage mental dans la civilisation moderne.* Trans. Paris, 1890.

Mandeville (B. de), *The Fable of the Bees.* London, 1724.

Manning (James), ' Notes on the Aborigines of New Holland ' ; in *Jour. and Proceed. Roy. Soc. N.S. Wales,* 1882, vol. xvi. Sydney, 1883.

Mansel (H. L.), *Prolegomena Logica.* Oxford, 1860.

Mantegazza (Paolo), *Rio de la Plata e Tenerife.* Milano, 1867.

—— ' Studii sull' etnologia dell' India ' ; in *Archivio per l'antropologia e la etnologia,* vol. xiii. Firenze, 1883.

Manu, The Laws of. See *Laws of Manu (The).*

Manual of the Laws of War on Land. Prepared by the Institute of International Law. Trans. (Appendix No. III. in Lorimer, *The Institutes of the Law of Nations,* vol. ii.) Edinburgh, 1884.

Manzoni (Alessandro), *Osservazioni sulla morale cattolica.* Firenze, 1887.

Marcellinus (Ammianus), *Rerum gestarum libri qui supersunt.* Ed. by V. Gardthausen. 2 vols. Lipsiae, 1874–75.

Marcgravius de Liebstad (G.), *Historia rerum naturalium Brasiliæ.* Lugduni Batavorum & Amstelodami, 1648.

Marculfus, ' Formularum libri duo ' ; in Migne, *Patrologiæ cursus,* vol. lxxxvii. Parisiis, 1851.

Marcus Aurelius, *Commentariorum libri XII.* Ed. by I. Stich. Lipsiæ, 1903.

Mareschalcus (Nicolaus), ' Annalium Herulorum ac Vandalorum libri septem ' ; in *Monumenta inedita rerum Germanicarum, &c.*, ed. by E. J. de Westphalen, vol. i. Lipsiae, 1739.

Marett (R. R.), *Anthropology.* London, 1912.

—— *The Threshold of Religion.* London, 1914.

Marillier (L.), *La survivance de l'âme et l'idée de justice chez les peuples non civilisés.* Paris, 1894.

Mariner (William), *An Account of the Natives of the Tonga Islands.* Compiled by John Martin. 2 vols. London, 1817.

Mariti (Giovanni), *Travels through Cyprus, Syria, and Palestine.* Trans. 3 vols. London, 1791–92.

Markham (A. H.), *The Cruise of the " Rosario " amongst the New Hebrides and Santa Cruz Islands.* London, 1873.

Markham (*Sir* C. R.), *A History of Peru.* Chicago, 1892.

—— ' A List of the Tribes in the Valley of the Amazon ' ; in *Jour. Anthr. Inst.* vol. xxiv. London, 1895.

—— ' On the Geographical Positions of the Tribes which formed the Empire of the Yncas ' ; in *Jour. Roy. Geo. Soc.* vol. xli. London, 1871.

Marquardt (J.), *Römische Staatsverwaltung.* 3 vols. Leipzig, 1873–78.

Marquette (Jacques), *Récit des voyages et des découvertes.* Albanie (N.Y.), 1855.

Marsden (W.), *The History of Sumatra.* London, 1811.

Marshall (Frederic), *International Vanities.* Edinburgh & London, 1875.

Marshall (H. R.), *Pain, Pleasure, and Æsthetics.* London, 1894.

Marshall (W. E.), *A Phrenologist amongst the Todas.* London, 1873.

Martensen (H.), *Christian Ethics.* [*General Part.*] Trans. Edinburgh, *s. d.*

—— *Christian Ethics. Special Part. Individual Ethics.* Trans. Edinburgh, 1881.

Martialis (M. V.), *Epigrammata.* 3 vols. Londini, 1822–23.

Martin (Henri), *Histoire de France depuis les temps les plus reculés jusqu'en 1789.* 17 vols. Paris, 1878.

Martin (K.), *Reisen in den Molukken, &c.* Leiden, 1894.

Martineau (James), *Types of Ethical Theory.* 2 vols. Oxford, 1891.

Martinengo-Cesaresco (*Countess* Evelyn), *Essays in the Study of Folk-Songs.* London, 1886.

Martius (C. F. Ph. von), *Beiträge zur Ethnographie und 'Sprachenkunde Amerika's zumal Brasiliens.* 2 vols. Leipzig, 1867.

—— *Von dem Rechtszustande unter den Ureinwohnern Brasiliens.* München, 1832.

Marx (Karl), *Capital.* Trans. Ed. by F. Engels. London, 1896.

Mas (S. de), *Informe sobre el estado de las Islas Filipinas en 1842.* Vol. i. Madrid, 1843.

Mason (F.), ' On Dwellings, Works of Art, Laws, &c. of the Karens ' ; in *Jour. Asiatic Soc. Bengal*, vol. xxxvii. pt. ii. Calcutta, 1868.

—— ' Physical Character of the Karens ' ; in *Jour. Asiatic Soc. Bengal*, vol. xxxv. pt. ii. Calcutta, 1867.

—— ' Religion, Mythology, and Astronomy among the Karens ' ; in *Jour. Asiatic Soc. Bengal*, vol. xxxiv. pt. ii. Calcutta, 1865.

Mason (O. T.), *Woman's Share in Primitive Culture.* London, 1895.

Maspero (G.), *The Dawn of Civilization.* Trans. London, 1896.

Maspero (G.), *Études de mythologie et d'archéologie égyptiennes.* 2 vols. Paris, 1893.

—— *Life in Ancient Egypt and Assyria.* Trans. London, 1892.

Massey (William), *A History of England during the Reign of George III.* 4 vols. London, 1865.

Mathew (John), ' The Australian Aborigines ' ; in *Jour. and Proceed. Roy. Soc. N.S. Wales,* vol. xxiii. London & Sydney, 1889.

—— *Eaglehawk and Crow.* London & Melbourne, 1899.

Mathews (R. H.), *Ethnological Notes on the Aboriginal Tribes of N.S. Wales and Victoria.* Sydney, 1905.

Matiegka (H.), ' Anthropophagie in der prähistorischen Ansiedlung bei Knovíze und in der prähistorischen Zeit überhaupt ' ; in *Mittheilungen der Anthropologischen Gesellschaft in Wien,* vol. xxvi. Wien, 1896.

Matignon (J.-J.), ' Deux mots sur la pédérastie en Chine ' ; in *Archives d'anthropologie criminelle,* vol. xiv. Paris, 1899.

—— ' Le suicide en Chine ' ; in *Archives d'anthropologie criminelle,* vol. xii. Paris, 1897.

Matthews (Washington), *Ethnography and Philology of the Hidatsa Indians.* Washington, 1877.

—— *Navaho Legends.* (*Memoirs of the American Folk-Lore Society,* vol. v.) Boston & New York, 1897.

—— ' The Study of Ethics among the Lower Races ' ; in *Jour. American Folk-Lore,* vol. xii. Boston & New York, 1899.

Maudsley (Henry), *Responsibility in Mental Disease.* London, 1892.

Maurer (Konrad), *Die Bekehrung des Norwegischen Stammes zum Christen thume.* 2 vols. München, 1856.

Maury (L. F. A.), *Histoire des religions de la Grèce antique.* 3 vols. Paris, 1857–59.

Mauss (M.), ' La religion et les origines du droit pénal ' ; in *Revue de l'histoire des religions,* vols. xxxiv.–xxxv. Paris, 1896–97.

Maximus Tyrius, *Dissertationes.* Ed. by F. Dübner. Parisiis, 1840.

May (Th. Erskine), *The Constitutional History of England since the Accession of George III.* 1760–1860. 2 vols. London, 1863.

Mayer (S.), *Die Rechte der Israeliten, Athener und Römer.* 2 vols. Leipzig, 1862–66.

Mayne (J. D.), *A Treatise on Hindu Law and Usage.* Madras, 1888.

Mayne (R. C.), *Four Years in British Columbia and Vancouver Island.* London, 1862.

Mazzarella (G.), *La condizione giuridica del marito nella famiglia matriarcale.* Catania, 1899.

Meade (H.), *A Ride through the disturbed Districts of New Zealand.* London, 1870.

Meakin (Budgett), *The Moors.* London, 1902.

Meares (John), *Voyages made in the Years* 1788 *and* 1789 *from China to the North-West Coast of America.* London, 1790.

Medhurst (W. H.), ' Marriage, Affinity, and Inheritance in China ' ; in *Trans. Roy. Asiatic Soc. China Branch,* vol. iv. Hongkong, 1855.

Medwin (Thomas), *The Angler in Wales.* 2 vols. London, 1834.

' Meghilla ' ; in *Le Talmud de Jérusalem,* trans. by M. Schwab, vol. vi. Paris, 1883.

Mehring (G. von), *Die Frage von der Todesstrafe.* Stuttgart, 1867.

Meier (M. H. E.) and Schömann (G. F.), *Der attische Process.* Ed. by J. H. Lipsius. Berlin, 1883–87.

Meiners (C.), *Allgemeine kritische Geschichte der Religionen.* 2 vols. Hannover, 1806–07.

—— *Grundriss der Geschichte der Menschheit.* Lemgo, 1785.

—— *History of the Female Sex.* Trans. 4 vols. London, 1808.

—— *Vergleichung des ältern und neuern Russlandes.* 2 vols. Leipzig, 1798.

Meissner (B.), *Beiträge zum altbabylonischen Privatrecht.* Leipzig, 1893.

Mela (Pomponius), *De chorographia (situ orbis) libri tres.* Ed. by C. Frick. Lipsiae, 1880.

Mélusine. Revue de mythologie, littérature populaire, traditions et usages. Ed. by H. Gaidoz. Paris.

Melville (H.), *Typee.* London, [1892].

Mémoires de l'Institut Royal de France, Académie des Inscriptions et Belles-Lettres. Paris.

Memoirs of the American Folk-Lore Society. Boston & New York.

—— *of the American Museum of Natural History.* New York.

—— *of the International Congress of Anthropology.* Ed. by C. Staniland Wake. Chicago, 1894.

Ménabréa (Léon), *De l'origine de la forme et de l'esprit des jugements rendus au moyen-âge contre les animaux.* Chambéry, 1846.

Mencius, ' The Works of ' ; in Legge, *The Chinese Classics*, vol. ii. Oxford, 1895.

Mendelsohn (S.), *The Criminal Jurisprudence of the Ancient Hebrews.* Baltimore, 1891.

Menger (Anton), *The Right to the Whole Produce of Labour.* Trans. London, 1899.

Merker (M.), *Die Masai.* Berlin, 1904.

Merolla da Sorrento (J.), ' A Voyage to Congo.' Trans. ; in Pinkerton, *Collection of Voyages and Travels*, vol. xvi. London, 1814.

Merzbacher (G.), *Aus den Hochregionen des Kaukasus.* 2 vols. Leipzig, 1901.

Methodist Magazine. London.

Methodist Magazine. New York.

Methodius (*Saint*), ' Opera omnia ' ; in Migne, *Patrologiæ cursus*, Ser. Graeca, vol. xviii. Parisiis, 1857.

Metz (F.), *The Tribes inhabiting the Neilgherry Hills.* Mangalore, 1864.

Meursius (J.); ' Themis Attica, sive de legibus Atticis ' ; in Gronovius, *Thesaurus Græcarum antiquitatum*, vol. v. Lugduni Batavorum, 1699.

Meyer (Eduard), *Geschichte des Alterthums.* Vol. i. Stuttgart, 1884.

Meyer (H. E. A.), ' Manners and Customs of the Aborigines of the Encounter Bay Tribe ' ; in Woods, *Native Tribes of South Australia.* Adelaide, 1879.

Meyrick (F.), *Moral and Devotional Theology of the Church of Rome. No. I. S. Alfonso de' Liguori's Theory of Truthfulness.* London, 1855.

Michaelis (J. D.), *Commentaries on the Laws of Moses.* Trans. 4 vols. London, 1814.

Michelet (J.), *Origines du droit français.* Paris, [1900].

Middleton (C.), *A Free Inquiry into the Miraculous Powers, Which are supposed to have subsisted in the Christian Church.* London, 1749.

Mielziner (M.), *Die Verhältnisse der Sklaven bei den alten Hebräern.* Kopenhagen, 1859.

Migne (J. P.), *Patrologiæ cursus completus.* 221 vols. Parisiis, 1844–64.

—— *Patrologiæ cursus completus. Series Græca.* 162 vols. Parisiis, 1857–66.

Miklosich (Franz), ' Die Blutrache bei den Slaven ' ; in *Denkschriften der kaiserlichen Akademie der Wissenschaften, Philosophisch-historische Classe*, vol. xxxvi. Wien, 1888.

Miler (E.), ' Die Hauskommunion der Südslaven ' ; in *Jahrbuch der internationalen Vereinigung für vergleichende Rechtswissenschaft und Volkswirtschaftslehre zu Berlin*, vol. iii. Berlin, 1897.

Mill (James), *Analysis of the Phenomena of the Human Mind*. Ed. by J. S. Mill. 2 vols. London, 1869.

—— *A Fragment on Mackintosh*. London, 1835.

Mill (John Stuart), *An Examination of Sir William Hamilton's Philosophy*. London, 1865.

—— *Principles of Political Economy*. 2 vols. London, 1865.

—— *Utilitarianism*. London, 1895.

Millar (John), *The Origin of the Distribution of Ranks*. Edinburgh, 1806.

Millingen (J. G.), *The History of Duelling*. 2 vols. London, 1841.

Mills (Charles), *The History of Chivalry*. 2 vols. London, 1826.

Milman (H. H.), *History of Latin Christianity*. 9 vols. London, 1867.

Milton (J.), *Poetical Works*. Ed. by D. Masson. 3 vols. London, 1874.

Mind. A Quarterly Review of Psychology and Philosophy. London.

Mindeleff (C.), ' Navaho Houses ' ; in *Ann. Rep. Bur. Ethn.* vol. xvii. Washington, 1898.

Missions Catholiques (Les). Lyon.

Missions-Blatt aus der Brüdergemeine. Hamburg.

Mitchell (T. L.), *Three Expeditions into the Interior of Eastern Australia*. 2 vols. London, 1839.

Mitford (A. B.), *Tales of Old Japan*. 2 vols. London, 1871.

Mittermaier (C. J. A. von), ' Beyträge zur Lehre vom Verbrechen des Kindesmordes ' ; in *Neues Archiv des Criminalrechts*, vol. vii. Halle, 1824–25.

—— *Grundsätze des gemeinen deutschen Privatrechts*. 2 vols. Regensburg, 1847.

—— *On the Effect of Drunkenness on Criminal Responsibility*. Trans. Edinburgh, 1841.

—— *Die Todesstrafe*. Heidelberg, 1862.

Mittheilungen der Anthropologischen Gesellschaft in Wien.

—— *der Geographischen Gesellschaft (für Thüringen) zu Jena*.

—— *der Geographischen Gesellschaft in Hamburg*.

—— *der kais. und könig. Geographischen Gesellschaft in Wien*.

—— *des Vereins für Erdkunde zu Halle a. S.*

—— *des Vereins für Erdkunde zu Leipzig*.

Mockler-Ferryman (A. F.), *British Nigeria*. London, 1902.

Modigliani (Elio), *Un viaggio a Nías*. Milano, 1890.

Mökern (Ph. von), *Ostindien*. 2 vols. Leipzig, 1857.

Möller (P.), Pagels (G.), and Gleerup (E.), *Tre år i Kongo*. 2 vols. Stockholm, 1887–88.

Moerenhout (J. A.), *Voyages aux îles du Grand Océan*. 2 vols. Paris, 1837.

Moffat (Robert), *Missionary Labours and Scenes in Southern Africa*. London, 1842.

—— The same work. London, 1846.

Molina (Christoval de), ' The Fables and Rites of the Yncas ' ; in *Narratives of the Rites and Laws of the Incas*. Trans. and ed. by C. R. Markham. London, 1873.

Molina (J. J.), *The Geographical, Natural, and Civil History of Chili*. Trans. 2 vols. London, 1809.

Moll (Albert), *Die Conträre Sexualempfindung.* Berlin, 1891.
Mommsen (Theodor), *History of Rome.* Trans. 5 vols. London, 1894.
—— *Römisches Strafrecht.* Leipzig, 1899.
Monier-Williams (Monier), *Brāhmanism and Hindūism.* London, 1887.
—— *Buddhism.* London, 1890.
—— *Hinduism.* London, s.d.
—— *Indian Wisdom.* London, 1893.
Monrad (H. C.), *Bidrag til en Skildring af Guinea-Kysten og dens Indbyggere.* Kjøbenhavn, 1822.
Montaigne (M. de), *Œuvres.* Ed. by J. A. C. Buchon. Paris, 1837.
Montefiore (C. G.), *Hibbert Lectures on . . . the Religion of the Ancient Hebrews.* London, 1892.
Montesquieu (C. de Secondat de), *Œuvres.* Paris, 1837.
Montgomery (James), *Journal of Voyages and Travels by D. Tyerman and G. Bennet.* 2 vols. London, 1831.
Month and Catholic Review (The). London.
Mooney (James), ' Myths of the Cherokee ' ; in *Ann. Rep. Bur. Ethn.* vol. xix. pt. i. Washington, 1900.
Moorcroft (William) and Trebeck (George), *Travels in the Himalayan Provinces of Hindustan and the Panjab.* Ed. by H. H. Wilson. 2 vols. London, 1841.
Moore (Charles), *A Full Inquiry into the Subject of Suicide, &c.* 2 vols. London, 1790.
Moore (Samuel), *The Public Acts in force ; passed by the Legislature of Barbados,* 1762–1800. London, 1801.
Moore (Theofilus), *Marriage Customs, &c. of the Various Nations of the Universe.* London, 1814.
More (*Sir* Thomas), *Utopia.* Trans. ed. by E. Arber. London, 1869.
Morehead (C. S.) and Brown (Mason), *A Digest of the Statute Laws of Kentucky.* 2 vols. Frankfort (Ky.), 1834.
Morgan (C. Lloyd), *Animal Life and Intelligence.* London, 1890–91.
Morgan (L. H.), *Houses and House-Life of the American Aborigines.* Washington, 1881.
—— *League of the Ho-de'-no-sau-nee, or Iroquois.* Rochester, 1851.
Morley (John), *Voltaire.* London, 1886.
Morrison (W. D.), *Crime and its Causes.* London, 1891.
Morselli (E.), *Il suicidio.* Milano, 1879.
Mort de Garin le Loherain (La). Ed. by É. du Méril. Paris, 1846.
Morte Darthur. London, 1868.
Moschus (Joannes), ' Pratum spirituale ' ; in Migne, *Patrologiæ cursus,* Ser. Graeca, vol. lxxxvii. Parisiis, 1860.
Moseley (H. N.), *Notes by a Naturalist on the " Challenger."* London, 1879.
—— ' On the Inhabitants of the Admiralty Islands, &c. ' ; in *Jour. Anthr. Inst.* vol. vi. London, 1877.
Mosheim (J. L. von), *Institutes of Ecclesiastical History.* 3 vols. London, 1863.
Mouhot (H.), *Travels in the Central Parts of Indo-China, &c.* 2 vols. London, 1864.
Mozley (J. B.), *Sermons preached before the University of Oxford.* London, 1883.
Müller (C. O.), *Dissertations on the Eumenides of Æschylus.* Trans. London & Cambridge, 1853.

Müller (C. O.), *The History and Antiquities of the Doric Race*. Trans. 2 vols. London, 1830.

Müller (Friedrich), *Allgemeine Ethnographie*. Wien, 1879.

—— *Reise der österreichischen Fregatte Novara um die Erde*. *Ethnographie*. Wien, 1868.

Müller (Friedrich Max), *Anthropological Religion*. London, 1892.

—— *Physical Religion*. London, 1891.

Müller (J. G.), *Geschichte der Amerikanischen Urreligionen*. Basel, 1867.

Müller (Josef), *Das sexuelle Leben der alten Kulturvölker*. Leipzig, 1902.

—— *Das sexuelle Leben der christlichen Kulturvölker*. Leipzig, 1904.

Müller (W. J.), *Die Africanische, Auff der Guineischen Gold-Cust gelegene Landschafft Fetu*. Hamburg, 1673.

Mürdter (F.), *Geschichte Babyloniens und Assyriens*. Ed. by F. Delitzsch. Calw & Stuttgart, 1891.

Muir (John), *Additional Moral and Religious Passages metrically rendered from the Sanskrit*. London, [1875].

—— *Original Sanskrit Texts*. 5 vols. London, 1868–84.

—— *Religious and Moral Sentiments metrically rendered from Sanskrit Writers*. London, 1875.

Muir (William), *The Life of Mahomet*. 4 vols. London, 1858–61.

Muirhead (J. H.), *The Elements of Ethics*. London, 1897.

Munzinger (W.), *Ostafrikanische Studien*. Schaffhausen, 1864.

—— *Ueber die Sitten und das Recht der Bogos*. Winterthur, 1859.

Muratori (L. A.), *Dissertazioni sopra le antichità Italiane*. 5 vols. Milano, 1836–37.

—— *Rerum Italicarum scriptores*. 25 vols. Mediolani, 1723–51.

Murdoch (John), ' Ethnological Results of the Point Barrow Expedition ' ; in *Ann. Rep. Bur. Ethn.* vol. ix. Washington, 1892.

Murray (A. W.), *Forty Years' Mission Work in Polynesia and New Guinea*. London, 1876.

Murray (J. A. H.), *A New English Dictionary*. Oxford, 1884, &c. *In progress.*

Murray (J. Clark), *An Introduction to Ethics*. London, 1891.

Musters (G. C.), *At Home with the Patagonians*. London, 1873.

Nachtigal (G.), *Sahara und Sudan*. 3 vols. Berlin, 1879–89.

Nadaillac (*Marquis* de), ' L'anthropophagie et les sacrifices humains ' ; in *Revue des Deux Mondes*, vol. lxvi. Paris, 1884.

Nägelsbach (C. F. von), *Homerische Theologie*. Ed. by G. Autenrieth. Nürnberg, 1884.

—— *Die nachhomerische Theologie des griechischen Volksglaubens bis auf Alexander*. Nürnberg, 1857.

Nansen (F.), *Eskimo Life*. Trans. London, 1893.

—— *The First Crossing of Greenland*. Trans. 2 vols. London, 1890.

' Nârada,' trans. by J. Jolly ; in *The Sacred Books of the East*, vol. xxxiii. Oxford, 1889.

Narrative of the Chinese Embassy to the Khan of the Tourgouth Tartars. Trans. from the Chinese by Sir G. T. Staunton. London, 1821.

Narratives of the Rites and Laws of the Yncas. Trans. and ed. by C. R. Markham. London, 1873.

Nassau (R. H.), *Fetichism in West Africa*. London, 1904.

Nation (The) ; a Weekly Journal. New York.

'National Personality'; in *The Edinburgh Review*, vol. cxciv. London, 1901.

'Nationality'; in *The Home and Foreign Review*, vol. i. London, 1862.

Natorp (Paul), *Die Ethika des Demokritos*. Marburg, 1893.

'Naturalization Act, 1870 (The)'; in Chitty, *Statutes of Practical Utility*, vol. i. London, 1894.

Nature ; a Weekly Illustrated Journal of Science. London.

Naudet (—), 'Des secours publics chez les Romains'; in *Mémoires de l'Institut Royal de France, Académie des Inscriptions et Belles-Lettres*, vol. xiii. Paris, 1838.

Navarette (D. F.), 'An Account of the Empire of China' Trans; in Awnsham and Churchill, *Collection of Voyages and Travels*, vol. i. London, 1704.

Neale (E. V.), *Feasts and Fasts*. London, 1845.

Neander (Joseph), *General History of the Christian Religion and Church*. Trans. 9 vols. Edinburgh, 1847–55.

Nelson (E. W.), 'The Eskimo about Bering Strait'; in *Ann. Rep. Bur. Ethn.* Washington, 1899.

Nelson (J. H.), *A View of the Hindū Law*. Madras, &c., 1877.

Nennius, *The Irish Version of the Historia Britonum of*. Ed. and trans. by J. H. Todd. Dublin, 1848.

Nepos (Cornelius), *Vitæ excellentium imperatorum*. 2 vols. Londini, 1822.

Neubauer (A.), 'Notes on the Race-Types of the Jews'; in *Jour. Anthr. Inst.* vol. xv. London, 1886.

Neues Archiv des Criminalrechts. Halle.

Neumann (K. F.), *Die Völker des südlichen Russlands*. Leipzig, 1847.

Nevill (Hugh), 'Vaeddas of Ceylon'; in *The Taprobanian*, vols. i.–ii. Bombay, 1887–88.

New (Charles), *Life, Wanderings, &c. in Eastern Africa*. London, 1874.

New Englander (The). New Haven.

Newbold (T. J.), *Political and Statistical Account of the British Settlements in the Straits of Malacca*. 2 vols. London, 1839.

Newman (F. W.), *Anglo-Saxon Abolition of Negro Slavery*. London, 1889.

Newman (J. H.), *Apologia pro vita sua*. London, 1873.

Nicolaus I. (*Pope*), 'Epistolae et decreta'; in Migne, *Patrologiæ cursus*, vol. cxix. Parisiis, 1852.

Nieboer (H. J.), *Slavery as an Industrial System*. The Hague, 1900.

Niebuhr (C.), *Travels through Arabia*. Trans. 2 vols. Edinburgh, 1792

Nielsen (F.), *Tertullians Ethik*. Kjøbenhavn, 1879.

Nietzsche (F.), *Also sprach Zarathustra*. 4 vols. Chemnitz & Leipzig, 1883-91.

Nisbet (Hume), *A Colonial Tramp*. 2 vols. London, 1891.

Njála. Ed. by Det Kongelige Nordiske Oldskrift-Selskab. 2 vols. Köbenhavn, 1875–89.

Nonius Marcellus, *De proprietate sermonis*. Lipsiae, 1826.

Noodt (G.), *Opera omnia*. 2 vols. Lugduni Batavorum, 1767.

Nordenskiöld (A. E.), *Den andra Dicksonska expeditionen till Grönland*. Stockholm, 1885.

—— *Vegas färd kring Asien och Europa*. 2 vols. Stockholm, 1880–81.

Nordström (J. J.), *Bidrag till den svenska samhälls-författningens historia*, 2 vols. Helsingfors, 1839–40.

Noreen (Ad.), *Spridda studier. Andra samlingen*. Stockholm, 1903.

Norman (Henry), *The Real Japan.* London, 1892.

North Indian Notes and Queries : a Monthly Periodical. Ed. by W. Crooke. Allahabad.

Norton (A.), *Tracts concerning Christianity.* Cambridge, 1852.

Nowack (Wilhelm), *Lehrbuch der hebräischen Archäologie.* 2 vols. Freiburg i. B. & Leipzig, 1894.

Numa Praetorius, ' Die strafrechtlichen Bestimmungen gegen den gleichgeschlechtlichen Verkehr ' ; in *Jahrbuch für sexuelle Zwischenstufen,* vol. i. Leipzig, 1899.

Nuñez Cabeza de Vaca (Alvar), ' Naufragios y relacion de la jornada que hizo a la Florida' ; in *Biblioteca de autores españoles,* vol. xxii. Madrid, 1852.

Nyrop (K.), ' Navnets magt ' ; in *Mindre Afhandlinger udgivne af det Philologisk-historiske Samfund.* Kjøbenhavn, 1887.

—— *Romanske Mosaiker.* Kjøbenhavn, 1885.

Nys (Ernest), *Le droit de la guerre et les précurseurs de Grotius.* Bruxelles & Leipzig, 1882.

—— *Le droit international.* 2 vols. Bruxelles & Paris, 1904–05.

Oberländer (R.), ' Die Eingeborenen der australischen Kolonie Victoria ' ; in *Globus,* vol. iv. Hildburghausen, 1863.

Oehler (G. F.), *Theology of the Old Testament.* Vol. i. Trans. Edinburgh, 1874.

Oldenberg (H.), *Buddha.* Trans. London, 1882.

—— *Die Religion des Veda.* Berlin, 1894.

Oldfield (A.), ' On the Aborigines of Australia ' ; in *Trans. Ethn. Soc.* new ser. vol. iii. London, 1865.

Olivecrona (K.), *Om dödsstraffet.* Upsala, 1866.

Olmsted (F. A.), *Incidents of a Whaling Voyage.* New York, 1841.

Open Court (The). Chicago.

Oppert (J.), ' La condition des esclaves à Babylone ' ; in *Académie des Inscriptions et Belles-Lettres—Comptes rendus des séances de l'année* 1888, ser. iv. vol. xvi. Paris.

—— and Ménant (J.), *Documents juridiques de l'Assyrie et de la Chaldée.* Paris, 1877.

Origen, *Opera omnia.* 7 vols. (Migne, *Patrologiæ cursus,* Ser. Graeca, vols. xi.–xvii.) Parisiis, 1857–60.

Original-Mittheilungen aus der ethnologischen Abtheilung der königlichen Museen zu Berlin. Berlin.

Orosius (P.), ' Historiarum libri septem ' ; in Migne, *Patrologiæ cursus,* vol. xxxi. Parisiis, 1846.

Orpen (J. M.), ' A Glimpse into the Mythology of the Maluti Bushmen ' ; in *The Cape Monthly Magazine,* new ser. vol. ix. Cape Town, 1874.

Ortolan (J.), *Éléments de droit pénal.* Paris, 1859.

Osenbrüggen (E.), *Das Alamannische Strafrecht.* Schaffhausen, 1860.

—— *Studien zur deutschen und schweizerischen Rechtsgeschichte.* Schaffhausen, 1868.

Ostfriesische Land-Recht (Das). Aurich, [1746].

Ottoman Penal Code (The). Trans. by C. G. Walpole. London, 1888.

Ovidius Naso (P.), *Opera omnia.* 9 vols. Londini, 1821.

Oviedo y Valdés (G. Hernandez de), ' Summario de la natural historia de las Indias ' ; in *Biblioteca de autores españoles,* vol. xxii. Madrid, 1852.

Paget (John), *Hungary and Transylvania.* 2 vols. London, 1839.

Paley (W.), *Complete Works.* 4 vols. London, 1825.

Palgrave (W. G.), *Narrative of a Year's Journey through Central and Eastern Arabia.* 2 vols. London & Cambridge, 1865.

Palissot de Montenoy (Charles), *Les philosophes.* Paris, 1760.

Pallas (P. S.), *Travels through the Southern Provinces of the Russian Empire.* Trans. 2 vols. London, 1802–03.

Palmer (Edward), ' Notes on some Australian Tribes ' ; in *Jour. Anthr. Inst.* vol. xiii. London, 1884.

Panchatantram. With an English translation and a Glossary. 5 pts. Madras, 1891–93.

—— See *Pantschatantra.*

Panjab Notes and Queries, a Monthly Periodical. Ed. by R. C. Temple. Allahabad.

Pantschatantra. Trans. into German by Th. Benfey. 2 vols. Leipzig, 1859.

Paramo (L. de), *De origine et progressu Sanctæ Inquisitionis.* Matriti, 1598.

Pardessus (J. M.), *Collection de lois maritimes antérieures au XVIII⁰ siècle.* 6 vols. Paris, 1828–45.

—— *Loi Salique.* Paris, 1843.

—— *Us et coutumes de la mer.* 2 vols. Paris, 1847.

Paris (Gaston), *La poésie du moyen âge.* Paris, 1885.

Park (Mungo), *Travels in the Interior Districts of Africa.* 2 vols. London, 1816–17.

—— The same work. Edinburgh, 1860.

Parker (E. H.), ' Comparative Chinese Family Law ' ; in *The China Review,* vol. viii. Hongkong, 1879–80.

Parker (E. S.), *The Aborigines of Australia.* Melbourne, 1854.

Parker (*Mrs.* K. Langloh), *The Euahlayi Tribe.* London, 1905.

Parker (Theodore), *The Collected Works of.* Ed. by F. P. Cobbe. 14 vols. London, 1863–71.

—— *A Sermon of War.* Boston, 1846.

Parkinson (John), ' Notes on the Asaba People ' ; in *Jour. Anthr. Inst.* vol. xxxvi. London, 1906.

Parkinson (R.), *Zur Ethnographie der nordwestlichen Salomo Inseln.* Berlin, 1899.

Parkman (Francis), *The Jesuits in North America in the Seventeenth Century.* London, 1885.

Parkyns (M.), *Life in Abyssinia.* 2 vols. London, 1853.

Parliamentary History and Review ; containing Reports of the Proceedings of the Two Houses of Parliament during the Session of 1825–26. London, 1826.

Parry (W. E.), *Journal of a Second Voyage for the Discovery of a North-West Passage from the Atlantic to the Pacific.* London, 1824.

Partridge (Charles), *Cross River Natives.* London, 1905.

Patetta (F.), *Le ordalie.* Torino, 1890.

Paul (Hermann), *Grundriss der germanischen Philologie.* Ed. by H. P. 2 vols. Strassburg, 1889–93.

—— The same work. 3 vols. Strassburg, 1896–1900.

Paulhan (F.), *L'activité mentale et les éléments de l'esprit.* Paris, 1889.

Paulitschke (Ph.), *Ethnographie Nordost-Afrikas.* 2 vols. Berlin, 1893–96.

Paulsen (F.), *System der Ethik.* 2 vols. Berlin, 1894.

Pauly (A. F. von), *Real-Encyclopädie der classischen Alterthumswissenschaft.* 6 vols. Stuttgart, 1842–62.

Pausanias, *Descriptio Græciæ.* Ed. by L. Dindorfius. Parisiis, 1845.

—— See Frazer (*Sir* J. G.).

Payne (E. J.), *History of the New World called America.* 2 vols. Oxford, 1892–99.

Peacock (Mabel), ' Executed Criminals and Folk-Medicine ' ; in *Folk-Lore*, vol. vii. London, 1896.

Pearson (Charles H.), *National Life and Character.* London, 1893.

Peirce (L.), Taylor (M.), and King (W. W.), *The Consolidation and Revision of the Statutes of the State [Louisiana].* New Orleans, 1852.

Peltzer (A.), *Deutsche Mystik und deutsche Kunst.* Strassburg, 1899.

Penny (Alfred), *Ten Years in Melanesia.* London, 1887.

Percival (Peter), *The Land of the Veda.* London, 1854.

Percival (Robert), *An Account of the Island of Ceylon.* London, 1803.

Perelaer (M. T. H.), *Ethnographische beschrijving der Dajaks.* Zalt-Bommel, 1870.

Perez (Bernard), *The First Three Years of Childhood.* Trans. London, 1892.

Perham (J.), ' Petara ' ; in *Jour. Straits Branch Roy. Asiatic Soc.* no. 8. Singapore, 1882.

—— ' Sea Dyak Religion ' ; in *Jour. Straits Branch Roy. Asiatic Soc.* no. 10. Singapore, 1883.

Perrin du Lac (F. M.), *Voyage dans les deux Louisianes et chez les nations sauvages du Missouri.* Paris, 1805.

Perrot (Nicholas), *Memoire sur les mœurs, coustumes et relligion des sauvages de l'Amerique septentrionale.* Ed. by R. P. J. Tailhan. Leipzig & Paris, 1864.

Perry (G. G.), *A History of the English Church. First Period.* London, 1881.

Pertile (Antonio), ' Gli animali in giudizio ' ; in *Atti del Reale Istituto Veneto di scienze, lettere ed arti*, ser. vi. vol. iv. Venezia, 1884–85.

Pertuiset (E.), *Le trésor des Incas à la Terre de Feu.* Paris, 1877.

Perty (Max.), *Ueber das Seelenleben der Thiere.* Leipzig & Heidelberg, 1876.

Pertz (G. H.), *Monumenta Germaniæ historica.* Leges. 5 vols. Hanno-verae, 1837–75.

Peschel (O.), *The Races of Man.* Trans. London, 1876.

Petherick (John), *Egypt, the Soudan and Central Africa.* Edinburgh & London, 1861.

—— and Petherick (*Mrs.*), *Travels in Central Africa, and Explorations of the Western Nile Tributaries.* 2 vols. London, 1869.

Petitot (C. B.), *Collection complète des Mémoires relatifs à l'histoire de France.* 130 vols. Paris, 1819–29.

Petitot (É.), *Les Grands Esquimaux.* Paris, 1887.

Petrie (W. M. Flinders), *Religion and Conscience in Ancient Egypt.* London, 1898.

Petroff (Ivan), ' Report on the Population, Industries, and Resources of Alaska ' ; in *Tenth Census of the United States.* Washington, 1884.

Pfeiffer (Ida), *A Lady's Second Journey round the World.* [Trans.] 2 vols. London, 1855.

Pfleiderer (Otto), *Philosophy and Development of Religion.* Trans. 2 vols. Edinburgh & London, 1894.

Philip (Robert), *The Life and Opinions of the Rev. William Milne.* London, 1840.

Philo Judaeus, *Opera.* Ed. by Th. Mangey. 2 vols. London, 1742.

Piedrahita (L. Fernandez de), *Historia general de las conquistas del nuevo reyno de Granada.* Amberes, [1688].

Pierotti (Ermete), *Customs and Traditions of Palestine.* Trans. Cambridge, 1864.

Pike (L. Owen), *A History of Crime in England.* 2 vols. London, 1873–76.

Pindar, *Carmina.* Ed. by C. I. T. Mommsen. Berolini, 1864.

Pinel (Ph.), *Traité médico-philosophique sur l'aliénation mentale.* Paris, 1809.

Pinkerton (John), *A General Collection of Voyages and Travels.* 17 vols. London, 1808–14.

Pitcairn (Robert), *Criminal Trials in Scotland.* 3 vols. Edinburgh, 1838.

Pitcairn (W. D.), *Two Years among the Savages of New Guinea.* London, 1891.

Placucci (M.), *Usi e pregiudizj dei contadini della Romagna.* Ed. by G. Pitrè. Palermo, 1885.

Plato, *Dialogues.* Trans. by B. Jowett. 5 vols. Oxford, 1892.

—— *Opera.* 3 vols. Parisiis, 1846–73.

Plautus (T. M.), *Comœdiæ.* 5 vols. Londini, 1829.

Pliny, the Elder, *Historia naturalis.* 13 vols. Londini, 1826.

Pliny, the Younger, *Epistolarum libri decem.* Ed. by N. E. Lemaire. 2 vols. Parisiis, 1822–23.

Ploss (H. H.), *Das Kind im Brauch und Sitte der Völker.* 2 vols. Stuttgart, 1876.

—— *Das Weib in der Natur- und Völkerkunde.* Ed. by M. Bartels. 2 vols. Leipzig, 1902.

Plowden (E.), *The Commentaries or Reports of.* Trans. 2 parts. Savoy (London), 1661.

Plutarch, *Romane Questions.* Trans. ed. by F. B. Jevons. London, 1892.

—— *Scripta moralia.* 2 vols. Parisiis, 1839–41.

—— *Vitæ.* Ed. by Th. Dœhner. 2 vols. Parisiis, 1846–47.

Pogge (Paul), *Im Reiche des Muata Jamwo.* Berlin, 1880.

Poircy (L. de), *Histoire naturelle et morale des Iles Antilles de l'Amerique.* Ed. by C. de Rochefort. Rotterdam, 1681.

Polack (J. S.), *Manners and Customs of the New Zealanders.* 2 vols. London, 1840.

Polak (J. E.), *Persien.* 2 vols. Leipzig, 1865.

—— ' Die Prostitution in Persien ' ; in *Wiener Medizinische Wochenschrift,* vol. xi. Wien, 1861.

Pollock (*Sir* Frederick), *Essays on Jurisprudence and Ethics.* London, 1882.

—— ' The King's Peace ' ; in *The Law Quarterly Review,* vol. i. London, 1885.

—— *The Law of Torts.* London, 1897.

—— *Oxford Lectures.* London, 1890.

—— and Maitland (F. W.), *The History of the English Law before the Time of Edward I.* 2 vols. Cambridge, 1898.

Pollux (Julius), *Onomasticum.* 2 vols. Amstelædami, 1706.

Polo (Marco), *The Book of, concerning the Kingdoms and Marvels of the East.* Trans. ed. by H. Yule. 2 vols. London, 1871.

Polybius, *Historiarum reliquiæ.* 2 vols. Parisiis, 1839.

Pommerol (Jean), *Among the Women of the Sahara.* Trans. London, 1900.

Pool (J. J.), *Studies in Mohammedanism.* Westminster, 1892.

Poole (R. Lane), *Illustrations of the History of Medieval Thought in the Departments of Theology and Ecclesiastical Politics.* London, 1884.

Poole (S. Lane). See Lane-Poole (S.).

Popović (Georg), *Recht und Gericht in Montenegro.* Agram, 1877.

Popular Science Monthly (The). New York.

Porphyry, *De abstinentia ab esu animalium.* Ed. by R. Hercher. Parisiis, 1858.

Porter (G. R.), *The Progress of the Nation from the Beginning of the Nineteenth Century to the Present Time.* London, 1843.

Post (A. H.), *Afrikanische Jurisprudenz.* 2 vols. Oldenburg & Leipzig, 1887.

—— *Die Anfänge des Staats- und Rechtslebens.* Oldenburg, 1878.

—— *Die Geschlechtsgenossenschaft der Urzeit und die Entstehung der Ehe.* Oldenburg, 1875.

—— *Die Grundlagen des Rechts.* Oldenburg, 1884.

—— *Grundriss der ethnologischen Jurisprudenz.* 2 vols. Oldenburg & Leipzig, 1894–95.

—— *Studien zur Entwicklungsgeschichte des Familienrechts.* Oldenburg & Leipzig, 1890.

Potgiesser (J.), *Commentariorum juris Germanici de statu servorum veteri perinde atque novo libri quinque.* Lemgoviae, 1736.

Potter (John), *Archæologia Græca.* 2 vols. Edinburgh, 1832.

Powell (J. W.), ' Outlines of Sociology ' ; in *The Saturday Lectures delivered in the Lecture-Room of the U.S. National Museum.* Washington, 1882.

—— ' Sociology ' ; in *The American Anthropologist,* new ser. vol. i. New York, 1899.

—— ' Wyandot Government ' ; in *Ann. Rep. Bur. Ethn.* vol. i. Washington, 1881.

Powell (Wilfred), *Wanderings in a Wild Country ; or, Three Years amongst the Cannibals of New Britain.* London, 1883.

Powers (Stephan), *Tribes of California.* Washington, 1877.

Prain (David), ' The Angami Nagas ' ; in *Revue coloniale internationale,* vol. v. Amsterdam, 1887.

Prejevalsky (N.), *Mongolia.* Trans. 2 vols. London, 1876.

Preller (L.), *Griechische Mythologie.* Vol. i. Ed. by Carl Robert. Berlin, 1894.

Prem Ságar ; or, the Ocean of Love. Trans. by E. B. Eastwick. Hertford & London, 1851.

Prentiss (G. L.), ' Infant Salvation and its Theological Bearings ' ; in *The Presbyterian Review,* vol. iv. New York, 1883.

Presbyterian Review (The). New York.

Prescott (W. H.), *History of the Conquest of Mexico.* Ed. by J. F. Kirk. London, 1887.

—— *History of the Conquest of Peru.* 3 vols. London, [1890].

Preuss (Theodor), *Die Begräbnisarten der Amerikaner und Nordostasiaten.* Königsberg, 1894.

Prexl (R.), ' Geburts- und Todtengebräuche der Rumänen in Siebenbürgen' ; in *Globus,* vol. lvii. Braunschweig, 1890.

Price (Richard), *A Review of the Principal Questions in Morals.* London, 1787.

Prichard (H. H.), *Through the Heart of Patagonia.* London, 1902.

Pridham (Charles), *An Account of Ceylon.* 2 vols. London, 1849.

Priestley (Joseph). See Hartley, *Theory of the Human Mind.*

Prince (O. H.), *A Digest of the Laws of the State of Georgia.* Athens (U.S.), 1837.

Pritchard (W. T.), *Polynesian Reminiscences.* London, 1866.
Proceedings of the Royal Geographical Society and Monthly Record of Geography. London.
—— *of the Royal Irish Academy.* Dublin.
—— *of the Royal Society of Edinburgh.*
—— *of the Society of Biblical Archæology.* London.
Procopius, ex recensione G. Dindorfii. 3 vols. Bonnae, 1833–38.
Proudhon (P.-J.), *La guerre et la paix.* 2 vols. Bruxelles, [1861].
Proyart (L. B.), ' History of Loango, &c.' Trans. ; in Pinkerton, *Collection of Voyages and Travels*, vol. xvi. London, 1814.
Ptan-Hotep, ' The Precepts of.' Trans. by Ph. Virey ; in *Records of the Past*, new ser. vol. iii. London, *s. d.*
Puchta (G. F.), *Cursus der Institutionen.* 2 vols. Leipzig, 1875.
Pufendorf (Samuel), *De jure naturæ et gentium.* Amstelodami, 1688.
Purcell (B. H.), ' Rites and Customs of Australian Aborigines ' ; in *Verhandl. Berliner Gesellsch. Anthrop.*, 1893.

Quarterly Review (The). London.
Quatremère (E. M.), ' Mémoire sur les asiles chez les Arabes ' ; in *Mémoires de l'Institut Royal de France, Académie des Inscriptions et Belles-Lettres*, vol. xv. pt. ii. Paris, 1842.
Quintilian (M. F.), *Declamationes quæ supersunt CXLV.* Ed. by C. Ritter. Lipsiae, 1884.
—— *Institutionis oratoriæ libri duodecim.* Ed. by C. Halm. 2 vols. Lipsiae, 1868.
Qur'ân (The). Trans. by E. H. Palmer. 2 vols. (*The Sacred Books of the East*, vols. vi. and ix.) Oxford, 1880.

Rabbinowicz (I. J. M.), *Législation criminelle du Talmud.* Paris, 1876.
Radde (G.), *Die Chews'uren und ihr Land.* Cassel, 1878.
Radloff (W.), *Das Schamanenthum.* Leipzig, 1885.
Raffenel (Anne), *Nouveau voyage dans le pays des nègres.* 2 vols. Paris, 1856.
Raffles (T. S.), *The History of Java.* 2 vols. London, 1817.
Rájendralála Mitra, *Indo-Aryans.* 2 vols. London & Calcutta, 1881.
Ralston (W. R. S.), *The Songs of the Russian People.* London, 1872.
Rambaud (A.), *Histoire de la civilisation française.* 2 vols. Paris, 1893–94.
Ramsay (W. M.), *The Church in the Roman Empire before A.D. 170.* London, 1903.
—— *The Cities and Bishoprics of Phrygia.* 2 vols. Oxford, 1895–97.
—— *The Historical Geography of Asia Minor.* London, 1890.
Ramseyer (F. A.) and Kühne (J.), *Four Years in Ashantee.* Ed. by Mrs. Weitbrecht. London, 1875.
Ranking (John), *Historical Researches on the Conquest of Peru, Mexico, &c.* London, 1827.
Rattray (R. S.), *Some Folk-Lore Stories and Songs in Chinyanja.* London, 1907.
Ratzel (F.), *The History of Mankind.* Trans. 3 vols. London, 1896–98.
Ravenscroft (A. G. B.), ' Some Habits and Customs of the Chingalee Tribe ' ; in *Trans. Roy. Soc. South Australia*, vol. xv. Adelaide, 1892.
Rawlinson (George), *The Religions of the Ancient World.* London, *s. d.*

Read (C. H.) and Dalton (O. M.), *Antiquities from the City of Benin*. London, 1899.

Reade (W. Winwood), *Savage Africa*. London, 1863.

Réal de Courban (G. de), *La science du gouvernement*. 8 vols. Aix-la-Chapelle, &c., 1761–65.

Recopilacion de leyes de los reinos de las Indias. 4 vols. Madrid, 1841.

Records of the Past. London.

Rée (Paul), *Die Entstehung des Gewissens*. Berlin, 1885.

—— *Der Ursprung der moralischen Empfindungen*. Chemnitz, 1877.

Reed (*Sir* E. J.), *Japan*. 2 vols. London, 1880.

Rehme (Paul), ' Das Recht der Amaxosa ' ; in *Zeitschr. f. vergl. Rechtswiss.* vol. x. Berlin, 1892.

Reichard (Paul), ' Die Wanjamuesi ' ; in *Zeitschr. der Gesellschaft für Erdkunde zu Berlin*, vol. xxiv. Berlin, 1889.

Reid (A. P.), ' Religious Belief of the Ojibois or Sauteux Indians ' ; in *Jour. Anthr. Inst.* vol. iii. London, 1874.

Reid (Thomas), *An Inquiry into the Human Mind*. London, 1785.

Rein (J. J.), *Japan*. Trans. London, 1884.

Rein (Wilhelm), *Das Criminalrecht der Römer*. Leipzig, 1844.

Reinhard (F. V.), *System der Christlichen Moral*. 5 vols. Wittenberg,1805–15.

Remy (Jules), *Ka Mooolelo Hawaii*. Paris & Leipzig, 1862.

Renan (Ernest), *Hibbert Lectures on the Influence of the Institutions, Thought and Culture of Rome, on Christianity*. London, 1885.

Rengger (J. R.), *Naturgeschichte der Säugethiere von Paraguay*. Basel, 1830.

Renouf (P. Le Page), *Hibbert Lectures on . . . the Religion of Ancient Egypt*. London, 1884.

Renton (A. W.), *Encyclopædia of the Laws of England*. London, [1897, &c.].

Report on the Work of the Horn Scientific Expedition to Central Australia. Ed. by B. Spencer. Part iv. London & Melbourne, 1896.

Reports of the Cambridge Anthropological Expedition to Torres Straits. Ed. by A. C. Haddon. Vol. v. Cambridge, 1904.

Réville (Albert), *Hibbert Lectures on . . . the Native Religions of Mexico and Peru*. London, 1884.

—— *Prolegomena of the History of Religions*. Trans. London, 1884.

—— *La Religion Chinoise*. Paris, 1889.

—— *Les religions des peuples non-civilisés*. 2 vols. Paris, 1883.

Réville (André), ' L'abjuratio regni ' ; in *Revue historique*, vol. l. Paris, 1892.

Revised Statutes of the State of North Carolina (*The*), *passed by the General Assembly at the Session of* 1836–7. 2 vols. Raleigh, 1837.

Revue Celtique. Paris.

—— *coloniale internationale*. Amsterdam.

—— *de législation et de jurisprudence*. Paris.

—— *de l'histoire des religions*. Paris.

—— *des Deux Mondes*. Paris.

—— *historique*. Paris.

—— *historique de droit français et é ranger*. Paris.

—— *internationale de sociologie*. Ed. by R. Worms. Paris.

—— *scientifique*. Paris.

Rheinisches Museum für Philologie. Frankfurt a. M.

Rhŷs (John), *Celtic Folklore*. 2 vols. Oxford, 1901.

Ribbe (Ch. de), *Les familles et la société en France avant la Révolution.* Paris, 1873.

Ribeiro de Sampaio (F. X.), *Diario da viagem.* Lisboa, 1825.

Ribot (Th.), *The Psychology of the Emotions.* [Trans.] London, 1897.

Richardson (C. H.), ' Observations among the Cameroon Tribes of West Central Africa ' ; in *Memoirs of the International Congress of Anthropology.* Chicago, 1894.

Richardson (James), *Narrative of a Mission to Central Africa performed in the Years* 1850–51. 2 vols. London, 1853.

Richardson (John), *Arctic Searching Expedition.* 2 vols. London, 1851.

Richmond (Legh), ' A Sermon on the Sin of Cruelty to the Brute Creation ' ; in *The Methodist Magazine,* vol. xxx. London, 1807.

Richter (W.), *Die Sklaverei im Griechischen Altertume.* Breslau, 1886.

Rickaby (J.), *Moral Philosophy.* London, 1892.

Ridley (William), *The Aborigines of Australia.* Sydney, 1864.

—— *Kámilarói, and other Australian Languages.* N. S. Wales, 1875.

—— *Kamilaroi, Dippil, and Turrubul.* N. S. Wales, 1866.

Riedel (J. G. F.), *De sluik- en kroesharige rassen tusschen Selebes en Papua.* 's-Gravenhage, 1886.

Rigveda (Der). Trans. into German by A. Ludwig. 6 vols. Prag, 1876–88.

Rink (H. J.), *Danish Greenland.* Ed. by R. Brown. London, 1877.

—— *The Eskimo Tribes.* Copenhagen & London, 1887.

—— *Tales and Traditions of the Eskimo.* Edinburgh & London, 1875.

Risley (H. H.), *Census of India,* 1901. *Vol. I. Ethnographic Appendices.* Calcutta, 1903.

—— *Tribes and Castes of Bengal. Ethnographic Glossary.* 2 vols. Calcutta, 1891.

Ritchie (D. G.), *Natural Rights.* London, 1895.

Ritson (Jos.), *An Essay on Abstinence from Animal Food as a Moral Duty.* London, 1802.

Ritter (B.), *Philo und die Halacha.* Leipzig, 1879.

Rivers (W. H. R.), *The Todas.* London, 1906.

Rivier (Alphonse), *Précis du droit de famille romain.* Paris, 1891.

Rivière (Armand), *L'Église et l'esclavage.* Paris, 1864.

Rivista italiana di sociologia. Roma.

Roberts (George), *The Social History of the People of the Southern Counties of England in Past Centuries.* London, 1856.

Robertson (*Sir* G. Scott), *The Káfirs of the Hindu-Kush.* London, 1896.

Robertson (H. A.), *Erromanga, the Martyr Isle.* Ed. by J. Fraser. London, 1902.

Robertson (John M.), *Patriotism and Empire.* London, 1899.

Robertson (William), *The History of America.* 2 vols. London, 1777.

—— *The History of the Reign of the Emperor Charles V.* 4 vols. London, 1806.

Robinson (A.), *Life in California.* New York, 1846.

Robinson (Cecilia), *The Ministry of Deaconesses.* London, 1898.

Robinson (Edward), *Biblical Researches in Palestine.* 3 vols. London, 1867.

Rochas (V. de), *La Nouvelle Calédonie et ses habitants.* Paris, 1862.

Rochefort (C. de). See Poircy (L. de).

Rochholz (E. L.), *Deutscher Glaube und Brauch im Spiegel der heidnischen Vorzeit.* 2 vols. Berlin, 1867.

Rochon (A. M.), *A Voyage to Madagascar and the East Indies.* Traps. London, 1793.

—— The same work. Trans. ; in Pinkerton, *Collection of Voyages and Travels,* vol. xvi. London, 1814.

Rockhill (W. W.), *The Land of the Lamas.* London, 1891.

—— ' Notes on Some of the Laws, Customs, and Superstitions of Korea ' ; in *The American Anthropologist,* vol. iv. Washington, 1891.

Rogers (Ch.), *Social Life in Scotland.* 3 vols. Edinburgh, 1884–86.

Rohde (Erwin), ' Paralipomena ' ; in *Rheinisches Museum für Philologie, neue Folge,* vol. xv. Frankfurt a. M., 1895.

—— *Psyche.* Freiburg i. B. & Leipzig, 1894.

Romanes (G. J.), *Animal Intelligence.* London, 1895.

—— ' Conscience in Animals ' ; in *The Quarterly Journal of Science,* vol. xiii. London, 1876.

—— *Mental Evolution in Animals.* London, 1883.

Romanische Forschungen. Erlangen.

Romans de Raoul de Cambrai et de Bernier (Li). Ed. by E. Le Glay. Paris, 1840.

Romilly (H. H.), *From my Verandah in New Guinea.* London, 1889.

—— *The Western Pacific and New Guinea.* London, 1887.

Romilly (Henry), *The Punishment of Death.* London, 1886.

Rorarius (Hieronymus), *Quod Animalia bruta ratione utantur melius Homine.* Paris, 1648.

Roscoe (J.), ' The Bahima ' ; in *Jour. Roy. Anthr. Inst.* vol. xxxvii. London, 1907.

Rosenbaum (Julius), *Geschichte der Lustseuche im Alterthume.* Halle, 1845.

Rosenberg (C. F. V. M.), *Nordboernes Aandsliv.* 3 vols. Kjøbenhavn, 1878–85.

—— *Traek af Livet paa Island i Fristats-Tiden.* Kjøbenhavn, 1894.

Rosenberg (H. von), *Der malayische Archipel.* Leipzig, 1878.

Roskoff (G. G.), *Geschichte des Teufels.* 2 vols. Leipzig, 1869.

Ross (B. R.), ' The Eastern Tinneh ' ; in *Smithsonian Report,* 1866. Washington, 1867.

Ross (John), *History of Corea.* Pasley, [1879].

Rossbach (A.), *Untersuchungen über die römische Ehe.* Stuttgart, 1853.

Rossi (P.), *Traité de droit pénal.* 3 vols. Genève, 1829.

Roth (H. Ling), *The Aborigines of Tasmania.* London, 1890.

—— *Great Benin.* Halifax, 1903.

—— *The Natives of Sarawak and British North Borneo.* 2 vols. London, 1896.

—— ' On the Origin of Agriculture ' ; in *Jour. Anthr. Inst.* vol. xvi. London, 1887.

—— ' On Salutations ' ; in *Jour. Anthr. Inst.* vol. xix. London, 1890.

—— ' On the Signification of Couvade ' ; in *Jour. Anthr. Inst.* vol. xxii. London, 1893.

Roth (Rud.), ' Brahma und die Brahmanen ' ; in *Zeitschr. der Deutschen Morgenländischen Gesellsch.* vol. i. Leipzig, 1846.

—— ' On the Morality of the Veda.' Trans. ; in *Journal of the American Oriental Society,* vol. iii. New York, 1853.

Roth (Walter E.), *Ethnological Studies among the North-West-Central Queensland Aborigines.* Brisbane & London, 1897.

Rothar (King), 'Edictus'; in Pertz, *Monumenta Germaniæ historica*, Leges, vol. iv. Hannoverae, 1868.

Rouse (W. H. D.), *Greek Votive Offerings*. Cambridge, 1902.

Rousseau (J. J.), *Œuvres complètes*. 4 vols. Paris, 1837.

Rowlatt (E. A.), 'Report of an Expedition into the Mishmee Hills'; in *Jour. Asiatic Soc. Bengal*, vol. xiv. pt. ii. Calcutta, 1845.

Rowley (Henry), *Africa Unveiled*. London, 1876.

—— *The Religion of the Africans*. London, [1877].

Rowney (H. B.), *The Wild Tribes of India*. London, 1882.

Rühs (F.), *Handbuch der Geschichte des Mittelalters*. Berlin, 1816.

Rüppell (E.), *Reise in Abyssinien*. 2 vols. Frankfurt a. M., 1838–40.

Ruskin (John), *The Works of*. 11 vols. Keston, Orpington, 1871–83.

Sabatier (Paul), *Life of St. Francis of Assisi*. Trans. London, 1894.

Sachau (E.), *Muhammedanisches Recht nach Schafiitischer Lehre*. Stuttgart & Berlin, 1897.

Saco (*Don* J. A.), *Historia de la esclavitud*. 3 vols. Paris & Barcelona, 1875–78.

Sacred Books of the East (The). Ed. by F. Max Müller. Oxford, 1879, &c.

'Sad Dar,' trans. by E. W. West; in *The Sacred Books of the East*, vol. xxiv. Oxford, 1885.

Sagard Théodat (G.), *Le grand voyage du pays des Hurons*. Paris, 1632.

Sahagun (F. Bernardino de), *Historia general de las cosas de Nueva España*. 3 vols. México, 1829–30.

Sainte-Palaye (De la Curne de), *Mémoires sur l'ancienne chevalerie*. 3 vols. Paris, 1781.

St. John (Bayle), *Adventures in the Libyan Desert*. London, 1849.

—— *Village Life in Egypt*. 2 vols. London, 1852.

St. John (Spenser), *Life in the Forests of the Far East*. 2 vols. London, 1863.

Saint Louis, *Les Établissements de*. Ed. by Paul Viollet. 4 vols. Paris, 1881–86.

Saint-Simon (*Duc* de), *Mémoires complets et authentiques*. 40 vols. Paris, 1840–41.

Sale (George), 'Preliminary Discourse'; in Wherry, *A Comprehensive Commentary on the Qurán*, vol. i. London, 1882.

Salt (H. S.), *Animals' Rights*. London, 1900.

Salt (Henry), *A Voyage to Abyssinia*. London, 1814.

Salvado (R.), *Mémoires historiques sur l'Australie*. Paris, 1854.

Salvioli (G.), *Manuale di storia del diritto italiano*. Torino, 1892.

Samuelson (James), *The History of Drink*. London, 1880.

Sandys (Edwin), *The Sermons of*. Ed. by John Ayre. Cambridge, 1841.

Santos (Joano dos), 'History of Eastern Ethiopia.' Trans.; in Pinkerton, *Collection of Voyages*, vol. xvi. London, 1814.

Sarasin (Paul and Fritz), *Ergebnisse naturwissenschaftlicher Forschungen auf Ceylon*. 3 vols. Wiesbaden, 1887–93.

Sarbah (J. M.), *Fanti Customary Laws*. London, 1897.

Sartori (Paul), 'Die Sitte der Alten- und Krankentötung'; in *Globus*, vol. lxvii. Braunschweig, 1895.

—— 'Ueber das Bauopfer'; in *Zeitschr. f. Ethnologie*, vol. xxx. Berlin, 1898.

Sarytschew (G.), ' Account of a Voyage of Discovery to the North-East of Siberia, the Frozen Ocean, and the North-East Sea.' Trans. ; in *A Collection of Modern and Contemporary Voyages and Travels*, vols. v.–vi. London, 1807.

Satapatha-Brâhmana (*The*). Trans. by J. Eggeling. 5 vols. (*The Sacred Books of the East*, vols. xii., xxvi., xli., xliii., and xliv.) Oxford, 1882–1900.

Sauer (M.), *An Account of a Geographical and Astronomical Expedition to the Northern Parts of Russia performed by J. Billings.* London, 1802.

Savage (T. S.), ' Observations on the External Characters and Habits of the *Troglodytes Niger* ' ; in *Boston Journal of Natural History*, vol. iv. Boston, 1844.

Sayce (A. H.), *Hibbert Lectures on . . . the Religion of the Ancient Babylonians.* London, 1887.

Scaramucci (F.) and Giglioli (E. H.), ' Notizie sui Danakil ' ; in *Archivio per l'antropologia e la etnologia*, vol. xiv. Firenze, 1884.

Schaafhausen (H.), ' Die Menschenfresserei und das Menschenopfer ' ; in *Archiv für Anthropologie*, vol. iv. Braunschweig, 1870.

Schadenberg (Alex.), ' Ueber die Negritos in den Philippinen ' ; in *Zeitschr. f. Ethnol.* vol. xii. Berlin, 1880.

Schaff (Philip), *History of the Christian Church : Ante-Nicene Christianity*, A.D. 100–325. Edinburgh, 1884.

Scherman (L.), ' Eine Art visionärer Höllenschilderung aus dem indischen Mittelalter ' ; in *Romanische Forschungen*, vol. v. Erlangen, 1890.

—— *Materialien zur Geschichte der Indischen Visionslitteratur.* Leipzig, 1892.

Scherzer (K. von), *Reise der Oesterreichischen Fregatte Novara um die Erde.* 3 vols. Wien, 1861–62.

Schiaparelli (E.), *Del sentimento religioso degli antichi egiziani.* Torino, 1877.

Schinz (Hans), *Deutsch-Süd-West-Afrika.* Oldenburg & Leipzig, 1891.

Schmidt (Bernhard), *Das Volksleben der Neugriechen und das hellenische Alterthum.* Leipzig, 1871.

Schmidt (C. C.), *Jahrbücher der in- und ausländischen gesammten Medicin.* Leipzig.

Schmidt (Emil), *Ceylon.* Berlin, [1897].

Schmidt (Leopold), *Die Ethik der alten Griechen.* 2 vols. Berlin, 1882.

Schneider (Wilhelm), *Die Naturvölker.* 2 vols. Paderborn & Münster, 1885–86.

—— *Die Religion der afrikanischen Naturvölker.* Münster i. W., 1891.

Schoemann (G. F.), *Griechische Alterthümer.* 2 vols. Berlin, 1855–59.

Schoen (J. F.) and Crowther (Samuel), *Journals of, who accompanied the Expedition up the Niger in* 1841. London, 1842.

Schönwerth (Fr.), *Aus der Oberpfalz. Sitten und Sagen.* 3 vols. Augsburg, 1857–59.

Schomburgk (*Sir* Robert H.), ' Journal of an Expedition from Pirara to the Upper Corentyne ' ; in *Jour. Roy. Geo. Soc.* vol. xv. London, 1845.

—— ' On the Natives of Guiana ' ; in *Jour. Ethn. Soc. London*, vol. i. London, 1848.

Schoolcraft (H. R.), *Historical and Statistical Information respecting the History, Condition, and Prospects of the Indian Tribes of the United States* (the title pages of vols. iv.–vi. read : *Archives of Aboriginal Knowledge, &c.*). 6 vols. Philadelphia, 1851–60.

—— *The Indian in his Wigwam.* New York, 1848.

Schopenhauer (Arthur), *Die beiden Grundprobleme der Ethik.* (*Sämmtliche Werke in zwölf Bänden,* vol. vii.) Stuttgart, *s. d.*

—— *Essays.* Trans. by Mrs. R. Dircks. London, *s. d.*

—— *Parerga und Paralipomena.* 2 vols. Berlin, 1851.

—— *Die Welt als Wille und Vorstellung.* 2 vols. Leipzig, 1859.

Schrader (E.), *Die Keilinschriften und das Alte Testament.* Ed. by H. Zimmern and H. Winckler. Berlin, 1903.

Schrader (O.), *Prehistoric Antiquities of the Aryan Peoples.* Trans. by F. B. Jevons. London, 1890.

—— *Reallexikon der indogermanischen Altertumskunde.* Strassburg, 1901.

Schröder (Richard), *Lehrbuch der deutschen Rechtsgeschichte.* Leipzig, 1898.

Schuermann (C. W.), ' The Aboriginal Tribes of Port Lincoln ' ; in Woods, *Native Tribes of South Australia.* Adelaide, 1879.

Schütz-Holzhausen (D. von), *Der Amazonas.* Freiburg i. B., 1895.

Schulchan Aruch oder Die vier jüdischen Gesetzbücher. Trans. by H. G. F. Löwe. 2 vols. Wien, 1896.

Schultz (H.), *Old Testament Theology.* Trans. 2 vols. Edinburgh, 1892.

Schultze (Fritz), *Der Fetischismus.* Leipzig, 1871.

—— *Vergleichende Seelenkunde.* Leipzig, 1892, &c.

Schurtz (H.), *Das afrikanische Gewerbe.* Leipzig, 1900.

—— ' Die Anfänge des Landbesitzes ' ; in *Zeitschr. f. Socialwissensch.* vol. iii. Berlin, 1900.

—— *Die Speiseverbote.* Hamburg, 1893.

—— *Urgeschichte der Kultur.* Leipzig & Wien, 1900.

Schuyler (E.), *Turkistan.* 2 vols. London, 1876.

Schwabenspiegel (Der). Ed. by F. L. A. von Lassberg. Tübingen, 1840.

Schwally (F.), *Das Leben nach dem Tode nach den Vorstellungen des alten Israel und Judentums.* Giessen, 1892.

Schwaner (C. A. L. M.), *Borneo.* 2 vols. Amsterdam, 1853.

Schwarz (W.), *Prähistorisch-anthropologische Studien.* Berlin, 1884.

Schweinfurth (Georg), *The Heart of Africa.* Trans. 2 vols. London, 1873.

Science. An Illustrated Journal. Cambridge (Mass.).

Scott (*Sir* Walter), ' An Essay on Chivalry ' ; in *Miscellaneous Prose Works,* vol. vi. Edinburgh, 1827.

Scotus Novanticus. See Laurie (S. S.).

Seaver (James E.), *A Narrative of the Life of Mrs. Mary Jemison, Who was taken by the Indians, in the Year,* 1755. Howden, 1826.

' Second Helvetic Confession ' ; in *Sylloge confessionum sub tempus reformandæ ecclesiæ.* Oxonii, 1804.

Seebohm (F.), *The English Village Community.* London, 1883.

—— *Tribal Custom in Anglo-Saxon Law.* London, 1902.

—— *The Tribal System in Wales.* London, 1895.

Seeger (Hermann), *Ueber die Ausbildung der Lehre vom Versuch der Verbrechen in der Wissenschaft des Mittelalters.* Tübingen, 1869.

—— *Der Versuch der Verbrechen nach römischen Recht.* Tübingen, 1879.

Seeley (J. R.), *Ecce Homo.* London, 1892.

—— *Natural Religion.* London & New York, 1895.

Seemann (B.), *Narrative of the Voyage of H.M.S. Herald during the Years* 1845–51. 2 vols. London, 1853.

—— *Viti.* Cambridge, 1862.

Selden (J.), *De Synedriis et Præfecturis Juridicis veterum Ebræorum*. Francofurti, 1696.

Selenka (Emil and Lenore), *Sonnige Welten. Ostasiatische Reise-Skizzen*. Wiesbaden, 1896.

Seligmann (C. G.), in *Reports of the Cambridge Anthropological Expedition to Torres Straits*, vol. v. Cambridge, 1904.

—— 'Sexual Inversion among Primitive Races'; in *The Alienist and Neurologist*, vol. xxxiii. St. Louis, 1902.

Sell (Edward), *The Faith of Islám*. London, 1896.

Semper (Karl), *Die Palau-Inseln im Stillen Ocean*. Leipzig, 1873.

Seneca (L. A.), *Opera quæ supersunt*. Ed. by F. Haase. 3 vols. Lipsiae, 1853–62.

Sepp (Johannes), *Völkerbrauch bei Hochzeit, Geburt und Tod*. München, 1891.

Serpillon (F.), *Code Criminel, ou Commentaire sur l'Ordonnance de* 1670. 2 vols. Lyon, 1784.

Servius Maurus Honoratus, *Commentarii in Virgilium*. Ed. by H. A. Lion. 2 vols. Gottingae, 1826.

Seth (James), *A Study of Ethical Principles*. Edinburgh & London, 1898.

Sextus Empiricus, *Opera Græce et Latine*. Ed. by I. A. Fabricius. 2 vols. Lipsiae, 1842.

Shaftesbury (Antony *Earl of*), *Characteristicks*. 3 vols. London, 1733.

Shakespeare (W.), *Works*. Ed. by A. Dyce. 9 vols. London, 1864–67.

Shand (A. F.), 'Character and the Emotions'; in *Mind*, new ser. vol. v. London, 1896.

—— 'The Sources of Tender Emotion'; in Stout, *The Groundwork of Psychology*. London, 1903.

'Shâyast Lâ-Shâyast,' trans. by E. W. West; in *The Sacred Books of the East*, vol. v. Oxford, 1880.

Shaw (Thomas), 'On the Inhabitants of the Hills near Rájamahall'; in *Asiatick Researches*, vol. iv. Calcutta, 1795.

Sheane (J. H. West), 'Some Aspects of the Avemba Religion'; in *Jour. Anthr. Inst.* vol. xxxvi. London, 1906.

Sherwill (W. S.), 'Notes upon a Tour through the Rájmahal Hills'; in *Jour. Asiatic Soc. Bengal*, vol. xx. Calcutta, 1852.

Shooter (Joseph), *The Kafirs of Natal and the Zulu Country*. London, 1857.

Short Treatise upon the Propriety and Necessity of Duelling (A). Bath, 1779.

Shortland (Edward), *Traditions and Superstitions of the New Zealanders*. London, 1854.

Shortt (John), 'An Account of the Hill Tribes of the Neilgherries'; in *Trans. Ethn. Soc.* new ser. vol. vii. London, 1869.

—— 'A Contribution to the Ethnology of Jeypore'; in *Trans. Ethn. Soc.* new ser. vol. vi. London, 1868.

—— *The Hill Ranges of Southern India*. 5 parts. Madras, 1870–76.

Shway Yoe (*i.e.* Sir J. G. Scott), *The Burman*. 2 vols. London, 1882.

Sibree (James), *The Great African Island. Chapters on Madagascar*. London, 1880.

Siculus Flaccus, 'De conditionibus agrorum'; in Goesius, *Rei agrariæ auctores*. Amstelredami, 1674.

Sidgwick (H.), *The Methods of Ethics*. London, 1901.

—— 'The Morality of Strife'; in *Internat. Jour. of Ethics*, vol. i. Philadelphia & London, 1891.

Sidonius (C. Sollius Apollinaris), *Epistulæ*. Ed. by P. Mohr. Lipsiae, 1895.

Siebold (H. von), *Ethnologische Studien über die Aino ʻuf der Insel Yesso*. Berlin, 1881.

Simancas (Jacobus), *De catholicis institutionibus liber*. Romae, 1575.

Simcox (E. J.), *Primitive Civilizations*. 2 vols. London, 1894.

Simmel (Georg), *Einleitung in die Moralwissenschaft*. 2 vols. Berlin, 1892-93.

——ʻ Die Verwandtenehe ʼ; in *Vossische Zeitung*, June 3rd and 10th, 1894. Berlin.

Simonde de Sismondi (J. C. L.), *Histoire des républiques italiennes du moyen âge*. 16 vols. Paris, 1826.

Simons (F. A. A.), ʻ An Exploration of the Goajira Peninsula, U.S. of Colombia ʼ; in *Proceed. Roy. Geo. Soc.* new ser. vol. vii. London, 1885.

Simson (Alfred), *Travels in the Wilds of Ecuador*. London, 1886.

Skeat (W. W.), *Malay Magic*. London, 1900.

—— and Blagden (Ch. O.), *Pagan Races of the Malay Peninsula*. 2 vols. London, 1906.

Skene (W. F.), *Celtic Scotland*. 3 vols. Edinburgh, 1876–80.

Skertchly (J. A.), *Dahomey as it is*. London, 1874.

Sleeman (*Sir* W. H.), *Rambles and Recollections of an Indian Official*. 2 vols. London, 1844.

Smaragdus, ʻ Via Regia ʼ; in d'Achery, *Spicilegium*, vol. i. Parisiis, 1723.

Smeaton (D. Mackenzie), *The Loyal Karens of Burma*. London, 1887.

Smellie (William), *The Philosophy of Natural History*. 2 vols. Edinburgh, 1790–99.

Smith (Adam), *An Inquiry into the Nature and Causes of the Wealth of Nations*. Edinburgh, 1863.

—— *The Theory of Moral Sentiments*. London, 1887.

Smith (Arthur H.), *Chinese Characteristics*. London, 1895.

—— *The Proverbs and Common Sayings of the Chinese*. Shanghai, 1888.

Smith (E. R.), *The Araucanians*. New York, 1855.

Smith (Erminnie A.), ʻ Myths of the Iroquois ʼ; in *Ann. Rep. Bur. Ethn.* vol. ii. Washington, 1883.

Smith (George), *Chaldäische Genesis*. Trans. by H. Delitzsch, ed. by F. Delitzsch. Leipzig, 1876.

—— *The Chaldean Account of Genesis*. Ed. by A. H. Sayce. London, 1880.

Smith (Gerrit), *Letter to Rev. James Smylie, of the State of Mississippi*. New York, 1837.

Smith (Goldwin), *Lectures and Essays*. Toronto, 1881.

Smith (R. Bosworth), *Mohammed and Mohammedanism*. London, 1889.

Smith (S. Percy), ʻ Futuna ʼ; in *Jour. Polynesian Soc.* vol. i. Wellington, 1892.

—— ʻ Uea ʼ; in *Jour. Polynesian Soc.* vol. i. Wellington, 1892.

Smith (*Sir* Thomas), *The Common-wealth of England*. London, 1635.

Smith (W. Robertson), *Kinship and Marriage in Early Arabia*. Ed. by S. A. Cook. London, 1903.

—— *Lectures on the Religion of the Semites*. London, 1894.

—— ʻ Sacrifice ʼ; in *Encyclopædia Britannica*, vol. xxi. Edinburgh, 1886.

Smithsonian Institution, Annual Reports of the Board of Regents. Washington.

Smyth (R. Brough), *The Aborigines of Victoria*. 2 vols. London, 1878.

Snorri Sturluson, *Edda*. Ed. by Þ. Jónsson. Kaupmannahöfn, 1875.

Snorri Sturluson, *Heimskringla. Nóregs Konunga Sögur.* Ed. by F.Jónsson. 4 vols. København, 1893–1901.

Snow (W. Parker), ' Remarks on the Wild Tribes of Tierra del Fuego ' ; in *Trans. Ethn. Soc. London,* new ser. vol. i. London, 1861.

—— *A Two Years' Cruise off Tierra del Fuego.* 2 vols. London, 1857.

Sociological Papers. Published for the Sociological Society. London.

Socrates, ' Historia ecclesiastica ' ; in Migne, *Patrologiæ cursus,* Ser. Graeca, vol. lxvii. Parisiis, 1859.

Söderblom (Nathan), *Gudstrons uppkomst.* Stockholm, 1914.

Solinus, *Collectanea rerum memorabilium.* Ed. by Th. Mommsen. Berlin,1864.

Sommerville (B. T.), ' Ethnographical Notes in New Georgia ' ; in *Jour.. Anthr. Inst.* vol. xxvi. London, 1897.

Sophocles, *The Plays and Fragments.* Ed. and trans. by R. C. Jebb. 7 vols. Cambridge, 1883–96.

—— *Tragœdiæ et Fragmenta.* Ed. by E. A. J. Ahrens. Parisiis, 1842.

Soppitt (C. A.), *A Short Account of the Kuki-Lushai Tribes on the North-East Frontier.* Shillong, 1887.

Soto (Dominicus), *De justitia et jure.* Lugduni, 1582.

South American Missionary Magazine (The). London.

Southey (R.), *History of Brazil.* 3 vols. London, 1810–19.

Sozomenus (Hermias), ' Historia ecclesiastica ' ; in Migne, *Patrologiæ cursus,* Ser. Graeca, vol. lxvii. Parisiis, 1859.

Spangenberg (——), ' Ueber das Verbrechen der Abtreibung der Leibesfrucht'; in *Neues Archiv des Criminalrechts,* vol. ii. Halle, 1818.

—— ' Ueber das Verbrechen des Kindermords und der Aussetzung der Kinder ' ; in *Neues Archiv des Criminalrechts,* vol. iii. Halle, 1819–20.

Sparrman (A.), *A Voyage to the Cape of Good Hope.* Trans. 2 vols. London, 1785.

Spartian, ' Vita Hadriani,' ed. by J. Centerwall ; in *Upsala Universitets Årsskrift,* 1870. Upsala, 1869.

' Speculum Saxonum ' ; in Goldast, *Collectio consuetudinum et legum imperialium.* Francofordiae ad Moenum, 1613.

Spencer (Baldwin) and Gillen (F. J.), *The Native Tribes of Central Australia.* London, 1899.

—— *The Northern Tribes of Central Australia.* London, 1904.

Spencer (Herbert), *Descriptive Sociology.* 8 vols. London, 1873–81.

—— *The Principles of Ethics.* 2 vols. London, 1892–93.

—— *The Principles of Psychology.* 2 vols. London, 1890.

—— *The Principles of Sociology.* 3 vols. London, 1879–96.

Spiegel (F.), *Erânische Alterthumskunde.* 3 vols. Leipzig, 1871–78.

Spieth (Jakob), *Die Ewe-Stämme.* Berlin, 1906.

Spinoza (B. de), *Opera philosophica omnia.* Ed. by A. Gfroerer. Stuttgardiae, 1830.

Spix (J. B. von) and Martius (C. F. Ph. von), *Reise in Brasilien.* 3 vols. München, 1823–31.

—— *Travels in Brazil in the Years* 1817–20. Trans. 2 vols. London, 1824.

Sproat (G. M.), *Scenes and Studies of Savage Life.* London, 1868.

Squier (E. G.), *Nicaragua.* 2 vols. London, 1852.

—— ' Observations on the Archaeology and Ethnology of Nicaragua ' ; in *Trans. American Ethn. Soc.* vol. iii. pt. i. New York, 1853.

Stäudlin (C. F.), *Geschichte der Vorstellungen und Lehren vom Selbstmorde.* Göttingen, 1824.

Stanley (A. P.), *Christian Institutions.* London, 1884.

Stanley (Hiram M.), *Studies in the Evolutionary Psychology of Feeling.* London, 1895.

Starbuck (E. D.), *The Psychology of Religion.* London, 1899.

Starcke (C. N.), *La famille dans les différentes sociétés.* Paris, 1899.

State Trials, Cobbett's Complete Collection of. Continued by T. B. and T. J. Howell. 33 vols. London, 1809–26.

Statutes of the United Kingdom of Great Britain and Ireland. 110 vols. Cambridge, London, 1762–1869.

Staunton (*Sir* G. Thomas), *An Inquiry into the Proper Mode of rendering the Word " God " in translating the Sacred Scriptures into the Chinese Language.* London, 1849.

Stavorinus (J. S.), *Voyages to the East Indies.* Trans. 3 vols. London, 1798.

Steinen (Karl von den), *Durch Central-Brasilien.* Leipzig, 1886.

—— *Unter den Naturvölkern Zentral-Brasiliens.* Berlin, 1894.

Steinmetz (S. R.), ' Gli antichi scongiuri giuridici contro i creditori ' ; in *Rivista italiana di sociologia,* vol. ii. Roma, 1898.

—— ' Continuität oder Lohn und Strafe im Jenseits der Wilden ' ; in *Archiv für Anthropologie,* vol. xxiv. Braunschweig, 1897.

—— *Endokannibalismus.* (Reprinted from *Mittheilungen der Anthropologischen Gesellschaft in Wien,* vol. xxvi.) Wien, 1896.

—— *Ethnologische Studien zur ersten Entwicklung der Strafe.* 2 vols. Leiden & Leipzig, 1894.

—— ' Die neueren Forschungen zur Geschichte der menschlichen Familie,' in *Zeitschr. f. Socialwissensch.* vol. ii. Berlin, 1899.

—— *Rechtsverhältnisse von eingeborenen Völkern in Afrika und Ozeanien.* Ed. by S. R. S. Berlin, 1903.

—— ' Suicide among Primitive Peoples ' ; in *The American Anthropologist,* vol. vii. Washington, 1894.

—— ' Das Verhältnis zwischen Eltern und Kindern bei den Naturvölkern ' ; in *Zeitschr. f. Socialwissensch.* vol. i. Berlin, 1898.

Steller (E.), *De Sangi-Archipel.* Amsterdam, 1866.

Steller (G. W.), *Beschreibung von dem Lande Kamtschatka.* Frankfurt & Leipzig, 1774.

Stemann (Chr. L. E.), *Den danske Retshistorie indtil Christian V.'s Lov.* Kjöbenhavn, 1871.

Stengel (Paul), *Die griechischen Kultusaltertümer.* München, 1898.

Stephen (A. M.), ' The Navajo ' ; in *The American Anthropologist,* vol. vi. Washington, 1893.

Stephen (H. J.), *New Commentaries on the Laws of England.* 4 vols. London, 1903.

Stephen (James), *The Slavery of the British West India Colonies delineated.* 2 vols. London, 1824–30.

Stephen (James Fitzjames), *A Digest of the Criminal Law.* London, 1894.

—— *A History of the Criminal Law of England.* 3 vols. London, 1883.

—— *Horæ Sabbaticæ.* 3 vols. London, 1891–92.

—— *Liberty, Equality, Fraternity.* London, 1873.

Stephen (Leslie), *The Science of Ethics.* London, 1882.

Stephens (Edward), ' The Aborigines of Australia ' ; in *Jour. & Proceed. Roy. Soc. N. S. Wales,* vol. xxiii. Sydney & London, 1889.

Stevenson (Matilda C.), ' A Chapter of Zuñi Mythology ' ; in *Memoirs of the International Congress of Anthropology.* Chicago, 1894.

Stevenson (Matilda C.), ' The Sia ' ; in *Ann. Rep. Bur. Ethn.* vol. xi. Washington, 1894.

Stewart (David), *Sketches of the Character, Institutions, and Customs of the Highlanders of Scotland.* Inverness, &c., 1885.

Stewart (Dugald), *The Philosophy of the Active and Moral Powers of Man.* 2 vols. Edinburgh, 1828.

Stewart (R.), ' Notes on Northern Cachar ' ; in *Jour. Asiatic Soc. Bengal,* vol. xxiv. Calcutta, 1855.

Stirling (E. C.), ' Anthropology ' ; in *Report on the Work of the Horn Scientific Expedition to Central Australia,* pt. iv. London & Melbourne, 1896.

Stobaeus (Joannes), *Florilegium.* Ed. by Th. Gaisford. 4 vols. Oxonii, 1822.

Stokes (J. Lort), *Discoveries in Australia.* 2 vols. London, 1846.

Stokes (W.), *All War inconsistent with the Christian Religion.* London, 1855.

Stoll (Otto), *Die Ethnologie der Indianerstämme von Guatemala.* Leiden, 1889.

Stone (O. C.), *A Few Months in New Guinea.* London, 1880.

Storch (Henri), *Cours d'économie politique.* 6 vols. St. Pétersbourg, 1815.

Storr (F.), ' Duel ' ; in *Encyclopædia Britannica,* vol. vii. Edinburgh, 1877.

Stout (G. F.), *The Groundwork of Psychology.* London, 1903.

Strabo, *Geographica.* Parisiis, 1853.

Strachey (William), *The Historie of Travaile into Virginia Britannia.* Ed. by R. H. Major. London, 1849.

Strack (H. L.), *Der Blutaberglaube in der Menschheit.* München, 1892.

Strafgesetzbuch für das Deutsche Reich (Das). Leipzig, 1876.

Strauss (D. F.), *Der alte und der neue Glaube.* Leipzig, 1872.

Strausz (Adolf), *Die Bulgaren.* Leipzig, 1898.

Stricker (W.), ' Ethnographische Notizen über den Kindermord und die künstliche Fruchtabtreibung ' ; in *Archiv f. Anthropologie,* vol. v. Braunschweig, 1872.

Strickland (Samuel), *Twenty-seven Years in Canada West.* 2 vols. London, 1853.

Stroud (G. M.), *A Sketch of the Laws relating to Slavery in the Several States of the United States of America.* Philadelphia, 1856.

Strutt (Joseph), *A Complete View of the Manners, Customs, Arms, &c. of the Inhabitants of England.* 3 vols. London, 1775-76.

Struve (B. von), ' Die Samojeden im Norden von Sibirien ' ; in *Das Ausland,* vol. liii. Stuttgart, 1880.

Strzelecki (P. E. de), *Physical Description of New South Wales and Van Diemen's Land.* London, 1845.

Stuhlmann (Franz), *Mit Emin Pascha ins Herz von Afrika.* Berlin, 1894.

Sturt (Charles), *Narrative of an Expedition into Central Australia.* 2 vols. London, 1849.

Suarez de Paz (Gonçalo), *Praxis ecclesiastica et secularis.* Salamanticae, 1583.

Suetonius Tranquillus (C.), *De vita Cæsarum.* Ed. by C. L. Roth. Lipsiae, 1886.

Sugenheim (S.), *Geschichte der Aufhebung der Leibeigenschaft und Hörigkeit in Europa.* St. Petersburg, 1861.

Sully (James), *Studies of Childhood.* London, 1895.

Sumner (W. G.), ' The Yakuts,' from the Russian of Sieroshevski ; in *Jour. Anthr. Inst.* vol. xxxi. London, 1901.

Suomi. Helsingfors.

Sutherland (Alex.), *The Origin and Growth of the Moral Instinct.* 2 vols. London, 1898.

Swan (James G.), *The Northwest Coast ; or, Three Years' Residence in Washington Territory.* New York, 1857.

Swettenham (F. A.), *Malay Sketches.* London & New York, 1895.

Swift (J.), *Works.* With notes by Sir W. Scott. 19 vols. Edinburgh, 1824.

'Tâ Hsio ' ; in Legge, *The Chinese Classics,* vol. i. Oxford, 1893.

Ta Tsing Leu Lee. Trans. by Sir G. Th. Staunton. London, 1810.

Tacitus (C. C.), *Opera omnia.* 11 vols. Londini, 1821.

Tallqvist (K. L.), ' Die assyrische Beschwörungsserie maqlû ' ; in *Acta Soc. Scientiarum Fennicæ,* vol. xx. Helsingfors, 1895.

Talmud de Jérusalem (Le). Trans. by M. Schwab. 11 vols. Paris, 1871–89.

' Tâo Teh King (The),' trans. by J. Legge ; in *The Sacred Books of the East,* vol. xxxix. Oxford, 1891.

Taplin (George), *The Folklore, Manners, Customs, and Languages of the South Australian Aborigines.* Ed. by G. T. Adelaide, 1879.

—— ' The Narrinyeri ' ; in Woods, *Native Tribes of South Australia.* Adelaide, 1879.

Taprobanian (The). Bombay.

Tasmanian Journal of Natural Science, &c. Hobart Town.

Taylor (Jeremy), *The Whole Works of.* Ed. by R. Heber. 15 vols. London, 1822.

Taylor (R.), *Te Ika a Maui ; or, New Zealand and its Inhabitants.* London, 1870.

Tedeschi (P.), *La schiavitù.* Piacenza, 1882.

Teit (James), ' The Thompson Indians of British Columbia ' ; in *Memoirs of the American Museun of Natural History,* vol. ii., Anthropology, vol. i. New York, 1900.

Tennent (*Sir* J. Emerson), *Ceylon.* 2 vols. London, 1860.

Terme (J.-F.) and Montfalcon (J.-B.), *Histoire des enfants trouvés.* Paris,1840.

Tertullian, *Opera omnia.* 3 vols. (Migne, *Patrologiæ cursus,* vols. i.–iii.) Parisiis, 1844.

Tettau (W. J. A. von), and Temme (J. D. H.), *Die Volkssagen Ostpreussens, Litthauens und Westpreussens.* Berlin, 1837.

Texte (J.), *Jean-Jacques Rousseau and the Cosmopolitan Spirit in Literature.* Trans. London, 1899.

' Thâi-Shang (The),' trans. by J. Legge ; in *The Sacred Books of the East,* vol. xl. Oxford, 1891.

Theal (G. M. M'Call), *History of the Boers in South Africa.* London, 1887.

Theognis, *Studies in, together with a Text of the Poems.* By E. Harrison. Cambridge, 1902.

Theologische Quartalschrift. Tübingen.

Thérou (*Abbé*), *Le christianisme et l'esclavage.* Paris, 1841.

Thesleff (A.), ' Zigenarlif i Finland ' ; in *Nya Pressen,* 1897, no. 331 B. Helsingfors.

Thiers (A.), *De la propriété.* Paris, 1848.

Thomas (N. W.), ' Baiame and the Bell-bird ' ; in *Man,* 1905. London.

—— *Kinship Organisations and Group Marriage in Australia.* Cambridge, 1906.

—— ' Religious Ideas of the Arunta ' ; in *Folk-Lore,* vol. xvi. London, 1905.

Thomas Aquinas (*Saint*), *Summa theologica.* 4 vols. (Migne, *Patrologiæ cursus*, Ser. Secunda, vols. i.–iv.) Parisiis, 1845–46.

Thomassin (Louis), *Dictionnaire de discipline ecclésiastique.* Ed. by J.-J. Bourassé. 2 vols. Paris, 1856.

Thoms (W. J.), *Anecdotes and Traditions, Illustrative of Early English History and Literature.* London, 1839.

Thomson (A. S.), *The Story of New Zealand.* 2 vols. London, 1859.

Thomson (Basil C.), *Savage Island.* London, 1902.

Thomson (J. P.), *British New Guinea.* London, 1892.

Thomson (Joseph), *Through Masai Land.* London, 1887.

Thon (August), *Rechtsnorm und subjectives Recht.* Weimar, 1878.

Thonissen (J. J.), *Le droit pénal de la république athénienne.* Bruxelles & Paris, 1875.

Thorpe (Benjamin), *Northern Mythology.* 3 vols. London, 1851.

Three Early Assize Rolls for the County of Northumberland, sæc. xiii. (*The Publications of the Surtees Society*, vol. lxxxviii.) Durham, 1891.

Threlkeld (L. E.), *An Australian Language as spoken by the Awabakal.* Sydney, 1892.

Thrupp (John), *The Anglo-Saxon Home.* London, 1862.

Thucydides, *Historia Belli Peloponnesiaci.* Parisiis, 1840.

Thunberg (Ch. P.), *Travels in Europe, Africa, and Asia, performed between the Years 1770 and 1779.* 4 vols. London, 1795.

Thurston (Edgar), ' Anthropology of the Todas and Kotas of the Nilgiri Hills ' ; in the Madras Government Museum's *Bulletin*, vol. i. Madras, 1896.

—— ' The Badágas of the Nilgiris ' ; in the Madras Government Museum's *Bulletin*, vol. ii. Madras, 1897.

Tickell (——), ' Memoir on the Hodésum ' ; in *Jour. Asiatic Soc. Bengal*, vol. ix. Calcutta, 1840.

Tiele (C. P.), *Elements of the Science of Religion.* 2 vols. Edinburgh & London, 1897–99.

—— *History of the Egyptian Religion.* Trans. London, 1882.

—— *Max Müller und Fritz Schultze über ein Problem der Religionswissenschaft.* Trans. Leipzig, 1871.

Tissot (J.), *Le droit pénal étudié dans ses principes.* 2 vols. Paris, 1860.

Tönnies (F.), ' Philosophical Terminology ' ; in *Mind*, new ser. vol. viii. London, 1899.

Toplady (A. M.), *The Works of.* London, 1853.

Torday (E.) and Joyce (T. A.), ' Notes on the Ethnography of the Ba-Huana ' ; in *Jour. Anthr. Inst.* vol. xxxvi. London, 1906.

—— ' Notes on the Ethnography of the Ba-Mbala ' ; in *Jour. Anthr. Inst.* vol. xxxv. London, 1905.

—— ' Notes on the Ethnography of the Ba-Yaka ' ; in *Jour. Anthr. Inst.* vol. xxxvi. London, 1906.

Torquemada (Juan de), *Veinte y un libros rituales y Monarchia Indiana.* 3 vols. Madrid, 1723.

Tout (Ch. Hill), ' Report on the Ethnology of the Siciatl of British Columbia ' ; in *Jour. Anthr. Inst.* vol. xxxiv. London, 1904.

—— ' Report on the Ethnology of the Stlatlumh of British Columbia ' ; in *Jour. Anthr. Inst.* vol. xxxv. London, 1905.

Toy (C. H.), *Judaism and Christianity.* London, 1890.

Transactions and Proceedings of the New Zealand Institute. Wellington.

Transactions of the American Ethnological Society. New York.
—— *of the Asiatic Society of Japan.* Yokohama.
—— *of the China Branch of the Royal Asiatic Society.* Hongkong.
—— *of the Ethnological Society of London.* New Series. London.
—— *of the Royal Soceity of Edinburgh.*
—— *of the Royal Society of South Australia.* Adelaide.
Travers (W. T. L.), ' On the Life and Times of Te Rauparaha ' ; in *Trans. and Proceed. New Zealand Inst.* 1872, vol. v. Wellington, 1873.
Tregear (E.), ' Easter Island ' ; in *Jour. Polynesian Soc.* vol. i. Wellington, 1892.
—— *The Maori-Polynesian Dictionary.* Wellington, 1891.
—— ' Niue ' ; in *Jour. Polynesian Soc.* vol. ii. Wellington, 1893.
Tristram (H. B.), *The Great Sahara.* London, 1860.
Trollope (Anthony), *South Africa.* 2 vols. London, 1878.
Tromp (S. W.), ' Uit de Salasila van Koetei ' ; in *Bijdragen tot de taal-, land- en volkenkunde van Nederlandsch-Indië,* vol. xxxvii. (ser. v. vol. iii.). 's Gravenhage, 1888.
Truman (B. C.), *The Field of Honor.* London, 1884.
Trumbull (H. Clay), *The Blood Covenant.* Philadelphia, 1893.
—— *The Threshold Covenant.* New York, 1896.
Trummer (C.), *Vorträge über Tortur, Hexenverfolgungen, &c. in der Hamburgischen Rechtsgeschichte.* 3 vols. Hamburg, 1844–49.
Tschudi (J. J. von), *Reisen durch Südamerika.* 5 vols. Leipzig, 1866–69.
Tucker (Abraham), *The Light of Nature pursued.* 2 vols. London, 1840.
Tuckey (J. K.), *Narrative of an Expedition to explore the River Zaire.* London, 1818.
Tuke (D. H.), *Chapters in the History of the Insane in the British Isles.* London, 1882.
—— *A Dictionary of Psychological Medicine.* 2 vols. London, 1892.
Turnbull (John), *A Voyage round the World, in the Years* 1800–1804. London, 1813.
Turner (George), *Nineteen Years in Polynesia.* London, 1861.
—— *Samoa.* London, 1884.
Turner (James), *Pallas Armata.* London, 1683.
Turner (L. M.), ' Ethnology of the Ungava District, Hudson Bay Territory ' ; in *Ann. Rep. Bur. Ethn.* vol. xi. Washington, 1894.
Turner (Sharon), *The History of England.* 12 vols. London 1839.
Tutuila (——), ' The Line Islanders ' ; in *Jour. Polynesian Soc.* vol. i. Wellington, 1892.
Twells (Leonard) and others, *The Lives of Dr. E. Pocock, &c.* 2 vols. London, 1816.
Twiss (*Sir* Travers), *The Law of Nations.* Oxford & London, 1875.
Tyler (Josiah), *Forty Years among the Zulus.* Boston & Chicago, [1891].
Tylor (*Sir* E. B.), *Anthropology.* London, 1895.
—— ' On the Limits of Savage Religion ' ; in *Jour. Anthr. Inst.* vol. xxi. London, 1892.
—— ' On a Method of investigating the Development of Institutions ' ; in *Jour. Anthr. Inst.* vol. xviii. London, 1889.
—— *Primitive Culture.* 2 vols. London, 1903.
—— ' Primitive Society ' ; in *The Contemporary Review,* vols. xxi.–xxii. London, 1873.

Tylor (E. B.), ' Remarks on Totemism ' ; in *Jour. Anthr. Inst.* vol. xxviii. London, 1899.
—— *Researches into the Early History of Mankind.* London, 1878.
—— ' Salutations ' ; in *Encyclopædia Britannica*, vol. xxi. London, 1886.

Uhlhorn (G.), *Die christliche Liebesthätigkeit.* 3 vols. Stuttgart, 1882–90.
Unger (F. W.), ' Der gerichtliche Zweikampf bei den germanischen Völkern'; in *Göttinger Studien*, 1847, Zweite Abtheilung : Philosophische, philologische und historische Abhandlungen. Göttingen.
Urquhart (D.), *The Spirit of the East.* 2 vols. London, 1838.
Usener (H.), *Götternamen.* Bonn, 1896.
Utiešenović (O. M.), *Die Hauskommunionen der Südslaven.* Wien, 1859.

Valerius Maximus, *Factorum dictorumque memorabilium libri novem.* 3 vols. Londini, 1823.
Valikhanof (—) and others, *The Russians in Central Asia.* Trans. by J. and R. Michell. London, 1865.
Vallon (Ch.) and Marie (A.), ' Des psychoses religieuses ' ; in *Archives de neurologie*, ser. ii. vol. iii. Paris, 1897.
Valroger (L. de), *Les Celtes.* Paris, 1879.
Vámbéry (H.), *Der Islam im neunzehnten Jahrhundert.* Leipzig, 1875.
—— *Travels in Central Asia.* London, 1864.
—— *Das Türkenvolk.* Leipzig, 1885.
Vangerow (K. A. von), *Lehrbuch der Pandekten.* 3 vols. Marburg & Leipzig, 1876.
Varro (M. Terentius), *De lingua Latina.* Ed. by M. Nisard. Paris, 1850.
—— *Rerum rusticarum libri tres.* Lipsiae, 1889.
' Vasishtha,' trans. by G. Bühler ; in *The Sacred Books of the East*, vol. xiv. Oxford, 1882.
Vattel (E. de), *Le droit des gens.* 2 vols. Neuchatel, 1777.
Velten (C.), *Sitten und Gebräuche der Suaheli.* Göttingen, 1903.
Vendîdâd (The). Trans. by J. Darmesteter. (*The Sacred Books of the East*, vol. iv.) Oxford, 1895.
' Venedotian Code (The) ' ; in *Ancient Laws and Institutes of Wales.* London, 1841.
Verhandlungen der Berliner Gesellschaft für Anthropologie, Ethnologie und Urgeschichte. Berlin.
Vierkandt (A.), *Naturvölker und Kulturvölker.* Leipzig, 1896.
Vigfusson (Gudbrand) and Powell (F. York), *Corpus Poeticum Boreale.* 2 vols. Oxford, 1883.
Vignioli (Tito), *Myth and Science.* London, 1882.
Villemain (A. F.), *Cours de littérature française. Littérature du moyen âge.* 2 vols. Paris, 1830.
Villot (E.), *Mœurs, coutumes et institutions des indigènes de l'Algérie.* Alger, 1888.
Vincentius Bellovacensis, *Speculum naturale.* Venetijs, 1494.
Vinnius (A.), *In quatuor libros institutionum imperialium commentarius.* Lugduni, 1747.
Vinogradoff (Paul), *Villainage in England.* Oxford, 1892.
Virgilius Maro (P.), *Opera omnia.* 10 vols. Londini, 1819.
Vischer (Wilhelm), *Kleine Schriften.* 2 vols. Leipzig, 1877–78.
Vishnu, *The Institutes of.* See *Institutes of Vishnu (The).*

Vishńu Puráńa (The). Trans. by H. H. Wilson. London, 1840.

Volkens (Georg), *Der Kilimandscharo.* Berlin, 1897.

Voltaire (F. M. Arouet de), *Œuvres complètes.* 70 vols. *S. l.,* 1785–89. (Quoted in vol. i.)

—— *Œuvres complètes.* 13 vols. Paris, 1836–38. (Quoted in vol. ii.)

Vos (H.), ' Die Verbreitung der Anthropophagie auf dem asiatischen Festlande ' ; in *Internat. Archiv f. Ethnogr.* vol. iii. Leiden, 1890.

Vossische Zeitung. Berlin.

Wachsmuth (Wilhelm), *Hellenische Alterthumskunde.* 2 vols. Halle, 1846.

Waddell (L. A.), *The Buddhism of Tibet.* London, 1895.

Wächter (C. G. von), *Beiträge zur Deutschen Geschichte.* Tübingen, 1845.

Waitz (Theodor), *Anthropologie der Naturvölker.* 6 vols. (vols. v. pt. ii. and vol. vi. by G. Gerland). Leipzig, 1859–72.

—— *Introduction to Anthropology.* Trans. London, 1863.

Wall (W.), *The History of Infant-Baptism.* 2 vols. Oxford, 1862.

Wallace (A. Russel), *The Malay Archipelago.* London, 1890.

—— *Travels on the Amazon and Rio Negro.* London, 1853.

Wallace (D. Mackenzie), *Russia.* 2 vols. London, 1877.

Wallin (G. A.), *Första Resa från Cairo till Arabiska öknen* 1845. Helsingfors, 1853.

—— *Notes taken during a Journey through Part of Northern Arabia, in* 1848. (Reprinted from *Jour. Roy. Geo. Soc.* vol. xx.) London, 1850–51.

—— *Reseanteckningar från Orienten åren* 1843–1849. Ed. by S. G. Elmgren. 4 vols. Helsingfors, 1864–66.

Wallon (H.), *Histoire de l'esclavage dans l'antiquité.* 3 vols. Paris, 1879.

Walter (Ferdinand), *Das alte Wales.* Bonn, 1859.

—— *Geschichte des Römischen Rechts bis auf Justinian.* 2 vols. Bonn, 1860–61.

Ward (Herbert), *Five Years with the Congo Cannibals.* London, 1890.

Ward (Robert), *An Enquiry into the Foundation and History of the Law of Nations in Europe, from the Time of the Greeks and Romans, to the Age of Grotius.* 2 vols. London, 1795.

Ward (W.), *A View of the History, Literature, and Religion of the Hindoos.* 4 vols. London, 1817–20.

Wardlaw (R.), *Four Sermons : Two on Man's Accountableness for his Belief, &c.* Glasgow, 1830.

Waronen (Matti), *Vainajainpalvelus muinaisilla suomalaisilla.* Helsingissä, 1895.

Wasserschleben (F. W. H.), *Die Bussordnungen der abendländischen Kirche.* Halle, 1851.

Waterland (D.), ' Sermon on Self-Love ' ; in *The English Preacher,* vol. i. London, 1773.

Watson (J. Selby), *The Reasoning Power in Animals.* London, 1867.

Wayland (Francis), *The Elements of Moral Science.* London, 1863.

Weber (A.), *Indische Streifen.* 3 vols. Berlin & Leipzig, 1868–79.

—— ' Eine Legende des Çatapatha-Brâhmaṇa über die strafende Vergeltung nach dem Tode ' ; in *Zeitschr. der Deutschen Morgenländischen Gesellsch.* vol. ix. Leipzig, 1855.

Weber (E. von), *Vier Jahre in Afrika.* 2 vols. Leipzig, 1878.

Webster (Hutton), *Rest Days.* New York, 1916.

Weddell (James), *A Voyage towards the South Pole.* London, 1825.

Wegener (H.), *Geschichte der christlichen Kirche auf dem Gesellschafts-Archipel.* Berlin, 1844.

Weinhold (Karl), *Altnordisches Leben.* Berlin, 1856.

—— *Die deutschen Frauen in dem Mittelalter.* 2 vols. Wien, 1882.

Welcker (F. G.), *Griechische Götterlehre.* 3 vols. Göttingen, 1857.

—— *Kleine Schriften.* 3 vols. Bonn, 1844–50.

Wellhausen (J.), *Prolegomena to the History of Israel.* Trans. London, 1885.

—— *Reste des arabischen Heidentums.* Berlin, 1897.

Welling (J. C.), ' The Law of Torture ' ; in *The American Anthropologist,* vol. v. Washington, 1892.

' Welsh Laws ' ; in *Ancient Laws and Institutes of Wales.* London, 1841.

Westcott (B. F.), *Essays in the History of Religious Thought in the West.* London, 1891.

Westcott (W. W.), *Suicide.* London, 1885.

Westermarck (Edward), " *L-'âr,* or the Transference of Conditional Curses in Morocco ' ; in *Anthropological Essays presented to E. B. Tylor.* London, 1907.

—— *Ceremonies and Beliefs connected with Agriculture, certain Dates of the Solar Year, and the Weather in Morocco.* (*Öfversigt af Finska Vetenskaps-Societetens Förhandlingar. Bd. LIV.,* 1911–1912. *Afd. B. N : o* 1) Helsingfors, 1913.

—— *The History of Human Marriage.* London, 1894.

—— ' The Magic Origin of Moorish Designs ' ; in *Jour. Anthr. Inst.* vol. xxxiv. London, 1904.

—— *Marriage Ceremonies in Morocco.* London, 1914.

—— ' Méthode pour la recherche des institutions préhistoriques à propos d'un ouvrage du professeur Kohler ' ; in *Revue internationale de sociologie,* vol. v. Paris, 1897.

—— ' Midsummer Customs in Morocco ' ; in *Folk-Lore,* vol. xvi. London, 1905.

—— *The Moorish Conception of Holiness (Baraka).* (*Öfversigt af Finska Vetenskaps-Societetens Förhandlingar. Bd. LVIII.,* 1915–1916. *Afd. B. N : o* 1) Helsingfors, 1916.

—— ' The Nature of the Arab *Ǧinn,* Illustrated by the present Beliefs of the People of Morocco ' ; in *Jour. Anthr. Inst.* vol. xxix. London, 1900.

—— ' Normative und psychologische Ethik ' ; in *Bericht über den III. Internationalen Congress für Psychologie in München.* München, 1897.

—— ' The Popular Ritual of the Great Feast in Morocco ' ; in *Folk-Lore,* vol. xxii. London, 1911.

—— ' The Position of Woman in Early Civilisation ' ; in *Sociological Papers,* vol. i., 1904. London, 1905.

—— ' Sul culto dei santi nel Marocco ' ; in *Actes du douzième Congrès International des Orientalistes,* Rome, 1899, vol. iii. pt. i. Florence, 1902.

Westgöta-Lagen. Ed. by H. S. Collin and C. J. Schlyter. (*Corpus Juris Sueo-Gotorum Antiqui,* vol. i.) Stockholm, 1827.

Wheaton (Henry), *Elements of International Law.* Ed. by A. C. Boyd. London, 1889.

Wheeler (G. C.), *The Tribe, and Intertribal Relations in Australia.* London, 1910.

Wheeler (J. D.), *A Practical Treatise on the Law of Slavery.* New York & New Orleans, 1837.

Wheeler (J. Talboys), *The History of India.* 4 vols. London, 1867–74.

Wherry (E. M.), *A Comprehensive Commentary on the Qurán*. 4 vols. London, 1882–86.

Whewell (William), *The Elements of Morality*. Cambridge, 1864.

Whitney (W. D.), ' On the Main Results of the later Vedic Researches in Germany ' ; in *Jour. American Oriental Soc.* vol. iii. New York, 1853.

Wichmann (Yrjö), ' Tietoja Votjaakkien mytologiiasta ' ; in *Suomi*, ser. iii. vol. vi. Helsingissä, 1893.

Wied-Neuwied (Maximilian Prinz zu), *Reise nach Brasilien in den Jahren 1815 bis 1817*. 2 vols   Frankfurt a.M., 1820–21.

—— *Travels in the Interior of North America*. Trans. London, 1843.

Wiedemann (Alfred), *The Ancient Egyptian Doctrine of the Immortality of the Soul*. Trans. London, 1895.

—— *Herodots zweites Buch mit sachlichen Erläuterungen herausgegeben von*. Leipzig, 1890.

——' Maâ, déesse de la vérité ' ; in *Annales du Musée Guimet*, vol. x. Paris, 1887.

—— *Religion of the Ancient Egyptians*. London, 1897.

Wiener (J.), Die alttestamentarischen Speiseverbote ' ; in *Zeitschr. f. Ethnol.* vol. viii. Berlin, 1875.

Wiener Medizinische Wochenschrift. Wien.

Wigmore (J. H.), ' Responsibility for Tortious Acts ' ; in *Harvard Law Review*, vol. vii., 1893–94. Cambridge (Mass.), 1894.

Wihtræd (*King*), ' The Laws of ' ; in *Ancient Laws and Institutes of England*. London, 1840.

Wilda (W. E.), *Das Strafrecht der Germanen*. Halle, 1842.

Wilken (G. A.), *Het animisme bij de volken van den Indischen Archipel*. Amsterdam, 1884–85.

—— *Huwelijken tusschen bloedverwanten*. (Reprinted from *De Gids*, 1890, no. 6.)   Amsterdam.

—— *Over de verwantschap en het huwelijks- en erfrecht bij de volken van het maleische ras*. (Reprinted from *De Indische Gids*, May, 1883.)   Amsterdam.

—— ' Plechtigheden en gebruiken bij verlovingen en huwelijken bij de volken van den Indischen Archipel ' ; in *Bijdragen tot de taal-, land- en volkenkunde van Nederlandsch-Indië*, ser. v. vols. i., iv.   's Gravenhage, 1886, 1889.

—— ' Het Strafrecht bij de volken van het maleische ras ' ; in *Bijdragen tot de taal-, land- en volkenkunde van Nederlandsch-Indië*, Land- en volkenkunde, 1883.   's Gravenhage.

—— ' Ueber das Haaropfer und einige andere Trauergebräuche bei den Völkern Indonesien's ' ; in *Revue coloniale internationale*, vols. iii.–iv. Amsterdam, 1886, vol. ii., and 1887, vol. i.   Amsterdam.

Wilkes (Charles), *Narrative of the United States Exploring Expedition during the Years 1838–42*. 5 vols. Philadelphia & London, 1845.

Wilkin (Anthony), in *Reports of the Cambridge Anthropological Expedition to Torres Straits*, vol. v. Cambridge, 1904.

Wilkins (D.), *Concilia Magnæ Britanniæ et Hiberniæ*. 4 vols. London, 1737.

Wilkins (W. J.), *Modern Hinduism*. London, 1887.

William the Conqueror (*King*), ' The Laws of ' ; in *Ancient Laws and Institutes of England*. London, 1840.

Williams (Charles), *Dogs and their Ways*. London, 1863.

Williams (John), *A Narrative of Missionary Enterprises in the South Sea Islands*. London, 1837.

Williams (Monier). See Monier-Williams (Monier).

Williams (S. Wells), *The Middle Kingdom*. 2 vols. New York, 1883.

Williams (Thomas) and Calvert (James), *Fiji and the Fijians*. London, 1870.

Wilson (Andrew), *The Abode of Snow*. Edinburgh & London, 1876.

Wilson (C. T.) and Felkin (R. W.), *Uganda and the Egyptian Soudan*. 2 vols. London, 1882.

Wilson (H. H.), ' A Sketch of the Religious Sects of the Hindus ' ; in *Asiatic Researches*, vol. xvi. Calcutta, 1828.

—— *Works*. 12 vols. London, 1862–71.

Wilson (J. Leighton), *Western Africa*. London, 1856.

Wilson (J. M.) and Fowler (Th.), *The Principles of Morals*. 2 parts. Oxford, 1886–87.

Wilson (James), *A Missionary Voyage to the Southern Pacific Ocean, performed in the Years* 1796–1798. London, 1799.

Wilson (M.), *Charity Mistaken*. St. Omer, 1630.

Wilson (*Sir* R. K.), *History of Modern English Law*. London, &c., 1875.

Wilson (S. G.), *Persian Life and Customs*. Edinburgh & London, 1896.

Windischmann (F.), *Zoroastrische Studien*. Ed. by F. Spiegel. Berlin, 1863.

Winroth (A.), *Offentlig rätt. Familjerätt : Äktenskapshindren*. Lund, 1890.

Winter (J.), *Die Stellung der Sklaven bei den Juden in rechtlicher und gesellschaftlicher Beziehung nach talmudischen Quellen*. Breslau, 1886.

Winterbottom (Thomas), *An Account of the Native Africans in the Neighbourhood of Sierra Leone*. 2 vols. London, 1803.

Winternitz (M.), ' Das altindische Hochzeitsrituell ' ; in *Denkschriften der kaiserlichen Akademie der Wissenschaften, Philosophisch-historische Classe*, vol. xl. Wien, 1892.

—— ' Einige Bemerkungen über das Bauopfer bei den Indern ' ; in *Mittheilungen der Anthropologischen Gesellschaft in Wien*, vol. xvii. Wien, 1887.

Wissmann (H. von), *Unter deutscher Flagge quer durch Afrika*. Berlin, 1889.

—— Wolf (L.), François (C. von), and Mueller (H.), *Im Innern Afrikas*. Leipzig, 1891.

Wissowa (Georg), *Religion und Kultus der Römer*. München, 1902.

Wlislocki (H. von), *Volksglaube und religiöser Brauch der Magyaren*. Münster i.W., 1893.

—— *Volksglaube und religiöser Brauch der Zigeuner*. Münster i.W., 1891.

Woldt (A.), *Kaptein Jacobsens Reiser til Nordamerikas Nordvestkyst* 1881–1883. Trans. Kristiania, 1887.

Wolff (Christian von), *Jus Gentium*. Francofurti & Lipsiae, 1764.

Wolseley (G. J. *Viscount*), *The Soldier's Pocket-Book for Field Service*. London, 1886.

Wood (John), *A Personal Narrative of a Journey to the Source of the River Oxus*. London, 1841.

Wood-Martin (W. G.), *Traces of the Elder Faiths of Ireland*. 2 vols. London, 1902.

Wood-Renton (A.), ' Moral Mania ' ; in *The Law Quarterly Review*, vol. iii. London, 1887.

Woods (J. D.), *The Native Tribes of South Australia ;* with an Introductory Chapter by J. D. W. Adelaide, 1879.

Woodthorpe (R. G.), ' Some Account of the Shans and Hill Tribes of the States on the Mekong ' ; in *Jour. Anthr. Inst.* vol. xxvi. London, 1897.

Worcester (Dean C.), *The Philippine Islands and their People.* New York, 1898.

World (The). By Adam Fitz-Adam. 4 vols. London, 1753–56.

Wrangell (F. von), *Narrative of an Expedition to the Polar Sea, in the Years 1820–1823.* Trans. London, 1840.

Wrede (A. von), *Reise in Ḥadhramaut.* Ed. by H. von Maltzan. Braunschweig, 1870.

Wrede (Richard), *Die Körperstrafen bei allen Völkern.* Dresden, 1898–99.

Wright (Julia McNair), *Among the Alaskans.* Philadelphia, 1883.

Wright (Thomas), *Essays on Archæological Subjects.* 2 vols. London, 1861.

—— *A History of Domestic Manners and Sentiments in England during the Middle Ages.* London, 1862.

Wundt (W.), *Ethics.* Trans. by E. B. Titchener and others. 3 vols· London, 1897–1901.

—— *Ethik.* Stuttgart, 1892.

Wuttke (A.), *Der deutsche Volksaberglaube der Gegenwart.* Ed. by E. H. Meyer. Berlin, 1900.

Wyatt (William), ' Some Account of the Manners and Superstitions of the Adelaide and Encounter Bay Aboriginal Tribes ' ; in Woods, *The Native Tribes of South Australia.* Adelaide, 1879.

Xenophon, *Scripta quæ supersunt.* Parisiis, 1838.

Yanoski (J.), *De l'abolition de l'esclavage ancien au moyen âge.* Paris, 1860.

Yarrow (H. C.), ' A Further Contribution to the Study of the Mortuary Customs of the North American Indians ' ; in *Ann. Rep. Bur. Ethn.* vol. i. Washington, 1881.

—— *Introduction to the Study of Mortuary Customs among the North American Indians.* Washington, 1880.

' Yasna (The),' trans. by L. H. Mills ; in *The Sacred Books of the East,* vol. xxxi. Oxford, 1887.

' Yasts (The),' trans. by J. Darmesteter ; in *The Sacred Books of the East,* vol. xxiii. Oxford, 1883.

Yate (William), *An Account of New Zealand.* London, 1835.

Ymer. Tidskrift utgifven af Svenska Sällskapet för Antropologi och Geografi. Stockholm.

Young (Thomas), *An Essay on Humanity to Animals.* London, 1798.

Zachariä (H. A.), *Die Lehre vom Versuche der Verbrechen.* 2 vols. Göttingen, 1836–39.

Zeitschrift der Deutschen Morgenländischen Gesellschaft. Leipzig.

—— *der Gesellschaft für Erdkunde zu Berlin.*

—— *für die Criminal-Rechts-Pflege in den Preussischen Staaten.* Ed. by J. E. Hitzig. Berlin.

—— *für Ethnologie.* Berlin.

—— *für geschichtliche Rechtswissenschaft.* Ed. by F. C. von Savigny and others. Berlin & Stettin.

—— *für Socialwissenschaft.* Ed. by J. Wolf. Berlin.

—— *für vergleichende Rechtswissenschaft.* Ed. by J. Kohler. Stuttgart.

—— *für Völkerpsychologie und Sprachwissenschaft.* Leipzig.

Zeller (E.), *A History of Greek Philosophy from the Earliest Period to the Time of Socrates.* Trans. 2 vols. London, 1881.

—— *Socrates and the Socratic School.* Trans. London, 1885.

Zeller (E.), *The Stoics, Epicureans and Sceptics.* Trans. London, 1892.

Zend-Avesta (Le). Trans. into French by J. Darmesteter. 2 vols. Paris, 1892.

Ziegler (Th.), *Social Ethics.* Trans. London, 1892.

Zimmer (Heinrich), *Altindisches Leben.* Berlin, 1879.

Zimmermann (W. F. A.), *Die Inseln des indischen und stillen Meeres.* 3 vols. Berlin, 1863–65.

Zimmern (Heinrich), *Babylonische Busspsalmen.* Leipzig, 1885.

—— *Babylonische Hymnen und Gebete in Auswahl.* Leipzig, 1905.

—— *Beiträge zur Kenntnis der Babylonischen Religion. Die Beschwörungstafeln Šurpu, &c.* Leipzig, 1901.

Zöckler (Otto), *Askese und Mönchtum.* 2 vols. Frankfurt a. M., 1897.

Zöller (Hugo), *Forschungsreisen in der deutschen Colonie Kamerun.* 3 vols Berlin & Stuttgart, 1885.

—— *Das Togoland und die Sklavenküste.* Berlin & Stuttgart, 1885.

Zscharnack (L.), *Der Dienst der Frau in den ersten Jahrhunderten der christlichen Kirche.* Göttingen, 1902.

SUBJECT INDEX

ABLUTIONS, i. 53–56, ii. 294, 295, 352–354, 358–359, 415, 416, 726
Abortion, i. 378, 408, 409, 413–417, ii. 705
Accessio, ii. 50
Accident, injuries due to, i. 217–240, 315, 316, 319, ii. 714 ; benefits due to, i. 318 *sq.* ; the future state of persons who have died by, ii. 238, 239, 241
Acts, i. 203–206
Adopted children, rules of inheritance relating to, ii. 46 ; maternal affection for, ii. 187–189
Adoption, of prisoners of war, i. 336 ; of unintentional manslayers, i. 484 ; the blood-covenant represented as a rite of, ii. 206 *sq.* ; marriage between relations by, ii. 369, 374, 375, 748–750, 752
Adultery, ii. 447–455 ; punishment of, i. 189, 311, 492, 521, 630, ii. 447–450, 452, 453, 558 ; self-redress in case of, i. 290–293, 491 *sq.*, ii. 447 ; as a ground for divorce or judicial separation, ii. 397, 455 ; supposed to injure the harvest, ii. 417, 747 ; stigmatised by religion, ii. 447, 448, 450, 453–455, 675, 676, 684, 686, 700, 717 ; refuge denied to persons guilty of, ii. 632 *sq.*
Aesthetic emotions, i. 326
—— judgments, i. 8
Affection. See Altruistic sentiment ; Conjugal, Filial, Fraternal, Marital, Maternal, Paternal, Social affection
Age, restrictions in diet depending on, ii. 319 *sq.* See Children, Old age, Old persons, Seniority
Agricultural tribes, the position of women among, i. 660 *sq.* ; slavery among, i. 673, 674, 681 ; social aggregates of, ii. 201 ; sympathy for domestic animals among, ii. 506, see Oxen

Agriculture, originally a feminine pursuit, i. 634, 635 n.[4], 637 ; moral valuation of, ii. 273–277, 280, 402
Albinos, religious veneration of, ii. 590
All Souls, ii. 550
All-father. See Supreme beings
Alliance, prohibition of marriage between relations by, ii. 369, 377
Alms, connection between sacrifices offered to gods and, i. 565–569 ; between fasting and the giving of, ii. 316–318 ; between offerings to the dead and, ii. 550–552 ; to be given with an ungrudging eye, and not before witnesses, i. 594. See Charity
Altruistic sentiment, the, its origin and development, ch. xxxiv. (ii. 186–228) ; i. 94, 95, 110–114, 129, 373, 468, 559, ii. 494–506, 510–514. See Conjugal, Filial, Fraternal, Marital, Maternal, Paternal, Social affection
Ancestors. See Dead
Anger, the nature and origin of, i. 21–23, 30, 38–42 ; in animals, i. 22, ii. 51 ; in children, i. 22 *sq.* ; towards inanimate things, i. 26, 27, 260–263, 315 ; appeased by repentance, i. 87 ; sympathetic resentment produced by the cognition of the signs of, i. 114 *sq.* ; injuries inflicted in, i. 290–298, 311, 316 *sq.* ; a cause of suicide, ii. 233
Animals, regard for the lower, ch. xliv. (ii. 490–514), i. 11 *sq.* ; anger in, i. 22, ii. 51 ; revenge taken upon, i. 26, 27, 251–253, 255, 256, 258 ; revenge taken by, i. 37 *sq.* ; self-regarding pride in, i. 39, ii. 137 *sq.* ; retributive kindly emotion in, i. 94 ; sympathetic resentment in, i. 112, ii. 52 ; killing of sacred, i. 227, ii. 603–606, 609 ; of totemic, ii. 210, 603, 604, 606 ;

3 I*

108–129 ; moral concepts springing from, i. 134–145 ; expressed in customs and laws, ch. vii. (i. 158–201) ; the resemblance between the phenomena which give rise to non-moral resentment and those which call forth, i. 315–319
Moral emotions, the moral concepts based on, chs. i. (i. 4–20), vi. (i. 131–157) ; the nature of the, chs. ii.–iv. (i. 21–107) ; the origin of the, ch. v. (i. 108–130) ; expressed in customs and laws, ch. vii. (i. 158–201) ; the resemblance between the phenomena which give rise to non-moral retributive emotions and those which call forth, i. 314–319 ; not determined by the cognition of free-will, i. 321–326
—— evolution, general characteristics of, ii. 743–746
—— ideals, i. 153 *sq.*
—— judgments, the emotional origin of, ch. i. (i. 4–20) ; the assumed objectivity of, i. 6–20, 104 *sq.* ; the general nature of the subjects of, chs. viii.–xii. (i. 202–313) ; why conduct and character form the subjects of, i. 314–320 ; the relation between free-will and, i. 320–326 ; the innate character the proper subject of, i. 326
—— law, the authoritativeness attributed to the, i. 14–17
" —— reason," i. 7 *sq.*
" —— truth," i. 17 *sq.*
Morbid impulses, injuries committed under the influence of, i. 298 *sq.*
Morning gift, ii. 385
Mos, i. 119, 122
Mother, children's affection for their, i. 534–538, 618, 659, ii. 194, 748 ; descent traced through the, i. 597, 598, 655 *sq.*, ii. 44–46, 54, 202, 203, 205, 206, 211, 220 ; committing suicide on the death of her only son, ii. 244 n.[3]. See Maternal affection, duties, rights ; Parents
Motives, ch. xi. (i. 283–302) ; i. 207–209, 316, 318
Mourners, delicate state of, ii. 283, 307 ; considered polluted, ii. 306, 307, 545 ; purificatory ceremonies of, ii. 354
Mourning costume, ii. 524, 545, 547
—— customs, ii. 283, 284, 298–308, 520, 524, 526, 528, 541, 542, 544–

548 ; forbidden in the case of suicide, ii. 247. See Death
Murder, manslaughter distinguished from, i. 294–298, ii. 633. See Homicide
Mutilation, as a punishment, i. 192, 195, 311, 312, 513, 518–523, ii. 8, 9, 12, 13, 74, 84, 123 n.[1], 143 n.[1], 447, 449 *sq.*
Mutton, abstinence from, ii. 322, 327
Mutual aid, i. 538–569

NAMES, certain superstitions relating to, i. 460, ii. 369 ; social influence of, ii. 203 *sq.* ; their influence on exogamy, ii. 369, 748 ; prohibition of mentioning dead persons', ii. 524, 545–547, 550 ; of mentioning supernatural beings', ii. 640–643
National conceit, ii. 170–174
Nationalism, i. 367–369, ii. 184, 185, 224 *sq.*
Nationality, the feeling of, ii. 183–185. See Patriotism
Negative commandments, why more prominent than positive commandments, i. 303
Negligence, i. 210, 211, 303–305
Negro slavery, i. 428, 429, 516–518, 683, 704–714, ii. 32 *sq.*
Negroes, not accepted as witnesses against white persons, i. 429 ; antipathy to, i. 713 *sq.* ; injuries inflicted upon white persons by, i. 713 *sq.* ; white persons prohibited from marrying, i. 714
New, fear of anything, i. 462 *sq.*
Nuns, sexual intercourse forbidden to, ii. 409, 412

OATHS, materialistic conception of, i. 58–61, 233 *sq.* ; the taking of, forbidden to the high priest, i. 58, ii. 638 ; to priestesses, ii. 638 ; contained in ordeals, i. 505 *sq.*, ii. 687–690 ; taken upon arms, i. 506, ii. 119–121 ; upon tent-poles, i. 588 n.[5] ; in connection with theft, ii. 62, 63, 66, 68 ; sworn by the eldest sister, i. 606 ; on the life of the king, ii. 637 ; supernatural beings appealed to in, ii. 67, 68, 120–123, 686–690, 699, 731 *sq.* ; prohibition of taking, ii. 99, 124 ; not considered binding if contrary to the good of the Church, ii. 100 ; methods of adding supernatural

who have refrained from, ii. 414
sq. ; danger attributed to, ii. 415,
446 ; prohibited in sacred places,
ii. 416, 752 ; abstained from in
connection with religious observances, ii. 416–420, 736, 752 ; admission into priesthood preceded
by abstinence from, ii. 419 ; regarded as a transmitter of hereditary sin, ii. 421 ; between unmarried persons, ii. 422–446, 675,
747 ; between persons of the same
sex, ch. xliii. (ii. 456–489), 752 *sq.* ;
between animals of the same sex,
ii. 456, 466, 475 n.² ; temporarily
forbidden to men who have eaten
human flesh, ii. 575. See Adultery, Incest, *Jus primæ noctis*,
Sodomy
Sexual inversion, congenital, ii. 465–
467 ; acquired, ii. 467–470
Shame, putting offenders to, i. 170 ;
a cause of suicide, ii. 233
Shaving, as a means of purification,
ii. 294 *sq.*
Sheep, stealing of, i. 187 *sq.*, ii. 14 ;
abstinence from killing, for food,
ii. 330. See Mutton
Shipwrecked persons, sacrifice of, i.
467 ; treatment of, ii. 25, 37 *sq.*
Sick persons, killing or abandoning
of, i. 391–393, ii. 542 ; kind treatment of, i. 546–548 ; suicide committed by, ii. 232 ; unkindness to,
punished by the supreme being,
ii. 672. See Disease
Sin, collective responsibility in the
case of, i. 48–57, 61–72 ; prayers
for remission of, i. 49, 54, 55, 228
sq., ii. 654, 655, 702, 707; materialistic conception and transference
of, i. 52–57, 61–65, 70, 71, 85, 86,
407, ii. 256 n.², 654 *sq.* ; committed
accidentally or unknowingly, i.
227–231, 233–235 ; the sense of,
ii. 361 ; sexual intercourse regarded as a transmitter of hereditary, ii. 421
Sister, the elder, respect for, i. 605,
606, 614 ; swearing by, i. 606 ;
curses of, i. 626, ii. 703
Slander, ii. 96, 98, 140–142, 700
Slavery, ch. xxvii. (i. 670–716) ; as a
punishment for crime, i. 45, 46,
494, 518, 675, 676, 681, 682, 685,
688–691, ii. 7, 8, 12, 13, 74 ; a
cause of suicide, ii. 233, 235, 241 ;
produces contempt for manual
labour, ii. 272, 273, 278

Slaves, sacrificed to gods, i. 66, 452,
455, 456, 467 *sq.* ; to dead persons,
i. 472, 474, 486, ii. 234 ; killing of,
i. 378, 421–429, 696, 707 ; of freemen by, i. 429, 430, 491 n.⁵ ; refuge
denied to, i. 427 ; granted to, i.
690, 692, 696, ii. 637 ; not allowed
as witnesses, i. 429, 697 ; bodily
injuries inflicted upon, i. 515–518,
524, 677, 707 ; upon freemen by,
i. 516–518 ; corporal punishment
inflicted upon, i. 522–524 ; children sold as, by their parents, i.
599, 607, 609, 611, 612, 615, 675,
681, 682, 684, 685, 689, 691 *sq.* ;
curses of, i. 716 ; proprietary
rights and incapacities of, i. 677,
684, 688, 690, 697, ii. 28, 31–33,
57 ; rules of inheritance relating
to, i. 679, ii. 46 *sq.* ; addicted to
falsehood, ii. 113, 129 *sq.* ; insults
offered by, ii. 142 *sq.* ; offered to,
ii. 143 ; marriages between freemen and, ii. 379 ; treatment of the
dead bodies of, ii. 527, 549 ; eaten,
ii. 559, 567 ; cursed by their
masters, ii. 703
Snakes, abstinence from eating, ii.
324. See Serpents
Social affection, i. 94, 95, 112–114,
559, ii. 197, 198, 226–228
—— aggregates, the evolution of, ii.
198–226
Socialism, ii. 69–71
Society, the birthplace of the moral
consciousness, i. 117–123
Sodomy, i. 188, ii. 460, 465 n.², 474–
476, 479–483, 486–489. See
Homosexual love
Solstices, fasting at, ii. 309 *sq.* See
Midsummer customs
Soma, ii. 591, 592, 707 *sq.*
Son, sacrificed to save the life of his
father, i. 455 *sq.* ; the parents' or
father's consent required for the
marriage of the, i. 607–609, 613,
615–618, 624 *sq.* ; mother committing suicide on the death of her
only, ii. 244 n.³ ; allowed to eat
only certain foods after the death
of his father, ii. 301 *sq.* See Children, Firstborn, Primogeniture,
Ultimogeniture
Sorrow expressions of, ii. 283, 308,
316, 528
Soul, the immateriality of the, ii.
595 *sq.* See Annihilation, Dead,
Future Life, Future state, Transmigration

THE END

PRINTED IN GREAT BRITAIN BY R. CLAY AND SONS, LTD.,
BRUNSWICK STREET, STAMFORD STREET, S.E., AND BUNGAY, SUFFOLK.